OXFORD PAPERBACK REFERENCE

A Dictionary of
Celtic Mythology

Dr James MacKillop is Emeritus Professor of English at Onondaga Community College (Syracuse, New York) and Past President of the American Conference for Irish Studies. He was also Professeur Invité at Université de Rennes II, Haute Bretagne, and Visiting Fellow in Celtic Languages at Harvard University. Descended from Jacobite soldiers who fought at Culloden Moor, he has lived most of his adult life in Upstate New York. He is author of *Irish Literature: A Reader* (1987), *Fionn mac Cumhail: Celtic Myth in English Literature* (1986), and *Contemporary Irish Cinema* (1999), all published by Syracuse University Press.

Oxford Paperback Reference

A Dictionary of

Celtic Mythology

JAMES MacKILLOP

OXFORD
UNIVERSITY PRESS

Great Clarendon Street, Oxford OX2 6DP

Oxford University Press is a department of the University of Oxford.
It furthers the University's objective of excellence in research, scholarship,
and education by publishing worldwide in

Oxford New York

Athens Auckland Bangkok Bogotá Buenos Aires Calcutta
Cape Town Chennai Dar es Salaam Delhi Florence Hong Kong Istanbul
Karachi Kuala Lumpur Madrid Melbourne Mexico City Mumbai
Nairobi Paris São Paulo Shanghai Singapore Taipei Tokyo Toronto Warsaw

with associated companies in Berlin Ibadan

Oxford is a registered trade mark of Oxford University Press
in the UK and in certain other countries

Published in the United States
by Oxford University Press Inc., New York

First published 1998

First issued as an Oxford University Press paperback 2000

British Library Cataloguing in Publication Data

Data available

Library of Congress Cataloging in Publication Data

Data available

ISBN 0–19–280120–1

10 9 8 7 6 5 4 3 2

Typeset in Ehrhardt
by RefineCatch Limited, Bungay, Suffolk
Printed in Great Britain by
Cox and Wyman Ltd., Reading, Berkshire

For my wife,
gu mo chéile, anns an lorgar mi fhéin

Consultant Editors

The author would particularly like to thank the following specialist advisors, who gave invaluable advice on Celtic language:

Professor Pádraig Oá Riain, University College, Cork *Old Irish*

Professor Derick S. Thompson, University of Glasgow *Scottish*

Professor D. Ellis Evans, Jesus College, Oxford *Welsh and Breton*

Acknowledgements

A generous grant for independent study from the National Endowment for the Humanities allowed this project to begin to emerge from drawers of citations. The British Council travel grant made it possible for me to visit the excellent collections in Northern Ireland as well as Emain Macha. Two sabbaticals from Onondaga Community College provided valuable time with particularly recalcitrant studies, like Cornish and Manx. A State University of New York Sabbatical Grant allowed for an important computer upgrade.

The Onondaga Community College Inter-Library Loan staff, especially Gail Rizzo, found hundreds of obscure articles and books, including an 1835 Manx dictionary. Also helpful have been the library staffs at the Harlan Hatcher Graduate Library of the University of Michigan, the Olin Library of Cornell University, the E. S. Bird Library of Syracuse University, the Widener Library of Harvard University, the New York Public Library, and the Library of Congress.

David Boeshaar gave invaluable word-processing instruction. Mary Helen Thuente agreed to finish the project for me when I wondered if I would live long enough to do it myself. Lois Kuter gave expert advice on Breton language and culture. Invaluable aid on specific questions was given by James Doan, Lucy McDiarmid, William Mahon, Maureen Murphy, Grace Neville, Séamas Ó Síocháin, Oighrig Rankin, and Margaret Spillane. Donna Woolfolk Cross, an empathic, marathon keyboard labourer, told me how to answer the question, 'When will the book be done?'

Contents

Abbreviations

ang.	anglicized
Bret.	Breton
Brit.	British
Corn.	Cornish
Gaul.	Gaulish
gen.	genitive
Ir.	Irish
L	Latin
MidE	Middle English
ModIr.	Modern Irish
OE	Old English
OIr.	Old Irish
ON	Old Norse
ScG	Scottish Gaelic
W	Welsh

Introduction

> History often resembles 'Myth', because they are both ultimately made of the same stuff.
>
> J. R. R. Tolkien
> Andrew Lang Lecture, 1938

Celts

Like the terms 'Slavic' or 'Germanic', 'Celtic' denotes one of the great families of Indo-European languages. 'Celtic' may also denote the culture and traditions of people speaking Celtic languages, though not necessarily their ethnicity, physique, or temperament. The earliest record of Celtic tradition, perhaps *c.*1000 BC, is found in the *Hallstatt[1] culture of the Danube Valley in what is today Austria. Before the second century BC Celtic languages were spoken in many parts of Europe, notably *Gaul and Britain, but also the Iberian peninsula, the Low Countries, the Alps, Germany, northern Italy, much of the Balkans, what is today the Czech Republic, Slovakia, Hungary, and Poland, and even *Galatia in Asia Minor. Because so many of the Celtic-speaking peoples were either conquered by or allied with the Romans, the Celtic languages came to have very low profiles. At the beginning of the eighteenth century scholars in France and Britain demonstrated that the Celtic languages had indeed survived among some hard-pressed populations at the margins of north-western Europe, the Irish, Scottish Gaelic, and Manx, who spoke *Goidelic or *Q-Celtic languages, and the Welsh, Cornish, and Bretons, who spoke *Brythonic or *P-Celtic languages. In the past three centuries the numbers of people speaking Celtic languages has declined precipitously; neither Cornish nor Manx can any longer muster a single living native speaker.

For many readers, however, the term 'Celtic' carries resonances and implications that obscure its designation of specific languages and literatures. Similar top-heavy connotations burden the denotation of a fourth family of European languages, the Romance. Something in the word 'Celtic' prompts an expectation in readers of a wide array of values and attitudes: mysticism, otherworldliness, impracticality, intense pitches of emotions, and a certain fey humour. This partially explains why occult bookstores commonly have 'Celtic' sections, even for books not originally written in Celtic languages, whereas such emporia never have 'Germanic' or 'Slavic' departments, even for books translated from Swedish or Russian. Sometimes the expectation is implicitly heroic. A Glasgow football team and the Boston basketball team both bear the name 'Celtic' although neither competes on linguistic ability. Alas, few stories translated from

[1] An asterisk designates a cross-reference to an entry on this subject.

Celtic languages, whether they are classed as myths, legends, or simply texts, ever fit the outlines of these cultural caricatures.

One reason for this perceptual aberration is that the Celtic-speaking peoples did not begin to call themselves 'Celts' until comparatively recent times.[2] The Greeks used the term *Keltoí* to denote the people north of what is today Marseilles. Gradually *classical commentators began to apply the term to peoples speaking apparently kindred languages, from the Iberian peninsula in the west to the *Galatians of Asia Minor in the east. For Julius *Caesar (first cent. BC) the term *Celtae* was restricted to the people of middle *Gaul, although other Roman writers used it to apply to many of the populations we now class as Celtic-speaking. Curiously, there is no record of classical commentators referring to the inhabitants of the British Isles as Celts, and the word 'Celt' has no counterpart in Old Irish or Old Welsh, as speakers of those languages did not see themselves as forming a linguistic community. The Celtic peoples often referred to themselves with the form *Gal-*, as we see in the words for *Gallia* (Gaul), Galatia, Galicia (provinces of both Spain and Poland), and Portu*gal*.

After having nearly been lost to history, the diverse people we now call 'Celts' are increasingly knowable to us from the material culture recovered by archaeologists. A place and date for the origin of the languages still eludes us, but the Danube Valley (named for the goddess Danu/*Ana) yields abundant evidence of early Celtic settlement. So much early Celtic art, especially in metal, survives that it is divided into two epochs or styles, the older Hallstatt, after the site in Austria, rougher and more angular, and the later *La Tène (*c.*500 BC onwards), named for a site in Switzerland, subtler and more fluid. Significant finds in the later twentieth century, such as that at Hochdorf, Germany (1978), provide information about burial practices, implying a belief that the well-born could reach the otherworld in a rich chariot. Workers at *Lindow bog in Cheshire (1984) found the body of an ancient Briton, who had been murdered or executed; an autopsy revealed his dietary habits, even his last meal. So much is now known about the everyday life of the ancient Celts, dress, housing construction, cuisine, and family that two folk parks, Butser Ancient Farm in southern England and Craggaunowen in western Ireland, may present informed living history displays to modern visitors.

To the Greeks the Celts were the principal barbarians of Europe, reaching the greatest extent of their influence in the second and third centuries BC. Classical culture paid little heed to the subtlety and refinements of the Celtic culture and instead focused on the threat of Celtic warriors. Despite going into battle naked, or clad only in gold neck-torcs, Celtic men at arms inspired fear in the hearts of their Mediterranean contemporaries. In 390 BC a Celtic army sacked Rome. But sacking meant only taking booty, not conquering or establishing an *imperium*. As the Celts moved west and north into new territories, they brought language, and artistic and religious practice, but they also mingled with older populations. Ethnically, then, the Celts of the Danube were very different, as well as different-looking, people from the Celts of the Rhondda and Boyne Valleys. The linguistic split between P-Celts and Q-Celts, today exemplified by

[2] See Malcolm Chapman, *The Celts: The Construction of a Myth* (London: Macmillan; New York: St Martin's, 1992).

the Welsh and the Irish, pre-dates the Celtic migration to the British Isles.

Celtic texts from Continental Europe are skimpy, as real literacy began with the introduction of Christianity to fifth-century Ireland, and its subsequent spread to other Celtic lands. Just how Celtic or how Christian are early texts from Ireland and Wales remains a matter of dispute. For much of the twentieth century the scholarly assumption was that Christian scribes, wittingly or unwittingly, had preserved much of pagan tradition. By century's end Kim McCone[3] and others challenged this view, asserting instead a greater role for classical learning as transmitted through the distinctive monasticism of Celtic Christianity.

'Celtic'

While the term 'Celtic', denoting ancient languages, was fairly widely known to learned writers of English—Milton uses it in *Paradise Lost* (1667)—the perception that the Brythonic and Goidelic languages were derived from ancient sources was slow in coming. Learned men generally ignored George Buchanan's assertion (1582) that Scottish Gaelic derived from ancient Celtic. But in France, where the memory of *Vercingetorix's resistance to Roman conquest has long animated intellectual fancy, several commentators saw elements of Celtic survival among the Bretons, in their isolated peninsula in the north-west. Paul-Yves Pezron established the modern denotation of the word with *Antiquité de la nation et la langue des Celtes* in 1703. Working concurrently with Pezron, the Welsh-born Edward Lhuyd or Lloyd (*c.*1660–1709), Keeper of the Ashmolean Museum, Oxford, applied close philological analysis to the languages of the British Isles in what would be today called 'field work'. His *Archaeologia Britannica* (1707) fixed the word 'Celtic' in the English lexicon. The pronunciation of the word remains ambiguous, however, a conflict between its Greek root, *keltoi*, and its path through French, where *celtique* is pronounced with a soft *c*: 'sell-TEEK'. Although many dictionaries, including the *OED*, prefer the soft *c* pronunciation, most students of Celtic culture prefer the hard *c*: 'KELL-tik', in acknowledgement of its Greek origin.

Although Celtic-speaking peoples lived in two of the most powerful and technologically advanced of world nations, Great Britain and France, their spheres were *terra incognita* to most educated persons, their languages rarely studied. This massive ignorance, sometimes wilful, fostered the acceptance of much chicanery. The Scottish writer James *Macpherson made prose translations of some passages from Gaelic ballads, and invented many more 'translations', presenting *The Poems of Ossian* (1760–3) as a lost epic of the Celtic people, a counterpart to Homer's *Iliad*. Although opposed by the gimlet-eyed but Gaelic-illiterate Samuel Johnson, Macpherson's *Ossian* achieved phenomenal success, being translated into all major European languages and attracting admirers as diverse as Napoleon, Goethe (also a translator), and Thomas Jefferson. Macpherson contributed to the fashionably morbid and self-consciously 'primitive' Celtic Revival of the late eighteenth century, which included the

[3] *Pagan Past and Christian Present in Early Irish Literature* (Maynooth: An Sagart, 1990).

Welsh-born Thomas Gray. While the movement popularized the Welsh and Irish word 'bard', it was emotionally and stylistically unrelated either to as-yet untranslated ancient texts or to still-flourishing literary traditions in living Celtic languages, such as Brian Mac Giolla Meidhre's [Brian Merriman] raucous and earthy *Cúirt an Mheán-Oíche* [The Midnight Court] (*c.*1780) or the wide-ranging poetry of the Scottish Alasdair Mac Mhaighstir Alasdair [Alexander MacDonald] (*c.*1695–*c.*1770).

During the nineteenth century, while the numbers of people speaking Celtic languages continued to dwindle, scholars—led by German philologists—compiled grammars and dictionaries of the Celtic languages, especially Old Irish, which has the most extensive manuscript literature. In both Ireland and Wales the great medieval codices, like the **Book of the Dun Cow* [*Lebor na hUidre*] and the **Black Book of Carmarthen* [*Llyfr Du Caerfyrddin*], were rediscovered, edited, and translated. In all Celtic countries, including the Scottish Highlands, *Cornwall, *Brittany, and the Isle of *Man, folklorists recorded and translated huge volumes of oral tradition, much of it of considerable antiquity.

By the mid-nineteenth century the perception that Celtic-speaking peoples, impoverished and despised though they were, were the inheritors of an ancient and little-known past began to penetrate learned consciousness. For many, the early Celts became exemplars of the medieval heroism Sir Walter Scott had fabricated in his popular historical novels earlier in the century. For others the Celtic world was an anodyne to and retreat from the ugliness and materialism begotten by the industrial revolution; thus the painter Paul Gauguin fled first to Brittany before departing for Tahiti. In his study of newly emerging Celtic texts, *Essai sur la poésie des races celtiques* (1854), Ernst Renan found the Celts reserved, inward-looking, deficient in political aptitude or initiative, fatalistic, and hopelessly wedded to lost causes. Reading many of the same materials, though only in translation, Matthew Arnold, in *On the Study of Celtic Literature* (1867), reduced Celtic traits to three: magic, melancholy, and a gift for style.

Putting aside the roastings that Renan and Arnold have suffered from Celtic nationalists over the years, we find that successive adaptations of ancient stories and characters have been equally subjective. Standish James O'Grady's inventive *History of Ireland* (1881) and his subsequent historical novels posit Celtic warriors that are at once Tory nationalists and model Victorian gentlemen. Pádraig Pearse imagined Cúchulainn as a beautiful boy bent on martyrdom (1916). And most influential of all, William Butler Yeats's *Celtic Twilight* (1893), was suffused with *fin de siècle* world-weariness. Elsewhere in his extensive corpus Yeats would adapt Celtic-derived characters and themes to express subtler and more complex emotions. Indeed it is largely because of Yeats, his peerless artistry, his towering prestige, and his extensive readership, that generally educated people first came to be expected to recognize allusions to 'Celtic mythology'. Examination of Celtic sources would not always gloss Yeats's allusions, however, as his sources were often eclectic; eventually he turned to Lady Gregory's tidy retellings of ancient stories, *Cuchulain of Muirthemne* (1902) and *Gods and Fighting Men* (1904). And Yeats could also confound the best-informed Celticists with his idiosyncratic inventions, like Clooth-na-Bare for *Cailleach Bhéire or King Goll for *Suibne Geilt [Mad Sweeney]. For most of the twentieth century adaptations of or allusions to Celtic mythology were found only in élite culture, like the many retellings of the Deirdre story (including an opera) or Saunders Lewis's intense drama *Blodeuwedd* (1948; translated as *Woman Made of Flowers*, 1985). By the century's end, however, Celtic mythology had also found its way into several more demotic forms, such as post-Tolkien fantasy fiction, Jim Fitzpatrick's illustrated epics, rock opera, New Age philosophizing, and Dungeons and Dragons gaming.

Literary Tradition

The reader who goes directly to Celtic-language texts, or their translations, encounters few or only oblique parallels to what enthusiasts and romantics since 1760 have claimed to be 'Celtic'. The medieval Irish and Welsh speak continually about such real-world issues as the nature of kingship and sovereignty. Usurpation is dreaded, and false claimants to titles or thrones are often dealt with brutally. Bloody vengeance is wreaked upon treachery, broken promises, and real and perceived insults. Most unchivalrously, warriors jockey for positions of prestige at dinner tables and easily come to blows over who deserves the *champion's portion, the finest cut of pork. Predatory monsters prey upon the unwary at crossroads, near dark pools, and in the recesses of remote hills. Adultery is common and portrayed surprisingly sensuously, given the reputation for prudery of Celtic peoples in the last two centuries, but cuckolded husbands show an unquenchable, almost Mediterranean, lust to assuage their injured pride. Yet love is sometimes fulfilled, wants can be satisfied, and bounty relished without care. An imagined world seen in vivid detail is always near at hand. Boats of white bronze sail on glassy seas, and seductive damsels entertain heroes for 300 years in what seems like an instant. The fullness of the Celtic record, from the evidence of ancient shrines to tales recorded from oral tradition in the late twentieth century, gives the fullness of life. There is not an emotion in all of it that cannot be known in our own lives.

The phrase 'Celtic texts' in this volume refers primarily to those written in the Irish and Welsh languages. Irish is the oldest written vernacular in Europe, with a literary tradition possibly beginning in the sixth century, with the coming of Christian scribes, that has produced hundreds of narratives. These survive in the great medieval codices beginning with the *Book of the Dun Cow* (before AD 1106), although internal evidence shows that many were composed centuries earlier. Written Irish-language literary tradition survived the coming of the Anglo-Normans (1169), the flight of the native aristocracy (1607), Cromwellian pogroms (the 1650s), to the eighteenth century. Welsh literary tradition, for all its artistic splendour, begins several centuries later, long after Christianity was well established, and exists in much smaller volume. A third, much more modest, written tradition exists in Gaelic Scotland, related to Old Irish, including the *Book of the Dean of Lismore* (1512–26), and continued by distinguished seventeenth- and eighteenth-century bards. All the Celtic countries produced huge bodies of oral tradition in which characters from written texts, notably *Fionn mac Cumhaill, can be portrayed very differently from how they are seen in written texts. Many oral-tradition narratives are undoubtedly centuries old, perhaps older than stories in written texts, but they did not begin to be collected on a large scale until the nineteenth and twentieth centuries. The focus in this volume is on written texts, with attention paid to oral tradition when it might illuminate a larger Celtic-language vision, such as the Manx *tarroo ushtey, which may be a survival of the ancient veneration of the *bull. Similarly, less attention is given to ancient Continental and Romano-British deities, known mostly from passages in classical commentators or from the close examination of archaeological remains, unless they suggest parallels with Irish and Welsh figures, such as *Ogmios and Irish *Ogma, *Epona and Welsh *Rhiannon, or Gaulish *Mercury and Irish *Lug Lámfota. Finally, a few Arthurian references exist here, mostly when they might have been mistaken for Celtic subjects, like *Tristan of Cornwall or *Iseult of Ireland, or when the Arthurian figures provide correlatives with Celtic characters, like *Perceval with *Peredur and *Peronnik. A fuller Arthurian dictionary would fill a volume larger than this one.

Myth and Tradition

Myth, like music, can never reveal its ultimate secret. But unlike music, there is far less agreement about just what 'mythology' is. Its etymological root in the Greek *mythos* (story, plot, speech) prompted Northop Frye to define 'myth' as 'a story in which some of the chief characters are gods'.[4] Stories of Zeus, Jupiter, and Thor, then, would unmistakably be myths, but Oedipus' search for the killer of Laius would not be. In everyday speech, of course, the tragic story of King Oedipus is one of the first examples many of us would think of if asked to name a myth. Then again, there are more *ad hoc* implicit definitions of 'myth', many of them pejorative, than most lexicographers are willing to itemize: not factual, unprovable, vainly wishful, wilfully uninformed, fabricated, fictional, subjective, naïve, and gullible. At the same time 'myth' has also come to denote those episodes or stories handed down within a culture that are continually retold or referred to for their resonant meaning. For example, in his history of Ireland R. F. Foster speaks of the 1689 siege of Derry, in which a small body of embattled Protestant settlers held out at great cost against their Jacobite, Roman Catholic attackers, an event still annually commemorated: 'This provided a story and a *myth* beloved of military historians of the time and ever since . . . [*italics mine*].'[5] Most readers can be expected to know what the author intends by this use of 'myth', even though few dictionaries endorse it. An episode or story can become a myth even when there is no ambiguity about whether the root narrative actually took place.

Not everything that anyone might call a 'myth' can be accommodated in this volume, however. There are no entries for the Siege of Derry, the Scottish Gaelic catastrophe at Culloden Moor, or the Duchess Anne, last ruler of Brittany, no matter what their resonances within the traditions of those Celtic countries. When we call something a 'myth' in the study of traditional literature, we expect that it be ancient rather than modern and that somebody at some time took it seriously. A myth differs from a 'folk-tale', a term equally

[4] *Fables of Identity* (New York: Harcourt, Brace, 1963), 30.

[5] *Modern Ireland, 1600–1972* (Harmondsworth: Allen Lane, The Penguin Press, 1988), 146.

difficult to define, in that a folk-tale often aspires to entertain. And a myth is entirely different from a *Märchen*, the Brothers Grimm reminded us, because a *Märchen* (which we carelessly translate as 'fairy tale') is not to be believed on the face of it.

At the beginning of the modern study of traditional literature in the eighteenth century, Gottlob Heyne (1729–1810) and Johann Gottfried Herder (1744–1803) determined that 'mythology' dealt with the origin of the world and the many creatures in it, the vicissitudes of vegetation, weather, eclipses, the discovery of fire, and the mystery of death. This means roughly that mythology is much like religion, especially other people's religion. The prestige accorded Heyne and Herder's point of view long made many learned commentators reluctant to describe Celtic traditions as a 'mythology'. Early Irish and Welsh texts were written by Christian scribes, often unmistakably hostile to the 'pagan' traditions that preceded them. Deities of the older religion are reduced to tantalizingly shadowy phantoms, like Ana, for whom the semi-divine *Tuatha Dé Danann are named, or *Mór Muman, territorial goddess of southern Ireland. Or they are historicized into kings, queens, or heroes, like *Conchobar mac Nessa or Rhiannon. Even with the certain divinities of the ancient Gauls or Britons, we do not have narratives in the native language, only brief comments from Greek and Latin writers and the physical evidence from archaeological survivals. The narratives from early Irish and Welsh traditions, on the other hand, no matter how corrupt their transmission may have been, contain countless parallels in motif, theme, and character with other Indo-European traditions we usually call 'mythology', not only Greek and Roman, but Norse, Slavic, Iranian, and Indian. They also demonstrate abundant parallels with continental Celtic religion, beginning with the Irish *Lug Lámfhota, the Welsh *Lleu Llaw Gyffes, and the Gaulish *Lugos.

The term 'Celtic mythology' has been in widespread use since the early twentieth century, usually describing old Celtic, medieval Irish, and Welsh sources. It does not usually apply to Scottish Gaelic, Manx, Cornish, or Breton traditions, but entries from those have been included here, especially when they provide parallels with personalities and motifs from earlier times. Entries are also made for materials that a conscientious but uninformed person might mistakenly think were mythological, like the Irish lovers *Liadain and *Cuirithir (often compared with the also historical Héloïse and Abelard); it seemed unwise to exclude them because they may have been historical figures. At the same time, legendary stories have accrued to figures we believe to be historical, like *Brian Bórama (Boru), *Llywelyn ap Iorwerth, and *Nominoë. Legends are popular, unauthenticated narratives thought to be historical, like those surrounding *Arthur and Charlemagne; although often differentiated from myths, Celtic legends are cited here. Similarly, the entire text of *Y *Gododdin*, attributed to *Aneirin (late sixth century), may be based on emotions experienced and expressed by breathing human beings, but its very antiquity and its proverbial place in Welsh tradition could lead the unwary reader to think it was 'mythological'. Place-names present a parallel challenge to readers. *Emain Macha, despite the fabulous stories attached to it, is today unambiguously identified with a hill-fort in Co. *Armagh, but *Emain Ablach existed only in the mind of a storyteller. There are also entries for animals (e.g. *boar), birds (*swan), plants, and trees (*alder, *yew) when they have continuing mythological associations. Finally, a large number of entries make reference to 'pseudo-history', especially the **Lebor Gabála* [Book of Invasions]. The compilers of this five-volume opus apparently thought they were writing the early history of Ireland, but like Raphael Holinshed (d. 1580) and other compilers of national chronicles, they used fabulous materials most credulously. In the *Lebor Gabála*, however, we can often find in the text a historical correlative transmogrified but still recognizable.

Spelling Methodology

Standardized spellings have not existed for many names and words in Irish tradition; Scottish Gaelic, Manx, Welsh, Cornish, and Breton present lesser problems. Even for such an often-cited figure as Cúchulainn, four or five variants, Cúchulain, Cú Chulainn, Cú Chulaind, Cuchulain, etc., are still widely used. The aim of this volume has been to follow the spellings of names and words most often used by learned commentators. The editor of this volume collected citations from various texts and commentaries, keeping count of the frequency of different spellings. Three works have been weighted as more influential or authoritative: Donnchadh Ó Corráin and Fidelma Maguire's *Gaelic Personal Names* (Dublin, 1981); Thomas F. O'Rahilly's *Early Irish History and Mythology* (Dublin, 1946); and The Royal Irish Academy's *Dictionary of the Irish Language* (Dublin, 1913–76). Sometimes, however, any of these three could be out of step with what the preponderance of learned commentators prefer. *The Dictionary of the Irish Language* has two additional drawbacks: (1) spellings are not consistent across volumes done by different editors, e.g. the entry for *túath* refers to the *Túatha Dé Danann* with a diacritical stroke over the first vowel, whereas elsewhere in the *Dictionary* and the preponderance of learned commentary the name is spelled without the diacritic: Tuatha Dé Danann. (2) Many of the names and words in the present volume do not appear at all in *The Dictionary of the Irish Language*. For that matter, not all the names in this volume appear in Ó Corráin and Maguire or O'Rahilly either.

Celtic spellings are generally to be preferred over anglicizations, unless it would be obfuscation or pedantry to prefer the Celtic. Thus there are entries for *banshee, *Deirdre, *Tara, and *sheela-na-gig. *Angus is not only an anglicization but from Scottish roots, yet it is far more recognizable to the general reader than the linguistically more authentic Aengus, Aonghus, Oengus, Oenghus, etc., as endorsed by James Stephens in *The Crock of Gold* (1912) and Liam O'Flaherty in *The Ecstasy of Angus* (1931). Similarly, several of the figures of Hiberno-English oral tradition, the *far darrig, *leprechaun, and the *pooka, are very rarely referred to in print as the fear dearg, leipreachán, or púca. The importance of well-received books determines spelling choice: thus *Lughnasa instead of the previously preferred Lugnasad because of Máire MacNeill's authoritative 1962 study; two books from the 1980s established Fionn mac Cumhaill as the preferred form. Following usage in these spellings is not an inconsistency; indeed, it is consistent with English practice with other European languages.

We refer to large Continental cities by their English forms—Cologne, Munich, Venice, Florence, Rome—although we are aware that Germans and Italians do not; but we follow local practice with less-well-known place-names.

Because of the antiquity of many sources, Old Irish is usually preferred to Modern Irish. Notable exceptions include texts that are themselves written in Modern Irish, like **Oidheadh Chlainne Tuireann* [The Tragic Story of the Children of Tuireann], of the several stories beginning *Eachtra* . . . [Adventure of . . .], while *Echtra* . . . is retained for older texts. Exceptions are made for the words sídh/sídhe [fairy mound] and ogham, as their use is already widespread in English, making them more recognizable than their Old Irish counterparts, síd/síde and ogum.

Pronunciation Guide

Most English speakers, having little opportunity to hear a Celtic language spoken, are likely to feel uncertainty in pronouncing many of the names and words included here. Broad and slender consonants and vowels, the voiced *g* in Irish, and the Welsh *-ll-* have no counterparts in English phonology. For these and other reasons, English speakers attempting to pronounce Celtic names without having worked with a native speaker or a good teacher are likely to mouth solecisms—except for those blessed with extraordinary talent. Additionally, Irish pronunciation in particular is not standardized. The name of the often-mentioned Ulster king Conchobar mac Nessa, for example, may be pronounced (roughly) 'KUN-khuh-var', 'KUNNA-khoor', or 'KRU-hoor', in different periods or places. Complicating matters further, the many variant spellings given at different entries, especially when they are in Classical or Modern Irish, call for different pronunciations. For these and other reasons, providing a pronunciation guide for each entry, much as many readers might wish it, was not a practical proposition. The general guide to pronunciation here is an attempt to allow readers to sound out words in some English contexts, such as rhymes in poems. It is insufficient to allow the user to pronounce with assurance these names and words in a broadcast or before learned assemblies.

GOIDELIC LANGUAGES

Old Irish

Vowels: most have the sound quality of Continental languages:

a, ai: g*a*ther
á, ái: l*aw*
áe, aí: *ai*sle
e, ei, éo, éoi: *e*nd
i: *i*t
í, íu, íui: *ea*ch
ía, íai: *Ia*n
o, oi: *o*dd
ó, ói: *o*de
óe, oí: *oi*l
u, úi: p*u*ll
ú, úi: sp*oo*n
úa, úai: *sewe*r

Consonants: those in initial positions are roughly like English, but those standing alone or in medial or final positions can be vastly unlike English:

b (initial): *b*eat; (medial or final): cle*v*er or clo*v*er
c, cc (initial): *c*at, never soft, eg. *c*ymbal
c (medial or final): di*g*
ch: German Ba*ch*, Scottish lo*ch*
d (initial): *d*art; medial or final: fa*th*er
dh: *th*ere
f: *f*ine
g (initial): gift; (medial or final): German magen
g may also be a guttural spirant, e.g. Cenél nEó*g*ain, pronounced like the Spanish ro*g*ó.
h: initial never pronounced; elsewhere used to change quality of adjacent consonant, ch-, dh-, th.
l, ll: *l*eap, ki*ll*er
m (initial), mb, mm: *m*other; (medial or final): cle*v*er
n, nd, nn: *n*ice
p (initial): *p*al; (medial or final): stu*bb*orn
r, rr: Italian se*r*a
s, ss (before *a*, *o*, *u* or after when final): *s*ong, never vi*s*ible or mea*s*ure; s, ss (before *e* or *i* or after when final): *sh*ine.
t (initial), tt: *t*ank; (medial or final): pe*d*al, sa*d*
th: *th*istle

Modern Irish

Spoken Modern Irish survives in three dialects, Ulster, Munster, and Connacht or Connemara, which is favored here. The most distinctive difference between Old and Modern Irish is the certain indication of aspiration of consonants with the addition of the letter *h*, or by a dot in the older Gaelic script.

a: f*a*ther
á: l*a*w
e: *e*nd
é: c*a*me
i: *i*t
í: *ea*ch
o: p*u*ll
ó: *o*de
u: p*u*ll
ú: sp*oo*n

Consonants:

b: *b*eat
bh (before or after *a* or *u*): *w*alrus, so*w*ing
bh (before or after *e* or *i*): sli*v*er, belie*v*e
c (before or after consonants): *c*limate, dis*c*
ch (before or after *a* or *u*): German Ba*ch*, Scottish lo*ch*
ch (before or after *e* or *i*): *h*it
d: much like dh

dh (before and after *a* and *o*): like Spanish rogó
dh (before and after *e* and *i*): roughly like English *y*
f: *fine*
fh: silent
g: *garland, girl*
gh (before and after *a* and *o*): like Spanish rogó
gh (before and after *e* and *i*): roughly like English *y*
l, ll: *leap, killer*
mh (before and after *a* and *o*): *walrus, sowing*
mh (before and after *e* and *i*): *sliver*
p: *pal*
ph: *flip*
r, rr: *ripe, sorrow*
s (before and after *a* and *o*): *song*, never *visible* or *measure*
s (before and after *e* and *i*): *shin, wish*
sh: *hope*
t (before and after *a* and *o*): *thought, thunder*
t (before and after *e* and *i*: with a y-sound, as the British pronounce *tune*
th: *hope*

Scottish Gaelic

While it resembles Modern Irish, especially the Ulster dialect, Scottish Gaelic contains more sounds, especially vowels when flanked by *m* or *n*, that have no counterpart in English. Only Breton (see below) presents the English speaker with greater challenge. Further, Scottish Gaelic vowels are more irregular than those in other Celtic languages; the *a* without diacritical markings, for example, may be pronounced like the vowel in English b*a*th, English c*u*p, or when before or after *m* or *n*, like French v*i*n. A fuller list of Scottish Gaelic irregularities would make this guide three times its length here.

Vowels:

a: b*a*th (British, and eastern US); c*u*p; (before and after *m*, *n*): French v*i*n
à: f*a*ther; (before and after *m*, *n*): French v*i*n
ai: *e*nd
ài: f*a*ther
ao: French n*eu*ve; also French m*u*se
aoi: k*ee*n
e: *e*nd
è, èi: f*a*re
é, éi: gl*a*de
ea: *e*nd
eà: *ya*rd
i: *ea*ch; also *i*t, t*i*ght
io: *i*t
o: p*o*t; *o*de
ò: m*o*re

oi: *o*de
u, ù, ùi: sp*oo*n

Consonants:

b: *b*eat
bh: *v*el*v*et, but sometimes a *u* in medial position, and sometimes silent, as in final position
c: *c*at
ch (before or after *a, o, u*): Scottish lo*ch*
ch (before or after *e, i*): German i*ch*
-chd: *d* becomes a *k* as in Scottish Lo*ch K*atrine
d: *t*ank (but softer than English or Scottish Gaelic *t*)
d (before or after *e* or *i*): *j*est
dh: similar to ch and gh, but silent in final position
dh (before or after *e* or *i*): *y*es
f: *f*ine
fh: silent, except for three words, *fhéin, fhuair*; in *fhathast* it is voiced as *h*.
g: *g*arland, *g*irl
gh: similar to ch, but may have the sound of English *y* before or after *e* or *i*; sometimes silent
l: in most positions not comparable to any sound in English
l, ll (before and after *e* and *i*): mi*ll*ion
m: *m*other (but with a nasal quality)
mh: *v*elvet, but more nasal than *bh*
n (in many positions): *n*ice
n (before and after *e* or *i*): pi*n*ion
n (after *c, g, m, t*): similar to *r*
ng: a*ng*le
p: *p*al
ph: *f*ine
r, rr: *r*ipe, ca*rr*y (but slightly flapped)
s (before and after *a, o, u*): *s*ong, never vi*s*ible or mea*s*ure
s (before and after *e, i*): *sh*in, wi*sh*
sh: *h*ope
t: almost aspirated, like the *th* in the Elizabethan mur*th*er [for murder]; before or after *e* or *i* it may have the sound of English *ch* as in *ch*in.
th (initial): *h*ope; elsewhere it may be silent or slightly aspirated

Manx

With very few exceptions, Manx is written to be pronounced with English phonetics.

BRYTHONIC

Welsh

Vowels: as with Irish, many of the sound quality of Continental languages; they are 'pure' and not diphthongized as vowels in English often are; the circumflex diacritical assures that a vowel is long, e.g. wˆ: sp*oo*n; the main accent usually falls on the penultimate syllable, as in eist-ÉDD-fod:

a: short as the *o* in p*o*t; long f*a*ther
ae, ai, au: *ai*sle, *aye-aye*
e: gl*a*de; also short, as in *e*nd
ei, eu, ey: t*ie*
ew: sk*ew*
i: k*ee*n; also short, as with *i*t
iw: *yew*
o: m*o*re; also kn*o*t
oe, oi, ou: *oi*l
u: (North Wales): French *u*ne; (South Wales): k*ee*n, *i*t
w: sp*oo*n; also p*u*ll
y: k*ee*n
yw: *yew*

Consonants:

b: *b*eat
c: *c*at, never *c*ymbal
ch: Scottish lo*ch*
d: *d*art
dd: *th*is, wea*th*er
f: *v*el*v*et
ff: *f*ine
g: *g*irl, *g*o
h: *h*ope (never silent)
l: *l*eap
ll: unvoiced lateral fricative unknown in English, approximately the *l* in ant*l*er, with more aspiration
m: *m*other
n: *n*ice
ng: si*ng*
p: *p*al
ph: *f*ine
r: ho*rr*id (trilled, as in British pronunciation)
s: *s*ong, never vi*s*ible or mea*s*ure
si: *sh*in
t: *t*ank
th: *th*in
w: *w*indo*w*; see also vowels, above

Cornish

Having lost its last native speaker in the eighteenth century, Cornish when spoken today tends to reflect English phonetics. Language revivalists recommend stress on the penultimate syllable, as in Welsh, and direct attention to the following vowel sounds:

ā: f*a*ther
au: l*aw*
aw: c*ow*
ay: gl*a*de
ē: gl*a*de
eu, ew: *yew*
ey: *eye*
ō: l*aw*
ou: sp*oo*n
ū: sp*oo*n
ü: k*ee*n
y: k*ee*n
yu, yw: *yew*

Breton

Influenced by French and possessing tricky patterns of nasalization of its own, Breton is likely to be the least familiar Celtic language to the English speaker. Historically closest to Cornish, it often retains the Brythonic pattern of stressing on the penultimate syllable of polysyllabic words, with dialectal variations. Vowels may be short or long without diacritical indicators:

a: f*a*ther, also b*a*th (British and eastern US pronunciation)
e: m*a*de (not a diphthong), also *e*nd
eu: German h*ö*ren
i: k*ee*n, also *i*t
o: *o*de, also c*o*t
ou: sp*oo*n, also p*u*ll
u: French m*u*r or German f*ü*hrer, also German f*ü*nf

Consonants:

b: *b*eat
ch: *sh*oe
c'h: Scottish lo*ch*, German Ba*ch*
d: *d*art
f: *f*ine
g: *g*o, *g*irl, never *g*in; (in final position): so*ck*
gn: o*ni*on
ihl: similar to Italian *gli*
j: mea*s*ure
k: *k*ale
l: *l*eap
m: *m*other
n: *n*ice
p: *p*al
r: comparable to the Welsh *r* in the north, more like the French *r* in the south, never like the English *r*
s: *s*ong

t: *t*ank
v: *v*el*v*et; may sound as a *w* or be silent in final position
w (after letter *i*): spi*v*
z: *z*one
zh: a spelling device to unify what was once spelled -*z*- in one part of Brittany and -*h*- in another

How to use this book

This volume has been compiled with the hope that anyone who could use a college dictionary—specifically my sophomore students in mythology—might find it accessible, without having to have recourse to a guide to symbols or abbreviations. Thus, esoteric and off-putting abbreviations, like '*LU*' for the *Book of the Dun Cow* [*Lebor na hUidre*] or '*ZCP*' for *Zeitschrift for celtische Philologie*, have been shunned. As this volume is titled a 'Dictionary' rather than an 'Encyclopedia', the editor has assumed users are looking for specific information in a hurry. Editorial policy thus favours brief entries over a variety of headings instead of inclusive, comprehensive, interpretive longer entries. This may mean that some users will sometimes have to link together several shorter entries to get the larger picture. Asterisks (*) indicate that more information about a cited name or term may be found in a separate entry. Translations appear in square brackets, e.g. *Lebor Gabála* [Book of Invasions], while parentheses indicate parallel forms, e.g. Brian Bórama (Boru), Eógan Mór (Mug Nuadat).

Technical language has, in general, been avoided, but a handful of specialist terms express concepts that do not find synonyms in everyday speech. They include:

agnomen an additional name given to a person, originally given to a Roman citizen, such as Publius Cornelius Scipio *Africanus*, to cite a distinction. Something like the agnomen survived to the modern world when Field Marshal Montgomery became First Viscount Montgomery *of Alamein* in recognition of his victory in World War II. Distinguish from **cognomen**.

cognomen a family name that accompanies a person's given name but does not serve the function of a modern surname, such as *Caesar* in Julius Caesar, who is not 'Mr Caesar'. Distinguish from **agnomen**.

chthonic pertaining to the underworld or underground.

eponym a historical or imagined person who gives his or her name to a city, region, nation, landform or era. Dub[h] is the **eponym** of Dublin.

euhemerism from the theory of Euhemerus (*c.*300 BC) that the gods are deified or inflated historical figures. A Celtic deity sometimes may be described as **euhemerizing** from an esteemed but mortal personage.

folk motif, see **international folk motif**.

international folk motif, **narrative type**, **tale type** from the classification system devised for world traditional literature by Antti Aarne and Stith Thompson. See Stith Thompson, *The Folktale* (New York: Henry Holt, 1936; repr. Berkeley and Los Angeles: University of California Press, 1977). A fuller treatment is found in Stith Thompson's six-volume *Motif-Index of Folk-Literature: A Classification of Narrative Elements in Folktales, Ballads, Myths, Fables, Medieval Romances, Exempla, Jest-Books and Local Legends* (Helsinki: FF Communications,

1932–6; Bloomington, Ind.: Indiana University Studies, 1932–6; revised and enlarged, Bloomington, Ind.: Indiana University Press, 1975, 1989).

matronymic a name signifying a female ancestor, usually a mother. Less common that the **patronymic**, it did not pass from generation to generation.

narrative type, see **international folk motif**.

patronymic a name signifying a male ancestor, usually a father, like ap Rhyˆs or mac Cumhaill. Before modern times patronymics did not serve the functions of surnames or family names.

scholiast an anonymous person, usually a copyist, who annotated or added to a manuscript of much earlier composition.

tale type, see **international folk motif**.

A

A. The first letter of the modern English alphabet was known as ailm [pine] in the *ogham alphabet of early Ireland.

Abac, Abhac. Irish for *Afanc.

Abaris the Hyperborean. One of the legendary 'People beyond the North Wind' in Greek traditions; by historical record he once disputed with Pythagoras. Eighteenth-century speculation made him a *druid, either Welsh or Scottish Gaelic. Modern scholarship suggests he was a central Asian *shaman.

Ábartach, Abarta, Ábhartach. [Ir., feat-performing one]. In the *Fenian Cycle he is the son of the King of the *Tír Tairngire [Land of Promise] and father of the unnamed beloved of the warrior *Cáel. He first appears in narrative as the *Giolla Deacair or 'Hard Gilly'. His daughter *Aífe (6) was changed into a heron by a jealous rival, *Iuchra (2). The name is sometimes also applied to *Céadach. Abartach yields the ModIr. surname O'Haverty.

Abcán, Abcan [Ir. *abcán, abhcán*, little dwarf]. *Dwarf poet of the *Tuatha Dé Danann who owns a bronze boat with a tin sail near the falls of *Assaroe.

aber. Welsh, Cornish, and Breton word for mouth of a river or estuary, the first element in countless place-names. See also OIr. INBER, ModIr. INBHEAR, ScG INBHIR, Manx INVER.

Aber Henfelen. Name for the sea between Wales and Cornwall, i.e. the Bristol Channel, in Welsh narrative.

Aberffraw [W *aber*, estuary]. Chief seat of the kings of *Gwynedd in Welsh narrative; south *Anglesey, 12 miles SE of Holyhead.

Abermenai. The estuary or strait that separates *Anglesey from the mainland of Wales.

Aberystwyth. Town at the mouths of the Ystwyth and Rheidol rivers; one of several traditional burial-places of *Taliesin.

Ábhartach. ModIr. for *Ábartach.

Ablach, Abhlach [Ir., having apple trees, like an apple tree]. *Ulster princess who was the mother of Eochaid mac Fiachnai (9th cent.). See also EMAIN ABLACH.

Abrat. See ÁED ABRAT; CENN ABRAT.

Abred [cf. W *abredu*, to transmigrate]. The innermost of the three concentric circles that represent the totality of being in the 'bardic' cosmogony of Llewelyn Siôn (16th cent.). Abred is also the stage of transmigration. See COSMOGONY.

Acallam na Senórach. ModIr. Agallamh na Seanórach, Agallamh na Seanóirí [Ir., the colloquy of the elders, old men]. An Irish narrative of the *Fenian Cycle composed between 1175 and 1200 and preserved in the 15th-century manuscript *Book of Lismore* and elsewhere.

The *Acallam* is set many generations after the death of *Fionn mac Cumhaill, the central figure of the Fenian Cycle. Two survivors, *Oisín and *Caílte, along with a few companions, are wandering glumly in northern *Leinster. At first Oisín departs for the north to visit his mother while Caílte and the others continue. After crossing the *Boyne River to Druim Dearg, they meet St *Patrick, with whom they discuss the values of pre-Christian Ireland. The focus of the colloquy is Fionn mac Cumhaill, who is also Oisín's father. As St Patrick travels west and south through Ireland, Caílte explains the names of the places they visit, much in the manner of the **Dindshenchas*. Sometimes Caílte can give an older name for a place than the one now in use. Some of this may reflect the juncture Irish society then faced, with the amalgamation of Norman invaders into Gaelic culture. Oisín joins the party and adds more of the heroic deeds of Fionn and the *Fianna, but Caílte is usually portrayed as the more important of the two pagans. Often the saint-pagan dialogue serves only as a frame to introduce stories of the Fianna. The narrative, in both prose and verse, has an Arthurian flavour, especially in the repeated mention of the generosity of Fionn. A general anti-clerical humour often portrays St Patrick as a bigot, pronouncing the doom of hell upon the Fenians. At times St Patrick seems more tolerant, willing to trade Christian learning for ancient lore. The temper of the work is cheerful, in spite of Caílte's loneliness, decrepitude, and regard for the lost heroic past.

Many critics regard the *Acallam* as one of the most successful works in Middle Irish.

Early ModIr. text: *Agallamh na Seanórach*, ed. Nessa Ní Shéaghdha (3 vols., Dublin, 1942–5); ModIr. text: *Agallamh na Seanóiri*, ed. Pádraig de Barra (Dublin, 1984); Myles Dillon, *Stories from the Acallam* (Dublin, 1970). See also Darrell Figgis's novel based on the story *Return of the Hero* (London, 1923; New York, 1930).

Accasbél. A *Partholonian, remembered for building the first guest-house in Ireland.

Achall. A daughter of the *Ulster warrior *Cairbre Nia Fer, she died in sorrow when *Conall Cearnach slew her brother; she gave her name to the hill of Achall near *Tara.

Achill. A large, mountainous island, 15 miles by 4, off the west coast of Co. Mayo. The hawk or crow of Achill was supposed to have lived for thousands of years, and could remember the remote past, which he details to *Fintan mac Bóchra. See Eleanor Knott, 'The Hawk of Achill . . . ', *Folk-Lore*, 43 (1932), 376–409.

Achtan. Variant of *Étaín (2); mother of *Cormac mac Airt.

Acunn. Hero in Scottish *Fenian narratives; gives his name to Kyle of Akin, the strait between the Isle of *Skye and Lochalsh. His brother was Riadh.

Adammair. Sometime husband of *Flidais, goddess of the wild in many early Irish narratives.

Adamnán, Adhamhnán, Adomnán, **Saint** [Ir., Little Adam]. Abbot of *Iona, *Argyllshire (now Strathclyde), 679–704; tenth in line of succession from Iona's founder, *Colum Cille (St Columba). Author of *Vita Columbae*, a Latin life of Colum Cille, in 690–700, nearly a century after the saint's death (*c.*597) and attributed, but unlikely, author of *Fís Adamnáin* [A Vision], a portrayal of heaven and hell that was widely read in medieval times and is sometimes cited as an anticipation of Dante. Credited with the founding of *Dunkeld, Tayside (until 1974, Perthshire), later an important centre of Celtic Christianity. Adamnán is the patron of the Diocese of Raphoe, Co. Donegal; feast-day 23 September.

Adar Llwch Gwin [W *llwch*, dust, powder; *gwin*, wine]. Magical birds of Welsh tradition, belonging to *Drudwas ap Tryffin, often equated with griffins. They were given to him by his wife, a fairy woman, and could understand human speech; they would also perform all that he commanded. In a contest with *Arthur, Drudwas ordered the birds to kill the first fighter to enter the battlefield. When Arthur himself was delayed from entering the fray, the birds attacked Drudwas himself, the first to arrive, tearing his flesh to pieces. In the poetry of the late medieval Beirdd yr Uchelwyr [Poets of the Gentry], the phrase Adar Llwch Gwin was a synonym for hawks or falcons and a metaphor for strong, brave men.

Addanc. Variant spelling of *Afanc.

adder stone. The glass balls or amulets possessed by the *druids, either for mysteries or for ornament, were known as 'adder stones' in several Celtic languages: Bret. glain neidr, ScG gloine nathair, W glain nadredd; but in Cornish it is millpreve. The stones were thought to have been formed during the summer by bubbles, blown from the mouth of the adder and hardened by sliding down the length of its back, forming a crystal ring, worn as an amulet. The adder is the only poisonous snake in the British Isles.

Adene. A variant of *Étaín favoured by W. B. Yeats.

Adhnúall [OIr. *adnúall*, sweet of sound]. One of many hounds belonging to *Fionn mac Cumhaill. He was once stolen by Arthur, son of the king of Britain. After a battle in Leinster, he made the circuit of Ireland three times before he returned to the battlefield to die where three *Fenians and their lovers were buried. See also BRAN (2); SCEOLANG.

Adná, Aidne [cf. Ir. *adnál*, very shameful, modest]. A legendary early explorer of Ireland, the son of *Bith, brother of *Cesair. He was sent on his mission by the pseudo-historical King Ninus of Syria.

Adonis. The handsome hunter of classical myth, lover of Aphrodite or Venus. Several Celtic parallels have been suggested for Adonis, esp. *Diarmait and *Angus Óg.

Adventures of . . . . See ECHTRA; EACHTRA.

Áeb, Áebh, Aobh [cf. OIr. *Oíb*, attractiveness, beauty]. Second of the three wives of *Lir and mother of the children of Lir in **Oidheadh Chlainne Lir* [The Tragic Story of the Children of Lir]. She was a foster-daughter of *Bodb Derg and a sister of Lir's third wife, *Aífe. In some texts she is known as *Niam or Albha. When she died Aífe became stepmother to the children. In some English-language retellings of the story the name Fingula, an anglicization of *Finnguala, one of Áeb's twin daughters, is perversely substituted for Áeb.

Áebhric, Ebhric, Evric. Young man, possibly a monk, at Erris [OIr. *Irrus Domnann*; ModIr. *Iorras Domhnann*], Co. Mayo, who heard the singing of the children of Lir in **Oidheadh Chlainne Lir* [The Tragic Story of the Children of Lir] and committed their story to writing. In some texts his name is anglicized as Evric, Eric, and Everett.

Áebinn. Variant of *Aíbell.

Áed, Áedh, Aodh [Ir., fire; cognate with L *aedes, aestus*]. The most common personal name in early Ireland; it was held by at least twenty saints and by numerous high kings and petty kings, as well as by a multitude of figures in saga and legend. Some figures are always known by the ModIr. and ScG spelling of *Aodh. The name is often anglicized as Hugh, and has given rise to more than a dozen surnames: Hay, Hayes, O'Hea, Hughes, McHugh, McCue, MacKay, etc. See also ÁEDA.

Áed 1. Son of Ainmire in the **Cycle of Kings* and father of *Domnall (1).

2. The son of Eochaid Lethderg, prince of Leinster, who was carried off to a *brugh, or palace of *fairyland, by two women of the *sídh who were in love with him and who held him captive for three years. At the end of this time Áed escaped and made his way to St *Patrick, who freed him from fairy domination. Patrick later restored him to humanity in his father's court. Folk motif: F379.1. See S. H. O'Grady, *Silva Gadelica* (London, 1892), 204–20.

3. One of the four children of Lir in **Oidheadh Chlainne Lir* [The Tragic Story of the Children of Lir].

4. A son of *Bodb Derg who sees the children of Lir but cannot help them.

5. A legendary king of the *Airgialla or Oriel who carried a shield which had one of the *badba perched on its rim; the shield is thus called dubgilla or dubh ghiolla [black servant].

6. King of *Tara in the 6th century who made war on *Brandub, king of *Leinster. Although he owned a magical cowl that would protect him in battle, a gift from *Colum Cille (St Columba), he left it behind and so perished.

7. The son of the *Dagda, seducer of the wife of *Coinche(a)nn, who then slew him. The Dagda did not avenge the murder, but he obliged Coinche(a)nn to carry the corpse until he had found a stone big enough to cover the remains.

8. The king of *Connacht. *Mongán took his shape to visit Áed's beautiful wife, Aíbell. Mongán substituted a temporarily transformed hag for Aíbell, to complete the deception.

9. Poet in the court of *Ulster king *Conchobar mac Nessa who was caught having an affair with Conchobar's strumpet wife *Mugain (2). Sentenced to death by the king, he asked that his mode of execution be drowning. Unbeknownst to Conchobar, Áed had the power to dry up any lake except Lough Laí, which lay before the house of the Ulster hero *Lóegaire Búadach. Outraged that a poet was to be killed, Lóegaire rushed out of his house as Áed was brought for execution. In doing so Lóegaire cracked open his own head but slew thirty of the execution party, and the poet went free.

10. Son of *Miodhchaoin in *Lochlainn, from whom *Brian (1), Iuchair, and Iucharba had to retrieve three shouts from the hill.

11. Another name for *Goll mac Morna, of the *Fenian Cycle.

Áed Abrat [Ir., light of the eye (?)]. The father of *Fand and usual father of *Lí Ban; in some stories *Eochaid (5) is Lí Ban's father. He took pride in his daughters' healing song. A son was the *Angus who invites *Cúchulainn to hear the song of Fand and Lí Ban.

Áed Álainn [Ir., the beautiful]. Husband of *Bébinn.

Áed Dub [Ir., dark fire]. Fulfilled the prophecy of the *druid *Bec mac Dé by killing *Diarmait mac Cerbaill.

Áed Finn, Fionn [Ir., Áed the fair]. The author of **Imram Curaig Maíle Dúin* [The Voyage of Máel Dúin's Boat]. He is described in one manuscript as the 'chief scholar in Ireland'. An Áed Finn is mentioned in the annals as having died in AD 777, a king of *Dál Riada, but no mention is made of his being a learned man.

Áed mac Fidga. Another name for *Goll mac Morna; see also CÚLDUB.

Áed Minbhrec, Minibhrec. A son of the *Dagda and a member of the *Tuatha Dé Danann. Wrongly accused of adultery by a jealous husband, Áed Minibhrec was murdered before his father's eyes. His sídh was near Ballyshannon, Co. Donegal.

Áed Ruad, Ruadh [Ir., red Áed]. Father of *Macha (2), who founded *Emain Macha. According to the annals, he once ruled Ireland for a seven-year term as third of a twenty-one-year sequence with his kinsmen (sometimes brothers, sometimes cousins) *Cimbáeth and *Díthorba. Seven magicians, seven poets, and seven lords of *Ulster guaranteed that the agreement would be kept. When Áed Ruad drowned in the waterfall named for him, *Assaroe [Eas Ruaidh], his daughter Macha was elected to rule in his place. At first Cimbáeth and Díthorba opposed her; she made peace with Cimbáeth and married him but killed Díthorba.

Áed Sláine, Slane. A king of *Tara, *c.* AD 600; a name cited in many genealogies. According to legend his mother, *Mugain Mór, territorial goddess of *Munster, gave birth to a trout before she bore him.

Áeda 1. [corrupt form of Áed, Áedán]. *Dwarf of King *Fergus mac Léti who accompanies *Eisirt to the realm of the *leprechaun of *Iubdán.

2. In the *Fenian Cycle the unwelcome suitor of the beautiful giantess *Bébinn (2), whom he slays while she is under *Fionn's protection.

Áedán, Aodhán [dim. of Áed]. A common name in early Ireland and Gaelic Scotland, borne by at least twenty-three saints and by many characters in history, legend, and saga. The name is often anglicized as Aidan or Edan. See also ÁEDA.

Áedán 1. The best-known clerical Áedán was the missionary sent by Iona to Christianize northern Britain and who founded the monastery at Lindisfarne, Northumberland.

2. A warrior who slew *Máel Fothartaig, son of *Rónán, king of *Leinster, at the king's request. He was himself later slain by one of the victim's sons. See FINGAL RÓNÁIN [How Rónán Killed His Son].

Áedán mac Gabráin, Gabhráin. Irish warrior who founded the kingdom of *Dál Riada in *Argyllshire (since 1974, Strathclyde); a close friend of *Colum Cille (St Columba). He extended his control eastward among the Picts; cited elsewhere as doing battle with the Saxons. His son *Eochaid Buide called himself 'king of the Picts'.

Aeife. See AÍFE.

áenach. Variant spelling of *aonach.

Aeneas. In classical mythology a Trojan prince, son of Anchises and *Aphrodite, hero of Virgil's *Aeneid*, the Latin epic. In both Ireland and Scotland the name *Angus was once thought to be a counterpart of Aeneas.

Aengus. A variant spelling of *Angus preferred by W. B. Yeats.

áer [Ir., cutting, incising]. The act of satirizing, lampooning, or defaming in Old Irish literature. Áer is the last weapon left to the hero on the battlefield; even when wounded and disarmed, he can respond with the power of the word, áer. Cf. ScG aoir.

Aeracura, Aericura, Heracura. Name for a Celto-Germanic goddess seen as a cult partner of Dis Pater in a stone statue found at Oberseebach, Switzerland; also venerated near Stuttgart, Germany. Aeracura may have been an earth goddess displaced by Dis Pater. Her name may be related to Hecate, the Greek goddess of the underworld. A male counterpart, Aericurus, is recorded in Northumberland.

Aerfen [W, renowned in battle]. A minor river-goddess of early Wales, whose name is linked to the River Dee.

Aeron. A god of battle or slaughter in early Wales, whose name seems derived from Agroná. The association of Aeron with the modern Scottish place-name Ayr is disputed.

áes dána, dáno [OIr., people of art]. People having the profession or trade of art, especially poets, in Old Irish literature.

áes sídhe, áes sí, aos sídhe [Ir., people of mound/ fairy hill]. One of many Irish names for the *fairies and, by implication, the *Tuatha Dé Danann.

Aeté. Corrupt form of *Aíde.

Aetern. An early form of *Edern.

Aethlenn. Corrupt form of *Eithne.

Afagddu, Yfagddu [W, utter darkness]. An alternative name for *Morfran.

Afallenau [W, apple trees]. A long series of vaticinatory stanzas ascribed to *Myrddin found in the **Black Book of Carmarthen* (*c.*1250). Each stanza begins with the formulaic phrase 'Afallen beren . . . ' [Sweet apple tree . . .] and usually runs from six to twelve rhyming lines. Myrddin speaks in the first person and tells of his flight from the battle of *Arfderydd (AD 573), his grief for his fallen lord, *Gwenddolau, and his mostly gloomy prophecies for the future of the Welsh people against their enemies. See A. O. H. Jarman, 'The Welsh Myrddin Poems', in R. S. Loomis (ed.), *Arthurian Literature in the Middle Ages* (Oxford, 1959), 20–30; A. O. H. Jarman, *Llyfr Du Caerfyrddin* (Cardiff, 1982), pp. xxxv ff.

Afallon [cf. W afallen, appletree]. The Welsh name for *Avalon, but *Ynys Afallon is *Glastonbury.

Afanc, Addanc [W, beavers]. A kind of water-monster in the whirlpool of Llyn yr Afanc on the River Conway in north Wales. Early reports of the monster are not specific about its shape, but it came to be thought of as a giant beaver, its name employing a word from the local dialect. It has also been described as a kind of crocodile. Many stories have been recorded about the Afanc, some as early as the 17th century. In the Welsh **Triads*, Afanc causes the flood that obliges *Dwyfan and Dwyfach to build an ark to save themselves and the animals. In this story Afanc resides in *Llyn Llion [Bala Lake?]. *Peredur may have slain it, although it continued to be the subject of tales. Akin to the Scottish *kelpie, the Irish and Scottish Gaelic *each uisce/uisge, and the Manx *glaistyn; see the Welsh CEFFYL DWFR [water horse]. See also CÌREIN CRÒIN. Folk motif: F420.1.4.

Ágach, Ághmach [Ir., contentious, warlike]. One of the *Fomorians, an enemy of the *Tuatha Dé Danann.

Agallamh na Seanórach, *Seanóirí.* ModIr. forms of **Acallam na Senórach.*

Agandecca. Character in James *Macpherson's *Poems of Ossian.* The fair-haired daughter of Starno, king of Lochlin, whom her father slew for having informed *Fingal of a plot which had been laid against his life.

Ághmach. ModIr. form of *Ágach.

Agnoman, Agno. An oft-cited ancestor of *Nemed mac Agnomain and *Crunnchu of the *Nemedians in the **Lebor Gabála* [Book of Invasions].

Agroná [Brit., goddess of slaughter]. An early British goddess who gave her name to the Welsh battle-god *Aeron.

Ahè. Variant form of *Dahut, villainess of the Breton story of the submerged city of *Ys.

Ahes. Breton goddess credited with the building of the Roman roads in *Brittany. She may be linked with the Welsh *Elen (1), also a patroness of roads. Distinguish from Ahès, another name for the selfish *Dahut.

Aí Arduallach, Aoi Arduallach [Ir. *aí*, poetic inspiration, learning, metrical composition; *arduallach*, arrogant]. Arrogant daughter of *Fionn mac Cumhaill who angered her father when she refused to marry the king of Scotland or any man who was not Irish.

Aí mac Ollamon; ModIr. Aoi [Ir., poetic inspiration, learning, metrical composition; son of master poet]. The poet of the *Tuatha Dé Danann. When Aí was in his mother's womb, a blast of wind shook the house and a druid prophesied the birth of a wonderful child. He was sent against the sons of *Carman.

Aíbell, Áebill, Aoibheall, Aoibhell, Aoibhil, Eevell, Ibhell; also Aíbinn, Eevin [Ir., radiance, spark, fire]. Old Irish goddess or fairy queen, associated with north *Munster, a patron of the O'Briens. Her fairy mound is at Craig Liath (also Craigeevil), near Killaloe, Co. Clare. Comparable to both *Áine and *Clídna, she was a rival of the latter for the affections of *Caomh. Clídna put her under a spell and changed her into a white cat. In other accounts, she accompanied *Brian

Bórama (Boru) to *Clontarf and became a lover of an attendant, *Dubhlaing, to Brian's oldest son.

Aíbell figures in many works of Irish literature including the 18th-century *Cúirt an Mheáin Oíche* or *Midnight Court* of Brian Merriman and *The Mock Aeneid* of Donnchadh Ruadh Mac Conmara (MacNamara). Also the name of the wife of *Áed (8).

Aíbgréne, Aíb Gréne, Aoibhgréine [Ir., radiance of the sun, ray of sunshine, sunny face]. The daughter of *Deirdre and Noíse in *Longas mac nUislenn* [The Exile of the Sons of Uisnech]. Later she was thought to marry Rinn, son of *Eochaid Iúil, king of the *Otherworld.

Aicher, Aichear [Ir., sharp, fierce, keen]. One of the musicians of the *Fianna in the *Fenian Cycle.

Aichlech mac Dubdrenn, Aichleach. The killer of *Fionn mac Cumhaill in battle at Áth Brea on the *Boyne River, according to *Aided Finn* [The Violent Death of Fionn]; see S. H. O'Grady, *Silva Gadelica*, ii (London, 1892), 96–9. Cf. the better-known death of Fionn at the hands of five warriors in **Cath Gabhra*.

Aidan. Common anglicization of *Áedán.

Aíde, Aeté. Second wife of *Énna (2), as recorded in the Irish *Dindshenchas. Her death, and the subsequent death of Énna's first wife, *Dub, are associated with the naming of *Dublin.

Aided [OIr., violent death; act of killing; unpleasant fate, plight]. A conventional, tone-defining first word in the title of number of Old Irish narratives. Plural Oitte; see also ModIr. OIDHEADH, OIDHE. See Daniel F. Melia, *Studia Hibernica*, 17/18 (1978), 36–57.

Aided Fergusa, *Fhergusa, Ferguso* [Ir., The Violent Death of Fergus]. One of the bawdiest of early Irish narratives, it includes many instances of sexual hyperbole and braggadocio. *Fergus mac Léti, the king of *Ulster, makes love to the tiny queen *Bebo and afterwards taunts her husband *Iubdán with the tale. See text in S. H. O'Grady, *Silva Gadelica*, ii (London, 1892), 244ff.

Aided Fraích. A chapter of the **Táin Bó Cuailnge* [Cattle Raid of Cooley], often the fifth. See Garrett Olmstead, 'On the Origin of the Aided Fraích Episode in the Táin Bó Cuailnge', *Études Celtiques*, 15 (1978), 537–47.

Aided Máele Fhothartaig maic Rónáin [Ir., The Death of Máel Fothartaig Son of Rónán]. Alternate title for **Fingal Rónáin* [Ir., How Rónán Killed His Son].

Aided Óenfhir Aífe [Ir., The Tragic Death of Aífe's Only Son; also The Tragic Death of Connla]. A short foretale of the **Táin Bó Cuailnge* [Cattle Raid of Cooley], dealing with *Cúchulainn's unwitting killing of his own son in combat. The story is an Irish instance of the international tale best known in the Persian narrative of Sohrab and Rustum (folk motif: N731.2).

The men of Ulster were assembled when they saw a boy coming on the sea in a boat of bronze with gilded oars. The men were awe-struck at the boy's powers to make birds do his will. They sent two champions to challenge him, but he defied them both. Only Cúchulainn seemed equal to the task. As he was summoned, his then wife *Emer begged him not to go because she said that the boy was the son of Cúchulainn's earlier encounter with *Aífe, and thus his only son. The hero disparaged such womanish talk and said that he would kill the boy for the honour of Ulster.

As the two challengers met, Cúchulainn demanded to know the boy's name and said his opponent would die if he would not tell. The boy responded with a stroke of his sword, shaving the older man's head. They began to wrestle, and Cúchulainn thrust at the boy so hard that his feet penetrated into stone up to his ankles. They went into the water, hoping to drown one another. At last Cúchulainn cast his spear, *Gae Bolga, into the boy, at which the latter cried, 'That is what *Scáthach did not teach me.' Because Scáthach had also taught Cúchulainn, the older man immediately knew the boy's identity. He took Connla in his arms, carried him ashore, and cast him before the Ulsterman. 'Here is my son,' he said.

See commentary by Jan de Vries, 'Das Motiv der Vater-Sohn-Kampfes im Hildebrandslied', *Germanisch-romanische Monatsschrift*, 3 (1953), 257- 74; de Vries' 'Nachschrift' in the same volume, 257–74, is expanded into 'Le Conte irlandais *Aided óenfhir Aífe . . .*', *Ogam*, 9 (1957), 122–38. Vernam E. Hull, 'The Death of Connla', *Zeitschrift für celtische Philologie*, 29 (1962/4), 190–1. Much of this story is used by W. B. Yeats in his poem 'Cuchulain's Fight with the Sea' (1892), where the son is known as Finmole, and in his play *On Baile's Strand* (1904); it is also retold in the ballad 'Sons of North Britain', as collected in *Nova Scotia. James *Macpherson transmogrified it in his 'Carthon' of the *Poems of Ossian* (1763).

Aideen, Aidín. Variants of *Étaín.

Aidne. Variant of *Adná.

Aífe, Aoife, Áeife, Eefa [Ir., pleasant, beautiful, radiant]. An ancient name in Ireland borne by many mythical and legendary heroines. T. F. O'Rahilly associates the name with the Gaulish goddess Esuvia. It is commonly anglicized as Eva.

Aífe **1.** An Amazonian chieftainess, 'the hardest woman warrior in the world', who lived in *Alba [Scotland], according to several early Irish narratives. The daughter of Ardgeimm, she was frequently in conflict with *Scáthach, who may be her double. Aífe cared for nothing so much as her horses and her chariot, and may have links with such Continental figures as *Epona. In the best-known story about her, a pupil of Scáthach, the great Ulster hero *Cúchulainn, vanquished her in combat and later begat the child *Connla upon her. Cúchulainn later unwittingly killed the son. The story of her encounter with Cúchulainn is told in *Tochmarc Emire* [The Wooing of Emer]; and the death of Connla is in **Aided Óenfhir Aífe* [The Death of Aífe's Only Son].

2. The third of the three wives of Lir in **Oidheadh Chlainne Lir* [The Tragic Story of the Children of Lir]. She was the daughter of *Ailill Aulomm and the sister of the children's mother, Áeb, and she became the cruel stepmother who transformed them into *swans.

3. The daughter of Dealbhaoth and lover of Ilbrec, she was transformed into a *crane by *Iuchra, a jealous rival. As an amphibian, she spent much of her time in the water, the realm of *Manannán mac Lir. When she died Manannán made her skin into the celebrated *crane bag, which contained marvellous treasures and belonged to a succession of Irish gods and heroes.

4. The daughter of Belchú, wife of the Ulster hero *Conall Cearnach; also known as Lendabair.

5. The daughter of Russ *Failge and the queen of a legendary king of *Ulster.

6. Daughter of *Ábartach in the *Fenian ballads, who was changed into a heron by her jealous rival *Iuchra (2).

Aífe Derg, Dearg [Ir., red Aífe]. Daughter of a king of *Connacht who had her marriage arranged by St *Patrick.

Aífe Foltfhind [Ir., Aífe of the fair hair]. A daughter of the king of *Ulster. See also MONGFHIND (Mong Bán) [fair mane].

Aige. The daughter of Broccaid mac Bricc, sister of *Faifne, who, through envy of her neighbours, was given a *síabair [distorter, enchanter, elf] who transformed her into a *fawn and sent her on a circuit all around Ireland. She was later slain by the warriors of Meilge, son of King *Cobthach (2), leaving only a bag of water that was thrown into a river bearing her name. *Faifne, Aige's brother, tried to avenge her death but was killed by Meilge.

Ail na Mírenn, Aill na Mureann. See UISNECH.

Ailbe, Ailbhe [cf. Ir. *albho-*, white; Gaul. Albiorix, world-king]. The name of both men and women in Old Irish narrative, including twelve warriors of the *Fianna in the *Fenian Cycle and two saints. Incorrectly anglicized as Albert or Bertie.

Ailbe **1.** Daughter of the fairy king *Midir.

2. Daughter of the high king Máel Sechnaill [Malachy] (d. 862) and the mother of Cerball, warrior-king of *Ossory.

3. Daughter of *Cormac mac Airt in **Echtrae Cormaic* [The Adventure of Cormac] who is granted to the strange warrior as the first of his wishes but later returned.

Ailbe, Saint. Patron of the church of Emly, Co. Tipperary. His death date is either AD 526, 531, or 541. According to tradition he was suckled by a wolf and acknowledged all his days a 'kinship with the milk'. Although modern commentators admit that his life is a 'confusion of vague legends', he retains his place in the calendar of saints, 12 September. He may be identical with the St Ailbe visited by St *Brendan in the *Navigatio*.

Ailbe Grúadbrecc [Ir., Ailbe of the freckled cheeks]. Daughter of *Cormac mac Airt and sister of *Gráinne. After Gráinne's infidelity to *Fionn mac Cumhaill and subsequent disgrace, the *Fenian leader wooed Ailbe and asked her a series of riddles; he asked her to live in the forest with him and be his wife. According to the testimony of Caílte, Ailbe was one of the four best lovers among the women of Ireland of his time. Her story is found in the *Tochmarc Ailbe*, trans. Whitley Stokes, in J. F. Campbell, *Leabhar na Feinne* (London, 1872), 151ff.

Aileach, Ailech, Oileach, Grianán Ailig [Ir., rock]. A great stone fort dating from perhaps early Christian times at Inishowen Head in north-east Co. Donegal, 5 miles W of [London]Derry, on the western entrance to Lough Foyle. Although the word grianán [sun porch] has an early association with the site, the structure is clearly not a sun porch; the names Grianán of Ailech and Greenan Elly are romantic attributions from the 19th century. In the Old Irish **Lebor Gabála* [Book of Invasions], it is Ailech Néit; also Aileach Ned. 'Capital' of *Ulster after the destruction of *Emain Macha, Aileach was once the equal of *Tara, *Cashel, *Cruachain, or *Naas. Standing on a high (803 feet) promontory, the ring fort commands one of the most spectacular panoramic views to be had from any man-made structure in the British Isles.

By tradition it was built by the *Tuatha Dé Danann and became one of their most important fortresses. When *Ith the *Milesian spy came to examine the country, he was slain by warriors who came from Aileach. The architect and stonemason of the fortress was Ringin. In some stories the fortress is thought to be occupied by Frigriun mac Rubai Ruaid and is called Aileach Frigrenn. According to some traditions *Nuadu Airgetlám is buried here. In Irish history Aileach became the seat of the *Uí Néill, when *Eógan (1), son of *Niall Noígiallach [of the Nine Hostages], seized it *c.*425; his line continued until *c.*1200. We cannot know today what Aileach looked like in ancient times, as it was 'reconstructed' by Dr Bernard of Derry *c.*1870.

Ailean nan Sop [ScG, Allan of the Straws]. A well-known character in Scottish Gaelic folk-tales. His birth was delayed for twenty-four months by the jealous wife of his natural father; thus he was born with a full set of teeth. See J. G. Campbell, *Witchcraft and Second Sight in the Highlands and Islands of Scotland* (Glasgow, 1902; repr. 1974), 45ff.

Aileel. A variant of *Ailill used by W. B. Yeats and other Anglo-Irish writers.

Ailenn. Variant of *Dún Aillinne.

Áilgesach, Áilgheasach. See ATHAIRNE ÁILGESACH.

Ailibhin. Variant of *Ainnle, especially in Scottish texts.

Ailill, Oilill, Ailell, Aleel [Ir., sprite, elf; cf. W *ellyll*]. An extremely popular name in early Ireland, borne by countless figures including at least two saints, ten warriors of the Fianna in the *Fenian Cycle, and a host of petty kings in genealogies. Perhaps the most widely known figure of this name is *Ailill mac Máta, the husband of *Medb in the **Táin Bó Cuailnge* [Cattle Raid of Cooley]. Eoin MacNeill once suggested that some Ailills, despite different epithets, may be identical or may have borrowed aspects of each other's histories. The name was once arbitrarily latinized as Elias and anglicized as Oliver.

Ailill 1. The leader of a Connacht war-party, he fought a battle with *Fothad Canainne, who had taken away his wife with her consent.

2. Son of *Eochaid Mugmedón and Mongfhind in **Echtra Mac nEchach Muigmedóin* [The Adventure of the Sons of Eochaid Mugmedón]. He accedes to the seniority of his half-brother, *Niall Noígiallach [of the Nine Hostages].

3. Father of *Étaín in **Tochmarc Étaíne* [The Wooing of Étaíne].

Ailill Áine, Áne. Father of the legendary *Labraid Loingseach, ancestor of the *Lagin, a historical people of early Leinster. Not to be confused with *Ailill Aulomm, who may have made love to *Áine, a fairy goddess.

Ailill Ánglonnach, Anguba [cf. Ir. *anglondach*, warlike, valiant]. The brother of *Eochaid Airem who is smitten with Étaín, Eochaid's wife. When Ailill fell ill the physician *Fachtna (1) told him that there were two pains in him that medicine could not cure: the pain of love and the pain of jealousy. While her husband was away, Ailill revealed his trouble to Étaín, who agreed to become his mistress, not for sin, but to save a member of the royal family (Ailill) from death. She did not want to deceive her husband in *Tara and thus made an assignation for a nearby hill-top. Étaín met with a man she believed to be Ailill, but it turned out to be her husband from a previous incarnation, *Midir, who wished to save her from dishonour. This story is told in the second part of **Tochmarc Étaíne* [The Wooing of Étaín].

Ailill Aulomm, Aulom, Ólom, Ólum, Olum [Ir., Ailill bare-ear]. The father of *Eógan (3) and foster-father of *Lugaid mac Con, fratricidal foster-brothers in a dynastic dispute. T. F. O'Rahilly (1946) believed that the widely known story of Ailill's having ravished the fairy goddess *Áine (1) and being slain by her was invented by later storytellers to explain his epithet. His story was probably the model for Maurice's impregnation of Áine (1), begetting *Gerald, Earl of Desmond. He was also the father of *Díchorb, *Aífe (2), and *Cian (3), and brother of *Lugaid Lága. Not to be confused with *Ailill Áine. See also ECHDAE [Ir. horse-god (?)], another husband of Áine (1).

Ailill Dubdétach, Dubhdédach [Ir., black tooth]. Monstrous brother of the beautiful *Delbcháem, who challenges and is slain by *Art mac Cuinn in *Echtrae Airt meic Cuinn*.

Ailill Érann. Another name for *Bolg or Bolga, an ancestor-deity of the *Fir Bolg in the *Lebor Gabála* [Book of Invasions].

Ailill mac Máta, mac Matach. The husband of *Medb in the *Táin Bó Cuailnge* [Cattle Raid of Cooley]. Although he is often described as being 'of Connacht', like his wife, the text of the *Táin* describes him as coming from Leinster, of the family of Russ Ruad. His patronymic distinguishes him from other Ailills, but it is not often used in the text of narratives. He appeared somewhat henpecked in the pillow-talk opening of the *Táin* but Medb praised him for many qualities, including bravery. Nevertheless, Ailill persisted in demanding that Medb should not have more possessions than he did. Their daughters are *Finnabair and *Faife.

In another story, *Táin Bó Fraich* [Cattle Raid of Fraich], Ailill is a stern father and wily king who opposes the marriage of his daughter Finnabair with *Fráech to the point of nearly killing the younger man, relenting only when Fráech kills a *dragon and recovers a ring swallowed by a *salmon.

He assists *Angus Óg to besiege *Ethal Anbúail, with whose daughter Angus Óg has fallen in love. He sends Nera on his quest in *Echtra Nerai* [The Adventure of Nera]. Later, Ailill is slain by *Conall Cearnach at Medb's urging when she finds her husband unfaithful.

Ailill Ochair Ága, Ochir Ága [Ir. *Ailill*, edge of battle]. The father of Máel Dúin in *Imram Curaig Maíle Dúin* [The Voyage of Máel Dúin's Boat]. Ailill was a warrior of the *Eóganacht of Ninuss (on the Aran Islands) who begot his son by seducing a nun who had come to strike the midnight bell; the mother died in childbirth and the son was fostered by a queen, a friend of the mother. Ailill was later killed by marauders from Laois.

Ailill Ólum, Olum, Ólom. Variants of *Ailill Aulomm.

Ailinn, Aillinn. The lover of *Baile in *Scél Baili Binnbérlaig* [The Story of Baile of the Clear Voice].

Ailinn. Variant of *Dún Aillinne.

Aill na Mureann, Ail na Mírenn. See UISNECH.

Ailleann. Variant of *Dún Ailinne.

Aillén, Ailléne, Ellén, Oillín [Ir. *ellén*, monstrous; cf. Ir. *ailill*, sprite; W *ellyll*, spirit]. Several figures in early Irish narrative bear this name, the best known of which was *Aillén mac Midgna.

Aillén 1. The brother of the fairy queen *Áine (1), he fell in love with a wife of *Manannán mac Lir. When Manannán became smitten with Áine, he agreed to hand over his then wife to Aillén so that he might be free to be with the fairy queen.

Aillén mac Midgna, Midna, Midhna. The 'burner' who brought destruction upon *Tara until he was slain by *Fionn mac Cumhaill on the latter's first visit there. Aillén was a fairy musician of the *Tuatha Dé Danann who resided at the *sídh *Finnachaid, also a home at different times to *Lir. Every *Samain [Halloween], Aillén would come to Tara playing on his timpán. After the men of Tara were lulled to sleep by his music, Aillén would spew forth flaming rock from his mouth and burn the dwelling to the ground. Each year Tara would be rebuilt, and for each of twenty-three years Ailill returned, until Fionn arrived on the scene. The hero first made himself immune to Aillén's musical charms by inhaling the poison of his own spear, whose point was so venomous as to forbid sleep. After this Fionn skewered Aillén with his poisoned point. T. F. O'Rahilly once argued that Aillén mac Midgna was really the *Fenian hero *Goll mac Morna, an assertion that has not found wide acceptance.

Aillén Trechenn, Trechend [Ir., triple-headed]. A triple-headed monster that came forth from its cave or mound at *Cruachain, Co. Roscommon, on the eve of *Samain [Halloween] to devastate Ireland. The creature harboured special aggression towards *Emain Macha and the Hill of *Tara. *Amairgin (2) dispatched the beast.

Aillinn. Variant spelling of *Ailinn.

Aillinne. Variant of *Dún Aillinne.

Aímend. According to early Irish legend, she was a daughter of a king of the *Corcu Loígde, a historical people. Circumstances imply she was a sun goddess.

Aimhirghin. ModIr. variant of *Amairgin.

Ainder, Ainnir [Ir., a young woman]. In the *Fenian Cycle, the daughter of *Barrán and wife of *Caílte.

Áindle. OIr. spelling of *Ainnle.

Áine (Ainé, an occasional corrupt form) [Ir., brightness, glow, radiance; splendour, glory, fame]. Name of a multitude of figures, both male and female, from early Ireland. Male bearers of this name appear to be historical and are cited in genealogies, especially of the Ciarraige family, who lived along what is now the Limerick-Kerry border in pre-Norman times. It is not now possible to know which Áine is commemorated in place-names such as Lios Áine 'Lissan', Northern Ireland, or Dún Áine 'Dunany', at the entrance to Dundalk Bay, Co. Louth.

Áine 1. The fairy goddess, patroness of love, desire, and fertility whose usual seat is at *Cnoc Áine or Knockainy in east Co. Limerick, near *Lough Gur. Many commentators have felt that this Áine draws much from *Ana, the goddess after whom the *Tuatha Dé Danann are named. T. F. O'Rahilly argued (1946) that the evidence of her name suggests she was originally a sun-goddess. Different sources speak of her father as *Fer Í [Ir., man of yew] or as *Eógabal, a foster-son of *Manannán mac Lir. Fer Í may be the father and Eógabal the grandfather, or Eógabal the father and Fer Í a brother; or they may be one and the same.

Áine has a series of lovers, both mortal and immortal. The best known of them is probably Maurice, Earl of Desmond, who fell in love with her at first sight. He gained control over her by seizing her cloak, and made her his bride. Their son was *Gerald, Earl of Desmond, who still lives, according to legend, deep in the waters of Lough Gur, reappearing every seven years to ride around it on a shining white horse. He may also swim across the lake in the form of a goose. Some Munster families claim descent from him. The story bears much resemblance to the Welsh Gwragedd Annwn. Áine may be an ancestor of the character known as Black Annis in Leicestershire folklore. Folk motifs: C30; C31; F302.2.

Áine was ravished by *Ailill Aulomm, by whom she became the mother of *Eógan, ancestor of the *Eóganacht. Although less well known, this story may have served as the model for Maurice's begetting of Gerald, Earl of Desmond. In some Eóganacht genealogies *Echdae [Ir., horse-god (?)] is described as the husband of Áine.

Many stories link Áine with Manannán mac Lir, the sea-god. Áine's brother Aillén (1) was in love with Manannán's then (but unnamed) wife, just as Manannán was in love with Áine. Áine's remedy for the unrequited passion was to have Manannán deliver his wife to Aillén so that the god could be with Áine. Manannán took her to *Tír Tairngire [the Land of Promise]. Variant texts assert that Manannán was either the father or husband instead of lover of Áine.

In the north of Ireland Áine was thought to be a mortal woman who was spirited away at night from her husband's side. In the south she was thought to have a neighbour named Grian, a goddess who dwelt at *Cnoc Gréine, a hill about 7 miles distant from Cnoc Áine. She is also linked to Cnoc Áine and the well Tobar Áine near Lissan, Co. [London]Derry, and Cnoc Áine near Augher, Co. Waterford. As Grian is also descended from Fer Í or Eógabal, some commentators believe she is the same figure as Áine under a different name. Áine is often thought to be a counterpart of both *Aíbell and *Clídna.

2. This lover of the *Fenian Cycle may be a different character, or she may be *Áine of *Cnoc Áine with a different genealogy. Her father is either Cuilenn, a smith, or a king of Scotland. In some versions she would sleep with no man but *Fionn, who wooed and won her, giving her two sons. In another version Áine and a sister, Milucra, both loved Fionn, but neither could have him. Milucra transformed Fionn into an old man, but Áine gave him a potion that restored his youth. Despite this kindness, Fionn would not marry Áine.

Ainge. A daughter of the *Dagda. When twigs Ainge was gathering were stolen by Gaible, son of *Nuadu, they became a forest springing up in every direction.

Ainnir 1. ModIr. variant of *Ainder.

2. In *Macpherson's *Ossian*, a Norseman from Lochlin and a barbarous fellow; the father of *Erragon, Trothar, and the hated Starno.

Ainnle, Áinle, Ánle, Áindle [Ir., hero, warrior, champion]. The name of several figures from early Ireland, most notably one of the three sons of *Uisnech, who followed his brother Noíse in eloping with *Deirdre to Scotland; thought to have a tenor voice, in contrast to his brother *Ardan, a baritone. *Macpherson based the character of *Sithallin on him.

Aireach. Variant spelling of *Erech Febria.

Airem, Aiream. Epithet of *Eochaid Airem.

Airennán. Variant spelling of *Erannán.

Airgetlám, Argetlám [Ir., silver hand]. An agnomen of *Nuadu.

Airgialla, Oirghialla, Oriel [Ir., those who have submitted (?), hostage-givers (?)]. One of three proto-kingdoms or realms in the north of pre-Nordic Ireland, along with *Ailech and *Ulaid. Airgialla territory was on a line from Lough Foyle to the mouth of the Newry River and included much of counties Armagh and Monaghan, and portions of Louth, Down, and Fermanagh, or the southern half of Northern Ireland and adjacent areas in the Republic of Ireland. Airgialla was early conquered by the *Uí Néill, who used the lands as a power-base for later expansion.

Airioch Feabhruadh. Variant spelling of *Erech Febria.

Airmid, Airmed, Airmedh [cf. Ir. *airmed*, measure of grain, dry measure]. Daughter of *Dian Cécht, the physician or leech of the *Tuatha Dé Danann, and sister of Miach. She assisted her brother in attempting to restore the real hand of *Nuadu after her father had made a silver substitute. Later, after her jealous father had killed her brother, Airmid attempted to classify the magical herbs that grew from his grave.

aisling, aislinge (older spelling, often with prose texts) [Ir., vision, dream]. A conventional form of Irish poetry, often employing patriotic themes in a fanciful setting; perhaps of late medieval origin but most widely practised from the 17th to 19th centuries, especially in Munster. According to the formula, (1) the poet is out walking when he meets a beautiful lady, usually Ireland personified; (2) he describes her appearance, often employing the rose and the lily in the imagery; (3) he begins a conversation with her. During the 18th century Jacobite poets were especially fond of the aisling. See Gerard Murphy, 'Notes on *Aisling* Poetry', *Eigse*, 1 (1939–40), 40–50. See also FÍS.

Aislinge Meic Con Glinne, *meic Conglinne* [Ir., Vision of Mac Con Glinne]. An Irish anticlerical satire composed in the 12th century, it uses the aislinge (but not the conventional form of Irish poetry cited above) to parody Irish institutions; it is known in two versions, one shorter than the other. The text, often compared to the work of Villon, attacks both ecclesiastical and literary establishments as well as abundance in a land of want.

The scholar Ainiér Mac Con Glinne, famous for his gifts of satire and eulogy, left his work in Roscommon and travelled to Cork in search of better food. The monastic guesthouse he visited in Cork was ill-kept and vermin-ridden. When Mac Con Glinne criticized the reception he received, the abbot, Manchín, ordered that he be beaten, stripped of his clothing, and sentenced to death. On the morning before the execution, Mac Con Glinne related a vision he had during the night. It was filled with images of food: a boat of lard sailing on a sea of new milk, and so on. The abbot then realized that Mac Con Glinne was just the man to drive out the demon of gluttony then inhabiting the local king, *Cathal (d. 742). In a droll exorcism, the narrator observed that the demon of gluttony would have consumed all of Ireland had it not been driven out by the wise scholar.

See Kuno Meyer, *Aislinge Meic Conglinne* (London, 1892); K. Jackson (ed.), *Aislinge Meic Conglinne* (Dublin, 1990). Austin Clarke retells a portion of *Aislinge Meic Con Glinne* in his drama *The Son of Learning* (1927).

Aislinge Óenguso. Old Irish narrative found in the **Book of Leinster* (*c.*1150), usually known in English as The Vision of Angus, which tells of the love of the god *Angus Óg and a *swan maiden. Angus Óg was a lover wasted by longing for a young woman he had seen only in a dream. When she disappeared from the dream, Angus searched for her for one year; later *Bodb Derg discovered that she was Cáer, daughter of *Ethal Anbúail. She spent alternate years in human and in swan form. Angus approached her during her swan year and was himself transformed into a swan with her. Together they flew off to Angus's palace at *Brug na Bóinne. On their way they chanted such wondrous music that none who heard it could sleep for three days and three nights.

A modern edition is by Francis Shaw (Dublin, 1934). The same narrative in oral tradition is usually titled *Angus Óg agus Caer.*

Aitheach-thúath, aithech-thuatha [Ir., vassals, rent-paying peoples]. According to the **Lebor Gabála* [Book of Invasions], they were pre-Gaelic people of Ireland who rebelled against the *Milesians, with short-lived success.

Aithechda, Aithechdae [Ir., vassal, peasant, churl, plebe]. According to the **Lebor Gabála* [Book of Invasions] a son of *Japheth, son of Noah, and ancestor of *Partholón. His is the oldest non-biblical name in the pedigree of post-diluvian invaders.

aithed, aitheda, aithedha [Ir., elopement, flight]. Name of a category of narratives in Old Irish literature; see also TOCHMARC [wooing].

Aithirne. Name of a kind of satire in Old Irish literature. The famous poet and satirist *Athairne Áilgesach takes his name from the concept.

Alator [Brit., he who rears or nourishes his people]. God of Celtic Britain, invoked in an inscription at Barkway, Hertfordshire, which links him with Gaulish *Mars.

Alba. The Scottish Gaelic and Modern Irish name for *Scotland; see also ALBU. See T. F. O'Rahilly, 'On the Name *Alba*', in *Early Irish History and Mythology* (Dublin, 1946), 385–7.

Alban. The Welsh and Cornish name for *Scotland.

Albha. Variant of *Áeb.

Albiorix. Occasional epithet of *Mars.

Albu. The Old Irish name first for all of Great Britain, or 'Albion', and later just for the northern part, *Scotland. The change in meaning came from the Irish settlement of *Dál Riada in *Argyllshire, whose inhabitants were known as Fir Alban [the men in Britain]. See also ALBA.

Alcluith. Ancient British name for a hill on the banks of the Leven where it meets the Clyde at Dumbarton, Scotland. It is identical with Dumbarton [ScG *dùn*, hill, fortress, mound; *breatann*, of the Britons] itself. The name was recorded as Alcluith in Bede's *History* (AD 731) and probably serves as a basis for *Macpherson's *Balclutha.

alder [OE *alor*]. A shrub or tree (genus *Alnus*) of the birch family that has special implications in Celtic tradition. The alder usually grows in wet ground, with small, pendulous catkins. Alders are especially associated with *Bran; at *Cad Goddeu, 'The Battle of the Trees', Gwydion guessed Bran's name from the alder twigs in his hand. The answer to an old *Taliesin riddle 'Why is the alder purple?' is 'Because Bran wore purple'. Bran's alder may be a symbol of resurrection. The name for the boy *Gwern, son of *Matholwch and *Branwen, means 'alder'. The place-name *Fernmag (ang. *Farney) means 'plain of the alder'.

In Ireland the alder was regarded with awe apparently because when cut the wood turns from white to red. At one time the felling of an alder was punishable, and it is still avoided. The alder was thought to have power of divination, especially in the diagnosing of diseases. Alder or *yew might be used in the *fé, a rod for measuring corpses and graves in pre-Christian Ireland. The letter F, third consonant in the *ogham alphabet, was named for the alder (OIr. fern). ModIr. fearnóg; ScG feàrna; Manx farney; W gwernen; Corn. gwernen; Bret. gwernenn. See also FAIRY TREE.

ale [OE *ealu*]. A favourite drink of the ancient Celts was fermented malt with hops, what we call ale when it has a heavier body than the Teutonic beer. Malaliach (or Samaliliath) the *Partholonian introduced ale-drinking into Ireland, and the ale of *Goibniu confers immortality on the drinker; Angus Óg drinks it. *Fand entertains *Cúchulainn with a bottomless vat of ale. *Conn Cétchathach [of the Hundred Battles] drank *dergfhlaith, the red ale or red sovereignty, as he had been bidden to by the goddess of *Sovereignty. Ale-bearers appear in many early Irish and Welsh narratives. OIr. linn, cuirm; ModIr. and ScG leann; Manx lhune; W cwrw; Corn. cor', cor'f, coref; Bret. laour. See also BRACIACA.

Aleel. Variant of *Ailill used by W. B. Yeats and others.

Alenecma. Name used by *Macpherson for *Connacht.

Alesia. Fortified settlement or oppidum of the Celts in eastern Gaul, in what is today Burgundy, according to *Diodorus Siculus (1st cent. BC). It was founded by *Hercules after his affair with the Gaulish princess *Galata. Base of *Vercingetorix's ill-fated resistance to Roman conquest in 52 BC.

Alisanos. Gaulish god of the rock, an animation of landscape feature, as recorded in Roman commentaries. He may be identical with Alisonos, who was invoked at *Alesia, a possible eponymous spirit of the site.

Allaid [cf. OIr. *allaid*, wild, undomesticated]. A druid in *Macpherson's *Ossian* (1760), called 'son of the rock', an allusion to his dwelling among rocks and caverns.

Allantide [MidE *Alhalwyn-tyd*, All-Hallow's Tide; cf. Corn. *aval*, apple]. Name in Cornwall for Halloween, counterpart of *Hollantide in Wales or Irish *Samain, which Cornish oral tradition steadfastly insists is (1) the *apple time, and (2) a feast sacred to an obscure 6th-century Cornish or Breton saint, *Arlan, Elwin, or Allen.

Allen, Bog of [Ir. *Móin Almhaine*]. The boggy, peat- (or turf-)filled plain that extends over much of central Ireland; it extends far beyond the environs of the Hill of *Allen in Co. Kildare.

Allen, Hill of [cf. OIr. *Almu*; ModIr. *Almhain, Almhaine* (gen.), *Almha, Almhuin, Allmhuinn*; thought to be named after a daughter of a warrior in the *Tuatha Dé Danann]. Also anglicized as Alvin. A hill in Co. Kildare, 676 feet high, about 6 miles NE of Kildare town. The Hill is conventionally portrayed as the home or 'palace' of *Fionn mac Cumhaill and his *Fianna in the *Fenian Cycle. Fionn won the residence by compelling his maternal grandfather, *Tadg mac Nuadat, to surrender it. *Nuadu Necht, an aspect of *Nuadu Airgetlám, had been an earlier resident of the Hill. Although archaeological evidence does not indicate the presence of any castle or palace, the Hill is thought to occupy the site of a prehistoric tumulus. The Hill of Allen is the site of an early 8th-century battle, during which *Fergal, the king of *Tara, was killed. In celebrations after the battle, the severed head of the retainer *Donn Bó sang in honour of Fergal's severed head; see Nora K. Chadwick, 'Geilt', *Scottish Gaelic Studies*, 5 (1942), 106–53; Pádraig Ó Riain, *Cath Almaine* (Dublin, 1978). In 1859–63 Sir Gerald Aylmer of Donadea built a tower here, a great 19th-century folly. Today, the Hill is locally called an 'island' because it is surrounded by bogland. See also ALLEN, BOG OF.

Allen, Saint. See ARLAN, SAINT.

Allmhuin. See ALLEN, HILL OF.

Allod, Allot. Sometimes named as the father of *Manannán; his patronymic, mac Lir, merely draws on the genitive, lir, of the Old Irish ler [sea].

Almha, Almhain, Almhaine (gen.), Almhuin, Almu, See ALLEN, HILL OF.

alphabet. See OGMA; OGHAM.

alp-luachra. An Irish instance of an international type of *fairy known as the joint-eater. The alp-luachra may be male or female; it inhabits the body of a human, much as a tapeworm in everyday life, and consumes most of the food the poor victim tries to eat. It may also sit beside the victim. Douglas Hyde recounts a story in *Beside the Fire* (London, 1890) of a man infested with thirteen alp-luachra. He was advised to eat a great quantity of salt beef while drinking nothing. He was then made to lie down with his open mouth above a stream until the fairies jumped out to quench their thirst.

Altclut, Alt Clut. Old name for *Dumbarton.

Althan. The chief bard of Arth or Art, king of Ireland in *Macpherson's *Ossian* (1760).

Althos. One of the sons of *Usnoth in *Macpherson's *Ossian* (1760).

Altrom Tige Dá Medar, *Altram Tige dá Medar* [Ir., The Nurture of the Houses of the Two Milk Vessels]. A late Middle Irish narrative of the *Mythological Cycle included in the 15th-century **Book of Fermoy*. Scholarly attention in the story has focused on the dispersal of the immortals, the *Tuatha Dé Danann, into the world of men, and on possible distant parallels with the French legend of the Holy Grail.

After their defeat at *Tailtiu and Druim Ligen, the remainder of the Tuatha Dé Danann, on the advice of *Manannán mac Lir, scattered themselves to the fairy mounds, hills, and plains of Ireland. They chose *Bodb as their king, but Manannán appointed them to their dwellings in the fairy mounds. He also instituted (1) *féth fiada [the veil of invisibility] to keep them from being seen; (2) the Feast of *Goibniu, to protect them against old age; and (3) the Pigs of Manannán, to be killed for food yet preserved for sustenance. Manannán also told them how to lay out their houses in the manner of *Emain Ablach. Shortly after this Manannán and others were invited to a banquet at *Brug na Bóinne by *Elcmar, a magician, and his fosterling, *Angus Óg. In the evening, after Manannán ordered the hall cleared, he told Angus Óg that Elcmar was not destined to occupy the splendid palace at Brug na Bóinne and that he, Angus, should expel him. After teaching Angus a powerful spell, Manannán also acknowledged that there was a God above gods, and retold the Old Testament story of the rebellion of the angels and the creation of man.

After Elcmar was expelled, Angus gave a banquet and asked that all present give him a child for *fosterage. All complied, including Manannán. Most interestingly, the wife of the steward at Brug na Bóinne bore a child named Eithne (see EITHNE (3)), of surpassing beauty and virtue. Eithne was courted by many suitors, including *Finnbarr, who insulted her with a lewd remark, for which he apologized. Because of the insult Eithne fasted for seven days, at which time she accepted milk from Angus's marvellous cow, brought from India, which she milked herself.

When news of Eithne's shame and unwillingness to eat reached Manannán, he summoned her to *Cruithín na Cuan in Emain Ablach. Manannán prepared food with his own hands, but Eithne would not eat it, preferring instead milk from his marvellous brindled cow, also brought from India. Manannán then diagnosed her ailment: when she was insulted the demon of the Tuatha Dé Danann left her and she could no longer partake of their food. She might, however, drink from the cows of India, as it was a land of righteousness. At this point she has partaken of the Nurture of the Houses of Two Milk Vessels, hence the title of the story. She remarked that henceforth the Trinity of Three Persons would be her god. From that time, through the many centuries to the coming of St *Patrick, Eithne lived only on the milk of the marvellous cows.

One day, after bathing in a river with friends, she realized that she had lost the power of *féth fiada* [*invisibility] and thus could not find her companions. She came instead to a church door, where she saw a cleric praising the Lord. After telling him her story, she decided to profess his faith. Not even Angus could dissuade her. St Patrick himself came to help Eithne to resist her former companions. She was lonely when they left her, and asked Patrick to baptize her and forgive her sins. Two weeks later she died and went directly to heaven. Patrick spoke an elegy, *marbnaid*, in her honour. *Ceall Eithne* at Brug na Bóinne is named after her. Eithne's companion, Curcóg, a daughter of Manannán, was in charge of the company of women at Brug na Boínne.

Some commentators see Eithne's unwillingness to eat fairy food as a parallel to the Greek Persephone's reluctance to eat the food of Hades. This Eithne (3) appears to be related to *Eithne (4) of oral tradition, the mortal woman who departed with *Finnbheara, king of the Connacht fairies. The text was edited and translated by Lilian Duncan, *Ériu*, 11 (1932), 184–225. Portions of the narrative were used by Austin Clarke in his prose romance *Sun Dances at Easter* (Dublin, 1952) and drama *The Moment Next to Nothing* (Dublin, 1958).

Alvin. Anglicization of Almhain, etc.; see ALLEN, HILL OF.

AM. See ANNO MUNDI.

Amadán [Ir., fool; cf. ScG *amadan*, OIr. *ammatán*]. A figure in Irish and Scottish Gaelic folklore who may assume both benevolent and malevolent roles. *Amadán Mór*, the Great Fool, is the *Perceval-like hero of several Irish folk narratives and a sometime leader of the fairy host in narrative and poetry. Amadán na bruidhne, the fool of the fairy mounds or palaces, is greatly feared because he may administer the *fairy stroke, causing paralysis, crippling, or death; he is most active in June. There does not appear to be a connection between the folk figure and the colloquial use of amadán in spoken Irish and English.

See EACHTRA AN AMADÁIN MHÓIR. A Scottish ballad version is 'Laoidh an Amadain Mhóir', in Alexander Cameron (ed.), *Reliquiae Celtique* (Inverness, 1892), 289–94. Additionally, Sheila J. McHugh postulates links between the *Amadán Mór* and Arthurian narrative in *'Sir Perceyvelle': Its Irish Connections* (Ann Arbor, Mich., 1946).

Amaethon, Amathaon, Amatha'on [W, great or divine ploughman; cf. W *amaeth*, agriculture, labour]. A ploughman and magician, the son of *Dôn, in early Welsh narrative. In *Culhwch ac Olwen* he was the only man who could till a certain difficult field. He taught magic to *Gwydion. Amaethon's theft of a dog and a roebuck from *Annwfn, the otherworld, caused a war between the ruler, *Arawn, and Gwydion, which culminated in *Cad Goddeu, the Battle of the Trees; Amaethon defeated Arawn before the battle was completed. Many authorities have suggested that Amaethon is derived from an agricultural god.

Amairgin, Amairgein, Amargein, Amargen, Amargin, Amergin, Amorgin, Amairgene, Amhairghin, Aimirgin [Ir., wondrously born]. Name borne by several figures in early Ireland, in myth and saga as well as in the genealogies of such families as the O'Moores of Laois. The two best-known figures bearing this name were poets.

Amairgin 1. Also known as Amairgin Glúnmar [big-kneed], the son of *Míl Espáine. A poet of the *Milesians, sometimes referred to as the first poet of Ireland. When the invading Milesians met the three divine eponyms of Ireland, *Ériu, *Banba, and *Fódla, Amairgin answered the request of Ériu that Ireland be named for her. He asked that the realm of Ireland be divided in two, and that the underground be given to the *Tuatha Dé Danann and the land above ground to the sons of Míl. He also arbitrated the division of the island of Ireland along the *Eiscir Riada in which the north was given to *Éremón and the south to *Éber Finn. At times he had the power to calm the wind; he compared himself to several powers in nature, the wind, the wave, the *bull, etc., in a poem composed the moment he set foot in Ireland. For this he is said to have introduced lyric poetry. In one recited poem he compares himself to many things, including a salmon, a sword, a plant, and a spear; this passage prompts several learned commentators to suggest he may have been borrowed by Welsh storytellers as a model for *Taliesin. His wife, Scéne, died before reaching Ireland; *Inber Scéne, or Inverskena, the ancient name for the Kenmare River in *Kerry, commemorates her. Morgan Llywelyn's popular novel *Bard: The Odyssey of the Irish* (Boston, 1984) treats of Amairgin (1).

2. A poet and warrior of the *Ulster Cycle, the father of *Conall Cernach, the husband of *Findchóem and thus the brother-in-law of *Conchobar mac Nessa; he shared in the upbringing of *Cúchulainn. He slew Aillén Trechend, the triple-headed monster that made raids on Ireland from its cave at *Cruachain. An 11th-century manuscript relates Amairgin's exchange with Athairne, his foster-father, about poetry and the seasons. Athairne was visiting one autumn, and when he came to depart Amairgin composed a poem counselling that autumn was not an appropriate time for farewells; two more poems followed for winter and spring. Finally, at the start of summer, Amairgin's poem announced: 'Summer is a good season for a long journey.' Amairgin also plays a role in *Fled Bricrenn [Briccriu's Feast], where he boasts of the praise he has received.

Amazon. Although the Amazons of Greek tradition are cited briefly in **Lebor Gabála* [Book of Invasions], the figures mentioned more often in this role include *female teachers of martial arts such as *Scáthach, *Aífe (1), and *Búanann. See also BERREY DHONE.

Ambrosius Aurelianus. Name in *Gildas (6th cent.) for the shadowy but historical Welsh figure *Emrys Wledig. See also MYRDDIN.

Amen. Name of the *cauldron of *Ceridwen in Welsh tradition.

Amergin. Variant of *Amairgin.

Amhairghin. Variant of *Amairgin.

Ammianus Marcellinus. Last of the great Roman historians (*c.* AD 330–*c.*390), although by birth a Greek and a native of Syrian Antioch. He is remembered by Celticists for his admiring but cautious descriptions of the Gauls, especially the tall, beautiful Gaulish women whose 'huge snowy arms' could strike like catapults when raised in anger. English translation in the Loeb Classical

Library, *Ammianus Marcellinus* (Cambridge, Mass. and London, 1935–9).

Amorgin. Variant of *Amairgin.

Amorica. Variant of *Armorica.

Amun. In *Macpherson's *Ossian* an Irish chieftain, the father of Feard who was slain in a single combat by *Cuchullin.

Ana, Anu, Anann (gen.) [Ir. wealth, abundance]. The principal goddess of pre-Christian Ireland, the mother or 'nourisher' of the *Tuatha Dé Danann, the 'people, tribe, or nation of Ana'. In **Sanas Cormaic* [Cormac's Glossary] (10th cent.), she is Ana, and Ireland may be known as the 'land of Ana'. A prosthetic *D-* changes Ana, Anu to Dana, Danu; some commentators advise that these forms are later scholarly inventions, while others point out that the name Dana has discrete associations and parallels. She is most probably the grandmother of *Ecne, a personification of knowledge and enlightenment. She may also be the mother of the three sons of *Tuireann, *Brian (1), *Iuchair, and *Iucharba; see OIDHEADH CHLAINNE TUIREANN [The Tragic Story of the Children of Tuireann].

Stories citing her name suggest she appeared in two aspects, beneficent and maleficent. In the former she gives prosperity to the province of *Munster, as can be seen in the mountains that bear her name, **Dá Chích Anann*, 'The Paps of Ana', two breast-shaped promontories 10 miles E of Killarney, Co. *Kerry. In her darker aspects she may be linked with *Áine of *Cnoc Áine near Lough Gur (without etymological connection), as Eleanor Hull asserted in *Folklore of the British Isles* (1928). Despite these pagan associations, her name is borne by the virgin St Ana whose feast-day is 18 January. The Welsh counterpart of Ana is *Dôn. See also MÓRRÍGAN; MÓR MUMAN.

Ana Life [Ir., Ana Liffey]. Name used to confer the status of goddess on the River Liffey that runs through Dublin. Found only in modern literature, it was used by Joyce to create Anna Livia Plurabelle in *Finnegans Wake* (1939).

Anaon [Bret. masc. pl., spirits of the dead; souls' society]. A Breton word for the afterworld. See also the Welsh ANNWFN.

Anbúail. See ETHAL ANBÚAIL.

Ancamna. Romano-Gaulish goddess commemorated at Trier in the Moselle valley, often consort of *Mars with the epithet Lenus. At Möhn north of Trier is the consort of *Smertrius, who may also be an aspect of Mars.

Andarta [Gaul., powerful bear (?)]. A Gaulish goddess whose name was invoked in inscriptions found at Berne, Switzerland, as well as in southern France; she may be a counterpart of *Artio.

Andraste, Andrasta [Brit., invincible]. British goddess invoked by the *female warrior Boudicca (1st cent. AD). She was worshipped in a sacred grove; hares were sacrificed to her.

Aneirin, Aneurin, Neirin [W form of Honorius; or W *an-*, very; *eur*, gold; *-in*, diminutive]. Welsh bard thought to have lived *c.* AD 600 in the 'old north', former Welsh-speaking territories now the Lowlands of *Scotland; sometimes called 'the British Homer', or 'Aneirin of the flowering muse'. The Welsh *Triads refer to him as 'Aneirin of flowing verse, prince of poets'. Aneirin and *Taliesin and three others whose works do not survive are **cynfeirdd* [oldest poets]. His compositions are contained in the 13th-century *Canu Aneirin.* Best known of his works is the lengthy **Gododdin*, an elegy for Welsh chieftains who fell at the Battle of *Catraeth at the hands of the Saxons. He occasionally carries the patronymic ap Caw; a Cornish variant of his name is Annear. See *Canu Aneirin: Poetical Work of Aneirin*, ed. Ifor Williams (Cardiff, 1938; repr. 1961). See also attributed BOOK OF ANEIRIN.

angau, angeu. A personification of death in early Welsh tradition. See also ANKOU; DEATH COACH; DULLAHAN; FAR DOROCHA; YANNIG.

Angharad, Anghared [W, much-loved one]. Name borne by several figures in early Welsh history.

Angharad 1. Daughter of Meurig ap Dyfnwallon and the wife of *Rhodri Mawr (7th cent.).

2. Daughter of Meredydd ab Owain and married to *Llywelyn ap Seissyllt, king of *Gwynedd (*c.* AD 1000).

3. Wife of William de Barri and the mother of *Giraldus Cambrensis (b. 1145).

Anglesey. An island and former county (until 1974) of north Wales, separated from the mainland by the Menai Strait or

Abermenai. The Welsh name for the island is Môn; this is confused with *Mona in some texts, a name usually referring to the Isle of *Man. The Roman historian Tacitus (1st cent. AD) describes an attack on the island under Paulinus; in his account heroic Roman soldiers drove howling priests and black-clad, screaming women from bloodstained groves, presumably the site of human sacrifices (*c.* AD 59–62). These fugitives are now identified with *druids. Great deposits of metalwork and other objects recovered from Llyn Cerrig Bach on Anglesey may be connected with the attempts of the insular druids to escape what seems to have been complete annihilation. In *The Myvyrian Archaiology* [sic] *of Wales*, compiled from medieval materials by Owen Jones (1801–7), Anglesey is associated with high birth, wise men, and relics. Since 1974 Anglesey has been part of the county of *Gwynedd.

Ánglonnach. See AILILL ÁNGLONNACH.

Anguba. See AILILL ÁNGLONNACH.

Angus, Óengus, Áengus, Aonghus, Aonghas; anglicized: Eenis, Neese, Niece, Nicholas, Enos; once wrongly thought a cognate of Aeneas. Angus, though an anglicization of Scottish origin, appears often in Irish contexts [Ir., unique strength, substance (?)]. A man's name, under one spelling or another, borne by many figures in early Irish and Scottish Gaelic traditions, most notably *Angus Óg, Óc, or mac-ind-Óc; the name is also borne by at least five Christian saints, and appears in the genealogies of numerous Irish and Scottish families.

Angus 1. The son of Áed Abrat and brother of *Fand and *Lí Ban, he sings of the healing to be given in the fairy world by his sisters and invites *Cúchulainn there. Angus disappears, but later returns when he learns that *Manannán mac Lir has abandoned Fand.

2. Also known as Óengus Céile Dé [Ir., client of God], or Angus the Culdee. An early Irish anchorite (*fl.* 800–50); author of the *Féilire,* a calendar of saints and festivals. His feast-day is 11 March.

3. A *Fir Bolg leader for whom, fancifully, *Dún Aonghusa on the *Aran Islands is named. Sometimes called Angus Bolg; often thought of as an ancestor of the *Déisi.

4. Chieftain of the *Déisi whose aggressions helped to bring about the expulsion of his people from their homelands. First Angus killed *Cellach, son of *Cormac mac Airt, with his spear, and second he put out the father's eye with the spear butt. Angus had been seeking revenge for Cellach's rape of his niece, but retribution visited upon the Déisi was more terrible. Sometimes known as 'Angus of the terrible spear'.

Angus mac Airt, son of Art mac Morna. One of the members of the *Fianna of *Fionn mac Cumhaill, often seen in the company of *Áed.

Angus mac Angus, more often **Óengus mac Óengusa**. Tenth-century Irish poet (d. 932), who is described in the annals as the chief poet of Ireland.

Angus mac Forgesso. Shadowy historical figure cited in early Scottish genealogies; the former (until 1974) Scottish county of Angus, also known as Forfarshire, was named after him.

Angus mac Natfraích, Nadfraich. A 5th-century leader of the *Eóganacht and king of *Cashel, reputedly baptized by St *Patrick. According to the well-known but apocryphal story, Patrick accidentally thrust his staff through Angus's foot during the ritual, causing him great pain. Noticing the mishap later, Patrick asked Angus why he did not cry out, and the king answered that he thought it was part of the ceremony.

Angus mac Nisse. Also known as St Macanisius. A saint of early Ireland (d. 514?) who was so pious that he refused to put the Scriptures in a bag; instead he carried them around the country on his back while crawling on all fours.

Angus Óg, mac Óg, mac Óc, mac Ócc, mac-ind-Óg, Óengus Óc, Angus of the Brug [Ir., young Angus, Angus son of youth; *mac Óc, mac Óg*, young son]. Angus Óg is the god of youth and beauty among the *Tuatha Dé Danann; he may also be the god of love, if any such god can be said to exist. His father was the *Dagda and his mother *Boand (the Boyne River), while she was still married to *Nechtan. To hide their infidelity, the parents asked *Elcmar to be the child's foster-father. In a lesser-known version, *Eochaid Ollathair (Dagda) seduced through trickery the wife of Elcmar, *Eithne (2) (perhaps another name for Boand), to produce the divine son, who was then fostered by *Midir. Angus Óg dispossessed either Dagda or Elcmar to assume his usual residence, *Brug na Bóinne [house, hostel of the Boyne], where trees were always in fruit and a cooked pig was always ready for the eating. In some versions Elcmar gains *Clettech Sídh in exchange for the loss of Brug na Bóinne. Popular tradition attributes to Angus Óg and to *Manannán mac Lir the bringing of cows from India to Ireland. Angus Óg drank the Ale of Immortality, and four swans circled over his head when he travelled. He was the protector of several heroes, most notably *Diarmait of the *Fenian Cycle; one of his important defences was a cloak of invisibility. He advised *Eochaid, who had eloped with his foster-mother, not to camp on his (Angus's) meadow, and punished the hero for ignoring him. Angus Óg was also the father of Maga, the ancestress of the Red Branch (see ULSTER CYCLE). He is sometimes credited with a son, Nemanach, and sometimes with a wife, Nuamaisi. He mates with *Eithne, the daughter of *Balor, to produce *Delbaeth (2). His magical sword is *Móralltach. In addition, Angus Óg is cited in numerous Old Irish narratives as well as in later folk and fairy lore.

In a widely known story Angus Óg is wasted by longing for a beautiful young woman he has seen only in a dream. The Old Irish version is known as *Aislinge Óenguso [Ir., The Dream of Angus], while the modern version is known as *Angus agus Cáer* [Ir. Angus and Cáer]. When she disappears from his dream, Angus Óg searches for her for a year; later, *Bodb Derg discovers that she was Cáer, daughter of *Ethal Anbúail. When the lovers are joined, they fly off together to Brug na Bóinne in the form of a pair of swans, chanting such wondrous music that no one who hears it can sleep for three days and three nights.

Angus Óg is the Irish counterpart to Continental Celtic divinity *Mabon-*Maponos. Scholarly speculation has made him the counterpart of such classical figures as Adonis, *Apollo, and Eros (Cupid). Because Angus Óg displaced his father, some commentators have suggested that he might be the counterpart of Zeus in displacing Cronus.

See Françoise Le Roux, 'Le Rêve d'Oengus', *Ogam*, 18 (1966), 132–50. Christian-J. Guyonvarc'h, 'Le Rêve d'Oengus', ibid. 117–31. Angus Óg has been a popular figure with Anglo-Irish writers. See W. B. Yeats, 'The Song of the Wandering Aengus' (1897) and 'The Harp of Aengus' (1900); Liam O'Flaherty, *The Ecstasy of Angus* (1931). In James Stephens's *The Crock of Gold* (1912), Angus Óg, calling himself 'Love' and 'Infinite Joy', contends with the Greek Pan for the favour of the young heroine; see also Stephens's *In the Land of Youth* (1924).

Angus Tuirmech, Tuirmheach [Ir., prolific (?); famous (?)]. Incestuous father of *Fiachu Fer Mara.

Anian. Variant spelling of *Einion.

animals. From the time of the earliest Celtic traditions at *Hallstatt and *La Tène, certain animals had continuous associations in iconography and in storytelling. Shape-shifting gods and heroes transformed themselves into animals. In Celtic Christianity some saints, such as St Pol of Brittany, were thought to have power over the animals, while others, Sts *Ailbe and *Ciwa, were thought to be suckled by animals (wolves), as was Bairre, an ancestor of *Amairgin. See BADGER; BEAR; BIRDS; BOAR; BULL; CAT; COCK; COW; DOG; OTTER; RAM; STAG; SWAN. The boar held a special place in Celtic iconography from earliest times, while the Continental Celts seem to have given most esteem to the horned, stag-like god *Cernunnos. Anne Ross devotes a lengthy chapter to divine animals in early Celtic art in *Pagan Celtic Britain* (London, 1967), 297–353. See also BIRDS; FISH.

ankou. A spectral figure portending death in Breton folklore, a counterpart of the Greek Thanatos. The ankou is usually the spirit of the last person to die in a community. Sometimes male, but more often female, the ankou is usually a tall, haggard figure in a wide hat with long white hair, or a skeleton with a revolving head who sees everybody everywhere. The ankou characteristically drives a deathly wagon or cart with a creaking axle and piled high with corpses; a stop at a cabin door means sudden death for those inside. Although roughly parallel to the driver of the *death coach in Irish folklore, the ankou appears to draw more from the Grim Reaper in medieval Christian folklore. The 19th-century writer Anatole le Braz suggested that the ankou is a survival of the prehistoric dolmen-builders of *Brittany. See also ANGAU; DULLAHAN; FAR DOROCHA; YANNIG.

Anlawdd Wledig [W *Anlawdd*, ruler or prince]. In early Welsh narrative the father of Goleuddyd and grandfather of Culhwch; also the father of *Eigr, the mother of the Welsh Arthur.

Ánle. OIr. variant of *Ainnle.

Anluan, Ánluan, Anlón [Ir., great hound (?), great warrior (?)]. Name borne by many figures in early Irish history, including an ancestor and a brother of *Brian Bórama (Boru). The best-known Anluan in narrative is a character in **Scéla Mucce meic Da Thó* [The Story of Mac Da Thó's Pig], a son of Maga and brother of *Cet. When Cet bragged to *Conall Cernach that his brother was even stronger than he was, Conall produced Anluan's head from his belt. In the **Táin Bó Cuailnge* [Cattle Raid of Cooley], he early rallied to the cause of *Medb of *Connacht.

Anna Livia Plurabelle. See LIFFEY.

Annals of the Four Masters. Usual English title for *Annála Ríoghachta Éireann* [Annals of the Kingdom of Ireland], a chronicle history of Ireland compiled 1632–6. Purporting to begin 'forty days after the Flood', in the year of the world 2242, the *Annals* are often only a record of names, dates, and battles, many of them fabulous, with occasional quotations from ancient sources; but they become more of a modern literary history as the timetable approaches the present. The *Annals* contrast with the narrative history of Geoffrey *Keating, compiled about the same time. The principal 'master' of the *Annals* was the Franciscan lay brother Micheál Ó Cléirigh (1575–1643), a native of Co. Donegal. The identity of the other three 'masters' is somewhat cloudy, as the introduction cites a total of six compilers, most of them Franciscans. The designation of 'Four Masters' was made *ex post facto* by Seán Mac Colgáin in Louvain about 1645. The industrious Ó Cléirigh, who is most often cited as the 'master' of the *Annals*, also compiled a version of the **Lebor Gabála* [Book of Invasions]. John O'Donovan produced the most recent edition entitled *Annals of the Kingdom of Ireland* (7 vols., Dublin, 1849–51). See also the study by Paul Walsh, *The Four Masters and Their Work* (Dublin, 1944); N. Ó Muraíle, 'The Autographed Manuscript of the *Annals of the Four Masters*', *Celtica*, 19 (1987), 75–95.

Annals of Tig[h]ernach. This oldest surviving native Irish historical record was purportedly compiled by Abbot Tigernach (d. 1088) at *Clonmacnoise on the *Shannon. Fragments of the manuscript are included in Rawlinson B488 and B502 at the Bodleian Library, Oxford. Although T. F. O'Rahilly (1946) and Paul Walsh (1947) have disputed the naming of the Annals of Tigernach, that name has persisted since Whitley Stokes used it with his translation, 1895–7. See Whitley Stokes, 'The Annals of Tigernach', *Revue Celtique*, 16 (1895), 374–419; 17 (1896), 6–33, 119–263, 337–420; 18 (1897), 9–59, 150–97, 267–303; repr. (Felinfach and Lampeter, Wales, 1993).

Annear. A Cornish variant of *Aneirin.

Annion. Variant spelling of *Einion.

Anno Mundi [L, year of the world]. The year since the creation of the world, according to biblical revelation, abbreviated AM. Medieval scholars were not uniform as to when this might have been. The Irish **Annals of the Four Masters* posited 5090 BC; e.g. 1000 BC would be 4090 AM. The influential Anglo-Saxon historian the Venerable Bede (8th cent.) suggested 3952 BC. Also widely cited were 5200 BC and 5198 BC.

Annwfn, Annwn [cf. W *an*, in; *dwfn*, the world]. The Welsh name for the *Otherworld, corresponding roughly to the *sídh and the *Tech Duinn [Ir., House of Donn] of Irish tradition. Details about its location and description vary; Annwfn might be on the surface or under the earth or the sea. It may be a great revolving castle, in Welsh *Caer Siddi, surrounded by the sea or by a series of fortified islands, where sickness and old age are unknown and there are both enchanting music and a fountain flowing with a liquid sweeter than wine. Conceived as *Caer Feddwid [W, Court of Intoxication or Carousal], it offers denizens a sample of sparkling wine. It may also be identical with *Caer Wydyr [W, Fortress of Glass] and *Gwales. In most of the *Mabinogi* Annwfn is next to *Pwyll, but in *Culhwch ac Olwen* it was beyond Scotland. Generally it is a place of delight with a magic cauldron and a well of sweet water.

There are two kings in Annwfn, mortal enemies: *Arawn, who appears more often and makes alliances with mortals, and *Hafgan. *Gwyn ap Nudd was placed over a brood of devils here so they would not destroy the human race. In Christian times Annwfn became confused with concepts of Hell [W *uffern*]. Cf. the Breton term Anaon; see also CŴN ANNWFN [The Hounds of Annwfn]. The

*Preiddiau Annwfn [Spoils of Annwfn] is the cauldron of *Arawn. Three shiploads of Arthur's men seek it in vain; only seven of them return. In the *cosmogony of Llywelyn Siôn (1540–*c.*1615), Annwfn is the abode of Cythrawl. See Patrick Sims-Williams, *Celtic Language, Celtic Culture*, ed. A. Matonis and D. Melia (Van Nuys, Calif., 1990), 57–81.

Anocitius. See ANTENOCITIUS.

Ánroth [Ir., travelling or glowing wheel]. A mythical ancestor of the *Eóganacht; in **Cóir Anmann* this Anroth is identified with Rothechtaid Rotha, the 'Great Traveller of the Wheel', a mythological king cited in early pedigrees.

Answerer. A translation of the name of the terrible sword owned by *Manannán mac Lir and others. The Irish name has many spellings; see FRECRAID.

Answering Stone. The English name for *Cloch Labhrais, found in Co. Waterford, and celebrated in Irish folklore.

Antenociticus, Anociticus, Antocidicus. A youthful male British god venerated in Roman times; one of his temples was at Condercum on Hadrian's Wall, near the modern town of Benwell, Northumberland. His frontal locks suggest a young *stag.

Anu. Variant of Ana.

Anubal. Variant spelling of Anbúail; see ETHAL ANBÚAIL.

Aobh. ModIr. spelling of *Áeb.

Aodh. ModIr. spelling of *Áed.

Aodhán. ModIr. spelling of *Áedán.

Aoi. ModIr. for *Aí.

Aoibheall, Aoibhell. ModIr. spellings of *Aíbell.

Aoibhgreine. ModIr. spelling of *Aíbgréne.

Aoibhil. ModIr. spelling of *Aíbell.

Aoibhinn. ModIr. variant of *Aíbell.

Aoife. ModIr. spelling of *Aífe.

aonach, aonaighe, áenach [ModIr., fair, assembly, meeting]. Category of celebration or fair such as those held on the first days of March, July, September, and December, at Millstreet, Co. Cork, about 20 miles W of Mallow Junction, in the early 20th century. The Old Irish equivalent, óenach, denotes medieval assemblies held periodically at *Tara, *Tailtiu, *Tlachtga, and *Uisnech, which included games and competitions rather than commerce. Distinguish from *festival, *féile, *feis.

Aonach Tailteann. See TAILTIU.

Aonbárr [Ir. *aonbárr*, unique supremacy]. Magical horse of *Manannán mac Lir who could gallop on land or sea. Also known as Énbarr, Enbhárr [*enbarr*, froth, foam].

Aonghus. ModIr. variant of *Angus.

aos Sídhe. ModIr. variant of *áes sídhe.

ap- [W *mab*, son]. Uncapitalized, unalphabetized prefix to Welsh patronymics, comparable to OIr. mac-; e.g. Gwyn ap Nudd is alphabetized thus, not as ap Nudd, Gwyn. Through mutation, it may also be spelled fab-, mab-, vab-. See also UA-.

Aphrodite. The Greek goddess of romantic love and beauty; mother of *Aeneas. Although she has no direct Celtic counterparts, her tragic love for Adonis has long been compared to that of *Deirdre for Noíse and *Gráinne for *Diarmait. See also her Roman counterpart, Venus.

Apollo. The Greek and Roman god of music, poetry, prophecy, sometimes of medicine, and, with the epithet 'Phoebus', of the sun. By the pattern of *interpretatio celtica* (see GAUL), the colonized Celts adopted him into their own pantheon, often combining his solar and healing powers. As in the instances of *Mercury, *Mars, and *Jupiter, Apollo's name often appears with those of indigenous gods. Sometimes this can mean that the cult of Apollo subsumed that of another god, so that the Graeco-Roman god with a recurring epithet or surname, such as Apollo Grannus, appears almost a distinct persona. In other instances Apollo may be closely linked with a native deity, particularly *Belenus, who retained some independent worship of his own. Or, third, the local deity may only be an aspect of Apollo whose name is not seen discretely. Without epithet or surname, Apollo is linked with at least two female cult-partners of native origin, *Damona in eastern France and *Sirona at the sanctuary of Hochscheid near Trier, Germany.

The cult of Apollo Grannus, a healing spring deity, was known widely on the

Continent, from *Brittany to what is now Hungary, even in Rome itself, with citations in Scandinavia and at Musselburgh, near Edinburgh. Important shrines called Aquae Granni are found at Aachen (Aix-la-Chapelle) and the Vosges of eastern France. *Sirona was his usual cult-partner.

The Roman historian Dio Cassius (2nd–3rd cent. AD) records that the emperor Caracalla vainly sought a cure from Grannus as well as from his Roman and Egyptian counterparts. The name Grannus/-os apparently corresponds to the ancient name for Grand in the Vosges. Speculative attempts to link the name philologically with the Irish *Gráinne or Grian [sun] are insupportable.

Two shrines in Gaul depicting Apollo Atepomarus [Gaul. *epo*, horse; i.e. great horseman, possessing a great horse] link the power of sun and horse, as are often united by the Continental Celts. Apollo is portrayed next to the Continental Celtic god *Cernunnos in a stele at Reims. The epithet Canumagus/Cunomagus [hound lord] exists on a shrine of Apollo found at Nettleton Shrub, Wiltshire. Apollo Citharoedus is Apollo the harp- or cithern-player. The Romano-Gaulish Apollo Moritasgus patronized a healing shrine at the provincial town of Moritsagus, coextensive with Mont Auxois, near Dijon, in north-eastern France; Damona is his cult-partner. At Essarois, near Châtillon-sur-Seine in eastern France, Apollo *Vindonnus [light, clear, white] presided over a temple made of *oak and stone, presumably promising a cure for *eye afflictions. The enigmatic Apollo Virotutis [benefactor of humanity (?)] also had two shrines. Elsewhere he is equated with *Angus Óg, *Belenus, *Lug Lámfhota, and *Maponos. See Jan de Vries, *La Religion des Celtes* (Paris, 1963), 82–3 and *passim*; W. J. Wedlake, *The Excavation of the Shrine of Apollo at Nettleton, Wiltshire, 1956–1971* (London, 1982).

apple [OE]. The pome fruit and tree (*Pyrus malus*) bearing this fruit is celebrated in numerous functions in Celtic mythology, legend, and folklore; it is an emblem of fruitfulness and sometimes a means to immortality. Wands of *druids were made from wood either of the *yew or of the apple. A name for the *Avalon of Arthurian tradition in certain medieval narratives, attributing Welsh origin, is Insula Pomorum, 'The Isle of Apples'. One gloss of the name for the magical Irish island *Emain Ablach is 'Emain of the Apples'. In the *Ulster Cycle the soul of *Cú Roí was confined in an apple that lay in the stomach of a *salmon which appeared once every seven years. *Cúchulainn once gained his escape by following the path of a rolled apple. An apple-tree grew from the grave of the tragic lover *Ailinn. In the Irish tale **Echtrae Conli* [The Adventure of Connla], *Connla the son of Conn is fed an apple by a *fairy lover [Ir. *leannán sídhe/sí*], which sustains him with food and drink for a month without diminishing; but it also makes him long for the woman and the beautiful country of women to which his lover is enticing him. In the Irish story from the *Mythological Cycle, **Oidheadh Chlainne Tuireann*, the first task given the Children of Tuireann is to retrieve the Apples of the Hesperides (or Hisbernia). *Afallennau* [W apple trees] is a 12th-century Welsh narrative poem dealing with *Myrddin. The Breton pseudo-saint *Konorin was reborn by means of an apple. OIr. uball, ubull; ModIr. ubhal, úll; ScG ubhall; Manx ooyl; W afal; Corn. aval; Bret. aval. See also ALLANTIDE; FAIRY TREE.

Aquae Sulis [L, waters of Sulis]. Roman name for the shrine at *Bath in west Britain, where the cult of *Sulis, equated with *Minerva, was merged with that of several native goddesses.

Aquitani. A Gaulish people who occupied what is now south-western France, from the Garonne to the Pyrenees, during Roman times.

Aran Islands. A chain of islands that run 15 miles across the mouth of Galway Bay on the west coast of Ireland. The three largest islands are Aranmore (or Inishmore), Inishmaan, and Inisheer, a total of 11,578 acres. Because the Irish language has survived here well into modern times, many Irish people think of the Islands as the most Irish (or Celtic) part of Ireland, a perception enhanced by the writings of J. M. Synge (1871–1909) and others. On the west coast of Aranmore lies *Dún Aonghusa, one of the most magnificent and dramatic prehistoric stone forts in all of Europe. The fort was named after a *Fir Bolg chief, *Angus (3), and strangely, considering its size, does not figure prominently in Island folklore. The Fir Bolg of the *Lebor Gabála* [Book of Invasions] fled here after their defeat at the First Battle of Mag Tuired (see CATH MAIGE TUIRED). The mysterious island in the Atlantic, *Hy-Brasil, is sometimes identified with the Aran Islands. A 'king' of the Islands in several Irish stories is *Ailill. These Irish islands are sometimes confused with the Scottish island of *Arran in *Argyllshire (since 1974, Strathclyde). See P. A. Ó Síocháin, *Aran, Islands of Legend* (Dublin, 1963).

Aranrhod. Variant spelling of *Arianrhod.

Arawn. Lord and king of *Annwfn, the Welsh *Otherworld, in several early narratives. Initially Arawn has a rival and archenemy *Hafgan, who is eliminated in an alliance with *Pwyll. Arawn and Pwyll struck up a friendship while hunting and agreed to change shapes and kingdoms for one year. No one discovered the ploy, not even Arawn's beautiful queen, whose chastity Pwyll respected. At the end of the year Pwyll disposed of Hafgan with a single blow. When he returned to his mortal shape, Pwyll learned that Arawn had been a just and wise king in his absence. The two remained strong friends.

Arawn owned a magic *cauldron [*Preiddiau Annwfn*, the Spoils of Annwfn), one of the treasures of Britain, which *Arthur coveted. He gave the pigs to *Pryderi, son of Pwyll, which were to play such an important part in Welsh legend. The theft of Arawn's animals by *Amaethon led to the Battle of the Trees, **Cad Goddeu*. In more recent Welsh legend, Arawn is displaced as ruler of the Otherworld by *Gwyn ap Nudd. Some commentators see a parallel between Arawn and *Tethra, a leader of the *Fomorians in Irish tradition. R. S. Loomis suggested that Arawn was an antecedent of the Arthurian figure Alain li Gros, a keeper of the Grail. See also *Pwyll*, the first branch of the **Mabinogi*.

Arberth. Residence or court of *Pwyll in early Welsh narrative. Outside the court was the *gorsedd, or 'throne mound', from which Pwyll first saw *Rhiannon on her magic horse. The mound apparently had ritual significance in early narrative, but it has been given new meaning in the folk celebrations of modern nationalists. Arberth may be on the site of the modern town of Narberth, *Dyfed (until 1974, Pembrokeshire).

Arca Dubh, Arcai Dubh Iasgair [ScG, black Arca/-i, the fisherman]. Villainous fisherman in Scottish Gaelic folklore, known as Black Arky in translated stories. He is the usual murderer of *Cumhall, father of *Fionn mac Cumhaill. In one version he tricks Cumhall out of his sword and kills him with it. In another he lures Cumhall to an island with a beautiful woman while he waits stealthily in the grass.

Arcaibh [ScG, among the orcs/boars]. A name for the Orkneys in Scottish Gaelic folklore; other names for the Orkneys are Inse Orc and Inistura.

ard, ard-. Irish and Scottish Gaelic word meaning 'high, lofty', 'above the ground, elevated'. Employed in many titles and names, especially place-names. Because the prefix is sometimes separate, e.g. Ard Macha, and sometimes joined, e.g. Ardmore, all entries with ard- in this definition are alphabetized letter by letter.

Ardagh [Ir., high field]. Common Irish place-name which survives in eight locations on the modern map. (1) A village in Co. Longford, 5 miles SSW of Edgeworthstown, near *Brí Léith, the home of *Midir; it is sometimes named instead of Brí Léith. (2) A village in Co. Limerick, 3 miles N of Newcastle, site of important archaeological finds from early Christian Ireland, including the celebrated Ardagh Chalice.

Ardan [cf. Ir. *Ardán*, pride]. One of the brothers of Noíse, the lover of *Deirdre. He was described as a baritone.

Ardar. In *Macpherson's *Ossian* (1760), the son of *Usnoth, the chief of Etha, and *Slissima, the sister of *Cuchullin. He was slain while still young by Swaran, the villainous king of Scandinavia.

Ard Caille [Ir., high division of land]. Site in north Co. Cork named in early poems as the burial-place of *Fionn mac Cumhaill; a more usual site is Luachair Dedad in western *Munster.

Ardee. A town in Co. Louth on the River Dee, 14 miles N of Drogheda. The name is an anglicization of Áth Fhirdiadh [Ir., the ford of Ferdia], marking the site of *Ferdiad's death in the **Táin Bó Cuailnge* [Cattle Raid of Cooley].

Ardfert [Ir. *Ard Fhearta*, height of the grave]. A village in Co. *Kerry, 6 miles NNW of Tralee, and a monastic centre in early Christian times. Home of St *Brendan, sometimes called 'Brendan of Ardfert'. See Francis

Nunan, *Ardfert-Brendan, Kerry's Ancient See and Shrine* (Tralee, 1966).

Ard Fostada na Féine [Ir., the height of the delaying of the fianna]. A hill in northern Co. Wexford in the Slaney valley, mentioned in several *Fenian narratives.

Ard Macha [Ir., height of Macha]. Irish name for the Christian metropolis now known as *Armagh; it is 2 miles E of the pre-Christian fortress of *Emain Macha.

Ardmore [Ir. and ScG, *ard mor*, great height]. A place-name that appears at least ten times in Ireland and Gaelic Scotland, the best-known of which is the village and early monastic site in south Co. Waterford. By tradition the abbey was founded by St *Declan (or Déaglán), chief saint of the *Déisi. Ardmore and its tall, round tower was so widely known as to appear in Breton legends as well as in Irish ones.

Ardnamurchan. A peninsula and adjoining inland region in NW *Argyllshire, since 1974 Strathclyde, including the westernmost point of mainland Scotland. The peninsula marks a division between the southern Inner Hebrides, Mull, Tiree, Coll, Colonsay, Oronsay, Islay, etc., from the northern islands, Muck, Eigg, Rhum, Skye, etc. From 1156 Ardnamurchan was the northern limit of *Somerled's jurisdiction.

Ardnurcher. See ATHNURCHER.

ard rí, ard rígh, ardríg [Ir., high king]. In many Irish narratives the ard rí of Ireland was portrayed as ruling all of the island from *Tara, where he was crowned. Countless legends and pseudo-histories claim that the title of ard rí existed from the earliest times, an assertion not supported in the early corpus of Irish laws known as the *Brehon Laws. Some informed modern commentators, including Francis J. Byrne (1973), have argued that the ard rí was pure fiction, created as political propaganda to support the claims of the Tara Dynasty of Co. Meath. The first claimant to the title of ard rí appears to be Máel Sechnaill (d. 862), known romantically as 'Malachy I'. Other commentators have suggested that some kind of sacral kingship might have existed at Tara in early times, even if it was not quite what later narratives imply. The term should not be understood to denote a national sovereign or over-king; it appears to have been an honorific title given to powerful local leaders. Among the figures known as ard rí are *Diarmait mac Cerbaill (d. 565), perhaps the last pre-Christian monarch of Ireland; Máel Sechnaill (d. 1022), the last to rule without unbroken opposition by powerful local princes; and Ruaidrí Ua Conchobair [Rory O'Connor] of Connacht, the last ard rí at the time of the Anglo-Norman Conquest (1169). See also BANAIS RÍGHE; TARA, FEAST OF.

Arduinna, Arduenna, Arduanna. Romano-Gaulish *boar-goddess of the Ardennes Forest; she is portrayed seated upon a boar. Also known as Dea Arduinna, Dea Arduenna. Often identified with *Diana.

Arecurius [L, the one who stands before the tribe]. God of Roman-occupied north Britain, invoked at Corstopitum, near the modern town of Corbridge, Northumberland.

Arfderydd, Arderydd. A battle remembered in several Welsh narratives as causing the madness of *Myrddin (or *Merlin). As a result he fled to the forests of Caledonia [W *Celyddon*, Scotland] where he lived in trees with wild beasts for half a century; in his frenzied condition he acquired the gift of prophecy. Arfderydd is mentioned in several Welsh narratives and documents; the Annals give its date as 573 or 575. Myrddin fought on the side of *Gwenddolau, who was slain by the sons of Eliffer, Gwrgi, and Peredur; Rhydderch of *Strathclyde was the victor in battle. The site of the battle is identified with the modern hamlet of Arthuret (derived from Arfderydd) in Cumberlandshire, on the River Esk, 8 miles N of Carlisle.

Argetlám. Variant of Airgetlám, a cognomen of *Nuadu.

Argoad, Argoadek [Bret. *Ar-Goad, Ar-Koad*, the woods, the forest]. The Breton name for the interior of the province of *Brittany as opposed to *Arvor, the coastal regions.

Argyll [Ir. *Airer Goídel*, country of the Gael; ScG *Oirer Ghaidheal*, country of the Gael; or ScG *erra Ghaidheal*, coastland of the Gael]. Formerly the southernmost county of Gaelic Scotland and closest to Ireland; since 1974 a north-west portion of Strathclyde. It occupies 3,110 square miles, including many islands and narrow peninsulas, nearly all of it mountainous. During Roman times the area was home to a British population called the *Epidii or 'horse people'. The region was once also known as Ergadia. After the 5th century AD the area was overrun with Gaelic settlers from Ireland, who established a kingdom at *Dál Riada. One of the richest collections of Scottish Gaelic traditional literature was gathered largely in Argyll: Archibald Campbell (ed.), *The Waifs and Strays in Celtic Tradition* (4 vols., London, 1889–91).

Arianrhod, Aranrhod, Arianrod [W, silver disk, wheel]. A renowned beauty of Welsh literature whose story may be based on that of an earlier moon goddess. Assumed to be the daughter of *Dôn, she was the sister and lover of *Gwydion; in the *Triads her father is given as *Beli. She claimed to be a virgin so that she might become the footholder of *Math. When the asserted virginity was tested, she gave premature birth to twins, *Dylan, who escaped into the sea, and *Lleu Llaw Gyffes, who became the object of his mother's scorn. Gwydion rescued the child and reared him carefully. According to folk tradition, there is a reef off the coast of *Gwynedd (formerly Carnarvonshire) called Caer Arianrhod that is the remains of an island castle where Arianrhod was tricked into giving Lleu the arms she intended to withhold. Caer Arianrhod is also a popular Welsh name for the constellation Corona Borealis. Arianrhod had other brothers, *Gilfaethwy and *Caswallon, with whom she did not have intimacies. R. S. Loomis suggested that Arianrhod may be a counterpart of the Arthurian figures Lunete and Morgawse.

arkan sonney. Also called 'lucky piggy' in English. The fairy pig of the Isle of *Man, usually described as white with red ears, like many Celtic supernatural animals. It can alter its size, but apparently not its shape. It is thought to bring luck, but is difficult to catch.

Arky, Black. See ARCA DUBH.

Arlan, Saint. Shadowy figure from early Cornish history; usually called 'Saint' although not listed in the saints' calendar. Through folk etymology he is thought to be the patron of *Allantide, Cornish *Halloween. He is often associated with Sts Allen and Elwin, whose names may be variants of his.

Armagh [Ir. *Ard Macha*, height of Macha]. City and district in Northern Ireland, home of the (papal) primate of Ireland, who bears the title Comharba Phádraig [successor of Patrick], the claimed antiquity of which has recently been challenged; it is also the residence of the head of the Church of Ireland. Although the site has been Christian in all of recorded history, its name in Irish, 'Height of Macha', acknowledges a pre-Christian past. According to the pseudo-history **Lebor Gabála* [Book of Invasions], Ard Macha was named for *Macha (1), wife of the mythical invader *Nemed. It is on high ground, 2 miles E of *Emain Macha [Ir. fortress of Macha], an important settlement in early Ireland, widely celebrated in Irish heroic literature. The excavations for St Patrick's (Protestant) Cathedral in 1840 uncovered many early carvings, especially figures of *bears.

In pre-conquest Ireland Armagh was the site of a centre of learning, sometimes described as a university, established by Ruaidrí Ua Conchobair [Rory O'Connor]. Following the Synod of Clane (1162), no one who was not an alumnus of Armagh could be *fer léiginn [Ir., master of studies] in any Irish monastic school. The advent of the Anglo-Normans in 1169, and their plundering of the school in 1184, 1185, and 1189, ended the tradition of learning at Armagh. The former (until 1974) county of Armagh, just south of *Lough Neagh, was the smallest of the six in Northern Ireland. Within its borders are several sites often mentioned in Irish narrative, including *Sliab Cuillinn [Slieve Gullion], a hill 5 miles SW of Newry, and *Sliab Fúait [Slieve Fuad], sometimes thought to be the residence of *Lir, near Newtown Abbott. See also **Book of Armagh* [*Liber Ardmachanus*]. Richard Sharpe, 'St. Patrick and the See of Armagh', *Cambridge Medieval Celtic Studies*, 4 (Winter 1982), 33–59; cf. B. K. Lambkin, 'Patrick, Armagh, and Emain Macha', *Emania* (Belfast), 2 (1987), 29–31.

Armes Prydain, Prydein [W, prophecy of Britain]. A 10th-century Welsh poem of 200 lines calling upon all Celtic peoples, as well as the Scandinavians of Dublin, to drive the Saxons from the Isle of Britain. Described by Nora Chadwick (1969) as 'the greatest of all Welsh patriotic poems', it also contains the first reference to *Myrddin (Merlin). See *Armes Prydein: The Prophecy of Britain*, ed. Ifor Williams, trans. R. Bromwich (Dublin, 1972, 1982); David Dumville, *Études Celtiques*, 20 (1983), 45–59.

Armorica, Amorica [cf. *armor*, on the sea]. Name for *Brittany in medieval times. It comprised two subdivisions: *Domnonia, north of the River Elorn, occupying what is today Côtes-du-Nord and Finistère, and *Cornouaille or Cornubia, S of the Elorn to the Ellé.

Army of the Trees. See CAD GODDEU.

Arnemetia [Brit., she who dwells over against the sacred grove]. British goddess venerated in Roman times at Aquae Arnemetiae, what is today Buxton Spa in north-west Derbyshire, the highest town in England (1000 feet), and long famous for its mineral waters. Her name incorporates the important term *nemeton [sacred grove].

Arrach, Arachd [ScG, spectre, apparition; mannikin]. Spectral monster of Scottish Gaelic folk tradition. It is often confused with Tarrach, from an t-arrachd, or it may be called Biast. (Cf. OIr. *arracht*, idol, idolatrous, image.)

Arran [Brit. *aran*, high place]. An island, 20 miles long by 8–10 miles wide, forming part of Strathclyde, Scotland; it is in the Firth of Clyde, about 50 miles due W of Glasgow. The island has been confused by many with the *Aran Islands of Ireland, including those medieval commentators who thought the *Fir Bolg might have fled here instead of to the west of Ireland. A minority of commentators have asserted it to be the model for *Emain Ablach, the otherworldly realm of *Mannanán mac Lir, the Irish sea-god. The most resounding local legends focus on the exile here of Robert the Bruce in the early 14th century. Scottish Gaelic was spoken on Arran until the late 20th century, despite the island's having become a popular holiday centre. See Robert McLellan, *The Isle of Arran* (New York, 1970).

Art [Ir., bear, in the sense of champion]. A name borne by several legendary heroes, of whom the best known is *Art mac Cuinn, as well as some figures in genealogies. The name is sometimes confused with *Arthur, which some nationalistic Welsh commentators link to the Welsh word arth, 'bear'. Despite this rather forced parallel, there does not seem to be any indication that Art is derived from Arthur.

Art Corb. A legendary ancestor of the *Déisi.

Art mac Cuinn. More often known in English contexts as Art Son of Conn; also as Art Óenfher [Ir., the lone one, the lonely]. Irish hero, he was the son of *Conn Cétchathach [Ir., of the Hundred Battles] and a principal figure of the adventure story **Echtrae Airt meic Cuinn*. Art was initially the object of the affections of the evil *Bé Chuma, who chose instead to live with Art's father Conn, sending the boy into exile for a year. Some time later, Art had returned and was playing a game of *fidchell with his stepmother. When he lost, she sent him in quest of the beautiful *Delbcháem. He won her and took possession of the Land of Wonder, only after slaying the girl's monstrous brother, mother, and father. On his return to Tara, Art's bride, Delbcháem, obliged Bé Chuma to leave the palace.

Art became the father of the illustrious *Cormac mac Airt through unusual circumstances. As he was travelling through Ireland, Art was the guest of Olc Acha the smith, who said he would be honoured if Art would lie with his daughter, *Étaín (2). Because he knew he would die in the battle at Mag Mucruma, Art asked that the girl take the child to his friend *Lugna in Connacht for fosterage. When she knew her time was near, Étaín set out for Lugna's residence, but delivered Cormac on the way, after which he was suckled by *wolves. Art was called Óenfher or 'the Lonely' after the death of his only brother *Connla. In variant texts Art is married to *Medb Lethderg. Art was slain by *Lugaid Lága at the Battle of Mag Mucrama; see CATH MAIGE MUCRAMA.

Art Mes Delmann. A legendary early king of the *Lagin.

Artaios, Artaius. An aspect of Gaulish *Mercury that appears to mean 'bear-god'. The *bear deity of the Continental Celts is usually thought to be the female *Artio.

Artemis. Greek goddess of open places and the hunt, counterpart of the Roman *Diana. One Celtic parallel is *Flidais, who drove a chariot drawn by deer. According to Greek tradition, one of the places to which Artemis travelled was the Celtic province of Galatia in Asia Minor.

Arthen [W *arth*, bear]. A regionalized bear- and river-god of early Wales. Several shadowy historical personages also bear this name, including a 9th-century king of *Ceredigion.

Arthfael, Arthmael, Arthfel [W *arth*, bear; *mael*, iron, mail, armour]. A name borne by several historical figures in early Wales, of whom Arthfael ap Noë, the 10th-century chief of *Gwent, is probably best known.

Arthur. The British hero 'King Arthur', of medieval international romance, legend, pseudo-history, and poetry. As Arthur was the most popular figure in European literature from the 12th to the 15th centuries, and because speculations about his origins and possible historicity have been endless, the study of his persona and associations fills libraries. The earliest written evidence for Arthur is in Welsh sources: *Gildas, who wrote the Latin history *De Excidio et Conquestu Britanniae* before AD 547; the 9th-century **Historia Brittonum*, formerly attributed to Nennius; and the *Annales Cambriae*, compiled *c*.950–1000. These fragments suggest to learned commentators that the beginnings of the Arthurian character lay in British (i.e. *Brythonic, antecedent to the modern Welsh) resistance to Saxon encroachments after the withdrawal of Roman forces (*c*.449–600). Welsh commentators, eager to accept Arthur as one of their own, have presented etymologies for Arthur's name to compete with several from other languages. Among the most plausible are arth [bear] = (g)wr [hero]; this is further supported by Arthur's association with the constellation Ursa Major, 'Great Bear'. A second nomination is arddhu, 'very black'; this is further supported by Arthur's association with theblack raven or chough. A writer who was not keen on the Welsh contributed most to what we now know as the dramatic character; this was *Geoffrey of Monmouth, whose widely read *Historia Regum Britanniae* (*c*.1136) freely adapted several Welsh sources, including Nennius and others now lost.

In the following century several writers, including Wace of Jersey, Layamon, and Chrétien de Troyes, added new dimensions both to the character of Arthur and to the whole of Arthurian literature; of these, Chrétien appears to have made the greatest use of Celtic sources. In this same century appeared the anonymous Welsh prose romance **Culhwch ac Olwen*, which despite its charm was apparently not known outside Wales until the 19th century. Other Welsh Arthurian narratives followed that have been conventionally bound with the **Mabinogi* since its first translation in 1848. These are known under their Welsh titles, **Breuddwyd Rhonabwy* [The Dream of Rhonabwy], **Owain* [The Lady of the Fountain], **Peredur*, and **Geraint ac Enid*. From the time of Geoffrey, according to T. G. Jones, Arthur tended to be folkloric in Welsh narrative and legendary in the *Triads. In Welsh tradition Arthur's activities are centred in south-east Wales and *Cornwall. Less well known is the Scottish claim for Arthur's identity, which in 1989 was supported by *Burke's Peerage*. Arthur's Seat (a place-name found elsewhere in Britain) is an 822-foot hill near the centre of *Edinburgh. And from the beginning of the 13th century the literary character of Arthur had a life of its own in nations beyond the Celtic lands.

Although the claims for the Celtic origin of Arthuriana made by R. S. Loomis in *Celtic Myth and Arthurian Romance* (1927) are now widely disputed, a number of striking parallels do exist between Celtic and Arthurian narratives. Examples include Irish, Scottish Gaelic, and Breton instances, as well as Welsh. Those figures most often thought to resemble Arthur include: *Fionn mac Cumhaill, *Conchobar mac Nessa, *Eochaid Airem, *Gwydion, *Angus Óg, and *Ogma. If these figures are not originals from which Arthurian copies were made, they certainly evoke a comparable ambiance and resonance. Some commentators have argued that post-12th-century Celtic narratives may themselves have been influenced by international Arthurian examples. Regardless of the merits of either side of the debate on origins, it must be admitted that a character called Arthur or Arthur of Britain also appears in Irish folklore collected from oral sources. He has little of the personality of the Arthur of Arthurian romance, and seems instead only to be a rapacious invader, much as another invader called 'King of the World' may evoke a peasant conception of the Holy Roman Emperor.

From the vast bibliography of Arthuriana a few items will be especially useful for Celticists. See the essays of K. H. Jackson, A. O. H. Jarman, I. L. Foster, R. Bromwich, and E. Hoepffner in R. S. Loomis (ed.), *Arthurian Literature in the Middle Ages* (Oxford, 1959); G. D. West, *An Index to Names in Arthurian Romances* (Toronto, 1975); Jean Markale, *Le Roi Arthur et la société celtique* (Paris, 1976); and *King Arthur: King of Kings* (London, 1977); Joy Chant, *The High Kings: Arthur's Celtic Ancestors* (New York, 1981). Also to be consulted are V. M.

Lagoria and M. L. Day (eds.), *King Arthur Through the Ages* (2 vols., New York, 1989); N. J. Lacy (comp.), *The Arthurian Encyclopedia* (New York, 1986); E. Reiss, L. H. Reiss, and B. Taylor (eds.), *Arthurian Legend and Literature: An Annotated Bibliography* (2 vols., New York, 1983); Rachel Bromwich and A. O. H. Jarman (eds.), *The Arthur of the Welsh* (Cardiff, 1991); and the *Bulletin Bibliographique* of the International Arthurian Society, published annually. See also MERLIN; AVALON; CAMELOT; TRISTAN; PREIDDIAU ANNWFN [The Spoils of Annwfn].

Artio, Dea Artio. The bear-goddess of the Continental Celts as represented in a small bronze found at Berne [bear city], Switzerland. Artio is depicted as seated before a huge bear that is near a tree. In her lap she holds a patera or saucer containing fruit, apparently in offering to the bear. Inscriptions elsewhere speak of Artaios, Artaius, masculine forms for 'bear-god', which are associated with Gaulish Mercury.

Arvor [Bret. *Ar-Mor*, by the sea]. The Breton name for the coastal regions of *Brittany as opposed to *Argoad, Argoadek, the name for the interior regions. The denoted area is not entirely coextensive with the northern department now known as Côte d'Armor, formerly Côte du Nord. See E. W. Rinder, *The Shadow of Arvor* (Edinburgh, 1896).

Asal, Asail (gen.). Variants of *Assal.

ash [OE *aesc*]. A tree regarded with awe in Celtic countries, especially Ireland. The ash may be any of the various trees of the genus *Fraxinus*, which usually grow quite tall and have close-grained wood; the mountain ash, *rowan, or quicken tree, a smaller tree of the genus *Sorbus aucuparia*, is usually considered separately in the Celtic imagination.

There are several recorded instances in Irish history in which people refused to cut an ash, even when wood was scarce, for fear of having their own cabins consumed with flame. The ash tree itself might be used in May Day (*Beltaine) rites. Under the Old Irish word nin, the ash also gives its name to the letter N in the *ogham alphabet. Together with the *oak and thorn, the ash is part of a magical trilogy in fairy lore. Ash seedpods may be used in *divination, and the wood has the power to ward off *fairies, especially on the Isle of Man. In Gaelic Scotland children were given the astringent sap of the tree as a medicine and as a protection against witchcraft. Some famous ash trees were the Tree of *Uisnech, the Bough of *Dathí, and the Tree of Tortu. The French poet who used Breton sources, Marie de France (late 12th cent.), wrote a lai about an ash tree.

OIr. nin; Ir. fuinseog; ScG fuinnseann; Manx unjin; W onnen; Corn. onnen; Bret. onnenn. See also FAIRY TREE; TREE.

Assal, Asal, Asail (gen.), Easal [cf. Ir. *asal*, ass]. A member of the *Tuatha Dé Danann who owned a magical spear, the Gáe or Gaí Assail, and seven magical pigs. His spear was the first brought into Ireland. It never failed to kill when he who threw it uttered the word 'ibar', or to return to the thrower when he said 'athibar' [cf. Ir. *ibar*, *yew tree, yew wood]. T. F. O'Rahilly observed that the *Gáe Assail was a lightning spear, like the weapon of Thor, which also returned to the hand that hurled it. When Gáe Assail had been taken to Persia, *Lug Lámfhota obliged the sons of *Tuireann, *Brian, Iuchair, and Iucharba, to retrieve it for him. Another task of those same children of Tuireann was to retrieve the seven magical pigs of Assal 'of the Golden Pillars', who could be killed and eaten and would be alive and ready to be slaughtered again the next morning. The bones of the pigs of Assal are in the *crane bag of *Manannán mac Lir. See OIDHEADH CHLAINNE TUIREANN [The Tragic Story of the Children of Tuireann].

Assaroe, Es Ruaidh, Es Ruad, Eas Ruadh, Easruadh, Eas Aodha Ruaidh, Easroe, Ess Ruaid, Ess Ruadh [Ir. *eas ruadh*, red cataract, falls]. A cataract formerly on the *Erne River, 1 mile W of Ballyshannon, Co. Donegal, that was once celebrated both for its abundance of *salmon and for its considerable beauty. Assaroe is one of the places where *Fionn mac Cumhaill is reputed to have caught the magic salmon; here the salmon bears the name 'Goll Essa Ruaid'. In modern times the cataract has been flooded by a hydroelectric project, and the salmon pass by on a fish ladder. One place-name story explains that the falls were named for *Áed Ruad, father of *Macha (3), eponym of *Emain Macha, who drowned here. Folk etymology suggests that the falls are named for Aodh Ruadh, Red Hugh O'Donnell (1571–1602), but the nearby Cistercian abbey of Assaroe was founded in 1178. Sometimes called Cathleen's Falls.

*Conall Gulban is also reputed to have lived here.

astrology [Gk. *astrologos*]. Students of the study of the purported influence of the stars on our lives profess to see evidence of astrological thinking in their reading of Celtic myth, but there is scant verbal evidence in early texts to demonstrate the widespread practice of astrology. The Irish term néladóir, 'cloud diviner', may be synonymous with 'astrologer'. Another Irish word, astralaíoch, is borrowed from the Greek. Reflecting Christian attitudes towards astrology, ScG speuradaireachd may also mean 'swearing loudly' or 'blasphemy'. Manx planartys; W sêr-ddewiniaeth, astroleg; Bret. hudsteredoniezh. See also DIVINATION.

Atepomaros [L, possessing a great horse (?)]. Gaulish epithet of *Apollo.

áth, àth. The Irish and Scottish Gaelic words for ford; fordable place of a river or stream, used in many place-names. Because the prefix áth-, àth- may be separate or joined with another word, all those with it are alphabetized here letter by letter.

Áth Cliath [Ir., ford of the hurdles]. Name used in many early Irish narratives for the place where *Dublin now lies. Baile Átha Cliath [Ir., town of the ford of hurdles] is the Irish name for the city of Dublin.

Áth Fhirdiad(h). [Ir., ford of Ferdia]. Ford of the River Dee in Co. Louth, 14 miles N of Drogheda, site of the combat between *Cúchulainn and *Ferdiad in the **Táin Bó Cuailnge* [Cattle Raid of Cooley]; coextensive with the town of *Ardee, Co. Louth.

Àth Fodhla, Fodla. A ScG version of *Atholl. See also FÓDLA.

Atha. In *Macpherson's *Ossian* (1760), this is *Cairbre's palace, which is described as being both in *Connacht and in Co. Antrim, on the banks of *Lough Neagh.

athach [ScG, giant, champion; monster; cf. OIr. *aithech*, boor, serf]. A monster or *giant of Scottish Gaelic folklore, thought to haunt gorges and lonely lochans or lakes. Comparable to the *bòcan, *d'reach, *fachan, or *luideag.

athair lus [Ir., father herb]. An Irish name for ground ivy, thought to have powers against the *fairies.

Athairne Áilgesach, Aithirne Áilghesach [Ir., importunate satirist; cf. OIr. *aithirne*, a kind of satire]. A court poet and satirist from the time of *Conchobar mac Nessa, known for his demanding tributes. He once asked for and received the eye of *Eochaid (6), a king from the midlands of Ireland. He continually exploited the tradition that a poet must not be refused a request. He sought *cows, women, and many other things from the people of *Leinster. These were given to him, and a bridge was built over the *Liffey (where the modern city of *Dublin lies) so that the cattle might be herded across, but the Leinstermen reneged on the promise to deliver the women. See AMAIRGIN (2) for his exchange with his foster-son about the appropriateness of the seasons for the composition of poetry. In some texts Athairne steals the three *cranes of *Midir. His altercation with Mesgegra/ Mesgedra, king of Leinster, is retold in Samuel Ferguson's poem 'Mesgedra' (1865).

Athena. Greek virgin goddess of wisdom, arts and crafts, and war. Suggested Celtic counterparts to her include *Brigantia/ *Brigit. See also MINERVA.

Athlone [Ir. *Áth Lúain*, ford of Lúan]. The principal ford of the River *Shannon, between the counties of Roscommon and Westmeath, 78 miles W of Dublin and 48 miles E of Galway. Because of its strategic position between east and west, Athlone has long figured prominently in Irish lore and history. *Cúchulainn sheared off the tops of three peaks near here. The first fortress at Athlone was built before the Anglo-Norman conquest. The city of Athlone, which lies on both sides of the river, was an English garrison from Elizabethan times.

Athnurcher, Athnurchar [Ir., ford of the cast or throw]. The site where *Cet slings a 'brain ball' at *Conchobar mac Nessa in Irish narrative. The modern parish at this locality on the borders of Co. Westmeath and Co. Offaly is known as Ardnurcher or Horseleap.

Atholl, Athole, Athol [ScG, the ford of *Fódla]. In ancient times Atholl was one of the four Pictish kingdoms, roughly equivalent with what was until 1974 Perthshire, now north-west Tayside. On the modern map Atholl is a mountainous, forested area at the south end of the Grampian mountains. The land is generally uncultivatable, but it has an extensive deer forest. Many Scotsmen perceive Atholl as a kind of impenetrable interior or 'heartland' of the Highlands.

Attecotti. Ancient, historical people of the British Isles, cited in Roman records; tentatively identified with invading populations from early *Ireland.

aughisky. Spelling used by W. B. Yeats and others for *each uisce.

August festival. See LUGHNASA.

Aulomm. See AILILL AULOMM.

Auraicept na nÉces [Ir., the scholar's primer]. Treatise on the origins and classifications of the Irish language, used in bardic schools of pre-Norman Ireland. Among the subjects discussed are the origin and order of the Latin and Irish alphabets, including *ogham, grammatical gender, verb forms, and elements of rhyme. Sometimes attributed to the 7th-century warrior and poet *Cenn Fáelad. The standard modern edition is by George Calder (Edinburgh, 1917). See also Anders Ahlquist, *The Early Irish Linguist* (Helsinki, 1983).

Aurmumu. OIr. name for East *Munster or *Ormond.

Avagddu, Avagdu. Anglicized spelling of Afagddu [W, utter darkness]; see MORFRAN.

Avalon [cf. OW *aballon*, 'apple']. The Elysium of the Arthurian legends where King *Arthur and other heroes went on their death, usually thought to lie on the western seas but sometimes identified with *Glastonbury. The English word derives from the Latin of *Geoffrey of Monmouth (12th cent.), Insula Avallonis, 'Isle of Apples'. In Welsh it is still known as Ynys Afallach, 'Isle of Apples'. Cf. Emain Ablach [Ir., fortress of apples], the true home of *Manannán mac Lir. In the Arthurian romance by Layamon (12th cent.) Argante is the queen of Avalon.

Avebury. Largest prehistoric monument in Britain, in north Wiltshire, 6 miles W of Marlborough. The earthworks with standing stones date from pre-Celtic times, *c.*4000–3000 BC. See Aubrey Burl, *Prehistoric Avebury* (New Haven, Conn., 1979); Michael Dames, *The Avebury Cycle* (London, 1980).

Avoca. Variation of the place-name oboxa, as found in Ptolemy's geography (2nd cent. AD), which is identical with the modern Avonmore, Co. Wicklow, 3 miles S of Rathdrum. Avoca was popularized in Thomas Moore's (1779–1852) song 'The Meeting of the Waters'. The waters are the Avonmore and Avonbeg rivers.

awenyddion, awenithion [cf. W *awen*, poetic or mantic inspiration]. The power of poetic insight, as described by Giraldus Cambrensis (12th cent. BC), although he thought it little more than soothsaying. Awenyddion might be conferred on a person in a mantic sleep. The receiver would become rapt in ecstasy, during which he or she might deliver oneself of speech that was not easily intelligible because the utterances are veiled, apparently contradictory, and highly figurative. The 18th-century figure Iolo *Morganwg used the word for a bardic pupil. See also IMBAS FOROSNAI; DÍCHETAL DO CHENNAIB; SOUS; TEINM LAÍDA.

ax, axe. An axe was thrown by Tuirbe Trágmar from his Hill of Axe in the full of flood-tide as a means of forbidding the sea to come beyond it. In the story **Fled Bricrenn* [Bricriu's Feast], the churl *Cráebruad (*Cú Roí in disguise) challenges the Ulster heroes to a beheading contest with an axe, a challenge which only *Cúchulainn will accept.

B

B.The second letter of the modern English alphabet was represented by beithe [*birch] in the *ogham alphabet of early Ireland.

Babal. A *Partholonian merchant in the *Lebor Gabála* [Book of Invasions] credited with the introduction of cattle into Ireland.

Bacchus. See DIONYSUS.

Bachlach [Ir., rustic, servant, labourer, etc.]. An Irish word often translated as 'churl', used to describe several figures in early narratives, most notably *Cráebruad in *Fled Bricrenn* [Briccriu's Feast] who challenges the *Ulster heroes to a beheading contest.

Bacorbladra, Bachorbladhra. A *Partholonian teacher in the *Lebor Gabála* [Book of Invasions] credited with being the first foster-father in Ireland.

Badb, Badhbh, Baobh, Bave [Ir., hooded or hoodie crow, the scald crow in Ireland or the Royston in England; crow or raven with implications of deadly, fatal, or dangerous]. Also Badb Catha [Ir., crow or raven of battle]. A supernatural woman, perhaps a goddess or demon, who frequents places of battle, both before and after conflict, in early Irish literature. In general she is an evil personality who delights in slaughter. She incites armies against one another and fills warriors with fury. She appears as a woman promising victory to the *Dagda before the Second Battle of *Mag Tuired. She is also a woman when she puts a spell on *Niam (1), but she is a 0*crow when she appears to *Cúchulainn. Badb is the daughter of either *Cailitin or *Ernmas and the wife or granddaughter of *Néit. Sometimes Néit is described as having two wives, *Nemain and Badb, but Badb's place may be taken by *Fea. Less commonly, Badb may be the wife of *Tethra.

Badb is one of a trio of battle-goddesses, the *Mórrígna, along with *Mórrígan and *Macha. *Nemain, perhaps an aspect of Badb, is sometimes also in the trio; she is another battle-goddess who is also married to Néit. In addition Badb appears to be closely related to the Gaulish battle-goddess whose name is reported as Bodua, Catubodua, or Cauth Bova. In later Irish folklore Badb appears to have lent much to the figure of badhbh chaointe [Ir., keening or weeping crow], a figure who haunts battlefields and may presage death. In this function she has much in common with the *banshee. Her name is commemorated in the Co. Kerry townland of Lisbabe [Ir. *lios baidbhe*, Badb's fort], near Aghadoe, named for the ancient ruin once thought to be Badb's residence. See also BÁNÁNACH; BOCÁNACH; WASHER AT THE FORD.

See Charles Donahue, 'The Valkyries and the Irish War Goddesses', *PMLA* 56 (1941), 381–409; Françoise Le Roux and Christian-J. Guyonvarc'h, *La Souveraineté guerrière de l'Irlande: Mórrígan, Bodb, Macha* (Rennes, 1983); Rosalind Elizabeth Clark, *Great Queens: Irish Goddesses from the Morrígan to Cathleen Ní Houlihan* (Gerrards Cross, 1990). Folk motifs: A132.6.2; A485.1.

Badenoch [ScG land of the wood clumps (?)]. A mountainous district in south-east Inverness-shire (since 1974, Highland), populated by Gaelic speakers until modern times. In the 18th century Badenoch was one of two centres of bogus Gaelic literature, including such writers as James *Macpherson, Ewan Macpherson, and Captain Morrison of Skye. The other school was that of Glenorchy.

badger. Any of various flesh-eating mammals that burrow in the ground; the most common species in the British Isles is *meles meles*. In the **Mabinogi* the heroes play a grim game called 'badger-in-the-bag', derived from the way the fierce badger is subdued and captured. *Pwyll captures *Rhiannon's rival suitor, *Gwawl, in a giant bag. In Irish tradition Grian turns the sons of *Conall into badgers; they were later killed by Cormac Gaileng. *Adamnán says in his life of St Columba (late 7th cent.) that a Pictish magus or holy man is named Brocan, 'badger'. Celtic words for 'badger' show considerable uniformity; OIr. brocc; ModIr. broc; ScG broc; W broch; Corn. brogh; Bret. broc'h.

Badh, Badhbh. ModIr. variants of *Badb. In east *Munster badb was once current for *banshee.

Badurn. An Irish king in early narrative. When Badurn's wife goes to the well one day, she sees two fairy women linked together with a bronze chain. When they see her approaching they go under the well, and she follows them, gaining entrance to the fairy mound.

Báetán mac Cairill. A king of *Ulster with a fortress at Knocklayd south of Ballycastle, Northern Ireland, who reigned from 572 to 581. Although his career has been obscured by synthetic historians, he does appear to have extended the suzerainty of *Dál Riada to Scotland and the Isle of Man.

bags. The assertion that the *Fir Bolg were the 'Men of the Bags' is no longer entertained by informed commentators.

baile. An Old Irish word meaning place or piece of land and a Modern Irish word meaning town or townland; it appears in innumerable Irish and Scottish place-names such as Baile Átha Cliath [Ir., town of the hurdle ford]; Dublin, or Baile an Mhóta [Ir., townland of the mound]: Ballymote. It is usually anglicized as 'Bally-'.

Baile, Baile Binnbérlach [Ir. *Baile*, (vision?) of the clear voice]. Heir to the *Ulster throne and tragic lover of *Ailinn of *Leinster in the 11th-century story *Scél Baili Binnbérlaig* [The Story of Baile of the Clear Voice]. Baile was making his way south from *Emain Macha when he was told, falsely, that Ailinn and been killed, and died himself of grief. Travelling north, Ailinn was told of Baile's death and she too perished at the news. After their deaths a *yew tree grew from his grave and an *apple from hers. Poets and seers cut down the trees; those from Ulster turned the yew into tablets for writing and the men of Leinster used the apple. Baile's name appears often in the writings of W. B. Yeats, most notably the poem 'Baile and Ailinn' (1901) and the play *On Baile's Strand* (1904); the play deals with *Cúchulainn, but Baile's Strand is near Dundalk, Co. Louth. Baile is also alluded to in *The Only Jealousy of Emer* (1919) and *The Death of Cuchulain*.

Baile Chuind Chétchathaig. An earlier text of **Baile In Scáil*.

Baile In Scáil [Ir., The Phantom's Frenzy; The Poetic Ecstasy of the Phantom]. An Irish adventure or **Echtrae* narrative composed before AD 1056. In a preliminary, *Conn Cétchathach [of the Hundred Battles] was mounting the ramparts at *Tara when a stone he trod upon screamed. The court poets explained, after a requested delay of fifty-three days, that the stone had come from *Inis Fáil to Tara, that it wanted to go to *Teltown where the games were held, and that any prince who did not find it on the last day of the week of the Fair at Teltown would die within the year. The number of cries uttered under Conn's feet signified the number of kings from his seed who would rule over Ireland. When Conn asked to know the number, his druid replied that he was not destined to tell.

Conn and some retainers set out, but were soon surrounded by a great mist so that they lost their way. A horseman approached them, inviting Conn to his dwelling. They went to a house 30 feet long with a ridgepole of white gold. In the house, in a room full of gold, they found a damsel seated in a chair of crystal and wearing a crown of gold. Upon a throne they saw the Phantom, whose like had never been seen in Tara. He revealed himself as *Lug Lámfhota, and the damsel as the *Sovereignty of Ireland, Lug's wife, who then served Conn with enormous portions of meat; though she is not named, commentators identify the 'wife' with the goddess *Ériu. When she served the red *ale, she asked to whom the cup should be given, and the Phantom answered her. He named every prince from the time of Conn onward, and then disappeared, along with his house. The gold cup and other vessels remained with Conn. None of the names mentioned in the prophecy appears in records as kings of Ireland.

An earlier text of the same story is *Baile Chuind Chétchathaig*. Many commentators see in *Baile In Scáil* a parallel with Perceval and the Holy Grail, especially in the question, 'To whom shall the cup be served?' Translated by R. Thurneysen, *Zeitschrift für celtische Philologie*, 20 (1935), 213–27.

Baile's Strand. The seashore around Dundalk, Co. Louth. It is named for *Baile Binnbérlach, the *Ulster heir and lover of

*Ailinn, and is the setting for W. B. Yeats's drama (1904).

Baillgel, Baillgheal, Ballgel [Ir., bright-limbed]. A lady of the *sídh in *Brega as mentioned in the *Fenian Cycle. This same name is borne by several personages named in genealogies.

Báine [Ir., whiteness, pallor]. A female figure or princess in early Irish place-name legends. She may be the daughter of Frigriu mac Rubai Ruaid, who gave his name to the great stone fort in Co. Donegal, *Ailech, Ailech Frigrenn, or Greenan Elly. In another story she is the daughter of *Tuathal Techtmar, ancestor of the kings of Ireland.

Báinleannán [Ir. *báine*, 'pale, white'; *leannán*, 'lover, paramour']. A female spirit who accompanies a number of questing heroes in Irish folk-tales recorded from oral tradition. See also FAIRY LOVER [Ir. *leannán sídhe/sí*].

baird. Gen. sing. or nom. pl. of *bard.

Baíscne, Baoiscne, Baoisgne, Bascna [cf. OIr. *baiscne*, 'large tree', 'stalwart' (?)]. A clan, one of the two great families in the *Fianna of the *Fenian Cycle. *Fionn mac Cumhaill headed the Clan Baíscne while *Goll headed the other, the Clan *Morna.

Bala Lake [W, place where river flows from the lake]. A lake in *Gwynedd (until 1974, Merionethshire), the largest stretch of inland fresh water in Wales, 4 miles long and half a mile wide, and the chief source of the River Dee. It was once the heart of the powerful, ancient Celtic people the *Ordovices, whose descendants became the leaders of *Gwynedd. The remains of an Ordovician hillfort, Caer Euni, lie 5 miles NE of Bala. At Llafawr, 2 miles from Bala, is the alleged burial-place of the 7th-century poet *Llywarch Hen. *Gwion Bach was immersed here and later transformed into *Taliesin. The giant *Tegid Foel [W, the bald] lived here with his wife, *Ceridwen. Known as *Llyn Tegid in much of Welsh tradition; also known as Pemble Mere; possibly identical with *Llyn Llion.

Balar. An OIr. variant of *Balor.

Balclutha. In *Macpherson's *Ossian* (1760), a city on the Clyde occupied by the Britons who opposed the Caledonians. Macpherson's apologists have hypothesized a Gaelic origin for the term, Baile Clutha, 'Town on the Clyde'. It may have been adapted from *Alcluith, as mentioned in Bede's *History* (8th cent.).

ball seirce [Ir., love spot, blemish]. A skin blemish on the forehead of *Diarmait Ua Duibne that made him irresistible to women.

ballad [OFr. *balade*]. The popular composition of anonymous ballads began after the 12th century in many countries in Western Europe, including the Celtic-speaking ones. 'Ballad' in Modern Irish is bailéad; ScG duanag, diminutive of duan: song, cf. òran: song, laoidh: verse, song, luinneag: ditty; Manx bannag; W baled, balad; Bre. gwerz.

Ballgel. Variant spelling of Baillgel.

Ballymote [Ir. *baile an Mhóta*, 'townland of the mount']. A town in Co. Sligo, 14 miles S of Sligo town; the late 18th-century *Book of Ballymote* [*Leabhar Bhaile an Mhóta*] was compiled here.

Balor, Balar, Bolar. Often called Balor of the Evil or Baleful Eye. A king of the *Fomorians who had an evil or basilisk eye, never opened except on the battlefield, when four men were needed to lift the eyelid. If an army looked at the eye that army was rendered powerless. Balor acquired the terrible eye when as a child he saw his father's druids brewing charms. When such theories were in fashion, he was thought to be the sun deity of the Celts. Often compared with the Welsh *Ysbaddaden Pencawr. Brian Ó Cuív, 'Lugh Lámhfhada and the Death of Balar Ua Néid', *Celtica*, 2 (1954), 64–6.

As he was the grandson of *Néit, Balor has the occasional patronymic Ua Néit. He is sometimes credited with a wife, the loathsome Caitlín or Céthlionn of the crooked tooth. His daughter was *Eithne, who mated with *Cian to produce the great hero *Lug Lámfhota. As Balor's death was prophesied to come at the hands of his grandson, he had a lifelong conflict with Lug, which finds its culmination in **Cath Maige Tuired* [The (Second) Battle of Mag Tuired], where the two meet in combat. In some versions Lug blinds Balor's eye with a spear made by *Goibniu, the craft god. In other versions Lug decapitates Balor and places the severed head on a pike, using the still potent eye to split rocks. In some stories Balor was a bandit or pirate on Tory Island. From this base he stole the fairy cow *Glas Ghaibhleann from its owner, *Gaibhlín.

The eminent folklorist A. H. Krappe once argued that the story of Balor and Lug represented the conflict between the Old Year or Winter against the New Year; see *Balor With the Evil Eye* (New York, 1927).

balores [Corn., chough]. *Crow-like *bird, species *pyrrhocorax pyrrhocorax*, with black feathers and red beak and feet. The bird, usually named with the definite article, An Balores, is an emblem for Cornish cultural identity. R. Morton Nance wrote a play in the Cornish language titled *An Balores* (1932). The chough is also associated with King *Arthur.

bán síde. OIr. spelling of *banshee.

banais ríghe [Ir., wedding-feast of kingship]. A ritual practised by early Irish kings in which they were united with the *sovereignty of the territory over which they ruled. The abundant evidence of the annals testifies that the practice was widespread, although details are not always precise. The ceremony appears to have comprised two main elements, the libation offered by the bride to her husband and the coition. At *Tara the ritual was called feis temrach.

bánánach. Preternatural female beings in early Irish literature who haunt the field of battle. See also BADB; BOCÁNACH.

Banba, Banbha. A poetic name for Ireland in early times, one of a divine trio of eponyms for Ireland along with *Ériu and *Fódla. Her father was *Delbáeth (2) and mother *Eirnin. A well-known fiction to explain how Ireland had three names appears in the **Lebor Gabála* [Book of Invasions]. When the advancing *Milesians met Banba at *Sliab Mis [Slieve Mish] she gave them her name, told them it was the name of the country, and begged that it remain so forever. The Milesians subsequently met Fódla and Ériu, who told them their names and made the same request; only Ériu's wish was granted. Banba was originally the name of either south *Leinster or the plain of *Meath containing *Tara before becoming a name for all of Ireland. In other narratives Banba is the daughter of *Cian and the wife of *Mac Cuill. The assertion that the name Banba is at the root of the place-name Banff, Scotland, is disputed.

Banbán [Ir., little pig]. Often called Banbán the hospitaller in the puzzling story of the death of *Diarmait mac Cerbaill.

Banbha. ModIr. spelling of *Banba.

Bangor [Ir. *bánchor*, 'white choir' (?); *beannchar*, 'pointed arrangement']. Name of at least six places in Ireland and Wales. Two of the best known are: (1) a town in Northern Ireland, 12 miles NE of Belfast, the site of a monastery founded by St *Comgall; (2) a hamlet in *Dyfed (formerly Cardiganshire), 4 miles E of Newcastle Emlyn on the River Teifi, one of several reputed burial-places for *Taliesin. See James Hamilton, *Bangor Abbey Through the Centuries* (Bangor, Northern Ireland, 1980).

banshee, badh [east Munster], banshie, bean sí, bean sídhe, ben síde; Scottish forms: bansìth, bean-shìth, bean sìth; Manx: ben shee [Ir., fairy woman, woman of the fairy mound]. A female wraith of Irish and Scottish Gaelic tradition thought to be able to foretell but not necessarily cause death in a household. Although *Fedelm in the **Táin Bó Cuailnge* [Cattle Raid of Cooley] seems to be an anticipation of the figure, observations and portrayals of the banshee in literature were not common before the 17th century. Since that time, the banshee has been depicted so often and so variously that generalizations about her appearance and role are difficult to make without many qualifications. She may be seen as a beautiful maiden weeping for the coming death of a loved one, or she may be a gruesome hag foretelling it. Lady Jane Wilde (1888) seems to be the first to opine that the beautiful banshee is more common in Ireland and the ugly more common in Scotland. In Scotland the figure is known as ban-sìth, bean-shìth, or bean sìth; closely related to it is the *baobhan sìth, which may embody elements of the succubus or vampire. The Manx ben shee seems closer to the Irish banshee. Both the beautiful and the ugly figures often wear white; in Meath she wears a white gown with red shoes. As oral tradition was continued by English speakers, the banshee tended to become confused with the White Lady of other folklores, as bean, 'woman', sounds like bán, 'white, fair-haired'. The banshee may also wear a grey cloak over a green dress. Her eyes are usually fiery red from continual weeping. The beautiful banshee has long hair which she strokes with a gold or silver comb. The wail of the banshee is most often compared with the keening of Irish mourners, and thus she is often known as an bhean chaointe, 'the keening woman'. Less flattering commentators have compared her sound to that of a dog baying at the moon. The banshee is most often a solitary person, although an assembly might wail at the passing of an especially noble or holy person.

The banshee appears to draw from the characterizations of *Áine and *Badb in earlier Irish literature, and like Badb she has associations with the hooded crow. In folk etiology the banshee was thought to be the spirit of a woman who died in childbirth, or of a murdered pregnant woman. Despite these sombre associations, a banshee's attentions to a family were thought to be a mark of high station, especially in Ireland, and several hundred families boasted of their own banshee. A Welsh counterpart is the *cyhyraeth. See also AÍBELL; ANGAU; ANKOU; CLÍDNA; DEATH COACH; GLAISTIG; WASHER AT THE FORD.

Patricia Lysaght, 'Irish Banshee Traditions', *Béaloideas*, 42–4 (1974–6); 'An Bhean Chaointe: The Supernatural Woman in Irish Folklore', *Éire-Ireland*, 14 (4) (Winter 1979), 7–29; *The Banshee: The Supernatural Death-Messenger* (Dublin, 1986).

ban-sìth. A ScG spelling of *banshee.

Baobh. Variant spelling of *Badb.

baobhan sìth [ScG, fairy woman]. A fearful female creature in Scottish Gaelic oral tradition. A kind of succubus, very dangerous and evil, she will suck dry of blood any man who takes her embrace. Distinguish from the death-presaging figure of Irish folklore, the *banshee, who is known as the ban-sìth, bean-shìth, or bean sìth in Scottish Gaelic tradition. Folk motifs: E251.3.3; F471.2.1.

Baoisne. ModIr. spelling of *Baíscne.

Baranton. The fountain of *Brocéliande, a forest in *Brittany.

Barbe, Saint. Legendary Breton saint who appears to be derived from a pre-Christian fire-goddess. She is the protectress of those who seek her aid in sudden death, especially from lightning, and a patroness of firemen. Although not on the Church's calendar of saints, she has been venerated at La Faouet on the last Sunday of June. Compare BRIGIT; BRIGID, SAINT.

Barc Breasail. See HY BRASIL.

bard [Ir. and ScG *bard*; W *bardd*; Bret. *barzh*; cf. L *bardus*; Gk. *bārdos*]. The current standard English definition of this Celtic word, denoting a poet of exalted status, i.e. the voice of a nation or people, dates from Thomas Gray's use of it in his poem 'The Bard' (1757). Although Gray's borrowing of the word seems to owe most to Welsh tradition, the role and status of the bard varied from one Celtic nation to another. Among the ancient Continental Celts, according to Roman commentators, the bards were singers and poets who occupied a lower status than the *vates (interpreters of sacrifice) or the *druids, who commanded the highest esteem. In Ireland the bard held a lower rank in the seven orders of *fili [poet], of which the highest was the *ollam; the bard had not mastered the 350 stories and twelve years of study required to become an ollam. In Wales the power and high position of the bard preceded and outlasted that of hereditary princes. The earliest bards, dating from the 6th century, included *Aneirin, *Taliesin, Blwchbardd, *Cian, and Talhearn Tad Awen; they were known as the *cynfeirdd [W, early or original poets], and their poetry as hengerdd. In following centuries, only the *pencerdd [W, chief poet or musician], whose training lasted nine years, was allowed to teach a bard in Wales. In time Welsh bards formed the Bardic Order or Bardd Teulu [W, household poet, poet of retinue], serving kings and princes for more than 1,000 years, forming a distinct segment of society with its own privileges. A bard might have assumed the role of the cyfarwydd [W, storyteller], although this is not certain. Great assemblies of bards began as early as 1176; the assembly later became known as *eisteddfod. A great flowering of Welsh bardic poetry came in the 12th and 13th centuries, concurrent with the zenith of native political power before the Anglo-Norman conquest. Bards of this time were known as gogynfeirdd [W, rather early poets]. Elements of Welsh bardic philosophy were mixed with Christian belief by Llywelyn Siôn in Barddas (late 16th cent.); see COSMOGONY. The 18th-century *Iolo Morganwg placed the seat of bardism in Glamorganshire in south Wales. In Gaelic Scotland a bard was a highly trained poet in the service of an hereditary chief. Bards were generally men of considerable status and authority in Celtic literature, although impoverished bardic scholars appear in a number of Irish narratives.

More than 1,000 bards are cited in Irish, Scottish Gaelic, and Welsh literatures, and there are numerous claimants to the titles of 'Bard of Ireland' and 'Bard of Wales'. Perhaps *Amairgin and *Dallán Forgaill were denoted by 'Bard of Ireland' more often than others. The title 'Last of the Bards' has been given posthumously to several poets, notably Fearflatha Ó Gnímh (*c*.1540–*c*.1640), bard of the O'Neills of Clandeboye, and Dòmhnall Mac Mhuirich (d. *c*.1745), the last with classical rather than vernacular training.

Bardsey. A small island (444 acres) in north Cardigan Bay, *Gwynedd. The Welsh name for the island is Ynys Enlli. According to the Welsh *Triads, *Merlin settled here to live in a glass house with the Treasures of Britain. St Cadfan founded a monastery here in the 6th century.

Barenton, Baranton. See BROCÉLIANDE.

Barinthus. The person who tells St *Brendan about the land promised to the saints.

baríoghan an bhrogla, banríon na bruig, bean ríghan na burgh. Irish phrases meaning 'queen of the fairy palace', denoting perhaps *Úna or Grian.

Barr, Saint [cf. ScG *barr*, 'top, uppermost, cream']. Saint and probable eponym of the Isle of *Barra in the Outer Hebrides. His feast, Là Féill Bharr, involving ritual horseback riding, was once celebrated on 27 September, later merging with the feast of St Michael, 29 September. His name and feast show him to be identical with Barra (Finnbarr) and, more generally, to have formed part of the cult of St *Finnbarr, whose feast in Cork, for example, fell on 25 September and, on Barry Island in South Wales, on about 26 September. The traveller Martin Martin (1703) records that a Catholic priest visited Barra and claimed never to have heard of St Barr, incurring the displeasure of the islanders.

Barra [cf. ScG *barr*, 'top, uppermost, cream']. An island and parish comprising the main island and several smaller nearby islands in the Outer Hebrides at the southern coda of the archipelago. The principal island is about 8 miles by 5, and today sustains a population of about 2,500, many of them bearing the surname MacNeill and claiming descent from the Irish hero *Niall Noígiallach [of the Nine Hostages]. Gaelic is still the first language of the many islanders, and thus Barra is perceived by some commentators as one of the most culturally pristine locations in Celtic Scotland. The inhabitants of Barra once spoke of the Otherworld as Roca Barraidh, an island on the dim western horizon.

See John Lorne Campbell (ed.), *The Book of Barra* (London, 1936).

Barrán [Ir. dim. of *barr*, 'tip, point, treetop']. Name borne by several early Irish figures, notably the father-in-law of *Caílte in the *Fenian Cycle.

Barrex, Barrecis [Brit., supreme (?), high god (?)]. A god of Roman-occupied Britain known from only one inscription at Carlisle, Cumberland. The Romans identified him with *Mars.

Barrow. A river of south-eastern Ireland, rising in the *Sliab Bladma [Slieve Bloom], providing a border between counties Kildare, Carlow, and Waterford from Laois and Kilkenny, and emptying, after a distance of 120 miles, in Wexford harbour. In early Irish stories it is known as Berba. In the valley of the Barrow, *Mac Cécht kills a supernatural being named *Mechi, son of *Mórrígan, and burns its three hearts, each one of which contains a serpent.

Basca, Bascna, Baskin. Variants of *Baíscne.

Bath. Resort town in Avon (before 1982, Somerset) 12 miles SE of Bristol whose medicinal waters have been known from prehistoric times. The ancient British worshipped a goddess here known as Sul or *Sulis and called the town *Aquae Sulis, identifying her with *Minerva. A divine couple known from Gaul, *Mars Leucetius and *Nemetona [Brit., goddess of the grove], were also worshipped here. In Welsh tradition Bath was thought to have been built by *Bladud, the father of *Lludd. Bath has rich associations in Arthurian literature, where it is known as Caer Bad, Caer Badum, Mons Badonis (in Nennius), and Bade (in *Chrétien de Troyes); it was the site of one of Arthur's greatest victories, against the Saxons. In recent years the town has been the subject of continuing archaeological investigation led by Barry Cunliffe; see his *Roman Bath Discovered* (London, 1971), etc.

battle fury. See CÚCHULAINN.

battle gods. See BADB; NÉIT; see also BOCÁNACH and BÁNÁNACH, the demons of battle.

Battle of . . . See CAD . . . [Welsh]; CATH . . . [Irish]. The Welsh title for *The Battle of the*

Trees is **Cad Goddeu*; the Irish for *The Battle of Moytura* is **Cath Maige Tuired*.

bauchan. Anglicization of *bòcan.

Bave. Anglicization of *Badb.

Bé Chuille, Becuille. Daughter of *Flidais, goddess of the wild, and one of the most witch-like women among the *Tuatha Dé Danann; often described as a *druidess.

Bé Chuma, Bé Cuma, Bécuma [Ir., woman of grief, sorrow]. Known as Bé Chuma of the Fair Skin in **Echtrae Airt meic Cuinn* [The Adventure of Art son of Conn]. Initially a wife of *Eógan Inbir in the *Otherworld, she is banished to the land of men for her sin with *Gaidiar son of *Manannán mac Lir. Once she is among mortals, *Conn takes her as a wife, but she lusts after his son *Art. When the druids complain that her wickedness has brought a curse upon the country, she has Art exiled as a remedy. When Art returns from a subsequent adventure with his new wife, *Delbcháem, Bé Chuma is forced to depart from Tara.

Bé Find. Variant of *Bébinn.

Bé Téite, Bétéide [Ir., wanton or luxurious woman]. A daughter of *Flidais and active woman in the *Tuatha Dé Danann.

Beag. ModIr. for *Bec.

Bealcu, Bealchu. Variant forms of *Bélchú.

Bealltuinn. ScG spelling for *Beltaine.

Bealtaine, Bealteine. ModIr. for the month of May; for a description of the pre-Christian feast, see BELTAINE.

bean chaointe. See BANSHEE.

bean nighe, nigheadaireachd [ScG, washerwoman, laundrymaid]. A female wraith of Scottish Gaelic folklore who washes blood-stained clothes when some person in the neighbourhood is about to die, usually in battle; a Scottish instance of the pan-Celtic *washer at the ford. The bean nighe is usually thought to be small and slender, often wearing green, sometimes with red webbed feet. She haunts desolate lakes and streams, and although she portends evil a person does better to see her before the bean nighe sees the mortal. Anyone rash enough to seize one of her hanging breasts and suck it may claim to be her foster-child and will be spared. The *Caointeag of the Isle of Islay and Kintyre is a fiercer and more formidable variation of the bean nighe; the *Cadineag of *Glencoe is gentler. In Ireland the role of the fearful washer or washer at the ford is subsumed in the *banshee. A Breton counterpart is the tunnerez noz.

bean ríghan na brugh, banríon na bruig. See BARÍOGHAN AN BHROGLA.

bean sídhe, bean sí. ModIr. spellings of *banshee.

bean sìth. ScG spelling of *banshee.

bear. Several species of this large mammal, family *Ursidae*, were common in western and northern Europe until modern times so that the bear was, along with the *boar, one of the most ferocious native beasts a person might encounter. Not surprisingly, then, the bear figured often in the Celtic imagination. Bears are found on Gaulish coins and statuettes. The bear-goddess *Artio, also known as Andarta, was venerated at what is now Berne ('bear city'), Switzerland. Another bear divinity was Matus or Matunus, venerated at Risingham, north of Hadrian's Wall. Names deriving from native forms for 'bear' are cited often in Welsh and Irish genealogies. The Welsh for bear is arth or arthen; cf. Bret. arzh, giving rise to the Gaelic personal name Art and possibly also *Arthur. Archaic OIr. for bear is math; OIr. and MidIr. mathgamain; ModIr. mathghamhain; ScG mathghamhainn. See also BEITHIR.

Béare. Legendary Castilian princess who married *Eógan Mór (Mug Nuadat), and for whom the *Beare peninsula is named.

Beare, Beara [Ir. *Béirre*, *Béarra*]. A peninsula in south-west Munster between Bantry Bay and the Kenmare River estuary, divided between Counties Cork and *Kerry. The peninsula is the home of the *sovereignty figure *Cailleach Bhéirre, the Hag or Old Woman of Beare, known from a 9th-century poem and often cited in the oral tradition. *Tech Duinn [Donn's House], the realm of *Donn (1) and thus of the dead, was thought to be on a rocky islet between the tip of the Beare peninsula and Dursey Island. Bear Island, formerly Beare Island, 1 mile S of Castletown Bearhaven, contains a standing stone associated with the Cailleach Bhéirre. By tradition peninsula and island are named for Beare, Spanish-born wife of *Eógan Mór (Mug Nuadat).

Bearrach. ModIr. spelling of *Berrach.

beauty spot. See BALL SEIRCE.

Bébinn, Bé Bind, Bé Find, Bébhionn, Bébind, Béfind, Befionn, Vivionn. [Ir., beautiful or fair woman]. A common name in early Ireland borne by several mythical and historical figures, including queens and abbesses. Although it has been anglicized as Vivionn/ Vivian, it is unrelated to that French and English name.

Bébinn, 1. An early Irish divinity who served as the patroness of birth and whose name was invoked, under different spellings, in oral tradition over many centuries. She is the sister of *Boand and the wife of either Áed Alainn, a divinity, or Idath, a mortal; she is the mother of *Fráech.

2. In the *Fenian Cycle she is a beautiful giantess of aristocratic bearing who seeks protection from *Fionn's *Fianna when an ugly giant pursues her. Subsequently the ugly giant breaks into the palace and kills her.

3. A daughter of *Elcmar.

Bebo. The wife of *Iubdán, a king of the *fairies, first mentioned in the 13th-century text of *Echtra Fergusa maic Léti* [The Adventure of Fergus mac Léti]; see FERGUS MAC LÉTI.

Bec, Beag, Becc [Ir., little, small]. Name borne by several figures in early Irish literature, both male (see below) and at least one female, a warrior from *Connacht.

Bec mac Buain. The keeper of a well of wisdom at Cahernarry (or Cahirnarry), Co. Limerick, according to **Feis Tighe Chonáin* [The Feast at Conán's House]. Bec's three daughters were guarding the well when *Fionn and two companions approached, looking for water. One of the daughters accidentally dropped some water from a bowl which fell into Fionn's mouth, giving him wisdom. The Norse scholar E. O. Turville-Petre once suggested that the episode reminded him of Odin's gaining of wisdom from the mead of Kvasir; *Myth and Religion of the North* (London and New York, 1964), 40–1.

Bec mac Dé Described as 'the best seer of his time', Bec could speak with nine men at once and answer all their questions with one reply. He prophesied that *Diarmait mac Cerbaill would be killed in the house of Banbán the hospitaller.

Becfola, Bec Fola, Becfhola [Ir., small dowry]. Wife of *Diarmait, king of *Tara, whose story is told in *Tochmarc Becfhola* [The Wooing of Becfola] in the *Cycle of Kings. Unhappy in her arranged marriage with Diarmait, Becfola lusted after the king's fosterling, Crimthann. On her urging the young couple planned to elope, but Crimthann did not arrive as he would not travel on a Sunday. Instead she met a fairy lover, *Flann ua Fedach, not known before and they spent the night together on an island in Lough *Erne, although they did not consummate their love. In the morning she returned to Tara; their time away appeared only an instant to ordinary mortals. Later Flann came in disguise, and they left together. See Standish Hayes O'Grady, 'Tochmarc Becfola', in *Silva Gadelica* (London, 1892), i. 85–7 (text); ii. 91–3 (translation). See also Myles Dillon, 'The Wooing of Becfola, and the Stories of Cano, Son of Gartnáin', *Modern Philology*, 43 (1945), 11–17.

Bed of Diarmait and Gráinne. Fanciful name given to the *dolmens or portal-tombs of Ireland because the lovers were thought to have slept on them in their flight from jealous *Fionn. See DIARMAIT; GRÁINNE.

Bedd Gelert, *Beth Gellert* (ang.) [W, grave of Gelert]. A well-known Welsh folk-tale about the loyal hound of 'Prince Llywelyn' (perhaps *Llywelyn ap Iorwerth, d. 1240; or *Llywelyn ap Gruffudd, d. 1282). One day the prince goes hunting, but his loyal hound Gelert does not answer the call. When the prince returns he finds blood on Gelert's mouth; assuming that the hound has attacked his child, in anger he kills it. Later the prince learns that Gelert had protected the royal child from the depredations of a wolf. To make amends, the prince erects a memorial in the hound's honour, Bedd Gelert [The Grave of Gelert]. Antecedents of the story can be found in Sanskrit, Mongolian, Persian, Russian, and the medieval Latin *Gesta Romanorum* (14th cent.). Beddgelert is the name of a village in *Gwynedd along the borders of the former counties of Carnarvonshire and Merioneth, 4 miles SSE of *Snowdon. William Robert Spencer (1769–1834) based his once widely known ballad, 'Beth Gelert', on the traditional story. See H. E. Lewis, *Bedd Gelert: Its Facts, Fairies and Folk-Lore* (Portmadoc, 1899). See also DOG.

Bedwyr [W, birch hero]. A Welsh Arthurian hero, the counterpart of and perhaps the origin for Bedivere, Beduers, Beduerus, etc., as well as Pellinor and Bellinor. The son of Pedrawg, Bedwyr was often seen in the company of *Cei. Bedwyr was the servitor of Arthur and was in charge of his liquor cabinet; he threw the sword Excalibur into the lake. Bedwyr accompanied *Culhwch on his quest for Olwen; in this story he is described as one-armed but unequalled in use of the lance. He was also a swift runner.

bee [OE *bēo*]. The honey-making insect with distinctive black and yellow colouring (order *Hymenoptera*) has attracted a small body of lore in Celtic languages. In both Ireland and Wales, bees are thought to hail from heaven and bring secret wisdom with them. Honey is listed among the attributes of *Munster. OIr. bech; ModIr. beach, seillean; ScG beach; Manx shellan; W gwenynen; Corn. gwenenen; Bret. gwenanenn. See H. M. Ransome, *The Sacred Bee* (London, 1937).

beer. See ALE.

Béfionn. Variant of *Bébinn.

beheading bargain. See FLED BRICRENN [Briccriu's Feast].

beisht kione, yn [Manx, the beast with the black head]. A sea-monster thought to reside off the south coast of the Isle of Man, dreaded by all who sailed the coast.

beithir [ScG, bear, serpent, wild beast; dragon (?)]. A word in early Scottish Gaelic narratives for an undetermined savage creature. It may be a translation of the Norse word for 'bear', but it may also mean 'thunderbolt'. The beithir may have a long tail, but it never appears to be the fiery winged dragon of Germanic tradition. In more recent oral tradition the beithir is a class of *fuath who haunts caves and corries (narrow circular valleys with high walls). It may also imply 'lightning' or 'serpent'. A mountain south of the entrance to Glencoe is named Ben Vair or Ben Vehir, thought locally to commemorate a beithir who took shelter in Corrie Lia.

Bel. See BELENUS.

Belatucadros [Romano-Gaulish, fair, shining one; bright, beautiful one]. God venerated in Roman-occupied north Britain, especially in what is now Cumberland and Westmorland; he seems to have been propitiated by the humbler soldier and non-Roman civilian. The different spellings of his name may testify to his worshippers' low rate of literacy. His name makes him comparable to *Belenus, while the Romans equated him with *Mars. His name may be another version of *Cocidius, and his altars are comparable to those of *Vitiris. Some commentators see him as a forerunner of *Bendigeidfran or Bran the Blessed.

Bélchú, Bealchu, Bealcu. As described in the *Ulster Cycle, a warrior of Connacht who comes upon the wounded *Conall Cernach after the defeat of *Cet. Conall is bleeding so badly that he asks Bélchú to kill him to spare further agony. Instead Bélchú takes him home and heals his wounds. Bélchú's three sons, noticing Conall's might, resolve to murder him before he recovers. Learning of their plan, Conall contrives to have the sons kill their own father instead, after which the hero slays all three, taking their heads with him back to Ulster.

Belenus, Bel, Belenos, Belinos, Belinu, Bellinus, Belus [Gaul., bright (?)]. Continental Celtic god whose cult stretched from the Italian peninsula to the British Isles. A principal shrine was at Aquileia on the Adriatic, and his worship was also associated with health-giving waters such as those at Aquae Borvonis (Bourbon-les-Bains, north-east France). His worship was also known in Aquitaine and what is now Austria. Several ancient commentators linked him with *Apollo, and some modern commentators classify him only as an aspect of Apollo; a shrine of Belenus at Inveresk, Scotland, is inscribed 'Apollini Granno'. The 19th-century attempt to link Belenus, under the spelling Bel, with the Phoenician Baal is now rejected. A tribal leader of pre-Roman Britain styled himself Cunobelinus or 'Hound of Belenus'. Belenus apparently gives his name to *Beli Mawr, a Welsh ancestor-deity, and may give his name to the fountain of Bérenton (formerly Belenton) at *Brocéliande in Brittany. The celebrations for the calendar feast of *Beltaine may or may not derive from the veneration of Belenus. In *Geoffrey of Monmouth (1136), Belenus is reduced to a mere mortal conqueror. Fanciful folk etymology links Belenus with Billingsgate, near the Thames in London. See J. Gourvest, 'Le Culte de Belenos en Provence occidentale et en Gaule', *Ogam*, 6 (1954), 257–62. See also BORVO.

Belgae. An ancient *P-Celtic people of northern Gaul whom Julius Caesar (1st cent. BC) described as the fiercest of all. Caesar also tells us that portions of these people settled in Britain in areas most accessible to the sea before the end of the 1st century BC. Irish commentators as early as Roderick O'Flaherty (1685) assumed that the Belgae could be identified with the *Fir Bolg of Irish pseudohistory. Caesar's assertion that the Belgae were of Germanic origin is now understood to be geographical (i.e. from east of the Rhine) rather than ethnic (i.e. Teutonic). Their settlement in Britain included what is now Hampshire and Wiltshire. T. F. O'Rahilly's argument (1946) that the Belgae were identical with the *Builg and *Érainn, early invaders of Ireland, is now rejected.

Beli, Beli Mawr [W, big, bright; Beli the great]. An ancestor deity who established several royal lines in Wales. Although he is probably an adaptation of the earlier deity *Belenus, he has sometimes been identified with the shadowy historical figure Beli ab Elfin/Elffin (d. 721). Beli Mawr is mentioned several times in the **Mabinogi* and is cited as the husband of *Dôn and father of *Arianrhod and *Caswallan. In **Cyfranc Lludd a Llefelys* his sons are named as *Lludd and *Llefelys. The Arthurian figure Pelle appears to have borrowed much from Beli Mawr. See Rachel Bromwich, *Trioedd Ynys Prydain*, 2nd edn. (Cardiff, 1978), 281, 545. See also BILE.

Belisama, Belesama, Belisma. A lake- and river-goddess venerated in Gaul and Britain. Roman commentators equated her with *Minerva. Ptolemy (2nd cent. AD) gives her name to the Ribble River in central England. She was also venerated at what is now Vaison (Vaucluse) in south-eastern France.

Bellinus. Variant of *Belenus.

Beltaine, Belltaine, Bealtaine, Beltain, Beltane, Beltine, Bealteine, Bealltuinn (ScG.), Boaldyn (Manx). Irish, Scottish Gaelic, and Manx words for the seasonal feast fixed at 1 May on the Gregorian calendar, or 15 May in Scotland. As the end of the dark half of the year, Beltaine is a survival of one of the four great Celtic calendar feasts, known in early Ireland as *Imbolc (1 February), Lugnasad (ModIr. *Lughnasa, 1 August), and *Samain (1 November). The day was also known as Cétshamain in Ireland. Its counterparts in Wales are *Cyntefin, Dydd Calan Mai, and Calan Mai, in Cornwall Cala' Mē, and in Brittany *Kala-Hañv. Beltaine may or may not derive from the veneration of *Belenus. It was a good day to begin great projects: both the *Partholonians and the *Milesians invaded Ireland on Beltaine, according to **Lebor Gabála* [Book of Invasions]. A great body of oral tradition is associated with Beltaine, of which the Beltaine *fires and Beltaine cakes or bannocks are the most significant. Great bonfires were built on Beltaine in Ireland and on the Isle of Man; in Scotland the fires might be on mountain-tops. The fires could be called teine éigin [need fire, or fire from rubbing sticks]. In Cornwall Cala' Mē bonfires were still known in the late 20th century. An important ritual required herdsmen to drive their cattle between two fires as a way of preventing contagion through the next year. In Scotland effigies of witches were burned in the fire as late as the 18th century. People danced around the fire *sunwise, to the right; on the Isle of Man they carried *rowan branches or twigs. Hearth fires were extinguished and rekindled as an act of purification.

Beltaine was a time for the ritual eating of certain kinds of food. The Beltaine cakes or bannocks were large, round, and flat, usually made from oats or barley. They were large enough to be broken into several portions, one of which contained a black spot made by charcoal. The person who drew by lot the piece with the black spot was the Beltaine carline or old hag; he or she might be subject to a mimed execution of being thrown into the fire or drawn and quartered.

Belus. Variant of *Belenus.

ben. The common English rendering of Irish and Scottish Gaelic words for mountain, crag, peak, crest, pinnacle, or summit; cf. OIr. benn; ModIr. binn, beann; ScG beinn. See also SLIAB; SLIEVE.

Ben Bulben, Benbulben, Benbulbin, Binn Gulbain, Beann Ghulban. A peak 1,722 feet high in Co. Sligo, 10–12 miles NW of Sligo town, adjacent to the village of Drumcliff, rich in legendary and literary associations. Ben Bulben takes its name from Conall Gulban, a son of *Niall Noígiallach [of the Nine Hostages], who was fostered here. It is the site where *Diarmait was killed in most versions of the wild *boar hunt of *Tóraigheacht Dhiarmada agus Ghráinne* [The Pursuit of Diarmait and Gráinne]. The baby Oisín of the *Fenian Cycle was found here. Remnants of the first castle of the O'Conors of Sligo may be seen at the foot. W. B. Yeats mentions Ben Bulben often in his poetry.

Ben Étair. See BENN EADER.

Ben Nevis. A mountain in the Scottish Highlands (until 1974, Inverness-shire), 5 miles ESE of Fort William, the highest peak in the British Isles, 4,406 feet, 24 miles in circumference at the base, often cited in Scottish Gaelic narrative. The folk etymologies, beinn neamh bhathais, 'mountain with head in clouds' or 'sky-touching peak', and others purporting to mean 'venomous one' or 'terrible' seem fanciful; it is more likely that the Ben was named for a nearby stream, also still called Nevis [water (?)].

ben shee. Manx spelling of *banshee.

ben síde, síth. OIr. spelling of *banshee.

Bendigeidfran, Bendigeid Fran, Bendigeit Vran, Brân Llyr [W *Brân*, (raven or carrion crow) the blessed]. Celtic sea-deity, later described as a king of Britain; a leading figure in early Welsh narrative. 'Bendigeidfran' or Brân 'the Blessed' is a form that may pre-date the introduction of Christianity, but it was preferred by Christian scribes who thought that Brân had helped to bring the faith to Wales; it is none the less the form used in translations of early secular narratives. Bendigeidfran is the son of *Lly^r, brother of *Branwen and *Manawydan and half-brother of *Efnisien. His son was *Caradog. Bendigeidfran is sometimes thought to be a giant; he could wade across the strait between Britain and Ireland. He possesses a magical horn of plenty that produces food and drink in abundance for the asking. Much of the action in *Branwen*, the second branch of the **Mabinogi*, takes place during his reign, and he plays a leading part in it. At his death from a poisoned spear he requests that his head be severed and placed in the White Hill in London, facing France, so that the country may be protected from invasion. The head, called Urdawl Ben [W., noble head] entertained its guardians at *Harlech for 87 years before it was buried. *Arthur was thought to have dug it up so that Britain might be defended by the valour of his warriors rather than by a talisman. After that the head presided over the otherworldly island of *Gwales. The Welsh **Triads* describe the severed head as one of Three Fortunate Concealments and also as one of Three Unfortunate Disclosures (because Arthur dug it up). Bendigeidfran may have an antecedent in the British god *Belatucadros, and has been compared with the Greek figures Cronus, because he once slept with fifty maidens, and Phoroneus. He may be the inspiration for, or prototype of, the characterization of Bron, the Fisher King, in Arthurian romance. See Helaine Newstead, *Brân the Blessed in Arthurian Romance* (New York, 1939, 1968); Rachel Bromwich, *Trioedd Ynys Prydain*, 2nd edn. (Cardiff, 1978), 284ff., 545.

bendith y mamau [W., mothers' blessings]. A Glamorganshire euphemism for the *fairies, known more often in Wales as *tylwyth teg. Euphemism is preferred to avoid kidnapping or fairy mischief. Cf. cwn bendith y mamau [W, dogs of the bendith y mamau] under CŴN ANNWFN.

Benén, Beanón, Benignus, **Saint** [L, benign]. A companion and psalmodist of St *Patrick, whose feast-day is 9 November.

Benn Eader, Eadair, Edair, Benn Étair meic Étgaith, Bineadar, Binn Eádair. Irish name for the Hill of Howth, 560 feet high, on the *Howth peninsula, 9 miles NE of Dublin. Benn Étair is cited in many stories as the easternmost point in Ireland. *Oscar is buried here with his wife, *Étaín (3). *Fionn mac Cumhaill kept ships here at the ready, and departed from here for the disastrous battle at *Gabhair. Probably named for ÉTAR (2), sometimes identified as the father of *Étaín Fholtfhind [fair-haired]. Sometimes known as Dún Étair.

Benntraige. A people of southern Ireland in pre-Christian times, perhaps a remnant of the tribe called the Coriondi by Ptolemy (2nd cent. AD). Although settled in what is now Wexford, a portion of these people migrated to what is now south-west Cork and gave their name to the Barony and Bay of Bantry.

ben-varrey. The Manx name for the mermaid. Her male counterpart is the dinnymara.

Beóthach [Ir., living]. The *Nemedian ancestor of the *Tuatha Dé Danann. In the pseudo-history **Lebor Gabála* [Book of Invasions], Beóthach was grandson of *Nemed and son of Iarbanél, who survived the rout at

Tory Island. He later died in a plague, but his clan left the dynastic wars of Ireland, after the defeat of the Nemedians, to migrate over northern Europe, where they perfected the arts of *divination, *druidism, and philosophy. His followers returned eleven generations later as the Tuatha Dé Danann.

Berba. Name for the River *Barrow in early Irish narrative.

Bérenton. See BROCÉLIANDE.

Bergusia. Female consort of *Ucuetis, a Gaulish hammer-god venerated at *Alesia in Burgundy, eastern France. She may have been a patron of crafts, on the evidence of an excavated underground room near their shrine, apparently the home of a crafts guild.

bérla ne filed, bélrae na filed [Ir., speech or jargon of the poets]. The esoteric speech of poets, a mixture of kennings, riddles, traditional metaphors, and allusions to myth and ritual. It was known to more than poets, as *Cúchulainn uses it when speaking to *Emer.

Berrach, Bearrach, Berrach **Brecc** [Ir., Berrach the freckled]. The daughter of Cass of Cuailnge and third wife of *Fionn mac Cumhaill; known as the most generous woman of her time in Ireland.

Berrey Dhone. A legendary witch, subject of several Manx ballads. She is sometimes represented as an amazon who can stride over mountains.

berries. The berries of the *rowan may confer immortality in several Celtic narratives.

Berwyn [W, white peak]. Range of mountains in north Wales on the border of *Gwynedd and *Powys (until 1974, Merioneth and Montgomeryshire); before the Anglo-Norman conquest this would all have been in Powys. The name Berwyn is also borne by a 5th-century saint and a minor character in **Culhwch ac Olwen*.

Bétéide. ModIr. for *Bé Téite.

Beth Gelert, Gellert. See BEDD GELERT.

biast, béist, biasd [ScG beast; cf. L bestia; OIr. bíast]. A Scottish Gaelic word that may describe any of several folkloric characters, the *arrachd, *fuath, or *muileartach.

Biast Bheulach, Biasd [ScG, prating beast]. A demon spirit or demonic ghost of the Isle of *Skye, usually in the area of the Odail Pass. Sometimes it bore the form of a man, sometimes of a man with only one leg; at other times it appeared to be a greyhound or beast prowling about. It emitted frightful shrieks, and seemed to be hunting for blood.

Bibracte. Important Gaulish archaeological site in eastern central France. At the time of the Roman conquest (52 BC), Bibracte was a fortified city high (2500 feet) on Mt Beuvray, near the modern town of Autun. Described in the histories of Julius *Caesar and defended by *Vercingetorix, Bibracte was first excavated in the 19th century. Five separate digs begun in the 1980s revealed thousands of domestic artefacts that argued for a more complex and sophisticated civilization in early Gaul than previous records had implied.

Bieuzy, Saint. Legendary Breton saint, patron of the holy well of Bieuzy whose waters have curative powers for mental illness, one of the most celebrated of all Breton holy wells.

Bile [Ir., scion, hero, noble warrior]. One of the leaders of the *Milesians in the pseudo-history **Lebor Gabála* [Book of Invasions]. To avenge the death of his son *Ith, Bile joined another son, *Míl Espáine, and forty others in the invasion of Ireland, but was drowned in the storm called down by a druid.

The 19th-century Celticists John Rhŷs (1840–1915) and M. H. d'Arbois de Jubainville (1827–1910) asserted that Bile was a god of darkness and death from the underworld, an opinion not shared by more recent commentators; he does, however, bear some relationship to the Roman deity *Dis Pater. See also BELI MAWR.

Bile, Bili (pl.). [Ir., large tree, tree trunk, mast]. A specially designated tree in early Ireland, believed to be the habitation of gods or elemental spirits. Under its branches many tribal chieftains or kings would be inaugurated. A chief's sceptre was made from a branch of his own tree, and a branch of his tree was symbolic of a king. It was sacrilege to fell or tamper with the chief's tree. The Bile Dathí was the Bough of *Dathí, an ash, one of the six wondrous trees of Ireland. The Irish practice may have had a counterpart in Gaul, as can be seen in the place-name Biliomagus [Gaul., plain of the sacred tree (?)].

Bind, Binde, Binn, Binne [Ir., melodious, sweet, sweetness]. A fairy woman of Irish folklore, the daughter of Modarn.

Bineadar. See BENN EADER.

Binn Eádair. See BENN EADER.

Binnbérlach. See BAILE.

Biobal. A *Partholonian merchant in the pseudo-history **Lebor Gabála* [Book of Invasions] who, with his partner *Babal, introduced gold into Ireland.

birch [OE *birce*]. The deciduous hardwood tree with slender branches and distinctive smooth white or grey bark, genus *Betula*, has attracted an extensive body of folk belief in Celtic countries. The *ogham alphabet of early Ireland associated the Roman letter B with birch. In Wales the birch tree is much associated with love; a lover's bower usually stands beneath a birch tree or in a birch bush. The maypole is usually made of birch; wreaths of birch may be presented as love tokens. The name *Bedwyr may mean 'birch hero'. On the isle of Colonsay in Gaelic Scotland, mothers put birch boughs over the cradles and carriages of babies to protect them from *fairies. ModIr. beith; ScG beithe; Manx beih; W bedwen; Corn. besewen; Bret. bezvenn.

birds. Birds are often depicted in Celtic tradition as symbols of divinity and as servants and messengers of the gods. The Continental Celts included representations of birds in temples and on coins, and more recent Celtic narrative is rich in bird symbolism. Birds and *bulls are linked in early Celtic imagery. Some Continental Celts portrayed birds joined with silver chains. The Irish goddesses *Badb, *Macha, and *Mórrígan are sometimes seen as *crows. The killing of birds was forbidden the Irish hero *Conaire. Several Irish figures were transformed into birds including *Angus Óg, *Cáer, and the *Children of Lir. *Éis Énchenn [bird-headed] was a grotesque adversary of *Cúchulainn. In Brittany the dead might return in the form of birds; the Breton *enfant-oiseau [infant-bird] was killed and eaten by his family. The symbol of Cornish cultural identity is the chough, An *Balores. The Irish word for bird is éan; ScG eun; Manx eean; W aderyn, edn; Corn. edhen; Bret. evn. Some of the most important birds in Celtic tradition are: *Adar Llwch Gwin, the *boobrie, *chough, *cock, *cornu, *crane, *crow, *duck, *eagle, *egret, goose, hawk, *jackdaw, ousel, owl, raven, and *swan. See also Anne Ross, 'Sacred and Magic Birds', in *Pagan Celtic Britain* (London and New York, 1967), 234–98.

Birog. The *druidess who helped *Cian to find and penetrate Balor's tower where he seduced *Eithne. She later saved the child of this union, *Lug Lámfhota, from drowning.

birth. The birth of many Celtic figures occurred under extraordinary circumstances, such as *Taliesin, who was conceived when *Ceridwen in the form of a hen unsuspectingly ate a grain of wheat. The story of *Cormac's birth is told in *Geineamhain Chormaic* and the birth of *Mongán is told in **Imram Brain* [The Voyage of Bran]. Stories of other unusual births, such as those of *Conchobar and *Cúchulainn, are summarized in their entries.

Bisclaveret, Bisclavaret. A word of purported Breton origin for werewolf, as found in the lays of Marie de France (12th cent.). Modern Breton words for werewolf are bleizgarv and den-bleiz.

Bith [Ir., world (?)]. In the pseudo-history **Lebor Gabála* [Book of Invasions], an apocryphal son of Noah who was denied entry to the Ark. With the counsel of his daughter, *Cesair, he built an idol who commanded him to build a ship and take refuge in it. Bith, Cesair, and others sailed for seven years before they reached Ireland, in a company of fifty women and only three men. Bith took one of Cesair's companions as well as sixteen other women and settled in the north, where he died before the Flood. Another son was *Adná. Reputed eponym of *Sliab Betha [Slieve Beagh] in Northern Ireland.

black. As in much of European tradition, black is the colour of evil, fear, and death among the Celts. The crow-goddess of the battlefield, *Badb, is much associated with blackness in Irish narrative. The killer of *Cumhall was the villainous *Arca Dubh [Ir., Black Arky], and a *one-eyed *giant called the Black Oppressor does battle with the Welsh hero *Owain. But black may have other associations. We see splendid Danish knights on parade, clothed in black, in **Breuddwyd Rhonabwy* [The Dream of Rhonabwy]. More mysteriously, black is seen in juxtaposition with red and white (folk motif: Z65.1), as in the stories of the Welsh *Peredur, the Irish *Deirdre, or the modern folktale 'The King of Ireland's Son'. The storytellers explain that black is the blackness of the raven and of a lover's black hair; white the colour of snow and the skin of the lover; red the colour of blood and either the lips or a spot on the cheek of the lover. A later and rather unlikely Christian exegesis is that the three colours evoke the Trinity; further, black is symbolic of the condemnation of God, red is for the Crucifixion, and white for the purification of the spirit.

Black Arky, Arcan. See ARCA DUBH.

Black Book of Carmarthen [W *Llyfr Du Caerfyrddin*]. The earliest complete manuscript of Welsh poetry, transcribed *c.*1250, and housed now in the National Library of Wales, Aberystwyth. The collection includes a large number of poems datable from the 9th to the end of the 12th centuries. Many of the poems sing the praise of heroes, including *Gwyn ap Nudd. A considerable number of poems are in the voice of *Myrddin. Carmarthen or Caerfyrddin is a former county (until 1974) in south Wales, now a part of *Dyfed. The Book is called 'black' because of its cover, not because it is a polemic or indictment. Ed. J. G. Evans (Pwllheli, 1906); ed. A. O. H. Jarman (Cardiff, 1982).

black dog. See DOG; MODDEY DHOO; MAUTHE DOOG.

Black Sainglend. See SAINGLIU.

blacksmith. See GOIBNIU, smith of the *Tuatha Dé Danann; *Gofannon, the smith of early Welsh narrative. See also SMITH.

blackthorn. This thorny shrub (*prunus spinosa*) was thought to provide protection against ghosts in Ireland (cf. ModIr. draighean) and has long been popular in lightweight walking-sticks. It should not be cut on 11 May or 11 November.

Bladma, Bladhma. *Milesian invader of Ireland for whom the *Sliab Bladma [Slieve Bloom] are named.

Bladmall. See BLEDMALL.

Bladud. In Welsh tradition, the fabled founder of *Bath who is sometimes named as the father of *Lludd. The 18th-century commentator John Wood (1742) rather fancifully suggested that Bladud might be identified with *Abaris the Hyperborean.

Blaí [Ir., exemption (?) covering (?)]. Sometimes with the epithet Blaí Dhearg, 'red'. The alternate name for the mother of *Oisín; the more usual name is *Sadb.

Blaí Briugu, Briuga [Ir., Blaí the hospitaller, the hospitable]. An *Ulster warrior renowned for his hospitality. He was a fosterer of *Cúchulainn, promising that if the child were entrusted to him neither contempt nor neglect would come to him. Blaí liked to sleep with different women, for which *Celtchair killed him.

Bláinid. See BLÁITHÍNE.

Bláithíne, Bláithin, Bláthine [Ir., floweret, blossom]. Identical with Bláthnat, Bláthnait, Bláthnad, Bláinid, Blánaid, Blanid. Lover of *Cúchulainn, who betrays her husband, *Cú Roí, for him. Her story was repeated often over the centuries, and the details vary from one version to another. She was a daughter either of *Conchobar or of *Midir. Cúchulainn first encounters her on a raid to the Otherworld, this time located in Scotland. With Cú Roí's aid, Cúchulainn carries off the magic cauldron, three cows, and a girl, Bláithíne, from the stronghold, but Cú Roí subsequently recovers them all. Cú Roí further humiliates Cúchulainn by thrusting him into the earth up to his armpits and shaving off his hair. A year later at *Samain, Cúchulainn makes a tryst with Bláithíne, who helps the Ulstermen to take Cú Roí unawares and kill him. This betrayal is revenged when Cú Roí's poet, *Ferchertne, sees Bláithíne standing at the edge of a sheer cliff, rushes forward, clasps her in his arms, and plunges to the beach below with her in his embrace. Bláithíne's sometimes attributed son, *Lugaid mac Con Roí, continues the enmity against Cúchulainn. See R. P. Joyce's novel *Blanid* (Boston, 1879); T. D. Sullivan's verse romance, *Blanaid* (Dublin, 1891). See also BLODEUEDD.

Blánaid, Blánid. Variants of *Bláithíne.

Blarney Stone [Ir., small field]. The famous stone, celebrated by travel agents and tavern owners, is housed at Blarney Castle, 6.5 miles NW of the city of Cork. One Cormac MacCarthy built the castle in the 15th century on the foundations of an English one from the previous century. For generations the MacCarthys maintained a bardic school, which withered away with the downfall of the Irish language. The tradition that a stone in the castle brings eloquence to those who kiss it is apparently modern, popularized by 'Fr. Prout' (F. S. Mahoney, 1804–66) and others. When Cormac faced a difficult lawsuit, the secret of the stone was revealed to him by *Clídna, a spirit-patron of the family. The stone was the first he faced upon waking in the morning. For fear that all of Ireland would kiss the stone and the entire nation would be overcome with facile speech, Cormac placed it in an almost inaccessible spot on the parapet.

Blaskets, The. A cluster of rocky islets off Dunmore Head at the tip of the *Dingle peninsula, 12 miles W of Dingle. Before the recent depopulation, the Irish-speaking islanders were much studied by folklorists. See Robin Flower, *Western Island* (1944). Three highly regarded Irish-language memoirs were written by islanders: Tomás O'Crohan, *The Islandman* (1929); Maurice O'Sullivan, *Twenty Years A-Growing* (1933); and Peig Sayers, *Peig* (1936, 1973).

Bláthine, Bláthnad, Bláthnait, Bláthnat. Variants of *Bláithíne.

bledlochtana [Ir., monsters]. Monstrous creatures who cry aloud so that their voices resound over the earth on the fourth day of the Battle of Mag Tuired; see CATH MAIGE TUIRED.

bledmall, bladmall, bledmail. [Ir., sea-monster]. Fearsome creatures of the deep which are alluded to in a number of early Irish narratives.

Bledri ap Cydifor. See CYFARWYDD.

Bleherus. See CYFARWYDD.

Bleiddwn, Bleiddyn [W., wolf cub]. Child of the brothers *Gilfaethwy and *Gwydion when they had changed into a wolf and a bitch.

Blodeuedd, Blodeuwedd [W., Flower Face]. Elfwife and betrayer of *Lleu Llaw Gyffes, whose story is told in *Math*, the fourth branch of the **Mabinogi*. When *Arianrhod curses Lleu by saying that he should have no wife of any race on earth, *Gwydion and *Math fashion Blodeuedd for him from the flowers of the *oak, broom, and meadowsweet. Her name, 'Flower Face', bears testimony to her beauty. She brings her husband little joy, however. While Lleu is absent she falls in love with a passing hunter, *Gronw Pebyr, with whom she plots to kill her husband. As Lleu is invulnerable, Blodeuedd has to find secret means by which his life may be taken. She tricks Lleu into a position that exposes him to Gronw, who kills him. As punishment for her betrayal, Blodeuedd is transformed into an owl by Gwydion. Blodeuedd may serve as a model for the Arthurian adulteresses Florie and Lore. See Saunders Lewis, *Blodeuwedd*, a verse play in Welsh (1947); trans. Gwyn Thomas in *Presenting Saunders Lewis*, ed. Alun R. Jones and Gwyn Thomas (Cardiff, 1983), 199–250; trans. Joseph Clancy as 'The Woman Made of Flowers', in *The Plays of Saunders Lewis*, i (Llandybie, 1985), 45–97. Alan Garner's popular novel *The Owl Service* (New York, 1979) also treats of Blodeuedd. See also BLÁITHÍNE.

blood. The Roman commentator Lucan (1st cent. AD) reported blood staining the trees of a Celtic sacred grove near Marseilles. *Badb, *Mórrígan, and *Macha send frogs, streams of blood, and rains of *fire to help defeat the *Fir Bolg at *Mag Tuired. After *Cúchulainn has drunk some of *Emer's blood while extracting a sling stone from her, he is forbidden to marry her. After Cúchulainn has killed Eochaid Glas, the hero sees a *banshee whom Eochaid had outraged bathe in his blood to wash away the shame. The blood of three kings is needed to ransom *Fionn mac Cumhaill.

Bloom. See BLADMA; SLIAB BLADMA [Slieve Bloom].

blue. The colour of the sky on a cloudless day, or azure, is often associated with *sovereignty or *kingship in Celtic tradition, especially in Ireland where the heraldic flag of Irish kings, surviving as the modern presidential flag, has a blue background. See also the many significant women named *Gormlaith [OIr. *gorm flaith*, blue sovereignty]. The Celtic words for blue do not always denote the same shades as are implied in English. OIr. and ModIr., ScG gorm; Manx gorrym; W glas; Corn. glas; Bret. glas.

Blue Men of the Minch. Creatures of Scottish maritime folklore known in Scottish Gaelic as Na Fir Ghorma [the blue men]. The Minch is the passage between the Outer Hebrides to the west and the mainland and Inner Hebrides to the east; it is known in Scottish Gaelic as *Sruth nam Fear Gorm* [Stream of the Blue Men]. They swam out to capsize passing ships, but could be thwarted by captains skilled at rhyming who could keep the last word. The Blue Men were thought to be especially active near the Shiant Islands in the Outer Hebrides. See Donald A. MacKenzie, *Scottish Folk-Lore and Folk-Life* (London and Glasgow, 1935), 85–98.

Boa Island. See ERNE waterway.

Boadach [cf. Ir. *búadach*, victorious, triumphant]. Described as the ruler of the Land of the Living, a variation of *Mag Mell [Pleasant Plain] by a *fairy woman in **Echtrae Conli* [The Adventure of Connla].

Boadicea, Boadicia. Variant spellings of *Boudicca.

Boaldyn. Manx word for *Beltaine.

Boand, Bóand, Boann, Bóann, Boanna, Bóinn, Bóinne (gen.) [Ir. *boänd*, *bóinn*, she who has white cows (?)]. Pre-Christian goddess of the *Boyne River and the river itself, the 70-mile principal waterway of eastern Ireland. Boand was a sister of *Bébinn and in most sources a wife of *Nechtan (1). She had an affair with the *Dagda to produce *Angus Óg, and to hide her adultery she asked *Elcmar to be the foster-father. In an alternate version Elcmar was married to Boand (or *Eithne (2), an alternate name for Boand), who succumbed to the blandishments of *Eochaid Ollathair (another name for the *Dagda) to produce Angus Óg. Her usual residence was *Brug na Bóinne, now called Newgrange.

Two different stories explain the origin of the river. According to one, Boand defied the magical powers of the Well of Segais, as a result of which the well rose up, mutilated and drowned the goddess, and, turning into a river, rushed seawards; see also the story of SINANN [Shannon] and the Well of Cóelrind. In another story Boand was forbidden to look into the well at Sídh Nechtán. When she violated this taboo the water rose up, followed her as she fled towards the sea, and drowned her. Boand may be identical with the British river-goddess worshipped in what is now Ilkley, Yorkshire. The River Boyne appears to be identical with the Bouvinda mentioned by Ptolemy (2nd cent. AD). Boand's lapdog is *Dabilla.

boar [OE *bār*]. The male wild pig, species *Sus scrofa*, has played a prominent role in the Celtic imagination for more than two millennia. The Celtic languages generally denote the wild boar by a different word from that meaning the domesticated pig. 'Boar' is torc in Old and Modern Irish as well as in Scottish Gaelic; baedd gwyllt in Welsh; bāth in Cornish. Only in Breton, hoc'h-gouez, and Manx, collagh muc, is it 'wild pig'. The boar was found all over Europe in early times and was, along with the bear, the most ferocious and aggressive animal a person was likely to encounter. From the time of *Hallstatt onwards, the boar was a favourite, if not the favourite, Celtic cult animal. It was represented on cult objects and coins from Central Europe to northern Britain, where the god *Vitiris was portrayed with a boar. Burials from the *La Tène period attest to the *champion's portion of a joint of pork, mentioned both by *classical commentators and Irish heroic narratives. On the *Gundestrup cauldron, a boar attends *Cernunnos and a large boar crest adorns the helmet of a horseman in a military procession. A Gaulish god *Moccus, found at Longres, France, and equated by the Romans with Mercury, epitomized the power of the boar. *Arduinna was the Romano-Gaulish boar-goddess of the Ardennes Forest. A northern British tribe in Roman times called themselves the Orci [people of the boar]. The boar was the best animal to hunt, admired both for its physical strength and for its heroic defence when cornered. It was thought to have great sexual power, and its food was fit for heroes. In Gaelic Scotland the boar's skin was thought an appropriate dress for a warrior, and a boar's head appears in the crest of the Clan MacKinnon.

Although the boar has been extinct in Ireland since the 12th century, it appears often in Irish narrative. The hermit Marbán has a pet white boar. *Tuan mac Cairill was transformed into a boar, among other things. Orc Triath was an otherworldly boar or pig in Irish tradition; Torc Triath was the king of the boars in the pseudo-history **Lebor Gabála* [Book of Invasions]. Torc Forbartach was a boar cited often in *Fenian stories, but he is kept separate from another one who killed *Diarmait Ua Duibne at any of several locations, most popularly *Ben Bulben (or Ben Gulban, etc.) in Sligo. Diarmait's father *Donn Ua Duibne had killed a bastard son who was transformed into this boar.

Boars are cult heroes in some Welsh stories. *Twrch Trwyth is the otherworldly boar or pig of Welsh tradition. His Breton counterpart is Tourtain. In *Manawydan*, the third branch of the **Mabinogi*, a gleaming white boar leads *Pryderi into an enclosure, where he cannot escape. In *Math*, the fourth branch, *Gwydion takes the form of a boar and his brother *Gilfaethwy a sow in order to produce *Hychdwn Hir. See also FRIUCH [Ir., boar bristles]; YSGITHRWYN PEN BEIDD; SCÉLA MUCCE MEIC DA THÓ [The Story of Mac Da Thó's Pig].

bobel vyghan, an [Corn., the little people]. A Cornish name for the *fairy.

bocaidhe [cf. OIr. *bocaide*, he-goat]. A ModIr. word for *fairy. The diminutive in west Donegal is *boctogaí.

bòcan [ScG], **bócan** [Ir.], **bauchan, bogan, buckawn.** A hobgoblin, sprite, or spectre chiefly known in Gaelic Scotland but also in Ireland, North America, and Australia. The bòcan could be a shape-shifter and a trickster; he was usually dangerous but sometimes helpful. Often a bòcan would attach itself to a family, such as the Coluinn (or Colann) gun Cheann [ScG, headless body] of the MacDonalds of Morar, west Highlands (until 1974, Inverness-shire). See also ATHACH.

bocánach [Ir., goat-like being; goblin]. A *goat-like supernatural being or demon who haunted the battlefield, often associated with the *bánánach. Bocánachs shrieked in the air when Cúchulainn fought *Ferdia.

boctogaí, bostogaí, buctogaí [Ir. var. of *bocaidhe*, fairies]. Word used in west Donegal for the *fairies who lived in the sea, especially on rocks and on the shore. They were thought less friendly to mortals than their counterparts on land. During rough weather their heads may be seen well up out of the water, each with long yellow hair down to the middle of her back. They were also called *bunadh beag na farraige, 'wee folk of the sea'.

Bod Fhearghais. See FÁL.

bodach [Ir., churl, clown; ScG, old or churlish person; cf. OIr. *botach*, serf, peasant]. A form of the bugbear or bug-a-boo in Scottish Gaelic and Irish folklore which in recent years has served only to torment naughty children. Some children's stories use the terms 'curmudgeon' or the name 'Nod' as a translation. In earlier times the bodach was more formidable; the bodach glas [ScG, grey or pale churl] foretells death in Walter Scott's *Waverley* (1814). See also the BWCI of Wales; BUGGANE of the Isle of *Man.

Bodach an Chóta Lachtna [Ir., churl or clown in the grey coat]. Character in a number of folk-tales in the *Fenian Cycle, some of which bear his name as a title. The Bodach is huge and ugly, but he helps the Fenians in a foot-race with a challenger, sometimes called 'Ironbones'. Although the Bodach is the swiftest of runners, he affects a lack of interest in the race and eats blackberries instead of competing. Later he is revealed to be *Manannán mac Lir in disguise. For a fuller account, see EACHTRA BHODAIGH AN CHÓTA LACHTNA.

bodachan sàbhail [ScG, frugal, saving little old man]. A barn kobold or helpful sprite who took pity on old farmers and threshed their grain for them.

Bodb, Bodhb, Bodhbh, Bov, Bove. Usually with the agnomen Derg, Dearg [Ir., Bodb the red]. A son (sometimes brother) of the *Dagda and his successor as leader of the *Tuatha Dé Danann. Bodb is described as having two residences, at Sídh ar *Femen on *Sliab na mBan [Slievenamon] in Tipperary and near Killaloe in Co. Clare, on the west bank of the Shannon. This has prompted some commentators to see two Bodbs, the one at Slievenamon being called 'Bodb of Munster' and the other, at Killaloe (also in Munster), 'Bodb Derg'. If that distinction is correct, it has not always been observed by storytellers, who use the residences interchangeably. After the defeat of the Tuatha Dé Danann by the *Milesians and the death of the Dagda, Bodb becomes the sovereign of his people. This displeases *Lir, who establishes his sídh on the opposite (east) coast of the island. Bodb's foster-daughter *Áeb becomes the wife of Lir and thus the mother of the Children of Lir whose story is told in **Oidheadh Chlainne Lir* [The Tragic Story of the Children of Lir]. After the children's stepmother Aífe changes them into *swans, Bodb punishes her by making her a demon of the air.

Famed for his wise judgement, Bodb helps *Angus Óg to discover the identity of the girl in his dreams, *Cáer. Bodb's best-known daughter is Mesca, but in some *Fenian stories he is described as the father of *Sadb, the mother of *Oisín. Another daughter is *Doirend. Bodb's goldsmith or artificer was Lén, whose workshop was at Lough Léin, the older Irish name for the Lake of Killarney. His pigkeeper *Friuch plays a leading role in the story of the begetting of the bulls at the beginning of *Táin Bó Cuailnge* [Cattle Raid of Cooley]; a second pig-keeper is the *one-eyed *Nár.

Bodhmall. A druidess who nurses the young *Fionn mac Cumhaill, the nephew born in her house, in folk-tales from oral tradition. Sister of *Muirenn, Fionn's mother.

Bodmin Moor. A hilly tract in central *Cornwall near the town of Bodmin, site of many megalithic ruins, described in some folk narratives as a spiritual centre of the Cornish people.

Bodua. A Gaulish war-goddess analogous with *Badb of Ireland. Also known as Cathubodua, Cauth Bova.

bog myrtle. Words used in Ireland to denote a shrub (species *Myrica gale*) having bitter fragrant leaves. Elsewhere in the English-speaking world it is known as sweet gale, sweet willow, or buck bean. In rural Ireland the bog myrtle was once carried as 'palm' in Palm Sunday processions, and it was proscribed as a cattle switch because it was thought to have been used as a scourge on Jesus. An infusion from its branch tips makes a yellow dye, and is also used in tanning. ModIr. roideog, roilleog; ScG roid; Manx roddagagh.

Bog of Allen. See ALLEN, BOG OF.

bogan. Variant spelling of *bòcan.

Boí. Variant spelling of *Buí.

Bóinn, Bóinne (gen.). ModIr. spelling of *Boand.

Bolar, Bola. Variant spellings of *Balor.

Bolcáin, Glenn or Glen Bolcan, Bolcáin. Valley of exiled madmen mentioned in several early Irish narratives, identified with Glenbuck, near Rasharkin, Co. Antrim. *Suibne lives here in *Buile Shuibhne* [The Frenzy of Suibne]. See Gearoid S. MacEoin, 'Gleann Bolcáinn agus Gleann na nGealt', *Béaloideas*, 30 (1962 [1964]), 105–20.

Bolg 1. Bolga, Bulga [Ir., lightning (?)]. Name borne by several shadowy figures in early Irish mythology and history of whom the most important appears to be the ancestor deity of both the *Corcu Loígde, a people of south-west *Munster, and the *Fir Bolg of the pseudo-history *Lebor Gabála* [Book of Invasions]. His name appears to record a movement of the *Belgae into Ireland. He was credited with the invention of the spear, in Old Irish bolga, bulga. He may have been a father of *Dáire mac Dedad, or Dáire may only have been one of his disguises. Bolg was also known as Ailill Érann.

2. In *Macpherson's *Ossian* (1760) the name for the southern part of Ireland.

bo-lol. A kind of apparition, bogey, or bugbear in Welsh folklore.

Bonduca. Spelling in Holinshed's *Chronicles* (1577) of *Boudicca.

boobrie. Fabulous giant water-bird who haunts the lakes and salt-wells of *Argyllshire (now Strathclyde). It has webbed feet and a harsh voice, and is capable of gobbling up sheep and cattle. See also EACH UISCE.

Book of . . . The pre-Gutenberg sources of much of Celtic tradition are found in the great collections of manuscripts compiled in monasteries and castles between 800 and 1500. Each collection or codex bore a title in Latin or one of the Celtic vernaculars. Most learned commentators today refer to these collections by an English title, often employing the place-name where it was either compiled or found; an exception is the **Book of the Dun Cow*, which is often referred to by its Irish title, *Lebor na hUidre*. The following list of Books is limited to sources of mythology, legend, and lore; many more exist, often dealing with genealogy, laws, and ecclesiastical matters.

Book of Aneirin. Welsh title, *Llyfr Aneirin*. Transcribed in the middle of the 13th century and now kept in the South Glamorgan County Library; 80 per cent of the orthography is 13th-century, while 20 per cent dates from the 9th and 10th centuries. The manuscript includes the famous poem **Gododdin* with the superscription, 'This is the Gododdin. Aneirin sang it.' To be distinguished from *Canu Aneirin* [The Poetical Works of Aneirin]. See *The Text of the Book of Aneirin*, ed. J. Gwenogvryn Evans (Pwllheli, 1908). *Llyfr Aneirin: Facsimile*, ed. and intro. Daniel Huws (Cardiff and Aberystwyth, 1989); Edward Anwyl, *The Book of Aneirin* (London, 1910); Brynley F. Roberts, *Early Welsh Poetry: Studies in the Book of Aneirin* (Cardiff, 1988). See also ANEIRIN, the 6th-century bard.

Book of Armagh. Latin name, *Liber Ardmachanus*. Includes materials in both Latin and Irish begun about 807 AD by Feardomnach in *Armagh, the seat of the primate of Ireland in what is now Northern Ireland. The passages in Irish are among the earliest we have. Many Latin passages deal with the life of St *Patrick, and were once revered as being in his own handwriting. An 11th-century insertion about *Brian Bórama (Boru) describes him as 'The Emperor of the Irish'. The manuscript is housed today at Trinity College, Dublin. Ed. J. Gwynn (Dublin and London, 1913); Patrician documents edited by E. Gwynn (Dublin, 1937) and again by L. Bieler (Dublin, 1979).

Book of Ballymote. Irish name, *Leabhar Bhaile an Mhóta*. Compiled *c*.1390 in the Sligo town of Ballymote. Although much of the material in this Book is historical, it also includes important literary and imaginative items, such as the key to the *ogham alphabet. There are bardic tracts on metre and grammar, stories of the birth of *Cormac, and tales of the loathly hag transformed to a beautiful woman, as well as the Irish version of the *Aeneid*. The manuscript is housed today at the Royal Irish Academy, Dublin. Edited and published by Robert Atkinson for the Royal Irish Academy (Dublin, 1887).

Book of Carmarthen. See BLACK BOOK OF CARMARTHEN.

Book of Conquests of Ireland. See LEBOR GABÁLA ÉRENN.

Book of the Dean of Lismore. James MacGregor, Dean of the isle of Lismore in Loch Linnhe, Strathclyde, formerly *Argyllshire, compiled this collection of poems in the early 16th century. Unfortunately, he chose to transcribe the Scottish Gaelic in a Scots phonological rendering of his own invention. In the 19th century Thomas MacLauchlan reconstructed the Scottish Gaelic spellings and translated them into English (Edinburgh, 1862). Alexander Cameron included material from the manuscript in his *Reliquiae Celticae* (Inverness, 1892–4). More recently the Scottish Gaelic Texts Society has issued collections of *Scottish Verse*, ed. W. J. Watson (Edinburgh, 1937) and *Heroic Poetry*, ed. Neil Ross (Edinburgh, 1939). The collection of heroic ballads is the earliest extensive corpus of these ballads in existence. This manuscript should be distinguished from the Irish *Book of Lismore* or *Book of Riabhach MacCarthaigh* [McCarthy] compiled at Kilbrittain, Co. Cork, in the 15th century. The Irish *Lismore*, edited by R. A. S. Macalister (Dublin, 1950), deals mostly with saints' lives, including that of St *Brendan.

Book of Deer, The. See DEER.

Book of the Dun Cow. Irish name, *Lebor* (or *Leabhar*) *na hUidre*; the Irish name is preferred by many learned commentators, who sometimes employ the abbreviation *LU*. The oldest manuscript written entirely in Irish, compiled before 1106 at the great monastic centre of *Clonmacnoise on the Shannon by, among others, a scribe named Máel Muire mac Céileachair. The codex contains texts of the *Mythological Cycle and the *Ulster Cycle, including a version of the epic **Táin Bó Cuailnge*. A vignette recorded later in a separate text explains the name of the codex. *Fergus mac Róigh is described as being summoned from his grave to recite the *Táin* to St *Ciarán of Clonmacnoise, who copied it down on the hide of a dark cow.

The manuscript disappeared after the Cromwellian conquest and reappeared in a bookshop in 1837; it is housed today in the Royal Irish Academy, Dublin. It has been published twice, first in facsimile, ed. J. T. Gilbert (Dublin, 1870), and second as edited by R. I. Best and Osborn Bergin (Dublin, 1929). Walter Wangerin's popular novel *Book of the Dun Cow* (New York, 1978) is unrelated to material in the codex.

Book of Fermoy. An Irish manuscript of the mid-15th century now housed in the Royal Irish Academy, Dublin. Includes the text of **Altrom Tige Dá Medar*. Fermoy is a small town in north-east Co. Cork, 16 miles E of Mallow.

Book of Hergest. See RED BOOK OF HERGEST.

Book of Hy Many. See BOOK OF UÍ MAINE.

Book of Invasions. See LEBOR GABÁLA ÉRENN.

Book of Lecan, sometimes called the *Great Book of Lecan* to distinguish it from the earlier **Yellow Book of Lecan* compiled by the same family of scribes in the same castle. Irish name, *Leabhar Mór Mhic Fhir Bhisigh Leacain*. Compiled *c*.1400; 600 pages contain genealogical material and a Book of Rights. Lecan is the name of a former castle, now in ruins, in the west of Co. Sligo, 2 miles N of Inishcrone. Published in edition by Kathleen Mulchrone (Dublin, 1937).

Book of Leinster. Irish name, *Lebor Laignech, Leabhar Laighneach*. Also known as *Book of Noughaval/ Oakvale, Lebor na Nuachongbála*. Compiled after 1150, this codex is the second best source of Irish myth and legend after the **Book of the Dun Cow*. Some of the material, such as the *Dindshenchas, the lore and history of places, dates from the 11th century. Also important are texts of the pseudo-history **Lebor Gabála* [Book of Invasions], a version of the **Táin Bó Cuailnge*, the *Deirdre story, and the **Bórama*. The surviving manuscript is divided between Trinity College and the Franciscan Library, Dublin. *Leinster, one of the five ancient provinces, constitutes much of eastern Ireland. First published in facsimile (Dublin, 1870), the *Book of Leinster* has been edited in six volumes by R. I. Best, Osborn Bergin, M. A. O'Brien, and A. O'Sullivan (Dublin, 1954–83).

Book of Noughaval/Oakvale. See BOOK OF LEINSTER.

Book of Rhydderch. See WHITE BOOK OF RHYDDERCH.

Book of Taliesin. Welsh name, *Llyfr Taliesin*. Manuscript compiled 14th century containing more than sixty poems attributed to the 6th-century *Taliesin, of which twelve were judged perhaps authentic by Sir Ifor Williams. The collection also includes the **Armes Prydain* [Prophecy of Britain], attributed to *Myrddin (Merlin); and **Cad Goddeu* [The Battle of the Trees]. The manuscript is now housed in the National Library, Aberystwyth. Edited by J. G. Evans (Llenbedrog, Tremvan, 1910, 1915). Distinguish from *Hanes Taliesin*, a tale of folk memory and literary invention about Taliesin as wonder-child. See Marged Haycock, 'Llyfr Taliesin', *National Library of Wales Journal*, 4 (Winter 1988), 357–86.

Book of Uí Maine. Irish name, *Leabhar Uí Maine*. Also *Book of Hy Many*. A smaller codex of the late 14th or early 15th century long in the possession of the O'Kelly family, a name borne by the descendants of the *Uí Maine sept that occupied in medieval times much of what is now Co. Galway and sections of Roscommon. The manuscript includes portions of the **Lebor Gabála* [Book of Invasions], poems, genealogies, and pedigrees. Edited by R. A. S. Macalister (Dublin, 1942).

borabu. The horn of the *Fianna. It was under a stone that Oisín found the horn, which was circled round like a sea-shell. A blast of the borabu could summon warriors from all parts of Ireland at any time.

Borach, Barach, Borrach [cf. OIr. *borrach*, proud, pretentious person]. Character in the *Deirdre story not named in the medieval text *Longas mac nUislenn* [Exile of the Sons of Uisnech]. On Conchobar's urging he prepares a feast which detains *Fergus, who was to be Deirdre and Noíse's surety for a safe return to *Emain Macha; when Fergus is delayed, Noíse is killed. Many modern retellers of the story have given the character much colour; James Stephens, *Deirdre* (London, 1923) makes him a shark-catcher.

bórama, bóraime, bóramha, boru, boromian tribute [Ir., tribute, cattle-tribute; prey; cattle-counting]. A tribute exacted by powerful chiefs or tribes from weaker ones. The best-known such tribute was the Leinster bórama paid by the *Lagin, because of their non-Goidelic origin, to the kingship at *Tara. The first king to demand the tribute was *Tuathal Techtmar. Imaginative narrative put the cost of this tribute at 5,000 cows, sheep, hogs, cloaks, bronze vessels, and ounces of silver; the cause of the tribute was explained as payment for the seduction of one of Tuathal Techtmar's daughter by *Eochaid (8), king of Leinster, who was already married to another daughter. Although often referred to over the centuries, the tribute was not paid after the 8th century.

The narrative titled *Bórama* deals among other things with the death of Eochaid's son; fifty captives were buried alive around the son's grave. The text is published and translated in S. H. O'Grady, *Silva Gadelica* (London, 1892). The sobriquet of *Brian Bórama or Boru (d. 1014) appears to be taken from the earthen ring-fort *Béal Bórama* [Pass of the Tributes] today called Béal Boru Fort, about a mile N of *Killaloe, Co. Clare. It is not clear whether Brian ever demanded tributes at the pass or was associated with the place for some other reason.

Borba [Ir. *borb*, fierce, harsh; arrogant]. An adversary of *Fionn mac Cumhaill in *Fenian folk-tales; the son of Sinsar.

Borbar, Borbaduthal [cf. ScG *borb-fhear*, fierce, passionate man]. In *Macpherson's

Ossian (1760), the father of Cathmor the Generous and of Cairbre the usurper. He was the brother of Colgulla, who rebelled against *Cormac, the king of Ireland.

Bormana. Female consort of *Borvo when the latter bears the name Bormanus. The usual consort of Borvo is *Damona.

Bormanus. Alternate name for *Borvo, especially as the consort of Bormana.

Bormo. Alternate name for *Borvo.

boromian, boromean tribute. See BÓRAMA.

bóromh. See BÓRAMA; BRIAN BÓRAMA.

Borrach. Variant of *Borach.

boru. Anglicization of *bórama; see also BRIAN BÓRAMA (Boru).

Borvo, Bormanus, Bormo [L, to boil, seethe, bubble]. Gaulish god of healing springs. At Vichy, France, he was portrayed equipped with a warrior's shield and helmet; the figure is seen seated, with a horned serpent rearing up towards him. His usual consort is *Damona, but when he is known as Bormanus his consort is Bormana. He was worshipped with Damona in a healing shrine at Bourbonne-les-Bains, France. His mother may have been *Sirona or *Dirona. The Romans equated Borvo with *Apollo. See also BELENUS, who also has the power to heal with spring waters.

Bosgeal [ScG, white palm]. In *Macpherson's *Ossian* (1760), the daughter of Colgar, a Connacht chief. She becomes the wife of *Cairbre and the daughter-in-law of Cormac.

Bosmin [ScG, smooth palm]. In James *Macpherson's *Ossian* (1760), the only daughter of *Fingal by *Clatha, the daughter of *Cathula.

bostogaí. Variant spelling of *boctogaí.

Boudicca, Boudica, Boadicea, Boadicia, Bonduca, Buddug [Romano-British, victory (?); cf. OIr. *búadach*, W *buddugol*, victorious]. A historical queen of the Iceni of eastern Britain at the time of the Roman conquest who has long attracted imaginative speculation. Tall, with a mass of bright red hair, she was virtually a giantess in Roman eyes. When her husband Prasutagus was killed, the Romans seized his territory, scourged Boudicca, and ill-treated her daughters. Infuriated and crying for vengeance, Boudicca raised a revolt of the Iceni and the Trinobantes, a neighbouring tribe, burning *Camulodunum (Colchester) and Londinium (London). When she was defeated, she took poison rather than fall into the hands of the Romans. Before dying she called out to the goddess Andraste [invincible (?)] (*c.* AD 61). So many legends accrued to the historical record that the ancient queen almost has a separate identity as the fabulous Boadicea. Her story is the basis of the drama by John Fletcher, *Bonduca* (*c.*1618), a ballad by William Cowper (1782), a poem by Tennyson, and the popular novel *Red Queen, White Queen* by Henry Treece (London, 1958). See the historical studies: Graham Webster, *Boudica: The British Revolt Against Rome* (1978); Antonia Fraser, *Boadicea's Chariot* (London, 1988); *The Warrior Queens* (New York, 1988). See also CARTIMANDUA.

boudig. One of two Breton words for fairy. See also KORRIGAN.

Bough of Dathí. English translation of bile Dathí, the ash tree belonging to *Dathí or Nathi, a nephew of *Niall Noígiallach [of the Nine Hostages], one of the six wondrous trees of Ireland. See also ASH; TREE.

Bove Derg, Bov the Red. See BODB DERG.

Boyhood Deeds of Cúchulainn, The. See TÁIN BÓ CUAILNGE [Cattle Raid of Cooley].

Boyhood Deeds of Fionn, The. See MACGHNÍMARTHA FINN.

Boyne River [Ir. *An Bhóinn*, Boand; (river of) the white cow (?)]. The principal waterway of *Leinster, eastern Ireland; the waters of the Boyne rise in the Bog of *Allen in Kildare and run north, west, and then east for 70 miles through counties Offaly, Westmeath, Meath, and Louth, emptying into the Irish Sea at Drogheda. The river takes its name from *Boand, the pre-Christian Irish goddess, and has been identified with the Bouvinda mentioned in Ptolemy's Geography (2nd cent. AD). It may also have borne the name *Eithne, Ethlinn, or Ethniu. The valley of the Boyne includes some of the most important archaeological sites in Ireland, including Newgrange (*Brug na Bóinne in Irish narrative), *Knowth, and *Dowth. The estuary of the Boyne was called *Inber Colptha in Old Irish narrative, the site of many heroic departures and landings. In **Altrom Tige Dá Medar* [Nurture of the Houses of the Two Milk Vessels], *Eithne loses her veil of invisibility while bathing in the waters of the Boyne, after which she dies in the arms of St *Patrick. At Slane, St Patrick lit the pascal *fire that would begin his challenge to the paganism of nearby *Tara and thus the Christianization of all Ireland. One of the many places *Fionn mac Cumhaill was thought to have caught the *salmon of knowledge was the 'Pool of the Boyne', Linn Féic; and one of the many places he was thought to have been killed was the Ford of Brea or Áth Brea on the Boyne. The valley is also rich in Christian associations, as it contains the early monastic ruins at Monasterboice and the 12th-century ruins at Mellifont.

The most resonant associations of the Boyne in the Irish imagination for the past three centuries has been with the defeat of Catholic forces under James II at the Battle of the Boyne, 3 miles W of Drogheda, 1 July 1690. This loss, together with another at Aughrim and the humiliating Treaty of Limerick (both 1691), quashed Catholic and nationalist aspiration until the rising of 1798. See Harry Boylan, *The Boyne: A Valley of the Kings* (Dublin, 1988). See also DUB CHOMAR; SHANNON; SINANN.

Bracan, Bracann. Alternative name for the father of *Muirenn, mother of *Fionn mac Cumhaill; the more usual name is *Tadg.

Brachan. Variant spelling of *Brychan.

Braciaca [cf. W *brag*, malt]. An obscure god of Roman Britain remembered in an inscription at Haddon House, Derbyshire.

Bragela [cf. ScG *bràigh gheal*, fair neck]. In *Macpherson's *Ossian* (1760), the wife of *Cuchullin. See also EMER.

Brahan Seer. Usual title for the 17th-century historical figure Kenneth MacKenzie, also known as Coinneach Odhar Fiosaiche [Sombre Kenneth of the Prophecies] and Kenneth Oaur. The Brahan Seer foretold the decline of the Highlands and the construction of the Caledonian Canal, as well as many specifics of Highland history, such as the location of cemeteries. His prophetic powers made a deep and lasting impact on the folk mind of Gaelic Scotland. Details of Kenneth's own life are not clear. He was thought to have lived either at Uig, Isle of Lewis, in the Outer Hebrides, or at Loch Ussie, near the Iron Age fort at Knockfarrel, a few miles W of Dingwall, Highlands (until 1974, Ross-shire). A small museum at Rosemarkie commemorates his work. See *The Prophecies of the Brahan Seer*, ed. A. MacKenzie (Inverness, 1877; Stirling, 1909).

Braint [W, privilege, right, honour, status]. A Welsh personal name, perhaps adapted from the goddess *Brigantia [high one (?)], which has also attached itself to a river in *Anglesey.

Bran. The word bran appears in all the living Celtic languages with the same spelling and near-uniformity in meaning: Ir. raven; W carrion crow; Bret. raven or crow. In Scottish Gaelic it acquires a suffix to mean raven: branfhitheach. In Scottish Gaelic and in Irish it is the name of *Fionn mac Cumhaill's dog (see Bran (2)). Not surprisingly, then, there are dozens of characters named Bran in Celtic narrative and history, including kings, poets, warriors, and at least one saint, St Bran Clane in Co. Kildare, whose feast-day is 18 May. There are two heroes named Bran in the *Fenian Cycle. The best-known Brans are probably the Irish Bran son of Febal (see BRAN MAC FEBAIL) and the Welsh Brân, known in the *Mabinogi/Mabinogion* as *Bendigeidfran.

Bran 1. Also known as Brân the Blessed, Brân Llyr; see BENDIGEIDFRAN.

2. One of two wonderful hunting dogs of *Fionn mac Cumhaill; the other was Sceolang [grey dog (?)], and a third, appearing less often, was Lomair. The story of how Fionn acquired the dogs is told differently in Ireland and in Scotland. In the Irish version, Bran and Sceolang are the children of Fionn's sister *Uirne (or Tuiren), who had been transformed into a dog by a jilted sweetheart of her husband, Illann (or Iollan). Uirne was restored to her human form, but her children remained canines. In the Scottish Gaelic version, the two dogs are unrelated to Fionn and are instead monstrous wild dogs that must be won in a contest with a baby-eating predator. Sceolang can be restrained only with Bran's gold chain; Bran was fastened for a long period at Oban, Strathclyde, formerly *Argyllshire.

Bran and Sceolang are celebrated in many stories for their extraordinary intelligence. Bran is favoured more by her master and is also a swifter runner; she can overtake geese in flight. Bran and Sceolang bring a young doe to Fionn's fortress, who is released from enchantment to become Fionn's beloved *Sadb, the mother of *Oisín. Later she is lured from the fortress and becomes a deer again; then Fionn will allow only Bran and Sceolang to hunt because they know Sadb and will do her no harm. Bran and Sceolang find the infant Oisín in the forest. With deep regret Fionn kills Bran when she is hunting a fawn, evidently the transformed Sadb whom she has not recognized. Fionn calls first to the fawn and then to Bran to run through his legs; when Bran passes, Fionn crushes her between his knees. Irish tradition has Bran buried at Carnawaddy [Ir. *carn an mhadra*, cairn of the dog], a cairn near Omeath, Co. Louth. Lough Brin in Co. *Kerry is thought to be named after Bran. See J. R. Reinhard and V. E. Hull, 'Bran and Sceolang', *Speculum*, 11 (1936), 42–58. See also ADHNÚALL; FAIRY DOG.

3. Legendary Breton hero thought to have done battle with the Norsemen. His story was much expanded in the free renderings of traditional Breton literature by Hersart de *La Villemarqué (1839). After dying in prison, Bran returns to life in the shape of a crow, the literal meaning of his name. Portions of his story parallel those of the Arthurian hero Tristram. The Breton village Kervran [Bret., Bran's village] is named after him.

4. In *Macpherson's *Ossian* (1760), a river in *Caledonia, perhaps identifiable with the actual river that falls into the Tay near *Dunkeld, Tayside (until 1974, Perthshire). Another Bran empties into Loch Luichart, mid-Highlands (until 1974, Ross and Cromarty).

Bran Galed. A Welsh hero celebrated for his horn, which flows with enough liquor to satisfy anyone.

Brân Llyr. Another name for *Bendigeidfran.

Bran mac Febail, Feabhail. Hero of the 8th-century adventure-voyage **Imram Brain* [The Voyage of Bran]. Bran falls asleep one day after listening to sweet music, after which he awakes and departs on a magical journey to the Otherworld, filled with bountiful delights. When he returns to the land of humans in Ireland, he announces that he is Bran son of Febal, but his listeners retort that Bran died many years before and that his story is ancient. Bran is able to tell what has happened to him, but then turns to dust. See also OISÍN.

Brandan, Brandon. Variants of *Brendan.

brandub, brannumh. A board-game of early Ireland often confused with *fidchell and *búanfach. Brandub, which may mean 'board', seems to have served as a model of the island of Ireland in miniature. See Eoin MacWhite, 'Early Irish Board Games', *Éigse*, 5 (1945), 25–35.

Brandub, Brandubh, Branduff [Ir., black raven]. A relatively common name in early Ireland, borne by at least two saints and a series of petty kings. The most memorable of these was Brandub king of the *Lagin (d. *c.*605), who wins *Mongán's wife, *Dubh Lacha, from him through a trick; Mongán recovers her a year later with another trick.

Branwen [W *bran*, raven, dark; *(g)wen*, fair, beauty; i.e. white or sacred raven]. Title character of *Branwen*, the second branch of the **Mabinogi*. The daughter of *Llŷr, Branwen is given in marriage to *Matholwch, king of Ireland, by her brother *Bendigeidfran. After an insult to the Irishmen by a half-brother, *Efnisien, Branwen is made to suffer at the hands of her husband's countrymen. Bendigeidfran, learning of this, makes war on Ireland and is killed. Branwen dies of sorrow. Branwen has been compared with *Rhiannon, as she is a giver of bracelets. Her name is confused with, but should be distinguished from, Bronwen [W *bron*, breast; *(g)wen*, fair]. She seems to be related to the Arthurian figures Brangwaine, Brangoene, Bringvain. See Proinsias Mac Cana, *Branwen, Daughter of Llŷr* (Cardiff, 1958); Rachel Bromwich, *Trioedd Ynys Prydain*, 2nd edn. (Cardiff, 1978); Derick S. Thomson, *Branwen verch Lyr* (Dublin, 1961, 1986).

Brasil, Brazil. See HY BRASIL.

Breaga. Son of *Breogan and uncle of *Míl Espáine in the pseudo-history **Lebor Gabála* [Book of Invasions]. He may be the eponym of *Brega/ Bregia, a petty kingdom of east central Ireland in early times.

Breagh. Variant spelling of *Brega.

Breas. Variant spelling of *Bres.

Breasail. See HY BRASIL.

Breatan, Breatain, Breatunn, Bretain. Irish and Scottish Gaelic words for Britain. In Irish Breatain usually refers to Great Britain, exclusive of Scotland, which is called Alba; Breatach more often means Briton. In Scottish Gaelic Breatunn usually refers to Great

Britain, but it may also denote the fortress at *Dumbarton, as in Dùn Breatann.

Breccán, Breacán [Ir. dim. of *brecc*, freckled, speckled]. A common name in early Ireland, borne by at least thirteen saints. The best-known Breccan in legend is a secular one, the Irish trader lost off the coast of Scotland and drowned in the whirlpool Corrievreckan whose name commemorates his death; Corrievreckan is between the islands of Jura and Scarba in the Inner Hebrides, Strathclyde, formerly *Argyllshire.

Brecheniauc. See BRYCHEINIOG.

Brecknockshire. See BRYCHEINIOG.

Brecon. See BRYCHEINIOG.

Breffny, Breffne, Breffni. Anglicized spellings of *Bréifne.

Brega, Breagh, Bregha, Bregia, Mag mBreg. The plain between the *Boyne and the *Liffey, coextensive with eastern Co. *Meath, a portion of north Co. Dublin, and a small piece of Co. Louth. This includes the sites of *Tara, *Brug na Bóinne, and *Knowth. The area took its name from *Breaga, son of *Breogan, but the dynasty of Brega claimed descent from *Áed Sláine. Brega emerged as a political unit when the old kingdom of *Mide dissolved in the 8th century, and it joined a reconstituted Mide at the end of the 11th. *Tailtiu the *Fir Bolg queen was thought to have cleared the forests of Brega. *Conaire was given the taboo of not going right-hand-wise around Tara nor left-hand-wise around Brega. Many commentators prefer the latinized form, Bregia.

Bregia. Latinized form of *Brega.

Bregon. Variant spelling of *Breogan.

Brehon, Brehon Laws [cf. OIr. *breithem*; ModIr. *breitheamh*, *breitheamain* (pl.), judge, arbiter; ScG *breitheamh*]. The brehon was a legal authority in early Ireland. His role appears to have derived from the **vates* described by Roman commentators, as did the fili, 'poet, seer'. Whatever his function in other societies, the brehon was not a judge in Ireland, as the administration of justice and preservation of law and order were responsibilities of the king. The brehon's function resembled that of the Roman jurisconsult; he was a specialist who knew, preserved, and to some degree developed the law from pre-Christian and Christian traditions. The occupation of brehon became hereditary, passed on to pupils or literary foster-sons. Exalted members of Scottish clans who served as brehons bore the title 'brieve'; in later times their functions were served by the doomster or dempster.

The treatises commonly known as Brehon Laws, some possibly as old as the 6th century, were textbooks. They were only law records, not collections of case law or statute law. A small number of famous decisions, usually in a legendary setting, are preserved in the texts, but there was no official registration of judgments. Important among these texts was the *Senchas Már* [Great Tradition]; see edition of some texts in *Zeitschrift für celtische Philologie*, 14 (1923) 334–94; 15 (1924), 238–76, 302–76; 16 (1926), 167–230; 18 (1929–30), 353–408. Many laws were attributed to the 7th-century warrior *Cenn Fáelad. Brehons continued to practise their law in Ireland until the reign of James I (1603–25).

See *Ancient Laws of Ireland* (6 vols., Dublin and London, 1865–1901); *Corpus iuris Hibernici*, ed. Daniel A. Binchy (6 vols., Dublin, 1978); Laurence Ginnel, *The Brehon Laws: A Legal Handbook* (London, 1844; Dublin, 1917); John MacNeill, *Early Irish Law and Institutions* (Dublin, 1934); D. A. Binchy (ed.), *Studies in Early Irish Law* (Dublin, 1936); Fergus Kelly, *A Guide to Early Irish Law* (Dublin, 1988). See also HYWEL DDA.

Bréifne, Breffny, Breffni, Breffne. Name for a region of early Ireland coextensive with the counties of Cavan and Leitrim, north central Ireland. See B. Hunt, *Folktales of Breffny* (London, 1912); M. Godley, *In the Land of Breffne* (London, 1925); *Bréifne: Journal of the Cumann Senchais Bhréifne* (Cavan), 1991– .

Breizh. The Breton name for *Brittany. *Breizh Izel* is western or lower Brittany; *Breizh Uhel* is eastern or upper Brittany.

Brendan, Brénainn, Bréanainn, **Saint.** [L *Brendanus*, from W *breinhin*, prince]. The most celebrated of seventeen Irish saints bearing this name is St Brendan of Clonfert (d. 577), the son of *Finnlug, called 'the Navigator'. Brendan founded the abbey of *Ardfert in his native *Kerry as well as *Clonfert, Co. Galway and others; his feast-day is 16 May. Details of Brendan's life are found primarily in two Latin texts, both composed several centuries after his death. The first is the *Vita*

Brendani [Life of Brendan], which survives in two versions and many variants; the second is the much better known *Navigatio Sancti Brendani Abbatis* [Voyage of the Abbot Saint Brendan]. The *Navigatio* was composed in the late 9th or early 10th century and was widely read all over Europe in the Middle Ages. It is an epic of the Old Irish Church, an amalgam of secular and religious learning, the last notable Hiberno-Latin literary production. It may be compared to **Imram Curaig Maíle Dúin* [The Voyage of Máel Dúin's Boat], in which there is a reference to St Brendan of Birr. This St Brendan, whose feast-day is 29 November, is described as a traveller on the western ocean; his story is evidently confused with that of St Brendan of Clonfert on several points.

Having been told of a Land of Promise to the west (See TÍR TAIRNGIRE) by Barinthus, St Brendan set sail with fourteen companions in a curragh, a small leather boat. This journey may have reached as far as Iceland, which was discovered by Irish monks and where there is today a small archipelago named Vestmannaejar [Irishmen's islands]. He returned after five years to much acclaim. A second voyage in a boat made of oak included a crew of sixty, and reached distant islands that partisan commentators have identified with Newfoundland, Florida, and the Bahamas. Among the many adventures of St Brendan are: (1) the visit to an island where the travellers are sheltered in a large building; (2) the visit to an island of sheep larger than cattle; (3) the landing on the whale Jasconius [cf. Ir. *iasc*, fish], mistaken for an island-an episode paralleled in the voyages of Sinbad; (4) the visit to the island of spirits in bird form; (5) the visit to the island of St *Ailbe, which offers a detailed description of the lives of a community of silent monks; (6) the voyage across the curdled sea; (7) the visit to the Island of Strong Men, inhabited only by boys, young men, and elders, who ate a purple fruit called scaltae; (8) the visit to the island of grape trees; (9) the voyage across a stream of clear water where the sailors could see to the bottom; (10) the sighting of a crystal column, possibly an iceberg; (11) the visit to an island of giant smiths; (12) the visit to a smoking and flaming mountain, perhaps a volcano; (13) the sighting of a man-shaped cloud on a rock mass, which was Judas reprieved from damnation on Sundays; (14) the visit to the island of Paul the hermit; (15) the visit to the island promised to the saints.

The work of several researchers in the late 20th century has implied much evidence of Irish travel to the New World, if not actually of St Brendan's voyage. Transatlantic voyages in curraghs, following St Brendan's directions, have been made three times, by Bill Verity in 1966 and 1970 and by Tim Severin in 1976–7, who published an account in *The Brendan Voyage* (New York, 1978). See also Frederick Buechner's popular novel *Brendan* (New York, 1987). *Vita Brendani* is in Charles Plummer's *Lives of Irish Saints* (Oxford, 1922). See *Navigatio Sancti Brendani Abbatis*, ed. Carl Selmer (Notre Dame, Ind., 1959); *The Voyage of Saint Brendan: Journey to the Promised Land. Navigatio Sancti Brendani Abbatis*, trans. John J. O'Meara (Portlaoise, 1985). See also Geoffrey Ashe, *Land to the West* (London, 1962). See also IMRAM CURAIG MAÍLE DÚIN.

Breoga. A *Partholonian of the **Lebor Gabála* [Book of Invasions] who helped civilize his people by having disputants settle quarrels in a single combat instead of going to war.

Breogan, Bregan. A leader of the *Milesians and the builder of a famous tower in the pseudo-history **Lebor Gabála* [Book of Invasions]. After travelling across the Mediterranean, the Milesians land in Spain (here, 'Land of the Dead'), where Breogan builds a tall tower at Brigantia (Braganza, Portugal?) to protect his territory. From this tower Breogan's son Ith sees Ireland across the sea and decides to set sail to investigate the island. Breogan is also the father of *Bile and *Fuad, the eponym of *Sliab Fúait (Slieve Fuad).

Breóthigernd, Breóthighearn. A wife of *Mongán.

Bres, Breas, Bress [Ir., shapely, beautiful (?); fight, uproar, din (?)]. Name borne by several mythological and legendary figures (sometimes by more than one in the same narrative), the best known of which is Bres the son of Elatha.

Bres 1. The son of *Elatha, sometimes Eochaid Bres: Bres the Beautiful, one of the leading characters of **Cath Maige Tuired* [The (Second) Battle of Mag Tuired]. Bres is conceived when his mother, *Ériu, a woman of the *Tuatha Dé Danann, is visited by a splendid and mysterious stranger later revealed to be *Elatha mac Delbaíth, a king of the rival *Fomorians. Bres grows rapidly as a child so that he is the size of a 14-year-old when only 7. None is more beautiful than he, and so he is called 'Bres the Beautiful'. When *Nuadu is deposed as king because of a physical deformity, the Tuatha Dé Danann make Bres the new king in the hope that his reign will bring peace between them and the Fomorians. But he is a poor king and neglects many of his responsibilities, for which he is humiliated in a satire by *Cairbre, a poet shabbily received at Bres's palace. After this Bres abandons the Tuatha Dé Danann, joins the family of his father, the Fomorians, and fights with them on the losing side at the Battle of Mag Tuired. He is also thought to have mated with Brigit (under the name Bríg[h]) to produce *Rúadán (2), who is killed when he himself tries to kill *Goibniu.

2. The son of *Balor as mentioned in **Oidheadh Chlainne Tuireann* [The Tragic Story of the Children of Tuireann]. When Bres greeted *Lug Lámfhota he compared the hero to the sun.

3. One of the real names of the *Finn Emna, the three Finns of Emain.

Bresal. See HY BRASIL.

Bresal, Bressal [Ir., strife (?); brave in conflict (?)]. A popular name in early Ireland, borne by several kings, a handful of legendary figures, and at least one saint.

Bresal Bélach. Early Irish personage thought to have built the wooden fortress Barc Bresail [Ir. *barc*, boat-shaped structure on land]. Bresal defeated *Cairbre Lifechair at the legendary battle of *Cnámross, perhaps with the aid of *Fionn mac Cumhaill.

Bresal Etarláim, Etarlám, Etarlann [OIr. *etarlám*, opportune (?)]. A *druid who gave *Fuamnach the spells that would banish *Étaín from *Midir in **Tochmarc Étaíne* [The Wooing of Étaín]. In some variants he is her foster-father; in others he is her lover, for which Midir kills Fuamnach.

Bress. Variant spelling of *Bres.

Bressal. Variant spelling of *Bresal.

Bretain. An OIr. word for *Britain, especially Britain exclusive of *Scotland [Ir. and ScG *Alba*].

Breton language. See BRITTANY.

Breuddwyd Macsen [Maxen] Wledig. Welsh title of 12th-century pseudo-historical tale known in English as 'The Dream of Macsen Wledig', 'Prince Maxen's Dream', etc. The historical figure at the centre of the story, *Macsen Wledig, is the Spanish-born Maximus, or Magnus, Clemens, a Roman emperor, AD 383–8. Although described as a usurper by Roman historians, he was a hero to the British (i.e. Welsh) for helping them to throw off the yoke of Gratian (383). His reign came to an end when he was slain by Theodosius the Great at Aquileia. His name is cited in *Gildas and Nennius (9th cent.), and he appears as the founder of many dynastic and ecclesiastical families.

Macsen Wledig, the Emperor of Rome, dreams one night of a lovely maiden in a wonderful, far-off land. Awakening, he sends his men all over the earth in search of her. With much difficulty they find her in a rich castle in Britain, and lead the Emperor to her. Everything he finds is exactly as in his dream. The maiden, whose name is *Elen (1), accepts and loves him. Because Elen is found a virgin, Macsen gives her father sovereignty over the island of Britain and orders three castles built for his bride. Elen is probably also based on a historical figure, Elen Luyddog of Segontium (Carnarvon), who was in reality Macsen's (Magnus's) wife. In Macsen's absence, a new emperor seizes power and warns him not to return. With the help of men from Britain led by Elen's brother *Cynan, Macsen marches across Gaul and Italy and recaptures Rome. In gratitude to his British allies, Macsen rewards them with a portion of Gaul that becomes known as *Brittany.

Some commentators see a link between this Welsh dream and the *aisling*, conventionalized dream poetry, often with political intent, in Irish tradition. Edited in Welsh by Ifor Williams (Bangor, 1928); English translations are included with several editions of the **Mabinogi/Mabinogion*.

Breuddwyd Rhonabwy [W, Dream of Rhonabwy]. Welsh title for the 12th- or 13th-century Welsh Arthurian narrative usually known in English as The Dream of Rhonabwy or Rhonabwy's Dream. Although its date is uncertain, *Rhonabwy* is the last wholly native narrative in Middle Welsh tradition, and the most consciously literary of all those included with the **Mabinogi/Mabinogion*. Internal evidence suggests it was never a part of the repertoire of traditional storytellers. The single surviving text is in the **Red Book of*

Hergest (1375–1425), but the purported setting is the reign of Madog ap Meredudd, prince of *Powys (d. 1159).

Prince Madog sends Rhonabwy and other warriors to seek the prince's rebellious brother, Iowerth, who has gone raiding in Lloegyr [England]. While the prince's historicity is supported by many documents, the brother's is not. Rhonabwy, with two companions, spends a night at the squalid lodgings of *Heilyn Goch [the red], whose floors are covered with cow dung and urine. There, sleeping on a yellow ox-hide, he is granted a vision of Arthurian Britain; in it the Arthurian figures are portrayed as giants while Rhonabwy and his contemporaries are contrasted as puny. Rhonabwy dreams that he is approaching a ford of the Severn when he is overtaken by two horsemen, each richly arrayed. The first gives his name as Iddawg, called the 'Embroiler', because he has helped provoke the Battle of *Camlan by distorting peaceful messages *Arthur had sent Medrawd [Mordred]. Accompanied by Iddawg, Rhonabwy finds Arthur and Bedwin the Bishop seated on an island in the river. Arthur asks Iddawg where he has found these 'little fellows' and speaks of his regret that these are the kind of men who now prevail in Britain. Rhonabwy then notices the stone in Arthur's ring which, he learns, will allow him to remember what he has seen.

The different heroes and companions that compose Arthur's army are minutely described. Although Arthur is to ride to do battle with his enemies from *Llychlyn [Norway] and Denmark, he is more concerned with the chess-like game of **gwyddbwyll* he is playing with *Owain son of Urien. During the progress of the game reports arrive of Arthur's knights harrying and disturbing the ravens of Owain, but Arthur responds only, 'Play the game'. Owain tells his men to raise his banner, whereupon the ravens begin to slaughter Arthur's men; this time it is Owain's turn to insist that the board-game continue. At last Arthur begs Owain to call off his ravens. Owain does so, and there was peace. Many men bring tribute to King Arthur. At this point Rhonabwy awakes, realizing that he has slept for three nights. Cited also in the story is *Cador, Arthur's nephew, the Duke of *Cornwall, who later appears in the chronicles of *Geoffrey of Monmouth (12th cent.), Wace (11th cent.), and Layamon (11th cent).

G. Melville Richards edited the Welsh text (Cardiff, 1948, 1972). English translations are included with many editions of the *Mabinogi/Mabinogion*. See the study of the narrative by J. A. Carson, *Philological Quarterly*, 53 (1974), 289–303. Mary Giffin treated the problem of dating the narrative, *Transactions . . . Society Cymmrodorion* (1958), 33–40.

Brezhoneg. Breton word for the Breton language.

Brí Léith [Ir. *brí*, hill]. A hill, *sídh, or *otherworldly residence, and route to the Otherworld, identified with the modern Ardagh Hill, 3 miles SW of Edgeworthstown, Co. Longford. Brí Léith was the residence of *Midir. *Angus Óg is sometimes described as being fostered here. In **Tochmarc Étaíne* [The Wooing of Étaín] the men of *Eochaid Airem want to destroy the hill in their search for the missing *Étaín. Celebrations of *Lughnasa were held here until recent times.

Brian, Bríon. A name known both in Ireland, where it has been very popular, and also in Britain, where it was introduced from *Brittany. The origin of the name is disputed but may be linked to the Brennus/Brenos cited in battle by Celtic raiders in the Mediterranean in late Roman times. The best-known Brian, from whom the O'Briens [Ir. Uí Bhriain] take their name, is *Brian Bórama or Boru.

Brian 1. A god of the *Tuatha Dé Danann, the first of the three sons, with *Iuchair and *Iucharba, of *Tuireann, whose story is told in **Oidheadh Chlainne Tuireann* [The Tragic Story of the Children of Tuireann]. Brian and his brothers kill *Cian, father of *Lug Lámfhota, for which they are punished by being sent on a quest for eight items that become the treasures of the Tuatha Dé Danann. Brian is later killed by Lug on the Isle of *Man.

2. Eldest son of *Eochaid Mugmedón and *Mongfhind in **Echtra Mac nEchach Muigmedóin* [The Adventure of the Sons of Eochaid Mugmedón].

Brian Bórama, Boru, Bóroimhe. Also bears the patronymic mac Ceinnéidigh. The victor of *Clontarf (1014), a historical high king of Ireland whose story is encrusted with legend. The cognomen Bórama derives from Béal Bórama, 'The Pass of the Tributes', an earthen ring fort 1 mile NW of *Killaloe [Ir. *Cill Dalua*, St Dalua's church], his birthplace, in Co. Clare. Brian's usual residence or 'palace' was at *Kincora [Ir. *ceann cora*, weir head] on the *Shannon, also near Killaloe. Brian became ruler of a small kingdom, *Dál Cais (also Dál gCais), or, in English, the Dalcassians, in east Clare, when his brother was killed in an ambush. Brian's first enemies were the Danes, headquartered in Limerick, and the *Eóganacht, seated at the acropolis of *Cashel, whose power was somewhat diminished under Danish pressure. He participated in the sack of Limerick in 968, and he vanquished Cashel in 978. In time Brian extended his will against neighbouring kingdoms as well as against the Norsemen who had settled in Ireland. By 988 he had become, in effect, king of southern Ireland, and in 997 he agreed with Máel Sechnaill [Malachy], the *ard rí [high king], to divide spheres of influence between them. Many Leinstermen opposed Brian's hegemony, but he proved the stronger, so strong that he could break his agreement with Máel Sechnaill and overcome him on the battlefield.

By 1005 he was, by his own description in the *Book of Armagh*, the emperor of the Irish. Brian did not, however, create a national monarchy or the institutions of such a monarch, but he did contribute to the idea of a kingship for the whole island. At Clontarf [Ir. *Cluain Tarbh*, bull meadow] Brian led forces from many parts of Ireland against the Norse and their Leinster allies. This was not an irredentist purge of foreigners, as Scandinavian settlers and traders remained in Ireland and eventually merged with the rest of the population. The great carnage was not forgotten by either side, however, and is described towards the end of the famous Icelandic saga *The Burning of Njal*. At Clontarf Brian was in advanced years, perhaps 74, and according to legend he was stabbed in his tent by a Danish intruder named Brodar or Brodir. Although Brian's prestige has always been great, some historians decry his destruction of dynastic principles of legitimacy, replacing it with a principle of submission to greater power. Brian was the third husband of *Gormlaith (1) (or Gormflaith), a much-divorced woman sometimes described as the 'Queen mother of Dublin'. A harp thought to belong to Brian, a symbol for Ireland, is housed at Trinity College.

See the historical study by Roger C. Newman, *Brian Boru: King of Ireland* (Dublin, 1983). Several popular novels also deal with Brian's story, the most recent of which is Morgan Llywelyn's *Lion of Ireland* (Boston, 1980). See also DALCASSIAN CYCLE.

Brianan, Brianain, Briannuil. Name for an unspecified divinity used in Scottish Gaelic exclamations. Although Brianan could be evoked for good or evil, he is more often asked to bring misfortune on enemies. Occasionally Brianan is called Brianan Buidhe [*Buidhe*, the Yellow].

Briccriu, Bricriu, Briccirne, Bricne [cf. Ir. *brecc*, speckled, freckled]. Usually accompanied by the epithets Neimthenga, Nemhthenga, 'bitter-tongued' or Biltenga, 'evil-tongued'. A warrior, troublemaker, and sometime poet in the *Ulster Cycle. In the well-known **Fled Bricrenn* [Briccriu's Feast], he incites the first three champions of Ulster, *Cúchulainn, *Lóegaire Búadach, and *Conall Cernach, to quarrel over the *champion's portion. He also instituted a rivalry of the champions of Ireland for the carving of Mac Da Thó's pig in **Scéla Mucce meic Da Thó*, which results in much bloodshed. But in the lesser-known *Táin Bó Flidais* [The Cattle Raid of Flidais], he is a poet and satirist- of bitter but not venomous tongue. His residence was Dún Rudraige, coextensive with the modern village of Dundrum, Co. Down; the lake and village of Loughbrickland, Co. Down, is thought to commemorate his name. Briccriu's patronymic, mac Carbada [son of Carbad], little cited in texts, links him with his brother, *Goll mac Carbada, the *one-eyed monster of the Ulster Cycle. Often compared with the foul-mouthed Thersites of the *Iliad*, the trickster Loki of Norse mythology, the malevolent *Efnisien of the second branch of the **Mabinogi*, and the pugnacious Sir *Kay of Arthurian legend.

Briccriu's Feast. See FLED BRICRENN.

Bricta. Variant form of *Brixia.

Bríd, Bride. Variant spellings of St *Brigid or *Brigit.

Bridei. A leader of the *Picts evangelized by St Columba (*Colum Cille). His dwelling was in the Great Glen of Scotland.

bridge. *Cúchulainn has to cross the Bridge of Leaps to reach the realm of *Scáthach. It is high, narrow, and slippery as an eel's tail; anyone failing to cross it will fall to sea-monsters below. Cúchulainn does cross, and on a second crossing kills a hag who opposes him.

Bridget. Variant spelling, especially popular on the Isle of *Man, of St *Brigid.

brieve. See BREHON.

Bríg, Brígh [Ir., high, noble, power (?)]. A daughter of the *Dagda whose son Rúadán is killed by *Goibniu. In her grief she gives the first mourning chant or keen [Ir. *caoineadh*] in Ireland.

Brigantes. A powerful confederacy of *Brythonic Celtic tribes centred in north Britain in Roman times. Their most important goddess was *Brigantia. During the reign of Claudius (AD 41- 54), their queen was *Cartimandua. An offshoot of the Brigantes settled in south Co. Wexford, Ireland.

Brigantia, Briganti [high one (?)]. British goddess at the time of the Roman occupation, a personification of the hegemony of the *Brigantes. She was concerned with river and water cults, and a centre of her worship was in what is now West Riding, Yorkshire. She is probably identical with the Gaulish goddess Brigindo, known only from inscription. The Romans equated her with *Minerva, while more recent commentators have seen a link with *Brigit. The River Brent, a tributary joining the Thames at Brentford, is named for Brigantia. The Welsh personal and place-name *Braint appears to be derived from Brigantia. See T. M. Charles-Edwards, 'Native Political Organization in Roman Britain, etc.', in Manfred Mayrhofer (ed.), *Antiquitates Indogermanicae* (Innsbruck, 1974), 35–45.

Brigid, Brighid, Bríd, Bride, Brigit, Bridget, **Saint.** Of the fifteen Irish saints bearing this name, the most important is St Brigid of Kildare (d. 525), one of the three patron saints of Ireland, along with St *Patrick and St *Colum Cille. Often referred to in popular tradition as 'Mary of the Gael', her feast-day is 1 February. Verifiable details of her life are scant, although her serious hagiographers elaborated the outline with many fabulous stories. She is thought to have been born in the middle of the 5th century at Faughart, near Dundalk, Co. Louth, and to have founded a religious house at Kildare, where she died. The name *Dubthach is traditionally ascribed to her father. Perhaps the most enduring legend attached to her is that she converted a pagan on his deathbed while holding a cross plaited from rushes on the floor; crosses of St Brigid, made of four stalks of rushes extending from a square, are still commonplace in Ireland. A second association is with *fire. *Giraldus Cambrensis reported (1184) that a company of nuns attended an 'inextinguishable' fire at Kildare in St Brigid's honour. Although it had been kept burning for 500 years, it had produced no ash; men were not allowed near the fire. Brigid was thought of as the 'mother' and exemplar of virgins. She was also a patroness of Leinstermen and was thought to favour them in times of war.

As her fame spread through the British Isles she was venerated in Scotland, Wales, on the Isle of Man, and in England, where there were nineteen churches dedicated to her before the Reformation. In the Hebrides she was thought to be the midwife of the Virgin Mary, and a special votive figure was made in her honour. A straw figure dressed in women's clothes was placed in a large basket and called 'Brigid's bed'. Commentators have long asserted that her persona is based on the cult of the pre-Christian goddess *Brigit. None the less, St Brigid remains on the Church calendar with the caution that most stories portraying her life are inauthentic. See also BARBE, SAINT. See Dorothy A. Bray, 'The Image of St. Brigit in the Early Irish Church', *Études celtiques*, 24 (1987), 209–15.

Brigindo. Goddess of eastern Gaul known only from inscriptions, thought to be identified with *Brigantia and *Brigit.

Brigit, Brighit, Brid, Briid, Brigid [Ir., the exalted one]. Pre-Christian Irish goddess of *fire, smithing, fertility, cattle, crops, and poetry. She was the daughter of the *Dagda and according to later tradition, the wife of *Senchán Torpéist, a purported author of the **Táin Bó Cuailnge* [Cattle Raid of Cooley]. The calendar feast of *Imbolc (1 February) was much associated with Brigit. **Sanas Cormaic* [Cormac's Glossary] (10th cent.) implies that Brigit is the name of three goddesses without giving extensive details of the other two. Brigit was the tutelary goddess of the province of *Leinster. She was probably worshipped at *Corleck Hill, near Drumeague, Co. Cavan, where a stone head thought to be hers once stood. Under the name Bríg[h], she is described as having mated with *Bres (1) to produce *Rúadán (2), who was killed when he tried to kill *Goibniu. At her son's death, Brigit lamented in the first keening ever heard in Ireland. She may be the grandmother of *Ecne, a personification of knowledge and enlightenment. Often compared with *Minerva, Vesta, *Brigantia, *Brigindo; historians also see a link with St *Brigid. See Séamas Ó Catháin, *The Festival of Brigit* (Dublin, 1995).

Brion. Variant spelling of *Brian.

Britain, Great Britain. The largest of the British Isles, including what is now called *England, *Wales, and *Scotland. Until Roman times the island's inhabitants were dominantly *Brythonic Celts, ancestors of the modern Welsh and Cornish. For that reason the word Prydain [W, Britain] in early Welsh narrative usually denotes all of Britain, not just the Welsh-speaking areas. The concept of Wales [W *Cymru*] as a nation distinct from Britain came later. The OIr. Bretain, ModIr. Breatain, ScG Breatunn, and Corn. Breten may mean all of Britain or Britain exclusive of Scotland. In Breton, the isle of Britain is Breizh-Veur or Enez-Vreizh. According to the Irish pseudo-history *Lebor Gabála* [Book of Invasions], Britain was named for the *Nemedian hero *Británul Máel. In many Welsh narratives Britain is known as the Island of the Mighty. See also ENGLAND.

Británul Mael, Briotán Maol [Ir., Bretan the crop-headed (?)]. According to the Irish pseudo-history *Lebor Gabála* [Book of Invasions], he was chief of one of the three surviving *Nemedian families, who migrated to *Britain, settled there, and gave his name to that island.

Brittany. Former duchy and province of north-western France on the Armorican peninsula, coextensive with modern French Departments of *Finistère, Côte d'Armor, Morbihan, Ille-et-Vilaine, and Loire-Atlantique (although the last is officially declared not a part of Brittany since the Vichy Regime, 1941). Occupying 18,630 square miles, the region is more than twice as large as Wales and more than half the size of Ireland. Brittany has been occupied by Celtic-speaking populations since pre-Roman times, but it takes its name from the *Brythonic people who fled the isle of *Britain in the 5th century. In Breton it is known as Breizh (cf. Breizh Uhel, 'east or Upper Brittany' (Fr. Haute Bretagne); Breizh Izel, 'west or Lower Brittany' (Fr. Basse Bretagne)); in Welsh it is Llydaw; Corn. Breten Vyghan; OIr. Letha; ModIr. An Bhriotáin; ScG Breatainn na Frainge; Manx Yn Vritaan. The coastal regions are known in Breton literature and folklore as *Arvor [Bret. *Ar-Mor*, sea], while the interior is known as *Argoad [Bret. *Ar-Goat, Ar-Koad*, woods, forest]. In early Christian times the region now called Brittany was divided among three petty kingdoms, *Domnonia in the north, *Cornouaille in the south and west, *Bro Waroch in the south and east. The *Fir Morca of early Irish myth, although sometimes placed in west Limerick, are Armoricans/Bretons.

In Welsh tradition the emigrants to Brittany were led by the legendary St *Cynan Meiriadog (or Meriadoc), who is described as a conqueror in **Breuddwyd Macsen Wledig* [The Dream of Macsen Wledig]. According to that story, the Roman emperor Macsen [Maximus] rewarded his British allies with a portion of Gaul then called Brytanieid. Macsen had married a British princess, Elen, whose brother Cynan had brought a British army to Rome. Cynan and his allies cut out the tongues of all the women of the province lest the language of the conquerors be corrupted, and thus they name it Llydaw [W *lled*, half; *taw*, silent]. Cynan is also described as the British invader in Breton legends, where he is known as Conan. With the subsequent influx of British ecclesiastics, the area increasingly became known as 'Brittany' instead of Armorica, although the two terms were interchangeable for many centuries.

A *P-Celtic language of the *Brythonic family, Breton is historically linked to both Welsh and the now extinct Cornish. On the testimony of *Giraldus Cambrensis (12th cent.), spoken Breton was more closely related to the Cornish of his day than to Welsh. But despite many lexical similarities, modern spoken Breton and Welsh are not mutually comprehensible. In 1907 scholars determined that Breton language and tradition should be divided into four parts. Three in the north and west are closely interrelated: KLT, named for Kernev (Cornouaille), Leon (or Léon), and Treger (Trégor, Tréguier). The G dialect of the south-west stands somewhat apart, taking its name from Gwened, Breton for Vannes, capital of Morbihan; the dialect is also known as Vannetais in French, Gwenedeg in Breton. The first great political leader of the Bretons, subject of many legends, was *Nominoë (9th cent.), who first accepted Frankish suzerainty but later revolted and restored Breton independence.

Although Giraldus Cambrensis speaks of 'tale-telling Bretons and their singers', no

Breton literature survives from before 1450. The Anglo-Norman writer Marie de France (1160–80) brought the purported Breton lai or lay, often employing Breton subject matter, into the mainstream of European literature. Breton folk-tales and songs were not collected until the 19th century. An attempt to fill the void of early Breton tradition was made by Hersart de *La Villemarqué's spurious, *Macpherson-like 'translations' in 1839. Traditional symbols of Breton national culture are the ermine, triscele or triskelion, and biniou (a distinctive Woodwind instrument).

See N. K. Chadwick, 'The Colonization of Brittany from Celtic Britain', *Proceedings of the British Academy*, 50 (1966); *Early Brittany* (Cardiff, 1969); Léon Fleuriot, *Les Origines de la Bretagne: l'émigration* (Paris, 1980). See also the Bibliography under 'Breton'.

Brittia. Name given by the Byzantine historian Procopius (5th cent.) to a fabulous island he recorded from the beliefs of the peasants of northern Gaul.

Brittonnic. See BRYTHONIC.

Brixia, Bricta. Obscure Continental Celtic goddess, consort of *Luxovius, the water-god of Luxeuil. Links to the Irish *Brigit are often suggested but have yet to be demonstrated.

Bro Waroch [Bret., the territory of Waroch]. A petty kingdom of early Christian *Brittany, founded by Waroch (*c.*577–94). The kingdom occupied the south-east, the wealthiest part of Brittany, which had been settled by the Veneti described by Julius Caesar. Two contemporary kingdoms were *Domnonia and *Cornouaille.

Brocéliande, Brécélien, Bréchéliant. Forest with fabulous associations of eastern *Brittany officially known since the French Revolution as the forest of Paimpont, the last remnant of the primeval forests, 25 miles SW of Rennes. Described by Nora K. Chadwick as 'the last stronghold of magic and the literature of magic in Europe', Brocéliande served as the scene of countless medieval and Renaissance narratives, Arthurian and non-Arthurian. One of the best-known sites in Brocéliande is the enchanted fountain or spring of Bérenton (also Baranton, Barenton; from Belenton, ultimately *Belenus [?]), usually presided over by a tall and beautiful queen; in some texts the guardian is Esclados le Roux, a menacing knight. The fountain was known for its storm-making powers; its water is always cold but never freezes in the winter. According to some Arthurian traditions, *Merlin was imprisoned in an *oak tree in Brocéliande by the maiden Vivien (or Niniane). The forest also served as a refuge for Christian clergy during the Viking raids. See Nora K. Chadwick, 'The Forest of Brocéliande', in *Early Brittany* (Cardiff, 1969), 292-354; Jean Markale, 'Brocéliande: mythe et réalité', in *Mélanges . . . offerts à Charles Foulon*, (Rennes, 1981), 185–91; *Brocéliande* (Paris, *c.*1984).

Brochan. Variant spelling of *Brychan.

Broich y Ddinas. See DINAS EMRYS.

Broichan. A Scottish *druid who challenged St Columba [*Colum Cille] and was bested. Broichan was a druid to King Brude and resented the incursion of the Christian evangelists. He caused a storm and darkness on Loch Ness so that navigation appeared impossible, until the saint gave orders that sails be unfurled; then everything became calm.

brollachan, brollochan, grollican [ScG, shapeless, deformed creature; senseless creature]. A shapeless, malevolent supernatural being in Scottish Gaelic folklore, a child of the *fuath [anglicized as vough, voght, etc.]. International tale type: 1137.

Bronwen. A Welsh personal name, sometimes seen as a variant of *Branwen.

Brown Bull of Cuailnge/Cooley. That bull desired by *Medb in the **Táin Bó Cuailnge*. Irish name: *Donn Cuailnge. See also BULL.

brownie. A friendly goblin or sprite of Scottish Gaelic folklore whose name seems to be known exclusively in the English form, which derives from the earlier 'little brown man'. The brownie wears a brown hood, attaches himself to families, and may reside in farmhouses or barns. He does the chores at night when people sleep; he has even been known to assist in childbirth. If criticized the brownie may revenge himself by breaking dishes, spilling milk, driving the cows astray, or spoiling the crops. Although always thought to be of Scottish Gaelic origin, the brownie is widely known in other parts of the British Isles and the English-speaking world. The brownie has much in common with the kobold of Germanic folklore and may be classed as a solitary *fairy, despite its benevolence. See also the Welsh PWCA/BWCI, the Manx FENODYREE, the Cornish PISKIE or pixie, and the Scottish Gaelic BODACH.

brú. Variant of *bruig; See also BRUIDEN.

brug, brugh. Variant spellings of *bruig.

Brug na Bóinne, na Bóinde, maic Ind Óc [Ir., hostel of the Boyne]. The otherworldly residence first of *Boand and of the *Dagda but later, more importantly, of *Angus Óg, Irish god of youth and poetry. It is usually identified with the great passage-grave of Newgrange, dating from 3200 to 2600 BC, but may include the nearby passage-graves of *Dowth and *Knowth, which are of comparable size and antiquity. All three are in the *Boyne valley, 2 miles NE of Slane, Co. Meath.

Brug na Bóinne offers hospitality to countless guests in hundreds of Irish stories. At times it is synonymous with the power and/or generosity of Angus Óg. It provided endless supplies of *ale, three trees that were always in fruit, and two pigs, one of which was living, the other cooked and ready to eat. In variant texts the great hero *Lug Lámfhota is sometimes described as buried here.

bruiden (OldIr.), bruidhean (ModIr.), bruighean (ScG). The Old and Modern Irish forms of this word signify different meanings. Bruiden, bruidne (pl.) may denote a hostel, large banqueting hall, or a house or mansion, which may or may not imply the Otherworld. A second Old Irish word, bruiden, almost certainly the same as the first, means 'fight, contest, or quarrel'. The ModIr. bruidhean, bruidnea (pl.) and ScG Bruighean are often used to denote the residence of the *fairies, but they may also mean 'hostel, caravanserai; castle or royal residence'. Anne Ross has asserted that the fear associated with the bruiden/bruidhean/bruighean may derive from the burning of human sacrifices in wickerwork images in pre-Christian times. See the following entries using bruiden/bruidhean in titles of Irish narratives as well as *Togail Bruidne Da Derga* and **Mesca Ulad*. See also BRUIG.

There were, in different narratives, five or six bruidne in early Ireland, including: (1) Of Da Derga among the men of Cualu in Leinster; it is usually placed along the River Dodder in Co. Dublin but is also identified with ruins at Stackallan Bridge, Co. Meath, in the *Boyne valley. See TOGAIL BRUIDNE DA DERGA. (2) Of *Forgall Manach beside Lusk, north of Dublin. (3) Of Da Réo in *Bréifne; also known as Bruiden Mic Cecht Da Réo. (4) Of Da Choca or Choga at Breenmore Hill, near Athlone, Co. Westmeath, where *Cormac met his death in *Togail Bruidne Da Choca* [The Destruction of Da Choca's Hostel]. (5) Of *Mac Da Thó after the character in **Scéla Mucce meic Da Thó* [The Story of Mac Da Thó's Pig]. In the latter we read a description of the bruiden: 'There were seven doors in each hall, seven roads through it, and seven fireplaces therein. There were seven cauldrons, with an ox and a salted pig in each. The person who came that way would thrust the fleshfork into the cauldron, and whatever he obtained with the first thrust he ate, and if he did not obtain anything with the first thrust he ate nothing'.

Bruidhean Bheag na hAlmhaine. Irish title for the *Fenian Cycle prose narrative known in English as The Little Brawl at [the Hill of] Allen. Here we read of an older *Fionn mac Cumhaill who can still perform feats of valour alongside his great-grandsons Eachtach and Illan. Ed. and trans. S. H. O'Grady, *Silva Gadelica* (London, 1892).

Bruidhean Chaorthainn, *an Chaorthainn.* Irish titles for the *Fenian prose narrative known most often in English as The Hostel, Palace, or Fairy Palace of the Quicken or Rowan Tree. The story has been collected from several oral sources in different parts of Ireland and the Scottish Highlands, where it is known as *Bruighean Caorthuinn*. As early as 1633 Geoffrey *Keating cited it as typical of the 'unhistorical' (i.e. magical, not to be believed) Fenian tales.

Midac (or Miodhac, etc.), the son of the villainous *Colgán of *Lochlainn [Norway], is a boy whom the *Fianna have raised as one of their own after they found him during the defeat of the invader. Upon reaching manhood Midac leaves the hospitality of the Hill of *Allen and takes up residence in his hostel 'of the Quicken or *Rowan Trees' on the *Shannon. Midac's dinner invitation to *Fionn and his men is only a lure to the enchanted trap. Once inside, the men find that they cannot cry out or raise themselves from their chairs. Midac's wish is to decapitate Fionn and bring his head to the *King of the World. Instead, the Fianna, led by *Diarmait, bring Fionn the head of the King and release the leader from enchantment.

P. H. Pearse edited an Irish version in *Sgéal Fiannaidheachta* (Dublin, 1908). A Scottish Gaelic text with translation is in *Leabhar na Feinne* (London, 1872); another Scottish version from a later oral source is titled *Fionn an Tigh a' Bhlàir-Bhuidhe* . . . , ed. J. M. L. (Glasgow, 1920). P. W. Joyce's translation in *Old Celtic Romances* (Dublin, 1879) has been often reprinted and is perhaps the most widely known.

bruig, bruigh, brug, brugh, brú [Ir., (farm-)house, abode; region, district; cultivated land]. Although this term may be translated as '(farm-)house, abode', etc., in much of Irish usage, it acquired associations with the spirit and fairy world as it was used in myths and folk-tales. In narratives collected from oral tradition it often denotes the interior of a fairy mound, especially a place where a number of *fairies live together, not just the home for a family. See also BRUIDEN; BRUG NA BÓINNE.

Bruighean Caorthuinn. ScG spelling for **Bruidhean Chaorthain.*

Brumo. In *Macpherson's *Ossian* (1760), the name for a place of worship in Craca, one of the Shetland Islands.

Brutus. Contrived eponym and progenitor of the British people, as found in *Geoffrey of Monmouth (1136). A leader of the Trojans, he dreams of the temple of Diana beyond the setting sun. After invading the island, he defeats the *giant Gogmagog and establishes law in the land named for him, Britain [W *Prydain*].

Brychan, Brachan, Brochan [cf. W *brych*, mottled, freckled]. Also known as Brychan ap Anllech, a 5th- or 6th-century chieftain of Irish stock who greatly extended his power when the Romans departed. The medieval kingdom of *Brycheiniog was named for Brychan, and he is sometimes cited with Brycheiniog as a sobriquet. Brychan is said to have had three wives and an enormous number of children, many of whom became saints, including St *Berwyn, St *Endellion and St *Keyne. Though hardly a saint himself, Brychan was once venerated on 6 April.

Brycheiniog, Brecheniauc. Romantic little Welsh kingdom centred in the Usk valley that remained independent of its neighbours from the 5th to the 10th centuries. Much of the same territory had earlier been the somewhat smaller kingdom of Garthmadrun, ruled by the celebrated King Tewdrig. Brycheiniog's royal pedigree claimed to be derived from a Princess Marcell [L Marcella], who married an Irishman and produced a son, *Brychan, eponym of the kingdom, who is often cited in early Welsh literature. Brychan's line continued to about 940, when the kingdom fell under the sway of *Deheubarth. From the 16th century until 1974 the region retained much of its historical identity as the county of Brecon or Brecknockshire; since that time the territory has been incorporated in the new county of *Powys.

Brynaich. A derisive Welsh term for the English, especially in 12th- and 13th-century poetry. The word is derived from 'Bernicia', the name for the petty kingdom of several centuries earlier that had been absorbed into Northumbria by the 12th century.

Brython, Brittonic, Brythonic. The branch of the Celtic languages that includes Welsh, Breton, and Cornish, the modern survivors of the *P-Celts; distinguish from Goídel, *Goidelic, and *Q-Celts (Irish, Scottish Gaelic, and Manx). The terms 'Brython', 'Brythonic', were coined by Sir John Rhy^s (1840–1915) to denote the Brittones, Romanized Britons in post-Roman times. Recent usage favours Brythonic for parent languages, Brittonic for modern languages.

Buachalla. See MES BUACHALLA.

Búadach. See LÓEGAIRE BÚADACH.

Búadnat, Buadhnat, Buanait [Ir., victorious lady (?)]. The daughter of the king of Norway [*Lochlainn] in the *Fenian Cycle.

Buan [Ir., lasting, enduring]. A name borne by a number of figures, both male and female, in early Irish narrative. One was the mother of *Baile Binnbérlach.

Búanann, Buanand, Buanann, Buanond [Ir., the lasting one]. An *amazonian warrior goddess called 'the nurse of warriors'. *Cúchulainn came to Britain to train with her and *Scáthach. Búanann was so helpful to *Fionn and his men as to be called 'the mother of the Fianna'. She may be compared conceptually but not etymologically with *Setlocenia. Probable counterpart of the Roman goddess *Minerva. *Mórrígan is given the patronymic Buan in the **Táin Bó Cuailnge* [Cattle Raid of Cooley].

búanfach [cf. Ir. *búan*, good; lasting]. Name for a board-game whose rules are lost to modern readers, perhaps comparable to *fidchell or *brandub. See Eóin MacWhite, 'Early Irish Board Games', *Éigse*, 5 (1945), 25–35.

bucca [Corn., hobgoblin]. Supernatural creature in Cornish folklore, related to the Welsh *pwca and the Irish *pooca. When it was still thought necessary to propitiate the bucca, fishermen left some of their fish on the sands for it, and others threw a few crumbs or drops of beer over their shoulders for it. In the 20th century the bucca has been a terror only for small children, and the word may now humorously describe a scarecrow. Two varieties of bucca are the bucca-dhu, bucca-boo, or bucca-hoo, the 'black spirit' and the bucca-gwidden or bucca-gwidder, the 'white spirit'. See also the Cornish KNACKER. Folk motif: V12.9.

Buchet. A hospitable man of *Leinster, the fosterer of *Eithne Tháebfhota, much celebrated for his generosity, whose story is told in **Esnada Tige Buchet* [The Melodies of Buchet's House].

buckawn. Anglicized spelling of *bòcan.

buctogai. Variant spelling of *boctogai.

Buddic, Buddug. Welsh forms of *Boudicca.

bugelnoz [Bret., night imp, goblin]. A supernatural creature in Breton folklore, known in the region of Vannes in south-central Brittany. He appears between midnight and morning to rescue victims from the devil by spreading his mouth over them.

buggane. A mischievous creature in Manx folklore. Each has a mane of black hair and torch-like eyes. Arch and naughty, the buggane can chase people and frighten. All of them are adept at shape-shifting. One attends an evil magician as his slave. Sometimes compared with the *cabbyl-ushtey, the Manx variant of the *each uisce. See also the POOCA of Ireland and the BÒCAN of Gaelic Scotland.

Buí, Boí, Búi. One of four wives of the Irish hero *Lug Lámfhota. Under this name she has associations with the megalithic monument at *Knowth, Co. Meath. She appears to be identical with the figure in Irish and Scottish Gaelic folklore known as *Cailleach Bhéirre or the Hag of Beare, after the *Beare peninsula in south-western Ireland.

Buic. See BUIDE MAC BÁIN.

Buide mac Báin [cf. Ir. *buide*, yellow; grateful]. In the **Táin Bó Cuailnge* [Cattle Raid of Cooley], Buide is driving *Donn Cuailnge [the Brown Bull of Cuailnge] when it first appears in the text. *Cúchulainn kills him, but the bull is driven off. Buide is the son of Bán Blai (also Benblai). In some texts Buide is called Buic [Ir., fool, half-wit].

Buile Shuibhne. Irish title of a 12th-century narrative of the *Cycle of Kings known in English as The Frenzy of Suibne, The Madness of Sweeney, etc. It is the third and best known of a trilogy about a 7th-century Ulster petty king, Suibne Geilt [Ir., mad Suibne or Sweeney], who lost his reason at the Battle of Mag Rath (or Moira) in 637. The first story, *Fled Dúin na nGéd* [The Feast of Dún na nGéd], deals with events before the battle, which itself is described in the second story, *Cath Maige Rátha* [The Battle of Mag Rath]. Many modern readers have found Suibne's wanderings across Ireland, from treetop to treetop, among the most affecting in early Irish literature. Although Suibne first resists and later accepts Christianity, his story contains many elements of pre-Christian mystery.

Suibne son of Colmán is a king of *Dál-nAraide in the former (until 1974) counties Antrim and Down of eastern Northern Ireland. He seeks to expel the evangelizing St Rónán from his kingdom, but his wife Eórann dissuades him. Angry at the sound of Rónán's bell, Suibne rushes from his castle, but Eórann grabs his cloak so that he goes through the door naked. The pagan king throws Rónán's psalter into a lake and is about to do violence to the saint when he is called to the Battle of Mag Rath. Rónán gives thanks to God for being spared but curses the king, asking that he may wander through the world naked, as he has come naked into his presence.

Rónán tries to make peace between the contending armies at Mag Rath without success. When he tries to bless the warriors, including Suibne, the king throws his spear at the saint; a second spear breaks against Rónán's bell, its shaft flying in the air. Rónán curses Suibne a second time, wishing that he may fly through the air like the shaft of his spear and that he may die of a cast spear. When Suibne tries to rejoin the battle he is seized with trembling and flees in frenzy like a wild bird. His feet barely touch the ground, and land at last on a *yew tree. After Suibne's withdrawal, his opponents are victorious. When a kinsman is unable to bring Suibne back among his people, the mad king flies to different parts of Ireland, settling for long intervals in the glen of madmen known as Glenn *Bolcáin.

His one faithful friend during this torment is Loingsechán, who may be a uterine brother or a foster-brother. Loingsechán rescues Suibne three times and keeps him informed about his family. Eórann, who has gone to live with Guaire, remains faithful to Suibne, even though he visits her and tells her she would be better off without him. On several occasions Suibne regains his reason, and once he seeks to return to his people, but Rónán prays that the king should not be allowed to come back and resume his persecution of the Church. The narrative is interspersed with a number of poems, some of them in Suibne's voice. Two of the most memorable, coming late in the narrative, are in praise of nature and of trees.

Suibne ends his wandering at the monastery of St Moling, Co. Carlow, whose monks fed and sheltered him and ask that his history be written. One night when Suibne is eating, Moling's cook's husband is jealous of the attention given the visitor. The husband's spear goes through Suibne's body, but not before he has accepted the faith. Many commentators see a link between the madness of Suibne and that of *Myrddin or *Merlin, who also begins a frenzied wandering after a battle; See WILD MAN OF THE WOOD. Among the modern writers attracted to Suibne's story are W. B. Yeats, whose 'Madness of King Goll' (1887) credits the madness to another king, and Flann O'Brien, whose title *At Swim-Two-Birds* (1939) translates a place-name in the original text. See also Seamus Heaney, *Sweeney Astray* (New York, 1984).

The standard modern edition is in the Irish Text Society, 12, ed. J. G. O'Keeffe (London, 1912). *Fled Dúin na nGéd* and *Cath Maige Ráth* were first edited by John O'Donovan (Dublin, 1848). Carl Marstrander re-edited *Fled Dúin na nGéd* in the Norwegian journal *Videnskabs-Selkabets Skrifter*, 2(6) (1909), and *Cath Maige Ráth* in *Ériu*, 5 (1911), 226–47.

Builg. A historical people who settled in south-eastern Ireland near the modern city of Cork in pre-Christian times. They were a division of the *P-Celtic *Belgae of Gaul and Britain. The Builg were also known as the *Érainn (latinized as Iverni or Ivernians). They also appear to be identical with the *Fir Bolg of the pseudo-history **Lebor Gabála* [Book of Invasions]. According to their own invasion legend, the heroic ancestor *Lugaid came from Britain to conquer Ireland. T. F. O'Rahilly devotes two chapters to sorting out relevant information in *Early Irish History and Mythology* (Dublin, 1946), 43–57, 78–84.

Buinne, Buino [Ir., circlet (?), bracelet (?)]. Faithless retainer of *Deirdre and Noíse in *Longas Mac nUislenn* [The Exile of the Sons of Uisnech]. Buinne, sometimes called Ruadh [the Red, or Rough Red], was a son of *Fergus mac Roich. Initially a brave defender of Deirdre and Noíse, Buinne accepts a bribe from *Conchobar and abandons the lovers. The bribe is all the land on the side of a mountain, which becomes a desert when Buinne tries to occupy it.

bull [MidE, OE, ON]. The male bovine animal has long been an important figure in the Celtic imagination, especially as an emblem of strength and virility, although less important than the *boar or *stag and less important than in other cultures, notably Persian, Syrian, Minoan, and Iberian. The word for 'bull' is remarkably uniform across Celtic languages: OIr. tarb; ModIr. and ScG tarbh; Manx tarroo; W tarw; Corn. tarow; Bret. tarv. Representations of the bull are found in Celtic art as early as the *Urnfield period (*c.*800 BC), often associated with the *egret. The divine bull of Celtic settlements in Asia Minor was known as Deotaros. The Gauls worshipped a three-horned bull known as *Tarvos trigaranus, one representation of which is found in the Cluny Museum, Paris. Bulls appeared on Gaulish coins, and may have been venerated in such names as Donnotaurus [Brown or Kingly Bull]. Figures of bulls are carved in stone near Burghead, Morayshire. Several heroes in Celtic stories wear bull horns, e.g. *Furbaide Ferbend.

The most celebrated bulls in Celtic literature are the brown (*Donn Cuailnge) and white (*Finnbennach) ones in the *Táin Bó Cuailnge* [Cattle Raid of Cooley]. The battle between them and the subsequent victory of the brown bull is the climax of the narrative. Many commentators have observed that both bulls are probably of divine origin. Two bulls associated with water appear in Celtic folklore, the Scottish Gaelic *tarbh uisge and the Manx *tarroo ushtey, comparable figures that are less malign than horses of the water. Another Scottish bull was thought to have defeated an English one, according to a tradition associated with a stone known as Clach nan Tarbh near Loch Lomond. In Christian times the bull was identified with St Luke the Evangelist, and in Renaissance physics the bull was linked with earth, one of the four elements.

Bulls were used in divination in both Ireland and Scotland. At *Tara a new king might be chosen in the tarbfheis, 'bull-feast' or 'bull-sleep', in which a bull was killed and a man ate his fill of its flesh, drank its broth, and then lay down to sleep. After an incantation had been chanted over him by four *druids, the dreamer would know the new king in his dream. In Scotland a person might answer an important question about the future (no king was to be selected) by wrapping himself in the warm, smoking hide of a newly slain bull in a remote place, such as near a waterfall. Upon going into a trance the person would have the answer. This method was known as taghairm, a term that might also apply to the roasting of cats.

bull feast. See BULL.

bunadh beag na farraige [Ir. *bunadh*, stock, family, host; *na farraige*, of the sea]. A name for the *fairies of the sea, sometimes translated idiomatically as 'the wee folk of the sea'. See also BOCTOGAI.

bunadh na croc, cnoc [Ir., stock, host, or family of the hill]. Another name for the *fairies.

Búrc Búiredach. Father of *Érne, the eponym of the *Erne waterway.

Burren, the [Ir. *Boireann*, great rock]. A barony in north-west Co. Clare, most of which is a 100-square-mile plateau of lunar-like limestone. Although it supports a sparse population in modern times, the Burren is home to a profusion of flowers and plants not found elsewhere in Europe. Also to be found are hundreds of ruined forts, megalithic tombs, caves, and underground streams.

Bussumarus [Romano-Gaulish, large-lipped]. A god of the Continental Celts whom the Romans identified with *Jupiter.

bwbach, bwbachod (pl.) [W, bogy, scarecrow, bugbear]. Welsh supernatural creature who may be helpful or mischievous in the household. The bwbach is a scold to teetotallers and dissenting ministers. Also used to describe a warrior as leader causing terror. Best known in the three Glamorganshires.

bwci, bwcïod (pl.), **bwca** [W, bogy, hobgoblin, ghost, spectre]. Welsh supernatural creature, a solitary *fairy or ghost, who may be helpful, mischievous, or awesome for the household. The bwci expects food, such as bread and bowls of milk, to be left for him; he can be vengeful to those who neglect him or tamper with his offerings. The bwci is often thought identical with the *pwca, although the latter spelling usually signals the character's friskier personality. One bwci who teases a farm maiden has the secret name of *gwarwyn a throt. See also BUCCA; BWBACH; BWGAN.

bwgan [W, goblin, bogey]. Welsh supernatural creature of fearful implications, a bogey or poltergeist.

C

C. The third letter of the modern English alphabet was known as coll [*hazel] in the *ogham alphabet of early Ireland.

Cabadius. Latinized variant of *Cathbad.

Cabal, Cafall, Caval, Cavall, Kawal. The hound of King *Arthur.

cabyll-ushtey. The Manx *each uisce or water-horse. Not as dangerous or greedy as its Highland counterpart, the Manx cabyll-ushtey appears in relatively few folk narratives. It might seize cows and tear them to pieces, stampede horses, or steal children. See also the Manx GLAISTYN, Welsh CEFFYL DWFR, and Scottish KELPIE and GLASHTIN. Folk motif: B17.2.1.

Cad Goddeu. Welsh title for a short, obscure poem of great antiquity preserved in the **Book of Taliesin* (13th cent.), known in English as The Battle of the Trees or The Army of the Trees. The poem is set during a war between *Arawn, king of *Annwfn, and *Amaethon, a ploughman, prompted by the latter's theft of a white roebuck, a whelp, and a lapwing. Central to the poem is the magician *Gwydion's use of a staff of enchantment to transform trees into fighting men. Although *Cad Goddeu* apparently contains implications of powers attributed to different trees, the larger meaning of the poem remains unexplicated. Robert Graves, though he professed to know no Welsh, 'translated' and rearranged the order of *Cad Goddeu* to support his thesis about the origin of the alphabet, which in turn was central to his 'grammar of poetic myth' in *The White Goddess* (New York, 1948); while Graves found a large lay readership, his views have been scorned by learned commentators on Welsh literature.

The Welsh text of *Cad Goddeu* was edited by J. G. Evans, *Book of Taliesin* (Llanbedrog, 1910), 23–7; see the translation by Patrick K. Ford, *The Mabinogi* (Berkeley, Calif., 1977), 183–7. Commentary: Marged Haycock, *Celtic Linguistics: Readings in the Brythonic Languages*, ed. Martin J. Ball et al. (Amsterdam, 1990), 297–332.

Cadan, Cadhan [Ir., wild goose]. An early hero whose wonderful dog killed a piast or monster near Derry, Northern Ireland.

Cadfan, Saint [W *cad*, battle; *ban*, summit]. Sixth-century Welsh saint who established a monastery on *Bardsey Island [W *Ynyn Enlli*], north Cardigan Bay.

Cadi Haf. See CALAN MAI.

cadineag. Scottish Gaelic *fairy or weeper, similar to the *bean nighe. It may be heard wailing in the darkness near a waterfall before catastrophe overtakes a clan; sometimes portrayed in stories of the massacre at *Glencoe, north Strathclyde, formerly *Argyllshire (1692). Perhaps identical with the *caoineag, *caointeach, and *caointeag.

Cadog, Cadoc, Catog, Catwg, **Saint** [W var. of *cadfael*, battle-prince (?)]. Sixth-century Welsh saint, one of the most celebrated of his nation, who founded a monastery at Llancarfan, Glamorganshire, and twenty other churches in south Wales, as well as others in *Cornwall and *Brittany. A grandson of *Brychan, he was murdered by invaders *c.*577. Sometimes called Cadog Ddoeth [W, the wise], he was the subject of many miraculous stories from the 11th and 12th centuries. The 'Wisdom of Cadog' consisted of witty apothegms that formed part of the lore to be learned by an aspiring *bard. By tradition Cadog was the teacher of *Gildas and *Taliesin. Feast-day 25 September.

Cador, Cadwr, Kadwr. The duke of *Cornwall in **Breuddwyd Rhonabwy* [The Dream of Rhonabwy] and a nephew of *Arthur; he also figures prominently in the Arthurian chronicles of *Geoffrey of Monmouth (12th cent.), Wace (10th cent.), and Layamon (12th cent.). He is killed in the last battle of Mount Badon.

Cadwaladr, Cadwalader [W *cad*, battle; *gwalader*, arranger]. Name borne by several figures in early Welsh history, most notably the prince and saint of *Gwynedd, sometimes called Cadwaladr Fendigaid [the blessed], who died at Rome, ?664 or ?681. His father was *Cadwallon.

Cadwallon [W *cad*, battle; *gallon*, scatterer (?), ruler (?)]. Name borne by several early Welsh figures, most notably the 7th-century political leader who invaded Northumberland (*c*.629) and drove the Irish from the north. Father of *Cadwaladr.

Cadwr. See CADOR.

Caeilte. Variant of *Caílte.

Cáel, Caol [Ir., slender]. The *Fenian hero and lover of *Créd/Credhe; he sometimes bears the agnomen An Iarann [Ir., of iron] and cognomen Ua Nemhnainn. While courting Créd in the company of the *Fianna, Cáel wins her by reciting a poem praising her possessions. After Cáel is killed at the battle of Ventry Harbour [**Cath Fionntrágha*] and his body was washed ashore, Créd lies down in his grave beside him, so great is her grief. The permanence of their love was cited by *Caílte in **Acallam na Senórach* [Colloquy of the Elders] and has been the subject of a number of poems in Irish and English.

Cáemgen, Cáomgen, Caoimhín, Cóemgen, **Saint** [Ir., beautiful born]. At least two saints bear this name, anglicized as Kevin, the better-known of whom was the founder and abbot (?498–618) of *Glendalough whose feast-day is 3 June. Cáemgen was celebrated for his chastity, and once resisted a temptress by falling propitiously into a bed of nettles—or by kicking her out of his *cave so that she fell into a lake and drowned. His name appears in a number of *Fenian stories.

Caemhoch, Saint. Variant form of *Mo Cháemóc.

Cáer [cf. Ir. *cáer*, globular mass, drop, mass of cast metal]. Beloved of *Angus Óg and a princess of *Connacht, a daughter of *Ethal Anbúail. Angus suffers from an ailment that can be cured only by a woman he has seen in a dream. When he finds her they become lovers; they are transformed into *swans and fly around a lake three times. She sometimes has the agnomen Iborm[m]eith [*yew berry]. International tale type 400, the swan maiden. See AISLINGE OENGUSO [The Dream of Angus].

Caer, Kaer. A Welsh word meaning 'wall; fort, castle, citadel' as employed in numerous place-names. Sometimes anglicized as Kaer. Entries relating to Caer are given letter by letter, whether 'Caer' is a separate word or a prefix.

Caercaradoc. Name for Salisbury in *Geoffrey of Monmouth and other medieval Arthuriana.

Caerdroea. Welsh for Troy, Ilium.

Caer Eiddyn. Variant form of *Din Eidyn, the Welsh name for *Edinburgh.

Caereni. A tribe of Roman-era Scotland, part of the Caledonian confederation. They occupied a territory coextensive with northwest Sutherland (until 1974) in the Highlands.

Caerfaddon. Welsh name for *Bath.

Caer Feddwid [W, city of carousal; court of intoxication, etc.]. Name for an *otherworldly city in Welsh and Welsh Arthurian narratives. See also ANNWFN; CAER SIDDI.

Caerfyrddin. Welsh name for Carmarthen.

Caer Iborm[m]eith. See CÁER (1).

Caerleon, Caerleon-on-Usk. Anglicized spelling of Caerllion ar Wysg, a residence of *Arthur, often identified with Camelot. The Romans built the fortress Isca near the site of the medieval walled city. Ruins of Isca seem to have encouraged *Geoffrey of Monmouth (12th cent.) to favour Caerleon as Arthur's seat. Here Arthur is described as massing his forces for the battle of Bedegraine and celebrating the subsequent victory. Caerleon Castle has a flight of 208 steps leading to a room thought to be used by *Merlin. The modern Caerleon is a modest urban district in south Monmouthshire on the Usk [W *Wysg*] River, 2.5 miles NE of Newport. Caerleon is sometimes confused with the English city of Chester [W *Caerllion Fawr*].

Caerliwelydd. Welsh name for Carlisle; see CAER LUEL.

Caerllion, Caer Llion. Welsh for *Caerleon. Caerllion Fawr is Welsh for Chester.

Caerlloyw, Caer Lloyw, Loyw. Welsh name for *Gloucester.

Caer Lludd, Ludd. An early Welsh name for London, alluding to the belief that *Lludd had helped to rebuild the walls of the city.

Caer Llundain, Llundein. London, in more recent Welsh.

Caer Loyw. Variant spelling of Caerlloyw: *Gloucester.

Caer Luel. Carlisle. See CAERLIWELYDD.

Caer Lundain, Lundein. Variant spellings of Caer Llundain: London.

Caernach. Variant of Cernach; see CONALL CERNACH.

Caerphilly. A town in south Mid-Glamorganshire, 7 miles N of Cardiff. In Welsh oral tradition it is the home of the Green Lady of Caerphilly, a wraith who takes the form of ivy when she is not walking through ruined castles. In more recent years the name Caerphilly has become better known for a distinctive cheese.

Caer Seint. One of *Bendigeidfran's assembly sites in the **Mabinogi*, a region in *Gwynedd opposite the island of *Anglesey. Nearby are the Roman ruins of Segontium.

Caer Siddi, Sidi [cf. Ir. **sídh*]. Another name for the otherworldly *Annwfn, especially when seen as an elysium. Sickness and old age are unknown in Caer Siddi. Enchanting music is heard there, and a fountain flows with a liquid sweeter than white wine. *Gwair was kept in a well-equipped prison here. Caer Siddi is sometimes identified with the islet of Grassholm off *Dyfed (until 1974, Pembrokeshire), as is *Gwales. See also CAER FEDDWID.

Caer Wydyr, Wydr [W, fortress of glass]. A name for *Annwfn, the Welsh Otherworld. See YNYS GUTRIN.

Caesair. Variant spelling of *Cesair.

Caesar, [Gaius] Julius. Roman general, statesman, and historian (100–44 BC) whose seven-volume *Gallic War* [*De Bello Gallico*] is a much-cited source for information on early Celtic ethnography and religion. Although much admired for his clarity of style, Caesar cannot be accepted without qualification: not only did he rely on the reports of subordinates, but he may have taken more from *Posidonius (*c.*135–*c.*51 BC) than from his own observations. As the conqueror first of the Gauls and then of the Britons, he had an understandably patronizing view of the Celts, finding them eager for battle but easily dashed by adversity. He also found them superstitious, given to submitting to *druids for arbitration in public and private affairs. As for religious beliefs, he was struck by their view that the soul did not perish at the death of the body. His vision of a Celtic pantheon is more troubling to modern commentators. Thinking that Celtic conceptions differed little from Roman, he assigned Roman names to native gods, ranking them in order of perceived preference: *Mercury, *Apollo, *Mars, *Jupiter, and *Minerva. Although it is not supported by any non-Roman evidence, Caesar enunciated clear differentiation of function among different Celtic gods as well as the existence of a universal pantheon.

Cafall. Welsh form of *Cabal.

Cahal. Anglicization of *Cathal.

Cahir More. Anglicization of *Cathaír Mór.

Cahirconree, Cahirconry, Caherconree [Ir. *cathair*, stone fort; *chonraoí*]. Iron-age stone fort on a 2,050-foot promontory, in the *Sliab Mis [Slieve Mish] mountains, *Dingle peninsula, Co. *Kerry, 8 miles SW of Tralee. The name of the fortress is thought to allude to *Cú Roí. According to an oft-told story, Cú Roí was betrayed by his wife *Bláithíne to *Cúchulainn at Cahirconree.

Cai. Variant spelling of *Cei.

Caibell. The story of Caibell and his friend Etar and the contest for their daughters depicts an enigmatic war between pre-Christian divinities little understood by later scribes. Caibell and Etar are rulers of the *sídh whose daughters are sought in marriage by two kings, who are offered a contest to settle the match. The idea of battle would pollute the sídh, however, and the sídh-folk have no wish to be visible to mortals lest that power be lost. The fight takes place at night, therefore, and the sídh-folk take the form of *deer. The struggle is so fierce that four hillocks are made of the hooves and antlers of the slain. Near the end, water bursts forth from a well and forms Lough Riach, which the storyteller says has the property of turning white sheep crimson, if they are cast in every seventh year at the proper hour. Of the combatants only Etar survives. This Irish story survives in the *Rennes* [Brittany] Dindshenchas; see the edition by W. Stokes, *Revue Celtique*, 16 (1895), 273 ff.

Caicer, Caicher, Caichér. *Druid of the *Milesians in the **Lebor Gabála* [Book of Invasions] who prophesied that his people would one day migrate to Ireland.

Cailb. The ugly female seer in the Irish story **Togail Bruidne Da Derga* [The Destruction of Da Derga's Hostel] who foretells the death of *Conaire. The description of her monstrous form includes an allusion to her sexual parts. When Conaire says that her name is insignificant, she stands on one foot and chants thirty-two different names.

Cailitin, Calatin, Calatín. Irish wizard or *druid, perhaps of *Fomorian origin, friendly to *Medb, who does battle with and is defeated by *Cúchulainn. Cailitin travels with his twenty-seven offspring, and may be called 'Clan Cailitin', but insists on being regarded as a single warrior as all have sprung from a single body. They study sorcery in *Alba [Scotland] and make every throw of their poisoned spears a direct, lethal hit. Each is mutilated, with the left hand and right foot missing. They almost succeed in drowning *Cúchulainn, before the *Connacht warrior *Fiachu mac Fir Fhebe rescues him. Later Cúchulainn dispatches him/them, but Cailitin's widow shortly afterwards gives birth to sextuplets, three sons and three daughters, all hideous and pernicious-looking. Among the children is *Badb, who is sometimes called a child of *Ernmas. Medb has the children trained in the black arts so that they may wreak vengeance on Cúchulainn. This they do by assuming different shapes and luring the hero into danger, including the battle in which he is slain. Cailitin is a character in W. B. Yeats's play *The Countess Cathleen* (1892).

Caillagh ny Groamagh. [Manx, old woman of gloominess, sullen witch]. A Manx weather-spirit and probable variant of the ScG *Cailleach Bheur. If 1 February (feast of St *Brigid, Bridget, or Bride; pre-Christian *Imbolc) is a fine day she comes out to warm herself, but if it is a wet day she stays inside. A fine 1 February, therefore, is a bad omen for the rest of the year. The tradition is clearly related to the American Groundhog Day, 2 February, centred in Pennsylvania. Her ill humour is attributed to her either having fallen into a crevice on Barrule, a mountain (1842 feet) on the Isle of Man, or having been thrown out to sea, after which she drifted back. Another name for her is Caillagh ny Gueshag.

Caillagh ny Gueshag [Manx, the old woman of the spells]. Another name for *Caillagh ny Groamagh.

Cailleac Buillia. W. B. Yeats's spelling of *Cailleach Bhéirre.

cailleach, caillech, cailliach, callech. Although the Modern Irish and Scottish Gaelic word cailleach means literally 'old woman', often in the pejorative sense, or 'hag', the word has many more connotations than this simple gloss would imply. The OIr. caillech, from which cailleach derives, meant literally 'veiled one', and could denote a nun, widow, or old woman. Thus the Irish sovereignty figure, *Cailleach Bhéirre, is best described by the resonant Irish term rather than the unsatisfactory English translations 'Nun', 'Hag', or 'Old Woman of Beare'.

In both Ireland and Gaelic Scotland, cailleach also denotes the last sheaf of a harvest and is the subject of many beliefs and practices. In Ireland farmers hold races at harvest time so that industrious farmers may call their last sheaf the 'corn maiden' while only slower workers are given the cailleach as their last sheaf, presumably a reproach for their procrastination and dilatory ways. The cailleach is kept during the year; some is given to the cattle and some shaken on the land to assure fertility in the coming year. Farm girls avoid tying the cailleach for fear that they shall never have a husband. In Scotland the cailleach is tied with a ribbon and hung up on a nail until spring. On the first day of ploughing it is given to the horse as a token of good luck. On the Isle of Lewis the cailleach was dressed as a woman and her apron filled with bread, cheese, and a sickle. Comparable customs of the old woman of the fields are found in Wales as well as in non-Celtic European countries.

Cailleach Beinne Bric [ScG, the old woman of speckled (trout, salmon, wolf, badger) mountain]. A ScG counterpart of the *Cailleach Bhéirre.

Cailleach Bhéirre, Béirre, Béarra, Bheare, Bhéara, Beare, Beara, Bhérri, Calliagh Birra [Ir., old woman, hag, nun of Beare]. The Irish *sovereignty figure, whose Scottish Gaelic counterpart is *Cailleach Beinne Bric. The Cailleach Bhéirre is usually associated with *Munster, especially the *Beare peninsula in south-western Ireland, between Bantry Bay and the Kenmare estuary, in counties Cork and *Kerry; also known as *Dígde, Díge, and *Duineach; a Connacht variant locates her at Slieve Daeane, a hill 4 miles SW of Sligo town. She also appears to be identical with *Buí or Boí, the wife of *Lug Lámfhota. As the allegorical sovereignty figure, she appears to a knight or hero as an ugly old woman asking to be loved. When she receives love, she becomes a beautiful young maiden. The Cailleach Bhéirre passes through at least seven periods of youth, so that each husband passes from her to death of old age. She had fifty foster-children in Beare. Her grandchildren and great-grandchildren were peoples and races. A note in the *Book of Lecan* (*c.*1400) says that the Cailleach Bhéirre was of the *Corcu Duibne, a people of south-western Ireland in pre-Norman times. The notion that she is a nun who has taken the veil is a Christian fiction, probably dating from the 8th century.

The Cailleach speaks in her own voice in a well-known dramatic monologue, widely translated under different titles. In the poem she says she is not the king's but the poet's mistress, and that she admires the plain of *Femen in Tipperary, which may have controlled power and wealth. See Jo Radner, 'The Hag of Beare: The Folklore of a Sovereignty Goddess', *Tennessee Folklore Society Bulletin*, 40 (1974), 75–81; Donncha Ó hAodha, 'The Lament of the Old Woman of Beare', in *Sages, Saints and Storytellers: Celtic Studies in Honour of Professor James Carney*, ed. Donnchadh Ó Corrain (Maynooth, 1989), 308–31.

The Cailleach Bhéirre has several counterparts in English, notably loathsome ladies in the Child ballad 'King Henry' and Chaucer's *Wife of Bath's Tale*. See Sigmund Eisner, *A Tale of Wonder: A Source Study of the Wife of Bath's Tale* (Wexford and New York, 1957). See also CAILLEACH BHEUR; CAITLÍN; CERIDWEN; SEAN-BHEAN BHOCHT. W. B. Yeats used the spelling Cailleach Buillia for this figure, and may also have implied her in his creation *Clooth-na-Bare.

Cailleach Bheur [ScG, the genteel old lady, hag]. A personification of winter in Scottish Gaelic folklore and a counterpart of *Caillagh ny Gueshag of the Isle of Man. The blue-faced Cailleach Bheur was a daughter of the pale winter sun of 1 November to 1 May. As she is born old and ugly (i.e. at the beginning of winter) and ends her time young and beautiful (i.e. as spring) she also presents a parallel with the ever-renewing *Cailleach Bhéirre and *Cailleach Beinne Bric. Known as *Cally Berry in *Ulster. Her watery form is known as Muileartach.

Cailleach Uragaig. The hag of isle of Colonsay, Strathclyde (until 1974, *Argyllshire). A spirit of winter, Cailleach Uragaig keeps a young girl captive and avoids the assaults of the girl's lover by turning herself into a permanently moist grey headland above the sea.

Caílte, Cailte, Caoilte, Caelte, Keelta, Kylta. Name borne by several figures, seven of whom were *Fenians, the best-known being Caílte mac Rónáin, sometimes described as a nephew of *Fionn mac Cumhaill, famous for his fleetness of foot. Caílte is a steward for Fionn and once helps him catch two of every kind of wild animal when *Gráinne asks for them. Caílte can kill *giants. He is also a golden-tongued reciter of tales and poems, and a favoured minstrel for an evening's entertainment. In the **Acallam na Senórach* [Colloquy of the Elders] Caílte survives until Christian times and speaks on behalf of the old values to St *Patrick. Several poems celebrating nature and the older values are attributed to Caílte. In the 8th-century **Imram Brain* [Voyage of Bran], Caílte discloses that Fionn was reincarnated by King *Mongán of the *Cycle of Kings. In later ballads on this theme Caílte is largely displaced by *Oisín. His father-in-law was Barrán and his daughter was Suain. He is known as Derglas in some Scottish Gaelic lore; his counterpart in *Macpherson's *Ossian* is Co-alt. Some modern commentators have asserted that the names Caílte and Oisín might both have been originally nicknames for Fionn, and that the personages grew out of aspects of the older hero.

Cain. This biblical figure appears in the **Lebor Gabála* [Book of Invasions], where he is the first to see Ireland.

Cain Wyry. Welsh for Keyne (or Cain) Virgin; see KEYNE.

Cainche, Caince [Ir., melody; songbird; bough, branch]. Also known as Cébha. In *Fenian ballads Cainche is the daughter of *Fionn mac Cumhaill. She mates with the enemy *Goll mac Morna to produce Feadha, who is killed by Fionn. Goll cites this murder as the reason for his final break with Fionn. Her name is anglicized as Keeva (or Keva) of the White Skin.

Cainder, Cainnear. Name borne by a daughter of *Medb as well as by a number of Christian saints.

Cainnlech, Cainnleach [Ir., shining, lustrous (?)]. A daughter of Gamgelta, she was the foster-mother of *Cormac Connloinges, whose slaying caused her death from grief.

Caíntigern, Caointiarn [Ir., gentle lady]. Name borne by several female figures in early Irish narrative, most notably the wife of *Fiachna mac Báetáin and mother of the hero *Mongán.

Cainwen [W *cain*, beautiful; *gwen*, fair]. A Welsh name for St *Keyne.

Caipre. Variant spelling of *Cairbre.

Cairbar, Carbar. Character in *Macpherson's *Ossian* (1760) borrowed from a number of Irish and Scottish Gaelic figures. He pursues *Dar-Thula (based in part on *Deirdre). Often referred to as 'Cairbar the Usurper'. He was an antagonist of *Oscar the son of Ossian. See also CAIRBRE CINN-CHAIT; CAIRBRE LIFECHAIR.

Cairbre, Cairbri, Cairpre, Caipre, Carbre, Carbry, Carpre, Coirbre, Coirpre, Corpre [Ir., charioteer (?)]. A common male name in early Ireland, borne by scores of figures in both legends and histories, including several saints. The best-known character with this name is probably *Cairbre Lifechair.

Cairbre 1. The son of *Niall Noígiallach [of the Nine Hostages]. He was the founder of a dynasty and gave his name to the barony of Carbury, Co. Kildare.

Cairbre Cinn-Chait, Caitchenn, Cattchenn [Ir., hard head (?), cat-head (?)]. According to the *Lebor Gabála* [Book of Invasions], when the Aithech-Túatha [plebeian races] overthrow the *Milesians they set Cairbre Cinn-Chait to rule over them, and he is sometimes therefore referred to as a usurper. During his reign there is only one grain on each stalk of wheat and one acorn on each oak, the rivers are empty of fish, and the cattle milkless, as nature refuses to condone his wrongful succession. None the less, he is an ancestor of the *Érainn. After Cairbre's death his son *Morann, who could have succeeded him, returns Ireland to the Milesians.

Cairbre Cuanach. An *Ulster warrior drowned during a battle with *Cú Roí mac Dáiri.

Cairbre Lifechair [Ir., of the Liffey; Liffey-lover]. An *ard rí [high king] of Ireland in the *Fenian Cycle, son of *Cormac mac Airt, and antagonist of *Fionn mac Cumhaill and his men. At the beginning of Cairbre's reign Fionn's *Fianna has power to rival the king's. When Cairbre's daughter Sgiamh Sholais [beauty of light] is to be married, the Fianna demand a tribute of twenty gold ingots, which, they say, is customarily paid to them on these occasions. Outraged, Cairbre seizes this opportunity to rally his allies and crush the Fianna. In doing so he splits apart the rival factions of the clans *Baíscne and *Morna, the latter joining him. In the final conflagration, described in **Cath Gabhra* [The Battle of Gabhair/Gowra], the Fianna are crushed but Cairbre, mortally wounded by *Oscar, puts a spear through Oscar's heart, thus dispatching the greatest Fenian warrior. In other stories the battle is named *Cnámross. His brother is *Dóel, and his most notable son is *Eochu Doimlén, father of the rapacious three *Collas; another son was *Fiachu Sraibthine. The story of his conception by Cormac upon *Eithne Tháebfhota is told in **Esnada Tige Buchet* [The Melodies of Buchet's House].

Cairbre Losc, Lusc [Ir., lame]. Father of *Daui Dalta Dedad.

Cairbre mac Ethne, Étaíne, Éadaoine. Son of *Ogma and *Étan (1), grandson of *Dian Cécht, and resident satirist of the *Tuatha Dé Danann. In **Cath Maige Tuired* [The (Second) Battle of Mag Tuired] he is treated rudely by *Bres and so composes a satire that causes the king's face to break out in red blotches, a disfigurement that allows a call for the latter's resignation. Later his satires break the morale of the *Fomorians in their battle with the Tuatha Dé Danann. He has the power to inflict the *glám dícenn upon his enemies.

Cairbre Músc. Legendary ancestor of the Múscraige, people of Muskerry, the name of several areas in Munster, including east of Lough Derg on the *Shannon. He may also be known as Angus (Óengus) Músc.

Cairbre Nia Fer, Niafer, Niaper. King of *Tara and antagonist of *Cúchulainn in the *Ulster Cycle, apparently because of a rivalry over *Conchobar's daughter *Fedelm Noíchrothach or Noíchride, whom he marries. Cúchulainn disdains *Emer's older sister *Fial (2) because of her relationship with Cairbre Nia Fer. Cúchulainn makes short work of him at Ros na Rígh. To avenge this killing *Erc (1) also engages Cúchulainn in battle. Cairbre is celebrated for his twelve daughters; his full patronymic is mac Rosa Ruaid. Cairbre's attributed brother is *Find File, mythical king of *Leinster.

caird. Variant spelling of *cerd.

Cairell. A son of *Fionn mac Cumhaill who was killed by his father's sometime rival, *Goll mac Morna.

Cairenn, Caireann [cf. L *Carina*]. Secondary wife, captured slave, of *Eochaid Mugmedón and mother of *Niall Noígiallach [of the Nine Hostages] and thus an ancestress of the *Uí Néill dynasty. Also called Cairenn Chasdub [of the dark curly hair]. She was a daughter of Sachall Balb [*balb*, stammerer, foreigner] of the Britons. Because she was hated by Eochaid's queen, *Mongfhind, she had to draw water for the household in her pregnancy until she delivered Niall. See **Echtra Mac nEchach Muigmedóin* [The Adventure of the Sons of Eochaid Mugmedón].

Cairpre. Variant of *Cairbre.

caisel, caiseal [cf. L *castellum*]. Although this word is often translated as 'castle', in a nod to its Latin root, it more often describes any large, non-ecclesiastical building made with drystone walls. Caisel Muman is the OIr. name for *Cashel.

Cáit Ní Dhuibhir [Ir., Kate, daughter of darkness (?)]. A poetic personification of *Ireland. See also RÓISÍN DUBH.

cait sith. See CAT SÌTH.

Caithbath, Caithbaid. In *Macpherson's *Ossian* (1760), the father of Semo and grandfather of *Cuthullin. He is based in part on *Cathbad of the *Ulster Cycle.

Caitlín, Ceithlenn, Cethlenn, Ceithlionn, Céthlionn. This Irish version (one of many) of the French name Catherine has been borne by thousands of historical personages since the 12th century. The best-known mythical or folkloric bearer of the name is Caitlín Ní hUallacháin [Ir., the proud], a family name known under many spellings from Kilkenny to Clare. As a personification of Ireland Caitlín Ní hUallacháin is fairly recent and has been much influenced by W. B. Yeats's play *Cathleen ni Houlihan* (1902), in which the tall, beautiful, and imposing Maude Gonne played the role. Within the play, however, Cathleen describes herself as the Poor Old Woman; see also SEAN-BHEAN BHOCHT; CAILLEACH BHÉIRRE; CERIDWEN. The name may also be transcribed Kathleen O'Hoolihan, etc.

The name Caitlín has also been applied to the buck-toothed wife of *Balor of the Evil Eye in some texts, even though he could have no associations with the Christian Catherine; she wounds the *Dagda at the battle of Mag Tuired; see CATH MAIGE TUIRED. See also Rosalind Elizabeth Clark, *Great Queens: Irish Goddesses from the Morrígan to Cathleen Ní Houlihan* (Gerrards Cross and Savage, Md., 1990).

Cala' Me. Cornish for May Day; see CALAN MAI; BELTAINE.

Caladbolg [Ir. *calad*, hard]. Also In Caladbolg. The lightning sword belonging to several early Irish heroes, notably *Fergus mac Róich. With it Fergus chops off the tops of three hills in *Meath. *Fergus mac Léti has a sword much like it called Caladhcholg. Several commentators have seen it as an anticipation of the Arthurian *Excalibur. See also CALEDFWLCH.

Caladfwlch. Variant spelling of *Caledfwlch.

Calan Awst. Welsh counterpart of *Lughnasa.

Calan Gaeaf. See HOLLANTIDE; SAMAIN; ALLANTIDE.

Calan Mai, Dydd Calan Mai, Galan Mai. Welsh terms for May Day, celebrated as the beginning of summer, although not to the extent of the Goidelic *Beltaine. In early Welsh literature *Gwyn ap Nudd and *Gwythyr fab Greidawl were thought to contend for the beautiful *Creiddylad each Calan Mai. Until the mid-19th century, bonfires were built and ghosts were thought to wander the countryside. The power of the *dyn hysbys [magician] would be stronger at this time. Calan Mai was always thought opportune for courtship and for celebrating the regeneration of nature. In north-east Wales the summer branch, a variant of the European maypole, was carried from house to house. Sometimes this procession would be accompanied by the Cadi Haf [*cadi*, effeminate male; *haf*, summer], or Yr Hen Gadi [the old *cadi*], a buffoonish figure with blackened face in a man's coat and a woman's petticoat who collected money in a ladle. Attempts by the Christian Church to associate Calan Mai with St Philip and St James obscured much of its pagan origin. See Trefor M. Owen, *Old Welsh Customs*, 3rd edn. (Cardiff, 1974).

Calatin. Variant spelling of *Cailitin.

Caledfwlch, Caladfwlch, Caledvwlch [W *caled*, hard]. Name for *Arthur's sword in several Welsh Arthurian narratives, one of many anticipations of *Excalibur. In **Culhwch ac Olwen* it is listed as one of Arthur's most cherished possessions and is used by Llenlleawg Wyddel to kill *Diwrnach Wyddel and his men. See also the Irish CALADBOLG.

Caledonii, Caledonians. A *P-Celtic people of ancient Scotland, part of the larger *Pictish population, who occupied land from the Tay valley to the Great Glen and gave their name to the Roman name for Scotland, Caledonia. The Caledonian confederation included peoples over an even wider area, as far north as Sutherland. As P-Celts, the Caledonii may have been more closely related to the Britons, who are ancestors of the modern Welsh, than they are to the *Q-Celtic Scots, who came from Ireland.

Caledvwlch. Variant spelling of *Caledfwlch.

calendar. The Celtic measurement of time appears to have assumed that darkness preceded light. Thus the Celtic calendar of pre-Christian times measured the year as beginning with the onset of winter. The Old Irish name for the first day of the new year is *Samain, usually assumed to be 1 November in the Julian and Gregorian calendars (but 11 November in Gaelic Scotland). The beginning of the light half of the year was *Beltaine, 1 May (or 15 May in Scotland). The dark half of the year was further divided by *Imbolc, 1 or 2 February; and the light half of the year was divided by *Lughnasa, 1 August (in Scotland sometimes as late as 29 September).

Key to our understanding of the Celtic measurement of time are the bronze tablets unearthed in 1897 at Coligny, 14 miles NNE of Bourg-en-Bresse (Ain) in eastern France, the most extensive document in the Gaulish language yet found (1st cent. AD) and now preserved at Lyons. They detail sixty-two consecutive months, approximately equal to five solar years. Months are thirty or twenty-nine days and are divided into halves. The lunar year of twelve months was adapted to the solar year by the intercalation of an extra month of thirty days every third year. Months are indicated either MAT [good or auspicious] or ANM [an abbreviation for *anmat*, not good]; remnants of this usage can be seen in the Welsh *Triads which list certain events as *mad* [fortunate] or *anfad* [unfortunate]. See A. and B. Rees, 'Light and Dark', ch. 3 of *Celtic Heritage* (London, 1961, 1973), 83–94; Kevin Danaher, *The Year in Ireland: Irish Calendar Customs* (Dublin, 1977); Paul-Marie Duval, 'Les Calendriers', in *Recueil des inscriptions gauloises*, iii (Paris, 1985); Garrett Olmsted, *The Gaulish Calendar* (Bonn, 1992).

Calgacus. Name given by Tacitus to the red-headed, sword-wielding native leader defeated by Julius Agricola at Mons Graupius in north-eastern Scotland (*c.* AD 78–84). Unless the name was invented by Tacitus, it is the oldest recorded for any Scotsman.

Callernish, Callanish. Archaeological site on the Isle of Lewis, Outer Hebrides, Scotland, containing one of the best-preserved *dolmens or 'druidical circles' to be found anywhere in Europe. It lies 16 miles W of Stornoway on the east coast of the island. In folk tradition the stones are thought to move and change their places when humans are not watching. They are referred to in Lewis Gaelic as *Tarsachan Chalanais* [the giants of Callanish], using a Norse word for 'giant'.

Calliagh Birra. *Ulster variant of *Cailleach Bhéirre.

Cally Berry. An Ulster version of the Scottish Gaelic weather spirit *Cailleach Bheur, except that here she is more likely to be a malignant, supernatural hag. See also CAILLEACH BHÉIRRE.

Calum Cille. See COLUM CILLE.

Camelot. The fabled residence of King *Arthur in medieval romances has been linked to many locations in England, Wales, Cornwall, and even Scotland. Among those with Celtic associations are *Caerleon, *Glastonbury, and *Tintagel Castle near Camelford, Cornwall. Sites in England often mentioned are Exeter and Cadbury (Somerset), where digs during the 1960s proved inconclusive.

Camlan, Camlann. *Arthur's last battle, fought after the peace secured at Mount

Badon, thought to be AD 537 or 539. The site has been variously identified: the Camel River at Camelford, *Cornwall; the Cam near Cadbury; near Salisbury; in Somerset; at Camboglanna in *Rheged on the western part of Hadrian's Wall, now called Birdoswald.

Camulodunum. Roman name, meaning 'Fort of Camulus', for two towns in occupied Britain, in Yorkshire and Exeter, the latter coextensive with the modern city of Colchester, which was the most important port city at that time. See CAMULUS.

Camulus, Camulos [Gaul., powerful (?)]. Important god of early Britain and Gaul, especially among the *Belgae and the Remi. The Romans equated him with *Mars; at Rindern, France, he was cited as Mars–Camulos on a stone with a corona of oak. Elsewhere he was portrayed with a *ram-horned head. Evidence of his popularity can be seen in several place-names notably *Camulodunum. Attempts to link him with the nursery character Old King Cole and *Fionn's father *Cumhall have been rejected by contemporary learned commentators.

Canada. See NOVA SCOTIA.

Canejach. Anglicization of *Caointeach.

Cano [Ir. *cana, cano*, wolf-cub; poet of the fourth degree]. A historical figure, son of a Scottish king, known in chronicle as Cano mac Gartnáin (d. 688), whose story seems to anticipate that of *Tristan in the Arthurian legends; in imaginative narrative his father's name is usually Gartnán. The story of his tragic love is found in *Scéla Cano meic Gartnáin* found in the **Yellow Book of Lecan* (14th cent.). Cano was in exile in Ireland when he was received in honour by one King Diarmait, whose daughter was already in love with him. After she had saved him from danger, he was travelling and visited the house of Marcán, whose young wife Créd also fell in love with Cano. At a feast she drugged all present except for Cano and herself and entreated his love. He refused to be her lover while he was still an exile, but as a pledge he gave her a stone which contained his life. Their attempts at a tryst were foiled by Créd's stepson Colcu. After a last attempt at Loch Créde was again frustrated by Colcu, Créd dashed her head against a stone. Cano died three days later after his return to Scotland. Rudolf Thurneysen argues for the parallel with Tristan in *Zeitschrift für celtische Philologie*, 43 (1924), 385–404, but D. A. Binchy in a more recent edition disagrees, *Scéla Cano Meic Gartnáin* (Dublin, 1963). See also Myles Dillon, 'The Wooing of Becfhola and the Stories of Cano, Son of Gartnán', *Modern Philology*, 43 (1945), 11–17.

Canola. Legendary discoverer of the harp in Ireland; she heard the sweet murmuring of the wind through sinews clinging to a whale's skeleton.

Canomagus. [L, hound lord]. Inscription found on a Romano-British shrine to *Apollo, Nettleton Shrub, Wiltshire. See also DOG.

cantref, cantred [W *cant*, hundred; *tref*, dwelling-place]. A division of land, as seen in early Welsh literature, containing 100 dwellings of hamlets. A cantref comprises two or more *commotes. Although the word 'cantred' is of Welsh origin, it has been used in translations of Irish texts.

Cantre'r Gwaelod, Cantref-y-Gwaelod [W, lowland hundred; cf. *gwaelod*, bottom]. Welsh *flood legend of great antiquity usually centring on the realm of *Gwyddno Garanhir in what is now *Cardigan Bay. In earliest versions of the story the land is called Maes Gwyddno, and is inundated when a well-maiden named Mererid neglects her duties. In the better-known version, dating from the early 16th century, evidencing Netherlandish influence, the legendary king *Gwyddno Garanhir reigns over sixteen cities ringed by an embankment with sluices. The drunken dike-keeper Seithenyn neglects his duties and allows the waters to flood the land, drowning all except the king. Yet the bell of Cantre'r Gwaelod's church is still thought to be heard on quiet evenings. The legend is also associated with other points of the Welsh coast, such as Tyno Heylyg further north, and bears striking similarities to the Breton legend of the City of *Ys. Modern perceptions of the story are influenced by popular 19th-century retellings in English, such as T. J. Ll. Prichard's poem 'The Land Beneath the Sea' (1823) and T. L. Peacock's novel *The Misfortunes of Elphin* (1829). See also Rachel Bromwich, 'Cantre'r Gwaelod and Ker-Is', in *The Early Cultures of North-West Europe*, ed. Cyril Fox and Bruce Dickens (Cambridge, 1950), 217–41; F. J. North, *Sunken Cities* (Cardiff, 1957).

Canu Heledd [W, the song of Heledd]. One of the longest and most unified of the early (9th or 10th cent.) narrative known as *englynion*, the oldest recorded Welsh metrical form. The central character and narrator is Heledd, the last surviving member of the royal house of *Powys, who laments the passing of the kingdom, especially of King *Cynddylan, who reigned in the early 7th century. Several commentators have posited the existence of an earlier version, which the anonymous author of the present text applied to the still lamentable conditions two centuries later. A lost text might explain why Heledd blames herself for the fall of Cynddylan's court at Pengwern in *Powys. The central poem of the cycle, *Stafell Cynddylan* [Cynddylan's Hall] is especially resonant. Ifor Williams included the text, with notes, in *Canu Llywarch Hen* (Cardiff, 1935). See also Jenny Rowland, *Early Welsh Saga Poetry* (Cambridge, 1990).

Caoilte mac Rónáin. See CAÍLTE.

Caoimhín. ModIr. spelling of *Cáemgen [Kevin].

caoineag [ScG, weeper]. A version of the *banshee known in the northern Highlands and in the Hebrides. The caoineag of the MacDonalds was said to be heard wailing after the massacre at Glencoe (1692). She may be identical with the *caointeach and *cadineag. See also FUATH.

caointeach, canejach [ScG, mourner, whiner]. A version of the *banshee who may also include elements of the *bean nighe as localized in the southern Highlands, especially what used to be *Argyllshire (since 1974, north Strathclyde). She has been described as a child or a very little woman in a short green petticoat with a high-crowned white cap. She may also wear a green shawl. A solitary *fairy, perhaps identical with the *caoineag and *cadineag; see CAOINTEAG. A Welsh counterpart is the *cyhyraeth.

caointeag. Name for the *caoineach in the isle of Islay and nearby Kintyre.

Caol 1. ModIr. spelling of *Cáel.
2. Another name for *Mac Lugach.

Ca-Olt. Hero in *Macpherson's *Ossian* (1760) based on *Caílte mac Rónáin.

Caolte. Spelling favoured by W. B. Yeats for *Caílte mac Rónáin.

Cáomgen. Variant of *Cáemgen [Kevin].

Caomh, Cóem [Ir. *caomh*, gentle, noble]. Legendary eponymous ancestor of the O'Keeffe family of Co. Cork and other counties of Munster. According to the stories, Caomh was a great athlete, a warrior against the Norsemen, and a lover, involved with both *Clídna and *Aoibhil.

Caoránach, Keeronagh. Name given to the monster banished to *Lough Derg (Co. *Donegal) by St *Patrick. Perceived as female, she was said to be the mother of *demons or devils. See also MUIRDRIS; OILLIPHÉIST.

Cape Breton Island. See NOVA SCOTIA.

Caractacus. Corrupt latinized version of *Caradog (1).

Caradog, Caradoc, Cradog, Caradawg, Caradawc, Caratach [Holinshed's *Chronicles*, 1577], Craddocke [in English ballads], Karadoc, Karadawg [cf. W *cariad*, love, amiability]. Name borne by several historical and imaginary figures of early Welsh tradition, of whom *Caradog (1) is the best-known. See also the Breton *Karadoc.

Caradog 1. Welsh name for an ancient British chieftain, the son of Cynfelyn, claimed by the Welsh as a national hero. Known to the Romans as Caractacus, he has been a character in Welsh oral tradition only since the 16th century. Trained by the Silures to defend western Britain from the Romans, Caradog led his people into battle over a period of eight years during the reign of Claudius (after AD 51). He was defeated on the slopes of a hill in Shropshire still known as Caer Caradog. After his defeat he fled to *Cartimandua, queen of the *Brigantes, who betrayed him. Caradog was taken to Rome, where his nobility so pleased the emperor that he pardoned and released him. In much of Welsh oral tradition the name of Caradog is a byword for bravery and nobility; sometimes called Colofn Cymry, 'Pillar of Wales/Cambria'. Under the name Caratach (from Holinshed) he is a character in Beaumont and Fletcher's *Bonduca* (*c.*1619). Under the latinized form Caractacus he is the title-character in a play by William Mason (1725–97) and of a dramatic cantata by Sir Edward Elgar (1897).

2. Often spelled as Caradawg; the son of *Bendigeidfran in *Branwen*, the second branch of the **Mabinogi*. Caradog is chief of the seven stewards left by Bendigeidfran (Bran the Blessed) during the expedition to Ireland. He dies of grief when the invisible *Caswallon slays the other six.

Caradog Freichfras, Breibras, Vreichvras [W short arms]. Welsh Arthurian figure, a son attributed to *Llŷr. In *Chrétien de Troyes he became Karadues Breibraz and in Breton, *Karadoc Brech Bras, Vreichvras [armstrong]. Known to be an eloquent and bold speaker, he is also virtuous and proud. Although unquestionably of Welsh origin, he appears more often in French legends and romances. Husband of *Tegau Eurfron, the paragon of virtue.

Caradog of Llancarfan. Twelfth-century Welsh historian, sometimes known by his patronymic ap Llefoed, who is cited as a contemporary of *Geoffrey of Monmouth. If he completed Geoffrey's work, the text has not survived. He is thought to be the author of the Latin *Vita Gildae*, Life of Gildas, which includes much Arthuriana. Llancarfan is a village in Glamorganshire.

Carantoc, Carannog, Crannog, **Saint.** Sixth-century Welsh saint formerly venerated in *Cardiganshire (now *Dyfed), his day being 16 May. He founded the monastery of Llangrannog, travelled in Ireland, and was venerated in Brittany as St Karentec. His medieval hagiographers included elements from secular fabulous narratives.

Carbar. Variant spelling of *Cairbar.

Cardiganshire [W *Ceredigion*, *Caredigion*]. Former maritime county (until 1974) of south Wales, now the northernmost third of *Dyfed, bordered on the west by Cardigan Bay. Named for Ceredigion, a son of *Cunedda. In Welsh legend a portion of Cardigan known as *Cantre'r Gwaelod was flooded to become Cardigan Bay. See also FLOOD; the Breton story of ffis; the Irish story of LOUGH NEAGH.

Caridwen. Variant spelling of *Ceridwen.

Carlingford Lough. Sea inlet, 10 miles long by 2 miles wide, between Co. Down in Northern Ireland and Co. Louth in the Republic of Ireland, 9 miles NE of Dundalk, Ireland. It is adjacent to the area where much of the action of the **Táin Bó Cuailnge* [Cattle Raid of Cooley] takes place. See M. G. Crawford, *Stories of the Carlingford Lough District* (Warrenpoint, Co. Down, 1913). Connected with Lough Neagh by the Newry Canal. The town of Carlingford lies on the south shore in Co. Louth.

Carman, Carmun. Malevolent female figure in early Irish tradition, perhaps a divinity. Together with her three sons, Dian [violent, fierce], Dub [dark, black], and Dothur [wicked, evil], she blighted the crops of Ireland until the superior magic of the *Tuatha Dé Danann drove her sons across the sea. She was held captive; later a festival, Óenach Carman, localized in Wexford, was held in her honour.

Carmarthenshire, Caermarthenshire [W, Caerfyrddin]. Former (until 1974) maritime county in south Wales, now the easternmost third of *Dyfed. See BLACK BOOK OF CARMARTHEN.

Carmun. Variant spelling of *Carman.

Carn Galver, Galva. Gentle giant of a well-known Cornish place-name story. Carn Galver is the playful and gentle giant protector of two villages, Morvah and Zennor, when he throws a stone and accidentally kills a small boy. He pines for the boy for seven years and dies of a broken heart; now commemorated in a logan- or rocking-stone, 5 miles NW of Penzance.

Carnac. One of the most extensive archaeological sites in any Celtic nation or all of Europe, near the village of Auray, Morbihan Department, on the south coast of Brittany. The site includes an alignment of upright megalithic blocks, among them *dolmens, *cromlechs, and menhirs, extending almost 2 miles in an approximately east–west direction. Many of the larger uprights are from 11 to 13 feet high. In Breton oral tradition Carnac is known as *Ty C'harriquet* [The House of the Gorics], after the gnomes peculiar to the area. In another Breton story, the pseudo-saint *Korneli created the monuments here by transforming his pursuers into blocks of stone. See G. E. Daniel, *Lascaux and Carnac* (London, 1955); Z. Le Rouzic, *Carnac: Légendes, etc.* (Vannes, 1924).

carpenter. See CRAFTSMAN.

Carpre. Variant spelling of *Cairbre.

Carraig Clíodhna. See CARRIGCLEENA.

Carras Dhoo, Carrasdhoo. Legendary robbers in Manx history who lured ships to the rocky shores of Maughold Head on the east coast of the island in the hope they would capsize. Although generally portrayed as murderers and villains, they are sometimes romanticized. See Esther Nelson, 'The Carras Dhoo Men', *Island Minstrelsy* (1837); Hall Caine, *The Manxman* (1897).

Carrigcleena, Carrig-Cleena [Ir. *carraig Chlíodhna*, Clídna's rock]. Name given to two large rocks thought to be sacred to *Clídna. The better-known of the two, 7 miles SSW of Mallow, Co. Cork, was once thought to be a door to the Otherworld. In peasant belief still current in the late 19th century, Clídna was thought to reside in a greensward in a circle of rocks; her benevolence would spare the area from blighted crops, diseased cattle, mischievous spirits, etc. The second Carrigcleena, also associated with Clídna, is off Inch Strand, 2 miles SE of Ross Carbery, Co. Cork.

Carril, Carrill. Variant spellings of *Cairell.

Carrog [W, torrent]. Name given to the monster of the Vale of *Conway, *Gwynedd.

Carrowmore [Ir. *ceathrú mhór*, big quarter]. Site in Co. Sligo, 5 miles NE of Tubbercurry, known for the *Fir Bolg 'burial mounds', a field of megaliths.

Carthach [Ir., loving person]. Name borne by many personages in early Ireland, both secular and ecclesiastical, of whom the best-known was the founder and eponym of the McCarthy [Mac Carthaigh] family in Munster.

Carthon, Carthonn. The son of Clessammor and Maona in *Macpherson's *Ossian* (1760) who is slain by his own father in a single combat. He appears to be based on *Connla, who was similarly killed by *Cúchulainn.

Cartimandua. Chieftainess of the north British people the *Brigantes at the time of Roman expansion (1st cent. AD). She repudiated her husband and took command of her people, but sought protection from the Romans and became in a sense their client. When *Caradog (Caractacus) fled to her in defeat, she betrayed him to the Romans. In worship she invoked Brigantia—'the high one'. Often compared with *Boudicca. See Ian Richmond, 'Queen Cartimandua', *Journal of Roman Studies*, 44 (1954), 50ff.

Cas Corach, Cascorrach, Cas Corrach [cf. Ir. *cas*, curled, skilled]. A harper of the *Tuatha Dé Danann who none the less is described as playing for St *Patrick. In the **Acallam na Senórach* [Colloquy of the Elders] he follows *Caílte to learn of the patriotic lore of the *Fenians.

Cashel [Ir. *caisel, caiseal*; L *castellum*]. The 200-foot acropolis of limestone known as the Rock of Cashel in central Tipperary is one of the best-known sites in Ireland, often mentioned in history and folklore, and visited by thousands of tourists annually. Actually, the place-name 'Cashel' is recorded elsewhere on the Irish map, and the one in Tipperary was once known as Caisel Mumhan [Cashel of Munster] to distinguish it. The *Eóganacht occupied the rock in perhaps the 5th century, before the alleged visit of St *Patrick, whose name is often associated with it. His first use of the shamrock as a Christian symbol is thought to have been here. In any case, Cashel is the only Irish royal seat to have a Latin-derived name, and for all its reputation it lacks the antiquity of *Cruachain, *Tara, or *Emain Macha. The legendary founder of the kingship of Cashel was *Corc mac Luigthig. The site was given to the Church at the beginning of the 12th century. The celebrated Cormac's Chapel, named for *Cormac mac Carthaig (d. 1138), was built there 1127–34. The larger gothic cathedral, now roofless and in disrepair, was begun in the 13th century. In folklore and history the use of 'Cashel' more often implies the rock, its earlier political associations or later ecclesiastical ones, rather than the small nearby town (pop. *c.*3,500) of the same name.

Cassivellaunus, Cassibela(u)nus. Roman name for a British chieftain north of the Thames who commanded the forces resisting *Caesar's second invasion (54 BC). He was defeated and sued for peace. Known as Cassibelen in Shakespeare's *Cymbeline* (1610–11), he may have contributed to the character of *Caswallon in Welsh literature. Sometimes thought of as the brother of *Lludd.

Caswallon, Caswallawn, Caswallan. Son of *Beli Mawr in the **Mabinogi/Mabinogion* who conquers Britain in Bendigeidfran's (Bran the Blessed's) absence, killing all but *Caradog (2) and righting the wrongs of *Branwen. His cloak of invisibility or veil of illusion allows him to wield his deadly sword without being seen. When he is crowned king in London, *Pryderi pays homage. His characterization may have drawn from the historical figure *Cassivellaunus. A brother of *Arianrhod and sometimes a brother of *Lludd. Rachel Bromwich (1954) has posited the existence of a lost saga dealing with Caswallon's wars in Britain.

cat. The domesticated feline has long played a role in the Celtic imagination, although not so prominent as that of the *dog or of several large wilder animals. Cat features adorning ancient carved heads may imply fearfulness. The cognomen of the Irish usurper *Cairbre Cinn-Chait means 'cat head'. There are several monster cats in Celtic tradition, including the *cat sìth of the Highlands and the *cath Paluc of Wales. *Aíbill was changed into a white cat by *Clídna. The Shetlands were known as Inisc Cat [Cat Islands] in earlier Scottish Gaelic tradition. The former shire of Caithness was apparently named for an ancient people whose emblem was the cat. In Scotland also, live cats were roasted in a brutal divination rite known as taghairm. In Irish folklore the *Kilkenny cats represented a mutually self-destructive enmity in a story that appears to have an origin in political experience. Elsewhere in Irish tradition black cats were thought to be lucky, and the blood of a black cat was thought to cure St Anthony's fire (erysipelas). See KING OF THE CATS. ModIr. cat; ScG, cat; Manx kayt; W cath; Corn. cath; Bret. kazh.

cat sìth. The fairy *cat of Scottish Gaelic tradition, described as being as large as a *dog, black, with a white spot on its breast, with an arched back and erect bristles. Highlanders commonly explained the cat sìth as a transformed witch, not a *fairy. The cat sìth may be related to the demonic cat sometimes known as 'Big Ears' summoned in the brutal divination ceremony known as the taghairm, in which cats were roasted alive for four days. See also CATH PULAC.

Catalin. Variant spelling of *Cailitin.

Catan, Saint. Legendary saint of 11th-century Scotland who gave his name to the *Clan Chattan, a supra-organization of clans claiming *Pictish origin.

cath. An Irish word meaning 'battle' which begins the title of many narratives and so classifies them by theme. The following entries employing Cath are alphabetized word by word rather than letter by letter. Cf. Old Celtic calu; W cad, 'battle'.

Cath Cnucha. See FOTHA CATHA CHNUCHA.

Cath Fionntrágha, *Finntrága.* Irish title for a narrative of the *Fenian Cycle known in English as The Battle of Ventry, The Battle of Ventry Harbour, The Battle of the White Strand, etc. The text derives from 15th-century recension, but references to it occur as early as the 12th century; the narrative, of little literary distinction, details at tedious length the invasion of Ireland by *Dáire Donn, the 'King of the World', and his repulsion by *Fionn mac Cumhaill and his *Fianna. The battle takes place at Ventry Harbour, Co. *Kerry, 4 miles W of *Dingle. Dáire has been identified by different commentators as a late Roman emperor, an emperor of the Holy Roman Empire, or even Charlemagne. He has invaded because (*a*) he wants to seek revenge for Fionn's dishonouring the French throne when he carried off the king's wife and daughter, (*b*) he lacks further worlds to conquer and so needs remote, poor Ireland, or (*c*) he has heard of Fionn's glory and so wants to challenge the great hero. The battle rages on interminably and serves as an example of the motif folklorists call 'the everlasting fight' (formula Z12, tale type 2300), becoming an omnium gatherum of Fenian energies. Variants of the narrative have been recorded in oral tradition, changing details considerably. In some Irish versions Dáire Donn is the king of Lochlainn, and in a Scottish version (recorded 1524) he is the king of Norway. The narrative may derive from an earlier text, *Cath Trága Rudraigi*, in which a large body of Norsemen invade Ireland at Dundrum Bay, Co. Down. In a pseudo-etymology, Rudraigi was thought to contain the word ruad [red, ruddy], making a parallel with Fionntráigi [white strand]. Texts have been edited three times: anonymously (Boston, 1856); by Kuno Meyer (Oxford, 1885); and by Cecile O'Rahilly, using Rawlinson B487 (Dublin, 1962).

Cath Gabhra [The Battle of Gabhair/Gowra]. Narrative from the *Fenian Cycle. Its distinction within the cycle is that it portrays the *Fianna in an unattractive light and shows their power coming to an end with the death of *Oscar. The reigning high king of Ireland,

*Cairbre Lifechair [of the Liffey] refuses to pay a tribute to the Fianna when his daughter Sgiamh Sholais [Ir., beauty of light] is betrothed to be married. Cairbre resolves that he would rather die in ridding the country of the Fianna than try to rule Ireland blighted by their immorality. He provokes the final conflict by killing *Fionn mac Cumhaill's servant *Ferdia, obliging the Fianna to declare war. The bloodbath is at Gabhair, coextensive with the modern Garristown in north-west Co. Dublin; variant texts place the battle near Skreen, Co. Meath. The pitched battle includes all the Fenians as well as the family of Sgiamh Sholais's suitor, a prince of the *Déisi (Co. Waterford). The climax of the action comes when a mortally wounded Cairbre casts his spear through Oscar's heart. Fionn weeps for the only time at the death of any Fenian, and he is killed by Aichlech. Oisín escapes. Some chronicles date the battle at AD 284. A rival story of the death of Cairbre names the battle as *Cnámross.

An early translation of the text of *Cath Gabhra* is vol. 1 of the *Transactions of the Ossianic Society*, by Nicholas O'Kearney (Dublin, 1853; repr. New York, 1980); trans. into French by H. d'Arbois de Jubainville (Louvain, 1884).

Cath Godeu. Corrupt form of **Cad Goddeu*.

Cath Maige Mucrama, *Muccrime*. Irish title for a narrative known in English as The Battle of Mag Mucrama and part of the *Cycle of the Kings. The work has been described by one commentator as a political scripture, a mixture of genuine history with symbolic fiction, whose function is to propagandize rather than to entertain. *Lugaid mac Con, returned from exile, defeats the kings of *Munster (his own brother *Eógan (3)) and of *Tara, and himself becomes the king of north and south. On the night before the battle, in which both men are slain, *Art mac Cuinn fathers *Cormac mac Airt, one of the most famous kings of early Ireland, and *Eógan (3) fathers *Fiachu Muillethan, the first of the *Éoganacht kings. Mag Mucrama is located west of Athenry, Co. Galway. See the most recent edition of text by M. O'Daly, Irish Texts Society, vol. 50 (London, 1975).

Cath Maige Ráth [The Battle of Mag Rath]. See BUILE SHUIBNE.

Cath Maige Tuired. Irish title for one of the key documents in the *Mythological Cycle whose title in English is usually The Battle of Mag Tuired; the place-name 'Mag Tuired' has many variants: Mag or Magh Tuireadh, Tured, Tuireadh, etc.; Moytura, Moytirra, etc. There are actually two battles associated with Mag Tuired, and although their narratives are confused, they are not identical, nor were they fought in the same place. The second is by far the more important of the two battles, and is the one more likely intended if only one is cited. From commentary in other texts we judge that the battles were separated by twenty-seven years (a magical number, three times nine); the first took place on *Beltaine (1 May, the first day of summer), while the second was on *Samain (1 November, the first day of the Celtic year). The place-name Mag Tuired is usually translated 'Plain of Pillars' (W. B. Yeats preferred 'Plain of Towers'), and is most often identified with an area still known as Moytirra near Lough Arrow, in south-east Co. Sligo near the Roscommon border. The area is filled with upright megalithic monuments, dating from 2000–2500 BC. The first battle should have taken place near Cong, Co. Mayo (Mag Tuired Conga). Other suggested sites include the Plain of Pillars north of Tuam, Co. Galway, and Ballysadsare, Co. Sligo.

The lengthy narrative preceding the action of the two battles of Mag Tuired is given in the pseudo-history or fictionalized history of the **Lebor Gabála* [Book of Invasions]. That document details the successive invasions of Ireland by five groups: (1) under *Cesair, a granddaughter of the biblical Noah; (2) the *Partholonians, who perished in a plague; (3) the *Nemedians; (4) the *Fomorians, not a separate invasion but euhemerized deities characterized as demonic pirates who constantly prey upon settlers and appear in strength at the Second Battle of Mag Tuired; and (5) the *Fir Bolg, mythologized extrapolations of the *Belgae or Builg, the *P-Celtic people who did indeed have some settlers in Ireland. The sixth invaders were the *Tuatha Dé Danann, euhemerized deities who had learned the arts of heathendom in 'the northern islands of the world' before they arrived in Ireland.

The First Battle of Mag Tuired, or *The Battle of Mag Tuired of Cong*. The focus of the First Battle is the invasion of Ireland by the Tuatha Dé Danann and their overcoming of the Fir Bolg. Although the text is later than for the Second Battle, the action is portrayed as happening twenty-seven years earlier. When the Tuatha Dé Danann land, they burn their ships on the beach to forbid retreat. They demand kingship from the Fir Bolg, who of course refuse, and enter into fierce battle. In the fighting the arm of *Nuadu, king of the Tuatha Dé Danann, is severed at the shoulder by *Sreng, a warrior of the Fir Bolg. To replace the loss, the physician *Dian Cécht with the help of the *smith *Credne makes Nuadu a wonderful new arm of silver; henceforth the wounded king is known as Nuadu Airgetlám [of the Silver Hand, Arm]. With only one natural arm Nuadu is no longer fit to be king, and so the title passes to *Bres, the son of a Danann woman and the Fomorian king *Elatha. The Tuatha Dé Danann sue for peace by offering the Fir Bolg half of Ireland, but this is refused. When the battle is renewed *Eochaid mac Eirc, king of the Fir Bolg, is overcome by thirst, but the rivers and streams are hidden from his vision by the druids of the Tuatha Dé Danann. While he is in vain search of water, the hapless Eochaid is slain with three companions, setting back the Fir Bolg cause. The battle continues with great slaughter, greater for the Fir Bolg. At last Sreng, now king in Eochaid's place, agrees to a peace that will allow him only *Connacht of all Ireland's provinces, while the rest of the Fir Bolg scatter to distant islands, *Aran (or *Arran, *Scotland), Rathlin, Islay in the Inner Hebrides, etc.

Learned commentators have not agreed on the significance of the *First Battle of Mag Tuired*. John Rhŷs and Henri d'Arbois de Jubainville thought the *First* to be only a retelling of the *Second Battle of Mag Tuired*. T. F. O'Rahilly thought the *First* was mythologized history, i.e. that there was a historical correlative to the story, while the *Second* was rationalized (by antagonistic Christian scribes) mythology, i.e. a war of the Irish gods. See T. F. O'Rahilly, *Early Irish History and Mythology* (Dublin, 1946).

The Second Battle of Mag Tuired. The focus of the Second Battle is between the now dominant Tuatha Dé Danann and the resurgent Fomorians [Ir. *Fomoire*]. Two of the principal combatants were *Lug Lámfhota of the Tuatha Dé Danann and *Balor of the Fomorians. The text is found in Harleian MS 5280, but the language suggests composition in the 9th or 10th centuries. Cross-references to the narrative are found in Irish literature from the 12th century on.

The narrative begins with a recounting of some of the action from the First Battle of Mag Tuired, followed by the story of Bres's conception. Bres was an odd choice to replace Nuadu as king of the Tuatha Dé Danann. He may have been 'the Beautiful', but his pedigree was strange. His father, Elatha, had been reared among the Tuatha Dé Danann, but he was king of the Fomorians. Once king himself, Bres proves oppressive, and the country falls under the sway of the alien Fomorians. The great *Dagda is reduced to building a fort for Bres, and Ogma to fetching firewood. Worse, Bres lacks the most esteemed mark of a good king: generosity. The Danann chiefs complain that 'their knives are not greased by him and however often they visit him their breath does not smell of ale'. There is no entertainment in the royal household. When the Danann poet *Cairbre comes to visit, Bres accommodates him in an outhouse. The poet responds with a satire that causes Bres to break out in red blotches. At the request of Tuatha Dé Danann leaders, Bres renounces his kingship and sets out to muster a Fomorian army in his support.

Meanwhile the previous king, Nuadu, is reinstated, his silver arm seeming less of an obstacle now. One day a hero comes to his door, *Lug Lámfhota, here called Samildánach [Ir., possessing many arts together]. When a doorkeeper tells Lug that he cannot enter unless he has an art, he describes himself as a carpenter, smith, champion, historian, sorcerer, physician, cupbearer, and brazier. When Lug passes a test of his merit at a board-game, Nuadu relinquishes his throne so that Lug may lead the Tuatha Dé Danann in battle. Under his direction the craftsmen fashion wondrous weapons, and sorcerers practise magic to be used in fighting.

Once the battle begins, the slaughter is great on both sides. The Tuatha Dé Danann gain an advantage when their dead are restored to life by Dian Cécht and his three children. Lug is able to use some of his magic to aid the armies when he assumes the characteristic posture of the sorcerer. Balor is a formidable enemy, as his baleful gaze can destroy an army. His eyelid is so mighty that it takes four men to lift it (cf. the eyelids of *Ysbaddaden in Wales). Balor has made short work of Nuadu when he meets Lug on the battlefield. The resourceful Lug puts a slingstone through Balor's eye which goes crashing out through the back of his skull, killing twenty-seven of Lug's own followers. The Fomorians are routed and expelled from Ireland forever. Bres is captured, but hopes to save his life by promising that the cattle will always be in milk and that there will always be good harvests. His offers are rejected, but he is spared in return for advice on the appropriate times for ploughing, sowing, and reaping. *Mórrígan announces the end of the battle, and the text ends with the prophecy by *Badb, the war-goddess, of the end of the world.

Elizabeth Gray edited and translated the text for the Irish Texts Society, vol. 52 (Dublin, 1982) and published a study of it, *Éigse*, 18 (1981), 183–209; 19 (1982–3), 1–35, 230–62. See also Kim McCone, 'A Tale of Two Ditties: Poet and Satirist in *Cath Maige Tuired*', in Donnchadh Ó Corráin et al. (eds.), *Sages, Saints and Storytellers* (Maynooth, 1989), 122–43; William Sayers, *Bulletin of the Board of Celtic Studies*, 34 (1976) 26–40; J. Fraser, 'The First Battle of Moytura', *Ériu*, 8 (1915), 1–63; Henry Morris, '[On] The First Battle of Magh Turedh', *Journal of the Royal Society of Antiquaries*, 58 (1928), 111–27; Padraic Colum, *Moytura: A Play for Dancers* (Dublin, 1963).

Cath Paluc, Balug, Balwg [W, Palug's cat]. A monstrous *cat of Welsh tradition, known to haunt Mona (*Anglesey) especially. According to the **Triads*, nine score warriors fell to make food for the cat. Cath Paluc may serve as a model for Chalapu of Arthurian tradition. See also the CAT SÌTH of Scotland.

Cathach Chatutchenn [Ir., bellicose, hard-headed]. A *female warrior who loved *Cúchulainn.

Cathair Chrofhind [Ir. *cathair*, fortress]. An alternate name for *Tara, used by the *Tuatha Dé Danann.

Cathaír Mór, Catháer Már, Cathaoir Mór, Catháeir Mór, Cahir More [see also Hiberno-Brittonic *catu-tegernos*, battle-lord]. A legendary ancestral king of *Leinstermen, thought to have reigned just before *Conn Cétchathach [of the Hundred Battles]. In the most common version of the story, Conn kills Cathaír and displaces him; in variants *Goll mac Morna or others do the killing. In **Esnada Tige Buchet* [The Melodies of Buchet's House], Cathaír's daughter *Eithne Tháebfhota is fostered to Buchet, while his twelve uncontrollable sons eat all Buchet's provisions; later Eithne marries *Cormac mac Airt and bears his son, *Cairbre Lifechair. His son *Failge is the eponym of Co. Offaly in Leinster. Another daughter was *Cochrann, the mother of *Diarmait Ua Duibne. *Fionn mac Cumhaill is often reckoned to have been born in his reign. The name is often translated as 'Charles', with which it has no etymological link. See the poem of James Clarence Mangan, 'The Testament of Cathaeir Mor' (1847).

Cathal, Cahal [Ir., strong in battle]. Common name in Ireland of the early Middle Ages, borne by hundreds of historical figures in genealogies but not by figures in imaginative narrative. The name is often translated as 'Charles', with which it has no etymological link.

Cathal Crobderg, Crobhdhearg [Ir., of the (wine-)red hand]. A king of *Connacht (d. 1224), thought to be the brother or son of the last high king of Ireland, Ruaidrí Ua Conchobair [Rory O'Connor]. Many legends have attached themselves to Cathal. After his conception out of wedlock, his father's legal wife and queen tried unsuccessfully to thwart his birth. He was spirited away to a distant area, but he could always be identified by a wine-red birthmark on his hand, which he covered with a glove. When a passing stranger told him that the throne of Connacht was vacant, Cathal ceased his hard farm labour, cutting rye, and went to assume his throne by showing his birthmark. See James Clarence Mangan's poem 'A Vision of Connaught in the Thirteenth Century' (*c*.1845).

Cathal mac Finguine, Fionghuine. Powerful *Munster king (d. 742), with a capital at *Glendamain, who is portrayed in **Aislinge Meic Con Glinne* [The Vision of Mac Con Glinne] as having a body inhabited by a demon of gluttony. In a verse composed many years after his death, Cathal was thought to have been visited by *Mór Muman, the *sovereignty goddess, but the author has confused him with his grandfather, also named Cathal.

Cathaoir. ModIr. spelling of *Cathaír.

Cathbad, Cathbhadh, Cabadius. Chief *druid of the court of *Conchobar mac Nessa and one of the leading figures of the *Ulster Cycle. He predicts the fate of *Deirdre before she is born. He teaches *Cúchulainn, who overhears him saying that the youth who takes up arms on a certain day will become the champion of Ireland but will die young. His daughter is *Findchóem, mother of *Conall Cernach. In some versions he is the real father of Conchobar. *Macpherson's character *Caithbath in *Ossian* (1760) seems based on Cathbad.

Cathleen. Anglicized spelling of a name usually spelled *Caitlín in Irish. Cathleen Ni Houlihan is W. B. Yeats's rendering of *Caitlín Ní hUallacháin. Cathleen's Falls is another name for *Assaroe.

Cathubodua [raven of battle]. Gaulish goddess known only from an inscription in Haute Savoie in eastern France; thought to be an anticipation of *Badb, the Irish war-goddess. Perhaps identical with Cauth Bodva.

Cathulla. King of Innistore in *Macpherson's *Ossian* (1760), whose residence was at Carric-thura. He was the father of *Clatho, the second wife of *Fingal.

Catoc, Catog. Variant spellings of *Cadog.

Catraeth [cf. L *cataracto*, waterfall]. Decisive 6th-century battle in British history in which Saxons crushed British (i.e. Welsh) chieftains. The site of the battle is coextensive with the ford of Catterick Bridge on the River Swale, 2.5 miles SE of Richmond, Yorkshire; remembered in the well-known Welsh poem, the **Gododdin* (6th cent.), attributed to *Aneirin.

cattle. See BULL; COW.

Cattle Raid of.... See TÁIN BÓ....

Cattwg, Catwg. Variant spellings of *Cadog.

Caturix [battle-king]. Sometime epithet of Gaulish *Mars.

cauldron. The cauldron was widely used in the Celtic nations from ancient to medieval times, as abundant archaeological and literary evidence testifies. The best-known surviving cauldron from ancient times is the ornately decorated silver one possibly made in Gaul and found at Gundestrup, Denmark, for which it is now named. It may be a Rosetta Stone for interpreting both mythology and literature; see GUNDESTRUP CAULDRON. Cauldrons were used for domestic and sacrificial as well as other ritual purposes. At the same time it is clear that the cauldron was a prestige possession and restricted for the most part to the homes of the rich. It could symbolize both plenty and the powers of resuscitation, and could have implied powers over fertility. The ruler of the *Otherworld characteristically has a cauldron in his role as dispenser of feasts. The *Bruidne or feasting-halls of Ireland were equipped with inexhaustible cauldrons. Not surprisingly, then, many commentators have seen links between the cauldron of Celtic tradition and the Arthurian Grail.

There are many famous cauldrons in Celtic narrative. The cauldron of the *Dagda was one of the treasures of the *Tuatha Dé Danann. The cauldron of Gwigawd was one of the treasures of Britain. The *Partholonians of Brea had the first cauldron in Ireland. *Cúchulainn twice brought magic cauldrons back from Scotland. *Ceridwen had a cauldron of inspiration or wisdom from which *Gwion Bach tasted before he became *Taliesin. A cauldron of regeneration attracts much attention in *Branwen*, the second branch of the Welsh **Mabinogi*. *Bendigeidfran obtains it mysteriously in Ireland, and gives it to Matholwch in compensation for the mischief of *Efnisien. Other cauldrons belonged to *Diwrnach of Ireland in the Welsh story of **Culhwch ac Olwen*; *Arawn, king of *Annwfn; and the historical king of early Scotland (Fifeshire), *Eochaid Buide.

Cause of the Battle of Cnucha. See FOTHA CATHA CHNUCHA.

Cauth Bodva. A Gaulish anticipation of *Badb, the Irish war-goddess. Perhaps identical with *Cathubodua.

Caval. Tennyson's spelling of *Cabal.

cave. The natural hollow in a mountain, hill, or cliff has been the subject of much speculation in the Celtic imagination. It is often the realm of the *fairy or a route to the *Otherworld. One tradition has *Oisín living in a cave for 300 years. Creatures who live in caves include the ciuthach (see *cughtagh of Scottish Gaelic tradition, the *buggane and *cughtagh on the Isle of *Man, and *Luchtigern in the famous cave of *Dunmore, Co. Kilkenny, Ireland. The name of *Forgall Monach's fortress, Lusca, employs an old word for cave. Caves were often entrances to the Otherworld. See John Rhŷs, 'Welsh Cave Legends', in *Celtic Folklore* (Oxford, 1891) 456–96. See also FINGAL'S CAVE; CRUACHAIN; LOUGH DERG (1). ModIr. uaimh; ScG uaimh; Manx ooig; W ogof; Corn. fogo, gogo, ogo; Bre. kev.

Caw o Prydyn, o Brydyn, Kaw (Bret.). Hero of Welsh Arthuriana who came from Prydyn [Britain] in Scotland to join Arthur's court. In **Culhwch ac Olwen* Caw attacks the great *boar *Ysgithrwyn Pen Beidd, splitting its head in two and taking its tusks. He collects the warm blood of the black witch and so shaves the *giant *Ysbaddaden.

cawr. The Welsh word for *giant.

Cayous. Variant spelling of Sir *Kay, the Arthurian figure.

Cé. A druid in the service of *Nuadu wounded at **Cath Maige Tuired* [The (Second) Battle of Mag Tuired]. *Cathaír Mór also had a druid with that name.

Céadach, Céadach Mór, Ceudach, Cétach [Ir., having a hundred (wiles)]. Familiar figure from Irish and Scottish Gaelic (where he is known as Ceudach) folklore, especially since the beginning of the 19th century. He is often an interloper in *Fenian tales, where he may disguise himself in skins. Although he always appears to want to join the Fenians, his reasons are unclear; he is often quarrelsome. Céadach is his usual name, but he may have many others, such as *Abartach. In a story recorded on Cape Breton Island, Nova Scotia, he gives himself the grand moniker Ceudach Mac Rìgh nan Collach, 'The Yearling Son of the King'.

In one of the best-known stories about him, Céadach is sent on a dangerous mission where he is expected to be killed; he returns a hero. Against the wishes of his beautiful wife, Céadach agrees to accompany the Fianna to war. The wife makes *Fionn mac Cumhaill agree to hoist sails if her husband does not return. Although he leads the Fianna to victory, Céadach is stabbed in the last battle. Before dying Céadach warns Fionn not to hoist the sails, because his wife's breath will blow a blast that would destroy everything for a hundred miles. When the wife receives the body, she takes her husband to a desert island where three brothers do daily battle with armies of *giants who return to life each night. The wife asks the brothers to use their magical power to restore Céadach, which they do. To repay them, Céadach kills all the giants and lies in wait at night to see how they are revived. When he sees an ancient hag sprinkling the giants with drops from a churn, he beheads her, making the island forever safe. See Alan Bruford, 'Gaelic Folk-Tales and Mediaeval Romances' (Dublin, 1969), 123–9.

Ceallach. ModIr. spelling of *Cellach.

Cearb [ScG, cutting (?), slaughtering (?)]. A malevolent spirit in Scottish Gaelic folklore, widely cited but little explained; thought to be a killer of men and cattle. Folk motif: F402.1.11.

Cearmaid. ModIr. spelling of *Cermait.

Cearnach. ModIr. spelling of the cognomen Cernach; see CONALL CERNACH.

Ceasair. Variant spelling of *Cesair.

Céatach. Variant spelling of *Céadach.

ceatharn. ModIr. form of *ceithern.

Cébhra. Variant form of *Cainche.

ceffyl dwfr, dŵr [W, water horse]. A malevolent horse-like creature inhabiting streams and lakes in Welsh folklore; a counterpart of the Ir. and ScG *each uisce/uisge, the Scottish *kelpie, and the Manx *cabyll-ushtey and *glaistyn; see also the AFANC.

Cei, Cai, Che, Kei. Sometimes with the patronymic ap Cynyr or vab Cynyr [son of Cynyr]. A character in Welsh Arthurian stories, a companion of *Arthur along with *Bedwyr, Cei is also the seneschal of Arthur's household and has a personality composed of unequal parts of courage and buffoonery. In the early poetry, such as the 12th-century **Black Book of Carmarthen*, he appears to be a great and admirable hero. In the later romances, however, he descends into a surly steward characterized by cruel, sometimes ridiculous behaviour. Even in the later material he can still initiate action. He is clearly a model for Sir *Kay in English Arthurian narratives. See also GLEWLWYD GAFAELFAWR. See Rachel Bromwich, *Trioedd Ynys Prydain*, 2nd edn. (Cardiff, 1978), 303–7, 547.

Ceingalad, Keingalet (Bret.), Grangalet, Gringolet, Guingalet (Fr.) [W, hard back (?), durable spine (?)]. Horse of the Welsh and Breton hero *Gwalchmai fab Gwyar, who contributes to the figure known as Gawain in English Arthurian romance and Gauvain in French Arthurian romance.

Ceinwen [W *cain*, beautiful; *gwen*, fair]. A Welsh form of St *Keyne.

Céis Chorainn, Chorrainn. A hill in Co. Sligo, much cited in *Fenian narratives.

Known in English as Keshcorran, the hill (1183 feet) is 4 miles SE of *Ballymote, near Lough Arrow. *Diarmait asked for Céis Chorainn as part of *Gráinne's dowry. In some versions of their story, the fugitive lovers lived here for a number of years and raised several children. Here *Caílte mac Rónáin earned his name, and *Fionn was bewitched by hags.

ceisnoidhe Uladh [Ir., nine days' affliction/pangs of the Ulstermen]. See NÓINDEN ULAD.

ceithern, ceithearn. OIr. word meaning 'band of fighting men', yielding ceithernach, ceathernach, anglicized as kern, kerne. ModIr. ceatharn, ceatharnach. See also FIANNA.

Ceithlenn, Ceithlionn. Variant spellings of *Caitlín.

Céitinn, Seathrún. Seventeenth-century Irish poet and historian usually known by his English name, Geoffrey *Keating.

Cellach, Ceallach [Ir., strife, contention (?); frequenter of churches (?); bright-headed (?)]. Name borne by many figures in early Irish history and legend. One was a nephew or son of *Cormac mac Airt, who raped a *Déisi princess and was slain by *Angus (4) in revenge. A second was the progenitor of the Kelly or O'Kelly family, Ir. Uí Chellaig, Ó Ceallaigh, etc.

Celliwig. Variant spelling of *Kelliwic.

Celtchair, Celtchar, Celtar, Keltchar. Often with the patronymic mac Uithechair, mac Uthechar, mac Cuthechair, mac Uthidir, etc.; sometimes Celtchair Mór [the Great]. A leading figure in the *Ulster Cycle, often included in catalogues of the most important fighters. Several stories describe him as huge and grey. He may boast of his killing, but in **Scéla Mucce meic Da Thó* [The Story of Mac Da Thó's Pig], Celtchair is humiliated when the warrior *Cet claims to have emasculated him in a previous encounter. He is the usual possessor of the lance known as *Lúin, whose lust for blood was so great that if it were not used it had to be dipped into a cauldron containing black fluid or poison or its shaft would break into flames. He killed *Blaí Briugu for sleeping with his wife, and later cleared the country of pests, including (with the help of his daughter Niam (2)) *Conganchnes mac Dedad and the black hound Dóelchu. One drop of the slain hound's blood ran along Celtchair's spear and went through his body. See Kuno Meyer (ed.), *Death Tales of Ulster Heroes* (Dublin, 1906); repr. in T. P. Cross and C. H. Slover (eds.), *Ancient Irish Tales* (New York, 1936, 1969), 340–3. See also 'Celtchair mac Cuthechair', in M. E. Dobbs, *Side-Lights on the Táin Age* (Dundalk, 1917); Kim McCone, '*Aided Cheltchair maic Uthechair*: Hounds, Heroes, and Hospitallers in Early Irish Myth and Story', *Ériu*, 35 (1984), 1–30.

Celtic. A subfamily of the Indo-European family of languages. In antiquity, speakers of Celtic languages could be found in what is today Turkey (the Galatians of St Paul's letters), the Balkans, and most of central and western Europe from the Danube valley to the British Isles, including large portions of northern Italy and the Iberian peninsula. In modern times the living Celtic languages have been Irish, Scottish Gaelic, and Manx (now extinct) from the Goidelic or *Q-Celtic branch, and Welsh, Cornish (now extinct), and Breton from the Brythonic, Cymric, or *P-Celtic branch. Despite stereotypes, the Celtic languages have been spoken by a wide variety of physical types, from short and dark to tall and fair.

Much controversy surrounds speculation on the meaning of the word 'Celt'. It appears to be derived from the Greek keltoí, used to denote a people north of what is now Marseilles. Julius *Caesar also reported that the Gauls described themselves as Celtae. The perception that the Celtic languages were all related was slow in coming, and thus the word 'Celtic' did not always denote all the Celtic-speaking peoples. *Classical commentators did not call the inhabitants of the British Isles Celts, and the word 'Celt' has no counterpart in Old Irish or Old Welsh, as speakers of those languages did not see themselves as forming a linguistic community. The term 'Celtic language' was not used in English with its present meaning until the beginning of the 18th century, first popularized by Paul-Yves Pezron's *Antiquité de la nation*, etc. (1706) and established the next year by Edward Lhuyd in *Archaeologia Britannica* (1707). See Malcolm Chapman, *The Celts: The Construction of a Myth* (London and New York, 1992).

Celyddon. Welsh name for the Caledonian Forest, i.e. Scotland.

cenél, cenéoil (gen.), cenéuil (gen.), ceníuil (gen.). An OIr. word usually glossed as 'race, tribe, nation, or kindred'. It was used to describe an aristocratic descent group in both early Ireland and Gaelic Scotland. Among the best-known groups under this distinction were the Cenél Conaill or *Tír Chonaill (Tirconnell or *Donegal) and the Cenél Eógain of *Tír Eógain (Tirowen or Tyrone). Cf. W cenedl [race, nation]. See DÁL; DERBFHINE. See also T. M. Charles-Edwards, *Early Irish and Welsh Kinship* (Oxford and New York, 1993).

Cenn Abrat, Cend Abrat, Cenn Febrat. Site of legendary battle in early Irish history in which *Lugaid mac Con is defeated by the southern Irish forces of the *Eóganacht, led by his brother *Eógan (3). Modern commentators have suggested that the legendary battle may be based on a historical defeat of the invading *Érainn by Eóganacht and their *Múscraige allies. Cenn Abrat is coextensive with the Ballyhoura mountains, Co. Limerick. Forced into exile in Scotland, Lugaid later returns to fight the decisive battle of Mag Mucrama; see CATH MAIGE MUCRAMA [The Battle of Mucrama]. See P. J. Lynch, *Cenn Abrat* (Limerick, 1911); Myles Dillon, 'Lecan Text of the Battle of Cenn Abrat', *PMLA* 60 (1945), 10–15; 'Death of Mac Con', *PMLA* 60 (1945), 340–5.

Cenn Cróich. Variant of *Crom Crúaich.

Cenn Fáelad, Cennfáelad. Seventh-century warrior and poet thought to have completed the writing of the *Brehon Laws. Sometimes credited with the writing of **Auraicept na nÉces* [Scholar's Primer]. A member of the *Uí Néill, he is the first poet to be quoted in the Annals.

Cenn Febrat. Variant spelling of *Cenn Abrat.

ceó druídecta, ceo draoidheachte. See FÉTH FÍADA.

ceo síth. See FAIRY MIST.

ceol síth. See FAIRY MUSIC.

Cera, Ceara [Ir., red, bright red (?)]. One of the wives of *Nemed in the **Lebor Gabála* [Book of Invasions], the pseudo-history of Ireland. She is thought to have given her name to Mag Cera [Carra], Co. Mayo.

cerd, caird. OIr. word meaning (*a*) craftsman, artisan; (*b*) handicraft, art, skill, accomplishment, feat. See CRAFTSMAN.

Ceredig Wledig, Gwledig [W, kind; rustic, rural]. Sixth-century ruler of *Dumbarton in the kingdom of Strathclyde, Scotland. He may be associated with the Coroticus who kidnapped St *Patrick's early converts to Christianity.

Ceredigion. Welsh name for *Cardiganshire, a former maritime county of Wales, since 1974 part of *Dyfed. In the 8th century Ceredigion joined with Ystrad Tywi to form the kingdom of Seissyllwg. Named for Ceredigion, a son of *Cunedda. A notable 9th-century king was Arthen.

Ceridwen, Cerridwen, Caridwen, Keridwen, Kyrridwen [W *gwen*, white, blessed (?)]. A shape-shifting keeper of a *cauldron of wisdom (called Amen) at the bottom of *Bala Lake (or Llyn Tegid) in north Wales. Her husband was Tegid Foel [W, the bald], and her children included the beautiful Creirwy and the odiously ugly *Morfran (also called Afagddu). When three magical drops from the cauldron intended for Morfran fell instead on *Gwion Bach, giving him unique wisdom and insight, she pursued him. Both pursuer and pursued changed shapes, Gwion Bach into a hare, Ceridwen into a greyhound, etc. Eventually Gwion Bach turned into a grain of wheat and Ceridwen swallowed him, becoming pregnant as a result. Nine months later the child born to her was *Taliesin. Ceridwen is often perceived as a witch or an unpleasant hag. See also CAILLEACH BHÉIRRE; CAITLÍN; SEAN-BHEAN BHOCHT; the Breton story of *Koadalan may present parallels. See *Ystoria Taliesin (=Hanes Taliesin)*, ed. Patrick K. Ford (Cardiff, 1992).

Cermait, Cermat, Cearmaid [Ir., honey-mouthed]. Son of the *Dagda killed by *Lug Lámfhota for his sexual transgressions with Lug's wife. Cermait's son *Mac Cuill later avenged his father by spearing *Lug.

2. A name given to *Ogma, a god of poetry and eloquence.

Cernach. Cognomen or epithet of *Conall Cernach.

Cerne Giant, the. Huge figure of a nude man cut in prehistoric times through turf to underlying chalk on a hillside near Cerne Abbas, 7 miles N of Dorchester, Dorset. Although of incalculable antiquity, the figure is often attributed to the British Celts who inhabited this region in pre-Roman times.

The figure holds a club measuring 167 feet in his right hand and extends his left arm. Cut in 2-foot-wide ditches, the whole figure is 200 feet from top to bottom; his erect phallus measures 30 feet. In recent centuries the hillside and figure itself were sites of fertility festivals and May Day celebrations. See Stuart Piggott, 'The Cerne Abbas Giant', *Antiquity*, 12 (1938), 323–31.

Cernunnos [L, the horned one]. An important (perhaps principal) god of the Continental Celts, a lord of nature, animals, fruit, grain, and prosperity. He is portrayed as having a man's body and the horns of a *stag; his figure is seen in a squatting position, and he wears or carries the sacred torc often associated with the Continental Celts. Although his name is known from only one inscription (and is there partially obliterated, '—ernunnos'), the evidence for Cernunnos' widespread worship is impressive; he is, for example, portrayed on the *Gundestrup Cauldron. More than thirty other representations survive, dispersed from what is today Romania to Ireland. There are convincing traces of him in the literary traditions of both Wales and Ireland; and in later illuminated manuscripts, figures evoking Cernunnos are symbolic of devilish and anti-Christian forces. The Breton pseudo-saint *Korneli, a patron of horned creatures, also shows traces of Cernunnos. In Gaulish representation he has a *ram-headed servant. Julius *Caesar identified him with the Roman god *Dis Pater. Later commentators have sought to link him with *Conall Cernach and the Hindu Pashupati, a 'lord of the beasts'. His posture has also been compared to that of Buddha, but it may only reflect the fact that Continental Celts squatted on the floor and did not use chairs. See P. B. Bober, 'Cernunnos: Origin and Transformation of a Celtic Divinity', *American Journal of Archaeology*, 55 (1951), 13–51; also the dissertation of Dorothea Kenny, 'Cernunnos' (UCLA, 1975), *Dissertation Abstracts*, 36 (1975), 3016A.

Cerridwen. Variant spelling of *Ceridwen.

ces noínden [Ir., difficulty of nine]. See NOÍNDEN ULAD.

Cesair 1, Cessair, Ceasair, Cesara, Kesair. Leader or queen of the first invasion of Ireland in the *Mythological Cycle. According to the curious reckoning of the **Lebor Gabála* [Book of Invasions], an attempt to mix Irish memory with biblical history, Cesair is a daughter of Bith, a son of Noah, and Birren who escapes to Inis Fáil (Ireland) just before the Flood; she has left her homeland in disgrace because she was denied admission to the Ark. An alternate version has her as the daughter of *Banba, one of the eponymous goddesses of *Ireland. She lands in Ireland at *Dún na mBarc (Co. Cork) on Bantry Bay with fifty women and three men, forty days before the *Flood. The three men divide the women among them, hoping to populate Ireland. Two of the men, including her helmsman, Ladra, die, leaving the full task to *Fintan mac Bóchra, a patron of poets, who feels inadequate to it and flees in the form of a *salmon. Abandoned, Cesair dies of a broken heart. According to the text, the origin of many obscure place-names may be traced to members of her retinue. Cesair is sometimes used as a poetic synonym for *Ireland. See John Carey, 'Origin and Development of the Cesair Legend', *Éigse*, 22 (1987), 37–48.

2. Daughter of the 'King of the Franks' who marries *Úgaine Mór and bears him twenty-five children.

Cet, Cét, Cett, Ceat, Ket, Keth [Ir., old, ancient, enduring]. A name borne by several figures in early Irish narratives, most notably the *Connacht warrior in the *Ulster Cycle whose patronymic is variously given as mac Mágu, mac Mágach, mac Maga, mac Matach, etc. In **Scéla Mucce meic Da Thó* [The Story of Mac Da Thó's Pig], he shames the Ulstermen by reminding them of how he has bested them in combat, emasculating *Celtchair, etc. He appears to be most deserving of the hero's portion until *Conall Cernach arrives. On another occasion he throws the calcified 'brain ball' of Mesgegra at *Conchobar mac Nessa, severely wounding him. Cet himself was killed by Conall Cernach. Later rulers of Connacht claimed descent from Cet in genealogies.

Cétach. MidIr. spelling of *Céadach.

Cétchathach. Cognomen or epithet of *Conn Cétchathach [of the Hundred Battles].

Cethern, Cethren [Ir., long-lived, lasting (?)]. Name borne by a number of figures in early Irish narrative, of whom Cethern mac Fintain is the best-known.

Cethern 1. Another name for the god of the *Otherworld.

2. Another name for *Cian, the father of *Lug Lámfhota.

3. The father of the druid *Mug Ruith.

Cethern mac Fintain, Finntain. In the **Táin Bó Cuailnge* [Cattle Raid of Cooley], he is a fighter for the *Connacht forces, but known as a man of generosity and a bloody blade. He has silver-grey hair and carries only a silver spike as a weapon. When he is wounded, the *Ulster forces take him to their camp. Although he kills the healers (fifteen or as many as fifty) who attempt to treat him, as he does not like their unfavourable diagnoses, the other Ulstermen listen patiently when he explains how he acquired his many wounds, one of which came from *Medb. *Cúchulainn helps to restore him with bone marrow and animal ribs. He goes back into battle, killing more Ulstermen before he himself falls. Cethern is also a teacher of *Fionn mac Cumhaill in the *Fenian Cycle. His father is *Fintan mac Néill.

Cethlenn, Céthlionn. Variant spellings of *Caitlín.

Cethor. Alternate name for *Mac Gréine, the husband of *Ériu.

Cethren. Variant spelling of *Cethern.

Cétshamain, Cétsamain [Ir., proto-spring]. Alternate names for *Beltaine.

Cett. Variant spelling of *Cet.

Ceudach. ScG spelling for *Céadach.

Ceugant, Ceugand [W *ceugant*, sure, true; infinity]. The last and outermost circle in Llewelyn Siôn's 16th-century *cosmogony. It is inhabited by infinity alone.

champion's portion. The choicest portion [OIr. *curadmír*] of the meat, beef, or pork was given to the hero of the hour, as described in several early Irish narratives. The antiquity of this tradition is attested by *Posidonius (1st cent. BC), who said that in earlier times the bravest hero at a feast was given the thigh; if another diner claimed the same piece of meat, the two men immediately arose and engaged in a single combat to the death. Also known as the hero's portion. ModIr. curadhmhír. See FLED BRICRENN [Briccriu's Feast]; SCÉLA MUCCE MEIC DA THÓ [The Story of Mac Da Thó's Pig].

changeling. The widespread belief that *fairies or other malevolent spiritual forces might secretly substitute one infant for another is amply represented in Celtic oral tradition. Ir. corpán sídhe, síodhbhradh, síofra; ScG tàcharan, ùmaidh; Manx lhiannoo shee; W plentyn a newidiwyd am arall. See also FAIRY STROKE.

chariot, charioteers. Warriors ride in chariots in early Irish and Welsh narratives because most of these were composed before the saddle was introduced. A grave in which chariots were buried with their owners has been found at Waldalgesheim, Germany. The Irish god most likely to be called 'the charioteer' is *Manannán mac Lir, but *Conall Anglonnach is also a charioteer. *Cúchulainn's faithful charioteer was Láeg. The name *Cairbre might mean 'charioteer'.

Chattan, Clan. Name for a loose federation of seventeen clans in Scotland that claimed *Pictish origin, mostly in Inverness, beginning in the 11th century. The clan takes its name from the title of the chief, Gilliechattan Mòr [Great Servant of St Catan], at Kilchattan Abbey, Isle of Bute.

Che. Variant spelling of *Cei.

chess. The usual but misleading translation for several early board-games played in Ireland and Wales, including *fidchell, *gwyddbwyll, and *búanfach.

Children of Dôn, etc. See DÔN, etc.

Children of Lir. See OIDHEADH CHLAINNE LIR [The Tragedy (or Exile) of the Children of Lir].

Children of Llŷr. An alternate title for *Branwen*, the second branch of the **Mabinogi*.

chough. A European bird of the *crow family, especially the red-legged or Cornish chough (sp. *pyrrhocorax pyrrhocorax*). Called An *Balores in Cornish, the chough has become a symbol of resurgent Cornish cultural identity. In narratives outside *Cornwall the chough is often confused with the crow and raven.

Chrétien de Troyes (*fl.* 1160–82). Earliest known writer of Arthurian romance, *Erec et Enide* (*c.*1170), *Lancelot* (*c.*1178), *Perceval* (*c.*1182), etc. Probably a native of Champagne, he almost certainly inherited most of his characters and incidents from the oral Celtic Arthurian tradition, but his portrayal of them, especially in matters of love and courtly behaviour, was original to him.

Chuailnge. Variant spelling of *Cuailnge; see also TÁIN BÓ CUAILNGE [Cattle Raid of Cooley].

Chwimlean, Chwibleian, Chwimbian, Hwimleian. Companion of *Myrddin [Merlin] and perhaps the model for such Arthurian figures as Viviane. See A. O. H. Jarman, *Bulletin of the Board of Celtic Studies*, 16 (1955), 71–6.

Ciabhán, Keevan [cf. Ir. *ciabhar*, head of hair, locks (collectively)]. The mortal lover of *Clídna who brought her to Ireland. After being expelled from *Fionn's *Fianna for being too much of a ladies' man, Ciabhán sets sail for distant lands. During a terrible storm at sea, a rider on a grey horse brings him to safety in *Tír Tairngire [The Land of Promise], which includes the city of *Manannán. While he is in the city, Ciabhán is invited to a great feast where some tricksters ask him to perform a seemingly impossible task of throwing nine straight willow rods into the rafters, catching them as they fall. To the amazement of all, Ciabhán performs the trick with ease. More importantly, Clídna, who has been watching, becomes smitten with him. A short while later she leaves with Ciabhán in his curragh to return to Ireland, landing at Glandore on the south coast. While Ciabhán goes inland hunting for a deer, Clídna lies sleeping in the curragh, where a great wave rolls over her and drowns her. In folk-tales Ciabhán's name is often anglicized as Keevan, and he is given the epithet 'of the curling locks'.

Cian, Kian [Ir., distant, enduring, long (time and space)]. Name borne by several heroes in early Irish narrative, of whom the most important is *Cian (1), the father of *Lug Lámfhota. There is also a Welsh Cian (See CIAN (2)).

Cian 1. The father of Lug Lámfhota and a leading figure in the *Mythological Cycle. There are two stories about how he came to father the hero. One is that his magical cow, *Glas Ghaibhleann, has been stolen by *Balor, and in revenge Cian seduces Balor's daughter, *Eithne. In another version Cian wins Eithne through long negotiation with the help of the *druidess *Birog in Balor's household. Three children are born from the union, two of whom are drowned at the order of their grandfather, with only Lug escaping.

Cian is himself a mysterious character, although little attention is paid to him. He may also be known as *Cethern (2) or *Dáire (1). He may be the son of *Dian Cécht or he may bear the patronymic mac Chainte. Born with a caul on his head, he is transformed into a pig as an infant by the stroke of a druidical wand. He can always shift his shape to a pig when he is in danger. In attempting to escape from the depredations of *Brian (1), Iuchar, and Iucharba (the sons of *Tuireann), he changes into a pig once more, but it is in vain; they stone him to death in human form. See OIDHEADH CHLAINNE TUIREANN [The Tragic Story of the Sons of Tuireann]. *Findchóem (2) is usually named as his wife.

2. One of the five famous poets of 6th-century Wales, of whom almost nothing is known. He is also known as Gwenith Gwawd [W, wheat of song]. See also TALIESIN.

3. The son of *Ailill Aulomm; he is cited in the genealogies of the O'Hara and O'Gara families and others. His son is *Tadg mac Céin, who has a vision of *Clídna.

Cian Cúldub [Ir., of the black hair]. A Leinster hero.

Ciar [Ir., dark, black]. Love-child of *Fergus mac Róich and Queen *Medb, whose descendants were thought to have founded *Kerry [Ir. *Ciarraighe*, *Ciarraí*].

Ciarán, Kieran [Ir., dark, black]. A name borne by at least twenty-six Irish saints, according to early sources, of whom St *Ciarán (1), founder of Clonmacnoise, is the best known.

Ciarán, Saint 1. Founder of the monastic settlement of *Clonmacnoise on the Shannon whose feast-day is 9 September (d. ?556). According to legend, St Ciarán copied down the text of *Táin Bó Cuailnge* [Cattle Raid of Cooley] from the dictation of *Fergus mac Róich, who had returned from the dead. The text was then written on hide thought to have come from his beloved cow and thus called the *Book of the Dun Cow*; the task of copying the *Táin* is more usually assigned to *Senchán Torpéist.

2. Of Seir or Saighir, sometimes called Ciarán the Elder, whose feast-day is 30 April; Ciarán has been much venerated in west Cork, and is the patron of the diocese of Ossory (Kilkenny).

Ciarnat [Ir., dark lady]. A mistress of *Cormac mac Airt of the *Ulster Cycle.

Ciarraí, Ciarraighe. ModIr. spelling of *Kerry.

Cichol, Cical [cf. Ir. *cicul*, astronomical cycle]. Sometimes with the cognomen Grichnos, Gricenchos, or Gricenchoss. A leader of the *Fomorians in the early Irish pseudohistory **Lebor Gabála* [Book of Invasions], who suffers a rare defeat at the hands of the invading *Partholonians.

Cicollius. Sometime epithet of Gaulish *Mars.

Cigfa. Wife of *Pryderi and daughter of Gwyn Gohoyw in the **Mabinogi*. After her husband's disappearance, she fears *Manawydan's sexual advances.

Cil Coed, Kilcoed. Father of *Llwyd the enchanter in the **Mabinogi*.

Cill Dalua, Dálua, Dá Lua, Da Lúa. See KILLALOE.

Cilydd. The son of Celyddon Wledig and father of *Culhwch. He sought a wife the equal of his own station. See CULHWCH AC OLWEN.

Cimbáeth, Cimbaoth, Kimbay. Legendary king of early Ireland, cited at the beginning of chronicle history and thought to have lived *c.* AD 300. He ruled for a seven-year term as part of a twenty-one-year cycle with his kinsmen (sometimes brothers, sometimes cousins) *Áed Ruad and *Díthorba. Seven magicians, seven poets, and seven lords of *Ulster saw to it that this agreement was kept. When Áed Ruad died, his daughter *Macha (2) was elected to rule. Cimbáeth and Díthorba opposed her at first, but Cimbáeth later made peace and married her, while she killed Díthorba. Macha (2) dominated Cimbáeth, and obliged him to build the royal fort of *Emain Macha.

Cináed, Cináeth, Cionaodh. A name borne by several figures in early Irish and Scottish Gaelic chronicle, of whom the best-known is certainly Cináed mac Alpín of *Dál Riada. According to chronicle, Cináed mac Alpín was the first king of Scotland, ruling from 844 until his death in 858. Cináed united the Scoto-Irish invaders in *Argyll (since 1974, Strathclyde), from his father's family, with the native *Picts, from his mother's family. His name is often anglicized Kenneth MacAlpin, and he is sometimes rather grandly called Kenneth I.

Cingciges, Cingcís [L *quinquagesima*, Pentecost, Whitsuntide, Whitsunday]. Irish words for Pentecost or Whit Sunday, to which several older beliefs have become attached; see FAIRY STROKE.

Circinn, Circenn, Girginn. One of the four principal *Pictish kingdoms, roughly coextensive with the modern counties of *Angus (Forfarshire) and Kincardine (since 1974, Tayside).

circumambulation. See SUNWISE TURN.

cìrein cròin, cìrean [ScG, grey crest]. A *sea monster in Scottish Gaelic folklore, thought to be the largest of all living creatures, capable of making a meal of seven whales. Known in songs and legends under several titles: mial mhòr a' chuain [the great beast of the ocean]; curtag mhòr a' chuain [the great whirlpool of the ocean]; uile bhéisd a' chuain [the monster of the ocean]. See also AFANC; LOCH NESS MONSTER; OILLIPHÉIST:

cities. As the indigenous populations of Celtic nations were country people, there were no metropolises founded by Celtic peoples. Most cities in Celtic lands were established by foreigners; the Romans built oppida in Celtic lands, and the Danes were the first inhabitants of Dublin. Despite this, there are a number of imaginary cities in the narratives of different Celtic lands. The Bretons speak of the underwater city of *Ys. The Irish speak of the city belonging to *Manannán mac Lir in the Land of Promise as well as the four cities of the *Tuatha Dé Danann: *Falias, *Findias, *Gorias, and *Murias. See also SUBMERGED CITIES.

Ciudach. A cave-dwelling spirit in Scottish Gaelic folklore also known on the Isle of Man and in parts of Ireland. Initially the character may have been a kind of admirable *giant; in stories recorded as far apart as Roscommon and Inverness, *Gráinne has an affair with Ciudach while she is on the run with *Diarmait. In later stories the Ciudach is a cave-haunting monster. See also CUGHTAGH.

Ciwa, Saint. Legendary Welsh saint thought to have been suckled by wolves. She had a great nail on one of her fingers and was called 'the Wolf Girl'.

Clachnahrie, Clachnaharry. Site of a 'battle' between the clans MacIntosh and Munroe in 1454, sparked by a series of insults and supposed insults, which has become the subject of a large body of Scottish Gaelic folklore. Clachnaharry today is a north-western suburb of the town of Inverness.

Claidheamh Soluis, Claíomh Solais [Ir., sword of light]. A symbol of Ireland attributed, in oral tradition, to *Cúchulainn. According to one story, an ugly *giant forced a poor widow to find the Claidheamh Soluis under the head of another giant. The unreformed ModIr. spelling Claidheamh Soluis, preferred by P. H. Pearse and other rebels of the 1916 Rising, is still more often seen than the reformed Claíomh Solais; also Cruaidín Catuchenn. See caladbolg.

clan. The English borrowing of this word from Scottish Gaelic obscures the more precise use of clann in both Irish and Scottish Gaelic as well as the existence of several other concepts of family and descent, such as *cenél, *dál, and *derbfhine; see also TUATH, which may be glossed as 'people' or 'tribe', and is predominantly territorial in meaning. In English, clan usually denotes a group with a common ancestor. It implies kinship, not territory. Its ultimate source is the Latin planta [plant, planting]. The OIr. clann is defined as 'children, family, offspring; a single child; descendants, race, [and finally] clan'. The ModIr. clann is also defined first as 'race' or 'children'. In ScG the first definition of clann is 'offspring' and 'children'. The W llwyth translates 'clan' more in the sense of tribe, while tylwyth implies family or shared ancestry. Bret. koskoriad denotes family or shared descent while klan, apparently borrowed from Scottish Gaelic via English and French, denotes a tribe or larger family. Attached to many a clan in Scotland is the sept [ScG *cinneach*], whose blood link to a common ancestor may be either distant or questionable. See also CORCU. Entries for individual clans, e.g. Clan *Baíscne, Clan *Chattan, Clan *Dedad, are found under their family names. See T. M. Charles-Edwards, *Early Irish and Welsh Kinship* (Oxford and New York, 1993).

Classical commentators. Among the ancient writers most helpful in understanding Celtic culture, religion, and myth are: *Ammianus Marcellinus, Julius *Caesar, *Diodorus Siculus, *Eusebius, *Pliny the Elder, *Polybius, *Posidonius, *Ptolemy, *Solinus, *Strabo, and *Tacitus.

Clatho. In *Macpherson's *Ossian* (1760), the daughter of *Cuthulla and the second wife of *Fingal. She bears the children Reyno, Fillean, and Bosmin. Fingal's first wife is Roscrana.

Cleena. Anglicization of *Clídna.

Clettig (gen.), e.g. Sídh Clettig, Sídh Chlettigh, Clettech (nom.), Cletech. *Sídh or enchanted residence of *Elcmar on the south bank of the *Boyne, near the pool of *Linn Féic. Elcmar takes it in exchange for *Brug na Bóinne from *Angus Óg. Later also a residence of *Muirchertach mac Erca.

Cliach. Harper, unsuccessful suitor of a daughter of *Bodb Derg, who uses magic to keep Cliach away from his door for more than a year.

Clídna, Clíodna, Cliodhna, Clíona, Cleena. An Irish goddess of great beauty, often called 'the shapely', much associated with Co. Cork. She is the counterpart of *Áine and *Aíbell and is sometimes called 'the Queen of the Munster Fairies'. According to the best-known story, she is one of three daughters of *Manannán's chief druid, *Gebann, and living contentedly in *Tír Tairngire [the Land of Promise] when *Ciabhán comes to win her heart. He takes her back to the land of mortals in Ireland, landing at Glandore [Ir. *Cúan dor*, harbour of gold] harbour in southern Co. Cork. While he goes inland to hunt, a great wave overcomes the sleeping Clídna, drowning her along with her fellow travellers, among them Ildathach, who was in love with her. In another account she drowns when she is lulled to sleep by the musician Iuchna. The wave is one of three mentioned under various names in Irish tradition, and is still remembered in Glandore harbour as *Tonn Chlíodhna. In *Tadg mac Céin's vision of her, she is the noblest and most desirable woman in the world; she has three brightly coloured *birds that eat *apples from an *otherworldly tree and sing so sweetly as to heal the sick with soothing sleep.

Although the drowning separates Clídna from her Ciabhán, she lives on and has a series of mortal lovers of high and low station. Among them are Earl Gerald FitzGerald (see GERALD), CAOMH (the eponymous progenitor of the O'Keeffe family), and a poor man named Teigue on Red Loch Island. She was also thought to be the seducer of many young boys at fairs. Her allure is associated with two rocks named *Carrigcleena, one near Mallow and the other offshore near Ross Carbery. She became the *fairy woman of the MacCarthy family, and is credited with telling them the secret of the *Blarney Stone. In the *Fenian stories her pedigree is changed so that she is one of the three beautiful daughters of Libra.

Among the representations of Clídna in literature is R. D. Joyce's 'Earl Gerald and His Bride', in *Ballads of Irish Chivalry* (Boston, 1872), 28–36. In this she steals the bridegroom from his wedding.

Cloch Labrais, Labhrais, Cloghlowrish [Ir., speaking, answering stone]. The oracular 'Answering Stone' of Co. Waterford, located near Ballykeroge, 6 miles NE of Dungarvan. According to legend, the rock split when it was asked to testify to a lie. A woman was rightfully accused of adultery by her husband. She claimed that she was no more guilty of sin with anyone than she was with a man seen at a distance, who was in fact her lover. Although her rhetorical ploy was not an untruth, the duplicity was more than Cloch Labrais could bear.

Clonard [Ir. *Cluain Ioraird/Eraird*, Iorard's meadow]. One of the great monasteries of early Ireland, founded by St Finnian (d. 549). Clonard became proverbial for the number of saints it fostered. The buildings were sacked many times, and most of the ruins disappeared in the early 19th century. Although Clonard is associated with the history of *Leinster, its site is today in Co. Meath, 4 miles E of Kinnegad. The Iorard for whom the meadow is named may have been a pagan chief who built the still-visible moat here. Unrelated to other sites named Clonard [Cluain Art, high meadow], e.g. Co. Dublin, Co. Wexford.

Clonfert [Ir., meadow of the grave]. Monastery founded in the 5th century by St *Brendan in east Co. Galway, 1 mile N of Ballinasloe. Although the buildings were often sacked over the centuries, the surviving doorway of the cathedral is thought to be one of the best works of the Hibernian Romanesque.

Clonmacnoise, Clonmacnois [Ir. *cluain moccu Nóis*, meadow of the sons of Nós]. Ireland's foremost early monastic settlement, founded by St Ciarán on 25 January 545. In the days of water transportation its location on the east shore of the Shannon was highly accessible, but today it lies on a backroad in Co. Offaly, 13 miles S of Athlone. As an ecclesiastical centre Clonmacnoise was rivalled only by *Armagh, but it was peerless as a focus of early Christian art and literature. The great codex the **Book of the Dun Cow* [*Lebor na hUidre*] was produced here. Although ravaged countless times by native and foreign enemies, Clonmacnoise was not abandoned until sacked by English troops in 1552. Much remains, however, including portions of nine churches, five high crosses, two round towers, and more than 500 early gravestones, many with inscriptions. Seven *ard ríthe [high kings] were buried here, including Ruaidrí Ua Conchobair (d. 1198), the last of that line. In more recent literature, Clonmacnoise is one of the most resonant names in invoking the lost glory of pre-conquest Ireland; see T. W. Rolleston's (1857–1920) 'The Dead at Clonmacnoise', translated from the Irish of Aongus Ó Giolláin. See also Doirin Doyle, *Clonmacnois* (Dublin, 1968).

Clonnach. A son of *Crom Crúaich, especially in later oral tales where the father is known as Crom Dubh and thought to be a pagan chief opposing St *Patrick rather than an idol or god.

Clontarf [Ir. *cluain tarbh*, bull meadow]. Site of the battle where *Brian Bórama (Boru) defeated the Danes on Good Friday, 1014. Today Clontarf is a northern suburb of metropolitan Dublin. See A. J. Goedheer, *Irish and Norse Traditions About the Battle of Clontarf* (Haarlem, Netherlands, 1938).

Clooth-na-Bare. W. B. Yeats's transmogrification of *Cailleach Bhéirre. Unlike her predecessor in Irish tradition, Clooth-na-Bare is not a *sovereignty figure. Instead, she seeks the deepest lake in which to drown her *fairy life as she has grown weary of it.

Clothach [Ir., famous, renowned]. The grandson of *agda, the 'good god'. A Christian saint whose feast is 3 May also bears this name.

Clothra, Clothru [Ir., famous (?); clapper (?)]. One of the four daughters of *Eochaid Feidlech whose siblings included *Medb, queen of *Connacht, *Eithne (5), and *Mugain (2), all of whom were married to

*Conchobar at different times, and their brothers *Finn Emna (the three Finns of Emain). She is the mother of the warrior *Lugaid Riab nDerg by the three Finn Emna, and of *Furbaide Ferbend. Later she commits a second incest with the incestuously begotten Lugaid to produce *Crimthann Nia Náir. Her murder, while pregnant, by her sister Medb is avenged by her son Furbaide. Although thought to be an immoral woman by Christian standards, incest only one of her sins, her name is cited in many genealogies, including that of St *Declan.

cluricaune, cluricaun, cluricane. English names for the household sprite known in Irish as clúracán, clúrachán, clutharachán. The cluricaune is one of three kinds of solitary *fairy in Ireland, the other two being the *leprechaun and the *far darrig. He appears to be an Irish instance of the figure from European folklore known as the buttery spirit (folk motif: F473.6.3). Although Dinneen's *Dictionary* (Dublin, 1927) defines the term only as 'dwarfish sprite', the cluricaune has been the subject of much commentary, the focus of which has been to distinguish it from the better-known leprechaun. The cluricaune is usually a withered little man, like the leprechaun, but he may have more of a pink tinge to his nose. As a solitary fairy, he is more likely to be dressed in red than in green. He shows no desire to do work of any kind and is dressed like a weekend gentleman with silver buckles on his shoes, gold lace on his cap, and blue silk stockings below his breeches. Like the leprechaun, he may know where gold is hidden, but he may carry in addition the spré na scillenagh [shilling fortune] or sparán na scillinge [purse of shillings], a purse flowing with silver. The cluricaune likes to enter a rich man's wine-cellar and drain the casks, but he will frighten away any servant who tries to join him. Although he prefers to stay indoors, he will, when venturing out, harness a sheep or shepherd's dog and ride it for his amusement, leaving them panting and mud-covered. Classed as a solitary *fairy.

Clydno Eiddyn. A prince of north Britain who came as a monk to Wales. His horse's halter was one of the treasures of Britain.

Cnámross, Cnámhros. Battle described in the **Book of Leinster* in which Bresal Bélach led the Leinstermen against *Cairbre Lifechair, king of *Tara, and killed him and his son *Eochu Doimlén. *Fionn mac Cumhaill and his *Fianna are described as assisting the victors. Cf. the better-known story of **Cath Gabhra* [The Battle of Gabhair/Gowra], in which Cairbre rids Ireland of the Fianna. Cnámross, coextensive with the modern hamlet of Camross, Co. Laois, was also the site of a defeat of the *Nemedians by the *Fomorians in the *Lebor Gabála* [Book of Invasions].

Cnobga, Cnobgha, Cnoba. Irish forms of *Knowth.

Cnoc Áine [Ir., hill of Áine]. A hill, its name anglicized as Knockainy, 3.5 miles E of Bruff, south of *Lough Gur, Co. Limerick, thought to be a dwelling-place of the fairy queen *Áine (1); nearby is a village of the same name. It is 7 miles from *Cnoc Gréine.

Cnoc Fírínne, Cnoc Frigrend [Ir., hill of 'truth' (?)]. A hill (949 feet) of volcanic origin in Co. Limerick, 2 miles E of Ballingarry, known in English as Knockfeerina, Knockfierna, etc. The hill is one of the most celebrated otherworldly sites in *Munster, and formerly had an annual *Lughnasa assembly. It was once thought to be the seat of a god named Donn Fírinne. Widely known in oral tradition, the hill is the scene of many episodes in *Fenian narrative.

Cnoc Gréine, Gréne [Ir., hill of Grian]. A hill in eastern Co. Limerick near Pallas Grean, thought to be sacred to Grian, a local pre-Christian divinity who may be *Macha in disguise and who has associations with the sun. It was attacked by the five sons of *Conall (1) and later by Conall (1) himself. In some stories the hill is known as Cnoc na gCuradh, 'Hill of the Heroes'. It is 7 miles from *Cnoc Áine.

Cnoc Meadha, Mheadha. A hill, Castlehacket, west of Tuam, Co. Galway, thought to be the residence of *Finnbheara, the king of the *Connacht fairies. Of two large cairns on the hill, one was thought to be the burial-place of Finnbheara and the other of Queen *Medb, whose name may be transformed in the name Cnoc Meadha. Known on some modern maps as Knockmagha, Knockma, or Knock Ma.

Cnoc na gCuradh. See CNOC GRÉINE.

Cnoc na Sídha. The 'hill of the fairies' could be any of hundreds of hills in Ireland; the one cited by W. B. Yeats appears to be in

Co. *Donegal, near the falls of *Assaroe.

Cnoc Sídhe Úna. A prominent hill (699 feet) in north Co. Tipperary, 2 miles E of Ballingarry. In folklore the hill is thought to be sacred to *Úna, a queen of the fairies. Known in English as Knockshegouna or Knockshigowna, the hill was once the site of *Lughnasa activities.

Cnú Deireóil [Ir., little nut of melody]. The *dwarf *fairy harper of *Fionn mac Cumhaill in the *Fenian Cycle. He is described as a little man with golden hair, perhaps 4 feet high, who claims to be a son of *Lug Lámfhota. Although he is associated with delight and play in many stories, his songs induce sweet slumber.

Cnucha [cf. OIr. *cnuchae*, hillock]. An early place-name coextensive with the modern Castle Knock, 4 miles W of Dublin's city centre, site of a great battle in the *Fenian Cycle in which *Fionn's father *Cumhall is killed. See FOTHA CATHA CHNUCHA [The Cause of the Battle of Cnucha].

coblynau, coblynnod [from Eng. *goblins*]. Welsh mine goblins, not unlike the *knockers of *Cornwall. Although usually seen as quite ugly and standing only 18 inches high, they are perceived as being friendly and helpful. They know where rich lodes of ore may be found. Sometimes known by the singular, coblyn. Folk motif: F456.

Cobthach, Cobhthach, Cofach, Covac [Ir., victorious]. A name borne by several legendary figures from early Irish history, especially from the southern half of the island, of whom *Cobthach Cóel Breg is the best-known. This Old Irish name yields the family name [O] Coffey, among others.

Cobthach 1. One of the legendary ancestors of the *Eóganacht, an important family of *Munster.

2. Father of Meilge who was responsible for the death of *Aige and is satirized by *Faifne.

Cobthach Cóel Breg [Ir., the slender of Breg]. A leading figure in that portion of Irish legendary literature known as the *Cycle of Kings. Cobthach seized power to become king of *Tara by killing his brother *Lóegaire Lorc, his brother's son *Ailill Áine, and sending Ailill Áine's son *Labraid Loingsech into exile. Many stories portray Cobthach as treating Labraid with wanton cruelty, such as forcing him to eat a mouse and its young, causing the boy to lose the power of speech. Labraid returned from exile in Gaul and burned Cobthach alive in 'an iron house' along with thirty allies. Cobthach may have been one of the early *Uí Néill.

cochall, cochull. See COHULEEN DRUITH.

Cochrann [Ir., red lady (?)]. Daughter of the legendary king of *Leinster, *Cathaír Mór, and mother of *Diarmait uá Duibne and *Oscar in the *Fenian Cycle. In ballads she is known as *Cróchnat.

Cocidius [cf. W *coch*, red]. A god worshipped in early Britain, especially in the north and west, whom the Romans compared with *Mars. He is sometimes represented as wearing a shawl or hood while at other times, in north Britain, he appears to have horns (cf. *horned god) and is associated with hunting. His shrine at Bewcastle, Cumberland, implies that he was a soldier's god. Cocidius may be identical with *Segomo, the war-god of the Continental Celts, and he may be associated with *Teutates [the ruler of the people], who was worshipped in Britain. Even more tentatively, Cocidius may be associated with *Belatucadros [fair, shining one] and *Mogons [the powerful one]. See D. B. Charlton and M. M. Mitcheson, 'Yardhope, a Shrine to Cocidius?', *Britannia*, 14 (1983), 143–53.

cock. Portrayals of the cock or rooster with Gaulish *Mercury may indicate that it was a sacred animal among the Continental Celts. Large birds, perhaps cocks, are also found in temples from northern Britain, here with human female figures. ModIr. coileach; ScG coileach; Manx kellagh ny giark; W ceiliog; Corn. cülyek; Bret. kilhog.

Codal. Foster-father of *Ériu.

Coed-Alun. See KOADALAN.

Coel [W, trust]. A 6th-century British (i.e. Welsh) king of Aeron (Ayrshire, Scotland) who is mentioned by *Taliesin. He has two agnomens, Hen [old] and Odebog [adulterous (?), hawkwood (?)]. By long-standing popular assertion he is the original for the Old King Cole of the nursery rhyme. In popular etymology he is the eponymous founder of Colchester. Pious medieval legend asserts that he is the father of *Elen (2), purported Welsh-born St Helen, mother of Constantine, 3rd-century Christian emperor.

Cóel Cróda. Variant spelling of *Coil Cróda.

Cóelrind, Well of. See CONNLA'S WELL.

Cóemgen. Variant spelling of *Cáemgen [Kevin].

Cofach. Variant spelling of *Cobthach.

cohuleen druith, cohullen [cf. Ir. *cochall*, hood]. In Irish folklore, a magical hood or cap worn by mermaids (or merrows) in order to survive under the waves. It is thought to be red and covered with feathers. If it is stolen, the mermaids cannot return beneath the water.

cóiced, cóigeadh, cúige [Ir., fifth]. A 'fifth' of Ireland, i.e. one of the five provinces before the English conquest; e.g. Cóiced Ulad: the fifth or province of Ulster. These included *Leinster, *Ulster, *Connacht, and *Munster; the fifth is usually *Meath (coextensive with the modern counties of Meath and Westmeath) including *Tara, but sometimes Munster is counted as two.

Coil Cróda, Cóel Cróda, Cródha [cf. ModIr. *ródha*, brave, valiant, heroic; OIr. *ródacht*, bloodthirstiness, cruelty]. A member of *Fionn mac Cumhaill's *Fianna, sometimes called 'Hundred Slayer'.

Coila. A spirit or muse of the poet's native Ayrshire addressed by Robert Burns in 'A Vision' (*c.*1790).

Coillnamham Fort [cf. Ir. *coill*, wood, forest; *náma(e)*, enemy]. Name for *Dún Aonghusa in the Aran Isles used by Liam O'Flaherty (1896–1984) and other Anglo-Irish writers.

Coimperta. Plural form of **Compert*.

Coinche(a)nn, Conchean. Slew *Áed (7) for having seduced his wife, and was later forced to carry the murdered man's corpse until he had found a stone big enough to cover it.

Coinchenn, Coinchend [Ir., dog-headed]. The monstrous, man-killing wife of Morgán and mother of the lovely *Delbcháem in **Echtrae Airt meic Cuinn* [The Adventure of Art Son of Conn]. She correctly fears that she will die if ever her daughter is wooed, and so she decapitates each suitor who comes to her daughter's door and decorates the bronze fence in front of her fortress with their heads. *Art kills her and puts her on a spike. She sometimes has the agnomen Cennfhata.

Coinneach Odhar Fiosaiche. ScG for 'Sombre Kenneth of the Prophecies', a nickname of the *Brahan Seer (Kenneth MacKenzie, 17th cent.).

Cóir Anmann. Irish title of a document that may be known in English as the Fitness of Names or the Elucidation of Names. The treatise elucidates the significance and associations of many personal names from early Ireland in much the same way as the *Dindshenchas deals with place-names. The title is also an epithet of *Ana. See Whitley Stokes, *Irische Texte mit Übersetzungen und Wörterbuch*, ser. iii, no. 2 (Leipzig: S. Hirzel, 1897), 285–444.

Coirbre. Variant spelling of *Cairbre.

Coire Brecain. See CORRIEVRECKAN.

Coirpre. Variant spelling of *Cairbre.

Colann gun Cheann, Coluinn gan Ceann, etc. [ScG, body without head]. A headless *bòcan of Scottish Gaelic folklore, thought to be a kind of tutelary spirit of the Macdonalds of Morar in the western Highlands (until 1974, Inverness-shire). The creature was thought to haunt a mile-long path from the river of Morar to Morar House. He was extremely hostile to people outside the family, but would not harm women or children. Folk motif: E422.1.1.

Colcu, Colga. Name borne by several figures from early Irish tradition, including a few saints. Perhaps the best-known Colcu was the stepson of *Créd, who thwarted her plans for an amorous dalliance with *Cano.

Colgán, Colga [cf. Ir. *colg*, sword]. *A villainous king of* *Lochlainn in several *Fenian *stories*, including **Bruidhean Chaorthainn* [The Hostel of the Quicken Trees], where his son Midac plays a leading role.

Coligny. Village in the department of Ain, Burgundy, eastern France, 14 miles NNE of Bourg-en-Bresse, where the Calendar of Coligny was found in 1897. The bronze plates of the calendar are some of the most extensive writings we have in any Continental Celtic language, and provide important evidence in understanding the early Celtic perception of time. See CALENDAR.

Colla [Ir., great lord (?), chief (?)]. Name borne by many shadowy figures from early Irish history, most notably the 'Three Collas', three brothers of the 4th century bearing the same name: Colla Uais [Ir., noble, distinguished, well-born], Colla Menn [notable (?); stammering (?)], and Colla Fo Chríth or Dachrích. All were the sons of *Eochu Doimlén, the son of *Cairbre Lifechair. The brothers murdered their uncle *Fiachu and established the kingdom of *Airgialla (Oriel) in north-eastern Ireland. They also attacked *Emain Macha, eliminating it as a centre of political power. In Scotland the Clan Donald, or MacDonald Lord of the Isles, traced its descent from both (1) Colla Uais, an Irish prince who ruled Scotland before the coming of *Dál Riada, and (2) *Conn Cétchathach [of the Hundred Battles]. T. F. O'Rahilly thought that Colla was but a nickname for each of the three sons of *Niall Noígiallach [of the Nine Hostages], e.g *Conall Gulban, *Énna (3), and *Eógan (1). See *Early Irish History and Mythology* (Dublin, 1946), 230–1.

Collen, Saint. Legendary 7th-century Welsh saint and eponym of Llangollen who was thought to have visited fairyland. After having been an abbot at *Glastonbury, Collen resigns and becomes a hermit nearby. After rebuking two men for speaking of *Annwfn, which the good saint considers infernal, Collen is invited to visit for himself. As he is not misled by the apparent grandeur of the place, he refuses to eat fairy food, denounces what he sees, and dashes all present with holy water. The scene disappears and Collen finds himself alone again. Folk motifs: D2031; F160.0.2; F382.2.

Colloquy. See YMDDIDDAN.

Colloquy of the Ancients, *Old Men.* See ACALLAM NA SENÓRACH.

Collumcille. Spelling used by W. B. Yeats and other Anglo-Irish writers for *Colum Cille.

Colmán [Ir., woodpigeon, ring-dove, dim. of L *columb*, dove]. Popular name in early Ireland borne by at least 234 saints, not to mention a host of shadowy figures in genealogies and chronicles. Suibne's father, though not a Christian, is named Colmán. A 6th-century poet was Colmán mac Léníni. Also known in Wales.

Colmcille, Colmkil. Variant spellings of *Colum Cille.

Colofn Cymry [W, the pillar of Wales/Cambria]. An epithet of *Caradog.

Colptha, Colpa [cf. Ir. *colpthae*, stout, sturdy, stalwart]. Fourth son of *Míl Espáine and *Scota, brother of *Amairgin and *Donn mac Míled, who drowned at the mouth of the *Boyne, giving the place-name *Inber Colptha to that locale.

Coluinn gan Ceann. Variant spelling of *Colann gun Cheann.

Colum Cille, Columb Cille, Columcille, Colmcille, Collumcille, Colmkil, Calum Cille, etc. [L *columba*, dove; Ir. *cill*, church, cell]. Although there are thirty-two saints named Colum/Columba, the best-known is the patron saint of Scottish Gaelic Christianity, *c.*521–97; he is also the third most celebrated saint in Ireland, after St *Patrick and St *Brigid. Colum Cille has a fixed place on the calendar of saints, 9 June, but a number of legends have accrued to his name in both *Scotland and Ireland. Born of the powerful *Uí Néill kindred in Gartan, Co. *Donegal, Colum Cille was descended from *Niall Noígiallach [of the Nine Hostages]; his ancestor was *Conall Gulban, who gave his name to the region, Donegal [Ir. *Tír Conaill*, Conall's land], as well as to *Ben Bulben [corrupted from *Beinn Ghulbain*]. Through his mother, *Eithne, he claimed descent from *Cathair Mór, king of *Leinster. He was baptized Crimthann but, according to one version, took the name Colum Cille through angelic intervention.

Although a less than pious youth, he took holy orders and studied at Moville and *Clonard. While still a deacon, but not yet a priest, he studied classical Irish poetry under the chief poet of Leinster. After ordination he lived in seclusion at Glasnevin, which is now within the northern city limits of *Dublin. After a plague devastated his community (*c.*544) he returned to his own region, founding a new community at *Doire [Derry, Londonderry], known for many centuries in Irish as Doire Choluim Chille in his honour; this was to be but one of thirty-eight monasteries he would establish in Ireland alone. His monasteries are associated with the copying of manuscripts.

Why he left Ireland is uncertain. He may have been involved in a dispute over the copying of manuscripts, or the dispute may have been over the rights of sanctuary; for two years a war had raged of which he was thought to be the instigator. For whatever reason, Colum Cille led a group of followers to found a monastery at *Iona (563), off the west coast of Mull, Strathclyde (until 1974, *Argyllshire). The island, previously known simply as Í [isle], became Í-Choluim Chille, later anglo-latinized to Iona. In part he wished to minister to the Irish-speaking settlers of *Dál Riada, as well as to evangelize the *Picts. Among his converts was Bridei or Brude of the Great Glen, Scottish Highlands (until 1974, Inverness-shire).

Among the legends attached to his name is an early encounter with a *Loch Ness monster; the open-jawed creature was thought to have submerged at his command. He is also thought to have killed the *suileach, a many-eyed eponymous monster of Lough Swilly, Co. *Donegal. *Mongán went to heaven under Colum Cille's cowl. According to a prophecy attributed to Colum Cille, Ireland would be destroyed by the Broom of Fanait when the festival of St John the Baptist fell on a Friday, which it did in 1096—without catastrophe.

Colum Cille returned to Ireland twice after settling at Iona, in 575 to serve as an intermediary between Dál Riada and Irish princes, and in 585 to speak on behalf of the bardic order then threatened with extirpation. In 597 he died and was buried at Iona, and in 878 his bones were returned to Ireland. The Danes stole them in 1127 but later restored them, after which they were lost.

Colum Cille's earliest biographer was St *Adamnán, who wrote a century after his subject's death. In the 20th century Colum Cille's career has been the subject of scholarly dispute, notably by W. D. Simpson, *The Historical St. Columba* (1927), who doubted the claim that the saint had been the apostle of northern Scotland. Two more recent studies are Ian Finlay, *St. Columba* (London, 1982) and Máire Herbert, *Iona, Kells, and Derry* (Oxford, New York, 1988). The mournful eulogy *Amra Choluimb Chille* [Colum Cille, the Wonderful Person], is often thought to be the oldest surviving work of Irish literature; see Whitley Stokes, 'The Bodleian Amra Choluimb Chille', *Revue Celtique*, 20 (1899), 30–55, 132–83, 248–89, 400–37; and Vernam E. Hull, 'Amra Choluim Chille', *Zeitschrift für celtische Philologie*, 28 (1961), 242–51; see also Fergus Kelly, 'A Poem in Praise of Columb Cille', *Ériu*, 24 (1973), 1–34. Robert Farren's poems *This Man Was Ireland* (New York, 1943) and *The First Exile* (London, 1944) both deal with Colum Cille.

St Columba's Day, 9 June, is celebrated in Scotland, Ireland, Australia, and New Zealand. The Scottish and English personal names Calum and Colin and the Irish personal name Colm are forms of Colum/Columba.

Colum Cúaillemech [cf. Ir. *cúaille*, stake, pole, post]. A *smith of the *Tuatha Dé Danann. See also GOIBNIU.

Columba, Saint. Latin name meaning 'dove' borne by thirty-two saints, of whom the most notable is known as *Colum Cille in Irish and Scottish Gaelic traditions.

Columban, Columbanus, **Saint.** An Irish saint (d. 615) who became a missionary on the Continent, founding abbeys at Luxeuil (near Fontaine, France) and Ebovium (modern Bobbio, Italy). Although sometimes called 'the Younger Columba', he should not be confused with *Colum Cille (St Columba).

Columcille. See COLUM CILLE.

Comala. In *Macpherson's *Ossian* (1760), the daughter of the villainous Starno, who falls in love with *Fingal.

Combert. Variant spelling of **Compert*.

Comgall, Comhghall, **Saint.** Name borne by at least ten Irish saints, of whom the best-known was the founder (d. 603) of the monastery in *Bangor, Northern Ireland. Comgall was known for his austere life; seven of his followers died of cold and hunger on his regimen. He may also have founded a monastery on the Scottish island of Tiree. In Irish legend he is thought to have offered King *Fiachna mac Báetáin the choice between victory in battle and eternal damnation or defeat in battle and eternal happiness.

Comhal. Character in *Macpherson's *Ossian* (1760), the father of *Fingal. Early in the action he is killed by the tribe of Morni. Apparently based on *Cumhall of the *Fenian Cycle.

commote, commot [W *cwmwd*]. In Wales, a territorial and administrative division, usually subordinate to a *cantref or cantred. Two or more commotes might make a cantref.

Compert, Combert, Coimperta (pl.) [Ir., conception, act of begetting, procreation]. Name for a genre of tales on the conceptions and births of heroes.

Comrac Liadaine ocus Chuirithir. Irish title for the 9th-century poem often known in English as 'The Meeting of Liadain and Cuirithir'. See LIADAIN.

Conachar. Variant spelling of *Conchobar.

Conaill, Clann or Cenél. See TÍR CHONAILL; CONALL GULBAN.

Conaing [OE *cynyng*, king]. A name borne by several figures in early Irish genealogies as well as secular and ecclesiastical history. Some commentators confuse Conaing with that of *Conand, the *Fomorian leader.

Conaire Mór, Már; Conare, Conary [cf. *cú*, hound, i.e. warrior]. Legendary high king of early Ireland, the leading figure of the story **Togail Bruidne Da Derga* [The Destruction of Da Derga's Hostel]. Conaire's birth was highly unusual. His mother is normally thought to have been *Mes Buachalla, the abandoned stepdaughter of *Étaín Óg, who was fostered by a poor cowherd. Her beauty does not go unnoticed, and she is visited by a divine figure, who gets her with child. Mes Buachalla is betrothed to *Eterscél, because it has been prophesied that a woman whose family is unknown to him will bear him a child; Conaire therefore sometimes bears the patronymic mac Eterscéle. An alternate version, found in **Tochmarc Étaíne* [The Wooing of Étaín] has *Eochaid Airem impregnate his daughter in unknowing incest; the child of that union is described as mating with Eterscél to produce Conaire.

Regardless of his parentage, Conaire is fostered by *Donn Désa, whose own sons, Fer Lé, Fer Gair, and Fer Rogain, become dangerous marauders. When Eterscél dies, a *bull feast is held which determines that Conaire will be the next king. On his way to accept the kingship, Conaire is visited by a man in bird form who gives his name as Nemglan and describes himself as 'king of Conaire's father's bird troop'. Nemglan warns Conaire of a series of 'observances' [Ir. *airmitiu*], chief among them that he should give birds a privileged place because he is of their kind, and also that he should not pass *Tara on his right hand nor *Brega on his left (i.e. not make a right-hand or *sunwise turn around Tara). But before he is the guest at Da Derga's Hostel, Conaire has broken all the observances. Marauders including his foster-brothers invade the house and decapitate him. At the end of the story his severed head thanks *Mac Cécht (2) for slaking his thirst. Apart from the story, the Gaelic-speaking settlers in *Dál Riada claimed to be the 'seed of Conaire Mór'.

Conall [Ir. *con, conda*, wolfish]. A very old and widely dispersed name borne both by legendary and by shadowy historical figures in early Irish history, of whom *Conall Cernach is probably the best-known. The name is sometimes confused with the unrelated name *Connla, Conlae, and it is anglicized as Connell.

Conall 1. A legendary warrior, the son of *Eochaid (4), who gives his name to the place-name Carn Conaill in Co. Limerick. When Conall's five sons attack the *sídh of Grian at *Cnoc Gréine, she pursues them and changes them into badgers, after which they are hunted, killed, and eaten by Cormac Gaileng. Hearing this, Conall goes to Cnoc Gréine and does battle with Grian. Then she pauses and asks Conall's true identity. 'Come here,' she says, 'that I may make a gift of prosperity to you.' She sprinkles magic dust on him, upon which he wanders off and dies at Carn Conaill, nearby.

2. A tale-telling traveller in oral tradition. When his sons accidentally kill one of his king's sons, Conall is sent in quest to *Lochlainn [Scandinavia]. Once there he is obliged to tell three tales, Scheherazade-like, to save himself. One story employs the motif of an encounter with a *one-eyed *giant. The third story reveals that he once saved the life of the king of Lochlainn, and so Conall himself is saved. In English versions of his story he bears the agnomen Yellowclaw.

Conall Anglonnach [Ir. *anglondach*, warlike, valiant]. One of the great charioteers and chariot fighters of the *Ulster Cycle.

Conall Cernach, Cearnach [Ir., of the victories, triumphant]. A leading hero of the *Ulster Cycle, approaching *Cúchulainn in power and resolve. He was a foster-brother and virtual twin of Cúchulainn, his frequent companion in adventure and whose death he avenged. Together with Cúchulainn and *Lóegaire, Conall is one of the three first champions of Ulster. Conall appears in several important narratives of the Ulster Cycle, including **Scéla Mucce meic Da Thó* [The Story of Mac Da Thó's Pig], in which he takes a leading role; the **Táin Bó Cuailnge* [Cattle Raid of Cooley], where he suffers the pangs inflicted by Macha; he assists *Fráech in *Táin Bó Fraích*, **Fled Bricrenn* [Briccriu's Feast], etc. Conall's father is *Amairgin the poet, and his mother is *Findchóem. Some commentators have suggested that Conall may be a euhemerized *horned god. He was given his name in an assault by his uncle that nearly killed the boy. His usual wife is *Lendabair, daughter of *Eógan mac Durthacht; elsewhere *Niam (1) is his consort; his son Rathend is drowned when fleeing with his father from *Ercol. *Fedelm Noíchrothach [the nine times beautiful] eloped with Conall, abandoning her husband *Cairbre Nia Fer; their love child was *Fiachna (1). Conall is capable of some extraordinary feats, such as swallowing a *boar whole, one that is so large as to require sixty oxen to pull it. He can be a killer. On *Medb's prompting, he kills *Ailill as he is committing an infidelity. In addition, he kills *Anluan and Mesgegra, whose brain he makes into the ball that *Cet throws at *Conchobar. In seeking vengeance on *Lugaid for the death of Cúchulainn, he is especially brutal. According to oral tradition, Conall is himself killed by Connachtmen including Cet at the town of Ballyconnell, Co. Cavan, which claims to take its name from him.

Conall Corc. Another name for *Corc mac Luigthig.

Conall Gulban [Ir., beak, sting]. Son of *Niall Noígiallach [of the Nine Hostages] and a founder of the kingdom of *Tír Chonaill (Co. *Donegal). Conall and his two brothers, *Eógan and *Énna (3), were, according to T. F. O'Rahilly, identical with the three *Collas who razed the *Ulster capital of *Emain Macha; see *Early Irish History and Mythology* (Dublin, 1946), 230. On his own Conall headed the Clann Conaill. The establishment of two kingdoms in north-west Ulster, Tír Chonaill by Conall and Tír Eógain [Tyrone] by his brother Eógan, were signal events in early Irish history. According to oral tradition, Conall Gulban gave his name to *Ben Bulben [corrupted from *Beinn Ghulbain*], Co. Sligo, when he was killed pursuing a giant who had abducted *Eithne Uchtsholas, daughter of the king of Leinster. His descendant was *Colum Cille. Sometimes reputed to be living at the falls of *Assaroe.

Conall mac Luigthig. Another name for *Corc mac Luigthig.

Conan, Conán. A name found with differing associations in three Celtic lands. In Ireland it is: Conán [hound, wolf] and is borne by two characters in the *Fenian Cycle, *Conán mac Morna and *Conán mac Lia, as well as by six saints and scores of minor characters in narratives. In Wales it is: Conan [to grumble, to mutter (?)] and is the name of Tegid Faol [the bald]. In Brittany Conan is the name for *Cynan, the British invader of the country; it was also borne by four counts of Rennes who reigned from the 10th to the 12th centuries. Despite much conjecture, there does not seem to be a link between any of the Celtic figures named Conan and the Conan of the pulp adventure fiction series of Robert E. Howard (d. 1936). Distinguish from *Conand.

Conán 1. King of *Cualu [Wicklow] and father of *Medb Lethderg.

Conán mac Lia, mac an Léith Luachra. The lesser-known of two Conáns in the *Fenian Cycle. The son of *Liath Luachra, from whom Fionn gained the *crane bag. Conán was a marauder opposing the Fenians for many years, but when he was overcome one day in Munster, he changed his allegiances and joined Fionn and his men, becoming a keen and hardy fighter. In some stories he mistreats Finnine, the sister of *Ferdoman, sometimes while described as her husband. To avenge his sister's honour, Ferdoman engages Conán in a duel in which they both die.

Conán mac Morna. The better-known of the two Conáns in the *Fenian Cycle. He is often cited with the agnomen Máel or Maol, which is usually translated as 'the Bald'. OIr. máel and ModIr. maol usually mean 'bald' but may also mean 'shorn'. In OIr. máel often implied servility, as servants would have their hair shorn or cropped. When applied to things, máel and maol imply bluntness.

Within the Fenian Cycle, Conán is often portrayed as the most comic figure, although he is not often a buffoon. His character has something in common with Thersites of the Tale of Troy, in that he is filled with bluster; in her retelling of the Fenian stories Lady Gregory called him 'Conan of the Bitter Tongue'. In that he is also a trouble-maker, he has something in common with Loki of Norse mythology. As he is fat and sometimes foolish, he has been compared with Shakespeare's Falstaff, except that he never runs from a fight. Mean and greedy, he is often detested by the bulk of the Fenians, but once he allies himself with Fionn the two of them are often seen together, sometimes almost as a team. Although bald, Conán has the fleece of a black sheep running down his back. Some stories describe him as wearing a black fleece as a wig. Often seen as the brother of *Goll mac Morna. In **Feis Tighe Chonáin* [A Feast at Conán's House], Fionn is entertained at Conán's house and tells many tales of the adventures of the Fenians. Ed. M. Joynt (Dublin, 1936).

Conand, Conann, Connan. The *Fomorian leader who resided on Tory Island (off Co. *Donegal), where his fortress was a great glass tower, Tor Conaind. He levied a tribute on the *Nemedians; they, in turn, attacked the island and stormed the tower. *Fergus Lethderg the Nemedian killed Conand before the Nemedian escape to Britain. Distinguish from *Conaing.

Conar. A king of Ireland in *Macpherson's *Ossian* (1760). He was the father of the *Cormac dethroned by *Carbar. As he was also related to *Fingal, he drew the Scottish hero into many Irish wars.

Conarán. A chief of the *Tuatha Dé Danann who appears in the *Fenian Cycle. At his bidding, his three ugly daughters punish *Fionn mac Cumhaill and some companions for hunting by using three holly-sticks to entrap them in a cave. Fionn's former enemy *Goll mac Morna comes to the rescue by killing two of the sisters and forcing the third to release the Fenians. Later, when the third sister tries to avenge her sisters, Goll kills her too. In gratitude Fionn awards Goll the hand of his daughter. In some versions of the story, Conarán's daughters are named Camóg [Ir., curl], Cúilín [curl at the back of the head], and Iarnach [iron instrument].

Conary Mor. Anglicization of *Conaire Mór.

Conchean. Variant of *Conche(a)nn.

Conchobar, Conchubar, Conchobhar, Conachar, Conchúr, Conor, Connor [Ir., wolf-lover (?), lover of hounds (?)]. A name borne by thousands of Irish figures over centuries of whom the best-known was the king of *Ulster in the times of the Red Branch, *Conchobar mac Nessa. The usual anglicization is Conor, as commemorated in the common family name O'Connor, which exists in six distinct divisions, each with its own eponymous progenitor. Since the 15th century Conchobar has been equated with the Latin name Cornelius, with which it has no etymological connection.

Conchobar Abratruad [Ir., of the red eyelashes]. An early king of the *Lagin, ancestors of the Leinstermen of eastern Ireland. In early pedigrees he is confused with the better-known *Conchobar mac Nessa.

Conchobar mac Nessa, Nes. King of *Emain Macha and thus of *Ulster during most of the action of stories in the *Ulster Cycle. In some translations, stories of the Ulster Cycle are called 'Red Branch' after Conchobar's principal residence or palace, *Cráebruad. Although usually an attractive figure, Conchobar is the creature of unsavoury lusts in his pursuit of the unwilling *Deirdre in *Longas mac nUislenn* [The Exile of the Sons of Uisnech]. Conchobar becomes king of Ulster through the machinations of his mother, Ness. His treatment of the Sons of Uisnech causes his son *Cormac Connloinges to abandon Ulster and join the forces of *Medb of *Connacht in **Táin Bó Cuailnge* [Cattle Raid of Cooley].

The story of Conchobar's birth and boyhood fuses different early narratives that are often included as foretales or *rémscéla* to the **Táin Bó Cuailnge*. His birth and conception set him apart from other men. Conchobar's mother Ness, daughter of *Eochaid Sálbuide, is impregnated by the druid *Cathbad who answers her question about what the hour was lucky for; 'Begetting a king upon a queen' is his reply. A rival version asserts that *Fachtna Fáthach is both Conchobar's father and Ness's husband. Some commentators suggest that Conchobar is named for the river where Cathbad sat, denying the more usual explanation given above. The boy Conchobar is reared by Cathbad until a new king of Ulster, *Fergus mac Róich, seeks Ness for his wife. Before giving her consent, Ness asks that Fergus give up the throne for a year and allow Conchobar to reign so that he may call his son the 'son of a king'. Conchobar becomes king, but at the end of a year Ness makes it difficult for Fergus to regain his title and so he departs. Despite his unusual access to royal power, Conchobar becomes a popular king, celebrated for his prudence and wise judgement. Following the wishes of his subjects, he sleeps with each bride of the kingdom on the first night of her marriage.

Conchobar has three residences or palaces, of which *Cráebruad [Red Branch], named for a beam across the ceiling, is best known. Red implies royalty, and Conchobar sits here most often. Cúchulainn is bred here. *Téte Brec* [Twinkling Hoard] houses the twinkling gold of his swords and other weapons. **Cráebderg* [Ruddy Branch] houses severed heads and other spoils of battle.

Because Conchobar suffers from the debilitating pangs of the Ulstermen, Ces *Noínden Ulad, inflicted by *Macha, he recedes from much of the action in *Táin Bó Cuailnge*. In some variants, Conchobar may have brought about the pangs by goading Macha to race, although her husband, *Crunniuc, is more often the culprit. He is almost killed by Fergus at the end of the *Táin*. The better-known story of his death has *Cet mac Matach wound Conchobar with the calcified brain ball of Mesgegra. The wound, sewn up on the advice of physician *Fíngein, is not fatal until much later, when the brain ball shakes loose. Later Christian interpolation has him dying on Good Friday after a druid tells him of the death of a just man.

Accounts of Conchobar's family are not consistent. His metronymic is 'mac Nessa' because Ness is always cited as his mother, but his father may be Cathbad or Fachtna Fáthach. His sisters include *Deichtine, the beloved of *Lug Lámfhota, and *Findchóem, the mother of *Conall Cernach. Among Conchobar's many wives are the four daughters of *Eochaid Feidlech, first *Medb [Maeve], a mismatch, *Eithne (5), *Clothra, and later *Mugain (2), who is most often named as his wife. Conchobar's sons include the aforementioned Cormac Connloinges as well as *Cúscraid Menn [the stammerer]; Furbaide Ferbend, the slayer of Medb; Follomain, his youngest, who leads the boy-corps in the *Táin Bó Cuailnge*; and *Glaisne. Among his daughters are *Bláithíne, the faithless wife of *Cú Roí, and *Fedelm Noíchrothach [the nine times beautiful] or Noíchríde [fresh heart], the wife of *Cairbre Nia Fer.

Several commentators have suggested that Conchobar may be one of many Celtic models for King *Arthur. His sword is Gorm Glas [Ir., blue-green]. His chief poet and entertainer is *Ferchertne (2).

Condatis [waters meet (?)]. A god worshipped in Roman-occupied Britain, much associated with the confluence of rivers. His shrines have been found between the Tyne and Tees rivers, Northumberland, Cumberland, and Durham, in the north of what is now England. His name is commemorated in many place-names, some as far away as Gaul. Condatis may be equated with *Mars.

Condere mac Echach. An *Ulster warrior known for his good sense and eloquence. He is the first to face the mysterious *Connla, the unacknowledged son of *Cúchulainn. When Connla says he could deal with Condere easily, the Ulster warrior backs off.

Cong [Ir. *Conga*; cf. OIr. *cuing*, isthmus]. Monastery in Co. Mayo at the north-east end of *Lough Corrib, established by St Féichín in the 6th century and rebuilt by the Austin canons in the 12th. It was reckoned to be on an isthmus in that it is between Lough Corrib and Lough Mask. Sometimes associated with the nearby plain known as *Mag Tuired [Moytura]. The last high king of Ireland, Ruaidrí Ua Conchobair, entered this monastery in 1183 and died here in 1198. The celebrated Cross of Cong, housed in the National Museum of Ireland, survived the destruction of the buildings. The ruins, partially restored in the 19th century, are in the south-east portion of the village of Cong.

Congal, Conghal [Ir., conflict, fight, attack]. Name borne by several figures from early Irish history and legend, most notably Congal Cáech [*One-eyed], a shadowy but historical 7th-century king of *Ulster. Congal was a leader of *Dál nAraide, a petty kingdom east of Lough Neagh, who became king of Ulster but was killed by the high king, *Domnall (1), at the Battle of Mag Rath [Moira] (637); cf. the account of Mag Rath in **Buile Shuibne*. Sir Samuel Ferguson dramatized this obscure ruler's reign in *Congal* (1872), the only epic poem in Anglo-Irish literature, much in the manner of George Chapman's Elizabethan translation of the *Iliad*. Another Congal was the foster-brother of *Máel Fothartaig in **Fingal Rónáin* [How Rónán Killed His Son].

Conganchnes mac Dedad, Dáire [Ir., horn-skinned]. Described as the brother or uncle of *Cú Roí. He avenges that hero's 'death', but he is really Cú Roí *revivus*. Later the figure known as Conganchnes is slain by *Celtchair mac Uthechair. *Niam (2), Celtchair's daughter, agrees to marry Conganchnes to learn the secret of his seeming invulnerability: that he can be killed only by having spear-points penetrate the soles of his feet and the calves of his legs. Later the blood from Conganchnes' dog Dóelchu kills Celtchair.

Conla, Conláech, Conlaí, Conlán, Conlaoch, Conle. Variant spellings of *Connla, a name borne by several figures in Irish history and legend.

Conmac, Conmacc, Conmhac [Ir., wolf's son]. The eponymous founder of *Connemara [Ir. *Conmaicne Mara*] is thought to be Conmac. Sources disagree whether this was Conmac, the by-blow of *Medb and *Fergus mac Róich, or *Lugaid Conmac, also known as Lugaid mac Con.

Conmaicne. A people of early Ireland, perhaps related to the *Lagin, who were dispersed to various parts of *Connacht and north-western *Leinster. The branch that settled west of *Lough Corrib, Co. Galway, the Conmaicne Mara [of the sea], gave their name to *Connemara. It was among the Conmaicne Réin, in eastern Galway, that the *Tuatha Dé Danann first appeared. T. F. O'Rahilly's assertion (1946) that the Conmaicne was non-*Goidelic is not widely accepted.

Conn [Ir., wisdom, sense, reason (?), cf. W **Pwyll*; pet-form of *cú/con*, wolf, hound (?)]. A name borne by dozens of figures in early Irish history and legend, especially among the ranks of powerful families, perhaps in evocation of *Conn Cétchathach.

Conn 1. One of the Children of Lir, the twin brother of *Fiachra in **Oidheadh Chlainne Lir* [The Tragic Story of the Children of Lir].

2. The son of Febal, and a member of the *Fianna of *Fionn mac Cumhaill.

Conn Cétchathach, Céadchathach [Ir., of the Hundred Battles, the Hundred-Fighter]. Shadowy king of Irish pre-history and ancestor, perhaps ancestor-deity, of Irish kings. Although described in the annals as having lived in the 2nd century, Conn bears a name sometimes applied to rulers of the *Otherworld. He is the first to hear from the *Lia Fáil [the Stone of Prophecy], allowing him to foresee how many of his line will occupy the kingship as well as the coming of St *Patrick. Along with his special role in kingship, he is also the eponymous ancestor of the *Goidels of the midlands who named the province of *Connacht (Connaught, Connachta, etc.) after him.

Conn's grandfather was the illustrious *Tuathal Techtmar, but his father is variously named, most often Fedlimid Rechtaid (or Rechtmar) or Óenlám Gaba; his mother may be *Medb Lethderg. The precocious Conn becomes king at *Tara by seizing power from *Cathaír Mór; by later interpolation he is aided by the *Fianna of *Fionn mac Cumhaill. Once in Tara, he mounts the ramparts each day lest the people of the *sídh or the *Fomorians should take Ireland unawares. In his early reign he is often at war with the petty kingdom of *Dál nAraide to the east of Lough Neagh; here he earns his epithet of 'Hundred Battles' or 'Hundred-Fighter'. His greatest rival is *Eógan Mór (also Mug Nuadat) of *Munster, with whom he divides Ireland. The division is made along a ridge of low mounds, known as *Eiscir Riada, running from Dublin to Galway Bay. Territory north of that line is known as Leth Cuinn: Conn's half, and south of the line is Leth Moga Nuadat: Mug Nuadat's (Eógan's) half. Invading Munster, Conn defeats Eógan, who then flees the country; Conn instals two rulers, Conaire and Maicnia, more disposed towards him. Eógan returns, stirs up a revolt against Conn, and is defeated and slain at the Battle of Mag Léna (near Tullamore, Co. Offaly). Stories of Conn's own death differ. He may have been killed by thirty Ulstermen, led by Tiobraide Tíreach, dressed as women.

We read of Conn's adventures in some well-known texts. In **Baile in Scáil* [The Phantom's Frenzy], Conn learns of the future of his line from the Lia Fáil, and meets a beautiful woman who is the *Sovereignty of Ireland. In **Echtrae Airt meic Cuinn* [The Adventure of Art Son of Conn], the fields of Ireland will bear no harvests and the cows will give no milk because Conn is mated with the disreputable *Bé Chuma. Previously, when he was married to the virtuous *Eithne Tháebfhota, daughter of Cathaír Mór, there were three harvests a year. When Conn's men kill *Eochaid Bélbuide, he compensates Eochaid's protector, *Fergus mac Léti, with a tract of land seized from the nobly born mother of one of the assassins, Dorn, who becomes Fergus's slave.

Conn is often mentioned in the *Fenian Cycle, although the stories there appear to be of later composition. Fionn mac Cumhaill is usually thought to have been born during the reign of Conn or that of his predecessor, Cathaír Mór. In some versions, Conn killed *Cumhall, Fionn's father, for his abduction of *Muirenn, Fionn's mother. Despite this, Fionn and his Fianna are often seen as Conn's allies. Among Conn's children are the aforementioned Art mac Cuinn as well as *Connla, who is seduced by a *fairy princess in *Echtrae Conli [The Adventure of Connla]. A daughter is Sárait, mother of three Cairbres. His grandson is the celebrated king *Cormac mac Airt. His druid was Máel or Corán. In Gaelic Scotland the *Lord of the Isles of the Clan Donald proudly claimed descent from Conn as well as from *Colla Uais.

Connacht, Connaught, Connachta, Connaght [Ir., descendants of Conn (?)]. A province of Ireland, the most westerly and smallest (6,610 square miles) of the four (the others being *Leinster, *Munster, and *Ulster) whose borders were drawn in the 17th century. In pre-conquest times, as *Cóiced Connacht*, it was one of five, when *Mide/*Meath is counted separately or Munster is counted as two. Within its borders are the counties of Galway, Leitrim, Mayo, Sligo, and Roscommon. In the Irish epic **Táin Bó Cuailnge* [Cattle Raid of Cooley], the ruler of Connacht is Queen *Medb [Maeve], whose royal residence is at *Cruachain (Co. Roscommon). For much of the narrative 'Medb' and 'Connacht' are almost synonymous. Elsewhere in the *Ulster Cycle, which includes the *Táin*, the great hero of Connacht is Cet mac Mágtach.

Roughly coextensive with the region known as Nagatae in *Ptolemy's geography (2nd cent. AD), Connacht is usually thought to be named for *Conn Cétchathach [of the Hundred Battles]. In mythic narrative, Connacht is given to *Sreng as part of the settlement after the defeat of the *Fir Bolg at the First Battle of Mag Tuired; see CATH MAIGE TUIRED. Other notable rulers of Connacht include: *Cathal Mór 'of the Wine-Red Hand', a personification of the province; *Crimthann Cass; *Eógan (2); *Guaire; and *Lairgnéan. The king of the Connacht fairies is *Finnbheara, who resides at *Cnoc Mheadha [Knockmagha], near Tuam, Co. Galway. Alenecma is the name for Connacht in *Macpherson's *Ossian* (1760). In Irish the phrase Iar [remote, west] Chonnacht refers to the barony of Moycullen, now reckoned to be a part of *Connemara. See also *The Annals of Connacht*, ed. A. Martin Freeman, *Revue Celtique*, 50 (1933), 1–23, 117–42, 272–88, 339–56; 51 (1934), 46–111, 199–301; also *Annála Connacht* (Dublin, 1944).

Connan. Variant spelling of *Conand.

Connemara [Ir. *Conmaicne Mara*, *Conmac's people of the sea; *Iarchonnacht*, western Connacht]. A region of west Co. Galway, west of *Lough Corrib; originally Connemara was roughly identical with the barony of Ballynahinch, but it is now reckoned informally to include portions of the barony of Moycullen to the east and Ross ('Joyce's Country') to the north. Because Connemara contains the largest surviving Gaeltacht [Irish-speaking community], many commentators have felt, rightly or wrongly, that the area is one of the most characteristic of traditional Irish culture. Despite exploitation by the tourist industry, Connemara remains a living reservoir of folk culture that has been tapped by many collectors. In the early 20th century James Berry (1842–1914) reshaped many of the narratives of Connemara, something in the manner of William Carleton; see G. M. Horgan (ed.), *Tales of the West of Ireland* (Dublin, 1964); see also Tim Robinson, *Connemara* (Galway, 1990).

Connla, Conla, Conláech, Conlae, Conlaí, Conlaoch, Conlán, Conle, Condla, Cúnla [Ir., great lord (?), great chief (?)]. Name borne by dozens of figures from early Irish legend and history, including characters in heroic narratives and ecclesiastics. One Connla is the hero of a bawdy modern Irish ballad. The name appears to be related to *Colla, and is sometimes confused with *Conall, to which it is not related.

Connla 1. The son of the Amazonian *Aífe in Scotland, fathered unawares by *Cúchulainn. The well-known story of Connla's death at his father's hands is told in **Aided Óenfhir Aífe* [The Death of Aífe's Only Son]. Scottish Gaelic traditions tell of Connla's nurturing at Dunsgàthaich, Isle of Skye. James *Macpherson retells the story as 'Carthon' in his *Ossian* (1760). In W. B. Yeats's poem 'Cuchulain's Fight with the Sea' (1892), Connla is known as Finmole.

2. The son of *Conn Cétchathach [of the Hundred Battles] seduced by a *fairy woman. His well-known story is told in **Echtrae Conli*

[The Adventures of Connla]; the title is sometimes translated to include the epithets 'the Bold', 'the Fair', or 'the Red'. Connla leaves the land of the living when the fairy woman promises him escape from old age and death; he will not return even with the promise of his father's crown. His story was retold by James Cousins in the play *The Sleep of the King* (Dublin, 1902; Chicago, 1973).

3. He for whom *Connla's Well is named.

Connla Cóel. Lord of an *otherworldly island visited by *Cúchulainn.

Connla's Well. A source of inspiration and knowledge in early Irish mythology, somewhat comparable to the well of Mimir in Norse tradition. The location of the well changes from text to text, and the identity of the Connla for whom it is named is not clear. It may be under the sea, in *Tír na nÓg [The Land of Youth], or in *Tír Tairngire [The Land of Promise]. One *Dindshenchas [lore of place-names] cites a Connla's Well near Tipperary. Over the well, whatever its location, were nine *hazel trees whose nuts contained wisdom, *knowledge, and inspiration. The nuts dropped into the well, and the *salmon swimming in it ate the nuts. The number of spots on each salmon indicated how many nuts it had eaten. Wisdom, knowledge, and inspiration came to the person who drank the water of the well or ate the salmon or the nuts. All were forbidden to visit the well except *Nechtan and his three cupbearers. *Sinann [Shannon], the granddaughter of the sea god *Lir, went to the well seeking wisdom. Although it is not clear which protocols she may have neglected, Sinann did not receive wisdom. Instead, the well rose up and drowned her. Her body washed up on the banks of the *Shannon, which was named for her. Connla's Well may be identical with the Well of *Segais, and is called the Well of Cóelrind in some texts. Magic wisdom gained from drinking the waters of a certain well is folk motif D1811.1.2.

Conor. Anglicization of *Conchobar.

Conquests, Book of. Non-standard translation of the Irish title **Lebor Gabála*.

consuriwr. The Welsh word for conjurer; see DYN HYSBYS.

Contortion of Cúchulainn. See ríastrad under *Cúchulainn.

Contrebus [L, co-habiter (?), he who dwells among us; cf. *treba*, dwelling]. A minor god worshipped in Roman-occupied Britain; a dedication to Contrebus survives at Overborough, Lancashire.

Conway [W *Conwy*]. Waterway of north Wales, starting from Lake Conway and running north to Beaumaris Bay in *Gwynedd; until 1974 it formed the boundary between the now extinct counties of Denbigh and Caernarvon. Near the town of Conway, at the west of the river's mouth, lies the site of Degannwy, court of the 6th-century king *Maelgwn Gwynedd. The waters of the Conway are thought to evoke the dying groans of *Dylan, the Welsh aquatic hero.

Cool. Anglicization of *Cumhall, father of *Fionn mac Cumhaill.

cooleen, coolun. Anglicizations of *cúilín.

Cooley [Ir. *Cuailnge*]. A peninsula in northeast Co. Louth, between Dundalk Bay and Carlingford Lough. It is here that many of the climactic scenes in the Irish epic **Táin Bó Cuailnge* [Cattle Raid of Cooley] take place.

copóg Phádraig [Ir., leaf of Patrick]. Irish name for the plantain or water-plantain (genus *plantago*), which was thought to ward off *fairies.

Corán. The *druid of *Connla.

Coraniaid, Coranians [cf. W *còr*, *corrach*, dwarf]. A magical and demonic people who invade and harass Britain in **Cyfranc Lludd a Llefelys* [The Story of Lludd and Lleuelys]. They have been identified in a general way with *fairies, but are far more malevolent than the *tylwyth teg of Welsh oral tradition. One of three invaders that threatened the kingdom of Lludd, they could hear sound carried on the wind.

Corb, Corbb [cf. Ir. *corbbaid*, defiles]. A god of the *Fomorians of the **Lebor Gabála* [Book of Invasions].

Corc mac Luigthig, Corcc mac Luigdech. [Ir. *corcc*, heart]. Also known as Conall Corc, Conall mac Luigthig. Traditional founder of the kingship of *Cashel, the fortress of Co. Tipperary, and ancestor of many kings of *Munster, about whom many legends have gathered. A swineherd foretells his coming to Cashel and to the kingship. During an initiation rite by his foster-mother *Fedelm (3) his ear becomes magically singed, giving him his name, Corc, which some early writers mistakenly thought meant 'red' or 'crimson'. Later he is sent to the king of the *Picts in Scotland, with a secret *ogham message on his shield that he should be killed. Fortunately, a scholar whom Corc had rescued from slavery alters the characters so as to provide a favourable introduction. Corc is warmly received and later marries the daughter of the Pictish king. On his return to Ireland he founds two dynasties, first at *Femen, second and more importantly at Cashel. According to tradition Corc, while trapped in a snowstorm, beholds a vision of a *yew bush growing over a stone with angels flying up and down before it. His druids tell him that the person who kindles a *fire on that stone will be king of Munster forever. The kingship of Cashel is controlled for many centuries by the *Eóganacht [the people descended from Eógan, he who was born of the yew].

Corca, Corco. Variant spellings of *Corcu.

Corcaguiney peninsula. See DINGLE.

Corcomroe. Tribal name lending itself to a barony and to a Cistercian abbey, founded 1180, now in ruins, in north Co. Clare, 2 miles S of the *Burren, 5 miles W of Kinvara. The locality is cited in many stories, not always with Christian associations. Máel Dúin, for example, consults a druid here when he first pursues his father's murderers (see **Imram Curaig Maíle Dúin*).

Corcu, Corco, Corca. An Old Irish word for population groups and, by extension, for the territories they occupied. It may be translated as 'clan'.

Corcu Baiscinn, Baiscind, Bascinn. A people settled north of the Shannon estuary in what is now Co. Clare, especially the south-western peninsula of the county, from earliest recorded history up to the 12th century. People of the Corcu Baiscinn were famous as sailors. The poet James Liddy titled one of his collections *Corca Bascinn* (Dublin, 1977).

Corcu Duibne. People of western Co. *Kerry, especially on both the north and the south shores of *Dingle Bay. In some writings *Corca Dhuibhne* denotes the Dingle peninsula specifically. The *Cailleach Bhéirre [Old Woman of Beare] was of the Corcu Duibne, but their (perhaps divine) ancestress may have been Dob[h]inia. *Cú Roí had his fortress in their territory. One of the highest concentrations of stones bearing *ogham inscriptions is found in land once occupied by the Corcu Duibne. Among the Corcu Duibne also was Gleann na nGealt, a valley filled with wild men.

Corcu Loígde, Lóegde, Laígde, Laoidhe. People of what is now south-western Co. Cork, who lived between the River Bandon and the sea in the southernmost area in Ireland. The ancient geographer Ptolemy (2nd cent. AD) may have identified the Corcu Loígde with the people he named *Iverni. They were a dominant power in south Munster before the rise of the *Eóganacht. In the pseudo-history **Lebor Gabála* [Book of Invasions], they are described as descending from Lugaid son of Dáire and thus from *Ith.

Corleck Hill. Sometimes known in Irish as *Sliabh na Trí nDée, Sliabh na nDée Dána* [Ir., hill of the three gods], a promontory near Drumeague, Co. Cavan, once known as 'the pulse of Ireland'. A stone head of *Brigit was once worshipped here, and the hill was the site of pagan worship on the feasts of *Imbolc, *Beltaine, *Lughnasa, and *Samain. The three gods of the Irish name are probably *Conn, *Dagda, and *Ogma, although earlier commentators suggested *Brian, *Iuchair, and *Iucharba. Near *Dub Chomar.

Cormac, Cormacc, Carmac [Ir. *corbbaid*, defiles (?); *mac*, son of]. Common Irish name borne by many figures both legendary and historical, including kings, ecclesiastics, and saints. The best-known Cormacs are probably the legendary king Cormac mac Airt; the glossator of **Sanas Cormaic* [Cormac's Glossary], Cormac mac Cuilennáin; and Cormac mac Carthaig, for whom 'Cormac's Chapel' at *Cashel is named. There does not appear to be one progenitor for the Irish and Scottish families named McCormick, MacCormack, etc.

Cormac 1. Son of a king of *Ulster named Lachtighe, grandfather of *Conaire Mór. He married *Étaín Óg but put her aside when she proved unable to bear sons. His daughter from a previous marriage, whom Étaín Óg sought to have killed, grew up to be *Mes Buachalla, wife of *Eterscél. He may be identical with *Cormac Connloinges.

2. A character in *Macpherson's *Ossian* (1760) described as the 'king of Ireland'. His daughter Ros-Cranna married *Fingal. The

son of *Arth, also king of Ireland, Cormac was dethroned and murdered by *Cairbre. The root of his characterization appears to be borrowed from *Cormac mac Airt.

Cormac mac Aililla. Another name for *Cormac Cas.

Cormac mac Airt. Also known as Cormac Ulf[h]ada [Ir., long beard] and Cormac Ua Cuinn (acknowledging *Conn Cétchathach, his grandfather). A legendary early king of Ireland at *Tara, perhaps the most famous of all early kings, and the first cited as having his seat at Tara. In the Annals he is described as reigning for forty years, with interruptions, AD 227–66. Cormac was thought to be so wise and just that during his reign calves were born after only three months' gestation, every ridge produced a sackful of wheat, the rivers abounded with salmon, and there were not enough vessels to hold the milk from the cows. Most of the episodes in the *Fenian Cycle occur during Cormac's reign, and *Fionn mac Cumhaill is sometimes described as being a part of his soldiery. In a sense, Fionn could be described as being a part of Cormac's cycle, especially as several non-Fenian stories centre on Cormac, including the magical and enticing **Echtrae Cormaic* [The Adventure of Cormac]. Convinced that Cormac was unhistorical, T. F. O'Rahilly (1946) argued that he was an idealization of the first *Goidelic king of *Tara. None the less, several important families of medieval Ireland, notably the *Uí Néill, claimed descent from Cormac.

Cormac was described as the grandson of the illustrious *Conn Cétchathach [Ir., of the Hundred Battles]. Conn's son *Art mac Cuinn fathers Cormac upon one *Étaín, the daughter of a *smith, before the battle of Mag Mucrama, in which Art is killed. Following Art's instructions, Étaín travels to *Connacht in her pregnancy so that the infant may be fostered by Art's friend there. But as she is near term, Étaín delivers Cormac in a brushwood along the way, during a thunderstorm. Shortly after his birth Cormac is spirited away by a wolf, who suckles him in its lair. The motif of the death of both parents is also found in Cormac's *Munster contemporary, *Fiachu Muillethan. Eventually, Cormac is fostered by *Lugaid mac Con, whom he replaces in the kingship by the power of his better judgement. But it is said of him that he will remain a lad until he has slept with *Medb (Maeve) Lethderg [half-red or red side; not to be confused with Medb of Connacht]. Medb, whose name appears to mean 'intoxicating' [cf. W *meddw*, drunk; Eng. *mead*], is described as having been the 'wife' of nine Irish kings, including Conn's father and Conn's son Art. She is a more specific instance of the *Sovereignty of Ireland figure seen in many stories; see FEIS TEMRO [feast of Tara]; BANAIS RÍGHE [marriage of kingship]. **Esnada Tige Buchet* [The Melodies of Buchet's House] tells how Cormac begets *Cairbre Lifechair upon *Eithne Tháebfhota, the daughter of *Cathaír Mór.

In perhaps the best-known story about him, *Echtrae Cormaic* [The Adventure of Cormac], the young king accepts a magical sleep-inducing bough from a warrior who is later revealed to be *Manannán mac Lir. In return for the magical bough, the mysterious warrior makes demands on Cormac, including the surrender of his wife, which the king cannot accept. When Cormac pursues the warrior he finds himself in a castle, where the warrior presents him with a wondrous golden cup that can be split apart with lies and put together again only with truths.

In the Fenian stories Cormac is represented as having a fairly close relationship with the central figure of the cycle, Fionn mac Cumhaill. Cormac accepts Fionn's hospitality at feasting. In some versions he is Fionn's father-in-law, the married daughter being either *Ailbe Gruadbrecc or *Gráinne. Gráinne's betrothal to Fionn is very much to Cormac's approval, but later, when she flees from Fionn with *Diarmait, Cormac shows restrained sympathy for the young lovers. The relationship between Cormac's son and successor, Cairbre Lifechair, and the Fenians is much poorer.

Cormac's power is sufficiently great to establish his half-brother Nia as king of *Connacht. But it is not sufficient to retain Cormac's kingship once he is disfigured. The episode is provoked when Cormac's nephew or son, *Cellach, rapes a maiden from the *Déisi. Seeking revenge, *Angus (4), the Déisi chieftain, spears Cellach and puts out Cormac's eye with the butt. Cormac is then obliged to abdicate in favour of Cairbre. Among the *Dál nAraide of northern Ireland, the story was told that their eponym, *Fiachu Araide, had driven Cormac from Tara, but that *Fiachu Muillethan of Munster had helped to restore him.

Later stories, interpolated by Christian commentators but widely popular in oral tradition, portray Cormac as somehow prescient about Christian values. In one story Cormac refuses to be buried on pagan ground. Cormac appears to be the basis of James *Macpherson's character named Cormac (see CORMAC (2)) in *Ossian* (1760). See Tomás Ó Cathasaigh, *The Heroic Biography of Cormac mac Airt* (Dublin, 1977); Vernam Hull (ed.), '*Echtra Cormaic mac Airt*, 'The Adventure of Cormac mac Airt'', *PMLA* 64 (1949), 871–83. Andrew J. Offutt used the heroic persona to create eight volumes of popular adventure fuction, the Cormac Mac Art series (New York, 1979–86).

Cormac Cas. Shadowy historical king of *Munster of the late 7th century and legendary ancestor of such *Dál Cais (or Dál gCais) families as the O'Briens and the McNamaras. He was a grandson of *Eógan Mór (Mug Nuadat) and a son of *Ailill Aulomm, and thus sometimes bears the patronymic mac Aililla. Slain by the invading Déisi at Carn Feradaig near the present city of Limerick, AD 713.

Cormac Connloinges, Conn Loingeas, CondLonges, Conloingeas. A son of *Conchobar mac Nessa, king of *Emain Macha, who goes into voluntary exile to protest the treacherous killing of the sons of *Uisnech, whose surety in passage he had been. In the epic *Táin Bó Cuailnge* [Cattle Raid of Cooley], he travels with the invading army of *Connacht under Queen *Medb [Maeve]. Later he prevents *Fergus mac Róich from killing Conchobar. Later still, Conchobar on his deathbed sends for Cormac to replace him in the kingship. As Cormac starts this journey of reconciliation he is murdered by a band of Connachtmen returning from a raid in *Ulster. He is sometimes thought to have married *Niam (2), daughter of *Celtchair, after her treacherous marriage to *Conganchnes. According to genealogical tracts, he later takes *Étaín (1) as a wife, presumably after the death of her usual mortal husband, *Eochaid Airem. Also a character in *Togail Bruidne Da Derga* [The Destruction of Da Derga's Hostel]. He may be identical with Cormac (1), husband of *Étaín Óg.

Cormac Gelta Gáeth. Legendary ancestor of *Leinstermen.

Cormac mac Carthaig. Twelfth-century king of *Munster who authorized the building of the Romanesque church at *Cashel called 'Cormac's Chapel' in his memory. Slain in 1138.

Cormac mac Cuilennáin. Late 9th-century (d. 908) scholar and king-bishop of *Cashel who is said to have compiled **Sanas Cormaic* [Cormac's Glossary]. Although Cormac could be an uncritical euhemerist, believing that all characters were historical, his Glossary is an invaluable source of information on early Irish tradition.

Cormac Ua Cuinn. Another name for *Cormac mac Airt.

Cormac Ulfhada, Ulfhota. Variant names for *Cormac mac Airt.

Cormac's Adventure in the Land of Promise. See ECHTRAE CORMAIC.

Cormac's cup. This golden cup could be split apart with lies and welded together with truths. A mysterious warrior, later revealed to be *Manannán mac Lir, gives it to *Cormac mac Airt in **Echtrae Cormaic* [The Adventure of Cormac].

Cormac's Glossary. See SANAS CORMAIC; named for *Cormac mac Cuilennáin.

Cormar. An attendant of *Cumhal in *Macpherson's *Ossian* (1760). His name is proverbial for a knowledge of the sea.

Cormoran. *Giant of Cornish folklore credited with building St Michael's Mount, a rocky islet near Marazion, 3 miles E of Penzance. Cormoran begins his work with white granite, but as he is lazy and dozes off, his wife, Cormelian, begins to build with green stone as it can be carried from a shorter distance. When Cormoran awakes he kicks Cormelian, who drops the green stone, forming the causeway to the mainland. The name Cormoran is also given to the giant in the English folk-tale of 'Jack the Giant-Killer'.

Cornavii. Name recorded by Ptolemy (2nd cent. AD) for a people living in what is now Caithness in northern Scotland. Speculation on the implications of the name include: people of the promontory, people of the horn, and people of the horned god.

Cornouaille. Petty kingdom in *Brittany from early Christian times; region retained the name until the Napoleonic redivision of local governments. The territory of

Cornouaille ran south of the River Elorn to the Elle, in what is today the south-west Department of *Finistère. While the name is similar to *Cornwall, Cornouaille does not appear to have been settled by Cornish emigrants, although Cornouaille does appear to be coextensive with the ancient British petty kingdom of *Cornubia. Bret. Kernev.

Cornovii. Ancient British tribe occupying much of the valleys of the Severn and the Dee near what is today the Welsh border. As their territory was often under attack and difficult to defend, the Cornovii worked more closely with the Romans than did other peoples; they were the only British people who gave their name to a unit in the Imperial auxiliary troop. They may have given their name to *Cornwall.

Cornu. Legendary great black bird that lived in St Patrick's Purgatory on *Lough Derg. According to oral tradition, Cornu was first a demon that St Patrick turned into a bird.

Cornubia. Ancient British kingdom in Armorica, the Breton peninsula, in Roman times. It occupied a territory coextensive with the later petty kingdom of *Cornouaille, south of the River Elorn to the Elle. Less frequently, Cornubia is a latinized name for early *Cornwall.

Cornwall. [Early Brit. *Cornovii*; Germ. *-wall*, foreigner; late Brit. *Cornouia*, latinized to *Cornubia*; cf. Corn. *Kernow*, W *Cernyw*; archaic Eng. *Kernyu*]. A county, earlier duchy, occupying 1,369 square miles on a peninsula in south-western England; with a population of about 450,000, Cornwall is the fifth largest Celtic culture in Europe. The region was a part of the kingdom of *Dumnonia in the 8th century. Prior to the 6th century Irish freebooters raided the peninsula, leaving settlements, and Irish missionaries later evangelized it. As the Duchy of Cornwall in medieval and early modern times, divided from England by the Tamar River, the region retained Celtic language and customs in spite of its powerful Saxon neighbours. The Cornish language [Corn. *Kernewek*] is *Brythonic and closely related to Welsh and to Breton (compare the words for 'oak': W derwen; Corn. derowen; Bret. dervenn). Some Cornish names appear as glosses in early Latin gospels. The gospels themselves began to be translated into Cornish as early as the 10th century, and mystery plays in Cornish survive from the 15th.

The language was spoken until the mid-18th and has been 'revived' by enthusiasts in the 20th. Collections of lore from Cornish tradition did not appear until the mid-19th century, with Robert Hunt's *Popular Romances of the West of England* (London, 1865) and William Bottrell's *Traditions and Hearthside Stories of West Cornwall* (Penzance, 1870). Several sites in Cornwall, such as *Tintagel and *Kelliwic, have rich Arthurian associations; and Cornwall is also the reputed home of King *Mark and *Tristan. See Bibliography under 'Cornish' for collections of Cornish traditions. Ir. An Corn; ScG A' Chòrn, Cornghall; Manx Yn Chorn; Bret. Kernev-Veur.

Coronation Stone. Another name for the Stone of Scone; see LIA FÁIL.

Coronians. Variant spelling of *Coraniaid.

Corotiacus. See MARS (Corotiacus).

Coroticus. See CEREDIG WLEDIG.

Corpre. Variant spelling of *Cairbre.

corrbolg. An Irish word for *crane bag.

Corrib. See LOUGH CORRIB.

Corrievreckan, Corry Vreckan [Ir. and ScG *coire brecáin*, cauldron of Brecáin (personal name)]. Name given to two whirlpools, the more celebrated of which is between the islands of Jura and Scarba in the Inner Hebrides; the second is between Rathlin Island and the mainland of north Northern Ireland. The Scottish Corrievreckan is named for Brecáin, Brecon, or Brechin, a hero described in the **Book of Ballymote* as having perished here with fifty ships. Both are known popularly as 'the cauldron of the old woman', a possible association with *Mórrígan.

corrigan. Variant spelling of *korrigan.

Corroi map Dayry. Welsh spelling of *Cú Roí mac Dáiri.

Corry Vreckan. Variant of *Corrievreckan.

Córus Cerda. See IMBAS FOROSNAI.

cosmogony. Also known as creation myth; a mythological explanation for the creation and evolution of the universe. Several ancient commentators, including Julius *Caesar, testify that the Celts had a cosmogony, but except for a line quoted in *Strabo (1st cent. AD) that the Celts believed in the indestructibility of the world, no traces survive, although Irish and Welsh flood legends imply a re-creation of the universe. Some tantalizing echoes of a cosmogony appear in the Scottish Gaelic of Cape Breton; see 'A Gaelic Tale of the Milky Way', recited by J. N. MacNeil, ed. and trans. J. Shaw, *Cape Breton's Magazine*, 19 (June 1978), 31.

Of lesser note are the purported bardic beliefs recorded by Llewelyn Siôn in *Barddas* (late 16th cent.). Siôn's vision contains elements borrowed from Christianity as well as from gnostic and probably also from Oriental traditions. Although *Barddas* has been scorned by learned commentators as representing the views of only one idiosyncratic individual, its text has been edited and translated by J. A. Williams ap Ithel, Society for the Publication of Ancient Welsh Manuscripts, No. 7 (Abergavenny, 1862).

cosmology. See COSMOGONY.

Country of . . . A translation of the Irish *tír*. For the Country of Youth, see TÍR NA NÓG.

Couril. A gnome of Brittany, much like the *goric, found especially around the ruins of Tresmalouen.

Courtship of . . . See TOCHMARC . . .

Covac. Anglicization of *Cobthach.

Coventina. Name for a British goddess worshipped during the Roman occupation. A well was dedicated to her near Hadrian's Wall at what is now Carrawborough, south Northumberland. Surviving reliefs portray her as a kind of water-nymph. Excavations at her well in 1876 uncovered a cache of 14,000 ancient coins.

cow. The mature female of cattle appears often in Celtic narrative and visual art, although not so differently from other European traditions. If cattle were once worshipped, as we believe, their earlier status attaches more to the male of the species; see BULL. Cattle were always valued possessions, among both human and otherworldly society; this was especially true of herding societies, such as that of early Ireland. The agnomen of *Brian Bórama (Boru) testifies to his wealth [Ir. *bórama*, cow-countings (?), i.e. tribute]. A bóaire [cow-noble, stock owner] was a freeman. No evidence of a cult of the cow survives, although it is suggested in the minor Continental goddess *Damona and the etymology of *Boand, goddess of the *Boyne. The Welsh *Triads speak of three prominent cows of Britain, implying a legend about cows not known to us.

Important female figures having strong associations with cows are Boand, *Brigit, *Flidais, *Mórrígan, and *Verbeia. The magical cow of Irish folk tradition was *Glas Ghaibhleann, and its counterpart in Scottish Gaelic tradition was *Glas Ghaibhnann. The hornless fairy cattle of the Scottish Highlands are the *Crodh Mara. The fairy cattle of Wales are known as *gwartheg y llyn. Otherworldly or fairy cows are usually thought to be white with red ears.

The Druimin Donn Dílis: The Faithful Brown, Whitebacked Cow, is a poetic name for Ireland. According to Irish place-name legend, three cows once emerged from the sea, Bó Finn [white cow], Bó Dub [black cow], and Bó Derg [red cow]. They scattered across the island, the black going south, the red going north, and the white going straight across; this accounts for the many Irish town names beginning 'Bó- '. The word for cow in both Old and Modern Irish is bó; ScG bò; Manx booa; W bu, buwch; Corn. bugh; Bret. ejen [the animal], bevin (the meat of the animal). See also BULL.

Cowshra Mend Macha. Anglicization of *Cúscraid Menn.

Craddock, Cradog. Variant spellings of *Caradog.

Cráebderg [Ir., ruddy branch]. One of three royal residences of *Conchobar mac Nessa. Severed heads and spoils of war were kept here. See also CRÁEBRUAD.

Cráebruad, Cráeb Ruad, Craobh Ruadh, Craob Rua, Crave Rua, Crevroe, etc. [Ir., red branch]. One of three royal residences of *Conchobar mac Nessa, and the one most often used for large assemblies. The hall appears to have taken its name from the large roofbeam or 'branch' which may have been painted. Weapons were not allowed in the hall, to reduce the incidence of contests between those assembled; instead, weapons were kept in the residence known as Téte Brec [Twinkling Hoard]. The usual English translation is Red Branch (cf. the third residence, Cráebderg [ruddy branch]). In 19th-century texts, the phrase 'Red Branch' might indicate both the royal residence and the warriors or 'knights' most often seen there. 'Red Branch Cycle' was sometimes used as a substitute for *Ulster Cycle. See Tomás Ó Broin, *Éigse*, 15 (1973), 103–13. The townland of Creeveroe or Creevroe, Northern Ireland, may echo the name of Cráebruad.

Craftine, Craftiny. Variant spellings of *Craiphtine.

craftsman. In the Celtic countries the concept of craftsman [Ir. *ceardaí, saor*; W *crefftwr*] would include artisan, carpenter, potter, or wright, but does not always include smith [Ir. *gabha*; W *gof*]. The craftsman or carpenter of the *Tuatha Dé Danann in Ireland is *Luchta, who frequently works with *Goibniu, a weaponmaker, wright, or smith, and *Credne, a metalsmith. Goibniu was known as *Gobbán Saor [Ir., Gobbán the wright or craftsman] in folk-tales. *Partholón in the *Lebor Gabála* [Book of Invasions], is the chief of every craft. The epithet of *Lug Lámfhota is *Samildánach [possessor of many talents or crafts]. Llassar Llaes Gyfnewid, the possessor of the *cauldron of regeneration in *Manawydan*, the third branch of the *Mabinogi*, was known for his craftsmanship.

Crageevil, Craglee. Anglicizations of *Craig Liath, the fairy residence of *Aíbell.

Craiftine. Variant spelling of *Craiphtine.

Craig Liath, Crageevil, Craglee, Craiglee, Creag Liath [Ir., grey rock]. A 40-feet rock about 1 mile from Killaloe, Co. Clare, with rich associations in Irish folklore. It was long thought to be the fairy palace of *Aíbell.

Craig y Ddinas [W, rock city, fort (?)]. Place-name given to two ruins in Wales: (1) a Roman camp 7 miles SW of the town of Caernarfon, *Gwynedd; (2) a British fort, 5 miles N of Barmouth, Gwynedd (until 1974, Merionethshire). The name has Arthurian associations, and is a supposed burial-site of the faithless *Blodeuedd.

Craignish. [ScG, rocky place]. A region on the west coast of north Strathclyde (until 1974, *Argyllshire), just south of the modern town of Kilmelfort that was once a reservoir of folklore; includes peninsula, loch, and castle. See *Craignish Tales*, the first volume of *Waifs and Strays in Celtic Tradition*, ed. A. Campbell (London, 1889).

Craiphtine, Craiftine, Craftine, Craftiny. A widely known harper of early Irish narrative; he is sometimes credited with the discovery of the harp, which he fashioned from a willow tree. Craiphtine is much associated with *Labraid Loingsech, a legendary early invader of Ireland, and may be, as some commentators have suggested, a double for him. By playing his harp, Craiphtine cures Labraid Loingsech of dumbness; he also reveals the secret of Labraid's deformity of equine ears. Craiphtine's music lulls to sleep the garrison at *Dind Ríg, allowing the capture of that fortress. Earlier Craiphtine sets music to the love-lay of *Muiriath and carries it to Labraid in exile. Craiphtine's own wife, Scenb, is unfaithful.

crane. The large wading bird with long legs, neck, and bill of the family *Gruidae* has widespread representation in Celtic tradition. It appears to have been perceived as a transformed human, usually a woman. Carved figures of cranes appear on Gaulish monuments dedicated to *Esus. The ancient Britons, reported Julius *Caesar (1st cent. BC), refused to eat the bird's flesh for fear that it had been human in an earlier life. Giraldus Cambrensis (12th cent.) observed the same taboo in Ireland. Representations of the crane appear in Celtic iconography as early as the *Urnfield period (*c.*800 BC), although the nature of possible early cults is imperfectly known. The crane of the Continental Celts may have had associations with healing. Those cranes not thought to be transformed humans were perceived as parsimonious and unpleasant. To see a crane was thought to be ill luck to a battle-bound warrior. In some representations the crane is confused with the *egret, also celebrated in Celtic tradition but with different associations.

A number of cranes are known in Celtic narratives, of whom the most important is probably *Aífe (3). She was transformed into a crane by a jealous rival, and *Manannán mac Lir, sometimes described as her 'husband', used her skin to make the *crane bag. *Midir of Brí Léith owned three cranes. A lone crane lives on the isle of Inishkea near Erris, Co. Mayo, and will remain there until the end of time. *Fionn mac Cumhaill is associated with cranes in several stories from oral tradition, and is the inheritor of the crane bag. St *Colum Cille was described as having transformed two women into cranes when he was evangelizing Scotland.

The *glám dícenn [Ir., poet's execration],

an extempore satire, required the speaker to stand on one foot with one arm extended and one eye closed, i. e. like a crane. The word for crane in Old Irish is corr; ModIr. corr mhóna; ScG còrra-mhonaidh; Manx coar; W garan; Corn. garan; Bret. garan. See Anne Ross, *Pagan Celtic Britain* (London, 1967), 279–92.

crane bag [Ir. *corrbolg*]. The celebrated bag of Irish tradition was made by *Manannán mac Lir and contained many treasures. Aífe (3) is transformed into a crane by a jealous rival, Iuchra; she subsequently spends 200 years in the household of Manannán mac Lir. When she dies, he uses her skin to hold things precious to him. These included his knife and shirt, the king of Scotland's shears, the king of *Lochlainn's helmet, the bones of *Assal's swine, and the girdle of the great whale's back. At high tide the treasures are visible in the sea, but at ebb tide they vanish. Modern commentators have speculated that the bag contained the letters of the *ogham alphabet used in writing before the introduction of Christianity. The ogham ciphers may have been suggested by the legs of flying cranes. The bag has many owners, including *Lug Lámfhota and *Liath Luachra (1), from whom it is obtained by *Fionn mac Cumhaill.

Crann Buí, Buidhe [Ir., yellow tree]. The yellow-hafted spear, one of three spears of the hero *Diarmait.

crannóg 1. [Ir. *crann*, tree, timber]. Ancient fortified lake dwellings built on pilings or an island, found in Ireland, Scotland, and Wales. There are more than 300 crannógs at Lough Gara, Co. Roscommon. See also DÚN; LISS; RATH.

2. Variant spelling of (St) *Carantoc (or Carannog).

Craobh Rua, Ruadh. ModIr. spelling of *Cráebruad.

Crarae. Chambered cairn or tombs on the west side of Loch Fyne, north Strathclyde (until 1974, *Argyllshire), the most impressive to be found in Scotland. Excavated 1955–7.

Crave Rua, Rue. Anglicizations of *Cráebruad.

creation myths, legends. See COSMOGONY.

Créd, Créde, Crédh, Credhe, Créidhe. A name borne by many famous ladies of Irish narrative and history, most notably by two unrelated tragic lovers. See CRÉIDE.

Créd 1. Fairy lover of the *Fenian hero *Cáel. A daughter of Cairbre, king of Ciarraige [*Kerry], she is wooed by Cáel, who wins her with the excellence of his poetry. Before *Cath Fionntrágha [the Battle of Ventry], she presents each of the Fenians with a special battle-dress. They are ineffective, though, and Cáel is killed. When Créd sees her lover in his grave, she takes her own life by lying beside him at his burial. Many love-songs are attributed to her, and one is recounted in **Acallam na Senórach* [The Colloquy of the Ancients].

2. The mistress of *Cano mac Gartnáin, a king of Scotland. A daughter of *Guaire, king of *Connacht, and wife of *Marcán, king of *Uí Maine, she is smitten with Cano when he pays a visit to the kingdom. After her tryst with Cano is thwarted, she dashes her head against a rock at Lough Crede. In later times the O'Connors of Connacht claimed her as an ancestress.

Credne, Creidne, Creidhne. Often with epithet, Credne Cerd [Ir., craftsman, artisan]. A divine artificer of the *Tuatha Dé Danann, usually working in bronze but also in brass and gold. Together with *Goibniu, the *smith, and *Luchta, the wright or carpenter, he was a part of na trí dée Dána [the three craft gods of the Danann]. The three of them make the weapons with which the Tuatha Dé Danann defeat the *Fomorians. Credne makes rivets for spears, hilts for swords, and bosses and rims for shields. See also CRAFTSMAN.

Creiddylad, Creuddylad, Creidylad, Creudylad, Crieddlad, Kreiddylat. Daughter of *Lludd Llaw Ereint, and sometimes called by the patronymic Ferch Lludd. In **Culhwch ac Olwen* she is referred to as 'the most majestic maiden who ever lived'. Each *Calan Mai [May Day] *Gwythyr fab Greidawl and *Gwyn ap Nudd contest for her. This came about because Gwynn had abducted her before she had a chance to sleep with Gwythyr, her intended. Gwyn's being the son of *Nudd (a double for Lludd) is never an issue in the story. *Arthur, disgusted with the enmity between Gwyn and Gwythyr, condemns them to continual combat. The Latin equivalent of her name is Cordelia.

Créide. Also known as Créide Fírálaind [Ir., Créide the Truly Beautiful]. Daughter of Fidech, she aids *Art in his search for

*Delbcháem in *Echtrae Airt meic Cuinn [The Adventure of Art Son of Conn]. May be the same name as *Créd.

Creidhne, Creidne. Variant spellings of *Credne.

Creidylad. Variant spelling of *Creiddylad.

Creirwy. Daughter of *Tegid the Bald and his wife *Ceridwen, she was described as 'the loveliest nymph of the earth'. Her brothers were the ugly *Afagddu and the handsome *Morfran. See also TALIESIN.

Cremthann. Variant spelling of *Crimthann.

Creones. Variant spelling of Cerones; see PICTS.

Crescent, Bloody. See CROM CRÚAICH.

Creuddylad, Creudylad. Welsh spellings of *Creiddylad.

Crevroe. Anglicization of *Cráebruad.

Crích Cualann [Ir. *crich*, boundary, territory, etc.]. Name in Old Irish narratives for *Cualu, running from the River Liffey to Arklow, roughly coextensive with the modern county of Wicklow, south-east of Dublin.

Cridenbél, Cridhenbhéal. An ugly, blind satirist in the household of the *Dagda, as described in **Cath Maige Tuired* [The (Second) Battle of Mag Tuired]. When Cridenbél demands the three best bits of Dagda's food, the ruler's health suffers. Dagda gives him three gold coins instead, and Cridenbél dies. When the satirist is cut open and the gold coins are found, the Dagda is presumed not to have poisoned him.

Crimhthann. Variant spelling of *Crimthann.

Crimthann, Crimthan, Criomthann, Criofan, Crimhthann, Cremthann, Criomhthann [Ir., fox]. One of the most popular names in early Ireland, borne by many kings of *Munster, at least ten figures in the *Fenian Cycle, and at least one saint. The best-known is probably *Crimthann Mór mac Fidaig, the pre-Patrician king. In addition, *Colum Cille was named Crimthann before he adopted a Christian name.

Crimthann 1. Fosterling of *Diarmait, the king of *Tara. Diarmait's wife *Becfola lusts after Crimthann and plans to elope with him, but cannot when he will not travel on Sunday.

2. A king of *Leinster raised to power by *Conn Cétchathach [Ir., of the Hundred Battles]. *Cumhall, *Fionn's father, makes war on both Conn and Crimthann, provoking the battle of *Cnucha.

Crimthann Cass. A king of *Connacht, the father of *Lóegaire, cited in **Echtrae Lóegairi* [The Adventure of Lóegaire].

Crimthann mac Énna. King of the *Lagin who expanded his power over neighbouring peoples in the 5th century. His father was Énna Censelach. According to the Annals, Crimthann was slain in either 483 or 485.

Crimthann mac Fidaig. See CRIMTHANN MÓR MAC FIDAIG.

Crimthann Már. Variant spelling of *Crimthann Mór mac Fidaig.

Crimthann Mór. Legendary ancestor of the Osraige [*Ossory], occupying a territory coextensive with the modern county of Kilkenny. Distinguish from *Crimthann Mór mac Fidaig.

Crimthann Mór mac Fidaig. Also Crimthann Már, Crimthann mac Fidig, Crimthann mac Fidhaigh, etc. Shadowy king of pre-Patrician Ireland, third in line before the *Lóegaire who disputes with the evangelist. He is described as being of *Munster stock and unrelated to other kings at *Tara; he would have just preceded *Niall Noígiallach [Ir., of the Nine Hostages]. Although his name appears in many Irish records, Crimthann's historicity is, in the words of T. F. O'Rahilly, 'unworthy of credence'. His reputed sister *Mongfhind is clearly supernatural. He perishes through the sorcery of another supernatural woman. The cannibalistic *Eithne Uathach [Horrible, Dreadful] is sometimes described as his daughter. The fortress built by the Irish near the River Dee in Britain, *Dind Traduí, sometimes carries the name *Dún Crimthainn in allusion to Crimthann Mór mac Fidaig. This should be distinguished from another fortress named Dun Crimthainn at *Howth named for *Crimthann Nia Náir. See also *Aided Chrimthaind Maic Fhidaig* [The Death of Crimthann mac Fidach], ed. Whitley Stokes, *Revue Celtique*, 24 (1903), 172–89.

Crimthann Nia Náir [Ir., honourable champion (?), reticent nephew (?), Nár's man (?)]. Son of *Lugaid Riab nDerg [Ir., red stripes], incestuously begotten with his mother *Clothra, who had lain with her brothers *Finn Emna to produce Lugaid; before this conception she visited the *Otherworld and ate divine food. In another story he is slain when he attempts to kill *Cúchulainn. A fortress at *Howth, *Dún Crimthann, was named for him; distinguish from another of the same name in Britain named for *Crimthann Mór mac Fidaig.

Criofan. ModIr. variant spelling of *Crimthann.

Crion. Breton gnomes thought to inhabit the ruins at Tresmalouen. They appear to be related to the better-known *gorics.

Croagh Patrick, Cro Patrick; also Cruachán Aigle [Ir. *Cruach Phádraig*, Patrick's stack or cone]. Ireland's Holy Mountain, a quartzite ridge, 2,510 feet high, rising above Clew Bay, 6 miles WSW of Westport, Co. Mayo. Popularly called 'The Reek', Croagh Patrick has long been the site of an annual pilgrimage held the last Sunday in July, a day associated with the *Lughnasa festival but locally called Domhnach Chrom Dubh [Crom Dubh's Sunday]. *Patrick is thought to have fasted forty days at the summit, and while there to have banished the serpents from Ireland. Lough na Corra near the south base of the mountain is thought to have been formed by a demon named Corra driven there by St Patrick. Several sites on the mountain are thought to be sacred to the saint.

Cróchan. Variant spelling of *Cruachain.

Cróchnat, Cróchnait [cf. Ir. *cróch*, saffron, red]. The mother of *Diarmait and *Oscar in *Fenian ballads. Elsewhere the mother of Diarmait is *Cochrann.

crodh mara [ScG, cattle of the sea]. The Highland fairy cattle or sea cattle, thought to inhabit fresh and salt water on the west coast of Scotland. They are less dangerous than the *each uisce. Hornless, they are generally of dun colour; those near Skye may be red and speckled but described as black. The bulls of the crodh mara may mate with mortal cows and will improve the stock. See also GWARTHEG Y LLYN, the fairy cattle of Wales. Folk motifs: B184.2.2.2; F241.2.

Croghan. Variant spelling of *Cruachain.

Crom Crúaich, Cromm Crúaich, Cróich, Cruach, Crooach, Kerman Kelstach [OIr., bloody crescent, crook], also known as Cenn Crúaich, etc. [bloody head, chief (?); lord of the mound (?)]. The chief idol of pagan Ireland as described in Christian accounts of pre-Patrician history. It was thought to stand in *Mag Slécht [the plain of adoration or prostrations], in Co. Cavan, near the present village of Ballymagauran; often associated with the Killycluggin Stone from Cavan, now in the National Museum, Dublin. The central idol was gold, surrounded by twelve others of stone. First worshipped by a shadowy king known as *Tigernmas, Crom is described as the principal god of every Irish people before the coming of St *Patrick. To him was sacrificed on each *Samain the first-born of every family and the first-born of every livestock.

Although St Patrick and other evangelists are described as smashing stone idols, the latter are not always named as Crom Crúaich. The portrayal of the cruel idol demanding human sacrifices may be an echo of the scriptural accounts of Tophet and Moloch, as Eoin MacNeill has suggested. Nevertheless, certain stones are still accorded magical powers in isolated parts of the Céltic world. The name 'Crom' lends itself to a mild oath, comparable to 'by Jove' or 'by Jingo', in both spoken Irish and English. In oral tradition Crom Crúaich was euhemerized to *Crom Dubh. The smashing of the idol is associated with both the last Sunday in July and the first Sunday in August, called the *Lughnasa, Garland Sunday, or Domhnach Chrom Dubh.

Crom Dubh, Cromm Dubh [Ir., black crescent]. A legendary pre-Christian Irish chieftain as euhemerized in oral tradition from *Crom Cruaich. According to the stories, St *Patrick overcomes Crom Dubh in evangelizing the island. The defeat of Crom Dubh is commemorated in the naming of Domhnach Chrom Dubh: Crom Dubh's Sunday, another name for *Lughnasa, or Garland Sunday, the last Sunday in July or the first Sunday in August.

cromlech [W *crom*, bent, bowed; *llech*, flat stone; Ir. *crom*, stooped; *leac*, flagstone]. Preferred Welsh and Cornish word for the prehistoric structure found in all Celtic countries consisting of a large flat stone supported by three or more upright stones; called *dolmen in English descriptions of sites in Ireland and Brittany. The word 'cromlech' may also describe a dolmen of more circular construction. When the word is borrowed into French usage, it may also describe a squared or circular assemblage of dolmens, as at *Carnac in *Brittany.

Crónánach [OIr., humming, purring, crooning; a performer of *crónán*, crooning, droning, humming, buzzing]. In the *Fenian Cycle, an enormous, black, misshapen churl who comes unbidden to *Fionn's hunting mound and reveals his destiny to him. He brought out two pipes 'so that wounded men and women in travail would have fallen asleep at the exquisite music which he made'. When light fell upon Crónánach in the morning he was transformed so that he had the beauty, charm, and demeanour of a high king. (In early Irish law the singers of crónán were bond or slave musicians.)

Cronk-y-Keillown. Another name for *Tynwald Hill.

Cronnchu. Variant spelling of *Crunniuc.

Crooach, Crooagh. Anglicizations of either *Crom Crúaich or *Cruachain.

crow. The several species of the large, raucous bird with glossy black plumage (genus *Corvus*) are often cited in Celtic narratives and usually have associations with war and death. The hooded or grey crow (genus *Corvus cornex*), carrion crow (*Corvus corone*), rook (*Corvus frugilegus*), and raven (genus *Corvus corax*) are not always perceived separately. Several figures take the form of the crow, including the Irish goddesses *Badb, *Mórrígan, and *Macha. When she perches on the shoulder of the dying *Cúchulainn, Mórrígan takes the form of a hooded crow. The crow-goddess *Cathubodua was an ancient Continental patroness of battle. *Cornu, a great black bird that may or may not have been a crow, was sent to St Patrick's Purgatory. The Welsh *Brân means crow; the Irish *Fuinche means scald-crow, *Morfran means great crow. The killing of a crow in winter, the spilling of blood on the snow, introduces the *black–white–red motif that sends such lovers as *Peredur and *Conchobar on their quests. ModIr. for crow is préachán or feannóg; hooded crow, feannóg dubh. ScG for crow is feannag; Manx craue, fannag; W brân; Corn. brān, cana; Bret. kavan.

Cruach. See CROM CRÚAICH.

Cruach Phádraig. Irish form of *Croagh Patrick.

Cruacha 1, Cróchan. The maidservant of the elder *Étaín, who accompanies her mistress when she is abducted by *Midir. The cave of *Cruachain in *Connacht is named for her, according to some commentators.

2. The mother of *Medb and therefore consort of *Eochaid Feidlech. The fortress of *Cruachain may have been named for her, according to some commentators.

Cruachain, Crúachu, Cruachan, Cruachain Aí, Crúachán, Croghan, Rathcroghan. Also known as Uaimh Chrúachan [Ir., the cave of Crúachu] and Druim na nDruadh [Ir., the ridge of the druids]. The great fortress of *Connacht as portrayed in many early narratives, including the **Táin Bó Cuailnge* [Cattle Raid of Cooley], where it is the seat of power for *Medb and *Ailill. The fortress of the stories is identified with Rathcroghan, an extensive archaeological site near Tulsk, north Co. Roscommon. In its antiquity and frequency of reference in Old Irish literature, Cruachain is the counterpart of *Tara in *Meath, *Emain Macha in *Ulster, and *Dún Ailinne in *Leinster.

The fortress of Medb and Ailill is usually described as both splendid and extensive, with seven compartments for residents. Thus in many stories a reference to Cruachain implies both the luxury and the power of the province of Connacht, which in modern times has been Ireland's poorest. Also celebrated in story is the cave at Cruachain, sometimes known as the 'Hell's Gate of Ireland'. In its fearful aspects it is well described in *Echtra *Nerai* [The Adventure of Nera]. From the cave issues forth Aillén (2), who devastates the landscape of Ireland. From the cave at Cruachain also comes a flock of white birds whose breath withers vegetation, as well as three predatory cats and a herd of wild pigs so numerous they cannot be counted.

Archaeologists have suggested that Rathcroghan was built by *Goidelic invaders who used it as their capital in subjugating the native population. The site is about 2 miles square, and contains a great number of earthworks of different kinds as well as mounds that may be passage-graves. There are also five concentric fortified circles. Different points in the site have been given fanciful names by amateur archaeologists over the years that are not necessarily supported by irrefutable evidence, 'Medb's Treasury', 'Medb's Mill', etc. One circular enclosure has been rather grandly named Reilig na Rígh [Ir., Cemetery of the Kings], although recent excavation has not shown it to be a burial place. A 7-feet-high standing stone is said to mark the grave of King *Dathí, the last pagan king of Ireland. At several points on the site are extensive *ogham inscriptions.

Cruachan, Falls of. A romantic cascade in Pass of Brander, at the head of Loch Awe in north Strathclyde (until 1974, *Argyllshire).

Cruachán Aigle. Variant form of *Croagh Patrick.

Crúaich. See CROM CRÚAICH.

Cruaidín Catutchenn. Another name for An *Claidheamh Soluis [the sword of light].

crúba leomhain. [Ir., lion's feet]. Irish name for vervain.

Cruinn, Cruinniuc. Variant spellings for *Crunniuc.

Cruithín na Cuan. A kind of city in the wondrous land of *Emain Ablach.

Cruithne 1. Beautiful daughter of the master smith Lóchán of Cuilleann. She is described as being so smitten with *Fionn mac Cumhaill that she becomes his 'wife' shortly after seeing the hero.

2. An Irish name for the *Picts.

Cruithni, Cruithnig. Irish names for the *Picts.

Crundchu, Crunnchu. Variant spellings of *Crunniuc.

Crunniuc, Cronnchu, Cruinn, Cruinniuc, Crundchu, Crunnchu. Sometimes with the patronymic mac Agnomain. A wealthy farmer of *Ulster in the *Ulster Cycle who marries *Macha (3). It is Crunniuc's boast that Macha can outrun a horse which brings her unfortunate contest when she is in the final hours of her pregnancy. Macha's subsequent curse brings on the debility of the Ulstermen.

Cruthin. Variant of Cruithne, an Irish name for the *Picts.

Cú, Cu. A son of Cáinte and brother of *Cian and Cethe.

Cú, Cú-. The Irish Cú, Cú- [hound] is a part of the names of several early figures, both legendary and historical. The names are alphabetized here letter by letter, regardless of whether Cú is separated; e.g. 'Culhwch' comes before 'Cú Roí'.

cuachag [ScG, girl (with curly hair); curl; cuckoo]. A kind of *fuath or water-sprite localized in the central Highlands (until 1974, Inverness-shire), Scotland. Loch Cuaich, 8 miles SW of Kingussie, is named for the cuachag. Like all the fuathan, it can be dangerous.

Cuailnge, Cualnge. Anglicized Cooley, Quelgny, etc. An early name for a hilly peninsula in *Ulster that is coextensive with the modern Cooley in north-eastern Co. Louth (in *Leinster), between Carlingford Lough and Dundalk harbour. This early place-name is cited in the title of the Irish epic **Táin Bó Cuailnge* [Cattle Raid of Cooley]. Much of the action takes place in Cuailnge, most notably *Cúchulainn's single-handed defence of Ulster against the armies of *Connacht.

Cualu, Cuala, Cualann. Name of a former territory in *Leinster from the River *Liffey to Arklow, roughly coextensive with modern Co. Wicklow, including the celebrated monastic centre of *Glendalough. The area takes its name from the Cualainn, an early people who were there in *Ptolemy's time (2nd cent. AD). Crích Cualann is the district of Cualu; Slige Chualann is the way or road to Cualu. See Henry Morris, 'Ancient Cualu: Where Was It?', *Journal of the Royal Society of Antiquaries of Ireland*, 68 (1937), 280–3.

Cúar, Cuare. One of two sons of the amazonian warrior and sorceress *Scáthach, of the Isle of *Skye.

Cuartag Mhòr a' Chuain [ScG, great whirlpool of the ocean]. An epithet of the fabulous beast *Cìrein Cròin.

Cubbie Roo. Ruined 12th-century stone castle on the isle of Wyre in the Orkneys, thought to be one of the oldest surviving medieval buildings in Scotland. Modern commentators have identified Cubbie Roo with Kolbein Hruga of the *Orkney Saga*.

Cubert son of Daere. Welsh hero whose name is cited by Culhwch to Arthur in a run of heroes' names in **Culhwch ac Olwen*. Modern commentators have suggested that he may be a counterpart of the Irish *Cú Roí mac Dáiri. See Patrick Sims-Williams, *Bulletin of the Board of Celtic Studies*, 39 (4) (May 1982), 608.

Cúcán. Diminutive of *Cúchulainn used in the **Táin Bó Cuailnge* [Cattle Raid of Cooley] and elsewhere.

Cúchulainn, Cú Chulainn, Cúchulain, Cú Chulaind, Cuchulinn, Cuculain Cúcán, etc. [Ir., hound of Culann; hound of the smith]. The greatest hero in early Irish literature and the principal hero of the *Ulster Cycle; along with *Lug Lámfhota and *Fionn mac Cumhaill, Cúchulainn is one of the three great heroes of early Ireland, all of whom may derive from a common source and may in fact be identical. The child of divine and human parents, Cúchulainn was first known as Sétanta and did not win the name by which we know him until he had performed heroic feats at the age of 7. Learned 19th-century commentators routinely compared him to *Hercules and Siegfried for feats of valour and supremacy over all contenders. Surviving stories about him are extensive, and he is the principal figure in **Táin Bó Cuailnge* [Cattle Raid of Cooley], the Irish epic. His characteristic quickness and small, dark stature have suggested to some commentators that Cúchulainn may be derived from Gaulish *Mercury, as described in *Caesar's commentaries (1st cent. BC). At one time he was thought to derive from the Gaulish god *Esus, although that assertion is now disputed. His birth-name, Sétanta, suggests a link with the early British people the Setantii, who were described by Ptolemy (2nd cent. AD). At times his portrayal suggests parallels with the earlier Celtic figure *Ogmios.

There are differing accounts of how Cúchulainn's mother *Deichtine happens to become pregnant with him. While she is grieving over the loss of a foster-son, she drinks some water with which a tiny creature passes into her mouth. Some versions assert that the creature is *Lug Lámfhota. Sleeping that night she dreamed she is visited by Lug. People hearing that she is pregnant did not know of a father, and think that she may have been violated by a drunken *Conchobar mac Nessa, her brother (or, in some versions, father). Conchobar gives Deichtine in marriage to *Sualtam mac Róich, but she is ashamed to enter his bed already pregnant. She becomes so sick that she spontaneously delivers the foetus within her, has her virginity restored, and so goes to her husband. The aborted foetus lives and is called Sétanta. For other versions of Cúchulainn's conception and birth, see DEICHTINE.

The leading men of Ulster wish to become foster-fathers to Sétanta. Rather than have them squabble over who should have precedence, Deichtine decides that seven of them should foster the child concurrently: (1) Sencha, to give eloquence and poetry; (2) *Blaí Briuga, to provide for material comfort; (3) *Fergus mac Róich, to take him on his knee; (4) *Amairgin, to be his teacher; (5) *Conall Cernach, to be his foster-brother and virtual twin; (6) *Findchóem, to be his wet nurse; and (7) Conchobar, to be his principal foster-father.

The story of Cúchulainn's boyhood deeds, as remembered by Fergus mac Róich, his tutor, forms a lengthy chapter early in the *Táin Bó Cuailnge*. At the beginning of these adventures, Cúchulainn still bears his name from birth, Sétanta. A key episode tells how he acquired his adult, heroic name while being fostered by Conchobar at *Emain Macha. The royal household has gone to visit a wealthy smith in *Cuailnge named *Culann, while Sétanta stays behind playing hurley. The guests at Culann's lonely mansion are making merry, knowing they are protected from intruders by a huge, ferocious dog. But in the midst of the laughter they hear a terrible sound. A late-arriving Sétanta, aged only 7, has killed the dog by smashing it against a doorpost. The guests cheer, but Culann is dismayed at the loss of his prized hound. Sétanta responds that he will raise another whelp to replace the guard dog, and will serve as the hound in the interim. The crowd applaud his generosity and call him the Hound: *Cú*, of Culann: *Chulainn*, the name he retained thenceforward.

Accounts of Cúchulainn's physical appearance differ, but he is most often seen as short, dark, beardless, and filled with high spirits. His hair is of three colours, brown at the roots, blood-red in the middle, and blond at the crown. In the *Táin* he is described as having four dimples in each cheek, each dimple being of a different colour: yellow, green, crimson, and blue. He has seven pupils in each eye, seven toes, and seven fingers, each with the grip of a hawk or gryphon. Despite these fearsome aspects of his appearance, he is conventionally described as handsome and attractive to women. Perhaps this is because readers of or listeners to early Irish literature did not necessarily visualize Cúchulainn as he was described. In any case, there is little in early literature to justify the somewhat Victorian representation of the hero in the much-photographed statue by Oliver Sheppard now housed at the General Post Office on O'Connell Street in Dublin.

In the *Táin* also, Fergus tells *Medb of Cúchulainn's superlative qualities. No raven is more ravenous, and no lion more ferocious. He can overcome all obstacles and barriers. In an aggressive burst of energy, he pounces on enemies in his distinctive *salmon leap, compared by modern commentators with the jump of a soccer player. Cúchulainn is also admired for his nimbleness and brilliance. Many Ulster warriors wish that Cúchulainn would get married so that their daughters would forget him. He chooses *Emer. Even before approaching her, Cúchulainn kills the three sons of *Nechtan, which results in the onset of his ríastrad [battle fury] (see below).

Emer's father *Forgall demands that Cúchulainn first be schooled by *Scáthach in distant Scotland before he is worthy of the daughter's hand. In truth, Forgall hopes that Cúchulainn will perish on the journey or be killed by Scáthach herself. Instead, Cúchulainn endears himself to the amazonian Scáthach and has a love affair with her colleague (or double) *Aífe. In Scotland he is also tutored by *Domnall Míldemail [the warlike] and his ugly daughter *Dornoll. When Cúchulainn returns from Scotland, he takes Emer as well as her sister by force along with much gold and silver. Despite such an unpromising beginning, Emer is usually seen as the hero's wife.

A number of other women are named as Cúchulainn's wives or lovers in different texts. After Emer the most commonly cited is *Eithne Ingubai, who may be but another name for Emer. He dallies with *Fand, the wife of *Manannán mac Lir; he consummates an affair with *Bláithíne (Blanid), the wife of *Cú Roí. He rewards *Étan (1) with a ring, so great is his pleasure in their night of lovemaking. Sometimes Cúchulainn is the object of love, as from the *female warrior *Cathach. He is also loved by *Derbforgaill, the tragic *swan maiden, and Uathach, Scáthach's daughter. But when *Mugain (2), queen of Ulster, bares her breasts before him and leads the beautiful women of Ulster to Cúchulainn, the hero averts his eyes. So great is his feeling from the episode that it takes three vats of iced water to cool him; the first he explodes, the second he boils, and the third he warms. His son is *Connla (1), unknowingly begotten upon *Aífe. In later literature he is ascribed a daughter, *Fínscoth.

Cúchulainn's chief weapon is his spear, the *Gáe Bulga. His usual sword is *Caladbolg, although in later oral tradition he is described as wielding the *Claidheamh Soluis [Ir., sword of light], which may also be known as Cruaidin Catutchenn. His favourite horse is the *Liath Macha [Grey of Macha], but he also likes *Saingliu or Dubh Sainglenn. His charioteer is Láeg. He has many associations with ravens and was once warned by two magical ravens, but he does not appear to have been a raven-god. Cúchulainn's homeland is *Mag Muirtheimne, a plain stretching north from the River *Boyne to *Cuailnge [Cooley] in what is today Co. Louth.

Before going into combat Cúchulainn goes through a transformation known as his ríastrad [battle fury, battle frenzy, contortion, warp spasm, etc.; gen. *ríastarthae*]. When this overtakes him, he becomes a fearsome figure such as has never been seen before. Every particle of him quivers like a bulrush in a running stream. His calves, hams, and heels shift to the front, and his feet and knees to the back, while the muscles of his neck stand out like the head of a baby. One eye is engulfed deep in his head, the other protrudes, his mouth meets his ears, foam pours from his jaws like the fleece of a three-year-old wether. The beats of his heart sound like the roars of a lion as he rushes to his prey. A column of dark blood spurts forth from his scalp and scatters in four directions, forming a mist of gloom. Then a projection emerges from Cúchulainn's head, like a horn but the size of man's fist; it is the *lón láith/laíd [light of the hero (?)], which signals that he is ready to fight.

Cúchulainn's best-known exploits are probably those recounted in Irish narratives summarized elsewhere in this volume. First among them is the Irish epic **Táin Bó Cuailnge* [Cattle Raid of Cooley], in which the hero single-handedly defends Ulster against the depredations of *Connacht, as led by Medb and *Ailill. A key episode in the *Táin* has Cúchulainn do battle at a ford with his friend *Ferdiad. In **Fled Bricrenn* [Briccriu's Feast] Cúchulainn is seen as the dominant Ulster hero, and he engages in a beheading contest with a challenging *giant. In **Aided Óenfhir Aífe* [The Tragic Death of Aífe's Only Son], Cúchulainn unwittingly kills his son,

Connla (1), whom he had begotten upon Aífe during his sojourn in Scotland. In *Serglige Con Culainn [The Wasting Sickness of Cúchulainn], the hero visits the Otherworld and is involved with Fand, the wife of *Manannán mac Lir. Cúchulainn's killing of the *one-eyed giant *Goll mac Carbada is widely commemorated in oral tradition.

Accounts of Cúchulainn's death vary. In the better-known, he is the victim of Medb's vengeance. When his allies and faithful horse are killed, Cúchulainn has himself chained to a pillar-post so that he may die standing up. He endures many wounds, but is not known to be dead until a raven alights on his head to take his eyes; oral tradition identifies this pillar-stone with one still standing in Knockbridge, Co. Louth. Sometimes the vengeance is of *Badb, whose father, *Cailitin, and all his male heirs Cúchulainn had killed. While he is being nursed from an illness by Niam (1), wife of Conall Cernach, who has become his mistress, Badb appears in the form of one of Niam's handmaidens and lures her away; she then assumes Niam's form and bids Cúchulainn begin the journey that will lead to his death. Another version of his death is told in *Brislech mór Maige Muirtheimne* [The Great Rout of Muirtheimne or The Death of Cúchulainn]. In this story Cúchulainn helps to bring about his end when he eats the meat of a cooked dog, as offered by three crones, in violation of a *geis [Ir., taboo]. Again, the hero's allies and horse are a part of the action; this death was thought to have taken place near Faughart, Co. Louth. In the fray *Lugaid mac Con Roí, the son of Cú Roí, sends a javelin through Cúchulainn's bowels but does not kill him. Cúchulainn retreats to a pillar, tying part of his armour to it so that, again, he may die standing up. Lugaid beheads Cúchulainn at the pillar, but is himself slain by *Conall Cernach who avenges his friend's death.

Editions of Irish stories about Cúchulainn may be found in Eleanor Hull, *The Cuchullin Saga* (London, 1898); Maria Tymoczko, *The Death Tales from the Ulster Cycle* (Dublin, 1981); T. P. Cross and C. H. Slover (eds.), *Ancient Irish Tales* (New York, 1936, 1969), 134–354. Among the many studies of the hero are Henri Gaidoz, 'Cúchulainn, Béowulf et Hercule', *Cinquantenaire de l'École Pratique des Hautes Études* (Paris, 1921), 131–56; Marie-Louise Sjoestedt, 'Légendes épiques irlandaises et monnaies gauloises; recherches sur la constitution de la légende de Cuchullin', *Études Celtiques*, 1 (1936), 1–77; Martin Huld, 'Cú Chulainn and his IE [Indo-European] Kin', *Zeitschrift für celtische Philologie*, 38 (1981), 238–41; Elizabeth Brewer, *From Cuchulain to Gawain* (Totowa, NJ, 1973). See further criticism under ULSTER CYCLE.

Accounts of Cúchulainn in English literature have reshaped the hero in many instances and, as they are more accessible than those in Irish, sometimes displace the original for some readers. Among the earliest was the character of *Cuchullin (sometimes Cuthullin) in *Macpherson's *Ossian* (1760). During the 19th century the works of Standish James O'Grady did much to romanticize the character for an increasingly nationalist readership; these include: *History of Ireland: Cuculain and His Contemporaries* (Dublin and London, 1880); *Cuculain: An Epic* (London, 1882); *The Coming of Cuculain* (London, 1894); and *The Triumph and Passing of Cuculain* (Dublin, 1920). The most widely read treatment in English is probably Lady Gregory's *Cuchulain of Muirthemne* (London, 1902; repr. Gerrards Cross, 1970). The most esteemed treatments in English are those of W. B. Yeats, especially the dramas *On Baile's Strand* (1904), *The Green Helmet* (1910), *At the Hawk's Well* (1917), *The Only Jealousy of Emer* (1919), and *The Death of Cuchulain* (1939), and the poems 'Cuchulain's Fight with the Sea' (1892) and 'Cuchulain Comforted' (1939). Some other English treatments are Suseen Varian, *Cúchulainn: A Cycle of Irish Plays* (Dublin, *c.*1910); Terence Gray, *Cuchulain: An Epic Drama of the Gael* (Cambridge, 1925); Morgan Llywelyn, *Red Branch* (popular novel) (New York, 1989); Kevin McCaffrey, *The Adventures of CuChulainn, Champion of Ulster* (juvenile fiction) (Dublin, 1989).

Cúchulainn's Leap. Place-name popularly ascribed to several sites in the Gaelic world. The most important Leap is a sheer-sided rectangular rock at Loop Head on the north side of the Shannon estuary, Co. Clare. According to the local story, Cúchulainn was fleeing an importunate female who did not leap as well as he did. Other place-names alluding to Cúchulainn are a bed, house, and grave, all near Anascaul on the *Dingle peninsula, Co. *Kerry, and the Cuchullin (or Cuillin) Hills in the south of the Isle of Skye.

Cuchullin, Cuthullin. Character in *Macpherson's *Ossian* (1760) based in part on the traditional hero *Cúchulainn. The son of Seuma and grandson of Cathbaid, Cuchullin is a wise and warlike druid. He is the brother of Slissama and the husband of Bragela. His strength is proverbial. In a memorable combat, he slays Feard.

cughtagh. Manx cave-dwelling spirit, once separate from but now apparently merged with the creature known as *buggane. The cughtagh may be a Manx relative of the ScG ciuthach.

Cuilenn, Cullen [Ir., wood of the holly tree]. A magical figure in the *Fenian Cycle. He is 'lord' or 'king' of a fairy mound or *sídh at *Sliab Cuilinn [Slieve Gullion] in Co. *Armagh. When *Fionn mac Cumhaill has been transformed into a feeble old man by taking a bath in a nearby lake, Cuilenn restores him and a colleague, Mac Reithe, with a drink from a golden cup that disappears as soon as the drink is finished. According to some stories, Fionn's supernatural knowledge comes from this drink. His daughters are *Áine (2) and Milucra.

cúilín, coolun, cooleen [Ir., hair or curl on the back of the head]. The custom in early Ireland of wearing the hair long and tied at the back of the neck has encouraged the use of Cúilín as an occasional poetic for Ireland; sometimes anglicized as Coolun, Cooleen, etc. This may be influenced by cúil-fhionn [fair-haired girl, attractive person, etc.]. There are several minor female figures named Cúilín, such as the daughter of *Conarán in *Fenian stories.

Cuimmíne, Cuimine, Cuimín, Cuimíne, Cumaine, Cumian [Ir., hypocoristic for Colum]. Name borne by several early Irish saints, the most notable of whom is Cuimmíne Fota, Fata, Foda, Fada [Long, Tall] (*c.*590–*c.*665), the founder of an abbey at Kilcummin, Co. Offaly. Cuimmíne's most important historical distinction is the introduction of the Roman computation of Easter; for this he was rebuked by the abbot of *Iona, who wished Christians to follow the Celtic computation favoured by *Colum Cille. A surviving hymn is attributed to him. In popular tradition he is thought to have been the product of an incestuous union between his father, *Fiachna (3), king of west Munster, and Fiachna's daughter, *Mugain (4). He is also the spiritual adviser of *Liadain who forbids her lovemaking with Cuirithir.

Cuimne, Cuimhne. Hag who helps *Mongán to retrieve his wife, *Dubh Lacha.

Cuirithir. The Abelard-like lover of *Liadain in the Irish story *Comrac Liadaine ocus Chuirithir*.

Culann, Culan, Cullan. A smith of the *Ulster Cycle who is best remembered for giving his name to *Cúchulainn. Culann was entertaining the nobles of Ulster when the late-arriving hero, still named Sétanta, killed the host's watchdog. In repentance Sétanta offered to replace the dog and serve watch himself in the interim, thus earning the name Cú [hound] Chulainn [of Culann]. Elsewhere in Ulster narrative Culann forged the sword, spear, and shield of *Conchobar mac Nessa. Some commentators have suggested that Culann may be a disguise for *Manannán mac Lir.

Cúldub, Cúldubh [Ir., black hair, black eye (?)]. Sometimes with the patronymic mac Fidga. A food-stealing villain killed by *Fionn mac Cumhaill in the *Fenian Cycle. Fionn slays him at *Sídh ar Femen [*Sliab na mBan], Co. Tipperary, as he is carrying a pig. He may be yet another persona of Fionn's antagonist *Goll mac Morna.

Culhwch ac Olwen. Welsh name for the 11th-century Arthurian narrative known in English as *Culhwch and Olwen*, also *Kilhwch*, *Kulhwch and Olwen*. *Culhwch* is one of the most important texts for the study of the Arthurian cycle because of its antiquity, its kinship with early Irish narrative, the roll-call of heroes associated with *Arthur, and its foreshadowing of themes which recur in later non-Celtic narratives. Whatever *Culhwch*'s interest as a story, it has attracted continuing attention because it is 'purely Celtic', i.e. lacking embellishments from Continental literature. Its main plot is known to folklorists as The Giant's Daughter, of which the most familiar in classical tradition is the story of Jason and Medea (Folk motifs: G530.2; E765.4.I.I.; H335). Although orthographical evidence suggests that the original narrative may have been composed before 1100, the only complete text is found in the *Red Book of Hergest* (*c.*1400); an incomplete text is found in the **White Book of Rhydderch* (*c.*1350–95).

The story begins when Cilydd, son of Celyddon Wledig [W *gwledig*, ruler, prince] seeks to marry a woman as well-born as himself. He chooses Goleuddydd, daughter of

Anlawdd Wledig. Pregnant soon after the wedding night, Goleuddydd becomes deranged and wanders through wild country, giving birth to her noble son in a pig-run and shortly afterwards dying. To find a new wife for himself, Cilydd kills the king of Doged and carries home his wife. In her unhappiness the step-mother curses Culhwch, prophesying that he will not touch woman until he has won Olwen, daughter of *Ysbaddaden, a crafty and powerful giant. Cilydd tells his son this task will be easy to accomplish if the boy will only seek help of King Arthur, a cousin; on meeting Arthur he should ask to have his hair trimmed. Hearing this, Culhwch, who has fallen in love with Olwen without having seen her, sets out for Arthur's court. Culhwch's arrival is evocative of *Lug Lámfhota's arrival at *Nuadu's court in **Cath Maige Tuired* [The (Second) Battle of Mag Tuired]. At first he is refused by Arthur's porter *Glewlwyd Gafaelfawr, but he persists until the king demands Culhwch be admitted. Culhwch asks that his hair be trimmed and recites a lengthy roll-call of Arthurian heroes including the children of *Dôn. So winning is Culhwch that Arthur agrees to help him in winning Olwen, and they are joined by *Cei, *Bedwyr, Cynddelig Cyfawydd, a guide, Gwrhyr Gwalstad Ieithoedd, an interpreter, and *Menw, an illusionist.

After a long journey Culhwch and Arthur meet the herdsman *Custennin, whose confidence is won with a gold ring; his wife proves to be the sister of Goleuddydd, Culhwch's mother. Both Custennin and his wife are concerned at reports that no one leaves Ysbaddaden's castle alive. None the less Culhwch, Arthur, and the company go on to the nearby castle, where Culhwch meets Olwen, whose name means 'flower track' because four white clovers spring up wherever she steps. Olwen accepts Culhwch's profession of love but says that she can not join him until he asks the permission of her father, Ysbaddaden. The giant is not receptive to guests. He throws three poisoned stone spears at Culhwch and Arthur's party, each one of which is turned back against the thrower. Thus wounded, Ysbaddaden hears Culhwch's entreaty. The father agrees to give his daughter's hand to Culhwch if he can accomplish forty apparently impossible tasks. Some are frivolous, such as finding honey nine times sweeter than that of the first swarm out of the hive. The first group of tasks require eight primary agricultural labours, such as ploughing waste land so that food might be grown, and five secondary labours to complete the ploughing. A second group of tasks pertain to the collaring and chaining of the great boar *Twrch Trwyth while enlisting the help of several foreign heroes. The boar must be made to yield his razor, scissors and comb. Culhwch agrees to each task rather insouciantly, and accomplishes thirteen of the original plus three not previously mentioned. The recitation of the tasks makes tedious reading, but handled by an exceptional storyteller they may have been engaging to early audiences. The hunting of Twrch Trwyth includes several place-name stories. Culhwch pursues the boar from Ireland to Wales, from Wales to Brittany, and from there to Cornwall. He seizes the razor and scissors at the mouth of the Severn, while Arthur's men capture the comb in Cornwall. These help the giant Ysbaddaden prepare for his daughter's marriage. At the end of the narrative Culhwch wins Olwen and spends the night with her.

The many names cited in *Culhwch ac Olwen* are perhaps more interesting to scholars today than is the narrative itself. Culhwch alone recites more than 200 names, including an invocation of Arthur's court. Some names appear frivolous, probably inventions of the author/redactor, such as the three maidservants Drwg [Bad], Gwaeth [Worse], and Gwaethaf Oll [Worst of All]. A handful of names are drawn from Irish sources. Some otherwise unfamiliar names imply a full but lost underlying tradition such as 'Teithi Hen son of Gwynnan, whose kingdom was overrun by the sea; he barely escaped and came to Arthur'. Because Teithi's knife can hold no haft, he becomes enfeebled and then dies. And the core of names represents characters deemed by modern commentators to be traditional.

Several stories in modern Irish oral tradition parallel *Culhwch ac Olwen* or The Giant's Daughter, most notably that tale known as The King of Ireland's Son. G. L. Kittredge noted that the motif of destiny sworn by an unhappy stepmother appears in a story collected from Co. Cork by Douglas Hyde in *An Sgéaluidhe Gaedhealach* (Dublin, 1901), 340–59. Ysbaddaden resembles the Irish *Balor in that his eyelids must be propped open. Many translations of *Culhwch ac Olwen* have been published in editions of the **Mabinogi*, e.g.

Patrick K. Ford, *The Mabinogi and Other Medieval Welsh Tales* (Berkeley and Los Angeles, Calif., 1977). Rachel Bromwich and D. Simon Evans (eds.), *Culhwch ac Olwen* (Cardiff, 1992). See also P. L. Henry, 'Culhwch and Olwen: Some Aspects of Style and Structure', *Studia Celtica*, 3 (1968), 30–8; Doris Edel, 'The Catalogues of *Culhwch and Olwen* and Insular Celtic Learning', *Bulletin of the Board of Celtic Studies*, 30 (1983), 253–67; Eric P. Hamp, 'Culhwch, the Swine', *Zeitschrift für celtische Philologie*, 41 (1986), 257–8; Rachel Bromwich et al. (eds.), *Arthur of the Welsh* (Cardiff, 1991), ch. 3. John Layard provides a Jungian reading in *A Celtic Quest: Sexuality and Soul in Individuation* (Dallas, 1975, 1985).

Cullan. Anglicized spelling of *Culann.

Cullen. Anglicized spelling of *Cuilenn.

Cumaine. Variant spelling of *Cuimíne.

Cumhall, Cumhal, Cumal, Cool [from the earlier Ir. *Umall*; initial C- elided from 'mac' in the patronymic mac Umaill/mac Cumhaill]. Father of *Fionn and leader of the Clan *Baíscne in the *Fenian Cycle. Cumhall sometimes bears the patronymic mac Trénmóir, although next to nothing survives of anyone with the name Trénmór. Cumhall desires *Muirenn, sometimes known as Muirenn of the White Neck, but she does not return his affections. Cumhall then abducts Muirenn, bringing down the vengeance of her father, *Tadg, and his protector, *Conn Cétchathach [of the Hundred Battles]. This also brings about the enmity between the Clan Baíscne, the descendants of Cumhall, and Clan *Morna, the descendants of Tadg and his warrior *Goll. In variant texts Cumhall fathers Fionn upon *Fuinche or Torba. In the best-known version of Cumhall's death, **Fotha Catha Chnucha* [The Cause of the Battle of Cnucha or Castletown], he is killed by Goll mac Morna. In other versions he is killed by Conn Cétchathach alone or by the keeper of the *crane bag [*corrbolg*]. In modern folktales, especially Scottish Gaelic versions, Cumhall is killed by the villainous *Arca Dubh ['Black Arky', etc.]. Muirenn gave birth to Fionn after Cumhall's death by retreating to the house of *Bodhmall, sometimes described as her sister. Cumhall's brother Crimnal is described as surviving the Battle of Cnucha and later joining the *Fianna. The assertion that Cumhall may be related to *Camulos or to King Cole of nursery rhymes has been rejected by contemporary learned commentators. James *Macpherson based the character of Comhal in *Ossian* (1760) on Cumhall. W. B. Yeats appears to have borrowed Cumhall in his poem 'The Blessed' (1897).

Cumian. Latinized spelling of *Cuimmíne.

Cunedda, Cunedag, Cynedda, Cunedda Wledig. Founder of Welsh dynasties. Cunedda is a shadowy personage of 5th-century Wales who, though described as historical by **Historia Brittonum* (8th cent.), is often perceived as legendary. Cunedda is reported as coming from southern Scotland, then a *Brythonic or *P-Celtic area, and driving the Irish from north Wales; his grandson *Cadwallon is described as completing the expulsion, although in fact elements of Irish settlement remained until a much later date. The kingdom he established came to be known as *Gwynedd. Cunedda brought with him eight sons, thus establishing dynasties in different parts of Wales that lasted until the death of *Dafydd, 1283. Most of his sons gave their names to different parts of north Wales, but one son, *Ceredigion, gave his name to *Cardiganshire; another son, *Einion, lent his name to lesser places. Cunedda may be compared to *Míl Espáine of Irish pseudo-history, who also established a dynasty with eight sons. See Geraint Gruffydd, *Studia Celtica*, 24/5 (1989–90), 1–14.

Cunobelinus [Romano-British, hound of Belinus]. British tribal leader at the time of the Roman invasion; he led the Catuvallaunians in southern Britain for forty years until shortly before the Claudian conquest, 43 BC.

Cunomaglus. Sometime epithet of Gaulish *Apollo.

cup. Although there does not appear to be a continuing association with cups or cup symbolism in different Celtic traditions, cups are mentioned prominently in several Irish and Welsh stories. The cup of *Cormac mac Airt would break when a lie was told. The *Fianna of *Fionn mac Cumhaill had a 'Cup of Victory' made of clay that they were frequently obliged to defend. There is a competition of cups of different worth, won by *Cúchulainn, in **Fled Bricrenn* [The Feast of Briccriu]. *Pryderi touched a magical cup in *Matholwch*, the third branch of the **Mabinogi*. The Welsh name *Heilyn means 'cup-bearer'. The prehistoric stone carvings containing distinctive 'cup and ring' symbolism do not appear to have Celtic associations, although they are found in all Celtic countries as well as throughout Europe and even outside Europe. R. W. B. Morris has studied the concentration of cup and ring carvings found at Achnabreck near Lochgilphead, Strathclyde (until 1974, *Argyllshire), Scotland; see *The Prehistoric Rock Art of Argyll* (Poole, 1977). A more general study may be found in Evan Hadingham, *Ancient Carvings in Britain: A Mystery* (London, 1974).

curadhmhír, curadmír, curad mír. Irish forms for *champion's portion.

Curcóg. A daughter of *Manannán mac Lir who is often seen as a companion of *Eithne. She once headed a company of women at *Brug na Bóinne.

curmudgeon. A common translation of the Irish and Scottish Gaelic *bodach, a hobgoblin.

Cú Roí, CúRoí, Curroi, Cú Ruí, Cú Raoi, Córroí, etc. [Ir., hound of the plain (?); hound of god (?)]. Usually seen as a hero of *Munster, Cú Roí is one of the most enigmatic figures in early Irish narrative; he may also be a divinity, king, chieftain, wizard, sorcerer, and traveller. His patronymic, mac Dáiri, may imply a divine origin, as Dáire (see DÁIRE (1)) is but another name for *Bolg. He is usually portrayed as an antagonist of *Ulster whose story is intertwined with that of *Cúchulainn at several points.

He became a fighter at the age of 7, and carries an immense rock in one hand and an axe in the other. It was said that Ireland could not contain him for his haughtiness. He seeks fir fer [the truth of men], a code of honour among warriors; thus he is often the severest judge of heroism. E. C. Quiggin once asserted that Cú Roí was the centre of a cycle of Munster mythology now lost. The several stories linking him with Cúchulainn are widely known. While raiding the *Otherworld, here located in Scotland, Cúchulainn is aided by Cú Roí, who appears as an uncouth stranger. They capture three marvellous cows, a cauldron, and a lady named *Bláithíne. When Cúchulainn refuses to share the booty, Cú Roí seizes the lot and thrusts the Ulster hero into the ground up to his armpits. As an additional ignominy, Cú Roí shaves off Cúchulainn's hair with his sword.

Cú Roí also appears in disguise, this time as a bachlach [ugly churl or herdsman], in a contest to determine who is the greatest of the three heroes, *Conall, *Lóegaire, and Cúchulainn. Cú Roí demands that first each of the heroes should cut off his head and second that he should cut off theirs. Conall and Lóegaire strike their blows, but the intruder merely picks up his head; neither will allow him to return the blow. Cúchulainn's blow also fails to slay the bachlach, but when the hero prepares himself to receive a blow in return, Cú Roí reveals his identity and proclaims Cúchulainn champion. See FLED BRICRENN [Briccriu's Feast]. Cú Roí wishes to do battle with Cúchulainn in the **Táin Bó Cuailnge* [Cattle Raid of Cooley], but *Medb dissuades him. Cúchulainn kills Cú Roí when aided by the betrayal of Cú Roí's wife, Bláithíne. The death does not go unavenged, however, as Cú Roí's poet, *Ferchertne (3), clasps Bláithíne in his arms and jumps off a sheer cliff on the *Beare peninsula with her in a deadly embrace.

Cú Roí's magical, impregnable fortress revolves on its axis each night so that the entrance can never be found after sunset, a distinction it shares with fortresses in other Celtic as well as in some Asian narratives. Cú Roí can control the rotation through a spell, even when he is in distant lands. Cúchulainn once helps to defend the fortress by defeating nine monstrous intruders. The fortress is usually associated with the Iron Age ruin on *Cahirconree in the *Sliab Mis (Slieve Mish) mountains about 10 miles SW of Tralee on the *Dingle peninsula, Co. *Kerry; Cahirconree, also Caherconry, etc., preserves the name of Cú Roí; the fortress is known as Cathair Chon-Raoí of Sliab (or Slieve) Mis in *Corcu Duibne in early Irish narrative. Additionally, he is sometimes thought to reside at *Temair Luachra, also in Co. Kerry. Cú Roí's best-known son is *Lugaid mac Con Roí or mac na Trí Con. His followers are the Clann *Dedad. Two figures who may be doubles for Cú Roí are Conganchnes mac Dedad and Lóch Mór. A Welsh figure briefly named in *Culhwch ac Olwen* appears to be a counterpart to Cú Roí; his name is variously rendered as *Cubert son of Daere, Chubert map Dare, or Corroi map Dayry. The Breton Esclados le Roux, guardian of a fountain in *Brocéliande, may also be a counterpart. A recent translation of *Aided Chon Roí* [The Tragic Death of Cú Roí], appears in *Two Death Tales from the*

Ulster Cycle, trans. Maria Tymoczko (Dublin, 1981).

curragh [Ir. *corrach*, wet bog, march, morass, low-lying plain]. Any extensive flat, boggy land in Ireland or the Isle of Man may be called a curragh. The best-known is called The Curragh or The Curragh of Kildare, about 5,000 acres, 6 miles by 2 miles, 2 miles E of the town of Kildare. The Curragh has often been mentioned in Irish narrative, notably in *Fenian tales, for more than 1,000 years. Prehistoric ruins include ring burial-mounds and the Race of the Black Pig, which may have been an ancient cattleway. More recent history has given The Curragh other associations; 350 unarmed United Irishmen were slaughtered here in 1798; it also includes the site of one of Ireland's most famous horse race-tracks and the training centre for the Irish military.

curse. *Macha put a curse upon the Ulstermen known as [ces] *noínden. See also GEIS.

Cú Ruí. Variant spelling of *Cú Roí.

Cúscraid, Cúscrid. *Ulster hero who bears the epithet Menn, Mend, Menn Machae [Ir., the stammerer, inarticulate one, of Macha]. Cúscraid is a son of *Conchobar mac Nessa who takes a leading role in **Scéla Mucce meic Da Thó* [The Story of Mac Da Thó's Pig], in which he is wounded by *Cet mac Mátach and slain by Mac Cécht. S. J. O'Grady changed the name to Cowshra Mend Macha in his imaginative *History of Ireland* (Dublin, 1878).

cù sìth [ScG, fairy dog]. The formidable fairy dog of Gaelic Scotland. Often represented to be the size of a yearling bullock, the cù sìth differs from other Celtic fairy dogs by being dark green. The cù sìth is shaggy and has paws as wide as a man's hand. Folk motif: F241.6. See also DOG; FAIRY DOG.

Custennin, Kistennin. Frequently appearing name in early Welsh tradition, the best-known of whom is the shepherd who helped *Culhwch to find Olwen in **Culhwch ac Olwen*. His son was *Goreu, the slayer of *Ysbaddaden.

Cuthullin. Variant spelling of *Cuchullin, the character in *Macpherson's *Ossian* (1760).

cŵn annwfn, annwn [W, dogs of annwfn, the Otherworld]. Otherworldly dogs or hell-hounds of Welsh tradition. Usually seen as a pack of small, red-grey or, alternatively, snow-white, red-eared spectral hounds. Near at hand they sound like beagles, but at a distance their sound is filled with wild lamentation. They terrify ordinary dogs and thus a dog howling at night is thought a bad omen. They are thought to come from the *Otherworld to hunt the souls of the living through the air; they seek to kidnap mortals and to lead the souls of the damned to infernal regions. Hunters who ride with them include *Arthur and the black-faced *Gwyn ap Nudd. The dogs may be known by many other names; in Welsh they are cŵn bendith y mamau [fairy dogs]; cŵn cyrff [corpse dogs]; cŵn wybr [sky dogs]; cŵn toili [toili dogs]. In English they may be known as Gabriel hounds, ratchets, or hell hounds. See also ARKAN SONNEY; CÙ SÌTH; DOG; FAIRY DOG. Motif E501.13.4.

Cycle of the Kings. One of four major cycles of Old and Middle Irish literature, known to some commentators as the Historical Cycle; it is distinguished from the other three by its focus on provincial and lesser kings, both legendary and historical, from the 3rd to the 7th centuries. The cycle is concerned not only with kings but also with *kingship. Critical commentators have found the cycle to be less magical than the *Mythological, less heroic than the *Ulster, and less romantic than the *Fenian. The phrase 'Cycle of the Kings' was coined by Myles Dillon, *The Cycles of the Kings* (Oxford, 1946), who allowed that there was more than one such cycle. Alan Bruford coined the phrase *Dalcassian Cycle in 1969 to refer to the stories of the 10th-century *Brian Bórama (Boru) and his family, which are so extensive and particular as to be separated from the rest.

Important personages mentioned in narratives of the Cycle of the Kings are *Baile and his lover Ailinn, *Becfola, *Cano (d. 688), *Conaire Mór, *Conn Cétchathach [of the Hundred Battles], *Cormac mac Airt (who also figures in the Fenian Cycle), *Domnall the son of Áed, *Fergus mac Léti, *Labraid Loingsech, *Lugaid mac Con, *Mongán, *Muirchertach mac Erca, *Niall Noígiallach [of the Nine Hostages], and *Rónán (1). Important narratives in the Cycle of the Kings include: **Buile Shuibne* [The Frenzy of Sweeney]; **Cath Maige Mucrama* [The Battle of Mag Mucrama]; **Echtra Maic nEchach Muigmedóin* [The Adventure of the Sons of Eochaid Mugmedón]; **Echtrae Airt meic Cuinn* [The Adventure of Art Son of Conn]; **Echtrae*

Conli [The Adventure of Connla]; **Esnada Tige Buchet* [The Melodies of Buchet's House]; **Fingal Rónáin* [How Rónán Slew His Son]; **Orgain Denna Ríg* [The Destruction of Dind Ríg].

cyclops. See ONE-EYED FIGURES.

cyfarwydd [W, storyteller; guide, leader; spell, magic]. Name given in medieval Welsh tradition to storytellers, all of whom are anonymous except for Bledri ap Cydifor (also Bledericus Walensis, Bleherus). The profession had disappeared before the oral composition of the **Mabinogi* was complete (12th cent.). The culmination of the cyfarwydd's tradition is the *Mabinogi*, where his role is described as offering pleasant tales to a patron. Although a member of the *bardic order, a cyfarwydd occupied a lower echelon. A cyfarwydd might borrow materials from other poets or printed sources and need not rely on his own imagination; his powers of dramatic presentation were especially esteemed. The survival of meanings associated with cognates of cyfarwydd imply that the storyteller might have played other roles; cf. cyfarwyddai [magician]; cyfarwyddyd [guidance, instruction, information, knowledge]. See Constance Bullock-Davies, *Professional Interpreters of the Matter of Britain* (Cardiff, 1966); Proinsias Mac Cana, *Learned Tales of Medieval Ireland* (Dublin, 1980); Patrick K. Ford, 'The Poet as *Cyfarrwydd* in Early Welsh Tradition', *Studia Celtica*, 10/11 (1975–6).

Cyfranc Lludd a Llefelys. An early Welsh narrative (?11th cent.) found in the**Red Book of Hergest* (*c*.1382–1410) and as a fragment in the **White Book of Rhydderch* (*c*.1325). The Welsh title translates literally as 'the meeting, battle, story, or adventure of Lludd and Llefelys', but the work is usually known in English simply as 'Lludd and Llefelys' (also Llevelys). It is a popular reworking of a pseudo-historical theme.

*Lludd, son of *Beli Mawr, was ruler of Britain, and his brother Llefelys was ruler of France. Lludd sought the aid of his brother when three plagues beset the land: (1) the Coraniaid [cf. W *còr*, dwarf], a crafty and demonic foreign people; (2) a fearful scream that was heard in every home in Britain at midnight of May Eve, *Calan Mai or Centefin, and scared people out of their senses; (3) the unaccountable disappearance of all provisions in the king's court every night, so that nothing not consumed by the household could be found in the morning. Lludd and Llefelys talked over these matters through a brazen tube, for the Coraniaid could hear everything that was said if once the winds got hold of it (a property also attributed to Math, son of Mathonwy). Llefelys suggested destroying the Coraniaid by mashing poisonous insects in water and sprinkling the solution over the foreigners to kill them; the insect would kill the Coraniaid, but the Britons would be immune. The scream, Llefelys explained, came from two dragons who fought each other once a year. They were to be killed by being intoxicated with mead that was to be placed in a pit dug in the very centre of Britain. Finally, the provisions, Llefelys explained, were being taken away by a giant wizard. Lludd overcame him in battle and made him a vassal. Thus Lludd and Llefelys freed the island of three plagues.

See Ifor Williams, *Cyfranc Lludd a Llevelys* (Bangor, 1922); Brynley F. Roberts, *Cyfranc Lludd a Llefelys* (Dublin, 1975).

cyhyraeth, cyheuraeth. Welsh spectral figure, comparable to the *caointeach of Gaelic Scotland or the Weeper of English tradition. Usually portrayed as an invisible, bodiless voice, the cyhyraeth may be heard groaning before death, especially multiple deaths caused by a disaster or epidemic. It is mostly associated with south Wales, east *Dyfed (until 1974, Carmarthenshire), and the three Glamorganshires, particularly near the Towy River. Like the Irish *banshee, the cyhyraeth will weep for natives who die away from home. It may once have been a goddess of streams.

cylch y tylwyth teg. Welsh for *fairy ring.

Cymidei Cymeinfoll, Kymideu Kymeinvoll. Giantess in *Branwen*, the second branch of the **Mabinogi*. She is the wife of the *giant Llassar Llaes Gyfnewid but is twice his size. Matholwch meets the husband and wife carrying the *cauldron of regeneration, and because of the disorders of their children, he determines to burn the parents in an iron house. Llassar and Cymidei escape to Britain, where they give the cauldron to *Bran in thanks for his hospitality. It is prophesied that Cymidei will give birth to a fully armed warrior. Proinsias Mac Cana thinks that Cymidei has the two attributes of the Celtic goddess: fertility and warlike vigour.

Cymru. Modern Welsh name for the principality or nation of Wales. In earlier tradition it was Cymry, anglicized as Kymry; but in Modern Welsh Cymry denotes the Welsh people. The Welsh language is Cymraeg.

Cynan. Name borne by numerous figures in early Wales, including saints, kings, and heroes, of whom two are most often mentioned.

Cynan Garwyn ap Brockfael. King of *Powys much praised (possibly) by *Taliesin.

Cynan Meiriadog, Meriadoc, Meriadach, **Saint**. Legendary 5th-century holy man who led Welsh migrants to *Armorica, founding *Brittany. In the Welsh story **Breuddwyd Macsen Wledig* [The Dream of Macsen Wledig], Cynan is a British general who leads his armies to Rome and is rewarded with the rights to Armorica/Brittany. In Breton legends he is known as Conan or Konan Meriedek.

Cynddylan, Cyndallan, Kyndylan. Prince of Pengwern in *Powys, late 6th and early 7th centuries, who is the subject of **Canu Heledd* [The Song of Heledd], the anonymous ninth cycle of poems once attributed to *Llywarch Hen. The speaker in the surviving poems is Heledd, thought to be Cynddylan's sister; often she laments Cynddylan's great hall, formerly filled with life, now ruined and empty. See Jenny Rowland, *Early Welsh Saga Poetry* (Cambridge, 1990).

Cyndeyrn. Name of several early Welsh saints; the Welsh form for St *Kentigern.

Cynedda. A variant form of *Cunedda.

Cynfeirdd [W, early, original poets]. Welsh name for the oldest poets, including *Aneirin and *Taliesin. See Joseph P. Clancy, *The Earliest Welsh Poetry* (New York, 1970); Rachel Bromwich and R. Brinley Jones (eds.), *Astudiaethau ar yr Hengerdd: Studies in Old Welsh Poetry* (Cardiff, 1978).

Cynon [W, great or divine hound (?)]. Name borne by many figures in early Welsh history, including saints, kings, and heroes. A king of *Gwynedd in 817 was Cynon. Cynon son of Clydno first tells Owain of the powerful knight who overthrows all challengers in **Owain*. A River Cynon flows 18 miles into the Taff, Glamorganshire.

Cyntefln, Cyntefyn. Alternative Welsh name for *Calan Mai or May Day; see also BELTAINE.

cythraul, cythrawl [W, hostile; devil, enemy]. Welsh word for the devil or other incarnation of evil in early narrative.

D

D. The fourth letter of the English alphabet is represented by dair [*oak] in the *ogham alphabet of early Ireland.

Dá Cheó, Cheo. See MAG DÁ CHEÓ.

Dá Chích Anann [Ir., two breasts of Ana; cf. ModIr. *cíoch*, breast]. Two round-topped hills, 2,273 and 2,284 feet, in Co. *Kerry, 3 miles S of Knockacappal and 17 miles SE of Killarney. The survival of this place-name into Modern Irish bears testimony of the association of the goddess *Ana with the province of *Munster. Locally the hills are referred to as 'The Paps'.

Da Derga's Hostel. The hotel, banqueting-hall, or **bruiden* of host Da Derga was thought to be near the River Dodder in south Co. Dublin. See TOGAIL BRUIDNE DA DERGA [The Destruction of Da Derga's Hostel].

dà shealladh. ScG for *second sight.

Dabilla. The lapdog of *Boand. According to place-name legend, the dog was dashed against two rocks in the sea on the east coast of *Brega; these have been identified with the 148-foot Rockabill or Rock-a-Bill rocks (OIr. *Da Billa*), 5 miles NE of Skerries, in north Co. Dublin.

Dadera. Variant spelling of *Do Dera, the fool killed by *Eógan (3).

Dáel Duiled. An *ollam or chief poet of *Leinster who engaged in and lost a riddle contest with the hermit Marbán.

Dafydd, Davydd [Hebrew, beloved, darling]. The most popular man's given name in Wales, counterpart of the English David, borne by countless figures in Welsh history. The patron saint of Wales, *Dewi Sant (*c.*520–*c.*589), is known as David in English; he is never known as St Dafydd.

Dafydd ap Gruffudd. Younger brother of Llywelyn ap Gruffudd, who is usually reckoned to be the last native prince of Wales, although Dafydd served for six months after him.

Dafydd ap Gwilym. Most admired medieval Welsh poet (*c.*1320–*c.*1370), who flourished in *Dyfed (formerly Cardiganshire). The object of his love-poetry was Morfydd. See *Gwaith Dafydd ap Gwilym*, ed. Thomas Parry (Cardiff, 1952); *Dafydd ap Gwilym: The Poems, Translation and Commentary*, ed. and trans. Richard Loomis (New York, 1981); Rachel Bromwich, *Dafydd ap Gwilym*, Writers of Wales Series (Cardiff, 1974).

Dagda, Dagda Mór, Daghda, Dagdae, Daghdha [Ir. *dag*, good; *día*, god (?)]. A leader of the *Tuatha Dé Danann and one of the principal gods of Old Irish tradition; often cited with the definite article, the Dagda; also known as *Eochaid Ollathair [father of all], Ruad Rofhessa [lord of great knowledge], and Deirgderc [red eye, i.e. the sun]. Sometimes, though not usually, seen as the son of *Eithne (1), who was also the mother of *Lug Lámfhota. The Dagda was proclaimed as the 'Good God', not for moral import, but rather because he was good, skilled, in so many endeavours: he was a warrior, an artisan, a magician, and an omniscient ruler.

Before going into battle he proclaimed, 'All that you promise I shall do for myself.' Among his two principal possessions were a huge *cauldron and a mighty club. The cauldron had been brought with the gods from Murias and was one of the four treasures of the Tuatha Dé Danann; it provided inexhaustible bounty for the Dagda's followers. The Dagda's club was so great that it had to be dragged on wheels, and left a track as deep as the boundary between two provinces. The size and potency of the club suggests parallels with the striker of the Gaulish *Sucellus and the hammer of Thor. In addition the Dagda possessed two marvellous swine (one always cooking, and still alive), and ever-laden fruit trees; these may imply powers over fertility.

For all his prowess, the Dagda was often portrayed as uncouth, even oafish, but benevolent. He dressed like a peasant with a tunic that came only to his rump, an effect some commentators describe as comic. His career as a spy against the *Fomorians was thwarted when they discovered his taste for porridge.

The Dagda is often seen married to *Boand, the river-goddess, although her usual husband is *Nechtan (1). Among his many children are the sons *Áed Minbhrec, *Bodb Derg, *Cermat, and *Midir, as well as the daughters *Ainge and *Brigit. His most celebrated child is *Angus Óg, the god of youth and beauty, according to a complex story told in two versions. Most commonly the Dagda mates with Boand adulterously, as she is then married to Nechtan, and the parents ask *Elcmar to be foster-father as a means of hiding the affair. In the alternate version the Dagda assumes the persona of Eochaid Ollathair to seduce *Eithne (2) (another name for Boand), cuckolding Elcmar, who has become her husband; in this version *Midir is the foster-father. *Brug na Bóinne first belongs to the Dagda, but it passes to his son Angus Óg. The Dagda's best-known tryst is with the *Mórrígan, the war-goddess, whom he met at *Samain (1 November). She is standing astride the river Unshin (or Uñius) in *Connacht, apparently tending to her washing. They have intercourse, and Mórrígan promises her assistance in a coming battle. Her washing is made of the heads and limbs of those about to die.

The Dagda takes an active role in **Cath Maige Tuired* [The (Second) Battle of Mag Tuired], in which he slaughters many of the rival Fomorians. Even his magical harp Úaithne helps to kill nine of the foe. But at the battle the Dagda is killed by the buck-toothed *Caitlín, wife of *Balor. In later folk tradition the Dagda is thought to have four great palaces in the depths of the earth and under hollow hills, and to have reigned for eighty years.

The Dagda's alternate names, Eochaid Ollathair [father of all] and Ruad Rofhessa [lord of great knowledge] testify to his high position in our reconstruction of the pre-Christian pantheon, but his precise role is not known. To the extent that he was an ancestor deity of the Irish, he is sometimes identified with *Donn (1), ruler of the dead and the *Otherworld. Speculation from the early 20th century asserted that he was a sky-god, a storm-god, an earth-god, or the sun itself. In addition, the Dagda has been thought to be a counterpart of Cronus, *Hercules, and *Dis Pater.

Dahut, Dahud. Also Ahés, Ahé. The foolish daughter of *Gradlon in the Breton legend of the city of *Ys. Despite repeated warnings, Dahut persisted in leading her people in nightly revelries with wild displays of pagan ritual, for which she and the city were punished. In Christianized treatments of the story, Dahut may be known as Keben, and portrayed as a sorceress and a female *druid. Sometimes equated with *Lí Ban.

Daigre, Daighre. Another name for *Dáire (4).

Dairbre. OIr. name for Valentia Island, Co. *Kerry; also known as Inis Dairbre.

Dáire, Dara [Ir., from root word meaning: fruitful, to make fruitful; fertile]. One of the commonest names in early Ireland, borne by innumerable historical and non-historical figures. Eoin MacNeill argued that the different figures bearing this name, despite different epithets, either are identical or have borrowed each other's qualities and histories so as to be essentially composite personalities: *Celtic Ireland* (Dublin and London, 1921), 61. Dara is a phonetic anglicization found in popular collections of folklore. Should be distinguished from **Doire* [Ir., oak grove], the Irish name for Derry (or Londonderry).

Dáire 1. Father of the five heroes known as *Lugaid; see LUGAID LAÍGDE. It was foretold that a son of Dáire would be king of Ireland, and so Dáire named each of his sons by that name. As these heroes are confused with *Lug Lámfhota, so too this Dáire may be identified with *Cian, father of Lug. This Dáire may also be the father of *Cú Roí mac Dáiri.

2. The son of Fergus of the Noble Judgement, ruler of *Tír Tairngire, visited by Conn in **Echtrae Airt meic Cuinn* [The Adventure of Art Son of Conn]. He may also be known as Dáire Degamra. His marriage to *Rígru Rosclethan is described as 'sinless'; his son is *Ségda Sáerlabraid.

3. The son of *Fionn mac Cumhaill. Dáire was swallowed by a monster or *dragon but cut himself out, liberating others along with himself. May be known as Dáire Derg, but should be distinguished from the Dáire Derg who opposed Fionn.

4. Daigre, Daighre. Musician of the

*Fianna Éireann in the *Fenian Cycle, celebrated in many stories for his melodiousness. Known in English stories as 'Dáire of the Poems'. See also CNÚ DEIREÓIL.

Dáire Derg, Dearg, Derc [Ir., Red Dáire]. Shadowy figure in the *Fenian Cycle. Usually he is the son of Gnáthaltach and the father of the three destructive *Fothads, whom *Fionn mac Cumhaill battles. Some commentators have asserted that Dáire Derg is identical with Morna, founder of the Clann *Morna, adversaries of Fionn in the Fenian Cycle. As Dáire Derg lost *one eye, he is also identified with *Goll mac Morna. In some narratives he is described as one of Fionn's ancestors. See also DÁIRE (3).

Dáire Donn. A minor *Fenian, a follower of *Fionn mac Cumhaill.

Dáire Donn, Durnmor, Durnmar. The so-called 'King of the World' in the *Fenian narrative **Cath Fionntrágha* [The Battle of Ventry]. Speculations on the model for Dáire Donn have included a late Roman emperor, the Holy Roman Emperor, or Charlemagne.

Dáire Dubh, Duff. A follower of *Fionn mac Cumhaill mentioned in several stories collected from oral tradition. His black tent stood apart from the rest, and few of the other warriors ever saw him.

Dáire mac Dedad. Ancestor-deity of the *Érainn and the *Corcu Loígde of early Ireland. T. F. O'Rahilly asserted that the god *Bolg was really Dáire under another aspect: *Early Irish History and Mythology* (Dublin, 1946).

Dáire mac Fiachna. Original owner of *Donn Cuailnge, the Brown Bull of Cuailnge or Cooley, in **Táin Bó Cuailnge* [Cattle Raid of Cooley]. After promising Donn Cuailnge to *Medb of *Connacht, Dáire overheard messengers, drunk at a feast, say he was a fool to hand over the bull. When Dáire then refused, Medb and her armies advanced into *Ulster to take Donn Cuailnge by force. In a sense, this otherwise obscure Ulster chief set in motion the war in Ireland's greatest epic. See also FIACHNA MAC DÁIRI, whose catching of the 'water worm' leads to Donn Cuailnge's conception.

Daireann, Dáireán, Dairenn. Modern Irish variants of *Doirend.

Dáirine. Daughter of *Tuathal Techtmar, a legendary king of early Ireland (?2nd cent. AD); younger sister of *Fithir. *Eochaid (8), king of Leinster, lusted after her but was obliged to marry Fithir instead; later he lied that Fithir had died, and so married Dáirine as well.

Daithi. Variant spelling of *Dathí.

dál [Ir., people, tribe; tribal territory]. Word prefixed to the names of early Irish and Scottish Gaelic proto-kingdoms; entries for such groups are given here alphabetized word by word. See also CENÉL; DERBFHINE.

Dál Cais, gCais. Sometimes anglicized Dalcassians, Dalcassia. Proto-kingdom of early Ireland occupying an area in east Co. Clare, concentrated near the monastery of *Killaloe, best remembered for producing the greatest king of early Ireland, *Brian Bórama (Boru). The people of Dál Cais, originally known as *Déisi, first settled in east Limerick. They began to move into Clare in the 8th century, but were not mentioned in the Annals until 934. Eventually they overthrew the *Eóganacht and seized the kingship of *Munster, which Brian used as a base for his adventures elsewhere in Ireland. After Brian's victory and death at *Clontarf (1014), the power of Dál Cais declined. Much of the area of the kingdom became known as *Thomond. The *Dalcassian Cycle is based on stories about the descendants of Brian. See J. V. Kelleher, 'The Rise of the Dál Cais', in E. Rynne (ed.), *North Munster Studies* (Limerick, 1967), 230–41.

Dál nAraide, nAraidi. Proto-kingdom of early Ireland occupying an area east of Lough Neagh coextensive with eastern Northern Ireland, from the Slemish mountains southwards to Newry. Their eponymous founder may be *Fiachu Araide, who is credited with driving *Cormac mac Airt from *Tara. *Conn Cétchathach [of the Hundred Battles] earned his epithet in waging war against Dál nAraide. *Congal Cáel, celebrated in Samuel Ferguson's poem *Congal* (1872), was king of Dál nAraide before he became king of all *Ulster. *Suibhne Geilt [Mad Sweeney] was also king here. The people of the petty kingdom were known as Dál nAraidi and thought to be Cruithin (*Picts) by their neighbours.

Dál Riada, Dalriada, Dál Riata. Proto-kingdom of Northern Ireland that later flourished in Gaelic Scotland. The Irish half of the kingdom, more often known as Dál Riata, after the mythological ancestor *Eochu Riata, was centred in north Northern Ireland, especially in the Glens of Antrim. When local military defeats caused it to cede ground, the kingdom expanded into what is now north Strathclyde (until 1974, *Argyllshire), led by *Áedán mac Gabráin, who was baptized by and associated with St *Colum Cille. The Irish invaders, who established a capital at *Dunadd, brought with them Gaelic language and culture as well as Christianity. An early king, *Fergus mac Eirc, also Fergus Mòr [ScG, the great], brought the *Lia Fáil [Ir., stone of destiny] from Ireland for his coronation and did not return it; in Scotland it came to be known as the Stone of Scone. The fortunes of the Scoto-Irish kingdom rose and fell during constant warfare with the neighbouring *Picts until *Cináed mac Alpín [Kenneth MacAlpine] united both forces into one Scottish kingdom north of the Clyde, 844–58. Although the influence of Dál Riada ceased after the 9th century, many Highland families claimed ancestry from Loarn son of Erc, one of the founders of the Scottish branch of the kingdom. See M. O. Anderson, 'Dalriada and the Creation of the Kingdom of the Scots', in D. Whitelock (ed.), *Ireland in Medieval Europe* (Cambridge, 1982), 106–32; John Bannerman, *Studies in the History of Dalriada* (Edinburgh, 1974).

Dalcassian Cycle. [Ir. *Dál Cais*]. Cycle of narratives from medieval Ireland centring on *Brian Bórama (Boru) and his son Murchad of the *Dál Cais (or Dál gCais). The name for this small cycle, a subdivision of the *Cycle of the Kings, was coined by Alan Bruford, although the anglicization 'Dalcassian', referring to the area around the Shannon estuary and to the O'Brien family, is much older. See Alan Bruford, *Gaelic Folk-Tales and Mediaeval Romances* (Dublin, 1969), 134–46.

Dallán Forgaill, Forgael [cf. Ir. *dall*, blind]. Fabled poet of 6th-century Ireland, perhaps the first to whom the title of any poem may be ascribed. He is thought to have penned *Amra Choluimb Chille* (*c.*580), a poem in praise of St *Colum Cille. Some narratives describe him as a 'Bard of All Ireland'. Dallán Forgaill may be identified with *Eochaid Éigeas and may be the model for *Forgoll, both of whom contend with *Mongán. The poet may have been the model for W. B. Yeats's fictional *Forgael in the drama *Shadowy Waters* (1906).

Dalny. Anglicized spelling of *Dealgnaid.

Dalriada. Variant spelling of *Dál Riada.

Damán. Father of *Ferdiad.

Damnonii. Variant spelling of Dumnonii; see DUMNONIA.

Damona [divine cow (?)]. Gaulish goddess, the usual consort of *Borvo and worshipped with him in the shrine at Bourbonne-les-Bains (north-eastern France); when Borvo is known as Bormanus, his consort is Bormana. Polyandrous, she is also the consort of *Apollo Moritasgus in Gaul. Several commentators have seen suggestions of the cult of the *cow in her worship.

Dana. See ANA; DANU; DÔN.

Danaans. Anglicized form of *Tuatha Dé Danann favoured by W. B. Yeats and others.

Danann. See TUATHA DÉ DANANN.

dandelion. The common plant or weed (*Taraxacum officinale*) with yellow blossoms and edible leaves was thought to have curative powers in the Celtic countries, especially for heart problems and diseases caused by fairies. Ir. caisearbhán or, when used as medicine, caol dearg; ScG am beàrnan Br'de; Manx lus y minnag; W dant y llew; Corn. dans-lew; Bret. c'hwervizon. See also FAIRY HERB.

Danu, Dana. Speculative name for the mother goddess of the Continental Celts based on the evidence of place-names, e.g. Danube (L *Dānuvius*; Hungarian *Duna*; German *Donau*); also a variant for the Irish *Ana (a prosthetic *d-* = *Ana*) and linked to the Welsh *Dôn. Other goddesses named Danu appear as far afield as Russia and India; in India's *Rig-Veda* the name of the goddess Danu signifies 'stream' and 'the waters of heaven'.

daoine maithe [Ir., good people]. One of several euphemisms for *fairies in Modern Irish folklore.

daoine sídhe, sí, sidh [Ir., people of the fairy mound]. One of several euphemisms for *fairies in Modern Irish and Scottish Gaelic folklore; the link with the fairy mounds may imply a descent from the *Tuatha Dé Danann. Deena Shee is a phonetic anglicization. The reformed Irish spelling is daoine sí.

daoine uaisle [Ir., noble people, gentry]. A euphemism for *fairies.

Daolghas. Irish hero whose story is told by *Fionn mac Cumhaill in **Feis Tighe Chonáin* [The Feast at Conán's House], in answer to the riddle, 'What man was the son of his own daughter?' When Daolghas lay dying, his daughter stooped to kiss him. As she did, a spark of *fire flew from his mouth to hers, making her pregnant. When she bore the child, she named him for her father.

Dara. Anglicization of *Dáire.

Dark Rosaleen. J. C. Mangan's translation (1847) of *Róisin Dubh, a personification of Ireland.

Daron. Shadowy early British goddess of the *oak whose name is commemorated by a rivulet in *Gwynedd.

Darthacht. Variant spelling of Durthacht, father of *Eógan mac Durthacht.

Dar-thula, Darthula. James *Macpherson's adaptation of the *Deirdre story as told in his *Poems of Ossian* (1760–3). Dar-thula is loved by the elderly Cairbar (*Conchobar) when she becomes smitten with the youthful Nathos (*Noíse). Dar-thula, Nathos, and his two brothers, Althos (see AINNLE) and Ardan, attempt to flee, but are driven back by a storm. The three brothers, sons of Usnoth (*Uisnech), are killed by the pursuing Cairbar, and Dar-thula commits suicide upon the body of Nathos. Credulous commentators gave Dar-thula a Scottish Gaelic etymology, *dart-'huile* [woman with fine eyes].

Dathí, Dathi, Da Thí, Daithí, Nath Í. Shadowy 5th-century king (*c.*445) of *Connacht, who may or may not have been the last pagan high king of Ireland; sometimes bears the patronymic mac Fiachrach. According to some annals, Dathí was the nephew of *Niall Noígiallach [of the Nine Hostages] and king of Connacht before he succeeded his uncle for a twenty-three-year reign. T. F. O'Rahilly believes that Dathí was only a raider to Britain whose story was concocted and interposed by later annalists. According to those stories, Dathí invaded first *Strathclyde and later Continental Europe, crossing the Alps; he was struck by lightning after occupying the tower of one *Formenus, 'king of Thrace', who lived in the Alps as a hermit. For more on this element of his narrative, see Samuel Ferguson, 'On the Legend of Dathi', *Proceedings of the Royal Irish Academy*, 2, 2nd ser. (1884), 167–84. A pillar at *Cruachain is thought to mark Dathí's grave, and the Bough of Dathí was one of the sacred trees of early Ireland.

The Dathí of tradition may be unrelated to the non-regal figure of the same name in W. B. Yeats's 'The Blessed' (1897). This Dathí is a wise or holy man who tells Cumhall that 'blessedness goes where the wind goes,/ And when it is gone we are dead.' See also Mary Genevieve Hogan, *The Legend of Dathi: An Analogue to the Chronicle Story of Arthur* (Washington, DC, 1933).

Daui Dalta Dedad, Daui Dallta Dedad, Duach Dallta Deadad [Ir., Blinder of Dedad]. King of *Tara, son of Cairbre Losc, who, according to the usual story, blinded his brother Dedad lest he aspire to the throne himself. In a variant he is the foster-son, dalta, of Dedad. Daui reigned for seven years until he was assassinated. Medieval redactors attempted to prove that Daui's assassination was coeval with that of Julius *Caesar.

Daui Ladrach, Duach Ladrach, Ladgrach, Laghrach [Ir. *ladrach*, crooked-toed, splay-footed]. An early king of Ireland, son of *Fiachu Tolgrach, known to be vindictive and a quick avenger of wrongs. He slew Airgetmar to gain the throne and was later betrayed by *Lugaid Laígde, who had helped in the ousting. Some time later Airgetmar's grandson *Áed Ruad murdered and displaced Lugaid.

Daurthecht. Variant spelling of *Durthacht.

David. English version of one of the most common men's names in Wales, after St David, who is known as *Dewi Sant in Welsh tradition; the usual Welsh equivalent is *Dafydd.

Davydd. Variant spelling of *Dafydd.

Ddraig Goch, Y [W, red dragon]. The red dragon, national symbol of Wales. Distinguish from gwiber, lit. viper or adder, a name for the winged serpent or *dragon not representative of the nation.

De Danann. See TUATHA DÉ DANANN.

Dea. Latin term used by some commentators when naming several Continental Celtic gods, Dea Arduinna (or Arduanna), Dea Artio, Dea Matrona, Dea Sequana, etc.; see ARDUINNA; ARTIO; MATRONA, etc.

dead, the. Celtic conceptions of the realm of the dead are often close to but are not synonymous with those of the *Otherworld. No detailed portrait of the realm of the dead is found in any Celtic tradition, although there is much in Celtic folklore to suggest a belief in the power of the dead to return to the world of the living. Named Celtic gods of the dead are rare. The Gaulish *Sucellus has some funerary aspects. The observations of classical commentators on Celtic belief in the afterlife are tantalizingly incomplete. Celtic warriors were said not to fear death. The 6th-century Byzantine historian Procopius tells a curious story about the island of 'Brittia' (Britain?) where the souls of the dead might be ferried. Often in Celtic tradition the realm of the dead is thought to be in the west. In recent times in Brittany the 'Bay of Souls' was thought to be at Raz, at the extreme western point of the peninsula. In Britain also the most westerly point of the Island, off Land's End in Cornwall, was thought to belong to the dead, but in the pseudo-history **Lebor Gabála* [Book of Invasions], Spain may be the land of the dead. The realm of *Donn (1), *Tech Duinn [Donn's House], on a rocky island in south-west Ireland, is sometimes the home of the dead. The Welsh conception that may include the realm of the dead is *Annwfn; a Welsh personification of death is *Angau, corresponding to the Breton bringer of death, *Ankou. The Breton religious festival known as pardon, of which there are many in honour of various saints and occasions, are perceived in learned opinion as Christianized celebrations of the dead; see Anatole le Braz, *The Land of Pardons* (New York, 1906). The Celtic deities most comparable to Hades or Pluto are the Irish figures *Bile and Donn (1). The Chthonic Donn bears a closer relationship to *Dis Pater. In the **Mabinogi*/Mabinogion, a magic *cauldron can rejuvenate the dead. See also ANGAU; ANKOU; DEATH COACH; DIS PATER.

Dealga. Variant spelling of *Delga.

Dealgnaid, Dealgnait, Dealgnat, Delgnat, Dalny, Elgnat. The wife of *Partholón whose affair with the slave Todga (or Topa) introduced adultery into Ireland. Dealgnaid seduced Todga while her husband was away hunting. In some versions the husband is predictably furious when he discovers the deception. In another, Todga placates him with a verse, saying that she should not have been presented with such temptation.

Dealra Dubh [cf. Ir. *dealramh dubh*, dark sheen, splendour, radiance]. An evil-minded opponent of *Fionn mac Cumhaill in several narratives from oral tradition. He never spoke a word that did not savour of censure.

deamhan aeir, aedhir. A demon of the air in Irish tradition. One such demon taunts the Children of *Lir.

Dearbhorgaill. ModIr. spelling of *Derbforgaill.

dearg. ModIr. for red; see also OIr. DERG. See DÁIRE DERG; LOUGH DERG.

Dearmid. Variant spelling of *Diarmait.

Deasmhumhain, Deasúin. Irish spellings of *Desmond.

deas-sail. Variant spelling of deiseal; see SUNWISE TURN.

death coach. Spectral vehicle in Irish folklore whose stopping at the door announced the death of a resident the next day. As the driver is headless and the horses are either black or headless, the death coach is sometimes called the headless coach. If it is seen passing it should not be stopped, as someone will die near the spot where it comes to rest. Sometimes the *banshee rides the coach or may fly in the air near it. At other times the headless phanton *dullahan drives. Fallen bridges offer no obstacle to the death coach. Although the death coach seems uniquely Irish, it is a variant on international tale type 335; see also the ANGOU of Wales; ANKOU of Brittany; FAR DOROCHA. While the death coach is found in Irish oral tradition, it is probably best known today from its recreation in the Disney film *Darby O'Gill and the Little People* (1958), based on the popular fiction of H. T. Kavanagh (1932).

Death of Aífe's Only Son. See AIDED ÓENFHIR AÍFE.

Death of Connla. See AIDED ÓENFHIR AÍFE.

Death of Fergus. Possible translation of two different Irish stories. See AIDED FERGUSA; and FERGUS MAC LÉTI.

Death of Máel Fothartaig Son of Rónán. English translation of *Aided Máele Fhothartaig maic Rónáin*, an alternate title for **Fingal Rónáin* [How Rónán Killed His Son].

Debility/Pangs of the Ulstermen. When *Crunniuc mac Agnomain made his pregnant wife, *Macha (3), run a footrace, many of the Ulstermen watching laughed at the distress of her labour. In revenge, Macha (3) cursed them unto nine times nine generations with the pains endured by women in labour, Ir. Ces *Nóinden Ulad; ceisnoidhe Uladh [nine days' affliction of Ulster]. The episode is retold at the beginning of **Táin Bó Cuailnge* [Cattle Raid of Cooley].

Decantae. Roman name for a British tribe in early Scotland. They occupied a territory coextensive with what was known until 1974 as Easter Ross in the central Scottish Highlands.

Decies. Anglicized name for a region in medieval Ireland, roughly coextensive with western Co. Waterford; named for the early Irish people, the *Déisi. One early record proclaimed that Decies ran from the River Suir to the sea and from Lismore to Credan Head. The area has also been known as Power Country as it was settled by the Power or de Paor family.

Declan, Déclán, Déaglán, **Saint.** Important saint of early Ireland, founder of the monastery of *Ardmore in what is now Co. Waterford; patron of the *Déisi and sometimes called 'the Patrick of the Déisi'. Details of his life are hazy; we are not certain that he lived before *Patrick or in the 6th century. Declan's ancestry could be traced back to the incestuous *Clothra. His traditional life contains chronological contradictions. He may have visited Rome twice, visiting *Dewi Sant [St David of Wales] on the second. Many miracles are attributed to him, and he was held in great veneration. His feast-day, 24 July, was observed throughout Ireland.

See *Life of St. Declan of Ardmore and Life of St. Mochuda of Lismore,* ed. and trans. P. Power, Irish Texts Society, vol. 16 (London, 1916).

Dectera, Dectora. Variant spellings of *Deichtine.

Dectire. Variant of *Deichtine.

Dedad, Clann Dedad, Fir Dedad. The subjects or followers of *Cú Roí mac Dáiri. Much evidence suggests that Clann Dedad is another name for the *Érainn, an important early non-Goidelic people of Ireland. In the *Táin Bó Flidais* [Cattle Raid of *Flidais] the Clann Dedad are listed as one of the three warrior races of Ireland along with the Clann Rudraige (i.e. *Ulaid) and the Gamanrad. D. Ó hÓgáin has suggested (1991) that the Dedad were fancifully associated with the Dee river in north-east *Leinster, and thus the famous ford of the river, *Áth Fhirdiad(h) [Ferdia's Ford] may be named for them instead of for the hero *Ferdiad [Ir., man of Dedad (?)], thought to have been killed here by *Cúchulainn, as reported in the **Táin Bó Cuailnge* [Cattle Raid of Cooley].

Dedannans. Anglicization of *Tuatha Dé Danann.

deena shee. Phonetic anglicization of *daoine sídhe.

deer. The familiar ruminant, swift-footed animal of European forests (*Cervidae*) has long played an important role in the Celtic imagination, especially the male of the species, the mighty horned *stag, which was an important cult animal in early times. The god of the Continental Celts, *Cernunnos, has the antlers of a stag; see also HORNED GOD. J. G. MacKay has reported on deer worship in early Scotland, especially in the Lochaber region of the Highlands (until 1974, Inverness-shire); see 'The Deer-Cult and Deer Goddess of the Ancient Caledonians', *Folklore*, 43 (1932), 144–74. The *sianach is a deer-monster of Scottish Gaelic tradition. In the vernacular tradition of Celtic countries deer commonly entice heroes into the realm of the gods. Sálbuide, son of the king of *Munster, died in a deer chase, along with thirty warriors, thirty attendants, and thirty deerhounds. In another Irish story a jealous woman turned 100 girls into deer. Both mortals and fairies may be turned into deer. *Lugaid Laígde, the *Érainn king, pursued a *fawn who was the divine personification of Ireland. *Shape-shifting *Mongán takes the form of a deer. *Aige was transformed into a fawn. When *Pryderi and Gilfaethwy in *Math*, the fourth branch of the **Mabinogi*, are turned into a stag and hind, they produce at the end of one year a fawn named *Hyddwn. J. Fife comments on the deer-hunting episode of 'Pwyll', the second branch: *Bulletin of the Board of Celtic Studies*, 39 (1992), 72ff. *Sadb mates with *Fionn mac Cumhaill under the form of a deer to produce *Oisín, whose name means 'Little Fawn'. The Irish goddess *Flidais drove a chariot drawn by deer. The king of the deer in Ireland was *Tuan mac Cairill.

An early Christian prayer-poem attributed to St *Patrick, 'The Deer's Cry' or 'St Patrick's Breastplate', speaks of the saint's escape from his enemies while in the form of a deer. In this instance Patrick has used the power to make himself invisible or to take animal form, *féth fiada, previously attributed to druids and pre-Christian religion. The short poem, often compared in structure and antiquity to the Anglo-Saxon 'Caedmon's Hymn', has been translated many times, recently by Malachi McCormick (Dublin, 1983).

The word for deer in OIr. is fiad; ModIr. fia, fiadh; ScG fiadh; Manx feeaih; W carw; Corn. carow; Bret. karv. See also FAWN.

Deer [ScG *doire*, forest; cf. *deur*, tear]. Monastery and village in north Aberdeenshire that has figured prominently in Scottish history. Although thought to have been founded in the 6th century by *Colum Cille [St Columba] and his Scottish disciple *Drostán, the site was occupied by the Cistercians in 1218–19. The Latin *Book of Deer*, *c.* 9th century, contains some added Gaelic entries, *c.*1130–*c.*1150, and so precedes that first great collection of Gaelic writing, the **Book of the Dean of Lismore*, by four centuries. Popular tradition asserts that Deer was named for the tear [*deur*] Colum Cille shed as he departed the site. See Kenneth H. Jackson, *The Gaelic Notes in the Book of Deer* (Cambridge, 1972).

Deering. Anglicization of *Diorruing.

Deheubarth [L *dextralis pars*, right hand, southern part]. Welsh name for the southern portion of Wales which can have different definitions during different periods of history. Often it is the counterpart of *Gwynedd, north Wales. Earlier it distinguished southern Wales from the *P-Celts of northern Britain, the 'men of the north', *Gwyˆr y Gogledd. Distinguish from *Dyfed, the south-west part of Wales.

Deichthe. Variant of *Deoch.

Deichtine, Deichtire, Deichter, Deicteir, Dechtire, Dechtere, Dectere, Dectera, Dectora. Mother of *Cúchulainn, daughter of *Cathbad the druid, lover of *Lug Lámfhota, usual sister of *Findchóem, and sometime sister or daughter of *Conchobar mac Nessa. The most familiar version of her conception of Cúchulainn is that, while grieving the loss of a foster-son, she drinks some water with which a tiny creature passes into her mouth; the creature may be Lug, or she may merely have dreamed of Lug. Before the child can be delivered, she is married to *Sualtam mac Róich. In a second version, Deichtine disappears with fifty maidens from the court of Conchobar mac Nessa. After a lapse of three years a flock of birds settles on the fields of *Emain Macha and lays waste the crops. When Conchobar and his retainers seek to drive off the birds, the birds lead them on to the magic mound of *Angus Óg on the *Boyne. At night the men come upon a splendid palace, where a noble youth is accompanied by fifty maidens. The maidens include Deichtine, and the noble youth is *Lug Lámfhota. On hearing the news, Conchobar asks to see Deichtine, but she sends him instead her newborn son Cúchulainn. In a third version Conchobar, as either Deichtine's father or brother, commits incest with her to father Cúchulainn.

The character of Dectora in W. B. Yeats's *The Shadowy Waters* (1900) appears to be based in part on Deichtine.

Deimne, Deimne Maol. Modern spellings for Demne, *Demne Máel.

deirbhfhine. Variant spelling of *derbfhine.

Deirdre, Derdriu, Deirdriu, Deirdri, Derdrend (gen.). Tragic heroine of the *Ulster Cycle whose well-known narrative is one of the '*Three Sorrows of Storytelling' of Irish tradition. The Irish text of her story, *Longas mac nUislenn* [The Exile of the Sons of Uisnech], exists in many versions, including those in the 12th-century **Book of Leinster* and **Yellow Book of Lecan*, and is a prologue or foretale [OIr. *rémscél*; ModIr. *réamhscéal*] of the epic **Táin Bó Cuailnge* [Cattle Raid of Cooley]. The story remained popular in the oral traditions of later centuries in both Ireland and Scotland. Within the Ulster Cycle Deirdre is not simply tragic and beautiful but is also a catalyst, an occasion of misfortune, bringing vengeance and misfortune on the nobility and warriors of the province. The many retellings of Deirdre's story in Anglo-Irish literature in the 19th and 20th centuries (see below) have made her the best-known figure from Celtic mythology in the world at large.

The etymology of Deirdre remains in doubt, despite persistent speculation. The common gloss 'troubler' seems unsupportable. The name may only be a diminutive of *der* [daughter, girl]; cf. *dér* [tear].

When the men of Ulster are feasting at the house of *Fedlimid mac Daill, chief storyteller to *Conchobar mac Nessa, the host's wife gives birth to a daughter, Deirdre. *Cathbad the druid at once prophesies that the girl-child will grow to be a woman of wonderful beauty, but that she will also cause great enmity, leading to the destruction of Ulster. The assembled warriors insist that she be put to death to avoid the curse. Conchobar orders that she be spared, and fostered at a distant stronghold under the care of Leborcham, a wise woman in the king's confidence. Conchobar adds that he intends to make the grown Deirdre his wife.

Deirdre's childhood is uneventful until one day she has a vision of her future. Her foster-father, a forester, is flaying a slaughtered calf outside in the snow when a raven lands to drink the blood. Deirdre turns to Leborcham and announces, 'Fair would be a man upon whom these three colours should be: his hair like the raven, his cheek like the blood, and his body like the snow.' In oral tradition the colours are sometimes attributed to the brow (black), lip (red), and teeth (white). (Cf. *black, white, and red symbolism, folk motif Z65.1.) Leborcham answers that the colours evoked a young man living nearby, *Noíse, a nephew of Conchobar and son of *Uisnech. Deirdre says she will not be well until she sees Noíse, and so Leborcham arranges that they meet. When Noíse first sees Deirdre he remarks, 'Fair is the heifer that goes past *me*.' Deirdre responds, 'Heifers are wont to be big where there is no bull.' To which Noíse replies, 'You have the bull of the province, the king of Ulster.' And then Deirdre admits, 'I will choose between the two of you, and I will choose a young bull like you.' Shortly thereafter Deirdre and Noíse elope, fleeing first across Ireland with Conchobar in pursuit and later to Scotland. Noíse's brothers Ardan and Ainnle go with them, hence the title of the story in Irish, *Longas mac nUislenn* [The Exile of the Sons of Uisnech]. Although the brothers are always a part of the narrative, no doubt an instance of Celtic *triplism, they are not usually given any character. In earlier texts of the story the exiles are accompanied by 150 warriors, 150 women, and 150 hounds.

For many years the lovers live happily together in the Scottish wilderness under the protection of a local king. In many stories they are thought to have lived near the shores of Loch Etive in north Strathclyde (until 1974, *Argyllshire). In some versions they are attributed one of two children, a daughter, *Aíbgréne, and, less often, a son, Gaiar. Noíse and his brothers build a house around Deirdre for safety. When a steward tells the local king of Deirdre's beauty he demands her for his wife, and the lovers and brothers have to flee to an island in the sea.

All the while Conchobar has been trying to retrieve the lovers with plots and treachery, but without success. He sends *Gelbann (in some texts, Tréndorn) to see if Deirdre's beauty has faded, but Noíse puts out his eye with a *fidchell piece. Pretending resignation, Conchobar invites Noíse and Deirdre back to Ulster, sending *Fergus mac Róich, one of the great heroes of Ireland, as a surety. Though fearing deceit, Deirdre consents, singing the famous 'Farewell to Alba' before joining the others in the boat. When they land in Ulster Conchobar uses a ruse to separate Fergus from Deirdre, Noíse, and his brothers. The king's men then attack, killing Noíse, his brothers, and the sons of Fergus who have stayed behind, but sparing Deirdre. In a variant text, Conchobar convinces *Maine (9), a Norse prince whose father has been killed by Noíse, that he should seek revenge by slaughtering the three brothers. In some versions Deirdre is so moved by Noíse's death that she throws herself on his grave and dies. More often she is described as being captured and brought back to Conchobar, her hands tied behind her back. For the next year Conchobar keeps her with him at *Emain Macha, but she never smiles or raises her head from her knee. She often rebukes Conchobar for killing what was dear to her. When asked what she hates most of what she sees, she answers Conchobar and *Eógan mac Durthacht, a royal retainer. Hearing this, Conchobar gives Deirdre to Eógan. Later, while riding in Eógan's chariot, Deirdre leaps out and dashes her head against a stone. In other versions she stabs herself with a knife, throwing it into the sea so that no one will be blamed. In oral tradition the lovers are thought to be buried next to each other at *Armagh; Conchobar drove two *yew stakes through the graves that later grew and intertwined. As a result of Conchobar's perfidy, many of his best warriors desert him for *Ailill and *Medb of *Connacht, and fight against him in the *Táin Bó Cuailnge* [Cattle Raid of Cooley], so bringing about Cathbad's prophecy at Deirdre's birth.

V. Hull edited *Longes mac nUisnig* (New York, 1949); cf. Whitley Stokes, 'The Death of the Sons of Uisnech', *Irische Texte*, ser. 2, 2 (1887), 109–84. See Raymond Cormier, 'Remarks on the Tale of Deirdriu and Noisiu and the Tristan Legend', *Études Celtiques*, 15 (1976–8), 303–15; Phillip O'Leary, 'The Honour of Woman in Early Irish Literature', *Ériu*, 38 (1987), 27–44. Deirdre's story has been especially popular with Anglo-Irish writers. Notable retellings of the narrative include: S. Ferguson, 'Death of the Children of Usnach' (1834) and *Deirdre* (1880); R. D. Joyce, *Deirdre* (1876); A. de Vere, *Sons of Usnach* (1882); W. Sharp, *House of Usna* (1900); H. Trench, *Deirdre Wedded* (1901); Lady Gregory, *Cuchulain of Muirthemne* (1902); George Russell, *Deirdre* (1906); W. B. Yeats, *Deirdre* (1906); J. M. Synge, *Deirdre of the Sorrows* (1909); J. Stephens, *Deirdre* (1923); John Coulter, *Deirdre of the Sorrows* (1944). Deirdre is transformed into a redeeming embodiment of love in Moireen Fox's [pseud. Móirín a Cheavasa] *The Fire-Bringers* (Dublin, 1920). See H. V. Fackler's study of this tradition, *That Tragic Queen: The Deirdre Legend in Anglo-Irish Literature* (Salzburg and Atlantic Highlands, NJ, 1978). Other popular treatments include: David Guard, *Deirdre: A Celtic Legend* (juvenile fiction) (Millbrae, Calif., 1977); Kevin McCaffrey, *Deirdre* (juvenile fiction) (Dublin, 1989).

A vitrified fort at Inverfarigaig on the eastern shore of Loch Ness was once known as Dún Dearduil [Deirdre's Fortress]. See also GRÁINNE; ISEULT.

Deirgderc [Ir., red eye]. An alternate name and epithet for both the *Dagda and *Eochaid (1), the sun-god.

Déise. Variant of *Déisi.

deiseal, deiseil. ModIr. and ScG words for *sunwise turn.

Déisi, Dési, Déssi, Déise [Ir., vassal or rent-paying tribes]. Historical people of early Ireland, who migrated from Co. Meath to both *Munster and south Wales, especially the south-western territories then occupied by the *Demetae later known as *Dyfed. Their alleged original homeland is commemorated in the barony of Deece, Co. Meath. Their region of settlement in counties Waterford and Tipperary came to be known as *Decies; here they became vassals of the Eóganacht. According to literary tradition, the Déisi of Meath are forced to migrate when they seek vengeance for the rape of a princess by *Cellach, son of *Cormac mac Airt. The Déisi chieftain spears Cellach and puts out Cormac's eye, thus disbarring him from kingship; he is replaced by another son, *Cairbre. After the Déisi settle in their Munster home, *Eochaid (9) leads them to Wales. St *Declan [Déaglán], founder of *Ardmore, was the principal saint of the Déisi.

Del Chliss. *Cúchulainn's spear, first belonging to *Nechtan (1) and used to kill the sons of *Nechtan Scéne. Formerly the name for the charioteer's goad, a split piece of wood.

Dela. *Fir Bolg leader; his five sons come from Greece to invade Ireland, later dividing the island into five parts.

Delbáeth, Delbáed, Delbaíth [Ir., fire shape]. Name borne by several shadowy figures in early Irish narrative whose identities are not always clearly discrete.

Delbáeth 1. *Fomorian king, father of *Elatha and grandfather of *Bres. Delbáeth (1) is also sometimes the father of *Eithne (1), instead of *Balor. Elatha mates with *Ériu, daughter of Delbáeth (2), to produce Bres.

2. Noble youth of the *Tuatha Dé Danann, son of *Angus Óg and *Eithne (daughter of *Balor); he fathered, by *Ernmas or *Eirnin, the three eponymous goddesses of early Ireland, *Ériu, *Fódla, and *Banba. Ériu mates with *Elatha, son of Delbáeth (1), to produce *Bres.

3. *Munster leader, seventh in line from *Ailill Aulomm. After being banished with his five sons, Delbáeth went to the cairn of *Fiachu (a common early Irish name) and kindled there a druidical *fire from which burst five fiery streams. He directed each of his five sons to a stream, thus explaining the origin of the five instances of the tribal and place-name Delbna.

Delbcháem, Delbchaen, Dealbcháem. [Ir., fair shape]. Mysterious and beautiful lover of *Art mac Cuinn in **Echtrae Airt meic Cuinn* [The Adventure of Art Son of Conn]. The daughter of Morgán, king of the Land of Wonder, and his terrible warrior wife, *Coinchenn; sister of the ugly *Ailill Dubdétach. After his stepmother *Bé Chuma impersonates Delbcháem to Art, she puts the latter under a *geis not to eat until he has brought Delbcháem from a mysterious island, intending thus to cause her death. Once there, Art learns from fair women how to escape the dangers before him and rescues Delbcháem from a high tower, killing her father and mother. Art subsequently banishes Bé Chuma from Tara.

Delga, Dealga. *Fir Bolg chieftain, builder of the fortress *Dun Delgan (Dundalk), later to belong to *Cúchulainn.

Delgnat. Variant spelling of *Dealgnaid.

Deluge. See FLOOD LEGENDS; SUBMERGED CITIES; DWYFAN AND DWYFACH; YS, LEGEND OF THE CITY OF.

Demetae, the [L]. One of the five principal tribes of pre-Roman and Roman Wales, according to the geographer Ptolemy (2nd cent. AD), occupying the south-western extremity of the country between the Rivers Teifi and Tywi, largely coextensive with the territory later known as *Dyfed. The Demetae appear to have offered little resistance to the Romans, and their homeland, known as Demetia, became a region of settled pastoralism. At the end of the 4th cent. AD Demetia was invaded by the *Déisi from Ireland. *Dewi Sant, patron saint of Wales, directed his main missionary activity towards portions of Demetia. The numerically superior Demetae eventually absorbed the Déisi.

Demne Máel. Boyhood name in classical Irish for *Fionn mac Cumhaill; *Deimne Maol is the ModIr. variant; Domhnach, Deima, etc., appear in oral tradition. Demne implies assurance or firmness and stability. Máel denotes short hair, and associations with *druidism and the *Otherworld. See J. F. Nagy, 'Demna Mael', *Celtica*, 14 (1981), 8–14, on the significance of this name; also J. F. Nagy, *The Wisdom of the Outlaw* (Berkeley, Calif., 1985).

demon [Gk. daimōn]. A Greek concept of an evil spirit, of second rank spiritually, borrowed by Christian commentators and applied subjectively to Celtic phenomena, such as the 'demons' driven from Ireland by St *Patrick. Almost any pre-Christian personalities may be described as demons, especially the *Fomorians and the *Tuatha Dé Danann. A large number of mischievous or malevolent figures from oral tradition may be called demons; these include *bocánach and the *Cornu of Ireland; the *ankou, *nain, and *youdik of Brittany. *Bodb changes *Aífe (2) into a 'demon of the air', a concept that appears in many translated texts although not expressed in an Irish phrase. See also DEVIL.

Deoch, Deocha, Deoca, Deichthe. Proud, vain princess of the 'South', i.e. *Munster, in **Oidheadh Chlainne Lir* [The Tragic Story of the Children of Lir]. The curse transforming the children into swans was prophesied to last until a Woman of the South should be joined with a man from the North. Deoch, daughter of the Munster chieftain *Fínghein, does indeed marry Lairgnéan, a prince of *Connacht. As Deoch speaks of her desire to possess the four singing swans, Lairgnéan resolves to get them, and the violence of his seizure undoes the magic which disguised them.

Der [OIr., daughter, girl (poetic)]. First syllable, sometimes separated, e.g. of many figures from early Ireland; alphabetized letter by letter.

derbfhine, derbfine, derbhfhine, dearbhfhine, deirbhfhine. Family group of four generations, the descendants of a common great-grandfather, in early Ireland and Gaelic Scotland; the normal property-owning unit and unit for dynastic succession, as any male member of a king's derbfhine—son, uncle, brother, nephew—might succeed him. In short, primogeniture did not prevail; property and power did not go automatically to the eldest legitimate male. See T. M. Charles-Edwards, *Early Irish and Welsh Kinship* (Oxford, 1993); Nerys T. Patterson, *Cattle-Lords and Clansmen: Kingship and Rank in Early Ireland* (New York, 1992); Liam Ó Buachalla, 'Some Researches in Ancient Irish Law', *Journal of the Cork Historical and Archaeological Society*, 52 (1947), 41–54, 135–48; 53 (1948), 1–12, 75–81; Donnchadh Ó Corráin, 'Irish Regnal Succession: A Reappraisal', *Studia Hibernica*, 9 (1971), 7–39. See also DÁL; KINGSHIP.

Derbforgaill, Dearbhfhorgaill, Derbhorgill, Derbforgaille, Dervorgilla, Devorgill, Devorvilla [Ir., daughter of Forgall]. Name borne by several personages in both myth and history.

Derbforgaill 1. Princess of *Lochlainn who suffers unrequited love for *Cúchulainn. Hearing stories of the hero's prowess but without having seen him, Derbforgaill and a servant take the forms of *swans to seek Cúchulainn. Not knowing their identity, the hero casts a stone at one swan, who, fallen to the ground, becomes Derbforgaill. He sucks the blood from her wound, saving her, but because he has tasted her blood, is forbidden carnal relations with her; Cúchulainn then gives Derbforgaill to his foster-brother (or foster-son) *Lugaid Riab nDerg. The marriage is happy, but Derbforgaill dies an ugly death. Provoked into a contest to prove her sexual allure, by seeing which woman can send her urine furthest through a pillar of snow, Derbforgaill wins, only to bring down the wrath of the other courtly women, who jealously mutilate and kill her. Cúchulainn vengefully slaughters 150 women of the household, but Lugaid perishes of grief or shock.

2. One of the most famous adulteresses of medieval Irish history. Wife of Tigernán Ua Ruairc [O'Rourke], she departed with *Diarmait mac Murchada [Dermot MacMurrough], perhaps willingly (1152), but returned home the next year. The resultant bitterness between the families led to the Anglo-Normans coming to Ireland, and thus the end of Irish freedom. In repentance, Derbforgaill founded the Nuns' church at *Clonmacnoise.

Derbrenn. First love of *Angus Óg and foster-mother of six children magically changed into pigs by their birth-mother. Hunted by 100 heroes, the six seek help from Angus Óg, who refuses it until they complete a series of magical tasks. When those are done within a year, *Medb hunts them, slaying all but one.

Derc Ferna. See DUNMORE.

Derdriu. Preferred OIr. spelling of *Deirdre.

derg. OIr. spelling of ModIr. dearg [red]. Derg implies red, ruddy, used as the colour for blood, flame; also the orange of tawny hue, as of ale, gold, etc. See also DÁIRE DERG; LOUGH DERG.

Derga. See TOGAIL BRUIDNE DA DERGA.

dergfhlaith, dergflaith [Ir., red sovereignty]. The red sovereignty or 'red ale' envisioned by *Conn Cétchathach [of the Hundred Battles]; the name puns on flaith [sovereignty] and laith [ale, liquor]. In Conn's dream, *Sovereignty gives dergfhlaith to him in lieu of sleeping with him; he and his descendants continue to drink of it.

Derglas. Another name, especially in Scottish Gaelic lore, for *Caílte.

Dér Gréine [Ir., sun tear]. Daughter of *Fiachna mac Rétach who marries *Lóegaire mac Crimthann; this is a partial reward for the hero's having helped Fiachna regain his abducted wife and daughter. See *Echtrae Lóegairi* [Adventure of Lóegaire].

Dering. Anglicization of *Diorruing.

Dermit, Dermot. Anglicizations of *Diarmait.

Derry. Anglicization of *Doire.

Dervorgill, Dervorgilla. Anglicizations of *Derbforgaill.

Désa. See DONN DÉSA.

deshel. Hiberno-English term for *sunwise turn.

Dési. See DÉISI.

Desmond [Ir. *Deasmhumhain, Desmuma*, South *Munster]. A territory in southern Ireland, recognized before the carving out of counties in the 17th century, coextensive today with Co. *Kerry and much of Co. Cork and Co. Limerick. In the 16th century Desmond was a theatre of armed resistance to English rule led by the Fitzgerald family or 'Geraldines', and has enjoyed rich romantic associations ever since. As the title of earl was in succession for several centuries, many historical figures could be called 'earl of Desmond', but the one most celebrated in story is *Gerald, also known as Lord Gerald or the Red Earl.

The name Desmond [Ir. *Deasmhumhnach*] was uncommon in Ireland until modern times, although it had gained some cachet, ironically, in England by the late 19th century; the ModIr. Deasúin appears to be a nationalist retranslation.

Desmuma. OIr. form of *Desmond.

dessel. OIr. word for *sunwise turn.

Déssi. See DÉISI.

Destructions. A class of tales in early Irish signified by the first word of the title, Togail (sing.), Togla (pl), e.g. The Destruction of Da Derga's Hostel; see TOGAIL BRUIDNE DA DERGA.

dét fis. The 'tooth of wisdom', cited in different rites.

Dēva, Deva [L goddess]. Roman name for the Celtic river-goddess who gives her name to the River Dee of North Wales and Chester, England.

Devenish [Ir. *Daimhinis*, ox island]. Site of ruined early island monastery in Lough *Erne, Co. Fermanagh, Northern Ireland. See Ann Hamlin, *Devenish* (Newry, 1979).

devil. The well-known creature from Jewish and Christian theology is sometimes aligned with characters in Celtic narrative; e.g. *Caoránach, the 'monster' of *Lough Derg, may be known as the mother of the devil. Aspects of *Donn (1), ruler of the dead, were used in portrayals of the devil in pious Irish folklore. The *earwig, a small centipede, is thought to be a disguise for the devil in Irish folklore. Speakers in Irish folklore conventionally refer to the devil as The Adversary, *An tÁibhirseoir*. In most other instances the Celtic languages employ cognates borrowed from Latin, English, and French, e.g. Ir. diabhal; ScG diabhal; Manx jouyl; W diafol, diawl, cythraul; Corn. dyawl; Bret. diaoul.

Devorgilla. See DERBFORGAILL.

Dewi Sant, Saint David. Patron saint of Wales, 520(?)–589(?), known for his asceticism and for his promotion of hard manual labour. Most information about his life dates from the Latin biography (*c.*1090) by Rhigyfarch (or Rhygyfarch; anglicized Ricemarch), although Dewi Sant is cited in the *Catalogue of Irish Saints* (*c.*900–1000) and **Armes Prydein* [Prophecy of Britain] (*c.*930). Rhigyfarch's account may be partisan, as he was the son of Bishop Sulien of Saint David's, *Dyfed (until 1974, Pembrokeshire); at that time this centre of Welsh Christianity was resisting domination by Canterbury and the Normans.

Born of a princely family at Vetus Rubus, *Ceredigion (Hen Fynyw, *Dyfed, formerly Cardiganshire), Dewi took holy orders as a young man and later studied under the Welsh Saint Paulinus on an island, perhaps Llanddeusant on *Anglesey. Much is written of his travels, which may have included Jerusalem. On pilgrimage in south Wales and the west of England, he founded twelve monasteries, most notably *Glastonbury. The healing waters at *Bath, although known to the Romans, are attributed to Dewi. After defeating an Irish chieftain named Boia, he settled at Glyn Rhosyn [L *Vallis Rosina*; also *Mynyw* or *Menevia*] in the far south-west corner of Dyfed, now called Saint David's. His community lived a life of extreme austerity. No cattle were allowed to assist the monks in the tilling of the earth. As they ate no meat and drank only water, Dewi's monks were known as the 'watermen'. Outsiders had to wait ten days at the gate before entry. Dewi is also described as having denounced the Pelagian heresy. His best-known miracle was preaching at the synod of Llanddewibrefi, where the ground rose beneath him so that all could see and hear him. In art he is represented as standing on a mound with a white dove on his shoulder.

The feast-day of Dewi Sant, 1 March, is a Welsh holiday, a time for patriotic and cultural celebration since the 18th century; it was a day for religious celebration until the Reformation. 1 March was also formerly a day for Welshmen to wear leeks on their person, as noted by Shakespeare in *Henry V* (1592). The Latin life of Dewi Sant appears in *Vitae sanctorum britaniae et genealiogiae*, ed. A. W. Wade-Evans (Cardiff, 1944); the Welsh life, *Buched Dewi*, was edited by D. Simon Evans (Cardiff, 1959); also *The Welsh Life of St. David*, ed. D. Simon Evans (Cardiff, 1988). See also Ernest Rhys, *The Life of Saint David* (Tregynon, 1927); TEILO.

dewin. The Welsh word for magician; see DYN HYSBYS.

Dhoya. Character in an early (1891) short story by W. B. Yeats. A *Fomorian giant abandoned by his comrades in Sligo, Dhoya marries a *fairy bride but loses her to her fairy husband in a chess game. Although essentially a dream vision of the author, Dhoya may draw elements from the story of *Eochaid Airem and *Étaín; see TOCHMARC ÉTAÍNE [The Wooing of Étaín]. The name Dhoya may have been borrowed from Pool Dyoya, the deepest part of Sligo Bay. See *John Sherman and Dhoya*, ed. R. J. Finneran (Detroit, 1969).

Dialogue of the Elders. See ACALLAM NA SENÓRACH.

Dian [Ir., swift, rapid; intense; strong]. Name borne by several figures in early Irish narrative.

Dian 1. Son of the malevolent *Carman who joined his two brothers in laying waste to Ireland.

2. Young chieftain of the *Fianna of *Fionn mac Cumhaill who was taken to the *Otherworld by the powers of the *sídh. On his return to the world of mortals he reported that he would prefer to be a slave of the *Fianna than a ruler in the Otherworld (an echo of Achilles' remark to Odysseus in the *Odyssey*).

Dian Cécht, Diancécht, Dían Cécht [Ir., rolling quickly forward (?); swift power (?)]. Principal healing god or physician of the ancient Irish and 'sage of leechcraft' (i.e. medicine) for the *Tuatha Dé Danann. Father of *Étan (1) and *Cian, thus grandfather of *Lug Lámfhota. In **Cath Maige Tuired* [The (Second) Battle of Mag Tuired] Dian Cécht's powerful healing spring can restore every mortally wounded man, except for the decapitated. More memorably, he makes a wonderful silver arm and hand with moving fingers for the wounded *Nuadu, who is afterwards called Nuadu Airgetlám [of the Silver Hand/Arm]. The arm is not sufficient, however, to qualify Nuadu for kingship. Later Dian Cécht's son Miach makes Nuadu an arm of flesh that allows him to ascend to power. In jealousy at his son's greater power, Dian Cécht then slays Miach. Dian Cécht is also jealous of his daughter *Airmid, who has sought to classify all magical healing herbs; he disrupts her ordering. The hero *Mac Cécht appears to be euhemerized from Dian Cécht.

Dian Cécht was known late into Christian times and his charms invoked at least until the 8th century. In modern folklore Dian Cécht's porridge is a cure for colds, sore throat, phlegm, and worms; it is made of *hazel nuts, *dandelion, woodsorrel, chickweed, and oatmeal.

Diana. Roman goddess of hunting, chastity, the moon, and open places; counterpart of the Greek *Artemis. Diana was worshipped widely in Roman Britain, and her name was venerated in many localities, including the Iron Age site of Maiden Castle, Dorsetshire. In Autun, France, Diana was regarded as a midday demon. Two possible Celtic counterparts are the Irish *Flidais, who drove a chariot drawn by *deer, and *Arduinna, the Gaulish *boar-goddess.

Diaring. Variant spelling of *Diorruing.

Diarmait, Diarmaid, Diarmuid, Diarmit, Dearmid, Dermot; sometimes anglicized as Jeremiah, Jerome, Darby [Ir., origin unknown]. One of the most common names in early Ireland, borne by scores of kings, saints, and heroes, the most notable of whom is *Diarmait Ua Duibne, the lover of *Gráinne.

Diarmait 1. King of *Tara, husband of *Becfola, whose story is told in *Tochmarc Becfhola* [The Wooing of Becfola]. Becfola lusts after Crimthann (1), Diarmait's fosterling, who refuses to elope with her because he will not travel on a Sunday. She later departs for the *Otherworld with Flann, but their affair is not consummated; she returns, unnoticed, in what seems an instant to ordinary mortals. Not to be confused with *Diarmait mac Cerbaill.

Diarmait mac Cerbaill, Cerrbeóil, Mac Cearbhaill, MacKerval. Historical *ard rí [high king] of Ireland, *c.*545–*c.*565/8, son of Fergus Cerrbél, a leader of the southern *Uí Néill, and reputedly the last pagan monarch. He was the last to celebrate the pagan ritual of *feis Temrach [the feast of Tara], i.e. of 'sleeping' with the local earth-goddess. The annals record that Diarmait was defeated by the northern Uí Néill at the Battle of Cúl Dremne, AD 561. He is better remembered for bringing curses from holy men, one that would leave *Tara desolate until Doomsday. A fanciful St *Rúadán (sometimes St Rónán) cursed Tara. Trouble began when one of Diarmait's retainers was killed by Áed Guaire, related in fosterage to St Rúadán. When Diarmait sent armed men to seize Áed, Rúadán concealed him, and so the king had the saint arrested and tried in his place. For this outrage, condemned by other clergy as well, St Rúadán declared that Tara should remain desolate forever.

Other legends describe three prophecies of Diarmait's death, one by a St Rónán, another by a St Ciarán (not identified as being of either Clonmacnoise or Seir), and a third by the druid *Bec mac Dé. Diarmait's troubles begin when he punishes *Flann mac Díma for adultery with his wife, *Mugain (3). Diarmait has Flann's fortress burned over his head, forcing him to seek refuge in a vat of water, where he drowns at *Beltaine. For this, according to St Rónán, a roofbeam will fall on Diarmait's head. St Ciarán foretells that Diarmait will die as Flann had. But Diarmait's own druid, Bec mac Dé, prophesies a threefold death: by drowning, burning, and having a roofbeam fall on his head. Diarmait will be killed, the druid says, by Áed Dub [Ir., Dark

Fire], Flann's kinsman, in the house of *Banbán the hospitaller. It will happen the night he wears a shirt grown from a single flax seed, drinks ale brewed from one grain of corn, and eats pork from a sow that has never farrowed. As these events seem easy to avoid, Diarmait dismisses the prophecy, even when Banbán invites him to a banquet; his wife, Mugain, however, accepts the prophecy and refuses to attend.

Seeing Mugain absent, Banbán offers his own daughter to be Diarmait's bed-partner for the night. Upon receiving a nightshirt, meat, and ale, Diarmait is not suspicious. When the girl tells him that the nightshirt has been made from a single flax seed, the pork has come from a sow that has not farrowed, and the ale has been brewed from a single grain of corn, the high king knows that the prophecy has been fulfilled. Before Diarmait can escape, Áed Dub meets him at the door, piercing him with his spear. Fleeing to the back of the house, wounded, Diarmait finds himself engulfed in flames; Áed Dub's men have set the house ablaze. Hoping to escape the conflagration, Diarmait leaps into a vat of ale; and a flaming roofbeam falls on his head. Bec mac Dé's prophecy is fulfilled. See F. J. Byrne, *Irish Kings and High-Kings* (London, 1973), 87–105.

Diarmait mac Murchada, MacMurrough, MacMorrogh, McMurrow. Twelfth-century king of Leinster best remembered for bringing the Anglo-Normans to Ireland, *c.*1169–70, and one of the most execrated names in Irish history. Diarmait eloped with *Derbforgaill (2), wife of Tigernán Ua Ruairc [O'Rourke], taking also her substantial dowry, while her husband was on pilgrimage; Derbforgaill may have gone willingly. A traditional date for this elopement is 8 March 1152 or 1156. Tigernán appealed to Tairdelbach Ua Conchobair [Turlough O'Connor], king of Connacht and *ard rí, for redress. Tairdelbach forced Diarmait to return Derbforgaill along with her dowry. Later the next ard rí, Ruaidrí Ua Conchobair [Rory/Roderick O'Connor], deposed and banished Diarmait, who fled first to Britain and later to Aquitaine. The Norman-Welsh Richard de Clare, Earl of Pembroke, popularly known as Strongbow, heeded the call, having been promised Diarmait's daughter Aífe. A year after a small preliminary force seized the Danish city of Wexford, May 1169, Strongbow led a large force of armed men to Waterford and Dublin, with the blessings of King Henry II and Pope Adrian IV. Diarmait died in 1171, a year after the taking of Dublin.

The story of Diarmait's treachery has inspired many popular retellings, including one by a president of the United States; see John Quincy Adams, *Dermot MacMorrogh, or the Conquest of Ireland* (Boston, 1832).

Diarmait Ua Duibne, úa Duibne, Ó Duibhne, O'Duinn, O'Dyna. Hero of **Tóraigheacht Dhiarmada agus Ghráinne* [The Pursuit of Diarmait and Gráinne] of the *Fenian Cycle, leading member of *Fionn mac Cumhaill's *Fianna, possessor of the **ball seirce* [love-spot], and one of the greatest lovers of early Irish literature. His father is usually named *Donn, sometimes Corc; his paternal grandfather is Duibne. His mother is usually given as *Cochrann, daughter of *Cathaír Mór, and sometimes as *Cróchnat. Regardless of his parentage, Diarmait is most linked with his divine fosterer and patron, *Angus Óg. Several of Diarmait's weapons are known by specific names: his great spear, Gáe Derg [red spear], Crann Buí [yellow shaft], the smaller Gáe Buide [yellow spear], and a sword, Nóralltach [great fury], also attributed to Angus Óg and Manannán mac Lir.

Shortly after his birth, Diarmait's father Donn takes him to be fostered by Angus Óg at *Brug na Bóinne. While there, Donn learns that his wife has lain in adultery with Roc, Angus Óg's steward. She gives birth to a child, whom Donn murders but whom his father, Roc, restores to life as a great *boar with a magical wand. Roc orders the boar to hunt Diarmait to death, which he accomplishes in *Tóraigheacht Dhiarmada agus Ghráinne*. In most versions the boar roams near *Ben Bulben, Co. Sligo, but other areas in both Ireland and Scotland have claimed him as well.

Another well-known story explains his *ball seirce, which made him irresistible to women. Already the handsomest of the Fianna, Diarmait is hunting with *Goll, *Conán mac Morna, and *Oscar when he comes upon a beautiful young girl living with an old man, his cat, and his wether (gelded sheep) in a hut in the forest. As they all sit down to eat, the old man's cat jumps up on the table, but none of the Fianna can take it off. The old man explains that the wether is the world and the cat death. After the four men have gone to bed, the beautiful young girl sleeps in the same room with them. Each of the men desires to make love with her, but she rejects all but Diarmait, declaring that she is Youth incarnate and that she will put a spot on her lover that no woman may see without loving him. Touching his forehead, she gives him the ball seirce.

The hero's best-known story is told in *Tóraigheacht Dhiarmada agus Ghráinne*, in which Diarmait elopes with young Gráinne while she is betrothed to the aged Fionn. The lovers are pursued all over Ireland for many years, until Diarmait is gored by a boar and allowed to die by Fionn. Diarmait also participates in the chase for *Ábartach [the Hard Gilly] and has adventures in the *Otherworld. His counterpart in the *Ulster Cycle is *Noíse, lover of *Deirdre. He is also compared with *Adonis of classical mythology and Osiris of Egyptian. The shadowy *Ferdoman of the Fenian Cycle may anticipate him.

díchetal do chennaib, *díchedul do chennaib, dícheadal do cheannaibh* [OIr., extempore incantation (?)]. A kind of incantation or spell composed by poets (*fili) and *druids of early Ireland. Various early sources describe it as being composed extemporaneously, often using the finger-tips, which may imply *divination. Commentators have suggested that *díchetal do chennaib* may have been a kind of clairvoyance or psychometry in which the seer conveys his message in quatrain or verse. The *ollam was required to be proficient in both the díchetal do chennaib and the *imbas forosnai. *Fionn mac Cumhaill is described as being especially proficient at díchetal do chennaib. St *Patrick allowed díchetal do chennaib to continue because it was judged harmless and did not involve pagan rites.

See also DIVINATION; TEINM LAÍDA; AWENYDDION.

Díchorb. Son of *Ailill Aulomm killed at the Battle of Mag Mucrama [*Cath Maige Mucrama*] in eastern Co. Galway, along with his uncle, *Art, son of Conn.

Dícuill, Dícuil. Historical Irish monk (*c*.775-*c*.850) who wrote on geography, astronomy, and metrics. Although he was resident at the Carolingian court, his writings show a first-hand knowledge of Ireland and Gaelic Scotland; he discourses knowledgeably on lands as distant as the Faroes and Ethiopia. His writings have been cited to support the discovery of Iceland by Irish monks, *c*.800. His principal work, [*Liber*] *De Mensura Orbis Terrae* has been edited three times, by C. A. Walckenaer (Paris, 1807), G. Parthey (Berlin, 1870), and J. J. Tierney (Dublin, 1967).

Dígde, Díge, Díghe, Díge, Dí [OIr., asking pardon (?); praying forgiveness (?)]. An early territorial goddess of *Munster whose identity merged with that of the *Cailleach Bhéire.

díguin. An Old Irish word whose fullest translation is 'violation of a man's protection through the wounding and slaying of another'. One of the gravest offences against a king or powerful magnate would be to harm or to murder someone under his protection.

Dil Maccu Crecga, Díl [Ir. *dil*, dear, beloved, precious, profitable]. Also Treth Moccu Creccai. A *druid of Osraige [*Ossory] in the invading army of *Lugaid mac Con who puts a spell on Lugaid's brother, Eógan (3). When Dil realizes that the royal Eógan is certain to be killed, he asks that his daughter Moncha be allowed to sleep with Eógan so that some of Dil's descendants may become king of *Munster. Eógan is killed, and nine months later Moncha gives birth to *Fiachu Muillethan, a name appearing often in *Eóganacht and *Munster genealogies.

Díle [Ir., flood]. Irish term for the biblical Flood, usually with definite article, An Díle.

Dillus Farfog, Farfawg, Varvawc [W, Dillus the Bearded]. Welsh *giant; one of the tasks of *Culhwch was to steal hair from Dillus's beard to make a leash for *Twrch Trwyth and *Drudwyn. Daunting though the task was, Culhwch accomplished it easily. See CULHWCH AC OLWEN. *Cei and *Bedwyr also make such a leash from Dillus's beard.

Din Eidyn. Historical citadel of the *Gododdin, comparable to *Dumbarton rock; widely presumed to be the extremity of the great Castle Rock in *Edinburgh, now obscured by Edinburgh Castle. Also known as Caer Eiddyn.

Dinadan, Dinaden. A knight of the Round Table in the Arthurian legends, usually Sir Dinadan. A satirist and one of the few wits of the Arthurian legends, Dinadan writes a lampoon against King *Mark and plays pranks on the other knights during a tournament in which *Lancelot takes part. In response, Lancelot appears with a dress over his armour, overpowers Dinadan, and carries him into a nearby forest, where he dresses him as a woman for punishment. Dinadan is later killed by Mordred. Commentators have not asserted a Celtic ancestry for him.

Dinas Emrys, Emreis [W, Ambrosius's fort]. Welsh name for the hill-fort on the southern fringes of Mount *Snowdon in *Gwynedd, with Arthurian and other legendary associations; also known as Braich y Ddinas. Named for *Emrys Wledig [the prince, landholder; (L Ambrosius Aurelianus], the boy-prophet who confronts Vortigern and his magicians on this site. Archaeological excavation has revealed settlement from Roman times, habitation during the 5th century, and evidence of what was once a nearby pool.

According to the best-known story, Vortigern's attempts to build a tower fail when materials disappear at night and walls collapse. His magicians recommend human sacrifice, with blood from a 'fatherless boy' to caulk the foundations. Before the boy can be killed he reveals the existence of an underground pool and two *dragons in a stone chest, continually fighting; the dragons are explained as the Britons and the Saxons, to whom Vortigern has sold his kingship. In **Historia Brittonum* (9th cent., formerly attributed to Nennius) the boy's name is Ambrosius Aurelianus; in *Geoffrey of Monmouth (12th cent.) he is *Merlin. Vortigern gives the fortress to the boy.

Dinas Vawr. Anglicized spelling of a fortress of bogus historicity invented by Thomas Love Peacock in the comic novel *The Misfortunes of Elphin* (1829). A poem within the novel, 'The War-Song of Dinas Vawr', portrays the delight of Welshmen in stealing sheep; later set to music it has almost the status of a folksong. Although Peacock does not posit a Welsh original, it should be dinas fawr (mawr) [big fort].

Dind Ríg, Dinn Ríg, Dinnrígh, Dinrígh [Ir., royal fort, fortress of kings]. Site of old earthworks, former citadel, on the west bank of the Barrow River near Leighlinbridge, Co. Carlow, with rich associations in early Irish literature. T. F. O'Rahilly (1946) asserted that Dind Ríg might have been known to Ptolemy (2nd cent. AD) as Dunon. Most often it is seen as the fortress of south *Leinster kings and their most ancient place. The *Fir Bolg king *Sláinge was thought to be buried here, and thus it is sometimes known as Duma Sláinge/Sláine. Dind Ríg is also known as Tuaim Tenba. In the best-known story, **Orgain Denna Ríg* [The Destruction of Dind Ríg], *Labraid Loingsech burns the citadel to the ground. Ramparts of the remaining earthworks are 237 feet in diameter. See *Orgain Denna Ríg*, ed. David Greene, in *Fingal Rónáin and Other Stories* (Dublin, 1955). Joseph Vendryes (trans.), 'La Destruction de Dind Rig', *Études Celtiques*, 8 (1958–9), 7–40.

Dindshenchas, Dinnshenchas, Dinnsheanchas, Dinnsheanchus, Dinn-Shenchus [Ir., lore of prominent places]. A collection of Old Irish local legends, in prose and verse, explaining the names and giving associations of famous rivers, fords, lakes, hills, and other places. Included also are stories of mythic and heroic figures who appear in lengthier narratives elsewhere; e.g. many stories are *Fenian. While most texts are imaginative, much information contained is factual; the Modern Irish word dinnsheanchas means 'topography'. The principal text is in the **Book of Leinster* (*c*.1150), but materials are preserved in many great Irish codices as well as in collections in Edinburgh and Rennes, France. See also CÓIR ANMANN.

See *The Metrical Dindshenchas*, ed. Edward Gwynn, Todd Lecture Series (5 vols., Dublin, 1903–35); *Poems from the Dindshenchas*, ed. Edward Gwynn (Dublin, 1900); 'Prose Tales in the Rennes Dindshenchas', ed. Whitley Stokes, *Revue Celtique*, 15–16 (1894–5); Charles Bowen, 'Studies in the Dindsenchas', dissertation (Harvard, 1972); Tomás Ó Concheanainn, 'The Three Forms of *Dinnshenchas Érenn*', *Journal of Celtic Studies*, 3 (1981), 88–101; 'A Pious Redactor of Dinnshenchas Érenn', *Ériu*, 33 (1982), 85–98.

Dingle [Ir. *An Daingean*, the fortress] peninsula, *c*.100 square miles in west Co. *Kerry, stretching from Tralee and the *Sliab Mis [Slieve Mish] mountains to the most westerly point in Ireland. The peninsula is also known as Corcaguiney [ModIr. *Corca Dhuibhne*], after a powerful early population, the *Corcu Duibne, while the name Dingle also applies to a substantial town (pop. 4,000) on the south coast and to Dingle Bay, south of the peninsula. Dingle is often perceived to be one of the most Irish parts of Ireland, containing one of the last Irish-speaking (Gaeltacht) areas and a multitude of megalithic and early historic remains. Dingle was the home of the great hero *Cú Roí and is the locale of many early Irish narratives, e.g. **Cath Fionntrágha*, set in Ventry harbour. The Witch of Dingle was said to be a sister of the *Cailleach Bhéire.

Dinn Ríg, Dinnrígh. Variant spellings of *Dind Ríg.

Dinnshenchas. Variant spelling of *Dindshenchas.

Dinny-Mara. Variant spelling of *dooiney marrey.

Dinoding, Dinodig. Former cantref (100 townships) in *Gwynedd (until 1974, Merionethshire), Wales. In the **Mabinogi*, *Lleu Llaw Gyffes marries *Blodeuedd and reigns here.

Dinrigh. Variant spelling of *Dind Ríg.

Diodorus Siculus. Sicilian-born classical historian (1st cent. BC), often cited for his commentaries on the Celts, especially the northern Gauls. His *Bibliotheca Historica* [Library of History] was a universal history, beginning with the earliest mythological times and running to the contemporary conquest of Gaul; of forty books thought to have been written, ten survive. See *The Library of History*, ed. and trans. C. H. Oldfather (Cambridge, Mass., and London, 1935).

Dionysus. Ancient Greek god of wine and fertility, worshipped in orgiastic rites; adapted from and identified with the earlier Lydian god Bacchus; known in Rome as both Bacchus and Liber. Some commentators see links between Dionysus and the Irish hero *Lug Lámfhota; see Michael Tierney, 'Lughnasa and Dionysus', *Éigse*, 10 (1963), 265–9.

Diorruing, Diorraing, Diaring, Dering, Deering. *Fenian hero, friend and attendant of *Fionn mac Cumhaill, member of his *Fianna, and a son of Dobar Ua Baíscne. Diorruing is credited with clairvoyance concerning both events happening concurrently at a distance and those that will occur in the future (i.e. *second sight); he need only shut his eyes and look into the darkness at the back of his head. At the beginning of **Tóraigheacht Dhiarmada agus Ghráinne* [The Pursuit of Diarmait and Gráinne], Diorruing tells the aged, lonely Fionn of the one woman in Ireland most worthy of him, *Gráinne.

Dioscuri [Gk., sons of Zeus]. In classical mythology the name given to Castor and Pollux (or Polydeuces) when spoken of as a team. The ancient historian *Diodorus Siculus (1st cent. BC) remarks that the Dioscuri were the gods most worshipped by the Celts in the west of *Gaul. An altar found at Paris portrays them amidst Celtic figures.

dìreach, dìthreach, direach [ScG *d'threach*, desert; uncultivated, solitary]. Creature in Scottish Gaelic folklore, a kind of *fachan, thus an ugly specimen of an ugly class. The d'reach is described as *giant with improbable deformities. One hand emerges from his chest; one leg is attached to his haunch; *one eye rests in his head; and one tuft of rigidly inflexible hair grows from that head. The d'reach haunts the deserted Glen Eiti (also Eite, Eitidh, Eitli; cf. ScG éitidh, éitigh, 'fierce, dreadful, ugly, dismal'), perhaps a distorted representation of Glen Etive, 8 miles S of Ballachulish.

Dirona. Variant spelling of *Sirona.

Dis Pater, Dispater, Dis. In Roman mythology, the god of the underworld and the dead, identified with Pluto (Gk. Hades), but often referred to as though having a separate personality. Julius *Caesar in *The Gallic Wars* (1st cent. BC) calls Dis the transcendent god among the Celts, one of the six in their 'pantheon', and asserts that all the Celts claimed him as their ultimate ancestor. Through *interpretatio romana* (see GAUL), we now ascribe the Roman name Dis Pater to the Gaulish deity, whose native name is unknown, just as we do with Gaulish *Mercury or *Mars. Several modern commentators have seen links between Dis Pater and nameable Celtic figures, especially *Donn (1), the god of the dead. Others cited include *Bile; *Cernunnos; the *Dagda; and *Taranis.

Díthorba, Dithurba. Legendary early king of Ireland, who ruled with his kinsmen (sometimes brothers, sometimes cousins) *Áed Ruad and *Cimbáeth. Each takes a seven-year term in a twenty-one-year cycle. Seven magicians, seven poets, and seven lords of *Ulster guarantee that the agreement will be kept. When Áed Ruad dies, his daughter *Macha (2) is elected to rule. Díthorba and Cimbáeth initially oppose her, but Cimbáeth makes peace with her and later marries her; she kills Díthorba. The five sons of Díthorba are forced by Macha to work as slaves in the building of *Emain Macha.

Dìthreach. Variant spelling of *Dìreach.

Diurán, Diuran. Sometimes Diurán 'the rhymer'. Poet and companion of *Máel Dúin on the fabulous **Imram Curaig Máele Dúin* [Voyage of Máel Dúin]. Among his adventures were: the plunge into the magic fountain that gives him lifelong youth and good health; cutting off the arm of the man holding the magical thread, thus allowing the crew to escape; and tearing off a piece of net from the pillar of silver, which he lays on the altar at *Armagh. This last is usually thought a Christian emendation of the original text.

Diviciacus. Variant spelling of *Divitiacus.

divination [L *divinus*, god]. Foretelling the future or discovering what is hidden or unknown, especially through intuitive, occult, or allegedly supernatural means; this includes vaticination, only foretelling the future through esoteric or occult means, but is distinct from prophecy, which does not always imply a magical motive. Abundant commentary from both Celtic and non-Celtic sources testifies to the widespread Celtic belief in divination under many forms. From the earliest times birds, especially the raven and the wren, were thought to have divining powers. Celtic New Year, 1 November (*Samain in Old Irish), was a popular time to practise divination, to see who would survive the winter or who would marry a young maiden. *Druids, both male and female, were thought adept at divination. In many stories heroes and heroines, notably *Deirdre, have their fate foretold at birth. To ignore such warning is to court disaster, as *Conaire Mór shows. Divination might take many forms: signs from nature, omens, and dreams. Astrology may have been practised; an early Irish word for astrologer appears to be nél(l)adóir 'cloud diviner'. At *Tara a new king was selected by using a *bull in a special rite called tarbfheis, 'bull feast'. Wood was thought to have special properties for divination. In early Ireland one could learn the future by casting *yew wands with *ogham inscriptions upon the ground. In *Fenian stories, wood shavings may help to find a missing or fugitive person. *Fionn mac Cumhaill and *Merlin are described as having special powers of divination.

See AWENYDDION; DÍCHETAL DO CHENNAIB; DYN HYSBYS; IMBAS FOROSNAI; SECOND SIGHT; SHAMANISM; SOUS; TEINM LAÍDA. See also Margaret E. Griffiths, *Early Vaticination in Welsh with English Parallels* (Cardiff, 1937).

divine horse. See EPONA.

divine land. Phrase used in English translations of Irish and Welsh stories whose reference cannot be made specific without knowing the preceding Celtic text. By implication the 'divine land' is a pleasant, even Elysian place, not the realm of the dead; see OTHERWORLD. In Irish stories 'divine land' most often refers to *Tír na nÓg [the Land of Youth], which is visited by several heroes, notably *Oisín. It may also refer to *Mag Mell [Pleasant Plain], *Tír Tairngire [the Land of Promise], *Tír na mBan [the Land of Women], and others. In Welsh contexts 'divine land' may refer to *Annwfn or *Caer Siddi.

Divitiacus, Diviciacus. Roman name for the west Gaulish (Aeduan) *druid of the Liger [Loire] valley known to Julius *Caesar (1st cent. BC) and cited by Cicero (1st cent. BC) for his knowledge of *divination.

Divonna, Divona. Another name for *Sirona.

Diwrnach Wyddel, Dyrnwch [W *Gwyddel*, Irish (-man)]. Irish owner of the magical *cauldron in **Culhwch ac Olwen*; a steward of King Odgar fab Aedd. Diwrnach is sometimes described as a giant, and his cauldron will not cook the food of a coward. Olwen's father, *Ysbaddaden Bencawr, demands that Diwrnach's cauldron be brought to Wales to provide food for his daughter's wedding feast. *Arthur asks Odgar to persuade Diwrnach to give it up willingly, but the steward refuses. After another failed attempt to wheedle Diwrnach, Arthur seizes the cauldron and takes it to Wales brimming with Irish treasure. The cauldron also appears in the second branch of the **Mabinogi* and **Preiddiau Annwfn* [The Spoils of Annwfn̦].

Do Dera, Dadara, Da Deara. The *fool of *Lugaid mac Con who put on the crown to impersonate him during the Battle of Cenn Abrat. Lugaid escaped, but Do Dera was killed by *Eógan (3), of *Munster.

Do Fhlathiusaib Érenn [Ir., tract on the kingship of Ireland]. A list of kings of Ireland from earliest times. See edition and translation by R. A. S. Macalister included in pt. v of *Lebor Gabála Érenn*, Irish Texts Society, vol. 44 (Dublin, 1956).

Dobar, Dobhar. Fanciful king of Siogar [Sicily (?); cf. OIr. *Sicil*, Sicily] in **Oidheadh Chlainne Tuireann* [The Fate of the Children of Tuireann], who owned wonderful steeds that travelled with equal ease over land and sea. *Lug Lámfhota commanded the children to bring back the horses and the king's chariot, which they did by killing Dobar with a poisoned spear.

Dobharchú, Dorraghow [Ir., otter]. In Irish folklore, the father of all *otters and 'king' of the lakes. His snout is so powerful it can break through a rock. A figure of fear on land, he can kill people and animals and drink their blood.

Dodder River [Ir. *Dothra*]. Small stream in Co. Dublin with headwaters in the Wicklow mountains, flowing 12 miles into Dublin Bay; 2.5 miles from city centre at Ballsbridge, a contemporary residential neighbourhood. The setting for **Togail Bruidne Da Derga* [The Destruction of Da Derga's Hostel] is the banks of the Dodder River. Farther upstream is *Glenasmole, where St *Patrick is reputed to have conversed with *Oisín. See Christopher Moriarty, *Down the Dodder: Walks, Wildlife, History, Legend* (Dublin, 1991).

Dóel [Ir., beetle, chafer]. Brother of *Cairbre Lifechair, whose story is told in *Longas mac nDuíl Dermait* [The Exile of the Sons of Dóel the Forgotten].

Dóelchu. The *dog of *Conganchnes mac Dedad whose dripping blood kills *Celtchair mac Uthechair.

dog, dogs. The domesticated canine has played many roles in the Celtic imagination for thirty centuries. The dog is portrayed on the *Gundestrup cauldron and is associated with the Gaulish deity *Sirona and the early British deity *Nodons, worshipped at the Romano-British temple in *Lydney Park on the Severn. Dog bones are found in ancient holy wells. The Celts appear to have inherited three associations with the dog from Mediterranean religions: healing, hunting, and death. Humans in different cultures have been impressed by dogs' ability to heal themselves with their saliva. The Gaulish mother-deity *Nehalennia is invariably portrayed as accompanied by a dog, suggestive of healing. The association with hunting exists in English as well, of course, usually with the more specific word 'hound'; but in Celtic languages the function tends to be more heroic. The title Cú- in the name of the greatest of Irish heroes, *Cúchulainn ['hound' of Culann], may be translated as the more general 'dog' as well as 'hound'. A leader of pre-Claudian Britain, Cunobelinus, is literally 'The dog/hound of Belinus'. The association with death, also known elsewhere in European tradition (cf. the black dog in Goethe's *Faust*, 1808), seems to be based on dogs' instincts for carrion. Surviving evidence does not suggest there was ever a Celtic dog-deity as there may have been for the wolf. The dog and the horse are the favourite domestic animals of Celtic *fairies.

Few dogs in narratives are given much characterization; they are usually portrayed only as faithful companions to master or mistress, and sometimes as figures of fear. Among the benign Celtic dogs are: *Ailbe, Mac Dathó's dog in **Scéla Mucce meic Da Thó* [The Story of Mac Da Thó's Pig]; *Bran and *Sceolang, the prime hunting-dogs (and nephews) of *Fionn mac Cumhaill, as well as *Adhnuall, his alternate; *Cabal (Cavall in Tennyson), hound of *Arthur; *Dabilla, the lapdog of the goddess *Boand; Dóelchu, the dog whose dripping blood kills Celtchar mac Uthechair; *Drudwyn, hunting-dog of Culhwch; *Failinis, hound of *Lug Lámfhota; Gelert, the greyhound who saves the prince's baby as told in **Bedd Gelert*; the unnamed dog of *Cadan who helps him kill the beast; the unnamed lapdog of the *Fenian hero *Cairill; the unnamed *fairy dog with a white ring around its neck that roams near Galway.

The more fearful dogs include *Coinchenn, the monstrous dog-headed wife of Morgán; *cù s'th, the black dog of the Highlands; *cwˆn annwfn, the Welsh hell-hounds; *gwyllgi, the Welsh spectral mastiff; *moddey dhoo and *mauthe doog, the great black dogs of the Isle of *Man; the dogs of *Crom Dubh, Coinn Iotair [Hounds of Rage] and Saidhthe Suaraighe [Bitch of Evil]; the unnamed large black dog thought to haunt the *Sliab Mis [Slieve Mish] in Co. *Kerry; *ki du, the Breton black dog who accompanies reincarnation; and the unnamed but great menacing black dogs thought to come forth from the quagmire in Brittany known as the

*Youdic. OIr. cú, madrad; ModIr. cú, madra; ScG cù, madadh, balgaire; Manx moddey, coo; W ci; Corn. ky; Bret. ki. See also ANIMALS. See F. Jenkins, 'The Role of the Dog in Romano-Gaulish Religion', *Collection Latomus*, 16 (1957), 60–76.

Dòideag. Celebrated witch of the Isle of Mull, to whom are attributed many evils. In oral tradition she caused the destruction of the Spanish Armada. It was once believed that Dòideag was one of three witches who caused the drowning of the historical MacGille Chaluim Ratharsaidh [Iain Mac Gille Chaluim of Raasay], on 19 April 1671, on his way home from visiting the Earl of Seaforth on the Isle of Lewis; MacGille's foster-mother had set Dòideag on this business. Also known in English as Black Dòideag of Mull.

Doire [OIr., oak grove]. Name given to many places on the early Irish map, the most famous of which is the monastic settlement reputedly established on the west banks of the River Foyle by St *Colum Cille after 544. The settlement was sometimes called Doire Choluim Chille in his honour as well as to erase its previous pagan associations, when the site was known as Doire Calgaich [Calgach's Oak Grove]. Doire is coextensive with the modern industrial city, the fourth largest in Ireland, of Derry, or, as the British have called it since the reign of James I, Londonderry.

Doirend, Doirenn, Doireand, Doirinn, Dairenn, Dairean, Daireann, Doireann. Name borne by several female figures in Irish myth, legend, and history, usually minor supporting characters in other figures' stories. One is the daughter of *Midir, the *fairy king. The most significant is the woman of the *sídh in the *Fenian Cycle, supposed daughter of *Bodb, who tempted and tormented *Fionn. She said she would be Fionn's wife if he would take her and be faithful to her for a year, and for half of the time after that. When Fionn refused, she gave him a cup of enchanted mead that drove him insane, causing him to rail against the Fianna, who deserted him. *Caílte persuaded the Fianna to return and by nightfall the madness left Fionn.

dolmen [Bret. *tol*, table; *men*, stone]. A large prehistoric monument found throughout the Celtic world, usually made of two or more large, rough stones set on end and capped with a huge single stone or several stones, especially in Brittany or Ireland; capstones may weigh as much as 40 tons. In Wales and Cornwall preferred usage favours cromlech [W *crom*, bent; *llech*, flat stone], although cromlech may also imply a more circular monument. Peter Harbison (1988) argues that the dolmen should more accurately be called the portal tomb or chamber, but the older, more popular usage persists.

In Ireland dolmens are often called 'Beds of *Diarmait and *Gráinne' from the belief that the fleeing lovers may have slept on them in their escape from *Fionn. In Irish folklore the stones were thought to induce barrenness in women who strayed near them. In Cornwall cromlechs/dolmens were thought to be the quoits or playthings of *giants, and the recesses in them the marks of giants' fingers. At many times they were thought to be druids' altars, or, more commonly, 'druids' tables', from the unfounded assumption that they dated from the time of the *druids. Modern archaeology suggests, however, that they were built as tombs by pre-Celtic peoples.

More than 161 dolmens may be found in Ireland; other outstanding examples are at *Callernish, Isle of Lewis, Outer Hebrides, and at *Carnac and *Essé in *Brittany. Comparable monuments are found as far away as Japan.

dolphin [L from Gk. *delphis*]. The porpoise-like marine, warm-water mammal appears often in early Celtic iconography but not later. It may be found on the *Gundestrup cauldron and on Gaulish coins, as at various pre-Christian British sites, notably *Lydney Park. The ModIr. word for dolphin is deilf; ScG an leumadair; Manx perkin; W dolffin, morwch; Bret. delfin.

Domhnach. ModIr. oral-tradition variant of *Demne Máel.

Domhnach Chrom Dubh [Ir., Sunday of Crom Dubh]. Another name for *Lughnasa.

Domhnall 1. [ScG, world-ruler (?)]. Anglicized as Donald. Name borne by many shadowy figures of medieval Scotland, most notably the leader who gives his name to the Clan Donald or the family of MacDonald of the Isles. This Domhnall, who flourished in the early 12th century, was the grandson of *Somerled (died *c.*1164). Domhnall's father

Raghnall was the actual forebear of the clan, although the name derives from the son. The spelling Domhnall is both the ScG equivalent of the OIr. *Domnall and the ModIr. spelling of that name.

Domnainn. Also Fir Domnann, Fir Dhomhnann, Domnannaig. One of three early invading Celtic peoples of Ireland, along with the *Lagin and *Galióin, sometimes known collectively as the Laginians. The Domnainn, like their allies, may have been *P-Celts from Great Britain; distinction between the three groups is now thought to be the invention of tendentious medieval historians. The *Dumnonii of pre-Roman Britain are usually thought to be cognates of the Irish Domnainn. Although they ultimately settled in what is today north-west Co. Mayo, allusions to their name exist in place-names in many parts of Ireland; the Irish name for Malahide Bay, Co. Dublin, Inber Domnann, asserts the insupportable belief that the Domnainn landed there. Several commentators have sought to link these actual people with different pseudo-historical peoples in the **Lebor Gabála* [Book of Invasions]; those with the *Fir Bolg are most supportable.

Domnall, Domnal, Domhnall, Dónal, Donal [Ir., world ruler (?)]. This ninth most popular name in early Ireland was borne by many a saint, hero, and *ard rí [high king]. The name is sometimes speciously given the biblical cognate of Daniel. See DOMHNALL, the ScG equivalent.

Domnall 1. Son of *Áed (1), son of Ainmire, and a historical *ard rí [high king] of Ireland (*c.*628–42) who plays a leading role in the *Cycle of Kings, most notably **Buile Shuibhne* [The Frenzy of Sweeney]. Domnall first became ard rí when his predecessor, Suibne Menn, was killed by *Congal Cáech of *Ulster. Congal also opposed Domnall but was defeated at Dún Cethern, whereupon he fled to Scotland. There he enlisted the aid of *Domnall Brecc, the king of *Dál Riada, the Irish kingdom in *Argyllshire (since 1974, north Strathclyde), which at that time included some territory in north-eastern Ireland. Spurred on by Congal, Domnall Brecc invaded Ireland with a large army but was defeated by the Irish king Domnall at the Battle of Mag Rath (Moira), 637. One political result of Mag Rath appears to be Dál Riada's loss of Irish territories. The battle also causes the madness of Suibne in *Buile Shuibhne*.

Because of the curse put upon *Tara by the (fanciful) St *Rúadán, Domnall moved his seat to *Dún na nGéd on the banks of the *Boyne. According to *Fled Dúin na nGéd* [Feast of Dún na nGéd], two terrifying spectres, male and female, appeared before a feast, devoured all the food provided for the assembly, and then vanished. The malignant milieu they left also helped to contribute to the Battle of Mag Rath and the madness of Suibne.

The text of *Fled Dúin na nGéd* was edited by John O'Donovan (Dublin, 1848), by Carl Marstrander in the Norwegian journal *Videnskabs-Selskabets Skrifter*, 2/6 (1909), and by Ruth Lehmann (Dublin, 1964).

2. King of *Decies in **Cath Gabhra* [The Battle of Gabhair/Gowra]. His son wanted to marry Sgiamh Sholais, the daughter of *Caîrbre Lifechair. He was killed by *Fiachra, a son of *Fionn mac Cumhaill.

Domnall Brecc, Breac [speckled, variegated]. King of *Dál Riada, the Irish enclave in north Strathclyde (until 1974, *Argyllshire), Scotland, who did battle with *Domnall (1) as part of an Irish dynastic dispute. Domnall Brecc was defeated at the Battle of Mag Rath (Moira), *c.*637, coincident with the madness of Suibne; see BUILE SHUIBHNE. Domnall Brecc's magical shield was penetrated by *Conall during the fighting.

Domnall Ilchelgach [Ir., of the many treacheries]. Historical Irish *ard rí [high king], d. 566, son of *Muirchertach mac Erca, ancestor of the *Uí Néill and MacLoughlin families.

Domnall Míldemail, Maeltemel [Ir., warlike, martial]. King of *Alba [Scotland] in the **Táin Bó Cuailnge* [Cattle Raid of Cooley]. *Forgall Monach sends *Cúchulainn to Domnall Míldemail under the pretence that the hero is to complete his military education; actually, Forgall fears that Cúchulainn may take the virtue of his daughter, *Emer. *Conchobar and *Lóegaire accompany Cúchulainn to Alba, where they learn a series of minor lessons. While the heroes are at their lessons, Domnall Míldemail's loathsome, misshapen daughter *Dornoll [Ir., big fist] falls in love with Cúchulainn, much to his chagrin. Angered at his rejection, she vows revenge. Domnall Míldemail then advises the heroes to further their studies with *Scáthach.

Domnannaig. See DOMNAINN.

Domnonia 1. Latin name for the British kingdom in *Brittany (Armorica), established in the 5th century AD. One of three kingdoms, along with *Cornouaille and *Bro Waroch, Domnonia covered most of northern Brittany, including, after 530, the province of Leon in the north-west. Its relationship with the British province of *Dumnonia (Devon and *Cornwall) is not certain. A portion of this kingdom became the pre-Napoleonic county of Domnonée. Today it embraces the Departments of Côtes d'Armor and *Finistère north of the River Élorn.

2. (of south-western Britain). See DUMNONIA.

Domnu. Goddess of the *Fomorians in the *Lebor Gabála* [Book of Invasions] and mother of the Fomorian leader *Indech. She may have been the mother of all the Fomorians, and as such would represent darkness and evil pitted against the forces of light and good, e.g. the *Tuatha Dé Danann.

Dôn. Welsh name for the Celtic mother-goddess, whose name in Continental Europe may have been *Danu; counterpart of the Irish *Ana, goddess of the *Tuatha Dé Danann. Surviving Welsh literature, especially the fourth branch of the *Mabinogi*, tells us more about Dôn than we can know about either Danu or Ana. Sister of Math fab Mathonwy, she bore at least five important children, the daughter *Arianrhod and the sons *Gwydion, *Gilfaethwy, *Gofannon, and *Amaethon; in the *Triads her husband is given as *Beli. She may have had powers over fertility. The Children of Dôn, representing light and good, are often seen in conflict with the Children of *Lly^r, forces of dark and evil. She lends her name to a Welsh phrase for the constellation Cassiopeia, Llys Dôn, 'Dôn's Court'. Dôn appears to have become confused with St Anne in Christian times. See Rachel Bromwich, *Trioedd Ynys Prydain*, rev. edn. (Cardiff, 1978), 327, 549.

Dónal, Donal. Variant spellings of *Domnall.

Donald. Anglicization of *Domhnall.

Donann. Variant spelling of *Tuatha Dé Danann.

Dond. Variant spelling of *Donn.

Donegal [Ir. *Dún na nGall*, fort of the foreigners/ Danes]. Known in Irish as *Tír Chonaill* [Conall's Land]. A county in the extreme north-west of the Republic of Ireland, the most westerly in *Ulster. Large (1,865 square miles), mountainous, and thinly populated, Donegal enjoys some of the most romantic associations of any Irish county. The Irish language survived here longer than in any county in Ulster, some pockets continuing until the end of the twentieth century. The Irish kingdom of Tír Chonaill, coextensive with most of modern Donegal, was founded by *Conall Gulban, son of *Niall Noígiallach [of the Nine Hostages], making much of the land subject to the *Uí Néill in early historical times. See Seán Ó hEochaidh (ed.), *Fairy Legends from Donegal* (Dublin, 1977).

Donn, Dond [Ir., dun brown; king, lord]. The name borne by kings, the ruler of the dead, and at least one famous bull appears to be a conflation of different words; the OIr. donn has eight definitions. The listing of six leaders of the *Tuatha Dé Danann with this name implies that many identities are confused and overlapping.

Donn 1. Irish god of the dead and the *Otherworld; simultaneously an ancestor-deity whose identity is confused with the *Dagda; may also be identified with Donn mac Míled, the son of *Míl Espáine, who sometimes retains a distinct personality (see below). To a lesser extent Donn (1) may also be confused with *Donn Fírinne and *Donn Ua Duibne; additionally, Donn (1) may also bear the name *Donn Tétscorach.

As a chthonic or underworld deity, Donn bears a relationship to several Mediterranean deities, most notably the Roman *Dis Pater, from whom he may derive through Gaulish intermediaries. He is a retiring, aloof deity who prefers to live in isolation away from the company of other gods. He is most associated with west *Munster, the province most often linked with the dead. The first of the invaders to land in Ireland, he resides at *Tech Duinn, 'Donn's House', or, more often in English, 'the House of Donn', described as a rocky islet near Dursey Island at the extreme western end of the *Beare peninsula. The dead live with him here. Some Christian commentators have speculated that the souls of the damned may linger for an undetermined time in Tech Duinn before departing for hell. Not surprisingly, aspects of Donn (1)'s character have been adapted to portrayals of the *devil in pious folklore. In later oral tradition Donn (1) was thought to cause storms and shipwrecks.

Donn mac Míled, the eldest son of *Míl Espáine and Seang, is portrayed as a character in the **Lebor Gabála* [Book of Invasions], but not always identified as Donn (1), god of the dead; his brothers are *Amairgin and *Colptha. When he offended *Ériu she prophesied that he would not be able to enter Ireland, and so he lived on the rocky islet at the end of the *Beare peninsula known in stories as Tech Duinn. Except that he is recorded as having drowned, all remaining elements of his characterization imply identification with Donn, ruler of the dead.

2. *Máel Fothartaig's foster-brother, who murders *Eochaid and his wife in revenge for the slaying of Máel Fothartaig.

Donn, House of. A translation of **Tech Duinn*. See also DONN (1).

Donn Ailéin. One of six leaders named Donn whom the **Lebor Gabála* [Book of Invasions] describes as a leader of the *Tuatha Dé Danann; probably should be identified with *Donn mac Míled and thus with *Donn (1).

Donn Bó. The singing severed head in the story of the Battle of *Allen. First known as a young warrior with a sweet singing voice, Donn Bó was killed in battle and decapitated. Later his head was found, cleaned, and taken to a feast at the Hill of Allen, where it/he sang in praise of *Fergal, also decapitated. This fulfilled his pledge, 'Wherever you may be tomorrow night, I will entertain you.'

Donn Cuailnge also Donn Tarb [Ir., brown bull]. The famous Brown Bull in the **Táin Bó Cuailnge* [Cattle Raid of Cooley], over whom the central conflict takes place. Originally a pig-keeper of *Bodb Derg named *Friuch [boar's bristle (?)] who contended bitterly with Rucht [boar's grunt (?)], the pig-keeper of Ochall. Their ferocious conflicts took them through various manifestations: as ravens, water beasts, *stags, warriors, phantoms, *dragons, and water worms, until they became transformed into the Brown Bull of Cuailnge and the White Bull of Connacht. They take different names through each shift of shape, and are known ultimately as Donn Cuailnge and *Finnbennach. The coveting of Donn Cuailnge by *Medb, queen of Connacht, sets the action of the *Táin* in motion, provoking war with *Ulster. At the end Donn Cuailnge meets and kills Finnbennach, but departs from the battle mortally wounded himself. Note also the possible Continental parallel in *Donnotaurus.

Donn Désa, Dond Déssa. Foster-father of *Conaire Mór and a champion hunter-warrior (see FIANNA). His three sons, Fer Lé, Fer Gair [near/convenient man (?)], and Fer Rogain [choice man (?)], thus became the foster-brothers of Conaire, who banished them from Ireland when they began marauding the countryside. Abroad they joined forces with *Ingcél Cáech, a fearsome British pirate. Later, they invaded Ireland to attack Conaire; see TOGAIL BRUIDNE DA DERGA [The Destruction of Da Derga's Hostel]. Another son of Donn Désa was Rumal, an early *Lagin king, the first to rule between the *Boyne and Tolka rivers.

Donn Fírinne, Fritgrinne, Fri(d)grinne [(folk etymology) the just, the righteous]. One of six chiefs of the *Tuatha Dé Danann who was described as taking mortals to his 'castle' at Knockfeerina, also Knockfierna [Ir. *Cnoc Fírinne*], in south-west Co. Limerick near Ballingarry. Käte Müller-Lisowski argued that this figure is derived from *Donn (1), the god of the dead: 'Donn of Cnoc Fírinne', *Béaloideas*, 18 (1948), 142–99.

Donn mac Midir. A ruler of a *sídh described in **Acallam na Senórach* [Colloquy of the Elders] who uses a woman disguised as a fawn to tempt *Fionn mac Cumhaill. Along with his men, Fionn pursues the fawn until it disappears into the earth; a heavy snowstorm follows, and when the men seek shelter they stumble in the sídh and enter it. They see a hideous, boorish churl [Ir. *aitheach*] pass by, carrying a pig on an iron fork, followed by a beautiful young woman. They try to overtake the churl and his beautiful companion, but succumb to a magical mist before they can reach them. When the mists clear, Fionn and his men find themselves before an impressive fortress, the *Otherworld residence of the churl. From the point of entering the sídh, this story is paralleled by an episode in **Feis Tighe Chonáin* [The Feast of Conán's House].

Donn mac Míled. Son of *Míl Espáine whose identity has become intertwined with that of *Donn (1), god of the dead. As a brother of *Éber Finn [Fair Éber] in the *Lebor Gabála [Book of Invasions], he is sometimes known as Éber Donn [Dark or Brown Éber]. A malevolent and envious figure, he drowns, victimized by his own anger, just as the *Milesian invasion takes place and thus is denied participation in the conquest he lusts for. Sometimes another of Míl's sons, *Erannán, is described as being the first to die.

Donn Tarb. Another name for *Donn Cuailnge. See also DONNOTAURUS.

Donn Tétscorach [Ir., abounding in furious horses (?)]. A son of *Donn Désa in *Togail Bruidne Da Derga [The Destruction of Da Derga's Hostel] speaks of riding the horses of Donn Tétscorach; probably another name for *Donn (1), ruler of the Otherworld.

Donn Ua Duibne, úa Duibne, Ó Duibhne, O'Duinn, O'Dyna. Father of the *Fenian hero *Diarmait Ua Duibne, whose vengeance causes his son to be pursued by a magical boar. Diarmait's mother, Cochrann (also Cróchnat), has committed adultery with a shepherd, bearing another son. *Angus Óg also raises this son, a half-brother. Perceiving this bastard child as a reproach, Donn kills him by crushing him between his legs. The shepherd father touches the corpse with a *hazel wand that revives him, and changes him into a boar who follows Diarmait until his dying day.

Donnotaurus. The existence of this half-Celtic, half-Latin name [cf. Ir. *donn*, brown, dark; L *taurus*, bull; Cont. Celtic *tarros* (?)] in Gaulish records implies a Continental parallel to the brown bull of *Ulster, *Donn Cuailnge.

Donu. Variant spelling of *Ana, the Irish mother-goddess; may also be equated with the Welsh parallel, *Dôn.

Donwenna. Variant spelling of *Dwynwen.

dooiney marrey, dinney-mara [Manx, sea-man]. The merman of the Isle of *Man, who bears a close relationship to the merrow of Irish tradition. He is sometimes portrayed as an affectionate father who romps with his children. More is written of *ben- varrey, the Manx mermaid. Classed as a solitary *fairy.

dooiney oie [Manx, night-man]. Benign, nocturnal spirit of the Isle of *Man who warns mortals of impending storms. He may shout his warning, speak while making a misty appearance, or use a loud horn; in either instance, farmers are warned to herd cattle and sheep into a shelter. Virtually indistinguishable from howlaa, who howls a warning but does not speak; alternatively, 'howlaa' may be what dooiney oie shouts.

Doomagh Crom Duff. Anglicized, phonetic rendering of Domhnach Chrom Dubh [Ir., Crom Dubh's Sunday], another name for *Lughnasa.

doomster. See BREHON.

Doon-. Anglicized, phonetic rendering of *Dún-.

Doon Buidhe. See DORNBHUIDHE.

Dooros, Forest of. See DUBROS.

Dord Fian, Fían [Ir. *dord*, buzzing, droning, intoning]. The war-chant or cry of the *Fianna of *Fionn mac Cumhaill. It is described in stories as being low on the musical scale, often delivered with a bass voice.

Dordmair. Alternate name for Dornoll.

Dorn [OIr., hand; fist]. Nobly born woman who becomes slave to *Fergus mac Léti and reveals to him the blemish that disqualifies him to hold the throne.

Dornbhuidhe [ModIr., yellow fist]. Name given to the *sídh of the mysterious Uainebhuidhe [Ir., yellow-green], who sings and is accompanied by magical birds.

Dornoll, Dornolla, Dordmair (gen.?) [Ir., big fist]. Loathsome daughter of *Domnall Míldemail in Scotland. A *druidess who trained heroes in the art of war, she and her father took *Cúchulainn, *Lóegaire, and *Conall Cernach as students. She fell deeply in love with Cúchulainn, who resisted her, earning her implacable hatred. She conjures up a vision of home to keep Cúchulainn from leaving for *Scáthach.

Dorraghow. Anglicization of *Dobharchú.

Dothra. OIr. and ModIr. word for the River *Dodder.

Dothur [Ir., Wicked, Evil]. One of the three malevolent sons of *Carman.

Douarnenez. Large bay in the far southwest of Brittany, under whose waters the submerged city of *Ys is thought to lie.

Douarnenez is also the name of a port city at the head of the bay.

Dougal, Dougall. Variant spellings for *Dugall.

Douthal. Bard in John Clark's bogus 'translation', *The Works of the Caledonian Bards* (1778), who is commissioned by King Morduth to retell the history of the kingdom. As Clark was an imitator of James *Macpherson (1736–96), Douthal can be seen as type for *Ossian.

Down Skayth. See DUNSCAITH.

Dowth [Ir. *dubad*, growing dark (?), turning black (?)]. Giant passage-grave (previously tumulus) of the *Boyne valley, the easternmost of the celebrated trio Newgrange (*Brug na Bóinne), *Knowth, and Dowth. With a diameter of 280 feet and height of 47–50 feet, it has approximately the same dimensions as the others. All are now dated between 2500 and 3200 BC, or earlier than estimates made in the early 20th century. While not easily accessible to visitors today, Dowth was so ill-treated by amateur antiquarians, the Office of Public Works, and vandals that one recent commentator described it as the 'flea market' of Irish passage-graves. Dowth contains two tombs with much ornate carving that has been less studied than the art of Newgrange or Knowth. As with the other two passage-graves, Dowth is sometimes seen as the home of *Angus Óg, but it generally plays a small role in the Irish imagination, most often as an allusion. See Michael J. O'Kelly, *Newgrange: Archaeology, Art and Legend* (Dublin, 1983).

Dozmare Pool, Dozmary Pool. A gloomy tarn or glacial pool 9 miles E of Bodmin, Cornwall, once thought to be the Lake of the Underworld because it is so deep. The celebrated Cornish ghost Jan/ John *Tregeagle was once condemned to empty it with a leaky limpet shell.

dragon [OFr. *dragon*, from L, Gk. roots]. The fabulous, winged, fire-breathing reptile plays an important role in the Welsh imagination but less so in Irish and other Celtic literatures; the presence of snakes in Wales and their absence in Ireland may account for this. The national symbol of Wales is Y *Ddraig Goch [the red dragon], to be distinguished from gwiber [viper], the word for dragon in other contexts. As in other European traditions, the dragon usually represents elemental power, often that of the earth. Celtic dragons often live at the bottom of deep lakes or guard trees. With the introduction of Christianity, the dragon comes to represent paganism, as in the story of St George. The agnomen of the Welsh-based Arthurian figure *Uthr Bendragon/Uther Pendragon [W, dragon's head (?), foremost leader (?)] signals the beast's admirable qualities. Linguistic evidence implies that many dragons in Celtic tradition are borrowed from non-Celtic sources, e.g. Ir. dragún; Manx dragane; Corn. dragon; Bret. dragon. ScG employs both dràgon and beithir, which may derive from the Norse for *bear.

Two dragons harass Britain every *Calan Mai [May Eve] midnight in **Cyfranc Lludd a Llefelys* [The Meeting of Lludd and Llefelys]. Lludd entombs two dragons at *Dinas Emrys. The Irish hero *Fráech kills a dragon at the beginning of the action of *Táin Bó Fraích* [The Cattle Raid of Fráech]. A dragon swallows Dáire (3), the son of *Fionn, but he escapes. A creature, perhaps a dragon, named *oilliphéist [Ir., great beast/worm], fled from St Patrick, thus cutting the *Shannon valley on his way. The Breton St Pol of Léon is sometimes pictured with a dragon. The dragon may be known as a 'firedrake' in some translations of Celtic stories. See J. J. Campbell, *The Celtic Dragon Myth* (Edinburgh, 1911; repr. New York, 1973).

draíocht, draoidheacht. This Irish term, whose literal translation is (1) druidic art, druidism, (2) witchcraft, magic; charm, enchantment, is a 'power' or 'talent' attributed to the *Tuatha Dé Danann in their ability to overcome the *Fir Bolg, who preceded them in Ireland. Cf. Ir. draoitheach, 'magician, wizard'; see also DRUID.

Dream of Angus** / Aonghus/Óengus, **The. See AISLINGE ÓENGUSO.

Dream of Macsen** (Maxen) **Wledig, The. See BREUDDWYD MACSEN.

Dream of Rhonabwy, The. See BREUDDWYD RHONABWY.

Drem son of Dremidydd [W, sight, aspect]. One of hundreds of figures cited in **Culhwch ac Olwen*, distinguished for the supernatural keenness of his sight. Probably the remnant of a lost tradition, Drem could see from Celliwig in Cornwall to the top of Mt. Blathaon in Britain (Scotland?) 'when the gnat would thrive in the morning sun'.

drochshúil, an droch súil, an. ModIr. for *evil eye; in ScG it is an droch shùil.

Droighin. River in *Alba [Scotland], sung of by *Deirdre: 'dear are its waters over clean sands'. Although not identified specifically with any contemporary body of water, it should be in north Strathclyde (until 1974, *Argyllshire).

Droimin Donn Dílis. Variant spelling of Druimin *Donn Dílis.

Drom, Drom- . Anglicizations of *Druim-.

Dromahair, Dromahaire, Dromohair, Drumahaire [Ir. *Droim Dhá Thiar*, ridge of the two demons]. Modern village in Co. Leitrim on the River Bonet (or Bonnet), which flows into the western end of Lough Gill, coextensive with the ancient seat of the Uí Ruairc [O'Rourke] kings. The adulterous *Derbforgaill (2) eloped with *Diarmait mac Murchada [MacMurrow], allegedly to this spot in 1152 or 1156. Dromahair is often cited in the poetry of W. B. Yeats.

Drostán. Sixth-century disciple of *Colum Cille from *Iona who helped his master found the monastery now called *Deer in north Aberdeenshire. The name is often confused with *Drust, the Pictish king, *Tristan the romantic hero, and others.

Drudwas ap Tryffin, Drutwas. Owner of the magical birds *Adar Llwch Gwin. The birds were a gift from Drudwas's wife, a *fairy woman; they could understand human speech and fulfilled all their owner's commands. In a contest with *Arthur, Drudwas gave orders to the birds to kill the first fighter to reach the battlefield; when Arthur was delayed Drudwas was torn to pieces by his own birds. See Rachel Bromwich, *Trioedd Ynys Prydain*, rev. edn. (Cardiff, 1978), 327ff., 549.

Drudwyn, Drutwyn [cf. W *drudwen*, starling]. Magical *dog used by *Culhwch to hunt the boar *Twrch Trwyth; usually referred to as Drufwyn, the 'pup' or 'whelp' of Greid son of Eri. Drudwyn was so strong that no leash could hold him except for one made of the beard of *Dillus Farfog.

druid, druidess [origin disputed; see second paragraph below]. An order of male and female priest-philosophers of pre-Christian Celtic society, known in Continental Europe, the Mediterranean basin, Great Britain, and Ireland; often thought to be comparable to Roman flāmines or the brahmins of India. According to classical commentators, druids in Gaul, and perhaps elsewhere, had authority over divine worship, officiated at sacrifices (including, perhaps, human sacrifices), exercised supreme authority over legislative and judicial matters, and educated élite youth along with aspirants to their order. They ate acorns to make themselves ready for prophecy. Druids paid no taxes and were not required to do battle. At important assemblies they took precedence in speaking before kings or chieftains, as was the case in the court of *Conchobar mac Nessa. Teaching and sacred knowledge was oral, pupils being required to memorize a great number of verses, spending as long as twenty years in study. Many lessons were taught in the form of riddles. Because of the lack of written texts, we must infer their teaching from non-druidical sources. The curriculum included astronomy and natural science. Druidical calculation of time perceived night or darkness as preceding day or light; see CALENDAR. Druids evidently held to a version of metempsychosis in which human souls do not die but are reborn under different forms; classical commentators saw parallels with Pythagoras. As healers they are associated especially with mistletoe and its ritual gathering. In Ireland druids practised a form of tonsure, airbacc giunnae [Ir., frontal curve of tonsure], which ran from ear to ear instead of being a circular form on the crown like the Roman and Christian pattern. Roman persecution led to the decline of the druidical order, especially after the slaughter on *Anglesey, AD 61, when it disappeared from Britain and Wales. Druids survived in Ireland until the coming of Christianity (5th cent.) and in Scotland, when the mantle of druidical magic passed on to Celtic Christian saints, while other aspects passed to the *filid who accommodated themselves to the new religion.

The oldest references to druids appear in classical texts, always in plurals, Gk. druidai, L druidae, druides. These presuppose the Gaulish form druvis, from druvids, although neither occurs in any Romano-Celtic inscriptions. The OIr. druí is sometimes translated as 'druid' but may also mean magician, wizard, diviner, or, in more modern poetry, poet, learned man. W dryw, 'seer' may be a cognate. From these, Kenneth H. Jackson hypothesizes a Gaulish original, druwids, 'wise man of the woods', 'very wise man'. The Indo-European root deru- implies being firm, solid, or steadfast, as a tree is, or it may be an affirmative prefix or element. Other commentators have seen a cognate in the second syllable with the Indo-European root wid-, 'to know'. Celtic words for 'oak' make an evocative sound: OIr. and ModIr. dair; ScG darach; Manx daragh; W derwen, dâr; Corn. derowen; Bret. dervenn. The root dru- from the Greek for 'oak' is implicit in the name of the druidical sanctuary in *Galatia (Asia Minor), *Drunemeton, as described by the ancient geographer *Strabo (1st cent. AD). *Pliny the Elder (1st cent. AD) observed that druids held oaks in high esteem, adorning them with flowers at religious ceremonies and worshipping them as symbols of *Jupiter; nevertheless, druidic association with the oak has not been proved beyond reasonable doubt. Modern consensus, for example, rejects the earlier speculative root dervovidos, 'knowledge of the oak'. The English word druid derives from the Latin druidae via the French druide, and is not borrowed from any Celtic language.

Classical commentators provide us with a substantial body of information about the druids, but it is neither consistent nor always supported by literary texts in Irish and Welsh. Julius *Caesar (1st cent. BC) describes druids as constituting a single learned caste, while his near-contemporaries Strabo and *Diodorus Siculus distinguish three learned orders: (*a*) druidae, philosophers and theologians, (*b*) vates or mantis, diviners and seers, and (*c*) bardi, panegyric poets. Although links between ancient Gaul and Ireland are tenuous, a similar division is recorded in early Ireland: (*a*) druídh, (*b*) filidh, seers, diviners, and (*c*) baird, poets. By the 7th century encroaching Christianity allowed the filidh to assume many of the functions and privileges of the druids, who were disappearing from the scene. *Tacitus (2nd cent. AD) observed that druids ruled it unlawful to build temples to the gods or to worship them within walls or under roofs. The classical attribution of human sacrifice in druidical practice, especially by being burned within a wickerwork figure, is not supported in Irish or Welsh texts.

Several druids figure prominently in the three great cycles of Old Irish literature, the *Mythological, *Ulster, and *Fenian. In the **Lebor Gabála* [Book of Invasions], the *Partholonians arrive with three druids, Fios [intelligence], Eólas [knowledge], and Fochmarc [enquiring]. In the same work the *druid of the *Nemedians, *Mide, an eponym for the province of Mide [Meath], lights the first *fire in Ireland, which lasts for seven years and from which every other fire is lit. Irish druids are portrayed as masters of *divination, including such powers as *díchetal do chennaib, *imbas forosnai, and *teinm laída. They also, reportedly, watched flame and smoke for signs and chewed raw flesh (cf. the magical thumb of *Fionn mac Cumhaill). Instead of oak, druids in Ireland favoured the wood of the *yew, hawthorn, and *rowan, especially for wands. *Ogham figures could be carved into these wands. At the introduction of Christianity they unsuccessfully disputed with St *Patrick and St *Colum Cille.

Much bogus scholarship, beginning with John Aubrey (1626–97) and continuing in the 18th and 19th centuries, asserted that druids had migrated to Britain from ancient India, but were nevertheless linked to North American Indians. This tradition also ascribed almost every remnant of prehistoric culture in Britain and Ireland to druidical influence, so that megalithic monuments such as Stonehenge, now known to be pre-Celtic, were called 'druid circles'. The phrases 'druids' tables' or 'druids' altars' denoted *dolmens. William Stukeley (1687–1765) established a religion based on his vision of druidism; adherents of his views still parade in Britain at the solstice and at changes of the season. Other romantic misinformation persists in print, e.g. Godfrey Higgins, *The Celtic Druids*, etc. (London, 1829; repr. Los Angeles, 1977). Another living heritage from the romantic misinterpretation of druidism is the *Gorsedd [W, throne, i.e. meeting of the bards] established by *Iolo Morganwg (*né* Edward Williams, 1747–1826) in 1792.

A full list of druids in Celtic history would be too extensive to include here, but among the names most often mentioned are: *Allaid in *Macpherson's *Ossian*; *Bresal Etarlám; *Broichan; *Caicer; *Cailitin; *Cathbad, among the most famous of all druids; *Corán; *Dáire (4); the historical *Divitiacus the Aeduan, cited by classical commentators; *Dil Maccu Crecga; *Duanach mac Morna; *Eliavres, a Breton; *Fer Doirich; *Fer Fidail; *Figol of the *Tuatha Dé Danann; *Finnéces; *Fíngen; *Fis; *Gebann; *Lóbais; Máel, druid of *Conn Cétchathach [of the Hundred Battles]; *Mide, druid of the *Nemedians and eponym of *Meath; *Morann; *Mug Ruith, second in renown to Cathbad; *Sithchenn in *Niall's *sovereignty story; *Tadg mac Nuadat of the *Fenian Cycle. Notable druidesses include: *Béchuille; *Birog; *Bodhmall; *Dornoll; *Dub[h], after whom *Dublin is named; the *Gallizenae.

Among the thousands of representations of druids in modern literature, the most significant artistically is Vincenzo Bellini's opera *Norma*, libretto by F. Romani (1821), in which the young heroine is torn between love and duty. See also T. D. Kendrick, *The Druids* (London, 1928, 1966); Françoise Le Roux, *Les Druides* (Paris, 1961; Rennes, 1986); A. L. Owen, *Famous Druids: A Survey of Three Centuries of English Literature on Druids* (Oxford, 1962); Stuart Piggott, *The Druids* (London, 1968, 1975); P. B. Ellis, *The Druids* (London and Grand Rapids, Mich., 1994); Paul R. Lonigan, *The Druids: Priests of the Ancient Celts* (Westport, Conn., 1996).

druid's fog. See FÉTH FÍADA.

Druim- [OIr., ridge]. Prefix in many OIr. place-names denoting a high, narrow land; often anglicized Drum- or Drom-; cf. ModIr. droim; ScG druim.

Druim Caín, Drumcain [Ir. *druim*, ridge; *caín*, fine, good, fair, beautiful]. Name for the hill of *Tara in the **Lebor Gabála* [Book of Invasions] and other early texts.

Druim Damgaire, Drom Damhghaire. Site of a failed siege begun by *Cormac ua Cuinn (mac Airt) against *Fiachu Muillethan of *Munster in **Forbais Dromma Damgaire* [the Siege of Knocklong]. Identified with a hill in SE Co. Limerick.

Druim Ligen, Lighean. Site of the second defeat of the *Tuatha Dé Danann by the *Milesians, here under the command of *Éremón. It is identified with the townland of Drumleene, near Raphoe, Co. *Donegal.

Druim na nDruadh [Ir., ridge of the druids]. Former name for Rathcroghan, Co. Roscommon, and therefore synonymous with the nearby ancient site of *Cruachain.

Druim Snechta, Sneachta [Ir., snow ridge]. Monastic site in Co. Monaghan, coextensive with the modern parish of Drumsnat, 5 miles WSW of Monaghan town, near Smithborough. One of the earliest literary codices, *Cín Dromma Snechta* [The Book of Drumsnat], containing an early draft of **Togail Bruidne Da Derga* [The Destruction of Da Derga's Hostel], now lost, was compiled here between the 8th and 10th centuries.

Druimin Donn Dílis [Ir., the faithful brown, white-backed cow]. One of several poetic names for *Ireland.

Drum, Drum-. See DRUIM-.

Drumcliff, Drumcliffe [Ir. *druim chliabh*, ridge of the baskets (?)]. Small fishing village 4 miles NE of Sligo in Co. Sligo on the Drumcliff River at the foot of *Ben Bulben, near the mouth of the Glencar valley. St *Colum Cille founded a monastery here in 575, of which no trace survives. Of later date are the lower part of a high tower and a fine high cross with scenes from the Scriptures as well as the shaft of an older cross. Poet-playwright W. B. Yeats is buried here, a site of his own choosing.

Drumsnat. Anglicized place-name for *Druim Snechta.

Drunemeton [Gk. *dru-*, *drus*, oak; *nemeton*, sacred place, sanctuary]. The 'oak sanctuary' of *Galatia, the Celtic province of Asia Minor, as described by *Strabo (1st cent. AD), the Roman geographer. A council of the Galatians met here. Site not yet fixed on the modern map.

Drust, Drustan. Name borne by several shadowy but historical kings of the *Picts, some of whom may have been antecedents of *Tristan, the Arthurian hero. The best-known is Drust son of Talorc, who reigned in northern Scotland about 780. The name Drust is distinctively Pictish and appears (along with such variants as Drustan, Drost, Droston) repeatedly as a royal name in chronicles of the Picts, as does Talorc and its variant Talorcan. The Welsh counterpart of this name is Drystan mab [son of] Tallwch (sometimes Trystan mab Tallwch), as recorded in the *Triads; Drystan, however, may be more fictional than historical, as he is also recorded as having a lover named Essylt [*Iseult]. A Latin form of the name, Drustanus, is inscribed on a stone near Fowey, Cornwall, locally known as the 'Tristan Stone'. None of the historical records suggests the outline of the Tristan and Iseult narrative, which appears to derive from the Greek story of Perseus and Andromeda. The Drust mentioned as a companion of *Cúchulainn in the 10th-century recension of *Tochmarc Emire* [The Wooing of Emer] appears to be a scribal interpolation; as the name does not appear elsewhere in the *Ulster Cycle, some commentators have suggested that Drust may have been the original hero of the story and was displaced when the episode was adapted to its present form. See also DROSTÁN. See Rachel Bromwich, *Trioedd Ynys Prydain*, rev. edn. (Cardiff, 1978), 329–33, 549; Rachel Bromwich et al. (eds.), *The Arthur of the Welsh* (Cardiff, 1991), ch. 10.

Drutwas. Variant spelling of *Drudwas ap Tryffin.

Drutwyn. Variant spelling of *Drudwyn.

Drych [W, mirror]. Name of a character in **Culhwch ac Olwen* noted for his handsomeness. Only *Arthur and Drych son of Cibddar were fairer than *Bedwyr.

Drystan mab Tallwch. Welsh adaptation of *Drust.

Du [W, black]. Magical horse cited in **Culhwch ac Olwen*. Culhwch needs both the help of the hero *Gwyn ap Nudd and Du, the horse of Moro Oerfeddawg, if he is to succeed in hunting the boar *Twrch Trwyth. See Rachel Bromwich, *Trioedd Ynys Prydain*, rev. edn. (Cardiff, 1978), 113, 536ff.

Du Traws [W, black oppressor]. The last adversary of *Owain, whom the hero must vanquish to gain his total rehabilitation. Du Traws has imprisoned twenty-four women and killed their companions; after his defeat by Owain he changes his nature.

Duach. A minor queen of Old Irish literature, foster-mother of *Lug Lámfhota and ancestress of *Tailtiu.

Duach Dallta Deadad. Variant spelling of *Daui Dalta Dedad.

Duach Ladrach. Variant spelling of *Daui Ladrach.

Duanach mac Morna [OIr. *dúanach*, given to song, fond of poetry]. *Bard and *druid in the court of *Fionn mac Cumhaill. He serenades *Gráinne at her pre-nuptial feast, when she is expected to marry Fionn, just before she elopes with *Diarmait.

Duanaire Finn [Ir. *duanaire*, verse anthology, maker or reciter of verses]. Usual title for a huge compilation of *Fenian verse made at Louvain (Belgium) in 1626–7, the English for which is 'The Poem Book of Fionn' or 'The Book of the Lays of Fionn'. Many poems are ascribed to Fionn's persona while others are attributed to *Oisín, Fionn's son, or take a Fenian setting amidst wild nature. Major themes are the celebration of nature and disputation with Christian repression of paganism. The verse derives from both the older, learned scribal tradition and also from the later, popular oral tradition; composed in Ireland, it was carried to the Catholic areas of the Netherlands at the flight of the Irish aristocracy ('Flight of the Earls', 1607-). An Irish mercenary in the Thirty Years War, Captain Somhairle Mac Domhnaill [Sorley MacDonnell], commissioned the compilation by the scribes, reputedly headed by Aodh Ó Dochartaigh, otherwise called Don Hugo Doharty. The manuscript is preserved in the Franciscan Library, Dublin. The Irish Texts Society published the text in three volumes, nos. 7, 28, and 43 of the series, over forty-five years: vol. i, ed. Eóin MacNeill (Dublin, 1908), vol. ii, ed. Gerard Murphy (Dublin, 1933), and vol. iii, ed. Gerard Murphy (Dublin, 1953). Gerard Murphy's 112-page introduction to the third volume contains a key study of Fenian literature.

Dub (OIr. black, dark]. Some names exist only in this spelling while others, especially from oral tradition, exist only in the ModIr. *Dubh.

Dub, Dubh **1.** [Ir., black, dark]. Legendary Irish *druidess, also known as Duibhlinn, who gave her name to *Dublin. When Dub learned that her husband, Énna (2), had taken a second wife, Áide or Aeté, she caused the drowning of her rival together with her family. In revenge, Margenn, a servant of Áide, cast a sling at Dub, killing her; she fell into a large pool at the mouth of the *Liffey, which came to be known as Dubh-linn, 'Dub's pool', or Dublin. Although the pool once assured the passage of ships to the port of Dublin, modern dredging has eliminated it.

2. One of the three malevolent sons of *Carman.

Dub Lacha, Dubh Lacha [Ir., black one of the lake (?); black duck (?)]. Beautiful daughter of *Fiachna mac Báetáin and wife of *Mongán, born the same night as her husband; celebrated for her white arms. *Brandub, who coveted her, deceived Mongán into giving his wife to him. Mongán, however, a son of *Manannán mac Lir, sought the help of the hag Cuimne in recovering her. Cuimne transformed herself into a beautiful woman and offered herself to Brandub in exchange; once Dubh Lacha was free, Cuimne reverted to her former shape, a rare instance of such a reversal. This tale is told in *Tóruigheacht Duibhe Lacha Láimh-ghile* [The Pursuit/ Rescue of Dubh Lacha of the White Arms], ed. Seamus Ó Duilearga, *Zeitschrift für celtische Philologie*, 17 (1928), 347–70.

Dub Sainglenn. See SAINGLIU.

Dubchomar, Dub Chomar, Dub Commair, Dub Combair, Dub Comair [Ir., dark confluence]. Name in heroic narratives for the confluence of the Blackwater tributary and the *Boyne River; the name of the modern town of Drumeague, Co. Cavan, echoes the older form. It is near the festival site of *Tailtiu as well as the modern town of Navan (see EMAIN MACHA). The 'dark' of the prefix in the place-name was described in folklore recorded as late as the 19th century as referring to a crime committed here; some commentators have suggested it may have been the murder of the 4th-century king of *Tara, *Eochaid Mugmedón, by the three *Collas. Near *Corleck Hill.

Dubgilla, Dubh Giolla [Ir., black servant]. Magical shield of legendary king *Áed (5) (Aodh) of *Airgialla (Oriel).

Dubglas [cf. W *glas*, blue]. An unidentified river in Britain cited in *Liber Brittonum* (9th cent., formerly ascribed to Nennius) and in Welsh narrative. Some commentators link it tentatively with the Lindsey in Lincolnshire.

Dubh. ModIr. spelling of *Dub.

Dubh Sainglenn, Sainglainn. See SAINGLIU.

dubhlachan. Variant spelling of *dullahan.

Dubhlaing. Legendary soldier at the historical Battle of Clontarf (1014), as an attendant to the oldest son of *Brian Bórama (Boru). He became the lover of the beautiful divinity *Aíbell, who prophesied he would die if not protected by the Cloak of Invisibility. She wrapped him in it, but he threw it off, going into battle and fulfilling her prediction. See also DÚNLANG Ó HARTAGÁIN.

Dubhros, Forest of. See DUBROS.

Dubhthach, Dubhtach. ModIr. spellings of *Dubthach.

Dublin [Ir. *dub(h)-linn*, dark pool]. The Irish capital was established by Norsemen, an outpost in 841 and a town perhaps in 988, but has always had Irish names. The story in the *Dindshenchas ascribes the name dub(h)-linn to the druidess *Dub(h), who on learning that her husband Énna has taken a second wife, Áide, drowns Áide and all her family. In revenge Margenn, a servant of Áide, casts a sling at Dub, killing her. She falls into a pool near the mouth of the *Liffey estuary, which is named for her.

While the pool once made the Liffey navigable to larger ships, modern dredging has eliminated it. Some commentators see allusions to the dark pool in *Ptolemy's (2nd cent. AD) name for the harbour, Eblana, as well as in the Latin name, Nigratherma. A Norse name for their settlement was Dyflinarski. The name of a nearby smaller pool has also been associated with the city; OIr. poll bec; ModIr. poll beag [small hole], anglicized Poolbeg. The usual Irish language name for the city, Baile Átha Cliath [Ir., settlement/ town of the hurdle ford], denotes the narrowest point on the Liffey, forded in pre-Norse times by the road between *Tara and Wicklow, near the Wood Quay area, west of the modern commercial centre. It was a 'hurdle ford' because of a causeway built of woven wicker, boughs, or hurdles. The ford was known by different names in Irish tradition, including Áth Liag Mairgene [Ford of Margenn's Sling Stone], after the killer of Dub(h).

As a town established by invaders, Dublin does not figure largely in early Irish tradition, although several important sites lie within the environs of modern metropolitan Dublin, including Da Derga's Hostel on the River *Dodder and *Cnucha [Castle Knock], scene of a significant *Fenian battle. James Joyce seized upon the little-known modern tradition that *Fionn mac Cumhaill's body lay stretched beneath the city of Dublin from the Head of *Howth in the east to Phoenix Park in the west. The Arthurian hero *Tristan visits Dublin after traversing the Irish Sea in a rudderless boat. Extensive excavation of Viking Dublin followed the accidental discovery of buried ruins at Wood Quay during construction of an office building in the mid-1970s. See J. M. Flood, *Dublin in Irish Legend* (Dublin, 1919); G. A. Little, *Dublin Before the*

Vikings (Dublin, 1957); Royal Irish Academy, *Dublin* (Dublin, 1988). See also MAG NELTA.

Dubric. Archbishop of *Caerleon in *Geoffrey of Monmouth's *Historia* (1136). Appointed by *Ambrosius Aurelianus, he crowned *Arthur as king.

Dubros, Dubhros, Dooros, **Forest of.** [Ir., dark wooded headland (?)]. Forest, once standing in what is now Co. Sligo, mentioned prominently in **Tóraigheacht Dhiarmada agus Ghráinne* [The Pursuit of Diarmait and Gráinne]. Here *Diarmait defeats the surly *one-eyed giant *Searbhán, who guards the magical quicken (*rowan) tree which the *Tuatha Dé Danann had brought with them from *Tír Tairngire [the Land of Promise]. *Gráinne desires the berries of the tree. While hiding in a tree in Dubros, Diarmait drops a berry on the board-game *fidchell, allowing his friend *Oisín to defeat *Fionn mac Cumhaill.

Dubthach, Dubhthach, Dubtach, Dufach [Ir. *dub*, black, dark]. Common name in early Ireland borne by heroes, kings, warriors, and saints, mostly male and some female. The modern Irish surname O'Duffy or Duffy derives from Dubthach.

Dubthach 1. Reputed father of St *Brigid; identical with Dugall Donn in Gaelic Scotland.

2. St Dubthach of *Donegal [*Tír Chonaill], whose feast-day is 5 February.

Dubthach Dóeltenga [Ir., chafer-tongued, given to backbiting]. Also **Dubtach Doél Ulad, Doellilad** [Ir., chafer, dung-beetle of Ulster]; also **Dubthach mac Lugdach,** a son of *Lugaid mac Casrubae; **Duffy Chafer-Tongue** in some English stories. An *Ulster warrior noted for his rancorous disposition; he shares with Briccriu the role of the Thersites of the *Ulster Cycle. Though he was an effective warrior, his companionship was often shunned by comrades in battle. He was given the loan of *Celtchar's lance, *Lúin*, but it was later found discarded. In the *Deirdre story, Dubthach assists *Fergus mac Roich in his attempts to take revenge on *Conchobar for the killings of the sons of *Uisnech. In the **Táin Bó Cuailnge* [Cattle Raid of Cooley], Dubthach kills *Maine (8), Conchobar's son; *Fiachna, the son of Conchobar's daughter *Fedelm Noíchrothach; and all the girls of *Emain Macha. Later he goes into exile in *Connacht with *Cormac and *Fergus mac Róich. He also appears in **Togail Bruidne Da Derga* [The Destruction of Da Derga's Hostel] and can be seen causing discord in **Fled Bricrenn* [Briccriu's Feast].

Dubthach Lánfhile. Legendary early Irish poet.

duck [OE *dūcan*]. The aquatic bird of the family *Anatidae* appears frequently in Romano-Celtic iconography and ritual and occasionally in early Irish tradition, but rarely elsewhere in the Celtic world. Like its fellow amphibian, the *swan, the duck can be seen as mobile in two elements. The duck is linked with the anthropomorphic goddess *Sequana of the source of the Seine near Dijon; she is portrayed standing in a boat with a duck's head on the prow; similar in design is a small bronze duck found at Milber Down, Devon. A figurine from Rotherly Down, England, shows a duck with a human head on the back, suggesting shape-shifting or metamorphosis. The ModIr. word for duck is lacha; ScG tunnag, lach; Manx thunnag; W hwyad; Corn. hōs; Bret. houad.

Dufach. Variant spelling of *Dubthach.

Duffy Chafer-Tongue. See DUBTHACH DOÉLTENGA.

Dugall, Dugal, Dugald, Dughall, Dougal [ScG *dubhghall*, dark stranger, i.e. Dane]. Shadowy but historical figure from 12th-century Gaelic Scotland, eldest and most important son of the powerful leader *Somerled. He was the progenitor of the Clan MacDhùghaill [MacDougall, MacDugald, etc.] of *Dunollie in north Strathclyde (until 1974, *Argyllshire), near Oban.

Dugall Donn [ScG, the brown]. Legendary father of St *Brigid in Scottish Gaelic genealogies; identical with *Dubthach (1) in Irish tradition.

Duibhlinn. See DUB (1).

Duibne, Duibhne. See DIARMAIT UA DUIBNE.

Duineach [Ir. *duine*, human being]. An alternative name for the *Cailleach Bhéire. A figurative translation of her name is 'has many followers'.

dulachan, dulacaun. Variant spellings of *dullahan.

Dul-Dána [Ir. *dul* (*daul*), poet; *dán*, gift]. Name

given to the baby *Lug Lámfhota by *Manannán mac Lir while he served as the hero's foster-father.

dullahan, dúlachan, dulacaun, dullaghan, dubhlachan [Ir. *dubh*, dark; cf. Ir. *lucharachán*, pigmy, puny creature; Ir. *lachan*, reed; ScG *lachan*, hearty laugh]. Headless phantom, on horseback or in horse-drawn coach, in Irish folklore. The dullahan rides a headless horse or may ride in a coach drawn by headless horses. His face is the colour and texture of mouldy cheese; his eyes make a bridge from ear to ear; his huge eyes dart like flies. But the dullahan can put on or take off this hideous head at will, or play ghoulish ball-games with it. His black horse has a head with flaming eyes and short-cropped ears that outdistances its body by six yards or more. His whip will flick out the eyes of those who watch him. Those opening their doors to hear the dullahan rumbling by will have basins of blood thrown in their faces. It is an omen of death to the houses where he pauses. Classed as a solitary *fairy. See also ANGAU; ANKOU; DEATH COACH; FAR DOROCHA; GAN CEANN.

duma [Ir., mound, tumulus, barrow]. An Irish word for burial-ground, an element in many ancient place-names, e.g. Duma na nGall [mound of the (foreign) hostages] at *Tara.

Duma Sláinge, Duma Sláine. Another name for *Dind Ríg.

Dumbarton [ScG *dùn Breatann*, fortress of the Britons]. Twin-peaked rock or boss, a volcanic plug of basalt, 240 feet high, on the banks of the River Leven near its confluence with the Clyde, 15 miles NW of Glasgow, which has had as long a history as any fortified place in Britain. It was the centre of the ancient kingdom of *Strathclyde and remained a fortified place until modern times. An eminent name here from late Roman times is *Ceredig Gwledig (Coroticus), whose soldiers were accused by St *Patrick of carrying off newly baptized members of his flock, apparently as slaves. Bede (early 8th cent.) called it the fortress of Altclut or Altcluit [rock of the Clyde], and described it as a munissima urbs [very strongly fortified place]. It was captured by two Irish Viking leaders in 870–1. The kingdom of Strathclyde retained its identity until its absorption into the kingdom of Scotland in the 10th century. Dumbarton is identified with Breatan in James *Macpherson's *Poems of Ossian* (1760–3). Adjacent to the rock is the modern town of Dumbarton; both rock and town are in the former (until 1974) Dunbartonshire, now part of Strathclyde. See I. M. M. MacPhail, *Dumbarton Castle* (Edinburgh, 1979).

Dumna. Name given by Ptolemy (2nd cent. AD) to the Hebridean Isle of Lewis, although he badly misplaces the island itself.

Dumnonia. Latin name for the south-west part of Britain, roughly coextensive with portions of the modern counties of *Cornwall and Devon. Its royal seat until the 7th century was *Tintagel. The *P-Celtic people known as the Dumnonii or Damnonii, who ranged as far north as southern Scotland, have been linked by some commentators with the *Domnainn (also Fir Domnann, early invaders of Ireland). See Charles Thomas, 'The Character and Origins of Roman Dumnonia', in Thomas (ed.), *Rural Settlement in Roman Britain* (London, 1966), 74–98; Aileen Fox, *The Dumnonii* (London, 1973).

Dumnonia (of Brittany). See DOMNONIA (1).

Dún, Dùn, Dún-. The Irish and Scottish Gaelic word for fortress, fortified place, royal residence, castle, etc., appears as a part of many place-names, sometimes as a separate word, e.g. Dún Scaith, and sometimes joined, especially when anglicized, e.g. Dundalk. Dún, Dùn, Dún- entries are thus alphabetized letter by letter instead of word by word. Cognate with the Continental Celtic -dunum, which is usually compounded in final position.

Dunadd [ScG, fort of the Add (valley)]. Rocky, isolated hill, 176 feet, in north Strathclyde (until 1974, *Argyllshire), 4 miles N of Lochgilphead, near the hamlet of Kilmichael Glassary, in the valley of the River Add. Once an important fortified place, Dunadd was the capital of the early Gaelic kingdom of *Dál Riada, *c.*500–843. The *Picts captured Dunadd in 736 in a temporary victory over the Scots. Few visible remains from Dunadd's early glory survive, most notably an incised boar of Pictish design and a right-footprint-shaped depression, thought to be the spot where kings of Dál Riada were invested with royal power.

Dún Ailinne, Aillinne, Ailinn, Ailleann, Ailenn. Ancient hill-fort, the largest in Ireland, on a hilltop near Kilcullen, Co. Kildare, 5 miles ESE of Kildare town. Enclosing an area of 34 acres, Dún Ailinne features a circular wall 450 yards in diameter that is sometimes 15 feet high. Recent excavations show occupation on the site from Neolithic times with traces of Iron Age use; other records indicate use as late as 1800. Dún Ailinne appears to have been the most important royal site in south *Leinster until the 7th century, and is now thought to have been the seat of the kings of Leinster. Yet it seems to have been used only in undetermined functions, and was not inhabited in any permanent fashion. The mythical Leinster king *Find File is thought to have lived here, and may have given his name to it. The site is popularly known as Knockawlin and Knockaulin. See also CRUACHAIN; EMAIN MACHA; TARA.

Dún Aonghusa, Óengusa, Aenghus, Aonghus, Angus. Huge stone fort perched on a cliff 200 feet above the sea on the south-west coast of Inishmore, the largest of the *Aran Islands. The fort, often described as one of the most magnificent structures of its kind in Western Europe, covers about 11 acres and comprises three concentric semicircles. The middle wall is covered by an abatis (or *chevaux-de-frise*) of jagged limestone uprights. The innermost semicircle has wall-walks and wall-chambers and a massive entrance-passage. Extensive restoration work, begun by the Office of Public Works in 1881, was ill-advised and made no record of the found state of the stone fort until that time. According to the **Lebor Gabála* [Book of Invasions], the *Fir Bolg built Dún Aonghusa and other stone forts on Aran Island; one of their chiefs, *Angus (3) (Aonghus, etc.), gives his name to the structure. It is also the last refuge of the *Fomorians. Curiously, Dún Aonghusa does not figure prominently in island folklore, although it is called Coillnamhan Fort in the fiction of island-born writer Liam O'Flaherty (1896–1984).

Dunatis. Continental god of fortified places.

Dunbarton. See DUMBARTON.

Dún Bolg [Ir., Bolg fortress]. Place-name of uncertain location, site of a legendary battle in which the men of *Leinster fought against payment of the tribute known as *bórama [cow-countings]. Young Leinstermen were smuggled into the camp of the *ard rí [high king], disguised as a tribute of food, hidden in baskets loaded on to 300 teams of twelve oxen each. Once inside the enemy encampment, the young Leinstermen emerged from their baskets and routed the ard rí's men. Alwyn and Brinley Rees, *Celtic Heritage* (London, 1961), 125–6, argue that this story demonstrates the function of Leinster among the five provinces in ancient Ireland: a food-providing yeomanry. It might possibly be identified with the place-name Dunboyke near Donard, Co. Wicklow.

Dunbristy [Ir. *dún briste*, broken fort]. An isolated rock off Downpatrick Head, Co. Mayo. Known in Irish folklore as Dún Geodruisge after the *giant thought to live on the rock. Geodruisge's castle, according to the story, was originally on the land, but was broken off and marooned by the curse of a woman from whom the giant had stolen cattle.

Dun Cow, Book of the. See LEBOR NA HUIDRE.

Dún Crimthainn 1. Irish fort on the Dee, also known as Dind Tradui; it was named for Crimthann Mór mac Fidaig, a shadowy pre-Patrician king in Ireland.

2. A fortress which may have once existed at *Howth, named for *Crimthann Nia Náir, a fabulous personality reputed to have visited the *Otherworld.

Dún Dá Bhenn [Ir., fortress of the two mountains]. In **Mesca Ulad* [The Intoxication of the Ulstermen] the men of *Ulster indulge themselves here lavishly for the first part of the night at this Co. Derry fortress before going on to Cúchulainn's fortress at *Dún Delgan.

Dún Delgan, Delga, Dealgan [Ir., Fortress of De(a)lga]. Fortress of *Cúchulainn in much of early Irish literature, identified with an ancient mound, popularly known today as Castletown Hill, which lies near Dundalk, Co. Louth, and close by *Baile's Strand. The town of Dundalk, established 1186, takes its name from the ModIr. Dún Dealgan, but is not identical with Cúchulainn's fortress. The *Fomorian (sometimes *Fir Bolg) chief Delga built the fortress, naming it for himself. Cúchulainn lived here as a child, before taking it as his own.

Dundrum [Ir. *dún droma*, fort of the ridge]. Village and small port on the southern coast of Northern Ireland, site of *Tonn Rudraige [Rudraige's Wave/ Surge], one of the three great waves of Ireland. Near here also was *Dún Rudraige, the residence of Briccriu.

Dunedin, Dùn Eideann. See EDINBURGH.

Dún Étair. Another name for *Benn Étair at *Howth.

Dún Geodruisge. See DUNBRISTY.

Dunkeld [ScG *dùn Chailleann*, fort of the Caledonians]. An ecclesiastical capital in the upper Tay valley, 15 miles NW of Perth, and centre of power in Scottish culture from the 9th century to the early Middle Ages. Reputedly founded by St *Adamnán, biographer of *Colum Cille [St Columba], before 700, Dunkeld became a leading centre of Celtic Christianity, especially after the demise of Iona (*c*.825), possibly the equal of Kells in Ireland. As its name implies, it was also a 'capital' of the *Caledonii, a *P-Celtic people. Remains of a pre-medieval stronghold are found on a crag north of the modern town of the same name. *Cináed mac Alpín [Kenneth MacAlpin] made Dunkeld one of two capitals, along with Scone, when he united the *Picts and Scots in 844. Remains of a late medieval cathedral (1318–1501) stand in the town.

Dúnlaing. Variant spelling of *Dúnlang.

Dúnlaith [Ir., lady of the fortress (?)]. Name borne by dozens of historical petty queens in early Ireland. The most significant in legend is the daughter of Regamon, the Connacht warrior.

Dúnlang, Dúnlaing. Name borne by countless early petty kings of *Leinster and *Munster. One legendary Dúnlang, king of Leinster, murdered twelve ladies of *Tara, and was executed in revenge by *Cormac mac Airt. Dúnlang's shirt was a treasure taken by *Ailill of Connacht in **Echtra Nerai* [The Adventure of Nera]; it was thought one of the Three Treasures of Ireland. The name is anglicized as Dowling or Dudley.

Dúnlang Ó hArtagáin, Dunlang O'Hartigan. Legendary warrior at the historical Battle of Clontarf (1014) who chose death over dishonour. A *fairy woman came to Dúnlang before the battle and offered him two years of life, and joy—'life without death, without cold, without thirst, without hunger, without decay'—if he would put off combat for a day. He refused the offer and fell valiantly in battle. See also DUBHLAING.

Dunmore [Ir. *dún mór*, big fortress]. Huge, three-chambered cave in Co. Kilkenny, about 6 miles N of Kilkenny city. Widely known in Old Irish literature and in folklore as the darkest place in Ireland, Dunmore was the home of the monster cat *Luchtigern. The cave was plundered in 928 by Godfrey and the Vikings of Dublin, who reputedly slaughtered more than 1,000 people; numerous human bones found in the cave are thought to bear testimony to this event. Also known as Derc Ferna.

Dún na mBarc [Ir., Fort of the Ships]. Point of landing on Bantry Bay, Co. Cork, for the first invasion of Ireland, led by *Cesair, according to the **Lebor Gabála* [Book of Invasions]. Identified today with Dunnamark Fort, Castle, House, and Falls, opposite Whiddy Island, near the town of Bantry, Co. Cork. Geoffrey *Keating's *History* (17th cent.) locates Dún na mBarc on Ballinskellig Bay, Co. *Kerry.

Dún na nGéd, nGedh. Seat of the *ard rí [high king], after *Domnall (1) abandoned *Tara because of the curse of St *Rúadán; an unspecified point along the *Boyne River. Here Domnall suffers the fright described in *Fled Dúin na nGéd* [The Feast of Dún na nGéd].

Dún na Sciath [Ir., Fortress of Shields]. The most important instance of this widely occurring early place-name is identified with a surviving circular hill-fort on the western shore of Lough Ennell near Mullingar, Co. Westmeath. In the **Lebor Gabála* [Book of Invasions] it is associated with Anind, son of *Nemed, who was said to flood the lake from his grave. After the abandonment of *Tara it became one of the residences of the *ard rí [high king].

Dunollie [ScG *Dùn Ollaigh*]. A rocky peninsula, 80 feet high, to the north of Oban harbour, north Strathclyde (until 1974, *Argyllshire), site of a fortress during the heyday of the Gaelic kingdom of *Dál Riada from the 5th to 8th centuries. The site may also have contained a Celtic hill-fort from an earlier period. Chronicles testify that it was burned by enemies in 686 and 698, sacked in 701, and replaced by major refortifications in 714. Remains of a castle begun in the 13th century also still stand. Dunollie was also the seat of the Clan MacDougall.

Dún Rudraige [Ir., Rudraige's (Rory's) Fort]. Residence of *Briccriu in **Fled Bricrenn* [Briccriu's Feast], near the modern town of *Dundrum, Northern Ireland.

Dunscaith, Dun Scaith 1, Dun Scaich [ScG *Dùn Scàith, Dùn Sgàthaich*]. Ruined fortress on the Isle of *Skye, 6 miles W of Isleornsay on the coast of Sleat; named for Sgàthach (see SCÁTHACH), the tutor and lover of *Cúchulainn, who lived on Skye. In local oral tradition it was built in one night by the *fairies. Used in late medieval times by the MacDonalds of Sleat. Once known as Down Skayth. See also DÚN SCÁTHAIG(E).

2. [Ir., Fort of Shadow, of Fear]. Another name for the *Otherworld, sometimes located on the Isle of *Man. When *Cúchulainn and his companions landed here they met with a series of challenges. First the men had to fend off odious serpents who swarmed from a pit at the centre of the fortress. Next they faced toads with sharp beaks who turned into dragons. Vanquishing these, the men procured an enchanted *cauldron along with gold, silver, a limitless supply of meat, and three magical crows who could pull their ship back to Ireland. The evil gods who protected Dún Scáith called up a storm that caused the Irish ship to founder. Although the men lost their treasure, they swam back to Ireland and lived to tell the tale.

Dún Scáthaig(e), Scáith, Scáthach [Ir., Scáthach's Fort]. A poetic name for all of the Isle of *Skye in some Old Irish stories; sometimes identified with the ruined fortress on Skye, *Dunscaith (1), 6 miles W of Ornsay.

Dùn Sgàthaich. See DUNSCAITH.

Dún Sobairche, Sobairce [Ir., primrose (?) fort]. Fortress cited in several OIr. narratives, coextensive with the modern village of Dunseverick, 4 miles N of Bushmills, on the north coast of Northern Ireland. Residence of King *Eochaid, who gave his daughter in marriage to *Rónán in the hopes that she would fall in love with *Máel Fothartaig in **Fingal Rónáin* [How Rónán Slew His Son]. The citation of Dún Sobairche in **Táin Bó Cuailnge* [Cattle Raid of Cooley] provokes questions; as *Medb captures the place after turning from the north, it could hardly be identical with Dunseverick. Gene Haley, geographer of the *Táin*, suggests the name here should be Dún Lethglaise, coextensive with modern Downpatrick, Northern Ireland.

Dunthalmo. Character in James *Macpherson's *Ossian* (1760–3): a cruel and ambitious prince who resides on the Tweed River. His daughter is Caolmhal.

Dunvegan [ScG *Dùn Bheagan, Bheagain*]. Castle, village, and bay in the north-west Isle of *Skye. While most of the present-day castle was constructed from the 15th to 19th centuries, its foundations date from the 9th. It has been occupied continuously-longer than any castle in Britain-by the same family, the MacLeods. The castle museum holds the famous 'fairy flag', thought to have been captured by the Saracens. The castle and environs have long been the focus of a considerable body of folklore. See Brenda MacLeod, *Tales of Dunvegan* (Stirling, 1950).

Duracht. Variant spelling of *Duthacht.

Durbhola, Durfulla. Daughter of the king of the merrows who marries a mortal; in some versions the human lover is a member of the Cantillon family. After a happy life among mortals, she died and was buried in the family ground on an island, which was then overrun by the sea. Thereafter, when members of the family died the body was left on the seashore until merrows carried it off.

Durrow [Ir. *darú*, oak plain]. Abbey and small village in Co. Offaly, 4 miles N of Tullamore, site of an early monastic centre founded in 551 by *Colum Cille [St Columba]. Here was kept the *Book of Durrow*, an illuminated manuscript of the Gospels, now in the library of Trinity College, Dublin.

Durthacht, Duracht, Daurthecht. Father of *Eógan, the *Ulster champion usually cited as the killer of *Noíse.

Duth-Maruno. A character in James *Macpherson's *Ossian*. A brave warrior, 'black and steady', from north of Caithness, who attended *Fingal in his last battle against the Morni.

dwarf, dwarfs [OE *dweorg*]. Not all adult persons of smaller than normal stature in Celtic literature are dwarfs. Several of the denizens of *fairy land, for example, are portrayed as smaller than most mortals, but they are not dwarfs. Allusions to non-fairy dwarfs are not especially common in the Celtic world, as compared with Norse or Arthurian traditions. The most celebrated is probably the satyr-like *fenodyree, a leading figure in the folklore of the Isle of *Man. Welsh dwarfs are more unattractive than those of Ireland or Gaelic Scotland. The Welsh word for dwarf, cor, lies at the root of Coraniaid, a plague upon Wales in **Cyfranc Lludd a Llefelys*. One of Culhwch's tasks is to retrieve the container of Gwyddolwyn the dwarf, which is needed to keep warm the black witch's blood. The shape-shifting *Eiddilig Gor is an enchanting dwarf. The Breton korr is easily identifiable in the roguish korrigans of Breton lore. By contrast in Ireland the dwarf harpist in the court of *Fionn mac Cumhaill, *Cnú Deireóil, has golden hair and sings sweetly. The benign *Áeda (1), dwarf of King *Fergus mac Léti, accompanies the dwarf bard *Eisirt to the realm of *Iubdán. *Abcán, a poet, and *Luchta, a wood-worker, were both dwarfs of the Tuatha Dé Danann. See also GENIUS CUCULLATUS.

The OIr. for dwarf is abacc; ModIr. abhac; ScG troich; Manx crivassan, trollag; W cor; Corn. cor; Bret. korr. See Vernon J. Harward, *The Dwarfs of Arthurian Romance and Celtic Tradition* (Leiden, 1958). See also GNOME.

Dwyfan and Dwyfach, Dwyvan and Dwyvach. Welsh equivalents of Noah or Deucalion who take their names from small rivers, as told in a *flood legend from the *Triads. A great flood was caused by the monster *Afanc, who dwelt in *Llyn Llion (possibly *Bala Lake). All humans were drowned except Dwyfan and Dwyfach, who escaped in a mastless boat. They built an imposing ship (or ark) called *Nefyd Naf Neifion, on which they carried two of every living kind. From Dwyfan and Dwyfach all of the island of Prydain [Britain] was repeopled. Dwyfach appears to take her name from the small Dwyfach [W, little Dwy] River of *Gwynedd (until 1974, Caernarvonshire) that flows into Cardigan Bay; Dwyfan would then derive from the river it enters, the Dwyfawr or Dwyfor [W, great Dwy].

Dwynwen, Dwyn, Donwenna. Patron saint (5th cent.) of lovers in Wales, whose feast-day is 25 January. Daughter of King Brychan of *Brecknockshire, *Powys, Dwynwen is most associated with the small island of Llanddwyn in *Gwynedd, on *Anglesey, where her name is commemorated in place-names, and also Glamorganshire. The best-known story about her dates from *Iolo Morganwg (*né* Edward Williams) in the early 19th century. Dwynwen was in love with a youth named Maelon but displeased him by rejecting his sexual advances. She prayed to God to release her from the liaison, even though her love was undiminished. God appeared and offered her a sweet drink, which quenched her passion but which proved to turn Maelon to ice once he had tasted it. Dwynwen was then granted three wishes, which were (1) to revive Maelon, (2) to become the patron saint of lovers, and (3) never to marry. She later became a nun. As a saint her name is also invoked in the curing of animals.

Dwyvan and Dwyvach. Anglicizations of *Dwyfan and Dwyfach.

Dydd Calan Mai, Calan Mai, Galan Mai. Welsh for May Day; see CALAN MAI; BELTAINE.

Dyddgu [W *dydd*, day; *cu*, dear, found beloved]. The unattained object of poet Dafydd ap Gwilym (*c.*1320–70) and subject of nine of his poems. A dark-haired, aristocratic, remote, and virginal woman, she contrasts with the poet's blonde sweetheart, *Morfudd. The woman who served as the basis for Dyddgu was the daughter of Ieuan ap Gruffudd ap Llywelyn, who lived at Tywyn in south *Ceredigion (Cardiganshire; since 1974, *Dyfed).

Dyfed, Dyved. A region of south-western Wales much associated with the action of the **Mabinogi*, the home of *Pwyll, and one of the most Irish-influenced areas of the principality. The modern county of Dyfed, created 1974, containing the former shires of Pembroke, Carmarthen, and Cardigan, is far more extensive than the ancient kingdom. The Romans called the region Demetia after the *P-Celtic people *Demetae, who had lived here from pre-Roman times. From late Roman times the area was invaded and settled by the *Déisi and by the 'sons of Liathán', the Uí Liatháin of what is now east Co. Cork, whose descendants formed the ruling dynasty until at least the 10th century. In Irish stories these invaders are described as the Déisi, from adjacent Co. Waterford, as led by *Eochaid (9). The first and third branches of the Mabinogi are set here, both concerning the family of Pwyll, Lord of Dyfed. *Pryderi, son of

Pwyll, who figures in all four branches, is born in Dyfed. A mysterious realm lies within or beside it, where Pwyll loses his companions while hunting and comes face to face with fearful *Arawn, king of the deathly realm of *Annwfn. In the third branch *Manawydan is given land in Dyfed when suddenly, following a thunderclap, it is left desolate, without creature or habitation. Later it is revealed that this enchantment was caused by *Llwyd in revenge for the treatment of *Gwawl; Llwyd then restores the land. Pendaran is the 'chief thunderer of Dyfed'. According to medieval materials collected in *The Myvyrrian Archaiology of Wales* (1801–7), giving characteristics of the people of different parts of the principality, those from Dyfed are serfs.

Dyflinarski. A Norse name for the settlement along the *Liffey that is now *Dublin. The area of Norse habitation would include only downtown streets, a fraction of the modern metropolitan city; all of the action of James Joyce's *Ulysses* (1922) takes place in what was Dyflinarski.

Dyfnwal Moelmud, Dyvnwal Moelmud. Legendary early (400 BC?) king of Wales, by reputation a benefactor and great law giver, the greatest before *Hywel Dda (10th cent.). He is the model for Dunwallo Molmutius in *Geoffrey of Monmouth's *Historia* (1136).

Dyfr [cf. W *dyfr*, waters]. Known for her golden hair, one of the Three Splendid Maidens at *Arthur's court; the other two were *Enid, the daughter of Yniwl, and *Tegau Eurfron, much celebrated by later poets for her beauty. According to the *Triads, she is the lover of *Glewlwyd Gafaefawr, Arthur's doorkeeper. Identical with the figure known as Dynwir in popular tradition.

Dying Gaul. A large bronze statue erected by Attalos I of Pergamon (3rd cent. BC) after his triumph over the *Galatians of Asia Minor. The warrior is portrayed reclining on his left arm, with head down; he is also naked, except for a metal torc around his neck, thus supporting the testimony of *Classical commentators that Celts went into battle naked, except for their weapons. His shield resembles those found in cemeteries in the Marne valley. The well-preserved original is in the Capitoline Museum, Rome; copies are housed in the Museum of Classical Archaeology, Cambridge University, as well as in Berlin and Stockholm.

Dylan [W, ocean, wave]. Welsh aquatic hero or sea demigod, the son of *Arianrhod daughter of *Dôn in the fourth branch of the **Mabinogi*; may carry the epithet Ail Ton, Eil Ton, Eil Tôn, Eilton, Eil Don [W, son of wave] or Ail Mor [W, son of the sea]. Described as dark, Dylan contrasts with his fair twin brother, *Lleu Llawgyffes.

Arianrhod gives birth to Dylan immediately after stepping over *Gwydion's magic wand. He takes to the sea as soon as he is baptized, and assumes the sea's nature; he can swim as well as any fish and no wave ever breaks under him. He is killed by a single blow from his uncle, Gofannon fab *Dôn. The rising tide rises to avenge the killing; the roar of the tide at the mouth of the *Conway River is thought to be the death-groan of Dylan. His name is also cited in the **Book of Taliesin* and the *Triads. Learned speculation asserts that Dylan may be based on an independent sea-divinity whose story became associated with Lleu Llaw Gyffes. See also ENDIL. Dylan may have served as a model for the Arthurian figure Dyonas, the father of the beautiful Vivien/Vivian. 'Dylan' was an uncommon given name in Wales before the career of poet Dylan Thomas (1914–53). See *Studia Celtica*, 24–5 (1989–90), 26–37.

dyn hysbys [W, wise man]. A title rather than a name, the most common term in Wales for a wizard, known in many districts. The soul of the *druid, too imperfect for Christian heaven and too good for hell, inhabits the body of the dyn hysbys. Among the powers of the dyn hysbys is the ability to know and reveal the unknown, especially events in the future pertaining to love and death. Such powers might also be applied to commonplaces, like finding money that has been lost or helping a Welshman to escape from an English gaol. He was said to possess the power of breaking spells by undoing the evil perpetrated by witches and others. A dyn hysbys might also undertake to heal an animal or human by using charms and incantations. His powers were especially efficacious on those days when the world of the spirits was thought to come closer to that of humans, such as *Calan Mai [May Day], St John's Day (24 June), and the eve of winter. There were three kinds of dyn hysbys: clerics, men who had learned their craft from esoteric books, and those who had inherited the power from their families. Other Welsh terms for wizard are: consuriwr [conjurer], dewin [magician], and swynwr [charmer]. The names of many dyn hysbys survive, and some were renowned beyond their time and place.

Dyna. See DIARMAIT UA DUIBNE.

dynon bach teg, dynion bach teg [W, fair little folk]. A Welsh term for the *tylwyth teg, the Welsh *fairies.

Dynwir. See DYFR.

Dyrnwch. Variant spelling of *Diwrnach.

Dyved. Anglicization of *Dyfed.

Dyvnwal Moelmud. Variant spelling of *Dyfnwal Moelmud.

E

E. The fifth letter of the modern English alphabet is represented by edad, [aspen] in the *ogham alphabet of early Ireland; edad is the fourth vowel in ogham.

each uisce, each uisge, aughisky. The malevolent water-horse of Irish [*each uisce*] and Scottish Gaelic [*each uisge*] folklore whose name has endured several anglicizations, e.g. aughisky; comparable to the *cabyll-ushtey and *glashtin of Manx folklore and *ceffyl dwfr of Welsh folklore. The water-horse inhabits salt water or large still bodies of inland water, and is thus distinguished from the *kelpie inhabiting running water. In all manifestations the each uisce is a fearsome creature who can deceive and torment mortals. A sleek and handsome steed, it almost offers itself to be ridden. The Irish each uisce is most likely to emerge from the water during the month of November (see SAMAIN), when it gallops along the sands or over fields. When humans bridle and saddle them, they make fine horses, as long as they do not catch sight of salt water. When this happens, the each uisce bounds into the water with its helpless rider on its back; the horse may later devour the rider. Only the human liver will be rejected, which then floats to the surface. An untamed each uisce might also devour mortal cattle. According to popular legend, St *Féchíne of Fore (d. 665?) compelled an each uisce to pull his chariot when his own horse had died.

The Scottish each uisge, even more terrifying, may appear as a gigantic bird or a handsome young man. Cautionary tales were once told how an each uisge once appeared as a pretty little pony to several little girls near Aberfeldy, Tayside (until 1974, Perthshire). As they mounted the pony, its back lengthened to accommodate them. Although the horse ran to and fro among the rocks, the children could not be unseated; next morning their livers floated to the top of a nearby lochan. A smith of the isle of Raasay vowed revenge when an each uisge devoured his beautiful daughter. Working with his son, he lured the each uisge with a roasted sheep and then held it tight in iron hooks until morning.

The each uisce or each uisge bears some relationship to the Welsh *afanc. It should not be confused with the beautiful, lake-dwelling horses *Cúchulainn captured and trained; he returned those to their mountain pool of his own volition when they were mortally wounded. The shoopiltee is a variant of the each uisce from the Shetlands. Folk motifs: B184.1.3; F234.1.8; F420.5.2.1; G303.3.3.1.3.

Eacha, Eachdha. ModIr. spellings of *Echdae.

Eachtach 1, Echtach. Daughter of *Diarmait Ua Duibne in lays from **Duanaire Finn* and in other oral traditions. After *Fionn mac Cumhaill's role in refusing to help Diarmait after he has been gored by the boar, Eachtach rallies her brothers for revenge against the *Fenian hero and wounds him severely.

2. Cognomen of *Illann (2).

3. One of the wives of *Lug Lámfhota.

Eachtra, *Eachtrae, Eachtrada* (pl.). The ModIr. word for 'adventure', the first word in the title of innumerable folk-tales, some of which are humorous and anti-heroic. Although ModIr. *Eachtra* is sometimes used interchangeably with the OIr. and MidIr. **Echtra*, the older form denotes an adventure of a specific type, often in the *Otherworld.

Eachtra an Amadáin Mhóir. Irish title translated as 'The Adventure of the Great Fool' or 'The Lay of the Great Fool'; ScG *Laoidh an Amadain Mhòir*. An Irish and Scottish Gaelic folk-tale usually thought to be part of the *Fenian canon, although Fenian names do not figure prominently in it. The name 'Great Fool' is given to the *Perceval-like hero by an adversary in combat; he bears it ironically.

The 'fool' of the title is the dispossessed son of a great king. In Irish versions, he may be the son of the king of *Munster, driven to the woods with his mother by an invading king of *Leinster, who slaughters the hero's father and other members of the royal household. While in the woods, the hero and his mother grow much hair on their bodies, like wild beasts. The boy grows only at night but, when he does, reaches the height of a giant. On behalf of his impoverished mother, he seizes turf, flour, and sheep from neighbours. Hearing of his power, the king, residing in the captured castle, sends the hero on two apparently dangerous quests; but the hero first tames a wild dog, making him a pet, and then slays a wild boar, taking his carcass for food. The hero then wins the king's beautiful daughter, sometimes known as Eilín Óg, but subsequently murders the other members of her family when he learns what they have done to his; she remains his faithful wife.

When the hero magically loses his shins in a dark glen, he can still run faster than other men on his stumps. Not incapacitated, he spears a swift white deer and captures a white dog running with it. But implored by his wife, he turns over the deer and the dog to a hunter named *Gruagach of the Castle of Gold, who claims them; this magnanimity wins an invitation to the castle for the hero and his wife. En route they encounter a champion named Maragach, who expresses his desire for the hero's wife. When Maragach learns that the hero will defend his wife's honour with nothing but his fists, he calls him a 'Great Fool' [*Amadán Mór*]. The Great Fool seizes Maragach's weapon and decapitates him. His legs are restored. Gruagach is later revealed to be the hero's brother. Together they successfully battle four giants.

Texts survive in Irish and Scottish Gaelic versions. See *Transactions of the Ossianic Society*, ed. John Daly, iv (Dublin, 1859); J. F. Campbell, *Popular Tales of the West Highlands*, iii (London, 1893); Jeremiah Curtin, *Hero Tales of Ireland* (London and Boston, 1894). Several commentators see links between this story and the development of the Arthurian hero *Perceval: See L. Muehlhausen, 'Neue Beiträge zum Perceval-Thema', *Zeitschrift für celtische Philologie*, 27 (1927), 1–30; Sheila J. McHugh, *'Sir Perceyvelle': Its Irish Connections* (Ann Arbor, Mich., 1946).

Eachtra an Ghiolla Dheacair, Variant title for **Tóraigheacht an Ghiolla Dheacair* [The Pursuit of the Hard Gilly/Difficult Servant].

Eachtra Bhodaigh an Chóta Lachtna. Irish title for a *Fenian tale dating from the 17th century, known in English as 'The Churl [or Clown] in the Grey [or Drab] Coat', 'The Adventure of the Churl in the Grey Coat', 'The Lay of the Churl in the Grey Coat', etc. Scottish Gaelic spelling for the same title is *Eachtra Bhodaig* . . . In most versions the action begins when the Fenians are challenged by a lone warrior named 'Ironbones', who describes himself as the 'Son of the King of Thessaly'. If the Fenians cannot defeat Ironbones in a contest, he will exact great tribute. Both sides agree on a foot-race from 'Bineader' [*Benn Étair/*Howth] to a point in south-west *Munster, even though the swiftest Fenian runner, *Caílte mac Rónáin, is away at *Tara. While looking for Caílte, *Fionn mac Cumhaill encounters a detestable *giant, the Bodach [churl, clown, lout, etc.] of the title, who agrees to run on the Fenians' behalf. Once in the race, the Bodach affects to be unconcerned with its outcome. He rises late in the morning and eats a leisurely breakfast, only to find that Ironbones has left ahead of him. The Bodach passes Ironbones twice before stopping to eat blackberries, allowing his opponent to take the lead. Another time he backtracks to fetch a coat he has dropped. Despite his desultory effort, the Bodach wins the race easily and is then revealed to be *Manannán mac Lir, the sea-god.

Standish Hayes O'Grady includes an Irish text and English translation, under the title 'The Carle in the Drab Coat', in *Silva Gadelica* (London, 1892). James Clarence Mangan adapted it as one of the earliest prose works (1840) of the Irish literary renaissance; see *The Prose Works of James Clarence Mangan*, ed. D. J. O'Donoghue (Dublin and London, 1904). Patriot leader Pádraic Pearse produced an Irish-language version, *Bodach an Chóta Lachtna* (Dublin, 1906).

Eadán, Edán. A chief of the *Milesians, who came from Spain to invade Ireland in the **Lebor Gabála* [Book of Invasions]. He participates in the slaughter of the *Tuatha Dé Danann, notably by slaying the esteemed *Fódla, wife of *Mac Cécht, at the Battle of *Tailtiu. When the sons of *Míl Espáine allotted land to the victors, Eadán apparently received portions of what is now Co. Sligo; he is described as establishing a fort at Ráth Rígbaird, now the hill of Knocknarea, east of the modern village of Easky. Eadán and his brothers Ún and Én were slain by *Éremón, another son of Míl, at Kilcomreragh near *Uisnech, Co. Westmeath.

Eadán, Eadan. Also variant spellings of *Étan.

Éadaoin. ModIr. spelling of *Étaín.

Eader. See BENN ÉTAIR.

Éadoin. Variant spelling of *Étaín.

Eadon. Member of the *Tuatha Dé Danann, known as the 'Nurse of Poets'.

eagle [L, MidE *egle*]. The large, diurnal bird of prey (genus *Aquila*) plays a surprisingly small role in Celtic mythology and iconography, compared to other European traditions. Gaulish examples appear copied from Roman models. In Irish and Welsh traditions the eagle is thought to be one of the oldest of animals; a Scottish Gaelic phrase describes it as *sàr-eun* [veritable bird]. *Culhwch consults the ancient eagle of Gwernabwy in his search for *Mabon. Several heroes, *Fintan mac Bóchra, *Lleu Llaw Gyffes, *Taliesin, and *Tuan mac Cairill, take the form of an eagle, often in a series of transformations; the transformation into a *salmon usually follows. In Irish folklore the hawk of *Achill tricks an eagle by sending it on a fruitless errand while the hawk eats the eagle's chicks. The eagles of *Snowdonia (W *Eryri) in Welsh tradition were thought to be oracles of peace and war; flying high signalled victory, but flying low, crying incessantly, implied defeat for the Welsh. In later tradition the eagle may be associated with St John the Evangelist, with the sign of Scorpio in the zodiac, or with water as one of the four elements. In Irish and Scottish Gaelic folklore Adam and Eve are thought to be extant as eagles. See ERYR PENGWERN [The Eagle of Pengwern]. ModIr. iolar; ScG iolaire; Manx urly; W eryr; Corn. ēr; Bret. erer.

Eairkyn Sonney. Variant spelling of *Arkan Sonney.

Ealadha. ModIr. variant spelling of *Elatha.

Ealcmhar. ModIr. spelling of *Elcmar.

Eamhain. See EMAIN MACHA.

Eamhain of the Apples. Manx variant of *Emain Ablach.

Éamonn an Chnuic [Ir., Edmund/Éamonn of the Hill]. Name in folk-tale and song for Edmund Ryan, a 17th-century Tipperary rapparee or patriotic bandit, whose reputation for daring outlived him. The rapparees were men evicted from their lands during the Cromwellian plantation who plundered those who had robbed them of their inheritance.

Earc. ModIr. variant of *Erc.

Earl of Desmond. See GERALD, EARL OF DESMOND.

earrach. The ModIr. and ScG word for spring, sometimes used to imply *Imbolc, the February festival.

earwig [OE *ēarwicga*]. The tiny insect with pincer-like appendages protruding from its abdomen, once thought to penetrate a person's head through the ear, was perceived to be a disguise of the *devil in Irish folklore. By custom they were to be killed as soon as they were seen. James Joyce draws on earwig lore in constructing the persona of HCE in *Finnegans Wake* (1939). ModIr. gaillseach; ScG fiolan; Manx gollage; W chwilen glust; Corn. gorlosten; Bret. garlostenn.

Eas Aodha Ruadh. See ASSAROE.

Eas Ruaidh, Easruadh. See ASSAROE.

Easal. Variant spelling of *Assal.

Easnadh. ModIr. spelling of *Esnad.

Easroe. Variant spelling of *Assaroe.

Éber, Eber, Heber, Ébir, Éibhear [disputed etymology: 1. from the biblical Eber, son of Salah, Gen. 11: 14; cf. OIr. *Éberda*, Hebrew. 2. Hiberno-Latin *Eberus*, *Ebernus*, Irishman]. Name borne by at least four characters in the **Lebor Gabála* [Book of Invasions], who are easily confused with one another. The most prominent is *Éber Finn, who is probably implied in the Old Irish phrase describing the genealogy of the Irish people, maicc Ébir, maicc Érimóin, 'sons of Éber, sons of Éremón'.

Éber Donn [Ir., Dark Éber]. Malevolent, envious older brother of *Éber Finn in the *Lebor Gabála* [Book of Invasions]. T. F. O'Rahilly argues in *Early Irish History and Mythology* (Dublin, 1946) that his name is a means of accommodating *Donn (1), the Irish god of the dead, with the pseudo-history of the invasion story. More often known as *Donn mac Míled, his story is now intertwined with that of Donn (1), although he retains a separate identity within the *Lebor Gabála*.

Éber Finn [Ir., Fair Éber]. Important leader of the *Milesian invasion of Ireland in the **Lebor Gabála* [Book of Invasions] and often-cited ancestor of the southern Gaels of Ireland. One of eight sons of *Míl Espáine and younger brother of *Éber Donn; sometimes confused with *Donn (1), the pre-Christian ancestor-deity. Éber participated bravely in the Milesian conquest of Ireland from the *Tuatha Dé Danann, but he was unhappy with the division of the spoils. In a decision arbitrated by the poet *Amairgin, Éber Finn would receive the south of Ireland and his brother *Éremón the north. Éber's displeasure came from his perception that he received the lesser half; seven chiefs went with Éremón to the north, while only six went to the south. In some texts Éremón receives the kingship in addition. The border between the divisions is usually thought to be *Eiscir Riada, an uneven ridge of low mounds between Galway Bay and the Dublin area. The names of other ancient mounds from Counties Galway, Limerick, and Wexford bear testimony to his rule. Éber was subsequently defeated and killed at Argetros, Co. Kilkenny, in an unsuccessful attempt to wrest power from Éremón. Éber's son-in-law was *Mug Nuadat [Ir., servant of Nuadu], also known as *Eógan Mór, an ancestor of the *Eóganacht of *Munster.

Éber Glúinfhinn [Ir., Éber White-Knee]. Ancestor of *Míl Espáine, eight generations before the *Milesians moved to Spain under the rule of *Bregon.

Éber Scot [Éber the Scot]. Fabricated eponymous ancestor of the Scotiae [i.e. Irish] and Scots, according to the **Lebor Gabála* [Book of Invasions]. In his quasi-biblical lineage, he is the son of Esru, son of Goídel, son of *Scota, who was a daughter of Pharaoh Nectanabes of Egypt.

Ebhric. Variant spelling of *Áebhric, the name of the monk who hears the story of the Children of Lir; see OIDHEADH CHLAINNE LIR [The Tragic Story of the Children of Lir].

Eblana. Name recorded in *Ptolemy's geography (2nd cent. AD) for the site of what is now *Dublin.

Ébliu 1, Éblenn, Éibhlear [OIr. *oíph*, sheen, beauty, radiance (?]. A sister of *Lug Lámfhota and wife of *Fintan mac Bóchra. Much associated with the province of *Munster, she is thought to have given her name to mountains south of Nenagh, Co. Tipperary.

2. *Ulster queen whose story is part of the lore of *Lough Neagh. She fled with her stepsons, *Eochu mac Maireda and *Ríb, to form a new kingdom on a plain; the flood that dashed their plans and drowned them became the Lough.

Ebudae. Name given by *Ptolemy (2nd cent. AD) to the Hebrides; some sources argue that Ebudae may refer only to the southern islands in the Hebrides, those nearest Ireland.

Eburones. Latin name for an ancient Continental Celtic people; it may be glossed as 'people of the *yew tree' (?). The Eburones occupied a territory that lay between the Rhine and Schelde rivers in what is today the borders of Belgium and the Netherlands.

Ecca. Variant form of *Eochu mac Maireda.

Éccell [Ir., concealed or unforeseen peril, trap, ambush (?)]. Brother of the terrifying *Ingcél Cáech, grandson of Conmac, a king of Britain, in **Togail Bruidne Da Derga* [The Destruction of Da Derga's Hostel].

Echaid, Echaidh. Variant spellings of *Eochaid and *Eochu.

Echbél [Ir., horse-mouth, horse-lipped]. Hippomorphic name borne by two figures in Old Irish narrative. One is a minor character in **Scéla Mucce meic Da Thó* [The Story of Mac Da Thó's Pig]; the second is an epithet of the obscure warriors Eichde (see ECHDAE), Echbél, and Errge Echbél.

Echdae, Echde, Eachdha, Eacha [Ir., horse-god (?); horse-like (?)]. Husband of the goddess *Áine (1), especially as cited in the genealogies of the *Eóganacht; see also AILILL AULOMM. *Cúchulainn and *Cú Roí carry off his three magical cows from Scotland.

Echid. Anglicization of *Eochaid.

Echraide [Ir., horse-rider]. Cognomen of *Étaín.

Echtach. Variant spelling of *Eachtach.

Echtge. Irish place-name, often cited in the writings of W. B. Yeats and Lady Gregory, for the range of mountains (1,243 feet) between

Counties Clare and Galway, between Loughrea and Lough Derg; usually known in English as Slieve Aughty (or Baughty). Place-name legend links the mountains with Echthge, a lady of the *Tuatha Dé Danann, who was given them as a dowry.
Lady Gregory acknowledged that Irish-speaking villages in these mountains, now abandoned, were the source of much of the folklore in her *Visions and Beliefs in the West of Ireland* (London, 1920).

Echtra, Echtrae, Ectra, Echtrai (pl.). The OIr. word for 'adventure', the first word in the title in a category of narrative that flourished from medieval to early modern times, especially during the 15th to 17th centuries. The thematic distinction of the *Echtra* is the setting of the hero's visit to the *Otherworld; his journey, whether in a coracle or underground, is but a subordinate framework. The *Echtra* should be differentiated from stories beginning with the word **Imram* [voyage], which tell of the hero's voyage and adventures to an Otherworld located on islands in the western ocean. These adventurous tales became so popular that *Echtra* came to be used in the titles of any romance. Although titles of OIr. narratives are sometimes given ModIr. spellings, the ModIr. **Eachtra* lacks the specificity of *Echtra* and may be used in titles of comic or anti-heroic stories that do not follow earlier convention.

In the *Echtra* the hero is often enticed by a beautiful woman or wonderful warrior telling of the marvels of a mysterious land, where every pleasure may be had and illness, grief, old age, and death are unknown. To reach this land the hero must usually cross either the western ocean or a plain in which he is lost in a magic mist. When the invitation to visit the marvellous land comes from a wonderful warrior, he will be revealed to be a member of the *Tuatha Dé Danann, the divine race of early Ireland, often *Lug Lámfhota or *Manannán mac Lir. Sometimes the hero never returns, but often he returns bearing gifts and great wisdom. The gravest danger facing the returning hero is that he will turn to dust as soon as his foot touches Ireland.

See David Dumville, '*Echtrae* and *Immram*: Some Problems of Definition', *Ériu*, 27 (1976), 73–94.

Echtra Fergusa maic Léti. Irish title for The Saga (or Adventure) of *Fergus mac Léti.

Echtra Mac nEchach Muigmedóin Irish title of an early 11th-century Irish narrative known in En.glish as The Adventure of the Sons of Eochaid Mugmedón, a part of the *Cycle of Kings. Texts survive in the **Yellow Book of Lecan* and the **Book of Ballymote*; it is not older than the 11th century. In it the most prominent son of Eochaid Mugmedón is Niall; we learn how he meets a female personification of Ireland and goes on to become the legendary king of Ireland, *Niall Noígiallach [of the Nine Hostages].

Eochaid Mugmedón, a wondrous and noble king of Ireland, has five sons, four, Brian, Ailill, Fiachra, and Fergus, by *Mongfhind, the daughter of Fidach, and one, Niall, by *Cairenn, a daughter of Sachell Balb, a British king. Mongfhind is filled with jealousy from the moment of Niall's conception, forcing the pregnant Cairenn to draw the water, hoping the labour would kill the child before birth. When Cairenn delivers a son, she is afraid to bring it into Tara and leaves Niall exposed to the birds. In fear of Mongfhind's anger, not one of the men of Tara will rescue the child until Torna the poet takes Niall to his bosom, fosters him, and foretells that he will become a great king. Upon reaching maturity Niall returns to Tara, where he finds his mother still drawing water for the household. Niall tells her to cease from such demeaning work to wear the royal purple henceforward because he is the son of the king. Mongfhind, predictably, is enraged, but she is taken to the breaking point when it appears that the common will favours Niall to succeed his father instead of her four sons. She demands that Eochaid Mugmedón choose his successor, but he refuses, giving the task instead to the wizard *Sithchenn, who devises a unique contest. He sets fire to a forge with the sons inside. Niall emerges first with the anvil and its block, prompting the wizard to exclaim, 'Niall vanquishes; and he will be a solid anvil forever.' The other sons make less satisfactory rescues: Brian, a sledgehammer; Fiachra, a pail of beer and the bellows; Ailill, a chest of weapons; and Fergus worst of all, a bundle of withered wood with a stick of *yew in it (symbolizing his sterility). Mongfhind finds these results grievously unacceptable, and bids her sons entrap Niall by pretending to quarrel, enticing him to settle the dispute, and then kill him. The sons comply and Niall is about to take the bait when Torna advises him, 'Let the sons of

Mongfhind be peaceful', a phrase which has survived as an Irish proverb.

Mongfhind says she will not abide by Sithchenn's test, and asks the wizard to make arms for the sons. He agrees, but gives the finest to Niall. Once armed, the five go hunting, wandering far astray. That night when they set about cooking their quarry they realize they need water, and send Fergus to fetch some. He finds instead, next to a well, a horrible hag, black as coal, with hair like the tail of a wild horse, smokey eyes, a crooked nose, green teeth that can cut oak, and green nails; she is covered in pustules and is in every way loathsome. She wants a kiss; otherwise, no water. Fergus refuses, saying he would rather perish of thirst. Fergus returns to tell his brothers, and one by one the others also go for water. Ailill and Brian refuse the kiss and return empty-handed, but Fiachra gives one small kiss, allowing him to see Tara and, later, to found a royal line in another part of Ireland; still, he does not return with water. Niall agrees to kiss the loathly lady, volunteers to lie with her, and then throws himself upon her, giving her a most passionate kiss. At this the hag is transformed into a wondrous beauty, clad all in royal purple, with bronze slippers on her white feet. She reveals herself as *Flaithius, the *Sovereignty of Erin, and grants Niall the water, kingship, and domination over the country for succeeding generations. When news of this reaches Mongfhind, she wants to know why the eldest son, Brian, has not received sovereignty. Her four sons answer that they acceded to Niall's seniority and kingship. Sithchenn confirms that Niall and his children will henceforward have the domination and kingship of Erin.

See text and translation by Whitley Stokes, *Revue Celtique*, 24 (1903), 190–207. The motif (D732) of the loathly lady transformed into gorgeous sovereignty is widespread in medieval literature, being best known in Geoffrey Chaucer's 'Wife of Bath's Tale' in the *Canterbury Tales* (1387–99). See Sigmund Eisner, *A Tale of Wonder: Source Study of the Wife of Bath's Tale* (Wexford, 1957).

Echtra Nerai. Irish title for an Old Irish narrative known in English as The Adventure of Nera. Although a part of the *Ulster Cycle, this tale of supernatural horror on *Samain, a time when demons were thought to be about, is set in *Connacht.

As the court of *Ailill and *Medb celebrates the feast of Samain at *Cruachain, Ailill offers a prize to any man brave enough to tie a withe around the leg of either of the two captives whose corpses have been left hanging on the gallows outside. After Nera fails in three attempts, one of the corpses offers some advice: use a peg. He then complains of thirst, for he has died thirsty. Nera carries the corpse on a circuitous search for water; when they find it, the corpse spits it upon an innocent household, all of whom die. At this Nera carries the corpse back to the gallows; but when he returns to Cruachain he finds all the residents decapitated and the court burned—or so it appears. He follows warriors into the cave of Cruachain (known conventionally as 'Ireland's gate to hell'), where he sees the ruler of the *sídh displaying heads on spikes. The denizens are clearly dead men, as each remarks to his neighbour that there must be a living man in the procession because it has become heavier.

The ruler of the sídh awards a home and wife to Nera, asking only that he provide a daily supply of firewood in return. Nera lives peaceably for a while until his wife tells him that Cruachain has not been destroyed as he imagined, but that it will be next Samain unless he warns his people to obliterate the sídh before that time. In his return to the mortal world he brings garlic, primrose, and golden fern to prove where he has been. Ailill welcomes him and gives him the prize, a sword, he had initially promised. In a year's time Ailill warns him to retrieve from the sídh what he most values. He brings out a brown bull calf that begins to fight with the famous *Finnbennach of **Táin Bó Cuailnge* [Cattle Raid of Cooley]. Nera's bull calf loses, but Medb swears that next time she must see the bull contest in person. The men of Cruachain, together with men of Ulster, commence battle on the sídh, but bring out three treasures as booty: the crown of Brión, the mantle of *Lóegaire in Armagh, and the shirt of Dúnlang in Kildare. Nera, his wife of the sídh, and their child are left inside, however, where they will stay until Doomsday.

See text by Kuno Meyer, *Revue Celtique*, 10 (1889), 212–28; 11 (1890), 210; repr. in T. P. Cross and C. H. Slover (eds.), *Ancient Irish Tales* (New York, 1936), 248–53. Several commentators have noted that the presence of Ailill, Medb, and Finnbennach indicates the storyteller's knowledge of *Táin Bó Cuailnge*. See also Dorothy M. Hoare, *The Works of*

Morris and Yeats in Relation to Early Irish Saga (Cambridge, 1938); Seamus Ó Duilearga, 'Nera and the Dead Man', in John Ryan (ed.), *Essays and Studies Presented to Professor Eoin MacNeil* (Dublin, 1940), 522–34. James Stephens employed elements of *Echtra Nerai* in his novel *In the Land of Youth* (London, 1924).

Echtrae Airt meic Cuinn. Irish title of a narrative usually known in English as 'The Adventure of Art Son of Conn', a part of the *Cycle of Kings. The sole surviving text, found in the *Book of Fermoy*, has long been thought to be derived from a lost original, based in part on the attention given to the legal and governmental system of early Ireland. The focus of the action is *Art, son of *Conn Cétchathach [of the Hundred Battles], legendary ancestor of Irish kings and noble families. Inconsistencies and obscurities mar the text.

After the death of his wife, *Eithne Tháebfhota, Conn Cétchathach goes out one day from *Tara to *Benn Étair [Hill of Howth]. On that same day the *Tuatha Dé Danann in council judge *Bé Chuma to be in sin with *Gaidiar, son of *Manannán mac Lir, and so she is banished from the *sídh and sent to live among the mortals of Ireland. Although she has never seen him, Bé Chuma already loves Art, son of Conn, and so sets out in a flimsy coracle to find him, landing at Benn Étair. She finds him quickly but misidentifies herself as *Delbcháem, daughter of Morgán, though admitting that she has come in search of the young prince. Even as she becames more enamoured of Art, and he of her, Bé Chuma asks Conn to ban him from Tara for a year (an action inexplicable in the text). Bé Chuma and Conn then arrive themselves at Tara as man and wife, and for the following year there is neither grain nor milk in all of Ireland. The *druids declare that Bé Chuma's wickedness and unbelief have brought this blight on the country, and that it can be removed only by the sacrifice made by a sinless couple, whose blood should be mixed with the soil of Tara.

Conn goes forth in search of the son of the sinless couple, sailing the coracle of Bé Chuma from Benn Étair through seas filled with monsters until he lands at the mysterious island of *Dáire (2), the wonderful son of *Fergus Fialbrethach [of the noble judgement] and his beautiful wife *Rígru Rosclethan [of the large eyes], daughter of Lodan from *Tír Tairngire [the Land of Promise]. Their son, *Ségda Sáerlabraid, sits in a crystal chair. Later Ségda dines with Conn as he is bound by *geis to do, just as his parents are bound to dine alone.

On the next day, when Conn makes his grim request to have Ségda for human sacrifice, his parents decline but the son consents, saying that the king of Ireland should not be refused. Although the parents ask that the boy be protected, Conn on his arrival at Tara accedes to the wishes of the druids, who insist on the boy's death. Before the druids can kill Ségda, a woman driving a cow enters the assembly and rescues the boy. She is revealed to be Rígru, the boy's mother, and before she departs she bids Conn to put Bé Chuma aside, which he will not do. She then prophesies that their state will grow worse.

Some time later, when the returned Art defeats Bé Chuma in a game of *fidchell, he lays a geis on her not to taste food in Ireland until she shall bring him the wand of *Cú Roí. After an extensive search she finds it at *Cahirconree on *Sliab Mis [Slieve Mish] and brings it to him. In a second game of fidchell, Bé Chuma wins; she bids Art taste no food until he has brought back Delbcháem the daughter of Morgán (whom Bé Chuma has previously impersonated). Art sails a coracle from the mouth of the *Boyne (*Inber Colptha) and finds a wonderful island inhabited by beautiful women, among them *Créide, the ravishing daughter of Fidech of the Long Hair. After a month and a fortnight Art tells Créide of his quest. She responds that the way will be long and fraught with difficulties, natural and supernatural. She predicts that when he reaches the maiden he will find a stronghold surrounded by a bronze fence festooned with heads of men killed by *Coinchenn [Dog-Headed], Delbcháem's fearsome mother. Thus forewarned, Art succeeds in his quest, slaying as he goes Delbcháem's terrible brother *Ailill Dubdétach [Black-Tooth].

When Art enters the fortress, Delbcháem is waiting for him in a sunroom. Saying she fears for his safety, she has her women welcome him and wash his feet. Coinchenn, who appropriately fears that she will die if ever her daughter is wooed, then enters; Art makes short work of her, placing her head on a vacant bronze stake outside the fortress. Then Morgán comes to avenge his wife, but he too loses his head. Art then takes hostages from Morgán's people, and also takes possession of the Land of Wonder and sets out with Delbcháem for Ireland. When they arrive at Benn Étair, Delbcháem bids Art to oblige Bé Chuma to leave Tara because it is she, Bé Chuma, who is blighting the land. Without farewell, then, Bé Chuma departs, and the nobles welcome Delbcháem and Art, who tells all present of his adventure.

See the translation by R. I. Best, *Ériu*, 3 (1907); repr. in T. P. Cross and C. H. Slover (eds.), *Ancient Irish Tales* (New York, 1936), 491–502.

Echtrae Brain maic Fhebail. Alternate title used by Myles Dillon (1946) for the narrative usually known as **Imram Brain* [The Voyage of Bran].

Echtrae Conli, *Echtra Connla, Conle.* Irish title of one of the most ancient (8th cent.?) of all Irish narratives, known in English as The Adventures of Connla, which survives in the **Book of the Dun Cow* [*Lebor na hUidre*] and the **Yellow Book of Lecan;* it is usually included in the *Cycle of Kings. The protagonist is *Connla (2), sometimes called 'the red' or 'the fair', a son of *Conn Cétchathach [of the Hundred Battles].

One day, as Connla walks with his father on the hill of *Uisnech, he sees a woman in rich garments who describes to him the wonder of *Tír na mBeó [the Land of the Living], and promises him eternal love and beauty without decay if he will remain with her there. Conn, who can hear the woman's voice but cannot see her, bids the druids block Connla's temptation by drowning out her voice. The woman then departs, but not before leaving Connla a magical apple; Connla touches no other food for a month, but his bites cannot diminish the apple. At the end of the month the mysterious lady coos even sweeter words about the land where Boadach rules but all the other denizens are women. Connla is torn between his love for his homeland and friends and the vision of what the woman promises. Eventually he relents and sails away with the woman in a coracle of glass, never to return.

The Land of the Living implied in the story bears a strong resemblance to *Mag Mell [the Pleasant Plain], folk motif F111; also, *Tír na mBan [the Land of Women], motif F112; and *Tír na nÓg [the Land of Youth], motif D1339.7. Several commentators have noted the parallels between *Echtrae Conli* and the lay of *Lanval* by Marie de France (12th cent.). Translated text, T. P. Cross and C. H. Slover (eds.), *Ancient Irish Tales* (New York, 1936), 488–90. See also Julius Pokorny, 'Conle's abenteuerliche Fahrt', *Zeitschrift für celtische Philologie*, 17 (1927), 193–205. James Cousins used the story as the basis of his play *The Sleep of the King* (Dublin, 1902; Chicago, 1973).

Echtrae Cormaic. Irish title for an Old Irish narrative known in English as The Adventure of Cormac or Cormac's Adventure in the Land of Promise [*Tír Tairngire]. Texts survive in the **Book of Ballymote*, the **Book of Fermoy*, and the **Yellow Book of Lecan*. The protagonist is *Cormac mac Airt, a legendary king of Ireland and grandson of *Conn Cétchathach [of the Hundred Battles].

One day at dawn, as Cormac mac Airt is walking the rampart at *Tara, he espies a warrior approaching who carries a branch with three golden apples. When he learns that the branch, when shaken, will produce a marvellous music that casts sleep upon all who hear it, Cormac asks to have it. The strange warrior agrees, asking in return the promise of three wishes, to which Cormac agrees. A year passes before the warrior asks his first wish, Cormac's daughter Ailbe, which Cormac grants. A month later he asks for *Cairbre Lifechair, Cormac's son, and again the father grants it. A third time the warrior asks for *Eithne (probably Eithne Tháebfhota), Cormac's wife. This Cormac will not allow; he pursues the warrior and his captives, including Eithne, until lost in a magical mist that falls upon the plain. After many adventures and sights Cormac comes to a castle where he is hospitably entertained by a handsome warrior. A pig is put on the spit for roasting as host and guests begin a unique storytelling contest. The pig cannot be cooked unless a truth is told for each quarter. When Cormac has to tell the fourth story, he relates how first his daughter, then his son, and finally his wife have been taken from him. At this the pig is found to be ready. Cormac protests that he usually dines with a company of fifty. The warrior sings a lullaby, putting Cormac to sleep; and when he awakes he finds fifty warriors around him, as well as his daughter, son, and wife.

The handsome host is given a golden cup whose craftsmanship startles Cormac. More importantly, it is a cup of truth, as the host demonstrates. He tells three lies and the cup breaks into three parts. He then tells Cormac that Eithne has lain with no man since she left Tara, nor has Ailbe, and that Cairbre has lain with no woman. The testimonies fuse the cup together, making it whole. At this the host reveals his true identity: he is *Manannán mac Lir, the sea-god; he is also the mysterious warrior who led them into the Land of the Living. He allows Cormac to keep the magical branch and cup for his lifetime, but that after that they must leave Ireland. Next morning Cormac, Eithne, Ailbe, and Cairbre find themselves at Tara again. Cormac uses the cup to test falsehood during his reign, but at his death it is not seen in Ireland again.

See translation by Whitley Stokes, *Irische Texte*, 3 (1) (Leipzig, 1891), 211–16; repr. in T. P. Cross (ed.), *Ancient Irish Tales* (New York, 1936), 503–7; Vernam Hull, '*Echtra Cormaic maic Airt*, "The Adventure of Cormac mac Airt"', *PMLA* 64 (1949), 871–83. Several commentators have noted the parallel between Cormac's visit to the Land of the Living and *Percevel's visit to Grail Castle. The motif of the testing cup of truth may be traced as far away as India; see Myles Dillon, 'The Hindu Act of Truth in Celtic Tradition', *Modern Philology*, 45 (1947), 137–40.

Echtrae Lóegairi, Láegairi. Irish title for an Old Irish narrative usually translated as the Adventure of Lóegaire. Texts are found in the **Book of Leinster* and the **Book of Fermoy*. It is distinguished from others of its type by having the mortal warrior lured away to the *Otherworld in order to take sides in an otherworldly conflict.

Early one morning a mysterious warrior approaches the king of *Connacht, *Crimthann Cass, and his retinue while they are assembled at *Énloch in Mag Aí (Co. Roscommon). The stranger identifies himself to Lóegaire mac Crimthainn, the king's son, as *Fiachna mac Rétach, who has come from the otherworldly realm of *Mag Dá Chéo. He asks help in retrieving his wife, who has been abducted by Eochaid son of Sál (*Eochaid (7)). Fiachna has already slain Eochaid, but his wife has fled to Eochaid's nephew *Goll son of Dolb, king of another otherworldly realm, *Mag Mell. As Fiachna has already been repulsed in seven attempts to recapture his wife, he seeks mortal help for the eighth, offering gold and silver to all who will go with him. Fiachna praises the beauty and valour of his people in two poems and then departs. Lóegaire takes fifty men, journeys to Fiachna's camp, joins the battle against Goll, and kills him. Asking to see the wife, Lóegaire learns that she is in Mag Mell, under guard. Lóegaire goes there, announces his victory over Goll, and demands the wife's release. She is then surrendered to him, but she laments her lost love for Eochaid, who was king of Mag Dá Chéo, and for Goll.

In reward for having his wife restored, Fiachna grants Lóegaire his daughter, Dér Gréine, and fifty maidens to his fifty men. The Connachtmen then stay in Mag Dá Chéo a year before returning home, having been warned by Fiachna not to dismount. They find their fellows still assembled. When the king's retainers come forth to greet Lóegaire, he tells them to stand back, saying that they have only returned to say farewell. Crimthann cries for his son not to leave, offering him the kingdom, gold, silver, steeds, and fair women. Lóegaire responds in a poem of praise of the Otherworld, its delightful music and the happiness of love. He then goes forth to the *fairy mound to live with Dér Gréine in the fort of Mag Mell; and there he still is.

Kenneth Jackson edited the text under the title 'The Adventure of Laeghaire Mac Crimthainn', *Speculum*, 17 (1942), 377–89. Mag Mell and Mag Dá Chéo of the story illustrate folk motif F111.

Echtrai. Plural form of *Echtra, Echtrae.

Echuid. Variant spelling of both *Eochaid and *Eochu.

Ecne, Ecna [OIr. *ecna*, *ecne*, wise, enlightened]. An early Irish personification of knowledge, enlightenment, and possibly also of poetry. His lineage implies his significance although he does not appear often in surviving literature. Ecne is usually thought to be the grandson of the great goddess *Ana, his mother having been impregnated by each of Ana's three sons.

Edaein, Edain, Édaín. Variant spellings of *Étaín; Edain was favoured by W. B. Yeats.

Edair. See BENN ÉTAIR, an Irish name for *Howth.

Edán. Variant spelling of *Eadán.

Édar, Edar. Variant spellings of *Étar.

Edern, Ederyn. A son of *Nudd, thus sometimes bearing the patronymic ap (or ab, fab, mab) Nudd, a recurrent figure in several early Welsh narratives. In *Culhwch ac Olwen *Culhwch cites him as one of Arthur's warriors. In *Breuddwyd Rhonabwy [The Dream of Rhonabwy] Edern leads the men of Denmark who are dressed in black. In *Geraint ac Enid Edern contests with Geraint when his *dwarf insults Arthur's wife, *Gwenhwyfar. The Welsh Edern appears to be identical with the pseudo-saint Edern of Brittany, whose cult was once important in *Finistère. R. S. Loomis (1927) speculated that the character of Edern may be the basis of such Arthurian figures as Isdernus, Ydier filz Nu, and Hiderus. Jean Markale (1986) has linked him with Yder de Northumbie in French Arthurian tradition.

Edinburgh [W *Eidyn, Eitin* (man's name); OE *burh*, fortress; cf. Sc. *burgh*, borough]. The Scottish capital, more specifically the imposing stone promontory (300 feet) today called Castle Rock, at the centre of the city, appears in many Celtic narratives. From earliest recorded history Castle Rock is described as impregnable, although the Angles succeeded in breaching it in AD 638. Its Latin name was Castellum Puellaram [Maidens' Castle], which appears to be based on 12th-century legend. Nothing is known of Eidyn or Eitin, the person who gave his apparently Welsh name to the rock and to the city. He is commemorated in the **Gododdin* (a 13th-cent. text about 7th-cent. events) where Edinburgh is known as Din Eidyn; it is known as Caer Eiddyn in other Welsh texts. Within the poem the defender of the Rock is Mynyddawg Mwynfawr [W, rich king of the castle]. The Scottish Gaelic name for the city, Dùn Eideann or Dùn Éideann [*dùn*, hill, fortress; *aodann*, slope], is often anglicized to Dunedin. In Arthurian narratives the Rock and city may be known as Danebroc or Tanebroc. Earlier etymologies linking Edinburgh to the OE Eadwinesburgh [Edwin's fortress] are now discredited.

Eefa. Anglicized spelling of *Aífe.

eel [MidE *ele*]. The snake-like marine or freshwater fish (order *Anguilliformes* or *Apodes*) does not play as important a role in the Celtic imagination as it does elsewhere. Often the eel appears malevolent. The Irish goddess *Mórrígan once came to *Cúchulainn in the form of an eel, but he repulsed her. Lake monsters may conventionally be referred to as eels. In the west of Ireland whistling eels were thought to foretell famine. Yet at other times eels might be benevolent, such as those thought to be the guardian spirits of wells and magic springs. Pilgrims at the sacred well of Tober Monachan, Co. *Kerry, were given the sight of a salmon and an eel, if their petition was to be granted. ModIr. eascann; ScG easgann; Manx astan; W llysywen; Corn. sylly; Bret. siliennn.

Eevell, Eevil. Anglicizations of *Aíbell.

Eevin. Anglicization of *Aíbell.

Efflam. Sixth-century Breton saint and *Arthur's legendary stepbrother. After Arthur has failed in several attempts to subdue a serpent, he is thirsty. Efflam assists him, first by defeating the serpent and second by causing a spring to rise; thought to have occurred at Saint-Michel-en-Grêve (Côtes d'Armor).

Efnisien, Efnysien, Efnissien, Evnisien, Evnissyen [W *efnys*, hostile enemy, unpeaceful). Malevolent and enigmatic son of *Euroswydd and Penarddun in the second branch of the **Mabinogi*, brother of the benevolent Nisien [W, peaceful], and half-brother of *Bendigeidfran, *Branwen, and *Manawydan. An easily insulted troublemaker, Efnisien causes much strife between Wales and Ireland. He disfigures the Irish horses, bringing war with the Irish, because he has not been asked for his consent when Bendigeidfran promises Branwen in marriage to the Irish king Matholwch. When it appears that Irish attempts to find reconciliation with the Welsh will succeed, he snatches *Gwern, Branwen and Matholwch's son, and throws him into a fire, renewing hostilities. But Efnisien can be heroic and self-sacrificing. He saves the life of Bendigeidfran and the Welsh invaders when he slaughters 200 Irishmen. And he sacrifices his life when he stretches out in the *cauldron of rebirth; as it is intended only to resuscitate the dead and Efnisien is still living, his martyrdom bursts it. Some commentators rationalize Efnisien's action by portraying him as a guardian of Welsh sovereignty, as embodied in Branwen. Others see him as an ill-tempered agitator like the Irish Briccriu; see FLED BRICRENN [Briccriu's Feast].

Efrawg, Evrawg, Evrawc [W *Efrog*, York]. Father of *Peredur in early Welsh narrative. He was slain in combat along with six of his sons, leaving Peredur and his mother without protection. The name Efrawg designates the site later called York in English.

egret [Old Provençal *aigreta*]. The long-legged wading bird (genera *Bubulcus, Casmerodius, Leucophoyx*) with characteristic long white tail-feathers played an important role in Celtic iconography as early as the *Urnfield period (*c.*800 BC), although not in later vernacular traditions. Three symbolic egrets appear in a temple of the Gaulish god *Esus. From earliest times egrets are portrayed with *bulls, probably reflecting the habit of the birds in life of perching on the back of the animal to eat its lice. In iconography they are also associated with the willow tree, as befits a bird that forages in marshes. Often egret, bull, and willow appear in combination. The egret may sometimes be confused with the *crane. ModIr. éigrit; Manx coar vane; W crychydd, crëyr; Bret. kribell-blu.

Éibhear. ModIr. spelling of *Éber.

Eibhlín a Rúin [Ir., Eileen my love]. Irish title for a well-known love ballad that may date from the 14th century but is usually ascribed to Cearbhall Ó Dálaigh (*fl.* 1590–1630) in honour of Eibhlín Caomhánach, the daughter of a nearby chief; usually titled 'Eileen Aroon' in English. The name Eibhlín entered Ireland with the Normans (12th cent.).

Eichde Echbél. See ECHBÉL.

Eiddilig Gor. *Dwarf and *shape-shifter of the Welsh *Triads, who could take any form he wished in escaping capture. Also known as one of the Three Enchanters of the Isle of Britain.

Eiddyn. See CLYDNO EIDDYN.

Eidiol. Another name for *Emrys Wledig.

Eidoel. Son of Aer and cousin of *Mabon in **Culhwch ac Olwen*. In order to find Mabon, Culhwch has first to free Eidoel from prison so that he may join in the pursuit.

Eidyn, Eitin. Apparently Welsh name for the person for whom *Edinburgh is named: Din Eidyn in the **Gododdin*. No traditions relating to him survive.

Eigr. Welsh antecedent to *Igerna of international Arthurian romance. One of the most beautiful women of Britain, she was the daughter of *Anlawdd Wledig and married to Gwrlais, Duke of Cornwall. *Uthr Bendragon became infatuated with her and, after being changed into the form of Gwrlais by *Myrddin, seduced her, begetting *Arthur.

Eil Ton, Eilton, Eil Don. Epithet of *Dylan.

Eildon Hills, Eildons. Three peaks, 1,327, 1,385, and 1,216 feet, in the Borders (formerly Roxburghshire) in south-eastern Scotland, especially rich in folkloric associations. Among the oldest are that both *Fionn mac Cumhaill and *Arthur are sleeping here, waiting to be recalled to action. They also contain prehistoric ruins of Celtic origin, including a cairn and a hill-fort.

Éile. ModIr. spelling of *Éle.

Eilean na hÒige. Scottish Gaelic name for *Tír na nÓg. In modern usage it may also refer to the island of *Eriskay.

Eilim. Variant spelling of *Éllim.

Eimhir. ScG variant of *Emer.

Einion, Eynon, Eniawn, Einyaun, Anian, Annion [W *einion*, anvil]. Name borne by scores of early Welsh figures of purported historicity (see below), as well as by several historical poets and bards, e.g. Einion ap Gwalchmai (*fl.* 1203–23), Einion ap Gwgan (*fl.* 1215), Einion ap Madog ap Rhahawd (*fl.* 1237), and priests, e.g. Einion Offeiriad (*fl.* 1330).

Einion Yrth, Eynon Urdd (corrupt). Son of the great king Cunedda Wledig, who flourished *c.*420. The small parish of Caerinion Fachan in south *Gwynedd (until 1974, Montgomeryshire) commemorates his name.

Éinne. Variant spelling of *Énna.

Éire. ModIr. spelling of *Ériu.

Éireamhón. ModIr. spelling of *Éremón.

éiric. ModIr. spelling of *éric.

Éirne. ModIr. spelling of *Érne.

Eirnin. Sometimes named as mother, by *Delbáeth (2), of the three eponymous goddesses of Ireland, *Banba, *Ériu, and *Fódla. More often the mother is *Ernmas.

Éis Énchenn, Ess Enchenn [Ir. *éis*, band, troop; *Énchenn*, bird-headed]. Grotesque *female adversary of *Cúchulainn. The hero encounters her while trying to depart from

*Scáthach and the land of shadow along a narrow ridge. She is a *one-eyed hag who first commands and then begs him to get out of her way. When he complies, clinging only by his toes, she strikes him, trying to knock him down the cliff. But he sees her in time and gives his *salmon leap upward, striking off the hag's head. She is revealed to be Éis Énchenn, mother of the last three warriors to die at Cúchulainn's hands: Ciri, Bir, and Blicne. Several commentators have discerned a parallel between Éis Énchenn and Kāli, the destructive mother-goddess of Hindu tradition.

Eiscir Riada, Eisgir Riada. [Ir. *eiscir*, esker, (glacial) ridge; *riada*, to travel by horse or chariot]. Traditional boundary dividing Ireland into two halves, north and south, running along a series of low sandhills from Galway Bay to *Dublin. In the pseudo-history *Lebor Gabála* [Book of Invasions], *Éber Finn takes the north; *Éremón takes the south. Elsewhere in early Irish tradition the northern portion is *Leth Cuinn, or Conn's half, attributed to *Conn Cétchathach [of the Hundred Battles], and the southern is *Leth Moga, or Mug's half, for *Mug Nuadat, better known as *Eógan Mór.

Eisirt. Court poet of *Iubdán, a ruler of *fairy land. To deflate his patron's boastfulness, Eisirt proclaimed that the men of *Ulster were giants; and to prove his point he journeyed to the court of *Fergus mac Léti, retrieving *Áeda (1), a *dwarf who seemed a giant to Iubdán's court. Eisirt then laid a demeaning *geis on Iubdán; the king must travel himself to *Emain Macha and be the first there to eat porridge in the morning. Eisirt then correctly predicted that Iubdán would fail and be imprisoned for a year and a day; his release would come only when he parted with his dearest possessions. Through his psychic powers Eisirt could tell that Fergus mac Léti was having an affair with his steward's wife and that his wife was having another with her stepson.

eisteddfod [W *eistedd*, to sit; *fod* (*bod*), to be]. An annual assembly of Welsh poets and musicians. The National Eisteddfod, established 1860, has become the principal cultural festival of the Welsh people, held each year in the first week of August, at venues alternating between north and south. Since 1880, the National Eisteddfod has been the charge of a professional association under the aegis of the Honourable Society of Cymmrodorion. The Welsh language has always predominated in proceedings, and was made the rule in 1937. Usually attended by crowds of 150,000, it is the model for cultural assemblies in other Celtic lands. Although the term is now coloured by 19th-century cultural revival, the origin of the eisteddfod can be traced to the *bardic order and can be traced with certainty to the 15th century and perhaps as early as 1176.

See Hywel T. Edwards, *The Eisteddfod* (Cardiff, 1990). See also GORSEDD BEIRDD YNYS PRYDAIN.

Eithlinn, Ethlenn. Variant spellings of *Eithne.

Eithne, Ethne, Ethna, Ethniu, Ethnea, Ethné, Ethnenn, Eithlinn, Ethlinn, Ethlenn, Athlenn. One of the most common women's names in early Ireland, borne by dozens of characters in myth and legend, several important queens, and at least nine saints. The two best-known are probably *Eithne (1), the mother of *Lug Lámfhota, and *Eithne Ingubai, the early mate of *Cúchulainn. Eithne is also a river name, surviving in the 40-mile Inny of counties Longford and Westmeath, as a rivulet in Co. *Kerry, and perhaps also applying to the *Boyne.

Eithne 1. Most often implied by variants Eithlenn and Ethniu. Usually described as a daughter of *Balor, king of the *Fomorians, and mother of *Lug Lámfhota; sometimes also described as the mother of the *Dagda and *Ogma. According to the *Lebor Gabála* [Book of Invasions], she was mated with *Cian, usually a son of *Dian Cécht, to promote an alliance between her people and the *Tuatha Dé Danann; in later tradition she is described as a virgin, and Lug's conception implies no political agenda. When a *druid tells Balor that his daughter will bear a grandson destined to slay him, he confines Eithne to a high tower on Tory Island, guarded by twelve women to keep her away from men. The plan might have worked if Balor had not desired to own *Glas Ghaibhleann, a magical cow that gave endless supplies of milk. In what appears to be the oldest version of the story, Balor steals the cow from Cian, who seeks revenge, with the help of *Biróg, a female *druid, by dressing himself as a woman, entering Eithne's tower on Tory

Island, and impregnating her, producing three children, one of whom was Lug. In a version better known in oral tradition Glas Ghaibhleann belongs to *Gaibhlín, a smith, who lives with his two brothers, Mac Samthainn and Mac Cennfaelaidh, the latter a lord of the district. When the cow is stolen Mac Cennfaelaidh seeks revenge with the help of a druid and a *fairy, gaining access to Eithne and impregnating her. Again Eithne gives birth to three children, but Balor attempts to kill all three by having them carried off in a blanket; two fall out but Lug survives. In a variant of this version Mac Cennfaelaidh also impregnates all twelve of the guardians, whose children become seals. In neither version does Lug thrive until taken back to Tory Island. In still another variant Eithne is the daughter of Delbáeth (1).

In the *Fenian Cycle, Eithne (1) was thought to have married *Nuadu Airgetlám, founding the family line that eventually produced *Fionn mac Cumhaill.

2. Wife of *Elcmar, an early ruler of *Brug na Bóinne, in an alternate version of *Angus Óg's birth. Seduced through a trick by *Eochaid Ollathair (the *Dagda), she conceived the divine son, Angus. Her name here may be a variant of *Boand (the *Boyne River).

3. Chief character of **Altrom Tige Dá Medar* [The Nurture of the Houses of the Two Milk Vessels]. A child of the wife of the steward of *Angus Óg, she refused the food of the *Tuatha Dé Danann and died embracing Christianity.

4. Sometimes known as Eithne (or Ethna) the Bride, the beautiful young woman who spends a year in the realm of the *fairies with *Finnbheara (or Finvara), the king of the *Connacht fairies, in a story known from oral tradition. Eithne is such a beautiful young bride that her proud husband holds many festivities in her honour. One evening as she is dancing, she falls in a swoon. Nothing will revive her, and she sleeps deeply through the night. In the morning she seems to revive but will speak only of a beautiful country she has visited and to which she longs to return. The next night her old nurse is set to guard her, but she too falls into deep sleep, and in the morning Eithne is gone. When she cannot be found it is clear the fairies have some role in her disappearance, and so her husband rides to Finnbheara's mound at *Cnoc Mheadha [Knockmagha, etc.], Co. Galway, to seek advice. Although the husband's castle is near Finnbheara's abode, the mortal does not fear the fairy king, leaving him offerings of wine and thinking him a friend. But when the husband approaches Finnbheara's rath, he overhears voices talking about his missing bride: that Finnbheara is happy now because he has her, and that her husband will never see her again unless he can succeed at the daunting task of digging a hole deep enough to let light into Finnbheara's underground dwelling.

The husband gathers workers from far and wide, but their work is discouraging. Every night when they cease digging the hole fills up and grows over with grass as if they have done nothing. On successive days he increases the number of workers, but to no avail. Then he hears a voice in the air advising that he sprinkle the earth with salt, which he does. He finds Eithne as beautiful as ever, but when he carries her back to the palace she will not speak or move, causing the household to fear she has eaten fairy food. Again the husband takes advice from friendly voices in the air. He removes the fairy girdle from around her waist and burns it, and puts the fairy pin holding it under a fairy thornbush, where no one will disturb it. She then sits up and stretches out her arms to him. Although she remembers everything that has happened, her year in fairyland seems but one night.

Eithne (4) bears some relationship with Eithne (3), who, in **Altrom Tiga Dá Medar* [The Nurture of the Houses of the Two Milk Vessels], is insulted by *Finnbarr, a member of the *Tuatha Dé Danann. In addition many commentators have seen a link between Eithne (4) and Eurydice of Greek tradition, rescued from Hades by Orpheus. In medieval versions of the story, known as *Sir Orfeo* or *King Orfeo* in English, Pluto [Hades] is known as the 'king of the fairies'. Folk motifs: F322, F322.2, F375. See Lady Jane Wilde, *Ancient Legends, Mystic Charms and Superstitions of Ireland* (2 vols., London, 1887).

5. Early wife of *Conchobar, daughter of *Eochaid Feidlech, and sister of *Clothra, *Medb, and *Mugain (2), sometimes also of *Éle. All the sisters were at one time married to Conchobar; Eithne came after Medb but before Mugain, who is most often portrayed in that role. She sometimes bears the epithet of Aittencháithrech or Aitencáithrech [having furze-like hair].

6. Wife of King *Rónán of *Leinster and

mother of *Máel Fothartaig in **Fingal Rónáin* [How Rónán Slew His Son].

Eithne Imgel. Mother of *Tuathal Techtmar.

Eithne Ingubai, In Gubai, Inguba, Ingube. Sometimes described as the wife of *Cúchulainn, instead of the more usual *Emer, with whom she may be confused; see SERGLIGE CON CULAINN [The Wasting Sickness of Cúchulainn]. In adaptations of OIr. narratives in English, Eithne is often described as Cúchulainn's mistress; see W. B. Yeats, 'Cuchulain's Fight with the Sea' (1892).

Eithne Tháebfhota, Táebfhada, Táebfhota, Thóebfhota [Ir., of the Long Side]. Daughter of the great king *Cathaír Mór, she is described as the queen of two other kings of different generations. In most Old Irish writing she is the wife of *Conn Cétchathach [of the Hundred Battles]. Her marriage was thought beneficial to the kingdom; until her death the fields gave three harvests a year. In **Esnada Tige Buchet* [The Melodies of Buchet's House] Eithne is in fosterage to Buchet when she spends a night with *Cormac mac Airt, Conn's grandson, to conceive *Cairbre Lifechair; and she appears to be Cormac's wife in **Echtrae Cormaic* [The Adventure of Cormac].

Eithne Úathach [Ir., horrible, dreadful]. Daughter of *Crimthann Mór mac Fidaig. She was reputed to eat the flesh of young infants to increase her growth so that she would be prepared for marriage more quickly.

Eithne Uchtsholas, Ucsholas [cf. Ir. *solas*, light]. A daughter of the king of *Leinster, she was abducted by a *giant, whom *Conall Gulban pursued, giving his name to *Ben Bulben, Co. Sligo, in the process.

Eithrial. Legendary early king of Ireland. During his twenty-year reign many plains were cleared in different parts of the island.

Eitin. Variant spelling of Eidyn, eponym of *Edinburgh [W *Din Eidyn*].

Elada. Variant spelling of *Elatha.

Elaine. Several female figures from Arthuriana bear this name, the most important of whom is Elaine of Corbenic, daughter of Pelles, the Grail King, mother of *Galahad and lover of *Lancelot. Her Welsh counterpart and possible source is *Elen.

Elatha, Elada, Elotha, Ealadha, Elathan (gen.) [OIr. *elada*, *elatha*, art, science, acquired skill, craft]. The handsome *Fomorian king who came from beneath the sea in a silver ship to mate with *Ériu and produce *Bres. Unlike most of his ugly people, Elatha was resplendent in shoulder-length golden hair. A brooch of gold adorned his chest, and he wore a cloak of gold with five wheels of gold on the back. He was easily able to seduce Ériu, although she was already married. He told her she would bear a son, gave her a golden ring, instructing her to give it to the boy upon maturity, and then sailed away. The son, Bres, grew up to become king of the *Tuatha Dé Danann. When Bres was rejected by the Tuatha Dé Danann, he and his mother sought help from the Fomorian Elatha, thus beginning the conflict that led to the Second Battle of Mag Tuired; see CATH MAIGE TUIRED. As Elatha is the son of *Delbáeth, he is sometimes known as Elatha mac Delbaíth.

Elcmar, Ealcmhar, Elcmaire (gen.), Elcmhaire (gen.) [OIr. *elcmar*, envious, spiteful]. Outwardly a magician, original master of *Brug na Bóinne and foster-father of *Angus Óg, to whom he ceded Brug na Bóinne. Although his true identity is not revealed, Elcmar is a pseudonym for *Nuadu Airgetlám. In a widely known story, *Boand (the *Boyne River) asks Elcmar to serve as foster-father to Angus Óg, conceived out of wedlock with *Eochaid Ollathair (identical with the *Dagda), as a means of hiding the adultery from her usual husband, *Nechtan. In an alternate version, Elcmar has been happily married to Boand (or *Eithne (2)), when Eochaid Ollathair begins to lust after her. Eochaid sends Elcmar on a journey which appears to him only a day and a night but is in reality nine months, during which time Eochaid becomes the lover of Boand (or Eithne (2)), fathering Angus Óg upon her. On his return, Elcmar knows nothing of the birth. Angus is then fostered by *Midir in *Brí Léith and, when he is old enough, brought to Eochaid Ollathair, who shows him how to gain possession of Brug na Bóinne. Angus will ask Elcmar to occupy the buildings for only a day and night as a ruse; this will be enough to establish permanent possession, so that Angus can hold it permanently. An alternate Christianized version of Angus' displacement of Elcmar is found in **Altrom Tige Dá Medar* [The Nurture of the House of the

Two Milk Vessels], in which Elcmar is expelled just as the evil angels were expelled from heaven. Elcmar then goes to live at Sídh *Clettig on the south side of the Boyne, where in other stories he is described as holding court. Some texts mention a daughter, *Bébinn (3). Elcmar is sometimes confused with Nechtan, Boand's usual husband, as he is also a pseudonym for Nuadu Airgetlám. In an unrelated story, *Cúchulainn is described as mutilating Elcmar while opposed in pursuit of the *salmon of wisdom.

elder tree [OE *ellaern*]. The small tree or bush, also called elderberry (genus *Sambucus*), having clusters of white flowers and red or blackish berry-like fruit, has many associations with the *fairy world in oral traditions of recent centuries in Celtic countries. On the Isle of *Man, where elder grows abundantly and is called tramman, it is commonly thought of as the '*fairy tree'. In Ireland many individual elder trees were thought haunted by fairies or demons. OIr. tromm; ModIr. trom; ScG troman, droman; W ysgawen; Corn. scawen; Bret. skavenn.

Éle, Éile. Daughter of *Eochaid Feidlech and usually seen as a sister of *Medb, *Clothra, *Eithne (5), and *Mugain (2).

Elen 1, Elen Luyddog, Helen [W *elen*, nymph, angel (?); *luyddog*, of the hosts]. British (Welsh) virgin princess dreamed of by *Macsen Wledig in **Breuddwyd Macsen Wledig* [The Dream of Macsen Wledig]. The probably historical figure Macsen (Magnus Maximus, d. AD 388) is thought to have grown impatient with imperial rule in 4th-century Britain and so to have taken an army to conquer Rome itself. Once established as emperor, Macsen dreamed of the beautiful Elen he had left behind. He then returned to Britain, found Elen to be a virgin, and married her; he also established three castles to fortify the country. Elen's two brothers, *Cynan and Gadeon, then helped Macsen to reconquer Rome. Recent scholarship deflates the dream somewhat. Elen was also historical, based on Elen the daughter of Eudaf, a British chieftain who held Segontium [Caernarvon]; she was already wife to the historical Magnus Maximus and travelled with him to the Continent. But the recent discovery of evidence of a British legion from Segontium as far away as the Balkans in AD 429 gives some plausibility to the larger scenario.

Elen (1) is often confused with *Elen (2), derived from St Helen, the mother of Constantine, in Welsh lore. One or the other is often thought to have given initiative to road-building, largely because surviving sections of a Roman road were called Sarn Helen. The name is more likely derived from *elin* [W, elbow, angle] as the roads are circuitous unlike normally straight Roman roads, or simply *Y Lleng* [W, The Legion]. The character of Elen does appear to have contributed to the persona of *Elaine of Arthurian tradition. See AHES, a Breton goddess of roads. See also Rachel Bromwich, *Trioedd Ynys Prydain*, rev. edn. (Cardiff, 1978), 341ff.; 550ff.

2, Helen. Historical saint (4th cent.), mother of Emperor Constantine, who was given a Welsh provenance through pious medieval imagination although no record implies she ever came near Britain. According to her Welsh pedigree she was the daughter of Coel Hen (the eponymous 'King' Cole of Colchester); in variant texts her father is Eudaf. She was thought to have discovered the True Cross in Jerusalem. Despite her being a generation too old to be identified with *Elen (1) (Luyddog), medieval hagiographers wilfully confused the two. More than 100 Welsh churches were named in her honour. See Charles Knightly, *Folk Heroes of Britain* (London, 1982).

elf, elves [OE *ælf*]. The familiar diminutive, magic-wielding creature that derives from Teutonic origin has only one close counterpart in the Celtic world, the Welsh *ellyll. Other parallels can be found only through forced analogy. The Irish *leprechaun makes an inexact analogue, although the *cluricaune and *dullahan and Cornish *piskie come closer. The Irish word *síabraid is sometimes translated as 'elf'. See also FAIRY. The English word elf translates inexactly into Celtic languages other than Welsh: ModIr. cluthar-achán, lucharachán; ScG s'thiche; Manx trollag; Corn. spyrys.

Elffin, Elphin. Spendthrift son of *Gwyddno Garanhir who discovers the baby *Taliesin in his father's fish-dam, or weir, rears him, and becomes his patron. Gwyddno, a wealthy man in the court of *Maelgwn Gwynedd, sees his riches diminishing but decides to give his feckless son Elffin one more chance to improve his circumstances by granting him the first haul of fish from his weir between *Aberystwyth and the Dyfi estuary on *Calan

Mai [May Day], when the catch will be especially valuable. Elffin, often thought unlucky, catches not one fish. He finds instead an infant in a basket, exclaiming, 'Dyma dâl iesin' [what a beautiful forehead]. The child answers, naming himself, 'Taliesin bid' [let it be Taliesin]. Elffin takes the child to court, and from that day forward his fortunes improve; he also fosters the boy until he is 13 years old. Much later, emboldened by his changed fortune, Elffin boasts to Maelgwn that his wife is the fairest in the kingdom, his horses the swiftest, and his poet the wisest. For this arrogance Maelgwn imprisons him, but in silver chains, respecting his noble status. Taliesin returns to exculpate Elffin and assists in his release. Taliesin also foils Maelgwn's plot to ruin the good name of Elffin's wife with *Rhun's failed seduction and, further, performs at court, besting all other poets present. Elffin is then released. His horses easily defeat those of Maelgwn, and Elffin's jockey drops his cap at a point where, Taliesin explains, a cauldron of gold would be found to compensate for the seemingly fruitless night at the weir.

The themes of a youth bound in chains and an otherworld cauldron are embedded in **Preiddiau Annwfn* [The Spoils of Annwfn]. Thomas Love Peacock retold Elffin's story in the humorous novel *The Misfortunes of Elphin* (1829).

Elgnat. Variant spelling of *Dealgnaid.

Eliavres. Breton sorcerer and *druid of notable deviousness. In order to further his scheme to sleep with the queen, he conspires to get the father of the [Breton] *Karadoc to copulate with a metamorphosed sow. The bestial union produces the fabled wild *boar Tourtain, a counterpart of the Welsh *Twrch Trwyth.

Elidyr, Elidor, Elidurus [W *elydyr*, bronze, fused metal, brass]. Character in a much-celebrated folktale recorded by *Giraldus Cambrensis in his *Itinerarium Cambriae* [Journey through Wales] (1188). The story is narrated by a priest, Elidurus, purporting to remember his childhood when he was known by his Welsh name, Elidyr. When playing the truant at age 12, he hid under a river bank where he met two little men who promised to lead him to a country of delights and sports. He was indeed most pleased with what he found: a country of perfectly formed little men and women with long blond hair to their shoulders, who ate neither fish nor fowl and dieted exclusively on milk with saffron. They took no oaths and detested lies. Neither did they practise any religion, simply loving the truth on their own. But they execrated mortal ambition, infidelity, and inconsistency. After a while Elidyr returned home, where his mother encouraged him to return to the delightful country to bring her back gold or jewels. He did her bidding, stealing a wonderful golden ball, but on his return home he dropped it accidentally; it was retrieved by people of the wonderful land who spat upon him for his theft. Elidyr was angry with his mother's greed, but he could never again find the entrance to the fairyland no matter how hard he tried. In reciting the story to Dewi II, the Bishop of St David's, Elidyr said that he remembered the language of fairyland being similar to Greek; this prompted Giraldus to editorialize that the ancient Britons had fled from Troy. In the end Elidyr still shed tears at his loss of the wondrous land. Folk motif: F370.

Elim. Variant spelling of *Éllim.

Ellan Vannin. The Manx name for the Isle of *Man. The island itself may also be called simply Mannin. See also Ir. Oileán Mhanann.

Ellén. Variant spelling of *Aillén.

Éllim mac Conrach, Eilim, Elim mac Conra. Shadowy early king of the *Dál nAraide in *Ulster who, with three confederates, murdered King *Fiachu and usurped the throne of *Tara. God punished this wickedness by sending a famine to Ireland. Éllim reigned for twenty years until Fiachu's son, *Tuathal Techtmar, avenged the killing and regained his heritage. Tuathal Techtmar would become one of the greatest of pre-Patrician Irish rulers.

ellyll, ellyllon (pl.) [W, fiend, ghost, goblin, elf, other-self]. Tiny, diaphanous creature from the Welsh *fairy world, the closest counterpart to the Teutonic *elf from the Celtic world. The ellyll is smaller than the *tylwyth teg, the better-known Welsh fairies. His usual food is the toadstool or 'fairy butter', a fungoid substance found in limestone crevices and under the roots of rotten trees. Queen Mab was the ruler of the ellyllon.

An ellyll could wield magic, as demonstrated in the story of Rowli Pugh collected near Cardiff by Wirt Sikes in the mid-19th century. Rowli Pugh is a poor farmer who feels himself cursed by misfortune. Other farmers flourish while his crops fail, his cattle grow thin. Even his wife Catti is sickly. An ellyll offers to help him, if only he will leave a candle burning in the night and will have his wife sweep the fire clean. They comply, and the ellyllon make good their promise. Each night, as Rowli and Catti go to bed, they hear the ellyllon at their merry work. Each morning all the household is in good order. This continues for three years. Crops burgeon, and cattle grow fat. Rowli and Catti also become healthier and stronger. But one night Catti becomes curious to see the ellyllon at their high-spirited work. She tiptoes downstairs to the kitchen to see the merry bustling. The infectious good humour of the works sets her to laughing, blowing out the candle. The ellyllon depart quickly, never to return. But Rowli and Catti retain their health and prosperity with hard work.

Usually classed as a solitary fairy. See Wirt Sikes, *British Goblins* (London, 1880), 13–17.

elopement. Translation of the Irish **Aithed*, first word of a category of tale from Old and Middle Irish, e.g. *Aithed Finn* [The Elopement of Fionn], etc. 'Elopement' is occasionally a mistranslation of **Tóraigheacht* [pursuit].

Elotha. Variant spelling of *Elatha.

Elphin. Anglicization of *Elffin.

Elta, Eltar, **Plain of.** See MAG NELTA.

Elthan. Variant spelling of *Elatha.

elves. See ELF.

Elwin. Obscure 5th-century Cornish saint, confused with or a variant of the well-known *Arlan.

Elysium, Elysian otherworld. See OTHERWORLD.

Elystan Glodrydd. Shadowy but probably historical ruler of medieval Wales. In an 11th-century division of the country into five parts, he received a region in east central Wales between the Wye and Severn rivers.

Emain Ablach, Emhain Abhlach, Emne (gen.), Emhnae (gen.), Eamhain of the Apples, Síth Emna [Ir. *emain*, brooch (?), twins (?); *ablach*, having apple trees]. Paradisiacal island off the coast of *Alba [Scotland], the home of *Manannán mac Lir, the Irish sea-god. As early as **Sanas Cormaic* [Cormac's Glossary] (9th cent.), Emain Ablach was erroneously identified with the Isle of *Man, supported by a confusion of Man and Manannán. Emain Ablach is, however, an imagined not a real place. In Manx tradition, where it is called Eamhain of the Apples, there is no identification with the Isle of Man. Neither can Emain Ablach be identified with the Scottish island of *Arran. The city or capital of the island is Cruithín na Cuan. *Bran mac Febail began his fabulous voyage after a mysterious woman presented him with a silver branch with white blossoms from the apple tree of Emain Ablach; her song of the richness and delight of the place sent him on his quest; see IMRAM BRAIN [Voyage of Bran]. Some authorities suggest that Emain Ablach may be glossed as the 'Land of Promise' because that is the announced goal of Bran's quest; it is also glossed as the Isle of Women; see TÍR TAIRNGIRE. Emain Ablach appears to be one of several Celtic contributions to the Arthurian concept of *Avalon.

Emain Macha, Eamhain Mhacha, Emhain, Emuin, Emania. Name borne both by an 18-acre late Bronze Age hill-fort in Co. Armagh, capital of the *Ulaid, and also by the mythical capital of *Ulster in the *Ulster Cycle, royal seat of *Conchobar mac Nessa, which is identified with the hill-fort; one of the most often cited place-names in early Irish literature.

The hill-fort, also called Navan Fort [ModIr. *An Eamhain*], lies at Navan, 2 miles W of *Armagh, Northern Ireland. An immense circular bank, now defaced, and ditch enclose a number of earth and stone works. At the summit rests a univallate tumulus, once a residential site subsequently used for ceremonial purposes. Excavation (1963–71) has established that the round house was begun *c.*700 BC and rebuilt nine times before 100 BC; the surrounding stockade was rebuilt six times. Emain Macha is probably identical with the Isamnion mentioned in Ptolemy's geography (2nd cent. AD). The survival of the skull of a Barbary ape at Emain Macha implies that the site was known far beyond Ireland. The residence was destroyed, or abandoned, when ravaged by the three *Collas from rival areas in Ulster, some time before the advent of Christian evangelization, perhaps in the 5th century. *Fergus Foga was the last king of Emain Macha. The abandoned hill-fort continued to be the site of an annual *feis [feast] through medieval times.

The Emain Macha of myth and legend is a far grander and more mysterious place than archaeological excavation supports. It contained the fabled palace of *Cráebruad [Red Branch], giving us the once popular name for the Ulster Cycle, the 'Red Branch' Cycle; the name is echoed in the village of Creeveroe, Co. Armagh. Two queens named Macha are associated with the founding of the fortress. The less well-known is *Macha (2), queen of *Cimbáeth, whom she dominated and obliged to build a residence in her honour. She marked out the area with her brooch, thus the folk etymology of emain as *eo*, bodkin + *muin*, neck = brooch, as authorized by Geoffrey *Keating (17th cent.). The better-known is *Macha (3), wife of *Crunniuc mac Agnomain. At a fair in Ulster Crunniuc boasts that his wife could beat a horse-drawn chariot in a foot-race, even though she was pregnant and near to her delivery. Macha cries out to be released from the bargain. A messenger tells her the child will die unless she complies. She succeeds in winning the race, giving birth to twins, a boy and a girl, at the finishing line; some commentators gloss *emain* as 'twins' from this episode. For her humiliation and her birth pangs she curses the men of Ulster with comparable suffering unto nine generations; women, young boys, and *Cúchulainn were exempted. Cráebruad was the best-known of the three great halls at Emain Macha; it had nine rooms of red *yew, partitioned by walls of bronze, surrounding Conchobar's apartment with silver ceiling and bronze pillars topped with gold. The second, *Cráebderg [ruddy branch], contained the treasure-house as well as the heads of slain enemies. The third, Téte Brec [twinkling hoard], held the weapons and armour. Weapons were not to be brought into Emain Macha, and the grounds contained a hospital for sick and wounded warriors. Bainche was the architect or stonemason of Emain Macha; Bairdéne the doorkeeper. The 1960s' excavations prompted a large-scale scholarly and popular interest in the site. The Navan Centre for visitors, with displays and multi-media show, opened in 1993. See J. P. Mallory, *Navan Fort: The Ancient Capital of Ulster* (Belfast, 1987). The serial publication *Emania: Bulletin of the Navan Research Group* (Belfast) began in 1986.

Emania. Latinized spelling of *Emain Macha.

Emer, Eimhir (ScG). Usual wife of *Cúchulainn and daughter of *Forgall Manach [the Wily] of Lusca [Lusk], in what is now north Co. Dublin; Cúchulainn's other wife is *Eithne Ingubai, who may be confused with Emer. Conventionally described as a female paragon, she possessed the six gifts of womanhood: beauty, voice, sweet speech, skill in needlework, wisdom, chastity. Her sister was *Fial (2) and her three brothers Scibar, Ibor, and Cat. Although Cúchulainn is smitten with Emer, and she with him, as soon as he comes to her father's fortress and beholds her, Forgall refuses his demand to marry her. As recounted in *Tochmarc Emire* [The Wooing of Emer], Forgall objects to Cúchulainn as a suitor for two reasons. His elder daughter, Fial, has to be married first, and more importantly, he feels the future hero of Ulster has not yet acquired a sufficient reputation and needs more training. He further suggests that Cúchulainn seek training with the warlike *Domnall Míldemail in *Alba [Scotland]. Domnall in turn tells Cúchulainn that his training would be best completed under the *female warrior *Scáthach, also in Alba, with whom the Ulsterman stays a long while. In the mean time Forgall tries to persuade *Lugaid mac Nóis, a *Munster king, to marry Emer, but he refuses the opportunity, fearing reprisals from the powerful Cúchulainn, who is, in addition, his foster-brother.

When Cúchulainn returns from Alba, eager to claim Emer, Forgall refuses him and locks him out of his fortress of Lusca. In a *salmon-leap Cúchulainn scales the wall and slaughters twenty-four of Forgall's men before he, in despair, jumps from the ramparts to his death. Cúchulainn then joyously departs with Emer, her foster-sister, and two loads of silver and gold. An ally of Forgall's, Scenmenn, tries to stop them, but Cúchulainn dispatches him quickly at a ford on the Ailbéne river, known later as Áth Scenmenn [Scenmenn's Ford]. Twice a victor, his prowess tested, Cúchulainn takes Emer to his fortress home of *Dún Delgan [Dundalk].

Their married life is not always blissful, for Cúchulainn loves many women, and still more love him. The most threatening of these affairs, causing the only jealousy of Emer, is with *Fand, wife of *Manannán mac Lir, as told in **Serglige Con Culainn* [The

Wasting Sickness of Cúchulainn]. After the adulterous pair have spent a month in love-making, Emer decides to kill her rival Fand. She finds their hidden trysting spot, but when she sees how much Fand loves Cúchulainn, she decides to give him up to her for the greater good. Fand, however, deeply impressed by Emer's magnanimity as well as her love, decides to return to her own husband, Manannán. And magically the affair vanishes from memory. Manannán shakes an enchanted cloak, ensuring that Fand and Cúchulainn never meet again; and Cúchulainn and Emer take potions of forgetfulness. In another story, **Fled Bricrenn* [Bricriu's Feast], Emer bears the epithet Foltchaín [of the fair hair] and arrives in the company of fifty women, seeking entrance to Briccriu's palace.

Cúchulainn has a vision of Emer's death before his own. He dreams that *Emain Macha is in flames and that she is thrown from the ramparts. But when he rushes home he finds her well and safe, although cautious of the dream's foreboding. He nevertheless returns to the road that will lead to the Pillar Stone and his own death. Emer then joins him in the grave.

Emer's name retains resonance in modern times. She is the model for *Bragela in James Macpherson's *Poems of Ossian* (1760–3). The Dun Emer Industries, a William Morris-inspired crafts movement founded 1902, later to include the Dun Emer Press and the Dun Emer Guild, commemorate her. Emer appears often in the writings of W. B. Yeats, where her name is pronounced 'EE-mer'; addition-ally, she is the mother of Cuchulain's [Cúchulainn's] son Finmole [see CONNLA], instead of *Aífe; she is a major figure in Yeats's drama *The Only Jealousy of Emer* (1919), prose version *Fighting the Waves*. See Somhairle MacGill-Eain [Sorley MacLean], *Dàin do Eimhir* [Poems to Emer] (Glasgow, 1943). See also *Tochmarc Emire* [The Wooing of Emer], in Eleanor Hull, *The Cuchullin Saga* (London, 1898), 55–84; T. P. Cross and C. H. Slover, *Ancient Irish Tales* (New York, 1936), 153–72; Thomas Kinsella, *The Táin* (London, 1970), 25–39.

Emergaid the Fair. Legendary Manx princess. When her father, the smith *Loan Maclibhuin, is killed, she marries the murderer, King *Olave II, Goddardson, founding the Manx royal line.

Emhain Abhlach. Corrupt variant of *Emain Ablach.

Emhain Macha, Emhain Mhacha. Corrupt variants of *Emain Macha.

Emhnae. Corrupt variant of *Emain Ablach.

Emne. Corrupt variant of *Emain Ablach.

Emrys Wledig [W *emrys*=L *ambrosius*, pertaining to the immortals; *(g)wledig*, prince]. Also known as Eidiol. Shadowy but historical 5th-century British commander known by *Gildas (d. 547) and **Historia Brittonum* (9th cent.) as Ambrosius Aurelianus. To Gildas Emrys was 'the last of the Romans', in that he led Romanized Britons against the Saxon invaders under Hengest. Recent scholarship asserts that there are two men named Emrys, possibly father and son, whose stories were conflated. The elder Emrys struggled for power with Vortigern [W *Gwrtheyrn*] after 430, while Ambrosius the younger (Aurelianus) began a new British resistance that Gildas regarded as a continuation of the earlier. Emrys was thought to be at the Battle of Mount Badon, dated perhaps 475, 480, or 519.

Emrys (Ambrosius) is the name *Historia Brittonum* gives to the mysterious boy who confronts Vortigern in the building of *Dinas Emrys [W Emrys/Ambrosius' fort]. Vortigern, retiring to the far reaches of his kingdom, tries to establish a new fortress in *Gwynedd but is disconcerted by the collapse of the foundation each time workers try to construct it. He is advised to caulk the stones with the blood of a 'fatherless boy'. When found, the clever boy astonishes the court magicians with his knowledge, and reveals that there is a pool under the foundations where two *dragons battle. The movement of the two dragons, one red (i.e. Wales) and the other white (i.e. Saxon invaders), shakes the foundations. In retelling this story centuries later, *Geoffrey of Monmouth in the *Historia* (1136) named the marvellous boy Ambrosius Merlin. See Rachel Bromwich, *Trioedd Ynys Prydain*, rev. edn. (Cardiff, 1978), 345 ff.

Emuin. Variant spelling of *Emain Macha.

Énbarr, Enbhárr [Ir. *enbarr*, froth, foam]. Enchanted horse of *Manannán mac Lir, the sea-god; also known as Aonbárr [ModIr. *aonbharr*, unique supremacy].

enchanter. See DYN HYSBYS; EIDDILIG GOR.

Enda. Anglicization of *Énna.

Endellion, Endelient, **Saint.** Legendary 6th-century Cornish saint with Arthurian associations. Daughter of the legendary King *Brychan, she was thought to be the foster-daughter of King *Arthur, who champions her by killing the man who has killed her cow, whose milk was her only food. She generously helps the cow-killer to come back from the dead. According to local lore, she chose her final resting-place by having her body put on an ox-cart and buried where the beast stopped. The parish and village of St Endellion lies in north Cornwall, 9 miles NW of Bodmin. There may be an evocation of the early British sea-god *Endil in her name. See E. Stark, *St. Endellion* (Redruth, 1983).

Endil. Obscure early British sea-deity, possibly a variant of *Dylan; his name may be evoked at the parish of St *Endellion in north Cornwall.

Enfant-Oiseau [Fr., infant-bird]. *Fairy personage of *Brittany who becomes victim of his family. He is washed by his sister, killed by his mother, and eaten by his father.

England. The dominant nation of the island of Great Britain should always be distinguished from *Britain, the *P-Celtic nation occupied by the Romans which England displaced. This is especially important in Welsh and Cornish literatures, as those peoples are direct descendants of the Celts displaced by the invading Angles, Saxons, and Jutes; the Welsh word for Britain, Prydein, may denote Wales. Other P-Celtic Britons inhabited southern Scotland, migrated to *Brittany, or fused with the invaders. ModIr. Sasana; ScG Sasunn; Manx Sostyn; W Lloegr, Lloegyr; Corn. Pow Saws; Bret. Bro-Saoz. Medieval Welsh poets used the term Brynaich, among others, to deride the English.

Englic. One of the wives of *Lug Lámfhota.

Eniawn. Variant spelling of *Einion.

Enid [cf. W *enaid*, life, soul]. Name borne both by a Welsh heroine and by her Arthurian counterpart. The Welsh Enid is the lover of *Geraint fab Erbin and a leading figure in *Geraint ac Enid* [Geraint and Enid]. Geraint once finds Enid weeping because he prefers the luxury of home life instead of the challenges of knighthood, but he mistakenly thinks that she is weeping for an absent lover. Thus when he takes her with him on a sequence of adventures, he forbids her to speak with him, which prevents her from warning him of dangers. Later they are reconciled. Her father was *Yniwl Iarll.

Alfred Lord Tennyson adapted this story in *Geraint and Enid* (1859). The most important Arthurian parallel is *Erec et Enide* by Chrétien de Troyes (d. 1180); in French and Continental Arthuriana, her husband is *Erec. In the German of Hartmann von Aue (*c*.1170–*c*.1215) she is Enite. To call a woman a 'second Enid' in the age of chivalry was to bestow upon her the highest compliment.

Énloch [Ir., bird lake]. Lake near Mag Aí and *Cruachain in what is today Co. Roscommon, Ireland. In early Irish literature the rulers of *Connacht led assemblies of notables at Énloch.

Énna, Énnae, Énda, Éanna, Éinne [Ir., bird-like (?)]. Name borne by dozens of heroes, kings, and saints of early Ireland, of whom the best-known was probably Énna (1).

Énna 1. St Énna of Aran, a shadowy but historical figure of the 6th century, whose feast-day is 21 March. After a youth spent in war-raiding, Énna entered the religious life, partially under the influence of his sister, St Fanchea (latinized from Fainche). He is thought to have visited Rome and to have founded churches in the *Boyne valley. Against advice to choose more fertile ground, he established the monastery of Cill Éanna or Cill Éinne [Killeany] on the eastern side of Aranmore in the Aran Islands. He was known for the austerity and sanctity of his life. St *Ciarán of *Clonmacnoise was a key disciple. He is the patron saint of the nationalist school for boys, Saint Enda's [Sgoil/Scoil Éanna], founded by Patrick Pearse in 1908. See Charles Plummer (ed.), *Vitae Sanctorum Hiberniae*, ii (Oxford, 1910), 60–75.

2. Husband of *Dub, for whom *Dublin is named.

3. One of three sons of *Niall Noígiallach [of the Nine Hostages], but less distinguished than his brothers; *Eógan (1) founded *Tír Eógain [Tyrone], and *Conall Gulban founded *Tír Chonaill. Together the three brothers might also be known as the Three *Collas.

Énna Airgthech, Airgthetch, Airgtheach [Ir., the plunderer]. Legendary king of *Munster remembered for having introduced the first silver shields in Ireland, which he distributed to his chieftains. These were produced near what is today Rathbeagh on the Nore River in north Co. Kilkenny.

Énna Cennselach, Censelach. Legendary ancestor of the kings of south *Leinster. In an anachronistic anecdote from medieval commentators he is described as having killed *Eochaid Mugmedón.

eó fis, fiosach, fios, feasach. Irish terms for the *salmon of knowledge.

Eoan. ModIr. variant of *Eógan.

Eochaí. Modern spelling of both *Eochaid and *Eochu.

Eochaid, Eochaidh, Eochaí, Echuid, Echaid, Echaidh, Eocho, Echid, Eochy [Ir., horse-rider (?), fighter on horseback (?), horse of conquest (?)]. *Eochu is a diminutive, and although the two forms are hopelessly confused in early manuscripts, some figures may be known only as Eochaid, some only as Eochu, and many may be known as both. Eochaid and Eochu together represent the second most common name in early Irish society; the thousands of bearers include kings, warriors, bards, and saints. Nevertheless, Eoin MacNeill (1921) asserted that all Eochaids of myth and legend, despite different epithets, are all either identical or have borrowed each other's qualities to become composites. The best-known bearers of the name are probably *Eochaid Airem, the lover of *Étaín, and *Eochaid mac Eirc, the *Fir Bolg chieftain.

Eochaid 1. Pre-Christian sun-god of the ancient Irish, horseman of the heavens, and god of lightning; his sword is a lightning bolt. He is usually described as *one-eyed, and sometimes carries the epithet Deirgderc [Ir., red eye], which is also borne by the *Dagda. This epithet may link him with *Lough Derg on the *Shannon. Euhemerizing medieval historians created *Eochaid mac Luchta from him and confused him with *Eochaid Ollathair (another name for the Dagda).

2. King of *Dún Sobairche [Dunseverick] who betrothed his daughter to *Rónán (1), a king of *Leinster. The story of the daughter's thwarted adultery with Rónán's son *Máel Fothartaig and the subsequent havoc is told in *Fingal Rónáin* [How Rónán Slew His Son]. In revenge, *Donn (2), Máel Fothartaig's foster-brother, murdered Eochaid, his wife, and son.

3. Sometimes named as the foster-father of *Lug Lámfhota instead of *Manannán mac Lir.

4. Father of the warrior *Conall (1), who gave his name to Carn Conaill, Co. Tipperary.

5. Father of *Lí Ban in some stories, displacing her usual father, *Áed Abrat.

6. A king from the midlands of Ireland tormented by the satirist *Athairne Áilgesach; the poet demanded and received in tribute Eochaid's one remaining eye. Possibly identical with *Eochaid mac Luchta.

7. The son of Sál, a character in *Echtrae Lóegairi* [The Adventure of Lóegaire]. Lóegaire learns that although *Fiachna mac Rétach has killed Eochaid, his wife's abductor, she still yearns for him; because of this she abandons her husband for Eochaid's nephew Goll.

8. Shadowy but perhaps historical king of *Leinster whose treachery with the daughters of *Tuathal Techtmar, the *ard rí [high king], caused his countrymen to pay the *Bórama, a heavy tribute. Eochaid desired *Dáirine, but could not have her until her elder sister *Fithir was married. Feigning love, Eochaid married the elder sister and took her back to his palace at Ráth Imil. In time Eochaid returned to Tara and said that Fithir had died, allowing him to have Dáirine as his own. But when she returned with him she found Fithir still alive, and both girls died of shame; in some texts Fithir dies first of shame and Dáirine dies of grief. Tuathal sought revenge, first by making war upon Leinster, in which Eochaid was killed, and secondly by levying the Bórama, an annual payment of 5,000 cows, 5,000 sheep, 5,000 hogs, 5,000 cloaks, 5,000 bronze vessels, and 5,000 ounces of silver. Although it was not usually paid without military threat, the Bórama is recorded until the early 8th century, or for more than 500 years.

9. Legendary, probably historical Irish king who led an Irish migration to south-west *Wales in the third century. In Irish stories, Eochaid is seen doing battle with *Cormac mac Airt seven times, resisting the attempts of the *ard rí [high king] to expel Eochaid's people, the *Déisi. While an Irish migration to *Dyfed certainly took place, historical records like **Historia Brittonum* (9th cent.) and **Sanas Cormaic* [Cormac's Glossary] (9th cent.) attribute it to the 'sons of Liathán', or Uí Liatháin, of nearby east Co. Cork. Sometimes known as Eochaid Allmuir.

10. Son of the *Leinster king Énna

Censelach who kills *Niall Noígiallach [of the Nine Hostages] in some accounts.

Eochaid Áenshúla, Aontsúla [of the *one eye]. Shadowy warrior of early Ireland, said to have fought on the side of *Conn Cétchathach [of the Hundred Battles] at the Battle of Mag Léna (Co. Offaly). The Sullivan/O'Sullivan [Ó Súilleabháin] family claims ancestry from Eochaid Áenshúla.

Eochaid Airem, Aireamh [Ir., ploughman, tiller]. Also known as Eochaid Óg [young]. A legendary *ard rí [high king] of *Tara and lover of the beautiful and divine *Étaín whose story is told in **Tochmarc Étaíne* [The Wooing of Étaín]. Eochaid seeks the most beautiful woman in Ireland and finds Étaín, not realizing that she is a member of the *Tuatha Dé Danann and already married to *Midir, with whom Eochaid's identity is confused. Eochaid was renowned for his horsemanship. His brothers were *Ailill Anglonnach and *Eochaid Feidlech, with whom he is often confused. He may have two or three daughters. In *Tochmarc Étaíne* Midir reveals that Étaín was pregnant before he ran off with her; Eochaid commits unwitting incest with this 'daughter' to produce yet another daughter, who marries King *Eterscél. In other texts Eochaid and the true Étaín produce the child *Mes Buachalla, who marries Eterscél. In either version Eochaid is an ancestor of Eterscél's child, *Conaire Mór.

T. F. O'Rahilly (1946) asserted that Eochaid Airem's first associations were with the small kingdom of *Tethba (parts of modern Cos. Longford and Westmeath) and *Mide (Co. Meath) and that only in pseudo-history did he become king of Tara. According to *Tochmarc Étaíne*, he acquires his epithet, Airem [ploughman], when he instructs Midir in the handling of oxen to build a road, an obligation put upon Midir when he loses a game of *fidchell. Previously oxen pulled their burdens with straps tied to their foreheads; Eochaid recommends they pull with their shoulders. In stories separate from *Tochmarc Étaíne* Eochaid is described as levying a road tax upon the people of Tethba, demanding that they build him a highway laid with tree trunks. A 2nd-century road fitting this description, laid with oak, was discovered in summer 1985. According to the story, however, the people of Tethba so resented the road that one *Samain they attacked Eochaid's residence, burning it and killing him.

Eochaid Allmuir. See EOCHAID (9).

Eochaid Ánchenn. Legendary ancestor of the *Lagin.

Eochaid Ballderg [Ir., red spot, mark, blemish]. Legendary ancestor of the *Dál Cais.

Eochaid Bélbuide, Béalbhuidhe [Ir., of the yellow lips; yellow mouth]. A lesser but heroic figure in the *Ulster Cycle. His slaying by the men of *Conn Cétchathach [of the Hundred Battles] required compensation for *Fergus mac Léti, his protector. See also EOCHAID BUIDE; EOCHAID SÁLBUIDE.

Eochaid Bres. Another name for *Bres (1), the son of *Elatha.

Eochaid Buide [Ir., the yellow]. Early Fifeshire king who designated himself Rex Pictorum [king of the *Picts]; a son of *Áedán mac Gabráin, the founder of *Dál Riada. Early chronicles ascribe to Eochaid the possession of a wonderful *cauldron 'from which no one ever departed unsatisfied'. See also EOCHAID BÉLBUIDE; EOCHAID SÁLBUIDE.

Eochaid Dála. Third husband of Queen *Medb of *Connacht. He became king of Connacht only with the consent of Medb and only if he married her.

Eochaid Deirgderc. See EOCHAID (1).

Eochaid Doimlén. See EOCHU DOIMLÉN.

Eochaid Echend. See EOCHU ECHEND.

Eochaid Éigeas, Eochu Rígéces [cf. Ir. *éces*, poet]. Poet of the *Ulaid who contends with *Mongán; may be identified with *Dallán Forgaill.

Eochaid Eúil. Variant spelling of *Eochaid Iúil.

Eochaid Feidlech, Fedlech, Feidleach [Ir. *feidlech*, enduring, constant]. Shadowy but historical king of *Tara, best remembered as the father of many celebrated daughters, including *Medb (whose mother may have been *Cruacha), *Clothra, *Eithne (5), *Éle, and *Mugain. Among the sons attributed to him are *Furbaide (1) and the Three Finns of Emain Macha, known collectively as *Finn Emna, who rose against him with the encouragement of *Conchobar mac Nessa;

although they knocked Eochaid unconscious, they were defeated. Eochaid Feidlech was the brother of *Ailill Anglonnach and *Eochaid Airem, with whom he is often confused. In **Togail Bruidne Da Derga* [The Destruction of Da Derga's Hostel], he is married to the beautiful *Étaín (1), taking the place of Eochaid Airem, as in *Tochmarc Étaíne* [The Wooing of Étaín]; the child of this union is *Étaín Óg. *Tuathal Techtmar, one of the most important of pre-Christian kings, claimed direct descent from Eochaid Feidlech through six generations.

Eochaid Glas. See EOCHU GLAS.

Eochaid Gunnat. Early king of the *Ulaid [Ulster-men]; imaginative medieval genealogists attributed the kingship of *Emain Macha to him.

Eochaid Inber. One of the three enemies of *Labraid Luathlám in **Serglige Con Culainn* [The Wasting Sickness of Cúchulainn] whom Cúchulainn dispatches easily.

Eochaid Iúil, Eúil. An Irish god of the *Otherworld, one of several, although not usually included in the ranks of the *Tuatha Dé Danann. *Fand, the sea-goddess, is sometimes described as married to him instead of to *Manannán mac Lir. His son Rinn was thought to have married *Aíbgréne, the daughter of *Deirdre and Noíse. In **Serglige Con Culainn* [The Wasting Sickness of Cúchulainn] *Lí Ban asked *Cúchulainn's aid against him along with two other warriors; later the *Ulster champion speared Eochaid Iúil when he took off his tunic to bathe.

Eochaid Lethderg [Ir., red side]. A king of *Leinster, father of *Áed (2).

Eochaid mac Eirc [son of Erc]. King of the *Fir Bolg who was the prototype of their kingship: 'No rain fell during his kingship, but only the dew; there was no year without harvest. Falsehood was banished from Ireland during his time, and he it was who first established the rule of justice there.' Eochaid was married to *Tailtiu, naming his palace in her honour and, in some versions, establishing an annual fair there (Teltown, Co. Meath) in early August to celebrate her further. He is sometimes also described as a king at *Tara. As he was king during the arrival of the *Tuatha Dé Danann, he resisted the invaders but became the first king to be killed with a weapon. As described in **Cath Maige Tuired* [The Battle of Mag Tuired] he was overcome by thirst and went in search of water, but the *druids of the Tuatha Dé Danann hid it from him. In this vain quest he was slain with three companions at a site today identified with both Ballysadare, Co. Sligo, and Eochy's Cairn, between Cong and Ballinrobe, Co. Mayo.

Eochaid mac Luchta, Muchtra. Fictitious king of *Munster during the time of *Conchobar mac Nessa, sometimes only of *Thomond (western Munster), euhemerized from *Eochaid (1), the sun-god; some texts describe him as sharing Munster with Cú Roí. He was given a pedigree going all the way back to *Íth son of Bregon by imaginative genealogists. In an echo of his derivation from Eochaid the sun-god, he is usually described as having only *one eye, a defect that would have disqualified him from kingship in any other province. *Temair Luachra is given as his residence, but it is also ascribed to Cú Roí. Possibly identical with *Eochaid (6). In some documents he is confused with Tétbannach mac Luchta.

Eochaid mac Maireda. See EOCHU MAC MAIREDA.

Eochaid mac Muchtra. See EOCHAID MAC LUCHTA.

Eochaid Mugmedón, Mug Mheadhón. Supposed late 4th-century king of Ireland, who with his son *Niall Noígiallach [of the Nine Hostages] makes two of the earliest verifiable rulers in Irish history. Eochaid earned his epithet, 'Lord of Slaves', from his many raids into *Britain, bringing back slaves to Ireland. According to the story **Echtra Mac nEchach Muigmedóin* [The Adventure of the Sons of Eochaid Mugmedón], one of these slaves was *Cairenn, daughter of a British king, who became the mother of Niall. Eochaid Mugmedón was king at *Tara for eight years, extending his sovereignty into what is today counties *Meath and Cavan. Powerful families, later rivals, traced their lineage back to Eochaid Mugmedón, the *Uí Néill through his son Niall Noígiallach, and the kings of *Connacht through his other sons, Ailill (2), Brian (2), and Fiachra (2). He was slain by the three *Collas at *Dub Chomar (*Corleck Hill, Drumeague, Co. Cavan).

Eochaid Óg. Another name for *Eochaid Airem.

Eochaid Ollathair, Ollathir [Ir., all-father, father of all]. Alternate name, in certain circumstances, for the *Dagda. Some imaginative genealogists have traced family pedigrees back to Eochaid Ollathair, just as they did with *Nuadu. In an alternate version of the birth of *Angus Óg, the god of youth and beauty, Eochaid seduces *Eithne (2) (another name for *Boand), the wife of *Elcmar; mother and father ask *Midir to foster the child. In the better-known version the Dagda under his own name seduces Boand, who is married to *Nechtan; the adulterers seek to disguise their deed by having Elcmar serve as foster-father. Eochaid Ollathair is often confused with *Eochaid (1), the sun-god.

Eochaid Riata. See EOCHU RIATA.

Eochaid Rond. See EOCHU ROND.

Eochaid Sálbuide [Ir., yellow heel]. Father of Ness and therefore grandfather of *Conchobar mac Nessa. See also EOCHAID BÉLBUIDE; *Eochaid Buide.

Eochaid ua Flainn, Flaind. Historical poet of the 10th century (*fl.* 950; d. 984 (?) 1004 (?)) best known for his poems preserved in the *Lebor Gabála* [Book of Invasions].

Eochair. Hero of the longest narrative (*c.*30,000 words) recorded from Irish oral tradition in the 20th century. Storyteller Éamon a Búrc of Kilkieran, Co. Galway, recited the tale of a binding spell, in which the hero Eochair is sent on an arduous quest, to Liam Costello in 1938; it was edited and published forty-four years later. See *Eochair, Mac Rí in Éirinn*, ed. and trans. Kevin O'Nolan (Dublin, 1982).

Eocho. Variant spelling of *Eochaid and *Eochu.

Eochu, Eocho, Eochy [Ir., horse-rider (?), fighter on horseback (?), horse of conquest (?)]. Diminutive of *Eochaid; although the two forms are hopelessly confused in early manuscripts, some figures may be known only as Eochu, some only as Eochaid, and many as both.

Eochu Áenshúla. See EOCHAID ÁENSHÚLA.

Eochu Airem. See EOCHAID AIREM.

Eochu Allmuir. See EOCHAID (9).

Eochu Ánchenn. See EOCHAID ÁNCHENN.

Eochu Ballderg. See EOCHAID BALLDERG.

Eochu Bélbuide. See EOCHAID BÉLBUIDE.

Eochu Bres. See BRES (1).

Eochu Buide. See EOCHAID BUIDE.

Eochu Dála. See EOCHAID DÁLA.

Eochu Deirgderc. See EOCHAID (1).

Eochu Doimlén, Domlén [Ir., grief (?)]. Son of *Cairbre Lifechair, brother of *Fiachu Sraibthine king of *Tara, and father of the rapacious Three *Collas. He was slain along with many of his family at the Battle of *Cnámross.

Eochu Echend [Ir., horse-head]. A king of the *Fomorians.

Eochu Eúil. See EOCHAID IÚIL.

Eochu Feidlech. See EOCHAID FEIDLECH.

Eochu Glas [Ir., green, greenish-blue]. Warrior portrayed only as an opponent of *Cúchulainn. In an early combat, Cúchulainn leaped to the edge of Eochu's shield, only to be blown away. Later Cúchulainn killed him with *Gáe Bolga, his deadly spear.

Eochu Gunnat. See EOCHAID GUNNAT.

Eochu Iúil. See EOCHAID IÚIL.

Eochu Lethderg. See EOCHAID LETHDERG.

Eochu mac Eirc. See EOCHAID MAC EIRC.

Eochu mac Luchta. See EOCHAID MAC LUCHTA.

Eochu mac Maireda, Maireadha; also known as Ecca. Divine figure from pre-Christian Ireland euhemerized into a mortal. His pedigree cites Mairid mac Caireda, an unmistakably divine figure; his stepmother is *Ébliu (2); his brother *Rib. Eochu is best known for giving his name to *Lough Neagh, or, in Irish, Lough nEchach. He was probably the ruler of the *Otherworld under the Lough. In Christian times, Eochu was portrayed in an invented legend as an unfortunate drowned by the expanding waters; fishermen were thought to be able to see his residence from the middle of the waters during calm weather.

Eochu mac Muchtra. See EOCHAID MAC LUCHTA.

Eochu Mugmedón. See EOCHAID MUGMEDÓN.

Eochu Óg. See EOCHAID AIREM.

Eochu Riata. Mythical ancestor of the *Dál Riada.

Eochu Rígéces. See EOCHAID ÉIGEAS.

Eochu Rond. King of the *Uí Maine who did battle with *Cúchulainn. Although he was a splendid horseman, Eochu was dispatched quickly by Cúchulainn's spear, *Gáe Bolga.

Eochu Sálbuide. See EOCHAID SÁLBUIDE.

Eochu ua Flainn. See EOCHAID UA FLAINN.

Eochy. Anglicization of *Eochaid and *Eochu.

Eodain. Variant spelling from modern oral tradition of *Étaín.

Eógabal, Eogabail, Eogabul, Owel. Foster-son of *Manannán mac Lir and parent of the regional goddesses *Áine (1) and Grian of Co. Limerick. In some accounts Eógabal is the grandfather of the goddesses, and *Fer Í the father; in others Eógabal is the father and Fer Í a brother. Áine's centre was *Cnoc Áine [Knockainy] and Grian's *Cnoc Gréine, 7 miles distant. He is also the grandfather (again through Fer Í) or father of the divine druid *Fer Fidail. In commenting on the confusion in family lines, T. F. O'Rahilly (1946) speculated that Eógabal should be identified both with Fer Í and *Eógan of *Munster's *Eóganacht. He was slain by *Ferches.

Eógan, Eogan, Eoghan, Eoan [Ir., born of the yew tree]. Spuriously anglicized as Eugene and Owen. One of the most common names in early Ireland, borne by dozens of kings, warriors, and saints, of whom the most cited are probably *Eógan (1), the son of *Niall Noígiallach [of the Nine Hostages], and *Eógan Mór of the *Eóganacht dynasty in *Munster.

Eógan 1. The son of *Niall Noígiallach [of the Nine Hostages], who sometimes bears the patronymic mac Néill Noígiallaig; founder of the kingdom of *Tír Eógain [Tyrone] in north-west *Ulster. Together with his brother *Conall Gulban and *Énna (3) constituted the rapacious Three *Collas, who destroyed *Emain Macha. He is thought to have seized the fortress of *Ailech some time in the 5th century (*c.*425 ?) and founded the line of kings there.

2. Legendary *Connacht king whose name is remembered in a place-name story. After he was killed fighting invading Ulster warriors, his body was buried facing the adversaries' territory under the presumption that his spirit would continue the defence of the homeland. To negate his power, Ulstermen exhumed his body and reburied it, face down, near Loughill; cf. ModIr. Leamhchoill, 'elm wood'.

3. Son of *Ailill Aulomm, and a legendary king of *Munster, to be distinguished from his grandfather, *Eógan Mór, an even better-known king of Munster. Eógan (3) gave his name to the *Eóganacht dynasty of Munster despite losing the struggle for succession. His dispute with his brother *Lugaid mac Con begins when the two of them hear wonderful music drifting down from a *yew tree over a waterfall; both brothers want the music-maker, *Fer Í, the son of *Eógabal, but he disappears before either can have him. Contention arises between the brothers until they meet in the Battle of *Cenn Abrat. Lugaid's fool, Do Dera, believes that his master will be defeated and killed, and so takes his place on the battlefield and dies in his stead. Although Eógan knows he has not killed his brother when he sees his distinctive white legs on a fleeing warrior, he cannot prevent Lugaid's escape to Scotland. Several commentators have suggested that the legendary Battle of Cenn Abrat may be based on the historical defeat of the invading *Érainn.

The brothers' fortunes are reversed when next they meet on the battlefield of Mag Mucrama (Co. Galway). Lugaid has raised a huge army, which includes Scottish allies and the blind *druid *Dil Maccu Crecga of Osraige [*Ossory], who puts a spell on Eógan. Once Dil senses that Eógan will not survive the battle, he asks the king to lie with his daughter Moncha, so that his descendants may become kings of *Munster. Nine months later Moncha gives birth to *Fiachu Muillethan, the beginning of the *Eóganacht dynasty. In the battle Eógan and six other sons of Ailill Aulomm fall, and Lugaid succeeds to the crown, later taking *Cormac mac Airt as a foster-son. Many commentators see a parallel between Eógan's fathering of Fiachu and *Art's fathering of Cormac, both with common women on the nights before they went to their deaths.

Eógan Inbir. An *otherworldly king, not a member of the *Tuatha Dé Danann, whose wife was *Bé Chuma. She cuckolded him with *Gaidiar, son of *Manannán mac Lir.

Eógan mac Durthacht. Aggressive king of *Fernmag [*Farney] in several early Irish stories. He is best remembered as the killer of *Noíse in *Longas mac nUislenn* [The Exile of the Sons of Uisnech], the *Deirdre story. Although Eógan has long quarrelled with Deirdre's adversary *Conchobar, he makes peace with the *Ulster king and agrees to carry out his treachery. Eógan initially pretends to welcome Noíse back to Ireland, but his greeting includes a mortal spear-thrust. In an alternate version the Norse prince *Maine is the killer. Later, when Deirdre admits that she hates Eógan equally with Conchobar, she is sent off in Eógan's chariot; from it she jumps, dashing her head against a stone. In **Scéla Mucce meic Da Thó* [The Story of Mac Dathó's Pig], Eógan mac Durthacht contests the right of the hero's portion. His family members include father Durthacht (also Darthacht), wife Findige, and daughter *Lendabair, the wife of *Conall Cernach.

Eógan mac Néill Noígiallaig. Occasional patronymic of *Eógan (1).

Eógan Mór [Ir., big, the great]. Legendary king of *Munster, also known as *Mug Nuadat, Eógan Fitheccach, and Eógan Taídlech. Although the *Eóganacht dynasty descended from him, it is named for his grandson *Eógan (3), son of Eógan Mór's son *Ailill Aulomm. His wife was *Béare, the Castilian princess, for whom the *Beare peninsula is named; his *fairy mistress was *Étaín of Inis Grecraige. Eógan Mór contended often with *Conn Cétchathach [of the Hundred Battles], with whom he divided Ireland along the *Eiscir Riada, running from Galway Bay to Dublin. The southern portion was known as Leth Moga [Mug's half] and the northern Leth Cuinn [Conn's half]. This did not end the dispute, however. Conn invaded Leth Moga and drove Eógan Mór from the country. For a period he was in Spain. Undaunted, he returned, raised an army and faced Conn once more at the Battle of Mag Léna, where he was slain. Mag Léna is coextensive with the modern village of Kilbride, near Tullamore, Co. Offaly. An attributed son was *Fiachna (2).

Eóganacht, Eoghanacht, Owenacht [Ir., people of Eógan, born of the *yew]. Great historical dynasty, or federation of dynastic groups, that dominated southern Ireland from the 5th to the 12th centuries. Although it claimed *Eógan Mór (also *Mug Nuadat) as an ancestor, the family takes its name from Eógan Mór's grandson *Eógan (3), whose son *Fiachu Muillethan became its first king. Some recent historians do not dismiss the family legend that it was established by Christianized Irishmen returning from Britain. The legendary founder of the dynasty is Corc mac Luigthig, who had a vision of a yew bush growing over a stone, leading him to the natural fortress of *Cashel, Co. Tipperary. While the Eóganacht's political power was centred at Cashel, its influence extended all over the province of *Munster, to the west as far as the *Aran Islands and the *Burren of Co. Clare and as far east as what is today Kilkenny. *Cnoc Áine [Knockainy], Co. Limerick, was also important to them, but their church was at Imblech Ibair [Emly], Co. Tipperary. They formed alliances with the Ciarraige [*Kerry] on the west and the Osraige [*Ossory] and Múscraige [*Muskerry] to the east. Together they may have beaten the invading *Érainn, as represented in the legendary Battle of *Cenn Abrat. At the beginning of the 12th century the fortress of Cashel was given to the Church in a stroke of political expediency.

Eóghan, Eoghan. Variant spellings of *Eógan.

eòlas [ScG, knowledge; cf. OIr. *eólas*, knowledge]. A charm or white magic cure for an ailment in man or beast. Hundreds of recipes have been recorded, particularly from Scottish Gaelic oral sources, including specific roots and herbs, and with them formulaic phrases should be repeated, e.g. eòlas nan sùl, a spell to banish a mote from the eye. In recent centuries the eòlas has acquired Roman Catholic associations and may invoke certain saints, St *Brigid, St Columba [*Colum Cille], St Michael [see LUG LÁMFHOTA], and St Peter. See Alexander Carmichael, *Carmina Gadelica* (5 vols., Edinburgh and London, 1928).

Eólas [OIr. *eólas*, knowledge, as learned from experience]. One of the chief *druids of the *Partholonians, along with his two brothers, *Fios [OIr. *fis*, ascertaining] and *Fochmarc [inquiry]. The brothers collectively are described as having three fathers and three mothers through joint parentage.

Eórann, Eorann. Wife of Suibne in **Buile Shuibne* [The Frenzy of Sweeney].

Epidii [L, people of the horse]. A British or *P-Celtic people of Scotland noted in *Ptolemy's geography (2nd cent. AD). Their homeland was beyond the Antonine Wall on the Kintyre peninsula, in what was until 1974 *Argyllshire. Several commentators have asserted that their name implies a worship of the goddess *Epona. Previously thought to be *Pictish. Sometimes named the Equidii.

Epona. Important goddess of the ancient Continental Celts, always linked to the horse; her name is implied by the expressions 'Divine Horse' and 'Horse-Goddess'. Epona's worship centred in the Alésia region of eastern Gaul [France], but was widespread on the Continent, usually in rural, domestic contexts, later spreading to Britain. She is commemorated in more surviving inscriptions and statues than any other early goddess. Most often she is portrayed on horseback, usually clothed and riding side-saddle, accompanied by a bird, dog, and foal. At thermal springs, such as Allerey and Saulon-la-Chapelle, she appears nude and nymph-like. A triple Epona was found at Hogondange in the Moselle valley, which may explain the occasional plural form of her name, Eponabus. Sometimes Epona is portrayed riding a great horned goose.

Epona's being female, modern commentators note, may acknowledge the role of women in agriculture and husbandry, but she is also linked to *Matres, the Romano-Gaulish fertility figures. Roman commentators noted her popularity with the cavalry, her statues being erected in stables, and her patronage extending to mules and donkeys. She was the only Celtic deity ever cited in the Roman pantheon, where her feast-day was celebrated on 18 December. Her worship appears to have been imported to Britain during Roman dominance, where her cult merged with that of *Macha and *Rhiannon, who is also portrayed holding and dispensing bags. Recent scholarship does not support her popular association with the great horse figure carved in the chalk bluffs at *Uffington in Berkshire. The *Epidii people of early Scotland, however, may have worshipped her. See René Magnen and Émile Thévenot, *Epona, déesse gauloise* (Bordeaux, 1953); Fernand Benot, *Les Mythes de l'outre-tombe; le cavalier à l'anguipède et l'écuyère Epona* (Brussels, 1950); K. Linduff, 'Epona: A Celt among the Romans', *Collection Latomus*, 38 (4) (1979), 817–37. Morgan Llywellen fabricates a love story for a blonde Epona in the popular novel *The Horse Goddess* (Boston, 1982).

Equidii. Occasional mistranscription for *Epidii.

Er 1. [cf. OIr. *ér*, noble, great]. A son of *Partholón.

2. [OIr., noble, great]. An eponymous ancestor of the *Érainn, created by genealogical fiction, purported to be the son of *Éber, son of *Míl Espáine.

Érainn. Historical population of early Ireland that first settled the island in perhaps the 5th century BC. Centred in what is now Co. Cork, the Érainn were identical with the Iverni or Everni noted by *Ptolemy (2nd cent. AD), adapting those names from the Érainn subdivision, the *Corcu Loígde. Scholars no longer believe that the Érainn were the aboriginal population of Ireland. Received opinion today asserts that the Érainn were preceded by the Cruithni [*Picts] and followed by the *Lagin and *Féni. T. F. O'Rahilly argued several provocative theses concerning the Érainn in *Early Irish History and Mythology* (1946): (*a*) that the Érainn were a *P-Celtic people who preceded the *Q-Celtic *Goídels who eventually dominated Ireland; (*b*) that they could be identified with the *Belgae who left what is today the Low Countries and crossed Britain to reach Ireland; (*c*) that the *Nemedians and *Fir Bolg of the pseudo-history **Lebor Gabála* [Book of Invasions] are based on them. Further, he thought that **Togail Bruidne Da Derga* [The Destruction of Da Derga's Hostel] was based on the memory of defeat by the Lagin.

Although many scholars doubt the Érainn's identification with the P-Celts, and therefore the British, O'Rahilly's views have not been overturned. Several important smaller groups were actually subdivisions of the Érainn, notably the already cited Corcu Loígde, the *Corcu Duibne of *Kerry, the *Déisi of Waterford, the *Múscraige [Muskerry], the Osraige [*Ossory], who allied themselves with the Q-Celtic *Eóganacht, and, in the north of the island, the *Dál Riada who colonized Gaelic Scotland and the *Ulaid who gave their name to *Ulster. Their principal ancestor-deity was *Dáire mac Dedad. The territorial goddess *Mór Muman [Great of Munster] apparently was first a goddess of the Érainn.

Erannán, Airennán. Youngest son of *Míl Espáine in the invasion legends of early Ireland. According to the **Lebor Gabála* [Book of Invasions] Erannán climbed a mast to reconnoitre the landscape but fell to his death. In the **Dindshenchas* *Donn mac Míled, Míl Espáine's eldest son, is the first to die.

Erc, Ercc, Erca, Earc [Ir., speckled, dark-red (?); a salmon (?)]. Common name in early Irish stories and in Scottish Gaelic and Irish genealogies, borne by both men and women; there is also a St Erc, an early bishop of Slane, Co. Meath.

Erc 1. A king of *Leinster, ally of *Medb of Connacht, and key adversary of *Cúchulainn, who kills Erc's father, *Cairbre Nia Fer. In revenge Erc casts his spear into one of Cúchulainn's favourite horses, *Liath Macha [Grey of Macha], just before Cúchulainn himself is killed by some of Erc's champions. Erc is subsequently killed by *Conall Cernach.

2. Father of *Eochaid mac Eirc, the admired king of the *Fir Bolg.

3. One of the women of the *Fianna in the *Fenian Cycle.

4. Father of *Fergus mac Eirc and *Loarn of the Scottish *Dál Riada. Many Highland genealogies trace family pedigrees back to Erc, and thus the phrase 'sons of Erc' might apply to many Scottish Gaelic families.

Ercol, Ercoil. *Connacht warrior and foster-father of *Medb as portrayed in **Fled Bricrenn* [Briccriu's Feast]. *Cúchulainn, *Conall Cernach, and *Lóegaire go to the court of Medb and *Ailill to seek their judgement as to which is the greatest warrior and thus most deserving of the hero's portion, but the royal couple send the three on to Ercol and his wife Garmuin. At first they hesitate, giving the three challengers a contest and sending them to *Samera, who tells them to return and test their worth in a single match with Ercol. Lóegaire advances first, but he soon flees when Ercol's gelding kills his horse. He disgraces himself further by lying that Ercol has first killed Conall and Cúchulainn to cover his cowardice. Conall is also put off by the death of his horse, and sees his son Rathend drowned in their flight. When Cúchulainn's turn comes, his horse *Liath Macha [Grey of Macha] makes short work of Ercol's gelding, after which Cúchulainn himself overcomes Ercol and binds him behind his chariot, taking him back to *Emain Macha. Several commentators have noted an echo of the name *Hercules in Ercol, although the humiliation behind the chariot is more evocative of Hector in the *Iliad*.

Erec, Erek. Hero of French and other Continental Arthurian romances, especially those of *Chrétien de Troyes (*c.*1180) and Hartmann von Aue (*c.*1170- *c.*1215), who rendered the name as Erek. After his marriage to *Enid, Erec gains in strength; the two become model lovers, partners, and rulers. Erec's Welsh counterpart is *Geraint.

Erech Febria, Aireach, Airioch Feabhruadh [cf. Ir. *erech*, laden, burdened]. One of the eight sons of *Míl Espáine in the **Lebor Gabála* [Book of Invasions]; in some versions Míl has only six sons, not including Erech and *Erannán. When Erech appears it is only to accompany his brother *Donn mac Míled in drowning during the invasion. His mother is Seang.

Erek. German spelling of *Erec.

Erem. Variant spelling of *Éremón.

Éremón, Eremon, Érimón, Éireamhóin, Heremon, Erem. First *Milesian (i.e. *Goidelic) king of Ireland, who established his capital at *Tara, according to the pseudo-history **Lebor Gabála* [Book of Invasions]. As one of the two most important sons, with *Eber Finn, of *Míl Espáine, Éremón takes a leading role in the Milesian conquest of Ireland, distinguishing himself in a defeat of the *Tuatha Dé Danann at *Tailtiu, as described in **Altrom Tige Dá Medar*. In victory, however, he enters into a dispute with his brother and ally, Eber Finn. The poet *Amairgin arbitrates the division of Ireland between the brothers, choosing a border following the *Eiscir Riada, a ridge of mounds between Galway Bay and *Dublin; Eber takes the south with six chiefs and Éremón the north and seven chiefs. Unhappy with this settlement, Eber attacks Éremón but is killed by him. This leaves Éremón as the sole ruler of a united island, but the feud is thought to have been continued by their descendants. Éremón establishes his capital at the hill of Temair (see TARA), named for his wife *Téa.

Perhaps because Éremón was cited in so many pedigrees and genealogies, the name, under different spellings, was borne by some later petty kings and noblemen. Éremón's uniting of the island led to his being compared to King David of Judea by exegetical medieval commentators. But modern commentators, especially those influenced by Georges Dumézil (1898–1986), find it more significant that Éremón, representing the north, acquires the whole island and the kingship. See Georges Dumézil, *Le Troisième Souverain* (Paris, 1949), 167–86.

Ergadia. Latin name for *Argyllshire, now (since 1974) in western Strathclyde.

Éri. Variant spelling of *Ériu.

éric, éraic. Old Irish term for a special kind of fine, wergild, or reparation in the laws of early Ireland. An éric might be imposed for any wrong, but it was mostly associated with homicide. The kinsmen of a murder victim might ask an éric of cattle or silver from the perpetrator, specified according to the rank of either killer or killed, or they might instead seek the death of the killer. The modern Irish word éiric, while derived from Old Irish, means, less specifically, 'reparation, retribution; compensation, reward'.

Eric. Bogus anglicization of *Áebhric, a character in **Oidheadh Chlainne Lir* [The Tragic Story of the Children of Lir].

Erin. Variant form of both *Ériu and *Ireland.

Eriskay. Small island, 3 1.5 miles, in the Outer Hebrides, between South *Uist and *Barra, known for the 'Eriskay Love Lilt', one of the most admired of all Scottish Gaelic songs. Marjorie Kennedy-Fraser (1857–1930) adapted this version, whose Gaelic title is 'Gràdh Geal mo Cridh' [Pure Love My Heart], from a folk original. The Gaelic name for the island, Eirisgeidh, is of Norse derivation. In modern usage the island may also be denoted by Eilean na hÒige [island of youth], a Scottish equivalent of *Tír na nÓg. See Calum MacNeill, *Aodannan Eriskay: Faces of Eriskay* (Glasgow, 1992).

Ériu, Éire, Éri, Erin. One of three sisters, divine eponyms and tutelary goddesses of Ireland, along with *Banba and *Fódla; sometimes Ériu is a personification of Ireland. According to an oft-cited passage from the **Lebor Gabála* [Book of Invasions] Ériu is chosen to give her name to Ireland itself. When the *Milesians invade Ireland, Ériu and her sisters greet them, each wanting the invader to name the country after herself. Asserting herself ahead of her sisters, Ériu meets the Milesians at *Uisnech, tells them that Ireland is the fairest land under the sun, and flatters them as the most perfect race the world has ever seen. When one of the leaders, *Donn mac Míled insults her, Ériu predicts that neither he nor his children will ever enjoy Ireland, and he subsequently drowns. The poet of the Milesians, *Amairgin, promises Ériu that the country will bear her name. Éire is the Modern Irish spelling for Ériu, and Erin is an anglicized form. Banba and Fódla have been poetic references for Ireland. Ériu is traditionally described as wearing circlets or rings, which may imply, along with the etymology of her name, an identification with the sun or moon.

Although the Ériu of the *Lebor Gabála* can be identified with the Ériu who mothers *Bres in **Cath Maige Tuired* [The Battle of Mag Tuired], these and variant texts present a conflicting picture of her pedigree. Her father is usually named as *Delbáeth (2), her mother either *Ernmas or *Eirnin; her foster-father is *Codal. She is usually married to *Mac Gréine (sometimes known as *Cethor), but she has a celebrated affair with *Elatha, son of Delbáeth (1), to produce Bres. While not named in **Baile in Scáil* [Phantom's Frenzy], she is thought to be *Lug Lámfhota's consort, a *sovereignty figure, in that narrative. She is later killed at the Battle of *Tailtiu by Suirge, where the Milesians slaughter all the kings and queens of the Tuatha Dé Danann.

Ériu is also named as the founder of the festival at *Uisnech. As a personification of Ireland, she may be the queen 'married' in the sacred ritual marriage of fled bainisi or *banais ríghe. See Julius Pokorny, 'Der Name Ériu', *Zeitschrift für celtische Philologie*, 15 (1925), 197–202; T. F. O'Rahilly, 'On the Origin of the Names *Érainn* and *Ériu*', *Ériu*, 14 (1946), 7–28.

Érne, Éirne. Legendary Irish princess, daughter of Búrc Búiredach, who gave her name to the *Erne waterway.

Erne. Waterway in Ireland flowing 75 miles NW from Lough Gowna in Co. Longford through Lough Oughter and Lough Erne, counties Cavan, Fermanagh, and Donegal, to Donegal Bay south of Ballyshannon. Two bodies of water are called Lough Erne, the smaller Upper to the south-east and larger Lower to the north-west. The entire region is rich in ruins of pagan Irish, Danish, and monastic origin. Most remarkable are three islands in Lower Lough Erne: Boa Island, which can be reached by bridge, containing a well-preserved, double-faced, phallic Janus figure and a smaller figure, the 'lusty man', so named from its origin on Lustymore Island; *Devenish Island, a 6th-century monastic settlement founded by St Molaise; and White Island, containing caryatid-like standing figures of Christian and apparently pagan origin, including a *sheela-na-gig. The fabled cataract of *Assaroe, now flooded for a hydroelectric project, was on the Erne. See W. F. Wakeman, *Lough Erne* (Enniskillen, 1870); John Charles Roy, *The Road Wet, the Wind Close* (Dublin, 1987).

Erni. Handmaiden and treasure-keeper for *Medb at *Cruachain.

Ernmas. Mother of divinities. According to some texts she is the mother of the divine eponyms of Ireland, *Ériu, *Banba, and *Fódla, but in other texts Eirnin is their mother. She is also named as the mother of the war-goddesses *Badb, *Macha, and the *Mórrígan; their father is usually thought to be *Cailitin, although Ernmas and Cailitin are not always linked. Additionally, she is often named as the mother of *Fiachna (4).

Erriapus. Name given to a local god in southern *Gaul, probably the equivalent of Gaulish *Mercury; another name for Mercury may have been *Lugos. A portrayal of his head, seen emerging from foliage, was found in the Garonne region of southern France.

Eryr Pengwern. Welsh title for a poem in the 9th-10th-century *Canu Heledd [Song of Heledd] cycle. The narrator, Heledd, describes the screaming birds of prey as they feast on the flesh of fallen warriors, especially that of her brother *Cynddylan. The exact location of Pengwern, probably in what is today England, has been the subject of much speculation. See Jenny Rowland, *Early Welsh Saga Poetry* (Cambridge, 1990).

Eryri [W, eagle top]. Welsh name for a mountainous region in north-west *Wales known in English as *Snowdonia. The name Eryri is sometimes misconstrued to refer specifically to Mount *Snowdon, the tallest peak in Wales (3,560 feet), which should be Yr Wyddfa in Welsh. Eryri was in the heart of the medieval kingdom of *Gwynedd and today lies in the reconstituted (1974) county of Gwynedd; from the 17th century until 1974 it was in Caernarvonshire. The white eagles once common in the region were thought to be emblems of national fortune. If they circled high, victory was imminent; if they flew low, crying incessantly, they warned of catastrophe for the Welsh. Such an eagle has been a logotype for clandestine Welsh nationalist groups in the late 20th century.

Es. Variant spelling of *Ésa.

Es Ruaid. An OIr. form of the cataract of *Assaroe.

Ésa, Esa, Ess, Es. In variants found outside the widely known texts of **Tochmarc Étaíne* [The Wooing of Étaín] and **Togail Bruidne Da Derga* [The Destruction of Da Derga's Hostel], Ésa is the daughter of *Eochaid Airem and *Étaín (1). In such versions she becomes the mother of *Mes Buachalla, the beautiful foundling who mothers *Conaire Mór.

Esclados le Roux [Fr. *le roux*, the reddish-brown]. Fearsome knight of *Brittany, sometimes named as the guardian of the fountain of Bérenton at *Brocéliande; more often it is an unnamed, tall, beautiful woman. Some commentators find Esclados a counterpart of the Irish hero *Cú Roí.

Esgair Oerfel, Esgeir Oerfel, Oervel [W, accursed ridge]. Imaginary place-name in Ireland as cited in the Welsh story of **Culhwch ac Olwen*. The ridge was so massive as to be visible from *Cornwall. *Twrch Trwyth, the fearful boar, ranges here.

Esnad, Easnadh [OIr., musical sound]. One of the beautiful *femmes fatales* responsible for the death of the *ard rí [high king], *Muirchertach mac Erca.

Esnada Tige Buchet. Irish title for a story known in English as 'The Melodies of Buchet's House'. A part of the *Cycle of Kings or Historical Cycle, the story dates from at least as far back as the 10th century and is preserved in five vellum manuscripts, including the **Book of Leinster* and the **Yellow Book of Lecan*. Buchet, a hospitable man of

*Leinster, fosters Eithne (*Eithne Tháebfota, though she is called simply Eithne here), the daughter of *Cathaír Mór, king of Ireland. Unhappily for Buchet, Cathaír Mór's twelve rapacious sons invite themselves to his house and consume all his larder and most of his livestock, leaving only seven cows and a bull. Cathaír Mór, now a withered old man, says he cannot control his sons, offers no redress, and tells Buchet to go away. He does so, fleeing with his wife, Eithne, and the remaining cattle, seeking out *Cormac mac Airt at *Kells. Already a powerful figure, Cormac is not yet king because (in a variant from the usual story) *Medb Lethderg, *Art's widow, has seized the kingship and kept Cormac away.

While watching Eithne one day, Cormac notices that the comely young girl sets aside the best portions of the rushes, water, and milk she has collected. When he asks her why she does this, she answers that it is to honour someone important, Buchet. Cormac is so charmed by this that he asks Buchet for Eithne's hand, but he cannot give it as her foster-father. So Eithne is carried off and spends the night with Cormac, during which she conceives *Cairbre Lifechair. Later she becomes Cormac's queen, for which he pays Buchet an enormous bride-price, including all that can be seen for a week from the ramparts of Kells. Buchet then returns to Leinster with huge herds. This prosperity funds the 'melodies' of the title, his warm and generous greeting to guests in his house: abundant food, drink, and entertainment. The best modern edition is in David H. Greene, *Fingal Rónáin and Other Stories* (Dublin, 1955).

Esras. One of the earliest *druids of the *Tuatha Dé Danann, best remembered for giving *Lug Lámfhota his spear, *Gáe Assail, that guaranteed victory in battle. He taught in Gorias, one of the four cities of the Tuatha Dé Danann, which is fancifully located in a 'northern isle of Greece'.

Ess. Variant spelling of *Ésa.

Ess Enchenn. Variant spelling of *Éis Énchenn.

Ess Ruaid. OIr. spelling of *Assaroe.

Essé. Village in Brittany, 17 miles SE of Rennes, best known for the nearby impressive megalithic *dolmens (or portal tombs) known locally as La Roche aux Fées [Fairies' Rock]. Long thought one of the finest megalithic monuments in any Celtic country, the dolmen at Essé is composed of forty-two stones, of which six weigh between forty and forty-five tons each. A massive portico leads to a low ceilinged corridor, which opens on to a large, high compartmented room. In popular etymology the town is thought to have been named for *Esus, the Gaulish god.

Essellt. Variant of the Welsh name *Essyllt; see ISEULT.

Essruadh. An Irish form of *Assaroe.

Essus. Corrupt variant of *Esus.

Essyllt, Essellt [W, that which is fair to view]. Welsh version of *Iseult, name of three characters in the *Tristan story. Other women named Essyllt are recorded in Welsh traditions and genealogies who appear unrelated to the Arthurian figure. See Rachel Bromwich, *Trioedd Ynys Prydain*, rev. edn. (Cardiff, 1978), 349ff., 551.

Esus, Hesus. Important god of ancient *Gaul, known both from Latin commentaries and from archaeological evidence; often mentioned in the company of the Gaulish gods *Taranis and *Teutates. Although the testimony of Lucan (1st cent. AD) has been challenged as biased against the Gauls and contrived to pander to metropolitan prejudices, it cannot be ignored. He portrays an 'uncouth Esus of the barbarous altars'. Human sacrifices are suspended from trees and ritually wounded; unnamed priests read omens from which way the blood ran from wounds. Ancient scholiasts linked Esus to both *Mercury and *Mars, the latter implying he might be a patron of war. Depictions of Esus as a woodcutter have prompted much imaginative speculation, but the earlier suggestion of a link between Esus and *Cúchulainn now seems ill-founded. One temple features three symbolic representations of *egrets; he is also associated with the *crane.

Although Esus' cult was thought confined to Gaul, the discovery of *Lindow Man, the body of an ancient human sacrifice found in Cheshire in 1984, implied to some commentators the propitiation of Esus in Britain. Although Esus was worshipped in many parts of Gaul, he appears to have been the eponymous god of the Esuvii of north-west Gaul, on the English Channel, coextensive with the modern French Department of Calvados. In popular etymology his name is commemorated in the Breton town of *Essé. See Waldemar Deonna, 'Les Victimes d'Esus', *Ogam*, 10 (1958), 3–29; Paul-Marie Duval, 'Teutatés, Esus, Taranis', *Études Celtiques*, 8 (1958), 41–58; Anne Ross, 'Esus et les trois "grues"', *Études Celtiques*, 9 (1960/1), 405–38.

Étaín, Édain, Éadaoin, Éadoin, Etaine, Edaein, Aideen, Aidín; Achtan is a variant only for Étaín (2); sometimes confused with *Étan [cf. OIr. *ét*, jealousy]. Name borne by dozens of figures from early Irish narrative, history, and genealogy, the most celebrated of whom is *Étaín (1), the heroine of **Tochmarc Étaíne* [The Wooing of Étaín]. St Étaín, patroness of Tumna, Co. Roscommon, is celebrated on 5 July. From the middle of the 13th century the name was common in the O'Connor, O'Hara, and O'Flanagan families.

Étaín 1. Beautiful heroine of **Tochmarc Étaíne* [The Wooing of Étaín], wife of *Eochaid Airem, and lover of *Midir, whose name is widely cited in Irish literature. Although her sometime epithet Echraide [horse-rider] suggests hippomorphic links with the Welsh *Rhiannon and possibly *Epona of the Continental Celts, she may have been originally a sun-goddess, as T. F. O'Rahilly asserted (1946). Étaín's divinity persists in *Tochmarc Étaíne* even though the story has her reborn as the daughter of the *Ulster king *Étar (1). Her identity is partially confused when Midir creates fifty women who look like her. When Eochaid Airem chooses one of these to replace his lost wife, she is revealed to be a daughter of the true Étaín from a previously unannounced pregnancy; Eochaid refuses to see this unnamed, incestuously begotten daughter, but according to *Tochmarc Étaíne* she mates with *Eterscél.

In **Togail Bruidne Da Derga* [The Destruction of Da Derga's Hostel] Étaín is portrayed somewhat differently. Here she is the divine daughter of Étar (1), who has saved herself to be the lover of *Eochaid Feidlech, a brother of Eochaid Airem, bearing him a daughter, *Étaín Óg. This second Étaín marries *Cormac of Ulster, who has a daughter from a previous marriage, *Mes Buachalla. In this version Mes Buachalla, not Étaín's offspring or double, marries Eterscél. In still other versions, Étaín and Eochaid Airem produce a daughter named *Ésa, whose daughter is Mes Buachalla. In genealogical tracts Étaín (1) is described as becoming the wife of the mortal king *Cormac Connloinges. Étaín's servant *Cruacha gave her name to *Cruachain, fortress home of Queen *Medb, who T. F. O'Rahilly asserts may have been a double for Étaín.

Throughout early Irish literature, Étaín's allure was proverbial, as one of Eochaid Airem's retainers explained: 'Every lovely form must be tested by Étaín, every beauty by the standard of Étaín.' Her name became known in English through the poetry of W. B. Yeats and the play by Fiona Macleod [pseud. of William Sharp], *The Immortal Hour* (published 1907), later the basis for Rutland Boughton's opera (1914) of the same title. See also Sir Samuel Ferguson, 'Aideen's Grave' (1865); E. H. Moore, *The Story of Etain and Otinel* (London, 1905); James H. Cousins, *Etain the Beloved and Other Poems* (Dublin, 1912); Moireen Fox [pseud. of Móirín a Cheavasa], *Midhir and Etain* (Dublin, 1920); Micheál Mac Liammóir, *Where Stars Walk* (1940, 1962).

2, Achtan. The mother of *Cormac mac Airt in unusual circumstance. *Art, son of *Conn, is travelling to the Battle of Mag Mucrama (Co. Galway) when he rests for the night in the house of the smith Olc Acha. The smith tells Art of the prophecy that great honour will follow if Art were to sleep with Olc Acha's daughter, Étaín. Anticipating that he will die the next day in battle, Art tells Étaín that if she conceives a child she should take it to be fostered by Art's friend *Lugna in *Connacht. She does become pregnant and so sets out for Lugna's stronghold, but falls into her labour pains along the Connacht borders, delivering the child in brushwood during a thunder-storm. A she-wolf takes the child away to its lair, and Étaín goes on to seek protection from Lugna. Later one of Lugna's retainers finds the child crawling on all fours and names him Cormac mac Airt.

3. In the *Fenian Cycle, a woman who gives gold and silver to St *Patrick; she is also identified as a wife of *Oscar.

Étaín Echraide. Occasional epithet for *Étaín (1).

Étaín Fholtfhind [Ir., of the fair hair]. A beautiful maiden identified by rival genealogies. She is either (*a*) the daughter of *Étar (2), living in the *fairy residence of *Howth, or (*b*) the daughter of *Gebann, chief druid of *Mannannán mac Lir, and sister of *Clídna.

Étaín of Inis Grecraige. Fairy mistress of *Eógan Mór; she resides on Inis Grecraige, today known as Beare Island in Bantry Bay. After Eógan is defeated by *Conn Cétchathach [of the Hundred Battles] at the Battle of Carn Buidhe, near the mouth of the River Roughty, by Kenmare, Étaín rescues him and his men and takes them to sea in her ships. Eógan later returns to the mainland to continue battle but is again defeated, after which he flees to Étaín's shelter on Inis Grecraige. Later still, he leaves Étaín's island and sets sail for Spain.

Étaín Óg, Óig. Daughter of *Étaín (1), with whom she is often confused. In **Togail Bruidne Da Derga* [The Destruction of Da Derga's Hostel], Étaín (1) mates with *Eochaid Feidlech to produce Étaín Óg, who marries Cormac (1), king of *Ulster. Some commentators think this Cormac identical with *Cormac Connloinges, who, in genealogical tracts, is thought married to Étaín (1). Cormac is disappointed that Étaín Óg bears him only one child, a daughter. Jealous and fearful, Étaín Óg demands that Cormac's retainers murder another daughter from a previous marriage. Charmed by the baby's laughter, the retainers refuse, leaving her instead in a cowshed. Upon maturity this child is named *Mes Buachalla [herdsman's fosterling], wife of *Eterscél and mother of *Conaire Mór. The name Étaín Óg should not apply to the other 'daughters' of Étaín (1) cited in **Tochmarc Étaíne* [The Wooing of Étaín]. Distinguish from *Ésa, yet another daughter of Étaín (1).

Etair. Genitive form of *Étar; see also BEN ÉTAIR.

Étan, Eadán. Name borne by several women in early Irish literature, most notably Étan (1), the wife of *Ogma. Sometimes confused with *Étaín.

Étan 1. Wife of *Ogma, the god of eloquence. Daughter of *Dian Cécht, a god of healing, she was attributed some powers as a patron of crafts. Usually thought to be the mother of *Tuireann and sometimes the mother of *Cairbre mac Ethne, the satirist.

2. Mistress of *Cúchulainn, to whom he gave a ring in appreciation of their lovemaking.

3. A woman of the *Fianna Éireann.

Étar 1, Édar, Etar, Edar, Etair. A king of *Ulster in **Tochmarc Étaíne* [The Wooing of Étaín], whose unnamed wife gives birth to the mortal incarnation of *Étaín. She drinks from a golden cup containing a fly, which is the transformed Étaín. Étar is described as the king of Inber Cichmaine, a place-name that occurs frequently on the map of early Ireland. The text indicates the non-existent kingdom of Echrad in north-east Ulster. This Étar appears to be identical with the king of the same name who fathers a divine Étaín in **Togail Bruidne Da Derga* [The Destruction of Da Derga's Hostel].

Étar 2, Édar, Etar, Edar, Etair. Father of *Étaín Fholtfhind, in some versions; probably the eponym of *Benn Étair, the Hill of *Howth.

Etarláim. See BRESAL ETARLÁIM.

Etarlann. See BRESAL ETARLÁIM.

Etarscéle. Variant spelling of *Eterscél.

Eterscél, Eterscéle, Etarscéle, Eterskel. King of *Tara who becomes the father of *Conaire Mór with one of three wives from rival stories. In **Tochmarc Étaíne* [The Wooing of Étaín] he mates with the abandoned, unnamed daughter *Eochaid Airem unwittingly begot upon the false Étaín, also his daughter. **Togail Bruidne Da Derga* [The Destruction of Da Derga's Hostel] describes him mating with *Mes Buachalla, the abandoned step-daughter of *Étaín Óg. And in variants he mates with *Ésa, yet another daughter of Eochaid Airem. Eterscél's own father may have been the incestuously begotten *Fiachu Fer Mara. Eterscél is succeeded as king of Tara by *Nuadu Necht.

Ethal Anbúail, Anubal, Anubhail. A *Connacht leader of the *Tuatha Dé Danann whose *sídh was at *Úaman; best remembered as the father of *Cáer, whom *Angus Óg loved. In different versions of the courtship, various divinities come to Angus's assistance. The *Dagda imprisoned him at *Cruachain and would not release him until he told where Cáer would be and explained her transformation into a bird.

Etherún, Etharún, Heithiurun, chief idol of the early Britons, according to the Metrical *Dindshenchas. The root of his name suggests a link with *Taranis, the thunder-god. See also ETIRUN.

Ethlenn, Ethlinn, Ethliu, Ethna, Ethné, Ethnea, Ethnen, Ethniu. Variant forms of *Eithne.

Etirun. A minor British thunder-god, according to the Irish *Dindshenchas. The root of his name suggests a link with *Taranis, the thunder-god. See also ETHERÚN.

Etlym Gleddyfcoch, Gleddyf Coch, Gleddyv Coch [W, red sword]. The noble youth who becomes a guide for *Peredur. After Peredur has overcome the 300 knights of the Countess of Achievement, he learns that she loves Etlym and so resigns her to him. Accompanied by Etlym, he goes forth to the Mound of Mourning, where he slays both the black serpent and 200 of the 300 knights guarding it. Later Peredur gives the magic stone found under the serpent to Etlym, who returns with it to his beloved.

Eubonia. Archaic name for the Isle of *Man.

Eugene [Gk., well-born]. Spurious anglicization of *Eógan; less commonly, for *Eochaid.

Euroswydd, Eurosswydd. Father by Panarddun of the malevolent *Efnisien and the benevolent Nisien.

Eusebius. Christian bishop and historian (264–340), born in Palestine, who wrote in Greek; known formally as Eusebius Pamphili, Bishop of Caesarea. Among several surviving works, his *Chronicle* [Gk. *Chronicon*], coordinating Christian and pagan events, was especially influential on the world-view of early Celtic Christian writers. See Alden A. Mosshammer, *The Chronicle of Eusebius and Greek Chronographic Tradition* (Lewisburg, Penn., 1979).

Eva. Occasional anglicization of *Aífe.

Ever Living Ones. Synonym for the *Tuatha Dé Danann.

Everallin [cf. ScG *aoibhir àlainn*, beautiful cheer]. In James *Macpherson's *Poems of Ossian* (1760–3), the wife of *Ossian. She is celebrated for her beauty, notably her characteristic brown hair and white bosom, in Book 4 of *Fingal*. Daughter of Branno and mother of *Oscar.

Everni. Latinized form of the *Érainn.

evil eye. A belief in the power of individuals to cast spells or cause harm, simply by looking, is world-wide; instances of the belief have been recorded in all Celtic countries, beginning as early as the *Ancient Laws of Ireland* and the *Annals of Connacht* for the years 1466 and 1467. Often a squint or very dark eyes were thought to indicate the presence of the evil eye; sometimes children conceived before their parents were married were thought to have the evil eye. While the power might belong to witches and other malevolent persons, some innocent persons possessed it unwillingly. A woman with an evil eye cast it upon *Conaire Mór. See also BALOR's deadly eye. Ir. súil mhillte, drochshúil; ScG droch shùil; Manx drogh hooil. See R. C. Maclagan, *Evil Eye in the Western Highlands* (London, 1902; repr. London, 1975); Alan Dundes (ed.), *The Evil Eye: A Folklore Casebook* (New York, 1981).

Evnisien, Evnissyen. Variant spellings of *Efnisien.

Evrawc, Evrawg. Variant spellings of *Efrawg.

Evric. Anglicization of *Áebric, the Irish monk who first hears and then retells the story of the Children of Lir in **Oidheadh Chlainne Lir* [The Tragic Story of the Children of Lir].

Excalibur [Celtic *kaleto-*, hard (?); W *Caledfwlch*; MedL *Caliburnus*; OFr. *Escalibor*]. King *Arthur's magical sword, given him by the Lady of the Lake; not to be confused with the sword he earlier drew from a stone and broke in combat. As long as Arthur carried Excalibur, he could not be defeated; but its scabbard, which preserved him from wounds, was stolen by his sister Morgan le Fay. The Arthurian conception of Excalibur, first presented in *Geoffrey of Monmouth's *Historia* (1136), has several parallels in Celtic traditions. The English spelling of the name is ultimately derived from the Welsh *Caledfwlch, which is cited in Welsh Arthuriana, such as **Culhwch ac Olwen*. Caledfwlch is nearly identical with the Breton Kaledvoulc'h and is comparable with the Irish *Caladbolg.

Exile of the Children of Lir, The. Variant translation of the Irish narrative **Oidheadh Chlainne Lir*, more often known in English as 'The Tragic Story of the Children of Lir'.

Exile of the Sons of Uisnech, The. English title for the early Irish narrative *Longas mac nUislenn*; see DEIRDRE.

Exploits of the Sons of Eochaid Mugmedón, The. Variant translation of the title of the early Irish narrative **Echtra Mac* *nEchach Muigmedóin* [The Adventure of the Sons of Eochaid Mugmedón].

eye [OE *ēage*]. Early Celts, in common with other Europeans, often anthropomorphized the sun as an eye. The Irish word for eye, súil, etymologically means 'sun'; its Welsh cognate, haul, 'sun' in Modern Welsh, denoted 'eye' in the older language. The proliferation of *one-eyed figures suggests an association with the sun. Several figures are noted for the power of their eye, notably *Balor, *Ingcél Cáech, and *Ogmios; *Cúchulainn had seven pupils in his eye during his battle fury. The Gaulish gods *Vindonnus (aspect of *Apollo) and *Mullo were thought to cure diseases of the eye. Ir. súil; ScG sùil; Manx sooill; W llygad; Corn. lagas; Bret. lagad. See also EVIL EYE.

eyebright, eye bright. Any of several flowing plants (genus *Euphrasia*) with white and purplish blossoms, thought in European folk medicine to be curative for diseases of the eye. In Irish, especially, it is known by several affectionate phrases, e.g. soilse na súil [light of the eye], radhaircín [little sight]. Ir. roisnín; ScG lus-nan-leac; Manx lus ny sooilley; W effros, arian gwynion, math o blanhigyn. See also FAIRY HERB.

Eynon Urdd. Corrupt form of *Einion Yrth.

F

F. The sixth letter of the modern English alphabet is represented by fern [*alder] in the *ogham alphabet of early Ireland.

fab, fab-. Mutated form of map, map- [cf. W *mab*, boy, son], used in patronymics; see also AP, ap-; VAB, vab-.

fachan, fachin. Grotesquely ugly supernatural figure in Scottish Gaelic folklore, counterparts of which are known in Irish tradition. The fachan is a variety of the better-known *athach, while the *d'reach is a more particular fachan. The fearsome creature has but one leg from its haunch, one hand protruding from its chest, *one eye, and rough, spiky hair; cf. the Irish FER CAILLE; FOMORIANS. There were no creatures haunting lonely gorges and lochs that credulous peasants dreaded more to meet. Sometimes classed as a *giant. See also BÒCAN; LUIDEAG.

Fachtna, Faghtna [Ir., malicious, hostile (?)]. Name borne by dozens of figures from early Ireland, mythological and historical, secular and religious, male and female.

Fachtna 1. Chief physician of *Eochaid Airem who diagnosed the illness of Eochaid's brother *Ailill Anglonnach in **Tochmarc Étaíne* [The Wooing of Étaín]. He knew that no doctor could cure Ailill's distress, his love for Eochaid's wife *Étaín, and so recommended that she give herself to him.

Fachtna Fáthach [Ir. *fáthach*, possessed of knowledge; wise, sagacious]. A *giant, king of *Ulster, sometimes described as the husband of Ness and the father of *Conchobar mac Nessa. The better-known version has *Cathbad the *druid impregnate Ness to become the father. After Fachtna's death his half-brother *Fergus mac Róich marries Ness and succeeds him as king.

Fáelán, Faolán, Foalán, Foilan [OIr. *fáel*, wolf]. Name borne by dozens of figures in early Irish history, mythology, and genealogy, including fourteen saints, and no fewer than ten members of the *Fianna of *Fionn mac Cumhaill, of whom the best known is *Fáelán mac Finn.

Fáelán mac Finn. Son of *Fionn mac Cumhaill and leading member of his *Fianna. Conceived by a foreign woman who came to be Fionn's lover, Fáelán was noted for his loyal devotion, both to his father, especially in resisting *Goll mac Morna, and also to his half-brother *Oisín.

Fáelchu, Foalchú [Ir., wolf, wolfhound]. Name borne by a few saints and one of the *Fianna of Fionn mac Cumhaill.

faery. Variant spelling of *fairy.

faeth fiadha. Variant spelling of *féth fiada.

Fafne. Variant spelling of *Faifne.

Faghtna. Variant spelling of *Fachtna.

fáidh. Modern Irish for *fáith.

Faife. A daughter of Queen *Medb of Connacht and her husband *Ailill, sister of the better-known *Finnabair.

Faifne, Fafne. Poet and satirist, a son of Broccaid mac Bricc. When his sister *Aige is killed by the warriors of Meilge, son of King Cobthach (2), Faifne sets about avengeing her by using satire to raise three blotches on the King. The King's son Meilge arrests Faifne for this offence and executes him; Meilge simultaneously protests his innocence in Aige's death, even though his warriors killed her.

Faílbe, Fáilbhe [cf. Ir. *failbe*, lively(?); wolf-slayer(?)]. Name borne by countless figures in early Irish history and genealogy as well as by several saints and clergymen. Faílbe Finn [Ir., the fair] is a character in **Serglige Con Culainn* [The Wasting Sickness of Cúchulainn].

Failge, Failghe [cf. Ir. *failgech*, having bracelets or rings(?)]. Name borne by many historical figures in early Ireland, most notably Russ Failge, son of *Cathaír Mór, and founder of the Uí Fhailge, who give their name to Co.

Offaly in *Leinster. His daughter was *Aífe (5).

Failias. Variant spelling of *Falias.

Failinis 1, Fáil Inis, Falinis. Invincible young hound or whelp owned by King Ioruaidhe who becomes the lapdog of *Lug Lámfhota. In reparation for killing *Cian, Lug's father, the children of *Tuirenn had to procure Failinis 'who shines like the sun on a summer day and before whom every wild beast falls to earth powerless'.

2. A legendary king of Iroda [Norway] cited in early Irish narratives.

fáinne sídhe, sí, fàinne s'th. See FAIRY RING.

fair. Common translation for the OIr. *óenach*, denoting public assemblies held periodically in medieval times at *Tara, *Tailtiu, *Tlachtga, and *Uisnech; unlike the English fair, the óenach did not include commerce. The ModIr. equivalent, aonach, denotes such assemblies as that held at Millstreet, Co. Cork, and all through the country in the early 20th century. ScG féill, margadh; Manx margey; W ffair; Corn. fēr; Bret. foar. Distinguish from *festival, *féil, *feis.

fair family, folk. Translation of *tylwyth teg, the usual Welsh name for *fairies.

Fair Mane, Tresses. Usual translation of *Mongfhind (2) (Mong Bán), a woman of the *Fenian Cycle. See also AÍFE FOLTFHIND [fair hair]; EITHNE (5); and ÉTAÍN FHOLTFHIND [fair hair]; *Emer bore the occasional epithet of Foltchaín [of the fair hair].

fairy, fairies, faery [L *fāta*; OFr. *faerie*]. The diminutive, supernatural beings in human form are frequently depicted in all modern Celtic traditions. In common with counterparts in other European traditions, Celtic fairies may be seen as clever, mischievous, and capable of assisting or harassing human endeavour. Discussion in English of such phenomena is hampered by an often indiscriminate use of the word 'fairy' to translate dozens of more precise terms from Irish, Scottish Gaelic, Manx, Welsh, Cornish, and Breton. More confusingly, 'fairy' has sometimes been used to describe (and implicitly to dismiss) many characters from ancient Celtic myth, legend, saga, and folklore. Yet the first citations of fairy lore appear in the writings of the learned elite, such as *Giraldus Cambrensis (*c.*1146–1223). These are few, however, and the great bulk of fairy lore was recorded in oral tradition in modern times. Although there is a quasi-orthodoxy in the portrayal of fairies, much in Celtic conceptions bears a striking resemblance to those found in English, Scandinavian (e.g. hulda-fólk), and Continental traditions. The lack of a single shared term for fairy implies the lack of a singular, discrete Celtic tradition: Ir. sídheog (unreformed), síóg (reformed), sheogue (anglicized), *boctogaí; ScG s'thiche; Manx ferrish; W y *tylwyth teg [W, fair family]; Corn. spyrys [Corn., spirit]; Bret. korriganez, boudig. Out of courtesy the fairy may also be known by a number of euphemisms: Ir. daoine maithe [good people], daoine sídhe, áes sídhe/aos sí [people of the mound], daoine uaisle [the noble people, gentry], bunadh na croc/bunadh na gcnoc [host/stock of the hills], bunadh beag na farraige [wee folk of the sea]; ScG daoine s'th [people of the mound]; Manx ny guillyn beggey [the little boys], ny mooinjer veggey [the little kindred], ny sleih veggey [the little people]; W *bendith y mamau [W, mother's blessings]; Corn. an bobel vyghan [the little people].

Celtic conceptions of fairies, which approach an orthodoxy, depict diminutive or pygmy persons. Fairies are often invisible or can become so at will, often by donning a magical cap. They prefer to live underground, especially under a hill, in a *cave or burrow, or in a heap of stones, such as the *raths of Ireland. Their preferred colour is green, not only for dress but sometimes for skin and hair as well; at other times they may favour the palest of whites. Fairies are not generally malevolent or harmful, but they are feared as abductors of children and as administrators of the *fairy stroke, which may render the victim speechless; the colloquial use of the word 'stroke' for cerebral haemorrhage alludes to this once widespread belief. If affronted, a fairy will retaliate with resolute vengeance; common fairy punishments are burning houses and despoiling crops. Some of their mischievous pranks are only tenuously linked to human provocations; these include curdling milk or milking cows in the field, snatching unwatched food, and soiling clothes left out to dry. Often fairies are seen as benevolent, taking money or food to give to the poor, providing toys for children, or counteracting the spells cast by witches.

Great distinction is made between solitary and social fairies, although the first commentators to note it were W. B. Yeats (1888) and James MacDougall (1910). The solitary fairy may elect to wear red, brown, or grey instead of the customary green. He or she avoids large gatherings and prefers to be left by himself or herself, disdaining the unbridled gaiety of social or trooping fairies. The solitary fairy is often associated with a specific household, place, or occupation, notably the shoemaking *leprechaun of Ireland. According to many stories the solitary fairy appears ominous to mortals and is easily irritated. None the less, such a fairy is not indifferent to human kind, and is more likely to interact with lives of men, women, or children. Solitary fairies generously lavish gifts upon mortals, but the consequences of accepting them may be dire. Faithful but suspicious Christians have accused solitary fairies of being in league with the *devil, a perception not widely shared; such fairies, however, may be on close terms with death. Among those fairies classed as solitary are the *banshee, *baobhan sith, *brownie, *bwci, *cadineag, *caoineag, *caointeag, *cluricaune, *dooiney marrey, *dooiney oie, *dullahan, *ellyll, *fairy lover [Ir. *leannán sídhe/sí*], *fenodyree, *fr'de/fridean, *glaistig, *gruagach, leprechaun, *piskie, *pooka, *pwca, *síabraid, *s'thich.

In defining the two divisions W. B. Yeats (1888) introduced the term 'trooping fairies' for those perceived to be in groups; they may also be known as social fairies, the sociable fairies, the fairy nation, or the fairy race. Although they may be friendly or sinister to humans, they are described as dancing and singing while in each other's company. Mortals may eavesdrop upon this celebration by entering a fairy mound [Ir. *sídh/sí*] or may find the evidence from *fairy rings, e.g. circular tracks left in grass or flower beds. Trooping fairies prefer green to other colours and may range more widely in size than the solitary; some may be so tiny as to have caps the size of heather bells while others may be large enough to have intercourse with humans. Although they may have higher spirits than the solitary fairies, they still may present a threat to mortals; especially to be feared is the fearsome Scottish Gaelic *sluagh, the host of unforgiving dead.

Fairyland, always perceived to embrace an enormous host, is always a monarchy, with queens, ruling without consort, appearing more often than mateless kings. Among the queens are *Aíbell, *Áine (1), *Clídna, and Grian; Queen *Medb of the **Táin Bó Cuailnge* [Cattle Raid of Cooley] becomes a fairy queen in oral tradition. Leading kings include *Cuilenn and *Gwyn ap Nudd; *Midir, a character from Old Irish literature, becomes a fairy king in oral tradition. Some fairy monarchs are married couples, such as King *Finnbheara and Queen *Úna, *Iubdán and *Bebo. In many respects the realm of the fairy seems heavenly or elysian. Time appears not to exist in fairyland, and neither is there any ugliness, sickness, age, or death. Mortals taken to fairyland may pass as much as 900 years there, thinking it only one night. Although no one dies in fairyland there appears to be a fairy birth, as there are many stories of fairy infants and children who require mortal mothers to nurse them. Fairy palaces (see Ir. BRUG; SÍDH / SÍ) are thought to be lavishly decorated in gold and silver, where the residents and their guests spend much time consuming immense banquets of the richest, most delicious food. Much time is given to dancing and music. Fairies favour two domestic animals, the *dog and the horse, although fearful dogs and cats are sometimes ascribed fairy powers (see FAIRY CAT; FAIRY DOG). Fairies ride in procession on their white horses, their manes braided and decorated with tinkling silver bells. See also GWLAD Y TYLWYTH TEG; MAG MELL; OTHERWORLD; TÍR NA MBAN; TÍR NA NÓG.

Although it was never the challenge to Christianity that witchcraft was and never accumulated a dogma, liturgy, or priesthood, the fairy faith was once far more than the literary conceit and narrative device it has been in recent times. Individual Christian clergymen offered accommodating rationales for lay adherence to fairy beliefs and practices. One was to suggest that fairies were descended from pre-Adamic beings or that fairies, who lacked human souls, might escort the souls of the faithful departed to the gates of heaven. Occasional clerical condemnation of fairy belief seems to be at the root of the thesis that fairies must pay a yearly tribute of their own children to the lords of hell. To spare their own children, fairies were thought to seek out human infants, especially the unbaptized. When mortal children were snatched for tribute, fairies would leave their own as substitutes; these 'changelings' were thought to bear a slight outward resemblance to the stolen child but were paler, more sickly, and more irritable. In the nineteenth century roads in Ireland were rerouted to avoid disturbing fairy mounds. Belief in fairies was still widespread in the early twentieth century, according to the testimony of W. Y. Evans-Wentz in *The Fairy Faith in the Celtic Countries* (London, 1911). An American-born believer in fairies, Evans-Wentz travelled all the Celtic countries on foot and collected material from all social classes, during which respondents spoke of their convictions without condescension or scepticism. In more recent times the fairy faith has fallen sharply, and many residents of all Celtic lands have found inquiries about such beliefs to be insulting. Nevertheless, as late as 1990 a privately funded Fairy Investigation Society maintained an office in Dublin, dedicated to collecting reports of fairy sightings while promising to protect the anonymity of the contributors.

Learned speculation on the origin of the fairy faith has centred on four theories. 1. Fairies embody a folk memory of a region's original inhabitants. When a new people seized a territory through force of arms or technological superiority, remnants of the conquered and displaced people would linger in caves and remote areas, preying upon their conquerors in the night. The survival in all Celtic countries of prehistoric monuments, apparently built by people of smaller stature, would support this perception. 2. Fairies are composed of the discarded gods and diminished heroes of the old native religion. While this thesis may explain the existence of fairies and fairy-like creatures in other traditions, its applications to Celtic instances requires several qualifications. The full nature of Celtic religion is not known. Characters in the oldest Celtic literature, e.g. *Lug Lámfhada, *Cúchulainn, and the *Tuatha Dé Danann, are now thought to be derived from the older faith, yet they are by no means fairies. When characters from the oldest literature reappear in fairy lore, specifically *Medb and *Midir, they are greatly transformed. In addition, many characters in fairy lore, such as the merrow or the *pooka, have no antecedents in the oldest Celtic literature but have many counterparts in international folklore.

3. Fairies are personifications of primitive spirits of nature. Earlier Celtic peoples, like pre-technological societies studied by modern anthropologists, may have endowed every object with a spiritual nature that was anthropomorphized over the centuries, especially after the arrival of Christianity. 4. Fairies embody the spirits of the dead. This view accommodates well the fearsome aspect of many solitary fairies and also explains the danger to mortals of eating fairy food, i.e. that they would be prevented from returning to the realm of the living. Further reading on these complex issues may be found in Katharine M. Briggs, *The Vanishing People* (London, 1978), 27–38, and in Lewis Spence, *British Fairy Origins* (London, 1946).

The *ash and the *birch were thought to have powers to resist fairy magic in different parts of the Celtic world. The *hazel, on the other hand, was thought so favoured by the fairies that it was not often burned; trooping fairies are described as dancing around or camping under the hawthorn. See ALP-LUACHRA, the joint-eater; BOCTOGAÍ; BUGELNOZ; BUGGANE; CNÚ DEIREÓIL, the fairy musician; CORANIAID, demonic dwarfs; ELF; ELLYLL, Welsh elves; ENFANT-OISEAU, sacrificial child-bird; FETCH, the doppelganger; FFERYLLT, alchemist or magician; GANCONER, the love-talker; GILLE DUBH; GÍRLE GUAIRLE; SPRIGGAN. See also Katharine M. Briggs, *An Encyclopedia of Fairies* (London and New York, 1976); *The Vanishing People: A Study of Traditional Fairy Beliefs* (London, 1978); Reidar Th. Christiansen, 'Some Notes on the Fairies and the Fairy Faith', *Béaloideas*, 39–41 (1971–3), 95–111, repr. in *Hereditas: Essays and Studies Presented to Professor Séamus Ó Duilearga*, ed. B. O. Almqvist (Dublin, 1975); Seán Ó hEochaidh, *Fairy Legends from Donegal*, trans. Maire MacNeill, ed. Séamas Ó Catháin (Dublin, 1977); Lucy Allen Paton, *Studies in the Fairy Mythology of Arthurian Romance* (Cambridge, Mass., 1903; repr. New York, 1960); Carolyn White, *A History of Irish Fairies* (Cork, 1976); William Butler Yeats (ed.), *Fairy and Folk Tales of the Irish Peasantry* (London, 1888); (ed.), *Irish Fairy Tales* (London, 1892); Yeats's 1888 and 1892 volumes were condensed in *Irish Fairy and Folk Tales* (New York, *c.*1935) and bound together as *Fairy and Folk Tales of Ireland* (Gerrards Cross, 1973). James Stephens's widely read *Irish Fairy Tales* (London and New York, 1920) is a highly individualized literary adaptation of traditional stories.

fairy blast. See FAIRY WIND.

fairy cat. See CAT S`TH; CATH PULAC; LUCHTIGERN; see also CAT.

fairy cow, cattle. See CW^N ANNWFN; CRODH MARA; GLAS GHAIBHLEANN; GWARTHEG Y LLYN;

the TYLWYTH TEG, Y owned the Speckled Cow of Hiraethog. See also COW.

fairy dart. Phrase used in Ireland to describe flint arrowheads found near *raths, ring-forts constructed in prehistoric times; the Irish original for the phrase, gáe sídhe, ga sí (reformed), is rarely used. 'Fairy dart' is also the colloquial name for the unexplained swelling of joints, hands, and feet thought to have been caused by malevolent fairies throwing the darts at humans.

fairy dog. Irish folklore depicts a large, unnamed fairy dog, with white rings around its neck, roaming near Galway. See BRAN and SCEOLANG; CÙ S`TH; CW^N ANNWFN; FARBHANN; GWYLLGI; MAUTHE DOOG; MODDEY DHOO; the unnamed black dog haunting *Sliab Mis [Slieve Mish] in *Kerry; the unnamed but menacing black dogs haunting the quagmire of *Youdic in *Brittany. See also DOG.

fairy grass. See FÉAR GORTACH.

fairy herbs. See DANDELION; EYEBRIGHT; FOXGLOVE; YARROW; others are ivy, plantain, polypody of oak, vervain.

fairy king. See FAIRY.

fairy land. See FAIRY.

fairy lover, mistress. The concept is commonly indicated in English by an anglicization of the ModIr. phrase leannán sídhe/sí [fairy lover], e.g. leannan shee, lannan shee, lannanshee, leanan sidhe, leanhaun shee, lianhan shee; OIr. lennán síde; Manx lhiannan shee. This most dramatic and poetic of all fairy stories concerns the doomed love between a mortal (usually male) and an immortal (usually female). The many Celtic instances of the story follow a fixed pattern found in international folklore. 1. The mortal loves the supernatural being. 2. The supernatural being consents to marry or to make love to the mortal subject to a certain condition, such as his not seeing her at specified time. 3. He breaks the taboo and loses her. 4. He then tries to recover her and sometimes succeeds, usually with great difficulty. In one familiar variation on the pattern, the fairy lover entices or seduces the mortal and pines for him when they are separated; i.e. she loves him deeply (though he may not have merited it) and is parted from him only by the conventions of her status. A second variation depicts a woman of dreadful power who seeks both the love of and dominion over mortal men. Male fairy lovers also exist in stories, characteristically well mannered and talkative but imperious.

Lady Wilde (1887) said that the 'leanan-sidhe' was the spirit of life, and inspirer of the singer and poet, and thus the opposite of the *banshee. W. B. Yeats (1888) thought the 'leanhaun shee' would inspire a poet or singer so intensely that its earthly life would necessarily be brief. The Manx lhiannan-shee is distinguished from her Irish counterpart in two aspects: (1) She haunts wells and springs, like Melusine. (2) She attaches herself to one man, to whom she appears irresistibly beautiful while remaining invisible to everyone else; if he yields to her seduction, she will drain him body and soul, like a vampire. Among the notable fairy lovers are *Créd (1), *Étaín of Inis Grecraige, *Niam, and the unnamed lover of *Connla in **Echtrae Conli* [The Adventure of Connla]; See also SÍN, the lover of *Muirchertach mac Erca. Folk motifs: A465.1.1; F301; F471.2.1. See also Rosalind E. Clark, *Great Queens* (Gerrards Cross, UK; Savage, Md., 1990).

fairy mist [Ir. *ceo sídhe*]. A mist that causes people to go astray.

fairy mistress. See FAIRY LOVER.

fairy music [Ir. *ceol sídhe*]. Music that lures people out of this world.

fairy palace. See BRUIDEN; BRUIG.

Fairy Palace of the Quicken Trees. Occasional translation of **Bruidhean Chaorthainn*.

fairy queen. See FAIRY.

fairy ring. A circle found in a lawn or pasture land thought to have been caused by dancing fairies. Scientific explanations for this widespread phenomenon are less poetic; the must usual is that it is caused by the spreading mycelia of a fungus (*Marasmius oreades*). The fairy ring may appear only as a depression in the grass but may also include sprouting mushrooms. If a human steps into the ring he or she is compelled to join the fairies in their wild dancing, which would seem to occur in a few minutes but in fact lasts for seven years or more. The unfortunate mortal dancer can be rescued by having someone outside the ring grab hold of his or her coat-tails. The concept is widely discussed in Celtic languages, usually by translations of the 'fairy ring': Ir. fáinne sídhe/sí; ScG fàinne s'th; Manx fainey shee; W cylch y tylwyth teg, twmpath chwarae. See also HUNGRY GRASS.

fairy rock, fairies' rocks. A phrase that might be applied to any of dozens of megalithic monuments found throughout the Celtic world, of which the best-known is probably the assembly of *dolmens known as *La Roche aux Fées* near *Essé in *Brittany.

fairy sleep [Ir. *suan sídhe*]. The sleep from which a person cannot awake until the appointed moment.

fairy stroke [Ir. *poc sídhe*]. Abrupt, seemingly inexplicable changes in mental or physical well-being of both humans and animals were once popularly attributed in many nations to the fairy stroke. Most often the fairy stroke denoted a paralytic seizure; the colloquial English usage of 'stroke' for cerebral haemorrhage derives from this once widespread belief. Sometimes it was held that the victim had been carried away and a simulacrum, e.g. an infant or aged fairy or carved figure, substituted. In Ireland the fairy stroke was thought synonymous with the ill omen or ill fate that hung over those born in the time of Pentecost; thus the Hiberno-English kinkisha, kinkesha [Ir. *Cincís, Cingcís, Cingcíse* (gen.), Whitsuntide evil destiny] is usually glossed as 'fairy stroke'. A person capable of directing such malicious power is known as the kinkishin or kinkeshin. Another Irish word that may translate fairy stroke is millteoireacht, (the act of) spoiling, destroying; e.g. Tá millteoireacht éigin air, 'he has been stricken in some mysterious way'. Tommy McArdle's film *The Kinkisha* (*c*.1978) treats of this theme in a modern setting.

fairy tree. Almost all kinds of tree found in the Celtic countries have been thought to have special powers or to serve as the abode of the fairies, especially the magical trio of *oak, *ash, and thorn. Next in rank are the fruit-bearing trees *apple and *hazel, followed by the *alder, *elder, holly, and willow. The esteem given different trees varies in different parts of the Celtic world; on the Isle of *Man, the phrase 'fairy tree' denotes the tramman [*elder]. D. A. MacManus devotes a chapter to Irish fairy trees in *The Middle Kingdom* (London, 1959).

fairy wind, blast. A sudden gust or blast of wind, or whirlwind, was thought in Ireland to have been caused by fairies. Several Irish phrases describe it: sídh/sí gaoithe, sídh/sí chóra, gaoth sídhe/sí, séideán sídhe/sí. The wind was sometimes thought to be caused by the passing of a fairy host; alternately, the wind may contain the host. Pious farm people would cross themselves when they saw the wind coming, as they were daunted to see a column of hay rise at one end of the meadow while the wind at the other end was perfectly still. Sometimes the wind was thought to be evidence that fairies were helping in farm labour. At other times the wind was thought to be the source of sudden illness. The fairy wind will rip the roof off a poor family's house and let the fairy host in, will protect fairy treasure from thieves, will silence mortal musicians playing fairy music, and can cause injury to humans or animals, especially the eyes.

fáith. Old and Middle Irish word for seer or prophet, describing both male and female examples; the powerful *Scáthach who taught *Cúchulainn is conventionally described as a ban-fháith [woman fáith]. Probably the Irish cognate of what *classical commentators represented in the word *vates. See also W GWELEDYDD; GWAWD; ModIr. fáidh.

Fál. Name cited in the *Dindshenchas for a ceremonial stone found at *Tara from pre-Christian through medieval times. Although it is known in Irish as Lia Fáil, literally 'Stone of Fál' or, idiomatically, 'Stone of Destiny', that term may also denote several other stones. Rival traditions claim that (*a*) the *Tuatha Dé Danann or (*b*) the *Milesians brought Fál to Ireland. Narrow and as tall as a full-grown man, Fál was conventionally described as a 'stone penis'. According to widely repeated tradition, Fál would roar or cry out under the feet of a legitimate king, or a man who aspired to kingship, who stepped upon it. A silent stone implied censure of the king who approached it. For this reason Fál became a learned and poetic synonym for Ireland and survives in several compounds, e.g. Inis Fáil [island of Fál]. The implicit sexual symbolism of Fál as a penis and Ireland as a woman has been the subject of widespread allusion, much of it covert. In 19th-century Irish oral tradition the stone was known as *Bod Fhearghais* [penis of Fergus], although which Fergus was not made clear; see FERGUS MAC RÓICH.

The absolute identity of the Fál of early Irish literature with the stone found today at Tara, called either Fál or Lia Fáil, is a matter of some argument; see LIA FÁIL.

Fálga. Mysterious small island to the east of Ireland whose grey inhabitants, Fir Fálgae, clad only in their shaggy hair, often threaten Irish heroes. One prominent king was Iuchna. Commentators as early as Rudolf Thurneysen (1921) have identified Fálga with the Isle of *Man.

Falias, Failias. One of the four cities of the *Tuatha Dé Danann, along with *Gorias, *Findias, and *Murias, whence they came to Ireland. Morfessa was the instructor of learning here. In their departure the Tuatha Dé Danann took the magical stone *Fál with them.

Falinis. Variant spelling for *Failinis (1).

Faltlaba. A warrior in the *Fianna of *Fionn mac Cumhaill, conventionally described as a superior tracker of prey.

Fanahan. Occasional anglicization of *Finnchú.

Fand, Fann [OIr. *fand*, tear; *fann*, weak, helpless person]. A renowned otherwordly beauty in early Irish literature, usually seen as the wife of *Manannán mac Lir and as the lover of *Cúchulainn in *_Serglige Con Culainn_ [The Wasting Sickness of Cúchulainn]. The hero first sees her in a vision, where she and her sister *Lí Ban whip him, bringing about his illness. Later, in waking consciousness, Lí Ban seeks Cúchulainn's friendship and tells him of her sister's love for him. After Cúchulainn's victory in battle on behalf of Lí Ban's husband *Labraid, the hero and Fand carry on a month-long affair. Later, when their tryst is interrupted by Cúchulainn's wife *Emer, both women ask to be rejected, thinking the other's love superior. Fand returns to her husband, whose cloak causes her to forget Cúchulainn and he her. Her father is *Áed Abrat and her brother *Angus (1); her mother is sometimes given as *Flidais, the woodland deity. In variant texts she is described as the wife of *Eochaid Iúil, one of Labraid's enemies vanquished by Cúchulainn.
The spellings 'Fand' and 'Fann' are not merely variants of one another, but are two discrete words of similar sound. The fuller etymology of the name remains contentious; see Christian J. Guyonvarc'h, 'Irlandais *Fand*, nom propre . . . ', *Ogam*, 11 (1959), 440. See also William Larminie, *Fand and Other Poems* (Dublin, 1892); Sir Arnold Bax [pseud. of Edward Trevor], *The Garden of Fand*, orchestral overture (1916, 1921). Fand may have contributed some characteristics to the Arthurian heroine Laudine.

Faolán. Variant spelling of *Fáelán.

far darrig, fear darrig, fir darrig, fir dhearga [Ir. *fear dearg*, red man]. Solitary *fairy from Hiberno-English oral tradition, known for mischievousness. This short, pugnacious, ugly red-clad figure specializes in practical jokes, some of which can be gruesome. He also has the ability to appear larger than he is and to release mortals trapped in fairyland. In *Donegal, where a mortal man was punished with macabre experiences for not producing a succession of stories, the far darrig is tall. In *Munster, according to T. Crofton Croker (1832), he is about 2.5 feet tall, wears a sugar-loaf cap, a wrinkled face, and has long grey hair.
Folk motifs: F233.3; F369.4; F375.

far dorocha, fear dorocha [Ir. *fear dorcha*, dark man]. A malevolent *fairy, the chief agent of mortal abduction. Usually portrayed as the butler-like servant of the fairy queen, he carries out her commands without emotion or waste of energy. With equal aplomb he may serve the queen her tea or retrieve on his black charger a desired mortal. Silently obedient to his queen, he is able to make all surrender their wills to his command. Although many have journeyed with the far dorocha to fairyland, few have returned with him. See ANGAU; ANKOU; DEATH COACH; DULLAHAN.

far gorta, fear gorta [Ir. *fear gorta*, man of hunger]. A benevolent *fairy from Hiberno-English oral tradition. This pale, emaciated figure goes through the land in famine time, begging and bringing good luck to the giver. He is so weak and thin he can barely lift his alms cup, and he has few clothes to cover his modesty, even in wintertime. Only the smug and selfish turn away from him in disgust. See HUNGRY GRASS [Ir. *féar gortach*].

far liath, leea, fear liath [Ir. *fear liath*, grey man]. Malevolent *fairy of Hiberno-Irish tradition, a personification of fog. He covers the land and sea with his mantle, darkening roads so that travellers unwittingly stumble over precipices to their deaths and obscuring rocks so that ships crash upon them.

farbhann, farvann [cf. ScG *farbhonn*, inner sole of a shoe; *farbheann*, mountain with cliffs]. Name given to a *fairy dog cited in Hebridean oral tradition. It was loosed upon a man named Hugh MacLeod of the Isle of Raasay when he stole a treasured cup from the realm of the *fairy.

Farney [ModIr. *fearnmhagh*, plain of alders]. Region in Co. Monaghan, Ireland, roughly coextensive with the old Irish kingdom of *Fernmag. The place-name Farney also appears in combination elsewhere on the Irish map; Farney Bridge and Farney Castle are both in Tipperary.

Farsa, Farsaid, Farsaidh, Farsaideb. See FÉNIUS FARSAID.

Faruach. Prince of the fanciful kingdom of Innia, extrapolated from reports of India. His exotic magic allowed him to build an entire ship with three blows of his axe upon his sling.

Farvann. Anglicization of *Farbhann.

fasting. Ritual fasting or hunger strike [OIr. *troscad*] is a frequently used device in Old Irish narrative, reflecting early Irish custom. According to the *Brehon Laws, ritual fasting is an established means of compelling justice and establishing individual rights. It was an infallible method of opening the fortress gates of a great warrior. Christian saints, according to tradition, fasted at the grave of *Fergus mac Róich before he rose from the dead and recited the **Táin Bó Cuailnge* [Cattle Raid of Cooley] to them. Even persons of lower station might compel redress of grievance by sitting before the door of the accused, refusing food until justice was paid. Not uniquely Celtic, ritual fasting is known as dharnia in Hindu tradition; it has been, however, a recurrent feature in Irish political life in the 19th and 20th centuries.

Fate of the Children of Lir, The. See OIDHEADH CHLAINNE LIR [The Tragic Story of the Children of Lir].

Fate of the Children of Tuireann, The. See OIDHEADH CHLAINNE TUIREANN [The Tragic Story of the Children of Tuireann].

Fate of the Sons of Uisnech. The. Translation of *Longas mac nUislenn* [The Exile of the Sons of Uisnech]; see DEIRDRE.

Fatha [cf. OIr. *fotha*, foundation, origin, source]. A minor member of the *Fianna of *Fionn mac Cumhaill.

Fáthach. See FACHTNA FÁTHACH.

Fathad Canaan. See FOTHAD.

fawn. Like the *deer and the *stag, the fawn exercised great power over the early Celtic imagination. The *Érainn king *Lugaid Laígde pursued a fawn, probably a divine personification of Ireland itself. *Aige and *Sadb were transformed into fawns. *Donn mac Midir used yet another woman transformed into a fawn to lure *Fionn mac Cumhaill and his men. But some fawns are male, like Fionn's son *Oisín, whose name is still the Irish word for fawn. The fawn appears to be an antecedent of the stag in the *Perceval legend. Folk etymology (wrongly) glosses the place-name *Uisnech as 'place of the fawn'. OIr. and ModIr. oisín; ScG laogh féidh, fiadh òg; Manx minjeig; W elain, hydd ifanc; Corn. yorghyk; Bret. menn-karvez.

faylinn. Archaic word, often presumed Celtic but of obscure origin, denoting the realm of the *fairy.

fé. Old Irish word for a rod of *yew or aspen, marked with an *ogham inscription, kept in pre-Christian graveyards to measure corpses and graves. As a reference it expresses woe, calamity, and ill omen. By tradition, no one would touch it except for the person whose job it was to measure.

fé fiada. Variant form of *féth fiada.

Fea. Shadowy Irish war-goddess sometimes seen as the second consort of *Néit instead of *Badb; the other consort is *Nemain. In some accounts she is a consort of *Nuadu.

Feabhal. Modern Irish spelling of *Febal.

Feacra. Anglicization of *Fiachra favoured by W. B. Yeats.

fear dearg. Irish spelling of *far darrig.

Fear Diadh. Variant spelling of *Ferdiad.

fear dorcha. Irish spelling of *far dorocha.

fear gorm. Scottish Gaelic for 'blue man', as in *Blue Men of the Minch.

fear gorta. Irish spelling of *far gorta.

féar gortach. See HUNGRY GRASS.

fear liath. Irish spelling of *far liath.

Fearadhach. Modern Irish spelling of *Feradach.

Feardhomhan. Modern Irish spelling of *Ferdoman.

Fearghal. Modern Irish spelling of *Fergal.

Fearghus. Variant spelling of *Fergus.

feast, feasts. See FESTIVAL; FÉIL; FEIS; FAIR.

Feast of Briccriu, The. Occasional translation of *_Fled Bricrenn_ [Briccriu's Feast].

Feast of Conán's House, The. See FEIS TIGHE CHONÁIN.

Feast of Dún na nGéd. English translation of _Fled Dúin na nGéd_; see DOMNALL (1).

Feast of Tara. See TARA.

Febal, Febhal, Feabhal [cf. W _gwefl_, lip]. Name borne by several minor figures in early Irish literature. The best-known is the father of *Bran mac Febail, the explorer in *_Imram Brain_ [The Voyage of Bran]; several commentators have suggested he may be identical with the eponym of Lough Foyle. Another was the father of Conn, a minor member of *Fionn mac Cumhaill's *Fianna.

Febrat. See CENN ABRAT.

February festival. See IMBOLC.

Féc's Pool, Fec's Pool. See LINN FÉIC.

Feccol Ferchertne [Ir. _ferchertne_, man of precise craft]. Legendary Irish builder and prophet, one of the nine prophets of *Brega. His slaves, sometimes known as the Men of Fex, are reputed to have built the hill of Slane, Co. Meath, as a burial-mound. See also FERCHERTNE.

Féchíne, Féchín, Féchin, Féichin [Ir. _fiach_, raven]. Name borne by several early Irish saints, notably St Féchíne of Fore (d. 665), who founded a community at Fobhar (anglicized, Fore) in Co. Westmeath. By tradition, St Féchíne of Fore had power over the water-horse, *each uisce, compelling one to pull his chariot when his mortal horse had died, later allowing the water-horse to return to its realm. St Féchíne of Fore's feast-day is 20 January.

Feda. A minor *Partholonian in the *_Lebor Gabála_ [Book of Invasions], distinguished only by being the first to die in Ireland.

Fedelm, Feidelm, Feidhelm, Fedelma. Name by many female personages, real and imaginary, in early Ireland, including prophetesses, queens, and saints.

Fedelm 1. The prophetess of *Cruachain in the *_Táin Bó Cuailnge_ [Cattle Raid of Cooley]. Her power of *imbas forosnai allows her to tell *Medb of Connacht that the foray into *Ulster will end in defeat. In the _Táin_ she is seen as an armed but beautiful blonde young woman riding in a chariot, with hair falling below her knees, gold-clasped sandals, and three irises in each eye. Patricia Lysaght (1986) has suggested that Fedelm anticipates the *banshee of later folk tradition.

2. Mother of *Brandub, the king of the *Lagin.

3. Woman of the *sídh in *Munster who gave *Corc mac Luightig, legendary founder of *Cashel, his name. While the child Corc was in her care, Fedelm was at work at her magic when one of her sisters in sorcery called out, 'I bless everything, except what's under the cauldron.' This caused an explosion that singed Corc's ear, giving him his name. Although modern lexicographers gloss corc as 'heart', early Irish writers thought it meant 'red' or 'crimson'.

Fedelm Noíchrothach [Ir., the nine times beautiful]. Identical with Fedelm Noíchride [Ir., fresh-heart]. A *female warrior noted for her great beauty. A daughter of *Conchobar mac Nessa, she abandoned her husband *Cairbre Nia Fer in favour of the great *Ulster hero *Conall Cernach. Her son *Fiachna 1 was killed by *Dubthach. She may have had a tryst with *Cúchulainn in the *_Táin Bó Cuailnge_ [Cattle Raid of Cooley], or he may have slept instead with one of her bondwomen.

Fedilmid. Variant spelling of *Fedlimid.

Fedlech. See EOCHAID FEIDLECH.

Fedlimid, Fedlimmid, Fedelmid, Feidlimid, Feidhlimidh, Felimid, Feidhlim, Fedilmid, Felim. Popular name in early Ireland, borne by mythological and historical figures, kings, saints, and many exalted ancestors in genealogies; usually a male name, it was also borne by some women. The best-known is probably *Fedlimid mac Daill, father of *Deirdre.

Fedlimid 1. King of *Munster who visits the house of Gulide, a bitter lampooner not known for his hospitality. While travelling in west Munster, Fedlimid was told by one of Gulide's daughters that the house was empty of food, the women were pregnant, the cows were barren and devoid of milk, the mice were active, and even the hard benches were rotten. Yet when Fedlimid actually arrived at Gulide's house, he stayed in comfort for three days, dining sumptuously each night. Possibly identical with *Fedlimid mac Crimthainn.

Fedlimid mac Crimthainn. Mid-9th-century bishop-king of *Munster who sought to become the ruler of all of Ireland. Early in his kingship he interfered with the successions at such distant ecclesiastical centres as *Armagh and *Clonmacnoise, the latter of which he sacked. On the secular front he did battle with the powerful *Uí Maine and *Uí Néill families. Before there was a paramount ruler of all of Ireland, he obtained the submission of a king of *Tara, *Niall Caille, and two years later seized Niall's queen, *Gormlaith (2), and her female retainers. Modern commentators have suggested that taking the king of Tara's mortal spouse implies possession of his other spouse, i.e. the *sovereignty of Ireland. Possibly identical with Fedlimid (1).

Fedlimid mac Daill. Father of *Deirdre and chief storyteller of *Conchobar mac Nessa in *Longas mac nUislenn* [The Exile of the Sons of Uisnech]. When Deirdre was born Conchobar's chief druid, *Cathbad, foretold that she would be seen as the fairest of women in Ireland but would bring death and ruin upon *Ulster.

fé-fíada. Variant form of *féth fiada.

Féichín. Modern Irish spelling of *Féchíne.

Feidelm, Feidhelm. Variant spellings of *Fedelm.

Feidhlimidh. Variant spelling of *Fedlimid.

Feidlech. See EOCHAID FEIDLECH.

Feidlimid. Variant spelling of *Fedlimid.

féil, féile [L *viglia, vigilia*, watchfulness; cf. W *gw^yl*, feast, holiday]. Old Irish word for feast-day or festival, especially if religious, rarely secular or pagan. See also FAIR; FESTIVAL; FEIS.

Féil Bhríde. See IMBOLC.

Féine. Modern Irish form of *Féni.

Feinius Farsaidh. Variant form of *Fénius Farsaid.

Féinn. Dative singular form of Fiann (pl. *Fianna) sometimes used in the nominative or as a substitute for Fianna. Although a solecism, it may also be confused with *Fenian Cycle or *Féni.

Féinne Cycle, Feinné Cycle. Bogus variant forms of *Fenian Cycle.

Féinnidh [Ir., Fiann member]. Shadowy second brother of *Fionn mac Cumhaill, cited in only one 14th-century text. The better-known brother is *Fíthel.

Feircheirdne. Modern Irish spelling of *Ferchertne.

feis, feiseanna (pl.)., fes [Ir. *foaid*, to spend the night with, to sleep with]. Although this word had as many as six definitions in early Irish, it usually has but two in English usage. (*a*) A feast or celebration, especially in honour of, or commemorating, the marriage of a king; this would include a symbolic marriage to a sovereignty figure. Important examples were held periodically at *Cruachain, *Emain Macha, and, most prominently, at *Tara. Distinguish from *fair; *féil; *festival. See also BANAIS RÍGHE. (*b*) A competitive musical convention, comparable to the *eisteddfod of Wales; the Feis Cheoil was founded in Dublin in 1897 to promote Irish music.

Feis Charmain. See CARMAN.

Feis Temro, Temhra, Teamhrach, Temrach. See TARA; KINGSHIP.

Feis Tighe Chonáin, Tige Chonáin. Irish title for a 14th- or 15th-century prose narrative of the *Fenian Cycle usually known in English as The Feast of Conán's House, or The Festivities in the House of Conán. While being entertained by *Conán mac Morna, *Fionn mac Cumhaill tells stories about himself, some of which have parallels in Norse traditions. In the most significant of the stories Fionn gives three versions of how he acquired supernatural knowledge by drinking a draft from the *Otherworld. (*a*) In the first, one of the daughters of *Bec mac Buain, the owner of a wisdom-giving well at Carn Feradaig (Cahernarry, Co. Limerick), accidentally spills the water into the mouth of Fionn and those of two of his companions.

(*b*) In a second, perhaps a variant of the first, also set at Carn Feradaig, Fionn and four companions follow an ugly churl [OIr. *aithech*] and a young woman into a magical mist. Once the mist clears, the men find themselves inside the churl's *Otherworldly palace, near which are two wells. Fionn drinks from both, giving him divine wisdom. The motif of the hero following a churl into the Otherworld has close parallels in the stories of *Donn mac Míled in **Acallam na Senórach* [The Colloquy of the Elders] and *Fer Caille in **Togail Bruidne na Derga* [The Destruction of Da Derga's Hostel]. (*c*) In the third version, Fionn finds himself turned into a feeble old man after bathing in a lake at *Sliab Cuilinn [Slieve Gullion, Co. Armagh]. Fionn's men then lay siege to the neighbouring sídh, until the lord, Cuilenn, offered a magical draft in his golden cup. This not only restores Fionn but gives him supernatural wisdom. Another memorable story allows Fionn to speak of the curious incest of *Daolghas. In answer to the question, 'What man was the son of his own daughter?', Fionn explains that as Daolghas was dying, his daughter stooped to kiss him; a spark from the fire flew from Daolghas's mouth to her, making her pregnant.

The supernatural wisdom from a magical liquid has suggested parallels with the Norse figures Sigurd and Odin. The standard text in Irish was edited by Maud Joynt, Mediaeval and Modern Irish Series, vol. 7 (Dublin, 1936). The only translation is the inaccessible and now antiquated one by Nicholas O'Kearney in *Transactions of the Ossianic Society*, 2 (1855). See also Rosemary Power, '"An Óige, an Saol agus an Bás"; *Feis Tighe Chonáin* and "Þórr's [Thor's] Visit to Útgarða-Loki"', *Béaloideas*, 53 (1985), 217–94; E. O. G. Turville-Petre, *Myth and Religion of the North* (London and New York, 1964), 41 ff.

Felim, Felimid. Variant forms of *Fedlimid.

female warriors and champions. Celtic traditions abound in assertive women, historical, mythological, and legendary. Some commentators have argued that the relatively equitable status accorded women in the *Brehon Laws of Ireland allowed for the emergence of strong women. Among the most notable figures are: *Aífe (1), 'the hardest woman in the world'; *Bec of *Connacht; *Boudicca, the historical British warrior, known to legend as Boadicea; *Cathach Chatutchenn, who loved *Cúchulainn; *Coinchenn, the monstrous Irish warrior-woman; *Creidne, champion of *Fionn's *Fianna; *Eis Enchenn, adversary of Cúchulainn; *Erc (3), a member of *Fionn's *Fianna; *Fedelm Noíchrothach, noted for her beauty; *Granuaile (Gháinne Ní Mháille), the 16th-century Irish sea-rover; *Medb, the protagonist of the **Táin Bó Cuailnge* [The Cattle Raid of Cooley]; *Scáthach, tutor of *Cúchulainn; *Luchtigern, the monster cat, was killed by a female warrior. See also LUIDEAG, the murderous Scottish female demon, and SOVEREIGNTY, LADY. See Antonia Fraser, *Boadicea's Chariot* (London, 1988); *The Warrior Queens* (New York, 1988); Miranda J. Green, *Celtic Goddesses, Warriors, Virgins and Mothers* (London, 1995).

Femen, Femuin (gen.), Femin (gen.), Femhen; also Mag Femin. Name used in early texts for a plain extending roughly from *Cashel to Clonmel in what is today Co. Tipperary. Proximity to the mountain known today as Slievenamon [Ir. **Sliab na mBan*, mountain of the women] has often linked the two place-names. Femen abounds in mythological and historical associations. It is the site of Síd ar Femen, home of *Bodb Derg, the son of the *Dagda. *Midir and *Étaín escape to the Sídh ar Femen in **Tochmarc Étaíne* [The Wooing of Étaín]; *Fionn mac Cumhaill is enchanted here. The plain of Femen was thought to control power and wealth in *Munster, which may explain the *Cailleach Bhéirre's interest in it. The historical king *Corc mac Luigthig founded an early dynasty here before establishing the *Eóganacht at Cashel. The plain of Femen includes Lough Béldracon, where *Angus Óg found *Cáer, the tall maiden.

Fena. Occasional anglicization for *Fianna; See also FÉNI.

Féne. Variant form of *Féni.

Féni, Féne. Name for the *Goídels, allegedly the third invaders of early Ireland, in their own language; the Féni followed the *Érainn and the *Lagin. Unlike their predecessors, the Féni are said to have migrated directly to Ireland from the Continent, not by way of Britain. In early Irish usage, the term Féni implies the old, aboriginal, purest population, i.e. free land-tillers, as opposed to servants or slaves; honorifically, Féni implies 'true' Irish. In the *Brehon Laws of early Ireland, the term *fénechas* denoted those laws applying to landed freeholders. Féni is unrelated to the term *fianna, although the neologism *Fenian was derived from a confusion between the two terms.

Fenian. Neologism coined in 1804 by charlatan scholar Col. Charles Vallancey. Although apparently derived from *Féni, a name for early, landed freeholders, Vallancey used it as an anglicization for *fianna. In many 19th-century writers, e.g. Sir Walter Scott, Fenian pertains to stories of *Fionn mac Cumhaill. The ambiguous reference to both fianna and Fionn persists in the naming of the *Fenian Cycle. In 1858 'Fenian' was adopted as an alternate name for the Irish Republican Brotherhood, a secret revolutionary society dedicated to the overthrow of English authority in Ireland. Never fully quashed, Fenian activity in the British Isles and North America peaked in 1866–7. In the 20th century 'Fenian' popularly denotes Republican anti-British activity, especially in the six counties of *Ulster, still a part of the United Kingdom.

Fenian Cycle, Fionn Cycle, Finn Cycle, Fianna Cycle, Finnian Tales, Fian Tales, Féinne Cycle, Feinné Cycle, Ossianic Cycle, Fianaigecht. A large body of verse and prose romances centring on the exploits of the mythic hero *Fionn mac Cumhaill and his warriors, the *Fianna Éireann, a kind of freelance militia, constituting one of four major cycles of early Irish tradition, along with the *Mythological and *Ulster Cycles and the *Cycle of the Kings. The Fenian is the most popular, extensive, and long-lived of the four, appearing first in 8th-century texts, and flourishing in both written and oral traditions in Ireland as well as in the oral traditions of Gaelic Scotland and the Isle of Man.

Although Fionn mac Cumhaill, his family, and followers were once thought to be historical, they are now understood to have their roots in pre-Christian religion. Many other elements in the narratives, however, such as the training of hunters and warriors, the service of armed men under various kings, and the conflict between old ways and the values of the new religion, Christianity, do reflect historical experience. Fenian stories have been recorded from all parts of Ireland and Gaelic Scotland, but internal references imply that episodes occur most often in *Leinster and *Munster. Fionn and his family, the Clan *Baíscne, are most often seen in conflict with the Clan *Morna, identified with *Connacht. From about the 11th century, texts attributed much of the action of the Fenian Cycle to the 3rd-century reign of *Cormac mac Airt and his son *Cairbre Lifechair. Fionn, his son *Oisín, grandson *Oscar, and leading members of the Fianna, such as *Caílte the great runner, and the handsome *Diarmait ua Duibne, are usually portrayed as living away from the centres of power, often at the isolated Hill of *Allen in Co. Kildare. This is because Fenian stories were perpetuated by a separate caste of storytellers from those who told narratives from the Ulster Cycle; this separateness also explains why several episodes and narratives from the Fenian Cycle run parallel with those in the Ulster.

Although enormously popular with Irish and Scottish Gaelic common people over many centuries, the Fenian Cycle has been less esteemed by critics and informed modern readers; Seán Ó Faoláin once called it 'the sow's ear' of Irish literature. Many stories have a breathless, *Boys' Own Paper* sense of adolescent adventure. Some of this quality was borrowed by James *Macpherson in his bogus 'translations', *The Poems of Ossian* (1760–3), concatenated texts of Scottish Fenian ballads passed off as a lost epic. Gerard Murphy (1953) points out, however, that Fenian stories from oral tradition are more exaggerated and cruder than those from the more restrained manuscript tradition. In their fullness, however, Fenian narratives depict a wide range of tone and emotion. Especially popular were stories of the *bruiden type, in which the heroes are magically entrapped in an enchanted castle or cave and cannot escape. Many Fenian stories describe Fionn and his heroes repulsing challengers and invaders, some of whom hail from distant lands, 'Spain', 'Greece', etc., and some who may be identified with various Scandinavians. This attributed service in the defence of Ireland explains the 19th- and 20th-century association of the word 'Fenian' with Irish nationalism. As early as the 12th-century **Acallam na Senórach* [Colloquy of the Elders], Oisín is portrayed as having survived the death of Fionn by several centuries, and now contends with St *Patrick about the values of pre-Christian society, stressing bravery, generosity, and freedom of the older order. The tone is both polemical and elegiac. In such narratives, the action of earlier generations is retold from Oisín's point of view, causing the entire Cycle to be called 'Ossianic', employing Macpherson's rendering of the name.

Important personages frequently mentioned in the Fenian Cycle, along with Fionn, his son Oisín, grandson Oscar, and his followers, the Fianna Éireann, include: *Ábartach, *Áeda (2), *Aicher, *Áine (2), *Baillgel, *Barrán, *Bébinn (2), *Cairbre Lifechair, *Cethern, *Cochrann, *Conán mac Lia, *Conán mac Morna, *Conarán, *Cormac mac Airt, *Crimthann, *Crónánach, *Cuilenn, *Cúldub, Cumhall mac Trénmóir, *Dáire (4), *Dáire Derg, *Dáire Donn, *Diarmait ua Duibne, *Doirend, *Eithne (1), *Erc (3), *Étaín (3), *Iuchra (2), *Liath Luachra, *Mongfhind (2) (Mong Bán), *Muirenn Munchaem, *Nuadu Airgetlám, *Nuadu Necht, *Tadg mac Nuadat, and *Uirne.

See also ACALLAM NA SENÓRACH [The Colloquy of the Elders]; BRUIDHEAN CHAORTHAINN [The House of the Quicken Trees]; BRUIDHEAN BHEAG NA HALMHAINE [The Little Brawl of the Hill of Allen]; CATH FIONNTRÁGHA [The Battle of Ventry]; CATH GABHRA [The Battle of Gabhair/Gowra]; DUANAIRE FINN [The Poem-Book of Fionn]; EACHTRA AN AMADÁIN MHÓIR [The Adventure of the Great Fool]; EACHTRA BHODAIGH AN CHÓTA LACHTNA [The Adventure of the Churl in the Grey Coat]; FEIS TIGHE CHONÁIN [The Feast at Conán's House]; FOTHA CATHA CHNUCHA [The Cause of the Battle of Cnucha]; MACGNÍMARTHA FINN [The Boyhood Deeds of Fionn]; TÓRAIGHEACHT DHIARMADA AGUS GHRÁINNE [The Pursuit of Diarmait and Gráinne]; TÓRAIGHEACHT AN GHIOLLA DHEACAIR [The Pursuit of the Hard Gilly/Difficult Servant].

Collections: John Campbell (ed.), *Leabhar na Féinne: Heroic Gaelic Ballads* (London, 1872); James MacDougall (ed.), *The Fians*, etc., *Waifs and Strays in Celtic Tradition*, iv (London, 1891); Kuno Meyer (ed.), *Fianaigecht* (Dublin, 1910); *Duanaire Finn: The Book of the Lays of Finn*, i, ed. Eóin MacNeill (London, 1908); ii, ed. Gerard Murphy (London, 1933); iii, ed. Gerard Murphy (Dublin, 1953); Neil Ross (ed.), *Heroic Poetry from the Book of the Dean of Lismore* (Edinburgh, 1939).

Studies: Bo Almqvist, Séamas Ó Catháin, and Pádraig Ó Héalaí (eds.), *Fiannaíocht: Essays on the Fenian Tradition of Ireland and Scotland* (Dublin, 1987); James MacKillop, *Fionn mac Cumhaill: Celtic Myth in English Literature* (Syracuse, NY, 1986); Gerard Murphy, 'Introduction', *Duanaire Finn III* (Dublin, 1953), pp. x–cxxii; Joseph Falaky Nagy, *The Wisdom of the Outlaw* (Berkeley, Calif., 1985); Cormac Ó Cadhlaigh, *An Fhinnuidheacht* (Dublin, 1938); Dáithí Ó hÓgáin, *Fionn Mac Cumhaill* (Dublin, 1988).

Fenians. See FIANNA.

Fénius Farsaid, Fenius Farsa, Feinius Farsaidh, Finius Farsaidib [Ir., Fénius the Pharisee]. Sometimes: Fénius the Ancient. Fabled linguist and ancestor of the *Milesians and thus of the Irish people. According to the **Lebor Gabála* [Book of Invasions], Fénius was a king of the *Scythians, contemporary with Moses; present at the Tower of Babel during the biblical separation of languages, he alone retained them all. His son *Niúl went to Egypt and married the Pharaoh's *Scota (2), producing the son *Goídel Glas, who fashioned the Irish language out of the seventy-two tongues then in existence, following Fénius' instructions. Fénius appears to be created from *Féni, a name for Ireland's earliest inhabitants.

fenodyree, fenoderee, finoderee, fynnoderee, phenodree, phynnodderee, phynodderree [Manx, hairy stockings (?)]. A short, dark, uncouth, supernatural creature of the Isle of *Man, one of the best-known members of the Manx *ferrishyn or *fairies; he is usually portrayed as naked but covered with body hair. Although customarily seen as an individual rather than a class, e.g. 'the fenodyree', his name is not usually capitalized. Comparable to the *brownie of Scotland, he is helpful and can perform tasks requiring enormous strength and endurance, like carrying a huge block of marble a long distance or harvesting an entire field of crops. In recognition of this second task he is sometimes called yn foldyr gastey [the nimble mower]. The creature was once thought handsome and known as uddereek, but was transformed into an ugly and solitary figure for courting a mortal girl from Glen Aldyn. Some commentators describe the fenodyree as satyr-like, more for his hairy legs than his sexual aggression. The *glashtin, known only in the southern Isle of Man, appears to be identical with the fenodyree. See Sir John Rhy^s, 'The Fenodyree and His Friends', *Celtic Folklore* (Oxford, 1891), 323–53.

Fer [OIr., man; husband]. The separable prefix Fer appears in the names of numerous figures from early Irish tradition, often as a kind of title, e.g. Fer Í [man of yew]; they are alphabetized here word by word. See also FIR [men].

Fer Caille [Ir., man of the wood]. A forbidding churl or herdsman [Ir. *bachlach*] of **Togail Bruidne Da Derga* [The Destruction of Da Derga's Hostel] who greets and entices *Conaire on his way to the hostel. Fer Caille is a dark figure with *one eye, one hand, and one foot, and he carries a black pig on his back; cf. the FOMORIANS and the ScG D`REACH and FACHAN. He is followed by a hideous woman. Several commentators have suggested he is a double for Da Derga. T. F. O'Rahilly (1946) sees a parallel between this episode and those of *Fionn in **Feis Tighe Chonáin* [The Feast at Conán's House] and *Donn mac Míled in **Acallam na Senórach* [Colloquy of the Elders]. R. S. Loomis (1927) once suggested Fer Caille was the model for several threatening dark herdsmen in Arthuriana, a line of influence given less credence today.

Fer Cherdne. Variant spelling of *Ferchertne.

Fer Diad. Variant spelling of *Ferdiad.

Fer Doirich [Ir., dark man (?)]. The dark *druid who transformed *Sadb into a *fawn because she refused his love. After meeting *Fionn mac Cumhaill, Sadb resumed human form; but when Fionn was away, Fer Doirich reappeared and changed her into a fawn a second time.

Fer Ferdiad. Variant of *Fer Fidail.

Fer Fí. Variant spelling of *Fer Í.

Fer Fidail, Fer Ferdiad. A *druid with supernatural powers killed by *Manannán mac Lir. Fer Fidail was either the son or grandson of *Eógabal and related to Fer Í. When Manannán became smitten with the beautiful *Tuag, he was frustrated to find she was kept under constant guard by hosts of women. He asked Fer Fidail to enter her chamber, which he did, dressed as a woman. He remained with her for three nights and, after singing a sleep-inducing song over her, left her slumbering on the shore of *Inber Glas (the mouth of the Bann River) while he looked for a boat. Suddenly a wave came to drown her, a wave identified in some versions as Manannán himself. For allowing Tuag to perish, Fer Fidail himself was killed, although the context implies that Manannán's jealousy was the greater cause. See also FER Í.

Fer Gair, Gar. Son of *Donn Désa, brother of *Fer Lé and *Fer Rogain, foster-brother of *Conaire in **Togail Bruidne da Derga* [The Destruction of Da Derga's Hostel].

Fer Hí. Variant spelling of *Fer Í.

Fer Í, Fí, Hí [Ir., man of yew]. Magical harper best known for his progeny. In **Cath Maige Mucrama* [The Battle of Mag Mucrama] he is seen playing in a *yew tree over a waterfall; he has the power to play so sadly as to make everyone weep, so merrily that everyone will laugh, and such a lullaby as to make everyone sleep. Whether he is the son or brother of *Eógabal is disputed in different texts; T. F. O'Rahilly (1946) asserted that Fer Í and Eógabal are identical. Fer Í was the foster-son of *Manannán mac Lir. He was the father of *Áine (1) of Knockainy, Co. Limerick, and her sister and possible double, Grian. See also FER FIDAIL.

Fer Lé. Son of *Donn Désa, brother of *Fer Gair and *Fer Rogain, foster-brother of *Conaire in **Togail Bruidne Da Derga* [The Destruction of Da Derga's Hostel].

fer léiginn [Ir., man of reading]. Twelfth-century Irish term that began to replace the earlier Latin scriba; an idiomatic English translation is 'master of studies'. In 1162 no one could be a fer léiginn in an Irish monastic church unless he were a graduate of *Armagh. Also used in Gaelic Scotland, e.g. the *Book of Deer*.

Fer Lí. Grandson of *Goll mac Morna, who vainly sought to avenge the latter's death. Fer Lí only wounded *Fionn mac Cumhaill but was killed himself.

Fer Rogain. Son of *Donn Désa, brother of *Fer Gair and *Fer Lé, foster-brother of *Conaire, in **Togail Bruidne Da Derga* [The Destruction of Da Derga's Hostel]. He speaks to *Ingcél, who foresees the slaughter. Fer Rogain interprets the vision without quite understanding it.

Feradach Fechtnach, Feradhach Finn Fechtnach, Fereadach Find Fechtnach, Fearadhach Fionn Feachtnach [Ir. *Finn Fechtnach*, fair fortunate]. Best-known of the several Irish figures of this name, shadowy early king of Ireland, celebrated for his military prowess and described as bearing two *bull horns on his head. The name Feradach Finn may be another name for *Morann, with whose story his own is confused. An attempt was made to murder the unborn Feradach, but his mother escaped to *Alba [Scotland], from which Feradach was invited to return from exile by Morann. Feradach's two sons divided the country between them upon their father's death. One son received her wealth, and her treasure, her cattle and her fortresses; the other received her cliffs and her estuaries, her mast (animal feed) and her 'sea fruit', her salmon, her hunting, and her venery. One son was *Fiachu Findfholaid, the father of *Tuathal Techtmar. See also FURBAIDE FERBEND.

Feramore, Feramorc. Anglicizations of *Fir Morca.

Ferann [Ir., land, domain, territory]. A son of *Partholón in the **Lebor Gabála* [Book of Invasions].

Ferchertne, Ferceirtne, Ferche(i)rtne, Fercherdne, Fercertniu, Feircheirdne, Fer Cherdne [Ir., man of precise crafts]. A personification of a descriptive idiom; the name may thus denote any number of admired personages in early Ireland, especially poets, the most cited (but not earliest) of whom is the bard of *Cú Roí. See also FECCOL FERCHERTNE.

Ferchertne 1. *Bard and faithful companion of the legendary *Leinster king *Labraid Loingsech. Allusions to him are found in other texts, including a 7th-century life of St *Patrick. To him are attributed verses on the destruction of *Dind Ríg, which are included in the narrative **Orgain Denna Ríg* [The Destruction of Dind Ríg], in which he is a character. He and harper *Craiphtine accompany *Labraid Loingsech into exile.

2. A son of Cairbre and chief poet and entertainer of *Conchobar mac Nessa.

3. Loyal *bard of *Cú Roí. When he learned that his master's wife, *Bláithíne, had treacherously brought about his death through her lover *Cúchulainn, Ferchertne clasped her in a deadly embrace and jumped off a precipice on the *Beare peninsula with her in his arms.

Ferches, Ferchess. A murderous figure, perhaps in many incarnations. One Ferches kills *Eógabal, the foster-son of *Manannán mac Lir. Perhaps the same Ferches kills Mac Con, the friend and retainer of *Fionn mac Cumhaill, who slays him in revenge.

Fercos. Variant spelling of *Fergos.

Ferdéadh. Variant spelling of *Ferdiad.

Ferdia 1. Variant spelling of *Ferdiad.

2. Servant of *Fionn mac Cumhaill whose murder at the hands of *Cairbre Lifechair provokes the climactic **Cath Gabhra* [Battle of Gabhair/Gowra].

Ferdiad, Fer Diad, Ferdia, Fear Diadh, Ferdiád, Ferdéadh [cf. *fer diad*, man of smoke]. Sometimes bears the epithet Conganchness [of skin like horn]. Friend and sworn brother of *Cúchulainn, beguiled by *Medb to fight against Cúchulainn in the war for the bull *Donn Cuailnge in **Táin Bó Cuailnge* [Cattle Raid of Cooley]. According to several texts, the two men had been closely bound to one another since they were given military training together by the amazonian *Scáthach on the Isle of *Skye. Even after his beguiling by Medb, who promises him her daughter among other things, Ferdiad is hesitant to fight Cúchulainn until he is driven to anger by the gibes and insults of Láeg, Cúchulainn's charioteer. The reluctant three-day battle between Ferdiad and Cúchulainn is, for many readers, the emotional climax of the *Táin*. Clad in impenetrable hornskins, Ferdiad is almost invulnerable, but Cúchulainn dispatches him with his spear, *Gáe Bolga, the weapon against which no man can stand. The ford in the River Dee where this was thought to have taken place was called *Áth Fhirdia(d) [ford of Ferdia], now Ardee, Co. Louth.

Modern commentators have asserted that the origin of Ferdiad's character pre-dates the composition of the *Táin*, even though he is assigned a father, *Damán, and a heritage. According to T. F. O'Rahilly (1946), Ferdiad's martial skills in defence of *Connacht suggest a link with the *Domnainn of what is now north-west Co. Mayo. In Dáithí Ó hÓgáin's view (1991), the Clann (or Fir) *Dedad may have fancifully been associated with the Dee River and Áth Fhirdia(d) before the *Táin* was composed. Not to be confused with Fer Ferdiad, another name for *Fer Fidail.

Ferdoman, Ferdomun, Feardhomhan, Fergiman, Fergoman. A recurring name in the *Fenian Cycle, in both older manuscript materials and in later oral tradition; may describe one figure whose story has been dispersed and partially lost, or a sequence of figures whose stories have been confused. Ferdoman is usually seen as the son of an important *Leinster family and as a young member of the *Fianna. He is a protector of his younger sister, Finnine or Finngheal (also sometimes Finn), who is mistreated or killed by *Conán mac Lia, sometimes described as her husband. Ferdoman avenges her in a duel in which both he and Conán are killed. According to different texts, Ferdoman also slays a monster, either a lake monster in Co. Offaly or a ferocious pig in Co. Donegal. Several elements, including his combat with the pig, suggest he is an anticipation of *Diarmait ua Duibne. See P. L. Henry, 'An Irish-Icelandic parallel *Ferdomun/ Karlsefni*', *Ériu*, 18 (1958), 158–9; Dáithí Ó hÓgáin, *Fionn Mac Cumhaill* (Dublin, 1988), 255–7.

Fergal, Fearghal [Ir., valorous]. Sometimes with the patronymic mac Máile Dúin, 'son of Máel Dúin'. A king of *Ailech better remembered in death than in life. After Fergal was defeated by a force of *Leinstermen near the Hill of *Allen, his head was severed, the hair washed, and combed, and set upon a pike. Shortly after this *Badb, the battle-goddess in the form of a raven, hovered over Fergal's head and that of the youth *Donn Bó, a youth celebrated for the sweetness of his song who had also been decapitated in battle. At the feasting by the victors that night, the severed head of Donn Bó began to sing the praises of Fergal. See Pádraig Ó Riain, *Cath Almaine* (Dublin, 1978); Nora K. Chadwick, '*Geilt*', *Scottish Gaelic Studies*, 5 (1942), 106–53; Whitley Stokes, 'The Battle of Allen [*Cath Almaine*]', *Revue Celtique*, 24 (1903), 41–70.

Fergiman. Variant spelling of *Ferdoman.

Fergna, Fergne. Name borne by at least a dozen minor figures in early Irish tradition, many of them physicians or leeches. One was a *Nemedian, the fourth physician in Ireland. Another was one of the three sons of *Partholón.

Fergoman. Variant spelling of *Ferdoman.

Fergos, Fercos. Given the patronymic 'son of Roach'. Irish-sounding personality cited without comment in a long list of warriors of *Arthur in **Culhwch ac Olwen*. See also FERGUS MAC RÓICH.

Fergus, Ferghus, Feargus, Fearghus [Ir., man-strength; virility; male outflow; semen (?); cf. L *virogustus*, choice of men]. Name borne by dozens of figures from early Irish history, genealogy, mythology, and legend, as well as in Scottish and Arthurian traditions, including kings, warriors, poets, and saints. The name may once have been a cultic attribute of kingship, implying equine associations, and was especially popular in the king lists of early *Ulster. The most often cited personage is probably *Fergus mac Róich, fabled reciter of the **Táin Bó Cuailnge* [Cattle Raid of Cooley].

Fergus 1. The least promising son of *Eochaid Mugmedón and *Mongfhind; see ECHTRA MAC NECHACH MUIGMEDÓIN [The Adventure of the Sons of Eochaid Mugmedón].

2. Sometimes Sir Fergus, a knight of King *Mark and friend of Sir *Tristram. Born a peasant, he wins Galiene, Lady of Lothian, after being knighted. Title character of a French verse romance by Guillaume le Clerc (*c*.1225).

Fergus Cerrbél. One of the great early kings of the *Uí Néill and father of *Diarmait mac Cerbaill, the last pagan monarch of Ireland.

Fergus Dubdétach [Ir., black-toothed]. Early king of *Tara. He drove out and replaced *Lugaid mac Con, and was himself defeated and replaced by *Cormac mac Airt. Cited in **Cath Fionntrágha* [The Battle of Ventry].

Fergus Fialbrethach [Ir., of the generous judgement]. Father of *Dáire (2) and husband of *Rígru Rosclethan in **Echtrae Airt meic Cuinn* [The Adventure of Art Son of Conn].

Fergus Fínbél, Fionbhéil, Finvel [Ir., wine mouth; fair mouth]. A poet, diplomat, and peacemaker, the best-known of the ten members of *Fionn mac Cumhaill's *Fianna named Fergus. He is sometimes thought to be Fionn's son. A constant companion, Fergus Fínbél was usually seen as Fionn's wisest counsellor and interpreter of dreams, and a favoured carrier of important messages. He was an admired maker of verses, i.e. poet, but not a *bard, and sings the war-ode *Rosg Catha* for *Oscar at the end of **Cath Gabhra* [The Battle of Gabhair/ Gowra]. He was once saved from an enchanted cave by *Goll mac Morna.

Fergus Foga [Ir., of the spear, i.e. lightning]. Shadowy king of early Ireland, sometimes credited with the invention of the spear. According to the *Lebor Gabála [Book of Invasions], he was the last member of the *Ulaid to rule at *Emain Macha, before he was slain by the ferocious Three *Collas. T. F. O'Rahilly (1946) asserted that he was identical with *Fergus mac Róich.

Fergus Lethderg [Ir., red side; half-red]. Ancestor of the British people, according to the **Lebor Gabála* [Book of Invasions], who dominated the island until the coming of the Saxons. Fergus was one of three sons of *Nemed, along with Iarbonél and Starn, who escaped the victorious *Fomorians by sailing to Britain. Earlier he slew a Fomorian chieftain, *Conand, at his tower, Tor Conaind, on the enemy stronghold of Tory Island (off Co. *Donegal). His offspring *Britán Máel gave his name to the British people.

Fergus mac Eirc, Erc, Erca; Fergus Mòr, the Great. Traditional Irish founding father of the early Scottish kingdom of *Dál Riada in what was (until 1974) *Argyllshire in the southern Highlands. As Fergus Mòr he is cited as a distant ancestor in countless Scottish genealogies, as well as that of the reigning British royal family. He asked his brother, *Muirchertach mac Erca, to send the coronation stone, *Lia Fáil, to Scotland so that he might be crowned sitting on it; he later refused to return it to Ireland. By oral tradition, this stone became known as the Stone of Scone, used in many subsequent coronations.

Fergus mac Léti, Léte, Léide, Leide, Leda. Mythical king of early *Ulster, probable double of the better-known *Fergus mac Róich, whose fantastic story, *Echtra Fergusa maic Léite* [The Saga (or Adventure) of Fergus mac Léti] exists in two widely divergent versions, one from the 7th or 8th century, and a burlesque, Rabelaisian one from the 13th. Suffering a disfigurement from fighting a sea-monster, Fergus was disqualified for his throne, even though his subjects revered him. The narrative includes the earliest portrayal of the *leprechaun, quite different from its appearance in modern popular literature.

When *Eochaid Bélbuide is slain by the men of *Conn Cétchathach [of the Hundred Battles], Fergus mac Léti, Eochaid's protector, demands compensation. He accepts a parcel of land and the mother of one of the assassins, Dorn, whom he treats as a menial. Shortly after this he makes a journey by the sea where there are water sprites, each with a small body, lúchorpáin [*leprechaun], who relieve him of his sword and carry his body to the water. Fergus awakes when his foot touches the water, and he seizes the sprites by the neck, demanding three wishes of them: that he be given the power of swimming under water in seas, pools, and lakes. The little men grant him this three-part wish by one of two means, either magical herbs in his ears or by winding a waterproof tunic over his head. But he will not be allowed his new power at Loch Rudraige [Dundrum Bay, Co. Down] in his own country. Despite this prohibition, Fergus tries, some time later, to swim under the waters of Loch Rudraige, where he encounters the fearsome monster *muirdris. At the sight of this creature, which alternately inflates and deflates itself like a bellows, Fergus's mouth is turned to the back of his head and he escapes to the land. Fergus's charioteer sees his transformation and notifies the wise men of the capital, *Emain Macha, who had now to decide the kingship. They esteem Fergus but feel they must follow the requirement that no man with such a blemish can be king. Their solution is to have only sympathetic nobles visit the palace and to banish all mirrors so that even Fergus will not know, solving the dilemma for seven years. But the enslaved noblewoman Dorn feels less compunction. One day when Fergus beats her with a whip because he thinks she is washing his hair too slowly, she taunts him for his deformity, whereupon he cuts her in two. Fergus then returns to Loch Rudraige to deal with the muirdris, roiling the water for two days and turning it red with blood. At the end Fergus emerges victorious with the head of the monster, but soon after drops dead from exhaustion.

The burlesque 13th-century version expands the roles of sprites or leprechauns, introducing their king, *Iubdán, his queen, *Bebo, and their court poet, *Eisirt. Fergus again encounters a sea-monster, now called *sínach, in Loch Rudraige, which turns his mouth to the back of his head, disqualifying him from the kingship. His secret is revealed by his wife, when they quarrel over the use of a bath stone. In a second encounter with the monster, Fergus slays it with his sword caladhcholg (see CALADBOLG), but not before it has torn out his heart.

Fergus mac Léti's identification with Fergus mac Róich comes from their both being kings of Ulster and swimmers, and from their possession of powerful swords. D. A. Binchy has suggested that, despite the fantastic elements in Fergus mac Léti's story and his associations with the leprechaun, elements in his story, especially the disputes over property at the beginning, imply ancient but contentious legal questions. Vivian Mercier in *The Irish Comic Tradition* (Oxford, 1962) gives credence to the long-held assertion that Jonathan Swift was influenced in the depiction of Lilliput in *Gulliver's Travels* (1726) by hearing a reading of the 13th-century version of *Echtra Fergusa maic Léti*. Eighth-century text: D. A. Binchy, 'The Saga of Fergus mac Léti', *Ériu*, 16 (1952), 33–48; thirteenth-century text, Standish H. O'Grady, *Silva Gadelica*, ii (London, 1892), 269–85; repr. in T. P. Cross and C. H. Slover (eds.), *Ancient Irish Tales* (New York, 1936), 471–87. See also D. A. Binchy, 'Echtra Fergusa Maic Léti', in Myles Dillon (ed.), *Irish Sagas* (Cork, 1959, 1968), 40–52. See also AIDED FERGUSA [The Death of Fergus].

Fergus mac Róich, Roich, Roech, Ro-ech, Roigh, Roi, Roth, Rosa Ruaidh, Rossa, MacRoy. One of the greatest of all *Ulster heroes, best known for (*a*) being tutor to *Cúchulainn; (*b*) losing his throne to *Conchobar mac Nessa through the treachery of Ness; (*c*) encouraging *Deirdre and Noíse to return to Ireland; (*d*) going into exile to join Queen *Medb's forces in *Connacht; and (*e*) revealing the story of the **Táin Bó Cuailnge* [Cattle Raid of Cooley] to the poet *Senchán Torpéist. Additionally, Fergus is characterized from his earliest portrayals as having great sexual energy, as implied in his earliest patronymic, Roach, possibly from Ro-ech [i.e. great horse]. He had huge genitalia, requiring seven women to satisfy him. *Fál, the upright stone at *Tara, was known in 19th-century oral tradition as Bod Fhearghais [Ir., Fergus's penis], perhaps implying Fergus mac Róich. His great sword is *Caladbolg.

Most of our perception of Fergus's persona is drawn from his description in the *Táin*, augmented by both earlier and later texts. Fergus is king of Ulster, resident at *Emain Macha, when he falls in love with Ness, the daughter of *Eochaid Sálbuide. She agrees to marry Fergus but only on condition that her son from a previous encounter, Conchobar mac Nessa, be allowed to become king for a year, almost as a trial. Fergus agrees to this, becoming also the foster-father of Conchobar, but Ness contrives with the nobles to prevent Fergus's return. In texts outside the *Táin*, an ambitious young Conchobar drives Fergus from Emain Macha, whence the older man allies himself with Tara, leading an unsuccessful rebellion against his former kingdom.

Fergus encourages the sons of *Uisnech, Noíse, Ardan, and Ainnle, to return with Deirdre from *Scotland, whence they had fled because *Conchobar had desired her, giving his honour as a pledge for their safety. Once the four are back in Ulster, he departs for a three-day banquet, under an obligation to a *geis put upon him. In Fergus's absence Conchobar, who has vouched for the lovers' safety, has the sons of Uisnech murdered and takes Deirdre, at last, for himself. Outraged at this dishonour, Fergus returns and burns Emain Macha to the ground. He and his warriors then depart for *Cruachain, where they join forces with Medb and her husband, *Ailill of Connacht, with whom he serves during most of the action of the *Táin*. He gives information about his former subjects, but is sometimes reluctant to oppose them in battle, once warning them of his arrival and leading his own forces on a detour south to give the Ulstermen time to assemble. None the less, he kills hundreds of Ulstermen with Caladbolg and would have slain Conchobar, if he had not been prevented from doing so by *Cormac Connloinges, Conchobar's son. To vent his rage and disappointment he is said to have struck off the tops of three hills in Co. *Meath.

Several stories outside the *Táin* link Fergus and Medb. In an obscure 7th-century verse Fergus is portrayed as deserting his own people because of his attachment to Medb. They are often seen as lovers, as in the best-known story of Fergus's death. When they are swimming together one day, the nude queen is sitting on his breast with her legs entwined around him. Medb's husband Ailill, understandably jealous, remarks ironically, 'It is delightful to see what the hart and doe are doing in the lake.' Hearing this, *Lugaid (1), a warrior-poet noted for his accuracy, despite his blindness, understands the allusion to hunting. He throws his lance so that it passes through the heart of Fergus and exits through his back. In the 7th-century version, Fergus dies near Larne, Co. Antrim, and thus the town of Carrickfergus is named for him. In the 10th- or 11th-century version, the lake is Finnloch (Lough Carrowmore, Co. Mayo).

This swimming episode links Fergus mac Róich with the lesser-known *Fergus mac Léti. The love-child who resulted from Fergus's union with Medb is *Ciar, whose descendants give their name to the Ciarraige, whence Co. *Kerry.

Although he is not the chief character in it, Fergus is usually thought to have preserved the *Táin*. According to references in different texts, dating from as early as the 12th century, full knowledge of the great cattle raid has passed from human memory when the *bard *Senchán Torpéist instructs his followers to wander until they are able to recover the tale to repeat it to perfection. They find Fergus's grave and call upon his spirit, in a three-day invocation, to reveal the *Táin* to them. He then comes forth from the mound, as mighty as in life, and tells the heroic story. Christian legends describe how Fergus recited the narrative to St *Brendan and to St Ciarán of *Clonmacnoise.

Fergus's most often-cited consort is *Flidais, the *Diana-like woodland deity, who left her former husband for him. Among his children are *Buinne, the faithless retainer; perhaps *Conmac, a love-child with Medb and later the founder of *Connemara; *Fiachra mac Fergusa; and *Illann (1), the defender of the sons of Uisnech. See also the Welsh FERGOS, son of Roch.

Fergus did not play a large role in Irish oral tradition, but he does appear frequently in works from the Irish Renaissance, especially by Katharine Tynan Hinkson, 'The Fate of King Feargus', and W. B. Yeats, 'Who Goes with Fergus', 'The Rose Upon the Rood of Time', *The Celtic Twilight*, etc. This dreamy, poetic, unwarlike Fergus owes little to the warrior of the *Táin* but draws instead from Sir Samuel Ferguson's mid-19th-century 'The Abdication of Fergus MacRoy'.

Fergus Mòr. See FERGUS MAC EIRC.

Fergus the Great. See FERGUS MAC EIRC.

Fernmag [Ir., plain of alders]. Small medieval kingdom in southernmost *Ulster, coextensive with the modern region known as *Farney, Co. Monaghan. At the time of the **Táin Bó Cuailnge* [Cattle Raid of Cooley], it was the realm of *Durthacht and his aggressive son *Eógan mac Durthacht.

ferrish, ferrishyn (pl.). The Manx word for *fairy, rough equivalent of yn sleigh beggey [the little people]. They are described as standing from one to three feet high and are less aristocratic than the fairies of Ireland and Wales, having no monarch. As trooping fairies, they like to hunt with their own red-eared white dogs. They are omniscient and also capable of stealing babies; thus the country people speak of them only in the most favourable terms.

fertility. The power to support vegetation and bring forth the young of living creatures was, in different Celtic traditions, dispersed between sacred objects and different personalities. The *cauldron often implies fertility in different Celtic traditions. Female deities may foster fertility more often than male deities, but either gender may pertain; there is no one fertility-god or goddess. *Rosmerta appears to be a fertility-goddess, and aspects of the representations of *Cernunnos imply fertility functions. The Romano-Gaulish trinity known as *Matres are both fertile mothers and virgins. Other figures associated with fertility include *Áine (1), *Brigit, *Cymidei Cymeinfoll, the *Dagda, and *Dôn. The *Fomorians of Ireland's pseudo-history **Lebor Gabála* [Book of Invasions] have associations both with blight and with fertility.

feryllt. Variant spelling of *fferyllt.

fes. Early Irish spelling of *feis.

festival [MedL *festivalis*]. Four days on the Celtic *calendar were occasions for mainline festivals: *Samain (November), *Imbolc (February), *Beltaine (May), and *Lughnasa (August). See also FAIR; FÉIL; FEIS.

Festivities in the House of Conán Alternate translation of the Irish title **Feis Tighe Chonáin* [The Feast at Conán's House].

fetch [OlE *feccan*]. English name for a kind of *fairy doppelganger known in Scotland and Ireland. If one sees this apparition in early morning, long life is assured; see it at night and the viewer will last only as long as the sod of turf in the fireplace. Michael Traynor, *The English Dialect of Donegal* (Dublin, 1953), notes that the word lacks an Irish translation in Irish contexts.

féth fíada, feth fiadha, fé fíada, faeth fiadha [OIr. *féth*, mist, fog; *fiada*, lord, master, possessor]. A magic mist or veil that usually renders those under it invisible; sometimes those under it may take animal form. Also known as ceó druídecta, ceo draoidheachte [druid's fog]. Féth fiada is usually thought to be a power of *druids and the *Tuatha Dé Danann, given them by *Manannán mac Lir after their defeat by the *Milesians. Eithne (3) had féth fiada but lost it when she partook of forbidden food; see ALTROM TIGE DÁ MEDAR [The Nurture of the Houses of the Two Milk Vessels]. The *Fenian hero *Caílte was wrapped in féth fiada when seeking a physician from *Angus Óg.

The power was thought to have passed to Christian saints, an attribution persisting in Scottish Gaelic oral tradition until recent times. In the celebrated prayer-poem 'The Deer's Cry' or 'St Patrick's Breastplate', attributed to St *Patrick, the saint turns himself and his companion Benén into wild *deer on their way to evangelize *Tara. The enemies who wished to ambush them saw only a deer with a *fawn.

Féthnat. A female musician to the *Tuatha Dé Danann.

Feunn Mac Cüail. A Scottish Gaelic variant of *Fionn mac Cumhaill.

Fex, Men of. See FECCOL FERCHERTNE.

fferyllt, feryllt [W, alchemist, magician; cf. W, *fferyll*, Virgil]. A name often translated as *fairy, although it derives from the Welsh name for the Roman poet Virgil (70–19 BC), often perceived as a magical figure in medieval Europe. *Ceridwen consulted the books of the fferyllt in preparing her *cauldron of inspiration from which *Gwion drank. See Juliette Wood, 'Virgil and Taliesin: The Concept of the Magician in Medieval Folklore', *Folklore*, 94 (1983), 91–104.

Fiacail mac Conchinn. Variant spelling of *Fiacclach mac Conchinn.

Fiacc. Widely known name in early Ireland, probably a diminutive of *Fiachra and *Fiachu, to which it usually refers. St Fiacc of Sletty is commemorated on 12 October.

Fiacclach mac Conchinn, Fiacchlach, Fiacail, Fiacail Fí mac Conchind. Also Fiacail mac Codhna, Fiachu mac Conga. Foster-father of *Fionn mac Cumhaill, as well as his uncle by marriage, he gave the hero a spear which never missed its mark. He advised Fionn in wooing. Certain that he was a faster runner than his foster-son, Fiacclach challenged him to a foot-race and weighted himself down with a handicap of twelve leaden balls. But as their race progressed, Fiacclach began to drop the balls and Fionn picked them up, reversing the handicap. Even with this switch of the burden, both runners finished at the same time. Fiacclach is the father of Moling Lúath, Fionn's foster-brother.

Fiacha. Variant spelling of *Fiachu.

Fiachaid Muillethan. Variant form of *Fiachu Muillethan.

Fiachna, Ficna [Ir., dim. of *fiach*, raven (?)]. Popular man's name in early Ireland, borne by dozens of mythical and legendary heroes, historical kings, and at least one minor saint. See FIACHRA and FIACHU, with which it is sometimes confused. The most often cited is probably *Fiachna mac Báetáin.

Fiachna 1. Son of *Conall Cernach and *Fedelm Noíchrothach, daughter of *Conchobar mac Nessa, who was slain by *Dubthach in *Táin Bó Cuailnge* [Cattle Raid of Cooley].

2. Cited as the son of *Eógan Mór of *Munster in the *Fenian Cycle, where he presents *Fionn mac Cumhaill with a fast black horse.

3. A west *Munster king who lay with his own daughter, *Mugain (4), to produce St *Cuimmíne Fota.

4. The only male child of *Ernmas, mother of Ireland's female eponyms, *Ériu, *Banba, and *Fódla.

5. An attributed son of *Fionn mac Cumhaill and lesser warrior of the *Fianna. During the action of **Bruidhean Chaorthainn* [The Hostel of the Quicken Trees], Fiachna holds off the *King of the World and takes many heads in so doing. His foster-brother is Innsa.

Fiachna Dub, Dubh [Ir., the dark]. Shadow rival of *Fiachna mac Báetáin and father of *Dub Lacha.

Fiachna Finn, Find. Variant name of *Fiachna mac Báetáin.

Fiachna Lurgan. Variant name of Fiachna mac Báetáin.

Fiachna mac Báetáin, Baetáin, Baodáin. Also Fiachna Finn, Find [Ir., the fair] and Fiachna Lurgan. Probably historical (d. 623/626) king of *Dál nAraide in *Ulster, to whom numerous legends have attached. In the best-known of them, he is cuckolded when his wife *Caíntigern sleeps with the sea-god *Manannán mac Lir to produce *Mongán. Different texts present three versions of how this happened: (*a*) Manannán appears in disguise on a battlefield in *Lochlainn offering victory to Fiachna for a night with his wife. Fiachna agrees, partially as Manannán takes Fiachna's form, and he achieves victory in battle. Manannán takes the child three days after birth. (*b*) Manannán bargains with Caíntigern, offering victory to Fiachna if she will lie with him, to which she agrees. Later Manannán informs Fiachna and grants his victory. (*c*) Fiachna is fighting in *Scotland while Manannán visits Caíntigern. Mongán often bears the patronymic mac Fiachna, despite his true paternity.

Stories of Fiachna's conception suggest another troubled paternity. His mother, a member of the rival Dál Fiatach, observes a wolf attacking sheep and wishes she could conceive a son who would give the same treatment to her husband's people. His father, Báetán, dislikes the infant Fiachna, claiming that the child resembles his mother too much, and so she rears him in a distant place. One day the child seizes a piece of meat from his playmates and takes it on a spit to his father's court. Báedán then sets a ferocious hound on the child, but Fiachna responds by putting the spit through the dog's heart. At the same time he grabs a hawk that has swooped after the meat in his other hand. This so startles his mother she can never conceive again.

Fiachna's occasional epithet Finn or Find [the fair] reminds readers of his contest with Fiachna Dub [the dark]. In many battles Fiachna Finn triumphs because his kinsman St *Comgall prays for him. Then Fiachna Dub also asks Comgall's favour. To resolve his dilemma, the saint asks Fiachna if he prefers victory in battle with eternal damnation or defeat in battle with eternal reward. Fiachna Finn chooses the latter and so is defeated and slain.

Historical records, which sometimes use the epithet Fiachna Lurgan, portray a celebrated warrior who did battle with the Saxons on their home ground in England. He may have been *ard rí [high king] for a period. Different records also suggest he was king in both Ireland and *Scotland.

Fiachna mac Dáiri. Linked to the conception of *Donn Cuailnge [the Brown Bull of Cooley] in a strange story. One day while he was fishing in *Cuailnge, Fiachna caught a 'water worm' who spoke, telling him that a great fight would come with the beast of *Connacht. Another water worm, found elsewhere in a river at the same time, advised Queen *Medb of Connacht to marry *Ailill, who did indeed become her husband. Both worms were then swallowed by two different cows, who subsequently gave birth to the famous *bulls, the worm advising Medb anticipating the white bull of Connacht, *Finnbennach, and Fiachna's worm anticipating Donn Cuailnge. See also DÁIRE MAC FIACHNA whose refusal to surrender Donn Cuailnge prompts Medb's aggression against *Ulster in **Táin Bó Cuailnge* [Cattle Raid of Cooley].

Fiachna mac Rétach. *Otherworldly king in **Echtrae Lóegairi* [The Adventure of Lóegaire] who seeks the assistance of a mortal warrior, *Lóegaire mac Crimthann, in retrieving his wife from abductors. When Lóegaire is successful, Fiachna rewards him with the hand of his beautiful daughter, *Dér Gréine.

Fiachra, Fiachrae, Feacra. Name borne by dozens of figures in early Ireland, including mythological and legendary kings and warriors as well as several historical kings and progenitors of important families. The best-known saint of this name is usually cited in a French spelling, St *Fiacre. It is not clear which personage is indicated by the anglicized spelling, Feacra, favoured by W. B. Yeats and others. See also FIACHNA and FIACHU, with which the name is often confused.

Fiachra 1. One of the Children of Lir, twin brother of Conn, in **Oidheadh Chlainne Lir* [The Tragic Story of the Children of Lir].

2. A son of *Eochaid Mugmedón as portrayed in **Echtra Mac nEchach Muigmedóin* [The Adventure of the Sons of Eochaid Mugmedón].

3. A son of *Fionn mac Cumhaill who kills *Domnall (2), the king of the *Déisi.

Fiachra Cáech. Alternate name for *Fiachra mac Fergusa.

Fiachra mac Fergusa. Son of *Fergus mac Róich, also known as Fergus Cáech [Ir., one-eyed]. See also ONE-EYED figures. In the *Deirdre story, *Longas mac nUislenn* [The Exile of the Sons of Uisnech], he tries vainly to save the life of the hero Noíse by throwing his body in front of a spear-thrust; but the spear impales both of them.

Fiachrach Tolgrach. Variant form of *Fiachu Tolgrach.

Fiachu, Fiacha. Pet-form of *Fiachna and Fiachra, with which it is often confused; a name borne by dozens of figures in early Ireland, including mythological and legendary warriors and kings, founders of dynasties, and saints, of whom *Fiachu Muillethan is the most often cited.

Fiachu 1. At his cairn *Delbáeth kindled a fire from which flowed five fiery streams.

Fiachu Araide. Early king of *Dál nAraide and possibly their eponymous founder. In the history of his people he is credited with temporarily driving the great *Cormac mac Airt from *Tara; later, Cormac joined forced with *Fiachu Muillethan and defeated Fiachu Araide.

Fiachu Broad Crown. See FIACHU MUILLETHAN.

Fiachu Fer Mara, Fermara, Fear Mara [Ir., man of the sea]. Fictional early king of Ireland invented by medieval genealogists. Fiachu's father, *Angus Tuirmech, lies with his own daughter while drunk. To conceal the shame of his incest, Angus takes the infant Fiachu, still dressed in royal purple, and puts him to sea in a small boat off the Donegal coast. He is rescued by fishermen who raise him under the name Fer Mara [man of the sea]. Despite or perhaps because of his fabulous origin, Fiachu's name is cited in many genealogies; he was thought to be the father of *Eterscél and thus the grandfather of *Conaire Mór. The incestuous birth and infant voyage is an Irish instance of the international tale type 933, most often associated with the fabricated story of the birth of Pope Gregory. R. S. Loomis (1927) noted that the story has striking parallels with that of the conception of the Arthurian figure Mordred.

Fiachu Findfholaid, Findolaid [Ir., fair property (?); white substance (?)]. Son of *Feradach Fechtnach who, upon his father's death, divided the wealth of Ireland with his brother, and became king of *Tara. The two divisions of wealth were: (*a*) wealth, treasure, cattle, and fortresses; and (*b*) cliffs, estuaries, mast (animal feed) and 'sea fruit', salmon, hunting, and venery. When this story is retold in *Fenian contexts, the *Fianna give Fiachu the sobriquet Finn [fair] and describe him as choosing the rivers, wastes, wilds and woods, and precipices and estuaries. Later, Fiachu is usurped by *Éllim mac Conrach leading vassal tribes from all four provinces of Ireland, *Connacht, *Leinster, *Munster, and *Ulster. Fiachu's son *Tuathal Techtmar avenges this murder by taking portions of all four provinces and creating *Mide (cf. MEATH).

Fiachu Finn. See FIACHU FINDFHOLAID.

Fiachu Flat-Head. See FIACHU MUILLETHAN.

Fiachu mac Conga. Variant form of *Fiacclach mac Conchinn.

Fiachu mac Fir Fhebe, mac Firaba. An *Ulster warrior who fought with *Medb and *Ailill against his own people in the **Táin Bó Cuailnge* [Cattle Raid of Cooley]. He came to the aid of *Cúchulainn when that hero was about to be drowned by the Clan *Cailitin. This Fiachu appears to be identical with the character of the same name in the *Fenian Cycle. He inherited a magical spear from *Cumall, the father of *Fionn mac Cumhaill, which when placed against the forehead filled a man with strength and battle fury. Eventually Fiachu ceded the spear to Fionn.

Fiachu Muillethan, Fiachaidh Muilleathan [Ir., broad crown, flat head]. Legendary ancestor of the *Eóganacht kings of *Munster, thought to be a contemporary of the illustrious *Cormac mac Airt. A widely known story explains the unusual circumstances of his birth and conception. The *druid *Dil Maccu Crecga wished to have grandchildren more celebrated than himself, and so he invited *Eógan (3) of *Munster to lie with his daughter Moncha. Shortly after, Eógan (3) died in battle. When the time for the delivery came, Moncha went with Dil to the River Suir in Tipperary, where the druid-father announced that any child born on this day would become the chief jester of Ireland; if his birth were delayed a day, he would become a most powerful king. Moncha sat on a stone in the river, suffering great pain, but the child's birth was delayed one day. In the delay the baby's head was flattened against the stone, giving rise to his usual sobriquet, Muillethan, 'broad-crowned or flat head'. Moncha perished in the difficult delivery, so that Fiachu lost both parents at birth, a fate he shares with Cormac

mac Airt; yet only Fiachu was known as fer dá líach [the man of two sorrows]. More importantly, Fiachu was the first member of the Eóganacht dynasty, and was cited in many genealogies. Many other stories link the Munster king with Cormac mac Airt. Fiachu Muillethan was first allied with Cormac mac Airt in regaining *Tara from *Fiachu Araide, but later Fiachu Muillethan defeated Cormac when he invaded Munster. This story is told in **Forbais Dromma Damgaire* [The Siege of Knocklong], where Cormac bears the patronymic ua Cuinn. In reward for assistance in defeating Cormac, Fiachu granted *Mug Ruith an extensive tract of land, Mag Féne, in what is now north Co. Cork, extending north from the Nagles mountains to the Ballyhoura hills.

Fiachu Sraibthine [Ir., lightning, sulphurous fire]. Son of *Cairbre Lifechair and early king of *Tara. According to the better-known version of his death, he was killed by his nephews, sons of his brother *Eochu Doimlén, the rapacious Three *Collas, who wished to take over the kingdom of *Airgialla (Oriel).

Fiachu Tolgrach, Fiachrach Tolgraig (gen.). Father of the vindictive *Daui Ladrach.

Fiacre, Saint. Historical (d. 670?) Irish saint, born Fiachra, who lived in exile at Breuil, Brie province, France: a patron of travellers and gardeners. The small hackney coach, the fiacre, derives more from the Hôtel de Fiacre, where one would be hired, than from his patronage; in *Portrait of the Artist as a Young Man* (1914), James Joyce facetiously makes Fiacre the patron saint of cab-drivers. Records indicate that in life Fiacre excluded women from his hermitage and chapel. He was long venerated for his miracles, and his shrine was established at Meaux by Anne of Austria, wife of King Louis XIII (1610–43).

Fial [Ir., modest, honourable, generous]. Name borne by several female personages of early Irish mythology and history.

Fial 1. Local divinity for whom the river Feale in counties Cork, *Kerry, and Limerick is named. Before the Feale enters the *Shannon, its name becomes the Cashen.

2. Elder sister of *Emer and daughter of *Forgall Manach. *Cúchulainn rejected Fial because of her relations with *Cairbre Nia Fer.

3. Wife of *Lugaid mac Ítha, legendary founding ancestor of several Irish families.

Fian, Fían. Singular of *Fianna.

Fian tales. See FENIAN CYCLE.

Fiana. Variant spelling of *Fianna.

Fianaigecht, Fíanaigecht [Ir., fian lore, adventures of the fianna]. Name preferred by some scholars for the *Fenian Cycle. Kuno Meyer used the word as the title for a collection of six previously unedited Fenian texts, Todd Lecture Series, vol. 16 (Dublin, 1910).

Fianchuibhe. Variant form of *Inis Fionnchuire.

Fianna, Fian (sing.), Fiana, Féinn, Fiantaichean (ScG.), Fenians, Fena, Fingallians [pl. of *fian*, warrior band; a band of (six?) warriors on the warpath; cf. L *venatio*, hunting; not related to **finn/fionn*, fair or **Féni*, the early people]. When capitalized, this group of words refers to the band of warriors and hunters led by the mythical hero *Fionn mac Cumhaill; this body may also be known as the Fianna Éireann and, less often, the Leinster Fianna. Not capitalized, the words may denote any bands of roving men whose principal occupations were hunting and war, or troops of professional fighting men under a leader, the rígfhéinnid [fian-king]; the *Brehon Laws indicate that bodies of nonsubject, landless men, who were not foreigners, did exist. They stood apart from the rest of society and were charged to defend the sovereignty of Ireland against external enemies, both natural and supernatural. These enemies may include the Norse, whose depredations in the 8th and 9th centuries deeply affect Irish literature. The fianna's responsibility seems to pre-date the Norse, but does not extend to the 12th-century Normans.

Perceptions about the nature of an early Irish fianna have shifted widely since the beginning of Celtic studies in the mid-19th century. These range from being chivalrous benefactors, i.e. Gaelic equivalents of the Knights of the Round Table or of the samurai, to being parasitic marauders, like the warlords of pre-Maoist China. An antecedent body may be the Gaulish *gaesatae from the Upper Rhone as described by the Greek historian *Polybius (2nd cent. BC). Because they were not a part of the Celtic settlements they defended, Polybius glossed their name as 'mercenaries', but a more likely translation is 'spearmen'; cf. OIr. gáe, 'spear'; ScG gath; W gwayw. Irish chronicles indicate that the first fianna were approximately contemporary with the gaesatae, as when they protected the *ard rí [high king] Fiachach. The influential theories of Georges Dumézil (1898- 1986) perceive a high status for the fianna. Dumézil sought to explicate much of European mythology against a threefold structure of early Indo-European society. In Alwyn and Brinley Rees's cogent application of Dumézil, *Celtic Heritage* (London, 1961), the fianna occupy Function III.

Membership in a fianna was exclusive but not hereditary. Applicants underwent rigorous initiatory ordeals requiring exceptional prowess and dexterity. In one a novice would stand in a waist-deep hole armed only with a shield and a *hazel stick while nine warriors cast their spears at him; to suffer a wound was to fail. In another his hair was braided after which he was pursued through the forest by the other warriors; if overtaken or wounded he failed. He would also be rejected if his weapons quivered in his hands, if his hair was disturbed by hanging branches, or if a dead branch cracked under his foot. He was also expected to make a running leap over a bough the height of his brow, to pass under one as low as his knee, and to be able to pull a thorn from his foot without slowing down. Additionally, he must be a prime poet versed in the twelve books of poesy.

Within the *Fenian Cycle, Fionn mac Cumhaill's men were first known as the Leinster Fianna, part of the Clan *Baíscne. Their rivals were the *Connacht Fianna and the Clan *Morna, led by *Goll mac Morna. After many skirmishes, the rivals joined to form the Fianna Éireann with Fionn as chief; in much of Irish literature Fianna and Fianna Éireann are virtually synonymous. Although centred around the Hill of *Allen in what is now Co. Kildare, the Fianna are described as wandering over all parts of Ireland and Gaelic Scotland. Among the leading members are Fionn's son *Oisín and grandson *Oscar and Fionn's love rival *Diarmait ua Duibne. The great runner Caílte mac Rónáin survives with Oisín until Christian times to tell later generations of the greatness of the Fianna. *Búanann was the 'mother of the Fianna'. *Fergus Fínbél was the most important poet, but it enjoyed several musicians, including *Aicher, *Cnú Deireóil, and *Dáire (4). *Borabu was the horn of the Fianna, and *Dord Fian its war-chant.

A full membership list of the Fianna would fill pages, but some names appear more often than others. At least ten are named Ailill or Crimthann, several are Illann/Iollann, and dozens are named Fáelán. Important women include: *Bébinn (2), the giantess; *Creidne, a *female champion; *Erc (3); and *Étan (3). Notable warriors are: *Ailbe; *Angus mac Airt; *Cáel; *Ciabhán; *Coil Cróda; *Conán mac Lia; *Conán mac Morna, a Falstaffian comic figure; *Conn (2); *Dian (2); *Diorruing, the faithful attendant; *Fáelán mac Finn; *Fáelchu; *Faltlaba; *Fatha; *Febal; *Ferdoman; *Fiachna (5); *Foltor; *Fothad Canainne; *Garaid; *Labraid Lámderg [red hand]; Liagan, another swift runner; *Mac Lughach, Fionn's lazy nephew, *Maine (10). The celebrated judge *Fíthel may have been a member.

Heroic and romantic portrayals of the Fianna began in Anglo-Irish and English literature as early as 1800, giving rise to the neologism *Fenian. Nineteenth-century writers like Sir Samuel Ferguson, Standish James O'Grady, and especially Lady Gregory in her *Gods and Fighting Men* (London, 1904) did much to enhance the chivalric identity of the Fianna. The name appears frequently in modern Irish contexts, such as the nationalist boy scouts founded by Countess Markievicz and Fianna Fáil, one of the Republic of Ireland's principal political parties. See Eoin MacNeill, 'Military Service in Medieval Ireland', *Journal of the Cork Historical and Archaeological Society*, 46 (1941), 6–15; Dáithí Ó hÓgáin, *Fionn mac Cumhaill* (Dublin, 1988). See also CEITHERN [Ir., fighting men].

fiannuigeach. See RÍGFHÉINNID, the leader of the *Fianna.

fiantaichean. Scottish Gaelic form of *Fianna.

Ficna. Anglicization of *Fiachna.

Fidal, Fidail. See FER FIDAIL.

fidchell, fidhcheall, fithchill [Ir., wood(en) wisdom; wood(en) intelligence]. A boardgame of early Ireland, often compared with but apparently distinct from chess. A precise description of play does not survive, but allusions to the game abound. The players sat on opposite sides of a square board. Playing pieces, described as 'smooth, speckled, and peaked', were pegged into positions in rows. The main object of the game seems to have been the capturing of one's opponent's pieces, if not his complete annihilation. Sometimes fidchell was played for mere amusement; sometimes the stakes were much higher, as in **Tochmarc Étaíne* [The Wooing of Étaín]. *Lug Lámfhota was said to have invented the game, and *Cúchulainn was a recognized champion: it is often described as a game of kings and is linked to the province of *Munster. Comparable to *brandub, *búanfach, and the Welsh board-game *gwyddbwyll [W, wood(en) wisdom]. See Eóin MacWhite, 'Early Irish Board Games', *Éigse*, 5 (1945), 25–35.

fideal [cf. ScG *fidealadh*, confused and irregular, intertwining; ScG *fideil*, entwine, twist]. An evil fresh-water creature in Scottish Gaelic folklore: the personification of the entangling bog grasses and water weeds in haunted Loch na Fideil near Gairloch, in the north-west Highlands, in what was (until 1974) Ross and Cromarty. The fideal is a subspecies of *fuath.

Fidelm. Variant spelling of *Fedelm.

fidhcheall. ModIr. spelling of *fidchell.

Figol. A *druid of the *Tuatha Dé Danann who boasts that he has power to resist the enemy *Fomorians; he pledges to rain down fire upon them, reduce their strength by two-thirds, and bind back their urine into their own bodies and that of their horses.

fili, file, filid (pl.), filidh (pl.). Member of a privileged, powerful caste of poets, diviners, and seers in early Ireland. To be distinguished from the lower-status *bard and the *brehon, whose learning dealt more with the law. Of the seven orders of fili, the *ollam is the highest and most often cited. The simple translation of 'poet' is misleading, as much of the writing of the fili in his guise as senchaid [historian] was in prose, including sagas and romances, historical narratives, panegyrics, topography (see DINDSHENCHAS), genealogies, and especially satires, for which he was feared; the ModIr. file, however, may be glossed as 'poet'. Although his calling was hereditary, each fili was attached to the household of a chief; being fili to the head of a clan was the prerogative of a particular family. Trained for at least twelve years in rigorous mental exercise, the fili might use an esoteric language, bérla na filed; his craft was filedecht. Some commentators have compared the status of the fili to the brahmin of India or to the Christian clergy of early modern Europe. See Gerard Murphy, 'Bards and *filidh*', *Éigse*, 2 (1940), 200–7; G. Turville-Petre, 'On the Poetry of the Scalds and the Filid', *Ériu*, 22 (1971), 1–22; Liam Breatnach, *Uraiceacht na Riar: The Poetic Grades in Early Irish Law* (Dublin, 1987).

Fínán, Fíonán. Name borne by as many as eleven early Irish saints, of whom the best-known is the early 7th-century Fínán Cam [squint-eyed], who founded a monastery at Kinnitty [Cenn Eitigh, Co. Offaly]. According to fabulous tradition he was conceived when his mother went swimming after dark and was impregnated by a *salmon. He was also described as introducing wheat to Ireland. To be distinguished from *Finnian and *Finnán.

Finbar. Variant spelling of both *Finnbarr, name borne by many saints and warriors, and *Finnbheara, king of the Connacht fairies.

Finbheara. Variant spelling of *Finnbheara.

Finchoom. Anglicization of *Findchóem.

Finchory, Isle of. Anglicization of *Inis Fionnchuire.

find, find-. Variant spelling for the OIr. finn, finn- [fair, white]. Names may incorporate either find- or finn- as a prefix, while others may employ the ModIr. fionn-.

Find [Ir., fair, white]. Shadowy ancient Irish personification of knowledge and wisdom, a prefiguration of *Fionn mac Cumhaill and possibly of *Fintan mac Bóchra. Although not cited in Old Irish narrative, his name is recorded as buvinda in *Ptolemy's geography (2nd cent. AD) and this can be argued to be an Irish cognate of the Continental Vindos and *Vindonnus, an epithet of *Apollo. Dáithí Ó hÓgain has argued that he contributes motifs of *knowledge and occult wisdom to several later figures whose names begin Find-, Finn-. See also FINN, FINN-. See *Fionn Mac Cumhaill* (Dublin, 1988), 3–26, 323–6.

Find File, Finn Fili [Ir., fair, white; poet, seer]. Mythical early king of *Leinster thought to have resided at *Dún Ailinne, the largest ring-fort in Ireland. Although modern commentators do not describe Find File as historical, poetry is attributed to him and his name is cited in genealogies. Various texts portray him as the brother of *Cairbre Nia Fer, king of *Tara, and son of a Ros Ruadh, giving him the occasional patronymic of mac Rosa or mac Rossa Ruaid. In **Táin Bó Cuailnge* [Cattle Raid of Cooley], *Medb tells her husband *Ailill that she had been wooed by Find File. Some of his characterization apparently derives from the ancient *Find, and he contributes some motifs to *Fionn mac Cumhaill. Despite the similarity of their names (Fionn is Find or Finn in Old Irish) and the names of their residences (the Hill of *Allen is Almu in Old Irish), they retain distinct identities in Irish-language contexts.

Findabair. Variant spelling of *Finnabair.

Findbair. Variant spelling of *Finnabair.

Findbarr. Variant spelling of *Finnbarr.

Findbennach. Variant spelling of *Finnbennach.

Findchóem, Finncháem, Fionnchaomh, Finchoom 1. Mythological Irish queen best remembered for her family relations: the mother of *Conall Cernach, stepmother of *Cúchulainn, daughter of *Cathbad and Ness, sister of *Conchobar mac Nessa and *Deichtine, and wife of Amairgin mac Eit.
2. Wife of the hero *Cian (1).

Findchú, Findchua. Variant spellings of *Finnchú.

Findchuire. See INIS FIONNCHUIRE.

Findéces. Variant spelling of *Finnéces.

Findias, Finias, Findrias. One of the four great mythical cities, along with *Falias, *Gorias, and *Murias, from which the *Tuatha Dé Danann were said to have emigrated.

Findige. Wife of the ferocious king *Eógan mac Durthacht of *Fernmag.

Findrias. Spelling of *Findias favoured by W. B. Yeats.

findruine (OIr.); fiondruine, fionndruine (MidIr.); findrinny, findrina, findriny [OIr. *findbruine*, white bronze (?)]. A precious metal often cited in early Irish manuscripts as having a value lower than gold but higher than bronze, thought to be an amalgam of silver and probably copper and perhaps even some gold. Some commentators suggest it was a counterpart of orichalch, orichalcum, esteemed by the ancient Greeks and Romans. The metal was sufficiently hard to be hammered into thin sheets and fine wires; well-born maidens are described as wearing sandals made of findruine.

Findthigearn. Variant of Fintigearnd, a wife of *Mongán.

Finegas. Anglicization of *Finnéces.

Finegím, Finegeen. Variant spellings of *Fíngein.

fingal. Old Irish word for the wounding or slaying of a relative, conventionally used in the titles of narratives telling of such events, e.g. **Fingal Rónáin* [How Rónán Slew His Son].

Fingal [cf. ScG *fionn gall*, fair foreigner]. Title character of James *Macpherson's six-part prose 'epic' *Fingal* (1762), now considered a part of *The Poems of Ossian*. Clearly based on *Fionn mac Cumhaill, despite Macpherson's denials, Fingal embodies many of the author's somewhat fey heroic ideals. He is the son of the giant *Comhal, and king of Morven, the land of the north-west Caledonians. His wives are Roscrana, mother of *Ossian, and Clatho, mother of Reyno, Fillean, and Bosmin, his only daughter. In *Fingal*, he travels to Ireland to aid *Cuchulain against Swaran, the vicious Scandinavian king of Lochlin, who is invading Ireland. After much struggle, Fingal succeeds in subduing and capturing Swaran. This narrative is continued in Macpherson's *Temora* (1763), also included in *The Poems of Ossian*. Elsewhere in the *Poems*, Fingal is a righter of wrongs and a defender of the oppressed. He dies in a battle near the River *Boyne.

Much as the name Fingal is associated with Macpherson, its use pre-dates the publication of *Ossian* by many centuries. A king named Fingal ruled the Isle of *Man, 1070–7; 'Fingal' was used in Scottish contexts for the character now known as Fionn mac Cumhaill as early as the 14th century. After Macpherson, Scottish commentators commonly substituted 'Fingal' for 'Fionn'. Distinguish from *Finngoll, cited in some of Fionn's pedigrees. See Derick S. Thomson, *The Gaelic Sources of Macpherson's Ossian* (Edinburgh, 1952); James MacKillop, *Fionn mac Cumhaill* (Syracuse, NY, 1986).

Fingal [place]. See FINGALL.

Fingal's Cave. An imposing basaltic cavern on the now uninhabited island of Staffa in the Inner Hebrides, 6 miles N of *Iona. Popular tradition, unsupported by the text of *The Poems of Ossian*, has associated the cave with James *Macpherson's character *Fingal. Felix Mendelssohn brought the cave to European attention by using the name 'Fingal's Cave' as the subtitle of his *Hebrides Overture* (1829). 'Fingal' is a part of more than twenty other place-names in the Scottish Highlands, e.g. Fingal's Grave, near Killin, Perthshire; Fingal's Seat, a mountain at the head of Portree Loch, Isle of *Skye; Fingal's Griddle, ancient remains north-west of Sunart, *Argyllshire, etc.

Fingal Rónáin, *Fionghal Rónáin* [Ir., How Rónán Killed His Son]. Tenth-century Irish narrative from the *Cycle of Kings, also known as *Aided Maíl Fhothartaig* [The Death of Máel Fothartaig Son of Rónán]. Although one of the grimmest stories in early Irish literature, *Fingal Rónáin* is also one of the most poetic and most admired. It does not concern gods, taboos, or enchantments but rather everyday human elements such as love and jealousy. The motif of mistaken sexual rivalry between son and father (folk motif: K2111) has parallels in the biblical story of Potiphar's Wife and the Greek story of Phaedra and Hippolytus. The text is preserved in the **Book of Leinster*.

Rónán, king of *Leinster, was the father of *Máel Fothartaig, one of the most celebrated young men in the province. When the handsome prince entered assemblies, men gathered around him. As he grew he became the darling of young girls and the lover of women. As the father was a lonely widower after the death of Eithne (6), the son exhorted him to marry again, perhaps to a mature woman. Against his son's advice Rónán chose the young daughter of *Eochaid (2), king of *Dún Sobairche [Dunseverick] in the north. When the old man brought home his bride, she immediately fell in love with the son and sent her maidservant to persuade him to visit his stepmother's bed. When Máel Fothartaig refused, the young wife [lit. 'girl-bride'] falsely accused him of trying to force his affections upon her. Rónán was initially doubtful, accusing his wife of lying and cursing her lips. At this moment Máel Fothartaig came in, and while drying his legs by the fire, spoke two lines of verse, which the youthful stepmother was able to match. To Rónán the exchange proved his son's guilt.

Rónán commanded one of his men, *Áedán (2), to cast his spear at the son. The shaft impaled Máel Fothartaig, a second caught his foster-brother *Congal, and a third killed the jester Mac Glas. As Máel Fothartaig was dying he protested his innocence and pledged to tell the truth. The son swore by the 'tryst of death' he was about to keep that he never wanted to lie with the queen, that Rónán was deceived, that Congal died unjustly because three times he had escorted the young queen home to prevent her from making further sexual propositions. Rónán lamented his deeds for three days. To seek vengeance, Congal's brother *Donn (2) went to Dún Sobairche and murdered the queen's family, beheading each one of them; he returned to Rónán's palace and threw the heads in the girl's lap, whereupon she stabbed herself. To finish the bloodshed, the two young sons of Máel Fothartaig killed their grandfather for having caused the death of their father.

David H. Greene, *Fingal Rónáin and Other Stories* (Dublin, 1955); David H. Greene, 'Fingal Rónáin', in *Irish Sagas*, ed. Myles Dillon (Cork, 1968), 162–75; T. P. Cross and C. H. Slover (eds.), 'How Rónán Slew His Son', *Ancient Irish Tales* (New York, 1936), 538–45. For links with other medieval literature, see R. E. Bennett, 'Walter Map's *Sadius and Galo*', *Speculum*, 16 (1941), 51–6. T. C. Murray reworks themes from the story in his drama *Autumn Fire* (1924), and William A. Fahey fictionalizes it, 'The Death of Ronan's Son', *Journal of Irish Literature*, 19 (2) (May 1990), 47–51.

Fingalian, Fingallian. Forms used, especially in Scottish contexts, for *Fenian, and in the *Fenian Cycle. The Fingalians are the *Fianna Éireann.

Fingall, Fingal [Ir. *finn gall*, fair foreigner]. Name once used for the portions of Co. *Dublin north of the *Liffey; gives the title of earl to the Plunkett family. There is also a Lough Fingal, having no *Fenian associations, in south Co. Galway, 4 miles NE of Kinvarra.

Fíngein, Fíngen, Fíngin, Fingen, Fingin, Finegín, Finghean, Finegeen, Fioneen [Ir., wine birth]. Name borne by dozens of figures from early Irish narrative and history, including kings and saints; differences in spelling are haphazard and do not indicate one bearer of the name over another. Equated with the English name Florence as early as the 13th century.

Fíngein. 1. Physician to *Conchobar mac Nessa; when *Cet struck Conchobar with a deadly, limed brain ball from Mesgegra, Fíngein advised the king that he would die if it were removed. Accordingly, the king was sewn up with golden thread and abstained thereafter from horse-riding and vehement passion. Fingein also healed *Cúchulainn at *Sliab Fúait [Slieve Fuad].

Fíngein Fisiocdha. Physician of the *Fir Bolg.

Fíngein mac Áeda, Aodha. Early king of *Munster (d. 619), ancestor of the O'Sullivan family, who, according to later scribes, was once seduced by the territorial goddess *Mór Muman.

Fíngein mac Luchta. A king of *Munster at the time of *Conn Cétchathach [of the Hundred Battles], who was visited each *Samain by a prophetess named Rothniam who told him all the occurrences of that sacred night and everything that would result from them for the next twelve months. Much of this story is told in *Airne Fíngein* [Fíngein's Night Watch], ed. Joseph Vendryes (Dublin, 1953).

Fingel. Mother of the marvellous child Noídiu.

Fingula. Name substituted for *Áeb, foster-daughter of *Bodb Derg and mother of the Children of Lir, in some English language versions of **Oidheadh Chlainne Lir* [The Tragic Story of the Children of Lir]. See also FINNGUALA, a daughter of Áeb and Lir.

Finian. Variant spelling of *Finnian.

Finias. Variant spelling of *Findias.

Finistère [Fr., land's end]. Department of the far west of *Brittany containing the largest population of Breton speakers; known as the diocese of Quimper and Léon in ecclesiastical records and in many folk-tales. Also noted for its prevalence of megalithic monuments, especially *dolmens (or portal-tombs).

Finius Farsaidh. Variant spelling of *Fénius Farsaid.

Finmole. Name used by W. B. Yeats for *Connla (1).

finn, finn- [Ir., fair, bright, white, lustrous, light-hued]. Most common OIr. spelling whose variant is *find, find-. Names may incorporate finn- or find- as a prefix, while others are encountered more often with the ModIr. *fionn, fionn-.

Finn, Finn-. Name borne by countless legendary and historical figures, both male and female. The personage most often implied by the name Finn is the hero of the *Fenian Cycle, Finn mac Cumhaill [ang. Finn MacCool], known in this volume under the ModIr. spelling *Fionn mac Cumhaill. The name Finn also appears to have been an honorific title, often coming in threes. A 16th-century poetic epithet for Ireland was . . . na dtrí bhFinn [Ir., of the three Finns], reflecting different heroic traditions from the midlands, *Leinster and *Munster. The triplet sons of *Eochaid Feidlech were known as the Three Finns of Emain Macha (see FINN EMNA), even though they had individual given names. Such *triplism may also derive from *Find, the early embodiment of knowledge recorded by *Ptolemy (2nd cent. AD).

Finn 1. An occasional variant for Finngheal or Finnine, the younger sister of *Ferdoman.

Finn Eamhna. ModIr. spelling of *Finn Emna.

Finn Éces. Variant spelling of *Finnéces.

Finn Emna, Eamhna [cf. OIr. *emnach*, pertaining to a pair; double]. Triplet sons attributed to *Eochaid Feidlech, also known as Trí Finn Emna [the Three Finns of *Emain Macha]; their given names, Bres, Nár, and Lothar, are usually ignored. Whatever Eochaid's historicity, the three Finns are more likely an echo of ancient *triplism originating in the *Find, a personification of knowledge. When their mother became estranged from Eochaid, she took them to Emain Macha, where she and *Ulster king *Conchobar mac Nessa exhorted them to rebellion against their father. When they began to mount their offensive they sought to enlist the support of their sister *Clothra, then reigning as queen of *Connacht. She not only resisted them but tried to dissuade them with sexual favours. Their war against Eochaid was fierce but unsuccessful, although Lothar knocked his father unconscious by flinging a stone. Ulster heroes pursued and captured them, removing their heads. Eochaid asked that their heads be buried with them but died himself, overcome by sorrow. The incestuous union of Clothra and her three brothers is thought to have produced the legendary king *Lugaid Riab nDerg.

Finn Faídech, Finn Faidheach [Ir., fair lamenting]. Name for the bell of St *Patrick, at whose sound the snakes fled from Ireland.

Finn File. Variant spelling of *Find File.

Finn mac Regamain. An early adversary easily slain by *Fionn mac Cumhaill.

Finn mac Rosa, Rossa Ruaid. Variant forms of *Find File.

Finn McCooil. Manx spelling of *Fionn mac Cumhaill.

Finn MacCool. Common anglicization of *Fionn mac Cumhaill.

Finn Varra, Varra Maa. See FINNBHEARA.

Finnabair, Finnabhair, Finnabher, Findabair, Fionnabhair, Fionnúir [Ir., fair eyebrows]. Beautiful daughter of Queen *Medb and her husband *Ailill mac Máta, sister of Faife. She was in love with the hero *Fráech, who would not pay her dowry. Ailill also feared that an alliance with Fráech would raise the enmity of rival kings. Without telling her daughter, Medb offered Finnabair's favours to many champions in the contest with *Ulster, as recounted in *Táin Bó Cuailnge* [Cattle Raid of Cooley]. *Ferdiad accepted the challenge but was killed in combat with *Cúchulainn. Later Fráech took on the invincible Cúchulainn and was killed, causing Finnabair to die of a broken heart. The etymology of the name Finnabair links it with the Welsh *Gwenhwyfar, the Arthurian *Guinevere, and the Anglo-Cornish Jennifer. Sometimes confused with *Lendabair, wife of *Conall Cernach.

Finnachad, Fionnachadh, Sídh Finnachaid [cf. OIr. *finnach*, overgrown with grass or shrub]. *Sídh or magical dwelling of both *Aillén mac Midgna and the sea-god *Lir. Modern commentators identify this with a site near Newtown Hamilton, Co. Armagh. Also known as Sídh Fionna.

Fínnachta, Finnachta, Fionnachta. Late 7th-century (*c.*675–95) *ard rí [high king] of Ireland, to whom many legends have accrued. By historical record he was the last ard rí to remit the *bórama tribute. As he was the nephew rather than the son of a previous ard rí, imaginative lore sought to explain his succession. In one version Fínnachta was originally a poor man whose generosity to a petty king caught in a storm brings him wealth and power. In a second he is also originally a poor man, but one who aids St *Adamnán, after having nearly trampled him on the road. Adamnán's tutor prophesies that Fínnachta will be ard rí and Adamnán his adviser until the king insults the saint. When Fínnachta pays the bórama tribute, he does so at the request of St Moling, which indeed insults Adamnán by denying the supremacy of his sept of the *Uí Néill. At Adamnán's urging, Fínnachta changes his mind and tries to capture Moling, which leads to the king's death from jealous rivals.

Finnán, Fionnán, **Saint.** [Ir., dim of *finn*, bright, fair, etc.]. Early bishop of Moville or Movilla, Co. Down, whose feast-day is 11 February; previously thought distinct from St *Finnian of Moville, feast-day 10 September, but now thought identical with him. Distinguish from *Fínán.

Finnbarr, Fionnbharr, Findbarr, Finbar [Ir., fair-topped, fair-haired]. Name borne by eight saints of early Ireland, most notably the founder and patron of the diocese of Cork, whose feast-day is 25 September; also St Finnbarr of Inis Doimle, 4 July; St Finnbarr, more often *Finnian, of Moville, 10 September. The saints should be distinguished from several minor legendary figures of the same name, e.g. the male of the *Tuatha Dé Danann making the lewd remark to *Eithne in **Altrom Tige Dá Medar* [Nurture of the House of Two Milk-Vessels]; see also BARR, SAINT and the unrelated FINNBHEARA, king of the fairies. See Pádraig Ó Riain, *Beatha Bharra: Saint Finbarr of Cork, The Complete Life* (London, 1994).

Finnbennach, Findbennach, Finnbhennach, Finnbennach Aí, Finnbhenach, Fionn Bheannach, Findbeenach [Ir., white horn]. Queen *Medb's white *bull in **Táin Bó Cuailnge* [Cattle Raid of Cooley], also known as the White Bull of *Connacht and as Whitehorn. According to a foretale to the epic, Finnbennach was originally a man named Rucht, swineherd to Ochall Ochne, who quarrelled with *Friuch, swineherd of *Bodb Derg. Their dispute was so bitter it survived their transformation into different forms: as ravens, water-beasts, *stags, *dragons, champions, water-worms, and finally as bulls. As a water-worm Rucht advised Medb to marry *Ailill; he was then swallowed by a cow and was begat as Finnbennach. But as he thought it unseemly to be born into the herd of a woman, he had himself born into the herd of Ailill. In maturity, Finnbennach's contest with *Donn Cuailnge, the Brown Bull of *Ulster, is central to the action of the epic; Finnbennach is eventually defeated, but not without severely wounding Donn Cuailnge.

Finnbheara, Fionnbharr, Finbheara, Fin Bheara, Fionvarra, Finvarra, Finvara, Fin Varra, Finn Varra Maa. King of the *Connacht *fairies with residence at *Cnoc Mheada [Knockmagha], west of Tuam, Co. Galway. Although fond of mortal women, he is usually cited with his wife *Úna (sometimes Nuala). Originally one of the *Tuatha Dé Danann, he settles at Cnoc Mheadha when his kind are driven underground by the *Milesians. The popularity of his stories in oral tradition led storytellers to think of Finnbheara as the king of all Irish fairies, not just of Connacht, and also as king of the dead. In one of the best-known stories, Finnbheara steals the most beautiful woman in Ireland, *Eithne (4) or Eithne the Bride, and keeps her with him, Persephone-like, for a year. He brings good crops to people in his region but his absence brings poor crops. He rewards a smith who is not afraid to shoe his three-legged horse. On one occasion he cures a sick woman, accepts food from her in recompense, but refuses salt. Lady Wilde collected many stories of Finnbheara in her *Ancient Legends, Mystic Charms and Superstitions of Ireland* (London, 1887). T. H. Nally's verse pantomime *Finn Varra Maa* (Dublin, 1917) conflates Finnbheara with *Fionn mac Cumhaill (here 'Finn MacCool') and makes him the Irish Santa Claus. W. B. Yeats cites him often, usually as Finvara, notably in the dramas, *The Land of Heart's Desire* (1894) and *The Dreaming of the Bones* (1919). Although his name is occasionally anglicized as Finbar, he should be distinguished from *Finnbarr. Folk motifs: F109; F160.0.2; F167.12; F184; F252.1.

Finnbhennach. Variant spelling of *Finnbennach.

Finncháem. Variant spelling of *Findchóem.

Finnchnes, Finnchneas [Ir., fair-skinned]. South *Leinster princess in the *Fenian Cycle known as the robe-maker of the *Fianna.

Finnchú, Findchú, Findchua, Fionnchú, Fanahan [Ir., fair hound, fair warrior]. Name borne by several early Irish Christian figures, most notably the 7th-century (d. 664) St Finnchú of Brí Gobann [later Brigown, near Mitchelstown, Co. Cork], about whom many legends have accrued. Stories of Finnchú's heroic self-mortification circulated widely during the Middle Ages and were collected in a later Irish-language biography. After a series of childhood miracles, such as turning the king of *Ulster's horses to stones, Finnchú became abbot of *Bangor, Co. Down, for seven years. Then he returned to the south of his birth and built a new monastery with the help of smiths at Brí Gobann [Ir., hillock of the smiths]. They made seven iron sickles for him, from which he hung, one sickle at a time under his armpit, both to ensure his place in heaven and to prevent the devil from stealing the soul of the recently departed. Finnchú was also a warrior who helped repel invaders, brandishing his crozier in battle and blowing fire from his mouth. See Whitley Stokes, *Lives of the Saints from the Book of Lismore* (Oxford, 1890), 84–98.

Finnéces, Finn Éces, Findéces, Finegas, Finnegas, Finnéigeas [Ir. *finn*, fair; *éices*, seer, scholar, sage, poet]. *Druid or seer who unwittingly helped *Fionn mac Cumhaill gain the power of *divination. Finnéces lives for seven years along the banks of the *Boyne, waiting for the *salmon of knowledge to appear at *Linn Féic [Fiac's Pool], near Rosnaree, Co. Meath. At this pool *hazel nuts fall into the water, giving *knowledge to salmon. Some oral variants put Finnéces at the falls of *Assaroe in north-western Ireland. When the 7-year-old Fionn comes to live as a pupil with him, Finnéces catches the salmon quite easily, as if it had been waiting for just such a moment. The druid gives the salmon to Fionn to cook, but instructs him not to eat any part of it. During the cooking Fionn scorches his thumb and thrusts it into his mouth, thus taking the salmon's power for himself. Several commentators have noted that 'Finnéces' means 'Finn the seer', which could also be a name for Fionn mac Cumhaill; additionally, the salmon of knowledge is sometimes known as *Fintan.

Finnén. An OIr. spelling of *Finnian.

Finngheal. Younger sister of *Ferdoman.

Finngoll [Ir., fair foreigner]. Shadowy legendary figure, cited only in some pedigrees of *Fionn mac Cumhaill. Distinguish from Macpherson's *Fingal.

Finnguala, Finnuala, Fionnghuala, Fionguala, Fionnuala, Finola [Ir., fair-shouldered]. Daughter of and most prominent child of *Lir, twin sister of *Áed (3), in **Oidheadh Chlainne Lir* [The Tragic Story of the Children of Lir]. These are the well-born children who are turned into swans by a cruel stepmother and wander the world in exile for 900 years. Some popular English-language retellings of the story capriciously name the mother as Fingula, clearly an anglicization of Finnguala, instead of Áeb. Nuala is a common diminutive of Finnguala, but in Irish oral tradition it becomes a substitute name for *Úna, the queen of the *fairies.

Finnian, Finian, Finnén [Ir. *finn*, fair, bright, etc.; cf. L *Vennianus*]. Name borne by several early Irish ecclesiastical figures, notably the two saints cited below. Possibly a pet-form of *Finnbarr; easily confused with *Fínán and *Finnán.

Finnian of Clonard, Saint. Sixth-century (d. 549) founder and abbot of the monastery of *Clonard, east of the modern town of Kinnegad, near the *Boyne River, Co. Westmeath. Later legend makes Finnian the 'tutor of the saints of Ireland', especially the 'Twelve Apostles of Ireland', i.e. founders of Irish monasteries of the next generation of saints. His feast-day is 12 December. See Whitley Stokes, *Lives of the Saints from the Book of Lismore* (Oxford, 1890), 75–83, 222–30; Kathleen Hughes, 'The Historical Value of the Lives of St. Finnian of Clonard', *English Historical Review*, 66 (1954), 353–72; Kathleen Hughes, 'The Cult of St. Finnian of Clonard from the Eighth to the Eleventh Century', *Irish Historical Studies*, 9 (1954), 13–27.

Finnian of Moville, Saint. [Ir. *mag bile*, plain of the large, venerated tree]. Sixth-century (d. *c.*579) bishop and founder of the abbey of Moville or Movilla, east of Newtownwards, Co. Down; sometimes called Finnian the Younger or Finnbarr (see FINNBARR). According to legends accruing to St Finnian, he entered the fortress of the pagan king *Tuan mac Cairill, hoping to convert him to Christianity. To do this Finnian listened to Tuan's stories, which included the invasions of Ireland (see LEBOR GABÁLA, The Book of Invasions) along with much of the rest of the pre-Christian history of the country. In other legends associated with Finnian of Moville, some of which confuse him with personages of similar name, he was (*a*) thought to have the power to change the course of rivers, and (*b*) embarrassed by a *Pictish princess whose advances he rejected. His feast-day is 10 September. Once thought distinct from Finnán of Moville, feast-day 11 February; the two are now thought to be identical. See John Ryan, *Irish Monasticism* (Dublin, 1931); Pádraig Ó Riain, 'Finnian or Winnian?', in P. Ní Chatháin and M. Richter (eds.), *Irland und Europa* (Stuttgart, 1984); 'Finnio and Winnian: A Question of Priority', in R. Bielmeier and R. Stempel (eds.), *Indogermanica et Caucasica* (Berlin and New York, 1994), 407–16.

Finnian tales. Variant form of *Fenian Cycle.

Finnine. Variant form of Finngheal, the younger sister of *Ferdoman, along with Finn (1).

Finnlug, Fionnlugh, Fionnlú, Finnloga (gen.) [Ir. *finn*, fair, bright, etc.; *lug*, light, brightness]. Name borne by numerous minor early Irish Christian figures, which is curious, as the name combines those of two of the best-known pagan figures, *Fionn mac Cumhaill and *Lug Lámfhota. Three of the most often mentioned are Finnlug, the father of St *Brendan, Finnlug of Doon (Co. Limerick), and Finnlug, the father of St *Finnian of Clonard. James Joyce cites the name as 'Fynlogue' in *Finnegans Wake* (1939), exploiting both the shadowy ambiguity and the possible associations with Fionn mac Cumhaill.

Finntan, Finntain (gen.). Variant spellings of *Fintan.

Finnuala. Variant spelling of *Finnguala.

finoderee. Variant spelling of *fenodyree.

Finola. Variant spelling of *Finnguala.

Fínscoth [Ir., wine blossom]. Daughter attributed to *Cúchulainn in stories composed later than the **Táin Bó Cuailnge* [Cattle Raid of Cooley].

Fintan, Finntan, Fintaan, Fionntan, Finntain (gen.) [proto-Celtic *vindo-senos*, white ancient

(?); *vindo-tenos,* white fire (?)]. Name borne by numerous figures in early Ireland, secular and ecclesiastical, including seventy-four saints and pseudo-saints and dozens of names cited in genealogies and pedigrees. The best-known Fintan, usually cited without patronymic, is *Fintan mac Bóchra.

Fintan I. The *salmon of knowledge is known as Fintan in many early Irish texts. At *Assaroe he sometimes bears the name *Goll Essa Ruaid [one-eyed of the red waterfall].

Fintan mac Bóchra, Bóchna. The only Irishman to survive the biblical *Flood, Fintan was a mythical seer whose name is cited in many texts. The Bóchra/Bóchna of his patronymic is never identified; it may refer to his mother or may imply the sea. He may be yet another figure derived from the shadowy *Find implied in *Ptolemy (2nd cent. AD). According to the pseudo-history **Lebor Gabála* [Book of Invasions], Fintan was one of three men who accompanied the lady *Cesair, whom he took as a wife, and her fifty women, forty days before the Flood. When the other two men died, all the women approached Fintan, who fled from them. A poem later ascribed to Fintan explains how he survived the Flood when all others perished by hiding in the hill of Tounthinna [Ir. *Tulach Tuindi, Tul Tuinne*] over the River *Shannon (near Portroe, Co. Tipperary). In another story Fintan details in a dialogue with the hawk of *Achill how he escaped the Flood. He had been 15 years old at the coming of the waters, but survived for another 5,500 years. In surviving he had been transformed into a one-eyed *salmon, an *eagle, and a hawk before resuming his own shape. The hawk responds that it also is very old and has witnessed many of the events Fintan describes, including the exploits of *Cúchulainn, the coming of Christianity, and the whole history of the Western world. Fintan is usually presumed to be a seer of great knowledge, partially because of his animal transformations and also because of his great age, and becomes a patron of history and poetry. His wife of later years is *Ébliu (1), the sister of *Lug Lámfhota. See Kuno Meyer (ed.), 'Colloquy between Fintan and the Hawk of Achill', in *Anecdota from Irish Manuscripts*, i, ed. R. I. Best et al. (Halle, 1907), 24–39.

Fintan mac Néill. Son of *Niall Noígiallach [of the Nine Hostages] and ruler over one-third of *Ulster at the time, achronologically, of *Conchobar mac Nessa. His son *Cethern mac Fintain was fostered by Conchobar and became a tutor of *Fionn mac Cumhaill.

Fintigernd, Findtighearn. A wife of *Mongán.

Finvara, Finvarra. Variant anglicizations of *Finnbheara.

Finvel. See FERGUS FÍNBÉL.

Fíonán. ModIr. spelling of *Fínán.

fiondruine. ModIr. spelling of *findruine.

Fioneen. Anglicization of *Fíngein.

Fionghal Rónáin. ModIr. spelling of **Fingal Rónáin*.

Fionguala. Variant spelling of *Finnguala.

fionn, fionn- [Ir., fair, bright, white, lustrous, light-hued]. ModIr. spelling of a concept whose OIr. and MidIr. spellings are *find and *finn. Of the several figures named *Find, *Finn, or Fionn, all but *Fionn mac Cumhaill are known here under the OIr. and MidIr. spellings.

Fionn Bheannach. ModIr. spelling of *Finnbennach.

Fionn Cycle. Variant form of *Fenian Cycle.

Fionn File. ModIr. spelling of *Find File.

Fionn Lú. ModIr. spelling of *Finnlug.

Fionn mac Cumhaill, Finn/Find mac Cumhaill/ mac Cumhail [OIr.], Finn MacCool [anglicized], Fionn Mac Cumhaill, Feunn Mac Cüail [ScG], Finn McCooil [Manx]; also Fingal, Finn Mac Cumhal, Finn mac Cumal, Find mac Umaill. Hunter-warrior-seer of Old and Modern Irish literatures, central hero of the *Fenian Cycle where he heads the Clan *Baiscne and the *Fianna Éireann, and subject of innumerable portrayals in thousands of narratives from both learned manuscript and later oral traditions. First known as *Demne Máel, he acquires the name Fionn [fair, light-haired] while still a youth. Fionn is usually seen as brave and admirable, especially in stories told in Ossianic frame (i.e. conventionally narrated by Fionn's son *Oisín or compatriot *Caílte), where he is a paragon of pagan Irish nobility: courageous and generous. Elsewhere, particularly in folk-tales from oral tradition, Fionn may become a crude, buffoonish bumbler. In the widely known story from manuscript tradition, *Tóraigheacht Dhiarmada agus Ghráinne* [The Pursuit of Diarmait and Gráinne], he is an ageing cuckold and jealous avenger. Long thought a historical personage, Fionn was ascribed the death date of AD 283 by chroniclers; his historicity was sanctioned by Geoffrey *Keating (*c.*1570– *c.*1650) and survived in popular perception until the 20th century. Fionn's stories are known in all parts of Ireland, Gaelic Scotland, the Isle of *Man, and Gaelic-speaking *Nova Scotia, and have migrated into the oral traditions and literatures of English-speaking peoples in North America and Australia. Internal references imply a base in *Leinster or eastern Ireland; Fionn's customary fortress or 'palace' is the Hill of *Allen [OIr. *Almu*; ModIr. *Almhain*] in Co. Kildare.

The glossing of Fionn as 'fair' implies links to a Continental Celtic divinity, *Vindonnus, whose name is commemorated in place-names from the Roman occupation. Gaulish vindos [white] and vindonos [fair] are employed in the several Vindonissas and Vindabonas; a Vindabona along the Danube lay on the site of modern Vienna. This same Continental divinity may explain the origin of the two other great Irish heroes, *Lug Lámfhota and *Cúchulainn, as well as Fionn's inexact counterpart in Welsh tradition, *Gwyn ap Nudd. Within Irish tradition, Fionn appears to have been anticipated by *Find, the ancient personification of wisdom implied by *Ptolemy (2nd cent. AD). Dáithí Ó hÓgáin has argued (1988) that Fionn's characteristic persona arose when Leinstermen revering Find in the *Boyne valley were driven from their homeland by the *Uí Néill of *Ulster. These families, especially the Uí Fháilghe, created Fionn the poet-warrior-seer who resides in the countryside and is ready to defend his people while not ruling them, out of the continuing enmity with the Uí Néill. Complete as early as the 6th century, Fionn was accommodated to Leinster genealogies by the 7th century. Informed commentators reject the assertion first put forth by Heinrich Zimmer (1891) that Fionn is of foreign, specifically Norse, origin.

Although Fionn's pedigree may have been fabricated, the names within it remain fixed even when the personalities behind them are thin. Fionn's father, always cited in the ubiquitous patronymic, is reported as having been killed before his son's birth, but the names of the perpetrators vary; (*a*) *Conn Cétchathach [of the Hundred Battles], protector of *Tadg (or Bracan) mac Nuadat, for Cumhall's having abducted Tadg's daughter *Muirenn Muncháem [of the white neck] and getting her with child; (*b*) *Goll mac Morna of the rival Clan Morna launching an ongoing clan rivalry, according to **Fotha Catha Chnucha* [The Cause of the Battle of Cnucha], the most widely known version; (*c*) *Liath Luachra, the keeper of the *crane bag [*corrbolg*]; or (*d*) the villainous *Arca Dubh, as in Scottish Gaelic folk-tales. Cumhall's death and his son's birth should take place during the reign of *Cathaír Mór. Cumhall's pedigree consists of little more than ciphers; he is the son of Trénmór [strong and big], the son of Sualt, the son of Ealtan, son of Baíscne. Through his maternal side Fionn claims his more important ancestor, *Nuadu Airgetlám, a king of the *Tuatha Dé Danann; or this may have been *Nuadu Necht, a Leinster manifestation of Nuadu Airgetlám. Nuadu's 'son' Tadg mac Nuadat may be but an alias for Nuadu himself; but Tadg taken as an entity is thought to be father of Muirenn. After Cumhall's death, Muirenn was unable to raise the baby and so had him nursed by her sister *Bodhmall, a *druidess. *Fiacclach mac Conchinn fostered Fionn, giving him a spear that never misses its mark; Fiacclach's son Moling Lúath is conventionally named as Fionn's foster-brother. Fionn's two named brothers are *Fíthel and *Féinnidh. Fionn's aunt (sometimes sister) is *Uirne, wife of *Illann (2), and mother of *Bran and *Sceolang. In lesser-known variant texts Fionn's mother's name is given as *Fuinche or Torba.

Two episodes dominate Fionn's childhood, the gaining of divine *knowledge and the earning of his usual name. When the boy was but 7 years old, he became a pupil of the *druid or seer *Finnéces, who had been waiting seven years to find the *salmon of knowledge at *Linn Féic [Fiac's Pool] along the Boyne (or in later tradition, the falls of *Assaroe in Co. Donegal). The name Finnéces means 'Finn the Seer' and may imply the old Find, or a double of Fionn himself. Finnéces caught the salmon and was roasting it on a spit when the boy touched the hot flesh; he then thrust his burnt thumb into his mouth, bestowing upon himself the divine knowledge that Finnéces sought. An alternate, less well-known version dating from the 8th century has Fionn gain knowledge when he catches his thumb in the door to an otherworldly house on *Sliab na mBan [Slievenamon], Co. Tipperary. The boy's name from birth was Demne Máel, implying shorn hair and associations with druids, poets, and craftsmen. After Demne Máel had won an athletic contest and killed a rival who challenged his victory, a spectator called out, 'Who is the fair boy?' [ModIr. *Cé hé an giolla fionn?*]; and thus he became Fionn the son of Cumhall.

Despite many shifts in portrayals of Fionn's character, certain aspects of his physical person remain constant. He is always tall, fair-haired, and conventionally handsome, with broad shoulders and a broad brow. No portraits of Fionn survive from Irish or Scottish Gaelic tradition, nor has he been the subject of any notable modern work of art. His usual residence is the Hill of Allen, Co. Kildare, a site associated with the families thought to have created his persona; but he is sometimes linked to *Dind Ríg, Co. Carlow. Fionn's favourite animal is the *dog; his companion dogs Bran and Sceolang are his transformed nephews. His standard, as recorded in later literature, is the likeness of the golden sun half-risen from the blue floor of the sea.

Like *Cúchulainn, Fionn benefited from an amazonian tutor, *Búanann, but he also learned from the male *Cethern mac Fintain. Along with his spear that never misses its mark, Fionn wields a famous sword, Mac an Lúin. In military and athletic prowess, Fionn excels at what all men must do. He is a superb runner and jumper, significantly in a milieu lacking cavalry or chariots. Along with other members of the fianna, Fionn sings out the war cry of *Dord Fian. His notable superhuman power is in *divination, specifically *díchetal do chennaib, of which he is a great practitioner; names for his special *knowledge are *fios and *imbas forosnai. Some commentators see Fionn's characteristic light, even shining hair as testimony to this unique luminous wisdom.

Encounters with a succession of females allowed Fionn to father innumerable progeny. The imposition of Christian monogamy may class some women as 'wives' and others as 'lovers', but Fionn lacks a constant mate, unlike Cúchulainn with *Emer. The most alluring woman in Fionn's life is the magical *Sadb, who first appeared as a *fawn and gave birth to his most notable son, *Oisín. Cormac mac Airt's daughter *Ailbe Chrúadbrecc ranks high among the hero's wives and Fionn is often described as the king's son-in-law. Other women listed as Fionn's wives are: *Berrach, often called his 'third wife'; *Cruithne (1), daughter of Lochán the smith; Daolach, cited only in *Duanaire Finn* (16th cent.); *Maigneis, who was unfaithful; *Smirgat (or Smirnat), daughter of *Fothad Canainne; *Taise and Téite. Fionn was betrothed to *Gráinne, who betrayed him for *Diarmait. Women who sought Fionn's love are the 'Daughter of the King of Greece' and Máer, a married woman. *Áine (2) would sleep with no man in Ireland except Fionn. Along with the oft-cited Oisín, the hero's sons include: *Cairell, a son killed by Goll; *Dáire (3); *Fáelán mac Finn; *Fergus Fínbél; *Fiachra (3); and *Fiachna (5). Among Fionn's daughters are *Aí Arduallach the arrogant, *Cainche, the mother of *Goll's children, and *Lugach; additionally, Fionn is the protector of the beautiful *Bébinn. Fionn's celebrated grandson is *Oscar, son of Oisín, and the 'Galahad' of the Fenian Cycle. Key members of Fionn's household are: *Duanach mac Morna, his *bard or *druid; *Cnú Deireóil, his harper; Lomna, his fool or jester; and the servant *Ferdia (2), murdered by *Cairbre Lifechair.

Decisive patterns emerge in the thousands of stories of Fionn as a hunter and warrior. Always a superb athlete, Fionn excells as a runner and swimmer, as well as in combat with a sword or spear. His favourite quarries are wild *boar and *deer. He is described as slaying a serpent in virtually every body of water in Ireland, as well as many in Scotland and the Isle of Man, but more place-names are cited from Leinster than elsewhere.

Numerous passes between mountains are thought to have been cut by his sword, and landmarks such as caves and 'fingerstones' (bare, vertical rocks) attributed to Fionn abound. At Glen Roy in Inverness-shire, Scotland, the 'Parallel Roads', horizontal markers from ancient glacial lakes, were attributed to Fionn. He is often seen as the victor in battles, but few are described in detail; the most extensive is the account of the repulsion of an invasion at Ventry Harbour, Co. Kerry, in **Cath Fionntrágha*. Other invaders to be repulsed come from the north, the Norsemen or Vikings from *Lochlainn. Within Ireland, Fionn's mortal adversaries are often identified with *Connacht, perhaps an inheritance of his father Cumhall's contention with Conn Cétchathach [of the Hundred Battles]. Over the centuries this rivalry is embodied in *Goll mac Morna. Other opponents, *Arca Dubh, *Borba, or *Dealra Dubh, are not rooted geographically. More celebrated are Fionn's several supernatural adversaries, especially *Aillén mac Midna, the 'burner' of *Tara, whom he kills to great acclaim, and Cúldub mac Fidga, a food-thief. In the extensive series of tales of the *Bruidhean type, Fionn and his men are trapped in a magical dwelling and cannot get out without help; a representative example is *Bruidhean Chaorthainn [The Hostel of the Quicken Tree]. Some of Fionn's supernatural adventures are clearly allegories, as in the 15th-century story of an encounter with an old man, a *ram, and a beautiful young woman. The ram who butts their food from the table and cannot be restrained is the world. The beautiful woman who rejects Fionn's advances, telling him that he has had her already, is youth. And the old man who easily ties up the ram is age itself, which subdues all. Many Fenian tales display a coarse humour, and in some of them from oral tradition he is portrayed as a slapstick figure himself; but in the most popular of these, of the *Céadach or comic helper tales, of which at least 128 survive, Fionn recedes into the background and his men take the brunt of the raillery. Fionn is most unattractive in *Tóraigheacht Dhiarmada agus Ghráinne* in which the old warrior is betrothed to the unwilling Gráinne, who runs off with the handsome young Diarmait, a member of the Fianna. Not only does Fionn's desire for Gráinne appear unsavoury, but he withholds use of his healing powers from her swain when he is gored by a *boar. Fionn appears at his most attractive in narratives that view him conventionally from some time after his passing; the longest and best-known of these is **Acallam na Senórach* [The Colloquy of the Elders]. Those 'elders' are Fionn's son Oisín and his compatriot Caílte, who also serve as conventional narrators in an immense body of literature from oral tradition. Perhaps the most impressive Irish collection is the **Duanaire Finn*, compiled at Louvain and Ostend in the 17th century.

Accounts vary concerning the manner of Fionn's death and also whether he was indeed mortal. Fionn's Fianna has worn out its welcome during the reign of Cormac's successor, *Cairbre Lifechair. Different factions begin to fight among themselves, and Cairbre provokes the climactic Battle of Gabhair/Gowra, **Cath Gabhra*, by killing Fionn's servant Ferdia (2); in this text five men murder Fionn at Garristown, Co. Dublin. In *Aided Finn* [The Violent Death of Fionn], *Aichlech mac Dubdrenn slays Fionn at Áth Brea, the Ford of Brea, on the Boyne; other stories have Fionn in mortal combat with Goll mac Morna at this same site. Scottish oral tradition places Fionn's death at Cill Fhinn, Perthshire. Rival Irish traditions have Fionn buried at *Ard Caille, north Co. Cork, or at Luachair Dedad, Co. Kerry. Fionn may have been reincarnated as *Mongán, or he may be a member of the Sleeping Army (Folk motif: E502), resting in a remote cave like *Arthur, Charlemagne, or Barbarossa, waiting until his people need him again.

See also: BRUIDHEAN BHEAG NA HALMHAINE [The Little Brawl of the Hill of Allen]; CATH GABHRA [The Battle of Gabhair/Gowra]; DUANAIRE FINN; EACHTRA AN AMADÁIN MHÓIR [The Adventure of the Great Fool]; FOTHA CATHA CHNUCHA [The Cause of the battle of Cnucha].

Fionn has been portrayed in English-language writing more than a hundred times from the 15th to the end of the 20th century in texts from the juvenile and popular to the most demanding. Among the most notable are: William Carleton, 'A Legend of Knockmany' (1845, often reprinted); James Joyce, *Finnegans Wake* (New York, 1939); Flann O'Brien, *At Swim-Two-Birds* (London, 1939); Standish James O'Grady, *Finn and His Companions* (London, 1892); Violet Russell, *Heroes of the Dawn* (Dublin, 1913); Gordon Snell, *The Cool MacCool* (Dublin, 1988); James Stephens, *Irish Fairy Tales* (London, 1920); Ella Young, *The Tangle-Coated Horse* (New York, 1929). Fionn is also the basis for James *Macpherson's Fingal in *The Poems of Ossian* (1760–3).

Studies: Reidar Th. Christiansen, *The Vikings and the Viking Wars in Irish and Gaelic Traditions* (Oslo, 1931); James MacKillop, *Fionn mac Cumhaill* (Syracuse, NY, 1986); Gerard Murphy, 'Introduction', *Duanaire Finn III*, Irish Texts Society No. 43 (Dublin, 1953), pp. x-cxxii; Gerard Murphy, *The Ossianic Lore and Romantic Tales of Medieval Ireland* (Dublin, 1955); Joseph Falaky Nagy, *The Wisdom of the Outlaw* (Berkeley, Calif., 1985); Dáithí Ó hÓgáin, *Fionn Mac Cumhaill* (Dublin, 1988).

See also FINGAL.

Fionn na Ghal [ScG, chief of valour (?)]. Hypothesized spelling of *Fingal.

Fionna, Sídh. Variant form of *Finnachad.

Fionnabhair. ModIr. spelling of *Finnabair.

Fionnachadh. ModIr. spelling of *Finnachad.

Fionnachta. ModIr. spelling of *Finnachta.

Fionnán. ModIr. spelling of *Finnán.

Fionnbharr. ModIr. spelling; may be variant for *Finnbarr or *Finnbheara.

Fionnchú. ModIr. spelling of *Finnchú.

fionndruine. ModIr. spelling of *findruine.

Fionnghula. ModIr. variant spelling of *Finnguala.

Fionnlugh. ModIr. spelling of *Finnlug.

Fionntan. ModIr. spelling of *Fintan.

Fionnuala, Fionuala. ModIr. spellings of *Finnguala.

Fionnúir. ModIr. spelling of *Finnabair.

Fionvara. Anglicization of *Finnbheara.

fios, Fios [OIr., ascertaining]. One of several early Irish terms for esoteric *knowledge, especially as embodied in the warrior-hunter-seer *Fionn mac Cumhaill. See also DIVINATION; IMBAS FOROSNAI [full knowledge]; and the enigmatic TEINM LAÍDA. Fios is also the name of one of the three *druids of *Partholón. In Modern Irish fios also denotes *second sight.

Fíothal. ModIr. spelling of *Fíthel.

Fir, Fir- [OIr., men; husbands]. The separable prefix Fir- is a part of the names of many groups in early Irish tradition, and is thus alphabetized here word by word. Cf. the singular *Fer [Ir., man]. Distinguish from fír [true, veracious].

Fir Bolg, Fir Bholg, Firbolg [Ir., men of Builg]. Mythical early invaders of Ireland, according to the pseudo-history *Lebor Gabála* [Book of Invasions], coming many generations after the *Nemedians and thirty-seven years before the *Tuatha Dé Danann, the race of pre-Christian divinities. Their brief period of power is marked by a secure *kingship and the rule of just laws. Descended from Nemed's son Starn, the Fir Bolg suffer oppression in 'Greece', where their forced labour includes carrying dirt in leather bags from the valleys to the bare hills; these same bags, refashioned into boats, allow them to escape. The bag motif prompted the fanciful gloss of their name, 'men of the bags', after bolg [bag, satchel, sack], which is now rejected. Instead, the Fir Bolg are mythologized from the *Builg and *Belgae and other *P-Celtic settlers in Ireland who preceded the *Q-Celtic *Goídels. Within the *Lebor Gabála* they take their name from *Bolg/Bolga, an ancestor deity.

The Fir Bolg leader in Greece is Semion, grandson of Starn and son of Stariat. But when the Fir Bolg return to Ireland, 230 years after Starn's departure, at *Inber Domnann [Malahide Bay, Co. Dublin] on the feast of *Lughnasa, their leader is *Dela, whose five sons divided the island. Gann and Sengann take two parts of *Munster; *Sláine (2) takes *Leinster; and Rudraige takes *Ulster, founding a dynasty. Unlike their predecessors, the Fir Bolg clear no plains nor form any lakes, as Ireland is by now prepared for agriculture. They are adept at war: an early king, Rinnal [cf. Ir. *rinn*, spear-point], is the first to employ weapons with points, i.e. iron heads. Curiously, they do not engage the predatory *Fomorians, as did the *Partholonians, Nemedians, and Tuatha Dé Danann, leading some to speculate that the Fir Bolg and Fomorians were identical, an otherwise insupportable assertion. Although the Fir Bolg prevail for only thirty-seven years, their era is distinguished by the rule of a great and generous king, *Eochaid mac Eirc, who establishes justice and provides that all rain will fall as dew and that every year will yield a harvest. His wife is *Tailtiu, in whose honour he establishes a famous festival. The invading Tuatha Dé Danann defeat the Fir Bolg at the First Battle of Mag Tuired, near Lough Arrow, Co. Sligo; see CATH MAIGE TUIRED. The beaten Fir Bolg flee to distant parts of the Gaelic world and are later associated with the Scottish coast, Rathlin Island, the province of *Connacht, and with the *Aran Islands; *Dún Aonghusa is named for their chief *Angus (3). In Irish and Scottish Gaelic folklore the Fir Bolg are grotesque helots and cave *fairies. In *Connemara their king is Bola. Literary adapters of the Fir Bolg outside Irish and Scottish Gaelic were often influenced by the earlier interpretation of them as subject workers carrying earth in bags to enrich hilltops. W. B. Yeats describes Forgael as a Fir Bolg in his play *The Shadowy Waters* (1905).

T. F. O'Rahilly's interpretation of the historical roots of the Fir Bolg invasion in *Early Irish History and Mythology* (1946), while widely cited, remains controversial. In his vision, the Fir Bolg represent the experience not of one people but of at least three of the P-Celtic invaders of Ireland who preceded the Q-Celtic Goídels: the *Érainn, the *Domnainn (or Fir Domnann), and *Galióin (another name for the *Lagin, founders of *Leinster). These P-Celts were linguistically related to the Belgae and Brythonic peoples of the Continent and Great Britain, but were eventually absorbed into the rest of the Irish population.

Other frequently cited members of the Fir Bolg include: *Delga, builder of Dún Delgan [Dundalk]; Fíngein Fisiocdha, their physician; and *Sreng, the champion who severed Nuadu's arm. See John Carey, '*Fir Bolg*: A Native Etymology Revisited', *Cambridge Medieval Celtic Studies*, 16 (1988), 76–83.

fir chlis, chlisneach [ScG *clis*, quick, lively, nimble]. Name for the northern lights or aurora borealis in Scottish Gaelic folklore; sometimes translated as 'the merry dancers'. Preceded in Gaelic by the article *na*.

fir darrig, fir dhearga. Plurals of *far darrig.

Fir Domnann. See DOMNAINN.

Fir Fálgae, Fhálchae. Mythical warriors who contend with *Cúchulainn and *Cú Roí when the heroes make forays into Scotland; speciously associated with warriors from the Isle of *Man.

fir gorm, na fir ghorma. ScG translation of *Blue Men of the Minch.

Fir Morca, Fir Mhorc, Feramorc, Feramore, Fermore. Legendary people of early Ireland, whose king was *Scoriath, conventionally described as big men who lived near Luachair Dedad in west *Munster. O'Rahilly (1946) argues that the name 'Fir Morca' is a folk etymology from 'Armorica', the Latin name for *Brittany.

fire. In common with other ancient people, the Celts appear to have perceived fire to be the earthly counterpart of the sun. Although there is no Celtic Prometheus, fire is seen as a purifying element, a gift from the sun to humankind that can cleanse, warm, and illuminate as well as destroy. Like other people of cold, dark northern Europe, Celts venerated fire in several festivals, especially at the new year, 1 November (*Samain) and the beginning of summer, 1 May (*Beltaine); vestiges of these celebrations have survived in modern times. Great bonfires were built on these days as well as at midsummer, Christianized as St John's Day after the purported birthday of John the Baptist. Celebrations also included the rolling of huge fire-wheels. The classical commentators Julius *Caesar and *Strabo (both 1st cent. BC) testify that the Celts used man-shaped wicker figures in ritual sacrifices; animal and human victims could be burned alive in them. A 9th-century commentator linked the sacrifices with the thunder-god *Taranis. The straw men burned in medieval and early Renaissance spring festivals may represent a survival of this sacrifice.

*Brigit, the Irish fire-goddess, was transformed into St *Brigid, the early Irish saint. The Breton St *Barbe was reputed to be descended from a fire-goddess. St *Patrick lit a paschal fire in Ireland, and *Dewi Sant lit a fire to claim Wales. In the Irish pseudo-history *Lebor Gabála* [Book of Invasions] *Mide, chief *druid of the *Nemedians, lit the first fire in Ireland, at *Uisnech, which blazed for seven years and was carried to every chief hearth of the island. In Irish folklore, fire was the best preventative against magic, *fairy or otherwise. The Irish name *Áed embodies another word for fire; *Delbáeth means 'fire shape'. OIr. teine; ModIr. tine, teine; ScG teine; Manx aile; W tân; Corn. tān; Bret. tan, tantad.

firedrake. See DRAGON.

First Battle of Mag Tuired. See CATH MAIGE TUIRED [The (Second) Battle of Mag Tuired].

fís, físi (pl.) [cf. L *visio*]. Name for a class of early Irish narrative, a kind of cosmic or metaphysical travel literature; convention makes *fís* the first word in the title, e.g. **Fís Adamnáin*. Distinguish from the later *aisling, which usually carries a political subtext.

Fís Adamnáin. Irish title for The Vision of Adamnán, a narrative description of the Christian afterlife that survives in three separate texts. Although attributed to the 7th-century *Adamnán, tenth abbot of *Iona, the oldest surviving text in the **Book of the Dun Cow* [*Lebor na hUidre*] is not earlier than the

10th century. On the midsummer feast of St John the Baptist, Adamnán's soul goes forth from his body (see SHAMANISM) and he is brought to heaven and hell. Guided by a guardian angel, Adamnán's soul crosses a wall of fire that surrounds the afterlife, but is not harmed by it. The Lord of Heaven, who lies beyond the human power to describe, is constantly praised by chanting angels and archangels. Between heaven and hell is a dark and dismal land where there is no punishment. The vision of hell includes descriptions of punishments suffered by those guilty of particular sins. Beyond hell lies a wall of fire, seven times more horrible, inhabited only by demons until the Last Judgement. Many commentators have noted the influence of the apocryphal *Book of Enoch* as well as an anticipation of Dante's *Divina Commedia*. Whitley Stokes provides text and translation in the hard-to-find *Fís Adamnáin* (Simla, India, 1870); cf. Ernst Windish, *Irische Texte*, ser. i (Leipzig, 1880), 165–96; Joseph Vendryes, *Revue Celtique*, 33 (1912), 349 ff.; summary translation, Myles Dillon, *Early Irish Literature* (Chicago, 1948), 133–9. See also Charles S. Boswell, *An Irish Precursor of Dante* (London, 1908); St John Seymour, 'The Vision of Adamnán', *Proceedings of the Royal Irish Academy*, 37(C) (1927), 304–12.

fish. Although representations of the sea creatures are found on certain Gallo-Roman altars, very few have played important roles in the Celtic imagination. Of these the most notable is the *salmon; see also DOLPHIN; EEL. The whale upon which St *Brendan and his followers land is *Jasconius.

Fisher King, Fisherman King. Name given the Grail keeper in Arthuriana; he has no specific Celtic antecedent. Variously identified as Amfortas, Alain, Bron, Pelles, or Pellinore. In Chrétien de Troyes (12th cent.) he is *Perceval's cousin; in the *Perlesvaus* (13th cent.) and Wolfram von Eschenbach's *Parzival* (13th cent.) he is Perceval's uncle; in the *Didot Perceval* (13th cent.), his grandfather.

fithchill. Variant spelling of *fidchell.

Fíthel, Fítheal, Fitheal, Fíothal, Fithil [Ir., calf (?); sprite, goblin (?)]. Celebrated judge at the court of *Cormac mac Airt in early Irish tradition, known for his infallible decisions. He may be a brother of *Fionn mac Cumhaill who left the *Fianna to join Cormac, or Fíthel the judge may have become confused with Fionn's brother of the same name. Fíthel as judge arbitrated disputes of the Fianna in general as well as those between Fionn and Cormac. Several collections of wise maxims attributed to him survive; see R. M. Smith, below. The 17th-century historian Geoffrey *Keating relates the story of the dying Fíthel giving advice to his son: (*a*) to avoid raising a king's child; (*b*) to keep dire secrets from his wife; (*c*) never to promote the son of a slave to higher station; (*d*) never to make his sister the trustee of his wealth. Fíthel's son did just the opposite, which jeopardized the son of Cormac, whom he was rearing. When extricated from his troubles, Fíthel's son pleaded that he was only testing his father's advice, which he had proved sound. See R. M. Smith, 'The *Senbriatha Fithail*', *Revue Celtique*, 45 (1928), 1–92; with addenda, 46 (1929), 268–71; 47 (1930), 30–8; 48 (1931), 325–31. Pádraig Ua Duinnín [Patrick S. Dinneen] based his Irish-language drama *Comhairle Fithil* (Dublin, 1909) upon Fíthel; translated as *Fitheal's Counsels* (Dublin, 1909).

Fithir [Ir., teacher (?)]. Elder daughter of the legendary king *Túathal Techtmar whose unhappy marriage to *Eochaid (8) brought humiliation to his kingdom, *Leinster. Preferring Fithir's comely younger sister *Dáirine, Eochaid used deceit to marry her as well; both daughters died, Fithir of shame and Dáirine of grief, or in other texts both of shame. Túathal waged war upon Eochaid, killing him and forcing Leinstermen to pay the heavy *bórama tribute.

Fitness of Names, The. See CÓIR ANMANN.

Fitzgerald, Earl. See GERALD, EARL OF DESMOND.

Five Peaks. See PUMLUMON.

Flag Fen. Archaeological site in Norfolkshire, eastern England, centre of intense ritual activity in the late Bronze Age (*c*.1200 BC). Excavations reveal an alignment of more than 2,000 *oak posts and more than 300 metal items, including daggers, swords, and spears. See Francis Pryor, 'Flag Fen', *Current Archaeology*, 119 (1990), 386–90.

Flaithinis, Flaith-inis [Ir., lordly, princely island]. An Irish expression denoting the Christian vision of heaven as a phantom island in the west. Cf. ModIr. na flaithis [heaven].

Flaithius, Flaitheas [Ir. *flaith*, sovereign, lord]. Name given to the loathly lady *Sovereignty goddess who prophesies to *Niall Noígiallach [of the Nine Hostages] that he will be a great king. Folk motif D732.

Flann, Fland [Ir., bright red, blood-red]. Name borne by countless figures in early Irish tradition, both male and female, including high kings, saints, abbots, poets, and scholars. The most often-cited is probably the 9th-century poet *Flann mac Lonáin.

Flann mac Díma. Hapless lover of *Mugain (3), wife of *Diarmait mac Cerbaill, king of *Tara. Jealous Diarmait set fire to Flann's house, during which the lover was burned, sought refuge in a vat of water, and drowned at *Beltaine. This death brought a curse upon Diarmait.

Flann mac Lonáin. Ninth- and tenth-century Irish poet, the earliest from whom any definite tradition survives; his death dates vary from 893 to 918/920. While little of his life can be documented, such as an association with the monastery at Terryglass, Co. Tipperary, his persona has attracted many stories. The bite of his satires caused him to be called the 'Devil's Son', and his avarice was reputed to have sent him to hell. In one story he contends with *Angus Óg, the pre-Christian god of poetry; and his knowledge of place-name lore was proverbial. After his death he rose to give his own elegy as well as elegies for the five people buried with him.

Flann ua Fedach [Ir. *fedach*, boughs, branches]. Lover who elopes with *Becfola in *Tochmarc Becfhola* [The Wooing of Becfola].

fled bainisi [Ir. *fled*, feast; *banais*, wedding]. Variant form of **banais righe*.

Fled Bricrenn, *Bricrend, Fleadh Bhricreann.* Irish title for an *Ulster Cycle narrative known in English as Briccriu's Feast. Composed as early as the 8th century, but probably drawing on ancient antecedents, the story exists in four variant texts written in the 11th century, one of which is in the **Book of the Dun Cow* [*Lebor na hUidre*]. The entire narrative merges two barely related motives: (*a*) Briccriu's inciting of competition for the *champion's portion [Ir. *curadhmhír*]; (*b*) the champion's bargain or beheading contest. An irascible mischief-maker, Briccriu's usual epithets are neimthenga, nemhthenga [poison-tongued], and biltenga [evil-mouthed].

The trouble begins when the Ulster heroes are reluctant to attend a party at the sumptuous new house Briccriu has built at Dún Rudraige [Dundrum, Co. Down], fashioned after the banquet hall at *Tara. The host's reputation is enough to deter them. But Briccriu threatens to set all Ulster in turmoil if they do not come: each father and son will be set against each other, even the two breasts of each woman will strike against each other until they are destroyed. Faced with such certain consequences, many acquiesce, but only on the condition that Briccriu himself should not enter the house. Undeterred, Briccriu sets about tempting the vanity of three heroes before they arrive. He goes first to *Lóegaire Buadach, urging him to claim the champion's portion of succulent milk-fed pork for himself because he is the most deserving. Then he taunts *Conall Cernach and *Cúchulainn in similar vein. When all three arrive in the hall, Briccriu withdraws as he has promised, asking only that the heroes decide among themselves who should have the champion's portion. The predictable tumult follows, ending only when the wise *Sencha mac Ailella divides the pork among the whole company.

Briccriu next turns his wiles to the consorts of the heroes. Seeing that *Fedelm Noíchrothach, wife of Lóegaire, has consumed much wine, he urges her to take precedence over all other women of Ulster by entering his hall first. With the same words he also tempts *Lendabair, wife of *Conall Cernach, and *Emer, wife of *Cúchulainn. Losing all pretence of dignity, the three women rush with their entourages to Dún Rudraige. Outside the door they compete in a boasting contest about their husbands, with the result that Conall and Lóegaire tear down the pillars of the house so that Fedelm and Lendabair may enter. But Cúchulainn simply lifts his side of the building, allowing Emer and her ladies a stately entrance, and also sliding Briccriu and his spouse into the mud among the dogs.

As the title to the champion's portion is still not settled, the three withdraw to *Connacht for a contest presided over by *Ercol. Cúchulainn's primacy is represented by a gold *cup, but the others do not accept the judgement, and so all return to *Emain Macha. Again they travel to seek an end to the dispute, this time to *Cú Roí in south-western

Ireland, who also judges Cúchulainn first, a verdict the others refuse. This stalemate leads to the most celebrated sequence in *Fled Bricrenn*, one in which Briccriu takes no part.

Back again at Emain Macha, the heroes are startled one evening by the entrance of a *giant, loathsome churl [Ir. *bachlach*] who shouts a daunting challenge: anyone present may cut off his head if he may do the same to them the following night. First Lóegaire and then Conall accept, lopping off the head easily, but when a headless churl returned the next night, they shirk their part of the bargain. At last Cúchulainn accepts the challenge; when the churl returned, Cúchulainn lowers his head, ready to accept the fatal blow. The huge churl raises his axe as high as he can, but brings down only the blunt edge, sparing Cúchulainn. The churl then calls out that Cúchulainn's bravery establishes his primacy over the other heroes, and reveals himself to be Cú Roí in disguise, who has returned to vindicate his judgement. From that day Cúchulainn is always awarded the champion's portion.

The ultimate unity of the two seemingly disconnected motives is often justified by reference to the classical commentator *Posidonius (1st cent. BC), who described both contests over status-conferring joints of pork and throat-slitting challenges among the ancient Celts. The beheading bargain (folk motif: M221) has been much commented upon, especially its links to the English romance *Sir Gawain and the Green Knight* (14th cent.). See Whitley A. Stokes, *Irische Texte*, ser. 2 (1) (1884), 164–217; George Henderson (ed. and trans.), *Fled Bricrenn: The Feast of Bricriu* (London, 1899); Kaarina Hollo, 'A Critical Edition of *Fled Bricrenn ocus Loinges mac nDuíl Dermait*', dissertation, Harvard University, 1992; T. P. Cross and C. H. Slover (eds.), *Ancient Irish Tales* (New York, 1936), 254–80; Edgar Slotkin, 'The Structure of *Fled Bricrenn* Before and After *Lebor na hUidre* Interpolations', *Ériu*, 29 (1978), 64–77. Eimar O'Duffy dramatized the narrative in *Bricriu's Feast: A Comedy in Three Acts* (Dublin, 1919).

Fled Gobnenn. See GOIBNIU.

Flidais, Fliodhais, Flidhais, Flidas [cf. OIr. *os*, deer]. Woodland goddess of venery and wild things, mistress to *stags, reputed to drive a chariot drawn by *deer; often compared to the Roman *Diana and Greek Artemis. She often bears the epithet foltchaín [fine or beautiful-haired]. Her magical *cow resembles the seven kine of *Mannanán, whose milk could sustain hundreds. Although she is cited as the mother of the witch-like *Bé Chuille and the wanton Bé Téite, and sometimes of *Fand, her husband is uncertain; he may be the shadowy Ádammair, who also takes her name as Ádammair Flidais, or Ailill Finn, a local king in what is today Co. Mayo. In any event, she is better known for her lusty affair with Fergus mac Róich, whose sexual appetite only she could satisfy; otherwise he required seven women. Her affair with Fergus is the subject of extensive oral tradition in Co. Mayo, where she may bear the name Muinchinn. In one story Fergus realizes he cannot trust her as she betrayed her husband, and he drowns her in a river flowing out of Carrowmore Lough.

The *Táin Bó Flidais* [Cattle Raid of Flidais] is sometimes seen as a preliminary to the epic **Táin Bó Cuailnge* [Cattle Raid of Cooley]. See Margaret E. Dobbs, 'On Táin Bó Flidais', *Ériu*, 8 (1916/17), 133–49.

flood, flood legends. Instances of the international flood theme (folk motifs: A1010–22) occur frequently in Celtic literatures. The biblical Deluge serves as a model for many instances and is cited as factual in the Irish pseudo-history, **Lebor Gabála* [Book of Invasions]; only *Fintan mac Bóchra survives it. Wales, although a mountainous country, has two flood stories: (*a*) *Cantre'r Gwaelod, the land of *Gwyddno Garanhir, flooded to make Cardigan Bay through the carelessness of Seithennyn, the drunken dike-keeper; (*b*) *Llyn Llion, the lake of the waves, whose overflowing forces *Dwyfan and *Dwyfach to escape in a hastily built ship. The Breton City of *Ys may be the best-known of all Celtic flood legends. See SUBMERGED CITIES. See also John Rhyˆs, 'Triumphs of the Water World', in *Celtic Folklore* (London, 1891), 401–55; F. J. North, *Sunken Cities* (Cardiff, 1957); Alan Dundes (ed.), *The Flood Myth* (Berkeley, Calif., 1988).

Foalán. Variant spelling of *Fáelán.

Foawr. Stone-throwing giants of Manx tradition, apparently derived from the *Fomorians of the **Lebor Gabála* [Book of Invasions]. Although ravishers of cattle, they are not ogres.

Fochmarc, Fochmart [Ir., inquiring]. One of the three brother *druids of the *Partholonians, along with *Eólas [knowledge] and *Fios [intelligence].

fód gortach. See HUNGRY GRASS.

fód seachráin. See FÓIDÍN MEARAÍ.

Fódla, Fódhla, Fodhla, Fótla, Fotla, Fohla. Irish goddess, one of the three divine eponyms of *Ireland, along with her sisters *Banba and *Ériu, and thus one of the poetic names for Ireland; she personifies the power of the land. A member of the immortal *Tuatha Dé Danann, she meets the invading, mortal *Milesians at Slieve Felim in what is now Co. Limerick and asks that Ireland be named for her; later she is revealed to be married to *Mac Cécht, a prominent warrior of the Tuatha Dé. Her mother is *Eirnin (sometimes Ernmas). The Highland Scottish placename *Atholl incorporates her name [ScG *Ath Fodhla*, the next Ireland]. Fódla is the conventional personification of Ireland in the poetry of Tadhg Dall Ó hUiginn (1550–1617). See OLLAM FODLA.

fóidín mearaí, mearbhaill; fóidín seachráin, fód seachráin [Ir. *fóidín*, clod of earth thrown up by flying feet; *mearaí*, craziness, distraction; *seachrán*, wandering]. An enchanted piece of turf bringing confusion to those who tread upon it; the condition is called being pixie-led or pixilated (see PISKIE) among the British Celts. See HUNGRY GRASS.

Foilan. Variant spelling of *Fáelán.

Foirbre. Variant spelling of *Furbaide Ferbend.

foldyr gastey [Manx, nimble mower]. Nickname of the *fenodyree.

Follamain mac Conchobair. Youngest son of *Ulster king *Conchobar mac Nessa in the **Táin Bó Cuailnge* [Cattle Raid of Cooley] who leads the ill-fated boy-corps against *Medb, warrior-queen of *Connacht while other warriors were suffering their disability. Despite heroic resolve, they were slaughtered to the last man. Earlier Follamain harassed *Cúchulainn on his first arrival at *Emain Macha.

Foltor, Foltlor. Lesser member of the *Fianna of *Fionn mac Cumhaill, son of the king of Innia, celebrated for his prowess in tracking or stalking over any terrain, even over water.

Fomorians, Fomoire, Fomóiri, Fomoraig, Fomhóraigh, Fomhoire, Fomorii, Fomor, Fomors, Fomoré, Fo-Muir, Foawr [Manx]. Malevolent euhemerized deities of the Irish *Mythological Cycle, known chiefly from two texts, the **Lebor Gabála* [Book of Invasions] and **Cath Maige Tuired* [The (Second) Battle of Mag Tuired], in which their portrayals are not coordinate. Although current scholarship agrees on their divine origin, earlier commentators often portrayed them as demonic pirates, probably reading the element *mór-* [phantom] as *muir* [sea]. Early Christian commentators traced the Fomorians to the biblical Ham, son of Noah. Later ecclesiastical storytellers made them either *giants or elves, with *goat- or horseheads and other misshapen features. While the origins of the Fomorians dates from pre-Christian times, their characterization has been coloured by generations of sea-raiders from the north, first from the Scottish islands and more extensively from the Norse lands; they are often linked to *Lochlainn [Scandinavia]. Rejected now is the earlier assumption that the Fomorians were primitive gods of fertility.

When they first appear in the *Lebor Gabála*, under their ferocious leader *Cichol against the beneficent *Partholonians, the Fomorians are portrayed as monstrous and fearful, each having only *one eye, one arm, and one leg; see the Irish FER CAILLE and the Scottish Gaelic FACHAN. Later in the text they are more anthropomorphic. While the Fomorians do not fit into the invasion sequence, they prey upon each successive invader, the Partholonians and the *Nemedians, until they are defeated by the *Tuatha Dé Danann. Curiously absent are Fomorian attacks on the invaders between the Nemedians of the Tuatha Dé Danann, the *Fir Bolg, prompting some commentators to speculate that the two are identical; later commentators reject this assertion. While associated with several locations, the Fomorians never appear to be settlers in Ireland but instead make raids from their fortress on Tory Island, north of Co. *Donegal. In general the Fomorians are wantonly cruel bullies, cutting the noses off those who would not pay them tribute. The Nemedians overcome the Fomorians in three battles until they themselves are defeated at *Cnámross (distinguish from *Fenian battle on the same site). The subsequent humiliations visited upon the Nemedians, especially an exacting annual tribute, cause them to rise up against their Fomorian masters, storming the fortress of Tory Island; they attack Tor Conaind, and the Nemedian champion *Fergus Lethderg slays the Fomorian chief *Conand. But the Fomorians prevail, and the disappointed Nemedians are scattered around the world.

In *Cath Maige Tuired*, the portrayal of the Fomorians draws more substantially on their divine origin. They intermarry freely with the Tuatha Dé Danann, the tribe of gods, implying that they are the marine counterparts of the latter. The Fomorian *Elatha mac Delbaíth, for example, mates with *Ériu of the Tuatha Dé Danann to produce *Bres, who inherits the leadership of the Tuatha Dé Danann from *Nuadu Airgetlám. The great champion of the Tuatha Dé Danann, *Lug Lámfhota, is the grandson of a Fomorian. Although the root of the conflict between the Fomorians and the Tuatha Dé Danann in *Cath Maige Tuired* is extraordinarily deep, the pretext within the narrative is the unsuitableness of Bres as king: he insults poets and demands humiliating tributes from the race of the gods made subject. Nuadu returns to power and Lug Lámfhota presents himself in court to aid the cause. The central conflict pits Lug against the Fomorian menace, *Balor of the Evil Eye, who is in fact Lug's grandfather. In an unexpected turn of events, Lug's sling stone drives Balor's eye back through his head, directing it towards his Fomorian comrades in arms and thus debilitating them. In the remainder of the story, the Tuatha Dé Danann rout the Fomorians and, amidst much slaughter, drive them back into the sea.

Other often-cited Fomorians include: *Ágach, an enemy of the Tuatha Dé Danann; *Cailitin, a wizard slain by *Cúchulainn; *Corb, a tribal deity; *Delga, builder of the fortress of *Dun Delgan [Dundalk]; *Domnu, the mother of them all; *Indech, a king killed at Mag Tuired; *Lóbais, *druid of the Fomorians; *Morc, who emigrated from Africa; *Néit, the war-god; *Searbhán, the *one-eyed keeper of *rowan berries, who is sometimes a Fomorian; *Tethra, a warrior-chief killed at Mag Tuired. The *goat-headed *Gaborchend may be derived from the Fomorians.

Under different guises, as demonic pirates or as spirits of the earth, as earlier commentators described them, the Fomorians have appealed to the imaginations of several writers in English. W. B. Yeats spoke often of the Fomorians, whose name he spelled either Fomor or Fomoroh. His sorceress Orchil in *The Shadowy Waters* (1905) and *Dhoya (1891), the abandoned giant, are both Fomorians. The *Foawr of Manx tradition, initially a local variant of the Fomorians, are stone-throwing giants. See also Alexander H. Krappe, *Balor with the Evil Eye* (New York, 1927).

Fontes Sequanae. See SEQUANA.

fool. Courtly society in medieval Ireland, Scotland, and Wales included jesters, buffoons, and mimics for entertainment; as conventional figures in early narratives they often, like King Lear's Fool, speak more wisely than their masters. *Lomna reports the adultery of *Fionn mac Cumhaill's wife. Mac Glas, fool of *Máel Fothartaig, is killed with his master. *Do Dera tries to save his master, *Lugaid mac Con, by impersonating him in battle. Irish distinguishes between the professional fool [OIr. *drúth*] and the more modern person of poor judgement [ModIr. *amadán*], although English does not. The Irish and Scottish Gaelic folk figure *Amadán Mór* [Big Fool] is heroic; see EACHTRA AN AMADÁIN MHÓIR [The Adventure of the Big Fool].

foot-holder. An officer in the court of medieval Welsh kings; Welsh laws designate a male foot-holder whose duty was to 'rub' the king. *Math's foot-holder in the **Mabinogi* is the female virgin *Goewin.

Forbaí, Forbay, Forbuide. Variant forms of *Furbaide Ferbend.

Forbais Dromma Damgaire, Droma Dámhghaire; Forbuis Droma Damgaire. Irish titles for the medieval narrative known in English as The Siege of Knocklong. Sometimes called the '*Táin* of the south', *Forbais Dromma Damgaire* portrays a legendary invasion of *Munster by a force from *Tara led by Cormac ua Cuinn (i.e. *Cormac mac Airt). To conquer the country, Cormac magically dries up all springs, rivers, and lakes. The Munster king *Fiachu Muillethan, a longtime rival of Cormac, seeks the help of his blind magician *Mug Ruith, who rallies the Munstermen and restores the waters. Fiachu defeats Cormac at Druim Damgaire in south eastern Co. Limerick, later called Cnoc Luinge [Knocklong]. In appreciation for his help Fiachu grants to Mug Ruith and his descendants an extensive tract of land in north Co. Cork known as Mag Féne. The historical undercurrent of the stories concerns the dynastic and territorial wars between the southern *Eóganacht and the *Érainn. The text has been translated into both French (1926–7) and English (1992); see M. L. Sjoestedt-Jonval, 'Forbuis Droma Damgaire', *Revue Celtique*, 43 (1926), 1–123, and 44 (1927), 157–86; Seán Ó Duinn, *Forbhais Droma Dámhgháire* (Cork, 1992).

ford, fords. Shallow river crossings were important to the early Celts before technology provided ferries and bridges. Ritona was a Continental Celtic goddess of fords worshipped at Trier, in what is now Germany. Many hand-to-hand combats take place at fords, notably that of *Cúchulainn and *Ferdiad in the **Táin Bó Cuailnge* [Cattle Raid of Cooley]. See also the spectral figure of Irish and Scottish Gaelic folklore, the *washer at the ford.

Fordruim. Early alternate name for *Tara.

Forgael. Fictional sea-king and protagonist of W. B. Yeats's drama *Shadowy Waters* (1906), of dubious Celtic antecedents. Although Yeats explained that Forgael was based on *Angus Óg yet was somehow also a member of *Fir Bolg, informed commentators link him to the fabled 6th-century poet *Dállan Forgaill.

Forgall. Variant spelling of *Forgoll.

Forgall Manach, Monach [Ir. *monach*, dexterous; capable of tricks]. Wily father of *Emer who opposes *Cúchulainn's courtship of her and demands that the hero undertake a series of tasks, as described in *Tochmarc Emire* [The Wooing of Emer]; he wants his elder daughter *Fial (2) married first. His task-setting has prompted some commentators to compare him with Eurystheus, task-master of *Hercules. The most important of Forgall's six fortresses was Luglochta Loga [Gardens of Lug] at Lusca, coextensive with the modern Lusk, in north Co. Dublin.

Forgoll, Forgall. The learned poet who recites the story of *Mongán.

Forménus, Formenius, Fearmenius. Alpine hermit and former king of 'Thrace' who calls down fatal lightning upon *Dathí when that Irish king destroys his tower hermitage. The Continental setting may signal a non-Irish origin; some commentators have suggested a model in Faramund, cited by the medieval French chronicler Fredegar.

Fortuna. The Roman personification of fortune, luck, and chance appears frequently in ancient Celtic iconography, although she is not recorded as having a Celtic name. She is usually portrayed with a characteristic wheel or a rudder on a globe, implying an instant, random change in direction. Her wheel may associate her with the Celtic sun-god, whose solar symbol is also identified with the wheel. She is often depicted with the Gaulish *Mercury and with *Rosmerta, goddess of prosperity; her worship may have contributed to the depiction of Celtic divinities, especially Rosmerta and *Nehalennia, a mother-goddess.

fosterage. Training and protection of sons and daughters by a distinguished, often powerful patron, not a family member. The English word 'foster', often connoting charity or altruism, inadequately describes this distinctive feature of early Celtic society, which survived in Gaelic Scotland until the 18th century. Described in the *Brehon Laws of early Ireland, fosterage began when a powerful man might have children by more than one woman in his household and primogeniture did not guarantee inheritance to an oldest, legitimate son. The fosterer might be a chieftain, especially in a distant province, a *druid, or later a monk; along with the arts of war, he would give instruction in poetry, music, and games. Children were fostered at the age of 7 until the perceived age of choice, 14 for girls and 17 for boys. In Christian times foster-children were also taught revealed belief and classical languages. In maturity, a former foster-child was a useful ally to his former patron. See Fergus Kelly, *A Guide to Early Irish Law* (Dublin, 1988).

Fotha Catha Chnucha. Irish title of a *Fenian Cycle narrative known in English as 'The Cause of the Battle of Cnucha', found in the 12th-century **Book of the Dun Cow* [*Lebor na hUidre*]. The action focuses on the death of *Cumhall, father of *Fionn mac Cumhaill, and explains the long-standing enmity between the rival clans *Baíscne, led first by Cumhall and later by Fionn, and Clan *Morna, led by *Goll mac Morna. Sometimes *Conn Cétchathach [of the Hundred Battles] takes Goll's place in the rivalry. The Cnucha of the title, later called Castle Knock or Castleknock, is today located on the grounds of Castleknock College near Phoenix Park, Dublin. See W. H. Hennessy, 'The Battle of Cnucha', *Revue Celtique*, 2 (1873), 86–93.

Fothad, Fothud, Fothadh [cf. *Votadini* (?), a Celtic people of early Scotland; cf. Ir. *fothad, fothud*, the founding or establishing; support, sustenance]. Name borne by many personages in early Ireland, mythological and ecclesiastical, especially the three *Connacht warriors of ancient origin who are enemies of *Fionn mac Cumhaill. They are the children of Mac Nia and the divine *Fuinche, daughter of their leader *Dáire Derg, who nurtures them with her three breasts. This *triplism implies divine origin. Best-known of the three is ferocious Fothad Canainne, who will not sit down to dinner without placing before him the heads of those he has recently slain. Yet Fothad Canainne is true to his love vows. After he carries off the wife of *Ailill (1) of Munster with her consent, he is pursued by the enraged husband and each man dies at the other's hand. But as he has promised to return to his lover after battle, Fothad comes back to meet her regularly, even after death, giving rise to the *Fenian poem translated by Kuno Meyer as 'The Tryst After Death', *Revue Celtique*, 15 (1910), 4–17. In later oral tradition Fothad is somehow joined to Fionn's *Fianna, and he is sometimes seen as the mate of the *Cailleach Bhéirre. His daughter is *Smirgat (or Smirnat). The other brothers are shadowy; Fothad Airgthech slew Fothad Cairthech and his death was reported by the *Fenian hero *Caílte. The trio are often cited by medieval pseudo-historians and genealogists, and Fothad Canainne is described as the ancestor of the Uaithne sept of north-eastern Limerick.

Fótla, Fotla. Variant spellings of *Fódla.

fountain. *Cormac mac Airt visits the Fountain of Knowledge in *Tír Tairngire [The Land of Promise]. For Lady of the Fountain, see OWAIN. See also the Fountain of Baranton in BROCÉLIANDE.

Four Ancient Books of Wales. Title of a once influential, now superseded, two-volume collection of poetry in Welsh with English translation, edited by William Forbes Skene (Edinburgh, 1868; repr. New York, 1982). The four cited are: **Black Book of Carmarthen*, **Book of Aneirin*, **Book of Taliesin* and the **Red Book of Hergest*.

Four Branches of the Mabinogi. See MABINOGI.

Four Masters. See ANNALS OF THE FOUR MASTERS.

foxglove. The healing powers, real and supposed, of the tall plant with distinctive white or purple flowers (genus *digitalis*) have been known since classical times. Poisonous if swallowed, it is applied externally for sprains, bruises, and bone ailments. In Gaelic and Welsh traditions its powers are thought to flow from the realm of the *fairy; its name means literally 'fairy fingers' [*méirini púca*] or 'fairy thimble' [*méaracán sídhe*] in Irish and 'banshee herb' in Scottish Gaelic [*lus-nam-ban-s'th*; cf. Ir. *lus na mban sídhe*]. Its prestige in Ireland is shown in the Hiberno-English word for foxglove, lusmore [Ir. *lus mór*, great herb]. Manx sleggan; W bysedd y cw^n [dog finger]; Corn. mannek lowarn [foxglove]; Bret. bruluenn.

Fráech, Fraích (gen.), Fraich, Fráich, Fraoch, Fróech [OIr. *fráech*, heather]. Name borne by dozens of personages from early Ireland, both legendary and historical. Previously Fráech mac Idaith was thought to be distinct from Fráech mac Fidaig (or mac Fiodach); more recent commentary has argued that the identity of the *Connacht warrior in the *Ulster Cycle Fráech persists through several narratives, even though the action is discontinuous and contradictory.

Hero of the 8th-century *Táin Bó Fraích* [Cattle Raid of Fráech], an antecedent to the action of the epic **Táin Bó Cuailnge* [Cattle Raid of Cooley], Fráech is the son of the divine *Bébinn, sister of *Boand, and the handsomest young man in all Ireland. So great is his reputation for masculine allure that *Finnabair, daughter of Queen *Medb and *Ailill, falls in love with him just hearing about him. Learning of this, Fráech seeks out Finnabair, whom he finds washing her hands in the river. She refuses to elope with him, but gives him a thumb ring she has received from her father and asks Fráech to seek his approval for the match. Ailill demands an exorbitant bridal price for Finnabair: all of Fráech's wealth, including the magical red-eared *cows he had received from his mother. Fráech refuses. Later while the young man is swimming, Ailill, fearful that Fráech might elope with his daughter steals the gift thumb ring and throws it into the water, where it is swallowed by a *salmon. He also commands that Fráech fetch some *rowan berries that will prolong life and cure illness. As Ailill knows, the berries are near the dwelling of a *dragon [Ir. *péist*], which he hopes will devour the swain. Fráech, with Finnabair's help, slays the dragon, but is wounded in the venture. One hundred and fifty maidens from the *sídh, clad in crimson and green, take him first to the *Otherworld, where he is healed, and then bear him back to Ailill's palace at *Cruachain. At a triumphal banquet, Ailill demands the thumb ring, which Fráech produces, having previously caught the salmon that swallowed it. With the ring restored, Ailill grants Fráech's wish, and Fráech agrees to bring his herd of cows to Cruachain.

In the second, seemingly unrelated part of *Táin Bó Fraích*, the hero returns to his fortress one day to find that his wife, three sons, and herd of magical cows have been abducted. In seeking them out he is aided by *Conall Cernach. They find the captives in a great fortress in the Alps, where a servant of Irish descent conveniently leaves a door open for the rescuers at night. Upon his return, Fráech then joins Medb and Ailill on the great cattle raid to retrieve the Brown Bull of Ulster. Within the action of the *Táin Bó Cuailnge*, Fráech is drowned in hand-to-hand combat with *Cúchulainn.

The popularity of Fráech's story persisted in several variant written texts from the 11th to the 14th centuries, continuing in Irish and Scottish Gaelic oral tradition, changing the names of characters and details of the action. Numerous commentators have seen an anticipation of the Old English *Beowulf* in Fráech's slaying of the dragon. The motif of the ring in the fish's belly is an Irish instance of the international tale type 736A. It has been edited several times: by Mary E. Byrne and Myles Dillon, *Táin Bó Fraích* (Dublin, 1933); Wolfgang Meid, *Táin Bó Fraích* (Dublin, 1967; rev. edn., 1974) and *Die Romanze von Froech und Findabair* (Innsbruck, 1970). See also J. F. Campbell, *The Celtic Dragon Myth* (Edinburgh, 1911; repr. New York, 1973; North Hollywood, 1981); Donald E. Meek, 'Táin Bó Fraich and other "Fraech" Texts; A Study in Thematic Relationships, (I-II)', *Cambridge Medieval Celtic Studies*, 7 (1984), 1–37.

Fragarach. Variant spelling of *Frecraid.

Fraích. Variant spelling of *Fráech.

France. See BRITTANY; GAUL.

Fraoch. Variant spelling of *Fráech.

Frecraid, Fragarach, Freagarach [Ir. *frecraid*, answerer]. Terrible sword of *Manannán mac Lir that could pierce any mail and whose every wound was fatal. It was brought by *Lug Lámfhota from *Tír na mBeó [the Land of the Living].

frenzy. See BUILE SHUIBHNE [The Frenzy of Suibne]; MONGÁN; CÚCHULAINN.

frìde, frid, fridean (pl.) [ScG *frìde*, gnome, pigmy, elf, rock-elfin]. Supernatural creature or *fairy of Scottish Highland folklore who lives in or under rocks and devours all spilled milk or crumbs. In a widely known story a piper and his dog follow the fridean into a winding cavern, his music still being heard by mortals above ground; the piper never returns, but the dog returns hairless and immediately dies. Folk motif: V12.9.

Friuch [Ir., boar's thistles]. Pig-keeper of *Bodb Derg at the beginning of the *Táin Bó Cuailnge* [Cattle Raid of Cooley], whose perpetual rivalry with Rucht, pig-keeper of Ochall Ochne, causes him to be transformed into *Donn Cuailnge, the much sought-after Brown Bull of *Ulster. Sometimes confused with *Nár, another swineherd of Bodb Derg.

Froech. Variant spelling of *Fráech.

Fuad, Fuadh, Fuait. *Milesian chief, son of *Breogan, for whom *Sliab Fúait [Slieve Fuad] in Co. Armagh is named.

Fuamnach, Fúamnach, Fuamach [cf. OIr. *fúamnach*, lamentation of the fair-skinned vocal woman]. First wife of *Midir who seeks to destroy her husband's second wife, the beautiful *Étaín. She takes a potion from *Bresal Etarláim, usually described as her foster-father, she transforms Étaín into a fly (or butterfly). See TOCHMARC ÉTAÍNE [The Wooing of Étaín].

fuath, fuathan (pl.), vough [ScG, hatred, aversion; cf. OIr. *fúath*, hate; likeness]. Generic term for a class of spectral monsters in Highland Gaelic folklore, usually having a close connection with water, lochs, rivers, and often the open sea. Sometimes known as the arrachd or fuath-arrachd. A fuath is the mother of the *brollachan. Highland subspecies of the fuath include the *beithir, *fideal, *peallaidh, and *ùruisg. Vough is a phonetic anglicization. See also ARRACH; GLAISTIG. Folk motifs: F420.5.2; F470.

Fuinche, Faince, Fuince [cf. Ir. *fuinche*, claw, talon; *fuinche*, scald-crow, black fox]. Name borne by many female personages in early Ireland, historical and legendary, including fourteen saints, but most notably by the divine daughter of *Dáire Derg and mother of the three *Fothads by a warrior named Mac Nia. She was said to have three breasts, like the legendary saints Fainche Tré-Chíchech and Ardmáer Tréchíchech or the Welsh saint Gwenn Teirbronn. In lesser-known variant texts she is cited as the mother of *Fionn mac Cumhaill.

Furbaide, Foirbre, Forbaí, Forbay. Name borne by at least two personages from early Irish narrative, of whom *Furbaide Ferbend is the better-known.

Furbaide 1. Son attributed to *Eochaid Feidlech, cited for his extraordinary birth 'through the side of his mother', i.e. Caesarian, like *Goll mac Morna, Buddha, the Egyptian god Set, and Julius *Caesar.

Furbaide Ferbend, Ferbenn, Fur Bend [Ir., the cut one]. Sometimes called Furbaide the Horned in English texts. *Ulster warrior, son of *Conchobar mac Nessa, protégé of *Cúchulainn, who kills *Medb, queen of *Connacht, with his sling loaded with hard cheese while she is bathing in *Lough Ree in the *Shanonn, Co. Roscommon; this avenges Medb's murder of *Clothra, Medb's sister and Furbaide's mother, at the same place. Furbaide had been cut from his dying mother's womb. He is portrayed with *bull horns, as is *Feradach Fechtnach; in the **Dindshenchas* he has three horns. Some commentators assert that the horns echo the ancient Celtic god *Cernunnos.

Fursa, Fursu, Fursey. Name borne by numerous early Irish ecclesiastics, such as the monk who evangelized East Anglia and later founded a monastery near Paris. To this 7th-century Irish saint (feast-day 16 June) is ascribed the horrific vision of the Christian afterlife, cited by the Venerable Bede (731) and often thought to have anticipated Dante's *Divina Commedia* (14th cent.). See Charles S. Boswell, *An Irish Precursor of Dante* (London, 1908); William W. Heist, *Vitae Sanctorum Hiberniae* (Brussels, 1965); Pádraig Ó Riain, 'Les Vies de Saint Fursy: les sources irlandaises', *Revue du Nord*, 68 (1986), 405–13; 'Sanctity and the Politics of Connacht c. 1100: The Case of St. Fursa', *Cambridge Medieval Celtic Studies*, 17 (1989), 1–14.

fynnoderee. Variant spelling of *fenodyree.

G

G. The seventh letter of the modern English alphabet is represented by gort [ivy] in the *ogham alphabet of early Ireland.

ga-. Variant spelling of *gáe- [Ir., spear, javelin].

Gabála, Lebor. See LEBOR GABÁLA.

Gabhair, nominative form of Gabhra (gen.); anglicizations: **Gowra, Gavra.** Site of the Battle of Gabhair/Gowra, portrayed in the Irish narrative **Cath Gabhra*, the climactic action of the *Fenian Cycle, which brings an end to the power of the *Fianna; coextensive with modern Garristown in north Co. Dublin. Variant texts place the action at Skreen, Co. Meath.

Gabhála, Leabhar. See LEBOR GABÁLA.

Gabhra. Genitive form of *Gabhair, as in **Cath Gabhra* [The Battle of Gabhair/Gowra].

Gaborchend, Gaborchind (pl.). Monstrous *goat-headed people of early Irish folklore.

Gadelus. Latinized form of *Goídel Glas.

gáe, gae, gaí, gai, ga. Irish word for spear, javelin; the spears of many Irish warriors have specific names and appear almost personified.

Gáe Assail [spear of Assal]. Lightning spear of *Lug Lámfhota, which returns to the hands of the thrower; named for a previous owner. It would bring certain death to the victim if the wielder uttered the word ibar [*yew] as he cast forth. The sons of *Tuirenn fetched it for Lug. One of the four treasures of the *Tuatha Dé Danann.

Gáe Buide, Buidhe, Boi [yellow spear]. Smaller spear of *Diarmait Ua Duibne that once belonged to *Manannán mac Lir. His larger spear was *Gáe Dearg.

Gáe Bulga, Bolga, Bulg, Bolg. Terrible weapon of the *Ulster Cycle, which entered the victim at one point but made thirty wounds within. Deeply notched and characterized by lightning speed, Gáe Bulga was made from the bones of a sea-monster killed in a duel with another monster of greater size. Although usually the possession of *Cúchulainn, received from his female tutor *Scáthach, Gáe Bulga also appears in the hands of other heroes. How it was used is still a matter of some conjecture. When Cúchulainn uses it to kill *Ferdiad, he casts it from the 'fork of his foot', i.e. between his toes. Also used to kill *Connla.

Gáe Derg, Dearg [red spear]. Greater spear of *Diarmait Ua Duibne, used against a witch-woman who threw darts at him from the sky. Diarmait also had Gáe Derg with him in his fatal *boar-hunt with *Fionn mac Cumhaill. His smaller spear is *Gáe Buide.

gáe sídhe, sí. See FAIRY DART.

Gáedel, Gaedhal. Variant forms of *Goídel Glas.

Gael. Name of disputed origin for the Irish and Scottish Gaelic peoples, speakers of related *Goidelic, *Q-Celtic languages. An insupportable popular perception persists that the name for the Gaelic people is somehow derived from *Goídel Glas, the inventor of the Irish language in the medieval pseudo-history **Lebor Gabála* [Book of Invasions]. OIr. Goídel is the word both for the supposed eponymous ancestor of the Irish language and for an Irishman or Scottish Highlander. Gael is indeed a modern form, in both Irish and English contexts, for Goídel, and Gael is the reformed ModIr. word for Irishman; cf. unreformed, Gaedheal. Learned commentators argue, however, that the OIr. Goídel predates the composition of the *Lebor Gabála* and derives from the OW word for Irishman, Gwyddel, which may derive from the OW gwydd [wild]. A third popular perception, that Gael is a variant of the Celtic phoneme -gal-, the name for the Celtic people as found in *Gaul, Galicia, *Galatia, etc., is simply a misreading. Lastly, the *Oxford English Dictionary*, 2nd edn. (1989) cites the oldest use of Gael in English (1596), deriving from the ScG

Gàidheal and denoting a Scottish Highlander.

Gaeltacht. Irish name for the surviving Irish-speaking areas as well as for the Irish-speaking people taken as a whole. See also GAIDHEALTACHD.

Gaesatae, Gaesati [cf. OIr. *gáe*, spear, javelin]. Name used by the classical commentator *Polybius (2nd cent. BC) for ancient Celtic warriors who served outside the tribal system. His descriptions are vivid: they throw off their clothes to fight naked in battle, their blond, lime-hardened hair standing erect, their golden bracelets glinting in the sun. Modern commentators dispute Polybius' contention that the Gaesatae were mercenaries. They are commonly seen as anticipations of *fianna of early Ireland, especially the Fianna Érainn of *Fionn mac Cumhaill. Their nakedness at going into battle was not unique, as other ancient Celtic warriors are recorded as following the same practice, apparently from the belief that nakedness would provide magical protection from the gods.

gaí, gai. Variant spellings of *gáe.

Gaiar. The only son of *Deirdre and *Noíse. See GAIDIAR.

Gaiblín, Gaibhlín, Gaibhle, Gaibhleen, Goibhleann, Gavida. Possible owner of *Glas Ghaibhleann, the magical *cow; lived in Co. Cavan. He may be a folk derivative of *Goibniu, the ancient craft-god.

Gaidhealtachd. ScG term for those regions in *Scotland where Gaelic is still spoken. See also GAELTACHT.

Gaidiar. Son of *Mannanán mac Lir in **Echtrae Airt meic Cuinn* [The Adventure of Art Son of Conn] whose adultery with *Bé Chuma caused her to be expelled from *Tír Tairngire [the Land of Promise]. See GAIAR.

Gaileoin, Gáileóin, Gáilióin, Gailioin. Variant spellings of *Galióin.

Gáirech, Garach. Site of the last battle in the **Táin Bó Cuailnge* [Cattle Raid of Cooley] in which the men of *Ulster, led by *Cúchulainn, finally overcame the forces of *Connacht led by Queen *Medb; identified with the modern Garhy near Mullingar, Co. Westmeath.

Galahad, Galaad. Morally immaculate Grail-questing hero of the Arthurian legends. Although Galahad does not have an obvious parallel in Celtic literatures, enthusiasts have posited a Welsh etymology for his name: gwalch [hawk, falcon, crested one]; cad [battle]. See Rachel Bromwich, *Trioedd Ynys Prydain*, rev. edn. (Cardiff, 1978), 353ff.

Galam, Galamh, Golam, Golamh. Birth-name of *Míl Espáine.

Galan Mai. Mutated form of Calan Mai and Dydd Calan Mai [W, May Day]; see BELTAINE.

Galata. Gaulish princess described in Greek mythology. According to *Diodorus Siculus (1st cent. BC) and others, Galata mated with Heracles to produce the race of warlike mercenaries, the *Galatians.

Galatia. Ancient district in central Anatolia, between the Halys (now Kizilirmak) and Sangarius (Sakarya), settled by Celtic peoples from the 3rd century BC until they were absorbed into Hellenistic civilization. Culturally much like the Celts of Continental Europe, their name is a variant of *Gaul. The Galatians clung to their language and customs despite being distant from the centres of Celtic civilization. The neighbouring Greeks accommodated them by explaining that they derived from *Heracles and his Gaulish lover *Galata. Their country was the site of one of several shrines known as *Drunemeton. Evangelized by St Paul in the Epistle to the Galatians. As late as the 5th century St Jerome reported that the language of Ancyra (Ankara) was similar to that spoken near Treves (Trier) in the Moselle valley, of what is today Germany and France. See Stephen Mitchell, *Land, Men and Gods in Asia Minor* (2 vols., Oxford, 1993).

Galióin, Gálioin, Gaileoin, Gáileóin, Gáilióin, Gailioin, Galeoin, Gálian, Galion, Galioin. Historical invaders of Ireland with mythic and legendary associations. Linked to the more prominent *Lagin, they settled in north *Leinster, especially in what is today counties Wicklow, Kildare, and Cavan, but they ranged as far to the west as Co. Mayo. In the pseudo-history **Lebor Gabála* [Book of Invasions] the Galióin are a subdivision of the *Fir Bolg, under their king *Sláinge, who is killed at the great Leinster fortress *Dind Ríg (Co. Carlow). In the **Táin Bó Cuailnge* [Cattle Raid of Cooley] Medb is awestruck by the might of 5,000 assembled Galióin and refuses them as allies, as they would likely gain greater glory.

Fearful that as freebooters they might lay waste to her kingdom of *Connacht, she is about to have them slaughtered when her husband *Ailill objects. *Fergus mac Róich counsels that individual Galióin soldiers be scattered among her ranks, which is how they serve in the assault on *Ulster.

Gall. General name for a foreigner in early Irish literature, who may be at different times (*a*) a Gaul, (*b*) a Scandinavian invader, (*c*) an Anglo-Norman or Irishman of Anglo-Norman descent. In Scottish Gaelic the term denotes (*a*) a Lowlander, (*b*) any foreigner.

Gallizenae. Virgin *druidesses of the Isle de Sein, off Pointe du Raz, *Finistère, western *Brittany. They had the power to predict the future, to calm the winds, and to take the forms of different animals.

galloglass, gallowglass [Ir. *gall*, foreigner, esp. Norseman; *óglach*, youth, warrior]. Foreign soldiers in Irish service from medieval to early modern times, characteristically heavily armed. Although their name implies Norse origin, they more likely came from Norse-influenced areas in the Hebrides and Gaelic Scotland. Although their often humdrum existence is attested to in numerous Irish records, their lives have been the focus of romantic fiction; see Howard Breslin, *The Gallowglass* (New York, 1958).

Gamanrad, Gamhanra. Warrior sept or family of early Ireland, associated with the area near Erris, Co. Mayo, *Connacht; although historical, they are associated with the pseudo-historical *Fir Bolg.

gan ceann, gan-ceann [Ir., without a head]. Headless, somewhat threatening Irish *fairy, comparable to the *dullahan. Unlike other fairies, he fears gold; a gan ceann would have overtaken a boat for America if not for a gold pin dropped in his path. Confused with but very different from the *ganconer.

ganconer, gancanagh, gean-cannach, geancánach. Amorous *leprechaun-like but false *fairy of Irish folk tradition, sometimes known in English as the 'love talker'. Always seen with a pipe [Ir. *dúidín*, dudeen] in his mouth, the ganconer haunts lonely valleys, speaking his love to milkmaids and shepherdesses, then abandoning them, leaving them to pine for death. Portrayed in Ethna Carbery's poem 'The Love-Talker', *Four Winds of Erin* (Dublin, 1902). W. B. Yeats records ganconers who play at hurling, *Irish Fairy and Folk Tales* (London, 1893). Confused with but very different from the *gan ceann. Folk motif: F301.2.

Gann. Leader of the *Fir Bolg invasion, son of *Dela; together with his brother Sengann takes the two parts of *Munster.

gans an howl [Corn., with/by the sun]. Cornish phrase for a *sunwise turn.

Gaodhal Glas. Variant spelling of *Goídel Glas.

Gaoine. Another name for *Mac Lugach.

gaoth sídhe, sí. Irish phrases for *fairy wind.

Garach. Variant spelling of *Gáirech.

Garad, Garadh, mac Morna. Sometimes with the epithet Glúndubh [Ir., black knee]. A leader of the *Connacht *fianna in the *Fenian Cycle. Although Garad is a frequent opponent of *Fionn, his daughter *Maigneis becomes Fionn's second wife. At *Cath Gabhra [The Battle of Gabhair/Gowra] Garad wounds *Oscar.

Garanhir. Epithet of *Gwyddno Garanhir.

Garb, Garbh [Ir., rough, coarse, rugged, rude]. Name borne by several personages, male and female, historical and legendary, human and animal, in early Irish tradition. Most notable is the two-headed monster of Glenn Rige, Co. Down, slain by *Cúchulainn.

Garb mac Stairn. Champion of purported Scandinavian origin in a late (17th cent.?) *Ulster Cycle narrative. When he demands tribute from *Tara, all comply except *Cúchulainn. *Briccriu chides Garb and then begins a week-long combat with him that ends when Cúchulainn beheads Garb with a single stroke from his sword. The name Garb[h] mac Stairn is cited for strength in Scottish Gaelic proverbs. James *Macpherson drew on Garb mac Stairn in the creating of the arch-villain Swaran in the *Poems of Ossian* (1760).

Gareint. Variant spelling of *Geraint.

Gareth. Hero of Arthurian romance, son of Lot and Morgawse, sponsored by *Lancelot and later mistakenly struck down by him. Known as Beaumains in Sir Thomas Malory (*c.*1470). Although the name Gareth may be of Welsh origin, an earlier speculation, gwaredd [benign, gentle], is now rejected. The French spelling is Gaheriet.

Gargam [Bret., curved thigh]. Kind of *giant in Breton oral tradition thought to roam at night. Nicknamed 'lame' [Fr. *boiteux*], he appears to have contributed to the giant Gargantua of Rabelais's celebrated satire (1532). His probable Welsh counterpart is Gwrgwnt.

Garlach Coileánach, An [Ir. *garlach*, child, brat, urchin; *coileánach*, mischievous, whelp, puppy]. A nimble-witted boy appearing in numerous Modern Irish folk-tales. When he is introduced, he is usually illegitimate, naked, and starving. He may labour as a cowherd. Through his resolve and inventive mind, he usually attains great wealth.

Garland Sunday. See LUGHNASA.

Garmuin, Garmna. Wife of *Ercol in **Fled Bricrenn* [Bricriu's Feast].

Garret Óg, 11th Earl of Kildare. See MULLAGHMAST.

Garwen. Woman's name cited in Welsh lyrics from the 9th century and later in medieval English poetry, evocative of beauty and nobility. Daughter of the obscure king Henin or Henyn, she may be identified with Wyrwein, one of *Arthur's three mistresses.

Gathelus. Variant form of *Goídel Glas.

Gaul [L *Gallia*]. English name for the land in antiquity populated by *P-Celtic-speaking peoples, south and west of the Rhine, west of the Alps, and north of the Pyrenees, approximately coextensive with the modern nations of France, Germany west of the Rhine, Belgium, and western Switzerland. The culture and language of the Celts extended across the Alps into Cisalpine Gaul [L *Gallia Cisalpina*], what is today northern Italy down to the Apennines; at various times Celtic dialect was also spoken in much of northern Europe, from Austria, Hungary, the Czech Republic, Slovakia, much of the Balkans, to *Galatia in what is today Turkey. Little can be known about the Gauls from the meagre surviving documents in the Gaulish language, but we can see obvious parallels with Welsh, Cornish, and Breton as well as more remote links to Old Irish. Most of what we know about Gaul derives from the sometimes prejudiced views of *classical commentators, beginning with Julius *Caesar, who conquered the country 59–50 BC. The historical leader of Gaulish resistance, *Vercingetorix, has been the focus of many legends. Recent archaeological evidence has demonstrated that the Gauls were far less barbaric than the conquering Romans implied.

Most gods of Gaul are known to us by Roman names. *Tacitus (2nd cent. AD) used the phrase *interpretatio romana* for the process under which the Romans described the gods of the Celts as if they were indeed Roman divinities. Thus a native god whose name is lost to us is now referred to as Gaulish *Mercury, Gaulish *Mars, etc. Iconographic evidence shows that the ancient Gauls acceded to this forced identification by portraying their gods with Roman affects. Modern commentators have coined the phrase *interpretatio celtica* to describe the reverse phenomenon in which the Celts adapted Roman gods into their own belief systems, venerating the god under a Latin name but adding a Celtic epithet. Caesar determined six principal gods of the Gauls and ranked them as he perceived a Gaulish pantheon: Mercury, *Apollo, Mars, *Jupiter, *Minerva, and *Dis Pater (Pluto). Modern commentators doubt that the Gauls clearly differentiated the functions of particular gods or of any pantheon that was propitiated throughout their culture. The names of other native gods survive in inscriptions at various shrines and in other classical commentators, but these also are called into question. The god *Teutates cited by Lucan (1st cent. AD) may simply derive from the 'god of the tribe'; cf. teutā, 'tribe'; OIr. túath, 'people, tribe, nation'.

See Olwen Brogan, *Roman Gaul* (Cambridge, Mass., 1953); Jean-Jacques Hatt, *Celts and Gallo-Romans*, trans. James Hogarth (London, 1970); J. L. Brunaux, *The Celtic Gauls: Gods, Rites and Sanctuaries* (London, 1978); H. D. Rankin, *Celts and the Classical World* (London, 1987); Pierre-Yves Lambert, *La Langue gauloise: description linguistique, commentaire d'inscriptions choisies* (Paris, 1994). See also Bibliography under 'Ancient and Continental'.

2. Alternate spelling of *Macpherson's Goll 2.

Gauvain. French form of *Gawain.

Gavida. Anglicization of *Gaiblín.

Gavrinis, Gavr'inis, Gavr'Innis [Bret., island of *goats]. Site of the most lavishly decorated megalithic tomb (*c.*3500 BC) in Europe; a small island in the Gulf of Morbihan, off the south coast of *Brittany, 7 miles SW of Vannes. Often compared with the passage grave at Newgrange, Co. Meath, the Gavrinis tomb is smaller (20 feet high, 164 feet round), older, and more decorated. The island was once the destination of Christian pilgrimages and features prominently in Breton folklore. The islet of Er-Lannic just south of Gavrinis contains two stone circles.

Gawain, Gawayne, Gawen, Gavin, Gauvain (Fr.) [cf. W *gwalchmai*, hawk/falcon of May; *gwalch(g)wyn*, white hawk/falcon; Bret. *Walchmoe*; L Gualganus]. The principal hero of Arthurian romances, nephew of *Arthur, son of Lot and Morgawse of Orkney whose links to the Celtic world have been extensively commented upon. His name in Welsh is *Gwalchmai fab Gwyar [son of Gwyar, the Welsh name for Lot in **Culhwch ac Olwen*]. The anonymous *Sir Gawain and the Green Knight* (written *c.*1370), the masterpiece of Middle English Arthuriana, contains unmistakable parallels with the beheading contest in the latter half of **Fled Bricrenn* [Briccriu's Feast]. A character very much like Gawain appears in the early Modern Irish romance *Eachtra an Mhadra Mhaoil* [The Adventure of the Crop-Eared Dog] under the name Sir Bhalbhauidh. Additionally, the temptress wife in *Sir Gawain* shows parallels with *Pwyll and the wife of *Arawn.

geancánach, gean-cannach. Irish forms of *ganconer.

Gearóid, Gearóidh Iarla. See GERALD, EARL OF DESMOND.

Gearóid Óg, 11th Earl of Kildare. See MULLAGHMAST.

geasa. A plural form for *geis.

Gebann. Chief *druid of *Manannán mac Lir and father of the beautiful *Clídna. Variant texts give him as the father of *Étaín Fholtfhind instead of her usual father, *Étar.

Gebrinius. Probable name of a local divinity of Ubii people of eastern *Gaul. The name is linked with that of Gaulish *Mercury at a shrine (2nd cent. AD) near the modern German city of Bonn, where he is seen in full Roman guise.

Geena mac Luga. Anglicization of *Gíona mac Lugha.

geilt. Old Irish word meaning 'he who goes mad from terror', most often describing Suibne; see BUILE SHUIBNE [The Madness of Suibne].

geis, gessa (OIr. pl.), **geasa** (ModIr. pl.), **geiss, geissi, ges, gesa, geas.** The idiosyncratic taboo or prohibition placed upon heroes and prominent personages in Irish narratives. In certain contexts the imposition of a geis may require a positive demand or injunction or may specify other actions as forbidden or unlawful. In yet other contexts it may be synonymous with the English incantation or spell, and perhaps even a point of honour.

Many of the thousands of instances of an imposed geis initially appear capricious or wilful, until they are seen in a larger context. *Cúchulainn, for example, was forbidden to eat the meat of a *dog or hound; but he earned his name [*Cú*, hound; *chulainn*, of Culann] when he killed a ferocious dog. That so many gessa are imposed upon kings-e.g. that the ruler of *Tara should not have the sun rise above him while he was still in bed there-suggests the concept may have originated in early rituals of *kingship. Some are prescribed by *druids at birth. The breaking of a geis often brings instant death and sometimes also ill favour or destruction to the culprit's people.

Many gessa are imposed by women upon men. In several stories of the *Sovereignty figure (usually seen first as a disgusting hag), she defeats the hero in a game or asks him a riddle he cannot answer and rewards herself with a geis he initially finds impossible to perform. In several love stories, e.g. *Deirdre, *Gráinne, and *Diarmait, the heroine places the hero under geis to elope with her. See also GLÁM DÍCENN.

See John R. Reinhard, *The Survival of Geis in Medieval Romance* (Halle, 1933); Phillip O'Leary, 'The Honour of Women in Early Irish Literature', *Ériu*, 38 (1987), 27–44; 'Honour-Bound: The Social Context of Early Irish Heroic *Geis*', *Celtica*, 20 (1988), 85–107.

Gelbann, Gelban. Spy for *Conchobar mac Nessa in most versions of the *Deirdre story. Although the son of the king of *Lochlainn, Gelbann was dispatched by Conchobar to see if Deirdre's beauty had faded while she was on the run with her lover Noíse. Noticing Gelbann peering through the window, Noíse threw a *fidchell piece at him, putting out his eye. But Gelbann retorted that he would gladly surrender his other eye to gaze again upon Deirdre's beauty. In some versions of the story Conchobar's servant Tréndorn plays the spy.

Gelert, Gellert. See BEDD GELERT.

Genius Cucullatus, Genii Cucullati (pl.) [L *genius*, deity of generation or birth, guardian spirit; *cucullus*, hood fastened to cloak or coat]. Name ascribed to cultic images from Celtic shrines built during Roman occupation. Though the images vary in size from the *dwarfish to the *giant, they are identified by hooded outdoor garments. Closed from neck to knee as well as hooded, the cucullus was commonly worn by contemporary Celtic peoples and implied an affinity between the god/s and worshippers. Some modern commentators perceive a phallic shape to the garment; on some surviving figures the garment is removed to expose a phallus; on others the god's phallus is used as a lamp holder. Other commentators perceive female breasts through the robes as well as soft feminine faces under the hoods. Further associations with fertility arise from the Genii Cucullati portrayed carrying eggs. On the Continent the Genius Cucullatus is a solitary figure, while in Britain they are always represented in threes (see TRIPLISM), as in the well-preserved and much-photographed relief at Housteads on Hadrian's Wall. Elsewhere in Britain they accompany the prosperity deities *Mercury and *Rosmerta.

Gentle Annis, Annie. Weather-spirit thought to drive the southwesterly gales on the Firth of Cromarty in the Scottish Highlands. Her changeability implies treachery. Commentators have seen her as a Scottish incarnation of the *Cailleach Bhéirre and have sought to trace her name to *Ana. Folk motif: F430.

Geodruisge. Local variant of *Dunbristy.

Geoffrey of Monmouth. Welsh bishop (*c*.1090–1155) and pseudo-historian, author of the Latin *Historia Regum Britanniae* [History of the Kings of Britain] (1136), which euhemerizes Arthurian legends as well as many Welsh-language narratives. Little is known of Geoffrey's life; he was born near the town of Monmouth and on evidence of his writings he knew south-east *Wales well and must have visited *Brittany. An Augustinian at Oxford University, he became bishop of St Asaph, a see he may never have visited. His *Historia* purports to give an account of British history from the conception of Christ and culminating in the reign of *Arthur. While drawing on recognized sources such as Bede (early 8th cent.) and **Historia Brittonum* (9th cent.) and lost Welsh sources, Geoffrey claimed to have relied mainly on a 'most ancient' book given him by Walter Calenius, which is not cited by any other contemporary chronicler. The *Historia* creates Arthur as a romantic hero, despite Geoffrey's lack of interest in courtly love and fear of women. *Merlin also becomes a fuller dramatic character in Geoffrey's hands. See Lewis Thorpe (trans.), *History of the Kings of Britain* (Harmondsworth, 1966); J. J. Parry and R. A. Caldwell, 'Geoffrey of Monmouth', in R. S. Loomis (ed.), *Arthurian Literature in the Middle Ages* (Oxford, 1959), 72–93.

Georóid Iarla. Variant form of *Gerald, Earl of Desmond.

Geraid. A leading figure of the *Fianna of *Fionn mac Cumhaill.

Geraint, Gereint, Keraint, often with patronymic fab [son of] Erbin [cf. L *Gerontius*]. Welsh Arthurian hero usually portrayed with his wife, Enid. The putative historical model for the hero, the 6th-century (d. 580) king of *Dumnonia [Devon], would have been two generations younger than *Arthur, but in romance he is seen as Arthur's contemporary and cousin. Manuscripts of the 13th-century prose romance *Geraint ac Enid* are found in the **White Book of Rhydderch* (*c*.1325) and the **Red Book of Hergest* (*c*.1382–1410) and elsewhere. Along with **Owain* and **Peredur* it is part of **Tair Rhamant* [Three Romances]. Lady Charlotte Guest included it in her translation of *The Mabinogion* (1846), as have later translators.

Geraint sets the action in motion by avenging an insult to Arthur's wife, here called *Gwenhwyfar; he defeats the Knight of the Sparrowhawk, who is revealed to be *Edern mab Nudd. In thanks for his help against Edern, Geraint restores Yniwl to his kingdom near Cardiff, wins the king's daughter Enid as his wife, and returns to Arthur's court, where he receives a *stag's head as a reward. In time, Geraint inherits the kingdom from his father-in-law and rules it with Enid. Because he devotes more time to his wife than he does to jousts or battles, Geraint's subjects complain bitterly, which Enid inadvertently repeats to him. Geraint then treats Enid rather badly before setting out on a journey to prove his valour and strength. He performs extraordinary feats and slaughters warlike knights and ruffians in great numbers, but nearly kills himself in the attempt. Redeemed in the eyes of Enid and subjects, Geraint rules once more, despite his suspicions of her infidelity.

The corresponding 12th-century French romance *Erec* or *Erec et Enide* by *Chrétien de Troyes differs in ascribing the hero's cruelty to Enid to jealousy. Some commentators argue that the French version is closer to original sources, its hero's name deriving from the Breton Guerec. Alfred Lord Tennyson's once widely known *Geraint and Enid* (1859) in his *Idylls of the King* draws more from Chrétien than from the Welsh *Geraint ac Enid*.

See also GERENNIUS. See Rachel Bromwich, *Trioedd Ynys Prydain*, rev. edn. (Cardiff, 1978), 355–60, 551.

Gerald, Earl of Desmond, Gearóid Iarla, Georóid Iarla, Geróit Iarla [Ir., OGer. *Gearovald*, from *ger*, spear; *vald*, rule]. Historical (1338–98) Hiberno-Norman nobleman, composer of love poetry, who became 3rd Earl of *Desmond (i.e. south *Munster) in 1358, and around whom fabulous legends have accrued.

Gerald's conception was magical. His father, Earl Maurice, saw the beautiful otherworldly woman *Áine on the shores of *Lough Gur, Co. Limerick, which was family property. By seizing her cloak he gained power over her and then lay with her; in nine months Áine presented the son Gerald at the castle door. In maturity Gerald frequently showed his magical ability, but in many stories this power precipitates a mysterious departure. After astonishing his father by leaping in and out of a bottle, he took the form of a goose, waded into the nearby Camogue River, and swam away. More commonly, he grows to maturity and marries, but his wife is curious that he practises magic spells in a private room and asks to see them. In a twinkling he turns himself into a goldfinch who plays at his wife's bosom, until he is pursued by a predatory hawk, which she dashes against a wall, killing it. But the lady cannot find the goldfinch, and Earl Gerald is never seen again. He is thought to live in his castle at the bottom of Lough Gur, it and the entire household having sunk there.

As his family, the Geraldines, Fitzgeralds, or Mac Gearailts, were both highly Gaelicized and powerful, Earl Gerald's interactions with the *Otherworld are rife with political implications and have numerous parallels in English, French, and German traditions. Gerald's persona unquestionably grew more prominent in Irish tradition with the Geraldine (Kildare branch) rebellion of 1534 and the failed military career of the 2nd Earl Gerald of Desmond (d. 1583). The story of Gerald's conception has parallels in the affair between *Ailill Aulomm and Áine, and *Cnoc Áine [Knockainy], seat of Áine, is near Lough Gur. Gerald's story should be distinguished from that of Gearóid [ang. Garret] Óg, the 11th Earl of Kildare, who lies under the rath at *Mullaghmast, rising up every seven years to ride round the Curragh of Kildare on a horse shod with silver. International tale type: 766; folk motifs: A560; A571; D150.

See Patrick Kennedy, 'The Enchantment of Gearoid Iarla', in *Legendary Fictions of the Irish Celts* (London, 1866). Adapted retelling: R. D. Joyce, 'Earl Gerald and His Bride', in *Ballads of Irish Chivalry* (Boston, 1872). For poems attributed to Gerald, see Gearóid Mac Niocaill (ed.), 'Duanaire Ghearóid Iarla', *Studia Hibernica*, 3 (1963), 7–53. Commentary: Dáithi Ó hÓgáin, *The Hero in Irish Folk History* (Dublin, 1985), 78–86, 141–57, etc.

Gereint. Variant spelling for *Geraint.

Gerennius. Heroic figure in Cornish folklore, usually linked with Dingerein, an ancient earthworks between Gerrans and Carne in southern Cornwall. Learned speculation sees him as derived from the Arthurian *Geraint or any of several local saints and kings.

Germán, Germane. Prominent crew member of Máel Dúin in **Imram Curaig Maíle Dúine* [The Voyage of Máel Dúin's Boat].

Gerontius. See GERAINT.

ges, gesa, gessa. Variant spellings for *geis.

ghillie. Anglicization of the ScG *gille*; see GILLA; GIOLLA.

ghost. The earliest Celtic tradition does not evince any body of generalized lore in which any part of the dead gratuitously return to terrorize the living. Most Celtic ghost stories are local borrowings from other European traditions in post-medieval times. Celtic words for 'ghost' are often borrowings from other languages: Ir. anam [from L *anima*], sprid [Eng. spirit]; ScG tannasg; Manx scanjoon; W ysbryd; Corn. bucca gwyn [lit. white hobgoblin]; Bret. teuz.

giant, giantess. There is little to unite the men and women of great size in Celtic tradition except their enormous strength and stature. Irish and Cornish giants are often foolish and gentle, while those in Gaelic Scotland may be more astute. Heroes may sometimes take giant form, such as *Fionn mac Cumhaill in oral tradition or *Cú Roí; or giants may assist heroes, as Wrnach aids *Culhwch; or giants may exist only for puny men to vanquish. Notable male giants include: the *athach, *Bendigeidfran (Brân the Blessed), *Carn Galver, the *Cerne Giant, *Ciudach, *Cormoran, *Dhoya, *Dillus Frafag, *Diwrnach Wyddel, the *d'reach, the *fachan, *Fachtna Fáthach, *Foawr, *Gruagach, *Llassar Llaes Gyfnewid, *Searbhán, *Tegid Foel, *Ysbaddaden Bencawr. Giantesses include: *Bébinn (2), *Boudicca, and *Cymidei Cymeinfoll. The *Fomorians of pseudo-history are sometimes seen as giants. See John C. Grooms, 'Giants in Welsh Folklore and Tradition', dissertation, University of Wales, Aberystwyth, 1988.

Giant's Causeway. Popular name for a promontory of more than 40,000 curiously formed basaltic columns closely piled together projecting from the base of a lofty cliff into the sea on the north shore of Co. Antrim, 2.5 miles NE of Bushmills. While *Fionn mac Cumhaill, a giant in oral tradition, is often implied as the giant builder of the causeway, its Irish name, Clochan na bhFómharach [stones of the Fomorians], cites the *Fomorians of pseudo-history.

Gildas. Brythonic monk (*c.*495–*c.*570), born, according to tradition, near what is today Glasgow, contemporary of *Dewi Sant, whose *De Excidio Britanniae* [On the Ruin of Britain] (*c.*540–8) is the only early work covering the phase of history to which King *Arthur is usually assigned. His description of the battle at Mount Badon is most often cited. Gildas argued that the Brythonic defeat before the Saxons was occasioned by moral failure and that in repentance 'good men' should join monasteries; thus he sometimes bears the title 'saint', although later medieval writers thought the saint and the historian were two different people. Even though *De Excidio* is composed in an inventive Latin, Gildas is sometimes cited as a father of Welsh literary tradition; his name is also known in Cornish and Breton traditions; see Joseph Loth, 'Le Nom de Gildas dans l'Iˆle de Bretagne en Irlande et en Armorique', *Revue Celtique*, 46 (1929), 1–15; Pádraig Ó Riain, 'Gildas: A Solution to His Enigmatic Name', in Catherine Laurent and Helen Davis (eds.), *Irlande et Bretagne* (Rennes, 1994), 33–9. See also Michael Winterbottom (ed. and trans.), *The Ruin of Britain* (Chichester, UK, and Totowa, NJ, 1978); Michael Lapidge and David Dumville (eds.), *Gildas: New Approaches* (Woodbridge, UK, 1984).

Gilfaethwy, Gilvaethwy, Gilvarthwy (corrupt), usually with the patronymic fab [son of] Dôn. Brother of *Gwydion in the fourth branch of the **Mabinogi* whose unrequited love for the virginal *Goewin, foot-holder to his uncle Math, led him to rape her after following Gwydion's ruse. In punishment, Gilfaethwy and Gwydion were transformed successively into a pair of *deer, pigs, and wolves. Probably the model for the Arthurian figure Giflet (or Girflet) Filz Do.

gilla. OIr. word for (*a*) youth of an age to bear arms, (*b*) servant, messenger, gilly. Initially used with an epithet to describe servants, e.g. Gilla Decair [the Hard Servant] in **Tóraigheacht an Ghiolla Dheacair* [Pursuit of the Hard Gilly/ Difficult Servant]. From the 10th century on, Gilla became the first element in masculine proper names, e.g. Gilla Cóemáin (*fl.* 1025–75), the poet and chronicler, or the many-named Gilla Críst [Servant of Christ]. ModIr. giolla; ScG gille.

gille dubh, dhu [ScG, dark boy]. Scottish Gaelic solitary *fairy, clothed in leaves and moss, who lurks in the birch woods near Gairloch in the north-west Highlands in what used to be (until 1974) Ross and Cromarty; generally thought benevolent.

gillie, gilly. Anglicizations of *gilla, *gille, and *giolla.

Gilvaethwy. Anglicization of *Gilfaethwy.

giolla. ModIr. word for (*a*) youth, (*b*) page, gilly, manservant; cf. OIr. gilla. With an epithet this describes a specific servant in a story, e.g. Giolla Deacair or Giolla Dacker: see TÓRAIGHEACHT AN GHIOLLA DHEACAIR [The Pursuit of the Hard Gilly/Difficult Servant].

Gíona mac Lugha, Geena Mac Lugha. Champion of the *Fianna, sometimes described as a grandson of *Fionn mac Cumhaill. His men were insubordinate, thinking him lazy, vain, and selfish, until Fionn stiffened his resolve by teaching him the maxims of the Fianna, whereupon Gíona became a leader.

Giraldus Cambrensis, Gerald of Wales, Gerald de Berri. Medieval (*c.*1146–1223) Welsh clergyman whose writings in Latin about both Wales and Ireland are among the most extensive, detailed records we have on those countries. Although he was the son of a Welsh princess, Giraldus' ecclesiastical career was constantly thwarted by authorities; Henry II twice rejected his appointment to the see of St David's (1176 and 1198). Most important of his many books are two on Wales itself, *Itinerarium Cambriae* [The Story of the Journey Through Wales] (*c.*1168) and *Descriptio Cambriae* [A Description of Wales] (*c.*1198). His treatments of Ireland are more prejudicial, combining insupportable beliefs with detailed realistic observations; they include *Expugnatio Hibernica* [The Conquest of Ireland] and *Topographia Hibernica* [The Topography of Ireland] (*c.*1185). J. S. Brewer edited the eight volumes of his complete works, *Giraldus Cambrensi Opera* (London, 1861–91). The English translation by Sir Richard Colt Hoare (1806) has long been available from Everyman's Library (1908, 1976). Thomas Jones produced a Welsh version, *Gerallt Gymro: Hanes y Daith trwy Gymru a'r Disgrifiad o Gymru* (Cardiff, 1938), later reissued in a bilingual edition, *Gerallt Gymro: Gerald of Wales* (Cardiff, 1947). See also Michael Richter, *Giraldus Cambrensis and the Growth of the Welsh Nation* (Aberystwyth, 1972, 1976); Robert Bartlett, *Gerald of Wales, 1146–1223* (Oxford, 1982); Charles Kightly, *Mirror of Medieval Wales* (Cardiff, 1988).

Gírle Guairle. Nonsense name of a *fairy woman spinner in an Irish variant of the Rumpelstiltskin story. Gírle Guairle agrees to spin and weave for a mortal woman, if only she will remember her difficult name. At first the mortal woman forgets, but later, to Gírle Guairle's anger, she remembers.

glaestig. Variant spelling of *glaistig.

glain nadredd, neidr. Welsh and Breton terms for *adder stone.

Glaisne [Ir. *glas*, green, grey, grey-blue]. Among the many bearers of this name is a son of *Conchobar mac Nessa.

glaistig, glaestig, glastig; also maighdean uaine [green maiden]. Usually malevolent solitary female *fairy haunting lonely pools in Scottish Gaelic tradition. Sometimes half-woman, half-*goat, she may take the form of a beautiful woman, especially one already known to the male victim; after offering sexual favours like a camp follower, she leaves her male victim with his throat cut, every drop of blood sucked from him. Often compared to the Russian baba yaga, the glaistig none the less conflates characteristics of other Highland imaginary creatures, such as the *banshee (bean s'dhe, etc.), *fuath, and *ùruisg. In some variant stories the glaistig may be seen as benevolent, fond of children and a protector of old people.

glaistyn. Variant spelling of *glashtin.

glám dícenn, dichenn, díchend, dícin [Ir. *glám*, satire, lampoon; cf. *díchennaid*, destroys, slays outright]. A poet's execration; a special curse declaimed by a poet that required him to stand (like a *crane?) on one leg, to close one eye, and to extend one arm. No mere expression of opinion, the glám dícenn is a potent weapon of war, capable of blistering an opponent's face or of costing him his life. The victim of glám dícenn would be shunned by all levels of society. Comparable to a power wielded by early Arab poets called *hija*. See GEIS.

Glanis. Gaulish healing spring god venerated at the 4th-century BC shrine of Glanum in the Alpilles mountains of Provence, southern France. A triad of local mother-gods, the Glanicae, are also represented at the site, as were *Epona, Gaulish *Mercury, and *Rosmerta. The city gate at Glanum, the oldest to be found in *Gaul, contains sculpture portraying Gaulish captives. See F. Salviat, *Glanum* (Paris, 1979).

Glanum. See GLANIS.

Glas Ghaibhleann, Gaibhleann, Ghaibhnann, Ghaibhnenn, Ghoibhneann, Gavelen, Gaivlen, Glasgavelen [Ir. *glas*, green, greenish blue; of **Gaiblín* (?), of **Goibniu* (?)]. Celebrated, magical *cow, white with green spots, whose inexhaustible supply of milk signalled prosperity. The original owner is a matter of some dispute, possibly *Goibniu the smith or

Gaiblín, a farmer of Co. Cavan. After the cow was stolen by *Balor and taken to Tory Island (off Co. *Donegal), *Cian retrieved him, and along the way fathered the hero *Lug Lámfhota. Stories about Glas Ghaibhleann are widespread in later Irish and also Scottish Gaelic folklore, where the cow is known as Glas Gaibhnann. The phrase 'The grey cow slept there' colloquially describes a fine field. Additionally, the name of the village of Duncaneely, Co. Donegal, is thought to testify to the cow's owner there, Mac Cinnfhaolaidh [ang. MacKenealy].

Glasgerion, Glascurian. Legendary 10th-century Welsh *bard; the claim that he collected ancient poetry and laws, contributed to the *Gorsedd, and compiled the first Welsh grammar is not supported by any known records. Cited as Glascurian by Geoffrey Chaucer in the *Hous of Fame* (1372–86) and in the English ballad included in *Percy's Reliques* (1765), and given no. 67 in F. J. Child's catalogue.

glashtin, glashan, glaistyn, glastyn. Manx counterpart of the Irish *each uisce, Scottish *kelpie, and Welsh *ceffyl dwfr, the mischievous water-horse. Although the glashtin might take human form, he could not hide his horse's ears. Sometimes confused with the heavier, shambling *fenodyree, but more human in appearance. See also CABYLL-USHTEY.

glass. The transparent, brittle, man-made material has often provoked the Celtic imagination. The Welsh *Caer Wydyr [Fortress of Glass] implied a vision of the *Otherworld. Conand's Tower, the *Fomorian fortress on Tory Island (off Co. *Donegal), is made of glass. Fabulous Irish voyagers such as *Bran, St *Brendan, and *Máel Dúin encounter towers of glass. *Merlin goes to sea in a glass house. Welshmen used the name Ynys Wydrin/ Gutrin/Witrin [glass island] for *Glastonbury in pre-Saxon times, although the English place-name is not a translation of it. OIr. glaine; ModIr. gloine; ScG glaine; Manx gless; W gwydr; Corn. gweder; Bret. gwer.

glastig. Variant spelling of *glaistig.

Glastonbury. Small town in Somerset with ruined medieval abbey that has extensive Arthurian associations; one of several candidates as the model for both *Avalon and Camelot. Artefacts testify to Celtic settlement in the *La Tène era, but Glastonbury was also the site of the oldest British Christian community. Known as Ynys Wydrin/ Gutrin/ Witrin [glass island] through a fanciful etymology in early Welsh and also as Ynys Afallon [apple island] in Modern Welsh. See John Scott, *The Early History of Glastonbury* (Woodbridge, UK, 1981). R. F. Traharne, *The Glastonbury Legends* (London, 1967).

glastyn. Variant spelling of *glashtin.

glen, glen-. [OIr. *glenn*; ModIr. *gleann*; ScG *gleann, glenn*, valley]. Celtic loanword, prefix of dozens of place-names in Ireland and Scotland; cf. the Welsh GLYN.

Glen Bolcáin, Bolcan. See BOLCÁIN, GLENN.

Glenasmole, Glennasmole, Glennasmól, Gleann-na-Smól, Glen na Smole, Glenismole [Ir. *gleann na smól*, valley of the thrushes]. Valley at the headwaters of the River *Dodder in south Co. Dublin extending into Co. Wicklow, especially rich in *Fenian associations. *Oisín first fell to earth here on his return from *Tír na nÓg. The proximity to Dublin may explain the glen's frequent citation in romantic, nationalist Irish poetry; see W. H. Drummond, 'The Lay of Glennasmol', in *Ancient Irish Minstrelsy* (Dublin, 1852), 61–79.

Glencoe, Glen Coe [ScG *comhann*, narrow]. One of the most resonant names in the Highland imagination, a 10-mile long glen surrounding the River Coe in the western Highlands, in the north of the former (until 1974) *Argyllshire, south of Loch Leven, east of the town of Ballachulish. Although it was once known as the realm of the *Cadineag, all previous folkloric associations were displaced by the slaughter of the MacDonalds here, 13 February 1792, at the hands of the Campbells who had been their house guests. See John Prebble, *Glencoe* (London, 1966).

Glendalough [Ir. *Gleann Dá Loch*, valley of two lakes]. Celebrated early monastic site in Co. Wicklow, 8 miles N of Rathdrum. Founded by St *Cáemgen [Kevin] (d. 618), Glendalough's relative accessibility has invited many visitors for centuries; it is today one of Ireland's best-known tourist attractions. The valley also has *Fenian associations; *Fionn mac Cumhaill fought a Hydra-like serpent here. See Dora Sigerson Shorter, *A Legend of Glendalough and Other Ballads* (Dublin, 1921).

Glendamain, Glenndamain, Glendamnach (gen.), Glendomain, Glennamain, Gleanndamhain. One of three capitals of pre-medieval *Munster, rotating with *Cashel, Co. Tipperary, and *Cnoc Áine, Co. Limerick. It was the seat of such powerful kings as *Cathal mac Finguine. Identified with the modern village of Glanworth on the River Funcheon, north-east Co. Cork.

Glewlwyd Gafaelfawr, Gavaelvawr [W *gafael*, grasp, grip; *fawr (mawr)*, mighty]. Obdurate door-keeper at *Arthur's court. He refuses *Culhwch entry because the feast has already begun but relents upon Arthur's command. In some texts he is door-keeper only on New Year's Day, while in others he serves the full year; in still others he has higher status as keeper of the court. Often compared to *Cei [Kay]. See Rachel Bromwich, *Trioedd Ynys Prydain*, rev. edn. (Cardiff, 1978), 361–3.

Gloucester. The site of the English city of the east bank of the Severn appears often in early Welsh narrative, where it is known as Caer Loyw. The evil Nine Witches of Gloucester/Caer Loyw are dispatched with vengeance by *Peredur. A Roman fortress in the same place was known as Glevum.

Glwyddyn Saer. Shadowy Welsh figure, probably counterpart of the Irish craft-god *Goibniu. See also GOFANNON; GOBBÁN SAOR.

glyn. Welsh word for valley, first element in dozens of place-names; see GLEN, GLEN-.

Glyn Cuch [frown valley]. Valley in *Dyfed, south-western Wales, where *Pwyll encounters *Arawn while hunting at the beginning of the action in the first branch of the **Mabinogi*.

Glyn Rhosyn [rose valley; L *vallis rosina*]. Site where *Dewi Sant [St David] first lighted the ritual pascal fire, thus a Welsh counterpart to the Irish *Tara.

gnome [L *gnomus*]. This fabled race of treasure-guarding *dwarfs, a concept coined by Paracelsus (16th cent.), has few counterparts in Celtic tradition, only the *knocker of Cornwall and the *goric of Brittany. International folk motif: F456.

goat [OE *gāt*]. This horned, bearded, cloven-hoofed mammal (genus *Capra*) appears often in Celtic traditions, usually representing fertility or, later, sexuality and sexual aggression. Ancient deities with goat-horns are found in *Gaul and Britain. Gaulish *Mercury appears with a goat at the shrine of *Glanum in Provence. *Cernunnus, the antlered god, is pictured both with goat legs and riding on a goat. A small bronze image of a goat with huge horns was found in south-west Scotland in the 1970s. Many frightening creatures in folklore are wholly or partially goat: the Irish *bocanách; the Manx *goayr heddagh; Scottish *glaistig (half-woman) and *ùruisg (half-man). The monstrous goathead people [*Gaborchend Goborchind*, etc.] in Irish folklore possibly derive from the *Fomorians. On the other hand, the more benign Irish *pooka (or púca) takes its name from the word for he-goat, poc. The Welsh hero *Lleu Llaw Gyffes could be made vulnerable only when his feet were touching a billygoat. A goat was once enthroned in a mock ceremony at Mullinavat, Co. Kilkenny, while a similar ceremony, the three-day long Puck Fair, a modern survival of the *Lughnasa feast, still draws thousands to Killorglin, Co. Kerry, each August. Numerous place-names incorporate goat references, e.g. Ardgour [ScG *aird ghobhair*, goat heights], south-west of Fort William, Inverness-shire, and *Gavrinis [Bret., goat island], the great Breton archaeological site. OIr. gabor; ModIr. gabhar; ScG gobhar; Manx goayr; W gafr; Corn. gavar; Bret. gavr.

goayr heddagh. The ghostly *goat of Manx folklore.

Gobbán Saor, Goban Saer, Gobán Saor [Ir. *saor*, smith, wright]. A euhemerized version of the god *Goibniu who becomes the master craftsman of Irish and Scottish Gaelic folklore. As he was described in early texts as a great architect of the Christian era, the name Gobbán was borne by many monks. He was thought to have assisted workmen in the building of many monasteries and round towers. W. B. Yeats in *The Celtic Twilight* (1893) describes Gobbán as a legendary mason who is very wise. His name is associated with numerous place-name stories, such as Turvey Strand (now Fairview), Co. Dublin, where he was born and where his father, Tuirbe Trágmar, stopped the tide by throwing an axe; Goban Saor's Castle, a ruin near Fair Head, Co. Antrim; and Goban's Mountain-Top [Slieve Anieran], Co. Leitrim. Ironically, the early modern Hiberno-English slang term gubbaun was used in derision for an unskilled tradesman. See also GLWYDDYN SAER; GOFANNON.

goblin [MidHighGer. *kobolt*; OFr. *gobelin*]. This concept of the grotesque, malevolent, diminutive sprite originates outside Celtic tradition and is only applied to it figuratively. Only a few supernatural creatures from Celtic folklore are ever called goblins: the Welsh colynau [a translation of the English] and *bwgan, and the Irish *cluricaune and *dullahan. See also FAIRY. See Wirt Sikes, *British Goblins* (London, 1880).

Gobnenn (gen.), **Gobniu.** Variant spellings for *Goibniu; see also GOBBÁN SAOR.

Goborchend, Goborchind. Monstrous goat-headed people of early Irish folklore; see GOAT.

god, goddess. There is no pantheon in Celtic mythology. The very use of the English words 'god' or 'goddess', denoting a superhuman, immortal entity who is venerated and propitiated and who has power over human affairs, misrepresents surviving records. Yet language habits die hard; we conventionally speak of the *Dagda as the 'Good God' or *Cernunnos as the 'Horned God'. Escaping death is not sufficient to be considered divine; the *Tuatha Dé Danann of the pseudo-history **Lebor Gabála* [Book of Invasions] are usually seen as immortals but not as gods. Several personages from the Continental Celts, like *Borvo or *Glanis who were venerated at ancient healing springs, or the unnamed entities behind Gaulish *Apollo or *Mercury, probably were worshipped as gods; but our incomplete knowledge of them prevents us from knowing their importance to their societies or their relationship with one another. Informed opinion today, however, is more likely to find a shadowy divine figure behind the kings and warriors of heroic narrative than to look for a historical antecedent as earlier commentators were wont; see FIND; FIONN MAC CUMHAILL.

Gododdin, Y. Welsh title for the long poem (1,480 lines) attributed to *Aneirin (late 6th cent.), which contains the only full-length exposition in Welsh literature of the ideals of the heroic age. The single surviving text in the *Book of Aneirin* (mid-13th cent.) comprises a series of elegies for the heroes who fell at the disastrous Battle of *Catraeth (*c.*600) on the River Swale in Yorkshire. As the *Gododdin* does not form a continuous narrative it is not classed as an epic, but events of epic proportions lie behind it. Although no corroborating references to the battle exist outside the poem, the name Gododdin denotes a historical people and their territory, part of which was known as Manaw Gododdin, that extended south from the Firth of Forth and included a capital at *Din Eidyn (the Rock of Edinburgh?). A Brythonic or *P-Celtic people, the Gododdin spoke a language anticipating Welsh, even though they lived in what is today *Scotland. At the time of the action in the poem, they were resisting the encroachments of their English neighbours; the site of the battle may have been a waterfall [L *Cataracto*; W *Catraeth*] on a river separating the Anglian kingdoms of Bernicia and Deira, whose forces were not yet allied.

The *Gododdin* celebrates the heroic values of the early British/Welsh warrior aristocracy and laments their passing. While there is little attempt to describe the battle itself, early passages explain its background and setting. Sensing a threat to his kingdom, *Mynyddog Mwynfawr [W, the wealthy] gathered warriors to his capital at Din Eidyn, where they feasted for a year. After this he selected 300 mail-clad horsemen to be in the war party; accompanying foot-soldiers are not described. The text cites many names, but these cannot always be attached to the heroic characters portrayed. Once in battle, the British horsemen killed seven English infantry for each of their own who fell. The enemy numbers were too large and they were too well entrenched; all but two or three of the Gododdin war party were slain. Many stanzas applaud the fighting prowess and bravery of the British horsemen as well as their unyielding pride in the face of defeat. Such a noble end, the text implies, is the means of winning deathless fame.

Editions: Ifor Williams, *Canu Aneirin* (Cardiff, 1938); A. O. H. Jarman, *Aneirin: Y Gododdin* (Llandysul, UK, 1988). Translations: Joseph P. Clancy, *The Earliest Welsh Poetry* (New York, 1970); Desmond O'Grady, *The Gododdin* (Dublin, 1977); Anthony Conran, *The Penguin Book of Welsh Verse* (Harmondsworth, 1967). Studies: Kenneth H. Jackson, *The Gododdin: The Oldest Scottish Poem* (Edinburgh, 1969); Ifor Williams, *The Beginnings of Welsh Poetry*, ed. R. Bromwich (Cardiff, 1972); A. O. H. Jarman, 'Aneirin-The Gododdin', in *A Guide to Welsh Literature*, i (Swansea, 1976), 68–80. Thomas Gray (1716–71) adapted his ode *The Death of Hoel* from the *Gododdin*.

Goedal Glas. Corrupt spelling of *Goídel Glas.

Goewin, Goevin [W *goboyw*, sprightly]. Virgin foot-holder of *Math ap Mathonwy, daughter of Pebin, described as the 'fairest maid of the land and time'. When Goewin confesses that *Gilfaethwy has raped her, Math marries her to save her from shame and thus makes her his queen.

Gofannon, Govannon [W *gof, gofan*, smith]. Welsh divine smith, one of the children of *Dôn and a British counterpart to the Irish *Goibniu; he is best remembered as the uncle who kills his nephew *Dylan. *Culhwch's third task was to get Gofannon to sharpen the plough of *Amaethon. In some texts he is described as a *dwarf. See also GLWYDDYN SAER.

Gogynfardd (sing.), **Gogynfeirdd, Y** (pl.) [W, fairly early poet]. Name for courtly Welsh *bards or poets of the 12th to early 14th centuries, after *Llywarch Hen (9th-10th cents.) but before *Dafydd ap Gwilym (*fl.* 1320–70). Their poetry, often celebrating military feats, uses ancient diction and intricate forms. See Edward Anwyl, *The Poetry of the Gogynfeirdd* (Denbigh, 1909); Arthur Hughes and Ifor Williams, *Gemau'r Gogynfeirdd* (Pwllheli, UK, 1910); J. E. Caerwyn Williams, *The Poets of the Welsh Princes* (Cardiff, 1994).

Goibniu, Goibhniu, Goibne, Guibne, Goibnenn, Gaibnenn, Gobnenn, Gobniu [OIr. *gobae*, smith]. Smith of the *Tuatha Dé Danann and one of the three gods of craft, na trí dé dána, along with *Credne and *Luchta. Goibniu is seen most vividly in **Cath Maige Tuired* [The (Second) Battle of Mag Tuired], where he is a tireless armourer, providing *Lug Lámfhota with the spear that penetrates *Balor's eye. His keen tips are always lethal. T. F. O'Rahilly (1946) has argued, however, that as a god of thunder and lightning Goibniu may be identified with Balor, as both derive from a conception of the sun; the spear given to Lug may be derived from a thunderbolt. At times Goibniu was himself also a combatant. When the *Fomorian spy *Rúadán (2), the son of *Bres (1) and *Brigit, impaled Goibniu with one of his own spears, the smith took it from his body and dispatched the young man with it. This caused the mother, here known as Bríg[h], to wail the first keening heard in Ireland.

Genealogies disagree about Goibniu's lineage. He may be a grandson of the war-god *Néit, as is Balor, and one of the four sons of Esarg, along with Credne, Luchta, and *Dian Cécht, the healing god. In an alternate text he is the brother of the *Dagda, *Nuadu Airgetlám, Credne, and Luchta, with whom he helps to conquer Ireland for the Tuatha Dé Danann. In yet other texts Tuirbe Trágmar the axe-thrower, father of the *Gobbán Saor, is named as Goibniu's father. Sometimes Goibniu is named as foster-father of Lug Lámfhota instead of *Manannán mac Lir.

Along with his smithing, Goibniu was often seen as a healer; his name is invoked on an Old Irish charm to aid removal of a thorn. More significantly, he is host of an *otherworldly feast, *Fled Goibnenn*, where guests imbibed great quantities of an intoxicating drink now identified with *ale. Instead of getting drunk, those attending would be protected from old age and decay. Commentators see in this yet another link with Hephaestus, the Greek smith-god, who provides the other gods drink in the *Iliad*. Goibniu's forge, *Cerdchae Ghaibhnenn*, was usually thought to lie east of *Mullaghmast hill in Glenn Treithim along the Kildare-Wicklow border. The once abundant copper ore in this area allowed early metalsmiths to make shields and spear-points. Other traditions place the forge on the *Beare peninsula, Co. Cork, and elsewhere.

Much of Goibniu's characterization survives in the folk figure Gobbán Saor, with echoes also in *Gaiblín, owner of the fabulous *cow *Glas Ghaibhleann. His Welsh counterparts are *Gofannon and *Glwyddyn Saer. See Vernam Hull, 'The Four Jewels of the Tuatha Dé Danann', *Zeitschrift für celtische Philologie*, 18 (1930), 73–89.

Goídel Glas, Goidel, Gaodhal, Gaidel, Gaedheal, Gael, Gadelus, Gathelus [cf. W *Gwyddel*, Irishman]. Eponymous founder of the *Goidelic or Gaelic languages, according to the pseudo-history **Lebor Gabála* [Book of Invasions]. Son of a Pharaoh's daughter, *Scota (2), and *Niúl, a forebear of the *Milesians, Goídel barely survives infancy. The biblical Moses saves him when he was bitten by a snake; the resultant green mark gives Goídel his epithet glas [green]. Moses cures him with a touch of his rod and then prophesies that he and his descendants will be free from serpents and will live in a land where none are to be found. Following the instructions of his grandfather, *Fénius Farsaid, who was present at the separation of the languages at Babel, Goídel fashions the Irish language out of the seventy-two tongues then in existence.

Goidelic, Goidhelic, Gadhelic, Gaedhelic. Name for the group of *Q-Celtic languages comprising Irish, Scottish Gaelic, and Manx. Distinguish from *Brythonic or Brittonic, denoting the *P-Celtic languages of Britain. The Goidelic invaders of Ireland are often referred to as the *Féni in Irish texts.

Golam, Golamh, Galam, Galamh. Birth-name of *Míl Espáine.

Goll [Ir., blind of one eye; purblind]. Name borne by dozens of figures from early Irish tradition, not all of whom are *one-eyed or purblind. The best-known is certainly *Goll mac Morna of the *Fenian Cycle.

Goll 1. 'King Goll' of W. B. Yeats's poem 'The Madness of King Goll' (1887) has been fatuously traced to any number of petty Irish rulers. Contemporary informed opinion asserts that Yeats wilfully substituted the name Goll for Suibne/ Sweeney of **Buile Shuibne* [The Frenzy of Suibne].

2. also Gaul. Leading character in *Macpherson's *Ossian* (1760), the son of Morni. First a disputant of *Fingal, he later became that hero's most faithful friend. Wounded by having a large rock rolled upon his leg while bravely defending himself, Goll later fell sacrifice to his enemies.

Goll Essa Ruaid [Ir., of Ruad's waterfall, Assaroe]. Name applied to the *one-eyed *salmon caught by *Fionn mac Cumhaill at *Assaroe. This one, like the one caught on the *Boyne, is identified with *Fintan.

Goll mac Carbada. *One-eyed monster killed by *Cúchulainn, whose traditional enemy he was. T. F. O'Rahilly (1946) asserts that Goll was a sun-deity and lord of the *Otherworld, and that this combat parallels that of *Lug Lámfhota with *Balor and *Fionn mac Cumhaill with *Goll mac Morna. Goll bears the same patronymic as *Briccriu and may be his brother.

Goll mac Doilb, Dolb. A ruler of *Mag Mell (one of three) and nephew of *Eochaid, son of Sál; he is slain by *Fiachna mac Rétach when attempting to abduct his wife.

Goll mac Morna. Also known as Áed or Aodh mac Fidga. Leader of the *Connacht *Fianna in the *Fenian Cycle, adversary and later sometime colleague of *Fionn mac Cumhaill. Goll led the killers of *Cumall, Fionn's father, at the Battle of Cnucha [**Fotha Catha Chnucha*] at Castleknock in modern Co. Dublin, and thus wrested control of the Fianna of all Ireland. As he lost an eye in this encounter, 'Goll' may be a nickname and Áed [Ir., fire] the original name. Goll gave up his command of the Fianna in favour of Fionn when the young hero slew the mysterious 'burner', *Aillén mac Midgna, at *Tara. Unlikely as it may seem, Goll and Fionn were temporarily close allies. He freed Fionn's poet *Fergus Fínbél from an enchanted cave. When Goll rescued Fionn from the depredations of *Conarán's daughters, he was rewarded with the hand of Fionn's daughter *Cainche; other texts name Scandlach as Goll's wife. Goll is sometimes the brother of the boisterous *Conán Máel or mac Morna. Numerous later narratives describe a rising feud between Fionn's people, the Clan *Baíscne, Goll's Clan Morna, with dozens of different pretexts. Some versions assert that Goll killed *Cairell, Fionn's son. Others describe Fionn or one of Fionn's retainers killing Goll. Later Goll's grandson *Fer Lí attempts to avenge Goll by attacking Fionn, but only wounds him and is killed himself.

Modern commentators explain the seemingly odd motivation in Goll's character, as well as the proliferation of variant text, by arguing that he originated at a different time and place from Fionn and was later synchronized with the larger Fenian canon. T. F. O'Rahilly (1946) argued that his original name, Áed, identifies him with Aillén mac Midgna, the 'burner', a sun-deity and lord of the *Otherworld; thus the Fionn-Goll/Áed contest parallels that of *Cúchulainn-*Goll mac Carbada and *Lug Lámfhota-*Balor.

Goreu, Gorau [W *gorau*, best]. Slayer of *Ysbaddaden Pencawr in **Culhwch ac Olwen*. Goreu was one of twenty-four sons of *Custennin, his mother being an unnamed woman, the sister of *Igerna; this made him a cousin of *Arthur. When Ysbaddaden killed both his father and his many brothers, Goreu escaped when his mother hid him in a cupboard. While still a boy, he distinguished himself as an ally of Culhwch, once fighting through three courtyards of men, winning for himself the title of 'The Best' [*gorau*]. His beheading of Ysbaddaden avenged both his father and his brothers. See Rachel Bromwich, *Trioedd Ynys Prydain*, rev. edn. (Cardiff, 1978), 364–7.

Gorias. A mythical city 'somewhere in the northern isles of Greece', whence the *Tuatha De Danann brought their treasure. *Esras of Gorias gives *Lug Lámfhota his invincible spear.

goric. A kind of Breton *gnome, thought to inhabit *dolmens and other megaliths.

Gormal. Corrupt form of *Gormshuil.

Gormfhlaith. Variant spelling of *Gormlaith.

Gormla. Corrupt form of *Gormshuil.

Gormlaith, Gormfhlaith, Gormleith [Ir. *gorm*, illustrious, splendid; blue; *flaith*, sovereignty]. Name borne by dozens of early Irish noblewomen and abbesses. The most often cited is *Gormlaith (1), wife of *Brian Bórama (Boru). See GORMSHUIL MHÓR NA MAIGHE.

Gormlaith 1. Daughter of the king of *Leinster whose third husband was *Brian Bórama (Boru). Sometimes called 'The Queen Mother of Dublin', she is described in texts as a beautiful, powerful, intriguing woman, skilled at manipulating men. A notorious divorcee, she had four husbands: (1) the great Máel Sechnaill II [Malachy]; (2) Olafr Kvaran [Amhlaobh, 'the Shoe'], the Norseman by whom she bore Sitric [Sigtryggr], first king of Dublin; (3) Brian Bórama, who put her aside for favouring the Danes before the Battle of Clontarf (1014); and (4) Ospak, a Norseman from the Isle of *Man whom she hoped to move against Brian.

2. Queen of Niall Caille at *Tara who was abducted, with all her women of her court, by *Fedlimid mac Crimthainn in 840.

3. Daughter of Flann, queen of *Niall Glúndub, for whom the O'Neill family is named; distinguish from the earlier *Uí Néill.

Gormshuil Mhór na Maighe, Gormal, Gormla [ScG *gormshuil*, blue-eye; *mhór*, big, great]. Celebrated witch of Lochaber in the Scottish Highlands. On the Isle of Mull she was known as Gormal of Mull, often a benefactor of local interests. Under the name Gormla she was a patron of Clan Cameron. Gormla's warning to Lochiel of the Camerons, against the treachery of the Duke of Atholl, during a dispute over ownership of Aird-Raineach, gave rise to the motto of that family: 'Come hither, come hither, / You shall get flesh, you shall get flesh.' See Alasdair Camshron, 'Gornshuil Mhór na Maighe', *An Gaidheal* (Mar. 1957). See also GORMLAITH.

Gorsedd Beirdd Ynys Prydain [W, Throne/ Assembly of the Bards of the Isle of Britain]. Society founded by *Iolo Morganwg in 1792 to celebrate Welsh poetry, music, and culture, its first meeting held at Primrose Hill, London, to remind the English of their Celtic antecedents. Although the word gorsedd is found in early Welsh texts, e.g. the gorsedd of *Arberth, the present celebration of the Gorsedd unquestionably begins with Iolo; he later encouraged the establishment of a gorsedd in each province of Wales. By the mid-19th century, the Gorsedd had become a part of the national *Eisteddfod. Membership in the Gorsedd was about 1,300 at the end of the 20th century. A Breton Gorsedd, Gorzez Breizh, was founded in 1901; the Cornish, Gorseth Kernow, in 1927. See Geraint Bowen, *Hanes Gorsedd y Beirdd* (Felindre, UK, 1991); Dillwyn Miles, *The Secret of the Bards of the Isle of Britain* (Llandybie, UK, 1992).

Grace O'Malley. See GRANUAILE.

Gradlon, Gralon. Father of the reprobate daughter *Dahut (or Ahè) and ruler of the doomed city of *Ys in the celebrated Breton legend. Despite his association with Douarnenez, a statue was erected to Gradlon in the city of Quimper, between the two towers of the cathedral. It was removed and beheaded during the French Revolution but has since been restored.

Gráinne [cf. Ir. *grán*, grain; she who inspired terror (?)]. Daughter of *Cormac mac Airt who elopes with *Diarmait Ua Duibne while betrothed to *Fionn mac Cumhaill, thus providing the central action of **Tóraigheacht Dhiarmada agus Ghráinne* [The Pursuit of Diarmait and Gráinne]. Although earlier versions of the story do not survive, medieval references indicate that Gráinne was initially married to Fionn, who put her aside for a sister, *Ailbe, when she proved unfaithful. Clearly comparable to *Deirdre of the *Ulster Cycle, she has been less celebrated in literature, perhaps because of folk variants of the story that have her married to Fionn after Diarmait's death. Lady Gregory dramatized her most favourably in *Grania* (1912). See also ISEULT. For Ráth Gráinne, see TARA.

Gráinne Mhaol Ní Mháille. See GRANUAILE.

Gralon. Variant spelling of *Gradlon.

Grania. Anglicization of *Gráinne; see also GRANUAILE (Gráinne Mhaol Ní Mháille).

Grannus, Grannos. Widely known epithet of Gaulish *Apollo.

Granuaile. A personification of *Ireland, based on the career of Gráinne Mhaol [of the cropped hair] Ní Mháille, or Grace O'Malley (*c.*1530–1603), celebrated pirate of the Mayo coast. Although contemporary records testify to her extraordinary, swashbuckling career, Granuaile is almost as much a creature of folklore as of history. The 18th-century *Munster poet Seán Clárach mac Domhnaill first used her name as a metaphor for Ireland, and in most subsequent portrayals little distinction was made between legendary and historical episodes. In one characteristic story, she rises from giving birth to a son to do battle with Turkish corsairs. Her raids take place as far afield as Scotland and also land her in prison. Most famously, she meets with Elizabeth I while barefoot and dressed as an Irish chieftain; ever resolute, she holds her head higher than the queen's, being taller, and converses with the monarch in Latin. Innumerable legends have accrued to her persona, of which the most widely known is her demand that *Howth Castle always have its gates open to hungry travellers, to which she forced the proprietors to accede after she herself was denied entry at dinner-time. Subject of more than a dozen popular novels, beginning with W. H. Maxwell's *The Dark Lady of Doona* (London, 1836), and of one thorough and reliable study, Anne Chambers, *Granuaile! The Life and Times of Grace O'Malley* (Dublin, 1979).

Gray/Grey **of Macha.** See LIATH MACHA.

Grianán Ailigh, Ailech, Aileach. See AILEACH.

grógach. Variant spelling of *gruagach.

grollican. Variant form of *brollachan.

Gronw Pebyr, Pefr [cf. W *pybyr*, staunch, strong]. Hunter from Penllyn near *Bala Lake who has an adulterous affair with *Blodeuwedd in the fourth branch of the **Mabinogi*. A year after he fails to kill Blodeuwedd's husband, *Lleu Llaw Gyffes, Lleu kills him in the manner Gronw intended for him, but only after Gronw begs for reconciliation.

gruagach, gruacach, grógach [OIr. *grúacach*, hairy, long-haired; goblin, wight, enchanter; wizard-like]. Solitary *fairy of Irish and Scottish Gaelic traditions, sometimes seen as a *giant or ogre. His characteristic long hair links the gruagach to the woodwose or *wild man of the woods. In Scotland the term gruagach may sometimes also refer to a fairy woman dressed in green or to a slender, handsome man.

Guaire, Guairy, Guary, Guairi, Guare [noble, proud]. Name borne by many figures in early Irish tradition, most notably Guaire Aidne, king of *Connacht (d. 663), much celebrated as a paragon of hospitality and generosity, called 'Guaire of the extended hand'. His daughter *Créd (2) became the lover of *Cano. A favourite allusion of W. B. Yeats, Guaire appears in the poem 'The Three Beggars' and is the title-character of the play *The King's Threshold* (1904). One of the most photographed castles in Ireland, Dún Guaire, 1 mile E of Kinvara, Co. Galway, is named for him; erected in 1520, it lies on the site of a 7th-century fortification attributed to Guaire.

Guennolous. Latinized version of *Gwenddolau.

Guénolé, Guénole, Gwénnolé. Virtuous but Jeremiah-like holy man of the Breton city of *Ys who tried to reform the sinful *Dahut (or Ahè).

Guibne, Guibniu. Variant spellings of *Goibniu.

Guinevere, Guenevere, Guinièvere. Wife of King *Arthur in the Arthurian legends whose illicit and ongoing relationship to *Lancelot helps to bring about the downfall of Arthur's court. Her Welsh counterpart or antecedent is *Gwenhwyfar.

Guir, Guirr. See LOUGH GUR.

Guivarc'h. Breton name for King *Mark.

Gullion, Slieve. See SLIAB CUILINN.

Gundestrup Cauldron. One the most celebrated works of early Celtic religious art was uncovered in a peat bog near the village of Gundestrup, Jutland peninsula, Denmark, in 1880, and is now housed in the museum at Århus. Made of 96 per cent pure silver and originally gilded, the vessel stands 14 in. high, is 25.5 in. in diameter, will hold 28.5 gallons, and weighs nearly 20 pounds. Dismantled when found, the cauldron comprises thirteen parts: a plain base plate, and five inner and seven outer plates decorated with mythological scenes. While the origin and date of the cauldron are still unsettled, commentators generally agree that it was carried, possibly by Teutonic looters, to Gundestrup from a distant place. It may have been transported from *Gaul, but stylistic details on the vessel suggest it may have been manufactured as far away as the Balkans, in Thrace or what is now Romania. Many elements depicted, such as torcs, snakes with *ram heads, or the *boar-headed war trumpet known as the carnyx, are certainly Celtic; other details and motifs are so exotic as not to seem European.

The plates depict gods, conventionally seen as larger than humans, ordinary mortals, and animals. The seated *horned god is now commonly accepted as an illustration of *Cernunnos. A tall divine figure holding a man over a vat of water is thought to be *Teutates accepting human sacrifice. A female divinity flanked by wheels, as if riding in a cart, has been compared with the Irish *Medb. The mortals include a troop of infantry in close-knit short trousers and a company of cavalry with a sacred tree. Three sword-bearing warriors are about to execute three huge *bulls (see TRIPLISM). Other animals depicted, such as leopards, were unknown in the Celtic world.

Although much studied and, more recently, photographed and reproduced, the Gundestrup Cauldron remains enigmatic to many commentators. The most controversial of them, Garrett S. Olmsted, has asserted that the scenes on the plates anticipate the action of the Irish epic **Táin Bó Cuailnge* [Cattle Raid of Cooley]. See Garrett S. Olmsted, 'The Gundestrup Version of the *Táin Bó Cuailnge*', *Antiquity*, 50 (1976), 95–103; *The Gundestrup Cauldron*, Collection Latomus no. 162 (Brussels, 1979); A. Bergquist and T. Taylor, 'The Origin of the Gundestrup Cauldron', *Antiquity*, 61 (1987), 10–24; Paul Jacobsthal, *Early Celtic Art* (Oxford, 1944).

Gur, Lough. See LOUGH GUR.

Gwaelod. See CANTRE'R GWAELOD.

Gwair, Gweir [W *gwair*, hay]. Mysterious prisoner of *Caer Siddi, another name for the *otherworldly *Annwfn in the pre-Norman poem **Preiddiau Annwfn* [The Spoils of Annwfn]. The Welsh *Triads cite him as one of the three exalted prisoners of the Isle of Britain, along with *Mabon. Goreu is said to have released him. Some commentators have suggested that Gwair is a title rather than a name and may refer to any of several characters in the **Mabinogi*, including Mabon. See Marged Haycock, *Studia Celtica*, 18/19 (1983–4), 52 ff.

Gwalchmai fab Gwyar, Gwalchmei [W *gwalch*, hawk; *mai/mei*, of May (?)/of the plain (?)]. Welsh counterpart or antecedent of *Gawain, here a nephew of *Arthur. In **Culhwch ac Olwen* he rides his horse Ceingalad while accompanying the hero. He acts the peacemaker between *Tristan and *March ap Meirchion. But according to the Welsh *Triads he has no links with Arthur at all. See Rachel Bromwich, *Trioedd Ynys Prydain*, rev. edn. (Cardiff, 1978), 369–75, 552.

Gwales [cf. W *gwales*, shelter, lair]. Name for an *otherworldly island off the south-west coast of *Dyfed (until 1974, Pembrokeshire), often identified, like *Caer Siddi, with the actual tiny islet (21 acres) of Grassholm, 6.5 miles W of Skomer Island. *Bendigeidfran's severed head presided over eighty years of joyous feasting here before it was removed to Gwynfryn in London; the feast was attended by the seven survivors of the war with Matholwch, who were oblivious to the passing of time until Heilyn fab Gwyn ended the spell by opening the door. Along with its assumed identity with an actual place, Gwales is also an example of *Annwfn, the Welsh Otherworld. See also HARLECH.

gwartheg y llyn [W *gwartheg*, cattle]. The *fairy cattle of Wales, counterparts of the *crodh mara of Gaelic Scotland, except that they are usually thought to be milk-white themselves. On the happy circumstance that they are joined with an earthly herd, they will give top-quality milk, cream, and butter in abundance.

gwarwyn a throt [W, the white-naped one with the trot]. Hidden or secret name once current in Monmouthshire (since 1974,

*Gwent) for the *tylwyth teg [fair folk] or Welsh *fairies.

gwawd. Initially a cognate of the Irish *fáith [seer, prophet], this Welsh word came to mean satire or mockery. Some early sources also used it for panegyric and praise poetry. See also GWELEDYDD; GWIDDON.

Gwawl ap Clud [W, light (?); wall (?); hedge (?)]. Rival suitor to *Pwyll for *Rhiannon, and son of the goddess Clud in the first branch of the *Mabinogi*. Although he appears almost feeble-witted, he is nearly successful. Pwyll wreaks vengeance in the game of badger-in-the-bag, killing Gwawl. Later, Llwyd the enchanter retaliates on Gwawl's behalf. Probably a native of Clydeside.

gweledydd. Welsh word for seer or prophet, the counterpart of the *fáith and the Latin *vates. See also GWIDDON [witch]; GWAWD.

Gwenddolau, Gwendoleu, sometimes with the patronymic fab Ceidio. Probably historical 6th-century Welsh chieftain of the Old North (former Welsh-speaking petty kingdoms of what is now the Scottish Lowlands) slain at the Battle of *Arfderydd (573/5). So traumatized by his death was his retainer *Myrddin (or *Merlin) that he went mad, became a *wild man of the woods, and received the gift of prophecy. His name may be commemorated in the place-name Carwinley [*Caer Wenddolau*, Gwenddolou's Fort], near Longtown, Cumberlandshire. *Geoffrey of Monmouth (12th cent.) latinized his name as Guennolous. See Rachel Bromwich, *Trioedd Ynys Prydain*, rev. edn. (Cardiff, 1978), 379ff.

Gwenhwyfar, Gwenhwyvar [W *gwên*, white, fair; *(g)wyf*, smooth, yielding (?)]. Welsh counterpart and possible antecedent of *Guinevere, wife of King *Arthur. *Geoffrey of Monmouth (12th cent.) reported that she was of noble Roman stock and had been brought up in a Cornish court. *Giraldus Cambrensis claimed to have seen Arthur and Gwenhwyfar's bodies exhumed in 1192 with the notation that she was a second wife. Like Guinevere, she is an adulteress, but with Medrod, the counterpart of Mo(r)dred, after which she becomes a nun. Several commentators have suggested that the name Gwenhwyfar is philologically related to the Irish *Finnabair.

Gwénnolé. Variant form of *Guénolé.

Gwent. A gwlad or region of south-eastern *Wales, a borderland between Wales and England. Deriving from the administrative system of the Romans, Gwent was an independent kingdom from the 5th to the 11th centuries; during some of that time it was united with *Morgannwg to the west. The region was sometimes divided into two parts, Gwent Uwch Coed [W, upper wood] to the north-west and Gwent Is Coed [lower wood] to the south-east. *Merlin was found at the fountain of Galabes in Gwent, according to *Geoffrey of Monmouth (12th cent.). From 1536 to 1974 much of the territory of Gwent constituted the county of Monmouth, which was assumed to be part of England. After 1974 Gwent was re-formed as a county of Wales, but with different boundaries from those of the medieval kingdom.

Gwern [cf. W *gwernen*, *alder tree]. Son of *Branwen and *Matholwch in the **Mabinogi* slain when thrown into the fire by the vile *Efnisien.

Gwernabwy, Gwern Abwy [cf. W *gwernen*, *alder tree]. Owner of the celebrated *eagle that *Culhwch consults in his search for *Mabon.

gwiddon. Welsh word for witch, hag, sorceress. See GWAWD; GWELEDYDD; FÁITH; VATES.

Gwion Bach, Gwyon Bach. Name of the servant in *Hanes Taliesin* [The Tale of Taliesin] who wins the gift of poetic inspiration intended for *Morfran and becomes, when reborn from the shape-shifting goddess *Ceridwen, *Taliesin. His many transformations are often compared with those of *Tuan mac Cairill.

gwlad. Welsh word for land or country, may be used both for the independent, small kingdoms in Wales before the English conquest (1282) or a definable cultural region where people sharing a common dialect or set of customs may have dwelt for a long period. See T. M. Charles-Edwards, *Early Irish and Welsh Kinship* (Oxford, 1993).

Gwlad y Tylwyth Teg. Welsh phrase for *fairy land, which colloquially may also denote sleep or the grave.

Gwreg Houarn, Ar [Bret., the iron woman]. Nickname for the *Venus of Quinipily.

Gwrhyr Gwalstawd Ieithoedd. *Shamanistic Welsh figure who talks to animals and accompanies *Culhwch.

Gwri sometimes with the epithet Gwallt Euryn [golden hair]. Name given to the child of *Rhiannon and *Pwyll in the *Mabinogi* by his adoptive father, *Teyrnon Twrf Liant. He is later renamed *Pryderi.

gwyddbwyll. Early Welsh board-game, often compared to the Irish *fidchell and *búanfach. While the word is commonly translated as 'chess', we lack sufficient information about how it was played to know how it might compare with that game, even though narrative descriptions tell us *Peredur and *Macsen play it; in **Breuddwyd Rhonabwy* [The Dream of Rhonabwy], *Arthur or *Owain play gwyddbwyll on a silver board. Rachel Bromwich discusses the game in *Trioedd Ynys Prydain*, rev. edn. (Cardiff, 1978), 246.

Gwyddno Garanhir, Gwyddneu Garanhir, Gwythno Garanhir [*garanhir*, long-shanked]. Mythical regional ruler of early Wales whose name appears in a number of disconnected stories. At the time of the flooding of *Cantre'r Gwaelod, his kingdom was along Cardigan Bay. The name Caer Wyddno was given to rocks eight miles from Aberystwyth. In the *Hanes Taliesin*, the baby *Taliesin floats into his fish weir between *Aberystwyth and the River Dyfi and is rescued by Gwyddno's feckless son *Elffin. Gwyddno is probably identical with the Gwyddneu who owns the basket providing inexhaustible supplies of food in **Culhwch ac Olwen*; *Ysbaddaden Pencawr sends Culhwch to retrieve it for a wedding feast. See Rachel Bromwich, *Trioedd Ynys Prydain*, rev. edn. (Cardiff, 1978), 397–400, 554.

Gwydion. Prominent figure in the fourth branch of the *Mabinogi*. Son of *Dôn and brother of *Gilfaethwy, Gwydion is a powerful magician like his uncle, Math, who gives his name to the fourth branch. Through his magic he contrives a war between Math of *Gwynedd and *Pryderi of *Dyfed by having his brother Gilfaethwy sleep with the virginal *Goewen, Math's foot-holder. Learning of this treachery, Math transforms Gwydion and his brother into, successively, a *stag and hind, a *boar and sow, and a male and she-wolf. Restored again to human form, Gwydion fashions a wife out of flowers, *Blodeuwedd, for his protégé *Lleu Llaw Gyffes, who may have been his incestuously begotten son. He transforms the *trees into warriors in **Cad Goddeu* [The Battle of the Trees]. Brother of *Arianrhod and father of *Bleiddwn, *Hychdwn Hir, and *Hyddwnn. See Rachel Bromwich, *Trioedd Ynys Prydain*, rev. edn. (Cardiff, 1978), 400–2.

gwyllgi. Fearsome, huge, spectral mastiff in Welsh oral tradition. See DOG; FAIRY DOG.

Gwyn ap Nudd, Gwynn [W *gwyn*, white, fair, holy]. Mythological king of Welsh tradition whose stature diminishes over the centuries with the advance of Christianity. In the oldest literature he is a ruler of *Annwfn or the *Otherworld and has within him the ferocity of *demons or fiends. Despite the meaning of his name, Gwyn bears a blackened face while leading the pack of *fairy dogs known as *cwˆn annwfn. *Culhwch must enlist his support in the hunt for the great *boar Twrch Trwyth in **Culhwch ac Olwen*. In the same poem *Arthur condemns Gwyn to a continual combat with *Gwythyr fab Greidawl for the love of *Creiddylad each *Calan Mai [May Day] until the end of time. Gwyn has abducted Creiddylad, the daughter or *Lludd Llaw Ereint, a double for Gwyn's father, *Nudd, a point unheeded in the story. After the 16th century Gwyn becomes the king of the *tylwyth teg [fair folk], i.e. *fairies. As commonly noted, the name Gwyn ap Nudd is philologically related to that of *Fionn mac Cumhaill, who is descended from *Nuadu (Airgetlám or Necht). T. F. O'Rahilly speculated (1946) that both Gwyn and Fionn are identical with the divine hero *Lug Lámfhota. *Gwyn ap Nudd* is the title of one of the most notable poems of the Welsh writer H. Elfed Lewis (1860–1953). See Idris L. Foster, 'Gwynn ap Nudd', in *Duanaire Finn*, iii, ed. Gerard Murphy, Irish Texts Society, no. 43 (Dublin, 1953), 198–205; Jenny Rowland, *Early Welsh Saga Poetry* (Cambridge, 1990).

Gwynedd, Gwyneth (ang.), Venedotia (L), North *Wales. Before Wales's subdivision into shires in the 16th century, Gwynedd might refer to much of the northern third of the principality north and west of the Dyfi/ Dovey River. Ancient and medieval Gwynedd is not identical in area with the 1,488-square-mile modern county of Gwynedd reconstituted in 1974 from the former shires of *Anglesey, Caernarvon, Merioneth, and parts of Denbigh. Although little is known of its beginnings, the first kingdom of Gwynedd was established after the departure of the Romans. According to *Historia Brittonum* (*c*.830) *Cunedda founded the royal line which later included *Maelgwn Gwynedd (6th cent.) and *Rhodri Mawr (d. 877), who extended his authority over *Ceredigion, *Powys, and *Ystrad Tywi. Rhodri's hegemony did not survive, but for much of medieval history Gwynedd, with a royal seat at Aberffraw, dominated its neighbouring petty kingdoms. Welsh native political power reached an apogee under *Llywelyn ap Iorwerth of Gwynedd (1173–1240), and consequently the main thrust of the English conquest of Wales under Edward I, (1277–82) was towards Gwynedd. The fabled Mount *Snowdon lies in Gwynedd, and much of the terrain is mountainous, making access by foot challenging. This relative remoteness has not prevented Gwynedd from participating in Welsh literary heritage. The wizard children of *Dôn reside here. The *Hanes Taliesin* [Tale of *Taliesin] moves the adventures of that 6th-century poet from the Old North (former Welsh-speaking areas in Lowland *Scotland) to Gwynedd. While much of the action of the **Mabinogi* takes place in *Dyfed, Math son of Mathonwy, so dominant in the third branch, is a Gwynedd man; *Lleu Llaw Gyffes becomes Lord of Gwynedd in the fourth branch. See Wendy Davies, *Wales in the Early Middle Ages* (Leicester, 1982).

Gwŷr y Gogledd [W, men of the north/left]. Welsh name for the *P-Celtic north Britons, ethnically and culturally antecedent to the Welsh, in territories that ceased to be a part of *Wales. Many of these peoples lived in extinct kingdoms, *Gododdin, *Rheged, *Strathclyde, coextensive with what is now the Lowlands of *Scotland.

Gwythyr fab Greidawl, Gwythur ap Greidawl [W, victor, son of scorcher]. Eternal combatant with *Gwynn ap Nudd. Gwythyr was the intended of the beautiful *Creiddylad, daughter of *Lludd Llaw Erient when Gwyn abducted her before the lovers could sleep together. Gwynn defeated Gwythyr's rescuing force and treated some of Gwythyr's retainers most savagely. So bitter was the enmity between the two men that *Arthur condemned them to do battle with one another each *Calan Mai [May Day] until doomsday.

H

Hafgan, Havgan [W, summer white (?)]. *Otherworldly rival of King *Arawn of *Annwfn, whom he was destined to fight each year. Arawn convinced *Pwyll to take his own shape one year, advising him to give but one blow to Hafgan as a second would revive him; Pwyll succeeded and returned to the realm of mortals. Hafgan is often thought to have contributed to the conception of the Green Knight who challenges *Gawain and to the Arthurian figure Gromer Somer Joure.

Hag of Beare, Beara. See CAILLEACH BHÉIRRE.

Halloween. See SAMAIN; HOLLANTIDE; ALLANTIDE.

Hallstatt. Archaeological site in upper Austria that has given its name to the first assuredly Celtic cultural epoch. Specifically, Hallstatt denotes a salt-mining complex overlooking the lake of the same name, extensively excavated between 1846 and 1899.

Synonymous with the early Iron Age, Hallstatt culture flourished in four phases, A, B, C, and D, from as early as 1200 BC to as late as 600 BC; its influence was widespread in Europe from *c.*800 BC to 450 BC, following the *Urnfield culture and being superseded by the *La Tène style. Hallstatt art is generally severely geometrical, admired more for its technical than for its aesthetic achievements. Extravagant, almost baroque, Hallstatt felt little of the Greek orientalizing influence. The typical bird motif probably derives from Italy; plant patterns are rare. See August Aigner, *Hallstatt* (Munich, 1911); J. V. S. Megaw, *Art of the European Iron Age* (New York, 1970).

Hanes Taliesin. See TALIESIN.

Harlech. Ancient coastal town of *Gwynedd (until 1974, Merionethshire), near which are the ruins of Harlech Castle (13th cent.), both of which enjoy abundant mythological and historical associations. In the **Mabinogi*, Harlech is one of the seats of *Bendigeidfran and his sister *Branwen, and where later his severed head presides over an *otherworldly feast. See also GWALES.

Havgan. Anglicization of *Hafgan.

hazel [OE *hæsel*]. Both the wood and the edible nuts of this bush or small tree (genus *Corylus*) have played important roles in Irish and Welsh traditions. Hazel leaves and nuts are found in early British burial mounds and shaft-wells, especially at Ashill, Norfolk. The place-name story for Fordruim, an early name for *Tara, describes it as a pleasant hazel wood. In the *ogham alphabet of early Ireland, the letter C was represented by hazel [OIr. *coll*]. It also represented the ninth month on the Old Irish calendar, 6 August to 2 September. Initiate members of the *Fianna had to defend themselves armed only with a hazel stick and a shield; yet in the *Fenian legends the hazel without leaves was thought evil, dripping poisonous milk, and the home of vultures. Thought a *fairy tree in both Ireland and Wales, wood from the hazel was sacred to poets and was thus a taboo fuel on any hearth. Heralds carried hazel wands as badges of office. Witches' wands are often made of hazel, as are divining rods, used to find underground water. In Cornwall the hazel was used in the millpreve, the magical *adder stones. In Wales a twig of hazel would be given to a rejected lover.

Even more esteemed than the hazel's wood were its nuts, often described as the 'nuts of wisdom', e.g. esoteric or occult *knowledge. Hazels of wisdom grew at the heads of the seven chief rivers of Ireland, and nine grew over both *Connla's Well and the Well of *Segais, the legendary common source of the *Boyne and the Shannon. The nuts would fall into the water, causing bubbles of mystic inspiration to form, or were eaten by *salmon. The number of spots on a salmon's back were thought to indicate the number of nuts it had consumed. The salmon of wisdom caught by *Fionn mac Cumhaill had eaten hazel nuts.

The name of the Irish hero *Mac Cuill

means 'son of the hazel'. W. B. Yeats thought the hazel was the common Irish form of the tree of life. OIr. and ModIr. coll; ScG calltunn, calltuinn; Manx coull; W collen; Corn. collwedhen; Bret. kraoñklevezenn.

Heber. Variant spelling of *Éber.

Heilyn fab Gwyn [W *heilyn*, cup-bearer]. Reveller on the *otherworldly isle of *Gwales who ended the feasting by carelessly opening the door.

Heilyn Goch [W *heilyn*, cup-bearer; *coch*, red]. Keeper of the filthy lodgings where Rhonabwy has his dream in **Breuddwyd Rhonabwy* [The Dream of Rhonabwy].

Heinen Fardd. Chief poet in the court of *Maelgwn Gwynedd who was disgraced by *Taliesin.

Heithiurun. Variant form of *Etharún.

Heledd. Perhaps historical (7th cent.?) female narrator of the 9th- or 10th-century **Canu Heledd* [Song of Heledd], last surviving member of the *Powys dynasty, who laments the loss of her family and lands, and especially of her king, *Cynddylan.

Heracura. Variant form of *Aeracura.

Hercules, Heracles. Images of the Graeco-Roman hero become divinity survive in two modes in Celtic Europe. In many instances he is simply borrowed from Mediterranean iconography: bearded, muscular, wielding a mighty club. Elsewhere the colonized natives appear to have adapted him through *interpretatio celtica* (see GAUL) to suit their own religious needs. At Aix-les-Bains in southern Gaul the local god *Borvo was venerated with bronze statuettes, apparently testifying to his power to combat illnesses. Names of several local Celtic deities, notably *Segomo, are linked as epithets to Hercules. The figure of *Smertrius, sometimes seen as an aspect of *Mars, resembles Hercules. In a widely cited story from the Greek writer Lucian of Samosata (2nd cent. AD), Hercules is equated with a Gaulish god known only in this text, *Ogmios. While travelling in southern Gaul, near the modern city of Marseille, Lucian encountered a drawing of a bald, ageing man pulling a band of smiling men attached to him by chains from their ears to his tongue. This was Ogmios, god of eloquence, he was told, identified with Hercules because of his great strength, supported visually with a distinctive bow and club. Many modern commentators see echoes of Hercules in the club-carrying *Cerne Abbas giant, and there may be an echo of Hercules' name in the person of *Ercol, who is dragged behind *Cúchulainn's chariot in **Fled Bricrenn* [Briccriu's Feast]. Cúchulainn himself has been called the 'Celtic Hercules' since the mid-19th century, not only because of his prowess and strength but also because his taskmaster, *Forgall Manach, bears some resemblance to the role of Eurystheus in the story of Hercules/ Heracles.

Heremon, Heremhon. Variant spellings of *Éremón.

Hergest. See RED BOOK OF HERGEST.

Herla, King. Traditional early British king whose story is told in the Latin text *De Nugis Curialum* by Walter Map (*c*.1140-*c*.1209). One day, while rising, King Herla meets a *dwarfish king with *goat's hooves who invites himself to Herla's wedding and bids Herla come to his in one year from the day. When Herla goes underground through the mouth of a great *cave to the king's realm, he is given a tiny bloodhound and told not to put it down until the *dog leaps down of his own accord. Returning to his own kingdom, Herla asks an old shepherd about the welfare of his queen, but the old man cannot understand him. Two hundred years have passed, and the Saxon tongue has supplanted the British in the land of the Britons. The old shepherd, however, has heard of King Herla, who was thought to have disappeared long ago. Some of Herla's retainers leap to the ground to see what has happened, but they instantly vanish in a puff of dust. Herla and a small band are still thought to wander in England, waiting for the tiny dog to leave his hand. Although Herla's story is probably of Germanic origin (the Saxon-derived term Herlethingi denotes a phantom train of soldiers bearing sumptuous gifts across the countryside), it is often compared with the Irish adventures of *Oisín in *Tír na nÓg. International tale type: 766 (variant); folk motifs: C521; C927.2; C984; EE501.1.7.1; F241.1.0.1; F377; F378.1; F379.1. See Walter Map *De Nugis Curialum*, ed. F. Tupper and M. B. Ogle (London, 1924).

Hesus. Variant form of *Esus.

Hi. Variant form of *Iona.

himbas forosnai. Variant spelling of *imbas forosnai.

Historia Brittonum [L, History of the Britons]. Early 9th-century chronicle of British and Welsh history, chapter 56 of which tells of *Arthur, '*dux bellorum*', and his twelve victories. Formerly ascribed to one Nennius, *Historia* is now seen, thanks to the work of David Dumville, to be a compilation from a number of disparate sources. See Arthur W. Wade-Evans, *Nennius's History of the Britons* (London, 1938); *Historia Brittonum*, ed. D. N. Dumville (Cambridge, 1985).

Historia Regnum Britanniae. See GEOFFREY OF MONMOUTH.

Historical Cycle. See CYCLE OF THE KINGS.

Hochscheid. See SIRONA.

Hollantide, Calan Gaeaf. Welsh calendar festival for 1 November, a counterpart of Irish *Samain, Cornish *Allantide, and Breton Kala-Goañv. A remnant of the old Celtic New Year, Hollantide was a time of ghostly visitation, divination games, bonfire burning, and post-harvest merrymaking, traditions which largely vanished in the 19th century to be replaced by the wassailing common to the other holidays. As dark preceded light on the Celtic *calendar, the dark time, i.e. of death, comes before the celebrations of spring and summer. At such a time Welsh people might encounter the apparitions known as Y *Ladi Wen [the white lady] and the *hwch ddu gota [bob-tailed black sow]. On the night before Hollantide it was believed that those who were going to die in the coming year could be seen through the church-door keyhole. Less ominously, young people sewing hemp at crossroads at night could make their future sweethearts appear. See Trefor M. Owen, *Welsh Folk Customs*, 3rd edn. (Cardiff, 1974).

hooded crow, hoodie. See CROW.

horned god. Depictions of early Celtic deities bearing horns are usually thought to be *Cernunnos when no other name is given; at some sites, however, Gaulish *Mercury and Silvanus as well as *Cocidius are represented with horns. The Irish heroes *Feradach Fechtnach and *Furbaide Ferbend bear horns, as does the monstrous creature from the Scottish Gaelic folklore, beannach-nimhe [horned poison].

hound. See DOG.

howlaa. See DOOINEY OIE.

Howth [ON *höfuth*, headland]. Peninsula jutting into the Irish Sea 9 miles NE of Dublin, scene of many actions in early Irish literature; by extension Howth is also the name of a 19th-century fishing village and a modern, fashionable suburb. In the oldest literature the locale is more often known as *Benn Étair, the Old Irish name for the Hill of Howth (560 feet). *Crimthan Nia Náir built one of his two fortresses, Dún Crimthainn, here. The first church on the site was built by the fabled King Sitric [Sigtryggr] as early as 1042. Howth Castle, begun 1564 and remodelled many times, is the subject of many legends, the best-known of which is that *Granuaile [Gráinne Ní Mháille], having been denied entrance at dinner-time, assured that its gates would evermore be open to the hungry traveller. James Joyce uses Howth Castle and environs as one of the many manifestations of HCE in *Finnegans Wake* (1939). *Oscar and *Étaín (3) are thought to be buried here. See *The Book of Howth: Calendar of the Carew Manuscripts*, ed. J. S. Brewer and W. Bullen (London, 1871); Whitley Stokes, 'The Siege of Howth', *Revue Celtique*, 8 (1887), 47–64.

hungry grass [Ir. *féar gortach, fód gortach*]. A belief in Irish oral tradition of unknown antiquity, perhaps from Famine times (*c.*1846–8), of an enchanted tuft of grass that leaves those unfortunates who tread upon it with a hunger that cannot be satisfied. A lesser-known tradition speaks of the fear gortach [hungry man] who begs for alms and rewards those who favour him. Also known as fairy grass. A frequent allusion in 20th-century Irish literature, e.g. Donagh MacDonagh's poems *The Hungry Grass* (London, 1947), and Richard Power's novel *The Hungry Grass* (London and New York, 1969). See also FÓIDÍN MEARAÍ.

hwch ddu gota [W, bob-tailed black sow]. Spectral pig, an embodiment of the Christian devil, thought to be seen at *Hollantide, the Welsh equivalent of *Samain and Halloween. It would arise from the last embers of a bonfire and catch the laggard participant in the festivities.

Hy Brasil, Brazil, Breasil, Breasail, Breasal, Brasil [cf. OIr. *Í*, island; *bres*, beauty, worth; great, mighty]. Mysterious island, an earthly paradise, once thought to lie at the same latitude as Ireland but far out to sea. Although perhaps of Irish origin, the concept of Hy

Brasil clearly owes much to the older European myth of the lost Atlantis. Some commentators speculate an Irish antecedent in Barc Bresail [OIr. *barc*, boat-shaped structure found on land], a wooden fortress built in *Leinster by *Bresal the 'High King of the World' and destroyed by *Tuathal Techtmar. The island Hy Brasil appears, under many different names, on medieval maps, and was the subject of cartographer Angelinus Dalorto's thesis *L'Isola Brazil* (Genoa, 1325). Dalorto's spelling influenced the naming of the South American nation Brazil, although maps after Columbus's time still showed an island of approximately that name west of Ireland. Regardless of its origin, Hy Brasil is often cited in Irish tradition, sometimes being associated with the *Aran Islands. The *Tuatha Dé Danann were thought to have fled there after their defeat by the *Milesians. In *The Celtic Twilight* (1893), W. B. Yeats reports speaking to fishermen who claimed to have sailed out as far as 'Hy Brazil'; they describe an island without labour, care, or cynical laughter where one can enjoy the conversation of *Cúchulainn and his heroes. See T. J. Westropp, 'Brasil and the Legendary Islands of the North Atlantic', *Proceedings of the Royal Irish Academy*, 30 (1912), 223–60; William Larminie's poem 'The Finding of Hy Brasil', in *Glanus* (London, 1889), 72; Eamon de Buitléar's film *Hy Brasil* (1972) suggests identification with the Azores. See also TÍR NA NÓG; EMAIN ABLACH.

Hy Many. Anglicization of *Uí Maine.

Hychdwn Hir [W, tall piglet]. Offspring of *Gwydion and *Gilfaethwy when they were in the shape of a *boar and sow.

Hyddwn [W, little *stag]. Offspring of *Gilfaethwy and *Gwydion when they were in the shape of a *stag and hind.

Hywel Dda, ap Cadell [W *hywell*, eminent, prominent; *dda*, good]. Historical (d. 950) Welsh king, grandson of *Rhodri Mawr, famed for establishing a native system of laws, counterparts of the Irish *Brehon Laws. The laws survive in seventy manuscripts, most dating from before the 16th century, when they were still in practice. Hywel appears to have been the only Welsh king to strike coins bearing his own image. See *Ancient Laws and Institutes of Wales*, ed. Aneurin Owen (2 vols., London, 1841, 1900; 1983); Meville Richards, *The Laws of Hywel Dda (The Book of Blegywryd)* (Liverpool, 1954).

I

I. The ninth letter of the modern English alphabet is represented by ibar [*yew] in the *ogham alphabet of early Ireland.

Í [OIr., island]. The word for island usually designates *Iona in early Irish texts.

Í Breasail, Í Breasil. Speculative Irish forms for *Hy Brasil.

Í Choluim Chille. OIr. name for *Iona.

Iarchonnacht, Iar Chonnacht [west Connacht]. Irish name for *Connemara.

Iarll y Cawg [W, knight of the fountain]. A title for **Owain*.

Iarmumu. OIr. name for West *Munster.

iath nAnann. Irish phrase meaning 'land of Anann', a poetic name for *Ireland. Anann is the genitive form of *Ana. Cf. íath, 'land, country, territory, estate'.

Ibhell. Variant of *Aíbell.

Icolumkill. Anglicization of Í Choluim Chille, i.e. *Iona.

ierna. Variant form of *Iverni.

Igerna, Igerne, Igraine, Igrayne, Ygerne, Yguerne. Mother of *Arthur in Arthurian romance. Wife of the Duke of Cornwall (variously, Gorlois or Hoel), she conceives Arthur by Uther Pendragon [*Uthr Bendragon], who appears in the likeness of her husband with the help of *Merlin's magic. After the death of her husband, she marries Uther. Her Welsh antecedent is *Eigr, one of the most beautiful women in Britain.

Ildánach, Ildána [Ir. *il*, many; *dán*, art]. From *Samildánach, a sobriquet meaning 'all-crafts', 'of many trades', or 'master of all the arts', applied to *Lug Lámfhota.

Iliann. Corrupt spelling of *Illann.

Illann, Illan, Iollan, Iollann, Iliann. Name borne by several early Irish kings, learned men, and warriors, the last found frequently among the *Fianna; *Fionn mac Cumhaill had a son named Illann/ Iollann, and some texts assert that *Goll mac Morna may have first been named Illann.

Illann 1. Son of *Fergus mac Róich who defends Noíse and his brothers in the *Deirdre story.

2, sometimes Iollann Éachtach [ModIr. wonderful, powerful]. Husband of *Uirne (or Tuiren), who turns her into a *dog.

imbas forosnai, himbas forosnai, imbus for osna, imus for osna [Ir. *imbas*, great knowledge, poetic talent, inspiration; *forosnai*, that illuminates]. A special gift for prophetic knowledge or clairvoyance thought to be possessed by poets, especially the *ollam as the highest rank of *fili, in early Ireland. Descriptions of the ritual allowing the poet to exercise his imbas forosnai are found in the 10th-century **Sanas Cormaic* [Cormac's Glossary]. The poet chews a piece of the red flesh of a pig, *dog, or *cat, and then puts it on a flagstone near the door and chants an invocation over it to unnamed gods. He chants over his two palms and asks that his sleep not be disturbed, and then puts his two palms on his cheeks and sleeps. Men guard him that he may not be disturbed or turned over. At the end of three days and nights the poet may judge whether imbas forosnai has come to him. The amazonian *Scáthach makes prophecies through imbas forosnai, and in the **Táin Bó Cuailnge* Medb asks *Fedelm whether she has acquired it. Of all Irish figures, *Fionn mac Cumhaill demonstrates imbas forosnai most consistently. St *Patrick was thought to have abolished imbas forosnai as a denial of baptism, but a counterpart in Christian contexts was known as córus cerda [the gift of poetry]. This power appears to be a combination of *fios [occult power] and *teinm laída. See Rudolf Thurneysen, '*Imbas Forosnai*', *Zeitschrift für celtische Philologie*, 19 (1932), 163–4; Nora K. Chadwick, 'Imbas Forosnai', *Scottish Gaelic Studies*, 4 (2) (1935), 97–135. See also AWENYDDION; DIVINATION; SHAMANISM.

Imbolc, Imbolg, Óimelc, Oimelc, Oímelg. Old Irish name for a seasonal feast of pre-Christian origin fixed at 1 February on the Gregorian calendar. One of the four major Celtic calendar feasts known in Old Irish as *Samain (1 November), *Beltaine (1 May), and Lugnasad (ModIr. *Lughnasa, 1 August). The natural phenomenon at the root of Imbolc is thought to be the visibly perceptive lengthening of daylight, and therefore the anticipation of spring; the alternate name for the day, Óimelc, is thought to denote the time of ewes coming into milk, also a signal of spring. From earliest times Imbolc was associated with *Brigit, the fire-goddess, and after Christianization with St *Brigid of Kildare, eventually becoming known as St Brigid's Day. The saint, it should be pointed out, was often seen as the patroness of sheep, the pastoral economy, and *fertility in general.

Unlike the other calendar feasts, celebrations acknowledging Imbolc's pagan origins have not persisted in popular tradition. The Scottish Gaelic name for the day, Là Féill Bhr'de, and the Irish Lá 'il Bríde, retain the link to St Brigid, but the common Irish and Manx names acknowledge the further Christianization of Imbolc as Candlemas Day, and associates it with the Blessed Virgin Mary: Ir. Lá Fhéile Muire na gCoinneal; Manx Laa'l Moirrey Ny Gainle. There are also echoes of Imbolc as an anticipation of spring in the American secular celebration Groundhog Day. See Joseph Vendryes, 'Imbolc', *Revue Celtique*, 41 (1924), 241–4; Dorothy A. Bray, 'The Image of Saint Brigit in the Early Irish Churches', *Études Celtiques*, 24 (1987), 209–15; Séamas Ó Catháin, *The Festival of Brigit* (Dublin, 1995); Eric Hamp, *Studia Celtica*, 14/15 (1979–80), 106–13.

Imchad. Cruel husband of *Uirne in older texts.

Imram, Immram, Imrama (pl.)., Iomramh (ModIr.) [Ir., the act of rowing, sea voyaging]. Conventional first word, usually translated as 'voyage', in the titles of a class of Old and Middle Irish narrative in which travellers reach an *Otherworld supposedly in the islands of the Western ocean. Compare stories beginning **Echtra* . . . , where interest focuses on a scene in the Otherworld and the voyage is a subordinate framework. The imram is undertaken voluntarily; an often involuntary voyage of greater duration is the Longas [exile]. Medieval lists cite seven Imrama, of which three survive; the same lists categorize **Imram Brain* as an Echtra.

Imram Brain. Irish title for the 7th- or 8th-century narrative known in English as The Voyage of Bran Son of Febal, or Bran's Voyage to the Land of Women; also *Echtrae Brain Maic Fhebail*. Several extant texts are found in Ireland, including the 11th-century **Book of the Dun Cow*, and the **Book of Leinster*, both thought to be derived from a lost manuscript compiled at the monastery of *Druim Snechta (Co. Monaghan). One of the oldest Irish narratives, *Imram Brain* is quite long and contains many digressions; at its core is the familiar European story (international folk motifs: F111; F112) of the mortal lured to the *Otherworld by a beautiful, divine woman.

One day Bran [raven] mac Febail is walking near his dún [stronghold] when he hears sweet music coming behind him that lulls him to sleep. When he awakes he has a silver branch in his hand covered with silver-white *apple blossom, which he carries back with him to the stronghold. As he shows the wondrous branch to his people, a beautiful woman in strange clothing appears before him, singing of Emne (i.e. *Emain Ablach), the island where there is no grieving, winter, or want, where the golden horses of *Manannán mac Lir prance, and where games and sport continue without cease. (Emne/ Emain Ablach is known in English under different names, the Land of Promise and the Isle of Women.) She bids Bran seek out that island, and when the song is done she disappears, the apple branch falling into Bran's hands, which cannot hold it.

The next morning Bran sets out with a fleet of currachs, three foster-brothers, and twenty-seven warriors. They row far across the sea until they come upon a warrior driving his chariot as if he were on land. Greeting them, he identifies himself as Manannán and sings further of Emain Ablach, urging Bran and his men to visit it. Though Bran feels he is rowing over the sea, it is for Manannán the flowery land of *Mag Mell [Delightful Plain], where leaping *salmon are calves and lambs. Then, in a sudden Christian interpolation, the sin of Adam is recalled and the death of Christ is foretold. Returning to the pre-Christian milieu, Manannán tells that he will become the lover of *Caíntigern who will bear him the son *Mongán, how the son will live and how he will die. And he tells Bran that if he keeps rowing he will reach Emain Ablach before sunset. Bran and his men follow this advice, but before reaching their goal they pass the Island of Merriment or Delight, whose inhabitants are so given to giddy shouting and laughter they will not answer enquiries. When Bran puts one of his men ashore, he too joins in the hilarity.

Finally arrived at Emain Ablach, Bran is greeted by the leader of the women but is reluctant to go ashore. She throws a ball of thread that entangles his hands and draws him towards the great hall on the many-coloured island. Each of the men is given a bed, a female companion, and an endless supply of food until they begin to lose any sense of time. Eventually one of the shipmates, *Nechtan mac Collbrain, speaks of his homesickness for Ireland, and urges Bran to leave with him. Bran's lover warns against this, telling him that only sorrow will come of it. When it is clear that he will leave with all his men, she counsels him to retrieve the man left on the Island of Merriment so that his company will be complete, and that when they all return to Ireland they should look at it and call out to friends but that no one should actually touch the land. The first point they see is called Srub Brain, usually identified with Stroove Point on Lough Foyle, Co. *Donegal, although Kuno Meyer (1895–7) thought it should be in south-western Ireland. Bran calls out his name, 'Bran son of Febal', to people on the shore; they answer that they do not know him, only that the tale of his voyage is one of their ancient stories. Nechtan, who has longed to return to Ireland, then jumps from the currach and wades through the surf; but as soon as his foot touches land his entire body crumbles into dust as if he has been in his grave 500 years. Bran stays long enough to tell his countrymen of his adventures by writing them in *ogham on wooden sticks and casting them, and then he sails away with his companions, never to be seen again.

Among the many digressions from the main action is the report by the *Fenian hero *Caílte that Mongán, son of Manannán mac Lir, is actually a reincarnation of *Fionn mac Cumhaill.

Myles Dillon (1948) argued that the narrative should be classed as an *Echtra rather than an Imram because it is principally a visit to the *Otherworld. Only the manuscript in the *Book of Leinster* includes the word *Imram* in the title. Although the redactor of the narrative inserts many Christian motifs, the core of the narrative is probably pre-Christian and pre-Fenian as well. International tale types: 470; 766 (variant); folk motifs: F111; F112; F302.3.1; F373; F377. Texts and translations: Kuno Meyer and Alfred Nutt, *Immram Brain: The Voyage of Bran* (2 vols., London, 1895–7); Anton G. van Hamel, *Immrama* (Dublin, 1941), 1–19; Séamus MacMathúna, *Immram Brain: Bran's Journey to the Land of Women* (Tübingen, 1985). See also Proinsias MacCana, 'Mongán mac Fiachna and "Immram Brain"', *Ériu*, 23 (1972), 102–42; 'On the Prehistory of Immram Brain', *Ériu*, 26 (1975), 33–52; 'The Sinless World of Immram Brain', *Ériu*, 27 (1976), 95–115.

Imram Curaig Maíle Dúin. Irish title for the narrative known in English as The Voyage of Máel Dúin's Boat; also *Imram Maíle Dúin*, The Voyage of Máel Dúin. Although probably composed in the 8th century, the story survives in 10th-century fragments in the **Book of the Dun Cow*, the **Yellow Book of Lecan*, Egerton MS 1782, and Harley MS 5280.

Máel Dúin is the love-child of a nun, fostered by a queen and three princes. In a taunt one day he learns both of his illegitimacy and that his father, Ailill Ochair Ága [edge of battle] has been killed by raiders. Not knowing how to avenge him, Máel Dúin consults a *druid, who tells him to build a boat of three skins and to take only seventeen companions. He sets about following this advice when three foster-brothers swim out to join, portentously violating the druid's *geis. They voyage all day until midnight before they land on the first two of what are to be thirty-one islands, each the site of a fabulous adventure. These include massive ants and birds, a beast who can turn his skin round like a mill, demon horses, fighting horses, and a cat guarding treasure who can turn men to ashes. One island is divided by a brass wall, with black sheep on one side and white on the other. Some of their discoveries are happier, like the severed branch of the *apple tree that satisfies the crew for forty days. Most often, though, they face dangers, both aggressive and seductive. On one island stones are thrown at the currachs as the men make their escape. On the Island of Smiths, a red-hot iron bar comes flying their way and sets the entire sea to boiling. A primal chorus draws travellers against their will on the Island of

Laughter and the Island of Weeping. On the Island of Women the queen warmly greets Máel Dúin, offering her seventeen daughters as bed-partners to the crew. Offering the men uninterrupted pleasure and perpetual youth, she induces them to stay forever, but after three months they try to return to their boat. She throws a ball of thread after them, magically preventing them from leaving; three times she holds them back for periods of three months each. On the fourth attempt the crewman and poet Diurán catches the thread and then allows his arm holding it to be severed, allowing them all to escape.

Often the narrative employs surreal imagery, suggestive of the *Otherworld, like seas of green glass, intoxicating fruit, silver nets, silver columns, and an island on a pedestal with a door at its base. Máel Dúin and his crew, Diurán and *Germán most prominently, are driven with vengeance as their quest. At a turning-point in the narrative, however, they encounter an old monk, clothed only in his own overgrown hair, who says he is a survivor from the time of St Brendan of Birr (d. 565 AD); he asks them to forgive the slayer of Ailill Ochair Ága. They agree, and in due time reach the island of their former enemies, where they are made welcome. After telling the story of their wanderings, Máel Dúin and his men return to Ireland.

The Egerton MS cites Áed Finn, 'chief scholar of Ireland', as the author, an assertion given little credence today. Despite the rich imagination of the author, modern commentators see links between Máel Dúin's adventures and those attributed to St *Brendan of Clonfert in the 9th-century *Navagatio Brendani*, the **Imram Brain* [Voyage of Bran], various feats of *Cúchulainn, pre-Christian Irish myth, classical mythology, and medieval bestiaries.

Whitley Stokes, 'The Voyage of Mael Duin', *Revue Celtique*, 9 (1889), 452–92, and 10 (1889), 50–94; A. G. van Hamel, 'Immram Curaig Maíle Dúin', in *Immrama* (Dublin, 1941), 20–77; H. P. A. Oskamp, *The Voyage of the Máel Dúin: A Study* (Groningen, 1970); M. Aguirre, *Études Celtiques*, 27 (1990), 203–20. P. W. Joyce's translation, 'The Voyage of Maildun', in *Old Celtic Romances* (London, 1879), inspired Alfred Lord Tennyson's late poem 'The Voyage of Maeldune'. Twentieth-century poets adapting the narrative are Louis MacNeice in the radio play *The Mad Islands* (London, 1962, 1964) and Paul Muldoon, 'Immram', in *Why Brownlee Left* (London and Winston-Salem, 1980). Two popular prose retellings are Michael Scott, *A Celtic Odyssey* (London, 1985) and Patricia A. McDowell, *The Voyage of Mael Duin* (Dublin, 1991).

imus for osna. Corrupt form of *imbas forosnai.

inber, indber. OIr. word for river mouth, found as the first element in innumerable place-names. Cf. ModIr. inbher, inbhear; ScG inbhir; Manx inver; W *aber [estuary, confluence]; Corn. aber; Bret. aber.

Inber Colptha, Colpa. The mouth of the *Boyne River, including the Boyne estuary, site of dozens of important events in early Irish history and mythology, most notably the landing of the *Milesians in the **Lebor Gabála* [Book of Invasions].

Inber Domnann. Malahide Bay, north Co. Dublin, named for the *Domnainn of the *Laginian invasion. Both the *Fir Bolg and *Tuathal Techtmar also invade Ireland here.

Inber Glas [green, greenish-blue harbour]. OIr. name for the long estuary at the mouth of the Bann River in what is today Co. *Derry, Northern Ireland. After the beautiful young *Tuag was drowned here, it was sometimes called Tuagh Inber.

Inber Scéne, Scénae. Perhaps imaginary place-name in south *Kerry, named for Scéne, wife of the poet *Amairgin (1), sometimes identified with the mouth of the Kenmare River. Some commentators link it with the *Shannon, on the testimony of early Spanish cleric Orosius (*Historia*, AD 417).

inbhear, inbher. ModIr. for *inber.

Indech, Inneach. *Fomorian warrior, son of *Domnu, who met misfortune at the Second Battle of Mag Tuired [**Cath Maige Tuired*]. In one version his blood and vitality are drained away from him by *Mórrígan before the battle so that she can show that her sympathies are with the *Tuatha Dé Danann. In a variant reading Indech is killed later in the battle by *Ogma. Indech's unnamed daughter is one of three females, along with the *Mórrígan and *Boand, with whom the *Dagda has ritual intercourse at *Samain.

Ingcél Cáech [Ir. *cáech*, *one-eyed]. Ferocious British (sometimes Cornish) pirate in early Irish literature; distinguished by his single eye, as broad as an oxhide and as black as a beetle, with three pupils in it. With the sons of *Donn Désa, *Fer Gair, Fer Lí, and *Fer Rogain, as well as the seven sons of *Medb named *Maine, he sacks Da Derga's Hostel in **Togail Bruidne Da Derga* [The Destruction of Da Derga's Hostel]. His brother is *Éccell.

inis. Irish word for island, first element in scores of place-names. Cf. ScG innis, *ynys.

Inis Ealga [noble isle]. Poetic nickname for *Ireland.

Inis Fáil [isle of destiny]. Poetic nickname for *Ireland.

Inis Fionnchuire, Findchuire, Fianchuibhe, Finchory. Imaginary underwater (under *Muir Torrain*) island populated by nymphs. In **Oidheadh Chlainne Tuireann* [The Tragic Story of the Sons of Tuireann], *Lug Lámfhota demanded that *Brian (1), Iuchair, and Iucharba retrieve the cooking-spit from here.

Inneach. Variant spelling of *Indech.

innis. ScG word for island, first element in scores of place-names. Cf. Ir. inis, W *ynys.

Intoxication of the Ulstermen. See MESCA ULAD.

Invasions, The Book of. See LEBOR GABÁLA.

Iollann. ModIr. spelling of *Illann.

Iolo Morganwg. Pseudonym of Edward Williams (1747–1826), Welsh poet, antiquarian, and founder of neo-druidism. Best remembered for having launched the cultural society gorsedd, or **Gorsedd Beirdd Ynys Prydain* [the Throne/Assembly of the Bards of the Isle of Britain], in 1792, Iolo remains a controversial figure. While thousands still devoutly practise neo-druidism, marching around the decidedly non-Celtic megaliths at Stonehenge, informed opinion has long since portrayed his antiquarianism as Iolo's own invention. He is the counterpart of the Scottish 'translator' James *Macpherson and the Breton revivalist Hesart de *La Villemarqué. A stonemason by trade, Iolo was deeply influenced both by late 18th-century antiquarianism and by the political radicalism attractive to many intellectuals following the French Revolution; he called himself 'the Bard of Liberty'. Critics have pointed out that he also had a lifelong addiction to the drug laudanum. Among his many publications were poems purportedly by the 14th-century Dafydd ap Gwilym, which have since been proved to be his own. See Stuart Piggott, *The Druids* (London, 1968); Prys Morgan, *Iolo Morganwg* (Cardiff, 1975).

Iomramh. ModIr. spelling of *Imram.

Iona, Hi, Icolumkill [OIr. *Í*, island; *Í Choluim Chille*, Colum Cille's island]. Anglo-Latinized name for the small island, 3.5 by 1.5 miles, SW of Mull in the Inner Hebrides, much celebrated in Scottish Gaelic tradition. The island was evangelized by St *Colum Cille *c.*563, who is popularly thought to have established a monastery there that appears to have been constructed some years after his arrival. A new monastery and nunnery were begun by the Benedictines in 1203 and have been restored in the 20th century. The chapel of St Oran (11th cent.) contains the burial-grounds of many Scottish, four Irish, and eight Norwegian kings. See F. Marian McNeill, *Iona: a History of the Island* (London, 1920); *An Iona Anthology* (Stirling, 1947); Shane Leslie, *Isle of Columcille* (London, *c.*1910); Fiona MacLeod [William Sharp], *Iona* (London, 1910); William Lindsay Alexander, *Iona* (London and Nashville, 1860); Máire Herbert, *Iona, Kells and Derry* (Oxford, 1988); Anna Ritchie, *Iona* (London, 1996).

Íor. ModIr. spelling of *Ír.

Ír, Ir, Íor. Third son of *Míl Espáne and the eponym for whom *Ireland is named, according to the pseudo-history **Lebor Gabála* [Book of Invasions]. As described in the narrative, Ír rows ahead of the pack of *Milesian invaders during a magical storm conjured up by the defending *Tuatha Dé Danann; his oar breaks and he falls back into the sea and drowns. T. F. O'Rahilly (1946) dismissed Ír as a genealogical fiction. Often confused with *Íth.

Ireland. Second largest of the British Isles, 32,595 square metres in area, largest of all Celtic lands; its modern population, between 4 and 5 million, is smaller than that of *Scotland, although the island may have contained more than 9 million in 1840. Ireland was divided into thirty-two counties in the 17th century, twenty-six of which formed an independent nation in 1922, first as the Irish Free State and, after 1949, as the Republic of Ireland, occupying 26,601 square metres, or 81.6 per cent of the total. Six counties remained a part of the UK in 1922 and were partitioned from the rest as Northern Ireland, a name with no currency before that time; all six, however, are coextensive with the ancient province of *Ulster, whose full borders embrace three more counties, now in the Republic.

According to widely known literary tradition, the Irish name for Ireland, Éire, derives from *Ériu, one of many feminine personifications of the country (see below); the dative and genitive forms of the name are Érinn, Érenn. At the same time the name is strikingly similar to that of the *Érainn, a people of early southern Ireland. According to the late medieval, biblicized pseudo-history *Lebor Gabála*, Ireland is named for *Ír, the first of the *Milesians. The Greek forms for Ireland as recorded in *Ptolemy (2nd cent. AD), Ierna, Iernē (elsewhere Ivernē), were latinized into Hibernia (also Iverna, Ivernia). Modern commentators have identified the *Iverni with the *Érainn of early Ireland, specifically the subdivision known as *Corcu Loígde. For a period in the early 20th century the anglicized term 'Ivernian' was coined to denote all the population of early Ireland. From Latin also come the terms Scotia for the island and *Scotti for its inhabitants, especially those in the north-east. When people from the north-east of Ireland invaded what they then called *Alba in the 4th century, that country came to be called *Scotland after them. Additionally, the ancient people known as the *Attecotti may also have been in fact from Ireland.

Celtic-speaking peoples were by no means the earliest inhabitants of Ireland. Radiocarbon dating indicates human habitation in what is now Co. Sligo as early as *c.*7500 BC, but the Celts did not arrive until the first millennium BC, specific dates for which are still under contention. This means that most of the best-known archaeological remains in Ireland, e.g. Newgrange (*c.*3200 BC), *Dowth, and *Knowth, were built by pre-Celtic peoples, even though they are frequently cited in Celtic tradition. Among the earliest Celtic-speaking peoples may have been the Priteni (or *Picts), who migrated west from Britain; the *Belgae, also found on the Continent and in Britain; the *Lagin, perhaps from Armorica [*Brittany] who may have invaded both Ireland and Britain simultaneously; and finally the *Gaels or *Goidelic-speakers. The language inherited from these invaders, Irish, is the most prominent of the *Q-Celtic family. T. F. O'Rahilly argued in *Early Irish History and Mythology* (1946) that only the last invaders, the Goidelic-speakers, were Q-Celts and that all the earlier peoples were *P-Celts, a controversial assertion that has little or no acceptance despite the enormous influence of his study. Shadowy parallels for the early populations of Ireland are found in the *Lebor Gabála*, which applies the name Milesian to the Q-Celtic ancestors of the modern Irish.

Unique among Celtic countries are Ireland's many poetic personifications and characterizations, most of them female. Among the oldest is iath nAnann [land of Ana], in the 10th-century **Sanas Cormaic* [Cormac's Glossary], alluding to *Ana, the pre-Christian earth-goddess. Perhaps as old are the three beautiful divinities of the *Lebor Gabála*, *Ériu, *Banba, and *Fódla. Also from the *Lebor Gabála* is the first invader, *Cesair, a woman whose name can be a poetic synonym for Ireland. Two early modern personae, *Cáit Ní Dhuibhir and *Róisín Dubh [Dark Rosaleen], depict a lovely maiden in distress. Not all personifications have radiated sexual allure, however. The loathsome *Cailleach Bhéirre [hag of Beare] proffers the forbidding face of *sovereignty; she appears reincarnated in *Sean-bhean Bhocht/*Shan Van Vocht, 'the Poor Old Woman', an emblem of the United Irishmen's rising in 1798 and frequently cited since then. A weakened Ireland could still be nurturing as in *Druimin Donn Dílis [faithful, brown, white-backed *cow]. Yet other female figures are powerful and commanding, like *Granuaile, based on the historical 16th-century Mayo coast pirate, Gráinne Mhaol Ní Mháille, and *Caitlín Ní hUallacháin [Cathleen Ni Houlihan], much evoked by 19th- and 20th-century nationalists. The two most important non-female metaphors for Ireland are *Fál or *Lia Fáil, the phallic stone of *Tara, and *Claidheamh Soluis [sword of light; reformed spelling Claíomh Solais]. Two common poetic nicknames are *Inis Ealga [noble isle] and *Inis Fáil [island of destiny], alluding to the stone Fál. In Geoffrey *Keating's history (17th cent.) Ireland is Muicinis [pig island].

Although Ireland is nearly bisected on an east-west axis by the *Shannon River, the historical imagination has favoured a north-south division along a nearly invisible line called the *Eiscir Riada that runs from outside Galway City into what is today *Dublin. Two stories explain this bifurcation. In the better-known version, *Conn Cétchathach [of the Hundred Battles] claimed the land north of Eiscir Riada, while *Eogan Mór (also known as Mug Nuadat) took the south; all territory was consequently either *Leth Cuinn [Conn's half] or *Leth Moga [Mug's half]. A division along the same line, Eiscir Riada, is made in the *Lebor Gabála*, with *Éber Finn taking the north and *Éremón taking the south. The north-south division persists in the alignment of Ireland's five provinces. Initially Ulster (earlier Ulaid) and *Connacht are mostly north of the Eiscir Riada, while *Leinster (Lagin) and *Munster (Mumu), so large as to be counted as two-east and west- are south. When *Mide is counted as the fifth province (and thus Munster as one), it also lies north of Eiscir Riada. Although the composition of each province reflects centuries of migration and settlement patterns, part 2 of the Welsh **Mabinogi* offers a different origin story: all the men of Ireland are slain except for five pregnant women whose sons establish the five provinces of Ireland.

While Ireland was not conquered by the Romans, it drew closer to the rest of Europe with Christian evangelization, putatively led by St *Patrick, beginning in the 5th century. Subsequently, early Irish writing was expressed in an adaptation of the Roman alphabet. As well as being the oldest written vernacular in Europe, the Irish language [OIr. *Goídelc*; ModIr. *Gaedhealg*; reformed ModIr. *Gaeilge*] survives in the largest volume of early texts of any early European language, more than 600, many of which have never been edited or translated. Some, not all, are bound in great early codices like the **Book of the Dun Cow* [*Lebor na hUidre*] (*c*.1100), **Book of Leinster* [*Lebor Laignech/na Núachongbála*] (*c*.1160), and **Yellow Book of Lecan* [*Lebor Buide Lecáin* (*c*.1390). From the advent of Christianity in the 5th century until the arrival of the Anglo-Normans in 1169, writing, in Irish or Latin, was largely an ecclesiastical franchise. Native-born clergymen absorbed pre-Christian narratives and in time made their own use of them.

Thus much of what is called 'Celtic mythology' in this volume has been transmitted to us by scribes unsympathetic with, if not hostile to, the religious traditions that had fostered the original traditions. Not surprisingly, some 19th- and early 20th-century commentators argued that heroic stories from early Irish literature did not constitute a 'mythology' because they had been compromised in transmission. Clearly, the characters of some divinities, notably *Ana for whom the *Tuatha Dé Danann are named, are nearly lost. Some heroes, such as *Lug Lámfhota and *Fionn mac Cumhaill, were certainly originally divinities. Yet much of the unwritten pre-Christian original tradition has been retained, as is implied by the numerous parallels between Old Irish literature, 'Celtic Mythology', and classical, Norse, Slavic, Indian, and other Indo-European mythologies. Additionally, more recent archaeological finds in the British Isles and elsewhere co-ordinate many aspects of the milieu depicted in the four major cycles of early Irish literature, the *Mythological, the *Ulster, the *Fenian, and the *Cycle of Kings.

Written tradition in Irish survived the 12th-century reform of the Irish Church, which brought with it the introduction of orders of Continental monasticism, like the Benedictines and the Cistercians, and ended the native monasticism of Celtic Christianity. Prominent families, including gaelicized Normans, acted as patrons in the transmission of manuscripts down the departure of the native aristocracy, the 'Flight of the Earls', at the beginning of the 17th century. Increased anglicization diminished Irish literary tradition, yet manuscripts continued to be produced in large numbers, sometimes abroad, e.g. **Duanaire Finn* at Louvain in the Spanish Netherlands, through the 18th century and up to the middle of the 19th.

Proscription of the Irish language in commerce and legal affairs meant that its speakers, though they were still a majority of the population as late as 1800, were often illiterate and powerless. Lack of the ability to write did not prevent the survival of an enormously rich oral tradition, which began to be collected, translated, and published in the 19th century. T. Crofton Croker's first volumes, *Researches in the South of Ireland* (1824) and *Fairy Legends and Traditions of the South of Ireland* (1825), attracted European attention, including that of the Brothers Grimm and Sir Walter Scott. Over the next two centuries hundreds of other collectors would fill libraries with narratives, many of which are rooted in the oldest documents of Irish literary tradition. The voluminous files of the Irish Folklore Commission, compiled in the 20th century, are more extensive than collections from any other western European country. At the end of the 20th century, the wellsprings of this oral tradition had by no means been exhausted. Oral tradition has survived the calamitous decline of the Irish language. The 1911 census recorded that only 17.6 per cent of the population could speak Irish to any degree, certainly a smaller number at independence eleven years later. The Free State Government (which became the Republic of Ireland, 1949) made a knowledge of Irish a requirement for schools and for applications to civil service positions, a policy that continued until 1973, and also created financial and other incentives to native speakers to remain in the Gaeltacht or Irish-speaking regions. With the 21st century approaching, more than 1 million persons had some knowledge of Irish while no more than 100,000, about 3.3 per cent of the population of the Republic, spoke Irish as a primary language. Ir. Éire; ScG Éirinn; Manx Nerin, Yn Erin; W Iwerddon; Corn. Ywerdhon; Bret. Iwerzhon, Iwerzon, Iverdon. See also Bibliography under 'Irish'.

Irish World-Chronicle. A fragment of this early annal survives in Rawlinson MS B 488 of the Bodleian Library, Oxford, along with the **Annals of Tigernach*. Although the two works are of distinctly different origin, they were edited and published together by Whitley Stokes, *Revue Celtique*, 16 (1895), 374–419; 17 (1896), 6–33, 119–263, 337–420; 18 (1897), 9–59, 150–97, 267–303.

Irota, Iroda. OIr. names for Norway.

Írusán. Huge *cat, as large as an ox, known as the King of the Cats, widely known in Irish written and oral tradition. According to a well-known story, when *Senchán Torpéist, chief poet of Ireland, dared to satirize cats, Írusán came out of his cave at *Knowth to carry the poet away on his back; when they passed *Clonmacnoise St *Ciarán saved the poet by throwing a red-hot poker at Írusán and killing him.

Isbaddaden. Variant form of *Ysbaddaden Pencawr.

Iseult, Isolda, Yseult, Ysolt, Es(s)yllt (Welsh). Name borne by two figures in the Arthurian romance of Tristan and Iseult. (1) Iseult (Isolt) of Ireland falls in love (sometimes from a potion) with Tristan of *Cornwall, even though she has sworn vengeance against him for killing her father, while he escorts her to her betrothed, King *Mark. After many intrigues she dies beside her mortally wounded lover. (2) Iseult (Ysonde) of Brittany, or of the White Hands, makes an unconsummated marriage with Tristan through the ruse of bearing his beloved's name. Jealously she lies to Tristan about the other Iseult's presence on the vessel he has awaited, and so causes him to die in grief before his beloved reaches him. Often compared to the Irish figures *Deirdre and *Gráinne. See Rachel Bromwich et al. (ed.), *The Arthur of the Welsh* (Cardiff, 1991), chs. 12 and 13.

Isle of Destiny. Anglicization of Inis Fáil, a poetic nickname for *Ireland.

Isle of Women. Variant translation of *Emain Ablach.

Isolda. Variant form of *Iseult.

Íth, Ith. A leader of the *Milesians in the pseudo-history **Lebor Gabála* [Book of Invasions], the first of his people to reach *Ireland. Son of *Breogan in Spain, he sails to Ireland to settle a dispute among the *Tuatha Dé Danann, but his eloquence makes the disputants fear that he seeks to be king and so they kill him. His nephew, *Míl Espáine, avenges his murder with the invasion of Ireland. His name is commemorated in several places on the Irish map, e.g. Mag Ítha, Co. Donegal. Imaginative medieval genealogists placed his name in many pedigrees. The fictitious king *Eochaid mac Luchta traced his line to Íth. The mythic hero of the *Érainn, *Lugaid mac Con, was given *Goidelic heritage by inventing the patronymic and identity of *Lugaid mac Ítha. Often confused with *Ír.

Iubdán, Iubdan. *Fairy king of Irish tradition, known as early as the 16th-century text of **Echtra Fergusa maic Léti* [The Adventure of Fergus mac Léti]. For a king, he suffers many humiliations. *Eisirt, Iubdán's court poet, tells him that *Ulster is a land of giants to deflate his boasting, and to prove his point brings home a *dwarf, *Áeda (1), who seems a giant in the fairy court. Eisirt then lays a demeaning *geis on Iubdán, requiring him to travel to *Emain Macha so that he may be the first there to eat porridge in the morning. As Eisirt correctly predicted, Iubdán clumsily falls into the porridge, is captured, and is kept prisoner for a year. In the bawdy **Aided*

Fergusa [The Violent Death of Fergus], Fergus mac Léti has a grotesque adulterous affair with *Bebo, Iubdán's wife, his greatest concern being that his male member is larger than she is. Fergus tells Iubdán of his pleasure with Bebo, but not until the fourth time does Iubdán condemn his lust. Later, Fergus captures both Iubdán and Bebo and will not release them until Iubdán surrenders his most prized possession, which is revealed to be a pair of enchanted shoes, allowing the wearer to walk on water. When Fergus puts them on, the shoes swell to fit his feet.

Iuchair, Iuchar. Second son of *Tuireann in **Oidheadh Chlainne Tuireann* [The Tragic Story of the Children of Tuireann].

Iucharba. Third son of *Tuireann in **Oidheadh Chlainne Tuireann* [The Tragic Story of the Children of Tuireann].

Iuchra 1, also Luchra. Villain who transforms *Aífe (3), wife of *Manannán mac Lir, into a *crane. When she dies, Manannán makes the *crane bag of her skin.

2. Daughter of *Ábartach in the *Fenian ballads who turns her rival, Aífe (2), into a heron.

Iverni, Iverna, Ierna, Ivernians. The ancient geographer *Ptolemy (2nd. cent. AD) used the name Iverni for what he perceived to be a section of the Irish people. Modern commentators have deduced that he derived this from the *Érainn people of early Ireland, specifically their subdivision, the *Corcu Loígde of what is today Co. Cork. In the early 20th century the anglicized term 'Ivernian' was often used to denote the ancient Irish people as a whole. See also IRELAND.

J

jackdaw. Although resembling and related to the *crow, this common European bird (species *Corvus monedula*) is sometimes represented as talking in different Celtic traditions. Those of Kilgarvan, Co. *Kerry, Ireland, asked to enter the town so that they might escape the depredations of the crows. The king refused permission, on the advice of his *druid, but relented when the jackdaws found a missing magical ring that defended all of *Munster from a *Fomorian attack. ModIr. cág; ScG cathag-fhireann; Manx caaig, doochassagh; W corfran, jac-y-do; Corn. choga; Bret. palorez.

Jan Tregeagle. See TREGEAGLE.

Japheth. Third son of Noah in *Genesis* 5: 32. The Irish pseudo-history **Lebor Gabála* [Book of Invasions] often cites Japheth's name in seeking to co-ordinate barely remembered native history and the biblical story of creation. *Nemed, a mythical invader of early Ireland, is described as his descendant. Early genealogists also cite Japheth as an ancestor of historical families.

Jasconius [cf. Ir. *iasc*, fish]. Name for the whale upon which St *Brendan and his followers land.

javelin. See GÁE-.

Jephthah, Jephtha. According to the Old Testament Book of Judges, chapters 11–12, a judge of Israel who sacrificed his daughter to fulfil a rash vow. This episode was often cited in Celtic attempts to align native traditions with biblical narratives. On the Isle of *Man, Jephthah's daughter was substituted for *Eithne in the celebration of Laa Launys (*Lughnasa).

jeshal. The Manx word for the *sunwise turn.

jester. See FOOL.

jili ffrwtan, frwtan. Variant term for *tylwyth teg, the Welsh *fairy, especially applied to a proud little female of amorous disposition. An unglossable name, like Rumpelstiltskin or Tom Tit Tom.

John Tregeagle. See TREGEAGLE.

joint-eater. English term for the *fairy known in Irish as *alp-luachra.

Jove. Variant form of *Jupiter.

Jud-Hael [Bret. *hael*, noble, generous]. Legendary Breton chieftain from the time of the emigration from Great Britain. His enigmatic dream was interpreted by *Taliesin as meaning that his son would have a happier reign than he and would become one of the greatest men in Breton history. That son, Judik-Hael, fulfilled the prophecy.

Judik-Hael. Son of *Jud-Hael.

Julius Caesar. See CAESAR, JULIUS.

Jupiter, also Jove. The chief patriarch of the Roman pantheon, god of sky and thunderbolts, protector of oaths, was widely worshipped in Romano-Celtic religion, often with local epithets. Under the process of interpretatio celtica (see GAUL), the native populations of Roman colonies adapted the imperial god to local religious needs. Not surprisingly, *classical commentators described Jupiter as ranking lower in native esteem than Gaulish *Mercury, Gaulish *Apollo, and Gaulish *Mars, Celtic gods given Roman names under interpretatio romana. Evidence from non-Roman sources implies that the Continental Celtic *Taranis most resembles Jupiter, as does *Bussumarus, although it is not clear that either is identical with 'Gaulish Jupiter'. About 150 columns were erected to honour Jupiter, from eastern *Gaul through the Moselle and Rhine valleys. The upper figure is usually seen trampling a serpent-like anthropomorphic monster. Jupiter's placement here may be to put him as high as possible into the sky, his realm, or to link him with trees. Contemporary commentators give little heed to Sir John Rhyˆs's (1886) assertation that *Nodons, *Conchobar mac Nessa, *Conaire Mór, and *Cormac mac Airt could be related to Zeus, Jupiter's Greek counterpart.

K

Kadwr. Variant form of *Cador.

Kaer. Anglicization of the Welsh place-name *Caer.

Kaherdin, Kahedîn. A prince of *Brittany in Arthurian romance, whose father is variously named Jovel'n or Hoel. He befriends *Tristan and travels to *Cornwall with him. *Iseult of Brittany is his sister. R. S. Loomis (1927) argued that Keherdin had Welsh antecedents.

Kai. See the English Arthurian KAY and the Welsh CEI.

Kala-Goañv [Bret. *kala*, calend, convocation; *goañv*, winter]. The Breton expression for *Samain or 1 November.

Kala-Hañv [Bret. *kala*, calend, convocation; *hañv*, summer]. The Breton expression for *Beltaine or *May Day.

Kaledvoulc'h. Breton term for *Excalibur.

kannerezed nod. Breton equivalent of the *washer at the ford.

Karadawc, Karadawg. Breton spellings of the Welsh *Caradog.

Karadoc. Breton counterpart of the Welsh *Caradog whose name is associated with stories collected near Vannes in southern *Brittany. In the best-known, Karadoc's unnamed father is tricked into sleeping with a metamorphosed sow so that the *druid *Eliaves might sleep with Karadoc's mother. The result of Karadoc's father's bestial union is the fabled wild *boar Tourtain, counterpart of the Welsh *Twrch Trwyth.

Kathleen Ni Houlihan. Anglicization of *Caitlín Ní hUallacháin, a personification of *Ireland.

Kaw. Breton spelling of *Caw.

Kawal. Variant spelling of *Cabal.

Kay, Kai, Keerz, Keu. Seneschal of King Arthur in English romance, derived from the Welsh Arthurian figure *Cei, whom he resembles. The English Sir Kay is always a somewhat irascible and churlish retainer, even though he is Arthur's foster-brother and frequent companion in adventure. See H. J. Herman, 'Sir Kay: A Study of the Character of the Seneschal of King Arthur's Court', dissertation, University of Pennsylvania, 1960; Jürgen Haupt, *Der Truchsess Keie im Artusroman* (Berlin, 1971); Christopher Dean, 'Sir Kay in Medieval English Romances: An Alternative Tradition', *English Studies in Canada*, 9 (1983), 125–35.

Kean. Variant spelling of *Keyne.

Keating, Geoffrey. English rendering of Séathrún Céitinn (*c.*1570–*c.*1645/1650), Irish historian, poet, and priest whose celebrated history of Ireland is often cited. Born in Tipperary of Norman stock, Keating was educated at a local bardic school, Bordeaux, and Salamanca before returning to Ireland as a doctor of theology and parish priest. According to legend, his sermons so enraged sinful parishioners that Keating was obliged to live in a cave in the Glen of Aherlow, Co. Limerick. His multi-volume history, whose Irish title is *Foras Feasa ar Éirinn* [lit. A Sound Basis for Knowledge of Ireland], was compiled between 1620 and 1633; some commentators assert that the principal labour on it was between 1629 and 1631. In contrast to the **Annals of the Four Masters*, a bare recitation of dates and facts compiled about the same time, Keating's history is written in a continuous narrative and includes colourful and dramatic vignettes. Written in Modern Irish when that language was still spoken by privileged and learned classes, Keating's history is an admired model of Irish prose style. To a degree the history is polemical, being a partial response to such denigrators of Ireland as Edmund Spenser (*c.*1552–99) and *Giraldus Cambrensis (*c.*1146–1223). Keating is sometimes compared to the Greek historian Herodotus (5th cent. BC) because he comes at the beginning of Irish modern historiography, and also because his record includes events we judge mythological and legendary as well as the certainly historical. His was the last important European book of history to be circulated in manuscript rather than having been published. The text has been translated into English several times, the first in 1723. The modern edition was published in four non-sequential volumes of the Irish Texts Society, 4, 8, 9, and 15; David Comyn edited the first (London, 1902), and Patrick S. Dinneen edited the remaining three (London, 1908, 1914); reprinted, with an introduction by Breandán Ó Buachalla (London, 1987). Keating also wrote poetry and spiritual texts.

Keelta MacRonan. Anglicization of *Caílte mac Rónáin.

Keeronagh. Anglicization of *Caoránach.

Keerz. Variant form of *Kay.

Keeva ('of the white skin'). Anglicization of *Cainche.

Keevan. Anglicization of *Ciabhán.

Kei. Variant spelling of *Kay; see also CEI.

Keingalet. Breton spelling of *Ceingalad, the horse of *Gwalchmai fab Gwyar.

Kelliwic, Kelliwec, Celliwig [Corn., woodland]. One of King Arthur's 'Three Tribal Thrones of the Island of Britain', according to the Welsh *Triads. It is the only one in *Cornwall; the others are St David's in Wales and Pen Rhionydd in Scotland. Although it is often cited in Cornish tradition, Kelliwic's precise location is not known. Most likely candidates are Castle Killibury or Kelly Rounds, an Iron Age hill-fort near Wadebridge, which was also occupied in post-Roman times; another is the town of Callington. See Rachel Bromwich, *Trioedd Ynys Prydain*, rev. edn. (Cardiff, 1978), pp. lxxiiiff.; Geoffrey Ashe, *A Guidebook to Arthurian Britain* (London, 1980); Rachel Bromwich et al. (eds.), *The Arthur of the Welsh* (Cardiff, 1991), 234–8.

Kells [*Cenlis, Kenlis*, from Ir. *Cenannas*]. Several towns in Ireland and one in Scotland bear this name, but the one most often denoted is the market town and former monastic site [Ir. *Ceanannus Mór*, head fort] in Co. Meath, about 55 miles NW of Dublin. Home of the celebrated treasures of early Christian Ireland, the Book of Kells and the Crozier of Kells. Although the founding date of the monastery here is not known, it enters history about 804 after the successive sackings of *Iona and the massacre of the community caused the division of the Columban or Celtic Christian Church. The monastery is cited in many narratives, e.g. **Esnada Tige Buchet* [The Melodies of Buchet's House], in which *Eithne Tháebfhota lies with *Cormac mac Airt near here to conceive *Cairbre Lifechair. The next best-known Kells is the village in Co. Kilkenny, site of many an important Norman settlement. See Máire Herbert, *Iona, Kells and Derry* (Oxford, 1988).

kelpie, kelpy, waterkelpie [cf. ScG *colpach calpach*, heifer, bullock, colt]. The *fairy water-creature of Scottish folklore, initially thought to inhabit lonely, fast-moving streams and later any body of water. Usually thought to be a horse, sometimes human, the kelpie is most often described as at least mischievous and more likely malevolent. The creature entices travellers on to its back and then rushes into deep pools to drown them. His tail strikes the water in thunder and he disappears in a flash of lightning. In human form the kelpie is a rough, shaggy man who leaps behind a solitary rider, gripping and crushing him. Some stories depict a human-form kelpie as tearing people apart and devouring them. The kelpie might be forced, however unwilling, to serve mortal ends. A bold man named MacGregor captured a kelpie's magic bridle and refused pleas to restore it; instead, MacGregor used it to work magic. In a widely known story a nobleman named Graham of Morphie bridled a kelpie and obliged him to drag stones to build his new castle. When the castle was completed, Graham released the unhappy kelpie who dashed to the river, promising that the Laird of Morphie would never enjoy the fruits of his forced labour. And, indeed, misfortune dogged the Grahams of Morphie all their lives.

Although known all over Scotland, the kelpie appears to originate in Scottish Gaelic tradition and is clearly a counterpart of the Welsh *ceffyl dwfr and *afanc, the Irish and Scottish Gaelic *each uisce/uisge, and the Manx *cabyll-ushtey and *glaistyn. Nevertheless the kelpie also has counterparts in the Norse-influenced islands north of Scotland, in Shetland: shoopiltee, and in the Orkneys: tangie, tang. See Helen Drever, *The Lure of the Kelpie* (Edinburgh, 1937). Folk motifs: B184.1.3; D1311.11.1; F234.1.8; F401.3.1; F420.1.3.3; G302.3.2; G303.3.3.1.3.

Keltchar. Variant spelling of *Celtchair.

Kemoc. Anglicization of *Mo Cháemóc.

Kenneth MacAlpin. Anglicization of *Cináed mac Ailpín.

Kenneth Oaur (Coinneach Odhar). See BRAHAN SEER.

Kennock. Anglicization of *Mo Cháemóc.

Kentigern [W *teyrn*, monarch]. Also known as Mungo. Patron saint (d. 603) of Glasgow and early bishop of *Strathclyde around whom many legends have accrued. According to tradition, he is the grandson of *Urien of *Rheged and a relative of King *Arthur; his mother was Thenaw, the Christian daughter of King Lot of Lothian, brother-in-law of King Arthur. Kentigern survived two attempts to kill him. First, his mother was about to be executed for her pregnancy but escaped; she recited the psalter while standing in an icy stream. Later the child and his mother were set adrift in a coracle, but were miraculously saved. These associations with water may partially explain Kentigern's identification with the *salmon. According to a well-known story, King *Rhydderch found a ring he had given his wife on the finger of a sleeping knight. He removed it and threw it into the sea and asked his wife where it was. She turned to Kentigern for help, who proceeded to catch a salmon that had swallowed the ring. The ring and salmon are in the arms of the city of Glasgow. Kentigern was reputed to have baptized *Merlin before his death, a possible borrowing from the Irish **Buile Shuibne* [The Madness of Suibne] story. Kentigern is also credited with evangelizing Cumbria (Scottish Lowlands) and establishing the Welsh see of Llanelwy (or St Asaph). Stories about Kentigern indicate that he was austere and that he travelled widely in Wales and Ireland; his feast-day is 14 January. See LAILOKEN. See Joceline of Furness's 12th-century *Life of St. Kentigern*, in W. F. Skene (ed.), *Four Ancient Books of Wales* (Edinburgh, 1874); A. P. Forbes, *The Lives of St. Ninian and St. Kentigern* (Edinburgh, 1868). The saint's link to Merlin is in the Welsh poem *Lailoken and Kentigern*, ed. H. D. L. Ward, *Romania*, 22 (1893), 514–25. See also Rachel Bromwich, *Trioedd Ynys Prydain*, rev. edn. (Cardiff, 1978), 319–21, 548.

Kêr Iz, Is, -Iz, -Is. Breton name for the city of *Ys.

Keraint. Variant spelling of *Geraint.

Kerglas [Bret. *kêr*, house, mansion; *glas*, blue-green]. The castle of the evil magician who has stolen the lance in the Breton folk-tale *Peronnik.

Keridwen. Anglicization of *Ceridwen.

Kerman Kelstach. Anglicization of *Cromm Cruaich.

Kermaria [Bret. *kêr*, house; *Maria*, the Virgin Mary]. Early settlement site near Pont l'Abbé, southern *Finistère, western *Brittany, site of a standing stone of Gaulish origin. Some commentators have suggested this was the *omphalos of Brittany or Armorica. See PUMLUMON; TYNWALD; UISNECH.

kern, kerne. Anglicizations of *ceithern.

Kernow. Cornish name for *Cornwall.

Kernyu. Archaic anglicization of *Cornwall.

Kerridwen. Variant spelling of *Ceridwen.

Kerry [Ir. *Ciarraighe Ciarraí*]. South-westernmost county of Ireland, western *Munster, occupying, 1,815 square miles deeply indented by Dingle, Kenmare, and other bays. Kerry has rich associations in Irish mythology and folklore, is the reputed home of *Ana (or Danu), for whom the *Tuatha Dé Danann are named, and is also the realm of the *Cailleach Bhéirre. The county takes its name from *Ciar, a love-child of Queen *Medb and *Fergus mac Róich; his descendants settled west of the Abbeyfeale River. Kerry is a common invasion route in the **Lebor Gabála* [Book of Invasions], and it is here that the *Milesians meet the three goddesses *Ériu, *Fódla, and *Banba, who give their names to Ireland. Part of Kerry is coextensive with *Corcu Duibne of early Christian centuries. See T. Crofton Croker and Sigerson Clifford, *Legends of Kerry* (Tralee, 1972); T. J. Barrington, *Discovering Kerry* (Dublin, 1976).

Kesair. Anglicization of *Cesair.

Keshcorran. Anglicization of *Céis Chorainn.

Ket. Anglicization of *Cet.

Keth. Anglicization of *Cet.

Keu. Variant spelling of *Kay.

Keva ('of the white skin'). Anglicization of *Cainche.

Kevin. Anglicization of *Cáemgen.

Kevoca, Kevoge. Anglicizations of *Mo Cháemóc.

Keyne, Kayna, Kean [W *cain*, beautiful]. Fifth-century Welsh virgin, reputed founder of a church in *Anglesey, whose story was celebrated elsewhere in Britain. Thought to be one of the twenty-four children of King *Brychan Brycheiniog, her name in Welsh may be Ceinwen, Cainwen [white or blessed Cain] or Cain Wyry [Cain the Virgin]. William Camden (1551–1623) described her heritage in Somerset. At least three holy wells are ascribed to her: (1) Near Liskeard, eastern Cornwall, the most famous of all Cornish wells. Its waters provided mastery in marriage. If a husband drank from it before the marriage, he would rule the household; if the wife drank first she would have the upper hand. Celebrated in a poem by Robert Southey (1774–1843). (2) At Llangeinor, Glamorganshire. This place-name is a corruption of Llan Gain Wyry, 'church place of the virgin Cain/Keyne'. (3) That ascribed to her at Llangenny, near Crickhowell, *Powys, should belong to the lesser-known St Ceneu. St Keyne's feast-day is 8 October.

Ki Du [Bret., black dog]. The black *dog of Breton tradition. It accompanies the deceased during their sojourn in the *Otherworld and their rebirth in the body of another human or an animal.

Kian. Anglicized spelling of *Cian.

Kicva. Anglicized spelling of *Cigfa.

Kieran. Anglicized spelling of *Ciarán.

Kilhwch. Anglicized spelling of *Culhwch.

Kilkenny cats. The once well-known Irish folktale of the two cats who fight until only their tails and nails are left masks an allusion in medieval Irish history. At issue is the enmity between the Anglo-Norman or 'English' settlers in Ireland and the native Gaelic Irish who were separated by only a small stream in the town of Kilkenny, *Leinster. As they had the upper hand legally, the Anglo-Normans sought to preserve their privileged status with the Statute of Kilkenny, 1367. This attributed all lawlessness to the Irish, proscribed intermarriage between the two communities, prohibited the English from entertaining Irish minstrels, or even from riding horseback in the Irish manner.

Modern commentators now dismiss the once current explanation of the story as pertaining to actual rather than to metamorphic cats. This asserted that Hessian troops stationed in Kilkenny during the 1798 rebellion would tie two cats together by their tails, hang them over a line, and watch them fight to the death.

Killaloe [Ir. *Cill Dalua*, monastic church of Dalua, Dolua, Dá Lua, Da Lúa]. Small market town in Co. Clare on the west bank of the Shannon, site first of an important medieval ecclesiastical centre and later also of *Kincora, the fortress of *Brian Bórama (Boru). Killaloe's ecclesiastical importance as well as its links with the *Dál Cais pre-date Brian. It was also the capital of the mythical *Bodb Derg. Part of the ruins were moved from Friar's Island, formerly in the Shannon, when the 1929 hydroelectric project flooded the area. Distinguish from Killaloe, Co. Kilkenny.

Kiltartan [Ir. *Cill Tartain*, Tartan's Church]. River and barony in south-east Co. Galway, Ireland. Once the site of Coole Park (demolished 1941), the estate of Augusta, Lady Gregory (1852–1932), who used the name in titles of her collections of folklore, e.g. *Kiltartan History Book* (Dublin, 1909), *The Kiltartan Wonder Book* (Dublin, 1910), etc. 'Kiltartan English' or 'Kiltartanese' denote her attempts to record what she felt was the poetic diction of country people in the area; the phrases are sometimes used disparagingly today, implying a patronizing falsity.

Kimbay. Anglicization of *Cimbáeth.

Kincora [Ir. *ceann cora coradh*, weir's head]. Fortress, sometimes 'palace' or 'capital', of *Brian Bórama (Boru) on the west bank of the *Shannon in what is now Co. Clare. Although lacking the grandeur associated with *Emain Macha or *Tara, Kincora does share the military glories of Brian (d. 1014) and the *Dál Cais. Demolished by the 11th or 12th centuries, the ruins of Kincora are alleged to survive on the grounds of the Catholic church in *Killaloe. The esteem given Kincora by 19th-century Anglo-Irish writers, especially in the romantic nationalist 'Kincora' by James Clarence Mangan (1803–1849), has tended to favour the use of the anglicized form over the Irish.

king, kings. See ARD RÍ [high king]; CYCLE OF THE KINGS; KINGSHIP.

King of Ireland's Son. Usual English title of story from modern Irish oral tradition whose Irish title is *Mac Rígh Éireann*, also known as *A Son of a King of Ireland, Mac Rígh i nÉirinn.* Distinguished for giving a sustained Celtic instance of the folk motif of the grateful dead (E341); the story also furnishes an unusually high number of other international folk motifs. On a winter's day when the King of Ireland's Son shoots a raven, the young man is impressed that there is nothing redder than the raven's blood on the snow or blacker than a raven's feather. The combination of the three colours reminds the King's Son of feminine beauty (folk motif: Z65.1), and so he resolves to have a wife with hair as black as the raven's, skin as white as snow, and cheeks as red as blood. Learning that such a maiden lives in the east, he sets out to find her. But before he goes any distance, he comes upon the funeral of a man who has been prevented from being buried by unpaid debts. The King of Ireland's Son pays the man's debts, sees to it that he is properly buried, and sets out on his quest.

Soon the King's Son encounters a short green man who volunteers to join him in his search for the beautiful maiden, asking only that he have the first kiss from her when she is found. The King's Son agrees, and soon they are joined by extraordinary companions (motif F601) including: (*a*) a man with remarkable sight (F642); (*b*) a man with hearing so exceptional that he can hear grass grow (F641; F641.1); (*c*) a marvellous runner (F681.1) who keeps one leg tied to restrain himself from going too fast; (*d*) a powerful blower (F622), who holds one finger to his nose to keep from blowing houses down; (*e*) a mighty stone-breaker (F625), who can turn any rock to powder. Together these seven are invincible, overcoming all difficulties, conquering all *giants, striding across all rivers and other obstacles. They also acquire such useful magical objects as a cap of invisibility.

The palace of the princess of the eastern world turns out to be forbidding, surrounded with rings of the skulls of disappointed suitors on spikes. The princess, however, is more agreeable, and says she would marry the King of Ireland's Son if he can deliver her from enchantments. She gives him a pair of scissors and asks that he keep them until morning. This seems easy enough until she attempts to put an enchanted sleep pin under his pillow and steal the scissors; fortunately the short green man, with the aid of the magical cap, shoes, and sword, returns the scissors so that the King's Son makes good his promise. The second night the princess asks that the King's Son keep a comb, and again the short green man helps him keep his promise. But on the third night the princess raises the stakes, demanding not only that he return the comb in the morning but also that he should return the head of him who was combed with it, or he will lose his own head. During the night the princess's accomplice, the rígh nimhe [Ir., the king of poison], hides the comb in a rock, securing it further with sixty locks, and sits guard over it himself. Yet once again the short green man saves the King's Son, first by splitting the rock with one stroke and second by severing the head of the rígh nimhe. This turn of events infuriates the princess, and so she imposes yet another contest, that a runner must bring back three bottles of healing balm from the western world and beat the princess's own runner set on the same task, or the King of Ireland's Son will lose his head. The swift runner serving the King's Son gets to the well and is half-way back when he is stopped by the princess's runner, a hag, who tricks him into sleep. Further, she puts his head on a horse's skull, spills out his balm, and leaves him snoring. But the other extraordinary companions come to the rescue. The man who can hear grass grow reports the condition of the King of Ireland's Son's runner, and that the hag is about to return instead. The superior marksman shoots the horse's head from beneath the sleeping runner's head. The remarkable blower takes his finger away from his nose and blows the hag as far back as the western world. Thus freed, the King of Ireland's Son's runner revives from his sleep, runs back to fill his bottles, and arrives back to win the race. Even more tests follow, all satisfied by the extraordinary companions, until at last the princess of the east agrees to marry the King of Ireland's Son.

The short green man then demands the first kiss, as had been promised at the beginning of the quest, and so takes the princess off to a room by himself. That room is filled with serpents, which the green man exterminates. Had the King of Ireland's Son spent his first night alone with his bride, he would have been killed by the serpents. Now that the princess is safely delivered to the King of Ireland's Son, the short green man reveals himself as the dead man whose debts the Son had graciously paid at the beginning of his journey. He then disappears and is not seen again.

In addition to the folk motifs already cited, the story also includes: the green man as revenant (E422.2.2); the specially gifted companions (F601) who complete the hero's tasks for him (F601.1); the grateful dead who helps the hero win a princess (T66.1); previous bridegrooms who were killed on the bridal night (T170); the quest for water as healing balm (H1321); returning the balm-water in a race with a hag or witch (H1109.1); the serpent maiden (F582.1) who kills her bridegrooms and the grateful dead who gets rid of the serpents. The story has many parallels, including passages of *Culhwch ac Olwen*, and others as far as Czech folklore and an adaptation, *Travelling Companion*, by the Danish writer Hans Christian Andersen (1805- 75). Douglas Hyde provides a dual-language text of a version collected in Co. Roscommon, *Beside the Fire* (London, 1910), 18–47. Pádraic Colum's oft-reprinted juvenile novel *The King of Ireland's Son* (New York, 1916) employs this title but retells other stories.

King of the Cats. See ÍRUSÁN.

King of the Fairies. See FAIRY.

King of the World. Phrase describing several imperious invaders in Irish and Scottish Gaelic *Fenian stories, possibly modelled on a late Roman emperor, a Holy Roman Emperor, or Charlemagne. In *Cath Fionntrágha* [The Battle of Ventry] he is *Dáire Donn; elsewhere he is Sinsar.

Kings, Cycle of. See CYCLE OF THE KINGS.

kingship. The rituals and beliefs pertaining to the most important male personage in early and medieval society are most in evidence in Irish rather than in other Celtic traditions. The English word 'king' is an inadequate translation of the OIr. rí (cf. L *rex*), which denotes the leader of a tuath, the basic territorial unit of early Irish society. Neither Ireland nor any Celtic nation was a nation-state as England became in 1485; thus the Irish rí is sometimes more accurately translated as 'petty king'. The Irish *ard rí [high king], inaugurated at the feis temhra at *Tara, was not a national sovereign. The notion of a ruler of the whole island, often attested to in early literature, seems to have been propagated by native historians and learned commentators partisan to the great *Uí Néill dynasty, claimed descendants of *Niall Noígiallach [of the Nine Hostages]. Many other Celtic words for 'king', ScG r'gh, Manx ree, Corn. myghtern, Bret. roue, are likely to denote either a foreign or a fictional monarch; only W brenin denotes a native ruler. The Irish instances, however, posit the existence of a kingship from pre-Christian times.

Often in Celtic contexts, a reference to kingship implies a lamented but unrecoverable past. Gaulish kingship was in dissolution at the time of *Caesar's conquest, and the decline of kingship in Ireland coincided with the atrophy of the Gaelic social system before English encroachment, culminating in the 17th century. The longing for a monarch to deliver the country from the misery of foreign domination, so characteristic of 18th-century Irish poetry and subsequent oral tradition, does not find antecedents in earliest Irish traditions.

A king could be selected from a family group of four generations, the *derbfhine, and he must pass a ritual test. Any member of the derbfhine might serve, not only the eldest son of the previous ruler. A first set of rituals tested a candidate's fitness, e.g. a royal chariot ride in which he must prove a worthy passenger; a royal mantle that must be the right size; two stones, a hand's distance apart, must open sufficiently wide to give passage to the candidate; and, lastly, the stone of *Fál must voice its assent. The second means of selection was the *bull feast or bull sleep [Ir. tarbfheis] in which a bull was killed and a selected man ate its flesh and drank its broth; he then lay down to sleep, while four druids chanted an incantation over him, which would allow him to envision whoever was destined to be king. These two methods of selection are most associated with the kingship of Tara, but informed opinion asserts they were also employed elsewhere.

Celtic sacral kings were often insulated from the perils of the profane world and often found their conduct severely regulated by binding prohibitions (cf. Ir. *geis). Why the king should be so bound is not clear; it may be that he was being forced to avoid circumstances and behaviours that were thought harmful to previous kings, but some taboos appear somewhat capricious. The king of *Ulster, for example, was forbidden to drink the waters of Lough Swilly while the sun was setting, or to go into the plain of Mag Coba (Co. Down) in the month of March. The proscriptions appear to support his sacral status, as do comparable restrictions placed upon the Roman priest of *Jupiter known as flamen Dialis; to violate them brings a clear portent of the end both of the kingship and of the king's life.

The qualities of a rightful king ensure peace, prosperity, and security of the kingdom's borders. As such these qualities are not simply admirable but necessary. In Old Irish these qualities were listed as fír flaithemhan [Ir., truth of the ruler]. At the same time, kings found to be deficient in character or conduct bring misfortune to their people; thus the illiberal *Bres is deposed in **Cath Maige Tuired*. Even the otherwise admirable *Nuadu abdicated after losing his arm in battle, a physical impairment that implied a great inadequacy to his followers. Worse than the deficient king is the usurper, whose reign is thought to bring famine and drought. Usurpation causes the rapid impoverishment of *Dyfed in the Manawydan portion of the Welsh **Mabinogi*. These Irish and Welsh instances are antecedent, some Arthurian commentators believe, to the maimed Fisher King in the Grail Legend.

According to custom a sacral king is a young husband and his kingdom is his bride. A king's inauguration was known as the *banais ríghe [wedding feast of kingship], during which the king is ritually united with the *sovereignty over the territory he will rule. At *Tara this ritual was known as feis temrach. The ceremony appears to have comprised two main elements: (*a*) the libation offered by the bride to her husband, and (*b*) the coition. Whatever the exact nature of this ceremony, the elements of intoxication and sexuality are unmistakably present. In reporting the inauguration of a king it was said that he was wedded to (literally 'slept with') his kingdom. Both elements are present in the characterization of one of the most powerful queens of Old Irish literature, *Medb [she who intoxicates]. The power of the king to bring his barren kingdom to fruitfulness is thought to parallel, according to many commentators, the transformation of the sovereignty goddess from an ugly old hag into a beautiful, nubile maiden. See Proinsias MacCana, 'Aspects of the Theme of the King and the Goddess in Irish Literature', *Études Celtiques*, 7 (1955–6), 76–114, 356–413; 'Aspects of the Theme of the King and the Goddess', *Études Celtiques*, 8 (1958–9), 59–65; D. A. Binchy, *Celtic and Anglo-Saxon Kingship* (Oxford, 1970); F. J. Byrne, *Irish Kings and High Kings* (London, 1973); Marjorie O. Anderson, *Kings and Kingship in Early Scotland* (Edinburgh, 1980); T. M. Charles-Edwards, *Early Irish and Welsh Kinship* (Oxford, 1991); Nerys T. Patterson, *Cattle-Lords and Clansmen: Kingship and Rank in Early Ireland* (New York, 1992).

kinkeshin, kinkishin. See FAIRY STROKE.

kinship system. See DERBFHINE.

Kistennin. Variant spelling of *Custennin.

Kitter. Legendary, piratical Viking jarl or earl from Manx tradition. He was enticed into a stormy sea by the witch Oda; Kitterland, a rock on the South-West coast of the Isle of *Man, is named for him.

knacker. Variant spelling of *knocker.

Knock-. Anglicization of the Irish cnoc [hill, height], a prefix in innumerable Irish and many Scottish Gaelic place-names; the Welsh cognate is cnwc. See SLIAB [Ir., mountain, slieve].

Knockainy. See CNOC ÁINE.

Knockaulin, Knockawlin. Hill (600 feet) in Co. Kildare near Kilcullen, site of extensive Iron Age earthworks excavated in the 1960s and 1970s, and identified with *Dún Ailinne, seat of the early kings of *Leinster.

knocker, knacker. Cornish mine-spirits, thought to be the ghosts of the Jews who worked the mines in the 11th and 12th centuries; sometimes confused with the *bucca. For the most part the gnomelike knocker is thought harmless; out of sight of humans, it cannot endure the sign of the Cross. A counterpart of the Welsh *coblynau. Folk motifs: F456; F456.I.I; F456.I.I.I; F456.I.2.I.I; F456.I.2.2.I; M242.

Knockfeerina, Knockfierna. Hill (948 feet) in Co. Limerick E of Ballingarry, one of the most celebrated *Otherworld seats in *Munster, perhaps better known as *Cnoc Fírinne.

Knockfefin. Form preferred by W. B. Yeats for *Sliab na mBan [Slivenamon].

Knockfierna. Variant spelling of *Knockfeerina.

Knockhaulin. Variant spelling of *Knockaulin.

Knocklong, Siege of. See FORBAIS DROMMA DAMGAIRE.

Knockmagh, Knock Ma, Knock Maa. Anglicizations of *Cnoc Mheadha.

Knockmany [Ir. *Cnoc Meánach*; middle hill]. Hill (770 feet) near Augher, Co. Tyrone. Although the hill is the site of Annia's Cove, a passage-tomb, its greatest renown came in the writings of William Carleton (1794–1869), who retold a comic *Fenian narrative, 'The Legend of Knockmany' (*c.*1845).

Knocknagow. Oft-cited fictional Irish village created by Charles J. Kickham (1828–82) in *Knocknagow; or, The Homes of Tipperary* (1873); a site of sentimental and farcical, quasi-Dickensian occurrences.

Knocknarea [Ir. *cnoc na Ria, na Riaghadh*, hill of executions (?)]. Hill (1,083 feet) 4 miles SW of Sligo popularly associated with Queen *Medb. A cairn atop the hill has long been known as 'Maeve's Lump' or Miscaun Maeve [Ir. *Miosgán Méabha*]. Old Irish narrative literature attributes the cairn to Eógan Bél (6th cent.), the last pre-Christian king of *Connacht, who was killed in battle nearby.

Knockshegouna, Knockshigowna. Anglicizations of *Cnoc Sídhe Úna.

knowledge. This English word, which usually implies an erudition open to those who seek it, inadequately translates Celtic conceptions of knowing, which often imply esoteric, metaphysical perception. Among the Celts knowledge is inspired rather than being acquired gradually; often it is derived from dead ancestors. *Fionn mac Cumhaill touches the *salmon of knowledge and as a result possesses the thumb of *knowledge, which allows him both a vision of the future and the power to heal. When *Gwion Bach acquires knowledge intended for *Morfran he is reborn and named *Taliesin. The *hazel is often known as the 'nut of knowledge'. The 'well of knowledge' is *Connla's Well. Among the personifications of knowledge are: *Ecne, *Eólas, *Find, *Fios. See also DIVINATION; IMBAS FOROSNAI; TEINM LAÍDA.

Knowth [Ir. *Cnobga*]. One of the three great passage-tombs, 280 feet in diameter, 40–50 feet high, at the Bend of the *Boyne [*Brug na Bóinne], 1.7 miles NW of the better-known Newgrange and *Dowth. *Buí, wife of *Lug Lámfhota, has special associations with Knowth, and *Írusán, King of the Cats, lives in a cave here. The kings of northern *Brega were thought to live at Knowth in early Christian times, and the Hiberno-Norman baron Richard de Flemming claimed it *c.*1175. The only Boyne passage-grave never made open to the public, Knowth has been the subject of intense scrutiny, beginning in the mid-1960s. See George Eogan, *Excavations at Knowth 1* (Dublin, 1984); *Knowth and the Passage Tombs of Ireland* (London, 1986).

Koadalan [Bret. *koad*, wood; *alan*, male Christian name; cf. W *Coed-Alun*, wood-Allen]. Title and hero of an episodic Breton folk-tale of magical transformation and denied immortality; the action is so complex that some modern commentators have titled it 'The Saga of Koadalan'. Although collected from oral tradition in the 19th century, the narrative shows correlatives from medieval Welsh literature.

Knowing that his poor parents could not keep him, Yves Koadalan set out at 16 to seek his fortune. When a nobleman refuses to employ him because he admits he can read, Koadalan disguises himself by turning his coat inside out and applies again, this time claiming he cannot read. The noble takes the boy along and soon they are both ascending into the air, alighting near a beautiful castle, when Koadalan sees written on a leaf: 'He who enters here will never leave'. Despite his apprehension, the boy sleeps in a feather bed and is provided a serviette that gives all the food and drink he asks. He is also given three instructions: (*a*) always to keep a hot *fire under the pot; (*b*) to beat a thin mare with a holly stick; (*c*) never to open two doors in the castle. When Koadalan builds the fire under the pot, he is unconcerned at the apparent sighings and moanings of people in pain, but when he beats the mare, named Teresa, she begs his mercy. Koadalan spares her, and she rewards him by instructing him to go through the two forbidden doors where he would find three marvellous, red books that will allow him to become the greatest magician in the world. The boy follows her advice and is stunned by the secrets in the books. She also tells him to wash his hair in the courtyard spring, thus turning himself into a golden-haired prince. As Koadalan and Teresa are escaping from the castle, they are pursued by the mysterious noble man, now disguised as a black *dog, who vows to retrieve the magical books and bites into the mare's flesh. Wounded and tired, Teresa asks Koadalan to kill her and open her belly. Reluctantly he does, thus bringing forth a beautiful princess, the daughter of the King of Naples. But lovely as Teresa now is, she says that there is someone even more beautiful, the Princess of Spain, whom Koadalan will marry. Meanwhile, she promises to aid him whenever he calls her name three times.

Koadalan then departs for Spain, dressed as a prince. Upon his arrival he receives a warm welcome, as the king thinks he is his nephew, son of the king of France, whose looks and manners Koadalan has taken. The king denies having a daughter, but Koadalan learns that she is being kept in a tower. Through his magic from the three red books, Koadalan learns how to enter the tower, where he gets the princess with child. The king is surprised that his protected daughter could be pregnant, but when he learns that Koadalan is the father he allows the marriage; he then dies and Koadalan succeeds him on the throne.

But Koadalan soon tires of ruling, so he, his wife, and their child take a magical journey on the back of an *eagle, passing the castle of the great magician Foulkes (or Foukes). The older man had also desired the Princess of Spain and is jealous of Koadalan's having won her. Foulkes lures the three inside and, while they are sleeping, steals the three magical books and drops Koadalan down a deep well, where he lands in a forest. Recognizing the place where he had said good-bye to Teresa, Koadalan calls out three times to his faithful friend, who returns his three magical books and takes him and his family back to the poor country where he was born. No one in the town recognizes the handsome prince and his family, not even Koadalan's father and mother, now very old and still poor. The son builds his parents a magnificent castle, but they stay in their thatched cottage.

One day Koadalan urges his father to attend the fair at Lannion. When the father complains he has nothing to sell, Koadalan says he will find an excellent steer in his barn, but, no matter what price offered, he should never sell the rope holding it. The father asks an exorbitant price for the steer at the fair, which is met by three devils disguised as dealers. When the father refuses to sell the rope, the buyers ride the steer, which is transformed into a dog and finally into Koadalan himself, thus thwarting the devils. Again Koadalan asks his father to attend a fair, this time at Morlaix, to sell a horse but not the bridle.

Again the father asks an exorbitant price, which is met by three buyers. This time the father gets drunk after the sale and forgets to keep the bridle, and so the three devils are able to ride him. Koadalan seeks to escape them by becoming successively an *eel, a dove, and a golden ring; to pursue him the three devils assume the form of three great fish, three sparrowhawks, and three musicians. Finding himself on the finger of a maidservant, Koadalan as a golden ring asks to be thrown into a fire. The three musician-devils follow him, being consumed in the flames.

Returning to his home, Koadalan finds that his father has died, and his wife and son soon follow him. Although he is alone, Koadalan can fulfil all his wishes by reading his three red books. But he cannot avoid death. When he sees that the end is near, he devises a plan which might save him. He asks to be chopped up like sausage-meat and to be placed in an earthenware pot and buried under hot manure. A nursing mother is asked to sprinkle her milk upon him twice a day for six months; if this ritual is followed rigorously he will be restored. The nursing mother comes each day, but three days before the time is up she falls asleep, and Koadalan cannot be restored.

Modern commentators assert that the mare Teresa is an equivalent of *Rhiannon, and that Koadalan's escape from the three devils parallels the transformations of *Ceridwen and *Taliesin. F. M. Luzel, 'Koadalan', *Revue Celtique*, 1 (1870–1), 106–31; trans. Derek Bryce, *Celtic Folk-Tales from Armorica* (Llanerch, UK, 1985), 70–84. See also Jean Markale, *La Tradition celtique en Bretagne armoricaine* (Paris, 1984).

Konan Meriadek. Breton form of *Cynan Meiriadog.

Konomor. Semi-legendary Breton king, comparable in stature to the *Ulster Cycle's *Conchobar mac Nessa, is best known as a kind of Bluebeard. Konomor first reigned in *Cornwall and Devon before emigrating to Brittany, settling in the northern regions. In some documents he is known as Marcus Conomorus, thus confusing him with King

*Mark of Cornwall. He married three times, killing each of the wives when she became pregnant because he feared that a son would kill him. The fourth wife, Trifina (or Tryphina), survived him. Konomor decapitated her, but St *Gildas restored her head. Trifina's son Trémeur wreaked vengeance upon his father by destroying his castle.

Konorin. Pseudo-saint of Brittany who experiences a magical double birth. Brigands murder the first Konorin, an ordinary mortal, by dismembering and burning; all that remains of him is a mysterious *apple. A young virgin eats of this apple and becomes impregnated by it. Nine months later she gives birth to 'Saint' Konorin, who was known in tradition as the 'son of the apple, the fruit of wisdom'.

Korentin. Bishop of Quimper in the Breton legend of the City of *Ys. He possesses a fish which he may eat one day and then find whole the next.

Korneli. Pseudo-saint of Breton folklore associated with the megalithic monuments at *Carnac. According to local legend, Korneli was being pursued by vicious enemies in an ox-cart when he turned and placed a curse upon them, transforming them into rows of huge stones. Elsewhere Korneli has been the protector of horned animals, not just oxen, prompting some commentators to suggest that he is a Christianized remnant of the cult of the Celtic god *Cernunnos.

korrigan, corrigan [Bret. *korr*, dwarf]. Wanton, impish, sprightly female *fairy of Breton folklore who desires sexual union with humans. Thought to be descended from ancient *druidesses, korrigans are especially malicious towards celibate Catholic priests. Each korrigan has the power to enmesh the heart of the most constant swain and doom him to perish for love of her. In Christian folklore korrigans are portrayed most unfavourably, characteristically blamed for changeling substitutions. Found near wells, fountains, *dolmens, and menhirs, especially in the forest *Brocéliande, korrigans are none the less thought very beautiful, with golden hair, flashing eyes, and laughing lips. Known as Ozegan, Ozeganned (pl.) near Vannes in southern Brittany.

Kreiddylat. Variant spelling of *Creiddylad.

Kristof. Small boy who provokes much of the action in the Breton legend of the city of *Ys. After casting stones in the water with a crooked stick, Kristof catches a magical fish who offers riches in exchange for his liberty. Princess *Dahut mocks this exchange, and so the fish casts a spell on her, making her pregnant with a son who can claim no father. Dahut's father, *Gradlon, puts Dahut, Kristof, and the baby boy in a cask and sets them out to sea, when the magical fish causes first a palace and then a city to appear. During this time *Ys is engulfed because Kristof has taken away the protective *oak.

Kulhwch. Variant spelling of *Culhwch.

Kylta Mac Ronan. Anglicization of *Caílte mac Rónáin.

Kymidu Kymein-Voll. Anglicization of *Cymidei Cymeinfoll.

Kymon. Variant spelling of *Cynon.

Kymry. See CYMRU.

Kyndylan. Variant spelling of *Cynddylan.

Kynon. Variant spelling of *Cynon.

Kystennin. Variant spelling of *Custennin.

L

L. The twelfth letter of the modern English alphabet is represented by luis [*rowan, mountain ash] in the *ogham alphabet of early Ireland.

La Tène [Fr., the shallows]. Archaeological site at the eastern end of Lake Neuchâtel, Switzerland, whose name now describes late Iron Age Celtic culture. Discovered by an amateur archaeologist in 1858, the La Tène site, one of the glories of the barbarian world, marks a holy settlement of Celtic craftspersons and artisans from after 500 BC until the Roman conquest. The huge trove at La Tène includes 400 brooches, 270 spears, 27 wooden shields, 170 swords, as well as votive offerings: dogs, pigs, cattle, chariots, and human beings. La Tène culture, now classed in three phases, I, II, and III, developed from the interaction of the earlier, geometric *Hallstatt style and Etruscan and Greek influences from the Mediterranean. The typical La Tène style is characterized by S-shapes, spirals, and swirling round patterns symmetrically applied. While known in all parts of Celtic Europe, the La Tène style is especially evident in the art of the pre-Roman British Isles; atrophying under Roman domination, it persisted through Christianization in Ireland until the Norman conquest, 1169. See Paul Vouga, *La Tène* (Leipzig, 1923); Ruth and J. V. S. Megaw, *Celtic Art* (London, 1989).

La Villemarqué, Théodore Hersart de (1815-95). The founder of Breton literary tradition with *Barzaz Breiz* [Breton Bards] (Paris, 1839). As a pseudo-medievalist, La Villemarqué is often compared to the Scottish 'translator' James *Macpherson, but he is linguistically superior and more authentic, if bowdlerized. English translation: *Ballads and Songs of Brittany*, trans. Tom Taylor (London, New York, 1865, 1907; repr. Norwood, Penn., 1976). See Francis Gourvil, *Théodore Hersart de La Villemarqué* (Rennes, 1959); D. Laurent, *Aux sources du Barzaz Breiz: la mémoire d'un peuple* (As Meu, 1989). See also IOLO MORGANWG.

Laa Luanistyn, Luanys. Manx names for *Lughnasa.

Labhra. Variant spelling of *Labraid.

Labhraidh. ModIr. for *Labraid.

Labra. Variant spelling of *Labraid.

Labraid, Labhraidh, Labhra, Labra, Leabhra, Lowry [Ir., speaker]. Name borne by more than a dozen legendary figures from early Ireland and some ecclesiastics. The best-known is *Labraid Loingsech [seafarer, exile], also known as Labraid Móen [dumb, speechless].

Labraid Lámderg, Lámhdhearg [Ir., red hand]. A hero of *Fionn mac Cumhaill's *Fianna, even though he is reputed to be the son of *Bolg, ancestor of the *Fir Bolg. He accompanies *Oscar on adventures overseas.

Labraid Loingsech, Loingseach [Ir., seafarer, exile, mariner]. Also Labraid Móen, Máen, Maon [dumb, speechless] and Labraid Lorc [fierce]. Ancestor deity of the *Leinstermen whose story of the revenge of his father's death and the regaining of his kingdom is told in **Orgain Denna Ríg* [The Destruction of Dind Ríg]. Although the *Lagin, progenitors of Leinster, ranked Labraid 'a man higher than the gods', and his children include the deity *Nechtán (1), Kuno Meyer thought he might have been a historical king at the time of the Roman invasion of Britain. Pedigrees make him twenty-fifth in direct line from *Éremón, ancestor of the *Gaels, and he is the grandson of *Úgaine Mór, whose name appears at the head of many medieval genealogies.

Whatever the historical correlative for Labraid's persona, his reign signals the advent of the Lagin to dominance in eastern Ireland. The **Book of Leinster* dates Labraid's killing of Cobthach at 307 BC; in the **Annals of the Four Masters* the date is 431 BC. In stories subsequent to the action of *Orgain Denna Ríg*, Labraid extends his dominion over much of Europe, to Italy, and in another text as far as Armenia. From these adventures he brought back 2,200 foreigners with broad spears [laignib], thus the Lagin or Leinstermen. The influential Geoffrey *Keating (17th cent.) treated him as a historical figure.

In oral and written tradition of much later composition, Labraid was thought to suffer horses' ears, an affliction he shares with the Welsh *March ap Meirchion and King Midas of ancient Greek tradition. To keep this shame secret, he executed every barber who cut his hair. One young barber was spared on the pleadings of his mother, a widow. But he grew sick with the burden of the secret and so, on the advice of a *druid, told it to a tree, thus curing himself. Later, however, the tree was cut down and made into a harp on which Labraid's harper *Craiphtine played; in the midst of the music the harp revealed Labraid's secret. He felt immediate remorse for the barbers he had killed and henceforward owned up to his blemish.

See Thomas F. O'Rahilly, *Early Irish History and Mythology* (Dublin, 1946), 101–20; Francis J. Byrne, *Irish Kings and High-Kings* (London, 1973), 130-6; Brian Ó Cuiv, 'Some Items from Irish Tradition [horse's ears]', *Éigse*, 11 (1964-6), 167–87; Máirtín Ó Briain, [Irish text of 'Midas and the Ass's Ears'], *Béaloideas*, 53 (1985), 11–74. Pádraic Colum made Labraid a hero of juvenile fiction in *The Story of Lowry Maen* (New York and London, 1937).

Labraid Lorc [fierce]. Another name for *Labraid Loingsech.

Labraid Luathlám ar Claideb [swift sword-hand]. Ruler of *Mag Mell [Plain of Delight] who sends his beautiful wife *Lí Ban [paragon of women] to seek *Cúchulainn's help in **Serglige Con Culainn* [The Wasting Sickness of Cúchulainn].

Labraid Móen, Maon, Máen [dumb, speechless]. See LABRAID LOINGSECH.

Ladi Wen, Y. [W, the White Lady]. Spectral apparition of a woman dressed in white, known in Welsh oral tradition. A common bogy reputed to warn children about bad behaviour, Y Ladi Wen was most often seen at *Hollantide, 31 October-1 November.

Ladra, Ladhra, Ladru. *Cesair's pilot or helmsman in the first invasion of *Ireland, and first man to die there; with sixteen wives, he suffered from an excess of women.

Lady of the Fountain. See OWAIN.

Láeg, Laeg, Lóeg. Friend, messenger, and charioteer of *Cúchulainn who is killed by *Lugaid mac Con Roí with a spear intended for Cúchulainn.

Láegaire, Laoghaire, Laeghire. Variant spellings of *Lóegaire.

Laery. Anglicization of *Lóegaire.

Lagin, Laigin, Laighin, Laighnigh, Lagenians [people of Lug (?)]. Early Celtic people who invaded *Ireland before the advent of written records, giving their name to the province of *Leinster. They were placed second in the order of Celtic invaders, after the *Érainn. They settled not only in what is now Leinster but also in other parts of the island, including large portions of *Connacht. Thomas F. O'Rahilly (1946) argued unconvincingly that they were a *P-Celtic people and only adopted genealogies implying a *Q-Celtic origin after the dominance of the *Goidels in Ireland. Their ancestor deity, *Labraid Loingsech, was thought to have invited 2,200 foreigners back with him from the continent of Europe, who became the Lagin. According to their own invasion legend, they were Gaulish in origin and invaded Ireland from *Brittany (Armorica). The **Annals of the Four Masters* set this after 431 BC, the **Book of Leinster* after 307 BC. Contemporary scholarship suggests a much earlier date. They brought with them the *Domnainn and the *Galióin. See Thomas F. O'Rahilly, *Early Irish History and Mythology* (Dublin, 1946), 17–24, 101–20; Alfred P. Smyth, *Celtic Leinster* (Dublin, 1982).

Laidcenn, Laidcheann. Poet of *Niall Noígiallach [of the Nine Hostages] whose tangle with the troublesome *Eochaid (10) leads to Niall's death.

Laigin, Laighin, Laighead, Laighnigh. Variant forms of *Lagin.

Lailoken. Naked, hairy *wild man of the woods who demonstrates prophetic powers at the court of *Rhydderch Hael in *Strathclyde, the 6th-century Welsh-speaking kingdom of the Old North, i.e. the Scottish Lowlands. By critical consensus, much of the legend of Lailoken's life contributes to *Geoffrey of Monmouth's conception of *Merlin in the *Vita Merlini* (*c.*1149). In the 15th-century Scottish story known as 'Lailoken and Kentigern', the hairy wild man confesses to St *Kentigern that he is the cause of the deaths of those who perished at the battle of *Arfderydd (573/575). *Myrddin (Merlin) is recorded as having gone mad after this defeat. See H. D. L. Ward, 'Lailoken (or Merlin Silvester)', *Romania*, 22 (1893), 504–26; 'Lailoken and Kentigern' is translated, 514–525. Kenneth H. Jackson, *Béaloideas*, 8 (1938), 48–9; James Carney, *Studies in Irish Literature and History* (Dublin, 1955), 129–53; Basil Clarke, *Life of Merlin* (Cardiff, 1972).

Lairgnéan. Promised 'Man of the North' who marries *Deoch at the end of **Oidheadh Chlainne Lir* [The Tragic Story of the Children of Lir].

lake. See LOCH; LOUGH; LLYN.

Lammas Day. See LUGHNASA.

Lancelot. Lover of *Guinevere and father of Galahad. Although he is one of the most French of all Arthurian heroes, appearing first in *Chrétien de Troyes's *Erec* (*c*.1170), his roots may well be Irish. See Roger Sherman Loomis, 'The Descent of Lancelot from Lug', *Bulletin bibliographique de la Société Internationale Arthurienne*, 3 (1951), 67–73.

Land of Promise. Usual translation of *Tír Tairngire and occasional translation of *Emain Ablach.

Land of the Living. Usual translation of *Tír na mBeó.

Land of Youth. Usual translation of *Tír na nÓg.

Langarrow, Langona. Legendary lost city of Cornish folklore, thought to lie near the modern town of Perranporth on the north coast. Because of its greed and dissoluteness, Langarrow was thought to have been covered over by shifting sand dunes. The story probably reflects the actual covering of two churches of St Piran near Perranporth, though one has since been excavated. The story may have contributed to the Lyonesse story of Arthurian tradition. See also SUBMERGED CITIES.

Laoghaire. ModIr. spelling of *Lóegaire.

Laoi Oisín i dTír na nÓg. See OISÍN.

Laoidh an Amadain Mhòir. ScG title for **Eachtra an Amadáin Mhóir* [The Lay of the Great Fool].

Laoire. ModIr. spelling of *Lóegaire.

Leabhar. Modern Irish for **Lebor* [book] . . . ; see also BOOK OF . . .

Leabhra. Corrupt spelling of *Labraid.

leannán sídhe, leannán sí, leannan sighe, leanhaun shee. See FAIRY LOVER.

Leary. Anglicization of *Lóegaire.

Lebarcham, Lebhorcham. Variant spellings of *Leborcham.

Lebor Buide Lecáin. Irish title of the **Yellow Book of Lecan*.

Lebor Gabála Érenn, *Leabhar Gabhála.* Irish title for the 12th-century text usually known in English as The Book of Invasions or Book of Conquests [lit. book of the taking of Ireland]. A collection of pseudo-historical texts by various authors of different periods, arranged in a pattern of invasions, the *Lebor Gabála* purports to synchronize myths, legends, and genealogies from early Ireland with the framework of biblical exegesis. In the words of Alwyn and Brinley Rees, it is 'a laborious attempt to combine parts of the native teaching with Hebrew mythology embellished with medieval legend'. One modern commentator calls the *Lebor Gabála* a 'masterpiece of muddled medieval miscellany'. Compilers of the *Lebor Gabála* do not demonstrate a profound knowledge of the Bible itself but rely instead on biblical commentators and historians, especially *Eusebius (3rd cent. AD), Orosius (6th cent.), and Isidore of Seville (7th cent.). Informed by Latin learning, the surviving Irish text may have been based on a Latin original, an assertion now much disputed. Portions of the Irish text were contributed by a number of identifiable poets from the 9th and 10th centuries, the final compilation coming after the 11th century. Accepting biblical cosmology, the *Lebor Gabála* plays a role in the Irish *Mythological Cycle comparable to that of Hesiod's *Works and Days* (6th cent. BC) in Greek mythology.

The text begins the story of human history with the biblical Flood, which commentators date at 2900 BC or in the supposed 'year of the world' 1104 Anno Mundi. Dates for different invasions vary widely in different texts, as medieval authorities never agreeed on the date of Creation; the Venerable Bede (7th cent.) argued for 3952 BC and the Septuagint commentators (3rd cent. BC) determined 5200 BC, while later authorities opted for 4004 BC.

The *Scoti (i.e. Goidels, Irish) are assumed to have originated in *Scythia but to have taken their name from *Scota (1) or Scotia, the daughter of a Pharaoh. While in Egypt the Scoti know Moses and are invited to join the Exodus, a probable source of the long-standing canard that the Irish are a lost tribe of Israel. *Fénius Farsaid is described as being present at the separation of languages at Babel and leaving instructions for his grandson, *Goídel Glas, to forge the Irish languages out of the seventy-two tongues then in existence.

Modern readers have taken the greatest interest in iteration of the six mythological invasions (or seven, counting the *Fomorians) of Ireland, which incorporate tantalizing elements of bona fide ethnic history, greatly transformed. Additionally, the *Lebor Gabála* borrows from literary texts and, at times, explains narratives in them. Sorting out the distinctions between invention and fact remains an ongoing task for scholars of early Ireland. The ordering of the invasions, and the character of the invaders, is fixed:

(I) *Cesair, granddaughter of Noah, who was sent to Ireland to escape the Flood, accompanied by her father Bith, fifty women, and three men, who hoped vainly to populate the island. (II) *Partholón and the *Partholonians, descendants of the biblical Magog, arrived 312 years after the death of Cesair and settled eastern Irish plains before being wiped out in a plague. (III) *Nemed and the *Nemedians came from the Caspian Sea thirty years after the death of Partholón. After clearing twelve plains and forming four lakes, Nemed fought four battles with the Fomorians, winning three and losing the fourth, after which their remnants went into exile, some to return with later invasions. (IIIa) The Fomorians, not a part of the invasion sequence, but euhemerized deities who come to be portrayed as a dark and violent but magical race of pirates, whose home is Tory Island off the Donegal coast. They battle the Partholonians and the Nemedians before being defeated by the *Tuatha Dé Danann.

(IV) The *Fir Bolg are short, dark people who came to Ireland fleeing oppression. Sometimes they are thought to be a second wave of Nemedians or survivors of their invasion. Defeated by the invading *Tuatha Dé Danann, they settle on *Aran and Rathlin Islands. (V) The Tuatha Dé Danann, gods of the pre-Christian Irish pantheon reduced to human stature, arrived thirty-seven years after the Fir Bolg, whom they subjugated. Their defeat of the Fomorians ushered in the luminous era in which many early Irish mythological narratives appear to be taking place. (VI) *Míl Espáine and the *Milesians are mortal ancestors of the modern Gaels. Although his name means 'soldier of Spain', Míl is a Scythian who marries *Scota [L, Irishwoman] (1). His descendants leave Spain for *Kerry 297 years after the arrival of the Tuatha Dé Danann, defeat their predecessors, and push on to found *Tara. The Milesians still reign when the time-frame of Irish heroic literature ceases.

The first two invasions are the least grounded and most contrived of the seven. Many of the names in Cesair's retinue appear to have been invented to provide a gloss for place-names. Elements in her invasion are both erotic and comic. The three men of the company are charged with dividing fifty women among them and to populate the island. Two of the men die and Cesair's 'husband', *Fintan mac Bóchra, feeling inadequate to the task, flees in the form of a *salmon. The name Partholón is probably also an invention, as the letter P is unknown in earlier Irish; it appears to be an adaptation of Bartholomaeus, which Isidore of Seville and St Jerome glossed as 'son of him who stays the waters'. Good colonists, the Partholonians cleared four plains, settling on *Mag nElta [Moynalty], roughly coextensive with the modern city of *Dublin, from *Howth on the east to Tallaght in the south-west. The first battle on Irish soil pitted the Partholonians against the devilish Fomorians from the north. After introducing agriculture, the Partholonian colony swelled to 9,000 before all but one of them died in a plague. Only *Tuan mac Cairill (sometimes mac Stairn) survived to the time of *Colum Cille to tell of the invasions of Ireland.

Nemed and the Nemedians arriving thirty years after the Partholonians appear initially to be shadows of their predecessors, clearing land and forming lakes. As a people their greed for gold led them to disaster before they arrived in Ireland, when all but one of their thirty-four ships were lost in a vain pursuit of a tower of gold seen on the sea. This attack on a tower prefigures their brave but futile assault against the tower of the Fomorians on Tory Island (off *Donegal). Before this the Nemedians had bested the hated Fomorians three times, but were none the less reduced to vassalage, paying a humiliating tribute. After being decimated by the Fomorians, remnants of the Nemedians scattered across the world, returning generations later as the mythical Fir Bolg and Tuatha Dé Danann as well as the historical British. Some commentators link the Nemedians with the historical *Érainn.

Although not a wave of invaders themselves, the Fomorians [Ir. *Fomoire*] appear often in the text of *Lebor Gabála*, usually as rapacious raiders upon other settlers. When the Partholonians first encounter them under *Cichol, they are hideous, misshapen monsters with but *one eye, one arm, and one leg, but elsewhere they are more anthropomorphic. Their portrait in another important early Irish text, **Cath Maige Tuired* [The (Second) Battle of Mag Tuired], has them intermarrying with the Tuatha Dé Danann, the race of gods. Modern commentators believe they are euhemerized pagan deities, possibly marine counterparts of the Tuatha Dé Danann, whose characterization was heavily influenced by early sea marauders, first from the Scottish Isles and more substantially the Norse. Often they appear to be demonic but magical pirates, given to gratuitous cruelty. For unexplained reasons they do not prey upon the agricultural Fir Bolg, causing some earlier commentators to think the two groups identical, an assertion now rejected. Their climactic moment comes in *Cath Maige Tuired*, whose action is summarized in *Lebor Gabála*. After *Bres, who is part Fomorian, part Tuatha Dé Danann, makes an unsuitable successor to *Nuadu Airgetlám, king of the Tuatha Dé Danann, a great battle ensues between the two people. *Lug Lámfhota, the Tuatha Dé Danann champion, puts his slingstone through the magical eye of *Balor, thus turning his power against Balor's fellow warriors, disabling many of them. The Fomorians are subsequently routed and do not make trouble in Ireland again.

Perceptions of the Fir Bolg have changed as modern readers abandoned older, more fanciful interpretations of their name, e.g. 'men of bags' [cf. Ir. *bolg*, bag, sack], in favour of the view that their invasion is mythologized from the possible movements of such peoples as the Érainn, the *Domnainn, and the *Lagin, who may have come from the Continent and Great Britain. The Fir Bolg are supposed to have introduced iron-tipped weapons and also to have established an era of peace and prosperity, especially under their king *Eochaid mac Eirc, whose reign induced harvests every year and established the rule of law. After thirty-seven years the Tuatha Dé Danann, a race of gods, invaded and defeated the Fir Bolg at the first Battle of Mag Tuired, near Lough Arrow, Co. Sligo; see CATH MAIGE TUIRED. Thus subdued, the Fir Bolg fled to distant corners of the Gaelic world such as the Scottish coast, Rathlin Island, and the *Aran Islands. In folkloric memory they are grotesque, dark helots and cave *fairies, a perception partially coordinate with the misinterpretation of their name as 'men of bags'.

The divine origins of the Tuatha Dé Danann are implicit in the usual story of their arrival in Ireland, descending from a dark cloud on a mountain in the west, instead of by ship as other invaders had. Their very name, 'people of the goddess Danu/ Ana', may have been invented in the *Lebor Gabála*, but the phrase Tuatha Dé was earlier used to describe the old gods or to denote the Israelites in translations of the Bible. The complete origin of the name and the precise implications of it are still disputed. Unquestionably many members of the Tuatha Dé Danann pre-date the composition of the *Lebor Gabála*, having been the gods of pre-Christian cults. But from the *Lebor Gabála* onward they are portrayed as humans, if extraordinary ones. They excel all peoples of the earth in their proficiency in every art. After their defeat of the Fir Bolg at the First Battle of Mag Tuired, their only enemies are the Fomorians, also euhemerized deities. After the unhappy succession of the part Fomorian Bres to the throne of *Nuadu Airgetlám, the Tuatha Dé Danann decisively defeat the Fomorians at the epic Second Battle of Mag Tuired. The era that follows is the time when most of the action of the Mythological Cycle takes place. Leading figures include: the *Dagda, the 'good god', a king who specializes in druidical magic; *Angus Óg, the god of poetry; Lug Lámfhota, not only an important champion but a master of arts and crafts; *Dian Cécht, the principal healing god; *Brigid, the fire-goddess; *Boand, the goddess of the *Boyne who is also wife to the Dagda; *Ogma, a god of eloquence who is also a strongman and warrior; and the triad of war goddesses, *Badb, *Macha, and *Mórrígan. This happy reign comes to an end with the invasion of the mortal *Milesians, who defeat the Tuatha Dé Danann in two battles, *Tailtiu and

*Druim Ligen. Although the *Lebor Gabála* does not describe the Tuatha Dé Danann in defeat, popular sources from the 12th century on portray them as living in the world of the Milesians and their progeny, but unseen by them through the power of *féth fiada. Mortals live above the earth while the immortal Tuatha Dé Danann live first in cairns and barrows, later beneath the earth. The route to the realm of the immortal Tuatha Dé Danann is the *sídh. Any humans entering the world of the Tuatha Dé Danann encounter enchanted idylls such as *Mag Mell [Pleasant Plain], *Emain Ablach [Fortress of Apples], and, best known of all, *Tír na nÓg [the Land of Youth]. In time the underground Tuatha Dé Danann became identical with the *fairies.

Narratives of the Milesians are discontinuous, those dealing with their origins in Scythia and biblical lands highly contrived and fanciful, and those of their invasion echoing the coming of the *Q-Celtic *Goidels. The Milesians invent the Irish language; their early leader *Fénius Farsaid was present at Babel, gleaning the best from all existing tongues, and his grandson *Goídel put Fénius' knowledge into practice. Moses himself assured the Milesians that they would live in a land free of snakes. Memory of the druid *Caicer's prophecy that they would live in Ireland haunted the Milesians, and Míl Espáine led his people from Egypt towards their promised land but was killed in Spain while aiding his kinsmen there. He gave his name to his people through his many sons, some of them from his second wife, *Scota (1), the daughter of the Pharaoh. One son, *Íth, after climbing Breogan's tower in Brigantia [Braganza, Portugal], sees Ireland one cold night and resolves to go there; when he does, and is killed, eight sons of Míl vow revenge. They land at *Inber Scéne and win a swift victory over the Tuatha Dé Danann at *Sliab Mis before meeting three goddesses, *Banba, *Ériu, and *Fódla, each of whom asked that Ireland be named for her. Three kings of the Tuatha Dé at *Tara, *Mac Cuill, *Mac Cécht, and Mac Gréine, possibly husbands of the goddesses, promise to turn over the country to the invaders if only the latter will keep nine waves from shore for three days. It is a trick, and two sons of Míl are drowned, the others sailing *sunwise to the *Boyne estuary, where they land at *Inber Colptha, named for Colptha, a surviving son. The Milesians then crush the Tuatha Dé Danann in two battles, *Tailtiu [Teltown, Co. Meath] and *Druim Ligen, and spread their power over all of Ireland. Because Míl Espáine's widow, Scota (1), accompanies the invaders, they come to be known as the *Scotti or Scoti, which is indeed the Latin name for the Gaelic-speaking Irishmen as well as those Gaels who settled in what is now Scotland. Míl's son *Amairgin (1) becomes a leading poet, and two others, *Éremón and Éber, divide Ireland between them. In the first century of their rule a rebellion of the Aitheachthuatha [plebeian races] sets up the disastrous interregnum of usurper *Cairbre Cinn-Chait; after his death Cairbre's son *Morann returns the kingship to the rightful heirs. Although the Milesians are not mentioned prominently in *Ulster or *Connacht records, most Irish aristocratic families claimed descent from Míl Espáine.

Although the oldest surviving text of *Lebor Gabála* is in the 12th-century **Book of Leinster*, we have abundant evidence that the full text grew over many centuries and was added to by many hands. Summaries of *Lebor Gabála* narratives appear in the **Historia Brittonum* (formerly attributed to Nennius). The Scottish chronicler John Fordun (d. 1384) drew from *Lebor Gabála* in his five-volume *Chronica gentis Scotorum* [Chronicle of the Scottish People], often interpolating passages of shameless chauvinism. Some of the most important Irish historians before modern times struggled to make the *Lebor Gabála* history fit with information gathered elsewhere, including Geoffrey Keating (*c.*1570-*c.*1645), Micheál Ó Cléirigh (1575-*c.*1645) of the **Annals of the Four Masters*, and Roderick O'Flaherty (1629–1718). As late as the 18th century a historian as conscientious as Charles O'Conor (1710–91) was trying to accommodate the *Lebor Gabála* to post-Enlightenment times.

Although themes and characters from *Lebor Gabála* appear often in literature written by non-Gaelic authors (James Joyce employs many in *Finnegans Wake*, 1939), the pedestrian prose and digressive narratives have discouraged English or other adaptations. Two exceptions are Charles Maturin's little-read *The Milesian Chief* (London, 1812) and Jim Fitzpatrick's adult comic book, *The Book of Conquests* (London, 1978). The success of the Fitzpatrick book inspired the short-lived amusement attraction ultimately based on the *Lebor Gabála* called CeltWorld, in Tramore, Co. Waterford, in the 1990s.

The fullest text, edited and translated by R. A. S. Macalister, has been widely criticized: *Lebor Gabála Érenn*, 5 vols., Irish Texts Society, Nos. 34, 35, 39, 41, 44 (Dublin, 1938–56); repr. Irish Text Society (London, 1993), with a new introduction by John Carey. See also Myles Dillon, 'Lebor Gabála Érenn', *Journal of the Royal Society of Antiquaries of Ireland*, 86 (1956), 62–72; Vernam E. Hull, 'The Milesian Invasion of Ireland', *Zeitschrift für celtische Philologie*, 19 (1932), 155-60; Liam Ó Buachalla, 'The *Lebor Gabála* or Book of Invasions of Ireland: Notes on Its Construction', *Journal of the Cork Historical and Archaeological Society*, 67 (1962), 70–9; Alwyn and Brinley Rees, *Celtic Heritage* (London, 1961), esp. ch. 4, pp. 95–117; R. Mark Scowcroft, '*Leabhar Gabhála*, I: The Growth of the Text', *Ériu*, 38 (1987), 81–142; Anton van Hamel, 'On Lebor Gabála', *Zeitschrift für celtische Philologie*, 10 (1914), 97–197.

Lebor Laig(h)nech. An Irish title of the **Book of Leinster*.

Lebor na hUidre. Irish title of the **Book of the Dun Cow*.

Leborcham, Lebhorcham, Lebarcham, Levarcham. Nurse of *Deirdre and messenger of *Conchobar mac Nessa.

lefthandwise turn. See WITHERSHINS.

Leinster [OIr. *Lagin, Laigin*, people (of Lug?); ON *staðir*, steadings]. A province of *Ireland occupying much of the island east of the *Shannon, the second largest (7,850 square miles) of the four, including *Connacht, *Munster, and *Ulster, whose borders were drawn in the 17th century. In pre-conquest Ireland, as Cóiced Laigín, it had been one of five, when *Mide is counted separately or when Munster is counted as two. Within its borders are the counties of Carlow, Dublin, Kildare, Kilkenny, Laois (until 1922, Queens), Longford, Louth, *Meath, Offaly (until 1922, Kings), Westmeath, Wexford, and Wicklow. Much of the northern portion of the modern province, especially the megaliths, passage-graves, and pre-Christian religious sites of the *Boyne valley in counties Meath and Westmeath, was historically part of Mide and are not usually identified with Leinster.

From earliest times there were two royal seats for Leinster kings, the major one being the 34-acre hill-fort at *Dún Ailinne [Knockawlin], the largest in Ireland, near Kilcullen, Co. Kildare, and the second *Dind Ríg on the banks of the Barrow River, Co. Carlow, home to the kings of south Leinster. The earthworks at Dind Ríg are the foundation of what was once a large citadel; the story of its being burned to the ground by *Labraid Loingsech is told in **Orgain Denna Ríg* [The Destruction of Dind Ríg]. Remains of two of the most important Christian monastic sites, *Clonmacnoise (earlier in Mide) and *Glendalough, are also found in Leinster.

See *The Book of Leinster: Lebor Laighnech*, ed. R. I. Best, Osborn Bergin, and M. A. O'Brien (5 vols., Dublin, 1954-67); Alfred P. Smyth, *Celtic Leinster* (Dublin, 1982).

leipreachán. Preferred ModIr. form for *leprechaun.

Leirr. Manx form for *Lir (2).

Lendabair. Usually named as wife of *Conall Cernach of the *Ulster Cycle, daughter of *Eógan mac Durthacht. Conall's other wife is *Niam (1). Sometimes confused with *Finnabair.

lennan sídhe. Variant of *fairy lover.

leprechaun, leprecaun, lepracaun, leipreachán [cf. MidIr. *luchorpán*, small body; ModIr. *leipreachán*, *luprachán*]; parallel regional and archaic forms: lochramán, loimreachán, loragádán, lubrican, luchragán, luchramán, luprecan, lúracán, lurgadán, lurikeen. Male, solitary *fairy, a guardian of hidden treasure, of Irish literary and oral tradition whose original identity is now hopelessly obscured by two centuries of commercial and sometimes artistic transmogrification far from the roots of Gaelic culture. Contrary to popular perception, the leprechaun is by no means representative of the entire realm of the Irish fairy nor is he its most striking instance within Irish tradition. Obscured also are the now archaic regional variations, mostly pre-dating the mid-19th century. The leprechaun's dominance as perceived from outside Irish tradition derives from the great popular reception of the works of T. Crofton Croker, especially *Fairy Legends and Traditions of the South of Ireland* (1825), and prestigious literary adaptations, notably William Allingham's poem 'Lepracaun' (*c.*1870), Lady Wilde's *Ancient Legends . . . of Ireland* (1887), James Stephens' *Crock of Gold* (1912), and the American musical partially based on Stephens, *Finian's Rainbow* (1947).

The earliest anticipation of the leprechaun comes in the depiction of the water sprites, luchoirp or luchorpán, depicted in the 8th-century text Echtra Fergusa maic Léti [The Adventure of Fergus son of Léte]. In the narrative Fergus is sleeping in his chariot by the seaside when the sprites lift him up, separated from his sword, and carry him over the water. When he seizes hold of three of them, they promise to share their skills in swimming as a condition of their release. This portrayal, coupled with earlier glossaries stressing north *Leinster spellings, suggests that initially the leprechaun was an aquatic or at least amphibious creature. But several comparable terms from different parts of Ireland suggest other associations. From elsewhere in Leinster: loimreachán, lúracán. From *Connacht: lúracán. From *Munster: luchragán, lurgadán. From *Ulster: luchramán. Perhaps contributing to these conceptions are the monstrous lupracánaig of the pseudo-history **Lebor Gabála* [Book of Invasions], begotten by the biblical Ham as a result of the curse put upon him by his father Noah.

From the time of Crofton Croker's *Fairy Legends* (1825) the leprechaun has often been confused with two other solitary fairies known by Hiberno-English names, the *cluricaune, who drinks, smokes, and haunts cellars, and the mischievous *far darrig. Abundant evidence now exists to demonstrate that the leprechaun flourished in oral tradition before the 19th century. There are allusions to the figure in the place-names Knocknalooricaun [hill of the leprechauns] near Lismore, Co. Waterford, and Poulaluppercadaun [pool of the leprechaun] near Killorglin, Co. *Kerry. The anglicization lubrican appeared in 1604. The leprechaun recovered from Irish tradition lacks the high spirits and insouciance of his literary and commercial simulacra. Instead, he (there are no females) is often dour, even saturnine. Ugly and stunted with a face like a dried apple, the leprechaun may be querulous, sottish, and foul-mouthed. In his single best-known story, known in many variations, the leprechaun while busy shoemaking is seized by an ordinary mortal, demanding to known where the crock of gold is kept. If the mortal can keep his eyes on the leprechaun without being distracted, the gold will be his. The wily leprechaun, however, can always distract the mortal, often by appealing to his cupidity or gullibility so that the loser blames himself. Other motifs, such as the leprechaun's sitting on a toadstool, red Galway beard, green hat, etc., are clearly inventions, but some are borrowings from European folklore, especially the German household spirit, the kobold. Some portrayals of the leprechaun's adventures in the household may have entered Ulster folklore from the *brownie of Scottish settlers. See also GANCONER. Folk motifs: D1455; D1470; D1520; F369.4; F451.0.1; K415.

See D. A. Binchy, 'The Saga of Fergus, Son of Léti', *Ériu*, 16 (1952), 33–48; 'Echtra Fergusa maic Léti', in *Irish Sagas*, ed. Myles Dillon (Cork, 1968), 40–52; James Carney, *Studies in Irish Literature and History* (Dublin, 1955), 103–10; Diarmaid Ó Giollán, 'An Leipreachán San Ainmníocht', *Béaloideas*, 50 (1982), 126-50; 'The *Leipreachán* and Fairies, Dwarfs and the Household Familiar: A Comparative Study', *Béaloideas*, 52 (1984), 75–150.

Leth Cuinn [Conn's half]. Name for the parts of *Ireland north of *Eiscir Riada, the line running between Galway City and *Dublin, or the parts claimed by *Conn Cétchathach [of the Hundred Battles].

Leth Moga [Mug's half]. Name for the parts of *Ireland south of *Eiscir Riada, the line running between Galway City and Dublin, or the parts claimed by *Eógan Mór (also known as Mug Nuadat).

Letha. Shadowy place-name in early Irish narrative, sometimes implying the continent of Europe generally, sometimes *Brittany more specifically. See LLYDAW.

Leucetius. Epithet of Gaulish *Mars.

Levarcham. Variant form of *Leborcham.

Lewy. Anglicization of *Lugaid.

lhiannan shee. See FAIRY LOVER.

Lí Ban 1, Liban, Liaban, Libane [paragon of women]. *Otherworldly beauty, daughter of *Áed Abrat (or Eochaid (5)), sister of *Fand, wife of *Labraid Luathlám ar Claideb [swift sword-hand] of *Mag Mell [Pleasant Plain] who comes in a green mantle as her husband's emissary in **Serglige Con Culainn* [The Wasting Sickness of Cúchulainn]. Lí Ban (2) may be based on her.

2. Sanctified mermaid of *Lough Neagh, perhaps identical with Lí Ban (1). According to the **Annals of the Four Masters*, she was the

daughter of an *Eochaid, who none the less lived in the fresh waters of Lough Neagh. She was baptized by St Comgall, Bishop of *Bangor, in the 6th century and thus came to be known as St Muirgen [sea-born]. In a variant text she was first a woman who was transformed into a *salmon except for her head. Folk motifs: F420.5.1; V229.2.12.

Lia Fáil, Lia-fáil [Ir., stone of destiny]. Irish name for the ancient coronation stone reputed to sing, or to utter a shriek, when a king willed by destiny sits upon it. *Conn Cétchathach [of the Hundred Battles] was the first to sit upon Lia Fáil and foretell the future; he saw how many of his line would occupy the kingship as well as the coming of St *Patrick. Just which stone is the true Lia Fáil has been a matter of much contention; as the Irish antiquarian George Petrie (1790–1866) observed, 'It would be difficult to find a monument of antiquity with which so many national associations can be connected.' The Lia Fáil may be (1) identical with the phallus-like *Fál described by the *Dindshenchas as being found at *Tara from pre-Christian up to medieval times. The pseudo-history **Lebor Gabála* [Book of Invasions] speculates that the semi-divine *Tuatha Dé Danann brought Fál with them from northern Germany or that the *Milesians brought it with them from Spain. (2) An Irish stone at Tara that was taken to *Cruachain in *Connacht centuries ago. (3) An Irish stone standing at Tara until the rebellion of 1798, when it was moved from the 'Mound of Hostages' to 'Cormac's House'. Made of granular limestone not found in the area, this stone is 12 feet long, 6 feet of which stands above ground. It is the most obviously phallic monument from early Ireland. (4) The stone raised at 'Cormac's House' in 1798, now marked with the letters 'R.I.P.', may originally have served another function at Tara. (5) The Scottish Stone of Scone. Scottish historians from Hector Boece (1465–1536) have argued that while the Lia Fáil is of Irish origin, the Fál of the *Dindshenchas*, it was taken from either *Cashel or Tara to *Dunadd in *Dál Riada for the coronation of *Fergus mac Eirc. In 846 the Scottish king Cináed mac Ailpín [Kenneth MacAlpin] moved it to his capitals, first Forteviot and later Scone, where it was used in Scottish coronations until 1296 when it was seized by the English. And despite being recovered by Scottish nationalists in the mid-twentieth century, it lay under the English coronation chair until 1996, when it was returned to Scotland. See Tomás Ó Broin, *Celtica*, 29 (1990), 393–401.

Lia Luchar. Corrupt spelling of *Liath Luachra.

Liaban. Variant spelling of *Lí Ban.

Liadain, Líadan, Líadain, Líadaine, Liadhain, Liadin. Possibly historical woman whose tragic love for the poet Cuirithir, as told in the 9th-century *Comrac Liadaine ocus Chuirithir* [The Meeting of Liadain and Cuirithir], is widely seen as an anticipation of the doomed love of Héloise and Abélard; like the later French story, the basis may be historical. Liadain, a well-born young woman of the *Corcu Duibne in what is now *Kerry, was travelling in north *Connacht when she met a poet named Cuirithir mac Dobrchon [son of the *otter], whom she invited to visit her on her return. Being 'under spiritual direction' of St *Cuimíne Fota, Liadain was in effect a nun. Arriving in Kerry, Cuirithir asked the household fool Comgán to send word to Liadain. Making a pun on Cuirithir's patronymic, Comgán said that 'the son of the beast that stays at night under pools' had arrived. This was sufficient for Liadain, who rushed to greet her lover, but St Cuimíne forbade their cohabiting. When Liadain would not cease from pleading, the saint allowed them to spend one night together, but with a boy between them. Such a practice, called consortium, was a common ascetic exercise in early Ireland and elsewhere. On St Cuimíne's orders, Cuirithir became a monk and went on pilgrimage to the *Déisi of what is now Waterford. On the report that Liadain was about to visit him, Cuirithir crossed the sea in a coracle, never to return. Still longing for him, Liadain came to the flagstone where Cuirithir used to pray and remained upon it until she died and was buried underneath. See *Liadin [sic] and Cuirithir: a Love Story*, ed. Kuno Meyer (London, 1902); Gerard Murphy, *Early Irish Lyrics* (Oxford, 1962), 82–5, 208–11. The story also inspired Móirín a Cheavasa's poems *Liadain and Curithir* (Oxford, 1917).

lianhan shee. See FAIRY LOVER.

Liath Luachra I, Liath Luachair, Lia Luchar [Ir., grey of Luachair]. Keeper of the *crane bag [*corrbolg*] in the *Fenian Cycle, which will become one of the great treasures of the *Fianna. Described as a hideous warrior,

Liath Luachra of *Connacht becomes 'treasurer' of the Fianna after the death of *Cumhall while *Goll mac Morna is in command. The boy *Fionn mac Cumhaill kills him and takes his treasure from him. Liath Luachra is the father of *Conán mac Lia.

2, **Liathluachra.** A nurse of *Fionn mac Cumhaill, along with *Bodhmall, in oral tradition.

Liath Macha [Ir., grey of Macha]. Favourite horse of the *Ulster hero *Cúchulainn, the other being *Saingliu or Dubh Sainglenn. Both horses were magical, having risen out of a grey lake at *Sliab Fúait [Slieve Fuad], but each is credited as a gift from *Macha (which of the three is not specified) or the *Mórrígan, with whom Macha is sometimes confused. Cúchulainn catches and tames both horses by springing onto their backs. For an entire day they tear round the 'circuit' of Ireland but cannot throw off their boy rider, after which they are gentle. The horse is portrayed as showing extraordinary love for his master, refusing to be saddled and shedding tears of blood before Cúchulainn's final battle. Some accounts have Liath Macha dying with his master, taking eighty enemy warriors with him; others report that Liath Macha and Saingliu return to their lakes after Cúchulainn's death.

Lifechair. See CAIRBRE LIFECHAIR.

Liffey [Ir. *an life*]. Fifty-mile river of eastern Ireland, rising in Co. Wicklow, flowing through Kildare, and emptying into the Irish Sea in Dublin harbour. James Joyce's personification of the river in *Finnegans Wake* (1939) as Anna Liffey or Anna Livia Plurabelle is based on his idiosyncratic transliteration of *Abha na Life* [lit. the River Liffey]. See Brendan O Hehir, 'Anna Livia Plurabelle's Gaelic Ancestry', *James Joyce Quarterly*, 2 (1965), 158-66; John de Courcy, *Anna Liffey: The River of Dublin* (Dublin, 1989); Elizabeth Healy (ed.), *The Book of the Liffey* (Dublin, 1989).

Lindow Man. Name given to the body of a 4th-century BC well-born (with manicured nails) male, human sacrificial victim found in the peat bog at Lindow Moss, Cheshire, 1 August 1984. His well-preserved flesh has been subject to close scrutiny; his stomach reveals mistletoe pollen and recently eaten burnt oatcakes. His throat was cut, and he was bludgeoned, strangled, and drowned. Learned examination dismisses the suggestion that his death was a mere execution, favouring instead his sacrifice to different gods, perhaps *Esus, *Taranis, and *Teutates. See Don R. Brothwell, *The Bog Man and the Archaeology of People* (London, 1986; Cambridge, Mass., 1987); I. M. Stead et al., *Lindow Man: The Body in the Bog* (London and Ithaca, NY, 1986); Anne Ross, *The Life and Death of a Druid Prince: The Story of Lindow Man, an Archaeological Sensation* (London and New York, 1989).

Linn Féic. A pool in the River *Boyne near Slane, Co. Meath, one of the two locations where *Fionn mac Cumhaill encountered the *salmon of wisdom. Known today as Fiac's or Féc's Pool, it was named for one Fiac who drowned here. Coincidentally, this was also the site of the Battle of the Boyne (1690).

Lir 1. Father of the children changed into *swans in *Oidheadh Chlainne Lir* [The Tragic Story of the Children of Lir].

2. Genitive form of the OIr. ler 'sea' in the patronymic of the Irish sea-god *Manannán mac Lir; in Manx, Leirr. His granddaughter is *Sinann, goddess of the *Shannon. See also LLŶR.

liss, lis [OIr. *les, liss*, space about a dwelling enclosed by a rampart; ModIr. *lios*; akin to W *llys*, court]. The enclosed ground of an ancient dwelling, including what might have been originally a storage space enclosed by a circular mound or trench or both; more simply, the word describes what is perceived to have been the outer court or garth of an ancient chieftain's fortification. By extension a liss could be a ring-fort, and in oral tradition it becomes one of many words for a *fairy fort. First word in innumerable place-names, e.g. Lismore [*lios mór*, big liss]. See also DÚN; RÁTH.

Llassar Llaes Gyfnewid. Original possessor of the *cauldron of regeneration in the second branch of the *Mabinogi*. His wife is *Cymidei Cymeinfoll.

Llefelys, Lleuelys, Llevelys. Son of *Beli Mawr, co-protagonist of *Cyfranc Lludd a Llefelys* [The Tale of Lludd and Llefelys]. He becomes king of France by marrying the dead king's daughter, and later delivers the kingdom of his brother *Lludd from three plagues.

Lleu Llaw Gyffes, Lleu Llawgyffes, Llew [W, light/the fair one of the sure/steady hand]. Central figure of the fourth branch of the

Mabinogi, son of *Arianrhod, who conceives him only when *Math tests her virginity, and brother of *Dylan. *Gwydion, Arianrhod's brother, abducts and raises the child, who shows great strength by his first birthday and is able to go to court by himself on his second. Because Gwydion then presents the still unnamed child to his mother, embarrassing her, some commentators have suggested that Gwydion may be the actual father, an incest hidden by late redactors; certain internal references may support this argument. For whichever reason, Arianrhod is furious at the sight of the child, accusing Gwydion of 'pursuing her shame'. She curses the boy three times: he shall not have a name unless she give it to him; he shall not bear arms unless she equip him; and he shall not have a wife of the race of this earth. Gwydion cleverly overcomes all these obstacles, the third by creating the lovely *Blodeuwedd entirely from flowers. But for all her comeliness, Blodeuwedd does not become a good wife to Lleu. While he is absent, she entertains the wandering hunter *Gronw Pebyr and resolves to help him to follow the formulated steps needed to kill her husband. Wounded, Lleu Llaw Gyffes turns into an *eagle and after uttering a piercing shriek flies to a magic *oak tree. Gwydion finds and restores him to human form, and shames Blodeuwedd by changing her into an owl. Lleu Llaw Gyffes seeks out Gronw Pebyr, who begs reconciliation before he is killed in the same way he would have killed Lleu. Thereafter Lleu becomes lord of *Gwynedd, north Wales.

A virtuous, skilful, but naïve figure in the *Mabinogi*, Lleu's antecedents imply a larger character than we find in this literary context. Philologically he is connected to, and may be identical with, the Irish hero *Lug Lámfhota [of the long arm] and the ancient god *Lugos/Lugus, who, along with being the antecedent of both Lleu and Lug, was probably the Gaulish *Mercury of whom Julius *Caesar spoke (1st cent. BC). Lugos/Lugus gave his name to *Lug(u)dunum*, a place-name given to scores of sites on the Roman map. His fleeting associations with the *oak and *eagle also imply a divine origin. See W. J. Gruffydd, *Math vab Mathonwy* (Cardiff, 1928); Rachel Bromwich, *Trioedd Ynys Prydain*, rev. edn. (Cardiff, 1978), 408–10, 555; Valenté, *Bulletin of the Board of Celtic Studies*, 35 (1988), 1 ff.

Lleuelys, Llevelys. Variant forms of *Llefelys.

Llew. Variant form of *Lleu Llaw Gyffes.

Llewelyn. Variant spelling of *Llywelyn.

Llinon. Welsh name for the *Shannon River. Uncapitalized, the word llinon means 'spear', '*ash'.

Lloegr, Lloegyr. Welsh name for England; see PRYDAIN [Britain].

Lludd. Name borne by as many as six personages, some quite shadowy, from early Welsh tradition whose identities cannot be completely disassociated from one another.

Lludd 1. The son of *Beli Mawr, leading character of the medieval romance *Cyfranc Lludd a Llefelys* [The Tale of Lludd and Llefelys]. See Rachel Bromwich, *Trioedd Ynys Prydain*, rev. edn. (Cardiff, 1978), 424–7, 556.

2. Another name for *Nudd, influenced by alliterative assimilation from Nudd Llaw Ereint. As Lludd Llaw Ereint or Llawereint, he is the father of *Creiddylad [Cordelia].

3. Legendary founder of London [W *Caer Lludd*], whose name is also commemorated in 'Ludgate Hill'.

Llwyd, son of Cil Coed. Also called 'the enchanter', humiliated by *Pwyll in playing 'badger-in-the-bag' in the first branch of the *Mabinogi*; he later sought revenge against *Dyfed.

Llychlyn. Fabulous or infernal region beneath the waves in such early Welsh texts as *Breuddwyd Rhonabwy* [The Dream of Rhonabwy]. Like the Irish cognate *Lochlainn, Llychlyn comes also to mean Scandinavia, its definition in contemporary Modern Welsh.

Llydaw, Llydawr. The Welsh name for the Breton language. By folk etymology this derives from llew [half] and taw [silent], based on the story that the women of Brittany had their tongues cut out to keep them from corrupting the language of the conquerors. See also LETHA.

Llyfr Coch Hergest. See RED BOOK OF HERGEST.

Llyfr Gwyn Rhydderch. See WHITE BOOK OF RHYDDERCH.

Llyfr Taliesin. See BOOK OF TALIESIN.

llyn. Welsh word for lake, first element in

dozens of place-names. See also LOCH; LOUGH.

Llyn Cerrig Bach. Small lake in a rocky portion of the island of *Anglesey, north-western *Wales, once the centre of ritual activity in the late Iron Age. Twentieth-century excavations at Llyn Cerrig Bach, especially at the edge of a bog under an 11-foot sheer rock cliff, have revealed an enormous trove of uncorroded metal objects. Evidently thrown off the cliff over as much as 200 years, *c.* 2nd cent. BC-1st cent. AD, the objects include *cauldrons, chariots, harness and other fittings, musical instruments, chains for slave gangs, and ironworkers', tools. Most items appear well made as if possessions of the most privileged classes; some appear deliberately damaged before having been thrown in the lake. Unfounded speculation has suggested the objects may have been thrown by the *druids that *Tacitus tells of being slaughtered in AD 61. See Cyril Fox, *A Find of the Early Iron Age from Llyn Cerrig Bach, Anglesey* (Cardiff, 1946); P. Lynch, *Prehistoric Anglesey* (Anglesey, 1970), 249–77.

Llyn Llion. Fabulous 'Lake of the Waves' in early Welsh tradition, the overflowing of which caused the *flood from which *Dwyfan and *Dwyfach escaped only in a ship built by *Nefyd Naf Neifion. Also the home of the water-monster *Afanc, Llyn Llion may possibly be associated with the actual *Bala Lake.

Llyn Llyw. See SALMON.

Llyn Tegid. Welsh name for *Bala Lake in *Hanes Taliesin* [The Story of *Taliesin], when *Ceridwen and *Tegid Foel live on its shores.

Llŷr [W, sea]. Father of *Manawydan, *Bendigeidfran, and *Bronwen in the **Mabinogi*, although only Manawydan bears his name in patronymic. A shadowy figure in Welsh tradition, Llŷr is often assumed to be borrowed from the Irish *Lir (1), the patronym of the sea-god *Manannán, whose name also means 'sea'. A possible hint of Llŷr's foreign origin may come in the references to him as Llŷr Llediaith [half-language]. Many commentators have sought to trace Shakespeare's King Lear to Llŷr, but the route is tortuous; Shakespeare drew from Raphael Holinshed's *Chronicles* (1577), which in turn drew from *Giraldus Cambrensis' work, *Geoffrey of Monmouth's *Historia*, where the name Leir appears, and perhaps also from lost Welsh texts. See Rachel Bromwich, *Trioedd Ynys Prydain*, rev. edn. (Cardiff, 1978), 427–9, 556.

Llywarch Hen. Central figure of the *Canu Llywarch Hen* [The Song of Llywarch the Old], a cycle of poems (englynion, the oldest Welsh verse form) in monologues and dialogues, giving emotional peaks of a fuller narrative that has not survived. Llywarch characteristically laments his current state, hunch-backed, weary, and wretched, in contrast to the merriment and daring of his youth. The poems were formerly attributed to Llywarch, but Ifor Williams (1972) demonstrated that he is only the subject of them. See Ifor Williams, *The Beginnings of Welsh Poetry*, ed. Rachel Bromwich (Cardiff, 1972); Patrick K. Ford, *The Poems of Llywarch Hen* (Berkeley and Los Angeles, 1974); Rachel Bromwich, *Trioedd Ynys Prydain*, rev. edn. (Cardiff, 1978), 430–3; Jenny Rowland, *Early Welsh Saga Poetry* (Cambridge, 1990).

Llywelyn, Llewelyn, Llewellyn. One of the most popular of all Welsh men's names, borne by innumerable medieval and Renaissance princes and poets, of whom the best-known is probably Llywelyn ap Gruffudd (d. 1282).

Llywelyn I. Princely owner of the faithful hound *Bedd Gelert in the famous folk-tale of the same name, sometimes identified with either *Llywelyn ap Iorwerth or *Llywelyn ap Gruffudd.

Llywelyn ap Gruffudd, Gruffydd (*c.*1225–82). Last and only native-born Welsh noble to bear the title 'Prince of Wales', sometimes known as Y Llyw Olaf [The Last Prince]. Like his grandfather, *Llywelyn ap Iorwerth, the younger Llywelyn forced his will on fractious Welsh princes and, at least initially, maintained cordial relations with the English Crown. The death of Henry III in England and accession of Edward I (1272) changed that. Llywelyn was killed while resisting English invasion at a bridge near Builth, 11 December 1282, by a soldier who did not recognize him. His severed head was displayed in London. A frequent subject of *Gogynfeirdd poetry (13th-14th cents.), Llywelyn also enjoyed a rich reputation in Welsh oral tradition, many stories linking him to Llywelyn's Cave near Aberedw, *Powys (formerly Radnorshire). See David Stephenson, *The Last Prince of Wales* (Buckingham, 1983); J. Beverley

Smith, *Llywelyn ap Gruffudd, Tywysog Cymru* (Cardiff, 1986).

Llywelyn ap Iorwerth, ab Iorwerth, Fawr [W *mawr*, great] (1173–1240). Most powerful of all medieval Welsh princes, ruler of *Gwynedd, often known as Llywelyn the Great in English. A successful military campaigner, he also sued for Welsh rights against the English king John at the signing of the Magna Carta (1215). He none the less married John's natural daughter Joan, called Siwan in Wales. For all his worldly success, Llywelyn died in a monk's habit in the monastery of Aberconwy. Grandfather of *Llywelyn ap Gruffudd. His princely life has been the subject of two Welsh-language dramas, Thomas Parry's *Llywelyn Fawr* (1954) and Saunders Lewis's *Siwan* (1956), trans. as *The King of England's Daughter* (1985).

Loan Maclibhuin. In Manx legend, the swarthy smith of Drontheim [Norway?] who made the sword Macabuin for King *Olave II, Goddardson, of the Isle of *Man. Loan's daughter Emergaid the Fair later married Olave, founding the Manx royal line. See also LON MAC LÍOMTHA.

Loarn. One of the three sons of *Erc who founded the kingdom of *Dál Riada in *Argyll in the 5th century; the genealogies of many Scottish Highland families were traced back to him as an ultimate ancestor.

Lóbais. *Druid of the *Fomorians.

loch. OIr., ModIr., and ScG word for lake or arm of the sea. The anglicization lough- is now standard in Irish place-names, while Scottish place-names retain loch; see also LLYN.

Loch Ness Monster. One of Scotland's best-known tourist attractions, the monster, Orm, or Nessy, has a surprisingly ancient history. *Adamnán's life of *Colum Cille, written *c.*690, reports that the saint caused an open-jawed monster in River Ness to submerge and cease threatening a man swimming. See also AFANC; SEA MONSTER. See Frederick W. Holiday, *The Great Orm of Loch Ness* (London, 1968); Roy P. Mackal, *The Monster of Loch Ness* (Athens, Oh., 1980).

Lochlainn, Lochlain, Lochlan, Loughlan. Realm of dangerous invaders, often, but not necessarily, identified with Scandinavia, especially Norway. Sir John Rhy^s suggested (1886) that Lochlainn may initially have described the fabulous abode under lakes or waters of hostile, supernatural beings, like the *Fomorians of the **Lebor Gabála* [Book of Invasions]; the Welsh cognate *Llychlyn retains this implication. After the Viking invasions (8th cent.), Lochlainn came to describe the seemingly invincible Norsemen. In Modern Irish Lochlannach means both 'Scandinavian' and 'marauder, robber'. Cf. ScG Lochlann, 'Norway, Scandinavia'; Manx Loghlin, 'Scandinavia'. Invaders from Lochlainn, especially under King *Colgán, make frequent appearances in *Fenian stories. The most dangerous task *Lug Lámfhota gives to the sons of *Tuireann in **Oidheadh Chlainne Tuireann* is to retrieve three shouts from the hill of *Miodhchaoin in Lochlainn. There is much fascination with Lochlainn in Irish folklore, especially the city of Berbha or Berva [Bergen, Norway?], the home of *Lon mac Líomtha the *smith.

Lochlin. Realm of dangerous invaders in James *Macpherson's *Ossian* (1760), clearly based on *Lochlainn. Macpherson, however, places Lochlin in north Germany, between the Rhine and the Elbe.

lochramán. Variant spelling of *leprechaun.

Lóeg. Variant spelling of *Láeg.

Lóegaire, Láegaire, Lóeghaire, Laeghire, Laoghaire, Laoire, Lóegure, Leary. One of the most common names in early Ireland, borne by legendary heroes, kings, and saints, of whom the best-known is probably *Lóegaire Búadach of the *Ulster Cycle.

Lóegaire Búadach, Lóegaire Bern Búadach, Buadhach [Ir., victorious, triumphant]. *Ulster Cycle hero, who appears to be one of the three most prominent when he contends for the *champion's portion [Ir. *curadmír*] with *Cúchulainn and *Conall Cearnach in **Fled Bricrenn* [Briccriu's Feast]. Although his name is often cited in passing, the most important text describing Lóegaire comes from the 11th century. When the poet *Áed (9) was about to be drowned for his adultery with *Conchobar's wife, *Mugain (2), Lóegaire rushed from his house in anger to save him. He struck the crown of his head on a door lintel and was killed, but not before he slew thirty of the executioners and spared Áed's life. Lóegaire's mantle is one of the

Three Treasures of Ireland. Under the name Lóegaire Bern Búadach, almost a separate identity, he was the ancestor-deity of the Osraige [*Ossory], and was thought to have a famous sword.

Lóegaire Lorc [fierce]. Son of *Úgaine Mór killed at the beginning of **Orgain Denna Ríg* [The Destruction of Dind Ríg] and avenged by his son *Labraid Loingsech.

Lóegaire mac Crimthann. Hero of **Echtrae Lóegairi* [The Adventure of Lóegaire].

Lóegaire mac Néill. King of *Tara (427/8–462/3) who was converted to Christianity by St *Patrick. A son of *Niall Noígiallach [of the Nine Hostages], he is the earliest king of Ireland whose dates can be known with reasonable accuracy. When he was told that he would die between Ériu [Ireland] and Alba [Scotland], he refused to go to sea. When he was killed fighting the *Lagin he was between two hills named Ére and Alba in the plain of the *Liffey. See Gearóid S. MacEoin, 'The Mysterious Death of Loegaire mac Néill', *Studia Hibernica*, 8 (1968), 21–48.

loimreachán. Variant form of *leprechaun.

Lomair. Sometime sibling of *Fionn mac Cumhaill's dogs, *Bran (2) and *Sceolang.

Lomna. Fool of *Fionn mac Cumhaill who betrays the adulterous affair of one of his wives and is murdered for his indiscretion by her lover. Later, his severed head speaks at a feast.

lón láith, laoich [Ir., champion's light]. Light-beam projecting from *Cúchulainn's forehead as he goes into battle.

Lon mac Líomtha. Smith and teacher of smiths from *Lochlainn in the *Fenian Cycle, noted for his fearful appearance. He made Mac an Luin, the famous sword of *Fionn mac Cumhaill. His smithy was at what may now be Bergen, Norway. See also LOAN MACLIBHUIN.

Longas mac nUislenn [The Exile of the Sons of Uisnech]. See DEIRDRE.

loragádán. Variant spelling of *leprechaun.

Lord of the Isles. English translation of a title borne by rulers of the Hebrides from the time of *Somerled (d. 1164) to the 15th century; the title was first lost in a treaty with Edward IV of England, restored in 1476, and finally lost in 1493. After his defeat of the Norse in 1156, Somerled took the Gaelic title Rí Innse Gall [king of the Hebrides]; this was translated into Latin as Dominus Insularum in 1354 and from thence into English as Lord of the Isles. Sir Walter Scott's six-canto poem titled *The Lord of the Isles* (1815) is a romantic fiction set in the time of Robert the Bruce (*c*.1305–7).

Loucetius. Epithet of *Mars.

lough. Standard anglicization of the Irish loch used in place-names for lake or arm of the sea. See also LOCH; LLYN.

Lough Corrib [Ir. *An Choirb*; OIr. *Loch nOirbsen*, Oirbsiu's lake]. A lake of 70 square miles in *Connacht, counties Galway and Mayo, the second largest in Ireland. The Old Irish name for the Lough, *Loch nOirbsen*, alludes to *Oirbsiu or Oirbsiu Mór, an obscure epithet (denoting inundation) of the sea-deity *Manannán mac Lir, and possibly his original name. An oral story of later composition claims that Manannán drowned here. *Lug Lámfhota was thought to have a palace under Lough Corrib. Adjacent to *Connemara, the Lough Corrib region is also a reservoir of folklore and folk culture. See Sir William Wilde, *Lough Corrib, Its Shores and Islands* (Dublin, 1867), 3rd edn., abridged by Colm Ó Lochlainn (Dublin, 1936, 1955); Richard Hayward, *The Corrib Country* (Dundalk, 1954).

Lough Derg, Dearg I [Ir. *derg*, red]. Lake 6 by 4 miles, 4 miles NW of Pettigoe in south Co. *Donegal, also called St Patrick's Purgatory, long the focus of religious pilgrimage. No documentable evidence survives to prove that St Patrick (d. 493?) ever visited the lake, but a well-known legend has the saint banishing the monster *Caoránach to its waters, turning them red. Pilgrimage to the lake began well before the 12th century, with the institution of a cavern known as the Purgatory. Medieval legend assumed that St Patrick had descended into Purgatory through a cavern on Station Island in the lake. Today, thousands of pilgrims ferry to Station Island on weekends between 1 June and 15 August to spend a night in the cavern without sleep, along with three days of fasting and praying at the nearby modern basilica. See Shane Leslie, *Saint Patrick's Purgatory* (London, 1932); Alice Curtayne, *Lough Derg, St. Patrick's Purgatory* (London, 1945); Michael Haren and

Yolande de Pontfarcy, *The Medieval Pilgrimage to St. Patrick's Purgatory* (Enniskillen, 1988); Alannah Hopkin, *The Living Legend of St. Patrick* (London, 1989), 84–105. Michael Dames's highly speculative interpretation of the Lough Derg pilgrimage, *Mythic Ireland* (London, 1992), 22–54, must be read with caution and scepticism. See also Seamus Heaney's meditative poem *Station Island* (New York and London, 1985).

2. An expansion of the *Shannon River, 24 miles long and an average of 2 miles wide, above *Killaloe, between counties Clare and Galway on the west and Tipperary on the east. This Lough Derg was named for *Eochaid (1), a possible sun-god, who sometimes bore the epithet Deirgderc [red eye].

Lough Erne. See ERNE.

Lough Gur, Guir. Small lake 2.5 miles NNE of Bruff, Co. Limerick, widely known in Irish tradition for the wealth of neolithic remains to be found near its shores and under its waters. The light limestone soil of the area made it especially attractive to cultivators in earliest times. From Irish legend *Gerald, Earl of Desmond, is said to have disappeared here in 1398 and to ride out in the moonlight every seventh year. A cave on Rockadoon Island in Lough Gur is one of several sites suggested as the entrance to *Tír na nÓg [the Land of Youth]. See Claire Kelly, *Illustrated Guide to Lough Gur* (Blackrock, 1978); Seán P. Ó Ríordáin, 'Lough Gur Excavations: The Great Stone Circle (B) in Grange Townland', *Proceedings of the Royal Irish Academy*, 54C (1951), 37–74; 'Lough Gur Excavations: Neolithic and Bronze Age Houses on Knockadoon', *Proceedings of the Royal Irish Academy*, 56C (1954), 297–459. The lake is also the setting for Mary Carbery's well-known memoir, *The Farm by Lough Gur* (London, 1937) and Michael Quinlan's historical novel *A Place of Dreams: The Lough Gur People* (1993).

Lough Neagh [Ir. *Loch nEchach, nEathach*, Eochaid's lake]. Lake of 153 square miles in Northern Ireland, the largest body of fresh water in the British Isles, bordered by counties Antrim, Armagh, Down, and Derry. Surrounded by flat, sandy shores, the Lough has attracted numerous stories, especially *flood legends. Place-name stories trace the origin of the Lough to *Eochu (or Eochaid) mac Maireda whose *otherworldly palace lay beneath the waters; in Christianized versions Eochu was merely an unfortunate mortal who had fallen into the Lough. In a separate story, Eochu (sometimes Ecca in this version) had fallen in love with his stepmother, Ébliu (2), who had been fostered by *Angus Óg. Together with Eochu's brother *Ríb, the illicit lovers hoped to establish a new kingdom on a northerly plain. After a stranger killed their horses, Angus gave them a marvellous new one, but warned that they should not let it stop to rest and urinate. But once the party reached Ulster, they did allow the horse to urinate, which caused a spring to rise on the spot. Eochu then built a house next to the spring, and one day when a woman did not replace the cover on the spring, it overflowed the area, drowning Eochu and most of his family, forming Lough Neagh. A comparable story is told of *Lough Ree. The sanctified mermaid *Lí Ban (2), sometimes known as St Muirgen, swims in Lough Neagh. In early Christian times the petty kingdom of *Dál nAraide bordered the Lough. A widely known story of more recent, popular origin depicts *Fionn mac Cumhaill's creation of the Lough by picking up a clod of earth to throw at a fleeing *giant; the clod when thrown becomes the Isle of *Man. Known as Lake of the Roes in *Macpherson's *Ossian* (1760). See also SUBMERGED CITIES.

Lough Ree. Formed by the waters of the River *Shannon above *Athlone, Lough Ree lies between counties Roscommon, Longford, and Westmeath, 16 miles long and from 1 to 7 miles wide. The story of Lough Ree's formation duplicates that of *Lough Neagh, with some substitutions. *Eochu mac Maireda (sometimes called Ecca) had fallen in love with his stepmother, *Ébliu (2), and together with his brother *Ríb planned to form a new kingdom. *Midir killed their horses and then offered them another one, presumably *otherworldly, as compensation. When this horse urinated, it formed Lough Ree. Ríb, ModIr. Ríbh, may be the eponym of the Lough. *Furbaide Ferbend killed *Medb on an island in Lough Ree. In oral tradition Lough Ree was thought to contain both a monster and a *submerged city. According to the medieval biography of St Mochuda, the Lough Ree monster once devoured a man; it was sighted in the lake as late as 1960. As for the submerged city, a bishop hearing that it contained a cathedral went to visit it but never returned. See *Life of St. Declan of Ardmore and Life of*

St. Mochuda of Lismore, trans. Patrick Power. Irish Texts Society, 16 (London, 1914), 74–147.

Loughlan. Corrupt spelling of *Lochlainn.

love spot. See BALL SEIRCE.

Lowry. Anglicization of *Labraid.

lubrican. Archaic anglicization of *leprechaun.

Lucetius. Epithet of *Mars.

luchorpán. Earlier spelling of *leprechaun.

Luchra. Corrupt spelling of *Iuchra (1).

luchragán, luchramám. Variant spellings of *leprechaun.

Luchta, Luchtar, Luchtain, Luchtaine, Luchtine. Carpenter or wright [Ir. *sóer*], god of the *Tuatha Dé Danann, one of the three gods of craft [*trí dée dána*] of early Ireland, along with *Credne and *Goibniu. Luchta was thought adept at making shields and spear shafts. As the son of Lúachad, he sometimes has the patronymic mac Lúachaid.

Luchtigern [OIr. *lug*, light, brightness; *tigern*, lord; cf. *luch*, mouse]. Mouse-lord of Kilkenny, slain by a huge cat, Banghaisgidheach.

Lug Lámfhota; Lugh, Luga; Lámfada, Lámfhada, Lámhfhada [OIr. *lug*, light, brightness; *lámhfhada*, long-armed, long-handed]. May also bear the patronymics mac Céin, mac Ethlenn, Maicnia, and the epithets Samildánach and Ildánach. Celebrated chief of the *Tuatha Dé Danann and central hero of the *Mythological Cycle of early Irish literature; one of the three great heroes of Irish tradition, along with *Fionn mac Cumhaill and *Cúchulainn, whose supernatural father he is. Lug's usual agnomen, Lámfhada [long-armed], testifies to an ability to hurl a weapon a long distance or to use a sling, not to the actual length of his arm. His usual sobriquet, Samildánach [possessing many arts, crafts, trades], also Ildánach, suggests he may also have been a *fili or seer. Another patronymic was Maicnia [lad-warrior]. Although Lug may originally have been a god of the sun or of light, he was still thought to be historical as late as the 19th century. The ancient Luigni of what is now Counties Meath and Sligo claimed descent from him. Much of Lug's story is told in the 11th-century text (based on earlier materials) **Cath Maige Tuired* [The (Second) Battle of Mag Tuired], in which he kills *Balor, coincidentally his grandfather. A close counterpart and possible double of the Welsh *Lleu Llaw Gyffes [W, light of the sure/steady hand], Lug appears to share a divine origin with Fionn [Ir., fair] and Cúchulainn, both of whom may be his doubles.

Lug appears to be identical with the Gaulish *Mercury, modern commentators agree, for two reasons: (*a*) Julius *Caesar's (1st cent. BC) description of Mercury 'inventor of all the arts' translates Lug's sobriquet Samildánach; (*b*) the name *Lugos/Lugus for Mercury is implicit in several place-names, e.g. *Lug(u)-dunum*, which survive as Leiden, Lyon, Liegnitz, etc. At the Roman colony of what is now Lyon, Emperor Augustus inaugurated a festival on the first day of August, an anticipation of the later Irish August festival of *Lughnasa. Aspects of Lug's persona suggest even deeper rooting in the Indo-European imagination. Lámfhada [long-armed], for example, echoes the epithet of the Indian god Savitar, 'of the wide hand'. Lug's use of magic links him with both the Indian Varuna and the Norse Odin. Commentators disagree whether the cult arrived early or late in Ireland, but by the time of Christ he was the patron of a harvest festival at *Tailtiu [Teltown, Co. Meath].

The circumstances of Lug's conception and birth imply that he was destined for an extraordinary career. His grandfather *Balor, a *Fomorian, had been told he would be slain by his grandson and so tried to prevent his daughter *Eithne (1) from knowing men, but *Cian (sometimes *Cethern (2)), son of *Dian Cécht the healing god, seduced the girl with the help of the *druidess *Birog. Triplets were conceived, but Lug's two siblings were either drowned at birth or turned into seals. Some commentators see this as evidence of Lug's *triplism. Sometimes Lug is also attributed a sister, *Ébliu (1), wife of *Fintan mac Bóchra. Grandfather Balor was not spiteful, however, calling out to the nimble baby picking up an apple that he had long hands, thus giving him his name. Along with his divine lineage, Lug could boast divine fosterage from the sea-god *Manannán mac Lir, who none the less chided the boy for his blindness and stubbornness. Variant texts name *Goibniu the smith-god and *Eochaid (3) as foster-father and *Tailtiu or *Duach as foster-mother.

Always portrayed as youthful, handsome,

and athletic, Lug's dramatic character becomes most sharply focused in *Cath Maige Tuired*; he comes to the aid of the Tuatha Dé Danann, who fear that their maimed king *Nuadu may not be able to resist the invading Fomorians. When Lug first approaches the citadel at *Tara, he is refused for having no art. In successive knockings at the gate Lug identifies himself as a wright or builder, a smith, champion, harper, warrior, poet, historian, magician, physician (or leech), cupbearer, and brazier (or craftsman in metal), but is told that the Tuatha Dé Danann already have one. Then he asks if they have someone who could perform all these skills, Samildánach, and when Tara's denizens admit they do not, he is allowed to enter. Upon his arrival, Lug dazzles the court with two more feats by throwing a huge flagstone over a high wall and by playing a harp. Nuadu yields his throne to Lug, who successfully leads the Tuatha Dé Danann against the Fomorians in the central action of *Cath Maige Tuired*; Lug's piercing of Balor's magical, lethal eye determines their victory. In the same text Lug is credited with inventing *fidchell, the archaic board-game described as a game of kings; and he is also thought to have instituted horse-racing. Lug assists his spiritual son Cúchulainn in **Táin Bó Cuailnge* [Cattle Raid of Cooley], is revealed as the phantom in **Baile In Scáil* [The Phantom's Frenzy], and sometimes appears as the consort of *Sovereignty in oral tradition. He reigned for forty years.

As befits a champion whose agnomen, Lámfhada, speaks of an ability to wield power over distance, Lug's favoured weapon is his spear, about which there are differing stories. According to **Oidheadh Chlainne Tuireann* [The Tragic Story of the Children of Tuireann], Lug sent the sons of Tuireann (earlier Tuirill), *Brian, Iuchair, and *Iucharba, on seemingly impossible tasks as recompense, *éric, for killing his father, Cian. One of these tasks was to bring back the spear of *Assal, *Gáe Assail, then in Persia. In another text, the druid *Esras provided Lug with the spear. In any case, it is usually thought of as one of the four treasures of the Tuatha Dé Danann.

According to a verse in the *Dindshenchas, Lug had four wives. The two better-known are: *Buí, linked to *Howth and the *Cailleach Bhéirre; her sister *Nás, linked tenuously to Naas, Co. Kildare; the remaining two, Echtach (3) and Énglic, are cipherous names. An unnamed wife, perhaps a fifth or sixth, was unfaithful to Lug with *Cermait, the son of the *Dagda; Lug's vengeful killing of Cermait brought, in return, the revenge of Cermait's sons (see below). Lug was enamoured of *Deichtine, mother of Cúchulainn. Strangely, considering that many early Irish families cited Lug in their pedigrees, he is not credited with either sons or daughters, except for Fionn's harper, *Cnú Deireóil, who claimed to be Lug's son (perhaps facetiously). Lug's constant companion was his lapdog *Failinis.

In the most widely known story, Lug is killed by *Mac Cuill, *Mac Cécht, and *Mac Gréine, the divine sons of Cermait, in revenge for the killing of their father. This takes places near the hill of *Uisnech; when the sons attack, Lug flees to nearby Loch Lugborta, where he drowns and is buried in a cairn on the shore. Other place-name traditions link him to *Goll mac Morna, representing either that Lug kills him or that he is killed by him. Still other stories have Lug buried at *Brug na Bóinne [Newgrange] or *Luglochta Loga [the Garden of Lug], which was the fortress of *Forgall Monach, Emer's father. Allusions to the name Lug survive in dozens of place-names, perhaps also in Lughbhadh, Co. Louth.

Lug's prominence in early Celtic culture was reflected and adapted countless times in subsequent generations. Early Christian commentators coordinated Lug, the victor over the Fomorians, with the archangel Michael, the conqueror of Lucifer; thus there are echoes of Lug as far afield as Mont St Michel in northern France, the Michaelmas festival (29 September), and the popularity of the name Michael in Ireland. A continuing allusion to Lug persists in *Lugaid, the seventh most popular name in early Ireland. Lug's persona contributes to the legends of several saints, including the twenty-eight named Mo Lua. There are also several discernible links between Lug and the Arthurian hero *Lancelot, even though many of the most ambitious claims for the Celtic origin of Arthurian characters are now dismissed. Unlike Cúchulainn and Fionn mac Cumhaill, however, Lug has not sparked extensive re-creations in English and other non-Celtic languages. Earlier commentators suggested his name was present in lugh-chorpán [little Lugh-body], an etymology for *leprechaun. The name Lug is applied to a radio delivering

Dionysian messages in Brian Friel's *Dancing at Lughnasa* (1990). See also MORVAH.

See Anon., 'Le Dieu irlandais Lug et le thème gaulois Lugu-', *Revue Celtique*, 10 (1889), 238–43; John Carey, 'Nodons in Britain and Ireland', *Zeitschrift für celtische Philologie*, 40 (1984), 1–22; Roger S. Loomis, 'The Descent of Lancelot from Lug', *Bulletin bibliographique de la Société Internationale Arthurienne*, 3 (1951), 67–73; Máire Mac Neill, *The Feast of Lughnasa* (Oxford, 1962), 1–11; Pádraig Ó Riain, 'Traces of Lug in Early Irish Hagiographical Tradition', *Zeitschrift für celtische Philologie*, 36 (1977), 138–56; Joseph Loth, 'Le Dieu Lug, la terre mère et les Lugoves', *Revue Archéologique*, 2 (1914), 205–30. Folk motifs: A141; A151.1.1.

Luga. Anglicization of both *Lugaid and *Lug.

Lugach, Lughach. A daughter of *Fionn mac Cumhaill in ballads from the *Fenian Cycle, mother of *Mac Lughach.

Lugaid, Lughaid, Lúí, Luga, Lewy [from Ir. *lug*, light]. Seventh most popular name in early Ireland, borne by countless legendary warriors, illustrious forebears in genealogies, and saints. As in other instances of many personages bearing the same name, e.g. *Ailill, the different Lugaids appear to borrow from one another's conception, the most seminal being *Lugaid mac Con, the usurper of *Munster. Additionally, the motifs of incest and *triplism occur frequently in their stories.

Lugaid 1. Warrior-poet known for his accuracy, despite his blindness. When *Ailill learns of his wife *Medb's adultery with *Fergus mac Róich, he has Lugaid kill Fergus during the lovers' swim together.

2. Variant (though masculine) form for *Lugach (fem.), the daughter of *Fionn mac Cumhaill.

Lugaid Conmac. Sometime eponym of *Connemara, in place of the usual eponymous founder, *Conmac, a by-blow of *Medb and *Fergus mac Róich. Lugaid Conmac either emanates from, or is confused with, *Lugaid mac Con.

Lugaid Lága, Lágha, Lágae, Láigne. Faithful henchman of *Lugaid mac Con who served with him through defeat, exile, and restoration of power only to abandon his king when he abdicated in favour of *Cormac mac Airt. That Lugaid Lága should have earlier slain Cormac's father, *Art mac Cuinn, seemed not to trouble the young king. Lugaid Lága later won great esteem at the court of Cormac and was once listed as one of the five great warriors of Ireland, along with *Cúchulainn, *Lug Lámfhota, *Conall Cearnach, and *Fionn mac Cumhaill. A brother of *Ailill Aulomm, he is much associated with the Glen of Aherlow, Co. Tipperary. Lugaid was the protector of *Uirne, the mother of *Bran (2) and Sceolang, after she returned to human form. Modern commentators have suggested his characterization is a local *Munster adaptation of *Lugaid mac Con. Once thought to be the father of Fenian warrior *Mac Lughach.

Lugaid Laígde, Lóigde, Loígde, Láigde, Laoighdhe. The son of *Dáire (1) who once slept with the lady of *Sovereignty. Dáire had named all his sons (usually seven, sometimes five) Lugaid in response to the prophecy that a son of his with that name would become king of Ireland. Lugaid Laígde, who sometimes bears the patronymic mac Dáire, was, like nearly all the heroes named Lugaid, an ancestor of the *Érainn of *Munster. A *druid had further predicted to Dáire that his successor would have to catch a golden *fawn which would enter the assembly. When the entourage hunted the fawn, a magic mist settled between the brothers and the other hunters, allowing Lugaid Laígde to capture it. Following this he met an ugly sorceress who offered him warmth, food, and *ale, and further invited him to lie with her. Initially he refused, at which she told him that he had deprived himself of Sovereignty. He then relented, and in the morning she was transformed into the beautiful maiden Sovereignty herself. While the sovereignty story is widely known in medieval literature, modern commentators feel that this retelling owes most to a comparable version in the story of *Niall Noígiallach [of the Nine Hostages]. Elsewhere Lugaid Laígde is recorded as having killed *Daui Ladrach to become king, and subsequently having been killed by *Áed Ruad.

Lugaid mac Casrubae. Father of the sharp-tongued *Dubthach Dóeltenga in the *Ulster Cycle. May be confused with *Lugaid Riab nDerg.

Lugaid mac Con [son of hound]. Mythical leader of the *Érainn of *Munster, to be distinguished from the similarly named *Lugaid mac Con Roí. A leading figure of the *Cycle of Kings, Lugaid mac Con suffers defeat from the *Eóganacht under his foster-brother *Eógan (3) in the Battle of *Cenn Abrat, goes into exile in Scotland, and regains power at the Battle of Mag Mucrama [*Cath Maige Mucrama]. Annalists date Lugaid's reign in the 2nd century AD, but most stories about him date from centuries later, many of them influenced by the antagonistic *Uí Néill dynasties who saw his usurpation as a cause of drought and suffering.

Lugaid gained his patronymic, mac Con, when he was suckled by a dog while being fostered in the house of *Ailill Aulomm. Also in this household was Ailill's own son, Eógan (3), a constant adversary in later life. In their first encounter, at Cenn Abrat, Eógan was triumphant; Lugaid mac Con escaped only when his *fool, Do Dera, who looked very much like him, wore a crown to impersonate him and was killed. But recognizing Lugaid's white legs as he ran, Eógan pursued him.

Lugaid escaped to Scotland with twenty-seven companions, hoping to lie low. All agreed not to reveal their leader's identity. A Scottish king generously offered them a year's hospitality but was surprised at their orderliness and prowess with no chief. Two events broke the anonymity. First a poet arrived from Ireland with news of Eógan's mistreatment of the land, causing Lugaid's pointed distress. This signalled to the Scottish king, who then devised a test; he offered Lugaid several dead mice for dinner. Being a regal guest, Lugaid did not refuse, and his men followed his example in eating the rodents. The Scottish king then asked Lugaid to admit his identity, which he did. Mightily impressed, the Scottish king then joined with Lugaid to help him regain his throne, bringing with him a host of Scotsmen and Britons that extended from the coasts of Scotland to Ireland.

At the head of this allied army, Lugaid swept all opposition before him, culminating in the Battle of Mag Mucrama. On the night before the battle Lugaid's adversary *Art mac Cuinn, who was to die the next day, conceived *Cormac mac Airt. The blind *druid *Dil foretold defeat for Eógan (3) because Eógan's cause was unjust. Going down in defeat were not only Art and Eógan but also the seven sons of Ailill.

Lugaid then ruled *Tara for seven years and took the young *Cormac mac Airt in fosterage with him. Within a few years, when Lugaid made a false judgment in the confiscation of an old woman's sheep, he was expelled and Cormac made king in his place. Returning to the home of his fosterage, Ailill Aulomm kissed Lugaid in the pretence of welcome, but Ailill's poisonous tooth touched Lugaid's cheek and within three days half his face was eaten away. Shortly after, Ailill's retainers dispatched him at a waterfall of the Bandon River.

Later accretions to Lugaid's story include an inventive etymology for his patronymic, mac Con: that his mother while bathing was impregnated by an *otter [*cú dobráin*, water-hound]; later when Lugaid suffered from sleeplessness, his otter-father cured him by taking him beneath the waves. See also LUGAID CONMAC; LUGAID LÁGA; LUGAID MAC ÍTHA.

Lugaid mac Con Roí, mac Trí Con. Son of *Cú Roí and killer of *Cúchulainn in the Ulster Cycle, to be distinguished from the similarly named *Lugaid mac Con. Although his usual patronymic identifies Lugaid as son of Cú Roí, his alternative patronymic, mac Trí Con or mac na Trí Con, means 'son of three hounds', denoting *triplism, perhaps Cú Roí, Cúchulainn, and *Conall [strong as a wolf] Cearnach. These latter 'fathers' seem odd in light of Lugaid's subsequent encounters with them. Storytellers explained Lugaid's lifelong antagonism towards Cúchulainn because of his mother *Bláithíne's adultery with the *Ulster hero. Lugaid tries to kill Cúchulainn several times before he succeeds. Once he throws his spear and misses, killing Cúchulainn's charioteer *Láeg instead. In the *Táin Bó Cuailnge* [Cattle Raid of Cooley] he is ready to attack again, but seeing Cúchulainn badly wounded from his battle with *Ferdiad at the ford, Lugaid relents. Their final combat is described in a tale often known in English as 'The Death of Cúchulainn' or *Brislech mór Maige Muirthemne* [The Great Rout of Mag Muirthemne]. Lugaid first thrusts his javelin through Cúchulainn's bowels but does not kill him. Allowing the hero a death with more dignity, Lugaid permits Cúchulainn to stand by a pillar-stone while he decapitates him. Conall Cearnach subsequently dispatches Lugaid. See Whitley Stokes, *Revue Celtique*, 3 (1887), 175–85; A. G. van Hamel, *Compert Con Culainn and Other Stories* (Dublin, 1933), 69–133; T. P. Cross and

C. H. Slover, *Ancient Irish Tales* (New York, 1936), 333–40.

Lugaid mac Dáire. Name for any of the five or seven sons of *Dáire (1), especially *Lugaid Laígde. Although initially an emanation of *Lugaid mac Con, Lugaid mac Dáire is a name cited in many medieval pedigrees and genealogies. The *Corcu Loígde claimed descent from him.

Lugaid mac Ítha. An invented name, citing the *Milesian *Íth in the patronymic, for the *Munster hero *Lugaid mac Con, for use in genealogies. Husband of *Fial (3), he founded the families from which the O'Coffeys, O'Driscolls, and others derive.

Lugaid mac Nóis. A foster-brother of *Cúchulainn in the **Táin Bó Cuailnge* [Cattle Raid of Cooley], the son of Alamiach. *Emer's father *Forgall seeks to marry her off to Lugaid, a southern king, during Cúchulainn's absence. When Lugaid learns that Cúchulainn desires Emer, he refuses to have anything further to do with her.

Lugaid mac Trí Con. See LUGAID MAC CON ROÍ.

Lugaid Réoderg, Reo-derg. See LUGAID RIAB NDERG.

Lugaid Riab nDerg, Riabhdhearg, Réoderg, Reo-derg, Lugaid Sriab nDerg [Ir., red stripes]. *Ulster Cycle king and foster-brother (sometimes foster-son) of *Cúchulainn, best remembered for his tragic marriage to *Derbforgaill (1) of *Lochlainn. Although she was smitten with Cúchulainn, he could not marry her as he had inadvertently tasted her blood while sucking out a stone that had penetrated her womb. He passed her along to Lugaid Riab nDerg, and the two of them were quite happily married. Derbforgaill suffered a grotesque death, however. Court women goaded her into a test of sexual allure by seeing which woman could send her urine furthest through a pillar of snow; when she won, they jealously mutilated and killed her. On his return Cúchulainn slaughtered 150 of the courtly women, but Lugaid died of grief or shock.

Incest is a frequent motif in Lugaid Riab nDerg's story. He was begotten when his mother *Clothra lay with her three brothers, *Finn Emna [the three Finns of Emain]. Later Lugaid lay with his mother Clothra to produce *Crimthann Nia Náir. This incest may explain his sobriquet. Some texts describe his body as divided by two red lines, separating his head from his shoulders and cutting his trunk at the belt, reflecting the contributions of his three fathers. A prosaic but common alternative is that the red stripes were battle scars.

Modern commentators have argued that Lugaid Riab nDerg was invented to fill out the cast of the Ulster Cycle, aspects of his character being borrowed from other Lugaids. Most specious is his kingship, as he never appears to rule. The Annals record that he was killed by Three Red Heads of *Leinster, an apparent contrivance to counter the three Finns [white, fair] who fathered him. See LUGAID MAC CASRUBAE. See also Carl Marstrander, *Ériu*, 5 (1911), 201–18.

Lugaid Sriab nDerg. See LUGAID RIAB NDERG.

Lugh. ModIr. spelling of *Lug.

Lughaidh. ModIr. spelling of *Lugaid.

Lughnasa (unreformed ModIr.), **Lugnasad** (OIr.), **Lughnasadh, Lúnasa** (reformed ModIr.), **Lùnasdain, Lùnasdal, Lunasduinn** (ScG), **Laa Luanistyn, Laa Luanys** (Manx); also Lammas Day, Garland Sunday, Domhnach Chrom Dubh, Crom Dubh Sunday, Bilberry Sunday, Fraughan Sunday [Ir. *Lug; *násad*, assembly, festive or commemorative gathering]. Irish, Scottish Gaelic, and Manx names for the seasonal feast of pre-Christian origin fixed at 1 August in Ireland and on the Isle of Man, the first Sunday in August or the last Sunday of July in the Gregorian calendar; in Scotland the festival is renamed in honour of St Michael, Michaelmas, 29 September. One of the four great calendar feasts of Celtic tradition along with *Samain (1 November), *Imbolc (1 February), and *Beltaine (1 May). Long a harvest festival celebrating the ripening of grain and, after they became plentiful, the maturing of potatoes, Lughnasa commemorates *Lug Lámfhota, one of the most prominent heroes of early Irish literature. Lug seems most certainly derived from *Lugos/Lugus or Gaulish *Mercury, the god described by Julius *Caesar (1st cent. BC) as the most prominent in the Gaulish pantheon. At Lug(o)dunum (Lyon), a city named for Lugos/ Lugus, a celebration was held each 1 August in honour of the Emperor Augustus. According to early Irish tradition, however, Lug himself established the festival to honour his foster-mother *Tailtiu in *Brega, modern

Co. *Meath; Lug also led the horse-racing and martial arts contests. Soon Lughnasa celebrations were held in other parts of Ireland, at *Emain Macha for *Ulster and at *Tara for the whole of the island.

The Christian Church did not oppose the continuation of the festival marking the beginning of the harvest and the weaning of calves and lambs, but the different names applied to it obscured its pagan origin. Eventually it broke away from its fixed time of 1 August and might include many days, especially Sundays, from 15 July to 15 August. Comparable but much smaller fairs, not associated with Lug or Lughnasa, were held for Calan Awst [first of August] in Wales and at *Morvah in Cornwall. Lughnasa and its counterparts provided a time for horse-racing, horse-swimming, and games of hurling. Celebrants might enjoy climbing to the tops of nearby hills, both to pray and to gather bilberries. Others would assemble at lakes and holy wells. Lughnasa fairs might also include the buying and selling of goods, especially at Killorglin in Co. Kerry, Ballycastle in Co. Antrim, Ennistymon in Co. Cavan, and elsewhere. Máire MacNeill's landmark study, *The Festival of Lughnasa* (Oxford, 1962), details the persistence and extent of celebrations. See also Pádraig Ó Riain, 'Traces of Lug in Early Irish Hagiographical Tradition', *Zeitschrift für celtische Philologie*, 36 (1977), 138–56; T. J. Westropp, 'Marriages of the Gods at the Sanctuary of Tailltiu', *Folk-Lore*, 31 (1920), 109–41. Brian Friel's drama *Dancing at Lughnasa* (1990) draws thematically on festival traditions.

Luglochta Loga, Luglocht Logo [garden/cradle of Lug*]. Fortress belonging to *Forgall Monach at Lusca, coextensive with the village of Lusk, Co. Dublin. *Cúchulainn goes a-wooing here in the **Táin Bó Cuailnge* [Cattle Raid of Cooley].

Lugna [dim. of *Lug]. King of *Connacht who fostered the infant *Cormac mac Airt. After *Étaín (2) became pregnant by *Art mac Cuinn, she was instructed to have the child fostered by Lugna. When she delivered the baby boy, he was first taken by a she-wolf before Lugna assumed his responsibilities.

Lugnasad. Preferred OIr. form of *Lughnasa.

Lugos, Lugus, Lugoves (pl.) [raven (?)]. Probable actual name of the god the Romans called Gaulish *Mercury. The name survives in inscriptions found in Avenches, Switzerland, and is implicit in the Roman town name Lug[u]dunum, the basis of the modern Lyon, Laon, Leiden, Loudon, Liegnitz, Léon, Dinlleu, and Luguvalium, antecedent of Carlisle. He would also be the Gaulish counterpart of Irish *Lug Lámfhota and the Welsh *Lleu Llaw Gyffes. Another possible name for Mercury is *Erriapus. See E. van Tassel Graves, 'Lugus, The Commercial Traveller', *Ogam*, 17 (1965), 165–71; A. Zooa, 'The God *Lugus* in Spain', *Bulletin of the Board of Celtic Studies*, 29 (1980–2), 201–29.

Lúí. ModIr. spelling of *Lugaid.

luideag [ScG dim of *luid*, rag, slovenly person]. Murderous female demon of Scottish Gaelic oral tradition, related to the fearful *athach. Squalid in appearance as she was evil, the luideag haunted several pools on the Isle of *Skye, especially the Lochan of the Black Trout. Folk motifs: G11.3; G346.2.

Lúin, Luin [OIr. *lúin*, lance]. One of the most famous spears of early Irish literature, belonging most often to *Celtchar. To quench its thirst for blood, Lúin had to be dipped in a cauldron containing 'black fluid' or 'poison' from time to time; otherwise its shaft would burst into flame. *Mac Cécht uses it to kill *Cúscraid. *Dubthach Dóeltenga borrows it for **Cath Maige Tuired* [The (Second) Battle of Mag Tuired] but loses it soon after.

Lùnasdal, Lùnasdain, Lùnasdainn. ScG forms of *Lughnasa.

Luned [cf. W *eilun*, idol, icon, image]. Maiden who helps Owain overcome the Lord of the Fountain, her father, in the 13th-century prose romance **Owain*. The French and English Arthurian figure in **Yvain* and elsewhere, Lunete, Lynete, Lynette, etc., appears to be derived from her.

luprachán, luprecan, lúracán, lurgadán, lurikeen. Variant spellings of *leprechaun.

Luxovius [L *lux*, light]. Latin name for an ancient Continental god known from only one site, at the thermal spring sanctuary of Luxeuil in the Saône valley of eastern France. By his name and placement, Luxovius appears to embody a Celtic linking of light and water symbolism. His consort is Brixia or Bricta. At the same shrine is evidence for the worship of *Sirona, another deity of healing springs, and a sky-horseman bearing a solar wheel. See Émile Espériandieu, 'Le Dieu Cavalier du Luxeuil', *Revue Archéologique*, 70 (1917), 72–86.

Lydney Park. Romano-British shrine (3rd cent. AD) high on the precipitous west bank of the Severn River, 8 miles NE of Chepstow, Gloucestershire; the most important native dedication of such a place of worship to be found in all of Britain. Though no physical depictions of him survive, the shrine has long been thought to have centred on the cult of *Nodons, a British healing god often compared with the Irish *Nuadu Airgetlám. Situated in the Forest of Dean, the shrine is a large complex, much like classical sanctuaries of healing, with a long portico like a cloister divided into compartments to accommodate patients. Luxurious details in construction, such as the mosaic floors, testify to the wealth of the society that constructed and maintained the shrine. R. E. M. and T. V. Wheeler, *Report on the Excavations . . . in Lydney Park, Gloucestershire* (London, 1932).

M

M. The thirteenth letter of the modern English alphabet is represented by muin [vine] in the *ogham alphabet of early Ireland.

mab, mab- [W, son, boy]. Prefix used in Welsh patronymics; mutated forms: ap, ap-; fab, fab-; vab, vab-. Cf. Irish and Scottish *mac, mac-. See T. J. Morgan and R. Morgan, *Welsh Surnames* (Cardiff, 1985).

Mabinogi, *Mabinogion* [W, a tale of youth (?); see also MAPONOS, divine youth]. The preferred form, *Mabinogi*, is an abbreviation of the title *Pedair Cainc y Mabinogi* [Four Branches of the Mabinogi], namely the tales *Pwyll*, *Branwen*, *Manawydan*, and *Math*, which together form the masterwork of medieval Welsh literature. The form *Mabinogion*, first used by Lady Charlotte Guest in her three-volume translation, 1838–49, and also in the more authoritative translation of Gwyn and Thomas Jones (1949), has wide currency in English; it denotes twelve tales, not only the four branches of the *Mabinogi* but also **Culhwch ac Olwen*, **Breuddwyd Macsen Wledig* [The Dream of Macsen Wledig], **Cyfranc Lludd a Llefelys* [The Meeting/Adventure of Lludd and Llefelys], **Breuddwyd Rhonabwy* [The Dream of Rhonabwy], and stories of *Geraint, *Owain, *Peredur, and *Taliesin. The *Pedair Cainc y Mabinogi*, while drawing from extensive oral tradition and only loosely connected internally, was put together, possibly by a single hand, before the mid-12th century. The two surviving complete manuscripts are found in the **White Book of Rhydderch* and the **Red Book of Hergest*, while fragments survive in pre-15th century collections.

Part I. Pwyll, Prince of Dyfed. The first branch deals with Pwyll [W, wisdom, reason], prince or ruler of *Dyfed, a peninsula of southwestern Wales, his adventures in the *Otherworld, his marriage to *Rhiannon, and the birth of their son *Pryderi. The action begins one day when Pwyll is hunting near Glyn Cuch [glen scowl] and becomes separated from his companions. He sees a pack of hounds, not his own, running down a *stag; they are snow white with red ears, colours indicating otherworldliness. Just as he is about to drive them off, their owner appears and reproaches Pwyll for his discourtesy. The stranger's name is *Arawn, a king of *Annwfn; he speaks of being harried by a rival king, *Hafgan [summer white], and suggests that Pwyll can redeem himself by meeting Hafgan in a single combat in a year's time. Under the plan he suggests, Pwyll and Arawn will exchange shapes and kingdoms for a year. At the end, Pwyll in the shape of Arawn will have to lay Hafgan low with a single blow—because a second would allow him to revive.

Pwyll agrees to the adventure, although he does not realize what a year's imposture will entail. He is a wise and good ruler of Annwfn, but he has overlooked his obligations to Arawn's beautiful wife. When the time comes for them to go to bed together, Pwyll sets his face to the wall, says nothing, and does not so much as touch the wife, much to her surprise and disappointment. None the less, Pwyll is courteous to the wife in public during the day. In a year's time Pwyll meets Hafgan in a combat at a river ford. In one bold stroke, Pwyll and Arawn splits Hafgan's shield and knock him the length of an arm and a shield over his horse's rump. In deathly bravado, Hafgan asks for another blow to finish him off, but Pwyll remembers that he has been told he would regret a second blow. Arawn's men rejoice that his kingdom is now united. Pwyll then returns to Glyn Cuch, where he greets Arawn. The two kings thank each other for their stewardship and resume their own kingdoms in their own shapes. When Pwyll makes love that night to his own wife (not named), he is impressed to learn that Arawn has kept his part of the bargain and has remained celibate. Arawn has also been a just ruler in Pwyll's absence. As a reward, the mortal king acquires a new title: Pwyll Pen Annwfn [ruler of Annwfn].

Some time later Pwyll is sitting on a

magical mound named *Arberth. It was thought that those who sat on the mound would have a strange adventure—perhaps to see a wonder. Pwyll is not disappointed; he soon sees a woman dressed in brilliant gold brocade mounted on a majestic pale white horse. Neither he nor any of his men can determine her name. They set out to pursue her, but she is too fast for them; on a fourth attempt he speaks to her. Identifying herself as Rhiannon, daughter of Hyfaidd Hen, she says that she has been looking for him, lamenting that she is betrothed to another man against her will when she loves only Pwyll. Then Pwyll assents that he now loves only her as well. They agree to meet at a marriage feast a year from that night. When the year elapses, Pwyll arrives with a hundred men and begins the wedding feast at Rhiannon's father's palace. Shortly a tall, auburn-haired stranger, dressed in satin, with regal bearing, enters and asks a favour of Pwyll. To Rhiannon's chagrin he grants it, for the stranger is *Gwawl, her other suitor, and he is seeking her hand now. Pwyll is bound by the honour of his word, but Rhiannon will not marry Gwawl before another year has passed. Meanwhile, Rhiannon gives Pwyll a magical bag and tells him to make good use of it when the time comes. When a year has passed, another great wedding feast is held, this time with Gwawl in the place of honour. As the company is making merry, an old beggar clad in rags and clumsy shoes enters, asking a boon of Gwawl. All he needs is to have his bag filled with food. Gwawl cheerfully consents, but no matter how much food an attendant puts in the bag, it will not fill up. The bag cannot be filled, the beggar says, until a man wealthy in treasure and land gets in the bag and stamps it down with his feet. Rhiannon encourages Gwawl to check the voracity of the bag. Gwawl has only put his two feet in when the beggar, now revealed to be Pwyll, draws the bag over Gwawl's head and ties it. Pwyll then blows his horn and invites the other revellers to join him in a game of 'badger in the bag', using Gwawl as the bagged badger, striking and kicking him about the hall. When Gwawl agrees not to seek revenge, he is released and Pwyll and Rhiannon are happily married.

Some time later, after a period of barrenness, Rhiannon gives birth to a child who mysteriously disappears before the dawn of the next morning. The women of the household, fearing they will be punished, contrive to make it appear that Rhiannon has killed her own son. Pwyll will not put his wife away but instead agrees that she should be punished by sitting every day by the horse-block at the gate of the castle. She must tell her tale to every passing stranger and offer to carry them on her back.

Across Wales in *Gwent Is Coed, there lives a lord named *Teyrnon Twrf Liant, who raises horses. His prize mare foals every *Calan Mai [May Day], but no one knows what becomes of the offspring. One year Teyrnon determines to know the reason. On the night of the foaling he is waiting in the horse barn when a great, clawed arm comes through the window. Smiting off the arm at the elbow, he rushes outside to see what is behind it. As it is dark he can see nothing, but when he returns to the barn he finds an infant boy wrapped in a mantle of satin. Having no other children, Teyrnon and his wife raise the boy as their own, calling him *Gwri of the Golden Hair. The boy grows rapidly until Teyrnon and his wife recognize that he greatly resembles Pwyll. They take him to Pwyll's castle, where there is great rejoicing and Rhiannon is released from her undeserved punishment. Now that the son has been returned to his rightful parents he is named *Pryderi.

Part II. Branwen, Daughter of Llŷr. Despite its title, this tale deals more with the children of *Llŷr, the Welsh sea-god. In the family are *Bendigeidfran (or Bran [crow/raven?] the Blessed), his brave brother *Manawydan, and their beautiful sister *Branwen, as well as two half-brothers born of the same mother, malevolent *Efnisien and gentle Nisien. Branwen is forced into a marriage of convenience with *Matholwch, king of Ireland. After Efnisien has insulted Matholwch, a war ensues between the children of Llŷr and the Irish. Branwen dies and Bendigeidfran is killed, but his severed head is buried in London.

At the beginning of the action Bendigeidfran is made king of the Island of the Mighty (Britain) with his court and family at Harlech. While sitting on a nearby rock one day, Bendigeidfran sees thirteen ships coming from Ireland with a fair wind. They bring Matholwch, king of Ireland, seeking to make an alliance. Bendigeidfran and Manawydan agree to marry Branwen to Matholwch without her consultation. Initially all goes well. A great celebration is held in a tent because

Bendigeidfran cannot fit into a building. The next day Efnisien expresses his displeasure at not being asked for his permission by mutilating Matholwch's horses, cutting their lips, ears, and tails. When Matholwch seems astounded by this, Bendigeidfran explains that the deed was only a whim of his ill-natured half-brother and makes up the loss, horse for horse, adding gold and silver gifts. Most importantly, Bendigeidfran gives Matholwch a *cauldron of regeneration that will restore slain warriors to life overnight. Bendigeidfran explains that he has received the cauldron from *Llassar Llaes Gyfnewid, who had escaped from a fiery iron house in Ireland with his wife, *Cymidei Cymeinfoll. Matholwch acknowledges having heard of the story, and returns home with his entourage and bride.

During Branwen's first year as queen of Ireland she is loved and acclaimed, and she produces a son named *Gwern. In the second year, Matholwch's brothers incite him to seek revenge for Efnisien's old insult, and so Branwen is reduced to being a cook and her ears are boxed each day. When in three years no travellers carry this news back to Wales, Branwen trains a starling to take the news home for her. Upon reading her letter Bendigeidfran immediately prepares a great army to invade Ireland; the men go in ships, but Bendigeidfran is so huge that he is obliged to wade across. The Irish are befuddled by Bendigeidfran's size, but Branwen knows that her brother has come to save her.

The Irish flee across the River *Shannon and destroy the only bridge after them. This prompts Bendigeidfran to make of himself a human bridge, allowing his men to cross on his back. To make amends for misusing Branwen, Matholwch and the Irish offer to build a house big enough to hold Bendigeidfran. But in it they put a peg in each of a hundred columns, and from each of the pegs they hang a bag containing an armed warrior. The foul-mouthed Efnisien, making himself useful for once, asks the Irishmen what is in the bags. Hearing that they are filled with flour, he squeezes each bag until he has killed every warrior. But because of their ruse, the Irish cannot acknowledge their dead.

That night there is feasting shared by the Welsh and the Irish. The Irish confer their sovereignty on Gwern, Branwen and Matholwch's son. Both Welsh and Irish love the boy, all except Efnisien, who in a fit of jealousy thrusts Gwern headlong into the fire. Fighting erupts, with slaughter on both sides. Efnisien sees that the Irish plan to regenerate their dead in the cauldron, and so he hides himself among their corpses. When he is cast in the cauldron he stretches out and breaks it in four ways—and bursts his own heart as well.

In the end all the Irishmen are slain, and all the Welshmen perish except for seven, including *Pryderi, Manawydan, and Bendigeidfran, who is later mortally wounded with a poisoned spear in his heel. Bendigeidfran asks that his head be struck off and taken to Gwyn Fryn, facing France, where it will always provide protection for the Island of the Mighty. Along the way the head will provide company, uncorrupted, both at Harlech and at *Gwales. On her landing in Britain, Branwen can still see Ireland when she cries out, 'Dear Son of God—alas that I was born! Two good islands have been destroyed because of me.' At this she sighs deeply and her heart breaks.

In Ireland only five pregnant women survive, each bearing sons. After each is born he mates with different mothers, to produce the tribes who will become the five provinces of Ireland.

Part III. Manawydan, Son of Llŷr. The third branch continues the action of the second and borrows characters from the first. Manawydan and Rhiannon, Pryderi and *Cigfa all play leading roles in locales from south-western Wales to England. There is much magic in this branch, but also portrayals of the lives of tradesmen and the mock execution of a mouse.

After Pryderi and Manawydan have fled from Ireland in *Branwen*, they decide to live in Dyfed, where Pryderi is lord of seven cantrefs. He decides to ask his still-beautiful mother, Rhiannon, to marry Manawydan, while he chooses Cigfa for himself. The four live pleasantly in prosperous surroundings, until one night when they are at *Arberth after a feast; a mysterious mist suddenly overcomes them and leaves the land desolate. Initially they are able to support themselves hunting game until Manawydan speaks of his discontent and suggests they all move to Lloegyr [England], where they earn their living at trades. They turn to leather goods, making saddles, shields, and shoes of the highest quality, so that competitors can no longer sell their wares. The other tradesmen angrily seek to bring them harm, but each time Manawydan argues that they should go quietly and not cause trouble. At last they resolve to return to Dyfed and to live by hunting as before.

One day a gleaming white wild *boar charges them and is subsequently chased by their dogs. When the boar makes for a fort, the dogs follow. Pryderi, against Manawydan's advice, also enters the fort. Chiding Manawydan for allowing her son to enter what is probably an enchanted place, Rhiannon goes in search of Pryderi. Inside she finds him clinging to a bowl, unable to speak. Rhiannon too seizes the bowl, and the same fate befalls her. Shortly after, the fort disappears in a thunder-clap. Cigfa weeps to see her husband gone, but Manawydan reassures her that he will be a helpful companion for her. And, like Pwyll in Part I, he is a chaste respecter of a woman's vows to another man.

As a celibate couple, Manawydan and Cigfa go again to England and resume the trade of shoemaking. Once again Manawydan is a success, but the jealousy of English shoemakers forces the couple to return to Dyfed, where they fish and hunt before tilling the soil in three crofts sown with wheat. Before Manawydan can bring in a harvest, the first croft is devastated. The next night the second croft is ruined. Determined to get at the bottom of the mystery, Manawydan keeps watch on the third croft. When he sees an enormous host of mice ravaging the field, he catches one and announces that he will hang it. Cigfa objects that it is unseemly for Manawydan to trouble himself about vermin, but he retorts that he will murder them all if he can catch them. The next day Manawydan takes the mouse to a mound at Arberth for the execution, but before he can complete the task he is interrupted by three travellers, the first strangers he has seen in seven years. All argue that it is undignified to kill such a lowly beast as a mouse. The first traveller, a shabbily dressed scholar, offers a ransom of one pound. The second, a priest, offers a ransom of three pounds. The third, a bishop, offers a ransom of seven pounds, and when that is not enough, twenty-four pounds, and then his horses and seven loads of baggage and seven horses to pull the loads. When Manawydan still will not yield, the bishop asks whatever else he might want. 'The release of Rhiannon and Pryderi,' Manawydan begins, 'and the removal of the magic enchantment from the seven cantrefs of Dyfed.' The bishop admits that he will pay such a price because the mouse is his transformed pregnant wife. He and his family have been harassing Dyfed because the 'bishop' is really Llwyd, son of Cil Coed, a friend of Gwawl, whom Pwyll, Pryderi's father, has humiliated with the game of 'badger-in-the-bag' in Part I. The entrapment of Pryderi and Rhiannon plus the enchantment of Dyfed and the devastation of the crops were all forms of revenge. When Llwyd promises never to trouble Dyfed again, Manawydan releases the mouse, who is immediately transformed into the fairest young woman anyone has ever seen. Everything is restored and Rhiannon and Manawydan, Pryderi and Cigfa return to their former happiness.

Part IV. Math, Son of Mathonwy. The last branch is far and away the most complex, combining mythological, magical, and human elements. While the story is filled with abrupt transitions, it is usually the most appealing to a modern reader. Part of its attraction is the array of arresting characters, including the enchanter *Gwydion, the adulterous *Blodeuedd, and the heroic *Lleu Llaw Gyffes.

Math son of Mathonwy is the lord of *Gwynedd in the north and Pryderi is the ruler of the south, not only of Dyfed but also of portions of *Morgannwg, *Ceredigion, and *Ystrad Tywi. In Math's household are two nephews, Gwydion and *Gilfaethwy. As he has supernatural powers, Gwydion can discern that his brother is smitten with the beautiful *Goewin, a girl whose ceremonial duty is to hold the feet of the king, unless he be away for war. Gwydion proposes a complicated plan to allow Gilfaethwy to be with his heart's desire-part of which requires Math to go to war and leave his foot-holder behind. Gwydion promises to obtain some of the swine of Pryderi, animals new to the kingdom, whose meat is reputed to be sweeter than beef. With ten companions he sets off for Dyfed disguised as a *bard. Although this charms Pryderi, the king will not give up his swine until he has received comparable exchange. Gwydion conjures up twelve phantom steeds and twelve phantom hounds and then leaves immediately with his prizes. When the ruse fades the next morning, the two petty kingdoms are at war. This allows Gilfaethwy his moment with Goewin, but she is unwilling and he forces his affections on her dishonourably. The war is settled when Gwydion meets Pryderi in a single combat and kills him.

Shortly after this, Goewin confesses to Math that she is no longer a maiden. In response Math marries Goewin to save her from shame, but expresses his anger with the brothers Gilfaethwy and Gwydion, changing them successively into a pair of *deer, pigs, and wolves. Their sexes are changed as well. At the end of the first year as a hind and *stag they produce the fawn Hyddwn [little stag]. As a boar and sow they give birth to Hychdwn Hir [tall piglet]. As wolf and bitch they are parents to Bleiddwn [wolf cub]. After the three-year transformation, the two brothers resume their human form, are cleansed and anointed, and rejoin the court.

The need then arises for another virgin foot-holder. Gwydion suggests his sister, Arianrhod. But when put to Math's magical test of virginity, Arianrhod fails, and in the process gives birth to two sons. *Dylan, sturdy and golden-haired, immediately leaves for the sea and takes the sea's nature. The other infant is seized by Gwydion and nurtured under protection. When Gwydion takes the child to his mother, Arianrhod is angered to see this exposer of her deception. She upbraids Gwydion for bringing the child and says she will prevent its getting a name until she decides on an appropriate one herself. But later, while Gwydion has the boy in disguise as a shoemaker, Arianrhod admires the youngster's ability to throw a stone accurately and calls him Lleu Llaw Gyffes [light/ fair one of the sure/steady hand]. Angered at Gwydion's deception, Arianrhod says that Lleu cannot have weapons until she gives them to him. But when her palace appears threatened, she does indeed give weapons to the boy. Angered a third time, Arianrhod declares that Lleu cannot have a wife of any race on this earth. Gwydion and Math then contrive a wife from flowers and name her *Blodeuedd [flower face]. She and Lleu are immediately attracted to one another, and make love on the first night.

Math and Gwydion help the couple establish a household in the far cantref of Dinoding. Lleu and Blodeuedd live happily for a short while until he returns for a stay at Math's court. In the interim a hunter named *Gronw Pebyr stops nearby, and when he and Blodeuedd first see each other they fall deeply in love. As with her husband, Blodeuedd is quick to go to bed with her paramour. Knowing that their love is endangered, the adulterers feel they must kill Lleu Llaw Gyffes before he discovers. Wary of Lleu's near-invulnerability, Blodeuedd, feigning an interest in his welfare, asks him how he may be killed. Although most weapons cannot harm him, Lleu foolishly admits that he can be killed by a spear made over a year's time while most people are at prayer-and then only if it is thrown at him while he is bathing in a special kind of tub and one of his feet touches a billy-*goat. Blodeuedd and Gronw Pebyr then meet all the conditions. When Gronw Pebyr tries to pierce the hero, Lleu Llaw Gyffes utters a horrible scream, takes flight in the shape of an *eagle, and flies out of sight. Gronw Pebyr then adds Lleu's castle and lands to his own.

Math and Gwydion are depressed and anxious when they hear the news of adultery and attempted murder. With great difficulty they find Lleu Llaw Gyffes in eagle shape. Gwydion touches the eagle with his magician's wand and restores Lleu to human shape, finding him distressingly thin and weak. Gwydion also finds Blodeuedd and, to shame her, changes her into an owl, condemning her never again to show her face to the light. Gronw Pebyr offers retribution for the attempted murder, and Lleu asks to return whatever blow was given to him. Although Gronw Pebyr is allowed to hide behind a stone, Lleu Llaw Gyffes's thrust of the spear is so great as to pierce both the stone and the adulterer's back, killing him instantly. Lleu Llaw Gyffes regains possession of his land and rules it successfully. Thus end the four branches of the *Mabinogi*.

Standard text in Welsh: Ifor Williams, *Pedeir Keinc y Mabinogi* (Caerdydd [Cardiff], 1930; rev. 1959); R. L. Thomson, *Pwyll Pendeuic Dyuet* (Dublin, 1957); Derick S. Thomson, *Branwen Uerch Lyr* (Dublin, 1961).

Translations: Gwyn Jones and Thomas Jones, *The Mabinogion* (London, 1949); Jeffrey Gantz, *The Mabinogion* (Harmondsworth, 1976); Patrick K. Ford, *The Mabinogi and Other Medieval Welsh Tales* (Berkeley and Los Angeles, 1977); Sionas Davies, *The Four Branches of the Mabinogi* (Llanysul, UK, 1993).

Commentary: Edward Anwyl, 'The Four Branches of the Mabinogi', *Zeitschrift für celtische Philologie*, 1 (1896), 277–93; 2 (1898), 124–33; 3 (1900), 123–34; Catherine E. Byfield, 'Character and Conflict in *The Four Branches of the Mabinogi*', *Bulletin of the Board of Celtic Studies*, 40 (1993), 51–72; T. M. Charles-Edwards, 'The Date of the Four Branches of the Mabinogi', *Transactions of the Honourable Society of Cymmrodorion* (1970), 263–98; W. J. Gruffydd, *Math vab Mathonwy* (Cardiff, 1928); *Rhiannon* (Cardiff, 1953); *Folklore and Myth in the Mabinogion* (Cardiff, 1958); Pierre Yves Lambert, *Les Quatre Branches du Mabinogi et autres contes gallois du Moyen ge* (Paris, 1993); Proinsias MacCana, *Branwen Daughter of Lly^r* (Cardiff, 1958); *The Mabinogi* (1st edn., Cardiff, 1977; 2nd edn., 1992); Kenneth H. Jackson, *The International Popular Tale and Early Welsh Tradition* (Cardiff, 1961); Glyn E. Jones, 'The Mabinogi', in A. O. H. Jarman and G. H. Hughes (eds.), *Guide to Welsh Literature*, i (Swansea, 1976), 189–202; Charles W. Johnson (ed.), *Mabinogi: A Book of Essays* (New York, 1996).

See also Evangeline Walton's 4-vol. fantasy fiction retellings, *The Prince of Annwn* [pt. i] (New York, 1974); *The Children of Llyr* [pt. ii] (New York, 1971); *The Song of Rhiannon* [pt. iii] (New York, 1972); *The Virgin and the Swine* [pt. iv] (Chicago, 1936), later known as *The Island of the Mighty* (New York, 1970).

Mabon [youth (?); young god (?)]. Young man stolen from his mother, *Modron, when he was three nights old whom Culhwch is commanded to rescue in **Culhwch ac Olwen*. It is *Arthur, however, with the aid of animal wisdom, who finds him in prison in Gloucester. The Welsh *Triads describe him as one of the Three Exalted Prisoners, along with *Gwair, of the Isle of Britain. Later, in the hunting of *Twrch Trwyth, Mabon succeeds in retrieving the razor from behind the ear of the *boar. Only he can hunt the *dog Drudwyn. In a poem from the **Black Book of Carmarthen*, Mabon is named a servant of *Uthr Bendragon/Uther Pendragon. Learned commentators have long agreed that Mabon is derived from *Maponos [divine youth], a Celtic god of Roman-occupied Britain and *Gaul often linked to *Apollo, just as his mother Modron is derived from *Matrona, eponym of the Marne River. The name Mabon also appears elsewhere in early Welsh history and literature; of these, Mabon vab Mellt [son of lightning] is a doublet of Mabon son of Modron, while Mabon-Agrain (also Mabuz) is an Arthurian figure derived from him. W. J. Gruffydd argued (1958) that Mabon may be identified with or at least parallels *Pryderi (or Gwair) of the **Mabinogi*. See W. J. Gruffydd, *Folklore and Myth in the Mabinogion* (Cardiff, 1958); Rachel Bromwich, *Trioedd Ynys Prydain*, rev. edn. (Cardiff, 1978), 433–6, 557.

mac, mac- [Ir., ScG, son, son of]. First word of early Irish and Scottish Gaelic patronymics, e.g. Conchobar mac Nessa. When the mac- is lower- case, the patronymic is not a family name: Conchobar is not 'Mr mac Nessa'. Such figures are alphabetized under their given names, 'C' for Conchobar. Mac- is capitalized in two instances: (1) when it is the first element in the only name by which a personage is known, e.g. Mac Cécht; (2) when patronymics became family names under English influence, e.g. Macpherson. See also AP-; FAB; *MAB-; UA; UÍ; *VAB-.

Mac Cécht, Cecht **1.** [Ir., son of the plough]. King/warrior of the *Tuatha Dé Danann who, along with his brothers *Mac Cuill and *Mac Gréine, kills *Lug Lámfhota. Killer also of *Mechi, son of the *Mórrígan. Probably a euhemerization of the healing god *Dian Cécht, Mac Cécht is also the consort of *Fódla, an incarnation of Ireland. After the death of *Nuadu Airgetlám, Mac Cécht and his two brothers take the king's body for burial at *Ailech in Co. *Donegal. While there the three brothers decide to divide Ireland among themselves and ask the *Milesian *Íth, a stranger who has just arrived, to give judgement. Suspicious of Íth's pronouncements, the brothers kill him, prompting the Milesian invasion of Ireland. Mac Cécht is killed by *Éremón.

2. A champion of *Conaire Mór who joins his king on his fateful last journey in **Togail Bruidne Da Derga* [The Destruction of Da Derga's Hostel]. In a variant text it is Mac Cécht not *Conall Cearnach who takes the king's golden cup to search for water when he is thirsty.

Mac Cuill, Guill [Ir., son of *hazel]. A king/warrior of the *Tuatha Dé Danann, best remembered as the first of the three brothers who kill the hero *Lug Lámfhota, along with *Mac Cécht (1) and *Mac Gréine, in revenge for Lug's having killed their father, *Cermait. Often described as the husband of *Banba, an incarnation of *Ireland. In Christian Irish tradition Mac Cuill is portrayed as a champion of paganism against St *Patrick. Muirchú's Life of Patrick (7th cent.) describes the saint, with superior magical power, converting Mac Cuill to Christianity and setting him adrift, as a penance, in a rudderless, oarless coracle which bears him to the Isle of *Man, where he becomes a missionary. From the episode evolved the persona of St *Maughold of Manx tradition.

Mac Da Thó's Pig. See SCÉLA MUCCE MEIC DA THÓ [The Story of Mac Da Thó's Pig].

Mac Gréine, Gréne [Ir., son of the sun]. Sometimes also Cethor. King/warrior of the *Tuatha Dé Danann who, with brothers *Mac Cuill and Mac Cécht (1), kills *Lug Lámfhota. Possibly a euhemerized sun-god, he is also the usual consort of *Ériu, an incarnation of Ireland. He was killed by *Amairgin. Least cited of the three brothers, he has little other mythology of his own.

Mac Guill. Corrupt spelling of *Mac Cuill.

Mac-ind-Óg. See ANGUS ÓG.

Mac Lughach, Lughaid(h), Lewy; also known as Gaoine or Caol; sometimes with the epithet 'of the Terrible Hand'. Grandson of *Fionn mac Cumhaill and known for laziness, he does not appear in *Fenian literature until the 12th century. In one early text he is described as the son of *Lugaid Lága, but he is usually seen as the son of Fionn's daughter *Lugach. Trained by *Mongfhind (2), he initially shows little prowess and gets on poorly with fellow students. He later shows great strength and musicianship. Fionn's advice to him is cited widely in Fenian literature: never to meddle with a fool, and to be gentle with women, servants, poets, and the common people. He is thought to have planted the stones of Ireland in memory of his first love, Tuadh. In later texts Mac Lughach is one of Fionn's closest compatriots.

Mac Óc, Óg. Patronymics of *Angus Óg.

Macc Óc. See ANGUS ÓG.

Macgnímartha Finn, *Macghníomhartha Finn, Macgnímrada Finn.* Irish titles for the medieval *Fenian narrative known in English as The Boyhood Deeds of Fionn or The Youthful Exploits of Fionn. Incomplete texts evince influences from comparable stories of the boyhood of *Cúchulainn. After being reared in hiding, the youthful Fionn, then called Demne, goes through a series of adventures to prepare him for a career as a great chief. These include his winning of the *salmon of wisdom, his earning of his name when he is called Fionn [fair-haired one] during an athletic contest, and the attainment of his sword, his banner, and his aegis. Most mysteriously, he also acquires the *crane bag [*corrbolg*], implicitly the beginnings of Irish writing. Capping his adventures, he overcomes *Goll mac Morna to become unchallenged chief of the *Fianna, and then goes to *Tara to slay *Aillén the burner. See Kuno Meyer, 'Boyish Exploits of Finn', *Ériu*, 1 (1904), 180–90. See also Joseph Falaky Nagy, *The Wisdom of the Outlaw* (Berkeley, Calif., 1985). James Stephens adapts many of Fionn's boyhood adventures in his *Irish Fairy Tales* (London, 1920).

Macha. Irish *otherworldly woman with three identities and multiple associations. She may have originally been a goddess of the land; see ANA. Her associations with war link her to *Badb and *Mórrígan; as a trio they are called *Mórrígna. An association with horses suggests a derivation from *Epona (or euhemerization from another, unnamed horse-goddess) as well as links to *Rhiannon. Her high status in *Ulster implies that she may have been a *sovereignty goddess. While there are three Machas for purposes of storytelling, they may all derive from a single persona; each is attributed the same mother, *Ernmass. Georges Dumézil has argued that this provides a model for tripartite division (see TRIPLISM); see 'Le Trio des Macha', *Revue de l'Histoire des Religions*, 146 (1954), 5–17. T. F. O'Rahilly (1946) thought there was but one Macha with three attributed husbands. *Cúchulainn's horse *Liath Macha [grey of Macha] could, for example, be named for any of the three Machas. *Emain Macha may be named for any of the three. All may also take the form of a *crow. See also Françoise Le Roux and Christian-J. Guyonvarc'h, *La Souveraineté guerrière de l'Irlande: Mórrígan, Bodb, Macha* (Rennes, 1983).

Macha 1. Wife of *Nemed the invader in **Lebor Gabála* [Book of Invasions]. Although she is not richly characterized there, the text claims that she gives her name to *Emain Macha; she also gives her name to *Armagh [Ard Macha]. Congruent with Dumézil's theory, she is a prophetess.

2. Also called Mong Ruadh, Mongroe [Ir., red-haired]. The Ulster queen who marries her rival, *Cimbáeth, and dominates him. Macha is heir to the throne as the daughter of one of three kings, *Áed Ruad, *Díthorba, and Cimbáeth, who have agreed to serve in successive seven-year reigns. When Áed, her

father, drowns at *Assaroe, the others refuse her claim to the throne. When Díthorba dies (in some accounts, at Macha's hand) she denies the throne to his five sons and routs them in battle. She then marries Cimbáeth, but knows that her claim on the queenship is not secure. Going to *Connacht in disguise as a leper, she comes upon Cimbáeth's sons roasting a pig and joins them at dinner. Implying that she is sexually available, she leads them one by one into a wood where they expect to lie with her. Instead, she overpowers each one of them, ties them up, and drags them back to Ulster, where she sets them to building a noble fortress in her honour. She names it eo-muin because she marks out its perimeter with a clasp [*eo*] about her neck [*muin*]. Fulfilling Dumézil's schema, Macha (2) is a warrior.

3. The wife of *Crunniuc mac Agnomain who gives birth during a horse-race and brings the noínden [debility/birth pangs] to *Ulster. She appears one day to a wealthy, widowed farmer, Crunniuc, and begins keeping house for him. Before the first nightfall she has made a *sunwise ritual right-hand turn ensuring good fortune, before entering his bed. Soon he grows more prosperous because of their union, and she becomes pregnant by him. Crunniuc announces that he wants to go to the great assembly of the Ulstermen, but Macha warns him not to speak of her there. Not heeding her, he watches *Conchobar mac Nessa's chariots racing and immediately boasts that his wife can outrun them all. Stung by these words, the king has Crunniuc seized and demands that he prove his claim. Macha protests that she is pregnant, but to defend her husband, agrees. As she does she shouts that her name is Macha, daughter of Sainrith mac Imbaith [strange son of the ocean], and that a perpetual evil will descend upon Ulster because of this affair. Crunniuc's boast turns out to be justified, as she beats all horses easily, but as she crosses the finishing line she cries out in pain and gives birth to twins [Ir. *emain*], thus naming the spot Emain Macha [the twins of Macha], the capital of Ulster. In her crying out she also curses all who hear her, and all their descendants unto nine times nine generations, that they will suffer the pangs or debility [Ir. *noínden*] of childbirth for five days and four nights at the time of their greatest difficulty. Thus do the Ulstermen suffer, with three exceptions: small boys, women, and Cúchulainn because he is a son and avatar of the divine *Lug Lámfhota; he will later be required to defend Ulster single-handedly. In Dumézil's analysis, Macha (3) is the telluric goddess who brings fruitfulness and increase. See J. F. Killeen, 'The Debility of the Ulstermen: A Suggestion', *Zeitschrift für celtische Philologie*, 33 (1974), 81–6. See also TLACHTGA.

Macpherson, James (1736–96). Scottish 'translator' whose *Poems of Ossian* (1760–3), based in part on Gaelic oral tradition, purported to be a lost Celtic epic. Although titled *Poems*, Macpherson's work is in prose and was published serially under three titles, *Fragments of Ancient Poetry collected in the Highlands of Scotland* (1760), *Fingal* (1762), and *Temora* (1763). The *Poems'* authenticity was challenged from their initial publication, and the 'originals' Macpherson produced to back his claim were fabricated. None the less, his characterizations manifestly draw upon characters in Irish and Scottish Gaelic tradition; e.g. *Fingal is *Fionn mac Cumhaill, *Darthula is *Deirdre, and *Ossian is *Oisín. While modern readers often find Macpherson's prose insufferably turgid, the *Poems of Ossian* electrified 18th- and early 19th-century Europe, finding admirers as diverse as Napoleon, Goethe, who translated them into German, William Blake, Thomas Jefferson, Henry David Thoreau, and Brahms who, among many, set them to music. Bogus though he may have been, Macpherson drew learned attention to Irish and Scottish Gaelic traditions and caused the name *Oscar to be one of the most widely known from Celtic storytelling. See George F. Black, *Macpherson's Ossian and the Ossianic Controversy* (New York, 1926); Derick S. Thomson, *The Gaelic Sources of Macpherson's Ossian* (Aberdeen, 1952); 'Macpherson's *Ossian*: Ballads into Epics', in Bo Almqvist et al. (eds.), *The Heroic Process* (Dun Laoghaire, 1987), 243–64. His Breton counterpart is Hersart de *La Villemarqué. See IOLO MORGANWG.

Macsen Wledig. See BREUDDWYD MACSEN [The Dream of Macsen Wledig].

Madron. Variant spelling of *Modron.

Máel Dúin. See IMRAM CURAIG MAÍLE DÚIN.

Máel Fothartaig. *Leinster hero whose death is caused by his father in **Fingal Rónáin* [How Rónán Slew His Son].

Maelgwn Gwynedd (d. 547). Historical king of *Gwynedd, great-grandson of *Cunedda who ruled from a court at Degannwy, near the mouth of the *Conway River, north Wales. Oral tradition maintains that he became king by beating his rivals in a contest against the incoming tide in which he kept his feet dry with a floating chair. Early written records treat him harshly, especially *Gildas, who accused him of being excessively fond of listening to his own praise, of the heresy of Pelagianism, and of murdering first his own wife and then his nephew, whose wife he then married. In the *Hanes Taliesin*, composed many centuries later, *Taliesin was thought to have bested Maelgwn's court poets, notably *Heinen Fardd. See J. Wood, 'Maelgwn Gwynedd: A Forgotten Welsh Hero', *Trivium*, 19 (1984), 103–17; J. E. Caerwyn Williams, 'Gildas, Maelgwn and the Bards', in R. R. Davies et al. (eds.), *Welsh Society and Nationhood* (Cardiff, 1984), 19–34.

Maeve, Maev. Anglicizations of *Medb.

Mag, Mag-, Magh, Magh-. Irish word for plain, found in countless imaginary and actual place-names, often phonetically transliterated as Moy-, e.g. Mag Tuired = Moytura, Moytirra. *Magh* is the ModIr. spelling. See also TÍR [land].

Mag Dá Cheó, Cheo [Ir., plain of the two mists]. Place in early Ireland, located between *Cruachain and Athlone in the realm of the *Uí Maine [Hy Many], *Connacht, in what is today Co. Roscommon. A place of *otherworldly associations, Mag Dá Cheó is sometimes also linked with the otherworldly *Mag Mell.

Mag Mell, Magh Meall [Ir. *mell*, pleasant, delightful, e.g. pleasant plain]. Often-cited Irish *otherworldly realm frequently visited by mortal heroes. *Bran in the 8th-century **Imram Brain* [The Voyage of Bran] passes through Mag Mell on his way to *Emain Ablach; in this instance it is a part of the sea where *salmon romp like calves. Often in Irish tradition Mag Mell is a generic *fairyland, little distinguishable from Emain Ablach or *Tír na nÓg. At other times it appears to lie south-west of Ireland; sometimes it is confused with the actual place-name of *Mag Dá Cheó in Co. Roscommon. In different texts Mag Mell may have as many as three different rulers: *Labraid Luathlám ar Claideb [swift sword-hand], *Goll mac Doilb, and *Boadach. Inspiration for Sir Arnold Bax's tone poem *Moy Mell* (1917). Folk motif: F111. See also TÍR TAIRNGIRE.

Mag Mucrama. See CATH MAIGE MUCRAMA [The Battle of Mag Mucrama].

Mag Muirtheimne, Murthemne. Plain adjacent to the Irish Sea between Dundalk and Drogheda, i.e. the mouth of the *Boyne River; *Cúchulainn's inheritance.

Mag nElta, Moynalty, Senmag nEltair [old plain of bird flock]. Old Irish name for the expanse of land between Tallaght, Clontarf, and Howth, Co. *Dublin, coextensive with much of the modern city of Dublin. The *Partholonians of the **Lebor Gabála* [Book of Invasions] settle here.

Mag Slécht, Magh Sleacht, Moyslaught. Expanse of flat land in Co. Cavan, 1 mile NE of Ballmagauran. Best remembered as the site where *Crom Crúaich, an idol requiring human sacrifices at *Samain, was worshipped in pre-Christian times. Although Crom was thought to have bowed to St *Patrick's superior power, a festival known as *Domhnach Croim Dhuibh* [Sunday of Black Crom], held on the last Sunday in July, persisted until the early 20th century.

Mag Tuired, Magh Tuireadh, Turach, Moytura, Moytirra, Moy Turey [cf. Ir. *tuire*, pillar]. Fabled place-name, site of two battles between the Tuatha Dé Danann and their enemies, the First Battle with the *Fir Bolg, the Second Battle with the *Fomorians; see CATH MAIGE TUIRED [The (Second) Battle of Mag Tuired]. The better-known Second Battle is attributed to an expanse of flat land near the west shore of Lough Arrow, Co. Sligo, Kilmactranny parish, south of the village of Castlebaldwin. A nearby modern hamlet bears the name Moytura. A second expanse of flat land, still called the Plain of Moytura, lies in southern Co. Mayo, 3.5 miles NE of the town of Cong and 3 miles SW of Ballinrobe. Sir William Wilde, the 19th-century enthusiast, favoured the Mayo site as the 'true' Mag Tuired, while most modern commentators favour the Sligo site. Others have asserted that the First Battle of Mag Tuired took place in Mayo and the Second in Sligo. If the place-name may indeed be glossed as 'Plain of the Pillars', then archaeological evidence favours the Sligo site, where a tall stone column once stood with many other monuments. The once common translations of Mag Tuired as

'Plain of Weeping' and 'Plain of Reckoning' are insupportable. See Thomas F. O'Rahilly, 'Mag Tuired', in *Early Irish History and Mythology* (Dublin, 1946), 388–90.

Magh. Modern Irish for *Mag.

Maigneis, Maighnéis, Maignes, Maighnis, Maighean, Manissa. Second wife of *Fionn mac Cumhaill, for whom he is grieving at the beginning of **Tóraigheacht Dhiarmada agus Gráinne* [The Pursuit of Diarmait and Gráinne]. Daughter of *Garad mac Morna or Glúndub [black knee], she is also the sister of *Goll mac Morna.

Maine, Maini (pl.), Mane (ang.). Name borne by countless personages in early Ireland, especially legendary warriors and founders of dynasties and at least one saint. Most often cited are the seven sons of *Medb and *Ailill.

Maine 1–7, The Manes (anglicized pl.). The seven sons of Queen *Medb [Maeve] and her husband *Ailill mac Máta, according to what is clearly a later literary contrivance. The parents took this unusual measure in response to a *druid who told them that their enemy Conchobar would be killed by a son of this name. The seven sons were already born, however, and so Maine was used to replace their earlier identities. Additionally, each of the Maini may sometimes carry an agnomen, e.g. Maine Andaí. But these are not always clear, and their identities sometimes merge with one another and also migrate out of this context to characters called Maine in other stories. But none of the figures called Maine murdered Conchobar mac Nessa. What the druid did not explain to Medb and Ailill is that his prophecy applied to a different Conchobar, the son of an Arthur of Britain; and Maine Andaí did indeed dispatch him. The late medieval redactor of this story may have misread his sources. Later described as outlaws, the Maini join the hideous pirate *Ingcél Cáech in marauding around the British coast as well as invading Ireland in **Togail Bruidne Da Derga* [The Destruction of Da Derga's Hostel]. Elsewhere in the *Ulster Cycle the Maini are virtually Medb's henchmen, violently extending the interests of their mother.

8. A son of *Conchobar mac Nessa killed by *Dubthach Dóeltenga.

9. A Norse prince, killer of Noíse in variant texts of the *Deirdre story. Maine (9)'s father has been killed by Noíse and his brother, and so *Conchobar mac Nessa urges him to seek vengeance.

10. A member of *Fionn mac Cumhaill's *Fianna.

Maine Mílbél [Ir., honey-mouth]. A legendary *Munster hero.

Maine Mór mac Echach. Purported founder of the *Uí Maine tribe/family of medieval Galway and Roscommon.

Maive. Anglicization of *Medb.

Malalich, Samaliliath. *Partholonian who introduced the drinking of *ale into Ireland, as well as ordaining *divination, sacrifice, and ritual.

Man, Isle of [Manx *Mannin, Ellan Vannin*; cf. L *Mona*; OE *Maenig*; ON *Maun*]. Island of 220 square miles, of Celtic heritage, in the Irish Sea, a Crown dependency of the United Kingdom, with its own independent parliament, the Tynwald, which pre-dates the English parliament at Westminster. With a population of about 65,000 Man is by far the smallest of the six European Celtic cultures, even smaller in both population and area than the Highland settlement in *Nova Scotia. Although the island is English-speaking today, the last native speaker of Manx, Ned Maddrell, having died on 27 December 1974, traditional culture and lore are closely linked to that of *Ireland, 32 miles to the west, and Gaelic *Scotland. The story from Irish oral tradition that has *Fionn mac Cumhaill create the Isle of Man by ripping up a huge sod of earth, thus creating *Lough Neagh, and throwing it into the Irish Sea is a plausible metaphor, except that Man's ties are more to *Leinster than to the region around the Lough. After the Norse domination of the island, 8th-12th centuries, the kings of Man held sway over the Scottish Hebrides until the Battle of Largs (1283); see SOMERLED; LORD OF THE ISLES. The extensive Norse settlement merged with the native *Goidelic population that had come from Ireland several centuries previously, which means that ethnically the current population of Man is highly similar to that of Gaelic Scotland.

Although the original form of the name for Man is still a matter of some conjecture, contemporary informed opinion holds that the sea-god *Manannán mac Lir takes his name from the island, rather than the other way around. *Ptolemy's geography (2nd cent. AD) calls the island Manavia, even though the Romans in Britain used the term *Mona for Man, *Anglesey, the coast of Scotland, and another island, probably *Arran. Manannán's realm in Irish tradition, *Emain Ablach, is frequently confused with Man. Manannán has also played a dominant role in Manx tradition. The first recording of local oral tradition in the 18th century was John Kelly's *Manannán Beg, Mac y Leirr, ny slane coontey yeh Ellan Vannin* [Little Manannán, Son of Leirr (Lir), or an account of the Isle of Man]. More fancifully, the three-legged triskelion, the symbol of Man of undoubtedly ancient origin, is often popularly attributed to Manannán's facility for riding over the waves. Veneration of Manannán continued until the end of the 19th century.

Allusions to the Isle of Man appear commonly in Irish and to a lesser degree in Scottish Gaelic stories. The legendary Manx St *Maughold derives from *Mac Cuill of the Tuatha Dé Danann. The shaggy-haired *Fir Fálgae were speciously associated with Man, as was the *otherworldly *Dún Scáith. Additionally, the early physical culture of the Isle of Man, the Neolithic chambered tombs and the Bronze Age cairns and ring-forts, correlates with that found in Ireland.

The language of the earliest settlers is not known, although speculation favours *Brythonic. The Manx language [Manx *Gaelg*] clearly derives from Old Irish, but is more closely connected with Scottish Gaelic. Since it was first written, in a translation of *The Book of Common Prayer* (*c.*1625), Manx has been spelled as it would sound to English ears. Compare the words for 'fish': OIr. íasc; ModIr. iasc; ScG iasg; Manx eeast. Collections from oral tradition did not begin until the mid-19th century, e.g. Douglas Harrison, *A Mona Miscellany* (Douglas, 1869). Notwithstanding the distinctive *fenodyree, many characters in Manx folklore find parallels in Irish and Scottish Gaelic traditions, e.g. Finn McCooil and Oshin for *Fionn mac Cumhaill and *Oisín. OIr. Mana; ModIr. Manainn; W Manaw; Bret. Manev. See Bibliography under 'Manx' for collections of Manx traditions.

Manannán mac Lir, Mananaan, Mananaun, Manandán, Monanaun. Principal sea-deity and also *otherworldly ruler of Irish and *Goidelic traditions. Never a creature of a single cycle of Irish literature, Manannán appears often in all four cycles, the *Mythological, *Ulster, *Fenian, and *Cycle of Kings, as well as in later oral tradition. He is sometimes, but not usually, numbered as a lord of the *Tuatha Dé Danann. Clearly of divine origin, Manannán was never successfully humanized by Christian literary tradition, despite his portrayal in the 10th-century **Sanas Cormaic* [Cormac's Glossary] as a celebrated merchant and pilot of the Irish Sea. In the oldest Irish tradition Manannán rules the otherworldly *Emain Ablach, but rides out at will in his chariot over the waves as if they were solid land; his other realms are *Tír Tairngire and *Mag Mell. In later tradition he appears to be more of a trickster and magician.

The name Manannán may derive from earlier names for the Isle of *Man, not the other way around as commonly supposed. In Old Irish the island was Mana and Manand (gen.); cf. W Manaw. The Romans used the term *Mona for *Anglesey, the Isle of Man, the coast of *Scotland, and another island, probably *Arran. A gloss of Manannán might be 'he of the Isle of Man' or 'he of the Irish Sea'. In Irish tradition, however, Manannán does not reside on the Isle of Man but rather on Emain Ablach, an imaginary island near the coast of *Alba [Scotland] sometimes confused with the Isle of Man. The patronymic mac Lir means 'son of the sea', employing the genitive lir from the nominative ler [sea]. Manannán is not the son of *Lir whose children are turned into *swans in **Oidheadh Chlainne Lir* [The Tragic Story of the Children of Lir]. Additionally, Manannán's obscure epithet Oirbsiu or Oirbsiu Mór may have been an earlier name; it denotes inundation and survives in the place-name *Lough Corrib [*Loch nOirbsen*].

Through many texts over several centuries, some aspects of Manannán's person remain constant. Although a *shape-shifter, he is usually portrayed as a handsome and noble warrior, evocative of the classical gods Poseidon and Neptune, with whom he is often compared. He possesses a magical currach ('the wave-sweeper'), but most often he travels over the waves with a horse, *Énbarr or *Aonbárr, usually in a chariot but sometimes on horseback. Nor can the armour of any enemy withstand his enchanted sword *Frecraid [the answerer]. Among his supernatural powers is the ability to cast spells, *féth fiada, which he teaches to the *druids, and the ability to envelop himself in a mist that makes him invisible to his enemies, a facility shared by the Olympians in the *Iliad*. He often wears a great cloak that catches the light and can assume many colours, like the sea itself; with one sweep of it, Manannán can change destinies. An even more important possession is the *crane bag that holds all his possessions, including language. He also owns birds, hounds, and magical pigs that can be eaten on one day but will be alive the next so that they can be slaughtered and eaten again.

Accounts of Manannán's family differ from text to text. Despite his patronymic mac Lir [son of the sea], his father is usually thought to be the shadowy *Allod. Among his wives are *Fand [tears], herself a deity of water, and *Aífe (3), transformed into a *crane by *Iuchra (1), and from whose skin the *crane bag was made. More complicated is Manannán's relationship with *Áine (1), the sun-goddess become a *fairy patroness of love. In the best-known story Áine's brother *Aillén (1) is smitten with Manannán's then (unnamed) wife. Ostensibly to quieten Aillén, Manannán allows him the pleasures of his wife so that he, Manannán, may be with Áine, whom he has loved all along. Variant texts assert that Manannán is either the father or husband of Áine. Additionally, Manannán has numerous affairs, of which the best-known is with *Caíntigern, producing the shape-shifting king *Mongán. His best-known unrequited passion is for *Tuag, who is guarded by a company of women. He asks *Fer Fidail to disguise himself as a woman to retrieve her, but Tuag drowns at *Inber Glas (the mouth of the Bann River) and Manannán kills Fer Fidail. Manannán's own son is *Gaidiar; better known are his foster-sons: *Eógabal, *Fer Í, and (sometimes) *Lug Lámfhota. His daughter was *Curcóg. His chief druid was *Gebann, father of *Clídna.

Although Manannán is not the central figure in any single narrative, his appearances dominate the action of many stories. Among the oldest and most impressive episodes comes in the 8th-century **Imram Brain* [The Voyage of Bran], where the encounter with Manannán riding his chariot over the waves is one of Bran's first adventures. Manannán assists the Tuatha Dé Danann against the *Milesians in the **Lebor Gabála* [Book of Invasions] and is sometimes numbered among their ranks, although abundant evidence suggests he is of much older origin. In **Cath Maige Tuired* [The (Second) Battle of Mag Tuired] he teaches skills to Lug Lámfhota, his sometime foster-son, that lead to the defeat of the *Fomorians. In **Echtrae Chormaic* [The Adventure of Cormac] he assumes two different disguises. When his wife Fand has an affair with *Cúchulainn in **Serglige Con Culainn* [The Wasting Sickness of Cúchulainn], Manannán waves his magical cloak between them so that they completely forget one another. He has distinctly otherworldly power in **Altrom Tige Dá Medar* [The Nurture of the Houses of the Two Milk Vessels]. But in the comic 17th-century Fenian story **Eachtra Bhodaigh an Chóta Lachtna* [The Churl in the Grey Coat], his identity is revealed only after Manannán in the person of the bodach/churl leads the warriors on a merry chase.

No story tells of Manannán's death, but allusions are made to his decline when he refuses to accept the succession of *Bodb Derg. He is thought to have again assisted the Tuatha Dé Danann after their defeat by the Milesians when they dwindled into the small creatures who live under the earth. Memory of Manannán lingered vividly on the Isle of Man, where the first record of native lore, in the 18th century, was a ballad titled *Manannán Beg, Mac y Leirr, my slane coontey yeh Ellan Vannin* [Little Manannán, Son of Leirr, or an account of the Isle of Man]. As late as the 19th century, Midsummer Eve's veneration of Manannán saw people bringing rushes or green meadow grass to the top of [Mount] Barrule as the payment for 'rent'. Prayers directed to him were thought to bring fishermen a bountiful catch. Folk motifs: A132.7; A421.

Joseph Vendryes, 'Manannán mac Lir', *Études Celtiques*, 6 (1953–4), 239–54; David B. Spaan, 'The Place of Manannan Mac Lir in Irish Mythology', *Folklore*, 76 (1965), 176–95; Heinrich Wagner, 'Origins of Pagan Irish Religion', *Zeitschrift für celtische Philologie*, 38 (1981), 1–28.

Manawydan fab Llŷr, son of Llŷr [cf. W *Manaw*, Isle of Man]. Welsh hero of the **Mabinogi*, title character and protagonist of the third branch and brother of *Bendigeidfran and *Branwen, protagonists of the second branch. Although he wields magic well and is a skilled craftsman, Manawydan shows no hint of the divine characteristics present in his Irish counterpart, *Manannán mac Lir, the sea-god. In the third branch Manawydan is married to *Rhiannon, and together with

*Pryderi and *Cigfa he lives in exile in England, where he works first as a leather craftsman and then as a wheat farmer. See Ifor Williams, *Pedeir Keinc y Mabinogi* (Cardiff, 1930), 49–65; Patrick K. Ford, 'Prolegomena to a Reading of the *Mabinogi*, "Pwyll" and "Manawydan"', *Studia Celtica*, 16/17 (1981/2), 110–25.

Manissa. Anglicization of *Maigneis.

Mannin. Manx name for the Isle of *Man.

Manx. See MAN, ISLE OF.

Maol, Maol-. ModIr. spelling of *Máel, Máel-.

Maponos, Maponus [Romano-British, divine youth; great son]. Celtic god of Roman-occupied Britain, apparently associated with the powers of music and poetry. Although his cult seems to have been centred on north Britain (a shrine at Chesterholm, Northumberland, is inscribed 'Deo Mapono'), his name is also invoked at sites in what is now France as well, including perhaps the Gaulish inscriptions of Chamalières. As a patron of music and poetry, Maponos is often linked with Gaulish *Apollo, especially Apollo Citharoedus [harper or cithern-player]. Most commentators feel that Maponos contributes to the conception of the Welsh divine youth *Mabon, and Patrick K. Ford (1977) has asserted that Maponos is virtually identical with *Pryderi. Eric Hamp argues further that a true gloss of the word **Mabinogi* would be 'the (collective) material pertaining to the god Maponos'. The deity is also equated with the Irish *Angus Óg, especially when he is referred to by the patronymics Mac Óc, Mac Óg, Mac-ind-Óc, Macc Óc, etc. Additionally, Maponos probably contributed to the conception of the Arthurian figures Mabuz and Mabongrain. See Patrick K. Ford, *The Mabinogi* (Berkeley and Los Angeles, Calif., 1977), 3.

Marcán [Ir. *marc*, steed]. Name borne by many personages from early Ireland, most notably the cuckold king of the *Uí Maine, whose wife *Créd (2) has an affair with *Cano; many commentators have suggested that he contributes to the characterization of the Arthurian King *Mark of Cornwall. Distinguish from Marcán mac Cennetíg, the brother of *Brian Bórama (Boru).

March ap Meirchion, vab Meirchiawn [W *march*, horse]. Early Welsh legendary hero and an antecedent of the Arthurian King *Mark. The Welsh *Triads refer to him as one of the Three Seafarers of the Isle of Britain, and historical records show him as the son of a king of Glamorgan who granted lands to St Illtud. Allusions to March exist in **Breuddwyd Rhonabwy* [The Dream of Rhonabwy] and the gnomic poetry known as *Englynion y Bidiau*. More recent folklore places March at Castell March in Lly^n, Caernarvonshire, in north-western Wales. Here he shares the affliction of the Irish king *Labraid Loingsech of having horse's ears, making word-play with his name; in shame he grows his hair long to cover them and has his barbers murdered. In Welsh Arthurian stories March is the king of *Cornwall in the love triangle with *Tristan and *Iseult. The King Mark of international Arthuriana draws also from other antecedents. See John James Jones, 'March ap Meirchion: A Study in Celtic Folk-Lore', *Aberystwyth Studies*, 12 (1932), 21–33.

Mark, King. Cuckold king of *Cornwall in international Arthurian legends, an uncle of *Tristan and the betrothed of *Iseult. A cowardly, easily deceived, yet jealous ruler, there is little of the kingly about him. Usually sited at *Tintagel, Cornwall, Mark is also linked to numerous other places, including Lantyan near Fowey, Cornwall, and Lancien, Brittany. His abundant antecedents from the Celtic world include the Welsh *March ap Meirchion, the Irish *Marcán, and the Breton *Konomor (Marcus Conomorus); in Breton Arthuriana he is called Guivarc'h. In two Irish stories of love triangles he plays the same role as rulers greater than he: *Conchobar mac Nessa between *Deirdre and *Noíse and *Fionn mac Cumhaill between *Diarmait and *Gráinne.

Mars. Depictions of the Roman god of war in early Gaul and Britain are multiform and complex because of two opposed but concurrent forces. First, the imperial-minded Romans applied interpretatio romana (see GAUL), which prompted them to ignore the native names of indigenous gods and simply denote them with Latin names. Secondly, the colonized natives followed what we now call interpretatio celtica, adapting the conqueror's deities to local religious needs, often adding a distinctive indigenous epithet. Thus the Mars of the early Celtic world appears far less bellicose than his Roman antecedent, even though

Julius *Caesar (1st cent. BC) describes Mars as a popular war-god in Gaul and Lucan's *Pharsalia* (1st cent. AD) equates the unmistakably warlike *Teutates with Mars. Instead, abundant archaeological evidence implies the widespread worship of Mars in the Roman-occupied Celtic world. He became the primary healing god of Roman Britain, especially with the epithet Loucetius, Leucetius, Lucetius [L, light, bright], at the great healing temple of Aquae Sulis Minerva at Bath. Another epithet of the healing god Mars is Lenus, especially as found at Trier, Germany; but Lenus may have pre-dated Roman conquest, as dedications found in Britain speak of Lenus Mars. The animal most associated with Mars's iconography is the goose, which for the Celts evokes the protectiveness of an alert sentry as well as a certain measure of aggression.

Mars's worship sometimes appears to co-opt that of indigenous deities, so that his identity becomes mixed with that of presumably Celtic figures, whose names may appear independently or linked with his as an epithet. Such figures, widely known in the Celtic world, include: *Belatucadros, *Camulos, *Cocidius, *Condatis, *Mullo, *Nodons, *Ocelus, *Olloudius, *Rudianus, *Rudiobus, *Segomo, *Smertrius, *Teutates, and *Visucius. Additionally, Mars also bears other epithets that define the functions of his cult in specific locales, such as Albiorix, Caturix, Cicollius, Coriaticus, Nabelcus, Rigisamus, Rigonemetis, and Thincsus (this last of German origin).

See Émile Thevenot, *Sur les traces des Mars celtiques* (Bruges, 1955); Miranda J. Green, *The Gods of the Celts* (Gloucester, 1986), 110–17; Jan de Vries, *La Religion des Celtes* (Paris, 1963), 63–9; E. M. Wightman, *Roman Trier and the Treveri* (London, 1970), 208–17; G. Barroul, 'Mars Nabelcus et Mars Albiorix', *Ogam*, 15 (1963), 345–68.

Math. Son of Mathonwy in the **Mabinogi* and lord of *Gwynedd; he and his nephew *Gwydion are superb magicians.

Matholwch. King of Ireland in the second branch of the **Mabinogi*. After *Branwen is forced into a marriage of convenience with him, the malevolent *Efnisien mutilates his horses, provoking a war between Ireland and Wales.

Matres [mothers]. Latin title given to the many representations of motherhood, often as triads of figures (see TRIPLISM). The figures conventionally wear long garments, often with one breast bared. They usually carry baskets or cornucopias of fruit and bread, babies, and other unmistakable signs of their association with human and earthly *fertility; none the less, some commentators see them as virgins. Mother-goddesses elsewhere in early Europe combine the functions of war and death along with fertility. They are also linked to *Epona, the horse-goddess. See Miranda J. Green, *The Gods of the Celts* (Gloucester, 1986), 78–91; *Symbol and Image in Celtic Religious Art* (London and New York, 1989), 24–39, 188–205; S. Barnard, 'The *Matres* of Roman Britain', *Archaeological Journal*, 142 (1985), 237–43. See also MATRONA; SULEVIAE.

Matrona [divine mother]. Gaulish mother-goddess who gives her name to the Marne River of eastern France; a shrine to 'Dea Matrona' survives from near the river's source. While she appears here singly, triads of mother-goddesses, Matronae, appear in eastern Gaul in what is today the German Rhineland. Often thought to have contributed to the Welsh *Modron. See also MATRES.

Maughold, Saint. Legendary saint of the Isle of *Man whose character was drawn from the *Tuatha Dé Danann hero *Mac Cuill; attempts to link him with the Breton St Machutus (Maclovius, Malo) have been proved false. But he is probably identical with Bishop Mac Caille, celebrated on 25 April in the Irish martyrology. Although the subject of almost as many fantasies as St *Patrick, who was thought to have converted him, St Maughold was long celebrated on the Christian calendar, 27 April; he is ascribed the death-date of 498. Converted from being a bloodthirsty freebooter, he was sent to Man in a rudderless, oarless coracle; once a missionary he led an austere, exemplary life, being chosen bishop for his holiness. His name is linked to the only pre-Norse monastic foundation in the north-eastern portion of the island, east of Ramsey; from this come Maughold Head, the village of Maughold, St Maughold's Well, and St Maughold's Cross, an 8-foot standing-stone cross with biblical scenes and the Manx triskelion.

mauthe doog. Local variant of *moddey dhoo, the great black *dog of Manx folklore.

Sir Walter Scott employs this version in *Lay of the Last Minstrel*, canto vi (1805).

Maxen Wledig. See BREUDDWYD MACSEN [The Dream of Macsen Wledig].

May Day, May Eve. See BELTAINE; CALAN MAI.

Meadhbh, Méadhbh. ModIr. spellings of *Medb.

Meath [ModIr. *An Mhí*, the middle (place); *Contae na Mí*]. County of 903 square miles in the Republic of Ireland, north and west of Co. *Dublin. Not identical with nor coextensive with the ancient and medieval *Mide, from which the name Meath is derived. From the 8th to the 11th centuries, what is now Co. Meath was contained in the petty kingdom of *Brega. Many of the most celebrated sites of early Irish civilization, e.g. *Tara, *Brug na Bóinne, *Tailtiu, *Tlachtga, as well as much of the *Boyne valley, lie in Co. Meath.

Mechi. Son of *Mórrígan. According to the Dindshenchas, *Mac Cécht killed him on the River Barrow. Mechi was revealed to have three hearts, each with a serpent in it, which could have caused disaster for Ireland if they were not stopped. Mac Cécht burned him and threw the ashes into the river.

Medb, Meadhbh, Méadhbh, Maeve, Maev, Meave, Maive [Ir., she who intoxicates; cf. Gk. *methu*, wine; L *medus*, mead; W *meddw*, drunk]. Warrior-queen of *Connacht, leading figure in the *Ulster Cycle, and the most vibrant female personality in all of Celtic mythology. Once thought historical, Medb now appears to be the apotheosis of several forces and antecedents, including goddesses of territory, fertility, and *sovereignty; she seems to owe something to *Mór Muman of *Munster. Like a Gaulish mother-goddess, Medb is often portrayed with creatures, a bird and a squirrel, on her shoulder. By literary convention she is pale, long-faced, with long flowing hair, wearing a red cloak and carrying a spear that may be flaming. Like *Macha, she can run faster than any horse, and the sight of her is enough to deprive men of two-thirds of their strength. Medb dominates men, both by the force of her personality and by her sexuality. She is always governed by her own will. In the **Táin Bó Cuailnge* [Cattle Raid of Cooley] she demonstrates more conviction than her husband of the text, *Ailill mac Máta, and both leads Connacht forces and provokes the central action of the narrative. Her allure is ageless; she appears to be a beautiful young woman regardless of the chronology. Called 'Medb of the friendly thighs' by translators, she claimed that it took thirty-two men to satisfy her sexually; she boasted of having any lover she wished, 'each man in another man's shadow'. Many men are named as her 'husbands', but *Fergus mac Róich was her favourite lover.

In historicizing her, medieval scribes constructed a detailed biography for Medb. Her father was *Eochaid Feidlech, one of the most important pre-Patrician kings of *Tara according to the annals; her mother is sometimes named as Cruacha, for whom the fortress *Cruachain was named. Her sisters, each famous, were *Clothra, *Eithne (5), and *Mugain (2). All four sisters were at one time 'married' to *Conchobar mac Nessa, ultimately one of Medb's great enemies. Medb killed her sister Clothra while she was pregnant with Conchobar's child, treachery that would later bring about her own death. Among her brothers were *Finn Emna, the Three Finns of Emain Macha. The order and total number of Medb's husbands is not certain. Conchobar mac Nessa may have been first, but 'through pride of mind' she departed from his company; he still lusted for her and later violated her while she was bathing in the *Boyne. Three husbands became kings of Connacht: Tinde son of Connra Cas (killed by Conchobar), *Eochaid Dála, and the best-known, Ailill mac Máta (a mere boy at the time of their marriage); Eochaid, at the least, became king only because Medb consented to have him as a husband. Medb was led to Ailill by a 'water worm', who eventually became *Finnbennach, the White Bull of Connacht. For a woman with such a demanding military and administrative career, she was often pregnant herself. She gives the name *Maine to seven sons she bears to Ailill, under a misreading of a *druid's prophecy that a son with that name would kill Conchobar. Her best-known daughter, *Finnabair, has extensive stories of her own; two others are *Cainder and *Faife. Two love-children fathered by Fergus mac Róich give their names to the land; *Ciar is the eponym of Ciarraí [*Kerry], and *Conmac the eponym of Conmaicne Mara [*Connemara]. An adoptive son is Etarcomul.

Although her fortress is always named as

Cruachain [Co. Roscommon], Medb is usually seen elsewhere. In stories she was reared at Tara; in fact she was probably worshipped there. As a force from Ulster sought to displace the Connacht men, her cult had rivals from the north; this early power struggle may well explain the links between Medb and the Ulster hero Fergus mac Róich. The misty early Medb cannot always be directly linked to later literature. The Leinster queen *Medb Lethderg, also associated with Tara, appears as a separate character within narrative texts, but is probably identical with Medb of Connacht and may have preceded her.

Our most coherent portrait of Medb of Connacht comes from four Ulster Cycle texts: **Táin Bó Cuailnge* [Cattle Raid of Cooley], **Fled Bricrenn* [Briccriu's Feast], **Echtra Nerai* [The Adventure of Nera], and **Scéla Mucce meic Da Thó* [The Story of Mac Da Thó's Pig]. In the latter three she is a strident supporting player, but in the *Táin* she leads the action, beginning with her bickering pillow-talk with Ailill in the opening scenes over who owns the greatest bull. Sensing that she has greater determination than her husband, she takes command of her armies and its allies. Her judgement is not always prudent. In reviewing troops from the *Galióin sept of *Leinster, Medb is awestruck at their grace and power and fears that they may overshadow her own force. Her first thought is to slaughter them, but she is dissuaded by Ailill. Fergus recommends that they be dispersed among the Connacht men. Her adultery with Fergus continues throughout most of the narrative, Ailill once finding them *in flagrante delicto*. The cuckold eventually gets his revenge, arranging to have Fergus speared while the lover is swimming with his erring wife. Elsewhere in the action, two henchmen always do Medb's bidding: the steward Mac Roth, who spies on the Ulster forces, and the champion *Nadcranntail, who first brings *Donn Cuailnge [the great brown bull] home to her.

Medb's conflicts with *Cúchulainn, however, shape the human focus of the narrative. At first she thought she could dismiss him with the back of her hand, but she came to regard him as a worthy adversary. Her scheme to entrap him by inviting him to come unarmed to meet with her is thwarted by the charioteer Láeg. She is more successful motivating Cúchulainn's friend *Ferdiad to act against him; she first gets Ferdiad drunk, offers her beautiful daughter Finnabair as a wife, and taunts him for cowardice. But in the single most dramatic scene in the *Táin*, Cúchulainn overcomes Ferdiad, frustrating Medb once again. In face-to-face encounters Cúchulainn taunts and humiliates her, once shooting a pet bird from her shoulder. Once when he comes upon her alone during her menstruation, she has to plead with him to be spared; in sneering condescension he says that he will not be a killer of women and leaves. Her revenge is to set the children of *Cailitin against the Ulster hero, beginning a sequence of events that will eventually bring Cúchulainn down.

The story of Medb's own death comes from an 11th-century text, composed much later than the *Táin*. When Medb kills her pregnant sister Clothra, the child cut from the dying woman's womb, *Furbaide Ferbend, survives and lives on an island in *Lough Ree, Co. Roscommon. For unexplained reasons, Medb goes to live on the same island, where she goes bathing each morning. As an assembly is being held on the shores of the lake, Furbaide sees a beautiful woman going to bathe and learns that it is Medb, killer of his mother. He thereupon takes a hardened piece of cheese he has been eating, places it in his sling, and shoots it, hitting the queen squarely in the forehead and killing her. This curious death is not the only oddity in the text, as Furbaide had been thought the son of Eithne (5) in earlier accounts. Oral tradition, however, supports this version. The highest point of the island, where Medb is thought to have been killed, Inis Clothrand (today, Inchcleraun or Quaker's Island), is known as Greenan Hill, earlier Grianán Meidbe [Medb's sun-porch].

Medb does not, however, inspire a rich body of literature from oral tradition. She is sometimes described as a queen of the fairies. Many commentators, with scant evidence, assume she is an antecedent of Shakespeare's Queen Mab (*Romeo and Juliet*, I. iv). She is alluded to in dozens of place-names, notably the cairn called 'Maeve's Lump' or Miscaun Maeve [Ir. *Miosgán Méabha*] atop *Knocknarea, Co. Sligo.

See Tomás Ó Máille, 'Medb Cruachna', *Zeitschrift für celtische Philologie*, 17 (1927), 129–46; Vernam Hull, 'Aided Meidbe: The Violent Death of Medb', *Speculum*, 13 (1938), 52–61; Charles Bowen, 'Great-Bladdered Medb: Mythology and Invention in the *Táin Bó Cuailnge*', *Éire-Ireland*, 10 (1975), 14–34; Arthur

Gribben, 'The Masks of Medb in Celtic Scholarship', *Folklore and Mythology Studies*, 10 (Fall 1986), 1–19. Medb has been the subject of dozens of portrayals in modern literature, most unflatteringly as a minor character in James Stephens's *Deirdre* (1923). See also Eva Gore-Booth's unproduced verse drama 'The Triumph of Maeve', in *Poems of Eva Gore-Booth*, ed. Esther Roper (London, 1929). See also GUNDESTRUP CAULDRON.

Medb Lethderg, Leathdhearg [Ir., red-side, half-red]. Goddess of *sovereignty at *Tara and queen of *Leinster. Although portrayed as a separate character from *Medb of Connacht, she is her double and is probably older; Medb of Connacht may well be an emanation from Medb Lethderg. Daughter of Conán of Cualu [Dublin/Wicklow], she was the wife of nine successive kings of Ireland, including the father of *Conn Cétchathach [of the Hundred Battles], *Cormac mac Airt, who could not be considered a king until he had slept with her, and *Art mac Cuinn (the son of Conn).

menhir. See CROMLECH; DOLMEN.

Menw fab Teirgwaedd. Wizard who accompanies *Culhwch in **Culhwch ac Olwen*, using his power of invisibility at the court of *Ysbaddaden Bencawr. On *Arthur's behalf he participates in the hunting of the *Twrch Trwyth, going to Ireland to make sure that the treasures to be sought are between the beast's ears. He may take the form of a bird, and is named in the **Triads* as one of the Three Enchanters of the Isle of Britain.

Mercury. *Classical commentators used the name of this Roman god of commerce, travel, and thievery (Greek counterpart, Hermes) to denote what was apparently the most popular god in Roman-occupied *Gaul and Britain. Through their imperial-minded interpretatio romana (see GAUL), the Romans simply ignored the native divine name and substituted their correlative. The vast number of depictions and descriptions of him, however, give us an outline of his cult. Julius *Caesar remarks that Mercury was the inventor of all the arts, one of several reasons he is thought comparable to the Irish *Lug Lámfhota and the Welsh *Lleu Llaw Gyffes. Caesar also describes his money-making abilities; he is a god of commercial success and plenty. The Celtic propensity for *triplism is evident in his iconography, both triple-faced and triple-phallused. Several important shrines survive, most notable in the Vosges mountains of eastern France. Sometimes he is shown to be *horned, and sometimes he is the consort of *Rosmerta, an indigenous deity.

Despite the Roman indifference to providing Mercury with a native name, modern commentators favour two choices. One is *Lugos/Lugus, a name found in inscriptions and implicit in the Roman town name of Lug(u)dunum, the root of such modern sites as Lyon, Laon, Loudon, Leiden, Léon, and Liegnitz. Lugos also links Mercury more firmly with Lug Lámfhota, Lleu Llaw Gyffes, and the festival of *Lughnasa. A second possibility is *Erriapus, a deity of southern Gaul.

Additionally, at many sites Mercury takes on different epithets, implying almost a separate identity, notably *Artaios [*bear], *Moccus [pig, *boar], and *Visucius. Other epithets, denoting shades of differing identity, are Arvernus, Cissonius, and Gebrinius. And despite the lack of a shared epithet, Mercury may also be linked to *Teutates, the Gaulish war-god. Lastly, although never linked directly to *Cúchulainn, Gaulish Mercury may find echoes in that hero's first name, *Setanta. See Jan de Vries, *La Religion des Celtes* (Paris, 1963), 48–63; Paul-Marie Duval, *Les Dieux de la Gaule* (Paris, 1976), 69–71; Waldemar Deonna, 'Trois, superlatif absolu: à propos du taureau tricornu et de Mercure triphallique', *L'Antiquité Classique*, 23 (1954), 403- 28; J. Santrot, 'Le Mercure phallique du Mas-Agenais et un dieu stylite inédit', *Gallia*, 44 (1986), fasc. 2, pp. 203–28.

Merddin. Variant spelling of *Myrddin.

Merlin. Celebrated magician, prophet, and tutor of *Arthur in Arthuriana, drawn in part from the 6th-century Welsh fictional poet and prophet *Myrddin, known from the **Black Book of Carmarthen*; in Welsh translations of Arthurian texts Myrddin is made the equivalent of Merlin. As one of the oldest of Arthurian characters, with roots independent of the king himself, Merlin also draws from *Lailoken, the naked *wild man of the woods. Three works of *Geoffrey of Monmouth forged the conception of Merlin as he came to be known in Arthurian tradition. In several books of the *Historia Regum Britanniae* (1136), Geoffrey implies that Merlin has a demonic ancestry, his mother being a nun impregnated by an incubus. In Book VII, earlier known as *Prophetiae Merlini*, Geoffrey identifies Merlin with the boy-prophet Ambrosius Aurelianus (Latin name for *Emrys Wledig). Geoffrey's last work, the *Vita Merlini* (*c.*1149), depicts Merlin's adventures apart from King Arthur, some of which also appear in *Prophetiae Merlini*. Merlin is sometimes bested; Viviane/Nimiane (the Lady of the Lake) imprisons him in an *oak tree in the Breton forest of *Brocéliande. In late life he retires to the Isle of Bardsey with his pet *boar and the treasures of Britain. See SENCHA MAC AILELLA. See also Paul Zumthor, *Merlin le prophète* (Lausanne, 1943); A. O. H. Jarman, *The Legend of Merlin* (Cardiff, 1959); 'The Merlin Legend and the Welsh Tradition of Prophecy', in R. Bromwich et al. (eds.), *The Arthur of the Welsh* (Cardiff, 1991), 117–45; Basil Clarke, *Life of Merlin* (Cardiff, 1972); Théophile Briant, *Le Testament de Merlin* (Nantes, 1975); Nikolai Tolstoy, *The Quest for Merlin* (London and Boston, 1985); Carol E. Harding, *Merlin and Legendary Romance* (New York, 1989); Peter Goodrich (ed.), *The Romance of Merlin* (New York, 1990).

Mes Buachalla, Mess Buachalla, Messbuachalla [Ir., cowherd's fosterling]. Young woman, often portrayed as a foundling, whose ancestry is presented differently in different early Irish texts. In **Togail Bruidne Da Derga* [The Destruction of Da Derga's Hostel] she is named as the daughter of *Cormac and a woman who came in the form of a *bird; her stepmother, *Étaín Óg, wants her killed but is subsequently charmed by her. In **Tochmarc Étaíne* [The Wooing of Étaín], the action of which precedes *Togail Bruidne Da Derga*, her name does not appear, but she is implicitly the incestuously begotten daughter of *Eochaid Feidlech and his daughter, Étaín Óg; before the action is completed she marries *Eterscél and gives birth to *Conaire Mór. Outside these two texts, Eochaid Airem and Étaín (1) produce *Ésa, who becomes the mother of Mes Buachalla.

Mesca Ulad. Irish title for the *Ulster Cycle narrative preserved in the 12th-century **Book of Leinster* and elsewhere usually known in English as 'The Intoxication of the Ulstermen'. The narrator does not follow a definite plot but instead gives free rein to lengthy passages of description and runs of personal and place-names, as would have been the stock-in-trade of medieval storytellers. Set at *Samain, a time of wild revelry, turbulence, and disorder, *Mesca Ulad* shows the Ulster warriors in less than heroic form. After receiving two invitations to go feasting, the Ulstermen decide to resolve their dilemma by going to both. They spend the first part of the night in the far north, at *Dún Dá Bhenn, in what is today Co. *Derry. They then set out to cross Ulster to the east to spend the rest of the night at *Cúchulainn's fortress in *Dún Delgan [Dundalk, Co. Louth], when they lose their way. The most vivid passages portray drunken charioteers bounding southward towards *Kerry. Once the Ulstermen arrive, they are initially given hospitality by the *Munstermen, their traditional enemies. But there is a trap: the Munstermen have prepared an iron house set within wooden walls, under which piles of faggots have been turned into bonfires. The text, while fragmentary, allows that the Ulstermen did not perish. See William H. Hennessy, *Mesca Ulad* (Dublin, 1889); J. Carmichael Watson, *Mesca Ulad* (Dublin, 1983); Uáitéar Mac Gearailt, 'The Edinburgh Text of *Mesca Ulad*', *Ériu*, 37 (1986), 133–80; T. P. Cross and C. H. Slover (eds.), *Ancient Irish Tales* (New York, 1936), 215–38.

metamorphosis. See SHAPE-SHIFTING.

Michael, Saint. See LUG LÁMFHOTA.

Midchaín. Variant spelling of *Miodhchaoin.

Mide [OIr., middle, centre]. Central province and sometime petty kingdom of early Ireland, originally a designation of the hill of *Uisnech, then regarded as the central point in Ireland. Although the name of modern Co. *Meath is derived from Mide, the ancient name denoted large tracts of land between *Ulster, *Connacht, and *Leinster, including at times not only what is today counties Meath, Westmeath, Offaly, and Longford but also south Co. Louth and north Co. Dublin. Kings of Mide sat at *Tlachtga. *Tuathal Techtmar (2nd cent. AD) is thought to have created Mide as Ireland's fifth province [OIr. *cóicede*; ModIr. *cúige*] so that the *ard rí [high king] crowned at *Tara could be independent of the other four provinces. Subsequently, it is the province most associated with *kingship.

The pseudo-history **Lebor Gabála* [Book of Invasions] offers a different explanation for Mide's prominence. According to the text the province is named for Mide the *druid of the invading *Nemedians, who was the first to light a fire at Uisnech. During the seven years that this fire burned every other fire in Ireland was lit from it, which entitled Mide and his successors to a sack of grain and a pig from every house in the land. When other druids objected to this tax, Mide had their tongues cut out and burned them at Uisnech, winning the praise of his mother.

Midir, Midhir, Mider, Midar. Chieftain of the *Tuatha Dé Danann, conventionally portrayed as proud and haughty, ruler of the *otherworldly dwelling of *Brí Léith, husband of *Fuamnach, and lover of *Étaín Óg in **Tochmarc Étaíne* [The Wooing of Étaín]. A certain pride in his possessions brings Midir much grief. His magic *cauldron, one of the treasures of the Tuatha Dé Danann, is stolen by *Cúchulainn. And his three *cranes, symbols of stinginess and unpleasantness, were thought to have been stolen by the satirist *Athairne Ailgesach. The place-name story of *Lough Ree has Midir giving a magical but mischievous horse, whose urine forms the lake, to *Eochu mac Maireda and his brother *Ríb. In an extraordinary number of variant texts he is given roles played elsewhere by other figures. He is sometimes cited as the foster-father of *Angus Óg, instead of *Elcmar, advising his charge on the taking of *Brug na Bóinne [Newgrange]. He is sometimes the father or brother of the *Dagda, and sometimes the father of *Macha and *Bláithíne. Daughters unquestionably his include *Ailbe (1) and *Doirind.

Míl Espáine, Mílid Espáine, Míl Espáne, Míl Easpáine, Míle Easpáin, Míled, Mílead, Míleadh, Miles, Mille Easpain [Ir., soldier of Spain; cf. L *miles Hispaniae*]. Eponymous founder of the *Milesians, final mythic invaders of Ireland in the **Lebor Gabála* [Book of Invasions], and fictional ancestor of the Irish people. Born with the name Golam or Galam, Míl bore a distinguished pedigree, tracing his line through *Bile, grandfather *Breogan, twenty more Irish names, and thirteen Hebrew names back to Adam. Although his usual name, Míl Espáine (clearly a title), links him with Spain, descriptions of his early career place him in *Scythia, a region the subject of much fanciful speculation in early Irish literature. His service initially so pleases the king of Scythia that Míl is made army commander and marries the king's daughter Seang, who bears him two sons, *Donn and *Erech Febria, before dying an early death. Discovering a plot against him, Míl murders Seang's father and flees from Scythia in sixty ships to Egypt. There he serves Pharaoh Nectanebus as army commander in a successful war against the Ethiopians; on this point the authors of the *Lebor Gabála* had studied their sources, as there are indeed two pharaohs of the Thirtieth Dynasty named Nectanebus, 380–363 BC and 360–343 BC. Míl marries the Pharaoh's daughter *Scota (1) [L, Irishwoman], who bears him two sons while in Egypt, *Éber Finn and *Amairgin (1); a third son, *Ír, is born near Thrace, and a fourth, *Colptha, is born on an island in the Mediterranean. Remembering the *druid *Caicer's prophecy that he and his people would settle in Ireland, Míl departs from Egypt and sails west. But hearing that Spain is menaced by villains, he stops in his homeland and triumphs in many battles. Some time later Míl dies of unspecified causes, never reaching Ireland himself. His kin who do reach Ireland include his uncle *Íth, his wife Scota [Irishwoman] (1), and many of his sons. The number of sons attributed to him ranges as high as thirty-two, counting his by-blows from adventures in Spain and Scythia, but the most conventional number is eight, a distinction he shares with the Welsh *Cunedda. Disregarding their mothers, his most important sons are Éber and *Éremón, who later divide Ireland between themselves, and then Ír, Donn, Colptha, Amairgin (1), Erech Febria, and *Erannán. See also TUATHAL TECHTMAR.

Mileadha. Corrupt form of the name of the *Milesians.

Miles. Occasional anglicization of *Míl Espáine.

Milesians, Sons of Míl, Clanna Míled. Final mythic invaders of Ireland according to the pseudo-history **Lebor Gabála* [Book of Invasions] and fictionalized counterparts of the *Goidels, important ancestors of the Irish people. 'Milesian' is a Latinized form taken from their eponymous founder, *Míl Espáine, but sources outside the *Lebor Gabála* also suggest a link with ancient Miletus in Asia Minor.

Narratives of Milesian origins and wanderings in the Mediterranean appear fabulous and contrived, while those of their invasion of Ireland have correlatives in history; the two portions of the whole seem forcibly united. In the curious mélange of biblical and classical learning in the *Lebor Gabála*, the Milesians originate in *Scythia, a region the subject of much fantasy in early Irish tradition. Descended from Noah's son Japheth, the first Milesian leader was *Fénius Farsaid, who was present at Babel during the biblical separation of the languages. His son *Niúl married a pharaoh's daughter, *Scota [L, Irishwoman] (2), producing *Goídel Glas, who fashioned the Irish language, following Fénius' instructions. The Milesians were so intimate with the captive Israelites that none other than Moses had saved the life of the infant Goídel with a touch of his rod. The child had been bitten by a snake, and Moses pledged that Goídel and his descendants would live in a land without serpents. In subsequent generations the Milesians met with persecution in Egypt and so wandered to many lands, first to their homeland in Scythia, later for seven years in the Caspian Sea, and eventually to Spain, which they conquered and settled. Míl Espáine [Ir., soldier of Spain], the Milesian eponym and hero, joins the narrative in Egypt and leads his people through their irregular itinerary to Spain, where he dies unexplainedly. Míl, however, knows of the *druid *Caicer's prophecy that his people will live in Ireland, a country no Milesian has seen, although one sight of Ireland from afar will crystallize the resolve to go there. After *Breogan has built a high defensive tower at Brigantia (Braganza, north-east Portugal; cf. ruins at La Coruña, capital of Galicia, Spain), his son *Íth climbs it in the cold winter twilight and sees the promised island on the horizon.

The Milesian penetration of Ireland comes in two waves. Íth, who is also Míl's uncle, first leads 150 men on a scouting mission, landing in what is now Derry, proceeding to the fortress of *Ailech. There Íth meets three kings from the *Tuatha Dé Danann, the previous invaders, who are dividing Ireland among themselves. Suspicious of his attempts to advise them, the three have Íth treacherously slain while returning to his ship. After his body has been returned, his nine brothers join with the eight sons of Míl to invade Ireland and capture it. Two of Míl's sons are drowned before the invasion, *Erannán when he falls from a mast lookout and *Ír after his oar breaks while he is trying to get ahead of the other warriors; he later became an eponym (one of several) for Ireland itself. The expedition finally lands at *Inber Scéne, an estuary in south Co. *Kerry (probably Kenmare). *Amairgin (1), the poet and son of Míl, was the first to set foot on Ireland.

The Milesian conquest of Ireland is aided by unexpected allies. After defeating a Tuatha Dé force at *Sliab Mis (Co. Kerry), the Milesians meet three goddesses, each of whom asks that the island be named for her: *Banba, *Ériu, and *Fódla. At *Tara the invaders meet three kings, who were, according to some texts, the husbands of the goddesses: *Mac Cuill, *Mac Cécht, and *Mac Gréine. The three kings seek to put off the Milesians with a trick, asking to hold the country only three days more while the invaders stay nine waves from shore. Although the Milesians faithfully comply, the druids of the Tuatha Dé use spells to raise a storm to drive the invaders further from shore; but Amairgin, the leading spokesman, calms the waters with a verse. Another brother, *Donn mac Míled, rages against the Tuatha Dé and vows to slaughter all in Ireland, but a magical wind drowns him and his brother *Erech Febria on the south-west coast. Then *Éremón, first among the four remaining brothers, leads the Milesians *sunwise turn around Ireland to the *Boyne estuary at *Beltaine; *Colptha is the first to go ashore, and *Inber Colptha is named for him. The Milesians soon crush the Tuatha Dé Danann, first and more memorably at *Tailtiu [Teltown, Co. Meath], and later at *Druim Ligen. Éremón and *Éber divide Ireland between themselves, but they and Amairgin, the poet brother, continue to contend with one another; Colptha is not mentioned further in the narrative. Aiding the Milesians are the chieftain *Eadán and *Breaga, eponym of the kingdom of *Brega and son of *Breogan. Míl Espáine's widow, Scota (1), accompanies the invaders, giving her name to all the Irish people, the Scoti, as Gaelic-speaking Irishmen were known in Latin; later invaders from *Ulster would take the name across the 'Sea' or Strait of *Moyle to what is now Scotland. Milesian hegemony spread to all corners of Ireland. After a century of Milesian rule the Aitheachthuatha [Ir., plebeian races], composed of surviving elements of the *Fir Bolg, rebelled and set the usurper *Cairbre Cinn-Chait upon his disastrous reign. Cairbre's son *Morann, who could have succeeded him, returned the kingship to the Milesians. Although no mention is made of Milesians in early *Ulster or *Connacht narratives, eventually, through the influence of the *Lebor Gabála*, all Irish aristocrats could claim a common ancestor in Míl Espáine. Other notable Milesians include: *Fuad, son of Breogan, eponoym of *Sliab Fúait [Slieve Fuad]; and *Bladma, eponym of *Sliab Bladma [Slieve Bloom].

See Vernam E. Hull, 'The Milesian Invasion of Ireland', *Zeitschrift für celtische Philologie*, 19 (1932), 155–60; T. F. O'Rahilly, *Early Irish History and Mythology* (Dublin, 1946), 195–9. Charles Maturin employed elements of the invasion story for his historical novel *The Milesian Chief* (London, 1813), before reliable translations of the medieval texts had been produced.

Milisius. Latinized form of *Míl Espáine.

millpreve. Cornish version of the *druidical *adder stones.

Minerva. The name of the Roman goddess of wisdom, invention, and the martial arts was applied by imperial-minded interpretatio romana (see GAUL) to an indigenous deity of the colonized Celts. Julius *Caesar (1st cent. BC) estimated that, while Gaulish Minerva was one of the most esteemed of native gods, she ranked lower than *Mercury, *Apollo, *Mars, and *Jupiter. She was thought to teach the first principles of the arts. Her worship was also known in Roman Britain, where the geographer *Solinus (2nd cent. AD) described her sanctuary as possessing a perpetual fire, thus earning her the epithet Belisama [most brilliant]. More importantly, the cult of Minerva became conflated with that of the British healing goddess *Sulis, especially at the spring at Bath, known as Aquae Sulis in Roman times. The name of the indigenous goddess, Sulis-Minerva or Sul-Minerva, always takes first place in inscriptions. The large gilded bronze head of Sulis-Minerva that survives at Bath, ripped from its torso with helmet severed, indicates that the goddess was portrayed there in classical dress. Minerva also appears to contribute to the conception of the British goddess *Brigantia and the Irish fire-goddess *Brigit. See also ATHENA; SULEVIAE.

Miodhchaoin, Midchaín, Mochaen. Ogre-guardian of a hill in northern *Lochlainn. The three sons of *Tuirenn in *Oidheadh Chlainne Tuireann* are sent by *Lug Lámfhota to take 'three shouts' from him, which leads to their deaths. Miodhchaoin's sons are Áed (10), Conn, and Corc.

Mo Cháemóc, St Caemhoc, Kemoc, Kevoge, Kevoca. Disciple of St *Patrick who brings Christianity to the Children of Lir in **Oidheadh Chlainne Lir* [The Tragic Story of the Children of Lir].

Moccus, Moccos [cf. W *moch*, pigs; Ir. *muc*, pig]. Swine-god of the Continental Gauls, known from his invocation at Langres, France; may have been the guardian of *boar-hunters among the tribe of Lingones. Moccus is linked to and may be an aspect of Gaulish *Mercury.

Mochaen. Corrupt form of *Miodhchaoin.

moddey dhoo. The great black *dog of Manx tradition, sometimes thought to inhabit the halls of Peel Castle on the west coast of the island. Two descriptions have him (*a*) as big as a calf with eyes as large as pewter plates, or (*b*) as a large, dark spaniel with curled, shaggy hair. A local variant of his name is mauthe doog. Cited in Sir Walter Scott's novel *Peveril of the Peak* (1822).

Modron, Madron. Mother of the abducted child *Mabon in the Welsh story of **Culhwch ac Olwen* and, according to the *Triads, the mother of *Owain ab Urien as well. By long-standing learned agreement, her name is derived from that of *Matrona, Gaulish eponym of the Marne River, just as that of her son is derived from *Maponos. The episode of Mabon's abduction while three days old may be a vestige of the myth of the Great Prisoner, a son of the Great Mother who is taken away from the sulphurous powers of *Annwfn. In a folk-tale *Urien Rheged meets a mysterious unnamed *washerwoman at the ford of Rhyd y Gyfarthfa who declares herself the daughter of Annwfn; later she bears him the son Owain and the daughter *Morfudd. Modron appears to have contributed to the figures of the Arthurian women Morgan le Fay and Morgawse.

Mog Ruith, Mogh Ruith. Variant spellings of *Mug Ruith.

Mogons. Name applied to a native Celtic deity recorded in Roman times, often translated as 'the Great One'. The widespread instances of inscription, from north Britain through eastern *Gaul to what is now Germany, plus the wide variety in spellings, Mogunos, Mountus, Mogtus, etc., suggest to some commentators that Mogons may have been a title applied to several deities, such as

*Belatucadros or *Cocidius, rather than the signifier of a single god. His name is sometimes linked with the north British god *Vitiris. The name Mogons is discussed by Kenneth H. Jackson, *Language and History in Early Britain* (Edinburgh, 1953), 444.

Moingfhionn, Moingionn. ModIr. spellings of *Mongfhind.

Mona [orig. *monapia* (?), *monavia* (?), *menavia* (?)]. Roman name for the Isle of *Man, *Anglesey, part of the Scottish coast, and another island in the Irish Sea, probably *Arran, now popularly thought to refer only to Man. 'Mona's Isle' is a nickname for the Isle of Man.

Monanaun. Anglicized spelling from Hiberno-Irish oral tradition for *Manannán mac Lir.

Mong Bán. Variant form for *Mongfhind (2).

Mong Ruadh, Mongroe. Alternative names for *Macha (2).

Mongán [Ir. *mong*, head of long and abundant hair; cf. *moing*, mane, i.e. a poetic kenning for the sea]. Character in several fantastic narratives in the *Cycle of Kings whose persona is rooted in a historical (d. *c.*624) leader of *Dál nAraide. Although his seat was at Ráth Mór [ang. Rathmore] in Mag Líne [ang. Moylinny], near *Lough Neagh, Co. Antrim, Mongán is not a character in the *Ulster Cycle. The Annals record that he was well-spoken and fond of wooing women, and that he was killed with a stone by a Welshman named Artur ap Bicior. Key aspects of his story, such as his magical conception and his capacity for shape-shifting, appear to date from many years after his lifetime.

By historical record, Mongán was the son of powerful Dál nAraide king *Fiachna mac Báetáin and his queen, *Caíntigern, thus bearing the occasional patronymic mac Fiachna. In texts dating from the 8th century and after, the sea-god *Manannán mac Lir fathers Mongán by cuckolding Fiachna in three different ways: (*a*) Manannán appears in disguise on a battlefield in *Lochlainn offering victory to Fiachna in return for a night with Caíntigern. Fiachna agrees, especially as Manannán takes the husband's form, and he is rewarded with victory. Manannán takes the child three days after birth. (*b*) Manannán bargains with Caíntigern, offering victory to Fiachna if she will lie with him, to which she agrees. Later Manannán informs Fiachna and grants him victory. (*c*) Fiachna is fighting in *Scotland when Manannán disguised as a handsome stranger visits Caíntigern, telling her that he will protect her husband if she will lie with him. She agrees; soon afterwards the 'stranger' departs for Scotland, where he intervenes on Fiachna's behalf and tells him what has happened. Mongán's repeated associations with Manannán make word-play on their names, cf. *moing* [mane]. When he is three days old Mongán joins Manannán in *Tír Tairngire [the Land of Promise], where he gains esoteric *knowledge and develops the capacity to take the form of a *deer, *salmon, seal, *swan, and wolf. At 12 he leaves Tír Tairngire, and at 16 he returns to Ulster.

Accounts of Mongán's adult life name three different women as his wife: Fintigernd (or Findthighearn) [fair leader], Breóthigernd (or Breothigearn) [flame leader], and *Dub Lacha; texts vary on whether he has children. Fintigernd is most curious to hear about Mongán's adventures, and after he has stalled her request for seven years she asks him again to recount them while they are at the hill of *Uisnech during a shower of hailstones. Mongán and his wife find refuge in a beautiful house with a bronze roof, attended by seven men with seven vats of *ale. Driven to *buile* [frenzy; see BUILE SHUIBNE] by the ale, Mongán fills what seems like a night with stories; at light of morning the listeners know that a year has passed. The text does not provide the words Mongán speaks.

Another of Mongán's wives, Breóthigernd (perhaps another name for Fintigernd), almost becomes a prize in a dispute with the poet Forgoll. Every night through the whole of winter, Forgoll (perhaps modelled on *Dallán Forgaill) recites stories uneventfully at the palace of Ráth Mór until he claims to have seen the hero *Fothad Airgthech slain. Mongán confutes this, sending Forgoll into a rage. The poet challenges the king to prove Fothad has not been killed as he says or he will satirize him mercilessly. Further, he disdains all recompense except for the pleasure of Breóthigernd, who must sleep with him in three days unless Mongán can back up his challenge with evidence. By the morning of the third day Breóthigernd is understandably forlorn, but Mongán produces by sundown the *Fenian warrior *Caílte, who testifies that he has seen Fothad killed at the Olarba

[Larne] River in Co. Antrim, and identifies the site of the grave. More important than refuting Forgoll, Caílte addresses Mongán by the name *Find (i.e. the predecessor of *Fionn mac Cumhaill). The anonymous author of the text asserts that Mongán was indeed a reincarnation of Find, probably confusing what had earlier been a conceit in oral poetry.

In the most widely known of Mongán's stories, *Tóruigheacht Duibhe Lacha Láimh-ghile* [The Pursuit/Rescue of Dubh Lacha of the White Arms], we once again see a wife bargained to another man and an impostor sleeping with her. Of his three wives Mongán has the most sensual relations with *Dub Lacha [Ir., black duck], born on the same night as he to *Fiachna Dub, a rival of Mongán's father Fiachna mac Báetáin. She is smitten with Mongán and bares her breasts to him; they become husband and wife. After Fiachna Dub kills Fiachna mac Báetáin and divides Ulster, Mongán wreaks vengeance upon him with the help of *Brandub, king of *Leinster. Brandub's price for this 'friendship without refusal' is Dub Lacha. She goes to live with him but disavows sexual relations for a year, during which time Mongán visits her by using tricks and disguises, but Brandub finds them out. Mongán then seeks the help of the hag Cuimne in recovering his wife. Cuimne transforms herself into a beautiful princess of *Munster with a love-spot on her cheek, to be offered to Brandub in exchange for Dub Lacha. Once Dub Lacha is free, Cuimne reverts to her former shape, a rare instance of such reversal.

Forgoll (see above) is not the only poet with whom Mongán contends. According to another story, *Eochaid Éigeas (also Eochu Rígéces), chief poet of the *Ulaid, becomes the household poet of Fiachna mac Báetáin but fears the superior wisdom of the young Mongán. Putting on a disguise and joining three other youths, Mongán begins to goad Eochaid about the origin of six large pillar-stones and other ancient structures. The poet fails to answer three times and is put to shame. Blaming Mongán for this humiliation, Eochaid curses him with a sterility that will deny him any royal issue.

According to the Annals, Mongán foretells his own death. While he is walking on the shore with his mother, she picks up a beautifully coloured stone which he then says will be used to kill him. Horrified, she throws it into the sea far from shore, but the tide carries it back. Later, after Mongán has defeated an army of invading Britons and allowed them a safe retreat, one of the Britons, Artur ap Bicior, picks up the appointed stone and hurls it at Mongán's head, killing him.

Texts: Kuno Meyer and Alfred Nutt, *Immram Brain: The Voyage of Bran*, i (London, 1895–7), 16–17, 24–8; Séamus Mac Mathúna, *Immram Brain* (Tübingen, 1985), 54–6, 101–7; Eleanor Knott, 'Why Mongán Was Deprived of Noble Issue', *Ériu*, 8 (1915–16), 155–60; Séamus Ó Duilearga (ed.), 'Tóruigheacht Duibhe Lacha Láimhghile', *Zeitschrift für celtische Philologie*, 17 (1928), 347–70; T. P. Cross and C. H. Slover (eds.), 'Stories of Mongan', in *Ancient Irish Tales* (New York, 1936), 546–50. Studies: James Carney, *Studies in Irish Literature and History* (Dublin, 1955), 280–95; Proinsias MacCana, 'Mongán mac Fiachna and "Immram Brain"', *Ériu*, 23 (1972), 102–42.

Mongfhind, Mongfind, Mongfhinn, Mong-Finn, Mongfhionn, Moingfhionn, Moingionn [Ir., fair-haired]. Name borne by several female personages in early Ireland and often cited in pedigrees; the best-known is Mongfhind (1).

Mongfhind 1. Wife of *Eochaid Mugmedón and jealous stepmother of *Niall Noígiallach [of the Nine Hostages]. She forces Niall's mother, the bondswoman Cairenn, to do menial labour on her behalf. But in **Echtra Mac nEchach Muigmedóin* [The Adventure of the Sons of Eochaid Mugmedón], Niall makes love to a *sovereignty goddess and so assumes the *kingship ahead of Mongfhind's four sons. Although many records imply that she was a mortal woman, such as being sister of the pre-Patrician king Crimthann Mór mac Fidig, Mongfhind may have been originally a divinity. At one time prayers at *Halloween were addressed to her to ward off evil, especially by the women of *Munster. This was explained by the story that she had died at *Samain time by taking poison intended for Niall.

2. Often Mongfhionn, Mong-Fhinn; also Mong Bán. Nurse and teacher of the *Fianna Éireann, most notably *Diarmait Ua Duibne, *Gíona mac Lugha, and *Mac Lughach.

Mór Muman, Mór Mumhan, Mumain [Ir. *Muman*, of Munster]. Territorial goddess from early southern Ireland. She also has associations with the powers of the sun and of *sovereignty; she was thought so beautiful that every woman in Ireland was compared with her. Of deeply mysterious origin, perhaps a goddess of the *Érainn people before the advent of writing, she is apparently identical with *Mugain (1) and contributes to the characterization of *Medb and *Mórrígan. In time she became a patroness of *Munster in general, occasionally taking the name Mumain or Mugain alone, and patroness of the powerful *Eóganacht in particular.

In an attempt to historicize her, medieval scribes assigned extraordinary qualities to her. Mór knows exaltation or frenzy, lives for a while under enchantment, hears voices, can fly, yet wanders Ireland in rags for two years. More pertinent to a territorial goddess, she is thought to have enjoyed sexual intimacies with known historical figures. At *Cashel she persuades the wife of the reigning king, *Fíngein mac Áeda (d. 613), to have him lie with her. She bears him a son, Sechnasach, but, hearing voices, flees before he is born; Fíngein dies shortly after. She subsequently visits the two other Munster capitals of that time, *Glendamain in north-east Co. Cork and *Cnoc Áine in Co. Limerick. Mór's name lived on in Munster oral tradition and proverbs, in which her children are thought to have suffered misfortunes; she and Mugain (1) are also commemorated in place-names. See Proinsias MacCana, 'Aspects of the Theme of King and Goddess in Irish Literature', *Études Celtiques*, 7 (1955/6), 76–114, 356–413; 8 (1958/9), 59–65. See also CAILLEACH BHÉIRRE; DÍGDE.

Móralltach [Ir., great fury]. Great sword of *Diarmait Ua Duibne, sometimes attributed to *Angus Óg or *Manannán mac Lir.

Morann, Morand. *Druid adviser and counsellor of *Conchobar mac Nessa who prophesied the birth of *Cúchulainn.

Morc. *Fomorian chieftain who taxed and otherwise oppressed the *Nemedians after the death of *Conand. Unlike others of his ilk, Morc was thought to have come from Africa.

Morfran, Morvran [W, great crow; sea crow]. Hideously ugly son of *Tegid Foel and the goddess *Ceridwen, to whom she hoped to give the power of poetic inspiration. Her servant *Gwion Bach, later to become *Taliesin, receives it instead. He may also be known as Y Fagddu or Afagddu [utter darkness]. Morfran is also a warrior in Welsh Arthuriana; no one would strike him in battle because his ugliness made opponents fear he might be the devil. See Rachel Bromwich, *Trioedd Ynys Prydain*, rev. edn. (Cardiff, 1978), 463–4, 558.

Morfudd, Morfydd [cf. W *morwyn*, maiden]. Name borne by many women from early Welsh tradition, the best-known of whom is the most abiding love of the poet *Dafydd ap Gwilym (*fl.* 1320–70), though she was married to Y Bwa Bach. Another is a daughter of *Modron and *Urien.

Morgannwg. Name loosely applied to south-eastern *Wales that has had different definitions at different times. There was a petty kingdom of Morgannwg in pre-Norman Wales, which was sometimes allied to *Gwent, its neighbour to the east. In the **Mabinogi*, *Pwyll expands his kingdom by occupying portions of Morgannwg. After the Act of Union with England, 1536, when the region was joined with nearby Gower to form the county of Glamorgan, the name Morgannwg still pertained to the regional literary tradition that flourished, with interruptions, from the 14th century to the time of *Iolo Morganwg (1747–1826).

Morganwg, Iolo. See IOLO MORGANWG.

Moriath. Variant spelling of *Muiriath.

Moritasgus. Occasional epithet of Gaulish *Apollo.

Morna, Clan. Rival *Fianna to *Fionn mac Cumhaill's Clan *Baíscne. James *Macpherson's counterpart in the *Poems of Ossian* (1760–3) was Morni. See also CONÁN MAC MORNA; GARAD MAC MORNA; GOLL MAC MORNA.

Morna of the White Neck. Anglicization of *Muirenn Muncháem.

Mórrígan, Morrígan, Mórrigan, Morríghan, Mór-Ríogain, Morrígu, Morrigu [Ir., great queen; phantom queen (?)]. Goddess of war fury in early Irish tradition, usually spoken of with the definite article, 'the Mórrígan'. She is part of a trio of war-goddesses called the *Mórrígna, with *Badb and *Macha. *Nemain may sometimes also be part of the three, but perhaps she is an aspect of either Badb or the Mórrígan. Some commentators argue that Mórrígna is identical with Mórrígan, and that Badb, Macha, and Nemain are all aspects of her. As war-goddess she does not engage in combat herself but rather affects armies psychologically, especially by her frightful appearance. Her persona in several early Irish narratives, notably the *Táin Bó Cuailnge [Cattle Raid of Cooley], fuses her bellicosity with an alluring sexuality. Probably an emanation of the Irish earth-goddess *Ana, the Mórrígan has the power of prophecy and can cast spells. She has, additionally, the ability to transform herself into a bird, fish, or animal and from a beautiful young girl into a hag. Much associated with the *crow, the Mórrígan is often described as living in the cave of *Cruachain in Co. Roscommon, also home to Medb.

Like Badb and Macha, she is the daughter of *Ernmas. The Mórrígan may or may not be the wife/consort of the *Dagda, but regardless of her bond with him her copulation with him is widely known. At the great feast of *Samain she was washing herself, with one foot on either bank, at the River Unshin (or Uinnius; downstream, Ballysadare) 4 miles SE of Ballymote, Co. Sligo. After their love-making, she told the Dagda that the *Fomorians would soon attack the *Tuatha Dé Danann in a combat to be known as the Second Battle of Mag Tuired [**Cath Maige Tuired*]. She then began to harass the *Fomorian warrior *Indech, either to drain the valour and vitality out of him, as in one version (in which he is later killed by *Ogma), or to murder him immediately, passing out handfuls of his blood to gaping bystanders. The only son attributed to her is *Mechi, the father not named.

Whereas the Mórrígan is an ally of the Tuatha Dé Danann at Mag Tuired, she is a patron of *Connacht in the *Táin Bó Cuailnge*, signalled in part by her residence at the Connacht fortress of Cruachain. Early in the action she journeys across Ireland to bring a cow to the Brown Bull of Ulster, *Donn Cuailnge, and to warn him of what is to come. In the text she sometimes bears the epithet buan, evocative of the Amazonian *Búanann, but in her dealings with the Ulster hero *Cúchulainn she is a *femme fatale*. She first approaches him as a lovely young girl, clearly wanting him to make love to her, but he rebuffs her, saying that he 'does not have time for women's backsides'. She then comes to him as an *eel, a wolf, and a hornless, red heifer, to no avail. He breaks the ribs of the eel, puts an eye out of the wolf, and breaks the leg of the heifer. Later when she sees him in combat she approaches him as an old milch cow; when he asks for a drink she allows suckling from each of her three teats. Later she tells Cúchulainn that he will die when the calf of her cow is a yearling. To help matters along she breaks his chariot wheels. And at the end the Mórrígan appears on his shoulder as a hooded *crow, portending the scavenging of his corpse. The Mórrígan also contends with Cúchulainn in the short but baffling *Táin Bó Regamna*; see T. P. Cross and C. H. Slover (eds.), *Ancient Irish Tales* (New York, 1936), 211–14.

Not all of the Mórrígan's spells are made on the battlefield. After she lures away the bull of a blameless woman named Odras, wife of Buchat, living near *Tara, the poor mortal woman follows the bull into the cave of Cruachain, an entrance to the *Otherworld, where she falls asleep. Finding her, the Mórrígan changes her into a pool of water. Surprisingly, the Mórrígan did not attract much attention from storytellers in oral tradition, but she was sighted at Clontarf (AD 1014) and probably contributed to the conception of the *banshee. Her name is alluded to in half a dozen place-names, notably Dá Cích na Mórrígna [two breasts/paps of Mórrígan] near Newgrange, Co. Meath. She may be the old woman implied in the Hebridean whirlpool of *Corry-Vreckan, popularly known as the 'cauldron of the old woman'. Commentators have seen parallels between Mórrígan and the Sumerian/Babylonian earth-goddess Innini/ Innana/ Inanna as well as the Valkyries of Norse tradition, who also take avian form as *swans. Folk motif: A485.1. See also MÓR MUMAN; WASHER AT THE FORD.

See William M. Hennessy, 'The Ancient Irish Goddess of War', *Revue Celtique*, 1 (1870), 32–55; Charles Donahue, 'The Valkyries and the Irish War Goddesses', *PMLA*, 56 (1941), 1–12; Garrett E. Olmstead, 'Mórrígan's Warning to Donn Cuailnge', *Études Celtiques*, 19 (1982), 165–72; John Carey, 'Notes on the Irish War-Goddess', *Éigse*, 19 (1982/3), 263–75; Françoise Le Roux and Christian-J. Guyonvarc'h, *La Souveraineté guerrière de l'Irlande: Mórrígan, Bodb, Macha* (Rennes, 1983); Rosalind Clark, 'Aspects of the Morrígan in Early Irish Poetry', *Irish University Review*, 17(2) (1987), 223–36; Rosalind Elizabeth Clark, *Great Queens: Irish Goddesses from the Morrígan to Cathleen Ní Houlihan* (Gerrards Cross and Savage, Md., 1990).

Recent elaborations of the Mórrígan's persona in popular fiction include Patricia Finney, *The Crow Goddess* (London, 1978) and Pat O'Shea's popular novel *The Hounds of Mórrígan* (London, 1985).

Mórrígna, Mórrigna [Ir., great queens]. Name for a trio of war-goddesses, usually thought to consist of *Badb, *Macha, and *Mórrígan. *Nemain is sometimes named, either because she is a double for or substitute for Badb or for Mórrígan. Some commentators argue that Mórrígna is identical with Mórrígan and that Badb, Macha, and Nemain are all aspects of her. See Françoise Le Roux and Christian-J. Guyonvarc'h, *La Souveraineté guerrière de l'Irlande: Mórrígan, Bodb, Macha* (Rennes, 1983).

Morvah. Granite moor 6 miles NW of Penzance on the north-western slope of the furthest promontory of Land's End, Cornwall, containing distinctive megaliths, which was formerly the site of a *Lughnasa-like August festival. Morvah's most distinctive feature is the doughnut-shaped Men-an-tol [Corn., holed stone], which originally formed the entrance to a chambered tomb and which acquired a reputation for healing powers in oral tradition. In the 19th century three acres of the moor were set aside for the Morvah Fair on 1 August, a time for horse-racing, merrymaking, courtship games, and storytelling, featuring the hero Jack the Tinkard. The Morvah legend begins when Tom, a local *giant, uses an axle-beam and cartwheel to overcome an evil giant whose uprooted tree cannot save him in combat. Tom moves into the evil giant's castle, assumes his great wealth, marries, and has a family. Soon Tom is joined by yet another giant, Jack the Tinkard, who is initially hostile but eventually becomes an ally. Like the Irish hero *Lug Lámfhota, Jack is the master of many skills, which encourages Tom to allow him his daughter's hand. To make a home for his bride, Jack kills the giant of Morvah by taking the cover off an old mineshaft and letting his opponent fall into it. Jack's wedding and the union of Jack and Tom's families takes place on 1 August.

mouse lord. See LUCHTIGERN

Moy, Moy-. Phonetic anglicization of the Irish *Mag [plain] found in both imaginary and actual place-names, e.g. Moytura, Moytirra, see MAG TUIRED; Moynalty, see MAG NELTA.

Moyle, Sea of [Ir. *Sruth na Maoile*, stream of the bare, rounded summit]. Archaic and poetic name for the narrowest expanse of water between Northern Ireland and *Scotland, the Mull of Kintyre, usually known as the North Channel. When Northern Ireland was redistricted in 1974, the voting unit immediately adjacent to the North Channel, formerly in Co. Antrim, became known as Moyle.

Mug Nuadat [servant of Nuadu]. An alternative form of *Eógan Mór of the *Eóganacht. When Eógan claimed those parts of *Ireland south of *Eiscir Riada, between Galway and Dublin, that became known as *Leth Moga [Mug's half].

Mug Ruith, Roith, Mog Ruith, Ruth, Mogh Ruith [cf. OIr. *mug*, male servant]. Celebrated *druid of early Ireland, sometimes called the archdruid; sometimes described as *one-eyed or blind. Son of *Cethern (3), his patron was the goddess *Ana. T. F. O'Rahilly (1946) argues that Mug Ruith was originally a sun-god, as his one eye implies. Further, by merely blowing his breath he could dry up waters or raise tempests. Because he was a champion of paganism against Christianity, a learned Christian medieval interpolator made Mug Ruith an associate of *Simon Magus [Ir. *Símón Druí*], a bitter opponent of St Peter in later ecclesiastical legend. Together Simon Magus and Mug Ruith construct a flying machine, *roth rámach [Ir., rowing wheel], which was later seen at *Tlachtga, the fair named for Mug Ruith's daughter. In **Forbais Dromma Damgaire* [The Siege of Knocklong], *Fiachu Muillethan grants him a large tract of land in north Co. Cork. Mug Ruith was also associated with Valencia Island, Co. *Kerry.

Mugain, Mugan, Mughain. Name borne by several female personages in early Ireland, including at least one saint. Uncommon variant form: Mumain.

Mugain 1. Sometimes Mugain Mór [Ir., great]. Territorial goddess of the south of Ireland who is reputed to have given birth to a trout. She appears to be identical with the better-known *Mór Muman.

2. Strumpet wife of *Conchobar mac Nessa, king of Ulster, daughter of *Eochaid Feidlech, sister of *Medb. In an often

repeated episode, she and her maidens strip naked before *Cúchulainn as he is returning from battle on his way to *Emain Macha; though this is done ostensibly to stifle his battle fever, he is so consumed with passion upon seeing the women that it takes three vats of icy water to cool him down. Later she is caught in adultery with *Áed (9), a court poet. Conchobar sentences Áed to death by drowning, but he has the power to dry up any lake with a spell, all except Lough Laíg, near the house of *Lóegaire Búadach. In coming to Áed's help, Lóegaire himself is killed. In earlier Ulster stories Conchobar's wife is Eithne Aittencháithrech. See EITHNE (5).

3. Adulterous wife of *Diarmait mac Cerbaill. Her co-respondent, *Flann mac Díma, suffers more for their sin. Flann's house is burned and he is later drowned. This in turn brings about Diarmait's death. She is the mother of *Áed Sláine, ancestor of the people of *Brega.

4. Mother of St *Cuimmíne, who begot him in incest. Her name appears in the quatrain, 'This Mugain was his mother, he to her was a brother.'

Muicinis [pig island]. Name for *Ireland in Geoffrey *Keating's 17th-century history.

Muilearteach, Muileartach, Muilidheartach, Muireatach. The water form taken by the monstrous *Cailleach Bheur of Scottish Gaelic tradition, known in the *Duan na Muileartaich* [Heroic Poem/Ode of Muilearteach].

Muirchertach, Muircheartach, Moriartogh [Ir., skilled in seacraft, mariner]. Common man's name in early and medieval Ireland, cited countlessly in pedigrees and genealogies. The best-known bearer is the legendary *ard rí [high king] *Muirchertach mac Erca. The most common of many anglicizations are Murtaugh, Mortimer, and Monty.

Muirchertach mac Erca. Legendary 6th-century *ard ri [high king] of Ireland, a figure in the *Cycle of the Kings, and great-grandson of the putatively historical *Niall Noígiallach [of the Nine Hostages], to whom several fanciful tales have attached. He is thought to have sent the coronation stone, *Lia Fáil, to his brother *Fergus mac Eirc of *Dál Riada in *Scotland so that he might be crowned sitting on it; Fergus refused to return it. The best-known story about him portrays the romantic sequence of events that leads to his death. One day while Muirchertach is seated alone on his hunting-mound a beautiful damsel in a green mantle approaches, saying that she has been seeking him, and so fills him with love and desire that he declares he would give all of Ireland for one night of passion with her. She agrees under three conditions, that he never utter her name, that the mother of his children never be in her sight, and that the clerics of the house leave whenever she enters it. In accepting her demands Muirchertach asks what her name is so that he may avoid uttering it. Despite her loveliness, the damsel follows the loathsome *Cailb in uttering a string of ambiguous but threatening-sounding names, 'Sigh, Sough, Storm [Ir. *Sín*], Rough Wind, Winter-night, Cry, Wail, Groan'. To please the damsel, Muirchertach turns his queen and their children out of his residence at [Sídh] *Clettig near the *Boyne and instead brings in craftsmen and their wives to his drinking-hall. Seeing what has happened, with the beautiful damsel sitting at Muirchertach's right hand, St Cairnech curses his house and his reign. In her defence the damsel says that she believes in God and is a child of Adam and Eve; yet she can perform works of wonder, such as turning the Boyne water into wine or making pigs from ferns. These flow from her for seven nights until the eve of Wednesday after *Samain, when foul weather reminds the king of the onset of winter. The damsel responds, 'I am the Rough Wind . . . winter night is my time . . . Sigh and Wind, winter-night.' When Muirchertach speaks of the storm [Sín] raging outside, she responds sharply, asking why he has uttered her forbidden name and telling him that he is now doomed. Muirchertach admits that he thinks he is indeed doomed, as it has been foretold that he will die as he has killed his own grandfather by burning him in his house. His troubled sleep is now filled with visions of drowning and fire. An angry Sín then sets Muirchertach's house ablaze and surrounds it with phantom attackers led by the menacing Tuathal Máelgarb [rough-head]. In a futile attempt to escape Muirchertach climbs into a wine cask, but he drowns even as the fire falls upon his head and burns the upper part of his body.

See Whitley Stokes, 'The Death of Muirchertach mac Erca', *Revue Celtique*, 23 (1902), 395–437; repr. in T. P. Cross and C. H. Slover (eds.), *Ancient Irish Tales* (New York, 1936), 518–32.

muirdris. Original name for the fearsome sea-monster *Fergus mac Léti kills in Lough Rudraige, Dundrum Bay, Co. Down. In later texts the monster is called *sínach. See also CAORÁNACH; OILLIPHÉIST.

Muirenn Muncháem, Muireann Munchaomh, Muirne, Murna, Morna, Murine [Ir., cf. *muin*, back, neck; *cáem*, fair, beautiful]. Often called Muirenn/ Murna of the White Neck in English texts. Mother of *Fionn mac Cumhaill who bore her son after the death of his father, *Cumhall. Descendant of *Nuadu Airgetlám, Muirenn was the daughter of *Tadg mac Nuadat, who opposed her marriage to Cumhall and had him killed. In oral tradition Muirenn was thought to have been unable to raise her infant herself and so to have put him under the care of nurses, *Bodhmall, a *druidess and Muirenn's sister, and *Liath Luachra (2). Her sister is *Uirne, mother of *Bran (2) and Sceolang. Hera in Greek mythology is also known for her white neck.

Muireatach. Variant spelling of *Muilearteach.

Muiriath, Moriath. Daughter of *Scoriath in **Orgain Denna Ríg* [The Destruction of Dind Ríg] who marries *Labraid Loingsech and returns with him to his kingdom in *Leinster.

Muirtheimne. See MAG MUIRTHEIMNE.

Mullaghmast, Mullagh Mast, Mullamast [Ir. *mullach*, a hilltop; *maisten*, of Maiste]. Hill (563 feet) 1 mile W of Ballitore, Co. Kildare, rich in mythological and archaeological associations. In nearby Glenn Treithim [OIr. *Treichim*], the *smith-god *Goibniu was thought to have had his forge. Copper ore was mined here in ancient times to make swords and spears. A standing stone formerly at Mullaghmast, now in the National Museum, contains a three-armed triskele; commentators are divided over whether it was once sacred to the pagan goddess *Brigit or exemplifies very early Christian art. In the *ráth at Mullaghmast is thought to lie Gearóid [ang. Garret] Óg, the 11th Earl of Kildare, who emerges once every seven years to ride around the Curragh of Kildare on a horse with silver shoes. (His story is easily confused with that of *Gerald Fitzgerald, 3rd Earl of Desmond.) Two events from modern history have greater resonance in the popular imagination. The first was the treacherous slaughter by the English and their O'Dempsey allies of the chiefs of Laoighis (ModIr. Laois) and Uí Fháilghe on New Year's Day 1577. According to folk etymology, the English adventurer Maiste, eponym of mullach maisten, led the Irishmen to their deaths. The second was when Daniel O'Connell held a 'Monster Meeting' here on 1 October 1843.

Mullo [L, mule, horse]. Roman name for a native god worshipped in north-western *Gaul, not entirely separable from Gaulish *Mars, for whom his name is sometimes an epithet. His name survives in several shrines and inscriptions, most notably a circular temple at Craôn. Despite his name linking him to the mule and horse, Mullo was probably more associated with Mars as a healing god, especially of diseases of the eye. See P. Térouanne, 'Dédicaces à Mars Mullo découvertes à Allones (Sarthe)', *Gallia*, 18 (1960), 185–9.

Mumain. Variant of *Mugain; see also MÓR MUMAN.

Mumu. OIr. name for *Munster.

Mungo. See KENTIGERN.

Munster [OIr. *Mumu*; ON *staðir*, steadings]. A province of Ireland occupying much of the south and south-west of the island, the largest (9,317 square miles) of the four, including *Connacht, *Leinster, and *Ulster, whose borders were drawn in the 17th century. In pre-conquest Ireland, as Cóiced Muman, it was either one of five, when *Mide/*Meath was counted separately, or was divided into two provinces. Another division was into East Munster, Aurmumu [*Ormond], and West Munster, Iarmumu or Irmumu, reflecting real political and geographical polarization; and in the 12th century an actual partition of the province took place between the O'Brien kingdom of North Munster, Tuadmuma [*Thomond], and the MacCarthy kingdom of South Munster, Desmuma [*Desmond]. Within its borders are the counties of Clare, Cork, *Kerry, Limerick, Tipperary, and Waterford.

Much of the fortune of early Munster is tied to the great dynasty of the *Eóganacht. Early medieval Munster had theoretically three capitals serving in rotation, *Cashel in Tipperary, *Glendamain in Cork, and *Cnoc Áine in Limerick; Temair Luachra was a regional capital. Many territorial goddesses are linked to Munster, including *Mór Muman (or Mugain (1)), *Dígde, whose personality merges with a figure surviving much longer in popular tradition, the *Cailleach Bhéirre, *Áine, *Aíbell, and *Ana.

Murias. One of the four great cities of the *Tuatha Dé Danann, from whence came the great *cauldron of the *Dagda.

Murine. Anglicization of *Muirenn Muncháem.

Murna of the White Neck. Anglicization of *Muirenn Muncháem.

Murtaugh. Anglicization of *Muirchertach.

Murthemne. See MAG MUIRTHEIMNE.

Muskerry [Ir. *Múscraige, Múscraighe*]. Anglicized name for ancient and medieval petty kingdom of *Munster coextensive with north-west and central Co. Cork.

Mynyddog Mwynfawr [cf. L *montanus*, mountain; W *mwynfawr*, rich]. Ruler of the 6th-century petty kingdom of Gododdin who raises a war-band to make war on the Angles and Saxons in *Y *Gododdin*, with disastrous results. His capital is *Din Eidyn (probably Edinburgh). A speculative translation of his name is 'king of the mountain'; he is often known as Mynyddog the Wealthy in English texts. See Rachel Bromwich, *Trioedd Ynys Prydain*, rev. edn. (Cardiff, 1978), 467–9; Graham Isaac, *Bulletin of the Board of Celtic Studies*, 37 (1990), 111–13.

Myrddin, Merddin [W *myr/mor*, sea; *ddin*, hill]. Fictional 6th-century Welsh poet and prophet, antecedent of and counterpart to *Merlin, whose Arthurian conception begins with *Geoffrey of Monmouth (12th cent.). A member of the court of *Gwenddolou fab Ceido, Myrddin was so traumatized by his patron's death at the battle of *Arfderydd (573/5) that he fled to the Caledonian forests [W *Celyddon*, Scotland], where he became a *wild man of the wood for half a century, communing with animals and living in fear of *Rhydderch Hael, Gwenddolou's enemy; at the end of this torment, he received the gift of prophecy. A number of early mantic poems are attributed to Myrddin, including **Afallenau* [The Apple Trees]. Myrddin's exile, madness, and poetic gifts sometimes gain him the epithet Gwyllt or Wyllt [mad], and link him with the Irish figure Suibne Geilt [Ir., mad Suibne/Sweeney] of **Buile Shuibne* [The Frenzy of Suibne]. The oldest text referring to Myrddin comes in the 10th-century **Armes Prydain* [The Prophecy of Britain]. For most of Welsh Arthuriana after Geoffrey of Monmouth, Myrddin is often indistinguishable from Merlin, the most important difference being Myrddin's ongoing dialogue with another Old North figure inflated into a magical prophet, *Taliesin; this culminates in the 12th-century **Ymddiddan Myrddin a Thaliesin* [The Colloquy between Myrddin/Merlin and Taliesin] in which the two impart arcane *knowledge to each other. See EMRYS WLEDIG; LAILOKEN; SENCHA MAC AILELLA. See also A. O. H. Jarman, *The Legend of Merlin* (Cardiff, 1960); 'The Welsh Myrddin Poems', in R. S. Loomis (ed.), *Arthurian Literature in the Middle Ages* (Oxford, 1959), 20–30; Basil Clarke, *Life of Merlin* (Cardiff, 1972); Nikolai Tolstoy, *The Quest for Merlin* (London and Boston, 1985).

Mythological Cycle. A large body of pseudo-historical narrative, romance, and verse centring on the imagined successive invasions of early Ireland, culminating in the arrival of the semi-divine *Tuatha Dé Danann, their champion *Lug Lámfhota, their defeat of the *Fir Bolg, and their defeat by the mortal *Milesians. It is one of the four major cycles of early Irish tradition, along with the *Ulster and *Fenian Cycles and the *Cycle of the Kings. Somewhat awkward today, the phrase 'Mythological Cycle' was coined to describe those early stories that, in the absence of a Celtic cosmology, deal most with origins and the discernible remnants of pre-Christian religion; its first usage pre-dates the currency of 'Celtic mythology'. While many of the events of the Mythological Cycle appear to occur prior to the action of the other cycles, the composition of individual narratives is now dated after many Ulster and some Fenian stories. Manuscripts of Mythological Cycle narratives are found in the oldest codices, the **Book of the Dun Cow* (before 1106) and the **Book of Leinster* (12th cent.), with correlatives in the *Dindshenchas (12th cent.), but some narratives, such as **Oidheadh Chlainne Lir* [The Tragic Story of the Children of Lir], do not appear to have been composed until much later.

More than in the other three cycles, the narrative point of view in the Mythological

Cycle is accepting of wizardry and magical transformations. *Angus Óg, his lover *Cáer, and the Children of Lir are all turned into *swans, and *Étaín (1) becomes a butterfly. Allusion to magic also pervades the fictionalized history of Ireland, synchronized to agree with biblical revelation and known events from ancient world history. The invasion of history as told in the *Lebor Gabála* was thought to have begun with *Cesair, before the biblical Flood, and continued with five waves of invaders, the *Partholonians, the *Nemedians, the *Fir Bolg, the *Tuatha Dé Danann, and finally the *Milesians. Each had to contend with the hated predatory pirates lurking off the north-west coast, the *Fomorians. Despite the text's inventiveness, modern commentators have argued that the various invaders of the *Lebor Gabála* have correlatives, admittedly shadowy, in the waves of early Celtic peoples settling on the island. In **Cath Maige Tuired* [The (Second) Battle of Mag Tuired], a text of deep and mysterious resonances, the Tuatha Dé Danann, under the maimed king Nuadu Airgetlám [of the Silver Hand], do battle with the Fomorians, the champion Lug Lámfhota killing the monstrous giant *Balor.

Personages most often cited in the Mythological Cycle are firstly Lug Lámfhota, the Dagda, Nuadu Airgetlám, and Míl Espáine, but also: *Áine (1), *Ana, *Angus Óg, *Balor, *Boand, *Bres, *Bran mac Febail, *Brian (1), *Brigit, the *Cailleach Bhéirre, *Cairbre mac Ethne, *Cesair, *Clídna, *Cridenbél, *Dian Cécht, *Donn (1), *Donn mac Míled, *Eochaid Airem, *Eochaid mac Eirc, *Étaín (1), *Étaín Óg, *Fintan mac Bóchra, *Goibniu, *Iuchair, *Iucharba, *Lir, *Macha, *Manannán mac Lir, *Midir, the *Mórrígan, *Nemed, *Ogma, and *Partholón.

See also AISLINGE ÓENGUSO [The Vision of Angus], ALTROM TIGE DÁ MEDAR [The Nurture of the Houses of the Two Milk-Vessels], CATH MAIGE TUIRED [The (Second) Battle of Mag Tuired], LEBOR GABÁLA [Book of Invasions], OIDHEADH CHLAINNE LIR [The Tragic Story of the Children of Lir], OIDHEADH CHLAINNE TUIREANN [The Tragic Story of the Children of Tuireann], and TOCHMARC ÉTAÍNE [The Wooing of Étaín]. All commentary is addressed to individual narratives.

N

N. The fourteenth letter of the modern English alphabet is represented by nin [Ir., *ash] in the *ogham alphabet of early Ireland.

Naas. See NÁS.

Nabelcus. Sometime epithet of Gaulish *Mars. See G. Barroul, 'Mars Nabelcus et Mars Albiorex', *Ogam*, 15 (1963), 343–68.

Nadcranntail, Natchrantel. *Connacht champion in *Medb's service in **Táin Bó Cuailnge* [Cattle Raid of Cooley]. He takes a third of his army on a daring raid into *Ulster and finds the Brown *Bull in Antrim, driving it and its herd back home. He refuses to fight *Cúchulainn because the latter is a beardless boy, so Cúchulainn dons a false beard and quickly dispatches him.

nain. Fearsome, *demon-like creature of Breton folklore. Black and menacing, the nain peers down at travellers like a gargoyle. His hands are feline claws, his feet hooves like a satyr, and under his dark elf-locks his small red eyes gleam like carbuncles. While he haunts ancient *dolmens, especially in Morbihan, built by a vanished race, he may also encounter mortals on lonely heaths and unfrequented roads. Wednesday is his favourite day, and his great nocturnal festival is held on the first Wednesday in May. Nains were thought to have originated in the cabalistic alphabet carved in several megalithic monuments. Like the *gorics, nains are the guardians of hidden treasure.

Naísi. Variant spelling of *Noíse, lover of *Deirdre.

Nantosuelta, Nantosvelta. Gaulish raven-goddess whose worship is recorded in several locations, including Britain. Her iconography is puzzling. In her left hand she carries a saucer or patera, evidently used for sacrifice on an altar; in some instances the saucer is replaced by a small pot, which may be an evocation of the great Celtic *cauldron. In her left hand she carries what looks like a small house set at the end of a long pole. While the patera and house-on-pole may imply prosperity, well-being, and domesticity, her constant association with the carrion-eating raven evokes sombre associations with death. Her usual cult-partner is *Sucellus [L, the good striker]. See Salomon Reinach, 'Sucellus et Nantosvelta', *Revue Celtique*, 17 (1896), 45–9; E. Linckenheld, 'Sucellus et Nantosuelta', *Revue de l'Histoire des Religions*, 99 (1929), 40–92; Miranda J. Green, *Symbol and Image in Celtic Religious Art* (London and New York, 1989), 27, 42–3, 49.

Naoise. ModIr. spelling of *Noíse, lover of *Deirdre.

Nár [shame]. *One-eyed swineherd of *Bodb Derg, known for his aggressive disposition; it was said that he never attended a feast where he did not shed blood. His sometime epithet Tuathcháech was thought to mean 'having but one eye, and that an evil one'. Often confused with Bodb's other swineherd, *Friuch.

Nás, Naas, Nass. One of the four wives of *Lug Lámfhota. Through folk invention the town of Naas [ModIr. *Nás na Ríogh*, the assembly place of the kings] has been ascribed as her birth- or burial-place. The site of Naas, however, was a residence of the kings of *Leinster until the 10th century, thus a meeting-place for great assemblies.

Natchrantal. Variant spelling of *Nadcranntail.

Navan Fort. See EMAIN MACHA.

Neachtan. Variant spelling of *Nechtan (1) and *Nechtan (2).

Neamhain. ModIr. for *Nemain.

Neara. ModIr. spelling of *Nera; see ECHTRA NERAI [The Adventure of Nera].

Nechta Scéne. Variant spelling of *Nechtan Scéne.

Nechtan 1, Neachtan [cf. L *Neptune*]. This husband of *Boand was the only person, other than his three cupbearers, who could visit *Connla's Well, over which the nine *hazel trees dropped their nuts. When Boand broke this taboo, the well rose up and chased her, becoming the River *Boyne. Recent scholarship suggests that Nechtan may be but a pseudonym for *Nuadu Airgetlám, whose cult superseded this early divinity of waters. In the *Dindshenchas his father is described as *Labraid Loingsech. *Cúchulainn used Nechtan's spear, *Del Chliss, to kill the three sons of *Nechtan Scéne. The *sídh of Nechtan is identified with Carbery Hill, Co. Kildare. See Patrick K. Ford, 'The Well of Nechtan and *la gloire lumineuse*', in Gerald J. Larson et al. (eds.), *Myth in Indo-European Antiquity* (Santa Barbara, Calif., 1974), 67–74.

2, **Nechtan.** Member of the crew in **Imram Brain* [The Voyage of Bran] who is lonely for Ireland and decides to return home. Different texts describe him as the son of Collbrain. His characterization may draw on that of the Roman sea-god Neptune.

3, **Nechtan, Nichtan.** Historical 7th- and 8th-century *Pictish king who converted to Christianity and adopted Roman law *c.*710. Inviting Northumbrian architects to what is now Scotland, he built a shrine over the supposed relics of St Andrew, later to be the centre of the university town of St Andrews. He also helped to establish St Andrew as Scotland's patron saint. *Nechtansmere is named for him.

Nechtan Scéne, Nechta Scéne, Nechtan Scéine. The three warriors known as the sons of Nechtan Scéne, Fannell, Foill, and Tuchell, had murdered half as many *Ulstermen as there were living before they met *Cúchulainn in his very first combat. He used the spear *Del Chliss of *Nechtan (1) to dispatch them.

Nechtansmere, Dun of Nechtan. Site of a *Pictish victory over the Northumbrians, 685, after which King Unuist recovered lost territory. The spot is known as Linn Garan [pool of the *crane] in Scottish Gaelic and is identified with the ruin known as Dunnichen or Dunnechain, near Forfar, Tayside.

Nefyd Naf Neifion, Nefyed Nav Nevion [W *naf*, lord; *Neifion*, Neptune]. Builder of the ship that allows *Dwyfan and his wife *Dwyfach to escape the *flooding of *Llyn Llion. American popular novelist Lloyd Alexander anglicizes this name as Nevvid Nav Neivion in his Taran Wanderer series, *c.*1975-*c.*1985. See also the Irish NEMED.

Nehalennia, Nehalannia [leader (?); steerswoman (?)]. Latin name for a Celtic goddess of seafarers worshipped at two sites along the North Sea which have since been inundated by rising waters. Depicted as a young woman in distinctive (perhaps local) dress, a small round cap and short shoulder-cape, she is often seen seated in a chair with fruit baskets in her lap and besides, and most individualizing, nearly always accompanied by a *dog. Surviving evidence indicates she was patronized by wealthy patrons, Roman citizens who were Celts but perhaps also Germans. See A. Hondius-Crone, *The Temple of Nehalennia at Domburg* (Amsterdam, 1955); J. van Aartsen, *Deae Nehalenniae* (Middelburg, Netherlands, 1971); Miranda J. Green, *Symbol and Image in Celtic Religious Art* (London and New York, 1989), 10–16.

Neimheadh. ModIr. spelling of *Nemed.

Néit, Nét, Neith. Shadowy early Irish god of war, often grouped with the *Fomorians. He is usually portrayed as having two wives or consorts, *Badb and *Nemain. This does not make him an adulterer; rather, he may be married to either, or the identity of one consort may drift to the other or to their husband. Additionally, his two grandsons *Balor and *Goibniu stand on opposite sides of the epochal Second Battle of Mag Tuired [**Cath Maige Tuired*]; T. F. O'Rahilly (1946) thinks both Balor and Goibniu derive from conceptions of the sun and may ultimately be identical. Although a divinity, Néit is killed at Mag Tuired.

Nemain, Nemainn, Nemon, Neman, Némain, Neamhain, Nemhain [battle-fury, war-like frenzy]. Shadowy early Irish war-goddess, wife/consort of *Néit along with *Badb, whose identity she may share. Old Irish texts cite three goddesses of war, usually Badb, *Macha, and *Mórrígan, known collectively as *Mórrígna. When the name Nemain is substituted in the trio for either Badb or Mórrígan, commentators are inclined to see her as an aspect of either of them; alternatively, all three may be aspects of Mórrígan. At the same time, her name carries an echo of the Gaulish and British goddess *Nemetona.

Nemed, Nemed mac Agnomain, Nemhedh, Neimheadh, Nemedius [cf. OIr. *neimed*, holy, sacred; privilege, sanctity]. Eponymous leader of the *Nemedians, third mythic invaders of early Ireland, according to the pseudo-history *Lebor Gabála [Book of Invasions]. A *Scythian descended from the biblical Magog and son of *Japheth, Nemed landed in Ireland with only his wife *Macha (1), four sons and their wives, and twenty others. Macha died after twelve years and was buried at Ard Macha [*Armagh], which in this text is named for her. Another wife is named *Cera. Three of his sons are *Fergus Lethderg, Iarbonél the soothsayer, and Starn. After building his fortress at Rath Chinneich in south Armagh in one day, he slaughtered the scions who helped him lest they build a better one for someone else. Nemed led his people in three victories over the hated Fomorians, after which the Fomorians made vassals of them, exacting heavy tribute. Nemed died of the plague on Ard Nemid, now called Great Island, in Cork Harbour; tradition implies that Ard Nemid commemorates Nemed, but T. F. O'Rahilly (1946) asserts that the place-name derives from Nemed's shadowy namesake Nemed mac Sroibcinn. See Vernam E. Hull, 'The Invasion of Nemed', *Modern Philology*, 23 (1935), 119–23.

Nemedians. Mythical early invaders of Ireland according to the pseudo-history *Lebor Gabála [Book of Invasions], named for the eponymous founder *Nemed. They came third in succession after (1) *Cesair and (2) the *Partholonians, who preceded them by thirty years. Contemporary with the predatory *Fomorians, arbitrarily cited here as the fourth invaders, the Nemedians preceded the *Fir Bolg by eleven generations. Departing from *Scythia in thirty-four ships, all but one lost when the party greedily pursued a tower of gold seen on the sea, the Nemedians wandered the world for a year and a half before landing in Ireland at a site and time not made specific. Least remarkable and romanticized of the *Lebor Gabála* invaders, the Nemedians built two royal fortresses (in *Armagh and Antrim), cleared twelve plains, and formed four lakes. The chief druid of the Nemedians, *Mide, the eponym of *Meath, lit the first fire at *Uisnech, which blazed for seven years and lit every chief's hearth in Ireland. Their singular distinction was in battling the hated Fomorians, three times successfully under Nemed's leadership and once catastrophically at *Cnámross (to be distinguished from a *Fenian battle at the same site). Subjugated by the Fomorians, the Nemedians were forced to pay a humiliating annual tribute at Mag Cétne each *Samain. They sought vengeance by storming the Fomorian tower Tor Conaind on the heavily defended Tory Island (off *Donegal). The Nemedian hero *Fergus Lethderg killed the Fomorian champion *Conand, but the Nemedians were slaughtered, only thirty surviving to be scattered about the world. Fergus Lethderg went north to Scotland; his son *Britán Máel lived there until the arrival of the *Picts, giving his name to the British and the island of Britain. Iarbonél migrated even further across northern Europe; his son *Béothach founded a family which returned to Ireland, eleven generations later, as the *Tuatha Dé Danann. The grandson of Nemed's son Starn, Semion led descendants known as *Fir Bolg in 'Greece'. Other notable Nemedians include Anind, the son of Nemed whose grave flooded Lough Ennell near *Dún na Sciath, Co. Westmeath; *Fergna, the fourth physician in Ireland; and Figma, the chief poet and historian.

A few commentators see faint echoes of actual Irish history in the Nemed, as they do not in the invasions of Cesair and the Partholonians. T. F. O'Rahilly's influential but still controversial *Early Irish History and Mythology* (Dublin, 1946) identified the Nemedians with the *Érainn, a *P-Celtic people.

nemeton. A Gaulish word, apparently meaning 'sacred grove' or 'sanctuary', appears whole or in part in several place-names. In medieval times a sacred forest named Nemeton surrounded the Benedictine priory near Locronan, south-western Brittany. Buxton, Derbyshire, was Aquae Arnemetiae in Roman times. *Drunemeton [oak sanctuary] is recorded in early Spain and in *Galatia. W. J. Watson, *History of the Celtic Place-Names of Scotland* (Edinburgh, 1926), sees remnants of the word in Scottish locations, e.g. Duneaves, Perthshire. A particle of the word nemeton appears in the sometime epithet of Gaulish *Mars, Rigonmetis. See also NEMETONA.

Nemetona, Nemontana [goddess of the sacred grove; see NEMETON]. Gaulish and British goddess whose name appears in many ancient inscriptions. She was venerated by the Celto-Germanic people called the Nemetes, whose name shares her root name. At *Bath she was the consort of *Mars Loucetius. She is again paired with Mars at Grosskrotzenburg near Hanau and at Altripp near Speyer. The Roman imperial aristocracy invoked her name on a bronze tablet at what is now Klein-Winternheim near Mainz. Nemetona's link to Mars, a god of war, may be echoed in the name of an Irish war-goddess, *Nemain.

Nemglan. See CONAIRE MÓR.

Nemhain. ModIr. spelling of *Nemain.

Nemon. Variant spelling of *Nemain.

Nemontana. Variant spelling of *Nemetona.

Nennius. See HISTORIA BRITTONUM.

Nera, Neara. See ECHTRA NERAI [The Adventure of Nera].

Nét. Variant spelling of *Néit.

Newgrange. See BRUG NA BÓINNE.

Ní, Ní-. Irish feminine patronymic. Figures bearing this form are alphabetized under their first names, even when Ní is capitalized.

Ní Mháille, Gráinne Mhaol. See GRANUAILE.

Niall. Name borne by several legendary and historical kings of early Ireland; without epithet or agnomen the name usually indicates *Niall Noígiallach [of the Nine Hostages].

Niall Caille [cf. OIr. *caill*, wood, forest]. King at *Tara who was twice humiliated, first by submitting to *Fedlimid mac Crimthann in AD 838 and second when Fedlimid abducted Niall's queen *Gormlaith (2) with all her female retinue. Earlier he was known for his decisive victory over the Airgialla in 827, slaying many of their leaders and making them dependent upon Tara.

Niall Glúndub, Glún Dubh, Glúndubh [Ir., dark knee]. King who fell in battle against the Norsemen on the *Liffey, AD 919, and from whom the O'Neills take their name; see the earlier UÍ NÉILL.

Niall Noígiallach, Naígiallach, Naoighiallach [of the Nine Hostages; Nine Hostager]. Ancestor and eponym of the *Uí Néill dynasty that dominated Ireland for six centuries; according to tradition, leader of ambitious foreign conquests, and possible captor of St Patrick. Although Niall is sometimes cited as the first irrefutably historical *ard rí [high king], his story is filled with mythological motifs. The purported dates of his reign, often given as AD 379–405, are still matters of dispute. He should have lived a generation before the coming of St Patrick, traditionally 432, as Niall's son *Lóegaire was thought to have met with the saint; but James Carney has controversially put Niall's death as late as *c*.452. The different branches of the Uí Néill dynasty quarrelled incessantly, but agreed upon a common ancestor in Niall, whose persona and biography were embellished by many hands. Two stories explain his epithet noígiallach [nine hostager]. The older, more plausible, but less known version is that he took one hostage from each of the nine tuatha of the *Airgialla, among his first conquests. Medieval scribes probably invented the better-known version, that he took one hostage from each of Ireland's five provinces, *Munster, *Ulster, *Leinster, *Connacht, and *Mide, as well as from the Scots, Saxons, British, and French.

Niall was the son of a captured British slave *Cairenn and King *Eochaid Mugmedón, of Connacht origins, who already had four sons by his wife *Mongfhind (1). The story of how Niall acceded to the *kingship ahead of his brothers by lying with dame *Sovereignty, the loathsome hag become beautiful when made love to, as well as Mongfhind's cruelty to Niall and his mother, is told in **Echtra Mac nEchach Muigmedóin* [The Adventure of the Sons of Eochaid Mugmedón]. The *druid *Sithchenn devises plans to test Niall and his half-brothers and announces at the end of the story that Niall and his descendants will have dominion over Ireland. In a variant of this story, Mongfhind dreams that her four sons will contest among themselves for the kingship, with *Brian winning. When, according to this version, Eochaid dies and her four sons squabble with Niall without Brian's prevailing, she uses her powers of sorcery to entreat the men of Ireland to give the kingship to her brother *Crimthann. Meanwhile, her four sons agree to divide the island among themselves, and so she turns to poisoning. In one version she intends to poison her brother, who deftly asks her to take the drink first; both die. In another, she tries to poison Niall, but takes it herself by mistake. She dies at *Samain in both versions, which explains why at one time women of *Munster addressed *Halloween prayers to Mongfhind.

For all Niall's eminence in history and

genealogical rolls, little is recorded of his reign and foreign conquests. Irish raiders unquestionably plundered the British coast in late Roman times, but contemporary commentators reject the assertion made by William Ridgeway (1924) that Niall can be identified with the *Scotti [Irish] resisted by General Stilicho in 399. Irish texts describe his travel to *Letha [Brittany] and Italy to seek his kingdom, but he would have lacked the wealth and logistical support to conquer and administer foreign lands. Much more plausible are slave-raids to various parts of Great Britain; attached to this is the unproven assumption that one of Niall's captured slaves was the boy St *Patrick.

Four accounts survive of Niall's death, all of them in texts dating after the 11th century. In each Niall is pursued by *Eochaid (10), son of the *Leinster king Énna Cennselach. Eochaid's enmity begins when he is refused food by Laidcenn, Niall's poet, for which he burns Laidcenn's house and kills his son. In revenge, Laidcenn satirizes Leinster, depriving it of all foliage for a year, and Niall invades it. Eventually Eochaid is turned over to Niall by the Leinstermen, but kills Laidcenn with a stone, causing Niall to banish him for the rest of the ruler's life. Later, while Niall is abroad, Eochaid kills him (1) in *Scotland, while Niall is being entertained by *Pictish bards; (2) in the Alps (which may be a confusion with *Alba [Scotland]); (3) in the English Channel; or (4) by the River Loire in France. In all versions his body is returned to be buried at Ochann/Ocha [folk-etymologized into *och cáini*, sighing and weeping], now known as Faughan Hill, SW of *Kells and 3 miles S of the assembly at *Tailtiu.

Niall's place in Irish history was assured by the Uí Néill dynasty, founded by eight of his (perhaps) fifteen sons. Four sons established the northern branch, displacing the *Ulaid of Ulster, with small, powerful kingdoms in *Tír Chonaill [Donegal] and *Tír Eógain [Tyrone], and four other sons along with *Diarmait mac Cerbaill established the southern branch in the midlands, adjacent to *Tara, over the modern counties of *Meath, Westmeath, and Longford. They kept the kingship at Tara between them, deeply influencing the writing of history as well as the development of Christian institutions.

See Kuno Meyer (trans.), 'The Death of Niall of the Nine Hostages', *Otia Mersiana*, 2 (1900), 84–92; repr. in T. P. Cross and C. H. Slover (eds.), *Ancient Irish Tales* (New York, 1936), 514–17; William Ridgeway, 'Neill "of the Nine Hostages"', *Journal of Roman Studies*, 14 (1924), 123–36; T. F. O'Rahilly, 'Niall of the Nine Hostages', in *Early Irish History and Mythology* (Dublin, 1946), 209–34; James Carney, *The Problem of St. Patrick* (Dublin, 1961); F. J. Byrne, 'Niall of the Nine Hostages', in *Irish Kings and High Kings* (London, 1973), 70–86; Gearóid S. MacEoin, 'The Mysterious Death of Loegaire mac Néill', *Studia Hibernica*, 8 (1968), 21–48.

Niam, Niamh, Niav [Ir. *níam*, brightness, radiance, lustre]. Name borne by several female personages from Irish tradition, of whom the best-known is Niam (3), the lover of *Oisín.

Niam 1. Sometime wife of *Conall Cernach, his other consort being *Lendabair. She is better remembered, however, for nursing *Cúchulainn, during which time she becomes his mistress. She tries to stop Cúchulainn from leaving the fortress until he is healed, but *Badb, daughter of *Cailitin, puts a spell on Niam by impersonating one of her handmaidens and enticing her from the hero's bedside. The jealous Badb, seeking vengeance for Cúchulainn's killing Cailitin and all his male children, then takes Niam's shape and bids the hero rise from his bed and begin the journey that will lead to his death.

2. Daughter of *Celtchair who agrees to marry *Conganchnes mac Dedad to learn the secret of his seeming invulnerability. When she relates that her husband can only be killed with spears penetrating the soles of his feet and the calves of his legs, Celtchair quickly dispatches him. Later she marries *Cormac Connloinges, son of *Conchobar mac Nessa.

3. Lover of *Oisín. In the oldest texts she is the daughter of Óengus (Angus) Tech, king of *Munster, who elopes to Oisín to *Ulster for six weeks, where she is pursued by her father and his retainers, dying of fear. In a second version she is the daughter of Áed Donn of Ulster, and it is over her that Oisín fights his first battle. Her best-known incarnation comes in Micheál Coimín's 18th-century Irish-language text, where she is called Niamh Chinn Óir [of the Golden Head/Hair]. Here she leads Oisín to a lengthy sojourn in *Tír na nÓg [the Land of Youth], from which he returns to find himself greatly aged.

Niav. Anglicization of *Niam.

Nichtan. Variant spelling of *Nechtan (3).

Ninian, Saint [L *Niniavus* (?)]. Shadowy 5th-century missionary, reputed to have studied with St Martin of Tours (d. 397), who brought Christianity to southern Scotland before the arrival of *Colum Cille at *Iona; he may also have been earlier than St *Patrick. The ruined priory at Whithorn, Dumfries and Galloway, associated with his mission was a centre for pilgrimage until Reformation times. Ninian's name is cited in landmarks in south-western Scotland and on the Isle of *Man; the church of St Trinian's, mentioned often in Manx legends, is named for Ninian. Feast-day 16 September. See A. P. Forbes, *Lives of St. Ninian and St. Kentigern* (Edinburgh, 1874). Distinguish from Niniane, a variant form of Nimianae, Niviene, etc., names for the Lady of the Lake in the Vulgate Cycle of the Arthurian Legends.

Nisien [W, peaceful]. Kind brother of the malevolent *Efnisien.

Niúl. Son of *Fénius Farsaid, inventor of the Irish language, in the pseudo-history **Lebor Gabála* [Book of Invasions]. Husband of *Scota (2), he fathers *Goídel Glas, also important to the early history of the Irish language. According to the inventive text, Niúl is a renowned schoolmaster who gives his name to the Nile River.

Noble Island. Translation of Inis Ealga, poetic nickname for Ireland.

Nodons, Nodens. British god of healing, commemorated in the shrine (3rd cent. BC) at *Lydney Park on the Severn River, Gloucester. No physical depiction of Nodons survives, but votive plaques at the shrine indicate his associations with *dogs. Another figure appears to show a man hooking a fish. Nodons has been likened to *Mars the healer rather than Mars the warrior, as well as to Silvanus, a Roman god of the hunt. More importantly, Nodons is a cognate of and perhaps an anticipation of the Irish *Nuadu Airgetlám; additionally, his persona contributed to the Welsh figure *Nudd. See Françoise Le Roux, 'Le Dieu-roi Nodons/ Nuada', *Celticum*, 6 (1963), 425–46; John Carey, 'Nodons in Britain and Ireland', *Zeitschrift für celtische Philologie*, 40 (1984), 1–22.

Noínden Ulad. Abbreviated form of Ces Noínden Ulad [nine days' debility/pangs of the Ulstermen]. When *Crunniuc mac Agnomain forces his wife *Macha (3) to run a humiliating foot-race with a horse, she curses the watching *Ulstermen so that they will suffer the pain of giving birth, at times of their greatest difficulties, for nine times nine generations. Also known as ceisnoidhe/ces noínden Ulad [nine days' affliction]. The episode is retold at the beginning of the **Táin Bó Cuailnge* [Cattle Raid of Cooley]. Noínden Ulad may be an Irish instance of what anthropologists call couvade, the practice in many pre-technological societies in which the husband of a woman in labour takes to his bed as if he were bearing the child. See Vernam E. Hull (ed.), '*Noínden Ulad*: The Debility of the Ulidians', *Celtica*, 8 (1968), 1–42; Vernam E. Hull (ed.), 'Ces Ulad: The Affliction of the Ulstermen', *Zeitschrift für celtische Philologie*, 29 (1962/4), 305–14; Tomás Ó Broin, 'What is the "Debility" of the Ulstermen?', *Éigse*, 10(4) (1961/3), 286–99; 'The Word *Noínden*', *Éigse*, 13 (1969/70), 165–76.

Noíse, Naoise, Naísi. Lover of *Deirdre.

Nominoë. Historical 9th-century Breton chief and king inflated into the creator of the Breton nation by 19th-century nationalists. A man of modest origin, Nominoë was discovered by Charlemagne, who made him Count of Vannes, in south-eastern Brittany. Becoming Duke of Brittany (826) under Louis the Pious, he set about uniting all the Bretons when Louis died, which required ten years to achieve. In 845 he forced Charles the Bald to recognize Breton independence, within borders that remained until 1790. Subject of a ballad 'translated' by *La Villemarqué in *Barzaz Breiz* [Breton Bards] (1839).

Nova Scotia. Maritime province of Canada, home to the largest population of speakers of any Celtic language to be found outside Europe. Migration from the Highlands of Scotland to Nova Scotia began in the late 18th century, chiefly to the north-eastern portions of the province, most especially on Cape Breton Island. Although speakers of Scottish Gaelic established settlements elsewhere in Canada, those in Nova Scotia have maintained it most persistently. The 1931 census recorded 24,303 speakers, the bulk of them born in Nova Scotia. Although not a language of commerce or education, Scottish Gaelic was spoken in the home and often in churches. Many of the Scottish emigrants were from the poorest classes, although far fewer were victims of the Clearances than was once popularly supposed. Scottish literary tradition migrated as well, as the Nova Scotian settlers included several *bards. Oral tradition in Gaelic continued to the end of the 20th century; the huge repertoire of storyteller Joe Neil MacNeil (b. 1908) includes stories with many parallels with Scottish collections. The province is also home to many Irish and some Welsh immigrants; Cape Breton Island was named for Breton fishermen who plied its waters as early as the 16th century. See Charles W. Dunn, *The Highland Settler in Nova Scotia* (Toronto, 1953); Margaret MacDonell, *The Emigrant Experience: Songs of Highland Emigrants in North America* (Toronto, 1982); C. I. N. MacLeod, *Highland Scottish Folklore and Beliefs* (Antigonish, Canada, 1975); *Sgialachdan a Albainn Nuaidh* (Glasgow, 1969); *Bàrdachd a Albainn Nuaidh* (Glasgow, 1970); Joe Neil MacNeil, *Tales Until Dawn: The World of a Cape Breton Story-Teller*, trans. John Shaw (Kingston and Montreal, 1987).

Novembers Eve, 1 November. See SAMAIN; HOLLANTIDE; ALLANTIDE.

Nuachongbála. See BOOK OF LEINSTER.

Nuadu, Nuada, Nuadha, Núadha, Nuado, Nuda, Nuagha [Ir., cloud-maker (?); catcher (?)]. Name borne by several perhaps divine figures from early Irish tradition, of whom the best-known is *Nuadu Airgetlám; characters with other epithets may be only variations on a single persona. The name also survived to Christian times and was borne by at least two saints.

Nuadu Airgetlám, Argetlám, Airgedlámh, Argatlám, Airgettlámh, Argentlam, Aircetlaum, n-Argetlaim [of the silver hand/arm]. King of the mythical *Tuatha Dé Danann who leads his people into Ireland but is later disqualified from *kingship because of the 'blemish' of his severed arm. Dispute over the succession to replace him dominates the beginning of the action of **Cath Maige Tuired* [The (Second) Battle of Mag Tuired]. The initial conception of this deeply mysterious character apparently pre-dates the narratives of the *Mythological and *Fenian Cycles. None the less, he appears frequently in early Irish tradition, often taking markedly different aspects, perhaps also taking different epithets as well. His early British cognate is *Nodons, worshipped at the Romano-British shrine of *Lydney Park; and he clearly resembles the Welsh *Nudd, more certainly derived from Nodons, who sometimes bears the epithet Llaw Ereint [silver hand].

In earliest Irish tradition Nuadu is associated with the *Boyne as the consort of the river's eponym *Boand under his pseudonym *Nechtan (1); under yet another pseudonym, *Elcmar, he has an affair with her. In the south of Ireland he was so much associated with the *Eóganacht dynasty that its leading member, *Eógan Mór, has an alternative name of Mug Nuadat [servant of Nuadu]. Together with these incarnations, we also find Nuadu as a member of the Tuatha Dé Danann, bringing the stone of *Fál to Ireland. His sword is one of the four treasures of the Tuatha Dé Danann. But Nuadu's kingship is interrupted, as he relinquishes the sacred office twice. First, it is because he no longer meets the criterion of physical perfection, a rule of sovereignty. In the First Battle of Mag Tuired, a *Fir Bolg warrior named *Sreng severs Nuadu's arm, but his Tuatha Dé comrades carry him from the field. On the next day Nuadu challenges Sreng to tie up his own right arm to ensure a fair fight, but Sreng refuses. To prevent a fatal injury to Nuadu, the Tuatha Dé then offer Sreng and the Fir Bolg the province of *Connacht, which they accept. The ill-starred *Bres then becomes leader of the Tuatha Dé Danann, but after seven years *Dian Cécht makes a silver arm for Nuadu, and he is restored to the kingship for another twenty years. In his second reign Nuadu is daunted by the terrible power of *Balor and is thus replaced by *Lug Lámfhota, who brings victory to the Tuatha Dé Danann.

Nuadu may also play a role in the *Fenian Cycle, perhaps confused with Nuadu Necht, the Leinster ancestor-deity. He is thought to have married *Eithne (1) (elsewhere the mother of Lug Lámfhota) to found the family line that forms the maternal ancestry of *Fionn mac Cumhaill. Additionally, Nuadu was thought to be the original owner of the fortress at the Hill of *Allen [Almu, etc.], also attributed to *Tadg mac Nuadat, a 'son' who may be an alias for the father. Nuadu is one of three prophets of pre-Christian religion, along with *Goibniu and the shadowy Mathu. Another attributed consort is *Fea, a war-goddess. Oral tradition has him buried at *Ailech in Co. Donegal.

See A. H. Krappe, 'Nuadu à la main d'argent', *Revue Celtique*, 49 (1932), 90–5;

Françoise Le Roux, 'Le Dieu-roi Nodons/ Nuada', *Celticum*, 6 (1963), 425–46; John Carey, 'Nodons in Britain and Ireland', *Zeitschrift für celtische Philologie*, 40 (1984), 1–22.

Nuadu Necht [cf. Ir. *necht*, washed, clean, pure; taken from a folk etymology, possibly related to *Nechtan*]. Ancestor-deity of the *Leinstermen, and probably identical with the divine king known in the *Mythological Cycle as *Nuadu Airgetlám. He succeeds *Eterscél, father of *Conaire Mór, as king of *Tara. In the *Fenian Cycle Nuadu Necht is the original possessor of the Hill of Allen [Almu], which is also attributed to his 'son' *Tadg mac Nuadat; Tadg may be an alias for Nuadu himself. Nuadu is also a reputed ancestor of Fionn mac Cumhaill on the maternal side; son Tadg mac Nuadat is the father of *Muirenn, mother of Fionn, which means that Nuadu may be either the grandfather or great-grandfather of the hero. Nuadu Necht may contribute to the characterization of *Nechtan (1).

Nuagha. Corrupt form of *Nuadu.

Nuala. Diminutive of the name *Finnguala, sometimes used as an alternative for *Úna, wife of *Finnbheara, king of the *fairies.

Nudd, Lludd; sometimes with the epithet **Llaw Ereint** [W, silver hand]. Legendary Welsh hero, noted in the *Triads as one of the three most generous men in Wales, along with his two cousins, *Rhydderch Hael and Mordaf Hael. Although early genealogies treat him as a historical figure, he appears to be derived from the early British god *Nodons, worshipped at the shrine of *Lydney Park, and a cognate of the Irish divine king *Nuadu Airgetlám. His two sons are *Edern and *Gwyn ap Nudd. Confusingly, Nudd may also be known as Lludd, apparently from an alliterative assimilation with his sometime epithet N[-Ll-]udd Llaw Ereint. It is difficult, therefore, to separate him from the other figures named Lludd, such as the son of *Beli Mawr in *Cyfranc Lludd a Llefelys*.

nuts of knowledge/wisdom. See HAZEL.

O

O. The fifteenth letter of the modern English alphabet is represented by onn [Ir., ash, furze] in the *ogham alphabet of early Ireland.

oak [OE *āc*]. The mighty deciduous hardwood (genus *Quercus*) has played a prominent role in the Celtic imagination from ancient to modern times. The English word 'druid' (from the Latin plural druidae) derives in part from the root dru- [oak]; Celtic words for oak, e.g. OIr. and ModIr. dair, W derwen, share the same root. The ancient geographer *Strabo (1st cent. AD) reported that the important sacred grove and meeting-place of the *Galatian Celts of Asia Minor, *Drunemeton, was filled with oaks. In an often-cited passage from *Historia Naturalis* (1st cent. AD), *Pliny the Elder describes a festival on the sixth day of the moon where the druids climbed an oak tree, cut a bough of mistletoe, and sacrificed two white *bulls as part of a fertility rite. Elsewhere druids made their wands from only three woods: *yew, oak, and *apple. In Mediterranean culture the oak was sacred to both Zeus and *Jupiter, some aspects of which were no doubt transferred to the worship of Gaulish Jupiter. Britons under Roman occupation worshipped a goddess of the oak tree, *Daron, whose name is commemorated in a rivulet in *Gwynedd. According to the pseudo-history **Lebor Gabála* [Book of Invasions], the sacred oak of early Ireland was that of Mugna, probably located at or near Dunmanogoe, south Co. Kildare. Sacred associations of oaks survived Christianization, so that St *Brigit's monastic foundation was at Cill Dara [church of (the) oak, i.e. Kildare], and St *Colum Cille favoured Doire Calgaich [Calgach's oak grove, i.e. (London-)Derry]; see also DURROW [*darú*, from *dair magh*, oak plain]. In Welsh tradition *Gwydion and *Math use the flower of oak with broom to fashion the beautiful *Blodeuwedd. When *Lleu Llaw Gyffes is about to be killed by *Gronw Pebyr, his wife's lover, he escapes in *eagle form onto a magic oak tree. A sacred oak tree protects the Breton city of *Ys until the feckless boy *Kristof removes it, allowing Ys to be engulfed. The Arthurian figure *Merlin is imprisoned in an oak tree in the Breton forest of *Brocéliande by Viviane/Nimiane (the Lady of the Lake). In both British and Irish *fairy lore, the oak is one of three magical woods, along with *ash and thorn. OIr. and ModIr. dair; ScG darach; Manx daragh; W derwen, dâr; Corn. derowen; Bret. dervenn.

Ocelus. Latinized name of a presumably indigenous god known in three inscriptions dating from the Roman occupation. He is clearly linked to *Mars, and his name serves twice as an epithet for that divinity, once linked also with the epithet Lenus. Ocelus is twice invoked near the Welsh village of Caerwent, Gwent, where a much-reduced statue survives with only two pairs of feet showing, one pair human, one belonging to a goose.

Odhras. Modern spelling of *Odras.

Odras, Odhras, Odrus. Hapless mortal woman changed into a pool of water by the *Mórrígan.

óenach. OIr. word commonly translated as 'popular assembly' or 'fair'. Widely reported instances from early Ireland at *Tara, *Tailtiu, *Tlachtga, and *Uisnech describe games, races, and similar contests. The ModIr. word aonach denotes such assemblies as used to be held on the first days of March, July, September, and December at places like Millstreet, Co. Cork.

Óengus, Oenghus. Preferred Irish forms of *Angus.

ogham (ModIr.), **ogam, ogum** (OIr.), **oghum** (ScG). The earliest form of writing in Irish in which the Latin alphabet is adapted to a series of twenty 'letters' of straight lines and notches carved on the edge of a piece of stone or wood. Letters are divided into four categories of five sounds:

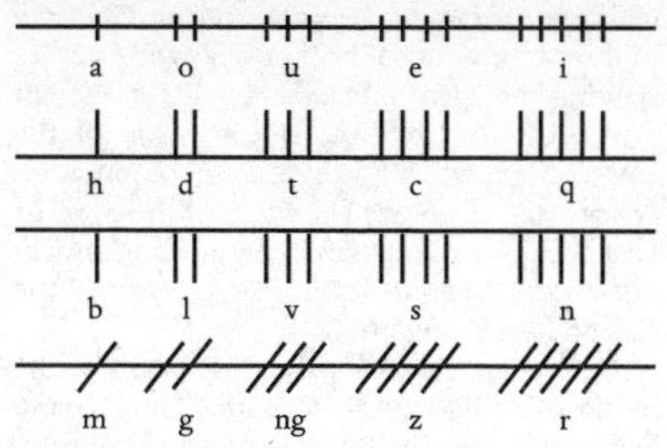

A twenty-first symbol, an upturned arrow, was used for the letter p in British inscriptions. Notches and grooves appear on one or both sides of a foundation-line [*druim*]. Each letter was named for a different *tree, e.g. a = ailm [pine], b = beithe [*birch], etc., as shown in separate entries in this volume. Designations for the letters q, v, and z, which are not used in Irish, support the now widely accepted interpretation of ogham as an expression of Irish through the Latin alphabet. The current view displaces many colourful speculations on ogham's origin: runic alphabet of Scandinavia, Chalcidic Greek, northern Etruscan, etc.

Ogham inscriptions date primarily from the 4th to 8th centuries and are found mainly on standing stones; evidence for inscriptions in wood exists, but examples do not survive. The greatest concentration of surviving ogham inscriptions is in southern Ireland; a 1945 survey found 121 in *Kerry and 81 in Co. Cork, while others are scattered throughout Ireland, Great Britain, and the Isle of *Man, with five in *Cornwall, about thirty in *Scotland, mainly in '*Pictish' areas, and more than forty in *Wales. South Wales was an area of extensive settlement from southern Ireland, including the migration of the *Déisi. Ogham was also used for Pictish. In Wales, ogham inscriptions have both Irish and Brythonic-Latin adjacent inscriptions.

Most ogham inscriptions are very short, usually consisting of a name and a patronymic in the genitive case. They are of linguistic rather than literary interest, because they show an older state of the Irish language than found in any other written sources. Many appear to be memorials to the dead, while others mark the border between two lands. Although the knowledge of ogham was never lost to scholars (at least one 19th-cent. grave-marker uses it), the notion that ogham was employed for occult or magical purposes dogs critical commentary. As late as the 1930s the eminent archaeologist R. A. S. Macalister proposed that ogham was part of the secret language of 'druidic freemasonry'. Seán O'Boyle suggested (1980) that the key to explaining ogham is harp notation. The god of rhetoric and eloquence, *Ogma, is an attributed creator; his name and the word appear to be philologically related.

See Damien McManus, *A Guide to Ogam* (Maynooth, 1991); Charles Thomas, *And Should These Mute Stones Speak?* (Cardiff, 1994); C. Mac Fhearaigh, *Ogham: An Irish Alphabet*, 2nd edn. (Indreabhan, 1996); Sabine Ziegler, *Die Sprache der altirischen Ogam-Inschriften* (Göttingen, 1994); Charles Plummer, 'On the Meaning of Ogam Stones', *Revue Celtique*, 40 (1923), 387–91; R. A. S. Macalister, *Corpus Inscriptionum Insularum Celticarum* (2 vols., Dublin, 1946–9); *The Secret Languages of Ireland* (Cambridge, 1937); Joseph Vendryes, 'L'Écriture ogamique et ses origines', *Études Celtiques*, 4 (1941–8), 83–116; L. J. D. Richardson, 'The Word *ogham*', *Hermathena*, 62 (1943), 96–105; R. Rolt Brash, *Ogham Monuments in Wales* (Felinfach, Wales, 1992); Kenneth H. Jackson, 'Notes on the Ogam Inscriptions of Southern Britain', in Cyril Fox and B. Dickins (eds.), *The Early Cultures of North-West Europe* (Cambridge, 1950), 197–213; 'Ogam Stones and Early Christian Latin Inscriptions', in D. S. Thomson (ed.), *Companion to Gaelic Scotland* (Glasgow, 1994), 220–1; Seán O'Boyle, *Ogam: The Poet's Secret* (Dublin, 1980).

Oghma. ModIr. spelling of *Ogma.

oghum. ScG spelling of *ogham.

Ogma, Oghma, Ogmae, Ogme. Orator-warrior of the *Tuatha Dé Danann, and one of its three principal champions along with *Lug Lámfhota and the *Dagda. Ogma is also the patron, perhaps of divine origin, of poetry and eloquence and the fabled inventor of the *ogham alphabet, philological cognate of his name. So esteemed is his eloquence that he sometimes bears the nickname or sobriquet of *Cermait [honey-mouthed], which occasionally causes him to be confused with a son of the Dagda of that name. Ogma may also bear the sobriquet of Grianainech [sun-countenance]. *Elatha is usually named as his father, with *Eithne (1) as his mother, and the Dagda a brother. His wife *Étan, daughter of

*Dian Cécht, gives him the sons *Tuireann and *Cairbre mac Ethne the satirist.

In **Cath Maige Tuired* [The (Second) Battle of Mag Tuired] and in the actions leading up to the battle, Ogma plays a leading role. At *Lug Lámfhota's first entrance to the Tuatha Dé court, Ogma engages him in a contest of strength requiring that the young hero throw a flagstone over the side of the royal hall; Ogma loses. During the oppressive reign of the ill-starred *Bres, Ogma is humiliated by having to do manual labour, carrying firewood. During the battle Ogma engages *Indech the Fomorian, although texts vary as to who killed whom.

The similarities between the name Ogma and that of *Ogmios, the Gaulish god of eloquence, suggest an affinity that commentators have been hard-pressed to delineate. The early 20th-century scholars Rudolf Thurneysen and Anton van Hamel disputed any link between Ogmios and Ogma. See Anton van Hamel, 'Aspects of Celtic Mythology', *Proceedings of the British Academy*, 20 (1934), 207–48.

Ogmios. Gaulish god of eloquence and letters known primarily from a single 2nd-century AD text, supported by some scattered inscriptions. The Greek writer Lucian of Samosata describes a picture of Ogmios he encountered in southern Gaul near the modern city of Marseille. In it Ogmios is a bald old man leading an apparently happy and willing band of men who are attached to him by chains connecting their ears with his tongue. Lucian's informant told him that Ogmios was identical with the Graeco-Roman hero become deity *Hercules, in part because of his great strength. Although Hercules is usually seen as a young, muscular man with a full head of hair, the picture did portray Ogmios with Hercules' bow and club. The German Renaissance painter Albrecht Dürer depicted this deity. Commonly compared with the Irish *Ogma. See Fernand Beno't, 'L'Ogmios de Lucien, la "tête coupée", et le cycle mythologique irlandais et gallois', *Ogam*, 5 (1953), 33–42; Françoise Le Roux, 'Le Dieu celtique aux liens de l'Ogmios de Lucien à l'Ogmios de Dürer', *Ogam*, 12 (1960), 209–34.

ogum. An OIr. spelling of *ogham.

Oidheadh Chlainne Lir. Irish title for the late medieval romance (MSS *c.*1500) usually known in English as The Tragic Story of the Children of Lir, or The Fate of the Children of Lir; it may also be known, with earlier spelling, as *Aided Chlainne Lir* [The Violent Death of the Children of Lir]. One of the Three Sorrows of Storytelling, along with *Longas mac nUislenn* [The Exile of the Sons of Uisnech] (see DEIRDRE) and OIDHEADH CHLAINNE TUIREANN [The Tragic Story of the Children of Tuireann].

After their defeat by the *Milesians at the battle of *Tailtiu, the *Tuatha Dé Danann begin to recede into their own world of mystery and imagination, of which they will be masters. At the same time they seek a new king so that they may not be ruled by their conquerors. Of the five candidates, *Bodb Derg of *Connacht is judged the strongest, which offends *Lir of the *sídh of *Finnachad (near the modern town of Newtown Hamilton, Co. Monaghan). The magnanimous Bodb is concerned at Lir's disappointment, especially when he is grieved by the death of his wife, and so offers the hand of one of his foster-daughters as bride. Lir chooses the eldest, *Áeb (or, in some versions, *Niam or Finnguala). She bears him four children, a twin son and daughter, *Áed (3) [fire] and *Finnguala [fair-shouldered]. She then bears twin sons, *Fiachra (1) and *Conn, but dies at their birth. When Lir is despondent at his wife's death, Bodb arranges for him to marry Áeb's sister Aífe (2), who honours and loves her sister's children, at least initially.

When Aífe proves childless, her view of the children darkens. Seized with an obsessive jealousy, she takes to her bed, feigning sickness for a year. Then she abruptly pronounces herself cured and declares she will visit Bodb Derg, taking the children with her; Finnguala resists, warned of evil portents in a dream. En route to Bodb's palace at *Killaloe in the west, Aífe begins to rage against the children for depriving her of her husband's love, and demands that her retainers slaughter them on the spot-Lough Derravaragh in Co. Westmeath. When the servants refuse, Aífe pushes the children into the water and transforms them with a *druidical wand (or sword) into four beautiful white *swans. Finnguala, who, like the other children, retains the power of speech, protests their blamelessness and asks Aífe how long their cruel punishment will last. The answer: 900 years in three sentences of increasing misery: 300 years in Lough Derravaragh, 300 years in the North Channel, the narrowest passage between Ireland and the

Mull of Kintyre in Scotland, sometimes called the Sea of Moyle, and 300 years on the west coast of Ireland between Erris and the small island of Inishglora, Co. Mayo. This will last, Aífe explains further, until a woman from the south, *Deoch daughter of Fíngen, king of *Munster, shall be joined with a man of the north, Lairgnéan, son of Colmán of *Connacht. Because Finnguala has asked for the term of the curse, no power of the Tuatha Dé Danann can lift it, but Aífe allows, in addition to the power of speech, their senses and faculties, and an ability to sing supreme among mortals. Aífe then proceeds to Bodb's palace at Killaloe, where her treachery is soon discovered, and she is punished by being transformed into a demon (sometimes vulture), condemned to wander through the air for ever.

In the children's early years of exile, Bodb, Lir, and other prominent figures come to hear them sing. The text includes many verse passages of their songs. At the end of each term, Finnguala reminds her siblings to move on. In time the people of Ireland forget them, but providentially their singing is heard by Áebhric, a young man living near Erris [Ir. *Irrus Domnann*, *Iorras Domhnann*], who records their story so that we may read it now. At the end of 300 years they return to the sídh of *Finnachad only to find it abandoned and desolate, and so they decide to settle on Inishglora until Mo Cháemóc, a disciple of St *Patrick, brings Christianity to the island. After hearing the evangelist's bell, the children begin to sing with it, thus making themselves known to him. Mo Cháemóc brings the children into his household, where they forget their suffering, and links them together with a silver chain.

Meanwhile, unbeknown to the children, the prophecy of Aífe is fulfilled. South and north are united as Deoch of Munster has married Lairgnéan, and they now reign in Connacht. A vain and haughty queen, Deoch covets the singing swans and demands that the king secure them for her. Lairgnéan tries to pull them away from Mo Cháemóc by their chain, but as he does they are returned to their human form, no longer as children but, reflecting their centuries of exile, as virtual pillars of dust. Mo Cháemóc baptizes them immediately, just in time to save their immortal souls.

Although the Children of Lir are commemorated in an early stone cross on Inishkeel islet on the Donegal coast, their story has had little influence on folklore and is widely known today because of its retelling in popular 19th-century anthologies, e.g. P. W. Joyce, *Old Celtic Romances* (London, 1879), and numerous schoolbook collections. Irish-language edition: Seán Ua Ceallaigh, *Trí Truagha na Scéaluigheachta* (Dublin, 1927), 42–64.

Oidheadh Chlainne Tuireann, *Aided Chlainne Tuirenn.* Irish title for the prose narrative of the *Mythological Cycle known in English as The Tragic Story of the Children of Tuireann or The Fate of the Children of Tuireann. Although the core of the story may have been composed as early as the 11th century, as interpolations from the **Lebor Gabála* [Book of Invasions] imply, the earliest surviving text is 16th-century, with more from the 17th. Within Irish literature *Oidheadh Chlainne Tuireann* is often classed as one of the *Trí Truagha na Sgéalaigheachta* [the Three Sorrows of Storytelling, or the Three Sorrowful Stories of Erin] along with the *Deirdre story and **Oidheadh Chlainne Lir* [The Tragic Story of the Children of Lir].

A child of *Ogma and *Étan (1), Tuireann fathers three sons, Brian (1), Iuchair, and Iucharba, upon the divine *Ana (also Danu) herself; variant texts cite great *Brigit as the mother. His paternity complete, Tuireann plays no part in the story. The action begins along the *Boyne while the *Tuatha Dé Danann are preparing for the great battle with the *Fomorians that will be known as Mag Tuired (see CATH MAIGE TUIRED). After scenes in which two physicians speculate on repairing *Nuadu's arm and *Lug Lámfhota is introduced, the action focuses on *Cian, Lug's father, who while travelling north becomes apprehensive about the approach of the three armed sons of Tuireann. Sensitive to the unexplained enmity between the families, Cian magically transforms himself into a pig and begins rooting the ground with a nearby herd. The most perceptive of the brothers, Brian, has spotted Cian before the transformation and so changes his brothers Iuchair and Iucharba into hounds to hunt the pigs, thus separating the magical pig, Cian, from the rest. Returned to human form, the brothers want to spare Cian, but Brian refuses, leading the brothers in stoning him after he is at least allowed the dignity of returning himself to human form. After finding his father's mangled body, Lug lays an *éiric [blood price] of retrieving magical treasures and of performing a dangerous feat. The treasures to be brought back are: (1) the three *apples of the Garden of the Hesperides; (2) the skin of the pig of King Tuis 'of Greece' that will cure all wounded and diseased persons and will turn water into wine; (3) an excellent poisoned spear currently belonging to Pisear, king of Persia, that will come to be known as *Gáe Assail; (4) two steeds able to pull a chariot over land or sea, belonging to Dobar, the king of Sicily; (5) seven pigs belonging to *Assal (in some texts Easal), king of the Golden Pillars, that can be eaten at night and will reappear in the morning; (6) the puppy or whelp *Failinis of the king of Ioruaidh (or Iruad); (7) the cooking-spit of the women of *Inis Fionnchuire (or Inis Findchuire, Finchory) beneath Muir Torrain, between Ireland and Britain; and, most enigmatically, (8) three shouts upon the hill of *Miodhchaoin (or Midchaín) in *Lochlainn. Through inexhaustible daring and resource, the three sons, Brian, Iuchair, and Iucharba, accomplish the first seven of Lug's tasks, but the eighth proves most exacting. Miodhchaoin and his three sons, Áed, Conn, and Corc, drive their spears through the three sons of Tuireann before they can return the attack. Miodhchaoin and his three sons are killed, but Brian, Iuchair, and Iucharba lie mortally wounded. Weakened though he is, Brian lifts his brothers' heads so that all three make feeble calls, fulfilling Lug's éiric. Iuchair and Iucharba then die, and Brian returns their bodies to their father. Tuireann pleads with Lug to save Brian with Tuis's healing pigskin, but the hero refuses, still angry at the way his father has been murdered. Tuireann buries his sons in a single grave and dies soon after himself. Lug values the treasure brought by the sons of Tuireann. Gáe Assail becomes his favourite sword, and Failinis his lapdog.

Although *Oidheadh Chlainne Tuireann* has been retold and reshaped in several popular collections, it has the poorest critical reputation of the Three Sorrows of Storytelling. Myles Dillon (1948) dismissed it as not being of primary interest or of great literary value, with interest only for a folklorist. See Richard O'Duffy, *The Fate of the Children of Tuireann* (Dublin, 1901); Rudolf Thurneysen, 'Tuirill Bicrenn und seine Kinder', *Zeitschrift für celtische Philologie*, 12 (1918), 239–50. Modern Irish-language text: Seán Ua Ceallaigh, *Trí Truagha na Scéaluigheachta* (Dublin, 1927).

oilliphéist, oillepheist [Ir. *oll*, great; *péist*, fabulous beast, reptile, monster]. *Dragon-like monster from Irish oral tradition. In the best-known story, the oilliphéist cuts the route of the *Shannon River when it hears that St *Patrick has come to drive out its kind. In a comic addition to the story, the oilliphéist swallows a drunken piper named Ó Ruairc [O'Rourke] who continues to play inside the monster, thus annoying it until coughed up and spat out. ScG counterpart: *uilepheist. See also CAORÁNACH; MUIRDRIS; SÍNACH.

Oímelc, Oímelg. Variant forms of *Imbolc.

Oirbsiu, Oirbsiu Mór, Oirbsean (gen.), Orbsen (gen.). An obscure epithet of the sea-divinity *Manannán mac Lir, possibly connoting inundation. It is alluded to in the place-name *Lough Corrib [OIr. *Loch nOirbsen*].

Oirghialla. Modern spelling of *Airgialla.

Oisín, Oissíne, Oisséne, Oiséne, Usheen [Ir. diminutive of *os*, deer]. Warrior and poet of the *Fianna, principal son of *Fionn mac Cumhaill, and sojourner in *Tír na nÓg with the beautiful *Niam; so much of later *Fenian literature revolves around Oisín, especially his dialogues with St *Patrick, that those stories are referred to as the Ossianic Cycle. Additionally, much later Fenian material is a recounting of earlier adventures as retold from Oisín's point of view. When the 18th-century charlatan James *Macpherson encountered Scottish Gaelic ballads constructed on this rhetorical frame, with Oisín as narrator, he fabricated a series of prose narratives purportedly derived from *Ossian [ang., of Oisín], whom he depicts as a historical figure.

Two stories are told of Oisín's birth, both with a *deer-mother. In the better-known version *Sadb comes to Fionn in the form of a doe, having been enchanted by *Fer Doirich the *druid. When the hounds *Bran and Sceolang chase the doe to the Hill of *Allen, Fionn gives her protection, and is delightfully surprised when she turns into a beautiful young woman the next morning. Soon they are married, Fionn abandons the chase and fighting, and Sadb is with child. But when Fionn returns to his old ways, Sadb is again enchanted by Fer Doirich and abandons the newborn Oisín to follow him. Seven years later Fionn finds a naked boy, Oisín, under a *rowan tree on *Ben Bulben. An alternative version, naming *Blaí as the mother, comes in two variants. In one she appears first in deer form, as Sadb does, but in the second she is a beautiful girl married to Fionn and later transformed into a deer by a malicious wizard while her husband is away. In the Blaí stories the mother again abandons her newborn, who is found later by the father, Fionn. Such stories are apparent rationalizations of traditions dating from at least the 9th century, explaining that father and son meet over a roasting pig in a forest and begin to contend with one another before they recognize each other's identity.

In much of older Fenian literature, Oisín is one of the half-dozen most important members of the Fianna, although not necessarily the leader; neither is he the esteemed poet of later tradition. The reputation for valour and bravery of his son *Oscar surpasses his own. In **Tóraigheacht Dhiarmada agus Ghráinne* [The Pursuit of Diarmait and Gráinne], Gráinne expresses a romantic interest in Oisín before she espies Diarmait; later Oisín sides with the fugitive lovers against his vengeful father.

Oisín plays a far larger role in later Fenian literature, in action set after the collapse of the Fianna at **Cath Gabhra* [The Battle of Gabhair/Gowra], focusing on two prolonged encounters, with St Patrick and with Niam. In the 12th-century text **Acallam na Senórach* [The Colloquy of the Elders], Oisín and *Caílte survive their comrade's destruction and live on to meet St Patrick. This was not the only portrayal of the saint's attempts at posthumous conversion to Christianity of pagan heroes, but it became the most widely known, inspiring an immense body of popular variations upon a theme, composed between the 13th and 18th centuries. While Caílte dominates more of the conversation with the saint in *Acallam*, the subsequent variations bring Oisín to the fore, apparently because the son inherits his father's mantle of nature wisdom and poetic invention. In these contentious dialogues with the saint, Oisín retells new adventures of the Fianna not found in the older literature, and continually champions the pagan nobility and generosity of Fionn against what he portrays as the cramped and joyless strictures of the new Christian dispensation.

Stories of Oisín's visit to the *Otherworld with a beautiful woman are widespread in the oral traditions of Ireland and Gaelic Scotland, but Micheál Coimín's [Michael Comyn's] literary version, *Laoi Oisín i dTír na nÓg* [Lay of Oisín in the Land of Youth], effectively displaces all others. Evidently drawing on abundant oral tradition, Coimín composed *Laoi Oisín* in Irish about 1750, a text circulating in manuscript for 100 years before it was edited and translated. In this version, Oisín is hunting one day with the Fianna when he is visited by a beautiful *fairy-like woman named Niamh Chinn Óir [of the Golden Head/Hair] on a white horse who tells him she loves him and wants him to accompany her to *Tír na nÓg [the Land of Youth] or Tír Tairngire [the Land of Promise]. In earlier versions (see NIAM (3)) she is merely a mortal woman who elopes with him. Travelling due west, Oisín slays a *giant so that when he arrives in Tír na nÓg he is awarded Niamh as a consort. They begin 300 years of love-making, which produces two sons, one confusingly named *Oscar (2), and a daughter. When Oisín then decides to return to Ireland, Niamh warns him not to dismount from his horse or he will find himself old, withered, and blind. What was once familiar to him now seems strange; he passes the Hill of *Allen [Almu] and finds it abandoned and overgrown. At *Glenasmole, Co. Wicklow, he answers the call of men trying to lift a stone into a wagon. As he stoops, his reins break; Oisín falls to the ground and is immediately transformed into the very aged man that Niamh had predicted. His white steed returns to the Otherworld. Whatever Coimín's reliance on oral tradition or the degree of his invention, his text of Oisín's story offers examples of two tale types, 470 and 766, and the folk motifs C521; C984; D1338.7; F302.1; F378.1. See also HERLA, KING.

Texts: *Laoi Oisín ar Thír na n-Óg*, ed. and trans. Tomás Ó Flannghaile (Dublin, 1907); 'The Lay of Oisín in the Land of Youth', trans. Bryan O'Looney, *Transactions of the Ossianic Society*, 4 (1861), 227–80; 'Ossian in Tir na n-Og', in *Blanaid and Other Irish Historical and Legendary Poems*, trans. T. D. Sullivan (Dublin, 1891), 115–42. Recent commentary: Máirtín Ó Briain, 'Some Material on Oisín in the Land of Youth', in Donnchadh Ó Corráin (ed.), *Sages, Saints and Storytellers* (Maynooth, 1989), 181–99. The most celebrated English-language adaptation of the story is William Butler Yeats's poem 'The Wanderings of Oisin' (1889). Others include T. W. Higginson, 'Usheen in the Island of Youth', in *Tales of the Enchanted Islands of the Atlantic* (1898), 25–31;

James Stephens, 'Oisín and Niamh', *Sinn Féin*, 26 (26 Feb. 1910), 2; John Varian, *Oisín the Hero* (1910).

Olave II [Norse *Olaf* (?)]. Legendary Manx ruler and founder of the island's royal line, also called Goddardson, the son of Goddard Crovan, renowned for his justice, strength, and for his great sword named Macabuin. When Olave inadvertently causes Macabuin to lose its enchantment, its maker, *Loan Maclibhuin, seeks vengeance; but Olave quickly dispatches him and marries his daughter Emergaid the Fair, and their children establish the royal line.

ollam, ollamh, ollave, ollav. A master or person holding the highest rank of any skill; in early Irish literature an ollam is usually an esteemed poet, the highest of the seven ranks of *fili. Before becoming an ollam, a candidate was required to train for twelve years and to master 350 tales. He had to be proficient in the forms of *divination known as *imbas forosnai, *díchetal do chennaib, and *teinm laída. A retinue of twenty-four men followed the ollam when he travelled, and he could always expect to receive the hospitality of the host; in law his rank was equal to that of a petty king, and the calling to the vocation was usually a family tradition. An even better protection than the law was his power of satire. As a part of the king's court, the ollam might combine the functions of poet, storyteller, and historian, including an accurate recitation of genealogies. By the first-hand testimony of Oxford antiquarian William Camden, the institution of the ollam survived up to the end of the 16th century. An equivalent rank in early Welsh tradition may be that of the *pencerdd. See P. A. Breatnach, 'The Chief's Poet', *Proceedings of the Royal Irish Academy*, 83 (1983), 37–79; Liam Breatnach, *Uraiceacht na Riar: The Poetic Grades in Early Irish Law* (Dublin, 1987).

Ollam Fodla, Ollamh Fodhla. Legendary king of *Tara thought to have established the fair [OIr. *óenach*] held there every three years at *Samain. Tenth *ard rí [high king] in line from *Éremón, he was esteemed for his poetry and wisdom; he is thought to have established the first code of laws and is one of several figures credited with the dividing of the country into five parts.

ollav, ollave. Phonetic anglicizations of *ollam.

Olloudius [L *ollo-vidios*, great tree (?)]. Roman name for a native Celtic god whose worship was known in both *Gaul and Britain, closely related to Gaulish *Mars, for whom his name is sometimes an epithet. Surviving artefacts suggest that his links to Mars are with healing, fertility, and peaceful protection rather than war. He is seen as a male figure with a small head and elongated body at a site in the English Cotswolds; here he wears a cap and cloak rather than armour and carries an offering saucer and a double cornucopia, implying prosperity. At Customs Scrubs, Gloucestershire, he is seen with sword, shield, and spear, but also with a cornucopia. Under the same spelling, Olloudius was worshipped by the Narbonenses near the present city of Antibes, France.

Olwen [W *ol*, footprint, track; *(g)wen*, white]. Daughter of *Ysbaddaden and beloved of *Culhwch.

O'Malley, Grace. See GRANUAILE.

omphalos [Gk, navel]. The centre of a culture, by analogy with the omphalos stone at Delphi in ancient Greece; see KERMARIA of BRITTANY; PUMLUMON of WALES; UISNECH of IRELAND; and, more figuratively, the TYNWALD of the ISLE OF MAN.

one-eyed figures. While the threatening giant with a single eye in the middle of his forehead like Polyphemus in Homer's *Odyssey* is widespread in world folklore (folk motif F531.1.1.1), not all Celtic instances of one-eyed figures match this paradigm. Most are found in Irish and Scottish Gaelic traditions. T. F. O'Rahilly argued (1946) that the single eye evokes the sun, as evidenced by the epithet, Deirgderc [red eye], of king *Eochaid (1). The lack of two eyes did not disqualify Eochaid from *kingship when kings could not have any physical shortcomings, such as *Nuadu's lacking an arm. Further, the single-eyed *Goll mac Morna, whose name goll literally means 'one-eyed', might also be called *Áed [fire]. In many *Fenian stories Goll's solar origin, if he has one, is obscured by having him wear an eye-patch, rationalizing the loss of the second eye.

Persons with a single eye may appear more menacing when they are also one-armed and one-legged. The *Fomorians of the pseudo-history *Lebor Gabála* [Book of Invasions] are made to appear more fearsome when described this way before a battle, while at other points in the text they appear to have both eyes, arms, and legs. *Fer Caille, the forbidding churl in **Togail Bruidne Da Derga* [The Destruction of Da Derga's Hostel], is described in the same way, as are the frightening *d'reach and *fachan of Scottish Gaelic oral tradition. And when early Irish poets sought to deliver their most threatening curse, the *glám dícenn [poet's execration], they stood on one leg (like a *crane?), closed one eye, and extended one arm. Other important one-eyed figures include: *Balor, whose eye could destroy; *Congal Cáech; *Dáire Derg; *Éis Énchenn, a one-eyed old hag, the only female listed here; *Eochaid Áenshúla, whose name means 'of the one eye'; *Eochaid mac Luchta; *Fiachra mac Fergusa; *Goll mac Carbada; *Goll mac Morna; *Ingcél Cáech, whose single eye has three pupils; *Mug Ruith; *Nár; *Searbhán the Surly; the sons of *Uar (1). Additionally, *Fintan (1), the *salmon of knowledge, also known as Goll Essa Ruaid, has but one eye.

O'Neill. See account under the distinctly different family *Uí Néill.

Oonagh, Oona. Anglicization of the name of *Úna, wife of *Finnbheara, king of the *fairies.

Orbsen. Genitive form of *Oirbsiu.

Ordovices [hammer fighters]. People of pre-Roman and Roman Wales, cited by the ancient geographer *Ptolemy (2nd cent. AD), whose territory extended from Herefordshire on the Welsh border to *Anglesey. The gloss of their name may link them with the prehistoric stone-axe 'factory' at Graig Lwyd in Caernarvonshire. *Tacitus (1st cent. AD) describes a Roman campaign against the Ordovices, AD 59, in which the legions were confronted with black-robed women with dishevelled hair like furies, brandishing torches. See Barry Cunliffe, *Iron Age Communities in Britain* (London, 1974).

Orgain Denna Ríg, *Denda Ríg*. Irish title for 9th-century Irish narrative of the *Cycle of Kings usually known in English as The Destruction/ Plunder of Dind Ríg. The text survives in three manuscripts, from Rawlinson B502 (or *Book of Glendalough*, *c.*1120–30), the **Book of Leinster* (12th cent.), and the **Yellow Book of Lecan* (*c.*1390), and the story was repeated by the historian Geoffrey *Keating (17th cent.). At the centre of the action is the arrival to power of *Labraid Loingsech, ancestor-deity of *Leinstermen.

Labraid has first to avenge the treachery against his father. Labraid's uncle, *Cobthach the king of *Brega (in what is now north Leinster), is so jealous of his brother, *Lóegaire Lorc, king of all Ireland, that he is wasting away, gaining the name 'the Meagre One of Brega'. Both are sons of *Úgaine Mór. Cobthach invites Lóegaire to come to his residence, after which he feigns death. When Lóegaire, following custom, lies upon what he thinks is the corpse, Cobthach thrusts a knife into his back so that it comes out through his heart. Not content with this, Cobthach then poisons Lóegaire's son Ailill Áne, thus taking the kingdom of Leinster from him. Little is expected of Ailill's son as he cannot speak, hence his name Móen Ollam [*móen*, dumb]. But when struck in the shin while playing hurley, he cries out, 'I am hurt', to the amazement of all watching, who exclaim, 'He is talking!' [*Labraid*], thus giving him his new name.

Later, at an assembly at *Tara, Cobthach asks who is the most generous ruler in Ireland, to which *Craiphtine the harper and *Ferchertne (1) the poet answer, 'Labraid'. Annoyed, Cobthach asks them both to leave, which they do, joining Labraid in exile in the west with King *Scoriath of *Fir Morca in *Munster, who makes them all welcome. Labraid is soon struck by the king's beautiful daughter *Muiriath, and she with him, but she is closely guarded by her parents and no suitor has yet been found worthy of her. Her watchful mother always sleeps with one eye open, fixed upon her daughter. At a feast Craiphtine plays 'sleep-music', which closes both the mother's eyes. In the morning the mother wakes and tells her husband, Scoriath, that he has had an unlucky sleep. 'Your daughter sleeps like a wife.' Angered, Scoriath threatens to kill all the *druids and poets until the lover is identified. Labraid tells Ferchertne to admit the truth, which Scoriath accepts joyfully, immediately ordering a feast. Not only does he give the hand of his daughter, but he promises to help Labraid in recovering the kingdom of *Leinster.

After Scoriath has rallied the men of Munster, Labraid and his allies attack *Dind Ríg (near Leighlinbridge, Co. Carlow), the capital of Leinster. Repulsed, they fall back upon the power of music, having Craiphtine play more sleep-music on the ramparts while the besiegers put their fingers in their ears. Muiriath, loving the music, listens and thus sleeps for a day as no one will wake her. But when the defenders sleep, Scoriath and the men of Munster come over the walls and slay the inhabitants.

Labraid assumes the throne of Leinster and lives for a while in peace with his murderous uncle Cobthach at Tara. After a while he invites Cobthach to come and visit him in a special house made for entertainment-with walls, floors, and doors made of iron. The Leinstermen have worked on it for a year, none of them speaking of what he has done, even to family members; thus the proverb about their reticence: 'Every Leinsterman has his own secret.' Cobthach arrives with thirty other kings in his entourage and with an abundance of suspicion. He refuses to enter the iron house until Labraid's mother and jester go in before him. Inside, Labraid tactfully observes that plenty of drink, food, and fire have been provided. As soon as Labraid has exited, his retainers slam the door shut, locking it with a heavy chain fastened to a pillar. A fire rises around the iron house, fed by 150 bellows, each with four workmen. As the walls turn red-hot, a warrior asks Labraid if he will save his mother. Hearing him, the mother calls out to Labraid to save his honour, as she will die anyway. And thus are Cobthach, thirty kings, and 700 men roasted alive. Lóegaire Lorc is avenged, but Labraid will have yet another exile, from which he returns with 2,200 foreigners with broad spears [*láigen*] to repopulate the province of Leinster.

Ferchertne the poet also appears to be the narrator of the action. The episode of the burning iron house has a parallel in the *Branwen* branch of the **Mabinogi*. The Fir Morca may not be in Munster or any part of Ireland but may instead be Armorica, i.e. *Brittany. In variant texts Labraid wanders as far away as Armenia and brings back 300 ships; in another he receives help from 'the king of the Franks' and lands in Wexford. The *Book of Leinster* records the death of Cobthach at 307 BC. See Kuno Meyer (ed.), *Rawlinson B 502, Facsimile Edition* (Oxford, 1909); Whitley Stokes, 'Orgain Denda Ríg', *Zeitschrift für celtische Philologie*, 3 (1901), 1–14; David Greene (ed.), 'Orgain Denna Ríg', in *Fingal Rónáin and Other Stories* (Dublin, 1958); Joseph Vendryes, 'La Destruction de Dind Ríg', *Études Celtiques*, 8 (1958/9), 7–40; Michael A. O'Brien (ed.), *Corpus genealogiarum Hiberniae* (Dublin, 1962); Heinrich Wagner, 'The Archaic *Dind Ríg* Poem and Related Problems', *Ériu*, 28 (1977), 1–16. Padraic Colum's *The Story of Lowry Maen* (1937) is a popular retelling.

Orghialla. Modern spelling of *Airgialla.

Oriel. Anglicization of *Airgialla.

Ormond [OIr. *Aurmumu*; ModIr. *Urmhumha*]. Anglicized name for the ancient territory of East *Munster, when the province was divided in pre-conquest times; it is coextensive with most of Co. Kilkenny and north Tipperary.

Oscar 1. **Osgar, Oscur, Osca** [Ir., deer-lover (?); cf. *os*, fawn]. A leading warrior of *Fenian narrative, 'the Galahad of the Cycle', the son of *Oisín and the grandson of *Fionn mac Cumhaill. As he does not appear in Fenian literature until the 11th century, some commentators have suggested that Oscar was originally an alternative form for Oisín. As a youth, Oscar is thought so maladroit that the other Fianna refuse to take him along on their adventures. Eventually, however, he becomes a focus for the idealization of storytellers; he is consistently the bravest, the most stalwart, the most frequently victorious. If a warrior is called for a single combat with a fearsome challenger, Oscar most readily serves. Oral-tradition texts have Oscar wrestling *Goll mac Morna to establish himself as the strongest of all the *Fianna. He engages in overseas adventures accompanied by *Labraid Lámderg [red hand]. In **Tóraighecht Dhiarmada agus Ghráinne* [The Pursuit of Diarmait and Gráinne], Oscar sympathizes with the fugitive lovers against his grandfather. *Étaín (3) is Oscar's usual consort, although he is a pale lover compared to Diarmait. Oscar's climactic moment in the Cycle comes in **Cath Gabhra* [The Battle of Gabhair/Gowra], when he mortally wounds the hated *Cairbre Lifechair, whose dying act is to thrust a spear through Oscar's heart. Oscar dies with a jest on his lips, provoking Fionn to weep as he does at no other point in the Cycle. The slain hero is then buried under a great cairn at *Benn Étair [Howth]. But Oscar's persona survives his death. In the Christianized story of the Fianna's escape from hell, Oscar is the critical rearguard, wielding an unbreakable thong so that his comrades can break free. Oisín tells St *Patrick in **Acallam na Senórach* [The Colloquy of the Elders] that only God can defeat Oscar.

2. Name of a second son born to *Oisín during his liaison with *Niam in *Tír na nÓg.

3. Character in James *Macpherson's *Poems of Ossian* (1760–3), based on Oscar (1). Son of *Ossian, grandson of *Fingal, he is killed in Book I of *Temora* when provoked at a dinner by Cairbar's druid Olla. Malvina is his grieving widow. The popularity of Macpherson's *Ossian* made the name Oscar widely known in Europe. After Marshal Bernadotte of France became King Charles XIV of Sweden, he and his wife, Désirée Cleary, daughter of a Dublin merchant, named their son Oscar, who became Oscar I of Sweden and Norway (1844–59).

Osraige, Osraighe. Irish names for *Ossory.

Ossian. Nominal narrator of James *Macpherson's *Poems of Ossian* (1760–3), based on the character of *Oisín as found in Scottish Gaelic ballad tradition; in the late 19th century the name Ossian displaced that of Oisín in popular retellings of *Fenian stories. Son of *Fingal and Roscranna, husband of Everallin, he was the father of *Oscar (3), whose mistress Malvina was also his companion in old age.

Ossianic Cycle, Ballads, etc. See FENIAN CYCLE. The immense popularity of James *Macpherson's *Poems of Ossian* from the late 18th century through much of the 19th century meant that 'Ossianic' once implied the whole spectrum of early Celtic culture.

Ossory [Ir. *Osraige, Osraighe*]. Anglicized name for a medieval kingdom roughly coextensive with the modern diocese of Ossory in Co. Kilkenny and adjacent areas.

Otherworld, otherworld. A realm beyond the senses, usually a delightful place, not knowable to ordinary mortals without an invitation from a denizen; the Celtic Otherworld sometimes subsumes the Mediterranean concept of the underworld, i.e. the realm of the *dead. Evidence from all areas of Celtic culture, from the ancient to all the vernaculars, demonstrates a belief in life materially surviving the expiration of the body. *Hallstatt-era (1200–600 BC) graves come supplied with food and equipment to allow the deceased to begin again in the next life. *Classical commentators agree that *druids taught the soul's immortality as well as its transmigration or metempsychosis. Early Irish and Welsh literary traditions extend the fragmentary outline from the ancient world. Transmigration of souls gives way to the widespread motif of *shape-shifting, and the happy afterlife becomes concurrent with mortal life. Both Irish and Welsh accounts are frequently ambiguous and contradictory about the place of the Otherworld. It may be unplaceable on human maps; or it may be identified with a remote island in or under the western seas. Sometimes an enterprising sailor reaching that remote island may enter the Otherworld. Or another adventurer may enter the Otherworld by travelling on land to enter mounds or dwelling-places of the divine; in Ireland these are known as *sídh (sing.), sídhe (pl.), places where the defeated semi-divine *Tuatha Dé Danann fled, and *bruiden. *Caves, especially the famous one at *Cruachain, are often thought to be routes to the Otherworld in all Celtic traditions, and so are some lakes. Curiously, entry to the Otherworld, by whatever means, never seems to be a reward for virtue or exemplary behaviour. More often, a mortal male invitee is asked by a beautiful otherworldly female who is inexplicably deeply in love with him; sometimes she takes the form of a *deer or fawn. In Brittany a fearful dark Otherworld is reached through the quagmire of *Youdic in the dismal bog of Yeun.

A number of early Irish adventurers' tales provide detailed descriptions of the Otherworld, which may go under different names. They include *Bran mac Febail in **Imram Brain* [The Voyage of Bran], *Connla (2) in **Echtrae Conli* [The Adventure of Connla], *Cormac mac Airt in **Echtrae Cormaic* [The Adventure of Cormac], Nera in **Echtra Nerai* [The Adventure of Nera], and *Tadg mac Céin. And despite its Latin text and Christian context, the voyage of St *Brendan also carries otherworldly resonances.

Many Irish and some Welsh visions of the Otherworld are Elysian, happy places overflowing with good food and drink, sport, beautiful and submissive women, enchanted music; special features are the pig slaughtered for dinner who appears restored ready to be eaten again the next morning, the *cauldron of plenty, and the prominence of the colour red. Sickness, age, and decay are banished.

Mortal visitors often find the Otherworld a source of wisdom and are impressed by the order and harmony there. The rulers of the Otherworld, not always named, appear wise, generous, and peace-loving, but they may be threatened by enemies and thus require the services of the mortal visitor, notably *Cúchulainn and *Pwyll. When mortal visitors sojourn in the Otherworld, they inevitably find that time there seems to pass in different duration, so that one year or even one day might be the same as 100 or 300 years in the lives of mortals. Among the happier Otherworlds are *Emain Ablach, *Hy Brasil, *Mag Dá Cheó, *Mag Mell, *Roca Barraidh, *Tír fo Thuinn, *Tír na mBan, *Tír na mBeó, *Tír na nÓg, *Tír Tairngire, and *Ynys Afallon. The Welsh *Annwfn, which may be known in different aspects, sometimes as the realm of the dead, often appears under other names: *Caer Feddwid, *Caer Siddi, *Caer Wydyr, and *Gwales, where *Bendigeidfran's severed head presides over a banquet; cf. *Harlech. Anaon is a Breton counterpart of Annwfn.

Yet not every visit to the Otherworld brings happy results, particularly when mortals travel there by their own choice. The more it is seen as the place of the dead, as in *Tech Duinn, the house of the unnerving *Donn (1), the more it is to be dreaded. *Arthur is nearly killed when he tries to retrieve the cauldron of plenty from Annwfn. This side of the Otherworld is reflected in an Irish name, *Dún Scáith [fort of shadow/fear]. The *Uffern, first found in the late 12th-century Latin writers Walter Map and *Giraldus Cambrensis, probably reflects Christian condemnation of pagan religion; derived from the Latin infernum, it has become the Welsh word for hell. Rulers of the Otherworld are not always named, but some who are include: *Arawn and his rival *Hafgan, *Cethern (1), *Eochaid Iúil, *Eógan Inbir and his wife *Bé Chuma, *Labraid Luathlám and *Lí Ban, *Mannanán mac Lir and *Fand, *Dáire (2) and *Rígru Rosclethan, and *Tethra. The craft-god *Goibniu hosts the otherworldly Fled Goibnenn, flowing with endless supplies of *ale.

David B. Spaan, 'The Otherworld in Early Irish Literature', dissertation, University of Michigan (1969); Christa Maria Löffler, *The Voyage to the Otherworld Island in Early Irish Literature* (2 vols., Salzburg, 1983); Alfred Nutt, 'An Essay Upon the Irish Vision of the Happy Otherworld and the Celtic Doctrine of Rebirth', in *Immram Brain* (London, 1895–7), i. 101–331; ii. 1–305; Proinsias MacCana, 'The Sinless Otherworld of *Immram Brain*', *Ériu*, 27 (1976), 95–115; Patrick Sims-Williams, 'Some Celtic Otherworld Terms', in Ann T. E. Matonis and Daniel F. Melia (eds.), *Celtic Language, Celtic Culture: A Festschrift for Eric P. Hamp* (Van Nuys, Calif., 1990), 57–81.

otter. The fish-eating, web-footed musteline mammal (genus *Lutra*) appears frequently in narratives of the modern Celtic languages but does not appear to have had comparable attention in ancient Celtic tradition. While biologically related to the *badger and the stoat, the otter is more often associated with the *salmon for its perceived skill in catching. *Ceridwen takes the form of an otter while in pursuit of *Taliesin, who had become a salmon. A late accretion to the story of the early Irish king *Lugaid mac Con portrays the king's mother being impregnated by an otter [*cú dobhráin*, water-hound] while bathing; later Lugaid's otter-father cures his sleeplessness by taking him under water. The epithet Dobharchon of *Cuirithir, lover of *Liadain, means 'son of the otter'. So highly prized was the skin of the otter in 10th-century Wales that it was thought equal to those of the *deer and the fox. The Highland bandit Rob Roy MacGregor (1671–1734) was reputed to have a sporran of otter skin. In the Hebrides, the liver of a newly killed otter gave the power to cure scalds and burns. The 'father' of otters in Irish folklore is *Dobharchú. Ir. madra uisce, dobharchú; ScG dòbhran, biast-dhubh; Manx moddey ushtey, dooarchoo; W dwrgi, dyfgri; Corn. dowrgy, dowrast; Bret. dourgi.

Owain, Owein, Owen [L *Eugenius*, wellborn]. Name borne by dozens of figures from early Welsh legend, romance, and history, most notably Owain ap Urien, hero of the 13th-century romance **Owain*, and Owain Glyndyfrdwy [Glendower], leader of the last successful Welsh resistance against English domination, 1401–6.

Owain, *Owein*. Thirteenth-century Welsh Arthurian prose romance, also known as *Lady of the Fountain* [W *Chwedyl Iarlles y Ffynnawn*], one of *Y *Tair Rhamant* [Three Romances], along with **Geraint ac Enid* and **Peredur*. Manuscripts are found in the **White Book of Rhydderch* (*c.*1325), the **Red Book of Hergest* (*c.*1382–1410), and elsewhere. Lady Charlotte Guest included the romance in her translation of the *Mabinogion* (1846), as have later translators, but it is not a part of the four branches of the **Mabinogi*.

One evening when *Arthur is in court at *Caer Llion, the knights begin to tell stories to amuse themselves. *Cynon son of Clydno speaks first, in a tale of a powerful Knight of the Fountain who overthrows all he confronts. Upon being challenged by *Cei, Owain goes in search of the Knight and slays him. Then with the help of a maiden named *Luned, who provides a magical ring and a stone of invisibility, he escapes the anger of the townspeople seeking to avenge the death of their lord. He subsequently marries the lord's widow, the beautiful Lady of the Fountain, Luned's mother, and rules the land for three years. Meanwhile, King Arthur and his knights have come in search of Owain. Upon arriving at the Fountain, King Arthur's men all challenge the new Knight of the Fountain (Owain) and are overthrown by him. Realizing their comrade's new identity, the knights are reunited with Owain, and the latter returns to Arthur's court after promising his wife, the Lady of the Fountain, that he will return after another three years. Owain is reminded of this promise when the Lady comes to King Arthur's court, removes the ring she has given him as a token to remember her, and charges him with betrayal. Overwhelmed with shame and remorse, Owain goes to live in the wild among beasts, allowing his hair to grow and his clothes to rot (see *wild man of the wood motif). An unnamed widow finds Owain and restores him to health. Owain then departs for his kingdom, but along the way meets a white lion who shares a slaughtered roebuck with him. The white lion is revealed to be Luned, kept in durance because of her love of Owain and his desertion. With the aid of Luned as lion, Owain does battle with several foes, including *Du Traws [the black oppressor] and Luned's tormentors. Owain is then restored to his kingdom, after which he is addressed as the Knight of the Fountain [W *Iarll y Cawg*].

Owain the Welsh Arthurian figure is generally thought to be based upon the 6th-century Owain ap Urien, who defended the kingdom of *Rheged against the encroachment of the Angles. He also appears in **Breuddwyd Rhonabwy* [The Dream of Rhonabwy], where he plays the board-game *gwyddbwyll with Arthur and is much associated with ravens. Owain ap Urien was a patron of *Taliesin and subject of a lament attributed to that poet. In the *Triads, Owain is described as the son of Urien and the semi-divine *Modron.

Like the other narratives of *Tair Rhamant*, *Owain* is paralleled in the works of *Chrétien de Troyes, **Yvain* or *Chevalier du Lion* (*c.*1178). Although the French version is much older than the *White Book* manuscript (*c.*1325), it is still an open question whether a lost Welsh original preceded Chrétien's composition. The best modern text is *Owein*, ed. R. L. Thomson (Dublin, 1968, 1975). See also R. L. Thomson, *The Arthur of the Welsh* (Cardiff, 1991), ch. 7; A. C. L. Brown, *Romanic Review*, 3 (1912), 147–72; Idris Llewelyn Foster, 'Owein', in R. S. Loomis (ed.), *Arthurian Literature in the Middle Ages* (Oxford, 1959), 196–9.

Owain Lawgoch [W, red hand]. Ancient ruler of Britain who survives in 'Sleeping Warrior' stories in Welsh folklore. In one story a simple drover named Dafydd loses his way to Owain's chamber and takes a lump of gold from it. Folk motif: E502.

Owel. Anglicization of *Eógabal.

P

P. The sixteenth letter of the modern English alphabet is represented by peith [Ir., tree or bush with edible berries; dwarf elder (?); gooseberry (?)] in the *ogham alphabet of early Ireland. Although thirteenth letter of the early Irish alphabet, P did not exist in the earlier ogham and entered the language through loanwords from Latin (through British), Romance, and Scandinavian sources.

P-Celts, P-Celtic. The division of Celtic languages into Q- and P-families depends on whether they retained the Indo-European qu- or substituted a p-. The substitution of p- for qu- probably took place in the first millennium BC in central Europe and spread to the west, but not as far as *Ireland or the Celtic areas of the Iberian peninsula. Gaulish was largely a P-Celtic language, with traces of Q-Celtic. The p-/q- split is clearest in cognates retaining the same roots, e.g. W *pen*, head and Ir. *ceann*, head. The Modern P-Celtic languages are Welsh, Cornish, and Breton; these are also called *Brythonic. The languages of ancient Britain and Scotland at the time of the Roman invasion were dominantly P-Celtic. See also BELGAE; BUILG; CALEDONII; ÉRAINN; PICTS.

Paimpont. Official French name, since the time of the Revolution, for the forest of *Brocéliande.

pangs/debility **of the Ulstermen.** When *Crunniuc mac Agnomain forced his wife *Macha (3) to run a foot-race with a horse, she cursed the watching *Ulster warriors unto nine times nine generations with the debilitating pains suffered by women in childbirth when they were in greatest difficulty. Known in Irish as [ces] *noínden Ulad [nine days' affliction of Ulster]. The episode is retold here at the beginning of the **Táin Bó Cuailnge* [Cattle Raid of Cooley].

Paps of Ana/Anu. See DÁ CHÍCH ANANN.

Parsifal. See PERCEVEL.

Parthalón. Variant spelling of *Partholón.

Parthanán. Agricultural demon, best known in the west of Ireland, who comes at harvest time to thresh all the grain left standing in the field; derived from *Partholón,

Partholón, Parthalón. Leader of the second mythic invasion of early Ireland, according to the medieval pseudo-history **Lebor Gabála* [Book of Invasions]. As the letter P was unknown in the earliest Irish, Partholón is a borrowed name, probably from Bartholomaeus, which St Jerome and Isidore of Seville gloss as 'son of him who stays the waters', i.e. a survivor of the biblical Flood; another possibility is Parthia, ancient name for northern Iran. Partholón's biblical pedigree makes him a descendant of Magog, who lived in the twenty-first year of the Patriarch Abraham. None the less, he is a prince of Greece who murders his father, Sera, and mother, hoping to inherit the kingdom for himself; the episode costs Partholón his left eye and marks him with bad fortune. He was, despite this, the 'chief of every craft'. After seven years' wandering he landed in Ireland with his wife, *Dealgnaid, three sons, and their wives; the complete list of Partholón's sons is more extensive: *Er (1), *Ferann [land, domain], *Fergna, Laiglinni, Orba [patrimony of land], Rudraige, and *Sláine [health] (1). His *druids, three brothers, are *Eólas [knowledge], *Fios [intelligence], and *Fochmarc [enquiring]. While Partholón is hunting one day, his wife Dealgnaid seduces the servant Todga, the first instance of adultery in Irish literature. Texts differ on Partholón's reaction, describing him either as flying into a rage or as being placated by her verse protest that she should not have been left alone with great temptation. After thirty years in Ireland Partholón dies near the modern town of Tallaght where, 120 years later, the remainder of his people perish in a plague. His name is not cited in later genealogies or pedigrees. A shard of his persona lives on as *Parthanán, the agricultural demon who comes at harvest time to thresh all the grain left standing. See

Kuno Meyer, 'Partholón mac Sera', *Zeitschrift für celtische Philologie*, 13 (1919), 141–2; Anton G. van Hamel, 'Partholón', *Revue Celtique*, 50 (1933), 217–37; Henry Morris, 'The Partholon Legend', *Journal of the Royal Society of Antiquaries*, 67 (1937), 57–71.

Partholonians, Parthalonians. Mythical early invaders of Ireland, according to the pseudo-history **Lebor Gabála* [Book of Invasions]; they are named for their leader, *Partholón [L Bartholomaeus]. Arriving from the eastern Mediterranean 312 years after the death of *Cesair, the leader of the previous invasion, the Partholonians are the first invaders after the Flood and precede the invasion of the *Nemedians by thirty years. They often do battle with the predatory *Fomorians, nominally the fourth invaders, who prey upon successive inhabitants of Ireland. Under their leader, *Cichol Gricenchos, the Fomorians appear hideously misshapen, with only *one eye, one arm, and one leg. A beneficent and productive people, the Partholonians clear four plains, form seven lakes, introduce agriculture, and are the first to divide the island into four parts. They also establish the first civilization, fostering law, *cauldron-making, crafts, *ale-brewing, and hospitality. Their impermanent settlement touches different parts of the island. Landing first at *Inber Scéne [Kenmare?] or Donegal Bay at *Beltaine time, they settle near *Assaroe but later cultivate *Mag nElta [Moynalty], the plain between *Howth, *Clontarf, and Tallaght, coextensive with the modern city of *Dublin. After flourishing for 520 years, their numbers reaching 9,000, all the Partholonians die of the plague within one week in May. In a widely known variant text, *Tuan mac Cairill survives to the time of *Colum Cille to tell the history of the invasions.

Frequently cited Partholonians, after Partholón's family and druids, include: *Accasbél, builder of Ireland's first inn or hotel; *Babal, a merchant who introduced cattle; *Bacorbladra, the first teacher and foster-father; *Biobal, a merchant who introduced gold; *Breoga, who instructed disputants to settle with a single combat instead of going to war; *Feda, the first member to die in Ireland; *Malaliach, who first brewed ale, later used in *divination, ritual, and sacrifice; Merbán, a champion; Muncnicán, a champion; and *Sláine, Ireland's first physician as well as Partholón's son.

Parzifal. See PERCEVEL.

Patrick, Pátraic (OIr.), Pádraig, Pádraic (ModIr.), **Saint** [L *Patricius*, well-born, patrician]. Evangelist to and national saint of *Ireland who flourished in the 5th century. Details of St Patrick's life have been traced to five documents, a *Confessio* and 'Epistle to Coroticus' attributed to him and thought reliable, and three memoirs/biographies written long after his death, that of Muirchú (late 7th cent.), Tírechán (late 7th cent.), and the anonymous *Bethu Phátraic* or *Vita Tripartita* [Tripartite Life] (*c*.896–901), which draws on the first two texts and adds much material. Learned opinion (see D. A. Binchy, 1962, below) now accepts the authenticity of the *Confessio* and 'Epistle' but regards the three later texts as unhistorical and deriving from native hagiographic tradition. None of these documents has allowed us to date St Patrick's mission with certainty. The once-accepted dates of 432–61 are now rejected, in part because '432' is a magical numerical formula, and 456–93 are now favoured. The uncertainty of Patrick's death-date, once given as early as 431, occasioned T. F. O'Rahilly's theory (1941) of the Two Patricks, the 'second' being a Gaul named Palladius, which has not gained wide acceptance. Further lives of St Patrick were written after the coming of the Anglo-Normans (1169), in which some of the more fabulous motifs attached to the biography were first given credence. Additionally, St Patrick is also a character in early Irish literary texts, such as **Altrom Tige Dá Medar* [The Nurture of the Houses of the Two Milk Vessels] and more importantly **Acallam na Senórach* [The Colloquy of the Elders], in which he makes contentious dialogue with the *Fenian heroes *Oisín and *Caílte. Subsequently St Patrick became a figure in a huge number of stories from Irish oral tradition, many of which remain alive in the popular imagination.

According to the *Confessio*, supposedly written in rough Latin in the author's old age, Patrick was a native of Roman Britain, the son of one Calpurnius, the deacon of the village of Bannaven Taberniae, which has been ascribed to Cumberland, Northampton, the Severn valley, the Isle of *Anglesey, and two points in southern Scotland, one near Hadrian's Wall and another near Carlisle. His original Celtic name is alleged to have been Succat. Captured by Irish raiders at 16, Patrick was sold into bondage to herd pigs and sheep for a chief named Milchú in 'a lonely place', possibly the north-west or the Slemish Mountains of Co. Antrim. During six years of slavery he thought often of the Christian message and realized he had a vocation to the priesthood. Then guided by a dream, he escaped and walked a very long way, presumably to the southern coast, where he found passage on a merchant craft with a pagan crew for a three-day voyage. Eventually he returned to his home in Britain. He does not say where he was trained, but tradition suggests he was the disciple of St Germanus of Auxerre. Later chosen to be bishop, he returned to Ireland to become 'a slave for Christ' among the people who had enslaved him. Other Christian missionaries, notably the Gaulish Palladius, would have preceded him, but St Patrick was more successful and left a more lasting heritage. In his own words, during a thirty-year mission he 'baptized thousands, ordained clerics everywhere and rejoiced to see the flock of the Lord in Ireland growing splendidly'. Given that 5th-century Ireland lacked cities and towns in the European sense, St Patrick could not be expected to have founded permanent churches, but he is traditionally thought to have established his see at *Armagh near the *Ulster 'capital' of *Emain Macha. The Primate of Ireland still resides there as Comharba Phádraig [the successor of Patrick], but recent scholarship (Sharpe, 1982) challenges Armagh's claim. By tradition alone he is thought to have died on 17 March at Sabhall [Ir., barn], coextensive with the town of Saul, near Downpatrick, Co. Down. The other text thought authentic, the Latin 'Epistle to Coroticus', beseeches a British chieftain to free Irish Christian captives. Lastly, the saint is thought to have composed the prayer-poem 'St Patrick's Breastplate' or 'The Deer's Cry', in which the saint avoids an ambush on the way to evangelize *Tara by turning himself and a companion, Benén, into a *deer and a *fawn, a Christian usage of the power of *féth fiada.

Other episodes in St Patrick's life, still in wide circulation at the end of the 20th century, lack reliable documentation. These include: the lighting of the first Paschal fire at Slane; the use of the three-leafed shamrock to explain the mystery of the Christian Trinity; the destruction of the idol *Crom Crúaich in Co. Cavan; the conversion of *Lóegaire mac Néill of Tara; the conversion of *Angus mac Natfráich of *Cashel, who did not cry out when Patrick punctured his foot during baptism because he thought it was part of the ceremony; the banishing of the monster *Caoránach, 'the mother of the devil', to *Lough Derg, Co. *Donegal, or the inauguration of pilgrimages there. The association with *Croagh Patrick, a place of pilgrimage in Co. Mayo, is cited in the memoir of Tírechán, a writer himself from north *Connacht. The most famous of all apocryphal attributions, the driving of snakes from Ireland, first appears in the credulous Anglo-Norman biographies of the 12th and 13th centuries; the absence of snakes on the island had been noted as early as AD 200 by the Roman geographer *Solinus.

Apart from the additional works of wonder and attributed magical powers (e.g. the *fairy herb plantain is known as capóg Phadraig [Patrick's leaf] in Irish), the most significant addition to St Patrick's persona comes in his contentious dialogues with the Fenian heroes Caílte and Oisín, first in *Acallam na Senórach* [The Colloquy of the Elders] and in the many poems in Fenian popular tradition, sometimes called Ossianic. Here St Patrick is sometimes on the losing end of arguments pitting the values of the lost pagan tradition, often embodied in *Fionn mac Cumhaill, against the discipline of the new faith, which is often portrayed as severe and joyless. Patrick's nickname in these dialogues is *Tálcend [adze-head], presumably making a pun on his bishop's mitre and his hard-headed unwillingness to hear the other side. Frequent mention is also made of his bell, Finnfaídech, which orders time.

See: *The Life and Writings of the Historical St. Patrick*, ed. R. P. C. Hanson (New York, 1983); *Four Latin Lives of St. Patrick*, ed. and trans. Ludwig Bieler (1971); *The Patrician Texts in the Book of Armagh*, ed. and trans. Ludwig Bieler (Dublin, 1979); *St. Patrick: His Writings and Muirchú's Life*, ed. and trans. A. B. E. Hood (Totowa, NJ, 1978); *Bethu Phátraic: The Tripartite Life of St. Patrick*, ed. and trans. Kathleen Mulchrone (Dublin, 1939); *The Tripartite Life of St. Patrick and Other Documents Relating to the Saint*, ed. and trans. Whitley Stokes (2 vols., London, 1887; repr. New York, 1965). Commentary: Ludwig Bieler, *The Life and Legend of St. Patrick* (Dublin, 1949); D. A. Binchy, 'Patrick and His Biographers: Ancient and Modern', *Studia Hibernica*, 2 (1962), 7–173; James Carney, *The Problem of St. Patrick*

(Dublin, 1961, 1973); R. P. C. Hanson, *Saint Patrick: His Origins and Career* (Oxford, 1968); Alannah Hopkin, *The Living Legend of St. Patrick* (London, 1989); Thomas F. O'Rahilly, *The Two Patricks* (Dublin, 1942, 1971); Richard Sharpe, 'St. Patrick and the See of Armagh', *Cambridge Medieval Celtic Studies*, 4 (Winter 1982), 33–59; cf. B. K. Lambkin, 'Patrick, Armagh, and Emain Macha', *Emania* [Belfast], 2 (1987), 29–31; David Dumville, *St. Patrick, A.D. 493–1993* (Woodbridge, UK, and Rochester, NY, 1993); George Otto Simms, *The Real Story of St. Patrick* (Dublin, 1993); E. A. Thompson, *Who Was St. Patrick?* (Suffolk, 1985; New York, 1986).

Patrick's Purgatory, Saint. See LOUGH DERG (1).

peallaidh. A regional variation on the *ùruisg in Scottish Gaelic tradition, especially associated with the town of Aberfeldy, 32 miles NW of Perth, which takes its name from the peallaidh. Although not a water-spirit, the peallaidh was thought to haunt rivers, lochs, or the seashore. Like the ùruisg, it is a subspecies of *fuath.

Pedair Cainc y Mabinogi [W, The Four Branches of the Mabinogi]. See MABINOGI.

Pen Annwfn [W, head of Annwfn]. Title won by *Pwyll for keeping his agreement with *Arawn in the first branch of the **Mabinogi*.

pencerdd [W *pen*, chief; *cerdd*, art]. A chief poet of early *Wales, requiring nine years of training in such subjects as grammar, metrics, and genealogy. Only a pencerdd could teach a *bard. As late as 1547, the poet Simwnt Fychan (*c.*1530–1606) received a written licence to become a pencerdd, a document which survives. Roughly comparable to the early Irish *ollam.

Pengwern. One of the three chief courts of medieval Wales, cited in the poem *Eryr Pengwern* [The Eagle of Pengwern] (9th–10th cents.). Previously identified with Shrewsbury, it is now thought to lie in Shropshire but has not been positively identified. See Jenny Rowland, *Early Welsh Saga Poetry* (Cambridge, 1990); Patrick Sims-Williams, *Welsh Historical Review*, 17 (June 1994).

Percevel, Perceval, Percival, Parsifal, Parzifal, Perchevael. The Grail hero of the Arthurian legends has numerous Celtic antecedents and/or parallels, including the *Amadán Mór, *Fionn mac Cumhaill, *Peredur, and *Peronnik. He first appears in *Chrétien de Troyes's *Conte del Graal* or *Perceval* (*c.*1182). Details of his life and circumstances are not consistent through various English, French, and German retellings of his story, but he is always a questing innocent, the bumpkin who becomes a hero. Richard Wagner described the character as a 'simpleton without guile' in his music drama *Parsifal* (1882). See Jessie L. Weston, *The Legend of Sir Perceval* (2 vols., London, 1906, 1909); R. B. Pace, 'Sir Perceval and the Boyish Exploits of Finn', *PMLA*, n.s. 25(4) (Dec. 1917), 598–604; Arthur C. L. Brown, *Origin of the Grail Legend* (New York, 1935); Sheila Joyce McHugh, *'Sir Perceyvelle': Its Irish Connections* (Ann Arbor, Mich., 1946); D. D. R. Owen, 'The Development of the Perceval Story', *Romania*, 80 (1959), 473–92; Ceridwen Lloyd-Morgan, 'Percival in Wales: The Late Medieval Grail Traditions', in Alison Adams et al. (eds.), *The Changing Face of Arthurian Romance* (Woodbridge, UK, 1986), 78–91.

Peredur. Welsh Arthurian hero of one of the 13th-century Three Romances, **Tair Rhamant*, which bears his name; the other two are **Geraint ac Enid* and **Owain*. Obviously related to the story of *Percevel, *Peredur* has been called 'the Grail legend without the Grail'. Manuscripts of the narrative survive in the **White Book of Rhydderch* (*c.*1325), the **Red Book of Hergest* (*c.*1382–1410), and two other collections. Lady Charlotte Guest included it in her translation of *The Mabinogion* (1846), although it is not one of the four branches of the **Mabinogi*.

After the death of his father, Efrawg [cf. ModW *Efrog*, York], Peredur, a seventh son, lives a quiet life with his mother; he none the less grows strong and swift. His mother does not want him to become a knight, fearing the dangers encountered, but nothing can keep him from the goal. Still, she instructs him in the knightly code, and he leaves home for *Arthur's court, expecting to be dubbed. Peredur's awkwardness and naïvety evoke amusement at court, but he soon establishes a reputation for a pure heart and valour. Gradually he also acquires skill and polish in hunting, war, and love. To avenge *Cei's insult to a *dwarf, he enters upon a long series of adventures, led by Etlym Gleddyfcoch [red sword], that bring out his innate chivalry. Two uncles continue his education. The first, who is lame, tells him never to ask about the significance of what he sees. At the court of the second, a fisher-lord, he sees a bleeding lance and a severed head upon a salver being carried in a procession. The head is that of Peredur's cousin, whom he is asked to avenge. He proceeds to the court of the witches of Caerloyw [Gloucester], who instruct him in weaponry. On another day, towards dusk, Peredur is greeted by a hermit in a snowy valley, when a *hawk attacks a wild duck and a *crow settles on the prey. The juxtaposition of the crow, the blood, and the snow, the *black-red-white motif, reminds him of the ideal of feminine beauty, as she will also combine these colours: black hair, white skin, red lips. But this love he will not know. After a return to Arthur's court, Peredur embarks on another series of adventures, culminating with his fourteen-year sojourn with the 'Empress of Constantinople' (Cristinobyl, etc.), an episode containing remnants of the *sovereignty story. In an abrupt return to Arthur's court, Peredur is berated by a loathly lady for failing to seek the meaning of the marvels he has seen at his second uncle's castle, which would have restored his king to health and his land to prosperity. After still more adventures, Peredur learns that the witches of Caerloyw had beheaded his cousin and wounded the first uncle, and that Peredur is fated to avenge them.

The relationship between Peredur and Percevel is extraordinarily complicated. Although *Chrétien's *Perceval* (*c*.1182) is earlier than the *Red Book* manuscript (*c*.1382–1410), the Welsh story is not necessarily a variation of the French. The order of events is different in the two stories, with the severed head replacing the Grail; the fourteen-year sojourn is not found in Chrétien. Independent references to Peredur exist in Welsh tradition before the writing of the *Red Book* (the *Annales Cambriae* put the death of Peredur, seventh son of Eilffer, in AD 580), and it is possible that *Peredur* is a retelling of lost Welsh material found in, or used by, Chrétien, conflated with native traditions about the hero.

See Idris Llewelyn Foster, 'Peredur', in R. S. Loomis (ed.), *Arthurian Literature in the Middle Ages* (Oxford, 1959), 199–205; Glenys Goetinck, 'Historia Peredur', *Llên Cymru*, 6 (1960/1), 138–53; *Peredur: A Study of Welsh Traditions in the Grail Legends* (Cardiff, 1975). See also PERONNIK.

Peronnik, Peronnique [Bret. *per-*, bowl]. Character in Breton folklore whose story parallels that of the Welsh *Peredur and the Arthurian *Percevel. Peronnik is a poor country orphan who, after many knights have failed, enters the castle Kerglas of the wicked magician Rogear in order to retrieve the stolen lance and cup. When he restores the purloined treasures to the rightful king, peace and prosperity return to the kingdom. Retold in the immensely popular collection by Émile Souvestre, *Le Foyer Breton* (Paris, 1853; much reprinted). See George Moore, *Peronnik the Fool* (New York, 1924).

Phantom's Frenzy. Usual English translation of the Irish title **Baile In Scáil*.

phenodree, phenodyree, phynnodderree, phynodderee. Variant spellings of *fenodyree.

phooka, phouka. Variant spellings of *pooka.

Picts [L *picti*, painted men]. Historical ancient people of the British Isles, perhaps the earliest to speak any form of a Celtic language in these islands. The Roman name, Picti, dates only from the late 3rd century AD and derives from a soldiers' nickname, apparently based on observing the tribal penchant for decorating bodies with tattoos, a custom not unknown to other Celtic peoples. While the Picts' name for themselves is not known, the *P-Celtic Preteni, Pretani and *Q-Celtic Cruithni, Cruithnig, Cruithne, Cruthin imply that if they did have one it would have included the elements -r-t-n-. The name for the Picts, therefore, may be at the root of the name Britain, although the Picts are not identical with the P-Celtic Britons conquered by the Romans. Because of their lack of surviving records and their apparent archaism, the Picts have been the subject of much scholarly speculation. At one time the Picts were thought to have been exotic intruders akin to the Basques of southern France, and to have resided primarily in northern and north-eastern Scotland; recent informed opinion rejects both notions. According to Kenneth H. Jackson (1980), the Picts had two languages, one P-Celtic, brought from the Continent by Gallo-Brittonic settlers, and the other which was non-Indo-European but absorbed some Celtic vocabulary. Further, the Picts settled throughout the British Isles including Ireland; T. F. O'Rahilly (1946) cites them as among the earliest inhabitants of that island. Custom tended to distinguish the Picts from their neighbours, e.g. descent was matrilinear, or reckoned through the female side: only sons of the Pictish royal lineage could succeed to kingship. The Picts also left an impressive artistic legacy of stylized carved memorial stones and crosses that have been much esteemed by modern aesthetes. Although the Picts are cited in Irish chronicles as late as the 8th century, they maintained a more lasting presence in Scotland. The Romans classified the Picts into two divisions, the Dicalydones [Double Caledonians], north and south of the Forest of Atholl barrier, and the Verturiones farther to the south. The initial migration of Q-Celtic *Scotti from Ireland to *Dál Riada during the 6th century and earlier seems to have caused little conflict, and the Irish saint *Colum Cille evangelized the Pictish king Bridei or Brudei. A more constant enemy were the Northumbrians, whom the Picts defeated at *Nechtansmere, AD 685. In another 200 years, however, the Picts were united with the Gaelic invaders by Cináed mac Ailpín [Kenneth MacAlpin] to form the nation of Alba, which would become Scotland. See T. F. O'Rahilly, 'Priteni, Pritani, Britanni', in *Early Irish History and Mythology* (Dublin, 1946), 444–52; F. T. Wainwright (ed.), *The Problem of the Picts* (Edinburgh, 1955; rev. Perth, 1980), esp. K. H. Jackson's 'The Pictish Language'; Sally M. Foster, *Picts, Gaels and Scots* (London, 1996); Isobel Henderson, *The Picts* (London, 1967); 'Pictish Art and the Book of Kells', in R. McKittrick et al. (eds.), *Ireland in Early Medieval Europe* (Cambridge, 1982); Anthony Jackson, *The Pictish Trail* (Kirkwall, Orkney, 1989); Lloyd and Jenny Laing, *The Picts and The Scots* (London, 1993); E. Nicoll (ed.), *Pictish Panorama* (Balgavies, 1995); A. Ritchie, *Picts* (Edinburgh, 1989).

piskie, pisky, piskey, pisgie, pigsie, pixie, pixy. The Cornish name piskie was metathesized in Somerset and Devon to pixie and pigsie. Cornish and west of England *fairy who haunts hills, rivers, and groves, misleading lonely travellers, thus giving us the English word 'pixilated'. The older, more genuinely Cornish conception envisages a wizened old man, sometimes in a green suit, who both threshes grain and rides a horse. Elsewhere, the figure may be either sturdy and earthy (in Somerset) or slight, white, and naked (in Devon). Piskies were introduced to English literary tradition by the letters of Ann Elizabeth Bray to Robert Southey, later published as *Traditions . . . on the Borders of the Tamar and the Tavy* (1838). See Enys Tregarthen, *The Piskey-Purse* (London, 1905); repr. in *Piskey Folk* (New York, 1940); repr. in *Pixie Folklore and Legends* (Avenal, NJ, 1995). Folk motif: F200.1. See also FÓIDÍN MEARAÍ.

Plain of Weeping, Plain of Reckoning. See MAG TUIRED.

Plinlimmon. Variant form of *Pumlumon.

Pliny the Elder (AD 23–79). Roman scholar, historian, and scientific encyclopaedist who gives us some of the closest examination of ancient *druids to be found among *classical commentators. Pliny's knowledge of the Celts came first-hand, for he served first in the army and later as governor of Gallia Narbonensis (southern Gaul, near modern Marseille). Although he was a highly prolific author, only his thirty-seven-part *Historia Naturalis* and letters survive. See *Natural History*, Loeb Classical Library (10 vols., Cambridge, Mass., and London, 1938–63).

Polybius (204–122 BC). Greek historian, author of forty books, most of which have not survived, dealing mostly with contemporary times, from 220 to 146 BC. After the Roman conquest of Greece, Polybius was taken to Rome for seventeen years as a distinguished prisoner, where he became acquainted with leading public figures, such as the younger Scipio Africanus. Thought to be among the most reliable of *classical commentators, Polybius speaks of Celtic mercenaries called the *gaesatae. See *Histories*, trans. W. R. Paton, Loeb Classical Library (6 vols., New York, 1922–7).

pooka, phouka, púca [Ir. *púca*; ON *pukki*]. Irish *fairy presented variously in a large body of lore collected in the 19th century. In the works of T. Crofton Croker (1825–7) the pooka is malevolent and demonic, spoiling blackberries, and taking the form of a horse and offering unsuspecting mortals a dangerous ride. In Lady Wilde's *Ancient Legends* (1887) the pooka is benevolent and helpful, like the Scottish *brownie. A common speculation links the pooka to the English folk figure Puck, although the Welsh *pwca is a more likely Celtic cognate. Cf. Corn. BUCCA, Manx BUGGANE. The 6′ 3¢ invisible rabbit in Mary Chase's Broadway comedy

Harvey (1944) is identified in the text as a pooka.

Poor Old Woman. Translation of *Sean-bhean Bhocht and *Shan Van Vocht, a personification of *Ireland.

Posidonius (*c.*135-*c.*51 BC). Syrian-born Roman philosopher and perhaps the most important commentator on Celtic affairs. He anticipates *bardic institutions and the *champion's portion. Other ancient commentators, including Julius *Caesar, clearly plagiarized him. See J. J. Tierney, 'The Celtic Ethnography of Posidonius', *Proceedings of the Royal Irish Academy*, 60 C(5) (1960), 189–275; repr. in a separate volume (Dublin, 1985); I. G. Kidd (ed.), *Posidonius*, 2nd edn. (2 vols., Cambridge and London, 1989).

Powys [L *pagenses*, (land of the) country-dwellers]. Ancient and medieval kingdom of eastern *Wales and now a county, re-formed in 1974, adjacent to the border with England. Believed to have developed from the territories of the ancient Carnovii, Powys reached its apogee during the reign of King Madog ap Maredudd (AD 1138–60), when its borders extended as far north as Pulford, near Chester, and east to the upper Severn. Esteemed for the welcome it extended to minstrels, Powys was called the 'Garden of Wales' in the poetry of *Llywarch Hen (9th-10th centuries). Evidence of the Powys dialect is found in the language of the second branch of the *Mabinogi*. Powys also provided the background for **Breuddwyd Rhonabwy* [The Dream of Rhonabwy], although the kingdom had disappeared by the time the text was composed. Powys is also the name of a castle near the town of Welshpool. The modern county of Powys was forged in 1974 from the former counties of Montgomery, Radnor, and Brecknock; it includes a great deal of territory never a part of medieval Powys and is the most thinly populated of all modern counties. The heroic elements of regional stories prompted Alwyn and Brinley Rees (1961) to see a link between Powys and *Ulster. See Wendy Davies, *Wales in the Early Middle Ages* (Leicester, 1982).

Preiddiau Annwfn, *Preiddeu Annwn.* Welsh title for a perhaps 9th-century short poem usually known in English as The Spoils of Annwfn. Although found in the *Book of *Taliesin*, it is no longer attributed to that 6th-century figure. *Arthur begins the action with an expedition on his ship Prydwen to capture the *cauldron of the chief of the *otherworldly realm of *Annwfn. The realm they visit is called *Caer Siddi [revolving fortress (?)], a four-cornered glass fortress contains youthful inhabitants much given to feasting and merrymaking, a wonderful fountain, a silent sentinel, and a doleful prisoner named *Gwair [hay]. Brilliant with a pearl-decorated rim, the cauldron is heated by the breath of nine maidens and will not cook the food of a coward. The expedition is a failure, however, and only seven return. Text: *Poems from the Book of Taliesin*, ed. J. Gwenogvryn Evans (Llanbedrog, Wales, 1915), 26–41. See also R. S. Loomis, *Wales and the Arthurian Legend* (Cardiff, 1956).

Priteni, Pritani, Preteni. Early *P-Celtic names for the *Picts. See also PRYDYN.

Prydain, Prydein. Welsh name for Britain, i.e. the Welsh-speaking island; contrast with Lloegr [England].

Pryderi. Son of *Pwyll and *Rhiannon and the only character mentioned by name in all four branches of the **Mabinogi*. He disappeared shortly after his birth and was found by *Teyrnon Twrf Liant and his wife, who called him *Gwri Gwallt-Euryn [golden hair]. In **Preiddiau Annwfn* [The Spoils of Annwfn] he appears with Pwyll, saying that the prison of *Gwair is well-equipped. Some of his story may have contributed to the conception of *Percevel in the Arthurian legends.

Prydyn. Early Welsh name for the *Picts. See PRYDAIN.

Ptolemy (*fl.* AD 139–61). Egyptian geographer and astronomer sometimes called Claudius Ptolemaeus to distinguish him from the several Egyptian kings also named Ptolemy. Better known as an astronomer, he was the most important theorist before Copernicus (1543). His *Geographia* retains a better reputation today, as it corrects the observations of his predecessors and includes some of the most reliable data to be found in the ancient world. Divided into eight books and illustrated with twenty-six maps, including a map of the then known world, the *Geographia* is primarily a catalogue of places, with their latitudes and longitudes, and a brief description of each continent, country, and people. See *Geography*, ed. P. J. Fischer (London, 1932); *Geographia* (3 vols., Hildesheim, 1966); T. G. Rylands, *The Geography of*

Ptolemy (London, 1893); *Geography of Claudius Ptolemy*, ed. Edward L. Stevenson (New York, 1932); Walter M. Ellis, *Ptolemy of Egypt* (London and New York, 1994).

Pumlumon, Plinlimmon [W *pum*, five; *lumon*, peaks (?), beacons (?)]. Mountain (2,468 feet) in central *Wales, 10 miles W of Llanidloes, whose springs provide the sources of the Severn and Wye rivers. Commonly perceived as the central point or *omphalos of Wales, comparable to *Uisnech in *Ireland and *Kermaria in *Brittany. The spelling Plinlimmon was favoured by Thomas Gray and other 18th-century Celtic revivalists.

Pursuit of . . . . English translation of **Tóraigheacht* . . . , a conventional first word in the title of a class of Irish narratives.

pwca [W, goblin]. Welsh solitary *fairy, a friskier version of *bwci, certainly related to, perhaps the inspiration of, the English folk figure Puck. See also POOKA [Ir. *púca*], the Cornish BUCCA, and the Manx BUGGANE.

Pwyll [W, wisdom; discretion, prudence]. Prince of *Dyfed, Welsh hero of the first branch of the **Mabinogi*, which usually bears his name. To pay for a discourtesy to *Arawn, ruler of *Annwfn, Pwyll agrees to take his form for a year and to meet Arawn's enemy *Hafgan. In that year he may share the bed of Arawn's wife but not make love to her. Pwyll keeps his agreement, killing Hafgan, chastely avoiding the wife, and winning the title Pen Annwfn [head of Annwfn]. Pwyll is dazzled by the beauty of *Rhiannon when she rides by on a white horse, but he is thwarted for one year by the trick of a rival suitor, *Gwawl. In the third year of their marriage, Rhiannon bears a son that is stolen and she is falsely accused of infanticide. For punishment, Rhiannon is obliged to sit by a horse-block for seven years, offering to give rides on her back to visitors. The child is later returned and named *Pryderi. Pwyll continues to rule from his palace *Arberth, and in due time is succeeded by his son, Pryderi.

Modern commentators are often unkind to Pwyll as a literary character, calling him 'foolish', 'spineless', and 'a bungling incompetent', especially for his treatment of Rhiannon when she is falsely accused. Like many Celtic heroes, however, he may have origins in the supernatural, as his title Pen Annwfn implies. The more likely root meaning of his name, 'wisdom', suggests links with the Irish figures *Midir of Brí Léith and *Conn [Ir., sense, wisdom, reason]. Roger Sherman Loomis (1927) thought that Pwyll's resistance to Arawn's wife may have contributed to the episode of the temptress wife in *Sir Gawain and the Green Knight* (14th cent.). See W. J. Gruffydd, *Rhiannon* (Cardiff, 1953); Kenneth H. Jackson, 'Some Popular Motifs in Early Welsh Tradition', *Études Celtiques*, 11 (1961-7), 83–9; Catherine A. McKenna, 'The Theme of Sovereignty in *Pwyll*', *Bulletin of the Board of Celtic Studies*, 29 (1980), 35–52.

Q

Q-Celts, Q-Celtic. The division of the Celtic languages into Q- and P-families depends on whether they retained the Indo-European qu- or substituted a p-. The substitution of p- for qu- probably took place in the first millennium BC in central Europe and spread to the west, but not as far as *Ireland or the Celtic areas of the Iberian peninsula. The p-/q- split is clearest in cognates retaining the same roots, e.g. Ir. *ceann*, head and W *pen*, head. The modern Q-Celtic languages are Irish, Scottish Gaelic, and Manx; these are also called Goidelic. The distinctions are not always absolute; Irish Q-Celtic speakers settled in *Dyfed, a Welsh-speaking or P-Celtic region. See GOÍDEL GLAS.

Quelgny. Variant anglicization of *Cuailnge; see TÁIN BÓ CUAILNGE [Cattle Raid of Cooley].

quicken tree. See ROWAN.

Quinipily, Quinipili. See VENUS OF QUINIPILY.

R

R. The eighteenth letter of the modern English alphabet was signified by ruis [dwarf elder] in the *ogham alphabet of early Ireland.

ram. Images of the male sheep appear frequently in ancient Celtic art from as early as *La Tène times (4th cent. BC). The reference implied by the ram, especially the ram's head, is not always clear. It may have been merely decorative, or it may have carried implications of fertility, as the ram (along with the *goat) had been linked to *Mercury in classical imagery. Romano-Celtic representations of rams with Mercury are found widely in what is now France and Great Britain. Images of rams with northern British war-gods imply sexual energy and aggression. Ram-horned heads appear in the worship of *Camulos. Ram-horned serpents, combining perhaps fertility and sexual aggression with regeneration, appear frequently and widely. In a later *Fenian allegory, *Fionn sees a ram representing the whole world. See also POOKA. Ir. reithe; ScG reithe, rùd; Manx rea; W maharen, hwrdd; Corn. horth; Bret. tourz.

ráth, ráith, rath. A circular earthen wall, usually fortified or palisaded, surrounding ancient Irish dwellings; more loosely, the fortified dwelling, presumably of an early chieftain or king, surrounded by such a wall. First element in innumerable Irish place-names, where it is sometimes translated as 'royal seat'; virtually interchangeable with the term *dún-. Thought to be the residence of *fairies in Irish oral tradition. See also LISS.

Ráth na Ríogh. Irish name for the Fort/Rath of the Kings at *Tara.

Rathcroghan. Variant form of *Cruachain.

raven. See CROW.

red-black-white symbolism. See BLACK.

Red Book of Hergest [W *Llyfr Coch Hergest*]. One of the most important of all medieval Welsh manuscripts (*c*.1382–1410), containing texts of the **Mabinogi* and the seven other narratives usually included in the *Mabinogion*. The *Red Book* also contains poetry of the *Gogynfeirdd, histories, grammars, and proverbs, but not religious works or laws. Most of the copying was done by the single hand of a conscientious worker, Hywel Fychan fab Howel Goch o Fuellt, who imposed an order upon the entire manuscript; internal evidence proves that he worked on other manuscripts as well. Lady Charlotte Guest drew on the *Red Book of Hergest* for her translation of *The Mabinogion* (1846); more recent translations also favour the *Red Book*, with reference to the **White Book of Rhydderch* (*c*.1325). The name Hergest refers to the mansion in Herefordshire where the book was kept from sometime after 1465 until 1634, when it was returned to Wales. Since 1701 it has been at Jesus College, Oxford.

Red Branch Cycle. See ULSTER CYCLE.

Red Hand. See UÍ NÉILL; LABRAID LÁMDERG.

Reilig na Rígh, Reilg na Ríogh, Relig na Rí [Ir., cemetery of the kings]. Fanciful name known since the 18th century for a large, ringed enclosure at *Cruachain, Co. Roscommon. The assertion that Reilig na Rígh is the burial place of the kings of *Connacht is not supported by modern archaeological evidence.

Rhedenfre, Redenvre, **Stag of.** See STAG.

Rheged. Welsh-speaking kingdom of the 5th-7th centuries in what is today *Scotland whose king *Urien was much praised by *Taliesin. The centre of the kingdom was the Eden valley around the modern city of Carlisle, but its precise boundaries and extent are unknown. Its influence reached to *Strathclyde in the north, *Gododdin in the east, and what is now Lancashire and Yorkshire in the south. In earlier times this was the territory of the Novantae.

Rhiannon, Riannon. One of the main female characters of the first, *Pwyll*, and third, *Manawydan*, branches of the **Mabinogi* whose persona derives from the pre-Christian goddesses *Rigantona and *Epona, the horse-goddess. Rhiannon, daughter of Hyfidd Hen, is betrothed to *Pwyll, prince of *Dyfed, after he has been dazzled by seeing her ride by on a white horse. At their wedding-feast, Pwyll fecklessly grants a favour to a suppliant, causing Rhiannon to be betrothed to *Gwawl, son of the goddess Clud and his rival in romance. In a year's time Pwyll returns with a cleverer and more deadly trick, the game of badger-in-the-bag, killing Gwawl. When the newly married Rhiannon arrives at *Arberth, Pwyll's palace, she dispenses precious gifts, evoking her divine origin as a bountiful goddess.

After a few years of marriage Rhiannon produces a son, who is stolen on *May eve, the night he is born. Falsely accused of the infant's murder, Rhiannon is obliged to do public penance for seven years by sitting at the horse-block outside the palace gate, offering all visitors a ride on her back. Then *Teyrnon, Pwyll's retainer, realizes that the child he has been fostering is royal, and returns him. Rhiannon calls the child *Pryderi [care] following her remark, 'I should be delivered of my care if that were true.'

In the third branch many years have passed, Pwyll has died, and Pryderi as ruler promises his mother as a wife to his comrade in arms *Manawydan. Soon disasters befall the country and the family. A magical mist ravages Dyfed, leaving only Pryderi, his wife, Rhiannon, and Manawydan still living. Then Pryderi and Rhiannon are held captive in *Annwfn, to be freed by Manawydan. The deadly mist is revealed to be the work of Llwyd the enchanter, a friend of Gwawl, seeking redress for the loss of Rhiannon to Pwyll. Manawydan then forces Llwyd to restore *Dyfed to its former verdancy.

There is little question of Rhiannon's anticipation in the shadowy British goddess *Rigantona, and her links to the horse-goddess *Epona also seem secure, as evidenced by her meeting with Pwyll and her punishment after Pryderi's abduction. She may also be related to *Macha (3), the Irish equine figure. The three *birds of Rhiannon, mentioned in the *Mabinogi*, are said to sing over the sea at *Harlech. In **Culhwch ac Olwen* they can wake the dead and lull the living to sleep. Roger Sherman Loomis (1927) thought Rhiannon's persona contributed to the Arthurian Ninian (The Lady of the Lake). See W. J. Gruffydd, *Rhiannon* (Cardiff, 1953); Kenneth H. Jackson, 'Some Popular Motifs in Early Welsh Tradition', *Études Celtiques*, 11 (1961–7), 83–9. The Anglo-American rock group Fleetwood Mac gave the name wider currency with the song 'Rhiannon' (1976).

Rhita Gawr, Rhitta Gawr [W *cawr*, giant]. Welsh *giant who boasted of the number of kings he had killed by wearing their beards. A place-name story explains that *Arthur killed him and commanded his men to place stones over the body, forming Gwyddfa Rhita [Rhita's Cairn], an archaic Welsh term for *Snowdon.

Rhodri Mawr [W *rhod*, circle, disc, orb, i.e. coronet, torque; *mawr*, great]. Historical (d. 877) monarch who united the small kingdoms of *Gwynedd, *Ceredigion, and *Powys under one ruler, thus assuming the style of Rex Brittonum [King of all Wales]. He successfully defended his realm against both the Danes and the English, but died while in flight in Ireland. Although the union did not survive his reign, Rhodri established an important dynastic family, for both north and south Wales. *Hywel Dda the lawgiver was his great-grandson.

Rhonabwy. See BREUDDWYD RHONABWY [The Dream of Rhonabwy].

Rhonwen [W *rhon*, pike, lance, figuratively: tall, slender; *(g)wen*, fair]. Welsh name ascribed to the daughter of Hengist, the semi-legendary 5th-century Saxon invader of Britain. *Geoffrey of Monmouth (12th cent.) substituted the name *Rowena.

Rhun [W *rhun*, grand, awful]. Name borne by dozens of historical figures from early Wales, of whom the best-known is the son of Maelgwn sent to seduce *Elphin's wife but foiled by *Taliesin.

Rhydderch 1. [W *rhi*, ruler; *dyrch*, exalted (?)]. Sixth-century (d. 570) Welsh king of *Strathclyde in what is now *Scotland; sometimes bearing the epithets Hen [old] and Hael [generous]. Cited in the *Triads as one of the three most generous men in the Isle of Britain, along with his cousins *Nudd Llaw Ereint and Mordaf, he is much associated with early stories of *Myrddin. He defeated *Gwenddolou fab Ceido at the battle of *Arfdderydd (573/5). St *Kentigern found the ring in the *salmon for Rhydderch. He is now identified with the latinized figures of Rodarchus and Rederech.

2. See WHITE BOOK OF RHYDDERCH.

Riannon. Variant spelling of *Rhiannon.

ríastrad, ríastradh, ríastarthae (gen.). See CÚCHULAINN.

Ríb, Ríbh. Brother of *Eochu mac Maireda, foster-son of *Ébliu (2), in two comparable place-name stories, of *Lough Neagh and *Lough Ree [*Loch Ríbh*]; Ríb may be the eponym of Lough Ree.

Rigantona [great queen; cf. OIr. *rígan*]. Hypothesized title or epithet for a shadowy goddess of Roman Britain, an antecedent of the Welsh *Rhiannon.

Rigasamus, Rigonemetis. Sometime epithets of Gaulish *Mars.

rígfhéinnid, ríghfhéinnidh [OIr. *ríg*, king; *féinnid*, warrior]. Irish name for the leadership of the *Fianna held by *Fionn mac Cumhaill.

Rígru Rosclethan, Roisclethan [of the large eyes]. Wife of *Dáire (2) and queen of *Tír Tairngire, called 'sinless' because she and her husband have intercourse only to produce *Ségda Sáerlabraid, whom *Conn hopes will remove the moral blight from Ireland. She saves her son from being sacrificed at *Tara by taking the form of a wailing woman with a lowing *cow. Additionally, Rígru also warns *Conn Cétchathach [of the Hundred Battles] that Ireland will remain a wasteland until he puts aside the evil *Bé Chuma.

Riothamus. Romanized name of several shadowy figures in 5th-century Britain. Geoffrey Ashe has suggested that two citations of the name in chronicles could be identified with the historical *Arthur. One Riothamus led a group of 12,000, emigrating from Britain to Brittany. Riothamus is also the name of a ruler of the Breton petty kingdom of Domnonia. See Geoffrey Ashe, 'The Historical Origins of the Arthurian Legend', in *The Vitality of the Arthurian Legend* (Odense, Denmark, 1988).

Roca Barraidh [cf. ScG *roc*, anything that tangles a fishing-hook; tops of seaweed that appear above the water]. Name current on the Isle of *Barra in the Outer Hebrides for an enchanted island on the dim western horizon, visible on rare occasions only to privileged fishermen. See also TÍR NA NÓG.

Roche aux Fées, La. See ESSÉ.

Róisín Dubh [Ir., dark little rose]. Personification of Ireland which may date from a 17th-century poem of that title attributed to Owen Roe MacWard. James Clarence Mangan's translation as 'Dark Rosaleen' (1847) is more widely known than the Irish original. See also CÁIT NÍ DHUIBHIR.

Rónán, Ronan [Ir., dim. of *rón*, seal]. Relatively popular name from early Ireland, borne by at least ten saints and several kings, the best-known of whom probably is *Rónán (1).

Rónán 1. Legendary king (d. 624) of *Leinster who kills his own son Máel Fothartaig in **Fingal Rónáin* [How Rónán Slew His Son].

2. St Rónán Finn (d. AD 664) of Magheralin who is described as cursing *Suibne in **Buile Shuibne* [The Frenzy of Suibne / Sweeney]. His feast-day is 22 May.

3. often **Ronan the Silent.** Irish anchorite who settled in *Brittany, where he became a Christian evangelist through the example of his charity and patience. In anticipation of St Francis of Assisi, stories portray him as keeping a tame pet wolf. The association has caused many commentators to confuse him with the even more shadowy St *Ruman of 6th-century Britain, who was accused of being a werewolf. Although not on the official calendar of saints, Rónán (3) has been venerated on 1 June. The town of Locronan in south-western Brittany, rich in both pre-Christian and early Christian associations, commemorates his name. The Breton-born Celticist and agnostic Ernst Renan claimed him as patron saint in 1889. See A. Thomas, *S. Ronan et la Troménie* (Paris, 1893).

4. Father and patronym of the *Fenian hero *Caílte mac Rónáin.

5. Sometimes confused with St *Rúadán (1).

Rosmerta [L, good purveyor, great provider]. Latin name for an indigenous Gaulish deity whose worship was known from what is today Germany to Britain. Frequently seen as a cult-partner of Gaulish *Mercury, her statues sometimes acquire his attributes, such as the purse of plenty and the caduceus. She also sometimes appears with the Roman goddess *Fortuna and may borrow artefacts from her icons. Other imagery implies *fertility and a patronage of motherhood. Additionally, however, she may also be seen by herself, especially in south-eastern France, implying that her cult may have pre-dated that of either Mercury or Fortuna. There may be an echo of her name in the epithet of Gaulish *Smertrius, a sometime epithet of Gaulish *Mars. See J. Alfs, 'A Gallo-Roman Temple near Bretton (Baden)', *Germania*, 24 (1940), 128–40; Colette Bémont, 'Ro-Smerta', *Études Celtiques*, 9 (1960–1), 29–43; 'À propos d'un nouveau monument de Rosmerta', *Gallia*, 27 (1969), 23–44; Jean-Jacques Hatt, 'Les Dieux gaulois en Alsace', *Revue Archéologique de l'Est et du Centre-Est*, 25 (1971), 187–276.

roth rámach [Ir., rowing wheel]. The fabulous flying-machine constructed by *Simon Magus and *Mug Ruith. It was sighted at the fair of *Tlachtga, named for Mug Ruith's daughter. In later legend roth rámach was seen as an engine of destruction that would come over Europe before Judgement Day as a punishment for the way in which each nation gave disciples to Simon Magus.

rowan [ON *reynir*]. The small deciduous tree (genus *Sorbus aucuparia*), also called the quicken tree or mountain ash, has rich associations in all modern Celtic literatures. Its distinctive clusters of white flowers and orange-red berries contribute to its reputation. In the *ogham alphabet of early Ireland the letter *L was signified by luis [rowan]. The *druids of Ireland favoured rowan, hawthorn, and *yew over the *oak, favoured by the druids of *Gaul. The semi-divine *Tuatha Dé Danann were thought to have brought rowan to Ireland from *Tír Tairngire [the Land of Promise]. In **Tochmarc Étaíne* [The Wooing of Étaín], the jealous *Fuamnach transforms *Étaín into a pool of water by striking her with a rod of rowan. *Ailill mac Máta sends *Fráech in search of rowan, just as *Gráinne demands that *Diarmait get some for her. Often the rowanberry was thought to foster rejuvenation: a man 160 years old could be returned to his prime with the honey taste of rowanberries. The happy dead rest under woven roofs of quicken or rowan boughs. The *salmon of knowledge [Ir. **eó fis, eó fiosach*] eats rowanberries. In all Celtic *fairy lore, the rowan was thought to offer the best protection against fairy enchantments and witchcraft. In the Isle of *Man twigs of rowan were made into crosses, crosh cuirn, and placed over doorways and hidden in the long tails of cattle to protect them from harm. On Man also rowan boughs were carried in *Beltaine [May Day] ceremonies. OIr. luis; ModIr. caorthann; ScG caorunn; Manx keirn, kern; W cerddinen; Corn. kerdhynen; Bret. kerzhinenn. See also the FENIAN story; BRUIDHEAN CHAORTHAINN [The Hostel of the Quicken Tree]; ASH.

Rowena [cf. OE *hreod*, banner; *wine*, friend]. Name ascribed to the daughter of Hengist, semi-legendary 5th-century Saxon invader of Britain; its possible Welsh antecendent is *Rhonwen. Sir Walter Scott used the name for the Saxon heroine of his novel *Ivanhoe* (1819).

Ruad Rofhessa. Another name for the *Dagda.

Rúadán, Ruadán, Rúadhán **1**, sometimes confused with *Rónán (5) [Ir. *rúad*, red-haired]. Sixth-century saint thought to have put a curse upon *Tara. Although he still finds a place on the calendar of saints, 15 April, Rúadán has very shaky historicity. His Latin life, written many centuries after his time, is now considered unreliable; many commentators describe Rúadán as a fanciful saint. Purportedly born in *Leinster, he was thought to have founded the monastery of Lothra, in what is now Tipperary. According to the story invented by later ecclesiastics, Rúadán cursed Tara because *Diarmait mac Cerbaill, its last king to celebrate the pagan *feis temrach [feast of Tara], insulted him in a Church/State dispute. Shortly afterwards, according to the story, Diarmait was struck by a roof-beam and Tara was abandoned. Abundant historical information elsewhere attests that Tara was not neglected, however, as it continued to be the site of the crowning of the *ard rí and of an annual *óenach [fair]. See Charles Plummer (ed.), *Vitae Sanctorum Hiberniae* (Oxford, 1910), ii. 240–52; Irish-language edn. *Bethada Náem nÉrenn* (Oxford, 1922), i. 316–29.

2. Son of *Bres (1) and *Brigit (under the name Bríg[h]) who failed in his attempt to kill *Goibniu, the *smith-god. When Goibniu slew him in revenge, Rúadán's mother lamented his death with the first keening heard in Ireland. Many commentators see a link between Goibniu's killing of Rúadán and that of the Welsh smith-god, *Gofannon, of his nephew *Dylan.

Ruan, Saint. Cornish variant of St *Ruman.

Rudianus. Shadowy southern Gaulish war-god, equated with *Mars, whose name is invoked in three locations in what is now southern France. At Saint-Michel-de-Valbonne an incised figure of a horseman is shown carrying five severed heads.

Rudiobus. Gaulish horse-god known from the excellent bronze figurines (1st cent. BC), including a prancing horse, inscribed 'sacred to the god Rudiobus', found at Neuvy-en-Sullias in the Loire valley of west central France. But rather than being an indigenous native god, Rudiobus may be an aspect of Gaulish *Mars.

Ruman, Ruan, **Saint.** Shadowy, perhaps 6th-century saint whose name survives in numerous place-names such as Romansleigh and Ruan Lanihorne, in Devonshire and Cornwall; Ruan is the Cornish version of his name. No reliable documents of his life survive, but in oral tradition he was thought both invulnerable to wolves and to be himself a werewolf. Although he was earlier identified with St *Rónán (3) of Brittany, 20th-century hagiography has argued for Ruman's discrete identity. Although not on the official calendar of saints, Ruman has been venerated on 30 August. See Gilbert H. Doble, *Four Saints of the Fal* (Exeter, 1930); *St. Rumon and St. Ronan* (Exeter, 1939); Paul Grosjean, *Analecta Bollandiana*, 61 (1953), 359–414.

S

S. The nineteenth letter of the modern English alphabet was signified by sail [willow] in the *ogham alphabet of early Ireland. The S symbol was frequently depicted in early Celtic art and was distinctive of the *La Tène period (*c*.450–50 BC). Modern commentators see in its double spiral associations with sky and solar cults.

Saar. Variant form of *Sadb.

Saba, Sabia. Variant forms of *Sadb.

Sadb, Sadhbh, Saba, Sabia, Sava, Saar. One of the most common women's names in early Ireland, of whom the most widely known is the *deer-mother of *Oisín, the *Fenian hero. In alternative texts the deer-mother's name is *Blaí.

Saingliu, Dub Saingliu, Sainglainn, Sainglend (gen.), Dubsainglend (gen.). *Cúchulainn's last and favourite horse, which exceeded all others in speed and beauty. See also LIATH MACHA.

Sainrith mac Imbaith. Father of *Macha (3).

salmon [L *salmō*]. The large fish with pinkish flesh (genus *Salmo salar*) has long played an important role in the Celtic imagination, usually as a repository of *otherworldly wisdom, especially in Ireland and Wales. A relief found in *Gaul shows a human head between two great salmon. In a Gallo-Roman altar a fish (probably a salmon) is shown talking into the ear of a human head. *Nodons, ancient British god of the Severn, is shown hooking a salmon. Although salmon swim from salt to fresh water to spawn, Irish and Welsh traditions often portray them as inhabiting wells, pools, waterfalls, or other fixed locations along important rivers like the *Boyne or Severn. Two salmon of wisdom or knowledge lived in Ireland, at *Linn Féic along the Boyne and at the falls of *Assaroe on the Erne, both caught by *Fionn mac Cumhaill. In the better-known story of the two, the *bard *Finnéces had been fishing for the salmon for seven years when the boy Fionn happened along. Finnéces thought his patience had paid off when he caught the salmon and began cooking it over a fire; but Fionn touched the cooking salmon with his thumb, burning it, and thrust it into his mouth, thus giving to himself the otherworldly wisdom Finnéces sought. Here the salmon bears a name, *Fintan (1). When Fionn spears the salmon on his own at the falls of Assaroe it is known as Goll Essa Ruaid [the *one-eyed fish of Assaroe]. A comparable Welsh salmon of wisdom swims under the name Llyn Llyw along the Severn and is 'the oldest of living creatures', 'the wisest of forty animals'; it tells *Culhwch where *Mabon is being held prisoner. Leixlip, Co. Kildare, on the *Liffey also has strong associations with salmon [ON *leax hlaup*, salmon leap; Ir. *Léim an Bhradáin*].

In Irish tradition salmon gain wisdom by eating the nuts of *hazel trees; the number of spots on the salmon's back shows how many nuts he has consumed. Nine hazels of wisdom grow at the heads of the seven chief rivers of Ireland and at *Connla's Well and the well of *Segais. In Osraige [*Ossory] salmon eat berries to the same effect. If salmon do not embody wisdom, they may carry important knowledge between persons, just as ravens delivered messages to the Norse Odin. The Welsh poet Dafydd ap Gwilym (*fl.* 1320–70) claimed that expressions of love for the beautiful Morfydd might be carried by salmon.

Humans and salmon interact in a variety of other ways. Several personages are transformed partly or completely into salmon, including *Amairgin (1), *Fintan mac Bóchra, and *Taliesin, just as Loki in Norse tradition once became a salmon to escape detection. *Tuan mac Cairill becomes a salmon that is caught by a woman, who eats him and then gives birth to him again in human form so that he may tell the early history of Ireland. For *Mongán, becoming a salmon is just one of his powers. The 'soul' of the hero *Cú Roí resides in a golden apple inside a certain salmon; to kill him, *Cúchulainn has first to kill the salmon with Cú Roí's own sword. The beauteous *Lí Ban (2) of *Lough Neagh becomes a salmon except for her head. The mother of St *Fínán Cam is impregnated by a salmon when she goes swimming after dark. *Ailill throws a ring into the water, which is swallowed by a salmon and retrieved by *Fráech (folk motif: 736A). St *Kentigern also finds a ring in a salmon, which explains the presence of salmon in the seal of the City of Glasgow.

Modern commentators have been at a loss to explain the mythic power of the salmon. Its swimming between salt and fresh water may have suggested the capacity to pass between worlds. The ability to swim against the stream over waterfalls easily excites human admiration; see SALMON LEAP. The Roman poet Catullus (1st cent. BC) equated the leaping salmon with an erect phallus. Pinkish salmon flesh may evoke human flesh. Seán O'Faoláin (1947) suggested that the Irish, lacking serpents, may have adopted the salmon as an alternative transformation of the sun-god. OIr. eó, eú, éicne, bratán, maigre, magar (as spawn); ModIr. bradán, diúilín (young salmon); ScG bradan, iasg geal [bright fish]; Manx braddan; W eog, samwn; Corn. ēok; Bret. eog. See Richard I. Best, 'The Tragic Death of Cúroí mac Dári', *Ériu*, 2 (1911), 18–35.

salmon leap. *Cúchulainn's aggressive, highly effective combat strategy is not fully explained in the texts where he exercises it. One modern commentator has suggested it may be comparable to the aggressive jump of soccer players.

Samain, Samhain, Samhuinn (ScG), Sauin (Manx) [cf. OIr. *sam*, summer; *fuin*, end]. Irish, Scottish Gaelic, and Manx names for the seasonal feast of pre-Christian origin fixed at 1 November on the Gregorian calendar. The most important of the four great calendar feasts of Celtic tradition, including, by their old Irish names, *Beltaine (1 May), *Imbolc (1 February), and Lugnasad (ModIr. Lúnasa/ *Lughnasa, 1 August); its counterparts are in Wales *Hollantide, in Cornwall *Allantide, and in Brittany Kala-Goañv. The antiquity of Samain is attested to by the Coligny *Calendar (1st cent. BC) which cites the feast of *Samonios*. The same source explains that to the ancient Gauls the period of dark precedes the light, supporting the commonly held belief that Samain is the equivalent of New Year's Day. Julius *Caesar (1st cent. BC) reported that the Gaulish *Dis Pater, god of death and winter's cold, was especially worshipped at this time of year. Other *classical commentators observed that *Teutates might be worshipped at this time by having sacrificial victims drowned in vats, whereas sacrifices to *Taranis were burned in wooden vessels. Samain's equivalents on the Christian calendar are All Saints' Day (introduced by Pope Boniface IV in the 7th cent. to supplant the pagan festival of the dead) and Halloween.

By abundant testimony, Samain was the principal calendar feast of early Ireland. Each of the five provinces sent assemblies to *Tara for a *feis held every third year. At *Tlachtga the lighting of the winter fires was a key part of the Samain ceremony. In part Samain ceremonies commemorated the *Dagda's ritual intercourse with three divinities, the *Mórrígan, *Boand, and *Indech's unnamed daughter. Just how much of this remembrance included *fertility rites, or what their nature might be, is not known; but in Irish and Scottish Gaelic oral tradition, Samain time was thought most favourable for a woman to become pregnant. At *Mag Slécht in Co. Cavan, human sacrifices might be offered to *Crom Crúaich, called the 'chief idol of Ireland' by early Christian scribes. Although the full nature of Crom Crúaich is not known, popular writers on early Ireland have taken to calling him Samain, implying that he gave his name to the seasonal feast; although at least one American encyclopaedia repeats this conjecture, it is unsupported by early Irish texts.

Authors of early texts are careful to point out when important action takes place at Samain. At this time the predatory *Fomorians would exact their tribute of grain, milk, and live children. Each year on this date *Aillén mac Midgna came to burn *Tara until *Fionn mac Cumhaill dispatched him. From *Cruachain in Co. Roscommon came the triple-headed monster *Aillén Tréchenn who wreaked havoc on all of Ireland, especially *Emain Macha and Tara, until he was eliminated by *Amairgin (1). *Cúchulainn encountered *otherworldly damsels at Samain time, and this was also the time *Cáer and *Angus Óg flew off in *swan form.

The different celebrations of Samain over the centuries explain some of the traditions still popularly attached to Halloween. Standing between the two halves of the Celtic year, Samain seemed suspended in time, when the borders between the natural and the supernatural dissolve and the spirits from the *Otherworld might move freely into the realm of mortals. Concurrently, humans might perceive more of the realm of the dead at this time, and looked for portents of the future in games. People might choose from small cakes called barmbracks [Ir. *bairín breac*, speckled loaf, i.e. with currants or raisins] containing a ring or a nut to determine who would be married and who would live singly. Bonfires were built in parts of Ireland and Gaelic Scotland. It was also a time to relax after the most demanding farm work was done. In counties Waterford and Cork, country lads visited farmers' houses on the night before Samain, oíche shamhna [Samain eve], collecting pence and provisions for the celebrations. In Cork the procession of young men blowing horns and making other noises was led by someone calling himself the White Mare, wearing white robes and the configuration of a horse's head. On the Isle of Lewis in the Outer Hebrides, though the inhabitants were Protestant, people gathered *ale and other provisions for a mock ceremony, calling Shoney of the sea to enrich their grounds in the coming year. Turnips were hollowed out with candles put inside.

See Françoise Le Roux, 'Études sur le festiaire celtique: Samain', *Ogam*, 13 (1961), 485–506; Alwyn and Brinley Rees, *Celtic Heritage* (London, 1961); F. Marian McNeill, *Hallowe'en: Its Origin, Rites and Ceremonies in the Scottish Tradition* (Edinburgh, 1970); Kevin Danaher, *The Year in Ireland* (Cork, 1972).

Samaliliath. Variant form of *Malaliach.

Samera. Character in **Fled Bricrenn* [Bricriu's Feast] who proposes a single combat to determine the *champion's portion.

Samhain. ModIr. spelling of *Samain.

Samhuinn. ScG spelling of *Samain.

Samildánach, Ildánach [Ir. *sam*, together; *il*, many; *dán*, art]. Master of all the arts, an epithet of *Lug Lámfhota.

Sanas Cormaic, *Chormaic*. Irish title of the document often known in English as Cormac's Glossary, traditionally ascribed to *Cormac mac Cuilennáin (d. 908), king-bishop of *Cashel. Entries list a large number of old and rare words, including names from Irish literature. Many of Cormac's judgements are reinterpreted by modern commentators; for example, he places *Manannán mac Lir on the Isle of *Man instead of on the *otherworldly *Emain Ablach. In many instances Cormac is an uncritical euhemerist; he readily cites as kings or heroes personages we believe to be of divine origin. None the less, *Sanas Cormaic* is a constantly cited source for information on the oldest traditions. See *Three Irish Glossaries*, trans. Whitley Stokes (London, 1862); *Sanas Chormaic*, trans. John O'Donovan, ed. Whitley Stokes (Calcutta, 1868); *Sanas Cormaic* [from text in the **Yellow Book of Lecan*], trans. Kuno Meyer (Halle, 1912). See also Paul Russell, 'The Sound of Silence: The Growth of Cormac's Glossary', *Cambridge Medieval Celtic Studies*, 15 (1988), 1–30.

Sauin. Manx equivalent of *Samain.

Sava. Anglicization of *Sadb.

Scáthach, Scáth, Scáthach nUanaind, Skatha [OIr. *scáth*, shadow, shade; shelter; under protection of]. Amazonian warrior with *otherworldly resonances in Old Irish literature who teaches martial arts to *Cúchulainn and other heroes. Some texts describe her as living in Alpi, which most commentators have understood as implying *Alba [Scotland]. Other texts link her specifically with the Hebridean Isle of *Skye, which is then called Dún Scáthaig(e)/Scáith for her. Cúchulainn completed his training under Scáthach, and from her he mastered his famous aggressive leap, the torannchless [thunder feat], and also received his spear, the *Gáe Bulga. In return he aided her against her enemy, *Aífe (1), who may be Scáthach's double. She granted him three wishes: to continue to instruct him most carefully; to give him her daughter Uathach [spectre] without paying the bride-price; and to predict his future career. Accounts of Cúchulainn's amorous adventures with Scáthach vary. Usually he is seen as having gained 'the friendship of her thighs', which may derive from now-forgotten sexual rites of warrior initiation. Earlier, while battling Aífe, he also slept with her, producing the son *Connla, who would follow Cúchulainn back to Ireland in seven years. Eventually he battles this son in **Aided Óenfhir Aífe* [The Tragic Death of Aífe's Only Son]. Additionally, he also enjoys intimacies with Uathach, Scáthach's daughter. Modern commentators see these sexual alliances as an indication not so much of Cúchulainn's lubriciousness as of the union of the apprentice with his heroic calling. Scáthach of the *Ulster Cycle should probably be distinguished from Scáthach daughter of Énna in the *Fenian Cycle; she lulls *Fionn mac Cumhaill to sleep with magic music in a *sídh. Her own son is Cúar. See Whitley Stokes, 'The Training of Cúchulainn', *Revue Celtique*, 29 (1908), 109–52; P. L. Henry, *Celtica*, 21 (1990), 191–207.

Scél Tuain meic Chairill. See TUAN MAC CAIRILL.

Scéla Cano meic Gartnáin. See CANO.

Scéla Mucce meic Da Thó, Scél Mucci maic Dáthó. Irish titles for a 9th-century *Ulster Cycle story implying that enmity between Ulster and *Connacht was of great antiquity; one of the few Ulster stories in which *Cúchulainn does not play a role. A wealthy landowner of *Leinster, Mac Da Thó [son of the two mutes (?)], has two animals that tickle his pride: a hound, *Ailbe, with the ferocity of ten armies that defends his properties all by himself, and a tame *boar that has been reared seven years and seven days on milk so that it may furnish a year-long feast. Interest in the hound prompts a bidding war between *Ailill and *Medb of Connacht and *Conchobar mac Nessa. Mac Da Thó cannot choose between the offers. Medb and Ailill offer 160 prize *cows with a prize chariot drawn by the two best horses in Connacht. Conchobar mac Nessa offers friendship, a military alliance, and cattle every year in perpetuity. With two such bellicose parties, Mac Da Thó fears to disappoint either. Following his wife's suggestion, he promises Ailbe to both Connacht and Ulster, if they will only come to claim it. By the time both arrive, Mac Da Thó has slaughtered his succulent pig, which takes sixty oxen to draw into Mac Da Thó's huge residence with seven doors and fifty beds.

The question of who should carve the pig dominates the rest of the story. *Briccriu, the mischief-making adviser, suggests that the pig should be divided according to 'battle victories'. One warrior after another claims the right to carve, but each has to yield to a rival with a stronger claim. The boasts and abusive retorts are among the liveliest dialogue in early Irish literature. Conflict is momentarily resolved when the Connacht hero *Cet mac Mágach shames and taunts the pride of Ulster and is about to carve the pig himself. At this moment *Conall Cearnach bursts in and challenges Cet to back away from the pig. He trumpets that he has never spent a day without slaying a Connachtman, never spent a night without plundering their property, and never slept without having a Connachtman's head beneath his knee. Cet responds that Conall may indeed be a better fighter but that his brother *Anluan is greater still, if only he were present now. 'But he is', Conall roars, flinging Anluan's severed head on the floor, blood flowing from the mouth. Conall then proceeds to carve the pig, allowing the choice portions for himself, leaving only the forelegs to the westerners. Enraged, the men of Connacht attack those from Ulster, and soon the bodies are heaped upon the floor and blood flows through the doorway. In their departure the men of Connacht, seeing that Mac Da Thó's hound Ailbe has favoured the other side, split it in two, leaving the head on a *yew tree, but the men of Ulster seek healing from the maidens of *Emain Macha.

The central motif of *Scéla Mucce meic Da Thó* dramatizes the contest for the *champion's portion [Ir. *curad-mír*], an echo of the kind of competition *Posidonius (1st cent. BC) described among the ancient *Gauls. See *Scéla Mucce Meic Dathó*, ed. Rudolf Thurneysen (Dublin, 1935, 1939); 'The Story of Mac Datho's Pig', trans. Kuno Meyer, in *Hibernica Minora* (Anecdota Oxoniensis) (Oxford, 1894), 51–64; repr. in T. P. Cross and C. H. Slover (eds.), *Ancient Irish Tales* (New York, 1936), 199–207; Cornelius G. Buttimer, 'Scéla Mucce Meic Dathó: A Reappraisal', *Proceedings of the Harvard Celtic Colloquium*, 2 (1982), 61–73; Arzel Even, 'Histoire du cochon de Mac Datho', *Ogam*, 5 (1953), 7–9, 50–4.

Sceolang, Sceolaing, Sceolan, Sceolán, Skeolan. One of *Fionn mac Cumhaill's favourite hunting *dogs, brother of the better-known *Bran (2), born of a human woman, *Uirne, Fionn's aunt (sometimes sister). Lomair is sometimes a third sibling.

Scoriath. King of *Fir Morca in **Orgain Denna Ríg* [The Destruction of Dind Ríg] who helps *Labraid Loingsech regain his kingdom and also gives him the hand of his beautiful daughter *Muiriath.

Scota 1 [L, Irishwoman]. Second wife of

*Míl Espáine in the pseudo-history *Lebor Gabála [Book of Invasions], the daughter of a pharaoh, Nectanebus, and one of several eponyms of the Irish [i.e. L Scotti] people. She bears Míl two sons, *Eber Finn and *Amairgin (1). After the death of Míl, she joins the Milesian invasion of *Kerry. Her name may have been commemorated at Glenn Scoithin [Scota's Glen], where a large boulder (35 feet high), *Leath Scoithin*, bears an *ogham inscription put in place by modern enthusiasts; the site, better known as Foley's Glen, lies by the stream Finglas near Tralee.

2. [L, Irishwoman]. Wife of *Niúl, the son of *Fénius Farsaid, and mother of *Goídel Glas. Like the younger and better-known *Scota (1), with whom she is often confused, Scota (2) is reputedly the daughter of an Egyptian pharaoh.

Scoti. Name used in the **Lebor Gabála* [Book of Invasions] for the Gaels or early Irish; elsewhere a variant spelling of *Scotti.

Scotia. Anciently a Latin name for *Ireland. After *Q-Celtic Gaelic Gaels invaded *Argyll and, centuries later, merged with the *Picts to form a single kingdom, it became an honorific Latin name for *Scotland. Also found in the **Lebor Gabála* [Book of Invasions] as a variant of *Scota (1).

Scotland [L *Scotti*, Irish]. Constituent country of the United Kingdom, occupying 30,405 square miles in northern Great Britain. Slightly smaller than *Ireland, it has the largest population of all Celtic lands, more than 5,200,000; yet not all Scottish persons are of Celtic heritage. Known as *Alba in ancient times, still its name in Scottish Gaelic, Scotland was not always distinguished from the rest of Britain until the Romans failed to conquer it and tried to close it off with walls, Hadrian's in AD 122 and the Antonine Wall further north in AD 138. The native populations of what was then Alba/Scotland, the *Caledonii or the *Picts, spoke *P-Celtic languages related to what was to become Welsh. One of the greatest poems from early Welsh tradition, *Y *Gododdin*, is represented as taking place partially in what is now Scotland; Kenneth Jackson (1969), perhaps mischievously, called it 'the oldest Scottish poem'.

Scotland takes its name from Irish [L *Scotti*] invaders who migrated in large numbers to *Argyll [ScG *Oirer Ghaidheal*, coast of the Gael], establishing the small kingdom of *Dál Riada. After many a century of armed struggle with the Picts and the Brythonic kingdom of *Strathclyde, the leader of the Q-Celtic, Goidelic *Scotti, *Cináed mac Ailpín [Kenneth MacAlpin] (d. 858), merged the three forces into one nation, called Scotland after its most powerful component. In the following centuries the Gaelic language [ScG *Gaidhlig*] spread across much of Scotland, except for parts of Norse-dominated Caithness and the islands of Orkney and Shetland to the north and the English-dominated regions like Roxburgh and Berwick to the south-east. But pressure against Gaelic began at the top of the power pyramid, as English became the language at court during the reign of Malcolm III, 1058–93, under the influence of his Wessex-born wife, (St) Margaret. Over the next nine centuries English and the English-related Scots dialect (the language of Robert Burns) superseded Gaelic gradually in all but the Hebrides and those parts of the Highlands beyond the Grampian mountains, i.e. the former counties (until 1974) of *Argyll, Inverness, Ross and Cromarty, Sutherland, and portions of Perthshire. Called the Gaidhealtachd [Gaelic-speaking area], this region occupies portions of the post-1974 counties of Strathclyde and Highland. The Act of Union (1707) with England somewhat diminished the Scottish sense of nationhood. Far more damaging to Highland culture was the failure of the Jacobite Rebellion (1745–6) and the subsequent suppression of the Gaelic language and culture of those who had supported it. Much of the 19th century saw mass migration from the Gaelic Highlands, some of it forced through clearances, in which crofters (tenant farmers) were driven from small farms to be replaced by herds of sheep. At the end of the twentieth century, Scottish Gaelic is spoken by about 65,000 people in Scotland and fewer than 5,000 in *Nova Scotia.

Although Scottish Gaelic passages, linguistically distinguishable from their Old Irish parent, appear in the 12th-century Gaelic notes to the 9th-century *Book of Deer*, the first extensive record of Scottish Gaelic tradition is found in the *Book of the Dean of Lismore* (1512–26), in which the spellings are rendered as they would sound phonetically in English, much as Manx is. The Scottish Gaelic bardic tradition continued into the 19th century under clan patronage, producing such distinguished poets as Iain Lóm (*c.*1625–*c.*1710),

Alastair Mac Mhaighstir Alasdair (*c.*1695–*c.*1770), Rob Donn (1714–78), and Donnachadh Bàn Mac-an-t-Saoir [Duncan Bàn Macintyre] (1724–1812). Despite the differences in geography and political history, not to mention the Norse invasions and the Reformation, much of Scottish Gaelic tradition remained linked to Ireland. Many Scottish Gaelic stories are parallels of Irish stories and have Irish settings. Characters in Irish stories, such as *Deirdre or *Cúchulainn, travel to Scotland and appear familiar with its geography, although often Scotland is seen as a place of magic and adventure, like other foreign countries. From medieval through to early modern times, commerce and social intercourse continued between Gaelic Scotland and Ireland: large numbers of Highland mercenaries, the *galloglasses [Ir. *gall*, stranger; *óglach*, soldier] migrated to Ireland, and Irish Franciscan missionaries resisted the tide of Calvinism in the Highlands. The now archaic English word for Scottish Gaelic, Erse [Irish], signals a historical perception of this unity. But in the mid-18th century the enormously popular 'translator' James *Macpherson (1736–96) promoted the still-persistent canard that Scottish Gaelic tradition was separate from and older than its Irish roots. Macpherson's *Poems of Ossian* (1760–3), drawing on unacknowledged Scottish Gaelic ballads, purported to be a lost epic, contemporary with the ancient classics. The widespread acceptance of this imposture promoted an international interest in Irish and other Celtic traditions. By the mid to late 19th century, informed collectors had assembled large collections of Scottish Gaelic tradition: John Francis Campbell, *Popular Tales of the West Highlands* (4 vols., Paisley, 1861); Archibald Campbell, *Waifs and Strays in Celtic Tradition* (4 vols., London, 1889–91); Alexander Cameron, *Reliquiae Celticae* (2 vols., Inverness, 1894). OIr. Albu, Alba; ModIr. Alba(in); Manx Nalbin; W Alban; Corn. Alban; Bret. Bro-Skos.

See also Charles W. J. Withers, *Gaelic in Scotland, 1698–1981: A Geographical History of a Language* (Edinburgh, 1984); Derick S. Thomson (ed.), *The Companion to Gaelic Scotland* (Oxford, 1983; Glasgow, 1994). See Bibliography under 'Scottish Gaelic' for collections of Scottish Gaelic traditions.

Scotti, Scoti. Originally one of several Latin names for Irish people (see IRELAND), especially those living in the north-east. The *Q-Celtic speaking invaders who crossed from *Ulster into *Argyll from the 6th century and earlier, founding the petty kingdom of *Dál Riada, readily applied the name Scotti to themselves. Three centuries later when these invaders, also known as *Gaels, became the dominant partners with the *Picts and the *P-Celts from *Strathclyde, their name easily extended to the entire kingdom of *Scotland. The kingdom is still also known as *Alba in Scottish Gaelic. Writers of the pseudo-history **Lebor Gabála* [Book of Invasions] claimed that the Scotti were descended from Queen *Scota of Egypt. Elsewhere in the same document the Scotti are confused with the Scythi of *Scythia.

Scythia. Name for an ancient region north of the Black Sea that held great attraction for the early Irish imagination. A homeland without definable borders, Scythia stretched from the Danube to the Caucasus, coextensive with modern Ukraine and Crimea. Although no Celtic remains have been found on Scythian territory, Scythian motifs have been traced in *La Tène art. Regardless of the tenuous links with the Celtic world, many Irish scribes, particularly the compilers of the pseudo-history **Lebor Gabála* [Book of Invasions], apparently assumed that Scythi was linguistically related to *Scotti [Irish people]. *Fénius Farsaid, fabled inventor of the Irish language, was thought to be king here. Scythia was also thought to be the homeland of the *Nemedians. See C. Scott Littleton, *From Scythia to Camelot: A Radical Reassessment of the Legends of King Arthur . . .* (New York, 1994).

sea-monster, water serpent. See AFANC; BEISHT KIONE, Y; BLEDMALL; CAORÁNACH; C`REIN CRÒIN; MUIRDRIS (or sínach); OILLIPHÉIST; SUILEACH.

Sean-bhean Bhocht [Ir., poor old woman]. Irish spelling of *Shan Van Vocht, a personification of *Ireland current in the 18th century, apparently derived from *Cailleach Bhéire. Under this spelling the phrase was also a pseudonym of Irish patriot Roger Casement (1864–1916).

Seanchán Toirpéist. ModIr. spelling of *Senchán Torpéist.

Searbhán, Searban, Searbhan, Sharvan. Surly ogre or *giant of **Tóraigheacht*

Dhiarmada agus Ghráinne [The Pursuit of Diarmait and Gráinne] who protects the magical *rowanberries in the forest of *Dubros, Co. Sligo. As he was so skilled in the arts of magic, Diarmait could not overcome him until he turned his own weapon, a club, against him. In some texts Searbhán takes the epithet Lochlonnach [Norseman], while in others he is described as a *Fomorian.

Second Battle of Mag Tuired (Moytura, Moytirra, etc.). See CATH MAIGE TUIRED.

second sight. The power to envisage events, frequently unpleasant, that have not yet taken place was widely accepted in vernacular Celtic tradition, especially in Gaelic Scotland. A person endowed with second sight might see a phantom funeral cortège passing down a road escorting a man then still robust and little expecting to die but who did die shortly afterwards. Having this power does not cause events to take place, nor does it bring any joy in seeing them. Some visions from second sight have taken place. The 17th-century *Brahan Seer, Kenneth MacKenzie, foresaw the decline of the Highlands and the building of the Caledonian Canal. Even those not endowed with full powers of second sight might see an occasional 'forerunner', like the bright light of a locomotive at night where no trains yet existed but where a railroad line was later to be constructed. The *Fenian hero *Diorruing was credited with second sight. Ir. *fios; ScG taibhse, dà shealladh [two sights]; Manx aa-hilley. See Norman MacRae, *Highland Second Sight* (Dingwall, Scotland, 1908).

Sédanda, Sedanda. Variant spellings of Sétanta, first name of *Cúchulainn.

Segais, Well of. Fabulous well or spring, thought to be the common source of both the *Boyne and the *Shannon rivers, and a source also for supernatural *knowledge. Like *Connla's Well, which it resembles and may be identical with, the Well of Segais is surrounded by nine *hazel trees, whose nuts fall in the water, feeding *salmon. When *Boand defies the magical powers of Segais, its waters rise up in anger, mutilating her, turning her into the River Boyne. At Connla's Well a comparable story is told of *Sinann and the Shannon. Although the Boyne and the Shannon do not have a common source, the name may come from a district adjoining the Boyne that is an affluent of the Shannon. Folk motif: D1811.1.2. See Vernam Hull, 'Early Irish *Segais*', *Zeitschrift für celtische Philologie*, 29, H. 3/4 (1964/5), 321–4.

Ségda Sáerlabraid [*sáer*, noble; *labraid*, speaker]. *Otherworldly son of the sinless rulers of *Tír Tairngire, *Dáire (2) and *Rígru Rosclethan, who had sexual relations only at the time of his conception. *Conn seeks Ségda in **Echtrae Airt meic Cuinn* [The Adventure of Art son of Conn] in hopes that he will bring *fertility back to the wasteland of Ireland. The boy gives unstinting affection to Conn and is even willing to make a sacrifice for him until he is rescued by his mother Rígru.

Segomo [victor; mighty one]. War-god worshipped in ancient *Gaul and perhaps also in Britain and Ireland. Because 'Segomo' is more a title than an actual name and exists as an epithet for both Gaulish *Mars and *Hercules, there is some ambiguity whether this figure is a discrete indigenous divinity or an aspect of one or both of those better-known figures. A statue of a mule, an animal associated with Mars, dedicated to Segomo survives at Neuvy-en-Sullias on the Loire River in west central France. A bronze horse from the shrine of Bolards, at Nuits-Saint-Georges in eastern France, may also be dedicated only to Segomo. The early Irish name Nia Segamoin [servant of Segomo] clearly echoes his one-time presence, and he may be identical with *Cocidius, a god worshipped in Roman Britain.

séideán sídh. See FAIRY WIND.

Seisyllwg, Seissyllwg, Seisylwch. Gwlad or petty kingdom of early medieval *Wales formed in the mid-8th century when King Seisyll ap Clydog of *Ceredigion forcibly united the southern gwlad of *Ystrad Tywi with his own. More than 100 years later in 871, Seisyllwg was united with *Gwynedd when Seisyll's great-great-granddaughter married *Rhodri Mawr. After a second brief period of independence, Seisyllwg was merged with the larger kingdom of *Deheubarth when *Hywel Dda annexed *Dyfed. The land area of Seisyllwg is coextensive with the modern (since 1974) counties of Dyfed and West Glamorgan.

Seithenyn. Drunken dike-keeper of the flooded city of *Cantre'r Gwaelod.

Selma. Palace of the Fingallians in James *Macpherson's *Poems of Ossian* (1760–3).

Sencha mac Ailella, Aillelea, Ailill [cf. Ir. *senchaid*, custodian of tradition; historian]. Peacemaker among the *Ulster warriors, an Irish counterpart of Nestor in the *Iliad* and possibly also of *Merlin in the Arthurian legends. Also chief judge and poet during the reign of *Conchobar mac Nessa. He offered to foster *Cúchulainn but was only his teacher of eloquence.

senchaid. See FILI.

Senchán Torpéist, Seanchán Toirpéist. *Connacht poet (*c*.570–617) reputed to have saved the *Táin Bó Cuailnge* [Cattle Raid of Cooley] from oblivion. According to a widely known story, he was trying vainly to piece together the narrative when *Fergus mac Róich appeared to him in a vision and recited the entire poem. Less fabulous narratives assert that he was the leader of the great bardic assembly and chief of the poets of Ireland after *Dallán Forgaill (*c*.540–96).

Senchas Már, *Mór*. See BREHON.

Senmag Étair. Variant form of *Mag nElta.

Sequana, Sequena, Dea Sequana. Goddess of the source of the River Seine whose healing shrine, Fontes Sequanae [L, springs of Sequana], dating from the 2nd century BC, is found north-west of Dijon, eastern France. Despite her Celtic origin, Sequana was clearly esteemed by the Romans, who enlarged Fontes Sequanae with two large temples. She is represented by a large bronze statuette of a draped young woman wearing a diadem, with arms outstretched as if to welcome suppliants and standing in a *duck-shaped boat.

Details in surviving figures imply much about the nature of Sequana's worship. Her devotees are depicted in heavy, hooded woollen cloaks, the kind worn by ordinary Celtic peasants. They bear her gifts of fruit, money, or pet animals. A large pot inscribed with Sequana's name is filled with silver and bronze body parts to be cured by her. Simultaneously, complete bodies, as well as coins and jewellery, are offered to her, presumably in the hope of a reciprocal cure.

Serglige Con Culainn agus Óenét Emire. Tenth- and 11th-century Irish narrative, known in English as The Wasting Sickness of Cúchulainn or The Sickbed of Cúchulainn and The Only Jealousy of Emer; it is most often referred to by the truncated title *Serglige Con Culainn*. The text in the 12th-century *Book of the Dun Cow* [*Lebor na hUidre*] combines two versions of earlier composition, causing some incoherence in the surviving narrative; as the full title suggests, what we have may derive from two earlier stories. Cúchulainn's wife is known first as *Eithne Ingubai and secondly as *Emer.

The men of *Ulster are assembled at *Mag Muirtheimne during *Samain when a flock of beautiful birds settles on a nearby lake. Learning that all the women desire the birds, one for each shoulder, Cúchulainn hunts them and gives two to each noble woman so that none is left for his wife. He promises her two different birds, who are linked with a golden chain and sing a sleep-inducing song. After only grazing them with his spear, Cúchulainn falls into a deep sleep while seated next to a pillar-stone. In a dream he sees two women, one in green, the other in red, laughing and whipping him, at first playfully but then so severely that all the strength drains from his body: thus his wasting sickness. Wakened, he asks to be carried to the Téte Brec [twinkling hoard] of *Emain Macha.

Here Cúchulainn lies prostrate for almost a year, until shortly before the next Samain, when an *otherworldly man appears next to his bed, offering a cure in a cryptic song. Identifying himself as *Angus (1), the son of *Áed Abrat, he invites Cúchulainn to come with him to Mag Cruachna (Co. Roscommon), where he will be healed and where Angus's sister *Fand is longing to be with him. Cúchulainn is then carried back to the pillar-stone where he was stricken, and there meets a beautiful woman. Dressed in green, she is one of the two who whipped him in his dream. Identifying herself as *Lí Ban [paragon of women], she says she means no further harm and instead seeks Cúchulainn's friendship. She brings greetings from her husband, *Labraid Luathlám ar Claidib [swift hand on sword] of Mag Mell, who promises him Lí Ban's beautiful sister Fand, now released from her husband *Manannán mac Lir, in return for only one day of service in fighting Labraid's enemies, Senach Siaborthe, *Eochaid Iúil, and *Eochaid Inber. Cúchulainn is intrigued with the offer, especially remembering Fand's renowned beauty, but as he is still on his sickbed he sends his charioteer *Láeg to investigate for him. Láeg sails with Lí Ban in a bronze boat to an island where they are greeted by Fand and her company of women, as well as by Labraid, who expresses his disappointment that Cúchulainn has not come. On his return Láeg regales Cúchulainn with descriptions of Mag Mell. After Láeg calls for her, Emer also visits Cúchulainn, urging him to rise from his sick-bed; she chides him for being weakened by 'woman-love', and calls for him to throw off his wasting sickness. He then arises, and finds that his weariness has passed from him. In another year, by the pillar-stone where he had slept, Cúchulainn again encounters Lí Ban, who bids him again to come to Mag Mell. Not wishing to respond to a woman's call, Cúchulainn again sends Láeg on his behalf, who travels over land this time; once there he again finds Labraid, together with a regent, Fáilbe Finn. On his return, Láeg again reports on the wonder of what he has found and tells Cúchulainn he would be a fool for not going forth.

Cúchulainn then harnesses his chariot for a ride with Lí Ban and Láeg to Mag Mell, where he receives an enthusiastic welcome. At Labraid's request he makes reconnaissance of the vast enemy encampment. Undaunted, Cúchulainn asks that Labraid and his retainers retreat so that he may prepare for battle alone. He stands solitary guard all night and at dawn falls into his ríastrad [battle fury], transforming his countenance into a vision of terror. So heated is the fury that he is immersed three times in a vat of cold water to help him overcome it. Thus resolved, Cúchulainn makes short work of Senach Siaborthe and Eochaid Inber; and he spears Eochaid Iúil as the latter bathes in the river. All of Mag Mell rejoices at the victory, none more than Fand, with whom Cúchulainn makes love continually for the next month. Bidding her farewell, Cúchulainn agrees to tryst with her by the *yew tree at Ibor Cind Tráchta, near the modern town of Newry, Co. Down. Emer learns of the assignation shortly after, although Cúchulainn and Láeg try to keep it from her. In her own fury, she leads fifty women with whetted knives to the appointed spot at the appointed time, seeking vengeance. But the unexpected follows. After hearing Emer's speech on men's lust for what they do not have and their rejection of the familiar, Cúchulainn pledges that he wishes to live with her for ever. Seeing their love, Fand asks to be abandoned. And when Emer sees the unselfishness of Fand's love, she asks to be left behind. Each woman would award her lover to the other. This impasse is resolved by the unanticipated arrival of Manannán mac Lir, Fand's husband, who takes her away with him. Cúchulainn, disconsolate, then wanders the mountains of *Munster, unwilling to drink or eat, until the *druids give him a vial of forgetfulness. Emer also drinks and forgets her jealousy. And Manannán shakes his cloak between Cúchulainn and Fand so that they may never meet again. The standard modern text in Irish was edited by Myles Dillon, *Serglige Con Culainn*, Mediaeval and Modern Irish Series, 14 (1953); translation, *Scottish Gaelic Studies*, 7 (1951), 47–88. See also A. H. Leahy, *Heroic Romances of Ireland*, i (London, 1905), 51–85; T. P. Cross and C. H. Slover (eds.), *Ancient Irish Tales* (New York, 1936), 176–98. Despite its title, W. B. Yeats's drama *The Only Jealousy of Emer* (1919), prose version *Fighting the Waves*, is not an adaptation.

Sétanta. The boyhood name of *Cúchulainn.

Setlocenia [goddess of long life; long-lived one]. Minor goddess of early northern Britain invoked at Maryport, Cumberland. She may be compared conceptually but not etymologically with the Irish *Buanann.

shamanism [Tungus *šaman*, ascetic; cf. Sanskrit *sramanás*, ascetic]. The religious practice purporting to communicate with good and evil spirits through a professional class of priest-seers was first studied by anthropologists among the peoples of western Siberia, especially the Tungus, in the late 19th century. Subsequently shamanism was found to have counterparts in the religions of the North American Indians and elsewhere on the globe. Many commentators have found indications of shamanistic ritual among the early Celts. Poets of early Ireland, for example, sometimes practised *divination while wearing cloaks of bird-feathers, much as Siberian shamans did. In **Fís Adamnáin* [The Vision of Adamnán] Adamnán's soul goes forth from his body on the midsummer feast of St John the Baptist (21 June, the solstice), much as shamans claim to have experience beyond the bodily. The Welsh Arthurian figure *Gwrhyr Gwalstawd Ieithoedd has the shamanistic power to speak the language of animals. See Daniel F. Melia, 'The Irish Saint as Shaman', *Pacific Coast Philology*, 18 (1983), 37–42; Paul R. Lonigan, 'Shamanism in the Old Irish Tradition', *Éire-Ireland*, 20(3) (Fall 1985), 109–29. See also AWENYDDION; DÍCHETEL

DO CHENNAIB; IMBAS FOROSNAI; SECOND SIGHT; SOUS; TEINM LAÍDA.

Shan Van Vocht. Anglicized spelling for *Sean-bhean Bhocht [Ir., the poor old woman], a personification of *Ireland current in the 18th century, perhaps derived from the *Cailleach Bhéire. A song titled 'Shan Van Vocht', dated from the rising of the United Irishmen, 1798, has been described as the 'Marseillaise' of Ireland.

Shannon [ModIr. *An tSionna*, the old one]. Principal river of *Ireland flowing 224 miles south-west from a spring under Cuilcach Mountain, Co. Cavan, to the Atlantic. In its last seventy miles the river becomes a wide estuary; between counties Roscommon, Longford, and Westmeath, it widens to form *Lough Ree, and above *Killaloe, between Clare, Galway, and Tipperary, it forms *Lough Derg (2). For much of its length the Shannon forms the border between *Connacht on the west and *Leinster and *Munster on the east and south, and thus in much of Irish literature the river's name implies a border. Surprisingly, considering its size and importance in Irish transportation and commerce, and its frequent citation in early Irish literature, the Shannon is less mythologized than the *Boyne. The goddess of the Shannon, *Sinann, is linked to the *Boand, goddess of Boyne, through the Well of *Segais. In stories from oral tradition, the Shannon was formed by the *dragon-like *oilliphéist [Ir., great beast] fleeing St *Patrick. Midach's enchanted Hostel of the Quicken Trees in the *Fenian story **Bruidhean Chaorthainn* is located on the Shannon. Much action along the river focuses on its principal ford *Athlone [the ford of Luan]. Along the Shannon's lower reaches, under the estuary, is thought to lie Shannon City, which appears above water every seven years; mortals who see it will die. See SUBMERGED CITIES. Known in Manx as *Yn hannon*; W *Llinon*. See Padraic O'Farrell, *Shannon Through Her Literature* (Dublin, 1983).

shape-shifting, shape-shifter, shape-changing, metamorphosis. The ability to change shape or appearance at will is an important mechanism in the myth and folklore of all the earth's peoples. Just as Zeus changed himself into a bull to seduce Europa, many Celtic deities and heroes take on different forms to suit their ends. Some of this may arise from the indistinct boundary between animals and anthropomorphic personae in Celtic religion. The older instances of shape-shifting by deities and heroes do not usually provoke fear or dread on the part of mere mortals, but the same practise by *fairies and lesser supernatural figures, like the Scottish *bòcan or Cornish *spriggan, implies threat. Even more to be dreaded was the power of certain creatures, such as witches, to transform humans into animals. Deities noted for shape-shifting include: *Angus Óg; *Arawn; *Cáer; the *Mórrígan; *Nodons; mortals: *Cian; *Cúchulainn; *Étaín; *Merlin; *Mongán; *Pwyll; *Taliesin; *Tuan mac Cairill; folk creatures: *bòcan; *each uisge; *Eiddelig Gor; *spriggan. Folk motifs: A1459; D610; F234.0.2.

Sharvan. Anglicization of *Searbhán.

shee. Manx form and anglicization of *sídh.

Sheela-na-gig, Sheila-na-gig [Ir. *Síle na gCíoch*, Sheila (Caecilia) of the breasts]. Stone carvings from medieval Ireland and elsewhere depicting a naked woman with her legs apart, revealing her vagina. Although the pose would often be considered obscene, many surviving examples are found in churches. In the British Isles most are found in Ireland, with smaller numbers in England, Wales, and Scotland; arguably some instances may be found in France. Although their precise origin, date, and significance have never been satisfactorily explained, speculations have not been wanting. They may be borrowed from French Romanesque depictions of the sin of lust, meant as a warning. They may be fertility figures, used as a cure for barrenness. Recent feminist commentators have suggested they may be reminders of the primal earth mother whose rule over life and death pre-dated Christianity. See H. Hickey, *Images of Stone* (Belfast, 1976); Jorgen Andersen, *The Witch on the Wall* (London, 1977); James H. Dunn, 'Síle-na-gCíoch', *Éire-Ireland*, 12(1) (1977), 68–85; Helen Lanigan Wood, 'Women in Myths and Early Depictions', in Eiléan Ní Chuilleanáin (ed.), *Irish Women: Image and Achievement* (Dublin, 1985), 12–24; Eamonn Kelly, *Sheela-na-gigs: Origin and Functions* (Dublin, 1997).

sheevra. Anglicization of *síabair.

sheogue. Phonetic anglicization of ModIr. *siόg* [*fairy], unreformed ModIr. *sídheóg*.

sí. Reformed ModIr. spelling of *sídh.

síabair, síabraid, siabhra, síofra, siabra, siabur, sheevra [Ir. *síabraid*, arouses to fury, enchants, distorts, bewitches]. Large, malicious *elf or *fairy of Irish tradition. One was thought to have tried to choke *Cormac mac Airt when that pagan king showed an interest in Christianity.

sianach [ScG, monster]. Large, malevolent, predatory *deer of Scottish Gaelic oral tradition.

sídh, sídhe, síodh, sí, síd (OIr.), síth (OIr.), s'th (ScG), side (gen.), shee (Manx, ang.); the form sídhe, commonly cited in English, is the unreformed ModIr. genitive singular. Irish, Scottish Gaelic, and Manx words for fairy mound and, by implication, the realm beyond the senses, the *Otherworld or, in oral tradition, the *fairy world. The fairy mound/sídh is a familiar landscape feature in *Goidelic culture: a round, flat-topped, manmade barrow, tumulus, or hillock of ancient origin apparently intended to bury or commemorate a mortal king or ruler. From long-standing oral tradition the fairy mounds/sídhe were thought to mark places where the semi-divine *Tuatha Dé Danann fled underground after their defeat by the mortal *Milesians. The *Dagda himself assigned a sídh to each member, both male and female. In much of earlier Irish written tradition, therefore, the sídh appears to be a palace or at least a fine residence, like *Finnachad, the sídh of *Lir in *_Oidheadh Chlainne Lir_ [The Tragic Story of the Children of Lir]. In early literature such residences, especially when they are named without the prefix sídh-, seem almost more this-worldly than otherworldly: *Brí Léith, [Sídh] *Clettig, *Femen, and [Sídh] *Úamain. Hundreds of others are cited in the literature, often bearing the name of their most powerful resident, e.g. Sídh Nechtain, dominated by *Nechtan.

In oral tradition the story of the Tuatha Dé Danann's defeat and migration underground became a means of accommodating international *fairy lore. The old divinities became the *áes síde [people of the fairy mound], invisible to most mortals at most times, *Samain and Midsummer's Eve being the chief exceptions. Humans favoured with *second sight could perceive them. On occasion persons from this hidden world might intrude into the realm of mortals, such as the woman of the sídh [Ir. *bean sídhe*] or *banshee who calls out in the night to foretell death. The sídh was not to be disturbed by grazing cattle, and most farmers would avoid both the sídh and perceived paths to and from it. In Modern Irish the word sídh, meaning 'fairy' instead of 'fairy mound', combines to make dozens of compounds, e.g. ceo sídhe [*fairy mist], ceol sídhe [*fairy music], sídh chóra, sídh ghaoithe, and séideán sídhe [*fairy wind], poc sídhe [*fairy stroke], corpán sídhe [*changeling], suan sídhe [*fairy sleep]. See Heinrich Wagner, 'The Origins of Pagan Irish Religion', *Zeitschrift für celtische Philologie*, 38 (1981), 1–28; Diarmuid A. MacManus, *The Middle Kingdom: The Fairy World of Ireland* (London, 1960); James A. MacDougall, *Folk and Fairy Lore in Gaelic and English*, ed. George Calder (Edinburgh, 1910); Dora Broom, *Fairy Tales from the Isle of Man* (Harmondsworth, 1951); Daniel Parry-Jones, *Welsh Legends and Fairy Lore* (London, 1953); Tomás Ó Cathasaigh, *Éigse*, 17 (1978), 137–55.

sídheóg. Unreformed ModIr. spelling of sióg [*fairy]; anglicized sheogue.

Síghle na gCíoch, Sígle na gCíoch. Irish forms of *Sheela-na-gig.

Síle na gCíoch, Síle-na-Gig. Irish forms of *Sheela-na-gig.

Simon Magus [L, sorcerer]. Character of biblical origin whose persona attracted a huge body of medieval legends, many of which entered Celtic literature; his Irish name is Símón Druí. In the *Acts of the Apostles* 8: 9–24 he is charged with trafficking in sacred things; thus the ecclesiastical crime of simony. More often he is seen as a disputant of Sts Peter and Paul, promising that he has the power to fly up to heaven on his own. The encyclopaedist Isidore of Seville (*c*.560–636) recorded that Simon had died during the reign of Emperor Nero (AD 54–68). In Irish tradition Simon Magus is much associated with *Mug Ruith, whose name may derive from his. Together they construct the fabulous flying-machine *roth rámach [Ir., rowing wheel], later an object of fear. Simon's three sons rape *Tlachtga, Mug Ruith's daughter; her delivery of triplets on a hill in Co. *Meath prompted the annual *fair [Ir. *óenach*] there.

Sín [Ir., storm]. *Femme fatale* in the story of *Muirchertach mac Erca.

sínach [Ir., stormy]. Later name for the sea-monster who fought with *Fergus mac Léti; in earlier texts it is *muirdris. See also CAORÁNACH; OILLIPHÉIST.

Sinann, Sinand, Sinend, Sinent, Sinainn, Sionnainn, Sionann. Goddess of the River *Shannon and granddaughter of *Lir (2), the sea-god. In her best-known story Sinann goes to *Connla's Well (sometimes the Well of Cóelrind) seeking esoteric *knowledge. Apparently because she has violated certain protocols, Sinann is denied knowledge. Instead, the well in its anger rises up and drowns her, her body washing up on the banks of a river, the Shannon, which is then named for her. A nearly identical story is told about *Boand [the *Boyne] at the Well of *Segais, which may be identified with Connla's Well.

Sinsar of the Battles. See KING OF THE WORLD.

síodh. Variant spelling of *sídh.

síodhbhradh. See CHANGELING.

síofra. See CHANGELING.

sióg. ModIr. word for a single *fairy; unreformed spelling sídheóg; anglicized sheogue.

Sionnainn, Sionann. Variant forms of *Sinann.

Sirona [divine star (?)]. Gaulish goddess of healing springs whose cult has been recorded at sites from Hungary to Brittany. As her statues appear both alone and with Apollo Grannus, she must have existed as a fertility and healing goddess from pre-Roman times but survived the fusion of Gaulish with Latin cults. The Treveri people of the Moselle valley, along the borders of modern France, Belgium, and Germany, took a special interest in Sirona's veneration. In their territory was built the rich healing shrine excavated at Hochscheid, between Mainz and Trier, which provides us with many artefacts of her worship. Seated next to Apollo in a maternal pose, Sirona has a *dog resting in her lap. On her head is a diadem, implying high status; she carries three eggs, an unmistakable fertility symbol, and a snake twines around her arm, its head towards the eggs. At nearby Sainte-Fontaine near Freyming, also in the Moselle valley, the Sirona figure bears edible grains and fruits, while at Mainz she holds grapes. At Mâlain in the Côte d'Or mountains of north-eastern France, Sirona again has the snake coiled on her right arm. Other shrines have been excavated at Niedaltdorf, Bitburg, and Wiesbaden in Germany, and Metz, Luxeuil, and Corseul (Brittany) in France. Sirona appears to be identical with the goddess known elsewhere as Divona and Dirona. Her cult was displaced by *Borvo in much of the Celtic world. See F. Jenkins, 'The Role of the Dog in Romano-Gaulish Religion', *Collection Latomus*, 16 (1957), 60–76. See also APOLLO.

síth. OIr. variant of *sídh.

Síth Emna. Variant form of *Emain Ablach.

Sithallin. Character in James *Macpherson's *Ossian* (1760–3), killed with his brother *Ardan by Swaran. Probably an adaptation of Ailibhin, usually written *Ainle, one of the sons of Uisnech.

Sithchenn, Sithcheann [Ir. *sith-*, long; *cenn*, head]. *Druid at the court of *Eochaid Mugmedón who devises two contests by which *Niall Noígiallach [of the Nine Hostages] becomes the successor to his father. See **Echtra Mac nEchach Muigmedóin* [The Adventure of the Sons of Eochaid Mugmedón].

s'thich [ScG, fairy, elf]. Wantonly mischievous sprite of Highland folklore, especially intrusive on women in birth pains and a thief of newborn infants. One of the most common figures in early Highland lore, the s'thich was denounced by a 17th-century clergyman of the Kirk for its peculiar, flint-like deadly weapons.

s'thiche, s'thichean. ScG words for the realm of the *fairy.

Skatha. Anglicization of *Scáthach.

Skeolan. Anglicization of *Sceolang.

Skye, Isle of [ScG *An t-Eilean Sgiathanach*, the winged isle]. Largest island (670 square miles) in Scotland's Inner Hebrides, often known as 'the Misty Isle', frequently cited in Irish and Scottish Gaelic narrative and well endowed with its own oral tradition. Known by *Ptolemy (2nd cent. AD) as Sketis, but badly misplaced on his map. Notable in early Irish literature as the home of *Scáthach [ScG *Sgàthaich*], the amazonian teacher of *Cúchulainn and other heroes. The Irish name for a fort on the island was Dún Scáthaig(e), implying that it was named for her. The ruin *Dunscaith (1), once belonging to the barons of Sleat, is attributed to her. See DUNVEGAN.

See also J. A. McCulloch, *The Misty Isle of Skye*, 3rd edn. (Stirling, 1927); Otta F. Swire, *Skye: The Island and Its Legends* (London, 1952).

Sláine 1. Sláinge, Slangia [Ir. *sláine*]. Son of *Partholón in the pseudo-history **Lebor Gabála* [Book of Invasions] and the first physician in Ireland. In the *Partholonian division of Ireland he takes *Leinster. See also SLÁINGE.

2. Leader of the *Galióin, a part of the *Fir Bolg, in the pseudo-history **Lebor Gabála* [Book of Invasions], who divides Ireland with his brothers, taking *Leinster for himself. In the Fir Bolg invasion he was thought to have come ashore at Inber Sláine, now the mouth of the Slaney River at Wexford Harbour. Sláine is usually thought to have been buried at the fortress of *Dind Ríg, Co. Carlow, which was once called Duma Sláine [Sláine's mound], but the *Dindshenchas records that he is buried at Slane, Co. Meath.

Sláinge, Sláine. Reputedly the first of the 142 kings of *Tara, reigning in the 20th century BC. See SLÁINE (1).

sleih veggey, yn [Manx, the little people]. Manx name for the *fairies.

sliab, slíab (OIr.), **sliabh** (ModIr.). Irish and Scottish Gaelic word for mountain or mountain range, first element in dozens of place-names; anglicized slieve. See CNOC . . . [hill; knock].

Sliab Betha, Sliabh Beatha, Slieve Beagh, Slabay. Range of high hills (highest 1,255 feet) on the borders of Co. Monaghan, Fermanagh, and Tyrone named for *Bith, early invader of Ireland according to the pseudo-history **Lebor Gabála* [Book of Invasions].

Sliab Bladma, Sliabh Bladhma, Slieve Bloom. Range of hills (highest 1,733 feet) on the borders of counties Offaly and Laois named for the Milesian invader Bladma. Action in many *Fenian stories takes place here. According to one text, *Muirenn takes refuge here while pregnant and thus gives birth to Demne (*Fionn mac Cumhaill) in the hills. See John Feehan, *The Landscape of Slieve Bloom* (Dublin, 1979).

Sliab Cuilinn, Cuillinn, Cuilind, Slieve Gullion. Imposing peak (1,893 feet), 5 miles SW of Newry, 8 miles W of Dundalk, Co. Armagh. One of the best-known promontories in all of Ireland, dominating the Gap of the North, gateway from *Ulster to the south, widely celebrated in Irish tradition. On the south slope lies a cruciform passage-tomb locally called Calliagh Birra's House (see CAILLEACH BHÉIRE). Eponym of the mountain is *Cuilenn, a lord of the *sídh in *Fenian narrative. Different versions of one story portray *Fionn mac Cumhaill weakened or diminished by his adventures here. In a representative version he bathes in a lake on Sliab Cuilinn and is transformed into a feeble old man. After Fionn's warriors lay siege to the sídh, Cuilenn comes forth with a golden cup whose contents not only restore the hero but give him and a companion supernatural *knowledge. Folklorist Michael J. Murphy commemorated the mountain in two widely known books, *At Slieve Gullion's Foot* (Dundalk, 1940) and *Mountain Year* (Belfast, 1964, 1987).

Sliab Echtgi. See ECHTGE.

Sliab Fúait, Sliabh Fuaid, Slieve Fuad, Slieve Fuadh. Highest point in the Fews [Ir. *Na Feadha*, the woods] mountains near Newtownhamilton, Co. Armagh, named for the *Milesian invader Fuad, son of *Breogan, and rich in mythological and legendary associations. Adjacent to the hill is *Finnachad, reputed residence of *Aillén mac Midgna and *Lir, father of the Children of Lir. *Conall Cearnach defends *Ulster from this point in the **Táin Bó Cuailnge* [Cattle Raid of Cooley]. *Fíngein (1), physician of *Conchobar mac Nessa, heals *Cúchulainn of his wounds on the mountain. Findlám, the herdsman of *Tara, has a house here. *Deirdre, *Fionn mac Cumhaill, and *Conán mac Morna all have adventures here. *Liath Macha [grey of Macha] and *Saingliu, Cúchulainn's horses, rose from a lake near the mountain.

Sliab Luachra, Slieve Logher. Mountain range on the borders of counties. Cork and *Kerry, near the sources of the River Sullane, site of both heroic and magical action in stories from oral tradition.

Sliab Mis 1, Slieve Mish. Range of mountains (highest 2,796 feet), 14 miles long, at the narrowest neck of the *Dingle peninsula, Co. *Kerry, with rich mythological and legendary associations. The invading *Milesians first defeat the *Tuatha Dé Danann here in the **Lebor Gabála* [Book of Invasions], and also first meet *Banba, an incarnation of *Ireland, in this same place. Here also is *Cahirconree, archaeological site thought to be the fortress of the hero *Cú Roí, many of whose adventures take place nearby; it is here that *Bé Chuma finds the wand of Cú Roí. In oral tradition the mountains are haunted by a man with a menacing black *dog.

2, Slemish Mountain. Peak (1,437 feet) in Co. Antrim, 4 miles SE of Broughshane, where, according to tradition, St *Patrick while a young captive tended sheep and swine.

Sliab na mBan, Sliab Ban Finn, Sliabh na mBan Fionn, Slievenamon, Slievenaman, Slieve-na-Man, Knockfefin [Ir. *na mBan*, of women; *Ban Finn*, of fair-haired women]. Mountain (2,368 feet) 10 miles E of *Cashel, 6 miles SE of Fethard, Co. Tipperary, sometimes called 'Ireland's Parnassus'. The mountain lies on the plain of *Femen [Ir., femininity], and the magical Sídh ar Femen is near the peak. According to oral tradition, Sliab na mBan is named for the women who race each other up the slopes for the privilege of lying with *Fionn mac Cumhaill. Other *Fenian stories recount that Fionn gets his thumb wisdom here when he catches it in the door-jamb of a cairn to the *Otherworld (instead of from the *salmon of wisdom, the more usual story). Fionn also kills *Cúldub here, as he is entering the mound carrying a pig. It is also at Sliab na mBan that Fionn chooses *Gráinne for his own, and where the *Fianna hunt *boar. Earlier *Bodb Derg was thought to keep supernatural pigs here that reappeared alive after they had been eaten. W. B. Yeats and others preferred to call the promontory Knockfefin. See James Maher, *Romantic Slievenamon, in History, Folklore and Song* (Mullinahone, 1954).

Sliab na Trí nDée, Sliabh na nDée Dána. Irish names for *Corleck Hill.

slieve. Phonetic anglicization of *sliab, sliabh [mountain].

Slieve Aughty. See ECHTGE.

Slieve Echtge. See ECHTGE.

Slieve Gullion. See SLIAB CUILINN.

Slievenamon, Slieve-na-Man. See SLIAB NA MBAN.

Slissima. Sister of *Cuchullin in Macpherson's *Ossian* (1760–3), and mother of Althan and Ardar.

sluagh, sluagh-síthe [ScG *sluagh*, people, folk; multitude; host, army]. Also sluagh na marbh [host of the dead]. Hosts of the unforgiven dead in Scottish Gaelic folklore, the most formidable of Scottish *fairy people. They may approach from any direction but the east, usually taking crescent form, like a flight of grey birds. They are said to be able to pick up a person bodily and transport him long distances through the air from one island to another. Although they can rescue a man from a dangerous rock cleft, they usually bode no good to mortals. They may be seen after dark and are said also to injure cattle. Their name appears in the Gaelic exclamation 'O shluagh!', a call for succour to the fairies.

Smertrius. Latin title rather than name for a Gaulish divinity sometimes linked to both *Hercules and *Mars, for whom Smertrius is an occasional epithet. Representations of the god were found in 1711 under Notre-Dame cathedral, along with figures of *Esus, *Cernunnos, and *Tarvos trigaranus; here he is a muscular god confronting a rearing snake while brandishing a club or firebrand. Near Trier, Germany, an enormous enclosure around a sacred spring provides him with the cult-partner *Ancamna; coins at the site imply it was in use before the Roman conquest. The word Smertrius is philologically related to *Rosmerta. A tribe known as the Smertae inhabited the northernmost Highlands of Scotland, in what used to be Sutherlandshire. See E. M. Wightman, *Roman Trier and the Treveri* (London, 1970), 223–4.

Smirgat, Smirnat. Daughter of *Fothad Canann and one of several women named as wife of *Fionn mac Cumhaill. After she has warned him that he will die if he drinks from a horn, he is careful to use a cup or bowl.

smith, smiths [OE *smith*]. Metalworkers were held in high esteem in Celtic countries, often thought to possess healing powers. In the early Scottish Highlands a smith might hold his hammer over the sick or infirm to frighten away illness. Archaeological evidence points to the existence of the cult of the smith-god in Roman Britain, figures with distinctive hammer and tongs, perhaps borrowed from the Latin divinity Vulcan. Smithcraft was also often related to an interest in alchemy as well as to initiations into men's societies. *Goibniu was the smith-god of the *Tuatha Dé Danann. OIr. gobae; ModIr.

gabha; ScG gobha; Manx gaaue; W gof; Corn. gōf; Bret. gov. See Miranda J. Green, *Small Cult-Objects from Military Areas of Roman Britain*, British Archaeology Reports (British Series), no. 52 (Oxford, 1978), 55–72. See also CULANN; CREDNE; GAIBLÍN; GLWYDDYN SAER; GOBBÁN SAOR; GOFANNON; LOAN MACLIBHUIN; LON MAC LÍOMTHA.

Snowdon [W *Eryri*]. Highest mountain (3,560 feet) in *Wales and England, 12 miles SE of Caernarfon, *Gwynedd, north-western *Wales, standing in a small range of peaks, sometimes known collectively as Snowdonia. Widely celebrated in Welsh oral tradition, the home of a famous *eagle and of the giant *Rhita Gawr. See J. E. Lloyd, 'The Mountains in History and Legend', in R. C. Carr and G. A. Lister (eds.), in *The Mountains of Snowdonia* (Cardiff, 1925).

Solinus, Caius Julius. Roman geographer (*fl. c.* AD 200) noted for his compendium, *Collectanea Rerum Memorabilium*, divided into fifty-seven chapters, each containing brief but unreliable sketches of the world as known to the ancients. His interest in social conditions, habits, and religious rites of different nations includes an account of the British goddess *Sulis/Sul and a note of the absence of snakes in Ireland.

Somerled [Norse, summer sailor (?)]. Historical (d. 1164) Scottish Gaelic leader, the first to be called *Lord of the Isles, around whose persona many legends have accrued. Although descended from Irish kings who had been in the Hebrides since the seventh century, Somerled may have been more Norse than Gaelic in culture; none the less, his buildings at *Iona show much Celtic influence in design. He had ambivalent relations with the kings of Scotland, having supported David I during an invasion of England in 1138, but supportive of an unsuccessful rebellion against Malcolm IV (1153). His major accomplishment was the recovery of the Hebrides and *Argyll from Norse influence, administered by the king of the Isle of *Man under Norse suzerainty. With Irish allies, he defeated the Norse in 1156 and again in 1158, after which the king of Man fled to Norway. His title, Rí Innse Gall [king of the Hebrides], borne by his successors, was translated into Latin, Dominus Insularum, in 1354, and from thence into English as Lord of the Isles. Somerled was killed near Renfrew in 1164, having led yet another rebellion against Malcolm IV. His son *Dugal was the progenitor of the MacDougalls, while his son Raghnall was the forebear of the MacDonalds of the Isles; his progeny became the Clan Donald. See W. D. H. Sellar, 'The Origins and Ancestry of Somerled', *Scottish Historical Review*, 45 (1966), 123–42. Subject of Nigel Tranter's historical novel *The Lord of the Isles* (London, 1983).

Sons of . . . . Occasional translation of the Irish *Uí-, e.g. *Uí Néill.

sous [Ir. *so-us, so-as, so-fiuss*, good knowledge]. Learning acquired by legitimate means as opposed to sorcery or the occult art of manticism or *divination. Among Christian scribes, sous might denote scientific inquiry, any skill trained in practice, and Christian learning, not excluding Christian revelation. It is the antonym of *díchetal do chennaib, *imbas forosnai, and *teinm laída. See also KNOWLEDGE.

Sovereignty, Lady; sovereignty, sovranty [MidEng. *souverein*]. The personification of the power and authority of a kingdom as a woman to be won sexually pre-dates literature written in any Celtic language. In the hierogamy [Gk *hieros*, sacred; *gamos*, marriage] described in a Sumerian hymn (2nd millennium BC), the king must mate with Inanna, queen of heaven and goddess of love and fertility, on New Year's Day in her residence. In the hymn the king is seen as an incarnation of Dumuzi, a shepherd-king and husband of Inanna, and thus the rite of hierogamy ends with his ecstatic sexual union with her, perhaps acted out in life with one of Inanna's sacred prostitutes. Correlatives and echoes to a kind of spiritual and/or physical sexual union between the male king and a divine female sovereignty are widespread in early Indo-European culture, as far away as India in the instances of Vishnu and Sri-Lakshmi. Within Celtic traditions, evidence of sexual-sovereignty rituals, involving horses, survives to late pre-Norman Ireland, as the shocked and disgusted observations of *Giraldus Cambrensis in *Topographia Hibernica* (1188) testify. Early Irish texts describe the ritual *banais ríghe [wedding-feast of *kingship], which included (1) a libation from the sovereignty bride and (2) the coition of the king with sovereignty herself. At *Tara for the installation of the *ard rí [high king], the ceremony was known as feis temrach [Ir. *foaid*, spends the night with] and fled bainisi.

Stories of a king's, or a potential king's, lovemaking with the goddess of Sovereignty are so widespread in early Ireland and elsewhere in Europe, such as Geoffrey Chaucer's 'Wife of Bath's Tale', as to merit their own international folk- motif number, D732. According to the conventionalized steps in the story, the male protagonist encounters an ugly hag who invites him to have intimate relations with her. Her repulsiveness, perhaps a metaphor for the responsibilities of both kingship and adulthood, initially put him off, but he eventually relents. On the morning after their lovemaking, the hag is transformed into a beautiful maiden. In Irish versions of the story, the hag sometimes defeats the male protagonist with a riddle he cannot answer and rewards herself with a *geis he finds impossible to perform; failing this he has no alternative but to perform sexual intercourse.

Proinsias MacCana has written (1982) that the sovereignty story in Ireland is by its very nature political and never far removed from the propaganda of an interested dynasty. According to **Echtra mac nEchach Muigmedóin* [The Adventure of the Sons of Eochaid Mugmedón], *Niall Noígiallach [of the Nine Hostages], nominal progenitor of the powerful *Uí Néill, makes love to Flaithius, the loathly hag, thus grasping power from his half-brothers. A similar story is told of *Lugaid Laígde, who takes precedence ahead of his brothers by making love to a hideous sorceress, again Dame Sovereignty in disguise. Thirdly, *Conn Cétchathach [of the Hundred Battles] also encounters Sovereignty in a story titled **Baile in Scáil* [The Phantom's Frenzy]. After Conn sets out from Tara, he finds himself in an otherworldly chamber with a ridge-pole of white gold. Seated upon a throne is *Lug Lámfhota, who embodies sacral kingship, while nearby on a crystal chair is a beautiful girl, his consort (unnamed, but identified by commentators with the goddess *Ériu). She asks who should serve the red ale [Ir. *derg-fhlaith*], making a pun on *ale [*laith*] and sovereignty [*flaith*]. Lug answers by naming all Conn's successors in the kingship. Here the sexual contact is only symbolic as Conn is offered the drink in a golden cup, whose implications are clear from other contexts.

Many other female personalities from early Irish literature also carry associations with sovereignty, often linked with specific territory. *Mór Muman embodies the sovereignty of *Munster just as *Medb Lethderg personifies it at Tara. *Macha, *Medb, and the *Mórrígan all have associations with sovereignty in older Irish literature, while the *Cailleach Bhéire is the foremost sovereignty figure from later and oral tradition. The colour *blue implies sovereignty, redoubled in the name *Gormfhlaith [blue sovereignty]. *Branwen is the only Welsh figure to have sovereignty affiliations. See also SHAN VAN VOCHT/SEAN-BHEAN BHOCHT. OIr. flaithius; ModIr. flaitheas, ceannas; ScG uachdaranachd; Manx ardreeriaght; W penarglwyddiaeth; Corn. sovranta, myghternsys; Bret. pennrouelezh.

Máire Bhreathnach, 'The Sovereignty Goddess as a Goddess of Death', *Zeitschrift für celtische Philologie*, 39 (1982), 243–60; Rosalind Elizabeth Clark, *Great Queens* (Gerrard's Cross, UK, and Savage, Md., 1990); Sigmund Eisner, *Tale of Wonder: Source Study for the Wife of Bath's Tale* (Wexford, 1957); Françoise Le Roux and Christian-J. Guyonvarc'h, *La Souveraineté guerrière de l'Irlande: Mórrígan, Bodb, Macha* (Rennes, 1983); Proinsias MacCana, 'Aspects of the Theme of the King and Goddess in Irish Literature', *Études Celtiques*, 7 (1955–6), 76–114, 356- 413; 'Aspects of the Theme of the King and the Goddess', *Études Celtiques*, 8 (1958–9), 59–65; Rhian Andrews, 'Rhai agweddau as sofraniaeth yng ngherddi's Gogynfeirdd', *Bulletin of the Board of Celtic Studies*, 27 (1976–8), 23–30; Proinsias MacCana, 'Women in Irish Mythology', in Mark P. Hederman and Richard Kearney (eds.), *The Crane Bag Book of Irish Studies (1977–1981)*, (Dublin, 1982), 520–4; Jo Radner, 'The Hag of Beare: The Folklore of a Sovereignty Goddess', *Tennessee Folklore Society Bulletin*, 40 (1974), 75–81; Catherine A. McKenna, 'The Theme of Sovereignty in *Pwyll*', *Bulletin of the Board of Celtic Studies*, 29 (1980), 35–52.

Spailpín Fánach, An [Ir., the itinerant labourer]. An Irish folk melody widely popular in the English-speaking world, sung to countless sets of words, including 'The Girl I Left Behind Me'.

sparáran na scillinge. See CLURICAUNE.

spear. See GÁE.

Spoils of Annwfn. English title for **Preiddiau Annwfn*.

spré na scillenagh. See CLURICAUNE.

spriggan. Dour, ugly warrior *fairy of Cornish tradition, where it is nearly as well known as the *piskie. Ghosts of old *giants, spriggans are now very small but may inflate themselves into monstrous forms; see SHAPE-SHIFTING. Found around cairns, cromlechs, and ancient barrows, they guard buried treasure, but are also responsible for bringing storms and the destruction of buildings and crops. Like piskies, they may also abduct children.

Sreng. *Fir Bolg warrior who cuts off the right arm of the *Tuatha Dé Danann king *Nuadu at the First Battle of Mag Tuired. Sreng was first a Fir Bolg ambassador known for his delaying tactics. On their initial meeting *Bres offered to divide Ireland between them, but as Sreng was impressed with the superiority of Tuatha Dé weapons he refused. He and the Fir Bolg went on to battle, where he severed Nuadu's arm. On the next day Nuadu asked Sreng to tie his right arm behind him so that they might have a fair combat, and again Sreng refused. To make peace the Tuatha Dé Danann then offered Sreng and the Fir Bolg the province of *Connacht as a peace settlement, which he accepted.

Sruth nam Fear Gorm. See BLUE MEN OF THE MINCH.

stag [OE *stagga*]. The fully grown male deer was an important cult animal among the Continental Celts and plays an important role in Celtic vernacular tradition, even though the Goidelic languages lack a single word to denote it. The *horned gods of the ancient Celts, notably *Cernunnos, have stag antlers. As monarch of the northern forests, the stag was admired for its speed and sexual aggression during the rutting season. Its antlers symbolized the changing seasons by being shed in autumn and regrowing in spring. The hardness of the antler clearly evoked male genitalia, and carved antlers were used to make phallic amulets. Representations of stags are found in Celtic art, beginning with rock carvings (7th cent. BC) and continuing with bronze figures and coins from the pre-Roman and Romano-Celtic periods. In the Camonica valley in the Italian Alps the stag is linked with sun imagery. The Celtic *Dis Pater described by *Caesar (1st cent. BC) may be a stag-god. The British god *Cocidius is accompanied by a stag.

In Welsh and Irish traditions the stag often entices humans into the *Otherworld. *Fionn mac Cumhaill often hunts an enchanted stag, the metamorphosed Irish god *Donn. Christianized, the stag becomes a guide to heaven and so is represented in cemeteries, such as at Mount Stewart Gardens in Co. Down, Ireland. But stags may also be associated with women. *Flidais, Irish goddess of wild things, is mistress of stags. The war-goddess *Mórrígan can take the form of a stag. The stag is one of the three transformations of *Tuan mac Cairill. In the first branch of the *Mabinogi*, *Pwyll hunts a stag that is the quarry of *Arawn, lord of *Annwfn. In the fourth branch *Gilfaethwy becomes a stag and *Gwydion a hind to produce *Hyddwn [W, little stag]. In *Culhwch ac Olwen*, the supernatural, speaking Stag of Rhedynfre (or Redynvre) helps Culhwch in the pursuit of the *boar Twrch Trwyth.

OIr. dam [also denotes ox]; ModIr. poc ['buck', also denotes the *ram], fia fireann [male deer]; ScG damh cabrach féidh; Manx tarroo-feeaih [lit. bull-deer]; W carw, hydd; Corn. carow; Bret. karv.

Stone of Scone. See LIA FÁIL.

Story of . . . . See SCÉLA . . .

Strabo. Greek geographer who flourished in Augustan Rome (*c.*58 BC-*c.* AD 24) whose seventeen-book *Geographia* provides much widely cited, descriptive information about early Celtic society. The standard modern translation is by H. L. Jones (8 vols.) in the Loeb Classical Library (New York, 1917–33). See also CLASSICAL COMMENTATORS.

Strathclyde [ScG *srath*, valley; cf. *cluden*, a pre-Celtic name for water]. *P-Celtic or British kingdom in *Scotland, from the watershed of the Clyde River down to perhaps the Anglo-Saxon kingdom of Mercia, flourishing from the 5th to the 8th centuries. Its capital was the great fortified rock of *Dumbarton. Although Strathclyde was subsumed into the new kingdom of Scotland (844) formed by *Cináed mac Ailpín [Kenneth MacAlpin], with *Picts and the *Scotti of *Dál Riada, its men played an increasingly important part in the life of the country. The name Strathclyde was reborn in 1974 when Scotland was rearranged by district; the new county of Strathclyde includes areas from the former shires of Ayr, Lanark, Renfrew, Dunbarton, Stirling, and Argyll.

Sualtam mac Róich, Sualdam. Mortal father or stepfather of *Cúchulainn; see also DEICHTINE.

suan sídhe. See FAIRY SLEEP.

submerged cities. An aspect of the various *flood legends is the belief that whole cities have been inundated, of which the best-known Celtic examples are *Ys in *Finistère from Breton tradition and *Cantre'r Gwaelod on *Cardigan Bay in Welsh tradition. In Ireland there are thought to be cities under *Lough Neagh, *Lough Ree, and the *Shannon River; Shannon City reappears every seven years and mortals who see it are doomed to die. Lancarrow in Cornish tradition is a city submerged beneath the sands. See also TÍR FO THUINN [Land Under Wave]. See also F. J. North, *Sunken Cities* (Cardiff, 1957).

Sucellus, Sucellos [L, the good striker; he who strikes to good effect]. *Gaulish god whose worship is recorded in several locations, including in Britain. A very masculine figure with curling beard and hair, he is conventionally depicted with a long-shafted hammer or mallet in his left hand, standing beside his cult-partner, *Nantosuelta. Critical opinion is undecided about the significance of the hammer, whether it is a weapon, a cooper's tool, or a fencing instrument. It may also be an emblem of power, like a wand or sceptre. Commentators have linked Sucellus with the Roman *Dis Pater and the Irish *Dagda. See Saloman Reinach, 'Sucellus et Nantosvelta', *Revue Celtique*, 17 (1896), 45–59; E. Linckenheld, 'Sucellus et Nantosuelta', *Revue de l'Histoire des Religions*, 99 (1929), 40–92; Miranda J. Green, *Symbol and Image in Celtic Religious Art* (London and New York, 1989), 46–54, 75–86.

Suibne Geilt, Suibhne [Ir. *geilt*, one gone mad from terror]. Main character of **Buile Shuibne* [The Frenzy of Suibne].

suileach. Multi-eyed, eponymous *sea-monster of Lough Swilly (Co. *Donegal) thought to have been dispatched by St *Colum Cille (521–95).

Suleviae. Latin name given to a triad of mother-goddesses known in many parts of the Roman-occupied Celtic world as well as in Rome itself. Iconographic and epigraphical evidence suggests that the goddesses were linked to cults of healing, regeneration, *fertility, and maternity. They were worshipped at three sites in Britain: Colchester, Cirencester, and Bath. This latter site suggests a connection with *Minerva, one of whose epithets is Sulevia, pl. Suleviae. See also MATRES.

Sulis, Sul [cf. L *sōl*, sun; Ir. *súil*, eye]. Latin name for an indigenous British goddess of healing springs whose worship was known as far afield as Hesse in Germany. During the Roman period her cult became conflated with that of Gaulish *Minerva, notably at Aquae Sulis, what is today Bath, England. Unlike the pattern with *Mars or *Mercury, where the local deity becomes attached to the Roman divinity as an aspect or epithet, the goddess at Aquae Sulis was always known as Sulis-Minerva or Sul-Minerva. The huge volumes of hot water pouring forth from the hot springs at Bath would have made it a destination for pilgrims long before Roman occupation, when the site was converted into a pool enclosed by a large building in classical style. See Barry W. Cunliffe, *Roman Bath* (London, 1969); Barry W. Cunliffe and P. Davenport, *The Temple of Sulis Minerva at Bath*, i: *The Site* (Oxford, 1985). See also SULEVIAE.

sunwise turn, circumambulation. A motion imitating the path of the sun, thought to bring good fortune or to ward off evil in most of Celtic tradition, as in early traditions elsewhere in Europe. A person makes a sunwise turn around an object, building, or monument by first heading towards the sun, i.e. south, always keeping the object passed at the right; clockwise. The belief in the powers of the sunwise turn appears in the oldest literature and continues through Christian to modern times. When *Medb begins her campaign against *Ulster in the **Táin Bó Cuailnge* [Cattle Raid of Cooley], her charioteer makes one sunwise turn to offset the prophesied evil. In medieval times the pious made 'holy rounds' by certain sacred stones, wells, *trees, *fires, etc. In 1703 Martin Martin observed that Hebridean fishermen first rowed their boats in a sunwise turn before setting out to sea. OIr. dessel; ModIr. deiseal; Hiberno-Eng. deshel; ScG deiseal; Manx jeshal; Corn. gans an howl.

swan [OE *swan, suan*]. The large, long-necked amphibious *bird (genus *Cygnus, Olor*) has played an important role in Celtic iconography and tradition from earliest times.

The long-necked water birds pull model wagons in art surviving from the *Urnfield (1500–800 BC) and *Hallstatt (1200–600 BC) eras. Swans are less common during Roman domination, but one is featured in a sculpture of three mothers and three children in a boat found at *Alesia in eastern France. A metal horse-goad from early Ireland found at Dunaverney, Co. Antrim, features swans with cygnets that can be turned in place, suggestive of augury. In early Irish literary tradition the swan is often depicted as the epitome of purity, beauty, and potential good luck. In Welsh stories swans are more likely to imply communication between the *Otherworld and the world of mortals, as when swans doff their feathers and frolic in a lake as maidens. Yet a certain sexual association, perhaps suggested by the phallic long neck, is often implied. *Derbforgaill (1) takes the form of a swan when she comes from *Lochlainn with her maidens to woo *Cúchulainn. Much earlier, a flock of destructive yet beautiful swans festooned with gold and silver chains ravages the area around *Emain Macha when Cúchulainn is conceived. In still another story Cúchulainn returns to Emain Macha with a flock of swans, again in gold and silver chains, wild *deer, and three severed heads. The chains of precious metal probably evoke the supernatural. Silver chains adorn *Cáer (1), the swan-maiden in love with *Angus Óg in **Aislinge Óenguso* [The Dream of Angus]. Not all humans taking swan form are female, however. In the third part of **Tochmarc Étaíne* [The Wooing of Étaín], the otherworldly *Midir is transformed into a swan and flies through a smoke-hole in the roof after he wins an amorous embrace with *Étaín, wife of *Eochaid Airem. King *Mongán also takes the form of a swan. Most memorably, the male and female children of Lir in **Oidheadh Chlainne Lir* [The Tragic Story of the Children of Lir] are transformed into swans, spend three watery exiles of 300 years each, are returned to human form, and are baptized Christians just before crumbling into dust. Irish oral tradition records the story of an old man who hides his money in the body of a swan he thinks dead, but it awakens and flies away with his hoard of coins. OIr. ela; ModIr. eala; ScG eala; Manx olla; W alarch; Corn. alargh; Bret. alarc'h. See Anne Ross, *Pagan Celtic Britain* (London, 1967), 234–42.

T

T. The twentieth letter of the modern English alphabet is represented by tinne [Ir., holly] in the *ogham alphabet of early Ireland.

taboo, tabu. See GEIS; see also WITHERSHINS.

tàcharan. ScG word for *changeling.

Tacitus, Cornelius (AD 55-*c*.117). Roman historian and biographer, often judged one of the most reliable of all *classical commentators. Of his five surviving volumes, the short *Germania* (*De origine situ moribus ac populis Germanorum*, written *c.* AD 98) is a trove of ethnographic information on peoples living north of the Alps, even though there is no evidence Tacitus had visited the regions. His comments on the Celts, while often cited, are incidental in the text. See *Agricola, Germania,* Loeb Classical Library No. 35 (Cambridge, Mass., 1968); *Agricola* (Cambridge, Mass., 1980); *The Histories* (London, 1993).

Tadg, Tadc, Tadhg [Ir., poet]. One of the commonest man's names in Irish, so that the phrase tadhg na sráide [Tadg on the street] is the equivalent of the English 'man on the street'. Thady is a common but now archaic transliteration. Spuriously anglicized as Timothy, Thaddeus, and Theophilus. The forms Teague and Taigue imply opprobrium for Catholics in Northern Ireland. The most often cited Tadg from early literature is *Tadg mac Nuadat, grandfather of *Fionn mac Cumhaill.

Tadg mac Céin. Son of *Cian (3), grandson of *Ailill Aulomm, who has the vision of *Clídna as the noblest and most beautiful of women, attended by three brightly coloured *birds. In adventures in the *Otherworld he comes to a mysterious island ruled by two sons of *Bodb, where a woman tells him that all the kings of Ireland from *Conn Cétchathach [of the Hundred Battles] live here. He also meets *Connla (2) and his *fairy woman as well as the *apple tree that lured him. Returning to the mortal world, Tadg realizes he has been gone a year. An earthly alliance with *Cormac mac Airt proves disappointing. In a campaign against *Ulster, Cormac promises allies as much land as they can circle in a chariot. When Cormac learns that Tadg has his sights on *Tara, he bribes Tadg's charioteer not to complete the circle, thus depriving him of the award. Learning of this, Tadg kills the charioteer. Tadg is also an ancestor-deity cited in *Munster and *Leinster pedigrees. See Standish Hayes O'Grady, *Silva Gadelica* (2 vols., London, 1892).

Tadg mac Nuadat. *Druid, son of Nuadu Necht and aspect of *Nuadu Airgetlám, and father of *Muirenn Muncháem, grandfather of *Fionn mac Cumhaill. Tadg opposes Muirenn's marriage to *Cumhall, fearing that the union will cause him to lose his ancestral seat, and so persuades *Conn to set Goll mac Morna upon him and kill him. In variant texts, Fionn overcomes Tadg to occupy the Hill of *Allen (Almu). Some commentators feel that Tadg is but an alias for Nuadu himself.

Taigue. See TADG.

Taillcenn, Taillkenn. Corrupt spellings of *Tálcend.

Tailtiu, Tailltiu, Tailte. Name for one of the three great fairs of early Ireland and the *Fir Bolg queen there commemorated. Although much of Tailtiu's character is fixed in the pseudo-history **Lebor Gabála* [Book of Invasions], she is apparently a much older figure and may be of divine origin. She is sometimes described as being the daughter of the 'king of Spain', but she may also be the child of the earth, e.g. Mag Mór [great plain]. Married to the last great Fir Bolg king, *Eochaid mac Eirc, who named his palace after her, she was also the foster-mother of the great hero *Lug Lámfhota. She led her people in the clearing of the forest, which by implication becomes all of *Brega or what is today Co. *Meath, some of Ireland's best farmland. Some commentators see in this identification evidence that she was originally a kind of earth goddess. But the work of clearing proves so onerous as to break her heart, in the words of the text. On her deathbed she asks that funeral games be held annually on the cleared ground. Lug leads the first games of horse-racing and martial arts at the time of *Lughnasa (1 August), singing a lamentation.

Coextensive with the modern hamlet of *Teltown, between Navan and Kells, the Tailtiu assembly or fair [OIr. *óenach Tailten*; ModIr. *Aonach Tailteann*] was celebrated intermittently from ancient times, and continued to be held even as late as about 1770; it was revived in the 20th century but then fell into abeyance again. In its early form Tailtiu was the principal assembly of the *Uí Néill federation, but presiding at the fair became the prerogative of the king of *Tara. Participants came from all parts of Ireland and also from Scotland, making Tailtiu the equal of Tara, *Tlachtga, and *Uisnech. The Tailtiu óenach was thought an optimal time to be married. The fair also was the occasion of the 'Teltown marriage', a chance espousal for a year and a day that could be ended simply by having the couple stand back to back, one facing north, the other south, and walk away from one another.

Important events taking place at Tailtiu unrelated to the óenach include *Éremón and the *Milesians' victory over the Tuatha Dé Danann, and the deaths of *Banba, *Ériu, and *Fódla. It was also described as the burial-place of the *Ulaid. See Máire Mac Neill, *The Festival of Lughnasa* (Oxford, 1962), 311–38; Daniel A. Binchy, 'The Fair at Tailtiu and the Feast of Tara', *Ériu*, 18 (1958), 113–38; Thomas H. Nally, *The Aonach Tailteann and the Tailteann Games* (Dublin, 1922); T. J. Westropp, 'Marriages of the Gods and the Sanctuary of Tailltiu', *Folk-Lore*, 31 (1920), 109–41.

Táin . . . [OIr., cattle raid]. Conventional first word in the titles of a class of Old Irish narratives. Although **Táin Bó Cuailnge* [Cattle Raid of Cooley] is often referred to in English as 'The *Táin*', other narratives also have titles beginning with the same word.

Táin Bó Cuailnge, *Cuálgne, Chuailge*. Irish title of the greatest work of classical Irish literature, an epic or epic-like saga and the key text of the *Ulster Cycle; known in English as The Cattle Raid of Cooley (Quelgny, etc.). The central action pits Queen *Medb (Maeve) of *Connacht against the *Ulster hero *Cúchulainn as well as *Finnbennach [the White Bull] against *Donn Cuailnge [the Brown Bull]. Initial composition in both prose and verse dates from the 7th and 8th centuries with texts surviving in the **Book of the Dun Cow* [*Lebor na hUidre*] (*c.*1100), the **Book of Leinster* [*Lebor Laignech*] (*c.*1160), and the **Yellow Book of Lecan* [*Lebor Buide Lecáin*] (*c.*1390). The many revisions and interpolations indicate a trend from the lean prose and sharp humour of the earlier passages to the bombast, florid alliteration, and sentimentality of the later.

Foretales. When the action of the *Táin* begins, the listener/reader is presumed to have had an introduction to characters and events that are the key to what follows. An explanation of these details is found in seven foretales or rémscéla that date from several centuries and are found in different codices. Preceding them is a 9th-century anecdote explaining that the *Táin* was recovered when *Fergus mac Róich returned from the dead and recited the text to the poet *Senchán Torpéist. The seven points of the rémscéla are (1) that *Conchobar mac Nessa became king of Ulster when his mother persuaded the previous king, Fergus mac Róich, to resign in his favour; Conchobar was none the less a popular king. (2) Ulster warriors suffered 'pangs' [Ir. **noínden*] like those of a woman in labour whenever they were in greatest difficulty. These were inflicted on them in a curse by Macha (3), when her husband, *Crunniuc, obliged her to run a foot-race just as she was about to give birth. (3) The story of Conchobar's frustrated love for the beautiful *Deirdre (*Longas mac nUislenn* [the Exile of the Sons of Uisnech]), whom *Cathbad tells will bring evil to Ulster. (4) The mysterious conception of *Cúchulainn, perhaps by *Lug Lámfhota, and his birth under the name *Setanta. At birth, Cúchulainn is thought to be the son of the mortal *Sualtam. (5) Cúchulainn's demonstrated skill with arms and his winning of *Emer, the daughter of *Forgall Manach. Later, the improvement of his fighting prowess while being tutored by *Scáthach and *Aífe in *Scotland. (6) Cúchulainn's unknowing slaying of *Connla, his child from an affair with Aífe; see AIDED ÓENFHIR AÍFE [The Tragic Death of Aífe's Only Son]. (7) The story of the begetting of Finnbennach and Donn Cuailnge.

The narrative. Medb, warrior queen of Connacht, disputes with her husband, *Ailill mac Máta, in their bedroom at *Cruachain [Rathcroghan, Co. Roscommon]. The issue is not romance but power. Who has the more valuable possessions, husband or wife? Ailill claims that his are greater because he has the white horned bull, Finnbennach, which was born in Medb's herds but has departed as it did not wish to be ruled by a woman. All her wealth seems worthless to Medb because she has no bull to match that of Ailill. *Bulls equalled wealth in this milieu; in pre-Christian Celtic culture they had been worshipped. Medb feels that the only way her wealth could appear to be more than that of her husband would be if she possessed the greatest bull in all of Ireland, Donn Cuailnge of the cantred of *Cuailgne [Cooley peninsula, north-east Co. Louth] in Ulster. She sends emissaries to bargain with the owner, *Dáire mac Fiachna, offering many treasures, including access to her own 'friendly thighs'. Dáire refuses, and so Medb resolves to take the bull by force.

Medb summons the armies of Connacht and *Leinster as well as those of the Ulster exiles, *Cormac Connloinges (a son of Conchobar) and Fergus mac Róich. Before the expedition gets under way, the Connacht army consults a mysterious prophetess, *Fedelm (1), who rides on the shaft of a chariot, weaving a fringe with a gold staff. When asked what she foresees, Fedelm responds, 'Crimson'. Medb and others challenge her vision, but Fedelm repeats it and adds a description of the deeds of Cúchulainn, the great Ulster champion. Medb's only consolation is a *druid's prophecy that she will return alive.

Camping on the first night, Medb reviews her troops. Noting that her Leinster allies are the most eager soldiers, she thinks for a moment of slaughtering them, lest they betray her. She instead distributes them among different battalions so that their threat is dissipated. Fergus mac Róich is appointed to guide the entire expedition, even though he has exiled himself from Ulster for his murder of the sons of *Uisnech (see DEIRDRE). He is uneasy in opposing his countrymen. Still, most of the Ulstermen still suffer under the birth pangs put upon them by Macha (3). Two excepted were Cúchulainn and his mortal father, Sualtam, who set out to meet the Connacht army at Iraird Cuillenn [Crossakeel, Co. Westmeath]. Cúchulainn sends his father back to warn Ulster, while he writes the message for the advancing army. To make sure it is read, Cúchulainn cuts an *oak sapling with a single stroke, and using only one arm, one leg, and one eye, he makes it into a hoop. He writes the message in the *ogham alphabet and fixes the hoop around a pillar-stone, before departing for a tryst with a girl, possibly *Fedelm Noíchrothach (daughter of Conchobar mac Nessa) or her bondwoman, near *Tara. The message reads, 'Come no further, unless you have a man who can make a hoop like this one, with one hand, out of one piece.' On the next night, Cúchulainn leaves another warning. He cuts the fork of a tree with a single stroke and casts it into the earth so that two-thirds of the stem is buried. On the branches he sets the heads of four Connachtmen so unfortunate as to have strayed from the army. Fergus says that it is *geis [Ir., taboo] for them to pass the tree with four heads, unless someone can pull it out. Medb commands Fergus to extract the tree, and after seven attempts he succeeds. When asked who could have put the tree so deep in the earth, Fergus answers that it could only have been Cúchulainn, his own foster-son and the foster-son of Conchobar. Following this, Fergus gives a long account of Cúchulainn's childhood deeds.

The Connacht army moves eastward, devastating *Brega [eastern Co. Meath] and *Mag Muirtheimne (Co. Louth). Fergus warns his comrades about Cúchulainn's vengeance, which comes quickly with the slaughter of one hundred soldiers. Medb can find no one to oppose him in combat. She then asks for a parley, but Cúchulainn refuses, slaughtering one hundred more men each night instead. Then Cúchulainn proposes terms: he will meet with one warrior at a ford of a river. Medb agrees, but Cúchulainn kills each of six adversaries, at which point Medb breaks the agreement.

Medb then departs, turning towards *Dún Sobairche [Dunseverick, Co. Antrim], which she plunders. Cúchulainn at first follows her, but then returns to his own country, where he finds *Buide mac Báin leading Donn Cuailnge, in the bull's first appearance in the narrative; Cúchulainn kills Buide, while others drive off the bull.

Lug Lámfhota, Cúchulainn's immortal father, comes and heals the hero of his accumulated wounds, telling him to rest for three days and nights. While Cúchulainn is regaining his strength, the fifteen-strong boy army of Ulster, not suffering the birth pangs from Macha, march out to battle. Though they wreak destruction on Connacht for a while, they are themselves destroyed. News of the boy army's terrible end brings on Cúchulainn's ríastrad [battle fury], during which he vows to seek vengeance upon Medb's army. Cúchulainn then begins a long series of single combats, in which he is always the victor. Medb persuades Fergus mac Róich to go against Cúchulainn, but once in the field they will not fight one another. By agreement, they yield to one another by turns.

At last Medb persuades *Ferdiad to enter the fray. A foster-brother of Cúchulainn, Ferdiad is threatened with disgrace if he refuses and is offered rich rewards if he consents-including the pledged troth of Medb's daughter *Finnabair. The four-day battle of the foster-brothers at the ford of *Áth Fhirdiad [Ardee, Co. Louth] constitutes the climactic action of the entire narrative. Neither combatant wishes to fight the other. Each night Cúchulainn sends Ferdiad leeches and herbs to heal his wounds, while Ferdiad sends a share of his food. They fight with darts, slender spears, heavy spears, and heavy swords, with neither gaining the advantage. At last Cúchulainn calls for the *Gáe Bulga, the mysterious weapon whose use he had learned from Scáthach, the woman warrior. It is a spear that enters a wound at one point but makes thirty points within. With the assistance of his charioteer *Láeg, Cúchulainn sets the Gáe Bulga against Ferdiad, killing him. In an instant Cúchulainn begins to lament the death of his foster-brother and friend, but he is prostrate from his own wounds.

While Cúchulainn lies recovering, single champions from Ulster come forth to oppose the Connacht army. Hearing them, Sualtam thinks his son in danger. Cúchulainn disabuses him, but asks him to return to *Emain Macha, the capital, to rouse the Ulstermen. Arriving at the palace, Sualtam calls out three times, but no one responds. The druid Cathbad tells Sualtam that he offends protocol by speaking unbidden. Turning away in anger, Sualtam falls on the sharp edge of his own shield and beheads himself. When his severed head is brought back on the shield, it roars out his earlier warning to the Ulstermen.

Hearing his call, Conchobar rouses the men of his kingdom, and the Ulstermen are released from their pangs. In the description of the armed companies' advance, the text here includes more than 500 lines of description of colour and armaments, all in anticipation for the climactic battle at Gáirech. As the battle begins, the Connacht army under Fergus's command breaks through the lines. Cúchulainn still lying ill from his wounds, the Ulster hero *Conall Cernach rises to the fore, taunting Fergus for opposing his kith and kin 'for the sake of a whore's [Medb's] backside'. Fergus turns to Conchobar and almost kills him, but cannot finish him off as he is a fellow Ulsterman. Cúchulainn, hearing of Conchobar's plight, rises up in a frenzy and enters the fray. Fergus, upon seeing him, withdraws from the fighting, as he had earlier promised.

This leaves Medb and Ailill alone on the battlefield. And though Cúchulainn comes upon her at a vulnerable moment, as she is relieving herself, he spares her and allows her to return home, unharmed, with Donn Cuailnge the brown bull in tow. The human battle is over.

When Donn Cuailnge comes to Cruachain, he gives out three mighty bellows, challenging Finnbennach the white-horned bull to fight him. All who have returned from battle watch the bulls at Tarbga [north-east Co. Roscommon] in a battle that lasts all day and into the dark. During the night the bulls fight all over Ireland, and in the morning Donn Cuailnge is seen passing Cruachain with Finnbennach on his horns. He gallops back to Ulster, scattering the white bull's entrails as he passes. When he comes to the border of Cuailnge, his heart breaks and he dies.

Medb and Ailill make peace with Ulster and with Cúchulainn, but their daughter Finnabair stays with the former enemy. The men of Ulster go to Emain Macha, celebrating great triumph.

Translations: Joseph Dunn, *The Ancient Irish Epic Tale Táin Bó Cúalnge* (London, 1914); Winifred Faraday, *The Cattle-Raid of Cualnge* (London, 1904); Christian-J. Guyonvarc'h, 'La Razzia des vaches de Cooley (version de Lebor na hUidre)', *Ogam*, 15 (1963), 139–60, 265–88, 393–412; 16 (1964), 225–30, 463–70 [incomplete]; Thomas Kinsella, *The Táin* (Dublin and London, 1969); Cecile O'Rahilly, *Táin Bó Cúailnge from the Book of Leinster* (Dublin, 1967); *Táin Bó Cúailnge: Recension I* (Dublin, 1978); Ernst Windisch, *Die altirische Heldensage Táin Bó Cúalnge nach dem Buch von Leinster* . . . (Leipzig, 1905).

Commentary: Rudolf Thurneysen, *Die irische Helden- und Königsaga bis zum siebzehnten Jahrhundert* (Halle, 1921); James Carney, *Studies in Irish Literature and History* (Dublin, 1955); David Greene, 'Táin Bó Cúailnge', in *Irish Sagas*, ed. Myles Dillon (Dublin, 1968), 93–104; Eleanor Hull, *The Cuchullin Saga of Irish Literature* (London, 1898); John V. Kelleher, 'The *Táin* and the Annals', *Ériu*, 22 (1971), 107–22; J. P. Mallory (ed.,) *Aspects of the Táin* (Belfast, 1992); *Studien zur Táin Bó Cuailnge* (Tübingen, 1993).

Adaptations and popularizations: Kenneth C. Flint, *A Storm Upon Ulster* (New York, 1981); Gregory Frost, *Táin* (New York, 1986); Augusta Gregory, *Cuchulain of Muirthemne* (London, 1902); Horselips, *The Táin* [rock music] (London, 1973); Mary Hutton, *The Táin* (Dublin, 1907, 1948); Liam MacUistin, *The Tain* [juvenile fiction] (Dublin, 1989); Joan Denise Moriarty, *The Táin* [ballet] (Dublin, 1981); Nuala Ní Dhomhnaill's five poems, sometimes subtitled the *Atáin*, offer feminist commentary, *Selected Poems/Rogha Dánta* (Dublin, 1988), 110–25.

Tair Rhamant, Y [W, Three Romances]. Conventional Welsh title for **Geraint ac Enid*, **Owain*, and **Peredur* seen as a trilogy. Manuscripts for the three romances survive whole or in part in the **Red Book of Hergest* and the **White Book of Rhydderch*, and are often included with modern translations of the **Mabinogi/Mabinogion*.

Taise 1, Tasha [Ir. *taise*, mild, gentle, kind, compassionate]. Beautiful daughter of Gilla Decair in **Tóraigheacht an Ghiolla Dheacair* [The Pursuit of the Hard Gilly/Difficult Servant] whose marriage to *Fionn mac Cumhaill releases the *Fianna from imprisonment by her father.

2. Daughter of a 'king of Greece' in love with *Fionn mac Cumhaill in *Fenian oral tradition.

Tálcend, Taillcenn, (corruptly) Taillkenn, Talkenn, Talkend [Ir. *tálcend*, adze-head; cf. W *talcen*, forehead]. Nickname for St. *Patrick in his contentious dialogues with the *Fenian heroes *Oisín and *Caílte. The unflattering implications of the word presumably play on the shape of Patrick's bishop's mitre and his hard-headed unwillingness to listen to the other side.

Taliesin [W *tal*, brow, forehead; *iesin*, radiant, beautiful]. Divine or divinely inspired poet of Wales, often thought to be historical (late 6th cent.) and to have flourished in the Old North, i.e. formerly Welsh-speaking regions of the Scottish Lowlands. Classed with *Aneirin as one of the two surviving *cynfeirdd [oldest poets], Taliesin was ascribed by Sir Ifor Williams (1944) twelve poems of the sixty in the **Book of Taliesin*, compiled *c*.1275. Two highly incompatible versions of Taliesin's life survive. In the older, supported by the ascribed twelve poems from the *Book of Taliesin*, he is the author of praise poems filled with realistic detail of chieftains like *Urien and *Owain who warred against the encroaching Angles, 550–600. The second version, developed much later and known chiefly in the *Hanes Taliesin* [Tale of Taliesin] or *Ystoria Taliesin* [History of Taliesin], places the poet further south, in *Powys, and portrays him as an immortal in the service of a series of princelings.

Highly folkloric but with traces of pre-Christian religious belief, the *Hanes Taliesin* was compiled by Llywelyn Siôn (1540-*c*.1615) and given wide readership by Lady Charlotte Guest in her translation of *The Mabinogion* (1838–49). In the days of *Maelgwn Gwynedd (6th cent.), the *shape-shifting goddess *Ceridwen lives at the bottom of *Bala Lake with her husband *Tegid Foel, after whom the lake [W *Llyn Tegid*] is named. She brews a magic *cauldron named Amen whose contents she intends for her own ugly son *Morfran [sea crow, also known as *Afagddu*, utter darkness], so that he may be gifted with poetic talent. Her wishes are thwarted when her servant, *Gwion Bach, catches three drops from the cauldron on his thumb and forefingers, which he thrusts into his mouth, giving himself the poetic gift. Enraged, Ceridwen sets after Gwion Bach, after which each of them undergoes a series of metamorphoses: he becomes a hare, and she a greyhound; he a *salmon, and she an *otter; he a bird, and she a hawk; he a grain of wheat, and she a hen who swallows him. Magically, this grain of wheat impregnates Ceridwen; what had been Gwion Bach is reborn from her womb as a creature of such great beauty that she cannot kill him and so casts him adrift on the sea. The infant drifts to the weir, near Aberystwyth, of *Gwyddno Garanhir, whose son *Elffin finds him on *Calan Mai [May Day], exclaiming as he opens the blanket, 'Dyma dâl iesin!' [what a beautiful forehead]. The child, although only three days old, answers with the words, 'Taliesin bid' [let it be Taliesin]. When he grows older the boy Taliesin accompanies Elffin to the court of Maelgwn Gwynedd at Degannwy (near the mouth of the *Conway river, north Wales), where he successfully overcomes the poets of the king's household by his magic and the demonstration of his superior poetic powers. This victory enhances the fortunes of the feckless Elffin, who fosters Taliesin until he is 13. Emboldened by his changed fortune, Elffin boasts to Maelgwn's court that his wife is the fairest in the kingdom, his horses the swiftest, and his poet (Taliesin) the wisest. For this arrogance Maelgwn imprisons him and sends his son the irresistible seducer, Rhun [grand, awful], to test Elffin's wife's virtue. But Taliesin saves his foster-father on all counts. He substitutes a female servant for Elffin's wife, and although the helpless girl succumbs to Rhun, Elffin is able to prove his wife is innocent. In a magnificent song of his origins from the time of Lucifer's fall, Taliesin sings so wonderfully as to release Elffin from his chains. Finally, Elffin's horses defeat Maelgwn's and a jockey drops his cap, following Taliesin's instructions, revealing a compensatory cauldron of gold.

Abundant references from Welsh tradition partially reconcile the seemingly historical 6th-century Taliesin of the Old North with the magical poet-seer of the *Hanes Taliesin*. In the second branch of the **Mabinogi*, for example, Taliesin is one of seven men to escape from Ireland after the death of *Bendigeidfran. From the 11th to the 13th centuries a large body of prophetic poems predicting the defeat of the Saxons and the Normans were ascribed to Taliesin. His name was frequently associated with that of *Myrddin [Merlin] rather than Aneirin. The two were thought to be in constant exchange of occult and arcane *knowledge, as in the 11th-century poem **Ymddiddan Myrddin a Thaliesin*. In *Geoffrey of Monmouth's *Vita Merlini* (*c*.1149), Merlin, as transformed from Myrddin, discourses with one Telgesinus, a Latinization which had little further life. Tradition has him buried both near Aberystwyth and at *Bangor. Taliesin remained little known outside Welsh tradition until the 19th century. Taliesin became a character in Thomas Love Peacock's satirical novel *The Misfortunes of Elphin* (1829), partially based on *Hanes Taliesin*, and was expanded into a more dramatic character in the novels of Anglo-Welsh fantasist Charles Williams (1886–1945). Welsh-American architect Frank Lloyd Wright (1869–1959) made Taliesin a personal culture hero, naming two estates, in Wisconsin and Arizona, for him. See KOADALAN; TUAN MAC CAIRILL.

Texts: *Canu Taliesin*, ed. Ifor Williams (Cardiff, 1960); *The Poems of Taliesin: English Version by J. E. Caerwyn Williams*, ed. Ifor Williams (Dublin, 1975, 1987). An unreliable version of *Hanes Taliesin* is found in vol. iii of Lady Charlotte Guest's *The Mabinogion* (London, 1849), 356 ff. Cf. Patrick K. Ford, 'A Fragment of the Hanes Taliesin by Llywelyn Siôn', *Études Celtiques*, 14 (1975), 449–58. A late version of the story by Elis Gruffydd is translated by Patrick K. Ford, 'The Tale of Taliesin', in *The Mabinogi and Other Medieval Welsh Tales* (Berkeley and Los Angeles, Calif., 1977), 164–81; *Ystoria Taliesin*, trans. Patrick K. Ford (Cardiff, 1992).

Studies: John Morris-Jones, 'Taliesin', *Y Cymmrodor* [London], 28 (1918), 1–290; Ifor Williams, *Lectures on Early Welsh Poetry* (Dublin, 1944); Rachel Bromwich, 'The Character of the Early Welsh Tradition', in Nora K. Chadwick (ed.), *Studies in Early British History* (Cambridge, 1959), 83–136; Marged Haycock, '*Llyfr Taliesin*', dissertation, University of Wales (Cardiff, 1983); 'Llyfr Taliesin', *National Library of Wales Journal*, 25 (1988), 357–86; A. O. H. Jarman and G. R. Hughes, *A Guide to Welsh Literature* (Swansea, 1976); Juliette Wood, 'The Folklore Background of the Gwion Bach Section of Hanes Taliesin', *Bulletin of the Board of Celtic Studies*, 29(4) (May 1982), 621–34.

Tara, Temair, Teamhair, Temuir; the anglicized Tara derives from the genitive form Teamhrach [Ir. *Temair*, dark one (?); spectacle (?); elevated place (?); assembly hall (?); free-standing eminence of wide prospect; the *Lebor Gabála* contrives the etymology *téa múr*, Téa's wall]. Hill (507 feet) in Co. Meath, 6 miles SE of Navan, where the Irish *ard rí [high king] is said to have had his seat. One of the most famous sites in the Celtic world, partially because of well-meaning but romantic misreadings of evidence by 19th-century poets and fiction-writers, Tara is unspectacular to visit, yet excavations there have yielded abundant and interesting information. According to the pseudo-history **Lebor*

Gabála [Book of Invasions], the mortal *Milesians named the site Temair after *Éremón's queen, *Téa, displacing the earlier name, *Druim Caín. Other names applied to Tara are: Cathair Crofhind, Druim Léith, and Fordruim. Forms of the name Temair survive elsewhere, e.g. Tara hill (831 feet), 4 miles NE of Gorey, Co. Wexford.

From the earliest Irish history Tara was an important centre of religious ceremony, sacred to *Medb, then considered a goddess, or to her double, *Medb Lethderg [red side]. It had been a burial site as early as the second millennium BC. Tara was the seat of kings who were also over-kings of the region and heads of the *Uí Néill federation, and thus the most powerful leaders in all Ireland. Central to each kingship was the ritual mating with the local earth-goddess in a ritual banquet, the feis temrach [feast of Tara] at *Samain time; see also KINGSHIP; BANAIS RÍGHE. The Uí Néill were named for *Niall Noígiallach [of the Nine Hostages], who had supposedly seized Tara from the *Leinstermen in the 5th century, before Christianization. As the Irish rule of descent (see DERBFHINE) did not foster an orderly distribution of property, Niall's many sons carved up what had been his hegemony. Later 'king of Tara' was only an honorary title for a ruler whose seat was often far distant. Beginning with *Sláinge, said to have reigned in the 20th century BC, the Annals list many monarchs of Tara, both pagan and Christian. The advance of Christianity may have led to the suppression of the highly pagan feis temrach; *Diarmait mac Cerbaill was the last to celebrate it. Later ecclesiastical writers invented the story of St Rúadán's curse upon Diarmait in a Church/State dispute. Testimony in the Annals implies that Tara was by no means abandoned even two centuries later. The Uí Néill continued to refer to their leaders as 'kings of Tara', although the site itself became overgrown. In time the hill also attracted one of the largest of the medieval *fairs [OIr. *óenach*; ModIr. *aonach*], held triennially at Samain, and comparable to those held at *Tailtiu, *Tlachtga, and *Uisnech; the legendary king *Ollam Fódla is thought to have begun the fair.

Much of the action of early Irish literature either takes place at Tara or touches upon it, but always from a distant narrative point of view, i.e. on the assumption that events portrayed had taken place in the past. The stories of *Conaire Mór depict a magical kingdom at Tara. The most important mythical king of Tara is *Cormac mac Airt, whose court may have been derived from Uí Néill ambitions or aspirations. The young *Fionn mac Cumhaill earns his first heroic distinction by slaying the 'burner', *Aillén mac Midgna, who comes to prey upon the 'palace' each year. *Lóegaire mac Néill is the king of Tara who meets St *Patrick.

Many features of the Tara site bear English names of modern provenance, some from an imaginative reading of the Dindshenchas; their long-term popularity makes them irresistible, even when there is scant evidence to shore up their purported associations. These include:

Adamnán's Cross. Upright stone attributed to St *Adamnán, St *Colum Cille's biographer, containing vague outlines of a female figure, possible a *Sheela-na-gig.

The 'Banqueting Hall' [Ir. *tech midchuarta, teach miodhchuarta*]. Rectangular earthwork, 750 by 90 feet, which does not match the descriptions of the five-sided banqueting hall in medieval literature. Recent scholarship favours an entrance-way for horses and chariots.

Cormac's House [Ir. *teach Cormaic*]. Small earthwork enclosed by the Fort/Rath of Kings (see below) at whose centre stands the Lia Fáil (see below). Named for the mythical king of Tara, Cormac mac Airt.

Fort/Rath of the Kings [Ir. *ráth na ríogh*]. Also known as the Royal Enclosure. Large, oval hill-fort, 950 by 800 feet, which nearly encircles three other earthworks (Cormac's House, the Mound of Hostages, the Royal Seat) and the Lia Fáil.

Fort/Rath of the Synods. Trivallate earthwork once thought to have been the site of a meeting between St Patrick and St *Brendan as well as other non-contemporaries. In the late 19th century British Israelites mutilated portions of the earthworks looking for the Ark of the Covenant. Later excavations showed timber palisades from the 1st and 3rd centuries AD.

Lia Fáil [stone of destiny]. Twelve-foot erect pillar-stone, 6 feet above ground, made of granular limestone, not quarried in the district, raised to honour the dead of the 1798 revolution. Found lying horizontally near the Mound of Hostages, it was moved to the centre of Cormac's House and is now marked with the letters 'R.I.P.' Assertions that it is identical with the ancient *Lia Fáil or mythical *Fál are less than convincing.

Mound of the Hostages [Ir. *dumha na ngiall*]. Small earthworks at the north end of the Fort/ Rath of the Kings. Records indicate that the 'Lia Fáil' now standing at Cormac's House (see above) should have been here before 1798.

Ráth Gráinne [Gráinne's fort, Gráinne's enclosure]. A burial-mound between the Banqueting Hall and the Sloping Trenches, fancifully thought to be the place whence *Gráinne eloped with *Diarmait while betrothed to *Fionn mac Cumhaill.

Ráth Lóegaire, Ráth Laoghaire [Laoghaire's fort, Leary's fort]. Large, univallate ring-fort associated with Lóegaire mac Néill, the king of Tara at the time of St Patrick.

Ráth Meidbe, Rath Maeve [Ir., Maeve's fort]. A univallate hill-fort, 750 feet in diameter, half a mile S of the centre of Tara. Although queen of *Connacht, *Medb is cited at Tara in **Fled Bricrenn* [Briccriu's Feast] and elsewhere.

Royal Seat [Ir. *Forradh*]. Small earthworks adjacent to Cormac's House (see above).

Sloping Trenches [Ir. *Claoin-fhearta*]. Two unusual ring-earthworks in the far north-west of the site.

See George Petrie, *History and Antiquities of Tara Hill* (Dublin, 1839); Josef Baudiš, 'On the Antiquity of the Kingship at Tara', *Ériu*, 8 (1916), 101–7; R. A. S. Macalister, *Tara: A Pagan Sanctuary of Ancient Ireland* (London, 1931); Seán P. Ó Ríordáin, *Tara: The Monuments on the Hill* (Dundalk, 1954, 1971); 'Tara', in G. E. Daniel (ed.), *Myth of Legend* (London, 1954), 49–59; D. A. Binchy, 'The Fair of Tailtiu and the Feast of Tara', *Ériu*, 18 (1958), 113–38; E. Estyn Evans, *Prehistoric and Early Christian Ireland, a Guide* (London, 1966); Francis J. Byrne, *Irish Kings and High-Kings* (London, 1973); Michael Herity and George Eogan, *Ireland in Prehistory* (London, 1977).

Taran [W *taran*, thunder]. Welsh hero, survivor of the battle between *Bendigeidfran and *Matholwch, and the father of Glunen/ Gluneu. He became the basis for Lloyd Alexander's Welsh-influenced series of juvenile fiction, *Taran Wanderer* (New York, 1980) and its sequels. Philologically related to *Taranis.

Taranis, Taranos, Taranus [W, Bret. *taran*, thunder]. One of the three principal divinities, along with *Esus and *Teutates, of *Gaul and Britain, according to the Roman poet Lucan (1st cent. AD) in his *Pharsalia*, on the subject of Julius *Caesar's conquest 100 years earlier. While each of the deities was propitiated with human sacrifice, according to Lucan, the cult of Taranis was crueller than that of the *Scythian *Diana; victims could be burned alive in wooden vessels. Speculation on the death of the 4th-cent. BC man found in *Lindow bog in 1984 has suggested that he may have been sacrificed to either Taranis or Teutates. A 9th-century commentary on Lucan describes Taranis as a 'master of war' and links him to *Jupiter. But from what we know, Taranis is only an embodiment of the natural force of thunder and lacks the complexity and wide-ranging functions of the Roman sky-god. Other commentators link Taranis to the Roman *Dis Pater and to the British *Etharún and *Etirun. Archaeological evidence does not, however, support Lucan's contentions. The name of Taranis survives on only seven altars, and although they range from Britain to the Balkans, their size and implied wealth does not match that of gods like Gaulish *Mercury, whose worship is much more widespread. See Paul-Marie Duval, 'Teutatés, Esus, Taranis', *Études Celtiques*, 8 (1958), 41–58; Miranda J. Green, 'Tanarus, Taranis and the Chester Altar', *Chester Archaeological Society*, 65 (1982), 37–44.

tarbfheis, tarbhfheis, tarb feis [Ir., bull feast]. See BULL; KINGSHIP.

tarbh uisge [ScG, water-bull]. Malevolent *bull of Scottish Gaelic tradition that emerges from the sea by moonlight to terrorize the countryside. A huge black monster, its head is as black as a thunder cloud, its nostrils redder than lightning, and its great bull neck breaks the waves. Calves born with split ears have been fathered by the tarbh uisge and so should be killed at birth before they bring disaster to the herd. See also TARROO USHTEY.

tarroo ushtey, theroo ushta [Manx, water-bull]. Malevolent *bull of Manx tradition, clearly adapted from the *tarbh uisge of Scottish Gaelic tradition. It lives in swamps and shallower pools, and sometimes roams the fields among the farm cattle; less malign than the *cabyll-ushtey.

Tarvos trigaranus, Tarvostrigaranus [bull with three cranes/egrets; three-horned]. Latin name for a presumably Celtic deity represented in two stone sculptures surviving in Paris and Trier, Germany. As his name implies, the figure is clearly a *bull, accompanied by three long-legged marsh birds, which may be either *cranes or *egrets, both of which have much resonance in Celtic tradition. In the Paris sculpture, uncovered under Notre-Dame cathedral in 1711, Tarvos trigaranus is represented with *Esus, *Cernunnos, and *Smertrius. While the Paris sculpture is dedicated to *Jupiter, a comparable representation in Trier is dedicated to *Mercury; the imagery is much the same but the name Tarvos does not appear.

Téa, Tea. Queen of King *Éremón, the *Milesian leader, for whom *Tara was named. The *Fir Bolg had called the site Druim Caín, but in renaming it the Milesians made it their own. According to the pseudo-history **Lebor Gabála* [Book of Invasions], Téa begged her husband to commemorate her with a rampart round her grave like the one she had seen before leaving Spain. Whatever the root meaning of Téa, it was taken to be an element in the name Temair; See TEMAIR LUACHRA, residence of the south *Munster kings.

Teach Miodhchuarta. Irish name for the 'Banqueting Hall' at *Tara.

Teague. See TADG.

Teamhair. ModIr. word for *Tara.

Teathbha. ModIr. spelling of *Tethba.

Tech Duinn, nDuinn [Ir., Donn's house]. An Irish name for the *Otherworld, specifically as the realm of the dead; it is the 'house' of *Donn (1), ruler of the dead. Although Tech Duinn as described in some texts lies beyond mortal geography, it is often identified with a rocky islet near Dursey Island at the extreme western end of the Beare peninsula, Co. Cork. When it is not sited so specifically, Tech Duinn is still linked with *Munster.

Tech Midchuarta. Irish name for the 'Banqueting Hall' at *Tara.

Teffia. Anglicization of *Tethba.

Tegau Eurfron, Eurvron. Golden-haired paragon of beauty and virtue in Welsh Arthurian tradition, one of the three splendid maidens of *Arthur's court, along with *Dyfr and *Enid; wife of *Caradog Freichfras. She was thought to have rescued Caradog from a poisonous snake, causing her to be bitten on the breast, which was removed and replaced with gold to save her life. Her cloak, a treasure of ancient Britain, could not be worn by any woman who had broken her marriage vow.

Tegid Foel, Tegyd Foël, Voel [W *teg*, beautiful; *foel*, bald]. *Giant of Pennllyn, husband of *Ceridwen in the folkloric *Hanes Taliesin* [Tale of *Taliesin], and eponym of *Llyn Tegid. His name is also cited in early Welsh genealogies and pedigrees.

Teilo [W form of Eludd]. Sixth-century Welsh saint, contemporary of *Dewi Sant, characterized by zeal and asceticism, active in south *Wales and *Brittany. Many wells, chapels, and churches bear his name, including the centre of his cult, Llandeilo Fawr, Carmarthenshire. Although his cult spread to Brittany, modern commentators reject *Geoffrey of Monmouth's (12th cent.) suggestion that Teilo was appointed archbishop of Dol there. A 12th-century *Life of Teilo* survives in two versions.

teinm laída, laéda, laeda, laído, laogha, laegda, láida [Ir., chewing or breaking open of the pith (?)]. An incantation of *divination used by the *fili and other poets in early Ireland. In the *Fenian Cycle it is invariably associated with the powers *Fionn mac Cumhaill gains by chewing on his thumb and chanting; T. F. O'Rahilly (1946) felt that it was Fionn's prerogative alone. The 10th-century **Sanas Cormaic* [Cormac's Glossary] cites teinm laída as one of the three ways of acquiring prophetic or hidden knowledge, along with *díchetal do chennaib and *imbas forosnai. Earlier speculation that teinm laída is derived from the Norse teinar-laigðir [thorn staves] and thus is anticipated in *Tacitus' *Germania* is now rejected. At present there is no learned agreement over just which procedures would bring teinm laída into motion, but some commentators argue that *fios [occult knowledge] and teinm laída combine in imbas forosnai. As with other forms of *divination, St *Patrick banned teinm laída as 'giving offerings to demons'. See also DIVINATION; SHAMANISM.

See T. F. O'Rahilly, 'Teinm Laeda', in *Early Irish History and Mythology* (Dublin, 1946), 336–40; Edward J. Gwynn, 'Athirne's Mother', *Zeitschrift für celtische Philologie*, 18 (1927), 156.

Teltown, Telltown. Hamlet in Co. Meath, Ireland, 4 miles SE of Kells, site of the ancient *Tailtiu celebration.

Temair. Ir. spelling of *Tara.

Temair Luachra, Temuir Luachra. Royal residence of the south *Munster kings, especially *Eochaid mac Luchta, possibly in *Kerry. Sometimes also thought to be the residence of *Cú Roí.

Temuir. Ir. spelling of *Tara.

Tène, La. See LA TÈNE.

tenm láida. Variant form of *teinm laída.

téte brec [twinkling hoard]. See CONCHOBAR MAC NESSA; EMAIN MACHA.

Tethba, Tethbae, Tethbe, Teathbha, Teffia. Region in pre-Norman *Ireland, coextensive with the modern counties of Longford and Westmeath. More specifically, Tethba adjoins the *Shannon, centring on the modern town of Granard, south of Lough Sheelin and north of the Inny River. See Margaret E. Dobbs, 'The Territory and People of Tethba', *Journal of the Royal Society of Antiquaries of Ireland*, 68 (1938), 241–59.

Tethra. Chief of the semi-divine *Fomorians, nephew of *Forgall Manach, who comes to be seen as a king of the *Otherworld. Seen as a Fomorian, Tethra wields the sword Orna savagely but is none the less killed at the Second Battle of Mag Tuired [**Cath Maige Tuired*]. Before the writing of the *Mythological Cycle, wherein this literary characterization was created, Tethra was evidently a divinity, probably of the sea. In later texts Tethra re-emerges as deity, now of the happy Otherworld, sometimes as the consort of *Badb in place of *Néit.

Teutates [*teuto-valos*, god of the tribe/people; cf. W *tud*, tribe; Ir. **tuath*, tribe]. One of the three principal divinities of *Gaul, along with *Taranis and *Esus, according to the Roman poet Lucan (1st cent. AD) in his *Pharsalia*, on the subject of Julius Caesar's conquest, 100 years earlier. As Lucan reports, each divinity was propitiated with human sacrifice; and a 9th-century commentary on Lucan claims that Teutates favoured drowning, especially on 1 November (*Samain). Modern commentators on the 4th-3rd cent. BC *Gundestrup Cauldron profess to identify Teutates with the figure plunging victims into a vat of water. Speculation on the 4th- cent. BC execution of the man found in *Lindow bog in 1984 has suggested he may have been a ritual sacrifice to Teutates or Taranis. A war-god, Teutates may be linked both to *Mars, who bears the epithet Mars Toutates from a site in Barkway, Hertfordshire, and to Gaulish *Mercury.

Despite the considerable number of inscriptions to Teutates in both Gaul and Britain, he remains a fairly shadowy figure, as his name is most likely a title, making him a tribal protector; such a title might be granted to any number of different divinities. The name of the Irish genealogical hero *Tuathal Techtmar may derive from the same stem. See Paul-Marie Duval, 'Teutatés, Esus, Taranis', *Études Celtiques*, 8 (1958), 41–58; *Les Dieux de la Gaule* (Paris, 1976), 29–31.

Teyrnon Twrf Liant, Teirnyon [Bryth. *Tigernonos*, great king; W *twrf liant*, roar of the sea]. Lord of *Gwent Is Coed in the first branch of the **Mabinogi* who, along with his wife, becomes a foster-parent of the child of *Rhiannon and *Pwyll, whom he names *Gwri Gwallt Euryn [Golden Hair]. When Gwri is in his fourth year, Teyrnon realizes his resemblance to Pwyll and restores him to his birth parents, who call him *Pryderi.

theroo ushta. Variant spelling of *tarroo ushtey.

Thincsus. Sometime epithet of Gaulish *Mars.

Thomond [OIr. *Tuadmumu, Tuadmumain*; ModIr. *Tuathmhumhain*]. Anglicized name for North *Munster, the petty kingdom of the O'Briens, which separated from the rest of Munster in the 12th century. From shortly after the conquest, 1169, until the reign of James I (1603–25) Thomond was considered a part of *Connacht. With the shiring of Ireland in the 17th century, most of Thomond became Co. Clare, but historically the name also refers to portions of adjacent counties Limerick and Tipperary.

three. See TRIPLISM.

Three Romances, The. See TAIR RHAMANT, Y.

Three Sorrows of Storytelling, Three Sorrowful Stories of Erin. See TRÍ TRUAGHA NA SGÉALAIGHEACHTA.

thumb of knowledge. See KNOWLEDGE; FIONN MAC CUMHAILL.

Tigernach, Tighearnach, Tiarnach [Ir. *tigern*, lord]. Name borne by a large number of early Irish ecclesiastics and saints, of whom the best-known are the Tigernach patron of Clones, Co. Monaghan, and Tigernach Ua Braoin (d. 1088) of *Clonmacnoise, who began compiling the **Annals of Tigernach*. The second name is sometimes anglicized as Tierney O'Breen.

Tigernmas, Tighernmas, Tiernmas. Legendary *ard rí of early Ireland, credited with the introduction of gold-smelting and the worship of *Crom Crúaich.

Tintagel [Corn. *dyn*, fortress; *tagell*, neck, constriction]. Picturesque site of a ruined castle on a 300-foot cliff, almost separated from the mainland, north shore of Cornwall, 5 miles NW of Camelford. Although Tintagel was actually the *Dumnonian royal seat before the 7th century, its legendary aura was mostly invented in medieval times. Earlier described as a monastic site, it does not figure in any saints' lives nor does it have a cemetery. In Arthurian associations alone Tintagel is the rival of *Glastonbury. *Uthr Bendragon/Uther Pendragon is usually thought to have conceived *Arthur here, upon *Igerna, then the wife of the Duke of Cornwall. In stories after the 12th century, Tintagel is the usual home of King *Mark. It inspired Sir Arnold Bax's symphonic poem *Tintagel* (1917). In the late 20th century, it is an enormously popular tourist destination. See Charles Thomas, *Tintagel Castle* (London, 1986); *Book of Tintagel: Arthur and Archaeology* (London, 1993); Oliver J. Padel, *The Arthur of the Welsh* (Cardiff, 1991), 229 ff.

Tír, Tír-. Irish word for land, first element in countless real and imaginary place-names, previously anglicized as Tyr-. See MAG [plain].

Tír Chonaill, Conaill, Tir Connell [Ir., land of Conall]. Kingdom named after *Conall Gulban, son of *Niall Noígiallach [of the Nine Hostages], part of the northern *Uí Néill federation, coextensive not only with modern Co. *Donegal but with most of the land from Lough Foyle to Ballysadare, Co. Sligo.

Tír Eógain, Eoghain, Tirowen [Ir., land of Eógan]. Kingdom named after *Eógan (1), son of *Niall Noígiallach [of the Nine Hostages], part of the northern *Uí Néill federation, coextensive with modern Co. Tyrone and portions of Derry and *Donegal, although the influence of Tír Eógain power was felt over many miles. In later centuries Tír Eógain was also the realm of the O'Neill family, a subdivision of Cenél Eógain named for *Niall Glúndub (d. 919).

Tír fo Thuinn, T'r fo Thuinn (ScG), Tír fa Thonn, Tir-fa-Tonn, Tir-na-Thonn [Ir. *tonn*, wave, i.e. Land under Wave]. Imagined realm under the seas, one of the many places where the *Tuatha Dé Danann would have fled after their defeat by the *Milesians. The 'Hard Gilly' leads the *Fianna here in **Tóraigheacht an Ghiolla Dheacair* [The Pursuit of the Hard Gilly/Difficult Servant]. In parts of Gaelic Scotland such as the isle of Tiree, Tír fo Thuinn might also be known as An tEilean Uaine [the Green Island]. See also OTHERWORLD; SUBMERGED CITIES.

Tír inna mBan. Variant form of *Tír na mBan.

Tír inna mBéo. Variant form of *Tír na mBéo.

Tír na mBan, inna mBan, na mban [*ban* (gen. pl.), women; i.e. Land of Women]. Imagined island populated only by beautiful, sexually inviting women, visited by many Irish heroes, notably Máel Dúin in **Imram Curaig Maíle Dúin* [The Voyage of Máel Dúin]. The women of the island provide a consort for every male visitor and serve only the best cuisine with the most enchanting music. Bran of **Imram Brain* [The Voyage of Bran] was summoned by the queen of Tír na mBan and stayed for many years, thinking but a single year had passed. This is an Irish instance of a widespread folk motif: F112. See also OTHERWORLD.

Tír na mBéo, na mBeo, inna Beo, Tir-nan-Beo, Tir-nam-béo [OIr. *béo*, living, quick]. The Land of the Living, a place of everlasting life, one of several distant lands settled by the semi-divine *Tuatha Dé Danann after their defeat by the mortal *Milesians; in much of Irish oral tradition it is an *otherworldly paradise, little distinguishable from *Tír na nÓg and *Tír Tairngire. *Lug Lámfhota brought his sword *Frecraid [answerer] from Tír na mBeó. Folk motif: D1338.7. See also YNYS AFALLON.

Tír na nÓg, Tir nan Òg (ScG), Tír na n-Óc,

Tir na n-Óg, Tir-nam-Oge, Tir na Nog; also Eilean na nOg (ScG) [Ir. *óg*, youth, i.e. Land of Youths]. Land of Youth, or the Ever-Young, in early Irish tradition. The most widely known of all the *otherworldly lands [Tír] from early Irish tradition, probably because of its portrayal in Micheál Coimín's 1750 Irish-language poem *Laoi Oisín i dTír na nÓg* [The Lay of *Oisín in the Land of Youth], wherein the *Fenian hero Oisín spends 300 years with the beautiful *Niamh of the Golden Hair without knowing sickness, age, or decay, and thinks it but a day until his return to the realm of mortals. Bran also visits the land in **Imram Brain* [The Voyage of Bran]. Earlier Tír na nÓg is one of the many lands thought to have been settled by the semi-divine *Tuatha Dé Danann after their defeat by the *Milesians. Although Tír na nÓg should lie beyond the confines of any map, it is often perceived to be west of Ireland. Long-standing oral tradition places its entrance at Liscannor Bay, Co. Clare, south of the cliffs of Moher. In 1861 Bryan O'Looney wrote that Tír na nÓg was a beautiful city surrounded by white breaking waves between Liscannor and Lahinch. It is also associated with a cave on Knockadoon Island in Lough *Gur and Rathlin Island, north of Co. Antrim. See David B. Spaan, 'The Otherworld in Early Irish Literature', dissertation, University of Michigan (Ann Arbor, 1969); Bryan O'Looney (trans.), 'The Lay of Oisín in the Land of Youth', *Transactions of the Ossianic Society*, 4 (1861), 227–80. T. Gwynn Jones partially reshaped the concept in his Welsh-language ode *Tir na n-Óg* (1910). Folk motifs: D1338.7; F172.1; F377; F378.1. See also OTHERWORLD; YNYS AFALLON; HERLA, KING; ROCA BARRAIDH.

Tír na Thonn. Variant form of *Tír fo Thuinn.

Tír Tairngire, Tairngiri, Tairn-Gire, Tir Tarraingthe [Ir. *tairgire*, *tarngaire*, prophecy, promise]. The Land of Promise, one of several *otherworldly paradises from early Irish tradition, much associated with *Manannán mac Lir, although he does not rule here. The goal of many *eachtrada [adventures] is to reach Tír Tairngire. St *Brendan is seeking it in his *Navigatio*, and *Cormac mac Airt visits the Fountain of Knowledge in **Echtrae Chormaic*. Manannán takes his three-day-old son *Mongán here to gain otherworldly knowledge; the latter stays for many years. The youthful *Ciabhán is taken here but, according to some texts, elopes with the beautiful *Clídna. After her adultery here with *Gaidiar, Manannán's son, *Bé Chuma is expelled. The *Tuatha Dé Danann bring the *rowan tree from Tír Tairngire. In **Echtrae Airt meic Cuinn* [The Adventure of Art Son of Conn], the rulers of Tír Tairngire are *Dáire (2) and *Rígru Rosclethan, called 'sinless' because they have intercourse only to produce their *otherworldly son *Ségda Sáerlabraid. Myles Dillon and Nora Chadwick (1967) see an Icelandic anticipation of Tír Tairngire in Ódainsakr [the field of the not dead] and Land lifanda manna [the land of living men]. See also EMAIN ABLACH; MAG MELL.

Tirowen. Anglicization of *Tír Eógain.

Tlachtga, Tlachta. One of the great assemblies or fairs [OIr. *óenach*; ModIr. *aonach*] of early Ireland, and the *druid's daughter for which it was named. Tlachtga, a sorceress, was the daughter of *Mug Ruith, the archdruid of Ireland, from whom she learned much secret wisdom; she travelled with him to the world's seats of learning and brought home magical stones from Italy. After having been raped by the three sons of *Simon Magus (often associated with her father), she gave birth to triplets (see TRIPLISM) on the hill in Co. Meath that was to bear her name. Like *Macha (3), she died of grief after the children were delivered; over her a fortress was built.

The fair or assembly of Tlachtga took place on a site now identified as Ward Hill (390 feet), 2 miles E of Athboy, 12 miles W of Tara, 8 miles SW of Tailtiu, Co. Meath, whose celebrations were comparable. Like *Uisnech, the Ward Hill site contains the ruins (much disturbed in Cromwellian times) of a massive ring-fort, consisting of four concentric banks and ditches, surrounding a 25-foot platform crowning the hilltop. The focus of the ceremonies, thought to have been begun by *Lug Lámfhota, was the lighting of the winter fires at *Samain [1 November]. Although the rulers of the intermittent kingdom of *Mide sat here, Tlachtga was often associated with the province of *Munster; the site lies in the contemporary county of *Meath, a part of modern *Leinster, in territory coextensive with the medieval kingdom of *Brega. The fabulous flying-machine constructed by Mug Ruith and Simon Magus, *roth rámach [Ir., rowing wheel], was sighted here. At Tlachtga in 1168 Ruaidrí Ua

Conchobair, last *ard rí [high king] of Ireland, presided over a national synod of kings and prelates; 13,000 horsemen are said to have attended.

Tochmarc [Ir., wooing]. Conventional first word in the title of a class of early Irish narratives. See also TÓRAIGHEACHT [pursuit].

Tochmarc Becfhola. See BECFOLA.

Tochmarc Emire. See EMER.

Tochmarc Étaíne. Irish title of a narrative from the *Mythological Cycle usually known in English as The Wooing of Étaín. Dating from perhaps the 8th or 9th centuries, mutilated and disconnected fragments of the story survive in the **Yellow Book of Lecan* [*Lebor Buide Lecáin*]. During the 1930s R. I. Best discovered long-missing pages, but the whole is still disconnected.

I. First we learn of Étaín's discovery by *Angus Óg, her involvement with *Midir, and her magical transformations. After the *Dagda wins the love of *Boand, tricking her husband *Elcmar (then lord of *Brug na Bóinne [Newgrange]), they give birth to Angus Óg, god of poetry and future lord of Brug na Bóinne. The child is given in fosterage to *Midir of *Brí Léith [near Ardagh, Co. Longford]. Later, when Angus reaches maturity and has taken possession of Brug na Bóinne, Midir comes to visit him. While a guest, Midir claims to have suffered an injury and demands as compensation the fairest maiden in all of Ireland, Étaín, daughter of *Ailill (3). Angus, with Dagda's aid, wins her for Midir by the Herculean task of clearing twelve plains, making twelve rivers, and delivering the equivalent of her weight in gold and silver.

Midir returns home with the prized Étaín but his first wife, *Fuamnach, understandably jealous, strikes her with a magical *rowan or quicken rod given by *Bresal Etarlám and turns her into a pool of water. Through heat and evaporation the pool becomes first a worm and then a purple fly (in some versions butterfly) of wonderful size and beauty that fills the air with fragrance and sweet music. Midir knows the fly as Étaín, and she stays by him. Fuamnach also knows the fly's identity and so causes a wind to drive her out to the rocks and waves of the sea. Étaín endures this misery for seven years until one day she alights upon the breast of Angus. He then carries her for some time in a sunlit crystal cage, but as soon as Fuamnach learns of it, she drives Étaín away again. She flies as far as a rooftop in *Ulster, after which she falls into a cup of the woman of the house, the wife of *Étar (1) of Inber Cichmaine, an Ulster king. She swallows the fly, and Étaín is reborn as the daughter of Étar. Although Étaín does not sense it, 1,012 years have elapsed since the time of her birth as daughter of Ailill (3) to her birth in the house of Étar.

II. In the second story 1,000 years have elapsed, the *Tuatha Dé Danann have retired to their fairy mounds, and the mortal *Milesians or Gaels now reign. Étaín is here married to the mortal *ard rí [high king] *Eochaid Airem, but her kindness almost leads her to betray him. When he becomes ard rí, the people refuse to pay Eochaid Airem tribute because he has no queen. As befits his station he seeks the most beautiful maiden in Ireland; his retainers find Étaín, daughter of Étar, for him, and he marries her. Alas, Eochaid's brother *Ailill Anglonnach is so smitten with Étaín's beauty that he falls sick with love for her, but he is shamed to speak it and thus no one can cure him. *Fachtna (1), Eochaid's chief physician, understands Ailill's distress and knows that only Étaín's love can cure it. Following his kingly duties, Eochaid leaves on a royal circuit of Ireland, leaving Étaín to attend to his dying brother; he asks that Ailill Anglonnach's grave be dug, lamentations be made for him, and that his cattle be slaughtered upon his death. Shortly after Eochaid departs Ailill Anglonnach confesses to Étaín the cause of his sickness. She responds that she is willing to heal him with her love, but not in her husband's residence; it would be better to tryst in a hilltop house outside the royal stronghold. But at the appointed hour a magical sleep comes upon Ailill, and an impostor in his likeness creeps into bed with Étaín. This occurs on three successive nights, by which time Étaín senses that she is not sleeping with Ailill, despite the love partner's appearance. She protests that it is not with him that she has made the tryst. The impostor then reveals himself to be Midir of Brí Léith, her husband from fairyland. He explains that he paid a great bride-price for her in gold and silver but that they have been parted by the jealousy of his first wife, Fuamnach. He has filled Ailill with longing for Étaín so that this meeting might be arranged. At last he asks Étaín to go away with him, but she refuses without the consent of her current husband, Eochaid Airem. When she returns to the stronghold Ailill is cured, and all rejoice that Étaín's honour has not been soiled by sleeping with her husband's brother.

III. The third story follows shortly upon the second. Midir's unfulfilled desire for Étaín prompts him to use trickery against her husband, Eochaid Airem. On a lovely summer day, Eochaid looks down from the ramparts at *Tara to see a warrior approaching; he wears purple and has long golden hair to his shoulders. Eochaid remarks that he does not know the stranger, but extends hospitality to him. The stranger says that he knows the identity of his host, and reveals himself as Midir of Brí Léith, challenging Eochaid to a game of *fidchell on a silver board with golden playing pieces. In three successive matches Eochaid is the victor, exacting rich prizes from Midir, including fifty horses and the building of a causeway across a bog in *Tethba. They agree that the winner may name the stakes in the fourth; and when Midir wins he asks to put his arms around Étaín and have a kiss from her. Eochaid is silent at first, but then agrees to grant the request in a month's time. On the appointed day Eochaid surrounds Tara with the armies and heroes of Ireland and secures the doors. Midir, appearing handsomer than ever, announces that Eochaid has given Étaín's very self to him, which makes her blush for shame. Eochaid sternly reminds him of the limits of the agreement and bids him take his embrace and kiss. Then, with his weapons in his left arm and Étaín clasped in his right, he rises up through the smoke-hole in the ceiling and flies away. The soldiers outside report seeing two *swans disappear in the distance.

Eochaid and his men resolve to have Étaín back, even if it means destroying every *sídh in Ireland. As Midir is thought to have flown to the sídh of *Femen in the south, Eochaid goes there, without success, and so destroys many others, at last going on to Midir's residence at Brí Léith, in the centre of Ireland. Midir responds by producing fifty women (in some accounts sixty) all in the shape of Étaín so that no one can tell who is the true queen. Eochaid asserts that he will know Étaín by the elegance with which she pours a drink; he then chooses who he thinks is his wife by this test, and resumes married life with her. But it is not Étaín. Midir, having bound Eochaid to no further recriminations, tells him that the true Étaín was pregnant when they left Tara, and thus the woman is his own daughter, another 'Étaín'; she should not be confused with yet another daughter, *Étaín Óg (see also below). Horrified at his deception, Eochaid Airem lays waste to Brí Léith, rescues the true Étaín, his wife, and returns with her to Tara. The child of Eochaid's incestuous union is put out to die, but she is found and raised by a herdsman and his wife; once mature, she has the stateliness of her royal forebears and is celebrated for her fine embroidery. King *Eterscél chooses her for his queen. Neither the 'daughter' Eochaid Airem chooses nor his (perhaps) incestuously begotten daughter are given names in the text. The suggestion that any child of Eochaid Airem should be mated with Eterscél conflicts with *Togail Bruidne Da Derga* [The Destruction of Da Derga's Hostel], where Eterscél mates with *Mes Buachalla, daughter of *Eochaid Feidlech, a brother of Eochaid Airem, and stepdaughter of Étaín Óg, yet another daughter of the true Étaín. Both Étaín and Mes Buachalla are described as being the 'mother' of *Conaire Mór; in each case Eterscél is the father. At this point, the narrative leads into *Togail Bruidne Da Derga*.

The standard text is by Osborn Bergin and R. I. Best, 'Tochmarc Étaíne', *Ériu*, 12 (1938), 137–96; and in response, Rudolf Thurneysen, 'Tochmarc Étaíne', *Zeitschrift für celtische Philologie*, 22 (1941), 3–23; Donnchadh Ó Corráin, 'Tochmarc Étaíne', in *Irisleabhar Mhá Nuad* (1962), 89–96; Christian-J. Guyonvarc'h translated the story into French, 'La Courtise d'Étain', *Celticum*, 15 (1966), 283–327; to which Françoise Le Roux added commentary, 328–75. Imaginative treatments in English include Lady Gregory's 'Midhir and Etain', in *Gods and Fighting Men* (London, 1904); Fiona MacLeod [pseud. of William Sharp], *The Immortal Hour* (published 1907), subsequently the basis of an opera of the same title by Rutland Boughton (1914); Moirin Cheavasa, *Midhir and Etain* (Dublin, 1920); and Patricia McDowell, *Daughter of the Boyne* (Dublin, 1992). Motifs within the story may be classed as F68 (Otherworld journeys) and F392 (marvellous creatures).

Togail, *Toghail* . . . [Ir., destruction]. Conventional first word in the titles of a class of early Irish narratives; Togla (pl.).

Togail Bruidne Da Derga, *Uí Derga.* Irish title for a narrative dating from at least the 11th century, composed possibly in the 8th or 9th centuries, usually known in English as The Destruction of Da Derga's Hostel. Although nominally a part of the *Ulster Cycle, the settings and character are in *Leinster. Texts are preserved in the **Book of the Dun Cow* [*Lebor na hUidre*] and the **Yellow Book of Lecan*. The beginning of the narrative appears to continue from **Tochmarc Étaíne* [The Wooing of Étaín], and contains a lush description of the resplendent princess of that story. The focus of the action, however, centres on the legendary king *Conaire Mór, the innocent victim of relentless fate.

Before Conaire Mór begins his just and prosperous rule at *Tara a number of seemingly unwarranted *gessa [taboos] are imposed upon him. He is told that: (*a*) birds must always be privileged in the kingdom; and he shall not (*b*) pass righthandwise [*deiseal*, i.e. *sunwise] around Tara nor lefthandwise [*túaithbel* i.e. *withershins] around *Brega; (*c*) hunt the 'crooked beasts' [*cláenmíla*] of Cerna; (*d*) stay away from Tara on any *ninth night; (*e*) sleep in a house from which the light of a fire is visible after sunset and into which one can see from the outside; (*f*) allow three red men to go before him into a red man's house; (*g*) allow plundering raiders to land during his reign; (*h*) allow a lone man or woman to visit his residence after sunset; (*i*) try to settle a quarrel between two of his subjects. In the course of the narrative, however, Conaire unintentionally violates every one of these. When his three foster-brothers, *Fer Gair, *Fer Lí, and Fer Rogain, sons or descendants of *Donn Désa, take to marauding, Conaire banishes them from Ireland. And when the three Ruadchoin of the *Cualu (south of the *Liffey) also begin marauding, he exiles them as well. At sea these exiles meet a band of reavers led by *one-eyed *Ingcél Cáech, a Briton, and together with the exiled sons of *Medb, all named *Maine, they ravage first Britain and then Ireland. In Britain they slay a local king along with Ingcél's parents and brothers. Setting sail for Ireland, they arrive first at *Howth, while Conaire is travelling to Da Derga's hostel (near either Bohernabreena, south Co. Dublin, or Glencree, Co. Wicklow). En route Conaire is enticed by the bizarre-looking *Fer Caille [man of the wood]. Once in the hostel Conaire is visited by a hideous female seer, *Cailbe, who prophesies that all of the defenders will be destroyed, except for what birds can take in their claws. Meanwhile, eager for both revenge and booty, the invaders land at Trácht Fuirbthi (Merrion Strand, Co. Dublin) and advance inland with 5,000 men. The hostel (see BRUIDEN), in many ways a magical dwelling, is usually described as having seven doorways, although some texts describe nine. Ingcél spies upon the hostel, describing the residents to his companions; Fer Rogain, Conaire's foster-brother, identifies the defenders from the descriptions and predicts which will survive. Three times the invaders set the hostel on fire, and three times the flames are extinguished. Many in the hostel are killed, the first being Lomna the fool, as he himself had predicted, but the defenders, including Conaire, slay many of the attackers. When all the available water is consumed Conaire dies of thirst, and two of the reavers decapitate him. At the end of the story Conaire's severed head thanks *Mac Cécht for searching all of Ireland to find water to slake his thirst.

Some modern commentators accept T. F. O'Rahilly's analysis that the action of *Togail Bruidne Da Derga*, for all its magical milieu (see BRUIDEN), is based on the historical triumph of the *Lagin over the *Érainn. The legendary king of Lagin is Donn Désa, foster-father of both Conaire and the first three marauders, while Conaire is king of the Érainn. John V. Kelleher has argued that *Togail Bruidne Da Derga* is alluded to in James Joyce's story 'The Dead', in *Dubliners* (1914). Texts: Whitley Stokes, *Revue Celtique*, 22 (1901), 9–61, 165–215, 282–329, 390–437 [from *The Book of the Dun Cow*]; Eleanor Knott, *Togail Bruidne Dá Derga* (Dublin, 1936) [from *The Yellow Book of Lecan*]; Jeffrey Gantz (trans.), 'The Destruction of Da Derga's Hostel', in *Early Irish Myths and Sagas* (Harmondsworth, 1981), 60–108. See also: T. F. O'Rahilly, *Early Irish History and Mythology* (Dublin, 1946), 117–30; Máirín O'Daly, 'Togail Bruidne Da Derga', in *Irish Sagas*, ed. Myles Dillon (Dublin, 1968), 107–21; Hadley Tremaine, 'The Three Saxon Princes at the Destruction of Da Derga's Hostel', *Éire-Ireland*, 4(3) (1969), 50–4; Tomás Ó Concheanainn, 'Notes on *Togail Bruidne da Derga*', *Celtica*, 17 (1985), 73–90; Henry Morris, 'Where Was Bruidhean Dá Derga?', *Journal of the Royal Society of Antiquities of Ireland*, 65(ii) (1937), 297–312; John V. Kelleher, 'Irish History and Mythology in James Joyce's "The

Dead" ', *Review of Politics*, 27 (1965), 414–33; M. West, *Cambridge Medieval Celtic Studies*, 20 (1990), 61–98.

tonn [Ir., wave]. Three great waves were thought to harass Ireland at intervals and are thus much spoken of in both written and oral tradition: Tonn Chlíodna [*Clídna's Wave] at Glandore, Co. Cork; Tonn Rudraige [Rudraige's Wave] at *Dundrum, Co. Down; and Tonn Tuaig/Tuaithe [Tuag's Wave] at *Inber Glas/Tuagh Inbir by the mouth of the Bann River, Co. [London-]Derry.

Tóraigheacht, *Tóraidheacht, Tóraidecht, Tóraigecht, Tóruigheacht, Tóraíocht* [Ir., pursuit]. Conventional first word in the title of a large group of early Irish narratives. See also TOCHMARC [wooing]; ECHTRA; EACHTRA [adventure].

Tóraigheacht Dhiarmada agus Ghráinne. Irish title for the greatest prose narrative in the *Fenian Cycle, usually known in English as The Pursuit of Diarmait and Gráinne. Although elements in the story date from at least as far back as the 10th century, texts survive only in Modern Irish, the oldest, from the 17th century, bearing evidence of the accretion of centuries. The love triangle of the ageing *Fionn mac Cumhaill, the comely young *Gráinne, and the handsome swain *Diarmait Ua Duibne immediately suggests parallels with the *Deirdre story from the *Ulster Cycle, another story of tragic elopement. However similar the two stories are now, medieval references suggest that the original story of Diarmait and Gráinne took different directions, i.e. that Gráinne was first married to and later divorced from Fionn, and that Fionn also wooed Ailbe, another daughter of *Cormac mac Airt.

Grieving for his wife Maigneis, Fionn mac Cumhaill complains to his retainers at the Hill of *Allen that a man without a wife cannot sleep well. Promising him that he can have any woman he wants, *Diorruing says that the most worthy in all Ireland is Gráinne, daughter of Cormac mac Airt at *Tara. Fionn immediately sends emissaries, who are told that Gráinne is willing if Fionn is worthy to be Cormac's son-in-law. But at the betrothal feast it is clear that Gráinne's affections lie elsewhere. Dismayed that Fionn is older than her father, Gráinne gives admiring glances at the younger members of the *Fianna, focusing on the dark curly-haired Diarmait, with whom she is soon smitten. In oral-tradition versions of the story she cannot resist his *ball seirce [love spot], which he modestly keeps covered with a cap. Gráinne gives a sleeping-potion to all present except Diarmait, whom she then urges to run away with her. At first he resists out of loyalty to Fionn, but when she threatens a *geis of destruction, he relents. The lovers flee across the *Shannon to a forest, where Diarmait builds a house with seven doors. Fionn and his men come in immediate pursuit, but some of the Fianna try to restrain their leader's hunger for vengeance. Fionn's own son *Oisín sends the hound *Bran to warn the lovers, and persuades a man with a great voice to call out an alarm. Diarmait ignores both cautions and instead plants three kisses upon Gráinne in full view of the enraged Fionn. Then in a flash the lovers make a magical escape, Gráinne rescued with a cloak of invisibility in the hands of *Angus Óg, Diarmait's foster-father, and Diarmait in a bold leap over the heads of Fionn and his men.

The route of the fugitive lovers takes many digressions, especially to west *Munster and to *Connacht. Innumerable folk variants in both Ireland and Scotland further take the lovers to all corners of the Gaelic world, as is testified by the common folk name for the *Dolmen as a 'bed of Diarmait and Gráinne'. But Diarmait is slow in his sexual approaches to Gráinne, outwardly out of respect to Fionn. In one of the most often-cited passages of the story, the two lovers are crossing a stream when a spurt of water splashes upon Gráinne's leg, prompting her taunt that it is more daring than he. Soon after their love is consummated, and in due time Gráinne becomes pregnant. This causes her craving of the red berries of the *rowan tree returned from *Tír Tairngire [the Land of Promise], now found in the forest of *Dubros, Co. Sligo, guarded by a *one-eyed, surly ogre named *Searbhán. Because Searbhán is so skilled in magical arts, Diarmait cannot overcome him by conventional means until he turns Searbhán's own weapon, an iron club, against him. Both Diarmait and Gráinne then feast on the berries, finding those on the highest branches to be the most delicious. While they are aloft, Fionn and the Fianna come to rest under the rowan tree, relaxing with the board-game *fidchell. When Diarmait's ally Oisín appears to be getting the worst of the match, the skilful lover aids him by adroitly dropping a rowanberry on the board to indicate the next best move, and so determines the outcome of three successive matches. Fionn angrily demands that Diarmait show himself, which he does, giving Gráinne three more kisses, before Angus Óg spirits her off to his residence at *Brug na Bóinne and Diarmait once more leaps over the heads of his pursuers and escapes.

After Diarmait has turned back further attempts to capture the lovers, Angus Óg negotiates a peace between them and Fionn. In some versions Fionn then contents himself with another daughter of Cormac. Diarmait and Gráinne settle near *Céis Chorainn [Keshcorran], Co. Sligo, where they raise four or five children and live peacefully. But one night while trying to sleep Diarmait is troubled by the cry of a hound on the scent, and so leaves his bed to follow it, despite Gráinne's warning of danger. Fionn has organized a *boar hunt near *Ben Bulben, which all the Fianna have joined. In some versions Fionn reminds Diarmait of his geis never to hunt pig because his half-brother had been magically restored under this form, yet Fionn clearly has reasons for wanting Diarmait to join the hunt, as he also knows that the lover will be killed by a boar. Foreseeing his doom, Diarmait none the less joins the chase with his old comrades, but finds his weapons useless. When the boar charges, he is mortally wounded. Seeing him dying amidst gore and blood, Fionn stands over him gloating that all the women of Ireland should see him now that his beauty has turned to ugliness. Diarmait reminds his older captain that he has the power to heal him by carrying healing water in his magical hands. Fionn's grandson *Oscar also pleads for help, which the older man then reluctantly provides; but on each of three attempts he lets the water drip through his hands, and thus Diarmait perishes.

Texts vary widely as to the outcome of the story. Sometimes Gráinne exhorts her sons to vengeance against Fionn; in other versions she mourns Diarmait until her own death; in still others she is reconciled to Fionn. Versions from oral tradition portray Gráinne unfavourably as a lewd woman, contrasting with Diarmait's chastity. In the Fenian ballads surviving in the 17th-century collection **Duanaire Finn*, Gráinne swallows her disgust for Fionn's age and his treatment of Diarmait, and marries him.

The love triangle between the older and younger man and the beautiful maiden has many correlatives in both Celtic and European literatures. The closest parallel in Irish tradition is, of course, the *Deirdre story from the *Ulster Cycle; in the popular imagination *Tóraigheacht Dhiarmada agus Ghráinne* has seemed less attractive because of Gráinne's hinted immorality and, in oral tradition, her marriage to Fionn after Diarmait's death. James Carney has argued that both stories derive from the late Roman love triangle of the ageing consort *Mars (Fionn), Venus (Gráinne), and her lover Adonis (Diarmait). The idea that the Fionn-Diarmait-Gráinne triangle contributed to the Arthurian romance of *Mark-*Tristan-*Iseult was suggested in the 19th century and argued convincingly by Gertrude Schoepperle in 1913.

The best modern edition and translation, superseding all others, is *Tóraidheacht Dhiarmada agus Gráinne*, ed. Nessa Ní Sheaghdha. Irish Texts Society, 48 (Dublin, 1967). See also R. A. Breatnach, 'The Pursuit of Diarmuid and Gráinne', *Studies* [Dublin], 47 (1958), 90–7; Alan Bruford, 'The Fenian Cycle: Pursuits', in *Gaelic Folk-Tales and Mediaeval Romances* (Dublin, 1969), 106–9; James Carney, *Studies in Irish Literature and History* (Dublin, 1955); A. H. Krappe, 'Diarmuid and Gráinne', *Folk-Lore*, 47 (1936), 347–61; Donald E. Meek, 'The Death of Diarmuid in Scottish and Irish Tradition', *Celtica*, 21 (1990), 335–61; Gertrude Schoepperle, *Tristan and Isolt: A Study of the Sources of the Romance* (London, 1913). Additionally, the tragic love story of Diarmait and Gráinne has been adapted more than a dozen times in English, including J. R. Anderson, *The Pursuit of Diarmuid and Graunia* (London, 1950); 9th Duke of Argyll, *Diarmid: An Opera* (1908); Austin Clarke, *The Vengeance of Fionn* (Dublin, 1917); Katharine Tynan Hinkson, 'The Pursuit of Diarmuid and Grainne', in *Shamrocks* (London, 1887), 1–54; E. R. Watters, *The Weekend of Dermot and Grace* (Dublin, 1963); William Butler Yeats and George Moore, *Diarmuid and Grania* (1901), with incidental music by Sir Edward Elgar.

Tóraigheacht an Ghiolla Dheacair. Irish title of the 16th-century comic *Fenian tale known in English as The Pursuit of the Hard Gilly/Difficult Servant. Found in both manuscript and oral tradition, the narrative is also known as *Eachtra* [Adventure] *an Ghiolla Dheacair*.

Gilla Decair [Ir., difficult servant] seems to

be a deformed churl when he appears before the *Fianna with his raw-boned mare, asking them to mount it. Fifteen, including *Conán mac Morna, agree; the animal finds new life and speedily carries them off through such inaccessible territories as *Tír fo Thuinn [Land Under Wave]. In one folk variant, the weight of the warriors breaks the animal's back. In the usual versions, however, Fionn and the rest of the Fianna must board a ship to seek out the missing men, arriving at last in *fairyland. The Hard Servant is revealed to be *Ábartach, a magician who wants the Fianna to help him against a rival king. The narrative ends with Fionn's marriage to *Taise of the White Arms, which releases the captured Fianna. All the Fianna forgive Ábartach except Goll, who demands fourteen of the finest women and the magician's own wife as compensation, to which he agrees; all the women disappear when the party arrives home.

Standish Hayes O'Grady, 'Pursuit of the *Gilla Decair*', *Silva Gadelica*, ii (London, 1892), 292–310. Hiberno-English oral version: Jeremiah Curtin (ed.), 'Gilla na Grakin and Fin MacCumhail', in *Myths and Folklore of Ireland* (London, 1890), 244–69. See also Carol T. Heffernan, 'Combat at the Fountain: The Early Irish *Pursuit of the Gilla Decair* and the Old French *Yvain*', *Éire-Ireland*, 17(4) (Winter 1982), 41–57; A. H. Krappe, 'La Poursuite du Gilla Dacker et les Dioscures celtiques', *Revue Celtique*, 49 (1932), 96–108, 216.

tree, trees [OE *treo(w)*]. The ancient Celts may have worshipped trees, as Eoin MacNeill asserted (1929), and certain trees are mentioned persistently in Celtic tradition: *alder, *apple, *ash, *birch, elm, evergreen, hawthorn, *hazel, pine, *oak, *rowan, thorn, willow, and *yew. The trees favoured by *fairies are ash, oak, and thorn. Many letters in the *ogham alphabet of early Ireland are named for trees. See also CAD GODDEU [The Battle of the Trees].

Tregeagle, Jan, John. Central figure in the best-known of Cornish ghost stories. While the historical Jan/John Tregeagle has been traced to an unremarkable steward of the Earl of Radnor, the figure in the ghost stories is portrayed as a Faust-like lawyer who sells his soul to the devil after having murdered his wife and stolen the estates of an orphan. While he is sometimes seen as a hostile *giant, not all stories portray him as malevolent; in one he is called up from the dead to bear witness at a trial. And he can get the worst of things; in one story he is condemned to drain the deep Dozmere Pool with a leaky limpet shell.

Trí Truagha na Sgéalaigheachta [The Three Sorrows of Storytelling; The Three Sorrowful Stories of Erin]. See the DEIRDRE story; OIDHEADH CHLAINNE LIR [The Tragic Story of the Children of Lir]; and OIDHEADH CHLAINNE TUIREANN [The Tragic Story of the Children of Tuireann].

Triads. The Celtic zest for triple groupings united with the need for mnemonic devices produced a pattern of versification to order learned traditions, precepts, and lore in both Ireland and Wales. In most instances a reference to the Triads implies the great *Trioedd Ynys Prydain* [Triads of the Isle of Britain] brought together during the 12th century and preserved in manuscripts from the 13th and 14th centuries. Perhaps because of the Welsh triadic verse form englyn, known since the 9th century, the volume of Welsh Triads is much greater than that of the Irish. Collections of Triads from different manuscripts deal with subjects as diverse as native learning, poetry, law, and medicine. The pervasiveness of both the triadic form and the knowledge recorded in its verses can be seen in the frequent citations found in the four branches of the **Mabinogi*. See *Trioedd Ynys Prydain*, ed. Rachel Bromwich, 2nd edn. (Cardiff, 1978); see also the editor's commentary, *Trioedd Ynys Prydain in Welsh Literature and Scholarship* (Cardiff, 1969); *The Triads of Ireland*, ed. Kuno Meyer (Dublin, 1906).

Trioedd Ynys Prydain. Welsh title for The Triads of the Isle of Britain; see TRIADS.

triplism. The resonant symbolism of the number three runs through Celtic tradition from earliest times. The Celts, like other Europeans, attached significance to nearly all frequently used numbers but gave the greatest to three. Triune and tripartite figures appear from the earliest times, while in *Wales and *Ireland traditional learning was formulated into the *Triad. No gloss in a Celtic language explains why this should be so, but commentators apply interpretations that have arisen in other European contexts. Pythagoras cites three as the perfect number, signalling beginning, middle, and end; a tripod or three-legged stool (as at Delphi) is stable and will not rock. Three can represent life: male, female, and progeny; time: past, present, and future; the visible world: sky, earth, and underground; space: before, behind, and right here. Some commentators, especially the influential Georges Dumézil (1898–1986), have suggested analogy with the tripartite division of early European society: farmers, warriors, and clergy. As Joseph Vendryes pointed out (1952) triune figures often have a single dominant personality and two ciphers; perhaps there is really only one person referred to, as can be seen in early Irish dynastic records that cite triplets all with the same name. A prime example in mythic literature is the three sons of *Uisnech: Noíse, the lover of *Deirdre, has a developed personality but his two brothers, Ardan and Ainnle, are distinguished only by the tones of their voices. At the same time, the reverse of Vendryes's thesis is also true; the three figures of the *Mórrígna, *Badb, *Macha, and the *Mórrígan, have much in common and are also easy to distinguish. Further, there are also three Machas.

A full account of Celtic instances of triplism would fill many pages, coming from all periods of Celtic culture, and a few citations must suffice here. Among the earliest are triple-faced heads, the best-known of which was found at Corleck, Co. Cavan. Gaulish *Mercury was both triple-faced and triple-phallused. Elsewhere in ancient sculpture, the mysterious hooded figure Genius Cucullatus appears singly among Continental survivals but forms a disciplined trio, Genii Cucullati, in Britain. The Roman poet Lucan (1st cent. AD) proposed that the Gaulish gods *Esus, *Taranis, and *Teutates were mentioned so often together as to form a triad. In early Ireland examples include the three *Fothads, the three sons of the *Dagda, and *Finn Emna or the Three Finns of Emain Macha. There are three female personifications of Ireland, *Ériu, *Banba, and *Fódla, and three gods of craft, *Credne, *Goibniu, and *Luchta. *Tlachtga is raped by the three sons of *Simon Magus and gives birth to triplets. *Ingcél Cáech has three pupils in one terrible black eye. *Branwen of the **Mabinogi* is one of three matriarchs. In Wales there are Three Exalted Prisoners and Three Generous Men of the Isle of Britain. The symbol of the Isle of *Man is the three-legged triskelion.

See Joseph Vendryes, 'L'Unité en trois personnes chez les Celtes', in *Choix d'études linguistiques et celtiques* (Paris, 1952), 233–46; Miranda J. Green, *Symbol and Image in Celtic Religious Art* (London and New York, 1989), 169–205.

Tristan, Tristram, Tristrem, Trystan. Cornish knight, lover of *Iseult, whose story became attached to the court of King *Arthur. Modern commentators trace several antecedents of Tristan's name, the earliest being the 'Tristan Stone', a monolith near Fowey, Cornwall, 30 miles S of *Tintagel, with a Latin inscription (6th cent.?) to Drustanus. The Welsh *Triads (12th cent.) associates Drystan, a name of apparent *Pictish origin, with a person named March. Drystan, in turn, has been linked to Drust or Drustan, an obscure Pictish king who died in 780. Marie de France's *Lai du Chèvrefeuil* (*c.*1160) depicts an already existing Tristan-Iseult union but does not place it at Arthur's court. About the same time Thomas of Britain *did* place the lovers within Arthuriana in his Anglo-Norman verse *Tristan*, most of which does not survive. Three later texts, Gottfried von Strassburg's *Tristan* (*c.*1210), Eilhart von Oberg's *Tristrant* (*c.*1175), and Béroul's *Tristan* (*c.*1170), shape the narrative as it has survived since medieval times. Tristan is sent to Ireland to bring back Iseult, betrothed to his uncle, King *Mark, whom the girl has never seen. Iseult's mother, hoping that her daughter will find love in an arranged marriage, prepares a potion which she entrusts to a nurse, Brangwain. En route the young people drink the potion by mistake and soon consummate their love. Many intrigues and digressions follow, but Iseult eventually returns to Mark while Tristan goes into exile. While abroad in *Brittany, Tristan marries but does not sleep with Iseult of the White Hands, who jealously tells her mortally wounded husband that the true Iseult is not on a vessel he is awaiting and so causes him to die of despair before he can finally be reunited with her.

While much of the prestige still accorded the Tristan story comes from its being seen as an important expression of the ideals of romantic love first propounded by the Provençal troubadours of the 12th century, the outlines of its love triangle have many international correlatives, notably in the medieval Arab story of Kais and Lobna. The often-cited Celtic counterparts are **Tóraigheacht Dhiarmada agus Ghráinne* [The Pursuit of Diarmait and Gráinne] and the *Deirdre story. See Gertrude Schoepperle, *Tristan and Isolt: A Study of the Sources of the Romance* (2 vols., London, 1913); Sigmund Eisner, *The Tristan Legend: A Study in Sources* (Evanston, Ill., 1969); Rachel Bromwich, 'Some Remarks on the Celtic Sources of *Tristan*', *Transactions of the Honourable Society of Cymmrodorion* (1955), 32–60; Raymond Cormier, 'Remarks on the Tale of Deirdriu and Noisiu and the Tristan Legend', *Études Celtiques*, 15 (1976–8), 303–15; Oliver J. Padel, 'The Cornish Background of the Tristan Stories', *Cambridge Medieval Celtic Studies*, 1 (1981), 53–81.

triune persons/gods. See TRIPLISM.

Trystan. Variant spelling of *Tristan.

Tuadmumu, Tuadnumain, Tuamumain. OIr. forms for North *Munster anglicized as *Thomond.

Tuag, Tuagh, Tuage (gen.). Beautiful young woman with whom *Manannán mac Lir is smitten. As she is guarded by women, Manannán asks the *druid *Fer Fidail to help him. The attempt fails, and both Tuag and Fer Fidail are killed. Tuag drowns at *Inber Glas, the mouth of the Bann River, which is sometimes known as Tuagh Inbir in her memory; *Tonn Tuaige [Tuag's Wave] also commemorates her.

Tuaim Tenba. Variant form of *Dind Ríg.

túaithbel. OIr. for *withershins.

Tuamumain. Variant form of *Tuadmumu.

Tuan mac Cairill, Cairell. The sole survivor of the *Partholonians who tells the story of the **Lebor Gabála* [Book of Invasions] to St *Finnian of Moville. The son of Starn and brother of *Partholón, Tuan somehow survives the plague that has killed his people and then lives through many generations under a series of metamorphoses as a *stag, a *boar, and an *eagle. Finally he is changed into a *salmon who is caught and eaten by the wife of Cairill, who gives birth to him again in human form so he may recite the early history of Ireland. See John Carey, 'Scél Tuain meic Chairill', *Ériu*, 35 (1984), 92–111. See also TALIESIN; GWION BACH.

tuath, túath. The basic territorial unit of early Irish society, consisting of a population group capable of maintaining from 700 to 3,000 soldiers in an emergency, and by extension, the land it occupied. The Royal Irish Academy *Dictionary of the Irish Language* (1948) spells this 'túath' and defines it: 'people, tribe, nation'. Dinneen's dictionary (1927) of Modern Irish reports that it now loosely means: 'a people or folk, the laity; the country (as opposed to city or town), a tract of land, territory, region'.

Tuatha Dé Danann, Dé Donann, de Danaan [Ir. *tuatha*, people, tribe, nation; *dé*, god; *danann*, of Ana (?); cf. *trí dee dána*, three gods of skill; *fir Tri nDéa*, men of the three gods]. Name found in the pseudo-history **Lebor Gabála* [Book of Invasions] for the principal family of euhemerized pre-Christian deities in Old Irish tradition. They were described as excelling over all peoples of the earth in their proficiency in every art. The phrase Tuatha Dé pre-dates the *Lebor Gabála*, describing both the Israelites in translations of the Bible (cf. L *Plebes Dei*) and the old gods. The origin of Danann is still disputed. In English and Irish the group may be known as Tuatha Dé for short; Dédanann, Dedananns, etc., while commonly seen, are non-standard. Also called 'the Ever-Living Ones', they are often implied by the phrase *áes sídhe [Ir., people of the sídh].

Although individual members of the Tuatha Dé unquestionably pre-date the *Lebor Gabála*, their literary characterization begins in that text, where they are synchronized with other invaders. The Tuatha Dé Danann arrive thirty-seven years after the *Fir Bolg, whom they displace, and 297 years before the *Milesians, who represent the *Q-Celtic, *Goidelic people, ancestors of the Irish. Overriding their conflicts with other invaders, the usual adversaries of the Tuatha Dé Danann are the other euhemerized deities, the *Fomorians. Glints of their divine origin persist in the literary portrayal of the Tuatha Dé Danann; unlike other invaders, who arrive by ship, the Tuatha Dé disembark from sombre clouds just before *Beltaine, settling on an obscure mountain in the west, causing a three-day eclipse. They are often associated with the west. A variant text has the Tuatha Dé arrive in ships, which were burned on the shore; the smoke from this conflagration also causes an eclipse. Descended through eleven generations from the *Nemedians, the Tuatha Dé were thought to have come from 'Greece' but to have learned magic and *druid lore, *draíocht, in remote northern lands. Their former homes were four magical cities: *Falias, *Findias, *Gorias, and *Murias. From them they take their principal treasures: from Falias *Fál or Lia Fáil, the stone of destiny, which cries out under a lawful king; from Findias the sword of *Nuadu, which allows no one to escape; from Gorias *Gáe Assail, the spear of *Lug Lámfhota, which guarantees victory; from Murias the *cauldron of the *Dagda, which leaves everyone satisfied. Shortly after their entry on the Irish scene, the Tuatha Dé defeat the Fir Bolg in the First Battle of Mag Tuired [Moytirra], near Lough Arrow, Co. Sligo; see CATH MAIGE TUIRED. After forming three lakes and introducing pigs into Irish agriculture, the Tuatha Dé Danann need only to quell the hateful Fomorians before establishing a golden era of peaceful prosperity.

Also euhemerized deities, the Fomorians are not a part of the invasion sequence and are sometimes characterized as demonic pirates; they harass previous settlers, the *Partholonians and the *Nemedians, from their fortress on Tory Island, off *Donegal. Although they are adversaries, the Tuatha Dé Danann intermarry with the Fomorians. Thus when the Tuatha Dé king *Nuadu is made unfit by losing his hand, his successor, *Bres, is the son of a Fomorian father. The great champion of the Tuatha Dé Danann, *Lug Lámfhota, is the grandson of the Fomorian juggernaut *Balor. After an epic struggle, Lug and the Tuatha Dé Danann triumph, as described in *Cath Maige Tuired* [The (Second) Battle of Mag Tuired], which, like the First Battle, takes place at Moytirra, near Lough Arrow, Co. Sligo. The text of *Cath Maige Tuired* exists independently of *Lebor Gabála* but is summarized in it. After the Second Battle of Mag Tuired, the Tuatha Dé Danann establish a capital at *Tara, which they call Cathair Crofuind. They are credited with building many of Ireland's (in fact) pre-Celtic ruins, including *Ailech.

The three sons of the Dagda, *Mac Cuill, *Mac Cécht, and *Mac Gréine, divide Ireland among themselves. Further, each takes wives who are eponyms for Ireland, Mac Cuill marrying *Banba, Mac Cécht marrying *Fódla, and Mac Gréine marrying *Ériu. Such *triplism is not only general in Irish myth but seems especially pertinent to the Tuatha Dé Danann, who are sometimes called Trí Dé Danann [the three gods of Danu/*Ana] and fir Trí nDéa [men of the three gods]. The phrase Tri Dée Dána [three gods of arts], from which Trí Dé Danann may be derived, describes *Brian (1), *Iuchair, and *Iucharba, who are also sons of Ana/ Danu and who appear in many episodes of *Lebor Gabála*; they are leading characters in *Oidheadh Chlainne Tuireann* [The Tragic Story of the Children of Tuireann]. Three other sons of Ana/Danu are *Goibniu the blacksmith, *Credne the artificer or silversmith, and *Luchta the wright or carpenter.

Leading figures of the Tuatha Dé Danann include: the Dagda, the 'good god', a king who specializes in druidical magic; *Manannán mac Lir, the sea-god; *Dian Cécht, the principal healing god; Lug Lámfhota, not only an important champion but a master of arts and crafts; *Angus Óg, the god of poetry and music; *Brigid, the fire-goddess and patron of poets; *Boand, goddess of the *Boyne and wife of the Dagda; the triad of war-goddesses, *Badb, *Macha, and *Mórrígan; *Ogma, a god of eloquence who is also a strongman and warrior; *Donn (1), ruler of the dead; and *Bodb Derg, a son of the Dagda and a later king. Artists among the Tuatha Dé Danann include *Cas Corach, harper; *Féthnat, a female musician; Aillén mac Midgna, the *fairy musician; the poets *Abcán and *Aí mac Ollamon; *Eadon, the 'nurse of poets'; the *druids *Esras and *Figol; satirists *Cridenbél and *Cairbre mac Ethne. Other names often cited are: *Áed Minbhreac, the son of the Dagda wrongly accused of adultery; *Assal, original owner of the spear *Gáe Assail; *Bé Chuille, a witch-like woman; *Bé Téite, a beautiful woman; *Colum Cúaillemech, another smith; *Conarán, a Tuatha Dé chief mentioned in the *Fenian Cycle; *Delbáeth (2), a noble youth; Echtge, a beautiful lady commemorated in the place-name *Echtge; *Eochaid Iúil, a god of the underworld; *Étaín, the great beauty; *Finnbarr, who makes a lewd remark to *Eithne (1); *Ethal Anbúail, a *Connacht leader. *Flidais, the goddess of beasts, is sometimes included.

Although the mortal Milesians, under *Míl Espáine, defeat the Tuatha Dé Danann twice, at *Tailtiu and *Druim Ligen, their struggle is far from epic. The fate of the Tuatha Dé after this is not a subject of the *Lebor Gabála* but rather of more popular materials that describe them surviving as immortals in the ancient barrows and cairns. The world is then divided in two, the surface going to the ordinary, mortal Milesians and their progeny while the Tuatha Dé live underground, the route to which is the *sídh. A war between immortals and mortals causes the Tuatha Dé to deprive the living of their milk and edible grain, for which restitution is later made. In some texts the Dagda is described as not having been killed at Mag Tuired so that he may now rule under the earth. Often his son *Bodb Derg is the king. Although mortals might consider ancient ruins to be places of fear, the underground Tuatha Dé are often portrayed as living in idyllic realms; one is *Mag Mell [Pleasant Plain]; another is *Emain Ablach [Fortress of Apples], a cognate of the Arthurian *Avalon; and the best-known is *Tír na nÓg [the Land of Youth]. A most important distinction was their power of *féth fiada, which could render them invisible, so that they could roam at will among mortals undetected. In many other respects, however, their world mirrors that of the mortals above. The Tuatha Dé Danann may have beauty and agelessness, but they still know quarrels, hierarchies, and intrigues. In time, the realm of the Tuatha Dé Danann becomes indistinguishable from that of the *fairies or the *áes sídhe. A 'king' of the fairies, *Finnbheara, is described as having first been a king of the Tuatha Dé Danann, but the prominent figures from the *Lebor Gabála* are not reduced to this status. A certain malevolence attributed to them may derive from a popular confusion with the predatory Fomorians. The reduced stature of such beings comes from living underground, away from the sun. Countless sites on the Irish countryside were thought to be their residences.

See also: John Carey, 'The Name "Tuatha Dé Danann" ', *Éigse*, 18 (1981), 291–4; 'A *Tuath Dé* Miscellany', *Bulletin of the Board of Celtic Studies*, 39 (1992), 24–45; Vernam E. Hull, 'The Four Jewels of the Tuatha Dé Danann', *Zeitschrift für celtische Philologie*, 18 (1930), 73–89; Gustav Lehmacher, 'Tuatha Dé Donann', *Zeitschrift für celtische Philologie*, 13 (1921), 360–4.

tuathal. ModIr. and ScG for *withershins.

Tuathal Techtmar, Túathal Techtmar, Teachtmhar, Teachmhar, Teachtmhair [Ir. *tuathal*, ruler of all the people, from Romano-Celtic *teuto-valos* (?); *techtmar*, possessing wealth (?), legitimate (?)]. Possibly historical but shadowy *ard rí [high king] of 2nd-century Ireland known mostly from genealogy, pedigree, and pseudo-history. Although documents purporting to tell of Tuathal's life, including the dates of his reign, AD 130–60, were not composed until after the 8th century, his two most important attributed achievements, leading *Goidelic invaders to Ireland and carving out the kingdom of *Mide from portions of other provinces, demonstrably did take place in pre-*Patrician Ireland. T. F. O'Rahilly asserted (1946) that his central presence in history is factual but much embroidered in retelling. Other commentators have been more doubtful, seeing him as an invented grandfather to the eminent heroic king *Conn Cétchathach [of the Hundred Battles]; the institution of the ard rí dates from a later time. Coordinating his contradictory chronology has presented problems for historians since the time of Geoffrey *Keating (17th cent.).

According to post-8th-century tradition, Tuathal invaded Ireland after an exiled birth and childhood in *Scotland to avenge the displacement of his father, *Fiachu Findholaid, but O'Rahilly felt that the Scottish exile was only a cover for his foreign origin. Fiachu had been murdered by *Éllim mac Conrach of the *Dál nAraide, a wickedness punished by God with famine. With an army mostly of foreigners, the 20-year-old Tuathal arrived at *Inber Domnann [Malahide Bay] and quickly conquered the nearby *Fir Bolg, *Domnainn, and *Galióin, eventually marching on *Tara, where he slew Éllim. In a 10th-century text Tuathal Techtmar is credited with the institution of the *boráma tribute from the subject *Laginian [*Leinster] peoples; the boráma usually consisted of 5,000 *cows, sheep, pigs, cloaks, bronze vessels, and ounces of silver, and was collected for many centuries. The pretext for the tribute was the disgrace *Eochaid (8) brought upon his kinsmen after he married Tuathal's daughter *Fithir and later came to desire her sister *Dáirine, bringing her into his household as well; the result was that Fithir died of shame and Dáirine died of grief. Tuathal would have imposed his will upon *Connacht, *Munster, and *Ulster as well to construct his own kingdom of *Mide. Although Mide certainly existed, Tuathal's association with it appears based on a misreading of etymology; the text describes him as making Mide [*mide*, middle, centre] from the 'neck' [*méide*] of each province. Mide also encompasses the territory around the hill of *Uisnech, perceived centre of

Ireland, where Tuathal Techtmar was thought to have founded the annual *óenach [fair], but probably did not.

Tuathal Techtmar claimed descent from *Eochaid Feidlech through six generations. His grandfather was Feradach Fechtnach, his mother *Eithne Imgel. The son who fathered Conn Cétchathach was Fedlim[m]id Rechtaid (or Rechtmar); another daughter was *Báine. See also MÍL ESPÁINE.

See Thomas F. O'Rahilly, 'Tuathal Techtmar', in *Early Irish History and Mythology* (Dublin, 1946), 154–70.

Tuathmhumhain. ModIr. spelling of *Thomond or North *Munster.

Tuireann, Tuirill, Tuirenn, Turenn; sometimes with agnomen Bicreo, Bicrenn. Son of *Ogma and *Étan (1) and the father of the three men who killed *Cian, the father of *Lug. See OIDHEADH CHLAINNE TUIREANN [The Tragic Story of the Children of Tuireann]. Rudolf Thurneysen, 'Tuirill Bicrenn und seine Kinder', *Zeitschrift für celtische Philologie*, 12 (1918), 239–50. See also TUIREN, etc.

Tuiren, Tuireann, Tuirrann. Variant forms of *Uirne, aunt of *Fionn mac Cumhaill. See also TUIREANN, etc.

Tuirill, Tuirill Bicreo, Bicrenn. Variant forms of *Tuireann.

Tuirn. Variant form of *Uirne.

Tuis. King 'of Greece' whose magical pigskin the sons of Tuireann must retrieve; see OIDHEADH CHLAINNE TUIREANN [The Tragic Story of the Children of Tuireann].

tunnerez noz [Bret. *noz*, night]. Probably a Breton instance of the death omen, the *washer at the ford.

Turenn. Anglicization of *Tuireann.

Twrch Trwyth [W *twrch*, male boar]. Magical but ferocious *boar that *Culhwch is required to hunt; the comb and razor lying between the ears of the beast are required to trim the hair of *Ysbaddaden Bencawr. This arduous task requires the assistance of *Mabon and *Arthur himself. In speaking to Arthur, the boar explains that he was once a king and that he has been changed into his present shape for committing some unspecified evil. More likely is the explanation that Twrch Trwyth is yet another manifestation of the divine boar from earliest Celtic mythology; allusion to him exists also in other early texts. See John Rhŷs, *Celtic Folklore* (Oxford, 1901), 509–15, 519–30, *et passim*; Rachel Bromwich and D. Simon Evans's annotations in *Culhwch ac Olwen* (Cardiff, 1992); John Carey, 'A *Tuatha Dé* Miscellany', *Bulletin of the Board of Celtic Studies*, 39 (1992), 41 ff.

tylwyth teg, y [W, the fair folk]. The most usual Welsh name for *fairies. They are often known by the euphemism *bendith y mamau [W, mother's blessings] to avert kidnapping, especially in Glamorgan. Although most stories about y tylwyth teg are recorded from oral tradition, references to them appear in writing as early as *Giraldus Cambrensis (*c.*1146–1223). They are described as fair-haired and as loving golden hair, and thus they covet mortal children with blond or fair hair. Their usual king is *Gwyn ap Nudd. In general y tylwyth teg are portrayed as benevolent but still capable of occasional mischief. Some of their later stories even profess improved behaviour and good morals, such as promising rewards of silver to young women who keep tidy houses. In distinction from other Celtic fairies, they are more often associated with lakes, especially at Llyn y Fan Fach in south *Wales. Another distinction is their fear of iron; unbaptized children should be guarded from y tylwyth teg by having a poker placed over the cradle. But like other fairies they are thought to possess magical cattle, the most famous of which is the Speckled Cow of Hiraethog. In one of the most commonly told stories of y tylwyth teg, a mortal young man seeks to marry a beautiful young daughter of the fairy host. She agrees, but only on the condition that he does not touch her with iron nor strike her with three unnecessary blows. *Gwlad y Tylwyth Teg is a Welsh name for fairyland.

The link with such lakes as Llyn y Fan Fach has implied to some commentators that the conception y tylwyth teg is derived from dark-skinned, short, early inhabitants of Britain who lived in crannogs, primitive lake dwellings; this coincides with one of the four general theories explaining the origin of *fairies. Smaller than y tylwyth teg are the *ellyll, who may have been adapted from the non-Welsh elves. Other names for y tylwyth teg include: dynon bach teg, *gwarwyn a throt, *jili ffrwtan, sili ffrit, sili-go-dwt, trwtyn tratyn. See Hugh Evans, *Y Tylwyth Teg* (Liverpool, 1944);

T. Gwynn Jones, *Welsh Folklore and Folk-custom* (London, 1930; Cambridge, 1979). Folk motifs: C433, F233.5.

Tynwald, Tynwald Hill, Cronk-y-Keillown. Manmade circular mound a few feet high near St John's Church, 3 miles from Peel, presumed to be as near as possible to the centre of the Isle of *Man; by tradition, earth was brought from every parish on the island to construct Tynwald. From earliest memory it has been a place for public ceremonials, including the reading of the laws passed by the House of Keys, the island legislature, and for the annual Tynwald Fair, held on 5 July, which was once thought of as Midsummer's Day. See also OMPHALOS.

Tyr, Tyr-. Sometime anglicization of the Irish *Tír, Tír- [land], e.g. Tyrone: see TÍR EÓGAIN.

U

U.The twenty-first letter of the modern English alphabet is represented by ur [blackthorn] in the *ogham alphabet of early Ireland.

Ua, Ua- [Ir., grandchild, spiritual descendant]. First word in early Irish patronymics, e.g. Ruaidrí Ua Conchobair. It is not a family marker; such persons are alphabetized under their given or first names. Plural form *Uí. See also AP-; MAB-; MAC; VAB.

Úaman, Sídh Úamain, Sídh Úamuin. *Connacht *sídh of *Ethal Anbúail, the father of *Cáer (1), lover of *Angus Óg.

Uar 1 [Ir., cruel (?); cf. *úar*, cold]. He and his three predatory, *one-eyed sons, Ill Omen, Damage, and Want, preyed upon *Fionn mac Cumhaill and the *Fianna from their fortress in *Munster. See also ONE-EYED figures.
2. A name sometimes substituted for one of the Three Sons of Tuireann, either *Brian (1) or *Iucharba, in *Oidheadh Chlainne Tuireann* [The Tragic Story of the Children of Tuireann].

Uathach [Ir., spectre]. Sometimes Uathach of the Glen. Daughter of *Scáthach and sometime lover of Cúchulainn. Initially, Uathach welcomes Cúchulainn when he comes to Scáthach for training. Scáthach later promises her to him without requiring the bride-price. Forgetful of his strength, Cúchulainn accidentally breaks her finger while she is serving him. Her scream brings her lover, whom Cúchulainn makes short work of; to make amends Cúchulainn takes his place, including becoming Uathach's lover.

Uchtdealb [ModIr., empty, mean-spirited breast]. Rejected mistress of Iollan Eachtach who transforms *Uirne into a dog.

Ucuetis. *Gaulish deity, usually seen with his consort *Bergusia, as in the shrine at *Alesia in eastern France (Burgundy). In some representations he bears a hammer, suggesting that he may be a divine patron of craftsmen.

Uffern [cf. L *infernum*, hell]. Name for the Welsh *Otherworld in the Latin texts of Walter Map (*c.*1140–*c.*1209) and *Giraldus Cambrensis (*c.*1146–1223); a semantic dismissal showing unmistakable Christian influence. Uffern has become the Welsh word for the Christian hell. See also ANNWFN.

Uffington White Horse. Figure of a horse, 364 feet long, cut through the sod to the white chalk below on the escarpment at the Iron Age fort of Uffington Castle, Oxfordshire (until 1974, Berkshire). With its distinctive taut, curvilinear style, the Uffington horse is one of the earth's largest pictorial works of art. Popularly supposed to represent the horse-goddess *Epona, the horse may be too early for that; stylistic evidence suggests that it dates from 50 BC while the cult of Epona appears to have arrived in Britain in post-Roman times. One of fourteen hill figures of white horses in southern England, this is by far the oldest. It was mentioned in medieval records as early as 1084. Popular scouring and cleaning, to keep the carved areas white and free of grass, continued from 1650 to the 20th century, usually accompanied with great festivities. Modern commentators are unsure which British people constructed the horse, possibly the Atrebates or the Dobunni, whose coinage featured a three-tailed horse.

Úgaine Mór, Ugaine Már, Ughaine, Úgoine, Ugainy, Ugony. Possibly a historical early Irish chieftain, frequently cited as the ultimate ancestor in medieval genealogies. Both *Labraid Loingsech of Leinster and *Conn Cétchathach [of the Hundred Battles] claimed descent from him. In stories composed hundreds of years after he would have lived, Úgaine is described as a foster-son of Queen *Macha who ruled at *Tara for forty years, extending his dominion over *Scotland, the Isle of Wight, and eventually over all of Europe. A story known in the 10th century, now lost, has Úgaine campaigning in Italy. He is described as marrying *Cesair (2), a 'daughter of the king of the Franks', who bore him twenty-five children. This Cesair (or Cessair) seems unrelated to the first invader of Ireland in *Lebor Gabála* [Book of Invasions]. Úgaine divided Ireland equally among his twenty-five children, but only two of them, *Cobthach and *Lóegaire Lorc, father of Labraid Loingsech, had any children themselves.

Uí [Ir., grandchildren, spiritual descendants]. Separated prefix in many early Irish tribal or family names. Singular form *Ua-, ModIr. Ó-, English O'-. See also AP-; MAC.

Uí Maine, Mhaine, Hy Many. Important and numerous early tribe/family of what is today eastern Co. Galway and southern Co. Roscommon. Although of non-*Goidelic origin, they created a Goidelic pedigree which included descent from Maine Mór, son of Eochu. Their king Marcán was the husband of *Créd (2), the lover of *Cano. An Uí Maine king, Eochu Rond, does battle with *Cúchulainn. The *Book of Uí Maine*, ed. R. A. S. Macalister (Dublin, 1942) is a late 14th-century miscellany containing genealogies and other materials. Hy Many is an anglicization. See John V. Kelleher, 'Uí Maine in the Annals and Genealogies to 1225', *Celtica*, 9 (1971), 61–112.

Uí Néill. Powerful dynasty, named for the assumed progenitor *Niall Noígiallach [of the Nine Hostages], whose several divisions and many members dominated Ireland for six centuries, from the middle of the 5th, coeval with the arrival of Christianity, until the Battle of Clontarf in 1014. Although Niall may have had as many as fifteen sons, eight established small kingdoms-four in the Northern Uí Néill [Uí Néill in Tuaiscirt] and four in the Southern Uí Néill [Uí Néill in Deiscirt]. Those in the north gained ground at the expense of the *Ulaid, who were driven eastward. Three of the sons, *Eógan (1), *Conall Gulban, and *Énna (3) (or Énda) are identical, T. F. O'Rahilly (1946) has argued, with the Three *Collas who reportedly destroyed the Ulidian capital of *Emain Macha. Two of the Northern Uí Néill kingdoms, *Tír Eógain [Ir., land of Eógan; Tyrone] and *Tír Chonaill [land of Conall; *Donegal] deeply affected Irish history. The southern branch of the dynasty, established by Diarmait mac Cerbaill, occupied the Irish midlands closer to *Tara, what is today counties *Meath, Westmeath, and Longford. Both branches of the dynasty federation remained antagonistic to the power even further south, the *Eóganacht. Meanwhile the two branches of the Uí Néill passed the high kingship [*ard rí] between themselves for the better part of six centuries. The Uí Néill influenced the writing of history and the development of Christian institutions. Not surprisingly, the great saint *Colum Cille was a member of the dynasty and allegedly a descendant of Niall himself.

The Uí Néill became increasingly identified with the province of Ulster, even though it was named for the much-diminished Ulaid. The heraldic symbol of the Uí Néill, the raised, severed red right hand, has been known locally from at least the time of De Burgo, Earl of Ulster during the Norman invasion, 12th-13th centuries. The red hand [ModIr. *lámh dearg*] became a symbol for all of Ulster at the beginning of the 17th century when James I created the Order of Baronets for the plantation of Ulster, selling each title for £1,000. Accommodating the colonizers, the O'Neill crest became attached to the Order, and thence to the province, and then more specifically to the Protestant and Unionist population of the province. Variations of the symbol, dexter hand appaumé gules in heraldic terms, can be found in the ancient civilizations of Assyria, Egypt, and Rome; it also occurs in the arms of Scottish Gaelic families. Stories purporting to identify the person whose hand is severed are aetiological fictions dating from later than the 17th century. Two versions remain popular: (1) A band of marauding Vikings, bent on plunder, are approaching the coast of northern Ireland when their leader promises that the first man to touch the strand with his hand or foot will take possession of it. A fierce sailor named O'Neill beats all rivals by cutting off his hand with one blow of his sword and throwing it forward to the sands. He is given possession of that part of Ireland and takes the 'Bloody Hand' as his crest. (2) Two rival Scottish clans race from Scotland to Ireland; whoever reaches Ireland first will possess the land. When the leader of the MacDonnells sees that he cannot get there in time, he cuts off his hand and throws it on the shore, thus claiming the land for himself. The Red Hand is also the crest of the MacDonnells of Antrim.

Despite the common misconception, the name O'Neill is not an anglicization of Uí Néill. Instead, many a family derives from the Uí Néill, including O'Doherty, O'Donnell,

O'Hagan, and others. The O'Neill family, a subdivision of Cenél Eógain in Tír Eógain, takes its name from *Niall Glúndub (d. 919). See Donncha Ó Corráin, *Ireland Before the Normans* (Dublin, 1972); F. J. Byrne, *Irish Kings and High Kings* (London, 1973).

uilepheist. Scottish Gaelic counterpart of the *oilliphéist.

Uirne, Tuirn, Tuireann, Tuirreann, Tuiren. Aunt of *Fionn mac Cumhaill and mother, through magical transformation, of his favourite hounds, *Bran (2) and *Sceolang; in variant texts she is Fionn's sister instead of being the sister of *Muirenn Muncháem, Fionn's mother. Uirne is accorded several different husbands in different texts. One of these husbands (sometimes a second as well) loves her imperfectly, even though Fionn had been promised by *Lugaid Lága that she would be well treated. In the oldest versions he is Imchad, a prince of *Dál nAraide (counties Antrim and Down); a first wife becomes jealous of Uirne and transforms her into a she-dog while pregnant, and she thus gives birth to Bran (2) and Sceolang. In later and folk variants, where her name is more likely to be Tuirn, she marries *Iollan (2) or Iollann Éachtach [ModIr., wonderful, powerful], whose discarded mistress is Uchtdealb [ModIr., empty or mean-spirited breast]. Again, she gives birth to Bran (2) and Sceolang. Uirne then returns to human form and marries Lugaid Lága. See John R. Reinhard and Vernam E. Hull, 'Bran and Sceolang', *Speculum*, 11 (1936), 42–58.

Uisnech, Uisneach, Uisneagh, Uishnach, Ushnagh, Ushney, Usna, Usnagh, Usnech, Usney, Uisnig (gen.), Uisnigh (gen.). Hill (602 feet) in Co. Westmeath, 12 miles W of Mullingar, that has played a significant role in the Irish imagination. Long thought of as the centre, navel, or *omphalos of the island, Uisnech contains a stone [Ail na Mírenn, stone of divisions] marked with lines showing where the borders of the five provinces (*Connacht, *Leinster, *Ulster, and *Munster considered as two) met; most of the hill was thought to be in the Connacht portion. As a ceremonial site Uisnech is second only to *Emain Macha. Although far from lofty, the top of Uisnech can be seen from great distances, which partially explains its continued use for the burning of ritual fires. In the pseudo-history *Lebor Gabála* [Book of Invasions], the *Nemedian *druid *Mide (eponym of *Meath) is credited with lighting the first fire there. Excavations in the early 20th century revealed huge beds of ash. Evidence from literary and oral tradition testifies that Uisnech was a favoured site for *Beltaine fires and druidical ceremonies, especially the driving of cattle. The legendary *Tuathal Techtmar (1st–2nd cent. AD) was thought to have founded the annual fair or óenach that continued to early modern times, which was also attributed to the goddess *Ériu. At its peak this was one of three great festivals of Ireland, along with *Tailtiu and *Tara. At Uisnech *Lug Lámfhota was killed by *Mac Cuill, *Mac Cécht, and Mac Gréine, the sons of *Cermat. Although Uisnech is always a place, not a person, Noíse and his brothers Ardan and Ainnle are called the 'sons of Uisnech' in the Irish title of the *Deirdre story, *Longas mac nUislenn* [The Exile of the Sons of Uisnech]. Nevertheless, James *Macpherson based the character *Usnoth on Uisnech. See also KERMARIA of BRITTANY; PUMLUMON of WALES.

Uisnig. Genitive of *Uisnech.

Uist [ScG *uibhist*]. Two large islands in the Outer Hebrides, North Uist [*Uibhist a Tuath*], 118 square miles, and South Uist [*Uibhist a Deas*], 141 square miles, where Scottish Gaelic continues to be spoken at the end of the 20th century. Although both islands are rich in archaeological sites comparable to the celebrated *Callanish of the Isle of Lewis, the Roman Catholic Southern island has been a greater reservoir of storytelling than has the Protestant North. See *Stories from South Uist, Told by Angus MacLellan*, trans. J. L. Campbell (London, 1961); Francis Thompson, *The Uists and Barra* (Newton Abbot, UK, 1974).

Ulaid, Ulaidh, Ulad (gen.). A people of early Ireland who gave their name to the province of *Ulster although they usually dominated only the eastern portion, with a capital at *Emain Macha; at various periods their hegemony extended as far south as the *Boyne and as far west as Co. Leitrim. Their power declined after the 5th century AD. The Ulaid called themselves Clanna Rudraige, a name thought to contain the particle ruad- [red]. See T. F. O'Rahilly, *Early Irish History and Mythology* (Dublin, 1946), 341–52; Francis J. Byrne, *Irish Kings and High Kings* (London, 1973), 106–10.

Ulidian. Adjectival form of *Ulaid, *Ulster.

Ulster [ON *Uladztir*; Ir. *Ulaid*, the people; ON *staðir*, steadings; cf. MedL *Ultonia*]. A province of Ireland occupying much of the north-east of the island, third largest (6,486 square miles) of the four, including *Connacht, *Leinster, and *Munster, whose borders were drawn in the 17th century. Known in pre-conquest Ireland as Cóiced Ulad, it had been one of five, when *Mide/*Meath is counted separately or when Munster is counted as two. Within its borders are the counties of: Antrim, *Armagh, Cavan, *Donegal, Down, Fermanagh, [London-]*Derry, Monaghan, Tyrone. Since the partition of 1922 'Ulster' has often erroneously been understood to imply only the six counties still a part of the United Kingdom: Antrim, Armagh, Fermanagh, [London-]Derry, Down, and Tyrone, or only 52.3 per cent (3,393 square miles) of the total original area. The name 'Ulster' is often used as the English equivalent of the Irish *Ulaid, even though that ancient people usually occupied only eastern portions of what became the province of Ulster.

The geographical focus of the *Ulster Cycle or Red Branch Cycle is *Emain Macha, the 18-acre hill-fort in Co. Armagh, the supposed court of King *Conchobar mac Nessa. Much of the action in the great epic of the Cycle, the **Táin Bó Cuailnge* [Cattle Raid of Cooley], takes place in Ulster, and the fortunes of the Ulstermen are championed by their greatest hero, *Cúchulainn, along with *Conall Cernach and *Lóegaire Búadach. See also the DEBILITY/PANGS OF THE ULSTERMEN; MESCA ULAD [The Intoxication of the Ulstermen]; for the Red Hand of Ulster, see UÍ NÉILL. See also *Annala Uladh: The Annals of Ulster*, ed. William H. Hennessy (Dublin, 1887–1901).

Ulster Cycle, formerly the **Red Branch Cycle.** A large body of prose and verse romances as well as the only Irish prose epic, **Táin Bó Cuailnge* [Cattle Raid of Cooley], centring on the traditional heroes of the *Ulaid in what is now eastern *Ulster. One of the four major cycles of Irish literature, along with the *Mythological and *Fenian Cycles and the *Cycle of Kings. In most Ulster Cycle stories, *Conchobar mac Nessa is king, reigning at his capital, *Emain Macha. *Cúchulainn is the supreme hero, *Deirdre a peerless tragic lover. Often compared with the Arthurian legends, the Ulster Cycle portrays a proud, even haughty people often at war with their neighbours, especially those in *Connacht. Set a century before the time of Christ, the Ulster stories posit an older world than any known in other European vernaculars. Ulster stories, both in Irish and in frequent English translation and adaptation, enjoy the greatest prestige of the four Irish cycles, often mixing beauty with sorrow in both romance and epic.

The name Red Branch Cycle, favoured by 19th-century translators and romantic nationalists, is an English rendering of *Cráebruad, the name for one of Conchobar's three residences, so called for the large red roof beam or 'branch' visible in the interior. This phrasing was supported by a reading of Clanna Rudraige, the name which the Ulaid, for whom Ulster was named, applied to themselves; Rudraige was thought to contain the element ruad [red]. The confusion existed only in the minds of commentators of the last three centuries. In early Ireland literature was not consciously divided into cycles, but instead was classed by tale type, such as the *Aided*: a story of a sorrowful death, or a **Tochmarc*: the story of a wooing. Thus not every story set in Ulster is a part of the Cycle, e.g. **Buile Shuibne* [The Frenzy of Sweeney] in the Cycle of Kings.

Narrative materials in the Ulster Cycle were transcribed as early as the 8th century, continued to be a part of living literature until the 18th, and extended to *Scotland and the Isle of *Man. Transmission was mostly through the pens of learned scribes rather than oral tradition. Although all recording of Ulster stories has taken place after the introduction of Christianity, their setting is always perceived to be a century before the birth of Christ. A certain bowdlerization and sanitizing must be assumed, but the prevailing religion of the stories includes sun worship and the veneration of natural objects. The belief in magic is ever-present, and pre-Christian divinities interfere in the affairs of mortal men and women. The society portrayed holds slaves without censure from the narrator and engages in frequent and brutal warfare, often for the possession of cattle. Physical evidence of the Ulaid's past glory would have been present to text redactors and copyists, as the ruins of Emain Macha still stood, as indeed they do to the present.

The prestige of the Ulster Cycle within Irish tradition does not rely on wealth or numbers.

Ulster was historically less affluent than regions further south, e.g. the *Boyne valley, *Brega, or the *Liffey valley, and stories from the Fenian Cycle were more widely known. Neither do the narratives present an idealized portrait of a life without pain or misery; literary Ulster may be pastoral but it lacks idyllic sentiment. Instead there is a grandeur of epic literature, of life lived to the fullest in extremes of bravery and love. Esteem for the Ulster Cycle passed into English during the 19th century, when nationalists searched ancient literature for heroes to replace those imposed on Irish children by English-run schools. The warriors of Emain Macha, who routinely decapitated slain enemies, came to be known as the 'Red Branch *knights*' in the poetry of Thomas Moore (1779–1852). Standish James O'Grady (1846–1928) extrapolated an even more heroic history, which in turn fostered widespread adaptation in English of Ulster stories during the generation of Lady Gregory, William Butler Yeats, and John Millington Synge.

Important personages frequently mentioned in the Ulster Cycle, along with the hero Cúchulainn, the king Conchobar mac Nessa, and the tragic lover Deirdre, include: *Achall, *Áed Ruad, *Amairgin (2) (mac Eit), *Baile, *Bec mac Dé, *Bélchú, *Blaí Briugu, *Bláithíne, *Briccriu, *Cairbre Cuanach, *Cairbre Nia Fer, *Cathbad, *Celtchar, *Cet mac Mágach, *Cethern mac Fintain, *Conall Cernach, *Condere mac Echach, *Cormac mac Airt, *Crunniuc, *Cú Roí, *Culann, *Cúscraid, *Dáire mac Fiachna, *Dubthach Dóeltenga, *Ébliu, *Fedelm Noíchrothach, *Fedlimid mac Daill, *Fergus mac Leti, *Fergus mac Róich, *Fiachu mac Fir Febhe, *Follomain mac Conchobair, *Fráech, *Friuch, *Furbaide Ferbend, *Garb mac Stairn, *Goll mac Carbada, *Lóegaire Búadach, *Lugaid mac Con Roí, *Lugaid Riab nDerg, *Macha, *Maine, *Medb, *Mórrígan, *Mugain (2), *Nera, *Scáthach, *Sencha mac Ailella, *Uathach.

See also AIDED FERGUSA [The Violent Death of Fergus]; AIDED ÓENFHIR AÍFE [The Tragic Death of Aífe's Only Son]; ECHTRA NERAI [The Adventure of Nera]; FLED BRICRENN [Briccriu's Feast]; *Longas mac nUislenn* [The Exile of the Sons of Uisnech] or the Deirdre story; MESCA ULAD [The Intoxication of the Ulstermen]; SCÉLA MUCCE MEIC DA THÓ [The Story of Mac Da Thó's Pig]; SERGLIGE CON CULAINN AGUS ÓENÉT EMIRE [The Wasting Sickness of Cúchulainn and The Only Jealousy of Emer]; TÁIN BÓ CUAILNGE [Cattle Raid of Cooley]; TOGAIL BRUIDNE DA DERGA [The Destruction of Da Derga's Hostel].

Studies: Alan Bruford, 'The Ulster Cycle', in *Gaelic Folktales and Mediaeval Romances* (Dublin, 1969), 93–105; Kenneth H. Jackson, *The Oldest Irish Tradition* (Cambridge, 1964); Rudolf Thurneysen, *Die irische Helden- und Königsage* (Halle, 1922).

Ultonians. Obsolete English form for *Ulstermen, after the medieval Latin *Ultonia*.

ùmaidh. A ScG word for *changeling.

Úna, Oonagh, Oona. Wife of *Finnbheara, king of the Irish *fairies, sometimes known as Nuala. She is thought the most beautiful of all women, with golden hair sweeping to the ground, and is the mother of seventeen sons. Sometimes she is thought to have a separate residence of her own of Cnoc Sídh Úna [Knockshegouna] in Co. Tipperary. Folk motif: F252.2.

underworld. See OTHERWORLD.

Urien, Urian. Sixth-century king of Welsh-speaking *Rheged in what is now Scotland who acquired an additional literary characterization in the Arthurian legends. His resistance along with his son *Owain, AD 550–600, earned him the high praise of *Taliesin, who called him Urien Rheged. His name appears in the Welsh *Triads, though not in any connection with *Arthur. In *Geoffrey of Monmouth's *Historia* (1136) he is made the king of Moray in northern Scotland. Later in the French *Claris et Laris* (13th cent.) he is credited as the father of *Yvain and Marine. And though he is often seen as the husband of Morgan le Fay, Malory (15th cent.) portrays him as dying fighting Morgan's son Mordred. See Jenny Rowland, *Early Welsh Saga Poetry* (Cambridge, 1990).

urisk. Anglicization of *ùruisg.

Urmhumhain. ModIr. name for *Ormond.

Urnfield period. Archaeologist's shorthand term for an era of Bronze Age culture in Central Europe distinguished by its burial practices, from the decline of Minoan and Mycenaean influence to the coming of *Hallstatt culture; dating ranges as early as *c.*1500 BC down to 800 BC, or partially contemporary, in different parts of Europe, with the rise of Hallstatt. Evidence of a new form of burial is found in the Danube valley in what is now Hungary. A body was cremated, its ashes placed in an urn, and the urns deposited in cemeteries known as 'urnfields'. The funeral practice spread westward to the area between the Elbe and the Vistula, to southern Germany, and across the Alps to Italy. By the 10th century BC the entire region shared cultural similarities. Some elements of urnfield may be found as far away as the Low Countries, the Iberian peninsula, and Britain. People of the urnfield culture or tradition may be regarded as proto-Celts as motifs from their art, such as the sun-wheel, appear again in Hallstatt, the first unmistakably Celtic culture.

ùruisg, urisk. Solitary *fairy of Scottish Gaelic tradition, a subspecies of the *fuath, half-man and half-*goat, but not satyr-like, despite appearances. In many ways, the ùruisg is a rougher, hirsute *brownie, given to helping at household chores, especially churning butter and cleaning, in spite of a reputation for good-humoured sloth. He has a taste for dairy products and is feared by dairy maids. Every manor house was reputed to have its resident ùruisg, and a seat in the kitchen close by the fire would be left vacant for him; he was lucky to have around. The ùruisg craves human companionship but almost always frightens people away with his unseemly appearance. He was also known to haunt lonely and sequestered places, notably a certain corrie near Loch Katrine. See also GLAISTIG; FUATH; PEALLAIDH. In spoken Scottish Gaelic the term ùruisg might also denote a diviner who foretells future events, or a savage-looking fellow.

Usheen. Anglicized spelling of *Oisín.

Ushnagh, Usna, Usnech, Usney. Variant forms of *Uisnech.

Usnoth. Character in James *Macpherson's *Ossian* (1760–3), drawn from *Uisnech of the *Ulster Cycle. Chief of Etho, a district on the west coast of Scotland, his sons Nathos, Althos, and Ardan/Ardar run off with *Darthula (*Deirdre).

Uthr Bendragon, Uther Pendragon, Uterpendragon [W *uthr*, terrible; *pen*, head; *dragon*, leader]. Father of *Arthur, begotten on *Eigr (or *Igerna), by means of an intrigue arranged by *Merlin. His name was known in Welsh tradition before the time of *Geoffrey of Monmouth (12th cent.).

V

vab, vab-. Mutated form of *mab, mab- [W, son of].

vates, vatis [cf. L *vātēs*, prophet, although probably of Celtic origin]. Word found in *Strabo (1st cent AD) and other *classical commentators for the interpreters of sacrifice and natural philosophy in Gaulish society. The vates were one of three ranks of men holding high positions of honour in the society; the other two were the better-known *bards and *druids. Vates might foretell the future through augury and the sacrifice of victims. Although apparently of lower status than the druids, the vates certainly had some religious power as well. The word vātēs is an exact cognate of the Irish *fáith [prophet, seer], although we lack evidence to suggest that their functions were identical. A near Welsh cognate is *gwawd.

vaticination. See DIVINATION.

Ventry, Ventry Harbour, **Battle of.** See CATH FIONNTRÁGHA.

Venus of Quinipily, Quinipili. Popular name given to a statue, 6 feet high, of unknown origin at Quinipily near Baud, *Brittany. Speculations on the provenance of the statue vary widely. It may be: (*a*) the survival from an ancient, local cult; (*b*) a representation of the Egyptian goddess Isis; (*c*) a copy of a statue from the cult of St Gildas; (*d*) a hoax of more recent creation than local tradition supposes. The statue was once thought to have healing properties. Denounced by ecclesiastical officials in the 17th century, it was thrown in a local river but later, by popular demand, restored. Known in Breton as Gwreg Houarn [Iron Woman].

Verbeia [cf. OIr. *ferb*, cattle]. Romano-British goddess of the River Wharfe in Wharfedale, Yorkshire. An altar in her honour survives at Ilkley, Yorkshire, near which was found a statue which may represent her: a figure in a pleated robe, with stylized features and an over-large head, and a large snake in each hand. She also appears to own a *cow.

Vercingetorix [L *ver*, over; *cinget*, warrior; *rex*, king]. Historical (d. 45 BC) Gaulish tribal chieftain who opposed Julius *Caesar's conquest of his country. Son of the king of the Arverni people, he lacked the support of other nobles but gained the confidence of the common people, who raised him to kingship in 52 BC. Eventually joined by other Gaulish tribes, he met with considerable success until Caesar besieged him at *Alesia. Forced to surrender, Vercingetorix was exhibited in Caesar's triumph, imprisoned in Rome, and eventually executed. Generally regarded as the first French national hero, his persona has attracted much legend-making. See Jean Markale, *Vercingétorix* (Paris, 1982; Monaco, 1995); Jean-Michel Thibaux, *Vercingétorix* (Paris, 1994).

Veteris. Variant spelling of *Vitiris.

Vindonnus, Vindonus [clear light, white]. Gaulish aspect of *Apollo, worshipped at a site coextensive with Essarois in Burgundy, eastern France. Bronze plaques found nearby depicting eyes suggest he was attributed curative powers for *eye diseases. Linguistically Vindonnus is linked with *Fionn mac Cumhaill.

Virotutis. Sometime epithet of Gaulish *Apollo.

vision. See AISLING; FÍS.

Visucius. Latin name for a shadowy deity of presumably Celtic origin whose name is known in inscriptions from Aquitaine in south-western France to the Gaul-German border. In some places a female consort, Visucia, forms a divine couple with him. Surviving evidence is ambiguous as to whether Visucius is a discrete figure or whether he is an aspect of both Gaulish *Mars and *Mercury.

Vitiris, Veteris, Vitris. Latin name for a British god of Roman Britain whose worship was popular among men, especially soldiers of the occupation army, even though his name does not appear to be derived from any god of Roman or Greek origin. Inscriptions of his name, found most frequently in north Britain, include a variety of spellings: Vitiris, Veterus, Vitris, Vetus, and Hvitiris. As his name is usually invoked in the plural, he may have taken tripartite form (see TRIPLISM). More than forty altars dedicated to Vitiris survive, many of them in Northumberland, some decorated with a serpent and a *boar. He may have been the north British *horned god. Sometimes linked with the British god *Mogons. See F. Haverfield, 'Early Northumbrian Christianity and the Altars of Di Veteres', *Archaeologia Aeliana*, 3rd ser., 15 (1918), 22–43.

voght, vough. Anglicizations of *fuath.

Vosegus. Gaulish god, personification of the Vosges mountains and forest of eastern France. May be identical with a local nature-deity, who was depicted wearing a great cloak with a piglet under his arm; the same god is associated with hunting-gear as well as with nuts, acorns, and pine-cones.

Voyage of . . . . See IMRAM. . . .

W

Wales [OE *wealh, wealas* (pl.), foreigner, i.e. a native Briton, not a Saxon]. Principality of the United Kingdom, occupying 8,016 square miles in Great Britain, west of England. Roughly a third the size of *Ireland or *Scotland, its population of about three million is somewhat less than that of the Republic of Ireland and a little more than half that of Scotland. The Welsh people are descendants of the *P-Celtic British conquered by the Romans in the 1st century BC, a cause for semantic ambiguity in many languages. In French the Welsh are still les Gallois [the Gauls]. Anglo-Saxons used the terms Brittas and Brittisc to denote both ancient Britons and surviving Welsh, but also employed the mixed forms Bretwalas, Bretwielisc [British foreigners]. From the earliest times the Welsh called themselves Y Gwir Frythoniaid [the true Britons], Brythoniaid, and Cymry. Cymry (also Kymry) derives from the Celtic combrogos [compatriot]; *Geoffrey of Monmouth's (12th cent.) asserted etymology tracing the root to an eponymous founder named Camber is clearly spurious. In Modern Welsh Cymry denotes the Welsh people, while Cymru denotes the principality or nation of Wales. Latinized forms such as Wallia and Gwalia were found in both English and Welsh contexts. The demarcation of Wales from ancient Britain is often dated by the Saxon victory at the Battle of Chester, *c.*615. Yet the memory of Welsh-speaking greater Britain persists in Welsh literature. The early medieval poem *Y *Gododdin*, widely known in Welsh tradition, commemorates the heroic deaths of Welsh warriors travelling from the lowlands of Scotland to what is today Yorkshire. In Welsh the phrase Gwŷr y Gogledd [men of the north/left] denotes the populations of such formerly Welsh petty kingdoms as *Rheged, Gododdin, and *Strathclyde.

The borders and constituent parts of Wales have not been constant over the centuries. Many a gwlad or petty kingdom flourished within the principality only to merge with its neighbour or fade from the scene. The most long-lasting of these were *Gwynedd in the north and *Dyfed and *Deheubarth in the south, names that were reborn in the Welsh map in 1974. Others include: *Brycheiniog, *Ceredigion, *Gwent, *Powys, *Seisyllwg, and *Ystrad Tywi. Additionally, south-east Wales was often known as *Morgannwg, an area later to become Glamorgan, and since 1974, West, Mid, and South Glamorgan. In medieval Wales the principality was divided among four bishoprics, *Bangor in the north-west, St Asaph north-east, Llandaff south-east, and St David's south-west. The centre or *omphalos where these bishoprics met is *Pumlumon [W, five peaks], also a source of the Wye and Severn Rivers. Long-term Anglo-Norman and English designs on Wales culminated in English conquest during the reign of Edward I (1272–1307) and the death of the last native-born Prince of Wales, *Llywelyn ap Gruffudd, in 1282. In 1301, after securing the English-Welsh border with a series of castles, Edward I made his own son (later Edward II) Prince of Wales, a title since borne by male heirs to the British throne. In spite of the failed rebellion lead by Owen Glendower [W *Owain Glyndŵr*] (1399–1415), Wales drew closer to England; by 1485 a partly Welsh prince, Henry Tudor [W *Tudur*], became Henry VII of England. Under his son, Henry VIII, Wales became an integral part of the Tudor kingdom, while retaining its identity as a principality. From the 16th century until 1974 Wales consisted of twelve or thirteen counties, sometimes excluding the English-influenced Monmouthshire. Of these, *Anglesey, *Cardigan, and *Carmarthenshire had significant local traditions. With the reconfiguration of 1974, Wales now has eight counties, including the lands of the former Monmouthshire as a part of Gwent; the other seven, while reviving names of older petty kingdoms, now occupy somewhat different territories from those of their medieval namesakes: Clwyd, Dyfed,

Gwynedd, Mid Glamorgan, Powys, South Glamorgan, West Glamorgan.

A leading member of the *Brythonic family, the Welsh language [*Cymraeg*] is a close relative of Breton and the now-extinct Cornish. Although Welsh literary tradition begins with the 6th-century *Cynfeirdd [early poets] *Aneirin and *Taliesin, surviving manuscripts date from several centuries later, e.g. the **Black Book of Carmarthen* [*Llyfr Du Caerfyrddin*] (*c.*1250), the **White Book of Rhydderch* [*Llyfr Gwyn Rhydderch*] (*c.*1325), and the **Red Book of Hergest* [*Llyfr Coch Hergest*] (*c.*1382–1410). Dispersed through these codices are manuscript copies of the four branches of the **Mabinogi*, the most highly regarded cycle of medieval Welsh prose literature. Lady Charlotte Guest collected and translated the *Mabinogi* along with seven unrelated medieval tales and romances from the same milieu in her *Mabinogion* (1838–49). Although the Acts of Union, 1536 and 1542, proscribed use of the Welsh language in official transactions, gravely diminishing its prestige and authority, the Welsh language thrived in domestic life. Welsh was also the language of literary traditions in different parts of the principality as well as the medium of a continuing oral tradition. Compulsory public education in English repressed Welsh further, but by the end of the 20th century almost 19 per cent of the population (about 500,000) claim that they can speak the language, a higher percentage and a higher total than in any other Celtic culture.

OIr. Bretain [not distinguished from Britain]; ModIr. An Breatain Bheag; ScG A'Chuimrigh; Manx Bretyn; Corn. Kembry; Bret. Kembre. See A. O. H. Jarman and G. R. Hughes, *A Guide to Welsh Literature* (2 vols., Swansea, 1976–9); see Bibliography under 'Welsh' for collections of Welsh traditions.

war-gods. See BATTLE GODS.

warp spasm. See CÚCHULAINN.

washer at the ford, washing woman. English name for a familiar figure in Irish, Scottish Gaelic, Welsh, and perhaps Breton oral tradition, who may appear locally under different names. A death omen, she is sometimes beautiful and weeping or may be ugly and grimacing. She washes bloody garments at the ford of a river and turns to tell the beholder that they are his or hers. The persona of the washer may be derived from the *Mórrígan, although *Badb can take on this role. In Irish oral tradition the washer is nearly synonymous with the *banshee, in Scottish Gaelic tradition is the *bean nighe, in Welsh *Modron, in Breton *tunnerez noz. Fiona Macleod [William Sharp] christianizes the figure as that of Mary Magdalene standing in the middle of a stream washing the souls who crave eternity in his *The Washer of the Ford* (Edinburgh, 1896).

wave, waves. See TONN; TÍR FO THUINN [Land Under the Waves].

white-black-red symbolism. See BLACK.

White Book of Hergest [W *Llyfr Gwyn Hergest*]. Welsh manuscript dating from the mid-15th century that was destroyed by fire sometime in the 19th century, perhaps 1810, 1840, or 1858. Among its contents were the *Laws* of King *Hywel Dda (d. 950). Distinguish from the **Red Book of Hergest* and the **White Book of Rhydderch*.

White Book of Rhydderch [W *Llyfr Gwyn Rhydderch*]. Great collection of medieval Welsh prose, copied on parchment *c.*1325, containing versions of the **Mabinogi* and all the other narratives included in the *Mabinogion*, except **Breuddwyd Rhonabwy* [The Dream of Rhonabwy], and many religious texts. In compiling her translation, *The Mabinogion* (1846), Lady Charlotte Guest relied on the later *Red Book of Hergest* (*c.*1382–1410). The transcriber of the *White Book* is not known, but dialect evidence suggests he was from *Deheubarth in south-western Wales. The name Rhydderch alludes both to Parc Rhydderch, a house where poetry was patronized, and to Rhydderch ab Ieuan Llwyd, master of Parc Rhydderch, who apparently owned the Book in the late 14th century. The *White Book*, now in two volumes, was rebound in white leather in 1940 at the National Library of Wales, where it is now kept. See J. Gwenogvryn Evans, *The White Book Mabinogion* (Pwllheli, 1907); Rachel Bromwich et al. (eds.), *The Arthur of the Welsh* (Cardiff, 1991), 9 ff.

White Horse of Uffington. See UFFINGTON WHITE HORSE.

White Island. See ERNE.

Whitehorn. Name for *Finnbennech, the White Bull of Connacht.

widdershins. Variant spelling of *withershins.

wild man of the wood, woodwose. The hairy, usually dirty, often naked wild man of the woods appears frequently in oral tradition and in art all over the British Isles from medieval times to at least the 19th century. Woodwose, wooser, and ooser are English names for him. He has something of the satyr or faun about him, without the lubricity. *Owain, *Lailoken, *Merlin, and Suibne (see BUILE SHUIBHNE [The Frenzy of Suibne]) have at times something of the wild man of the wood about them. See also GRUAGACH. See Kenneth H. Jackson, 'The Wild Man of the Woods', *Yorkshire Society for Celtic Studies* (1935); R. Bernheimer, *Wild Men in the Middle Ages* (Cambridge, Mass., 1952); Pádraig Ó Riain, 'A Study of the Irish Legend of the Wild Man', *Éigse*, 14 (1972), 179–206.

withershins, widdershins [MidHGer. *widersinnes*, counter-course]. To take a course opposite that of the sun, i.e. counterclockwise, lefthandwise, or to circle an object, building, monument by always keeping it on the left. A journey begun with such a turn is thought either unlucky or given to evil intentions in much of Celtic literature, as it is in much of older European popular tradition. In English, however, the belief is so uncommon that our only word for it, withershins, comes from Scottish regional usage. Cf. the antonym, SUNWISE TURN. OIr. túaithbel; ModIr. tuathal; ScG tuathal; Manx dy kiuttagh.

wolf. See ANIMALS.

woman, women. See FEMALE WARRIORS AND CHAMPIONS.

Women, Isle of. See EMAIN ABLACH.

Women, Land of. See TÍR NA MBAN.

woodwose. See WILD MAN OF THE WOOD.

Wooing of . . . . See TOCHMARC.

Y

Y. The Welsh definite article, e.g. Y Gododdin; see GODODDIN, Y

yannig, yannig an od. Spectral creature of Breton folklore, comparable to the *ankou. It emerges from the sea at night to hoot like an owl. Mortals should not heed the yannig's call, even when it asks for pity. At a third call it will be at the person's back, consuming him and turning him into a whiff of air.

yarrow [OE *gearwe*]. The plant with feathery leaves and strong-smelling white or pinkish flowers (genus *Achillea*) was known to both the ancient Greeks and Chinese for its attributed powers of healing and *divination. In most of the Celtic world yarrow is a *fairy herb. Practitioners in the Hebrides held a leaf of yarrow against the eyelids to see the person in one's thoughts. Yarrow roots were also used in snuff-making. In Irish tradition yarrow was known by honorific titles: lus na fola [blood herb] and lus na gcluas [ear herb]. The name *Emer may derive from an early Irish form for yarrow. ModIr. athair thalún [lit. earth creeper]; ScG eàrr thalmhuinn; Manx ayr; W milddail, llysiau gwaedlif; Corn. mynfel; Bret. mildelienn.

Yellow Book of Lecan [Ir. *Lebor Buide Lecáin*]. One of the great medieval Irish manuscripts, including the complete version of **Tochmarc Étaíne* [The Wooing of Étaín], **Aided Óenfhir Aífe* [The Tragic Death of Aífe's Only Son], *Scéla Cano meic Gartnáin* [The Story of *Cano mac Gartnáin], **Togail Bruidne Da Derga* [The Destruction of Da Derga's Hostel], and a version of **Orgain Denna Ríg* [The Destruction of Dind Ríg], as well as a version of **Táin Bó Cuailnge* [Cattle Raid of Cooley]. Although the *Yellow Book* was compiled at Lecán (now Lacken), near Inishcrone, Co. Sligo, *c.*1390, narratives within the collection can be dated centuries earlier from internal evidence; *Aided Óenfhir Aífe*, for example, appears to be 9th-century. See *The Yellow Book of Lecan*, ed. Robert Atkinson (Dublin, 1896). A selection of poems from the manuscript appears in *The Yellow Book of Lecan*, ed. Lambert McKenna for the Irish Texts Society (Dublin, 1939–40).

Yeun, Yeun-Elez, Yeunn Ellez. See YOUDIC.

yew [OE *ēow*]. The evergreen tree or shrub (genus *Taxus*) with dark green, needle-like leaves and red berries has commonly symbolized immortality in the Indo-European imagination as it is the longest-lived entity, often lasting more than 1,000 years, to be found in the European environment. It is still commonly planted in Christian churchyards and cemeteries. The *druids preferred yew for wand-making over their other favourite woods, *apple and *oak. The name of the Eburones, a Gaulish people residing between the Main and Rhine, means 'people of the yew', while several Irish and Scottish place-names allude to the yew, notably Youghall [*Eochaill*, yew wood] in Co. Cork. The Irish personal name *Eógan means 'born of the yew', so that the great *Munster dynasty could be glossed as 'people of the yew'. According to the foundation story of *Cashel, the Eóganacht capital, *Corc mac Luigthig has a vision of a yew bush, with angels dancing over it, before settling on the site. One of *Conchobar mac Nessa's residences at *Emain Macha, *Cráebruad, has nine rooms lined with red yew. *Suibne Geilt in **Buile Shuibne* [The Frenzy of Suibne] rests on yew trees during his flight. When *Eógan (3) and *Lugaid mac Con are disputing they hear the magical music of the yew tree over a waterfall; the musician is revealed to be *Fer Í [man of yew], the son of *Eogabal. Wielders of the spear *Gáe Assail are sure to kill their victims if they utter the word *ibar* [yew] as they cast. The agnomen of *Cáer (1), the *swan maiden, is Ibormeith [yew berry]. In oral variants of the *Deirdre story, King Conchobar mac Nessa drives yew stakes through the hearts of the dead lovers, which later grow and intertwine near a church. Yet not all stories of the yew imply power or vitality. A rod named *fé, made of yew or *alder, was used to measure corpses and graves. And *Fergus, the hapless brother of *Niall Noígiallach [of the Nine Hostages] in **Echtra Mac nEchach Muigmedóin* [The Adventure of the Sons of Eochaid Mugmedón], signals his sterility when he rescues from a burning forge only the 'withered wood' of yew, which will not burn. OIr. ibar; ModIr. iúr; ScG iubhar; Manx euar; W ywen; Corn. ewen; Bret. ivinenn.

yfagddu. Variant spelling of *afagddu.

Ygerne, Yguerne. Variant spellings of *Igerna.

Ymddiddan [W, colloquy, conversation]. First word in the title of a series of late medieval Welsh poems following the conventions of the ymddiddan cyfarch genre. Two speakers meet, of whom one is unknown to the other until, through the dialogue, they establish mutual identification. See Brynley F. Roberts, 'Rhai o gerddiymddiddan Llyfr Du Caerfyrddin', in Rachel Bromwich and R. Birnley Jones (eds.), *Astudiaethau ar yr Hengerdd/ Studies in Old Welsh Poetry* (Cardiff, 1978).

Ymddiddan Myrddin a Thaliesin. Welsh title for the 11th-century poem, found in the **Black Book of Carmarthen*, usually known in English as The Colloquy of *Merlin and *Taliesin. Both the prophet Myrddin and the supernatural poet Taliesin share their arcane knowledge and also speak informatively of recent battles in Wales. See *Ymddiddan Myrddin a Thaliesin*, ed. A. O. H. Jarman (Cardiff, 1951).

yn sleih veggey [the little people]. A Manx name for the *fairies.

Yniwl Iarll, Ynywl Iarll. Father of *Enid.

ynys, ynis. Welsh word for island, first element in dozens of real and imaginary place-names. Cf. the Irish *inis, Scottish Gaelic innis.

Ynys Afallon, Ynis Avallon, Ynis Avallach [cf. W *afall*, apple]. Happy island in the western ocean, a land of perpetual youth, fertility, feasting, and abundant sensual pleasure, where magical birds sing enchanted songs. Comparable to the Irish *Tír na nÓg and *Tír na mBéo, Ynys Afallon also contributed to the Arthurian conception of *Avalon and is still the Welsh name for that island. Under the influence of *Giraldus Cambrensis (12th cent.) and William of Malmesbury, Ynys Afallon has also become the Welsh name for *Glastonbury. Folk motif: D1338.7.

Ynys Enlli. Welsh name for *Bardsey Island.

Ynys Gutrin [glass island]. The water-girded island or fortress of glass in medieval Welsh romance, presided over by nine maidens. Apparently identical with Ynys Wydrin. During the 12th century Ynys Gutrin, through a false etymology, might also indicate *Glastonbury.

Ynys Wydrin, Ynys Witrin. Apparently identical wtih *Ynys Gutrin.

Ynywl. Variant spelling of *Yniwl Iarll.

Youdic. Fearsome entrance to infernal regions cited often in Breton lore. The actual Youdic is a deep pit in the flat, black quagmire of Yeun (also Yeun-Elez, Yuenn Ellez) in the Arrée mountains of *Finistère, north-western Brittany. Hapless mortals peering into Youdic risked being seized and dragged down by unseen forces below. Malevolent fiends, often taking the form of a great black *dog, are heard baying at night. Another sound heard floating on the night wind comes from the mad revels of lost souls. In Christian folklore the Youdic was thought to be a place for confining the possessed, but St Michael can save souls from falling in.

Youthful Exploits of Fionn. See MACGNÍMARTHA FINN [The Boyhood Deeds of Fionn].

Ys, Legend of the City of, also City of Is; in Breton Kêr Is, Kêr-Is, Kêr Iz, Kêr-Iz, Ker Is. How the legendary city of Ys came to be submerged under the Bay of Douarnenez in south-west Brittany is explained in the best-known narrative from Breton tradition. At least three versions survive; each portrays at least three characters: *Gradlon (or Gralon) Meur [the great], a pious, saintly king who has protected his city by building a protective dike; *Dahut (also Dahud, Ahè, Ahès), his wilful and wayward daughter; and the abbé Guénolé, founder of the first monastery in Brittany at Landévennec. In the oldest version Dahut secretly entertains her lover, and the two of them, excited by wine, steal Gradlon's key to open the dike, flooding the city.

The more familiar second version depicts Ys as a commercial centre so given to luxury as to arouse the ire of Guénolé, who, like the biblical Jeremiah, foretells ruin. Among the wickedest of Ys's citizens is Dahut, who has made a crown of her vices and has taken as pages the seven deadly sins. A small boy named *Kristof, whose encounter with a magical fish has provoked Dahut's scorn and thus caused her to be pregnant, removes the enchanted *oak tree protecting the city. One night at a feast a devilish stranger whispers his love into Dahut's ear and bids her take the key to the dike from around her sleeping father's neck. As soon as the key is put in the dike the sea begins to rush in, but Guénolé wakes Gradlon and urges him to flee. The king charitably takes his daughter with him on the steed Morvarc'h [horse of the sea] until he hears a voice crying out to cast aside his demon passenger or he also will be lost. With his heart breaking, Gradlon complies and the waters immediately recede, allowing him to reach Quimper safely. Dahut becomes a siren-like mermaid, calling out to sailors about to be wrecked, but Ys is submerged either at Douarnenez or under the Étang de Laval.

In the third version, from ballad tradition, Gradlon leads the people in extravagance of every kind, and he freely gives the dike's key to Dahut, who misuses it. When the city is flooded Dahut becomes a mermaid who haunts the waters at Douarnenez.

A statue of Gradlon was erected between the two towers of the cathedral in Quimper, damaged in 1793, and restored in 1859. The legend that church bells can still be heard ringing below the waters of the Bay of Douarnenez inspired Claude Debussy's overture *La Cathédrale engloutie* [The Sunken Cathedral]. In colloquial Breton Ys lends itself to a familiar pun with the modern capital of sin: Par [Bret., like] Is. See Charles Guyot, *The Legend of the City of Ys*, trans. Deirdre Cavanagh (Amherst, Mass., 1979); Rachel Bromwich, 'Cantre'r and Ker-Is', in Cyril Fox and Bruce Dickens (eds.), *The Early Cultures of North-West Europe* (Cambridge, 1950), 217–41.

Ysbaddaden Bencawr, Yspaddaden Penkawr, Isbaddaden [W, hawthorn (?); king of the *giants]. Father of Olwen in *Culhwch ac Olwen* who sets the young hero Culhwch on a number of impossible tasks before he will give up his daughter. Culhwch and his companions wound Ysbaddaden in the knee, stomach, and eye, but they cannot kill him until his daughter marries. *Caw shaves him, and eventually *Goreu son of *Custennin beheads him. Counterpart of the Irish *Balor.

Yseult. Variant spelling of *Iseult.

Ysgithrwyn Pen Beidd, Yskithyrwynn Penbeidd [W, white tusk, chief boar]. Fearsome *boar of **Culhwch ac Olwen*. *Ysbaddaden sends Culhwch to get his white tusk so that he may use it for shaving.

Ysolde, Ysolt, Ysonde. Variant spellings of *Iseult.

Yspaddaden Penkawr. Variant spelling of *Ysbaddaden Bencawr.

Ystoria Taliesin. See TALIESIN.

Ystrad Tywi. Medieval gwlad or petty kingdom of southern *Wales, occupying territory coextensive with the modern counties of West Glamorgan and *Dyfed. In the **Mabinogi*, *Pryderi expands his kingdom by seizing land from Ystrad Tywi. During the 8th century, three cantrefs of Ystrad Tywi merged with four from Ceredigion to form the more powerful *Seisyllwg.

Yvain, *Ywain, Ivain, Evein*. Arthurian romance (*c.*1178) by *Chrétien de Troyes, also known as *Chevalier au Lion*, which presents parallels with the Welsh Arthurian romance **Owain*. Yvain wins Laudine after killing her husband but then forgets her during a year at *Arthur's court and must undertake a series of adventures to regain her. The story is retold in *Ywain and Gawain*, an English 14th-century romance. See Robert W. Ackerman, F. W. Locke, and C. W. Carroll, *Ywain: The Knight of the Lion* (New York, 1977). See also TÓRAIGHEACHT AN GHIOLLA DHEACAIR [The Pursuit of the Hard Gilly/Difficult Servant].

Z

Zeus. See JUPITER.

Select Bibliography

General

ALMQVIST, BO, Ó CATHÁIN, SÉAMAS, and Ó HÉALAÍ, PÁDRAIG (eds.). *The Heroic Process: Form, Function and Fantasy in Folk Epic*. Dublin: Glendale Press, 1987.

ANWYL, EDWARD. *Celtic Religion in Pre-Christian Times*. London: Constable, 1906.

ASHE, GEOFFREY. *Mythology of the British Isles*. London: Methuen, 1990.

BAKER, W. BUCK. *Celtic Mythological Influences on American Theatre, 1750–1875*. Lanham, Md.: University Press of America, 1993.

BIRKHAN, HELMUT. *Germanen und Kelten bis zum Ausgang der Römerzeit*. Vienna: Böhlau, 1970.

BREKILIEN, YANN. *La Mythologie celtique*. Brussels: Marabout, 1981.

BRIGGS, KATHARINE. *An Encyclopedia of Fairies*. New York: Pantheon, 1976.

BRØGGER, NEILS CHR. *Heltr og Halvguder hog Kelterne*. Oslo: Ernst G. Martenens. 1961.

Cambridge Medieval Celtic Studies, 1981– .

Celtica (Dublin), 1946–60.

Celticum (Rennes), 1961– .

CHADWICK, HECTOR MUNRO, and CHADWICK, NORA KERSHAW. *The Growth of Literature*, 3 vols. Cambridge: Cambridge University Press; New York: Macmillan, 1932–40.

CHADWICK, NORA. *Celtic Britain*. London: Thames & Hudson, 1963.

—— *The Celts*. Harmondsworth: Penguin, 1970.

CHAPMAN, MALCOLM. *The Celts: The Construction of a Myth*. London: Macmillan; New York: St. Martin's, 1992.

CHARLES-EDWARDS, T. M. *Early Irish and Welsh Kinship*. Oxford: Clarendon Press; New York: Oxford University Press, 1993.

CHILD, FRANCIS JAMES. *English and Scottish Popular Ballads*, 5 vols. Boston and New York: Houghton Mifflin, 1883–98.

CLEMEN, CARL CHRISTIAN. 'Die Kelten', in *Religionsgeschichte Europas*, i. Heidelberg: C. Winters, 1926, 314–35.

COARER-KOLANDON, EDMOND. *Le Druidisme ou La Lumière de l'Occident*. Paris: Éditions et Publications Premières, 1971.

CUNLIFFE, BARRY. *The Celtic World*. New York: McGraw-Hill, 1979.

DAVIDSON, H. R. ELLIS. *Myth and Symbols in Pagan Europe: Early Scandinavian and Celtic Religions*. Syracuse, NY: Syracuse University Press, 1988.

DILLON, MYLES, and CHADWICK, NORA. *Celtic Realms*. London: Weidenfeld & Nicolson; New York: New American Library, 1967; repr. London: Cardinal, 1973.

DIXON-KENNEDY, MIKE. *Celtic Myth and Legend: An A–Z of People and Places*. London: Blandford, 1996.

DOAN, JAMES E. *Women and Goddesses in Early Celtic History, Myth and Legend*. Working Papers in Irish Studies, 87(4/5). Boston: Northeastern University, 1987.

DOTTIN, GEORGES. *Les Littératures celtiques*. Paris: Payot, 1924.

—— *La Religion des Celtes*. Paris: Bloud, 1904, 1908.

DUVAL, PAUL-MARIE. *Les Celtes*. Paris: Gallimard, 1977.

ELLIS, PETER BERRESFORD. *Dictionary of Celtic Mythology*. London: Constable, 1992.

ELUÈRE, CHRISTINE. *The Celts: First Masters of Europe*. London: Thames & Hudson, 1993.

Études Celtiques [Paris], 1936– .

FILIP, JAN. *Celtic Civilization and Its Heritage*, trans. R. F. Samsour, 2nd edn. Prague: Artia, 1977.

FOSS, MICHAEL. *Celtic Myth and Legends*. London: Michael O'Mara; New York: Barnes & Noble, 1995.

GASSOWSKI, JERZY. *Mithologia Celtow*. Warsaw: Wydaw-A Artystyczne i Filmowe, 1978.

Gazetteer of the British Isles. Edinburgh: Bartholomew, 1972.

GIMBUTAS, MARIJA. *The Goddesses and Gods of Old Europe, 6500–3500 BC: Myths and Cult Images*. Berkeley and Los Angeles: University of California Press, 1974.

GREEN, MIRANDA J. *Celtic Goddesses: Warriors, Virgins and Mothers*. London: British Museum, 1996.

—— *Celtic Myths*. London: British Museum, 1993.

GREEN, MIRANDA J. (ed.). *The Celtic World.* London, New York: Routledge, 1995.

—— *Dictionary of Celtic Myth and Legend.* London: Thames & Hudson, 1992.

—— *The Gods of the Celts.* Gloucester: Alan Sutton; Totowa, NJ: Barnes & Noble, 1986.

—— *Sun Gods of Ancient Europe.* London: B. T. Batsford, 1991.

—— *Symbol and Image in Celtic Religious Art.* London and New York: Routledge Chapman & Hall, 1989.

HAMEL, ANTON G. VAN. 'Aspects of Celtic Mythology', *Proceedings of the British Academy*, 20 (1934), 207–48.

—— *Mythe en historie in het oude Ierland.* Amsterdam: Noord-Hollandsche-Uitgevers Maatschappij, 1942.

HENDERSON, GEORGE. *The Survival of Belief Among the Celts.* Edinburgh: James MacLehose, 1911.

Herder Lexikon: germanische und keltische Mythologie. Freiburg: Herder, 1990.

HERM, GERHARD. *Die Kelten: das Volk aus dem Dunkel Kam.* Düsseldorf and Vienna: Econ, 1975; *The Celts: The People Who Came Out of the Darkness.* London: Weidenfeld & Nicolson; New York: St. Martin's Press, 1975.

HUBERT, HENRI. *The Greatness and Decline of the Celts*, trans. M. R. Dobie. New York: Knopf, 1934; repr. London: Constable, 1987.

—— *The Rise of the Celts*, trans. M. R. Dobie. New York: Knopf, 1934; repr. New York: Dorset, 1988.

JACOBS, JOSEPH. *Celtic Folk and Fairy Tales.* London: David Nutt, 1892.

—— *More Celtic Folk and Fairy Tales.* New York: G. P. Putnam's, 1895.

JACOBSTHAL, PAUL. *Early Celtic Art.* London: Oxford University Press, 1944.

JAMES, SIMON. *Exploring the World of the Celts.* London: Thames & Hudson, 1993.

Journal of Celtic Studies (Baltimore), 1949–58.

KIRFIL, WILLIBALD. *Die dreiköpfige Gottheit.* Bonn: F. Dümmler, 1948.

KIRK, ROBERT. *The Secret Commonwealth of Elves, Fauns, and Fairies.* 1961; repr. Stirling: Mackay, 1933; London: Folklore Society, 1976.

KRAPPE, ALEXANDER HAGGERTY. *Balor with the Evil Eye; Studies in Celtic and French Literature.* New York: Institut des Études Françaises, Columbia University, 1927.

KRUTA, VENCESLAS, FREY, OTTO-HERMAN, SZABÓ, MIKLÓS, and RAFTERY, BARRY. *The Celts.* London: Thames & Hudson; New York: Rizzoli, 1991.

LAING, LLOYD, and LAING, JENNIFER. *Celtic Britain and Ireland: The Myth of the Dark Ages.* Dublin: Irish Academic Press, 1990.

LAMBRECHTS, PIERRE. *Contributions à l'étude des divinités celtiques.* Bruges: De Tempel, 1942.

LANTIER, RAYMOND. 'Keltische Mythologie', in H. W. Haussig (ed.), *Wörterbuch der Mythologie.* Stuttgart: E. Klett. 1. Abt. (5. Lieferung, *c.*1966), 99–162.

LEACH, MARIA (ed.). *Standard Dictionary of Folklore, Mythology, and Legend.* New York: Funk & Wagnalls, 1950.

LE ROUX, FRANÇOISE. *Les Fêtes celtiques.* Rennes: Ouest-France, 1995.

—— *Introduction générale de l'étude de la tradition celtique.* Vol. xiii of *Celticum.* Rennes: Ogam, 1967.

—— and GUYONVARC'H, CHRISTIAN-J. *Les Druides*, rev. edn. Rennes: Ouest-France, 1986.

LINDSAY, JACK. *Our Celtic Heritage.* London: Weidenfeld & Nicolson, 1962.

Lochlann. A Review of Celtic Studies (Oslo), 1958- .

LONIGAN, PAUL R. *The Druids: Priests of the Ancient Celts.* Westport, Conn.: Greenwood Press, 1996.

LOW, MARY. *Celtic Christianity and Nature: the Early Irish and Hebridean Traditions.* Belfast: Blackstaff Press, 1996.

MACBAIN, ALEXANDER. *Celtic Mythology and Religion.* New York: Dutton, 1917.

MACCANA, PROINSIAS. *Celtic Mythology.* London: Hamlyn, 1970.

—— 'Conservation, Innovation in Early Celtic Literature', *Études Celtiques*, 13 (1972), 61–119.

MACCULLOCH, JOHN A. *Celtic. The Mythology of All Races*, iii. pp. 1–213. Ed. Louis H. Gray. Boston: Marshall Jones, 1918; repr. New York: Cooper Square, 1964.

—— *The Celtic and Scandinavian Religions.* New York: Hutchinson's Universal Library, 1948.

—— *Religion of the Ancient Celts.* Edinburgh: T. & T. Clark, 1911.

MACDOUGALL, JAMES. *Folk and Fairy Lore in Gaelic and English*, ed. George Calder. Edinburgh: Grant, 1910.

MACLEAN, MAGNUS. *The Literature of the Celts: Its History and Romance.* Edinburgh: T. & T. Clark; New York: Scribner's, 1912.

MACNEILL, JOHN [Eóin] and CARNEY, A. C. *Celtic and Teutonic Religions.* London: Catholic Truth Society, 1935.

MAIER, BERNHARD. *Lexikon der keltischen Religion und Kultur*. Stuttgart: Alfred Kröner, 1994.

MARKALE, JEAN. *Celtic Civilization*. London and New York: Gordon & Cremonesi, *c*.1978.

—— *Le Druidisme*. Paris: Payot, 1985.

—— *Mélusine, ou L'Androgyne*. Paris: Retz, *c*.1983.

—— *Petit dictionnaire de mythologie celtique*. Paris: Entente, 1986.

—— *La Tradition celtique*. Paris: Payot, 1979.

—— *Women of the Celts*, trans. A. Mygind, P. Hauch, and P. Henry. London: Gordon & Cremonesi, 1975.

MARX, JEAN. *Les Littératures celtiques*. Paris: Presses Universitaires de France, 1959.

MATONIS, ANN T. and MELIA, DANIEL F. (eds.). *Celtic Language, Celtic Culture: A Festschrift for Eric P. Hamp*. Van Nuys, Calif.: Ford & Baillie, 1990.

MATTHEWS, JOHN, and MATTHEWS, CAITLÍN. *Aquarian Guide to British and Irish Mythology*. Wellingborough, UK: Aquarian Press, 1988.

MINAHANE, JOHN. *The Christian Druids*. Dublin: Sanas, 1993.

MORDIERN, MEVEN. *Notennoù diwar-benn ar Gelted koz: o istor hag o sevenadur*, trans. Abherve [pseud., Fransez Vallée], 3rd edn. Brest: Skridoù Breizh, 1944.

MOREAU, JACQUES. *Die Welt der Kelten*. Stuttgart and Zurich: Klipper, 1958.

MOSCATI, SABATINO et al. (eds.). *The Celts*. London: Thames & Hudson, 1992.

NORTON-TAYLOR, DUNCAN. *The Celts*. Time-Life Emergence of Man Series. Amsterdam: Time-Life Books, 1975.

Ó CORRÁIN, DONNCHADH, BREATNACH, LIAM, and MCCONE, KIM (eds.). *Sages, Saints and Storytellers: Celtic Studies in Honour of Professor James Carney*. Maynooth: An Sagart, 1989.

O'DRISCOLL, ROBERT (ed.). *The Celtic Consciousness*. Toronto: McClelland & Stewart; New York: Braziller, 1981.

Ogam: Tradition Celtique (Rennes), 1948- .

OLMSTED, GARRETT S. *The Gods of the Celts and the Indo-Europeans*. Innsbruck: Verlag des Instituts für Sprachwissenschaft der Universität Innsbruck, 1994.

OOSTEN, JARICH G. *The War of the Gods: The Social Code in Indo-European Mythology*. London: Routledge, 1985.

O'RAHILLY, CECILE. *Ireland and Wales: Their Historical and Literary Relations*. London: Longmans, Green, 1924.

PERSIGOUT, JEAN-PAUL. *Dictionnaire de mythologie celtique*. Monaco: du Rocher, 1985.

POWELL, T. G. E. *The Celts*. London: Thames & Hudson; New York: Praeger, 1958.

PRICE, GLANVILLE (ed.). *The Celtic Connection*. Gerrards Cross, UK: Colin Smythe, 1991.

RAFTERY, JOSEPH (ed.). *The Celts*. Cork: Mercier Press, 1967.

REES, ALWYN and REES, BRINLEY. *Celtic Heritage*. London: Thames, 1961.

REINHARD, JOHN REVELL. *The Survival of Geis in Medieval Romance*. Halle: Niemeyer, 1933.

Revue Celtique (Paris), 1870–1934.

RHŶS, JOHN. *Lectures on the Origin and Growth of Religion as Illustrated by Celtic Heathendom*. The Hibbert Lectures, 1886. London: Williams & Norgate, 1887; 3rd edn., 1898.

RIVOALLAN, A. *Présence des Celtes*. Paris: Nouvelle Librairie Celtique, 1957.

ROLLESTON, T. W. *Myths and Legends of the Celtic Race*, 2nd edn. London: Harrap, 1911.

ROSEN-PRZEWORSKA, JANINA. *Religie Celtow*. Warsaw: Ksiazka i Wiedza, 1971.

SERBANSCO, GÉRARD. *Les Celtes et les druides*. Paris: la Ruche Ouvrière, 1968.

SJOESTEDT-JONVAL, MARIE-LOUISE. *Dieux et Héros des Celts*. Paris: Presses Universitaires de France, 1940; *Gods and Heroes of the Celts*, trans. M. Dillon. London: Methuen, 1949.

SNYDER, EDWARD DOUGLAS. *The Celtic Revival in English Literature, 1760–1800*. Cambridge, Mass.: Harvard University Press, 1923; repr. Gloucester: Peter Smith, 1965.

SPENCE, LEWIS. *A Dictionary of Medieval Romance and Romance Writers*. London: Routledge; New York: E. P. Dutton, 1913; repr. New York: Humanities, 1962.

SQUIRE, CHARLES. *Celtic Myth and Legend, Poetry and Romance*. London: Gresham, 1905; London: Constable, 1906; Chicago: Open Court, 1906.

Studia Celtica (Cardiff), 1966– .

SYKES, EGERTON. *Everyman's Dictionary of Non-Classical Mythology*. New York: Dutton, 1965.

SZABÓ, MIKLÓS. *The Celtic Heritage in Hungary*, trans. Paul Aston. Budapest: Corvina, 1971.

VENDRYES, JOSEPH. *Choix d'études linguistiques et celtiques*. Paris: Klincksieck, 1952.

—— *La Religion des Celtes*. [In] *'Mana': introduction à l'histoire les religions*, ii: *Les religions de l'Europe ancienne*, pt 3. Paris: Presses Universitaires de France, 1948, 237–320.

VRIES, JAN DE. *Keltische Religion*. Stuttgart: W. Kohlhammer, 1961; *La Religion des celtes*, trans. L. Jospin. Paris: Payot, 1963.

WAGNER, HEINRICH. *Studies in the Origin of the Celts and of Early Celtic Civilisation*. Belfast and Tübingen: Niemeyer (for the Belfast Institute of Irish Studies), 1971.

WESTWOOD, JENNIFER. *Albion: A Guide to Legendary Britain*. London: Granada, 1985; Bridgeport, Conn.: Merrimack, 1986.

WITHYCOMBE, ELIZABETH G. *The Oxford Book of English Christian Names*, 3rd edn. Oxford: Oxford University Press, 1986.

Zeitschrift für celtische Philologie (Halle, 1897–1941; Tübingen, 1953–), 1897– .

ZIMMER, HEINRICH, and MEYER, KUNO. *Die romanischen Literaturen und Sprachen, mit Einschluss des Keltischen*. Berlin and Leipzig: B. G. Teubner, 1909.

ZWICKER, JOHANNES. *Fontes historiae religionis celticae*. Berlin: de Gruyter, 1934–6.

Ancient and Continental Celtic

BROGAN, OLWEN. *Roman Gaul*. Cambridge, Mass.: Harvard University Press, 1953.

BRUNAUX, JEAN LOUIS. *The Celtic Gauls. Gods, Rites, and Sanctuaries*. London: B. A. Seaby, 1988.

DOTTIN, GEORGES. *La Langue gauloise; grammaire, textes et glossarie*. Paris: C. Klincksieck, 1920.

DRINKWATER, J. F. *Roman Gaul: The Three Provinces, 58 BC–AD 260*. London and Canberra: Croom Helm, 1983.

DUVAL, PAUL-MARIE. *Les Dieux de la Gaule*. Paris: Presses Universitaires de France, 1957.

—— *Recueil des inscriptions gauloises*, 3 vols. Paris: Centre National de la Recherche Scientifique, 1985; 1 vol., Paris: CNRS, 1986.

EVANS, D. ELLIS. *Gaulish Personal Names*. Oxford: Clarendon Press, 1967.

FAUDUET, ISABELLE. *Atlas des sanctuaires romano-celtiques de Gaule: les fanums*. Paris: Errance, 1993.

GRENIER, ALBERT. *Les Gaulois*. Paris: Payot, 1945, 1970.

HARMAND, JACQUES. *Les Celtes au second âge du fer*. Paris: F. Nathan, 1970.

HATT, JEAN-JACQUES. *Celts and Gallo-Romans*, trans. James Hogarth. London: Barrie & Jenkins, 1970.

HENIG, MARTIN. *Religion in Roman Britain*. New York: St. Martin's Press, 1984.

JULLIAN, CAMILLE LOUIS. 'Keltic Heathenism in Gaul', *Cambridge Medieval History*, 2 (1913), 459–71.

—— *Recherches sur la religion gauloise*. Bordeaux: Feret, 1903.

LAMBERT, PIERRE-YVES. *La Langue gauloise: description lingustique, commentaire d'inscriptions choisies*. Paris: Errance, 1994.

OLMSTED, GARRETT S. *The Gaulish Calendar: A Reconstruction*. Bonn: R. Habelt, 1992.

POBÉ, MARCEL, and ROUBIER, J. *The Art of Roman Gaul*. London: Gallery Press, 1961.

ROSS, ANNE. *Everyday Life of the Pagan Celts*. London: Batsford, 1970; repr. as *The Pagan Celts*, Totowa, NJ: Barnes & Noble, 1986.

—— *Pagan Celtic Britain*. New York: Columbia, 1967; 2nd edn., London: Constable, 1992.

THOMAS, CHARLES. *Celtic Britain*. London: Thames & Hudson, 1986.

WATTS, DOROTHY. *Christians and Pagans in Roman Britain*. London, and New York: Routledge, 1991.

WEBSTER, GRAHAM. *The British Celts and Their Gods under Rome*. London: Batsford, 1986; repr. as *Celtic Religion in Roman Britain*. Totowa, NJ: Barnes & Noble, 1987.

Irish

ANDREWS, ELIZABETH. *Ulster Folklore*. London: E. Stock, 1913; repr. New York: E. P. Dutton, 1919.

Annals of the Four Masters, 2nd edn., ed. John O'Donovan, 7 vols. Dublin: Hodges & Smith, 1856.

ARBOIS DE JUBAINVILLE, HENRY D'. *Cours de littérature celtique*, 12 vols. Paris: Fontemoing, 1883–1902. Vol. ii, *Le Cycle mythologique irlandais et la mythologie celtique*, 1884, trans. R. I. Best as *Irish Mythological Cycle and Celtic Mythology*. Dublin: Hodges Figgis; London: Simpkin, Marshall, 1903; repr. New York: Lemma, 1970.

BAUMGARTEN, ROLF. *Bibliography of Irish Linguistics and Literature, 1942–1971*. Dublin: Dublin Institute for Advanced Studies, 1986.

Béaloideas: The Journal of the Folklore Society of Ireland (Dublin), 1928– .

BEST, RICHARD IRVINE. *Bibliography of Irish Philology and Manuscript Literature, 1913–1941*. Dublin: Dublin Institute for Advanced Studies, 1969.

—— *Bibliography of Irish Philology and of Printed Irish Literature to 1912*. Dublin: HMSO,

1913; repr. Dublin: Dublin Institute for Advanced Studies, 1992.

Bjersby, Birgit M. H. *The Interpretation of the Cuchulain Saga in the Works of W. B. Yeats.* Uppsala Irish Studies Series No. 1. Uppsala: Uppsala University Press, 1950.

Bréifne: Journal of the Cumann Seanchas Bhréifne (Cavan), 1991– .

Bruford, Alan. *Gaelic Folk-Tales and Mediaeval Romances*. Dublin: Folklore of Ireland Society, 1969.

Butler, Hubert. *Ten Thousand Saints: A Study In Irish and European Origins*. Kilkenny: Wellbrook Press, 1972.

Byrne, Francis John. *Irish Kings and High Kings*. London: Batsford, 1973.

Campbell, J. J. (ed.). *Legends of Ireland*. London: Batsford, 1955.

Carney, James (comp.). *Early Irish Literature*. Cork: Mercier Press, 1966; binds together Eleanor Knott's *Irish Classical Poetry* (1957) with Gerard Murphy's *Ossianic Lore* (1955) and *Saga and Myth in Ancient Ireland* (1955) (see below).

Carney, James. *Studies in Irish Literature and History*. Dublin: Dublin Institute for Advanced Studies, 1955.

Christiansen, Reidar Thoralf. *Studies in Irish and Scandinavian Folktales*. Copenhagen: Rosenkilde & Bagger, 1931.

Clark, Rosalind Elizabeth. *Great Queens: Irish Goddesses from the Morrigan to Cathleen Ní Houlihan*. Gerrards Cross, UK: Colin Smythe; Savage, Md.: B & N Imports, 1990.

Coghlan, Ronan. *Dictionary of Irish Myth and Legend*. Bangor, NI: Donard, 1979; repr. as *The Pocket Dictionary of Irish Myth and Legend*, Belfast: Appletree, 1985.

Colum, Padraic (ed.). *A Treasury of Irish Folklore*. New York: Crown, 1954.

Condren, Mary. *The Serpent and the Goddess: Women, Religion, and Power in Celtic Ireland*. San Francisco, Calif.: Harper & Row, 1989.

Croker, Thomas Crofton. *Fairy Legends and Traditions of the South of Ireland*. London: John Murray, 1825; 2nd edn., London: John Murray, 1838.

—— *Researches in the South of Ireland Illustrative of the Scenery, Architectural Remains, and the Manners and Superstitions of the Peasantry*. London: John Murray, 1824; repr. New York: Barnes & Noble, 1969.

Cross, Tom Peete. *Motif Index of Early Irish Literature*. Indiana Folklore Series, vol. 7. Bloomington: Indiana University Press, 1952.

Cross, T. P. and Slover, C. H. (eds.). *Ancient Irish Tales*. New York: Henry Holt, 1936; repr., New York: Barnes & Noble, 1969.

Curtin, Jeremiah. *Hero Tales of Ireland*. London: Macmillan; Boston: Little, Brown, 1894.

—— *Irish Folk Tales*. Dublin: Talbot Press, 1944; repr. Dublin: Folklore Society of Ireland, 1967.

—— *Myths and Folk-Lore of Ireland*. London: Sampson Low; Boston: Little, Brown, 1890; repr. Detroit: Singing Tree, 1968.

Dames, Michael. *Mythic Ireland*. London: Thames & Hudson, 1992.

Danaher, Kevin [Caoimhín Ó Danahcair]. *Bibliography of Irish Folk Traditions and Ethnology*. Dublin: Mercier Press, 1978.

—— *Folktales of the Irish Countryside*. Cork: Mercier Press, 1968.

—— *The Year in Ireland*. Cork: Mercier Press, 1972.

de Bhaldraithe, Tomas. *English–Irish Dictionary*. Dublin: Oifig an tSolathair, 1959.

de Blacam, Aodh. *A First Book of Irish Literature*. Dublin: Talbot Press; Educational Company of Ireland, 1934.

—— *Gaelic Literature Surveyed*. Dublin and Cork: Talbot Press, 1929.

Delargy, J. H. 'The Gaelic Story-Teller. With Some Notes on Gaelic Folk-Tales', *Proceedings of the British Academy*, 31 (1945), 177–221.

Dillon, Myles. 'The Archaism of Irish Tradition', *Proceedings of the British Academy*, 35 (1947), 245–64; repr., as a monograph, London: D. Cumberledge, 1948.

—— *The Cycles of the Kings*. Oxford: Oxford University Press, 1946.

—— *Early Irish Literature*. Chicago: University of Chicago Press, 1948.

—— *Early Irish Society*. Dublin: Colm Ó Lochlainn, 1954.

—— (ed.). *Irish Sagas*. Cork: Mercier, 1968.

Dinneen, Patrick S. *Foclóir Gaedhilge agus Béarla: An Irish-English Dictionary*, rev. edn. Dublin: Educational Company, 1927.

Dinnseanchas (Dublin), 1961– .

Dottin, Georges. *L'Épopée irlandaise*. Paris: Le Renaissance du Livre, 1926; repr. Paris: Presses d'Aujourd'hui, 1980.

Drummond, William Henry. *Ancient Irish Minstrelsy*. Dublin: Hodges & Smith, 1852.

Dumézil, Georges. *Le Troisième souverain; essai sur le dieu indo-iranian Aryaman et sur la formation de l'histoire mythique de l'irlande*. Paris: G. P. Maisonneuve, 1949.

Éigse: A Journal of Irish Studies (Dublin), 1939– .

Ellis, Peter Berresford. *A Dictionary of Irish Mythology*. London: Constable, 1987.

Emania: Bulletin of the Navan Research Group (Belfast), 1986– .

Ériu (Dublin), 1904– .

Fitzgerald, Walter. *The Historical Geography of Early Ireland*. London: G. Philip, 1925.

Flood, Joseph Mary. *Ireland: Its Myths and Legends*. Dublin: Talbot Press, 1916; repr. Port Washington, NY: Kennikat, 1970.

Flower, Robin. *The Irish Tradition*. Oxford: Clarendon Press, 1947.

Gantz, Jeffrey (ed. and trans.). *Early Irish Myths and Sagas*. Harmondsworth: Penguin, 1981.

Glassie, Henry. *Irish Folktales*. New York: Pantheon, 1985.

Gose, Elliott B., Jr. *The World of the Irish Wonder Tale*. Toronto: University of Toronto Press, 1985.

Guyonvarc'h, Christian-J. (ed.). *Textes mythologiques irlandaises*. Rennes: Ogam-Celticum, 1981.

Harbison, Peter. *Guide to the National Monuments of Ireland*, rev. edn. Dublin: Gill, 1975.

—— See Killanin, Lord, below.

Heaney, Marie. *Over Nine Waves: A Book of Irish Legends*. London and Boston: Faber & Faber, 1994.

Heist, William. *Vitae sanctorum Hiberniae ex codice olim Salmanticensi nunc Bruxellensi*. Brussels: Société des Bollandistes, 1965.

Herbert, Máire. *Iona, Kells, and Derry*. Oxford: Clarendon Press, 1988.

Higgins, Jim. *Irish Mermaids: Sirens, Temptresses, and Their Symbolism in Art, Architecture and Folklore*. Galway: Crow's Rock, 1995.

Hogan, Edmund I. *Onomasticon Goedelicum, Locorum et Tribuum Hiberniae et Scotiae*. Dublin: Hodges Figgis, 1910.

Hull, Eleanor. *The Cuchullin Saga in Irish Literature*. Grimm Library No. 8. London: David Nutt, 1898; repr. New York: AMS Press, 1972.

—— *A Textbook of Irish Literature*, 2nd edn., 2 vols. Dublin: M. H. Gill, 1908.

Hyde, Douglas. *An Sgéuluidhe Gaodhalach*. London: David Nutt, n.d.; trans. as *Beside the Fire*, trans. Douglas Hyde. London: David Nutt, 1910.

—— *Legends of Saints and Sinners*. Every Irishman's Library. Dublin: Talbot Press; New York: F. A. Stokes, 1915.

—— *A Literary History of Ireland*. London: T. Fisher Unwin, 1899; repr. New York: Barnes & Noble, 1967.

—— *The Story of Early Gaelic Literature*. New Irish Library 6. London: T. Fisher Unwin: New York: P. J. Kennedy, 1903.

Jackson, Kenneth H. *The Oldest Irish Tradition*. Cambridge: Cambridge University Press, 1964.

Journal of the Royal Society of Antiquaries of Ireland (includes fromer *Kilkenny Historical and Archaeological Journal*) (Dublin), 1848– .

Joyce, Patrick Weston. *Old Celtic Romances*. London: Kegan Paul, 1879; repr. Dublin: Talbot Press, 1961.

—— *A Social History of Ancient Ireland . . .*, 2 vols. Dublin: M. H. Gill; London: Longman's, 1903; repr. New York: Benjamin Blom, 1968.

—— *The Story of Ancient Irish Civilisation*. Dublin: M. H. Gill; London: Longmans, 1907.

Joynt, Maud. *Golden Legends of the Gael*. Dublin: Talbot Press, 1920.

Kavanagh, Peter. *Irish Mythology: A Dictionary*, 3 vols. New York: privately printed, 1958; repr. Newbridge, Co. Kildare, 1988.

Keating, Geoffrey [Séathrún Céitinn]. *Forus Feasa ar Éririnn* [lit. 'A Sound Basis for a Knowledge of Ireland']. Vol. i, ed. David Comyn, Irish Texts Society 4, London: David Nutt, 1902. Vols. ii–iv, ed. Patrick S. Dinneen, Irish Texts Society 8, 9, 15. London: David Nutt, 1908, 1914.

Kelleher, John V. 'Early Irish History and Pseudo-History', *Studia Hibernica*, 3 (1963), 113–27.

—— 'Yeats' Use of Irish Materials', *TriQuarterly*, 4 (1965), 115–25.

Kennedy, Gerald Conan. *Irish Mythology: A Guide and Sourcebook*. Killala: Morrigan, 1991.

Kennedy, Gerry, and Smith, Daragh. *Places of Mythology in Ireland*. Killala: Morrigan, 1989.

Kennedy, Patrick. *Bardic Stories of Ireland*. Dublin: M'Glashan & Gill, 1871.

—— *Legendary Fictions of the Irish Celts*. London: Macmillan, 1866; repr. Detroit: Singing Tree, 1968.

Kennelly, T. Brendan. 'Modern Irish Poets and the Irish Epic'. dissertation, Trinity College, Dublin, 1967.

Killanin, Lord, and Duignan, Michael V. *The Shell Guide to Ireland*, 2nd edn. London:

Ebury Press, 1967, 1969. Rev. edn. by Peter Harbison. Dublin: Gill & Macmillan, 1989.

KILLINGER, KARL VON. *Sagen und Märchen aus Irland*. Stuttgart: F. O. Gotta'scher Verlag, 1848.

KNOTT, ELEANOR. *Irish Classical Poetry, Commonly Called Bardic*. Dublin: Colm Ó Lochlainn, 1957. Republished in James Carney's *Early Irish Literature* (see above).

—— *Pagan Ireland. Epochs of Irish History*. Dublin: M. H. Gill; London: David Nutt, 1904.

LEAHY, ARTHUR HERBERT. *Heroic Romances of Ireland*, 2 vols. London: David Nutt, 1905; repr. New York: Lemma, 1974.

LEAMY, EDMUND. *Irish Fairy Tales*. Dublin: Gill, 1906; repr. Dublin and Cork: Mercier, 1978.

Lebor Gabála Érenn: The Book of the Taking of Ireland, ed. and trans. R. A. S. Macalister. Irish Texts Society 34, 35, 39, 41, 44. Dublin: Educational Company of Ireland, 1938–56.

Lebor Laignech: The Book of Leinster, ed. Richard Irvine Best, Osborn Bergin, and M. A. O'Brien. Dublin: Dublin Institute for Advanced Studies, 1954.

Lebor na hUidre: The Book of the Dun Cow, ed. Richard Irvine Best and Osborn Bergin. Dublin: Royal Irish Society, 1929, 1970.

LE ROUX, FRANÇOISE, and GUYONVARC'H, CHRISTIAN-J. *La Souveraineté guerrière de l'Irlande: Mórrigan, Bodb, Macha*. Rennes: Ogam-Celticum, 1983.

LIESSEM, FRANZ J. *Irische Legende: Mysterien, Mythen, Metamorphosen*. Frankfurt a.M. and New York: Peter Lang, 1992.

LOGAN, PATRICK. *The Old Gods*. Belfast: Appletree, 1981.

MCANALLY, D. R. *Irish Wonders: Popular Tales as Told by the People*. New York: Ward Lock, 1888; repr. New York: Weathervane, 1977.

MACCANA, PROINSIAS. *Learned Tales of Medieval Ireland*. Dublin: Dublin Institute for Advanced Studies, 1980.

MCCONE, KIM. *Pagan Past and Christian Present in Early Irish Literature*. Maynooth: An Sagart, 1990.

MCGARRY, JAMES. *Place Names in the Writings of W. B. Yeats*. Gerrards Cross, UK: Smythe, 1976.

MACKILLOP, JAMES. *Fionn mac Cumhaill: Celtic Myth in English Literature*. Syracuse, NY: Syracuse University Press, 1986.

MACMANUS, DIARMUID A. *The Middle Kingdom: The Fairy World of Ireland*. London: Max Parrish, 1960; repr. Gerrards Cross, UK: Colin Smythe, 1973.

MACNEILL, EOIN [JOHN]. *Celtic Ireland*. Dublin: Martin Lester; London: Leonard Parsons, 1921.

MACNEILL, MÁIRE. *The Feast of Lughnasa*. Oxford: Oxford University Press, 1962; repr. Dublin: Comhairle Bhéaloideas Éireann, 1982.

MARKALE, JEAN. *l'Épopée celtique d'Irlande*. Paris: Payot, 1971.

MEYER, KUNO (ed. and trans.). *The Death-Tales of the Ulster Heroes*. Todd Lecture Series, vol. 14. Dublin: Hodges Figgis, 1906.

MURPHY, GERARD. 'Introduction', in *Duanaire Finn III*, Irish Texts Society No. 43. Dublin: Educational Company of Ireland, 1953, pp. x–cxxii.

—— *Ossianic Lore and Romantic Tales of Medieval Ireland*. Dublin: Colm Ó Lochlainn, 1955, 1961. Repr. in James Carney's *Early Irish Literature* (see above).

—— *Saga and Myth in Ancient Ireland*. Dublin: Three Candles, 1961. Repr. in James Carney's *Early Irish Literature* (see above).

NEESON, EOIN. *The First Book of Irish Myths and Legends*. Cork: Mercier Press, 1965.

—— *The Second Book of Irish Myths and Legends*. Cork: Mercier Press, 1966.

O'BRIEN, MICHAEL A. (ed.). *Corpus genealogiarum Hiberniae*, i [only issue]. Dublin: Dublin Institute for Advanced Studies, 1962.

Ó CÍOBHÁIN, BREANDÁN. *Toponomia Hiberniae: The Place Names of Ireland*. Dublin: An Foras Duibneach, 1978– [25 vols. projected].

Ó CORRÁIN, DONNCHADH, and MAGUIRE, FIDELMA. *Gaelic Personal Names*. Dublin: Academy Press, 1981.

O'CURRY, EUGENE. *Lectures on the Manuscript Materials of Ancient Irish History*. Dublin: James Duffy, 1861; republished Dublin: W. V. Hinch & P. Traynor. 1878; repr. (of 1861 edn.) New York: Burt Franklin, 1973.

—— *On the Manners and Customs of the Ancient Irish*, 3 vols. Dublin and London: Williams & Norgate; New York: Scribner's, 1873.

Ó DÓNAILL, NIALL. *Foclóir Gaeilge-Béarla*. Dublin: Oifig An tSoláthair, 1977.

Ó FOGHLUDHA, RISTEÁRD [RICHARD FOLEY]. *Dictionary of Irish Placenames*. Dublin: Brown & Nolan, 1935.

O'GRADY, STANDISH HAYES. *Silva Gadelica: A Collection of Tales in Irish with Extracts*

Illustrating Persons and Places. 2 vols., London: Williams & Norgate, 1892.

O'Grady, Standish James. *Early Bardic Literature, Ireland*. London: Sampson Low; Dublin: Ponsonby, 1879.

—— *History of Ireland: Critical and Philosophical*. London: Sampson Low; Dublin: Ponsonby, 1881.

—— *History of Ireland: Cuculain and His Contemporaries*. London: Sampson Low; Dublin: Ponsonby, 1880.

—— *History of Ireland: Heroic Period*. London: Sampson Low; Dublin: Ponsonby, 1878.

Ó hÓgáin, Dáithí. *Fionn mac Cumhaill: Images of the Gaelic Hero*. Dublin: Gill & Macmillan, 1988.

—— *The Hero in Irish Folk History*. Dublin: Gill & Macmillan, 1986.

—— *Myth, Legend, and Romance: An Encyclopedia of the Irish Folk Tradition*. London: Ryan; New York: Prentice-Hall, 1991.

O'Rahilly, T. F. *Early Irish History and Mythology*. Dublin: Dublin Institute for Advanced Studies, 1946.

Ó Riain, Pádraig. *Corpus Genealogiarum Sanctorum Hiberniae*. Dublin: Dublin Institute for Adanced Studies, 1985.

Ossianic Society, Transactions of, 6 vols. Dublin, 1853–61.

O'Sheridan, Mary Grant. *Gaelic Folk Tales*. Chicago: Henneberry, 1910.

Ó'Súilleabhain, Seán [Sean O'Sullivan]. *A Handbook of Irish Folklore*. London: Jenkins: Hatboro, Pa.: Folklore Associates, 1963.

—— and Christiansen, Reidar Thoralf. *The Types of the Irish Folktale*. Helsinki: Suomalainen tiedekatemia, 1963.

O'Sullivan, Patrick V. *Irish Superstitions and Legends of Animals and Birds*. Cork: Mercier Press, 1991.

O'Sullivan, Seán. *Folktales of Ireland*. Chicago: University of Chicago Press, 1966.

—— *Legends From Ireland*. Totowa, NJ: Rowman & Littlefield, 1977.

Patterson, Nerys T. *Cattle-Lords and Clansmen: Kingship and Rank in Early Ireland*. New York: Garland Press, 1992.

Peritia (Dublin), 1982– .

Plummer, Charles. *Bethada náem nÉrenn: Lives of Irish Saints*. Oxford: Clarendon Press, 1922.

—— *Vitae Sanctorum Hiberniae . . .*, 2 vols. Oxford: Clarendon Press, 1910.

Ridgeway, Sir William. 'Ireland and the Heroic Age' in *Early Age of Greece*, ii. Cambridge: Cambridge University Press, 1931, pp. 504–714.

Room, Adrian. *A Dictionary of Irish Place-Names*. Belfast: Appletree Press, 1986.

Royal Irish Academy Dictionary of the Irish Language. Dublin: Royal Irish Academy, 1913–76.

Saul, George Brandon. *The Shadow of the Three Queens: A Handbook Introduction to Traditional Irish Literature and Its Backgrounds*. Harrisburg Pa.: Stackpole, 1953. Revised and retitled, *Traditional Irish Literature and Its Backgrounds*. Lewisburg, Pa.: Bucknell University Press, 1970.

Smyth, Daragh. *A Guide to Irish Mythology*. Dublin: Irish Academic Press, 1988.

Spaan, David B. 'The Otherworld in Early Irish Literature', dissertation, University of Michigan, 1969.

Stanford, W. B. *Ireland and Classical Tradition*. Totowa, NJ: Rowman & Littlefield, 1976.

Stokes, Whitley and Ernst Windisch (eds.). *Irische Texte mit Übersetzungen und Wörterbuch*, 5 vols. Leipzig: S. Hirzel, 1880– 1909.

Studia Hibernica (Dublin), 1961– .

Táin Bó Cuailnge, trans. Thomas Kinsella. London: Oxford University Press, 1969.

Thuente, Mary Helen. *W. B. Yeats and Irish Folklore*. Totowa, NJ: Barnes & Noble, 1981.

Thurneysen, Rudolf. *Die irische Helden- und Königsage bis zum siebzehnten Jahrhundert*. Halle: Salle, 1921.

—— *Sagen aus dem alten Irland*. Berlin: Wiegandt & Grieben, 1901.

Walker, Joseph C. *Historical Memoirs of the Irish Bards*. Dublin, 1786; repr. New York: Garland Press, 1971.

Wilde, Lady Jane. *Ancient Legends, Mystic Charms and Superstitions of Ireland*, 2 vols. London: Ward & Downey, 1887.

Wilde, Sir William Robert Wills. *Irish Popular Superstitions: Readings in Popular Literature*. Dublin: McGlashan; London: W. S. Orr, 1852.

Williams, J[ohn] E[llis] Caerwyn. *Traddodiad llenyddul Iwerddon*. Cardiff: Gwasg Prifysgol Cymru, 1958; trans. and rev., with Patrick K. Ford, *The Irish Literary Tradition*. Cardiff: University of Wales Press; Belmont, Mass.: Ford & Ballie, 1992.

Wood-Martin, William. *Traces of the Elder Faiths of Ireland; A Folklore Sketch; A Handbook of Pre-Christian Traditions*. 2 vols., London and New York: Longmans, Green, 1902.

YEATS, WILLIAM BUTLER (ed.). *Fairy and Folk Tales of Ireland*, introd. Kathleen Raine. Gerrards Cross, UK: Colin Smythe, 1973 [reprints 1888 collection, pp. 1–289, and 1892 collection, pp. 299–389].

—— (ed.). *Fairy and Folk Tales of the Irish Peasantry*. London: Walter Scott; New York: Thomas Whittaker; Toronto: W. J. Gage, 1888.

—— (ed.). *Irish Fairy and Folk Tales*. New York: Modern Library, *c*.1935 [contains selections from 1888 and 1892 collections].

—— (ed.). *Irish Fairy Tales*. London: T. Fisher Unwin; New York: Cassell, 1892.

—— *Writings on Irish Folklore, Legend and Myth*, ed. Robert Welch, with glossary. Harmondsworth: Penguin, 1993.

Scottish Gaelic

ANDERSON, MARJORIE O. *Kings and Kingship in Early Scotland*. Edinburgh: Scottish Academic Press, 1980.

BLACK, GEORGE F. *Macpherson's Ossian and the Ossianic Controversy*. New York: New York Public Library, 1926, 1927; see also John J. Dunn, 'Macpherson's *Ossian* and the Ossianic Controversy: A Supplemental Bibliography', *Bulletin of the New York Public Library*, 75 (1971), 465–73.

BUCHAN, PETER. *Ancient Scottish Tales*, ed. John A. Fairley. Peterhead: Buchan Field Club, 1908; repr. Darby, Pa.: Norwood, 1973.

CAMERON, ALEXANDER (ed.). *Reliquiae Celticae*, 2 vols. Inverness: Northern Chronicle Office, 1894.

CAMPBELL, ARCHIBALD. *Records of Argyll: Legends, Traditions, and Recollections of Argyllshire Highlanders*, etc. Edinburgh and London: Blackwood, 1885.

—— (ed.). *Waifs and Strays in Celtic Tradition*, 4 vols. London: David Nutt, 1889–1891. See also John Gregorson Campbell, 1895 (below).

CAMPBELL, HECTOR. *Luirgean Eachainn N'll, Folktales From Cape Breton*, ed. and trans. Margaret MacDonell and John Shaw. Stornoway: Acair, 1981.

CAMPBELL, JOHN FRANCIS. *Leabhar na Feinne: Heroic Gaelic Ballads*, i [only issue]. London: Spottiswoode, 1872.

—— *Popular Tales of the West Highlands, Orally Collected*, 4 vols. Paisley: Gardner, 1861; repr. London: Gardner, 1890–3.

CAMPBELL, JOHN GREGORSON. *Clan Traditions and Popular Tales of the Western Highlands and Islands*, ed. Jessie Wallace and Duncan MacIsaac; vol. v: *Waifs and Strays in Celtic Tradition*. London: David Nutt, 1895; repr. New York: AMS, 1973.

—— *Superstitions of the Highlands and Islands of Scotland*, etc. Glasgow: J. MacLehose, 1900; repr. Detroit: Singing Tree, 1970; New York: Benjamin Blom, 1971.

—— *Witchcraft and Second Sight in the Highlands and Islands of Scotland*, etc. Glasgow: J. MacLehose, 1902; repr. Detroit: Singing Tree, 1970.

CARMICHAEL, ALEXANDER (comp.). *Carmina Gadelica*, rev. edn., ed. J. Carmichael Watson and Angus Matheson, 5 vols. Edinburgh and London: Oliver and Boyd, 1928; vol. vi, ed. Angus Matheson, Edinburgh and London: Scottish Academic Press, 1971.

DWELLY, EDWARD. *The Illustrated Gaelic-English Dictionary*, 8th edn. Glasgow: Gairm, 1973.

GRANT, K. W. *Myth Tradition and Story from Western Argyll*. Oban: Oban Times Press, 1925.

GRASSIE, JAMES. *Legends of the Highlands of Scotland, from Oral Tradition*. Inverness: J. Smith, 1843.

GUTHRIE, JAMES CARGILL. *The Vale of Strathmore: Its Scenes and Legends*. Edinburgh: Paterson, 1875.

HENDERSON, GEORGE. *The Norse Influence on Celtic Scotland*. Glasgow: James MacLehose, 1910.

LAUDER, THOMAS DICK. *Highland Rambles, and Long Legends to Shorten the Way*. Edinburgh: A. & C. Black, 1837.

—— *Legendary Tales of the Highlands*. London: H. Coburn, 1841.

LEACH, MACEDWARD. 'Celtic Tales from Cape Breton', in W. Edson Richmond (ed.), *Studies in Folklore in Honor of Distinguished Service Professor Stith Thompson*. Bloomington: Indiana University Press, 1957, pp. 40–54.

MACDONALD, ALEXANDER. *Story and Song from Loch Ness-Side*. Inverness: Northern Counties Newspaper, 1914; repr. Inverness: Gaelic Society of Inverness, 1982.

MACDONALD, T. D. *Gaelic Proverbs and Proverbial Sayings*. Stirling: Eneas MacKay, 1926.

MACDOUGALL, BETTY. *Folklore from Coll*. Glasgow: privately printed, 1978.

MACGREGOR, ALASDAIR ALPIN DOUGLAS. *The Peat Fire Flame: Folk Tales and Traditions of the Highlands and Islands*. Edinburgh: Ettrick Press, 1947.

MACGREGOR, ALEXANDER. *Highland Superstitions Connected with the Druids, Fairies, Witchcraft, Second-Sight, Hallowe'en, Sacred Wells and Lochs*, etc. Inverness: A. & W. Mackenzie, 1891; repr. Stirling: Eneas MacKay, 1922.

MACKAY, CHARLES. *Legends of the Isles and Highland Gatherings*, 2nd edn. London and New York: G. Routledge, 1857.

MACKENZIE, DONALD A. *Scottish Folk Lore and Folk Life*. London: Blackie, 1935.

MACKENZIE, WILLIAM COOK. *The Western Isles; Their History, and Place Names*. Paisley: Gardner, 1932; includes John Morrison's (1787–1834) *Traditions of the Western Isles*, pp. 77–249.

MCLAREN, MORAY. *The Shell Guide to Scotland*. London: Ebury Press, 1972.

MACLAUCHLAN, THOMAS (ed. and trans.). *The Dean of Lismore's Book*, introd. by W. F. Skene. Edinburgh: Edmonston & Douglas, 1862.

MACLENNAN, MALCOLM. *A Pronouncing and Etymological Dictionary of the Gaelic Language*. Edinburgh: John Grant, 1925; repr. Stornoway: Acair; Aberdeen: Aberdeen University Press, 1979.

MACLEOD, CALUM I. N. *Highland Scottish Folklore and Beliefs*. Antigonish, Can.: Formac, 1975.

—— *Sgialachdan a Albainn Nuaidh*. Glasgow: Gairm, 1969.

—— *Stories from Nova Scotia*. Antigonish, Can.: Formac, 1974.

MACNEIL, JOE NEIL. *Tales Until Dawn: The World of a Cape Breton Gaelic Story-Teller*, trans. John Shaw. Kingston and Montreal: McGill-Queen's University Press, 1987.

MACNEILL, NIGEL. *The Literature of the Highlanders*. London: Lamley, 1892. 2nd edn., with additional chapter by John MacMaster Campbell. Stirling: Eneas MacKay, 1929.

MACPHERSON, JAMES. *The Poems of Ossian*. Edinburgh: Geddes, 1896; published first serially under the title *Fragments of Antient Poetry collected in the Highlands of Scotland*, 1760–3.

MACRITCHIE, DAVID. *The Savages of Gaelic Tradition*. Inverness: Northern Counties Newspaper and Print, 1920.

MARTIN, MARTIN. *Description of the Western Islands of Scotland*. 1703; repr. Glasgow: T. D. Morrison, 1884.

MILLER, HUGH. *Scenes and Legends of the North of Scotland*, etc. Paisley: W. P. Nimmo, 1889; repr. New York: Arno Press, 1977.

MILLER, THOMAS DUNCAN. *Tales of a Highland Village (Glenshee), on the Royal Route*. Perth: Munro Press, 1925.

MORRISON, JOHN. See Mackenzie, W. C. (above).

PATTISON, THOMAS. *Selections from the Gaelic Bards*. Glasgow: A. Sinclair, 1866.

POLSON, ALEXANDER. *Our Highland Folklore Heritage*. Dingwall: G. Souter; Inverness: Northern Chronicle, 1926.

ROBERTSON, RONALD MACDONALD. *More Highland Folktales*. Edinburgh: Oliver & Boyd, 1964.

—— *Selected Highland Folktales*. Edinburgh: Oliver & Boyd, 1961.

ROSS, ANNE. *The Folklore of the Scottish Highlands*. London: Batsford, 1976.

Scottish Gaelic Studies (Aberdeen), 1928– .

[SHAW, DONALD] 'Glenmore' [pseud.]. *Highland Legends and Fugitive Pieces of Original Poetry*, etc. Edinburgh: privately printed, 1859.

SHEDDAN, HUGH. *The Story of Lorn, Its Islands and Oban*. Oban: Oban Times, 1938.

SKENE, WILLIAM FORBES. *Celtic Scotland; History of Ancient Alban*, 3 vols. Edinburgh: Douglas, 1886.

STEWART, WILLIAM GRANT. *The Popular Superstitions and Festive Amusements of the Highlanders of Scotland*. Edinburgh: Constable, 1823.

SWIRE, OTTA. *The Highlands and Their Legends*. Edinburgh: Oliver & Boyd, 1963.

—— *The Inner Hebrides and Their Legends*. London: Collins, 1964.

—— *The Outer Hebrides and Their Legends*. Edinburgh: Oliver & Boyd, 1966.

—— *Skye: The Isle and Its Legends*. New York: Oxford University Press, 1952.

THOMSON, DERICK S. (ed.). *The Companion to Gaelic Scotland*. Oxford: Basil Blackwell, 1983; 3rd edn., Glasgow: Gairm, 1994.

—— *Gaelic Sources of Macpherson's Ossian*. Aberdeen: Aberdeen University Press, 1952.

—— *An Introduction to Gaelic Poetry*. Edinburgh: Edinburgh University Press, 1990.

—— *The New English–Gaelic Dictionary*. Glasgow: Gairm, 1981.

Tocher (Edinburgh, School of Scottish Studies), 1971– .

Transactions of the Gaelic Society of Inverness, 1871– .

WARNER, GERALD. *Tales of the Scottish Highlands*. London: Shepheard-Walwyn, 1982.

WITHERS, CHARLES W. J. *Gaelic in Scotland, 1698- 1981: The Geographical History of a Language*. Edinburgh: John Donald, 1984.

Manx

BROOME, DORA. *Fairy Tales from the Isle of Man*. Harmondsworth: Penguin, 1951.

CALLOW, EDWARD. *The Phynodderee, and Other Legends of the Isle of Man*. London: J. Dean, 1882.

CASHEN, WILLIAM. *Manx Folk-Lore*. Douglas: G. & L. Johnson, 1912; repr. Folcraft, Pa.: Folcraft Library Editions, 1977.

CREGEEN, ARCHIBALD. *A Dictionary of the Manks Language*. Douglas: J. Quiggen, 1835.

FALCONAR, A. E. I. *Celtic Tales of Myth and Fantasy*. Port Erin, Isle of Man: Fannag Press, n.d. (*c*.1987).

FARGHER, DOUGLAS C. *Fargher's English-Manx Dictionary*. Douglas: Shearwater, 1979.

HARRISON, WILLIAM. *A Mona Miscellany: A Selection of Proverbs, Sayings, Ballads, Customs, Superstitions, and Legends Peculiar to the Isle of Man*. Douglas, 1869.

KELLY, JOHN. *The Manx Dictionary*. Douglas: Manx Society, 1866.

KILLIP, MARGARET. *The Folklore of the Isle of Man*. London: Batsford; Totowa, NJ: Rowman & Littlefield, 1976.

MOORE, ARTHUR W. *Folk-Lore of the Isle of Man*, etc. Douglas: Brown; London: David Nutt, 1891.

—— *A Vocabulary of the Anglo-Manx Dialect*. London: Oxford University Press, 1924.

RHŶS, JOHN. See under Welsh.

WOOD, WILLIAM. *Focklioar Galg-Baarla*. Glasgow: MacLaurin, *c*.1950.

Welsh

BARING-GOULD, SABINE. *A Book of South Wales*. London: Methuen, 1905.

BARNES, RONALD. *Great Legends of Wales*. Gerrards Cross, UK: Colin Smythe, 1991.

BARTRUM. PETER C. *A Welsh Classical Dictionary: People in History and Legend up to about ad 1000*. Aberystwyth: National Library of Wales, 1993.

BOWEN, EMRYS GEORGE. *Saints, Seaways and Settlements in the Celtic Islands*. Cardiff: University of Wales Press, 1969.

BROMWICH, RACHEL (ed. and trans.). *Trioedd Ynys Prydain: The Welsh Triads*. Cardiff: University of Wales Press, 1961; 2nd edn., 1978.

—— and BRINLEY JONES, R. (eds.). *Astudiaethau ar yr Hengerdd/Studies in Old Welsh Poetry*. Cardiff: Gwasg Prifysol Cymru, 1978.

Bulletin of the Board of Celtic Studies (Cardiff), 1921- .

COLEMAN, STANLEY JACKSON. *Lore and Legends of Flintshire*. Douglas, Isle of Man: Folklore Academy, 1956.

—— *Radnorshire in Lore and Legend*. Douglas, Isle of Man: Folklore Academy, 1956.

Cymmrodorion, Transactions of the Honourable Society of (London), 1892– .

DAVIES, TREFOR R. *A Book of Welsh Names*. London: Sheppard, 1952.

EARL, WILLIAM. *Welsh Legends; A Collection of Popular Oral Tales*. London: J. Badcock, 1802.

EMERSON, WILLIAM. *Tales from Welsh Wales*, etc. London: David Nutt, 1894.

EVANS, H. M. and THOMAS, W. O. *Y Geiriadur Mawr: The Complete Welsh-English, English-Welsh Dictionary*, 10th edn. Llandysul: Davies, 1981.

EVANS, HUGH. *Y Tylwyth Teg*. Liverpool: H. Evans, 1944.

GRUFFUDD, HEINI. *Welsh Personal Names*. Talybont: Cyhoeddwyd, 1980.

GRUFFYDD, WILLIAM JOHN. *Folklore and Myth in the Mabinogion*. Cardiff: University of Wales Press, 1958.

—— *Math vab Mathonwy*. Cardiff: University of Wales Press, 1928.

—— *Rhiannon: An Inquiry into the Origins of the First and Third Branches of the Mabinogi*. Cardiff: University of Wales Press, 1953.

HOWELLS, WILLIAM. *Cambrian Superstitions, Composing Ghosts, Omens, Witchcraft, Traditions*, etc. London: Longman, 1831.

JARMAN, A. O. H. and HUGHES, G. R. *A Guide to Welsh Literature*, 2 vols. Swansea: Christopher Davies, 1976–9.

JONES, MARY EIRWIN. *The Folktales of Wales*, 11th edn. Llandysul: Gomer Press, 1978.

JONES, THOMAS GWYNN. *Welsh Folklore and Folk-Custom*. London: Methuen, 1930; repr. Cambridge: D. S. Brewer; Totowa, NJ: Rowman & Littlefield, 1979.

LEWES, MARY L. *Stranger Than Fiction, Being Tales from the Byways of Ghosts and Folklore*. London: W. Rider, 1911.

The Mabinogi, ed. and trans. Patrick K. Ford. Los Angeles: University of California Press, 1977.

The Mabinogion, ed. and trans. Lady Charlotte Guest [Schreiber], 3 vols. London: Longmans, 1838–49.

The Mabinogion. ed. and trans. Gwyn Jones and Thomas Jones. London: Golden Cockerel Press, 1948; repr. London: Everyman's Library, 1949.

MARKALE, JEAN. *L'Épopée celtique en Bretagne*, 3rd edn. Paris: Payot, 1985.

OSBORNE, LINDA BARRETT. *The Songs of the Harp: Old Welsh Folktales*. New York: St. Martin's Press, 1976.

OWEN, ELIAS. *Old Stone Crosses of the Vale of Clwyd and Neighbouring Parishes*, etc. London: B. Quaritch, 1886.

—— *Welsh Folk-Lore: A Collection of Folk-Tales and Legends of North Wales, etc.* Woodall: Minshall, 1896.

OWEN, TREFOR MEREDITH. *Welsh Folk Customs*. Cardiff: National Museum of Wales, 1959.

PARRY, THOMAS. *A History of Welsh Literature*, trans. H. Idris Bell. Oxford: Clarendon Press, 1955.

PARRY-JONES, Daniel. *Welsh Legends and Fairy Lore*. London: Batsford, 1953; repr. New York: Barnes & Noble, 1992.

RADFORD, KEN. *Tales of South Wales*. London: Skilton & Shaw, 1978.

RHŶS, [SIR] JOHN. *Celtic Folklore, Welsh and Manx*, 2 vols. Oxford: Clarendon Press, 1902.

ROWLAND, JENNY. *Early Welsh Saga Poetry: A Study and Edition of the Englynion*. Cambridge: D. S. Brewer; Wolfeboro, NH: Boydell & Brewer, 1990.

SIKES, WIRT. *British Goblins: Welsh Folk-Lore, Fairy Mythology, Legends, and Traditions*, 2nd edn. London: Sampson Low, 1880; repr. Wakefield: EP, 1973.

SIMPSON, JACQUELINE. *The Folklore of the Welsh Border*. London: Batsford; Totowa, NJ: Rowman & Littlefield, 1976.

STEPHENS, MEIC (ed.). *The Oxford Companion to the Literature of Wales*. Oxford: Oxford University Press, 1986.

SULLIVAN, C. W., III. *Welsh Celtic Myth in Modern Fantasy*. Westport, Conn.: Greenwood Press, 1989.

Transactions of the Honourable Society of Cymmrodorion (London), 1892– .

TREVELYAN, MARIE. *Folk-Lore and Folk Stories of Wales*. London: E. Stock, 1909.

WILLIAMS, IFOR. *Lectures on Early Welsh Poetry*. Dublin: Dublin Institute for Advanced Studies, 1944.

Cornish

BARING-GOULD, SABINE. *Cornish Characters and Strange Events*. London and New York: J. Lane, 1909.

BOTTRELL, WILLIAM. *Traditions and Hearthside Stories of West Cornwall*. Penzance: W. Cornish, 1870; repr. Newcastle upon Tyne: Frank Graham, 1970.

COURTNEY, MARGARET ANN. *Cornish Feasts and Folk-Lore*. Penzance: Beare, 1890; repr. Wakefield: EP, 1973.

CROSSING, WILLIAM. *Tales of the Dartmoor Pixies: Glimpses of Elfin Haunts and Antics*. First published 1890; repr. Newcastle upon Tyne: Frank Graham, 1968.

DEANE, TONY, and SHAW, TONY. *The Folklore of Cornwall*. London: Batsford; Totowa, NJ: Rowman & Littlefield, 1975.

DEXTER, THOMAS FRANCIS GEORGE. *Cornwall: Land of the Gods*. Truro: Jordan's Bookshop, 1932.

ELLIS, PETER BERRESFORD. *The Cornish Language and Its Literature*. London: Routledge, 1974.

HARRIS, J. HENRY. *Cornish Saints and Sinners*. London and New York: J. Lane, 1906.

HUNT, ROBERT. *Popular Romances of the West of England; or, The Drolls, Traditions, and Superstitions of Old Cornwall*, 3rd edn. London: Chatto & Windus, 1881; repr. New York: Benjamin Blom, 1968.

JENKIN, ALFRED KENNETH HAMILTON. *Cornwall and the Cornish: The Story, Religion, and Folk-Lore of the 'Western Land'*. London and Toronto: J. M. Dent, 1933.

NANCE, R. MORTON. *An English–Cornish Dictionary*. Marazion: Federation of Old Cornwall Societies, 1952. *A Cornish–English Dictionary*. Marazion: FOCS, 1955. Repr. as single vol., Penzance: Cornish Language Board, 1978.

PADEL, OLIVER J. *A Popular Dictionary of Cornish Place-Names*. Penzance: Alison Hodge, 1988.

PENNY, GEORGINA. *Witchery of the West: Some Legends of Cornwall*. Penzance: Cornish Library, n.d.

QUILLER-COUCH, MABEL *Cornwall's Wonderland*. London and Toronto: J. M. Dent, 1914.

TREGARTHEN, ENYS. *Piskey Folk; A Book of Cornish Legends*. New York: John Day, 1940.

WEATHERHILL, CRAIG. *Myths and Legends of Cornwall*. Wilmslow, UK: Sigma Leisure, 1994.

WHITCOMBE, MARY ELIZABETH. *Bygone Days in Devonshire and Cornwall*. London: R. Bentley, 1874.

Breton

ANSON, PETER FREDERICK. *Mariners of Brittany*. London and Toronto: J. M. Dent; New York: E. P. Dutton, 1931.

BRETT, CAROLINE. *The Monks of Redon: Gesta Sanctorum Rotonensium and Vita Conuuionis*. Woodbridge, UK and Wolfeboro, NH: Boydell, 1989.

DELAPORTE, RAYMOND [REMON ar PORZH]. *Geriadur Brezhoneg–Saozneg/Breton–English Dictionary*, multi-volumed. Lesneven: Mouladuriou Hor Yezh, 1986– .

EVANS, CLAUDE. *A Dictionary of Old Breton*, 2 vols. Toronto: Prepcorp, 1985, a translation of Fleuriot (1964) (see below).

FALC'HON, FRANÇOIS. *Les Noms de lieus celtiques*. Rennes: Armoricaines, 1966.

FAVEREAU, Francis. *Dictionnaire du Breton contemporain: Geriadur ar brezhoneg a-vremen*. Morlaix: Skol Vreizh, 1992.

FLEURIOT, LÉON. *Dictionnaire du vieux breton*, 2 vols. Paris: Klincksieck, 1964; cf. Evans (1985) (above).

—— *Les Origines de la Bretagne: l'émigration*. Paris: Payot, 1980.

GOSTLING, FRANCES M. *The Bretons at Home*, 3rd edn. London: Methuen, 1925.

GOURVIL, FRANCIS. *Langue et littérature bretonnes*. Paris: Presses Universitaires de France, 1952.

GUYOT, CHARLES. *The Legend of the City of Ys*, trans. Deirdre Cavanagh. Amherst: University of Massachusetts Press, 1979.

HEARD, JOHN M. *Four Legends of Brittany*. Boston: B. Humphries, 1936.

HEMON, ROPARZ. *Dictionnaire Français–Breton*. Brest: An Liamm, 1974.

—— *Nouveau Dictionnaire Breton–Français*. Brest: An Liamm, 1973.

JACKSON, KENNETH H. *A Historical Phonology of Breton*. Dublin: Dublin Institute for Advanced Studies, 1967.

JOHNSON, WILLIAM BRANCH. *Folktales of Brittany*. London: Methuen, 1927.

LAURENT, CATHERINE, and DAVIS, HELEN (eds.). *Irlande et Bretagne: vingt siècles d'histoire*. Rennes: Terre de Brume 1994.

La VILLEMARQUÉ, HERSART DE. *Barzaz Breiz: chantes populaires de la Bretagne*. Paris: Charpentier, 1839. Translated by Tom Taylor as *Ballads and Songs of Brittany*. London and Cambridge: Macmillan, 1865, 1907, 1978; repr. Norwood, Pa.: Norwood Editions, 1976; also Henry Carrington, *Breton Ballads*. Edinburgh: privately printed, 1886.

LE BRAZ, ANATOLE. *The Land of Pardons*, trans. F. Gostling. New York: Macmillan, 1906.

LE GLEAU, R. *Dictionnaire classique Français–Breton*, multi-volumed. Brest: An Liamm, 1983- .

LUZEL, FRANÇOIS MARIE. *Celtic Folk-Tales from Armorica*, trans. Derek Bryce. Llanerch, Wales: Llanerch Enterprises, 1985.

—— *Contes populaires de la Basse-Bretagne*, 3 vols. Paris: Maisonneuve & Le Clerc, 1887.

—— *Guerziou Breiz-Izel: Chants populaires de la Basse-Bretagne*, 2 vols. Lorient: É. Corfmat, 1868–74.

MACQUOID, THOMAS ROBERT. *Pictures and Legends from Normandy and Brittany*. New York: Putnam, 1881.

MARKALE, JEAN. *La Tradition celtique en Bretagne armorique*. Paris: Payot, 1975.

RINDER, EDITH WINGATE. *The Shadow of Arvor: Legendary Romances and Folktales of Brittany*. Edinburgh: P. Geddes, 1892, 1897, 1919.

SÉBILLOT, PAUL-YVES. *Le Folklore de la Bretagne*. Paris: Payot, 1950.

SOUPAULT, R. *Bretonische Volksmärchen*. Dusseldorf: Diederichs, 1959; *Breton Folktales*, trans. Ruth Meuss. London: E. Bell, 1971.

SOUVESTRE, ÉMILE. *Le Foyer breton; contes et récits populaires*. Paris, 1853; much reprinted.

SPENCE, LEWIS. *Legends and Romances of Brittany*. London: Harrap, 1917.

Arthurian

ALCOCK, LESLIE. *Arthur's Britain*. London: Allen Lane, 1971.

ASHE, GEOFFREY. *A Guidebook to Arthurian Britain*. London: Longman, 1980.

BROMWICH, RACHEL, JARMAN, A. O. H., and ROBERTS, BRYNLEY F. (eds.). *The Arthur of the Welsh: The Arthurian Legend in Medieval Welsh Literature*. Cardiff: University of Wales Press, 1991.

Select Bibliography

BROWN, ARTHUR C. L. *The Origin of the Grail Legend*. Cambridge, Mass.: Harvard University Press, 1943.

Bulletin Bibliographique de la Sociéte Internationale Arthurienne (Paris), 1949– .

GLENNIE, JOHN STUART. *Arthurian Localities; Their Historical Origin, Chief Country, and Fenian Relations; with a Map of Arthurian Scotland*. Edinburgh: Hertford, 1869. The volume collects appendices from *The Early English Texts Society*, vols. 10, 21, 36, and 112.

GROUT, P. B. *et al.* (eds.). *The Legend of Arthur in the Middle Ages: Studies Presented to A. H. Diverres by Colleagues, Pupils, and Friends*. Cambridge: Brewer, 1983.

LACY, MORRIS J. (ed.). *The Arthurian Encyclopedia*. New York: Garland, 1985.

LITTLETON, C. SCOTT. *From Scythia to Camelot: A Radical Reassessment of the Legends of King Arthur, the Knights of the Round Table, and the Holy Grail*. New York: Garland, 1994.

LOOMIS, R. S. (ed.). *Arthurian Literature in the Middle Ages*. Oxford: Clarendon Press, 1959.

—— *Celtic Myth and Arthurian Romance*. New York: Columbia, 1927.

MACALISTER, R. A. S. *Two Arthurian Romances*. Irish Texts Society, No. 10. London: David Nutt, 1910.

MARKALE, JEAN. *Le Roi Arthur*. Paris: Payot, 1980.

MINARY, RUTH, and MOORMAN, CHARLES. *An Arthurian Dictionary*. Chicago: Academy Chicago Publishers, 1990.

TOLSTOY, NIKOLAI. *The Quest for Merlin*. London: Hamish Hamilton; Boston: Little Brown, 1985.

WEST, G. D. *An Index to Names in Arthurian Romances, 1150–1500*. Toronto: University of Toronto Press, 1975.

ZIMMER, HEINRICH. 'Keltische Beiträge', *Zeitschrift für Deutsches Alterthum und Deutsche Literatur*, 35 (1891), 1–173.

Subject Index